www.wadsworth.com

wadsworth.com is the World Wide Web site for Wadsworth and is your direct source to dozens of online resources.

At *wadsworth.com* you can find out about supplements, demonstration software, and student resources. You can also send email to many of our authors and preview new publications and exciting new technologies.

wadsworth.com
Changing the way the world learns®

Worldviews, Religion, and the Environment

A Global Anthology

Edited by
Richard C. Foltz
University of Florida

THOMSON
WADSWORTH

Australia • Canada • Mexico • Singapore • Spain
United Kingdom • United States

THOMSON
WADSWORTH

Editor in Chief: Holly J. Allen
Acquisitions Editor: Steven Wainwright
Development Editor: Eric Carlson
Assistant Editor: Kara Kindstrom
Editorial Assistant: Anna Lustig
Technology Project Manager: Susan DeVanna
Marketing Manager: Worth Hawes
Marketing Assistant: Justine Ferguson
Project Manager, Editorial Production: Belinda Krohmer
Print/Media Buyer: Judy Inouye
Permissions Editor: Elizabeth Zuber
Production Service: G&S Typesetters
Copy Editor: Jan Six
Cover Designer: Stephen Rapley
Cover Image: Stand of Trees, Texas © 2002 Dan Burkholder
Cover Printer: Transcontinental Louiseville
Compositor: G&S Typesetters
Printer: Transcontinental Louiseville

Printed in Canada
1 2 3 4 5 6 7 06 05 04 03 02

For more information about our products, contact us at:
Thomson Learning Academic Resource Center
1-800-423-0563

For permission to use material from this text, contact us by: **Phone:** 1-800-730-2214
Fax: 1-800-730-2215
Web: http://www.thomsonrights.com

Library of Congress Control Number: 2002104593

ISBN: 0-534-59607-X

Wadsworth/Thomson Learning
10 Davis Drive
Belmont, CA 94002-3098
USA

Asia
Thomson Learning
60 Albert Street, #15-01
Albert Complex
Singapore 189969

Australia
Nelson Thomson Learning
102 Dodds Street
South Melbourne, Victoria 3205
Australia

Canada
Nelson Thomson Learning
1120 Birchmount Road
Toronto, Ontario M1K 5G4
Canada

Europe/Middle East/Africa
Thomson Learning
Berkshire House
168-173 High Holborn
London WC1V 7AA
United Kingdom

Latin America
Thomson Learning
Seneca, 53
Colonia Polanco
11560 Mexico D.F.
Mexico

Spain
Paraninfo Thomson Learning
Calle/Magallanes, 25
28015 Madrid, Spain

To my daughter Shahrzad,
my nephew Adam,
and all of their generation

Contents

Part Two

Interpreting Tradition 77

Chapter 3

First Peoples 79

Chapter 4

South Asian Traditions 112

Chapter 5

Buddhism 161

Chapter 6

Chinese Traditions 208

Chapter 7

Japanese Traditions 246

Chapter 8

Judaism 279

Chapter 9

Chapter 10

Chapter 11

Part Three

Contemporary Perspectives 429

Chapter 12

Ecocentrism and Radical Environmentalism 430

Chapter 13

Ecofeminism 456

Chapter 14

Voices from the Global South 493

Preface

What do the various cultural traditions of the world say about human responsibility toward the natural environment? Western civilization has long seen nature as an adversary to be overcome and resources as existing only for the benefit of human beings. Consequently, many contemporary debates have sprung from the assertion that Western values, and Christianity in particular, are to blame for the present global crisis. Is this accusation valid? Are other traditions more eco-friendly? Is an ecological Christianity possible?

In an age when our very life support systems are in jeopardy, the relationship of humanity to nature needs to be re-addressed in spiritual as well as in material terms. The world of faith institutions has been giving increasing attention in recent years to environmental stewardship issues. All major Christian denominations in the United States (with the notable exception of the Church of Jesus Christ of Latter-day Saints) have issued formal declarations on the subject, as have Jewish, Muslim, and other religious groups. In some cases, this consciousness has manifested itself in sermons on the environment and in community-based environmental activities. In New York City, the cathedral of St. John the Divine has hosted numerous faith-based environmental initiatives, such as environmental justice outreach programs and an annual performance of Paul Winter's *Gaia Missa*. The cathedral is also home to the ecumenical National Religious Partnership on the Environment.

An academic discourse at the interface between religion and the environment has been emerging steadily for more than thirty years, represented by a veritable boom in scholarly literature, especially during the past decade. From 1996 to 1998, Mary Evelyn Tucker and John Grim organized a series of thirteen conferences on religion and ecology that involved more than 700 scholars and activists from around the globe. The first eleven conferences were hosted by the Center for the Study of World Religions at Harvard University, whereas the last two were in New York City at the American Museum of Natural History and the United Nations. To date, this has been the most comprehensive research project to examine the relation between worldviews and the environment from the standpoint of various religions. One outgrowth of these conferences is a series of books published by Harvard University Press. Another is an ongoing Forum on Religion and Ecology, featuring a Web site with bibliographies, outreach initiatives, and other resources (Contact information can be found in the Resources section at the end of this book.).

Another academic forum is the Religion and Ecology group, which has been flourishing since the early 1990s within the American Academy of Religion (AAR). This group now counts more than fifty members, with many more attending the group's panels at the AAR's annual meetings. Most members are educators; some already teach courses related to religion and the environment, and others are hoping to add the subject to their curriculum. Each year attendance increases, reflecting the growing awareness within the field of religious studies of the importance of including questions of values and worldviews in any discussion on the environment.

The religious dimension of the environmental crisis is also increasingly acknowledged by those working in other areas of environmental studies. Many scientists and policy makers now concede that in their work, they frequently run up against problems resulting from differences in culture and values. As a result, on campuses across the country there is an ever-increasing interest in adding environmental studies courses within the humanities to balance similar courses in the sciences and policy making. Many philosophy departments now offer courses in environmental ethics; religion scholars, however, have a distinct and perhaps broader perspective to offer, especially if they teach world religions.

Religion and ecology, a designation first coined only recently, may not, in fact, be the most accurate label for this new academic field. A biologist will certainly not understand the term *ecology* in the same way as religion scholars are now using it. And although some may understand that *religion* need not be restricted to the world's historically recognized faith systems, the use of the word probably conjures up unnecessary (and, in this case, undesirable) category restrictions in the minds of many people. I have therefore preferred to use the terms *worldviews* and *environment,* as being broader in scope than their alternatives religion and ecology. By worldviews, I mean the culturally constructed ways in which one sees the world and one's place in it, and by environment, I mean generally the biosphere of which we are all a part (although it is understood that cultural contexts are typically intertwined with specific ecosystem contexts). I hope that my colleagues will forgive me for this departure from convention and understand that in the end, we are all basically talking about the same thing.

Those of us who teach in this area have seen the extent to which the appeal of courses on worldviews and the environment is truly interdisciplinary. In addition to religion majors, one regularly encounters interested students from the sciences, economics, philosophy, humanities, political science—indeed, every major. Often in contrast to other areas within their academic experience, students see the environmental crisis as a topic with wide-ranging implications for their own lives and for the world they will participate in building for themselves and future generations.

Personally, I have been teaching a course on worldviews and the environment for the past four years at three different institutions: a private liberal arts college, an elite private research university, and a large public university. In all three cases, this has been my most successful course in terms of student interest, enthusiasm, input, and classroom dynamic. Many students come into the course deeply committed to environmental issues, whereas others are initially skeptical but soon come to feel the importance and relevance of the subject to their personal lives and to society at large.

The major obstacle in most cases, for students who don't personally consider themselves religious, is to concede the importance of religion in addressing environmental issues. This obstacle is soon overcome, however, as students come to understand that every human being possesses a worldview of some kind that informs his or her every decision (not always rationally) and that values and perspectives commonly thought of as religious often subconsciously drive the responses even of individuals who do not see themselves as religious in any traditionally understood sense. Students often ask on the first day of the course what religion could possibly have to do with the environment. By the end of the term, no one is asking that question. Rather, students have begun to think about how our values shape the choices we make and to see problems in terms of how different value systems allow these problems to occur. Likewise, they have begun to think about how different value systems can generate different responses by which these problems can be addressed.

One recurring criticism directed at scholars working in this field has been a frequent tendency to romanticize religious traditions through the presentation of apologetic (and sometimes highly selective) *eco-friendly* readings. To date the majority of available material in the field is somewhat idealistic in tone, and this is perhaps reflected in the selection of readings in this volume. Of course, it should be understood that religions are only one component (though often a major one) of any individual's or any society's overall worldview and the resultant value system that influences individual and group attitudes and decisions. Poverty and greed are two examples of forces that may override religiously or culturally instilled values; there are surely many others. (Anthropologists such as Roy Rappaport, who rely more on materialistic and evolutionary frameworks, are among those offering alternative emphases.) It would be a mistake to assume that one's religion or worldview is the only (or perhaps even the primary) factor in determining environmental behavior, just as it would be naive to claim that the generalized practice of an eco-friendly Christianity, Buddhism, or anything else would automatically lead to a rehabilitation of the biosphere. A study of worldviews and the environment does, however, at least assume that worldviews constitute a *significant* factor, worthy of attention and analysis.

I hope that the present volume will be perceived as a timely contribution to teaching what will surely be recognized as one of the most important new areas of academic inquiry for the twenty-first century. Indeed, my motivation to propose such a project emerged partly out of personal frustration at having to assemble photocopy packets every year for the course I teach. My goal has been to put together an anthology of sufficient scope and quality to serve as the main text for such a course.

This collection strives to be as inclusive as possible. It attempts to give voice to as wide a range as possible of the diverse sources of contemporary worldviews throughout the globe, Western and Eastern, Northern and Southern, women's and men's. I encourage readers to consider social class as a major factor in determining worldviews, although regrettably, because most scholarly work is the product of scholars (that is, educated and therefore privileged writers), differences in class perspective are not always easy to represent in a work such as this, at least firsthand. Also, with some hesitation, I have decided not to include examples of the many primary textual sources in which practitioners of various religions have sought ecological readings. Rather, in the interest of conserving already overtaxed space, I have chosen to present the interpretations themselves. Many of the articles, of course, do include substantial citations from the scriptural traditions they seek to interpret.

I have not included readings that expressly establish the reality of the environmental crisis, because this is an anthology about *ways of dealing* with the crisis, the existence of which is assumed. This is essentially an anthology of diverse environmentalist perspectives. Those seeking voices that are skeptical about the reality of the environmental crisis will have no trouble locating such material elsewhere.

The anthology is presented in three parts. Part One, "Environmental Crisis, Spiritual Crisis," contrasts the dawning of awareness, during the mid-twentieth century in Western theological circles, of the spiritual aspects of the environmental crisis (in non-Western cultures, the connection was perhaps never questioned in the first place) with a few more recent essays that evoke or discuss the contemporary dominant worldview that often makes the spiritual dimension of the environmental crisis difficult for Westerners to perceive. Part

Two, "Interpreting Tradition," samples some of the approaches that contemporary thinkers within and without various religious and cultural traditions have applied to addressing ecological problems. Part Three, "Contemporary Perspectives," goes beyond the realm of established traditions and looks at some of the emerging systems of thought in which environmental values are being explored.

The sixteen chapters lend themselves to structuring a typical semester. Of course, schedules vary among institutions, and instructors may pick, choose, and reorganize assignments to meet the needs of their own classes. Each chapter includes a topical overview, followed by four readings indicating the diversity of perspectives within each worldview, thus constituting a week's worth of reading. The readings have been selected for maximum readability, diversity, and discussion potential. I hope that the readings will inspire students to reflect critically on their own lifestyles and attitudes in terms of their received traditions, while helping to stimulate their perceptions and enliven their sentiments toward the world they live in. Discussion questions have been included for this purpose. For students wishing to pursue more in-depth research, suggestions for further reading appear at the end of each chapter.

The target audience for this text are undergraduates in an introductory course on religion (understood broadly as worldviews) and the environment. The choice and presentation of readings reflect an approach that is drawn more from religious studies than from philosophy; hence the absence of explicit references to the now very rich and closely related field of environmental ethics. However, no prerequisites or prior work in religious studies are assumed. Indeed, many students will presumably not initially perceive the connection between religion and environmental issues. The aim is to engage students as deeply as possible with each reading, so that they may bring their own creative and critical thought into this new and dynamic field of inquiry.

Inevitably, this collection gives short shrift to many important perspectives on the environmental crisis. In attempting to give global coverage of the world's major value systems, a degree of depth and breadth is necessarily sacrificed. Such are the inevitable pitfalls of undertaking a work of such broad scope. I do not expect my colleagues to be completely satisfied with the anthology I have put together here, but I do hope that they will find it useful. Any comments from the classroom on individual reading selections or on the structure of the anthology as a whole will be taken into consideration for future editions and will be greatly appreciated.

As always, my thanks go first and foremost to my wife, Aphrodite Désirée Navab, for her constant support and companionship that make everything else possible, and to our daughter Shahrzad for making it meaningful. I would like to thank Mary Evelyn Tucker and John Grim for opening the door to me several years ago into the expanding universe of the field they have been calling *religion and ecology,* a field that they themselves have played a major role in shaping. I hope that this book may be a tribute to their unflagging energy in bringing so many people from around the world into this discussion.

I am also grateful to the following friends and colleagues for their critical input on this volume: Christopher Chapple, Loyola Marymount University; Barbara Darling-Smith, Wheaton College; Irene Diamond, University of Oregon; Roger S. Gottlieb, Worcester Polytechnic Institute; Rebecca Kneale Gould, Middlebury College; Stephanie Kaza, University of Vermont; Lynn Ross-Bryant, University of Colorado; Lisa Sideris, Indiana University; Bron Taylor, University of Wisconsin; and Mark Wallace, Swarthmore College. A number of others, including John Cobb, Heather Eaton, and Holmes Rolston, have offered important specific suggestions. The Department of Religion at the University of Florida has been an amazingly supportive environment in which to work and teach, particularly in its encouragement of matters pertaining to environmental values.

I would also like to thank my students at the University of Florida, Columbia University, and Gettysburg College for many fruitful and stimulating discussions on the subject of worldviews and the environment. Finally, I am grateful to Peter Adams, my initial editor at Wadsworth, for the interest and enthusiasm he has shown for this project from the moment that the proposal crossed his desk, and to his successor Steve Wainwright, to Bob Kauser, Beth Zuber, Belinda Krohmer, Gretchen Otto, Jan Six, and everyone else who helped with the production of this book.

Gainesville, Florida
March 5, 2002

Introduction

Understanding Our Place in a Global Age

As we enter the third millennium, it might appear to the uninitiated eye that, overall, things are going rather well. Granted, poverty and injustice continue to exist worldwide, and old perceived "dangers" such as communism have been replaced by new ones such as Islamic fundamentalism. But if one is accustomed to measuring human well-being by the standard of the American way of life, the increasing availability on a global scale of life-enhancing products, such as cellular phones, private cars, televisions, computers, and processed food, and the apparent triumph of market capitalism and the trend toward democratic systems of government throughout much of the world are all positive signs.

Technology and science seem to be advancing by leaps and bounds, at a rate never before seen in human history; indeed, one feels at times overwhelmed by the attempt to keep up with all the latest innovations, although in a way that is also exhilarating. The 281 million humans fortunate enough to live in the United States of America have entered the millennium experiencing what they are told is an unprecedented period of prosperity, with the prospect for all of even better times to come. Against the backdrop of all these hopeful indicators, the voices of modern-day prophets forecasting doom and retribution sound jarring and out of place, even impertinent and, perhaps, unpatriotic.

Nevertheless, a closer look at the available data offers a disturbing alternate reading. Even within the privileged setting of the United States, the average American is working longer hours for less pay than in 1970. We spend more on health care than any other nation, but we are generally much less healthy than in many other societies. We waste more and more hours of the day in mindless and nerve-frazzling commutes to and from our places of work. We have the world's highest prison population. Our impressive economic figures are misleading; the skyrocketing profits that drive them are winding up in the hands of an ever smaller elite, as the gap between rich and poor steadily increases. It seems that the rising economic tide, which we were told throughout the 1980s would raise all boats, has in fact raised only the yachts, leaving the more numerous smaller vessels to flounder and sink. Nor do our economists' figures for the most part take into account the costs passed off as "externalities" onto our society as a whole and onto the ecological systems that support it. Amazingly, negative indicators such as cancer, lawsuits, and pollution even count as *positive* additions to the gross national product, because they generate economic activity.

Of course, the greatest costs of the American way of life are passed off onto the rest of the world. With less than 5 percent of the world's population, the United States consumes more than a third of the planet's resources and is responsible for the largest share of its environmental pollution. If we look more closely at the state of the so-called developing world, the realities are even more dire. China will soon surpass the United States as the world's most polluting nation and shows few signs of willingness to alter its course of industrialization. The Three Gorges Dam project on the Yangtze River, like the similar Narmada River project in India, is displacing millions of people, many of whom are poor and have nowhere to go.

Rising sea levels (a predicted effect of global warming) have put into question the very survival of hundreds of millions of people worldwide who live at or near coastlines. Human-induced climate change engenders ever more dramatic variations in weather patterns, resulting in drought and deluge, crop failures, and water-borne epidemics. Habitat destruction in the name of development has accelerated the rate of species loss and dramatically reduced biodiversity. Industrial agriculture's excessive use of chemicals and preference for monocultures has brought about a decrease in crop resistance to pests and disease and led to the degradation and loss of soil and water resources. On every continent, people living in poverty show the highest rates of population increase, multiplying the effects of their disproportionate suffering from economic deprivation and environmental degradation. For indigenous peoples everywhere, the added threat of global homogenization puts the survival of their own cultural traditions in jeopardy. Are we helpless in the face of all these undesirable results of "progress," or can we choose a better course?

The Significance of Differing Worldviews

In recent years, a growing number of voices from all societies have signaled the deteriorating state of the Earth and the recklessness of the course we are taking. Given the amount of data now available, it is increasingly difficult (and irrational) to maintain that these many problems have arisen by unforeseen accident rather than through the choices we have made and continue to make. Because so many of our choices appear to have been (and continue to be) bad ones, it is helpful to ask on what basis these choices are made.

In order to weigh the different possible outcomes of an action, we must have a *value system* that ranks these outcomes in terms of desirability. A random sample of opinions taken from any set of humans on Earth will likely demonstrate that value systems tend to be more arbitrary than universal. How one sees (or how one's group sees) the world and one's place in it constitutes one's *worldview.* A worldview includes assumptions about what matters and what does not, about what is more and what is less important. Although worldviews are most often deeply informed by what we in the Western tradition call *religions,* some of the assumptions that serve as a foundation for contemporary worldviews also reflect cosmologies and value systems that are not commonly thought of as religious. Thus, whereas Marxism is often characterized as a Judeo-Christian heresy (that is, a challenge arising from within and not from outside of a set of assumptions characteristic of that heritage) and therefore in some sense arguably religious, other worldviews, such as those derived from Darwinism, secular humanism, nationalism, or market capitalism, do not as obviously constitute what most people would recognize as religious systems. Probing more deeply, however, these systems turn out to have much structurally in common with established religions: rituals, dogmas, assumptions accepted on faith, and so on.

Worldviews differ dramatically, and for that reason, consensus between groups or individuals is rare, if not altogether impossible. In a small community, like a family or a village, consensus is often reached through a mutual recognition of shared interest and facilitated by a more or less shared worldview. In a large community, like a nation or the Earth as a whole, the common interest may be obscured by a plurality of issues, so that it is less apparent, and differences in basic assumptions make consensus difficult.

When differences in worldviews are not taken into account, misunderstandings often arise. It is all too easy to assume that one's own observations or interpretations are replicable by *any* thinking person confronted with the same set of data. The elusiveness of agreement on a course of action can then come as a surprise. An understanding of differing worldviews, on the other hand, arms one with the knowledge that the same data can appear differently to different people, depending on which respective worldviews they use to observe and analyze the data. Failing to acknowledge these differences and to accommodate them in the discourse equates to a tyranny of one worldview over others.

Regrettably, such failures have often taken place, as can be observed in the continued imposition of the worldview of post-Enlightenment Western science on peoples around the globe, at the expense of their native ways of knowing. Historian Richard Bulliet has pointed out that the dangerous alternative to a dialogue of civilizations is not, as political scientist Samuel Huntington has claimed, a clash of civilizations, but rather a *monologue* of civilizations.

The argument for a plurality of worldviews is not simply one of justice, however. The modernist vision of technology and progress that has been associated with the West since the industrial revolution has also been the vision that is most responsible for throwing the life-support systems of the entire planet out of balance and that in many ways continues to tolerate our doing so. Yet, if we Westerners would be able to stop shouting our own solutions long enough to hear the many and varied voices that we have these past five centuries been striving to silence, we might be surprised to learn that they are telling us much of value about the world that we either didn't know or had forgotten. We may even find that the solutions to our problems are already available—solutions that have existed for centuries, but the cultural blinders imposed by the dominant ideology have prevented us from seeing them.

But perhaps the best argument for studying a diversity of worldviews is that today, for the first time in the history of our species, we are confronted with a crisis that is in the interest of *all* of us to solve. Never before in the history of humankind has there been a crisis of such global proportions. We are all implicated in the environmental crisis, and we are all affected by it. Our common interest will be best served by making available the broadest array of tools and resources that the human species can muster. The hammers and screwdrivers of our Western worldview won't suffice for this one; we're going to need every tool in the box.

Obstacles to an Ecological Worldview

The historical precedents that have led to the fragmented (and therefore un-ecological) dominant worldview of today are discussed in several of the essays in this volume. No doubt the greatest obstacles impeding serious and meaningful discussion of the environmental crisis are the lack of a strong public conviction that such a crisis even exists and the lack of awareness of its magnitude. It needs to be acknowledged, however, that such public attitudes are not passively inherited, nor do they arise spontaneously or even freely. More and more, the prevailing worldview among the general public is shaped by the multi-billion dollar advertising and public relations industries—hardly disinterested enterprises!—which together probably constitute the most massive and successful apparatus for mind control in the history of the human species (Stauber and Rampton, 1995; Kilbourne, 1999). As economist David C. Korten notes in *When Corporations Rule the World,* "present-day corporations have no reservations about reshaping the values of whole societies to create a homogenized culture of indulgence" (Korten, 2001, p. 152). If, as philosopher David R. Loy suggests in his essay in this volume (see Chapter 2), the dominant religion in the world today is consumerism, then the advertising agencies are its missionary apparatus.

To cite only one of many recent examples of how advertising affects values pertaining to the environment, we may note that within the space of only a few years, the average American car buyer has been persuaded that all-terrain, four-wheel drive sport utility vehicles (SUVs—sometimes and perhaps more accurately referred to as "suburban assault vehicles") are more suitable than normal cars for simple city and highway driving. Relatively few new car buyers question whether the particular capabilities of these behemoths are actually appropriate to their needs or make the connection that by choosing a gas-guzzling class of vehicles craftily exempted from the government's Corporate Average Fuel Economy (CAFE) standards, they are personally helping to dramatically worsen the quality of the air they themselves must breathe, to raise temperatures in the climate they themselves must inhabit, and to reduce the likelihood that pristine natural treasures of their own national patrimony (such as the Arctic National Wildlife Refuge) will be preserved. Ironically, most ads claim that purchasing an SUV will enable consumers to escape into nature—the very freedom and natural beauty that their purchase is helping to destroy! The faith element in some of these advertisements even dares to be explicitly religious, as in a recent Lexus ad that promises to deliver heaven.

The significant point here—all too easily lost amid the seductive deceptions inherent to advertising—is that there are far deeper human values in play than mere status or fantasy fulfillment. The advertising industry's success in clouding the distinction between wants and needs has had devastating effects, not only on our environment and on our physical well-being but on our emotional and spiritual health. Value choices regarding the quality and integrity of the Earth's life-support systems, not to mention our legacy to future generations, are being made less on the basis of ecological realities and issues pertaining to human survival than as a result of the marketing process of manufacturing desires and selling products. Most dangerous of all, these choices are usually being made without public debate or individual reflection, for the process obscures these deeper value issues, often deliberately, to the point where the average consumer–citizen fails to perceive that they are there at all.

A related phenomenon that shapes our environmental values—usually negatively—is the mass media and how they mirror our world back to us through news reporting and entertainment. Our "ecological illiteracy," as educator David Orr calls it (Orr, 1992), is reinforced daily by the fragmented way that events are presented to us, most often as discrete occurrences without any relationship to other events. Although in some cases this may be merely negligence or shallow reporting, in others—for example, when global warming is repeatedly reported without any reference to the burning of fossil fuels—it is hard not to suspect that the connections are being intentionally suppressed. With the increasingly monopolistic control over the media by corporate interests, this kind of unseen censorship is becoming the rule.

Another related problem, richly detailed by Paul and Anne Ehrlich in their book *Betrayal of Science and Reason* (Ehrlich and Ehrlich, 1996), is that a too facile application of the principle of balanced reporting often leads the media to present fringe views (for instance, that global warming may not be anthropogenic) alongside those of mainstream science (that global warming is almost certainly caused by human activity) as if the two perspectives deserved equal weight. The result, therefore, is often not balanced reporting at all but rather the reinforcement of a particular worldview that is compatible with that of the media's corporate sponsors. This worldview, then, disproportionately influences the choices and decisions that we make as a society.

Furthermore, the line between advertising and reporting has become increasingly blurred through certain corporate "greenwashing" efforts, such as propaganda pieces (sometimes, though not always, identified as paid advertisements) appearing on the op-ed pages of major newspapers and magazines and pseudo-scholarly articles prepared in industry-funded think tanks by writers whose credentials are inappropriate or nonexistent. Furthermore, the timber, mining, and petroleum industries have taken to producing school textbooks, presenting their often sanitized views of science, economics, and other disciplines, which are frequently required for adoption as part of "charitable" donations to underfunded school districts. Propaganda campaigns are devised and carried out by highly paid public relations firms on behalf of their industrial clients, masquerading as citizens' groups such as the Wise Use movement or virtually any of the proliferating "Citizens for . . ." or "Citizens Against . . ." lobbies. Such phony grassroots movements have been dubbed "Astroturf movements" by journalists who have worked to expose them. Examples of Orwellian newspeak abound, as anti-environmental organizations adopt seemingly pro-environmental titles and language. The Global Climate Coalition (which seeks to cast doubt on the reality of anthropogenic global warming), the National Wetlands Coalition (which seeks to facilitate oil and gas drilling and development on wetlands), the Water Environment Federation (formerly the Federation of Sewage Works Associations), and the renaming of toxic sludge as "biosolids" (thereby exempting it from some environmental regulations merely because the new word doesn't exist in the written law) are all creations of public relations firms working on behalf of their wealthy corporate clients.

Amid such a confusing array of data, the sources of which are increasingly disguised or obscured, it becomes harder and harder to distinguish between information and disinformation, and even conscientious and well-meaning citizens are hard put to make properly informed choices. Again, it may be helpful in this regard to gain a better understanding of the assumptions on which our worldview is based, where those assumptions originate, and how valid they are.

Worldviews Can Change

It may seem like stating the obvious, but it is good to remind ourselves that worldviews can and do change. For example, many Western Christians today, if they were to undertake a scholarly study of the history of Christianity, might be challenged to find historical precedents for some of their most passionately cherished values and beliefs, and they might likewise find some of the concerns, preoccupations, and practices of earlier Christians to be alien, irrelevant, or even simply wrong. Similarly, contemporary Chinese and Japanese Buddhism have diverged in many respects from their models portrayed in the earliest Indian texts.

To take a more recent example, consider how dramatically certain formerly dominant attitudes in the United States concerning race and gender have changed within only a generation or two. This is not to say that racism and sexism have disappeared, but there are sanctions against them today that could scarcely have been imagined only fifty years ago. Many people now argue that an attitude shift of similar magnitude and speed will be required to face the worsening environmental crisis with any measure of success. Such a huge change often seems desperately unlikely, yet to women suffragists of the early twentieth century or to civil rights workers in the early 1960s, the situation must at times have appeared similarly hopeless.

What is required today—and urgently so—is a level of faith and commitment on a par with those earlier movements. One day, our descendants may regard our dependence on fossil fuels in the same way we regard our ancestors' dependence on slavery: as immoral, lazy, and unnecessary. That would represent a worldview change indeed!

Further Reading

Barnes, Michael, Ed., *An Ecology of the Spirit: Religious Reflection and Environmental Consciousness,* Lanham, Md.: University Press of America, 1990.

Berman, Morris, *The Twilight of American Culture,* New York: W. W. Norton, 2000.

Bowers, C. A., *The Culture of Denial: Why the Environmental Movement Needs a Strategy for Reforming Universities and Public Schools,* Albany, N.Y.: SUNY Press, 1997.

Carroll, John E., Paul Brockelman, and Mary Westfall, Eds., *The Greening of Faith: God, the Environment, and the Good Life,* Hanover, N.H.: University Press of New England, 1997.

Daly, Herman, and John Cobb Jr., *For the Common Good: Redirecting the Economy toward Community, the Environment, and a Sustainable Future,* 2d ed., Boston: Beacon Press, 1994 [1989].

Ehrlich, Paul, and Anne Ehrlich, *Betrayal of Science and Reason,* Washington, D.C.: Island Press, 1996.

Gottlieb, Roger S., *This Sacred Earth: Religion, Nature, Environment,* New York: Routledge, 1996.

Hessel, Dieter T., Ed., *Theology for Earth Community: A Field Guide,* Maryknoll, N.Y.: Orbis, 1996.

Hope, Marjorie, and James Young, *Voices of Hope in the Struggle to Save the Planet,* New York: Apex Press, 2000.

Kilbourne, Jean, *Deadly Persuasion: The Addictive Power of Advertising,* New York: Simon & Schuster, 1999.

Kinsley, David, *Ecology and Religion: Ecological Spirituality in Cross-Cultural Perspective,* Englewood Cliffs, N.J.: Prentice Hall, 1995.

Korten, David, *When Corporations Rule the World,* rev. ed., Bloomfield, Conn.: Kumarian Press, 2001.

Lasn, Kalle, *Culture Jam: The Uncooling of America,* New York: Eagle Brook, 1999.

Leach, William, *Land of Desire: Merchants, Power, and the Rise of a New American Culture,* New York: Pantheon Books, 1993.

Mander, Jerry, *Four Arguments for the Elimination of Television,* New York: William Morrow, 1977.
McCagney, Nancy, *Religion and Ecology,* Oxford, U.K.: Blackwell Publishers, 1999.
Orr, David, *Ecological Literacy,* Albany, N.Y.: SUNY Press, 1992.
———, *Earth in Mind,* Washington, D.C.: Island Press, 1994.
Rappaport, Roy A., *Ritual and Religion in the Making of Humanity,* New York: Cambridge University Press, 1999.
Robb, Carol S., and Carl J. Casebolt, *Covenant for a New Creation: Ethics, Religion and Public Policy,* Maryknoll, N.Y.: Orbis, 1991.
Roszak, Theodore, Ed., *Ecopsychology: Restoring the Earth, Healing the Mind,* San Francisco: Sierra Club Books, 1995.
Schumacher, E. F., *Small Is Beautiful,* New York: Harper, 1973.
Sheldrake, Rupert, *The Rebirth of Nature: The Greening of Science and God,* Rochester, Vt.: Park Street Press, 1994.
Stauber, John, and Sheldon Rampton, *Toxic Sludge Is Good for You: Lies, Damn Lies and the Public Relations Industry,* Monroe, Maine: Common Courage Press, 1995.
Tucker, Mary Evelyn, and John Grim, *Worldviews and Ecology: Religion, Philosophy and the Environment,* Maryknoll, N.Y.: Orbis, 1994.

Part One

Environmental Crisis, Spiritual Crisis

Environmental crises are nothing new. The Earth has seen at least five major extinction events in its long history; the most recent, around 65 million years ago, saw the end of the dinosaurs. Our own species has lived and adapted through ice ages, warming periods, and other types of climate change. Since the invention of agriculture some 10,000 years ago, humans have brought on environmental crises through deforestation (as in ancient China and Greece), salinization and depletion of once fertile lands through irrigated agriculture (as in Mesopotamia, the Indus Valley, and the Sonoran Desert), and other means.

What is new today is the *scale* of the crisis brought on by human activities. For the first time in the history of our species, we are affecting not just isolated parts of the planet but the entire system, everywhere, from the depths of the oceans to the heights of the stratosphere. We have penetrated the densest jungles and the remotest deserts. PCBs produced in North America are found in penguin fat in Antarctica. The French nuclear program has obliterated isolated ecosystems on islands in the South Pacific, rendering them forever uninhabitable. Tropical deforestation, the burning of fossil fuels, and other activities are changing the atmosphere and weather patterns of the entire planet. And scientists worldwide are virtually unanimous in warning us that these changes will affect future generations of humans and all other living species in ways we cannot even predict, though these changes are far more likely to cause problems than to bring benefits.

But most people feel that these are issues of technology and public policy. What have they got to do with religion? The essays in Chapter 1 address this question, taking up the common theme that the environmental crisis is merely a symptom—albeit a highly dramatic one—of a deeper spiritual crisis. The implication is that whatever may occur within the realms of technology and politics, the environmental crisis cannot and will not be resolved unless its spiritual dimensions are addressed. How is it, then, that we have largely failed to see this important connection? The selections in Chapter 2 respond to this question by explaining and deconstructing the modernist paradigm that has given us the fragmented worldview that prevails today.

Chapter 1

The Seeds of a Green Theology

PRIOR TO THE APPEARANCE of Rachel Carson's book *Silent Spring* in 1962, awareness of a developing ecological crisis was rare. Even rarer were those who saw in the impending crisis any ethical or religious aspects. For most people, environmental issues were primarily economic: how to ensure sustained forestry yields, how to avoid a recurrence of the tragic Dust Bowl phenomenon of the 1930s. One of the first Americans to foresee long-term environmental crisis, conservationist Aldo Leopold, remarked in *A Sand County Almanac* (1949) that while successful conservation requires an ethic expanded beyond human concerns, "philosophy and religion have not yet heard of it" (210). Indeed, until quite recently the otherworldly emphasis of Christianity was hardly questioned. As theologian Ludwig Feuerbach put it in the nineteenth century, "nature, the world, has no value, no interest for Christians. The Christian thinks of himself and the salvation of his soul" (Santmire 1985, 3).

Since the Middle Ages, many Christians have equated reverence for nature with paganism. Still in the mid-twentieth century, applying ethical considerations to the nonhuman world would have seemed nonsensical to most Westerners. The extent to which the essays in this chapter departed from the norms of their time can be judged from the response of some conservative Christians to Lynn White Jr.'s essay, "The Historical Roots of Our Ecologic Crisis," labeling him among other things as "a junior Anti-Christ, probably in the Kremlin's pay, bent on destroying the true faith" (Nash 1989, 92). It is remarkable that within the space of only a few decades since these essays were written, environmental values have gone from being classed as irrelevant or threatening to being accepted as mainstream—among theologians at least, if not always among practitioners—within most Christian denominations.

This section begins with what may be the earliest statement on religion and the environment in contemporary language, and it remains one of the strongest. Soil conservationist Walter Lowdermilk's essay "The Eleventh Commandment" was written on the heels of the author's fifteen-month research journey across the Near East and Europe, in which he sought to understand the role of ecological degradation in the decline of the great premodern civilizations. Lowdermilk's characterization of land stewardship as constituting a religious duty must have seemed quaint to many of his contemporaries, but in hindsight he appears to have been sowing the seeds for a major requestioning of modernist notions about agriculture (that is, the idea that the solution to world hunger is the application of industrial technologies to farming). In particular, his remarks about intergenerational justice and the folly of an economy that lives off its capital can now be seen to have been well ahead of their time.

Lowdermilk's essay, which was originally delivered as an address on Jerusalem radio, appeared in 1940, when Palestine was a British protectorate and the United States had not yet entered World War II. Yet apart from a few small details, this insightful and prophetic essay might have been written yesterday. Indeed, despite his professional expertise, even Lowdermilk may have been unable to imagine the magnitude of the devastation that industrial agriculture would yet cause to the soils, water, and air during the decades after his essay was written.

Lutheran theology professor Joseph Sittler's 1954 essay "A Theology for the Earth" was equally revolutionary. In it, Sittler rejected the received dualism by which most Christian theologians had separated humanity from the rest of the divine creation, and he argued instead that God, humans, and nature must be understood as a unity. Sittler developed this concept throughout the rest of his career, going so far in his later writings as to assert that God's purpose is nothing less than *cosmic redemption;* that is, the salvation not only of human souls but of all things in the universe. Sittler's work was a major inspiration behind the establishment in 1963 of the Faith-Man-Nature group, an assembly of theologians and clergy including Richard Baer, Philip Joranson, Conrad Bonifazi, Paul Santmire, Daniel Day-Williams, and others. Through a series of conferences held over the space of ten years, Faith-Man-Nature sought to articulate a Christian basis for environmental ethics.

The contemporary discussion on religion and the environment, which originated in a Western, Christian academic setting, was broadened by the contribution of an American-educated Shi'ite Muslim scholar from Iran, Seyyed Hossein Nasr. In his Rockefeller lectures at the University of Chicago in May 1966, Nasr, trained as a philosopher of science, drew attention to the spiritual origins of environmental abuse. Applying notions of the *perennial philosophy* associated with Fritjof Schuon, Titus Burckhardt, and others (in which timeless truths are seen as being expressed in a variety of historical, cultural, and philosophical traditions), Nasr argued that the imbalances in nature being brought about by human activities were rooted in "the destruction of the harmony between man and God." Modern humans, Nasr believed, had lost the sense of the sacred that enabled them to know their true place in the universe.

In a lecture before the American Academy of Sciences later that same year, historian of technology Lynn White Jr. took a somewhat different approach. He argued that in the case of Western Christianity, it was religion itself that had led to an estrangement between humans and nature, largely through the desacralization of nature in the christianization of medieval Europe. By removing animism's respectful constraints, White reasoned, "Christianity made it possible to exploit nature in a mood of indifference to the feelings of natural objects." Although White unfavorably contrasted the Christian attitude toward nature with that of paganism and some Eastern traditions, his essay called not for an abandoning of Christianity but rather for a more ecological reworking of it, perhaps in accordance with the nonhierarchical example of St. Francis of Assisi.

The Eleventh Commandment

WALTER C. LOWDERMILK

This article was written in the biblical land of Palestine as the author was completing a fifteen months' study of man's stewardship of land down through the ages in fifteen countries of the Old World. Traveling over 30,000 miles by train, airplane, automobile, boat and afoot, Dr. Lowdermilk, as Chief of Research of the Soil Conservation Service, surveyed the land as civilization has used it and passed it down to the present generation. His special interest was human use as it relates to soil erosion, soil and water conservation and flood control. His studies took him into Egypt, Algeria, Tunisia, Libya, Trans-Jordan, Palestine, Lebanon, Syria, Iraq, Italy, France, Holland, Scotland and England. As a background to this survey he previously had made five different explorations into the interior of northern China so that in "The Eleventh Commandment" he writes with a vivid world picture before him of the sins of civilization against Mother Earth.—Editor.

MOSES WAS INSPIRED TO DELIVER TO THE Children of Israel wandering in the wilderness of Sinai the Ten Commandments to regulate man's relation to his Creator and to his fellow men. These guides of conduct have stood the test of time for more than 3,000 years. But Moses, during those forty years in the wilderness, failed to foresee the vital need of the future for an additional Commandment to regulate man's relation and responsibility to Mother Earth, whose cultivation and production must nourish all generations.

If Moses had anticipated what we have seen in north China, Korea, north Africa, Asia Minor, Mesopotamia and our own United States; namely, the wastage of land due to man's practices of suicidal agriculture and the resulting man-made deserts and ruined civilizations, if he had foreseen the impoverishment, revolutions, wars, migrations, and social decadence of billions of peoples through thousands of years and the oncoming desolation of their lands, he doubtless would have been inspired to deliver an "Eleventh" Commandment to complete the trinity of man's responsibilities—to his Creator, to his fellow men, and to Mother Earth. Such a Commandment should read somewhat as follows:

"XI. Thou shall inherit the holy earth as a faithful steward, conserving its resources and productivity from generation to generation. Thou shalt safeguard thy fields from soil erosion, thy living waters from drying up, thy forests from desolation, and protect thy hills from over-grazing by thy herds, so that thy descendants may have abundance forever. If any shall fail in this stewardship of the land thy fruitful fields shall become sterile stony ground and wasting gullies, and thy descendants shall decrease and live in poverty or be destroyed from off the face of the earth."

But no such Commandment has been a part of man's attitude toward his occupation of the earth except in very limited areas. Man has generally been an exploiter, despoiler and destroyer of natural physical, plant and animal resources of the earth. He has brought upon himself the curse of destruction, impoverishment and desolation in vast areas.

Today literally billions of acres of originally productive lands throughout the world bear the curse of unfaithful stewards through the centuries, and their sins of land misuse are visited upon their descendants not only unto the third and fourth generations, but unto the tillers of exploited lands today. This curse upon the land, by generations of ignorance, neglect, lack of forethought, greed, or oppression, represents

Lowdermilk, W. C., "The Eleventh Commandment," *American Forests* 46 (Jan. 1940), pp. 12–15. Reprinted by permission.

a waste to humanity so stupendous as to exceed the comprehension of the human mind.

The world is now more fully occupied by the human race than ever before. Fully two billion souls must find their daily food from the land and waters of the earth. All lands have been occupied or possessed by nations. No free land remains.

In the face of the limited area now available to the human race, the idea that man is still destroying its usefulness by inconsiderate and wasteful methods, comes as a shock to thinking people. If man is making deserts out of productive lands, it is a matter not only of national, but of world-wide concern.

An international tragedy, emphasizing the lack of available lands for exploitation or colonization, is now taking place in the Mediterranean area. Countless refugees from Central Europe, with possessions confiscated, are fleeing from persecutions unparalleled in modern history. Their ships float for weeks, even months, unable to find a refuge. They are turned away from every port; there is no room for them on the land. But the refugees who have gained admittance to Palestine are carrying out the finest example of devotion to and reclamation of land that I have seen on three continents. What they are doing represents the possibilities of these wandering refugees if given a chance.

This overcrowded condition in a world of land hungry nations, whose soils are being impoverished by erosion and misuse while populations increase, demands a new conception of individual and national obligation to the earth and to posterity. When men are unfaithful stewards in their use of the land they bring a curse upon themselves and upon succeeding inhabitants. They find the very source of livelihood washed away, gradually and diabolically impoverishing them. Life becomes such a struggle for mere physical existence as to warp and crush the human spirit, bringing on revolutions, wars, migrations, or political and social decadence. In time the insidious forces of soil erosion and land wastage reach proportions beyond the control and resources of individual tillers of the soil; wearied and discouraged, they migrate, fight, or perish in the wrecks of misused land.

Travels through the morgues of former prosperous areas, now desolate and depopulated, are depressing to one who reads the Macbethan tragedy written far and wide on the landscape. It is appalling to see ruins of once great cities, of civilizations and flourishing cultures, strewn like weather beaten skeletons in the graveyard of their erosion wasted lands. In north Africa we found huge olive presses littering areas where today not an olive tree grows within the circle of the horizon. Stone wine presses were there in great numbers as the only indication of the land use before man-induced erosion had transformed its productivity into desolation. Thistles and thorn-bush are the inheritance of occasional Bedouin Nomads who are ready to fight for every water hole and blade of grass which appears after rains. They pitch their tents on the ruins of magnificent stone structures, whose floors were masterpieces of mosaics, whose porticoes were supported by massive columns and whose courts were beautified by marble statuary. Behind all these ruins is the stirring drama of hunger, invasion, and destruction of life. Death of fertile lands and of its people is a nameless tragedy written across landscape after landscape.

It fills one with consternation to visit regions which have lain desolate and unproductive for centuries with their beautifully cut stone dams completely silted up as at Kurnub, in the Negeb of Palestine, or terraces broken down as above Petra and Jerash, in Trans-Jordan, or aqueducts crumbled as in North Africa. Such areas were abandoned when the erosion wasted soils would no longer feed the inhabitants.

It was astonishing and revealing to find Mesopotamia literally covered with miniature mountain ranges of silt, some ten, twenty and up to fifty feet in height, piled beside the ancient irrigation ditches. This silt, the offspring of erosion in overgrazed watersheds, tells a story of the ceaseless struggles of millions of nameless toilers, before the potentially rich irrigated lands were allowed to revert again to desert, when due to wars or political decadence, the cleaning of silt from the canals was no longer continued. This valley, which formerly maintained from 30,000,000 to 50,000,000 people, supporting renowned civilizations of culture, refinement and learning, now maintains on a very low standard about 5,000,000, whose comforts and accomplishments are a sad commentary on the decadence of cultures.

The Negeb and Sinai region is believed to have supported fully 100,000 inhabitants, but now it scarcely suffices for 2,000 Bedouins. In Trans-Jordan studies by the American School of Oriental Research reveal an extensive ancient agriculture from more than a thousand years B.C. to the 7th century A.D. The loss of fertile soil and the resulting reduction of food supply from the lands of Trans-Jordan are greater than the proportional decrease in population. The food supply and the standards of living and embellished cities among the cultured ancients have little counterpart in the rough stone houses and wretched villages, and in the camps of illiterate Bedouins of today.

The staggering soil wastage of North China is unbelievable. Historical records show that mountain slopes of North China were once heavily forested. Populations increased and exceeded the carrying capacities of alluvial valleys, thereupon farmers cleared away the forests and pushed cultivation higher and higher up the slopes. Trees were cut, the fertile soils were dug up and planted to crops. In from three to twenty years, depending upon gradients of slopes, the soils were washed off and farmers abandoned these fields to clear new lands. finally, this shifting cultivation was pushed up slopes to the summits. Accelerated erosion cut great gullies, and bared the rocky flanks of the mountains. Today, hundreds of millions of acres have been seriously reduced from productivity to barren slopes and labyrinths of gullies. Perennial streams are gone; lowlands have been damaged by debris from the slopes; old irrigation systems have been clogged and put out of use, while floods far away in lowlands and deltas of the rivers rise to higher stages and cause enormous destruction of life and property.

Some students have attributed this disastrous loss of productivity, and desiccation, to adverse climatic change. But throughout northwest China I found temple forests as green emeralds in ugly settings of gully-riddled landscapes, reproducing themselves naturally in the present prevailing climate. In several remote areas I found the diabolic process at work where a virgin forest was being cleared, not for timber, but to get at the soil for food production. The deep soils were sowed to crops; soil erosion soon destroyed the fruitfulness of the sloping lands.

In spite of this vast destruction by increased populations hard pressed for food, the Chinese in the alluvial and rice growing areas are the world's best farmers. For 6,000 years they have farmed these lands which still produce four crops and more yearly. In west and south China, especially, they have level terraced all slopes by infinite labor and patience, and have shown what good stewardship of the land may be.

During five expeditions into North China prior to 1927, my experimental studies determined for the first time comparative rates and amounts of run-off and soil erosion from land within temple forests and adjoining like areas which had been cultivated and denuded. We found that often sixty times as much water, in the form of liquid mud, flowed from cultivated and barren areas as from the forest. The run-off from the latter was scarcely discolored, showing little or no erosion, while the storm run-off on denuded areas tore away the soil, causing permanent loss to the land.

On the basis of these measurements of widespread soil loss by erosion, my estimate is that soil has been removed to an average depth of from twelve to eighteen inches from hundreds of millions of acres of sloping lands in northwest China by man-induced erosion. By such diabolic processes areas formerly capable of supporting great populations in prosperity, now provide meagre existence for lesser numbers.

Until very recently, the desiccation and torrential flooding of inhabited areas was considered an act of a Supreme Being. That man may be a decisive factor to so-called vagaries of many natural phenomena is a recent conception. The rapid growth of this idea may be partly attributed to the fact that America has developed desiccated and unproductive lands more rapidly than ever before in the history of the world. Effects have followed so closely on the heels of causes that the reasons are glaringly obvious to students of land problems. Striking transformations have been visible to eye witnesses within a single generation. We have come to know soil erosion for what it is.

The exploitation of great areas, whether in America, Africa, Australia, or elsewhere, where farmers and stockmen have cleared and grazed new lands at a rate hitherto unknown, tell the same story. Within the memory of the present inhabitants of certain portions of the world, men have witnessed the transformation of fertile plains from luxuriant vegetation, into barren windswept desert-like lands, periodically whirling blizzards of fine soils to parts unknown, and leaving behind sandy hummocks. Stockmen tell of grazing paradises, which within their day have been depleted of vegetation and gouged with gullies. People who paid taxes for the building of irrigation dams and reservoirs have already seen some of them abandoned and useless, while other reservoirs are silting up at an alarming rate.

The vast virgin forests of all these newly exploited continents have largely disappeared under wasteful exploitation. It has been annihilation rather than rational cutting with a planned maintenance of the forest for permanent productivity, and for the control of erosion and flashy storm run-off. In a few countries such as Germany, Italy, and Japan, a high conception of the permanent value of natural resources for future national greatness has been developed as a vital policy of national planning. Germany and Japan are exemplary in forest and land conservation. Italy is rushing her program of conservation and reclamation as a basis for a greater empire.

Fortunately, though belated, a national movement for soil and water conservation has been initiated within the past few years which has aroused the American people to the menace of soil erosion. This enemy of civilizations had already destroyed or seriously impoverished 282,000,000 acres of American lands and impaired the productivity of 775,000,000 acres more. As a result, the United States has begun the largest and most comprehensive movement for soil and water conservation in the history of the world. But only a beginning has been made; it must be continued and enlarged.

If a nation would project itself into the future it must protect its lands from the ravages of soil erosion. When lands are impoverished, peoples lower their standards, both physically and spiritually. Soil erosion expresses itself as a deficiency disease of the land which begets deficiency of food, vitality and higher values for peoples and nations.

As we travel through those lands which have been farmed for centuries, and over which destructive armies have marched and nomads have run their herds, where peoples have risen to varying degrees of culture and have been thrown back again to primitive conditions, we are deeply moved by the futility, wastefulness and ineffable sadness of man's effort to adjust himself to the land. Everywhere in the ancient home of mankind one sees decadence, ruins, fragments of a greater past. It is an arresting tragedy. How can we make people realize that present day agricultural operations have everlasting significance for present and succeeding generations?

Soil erosion, the destroyer of land, has been diagnosed; its processes are known and its control is possible. The hope for the future lies in a realization that man has an obligation born of a higher economics, a moral obligation to bountiful Mother Earth which must nourish all present and future human beings as long as it lasts. It is nothing short of criminal for individuals of one generation to sacrifice the right of future man to survive because of traditions of special privileges to exploit the earth. The present and future well-being of a people calls for long range policies for the maintenance of productive lands and resources. These policies must be founded on what is right for the greatest number of people in the long run. It becomes a matter of social economics and national ethics. Practices of land use which work against the good of the whole must be regulated, whether by law or public opinion, to achieve a dual purpose: to maintain individual initiative, and to safeguard the integrity of resources.

Exploitation is self limiting and suicidal. It uses up the principal and makes no provision for future balancing of the national resources budget. Finally when a nation is reduced to desperation to supply food for its people, it will go to an expense far beyond any tax burden yet known to cultivate diminishing soils. Rock wall terraces in old lands prove the Herculean labor and expense to which people will go to maintain a food supply; the cost of such terracing of steep lands would amount to several thousand dollars per acre at labor wages today. Yet such works were carried out to survive. The economics of survival prevailed.

Land thus becomes, not a commodity, but an integral part of the corporate existence of a nation, even as its people. This principle justifies the safeguarding of soils and the restoration of denuded areas on a basis of national ethics and national economy. Economic considerations of today must be shot through with economics of a higher order to meet problems of sustained land use constructively for generations to follow.

Thus for the very endurance of civilization, an ethical approach to land use as a trusteeship, to be used and handed down in a productive condition to succeeding generations, becomes imperative. Man expresses his moral obligation to posterity as surely through the earth as through his social institutions. The fertile or sterile lands which are passed on to feed future civilizations are, apart from blood descendants, our most direct link with the future. The ethical motivation identifies the interests of the individual with those of one's own family of today and tomorrow, outward through local groups to the nation, and eventually to mankind. It draws support and depth from experiences of the past to long range vision and conservation for the future.

Each nation today needs to have many a Moses of land conservation, to instill in the national consciousness the principle of an Eleventh Commandment to regulate man's relation to the holy earth as a faithful steward, to conserve its productivity from generation to generation. Then fields will be protected from soil erosion, water brooks from drying up, and hills from overgrazing by herds, and future generations may be assured of abundance forever.

With the recognition of man's moral obligation to Mother Earth, each nation must assume the responsibility of taking over the reclamation of waste heritages by unfaithful stewards whose lands have become sterile stones and riddled with wasting gullies, and by intelligent land use bring them back to productivity as much as possible. When its resources are fully husbanded in the advanced knowledge of full conservation, the possibilities of the earth for increased populations are far beyond the imagination of mankind in general. If the vast energies of the human race could be directed toward a goal of conservation instead of destruction and despoliation, the good earth would respond with abundance of food for all.

Only by conservation in the fullest sense, of the basic resources of land, water, and the spirit of peoples, can we maintain the human values of wholesome standards of living, opportunity, freedom, justice, and faith in the destiny of our modern civilization. Only in conservation have we the assurance of continued progress in the search for that something which has led humanity out of the stone age to a modern mechanical age of development. Only by conservation can we be led on to a higher spiritual and physical development which will express itself in stewardship of the earth for the well-being of humanity for all time.

A Theology for Earth

JOSEPH SITTLER

IN MY OWN OPINION AS A TEACHER OF CHRISTian theology, I have felt a deepening uneasiness about that tendency in Biblical Theology, generally known as neo-orthodoxy, whereby the promises, imperatives, and dynamics of the Gospel are declared in sharp and calculated disengagement from the stuff of earthly life. For it is, after all, asserted that "the spirit beareth witness *with* our spirit that we are the children of God." This declaration, to be sure, dare not be understood merely as the Holy Spirit's seconding of the motion of the spirit of man. There are adequate denials of that interpretation throughout the Scriptures, particularly in the Fourth Gospel and in the very Epistle in which this statement occurs. But neither dare this activity of God's Spirit be interpreted as the Spirit bearing witness only *against* us, in total irrelevancy to our spirit. For there is a sort of *negative congruence* between the felt antinomies and ambiguities of man's spirit, and the ingressive activity of the Holy Spirit. The people that walk in darkness behold a great light. That light is not squeezed out of darkness by virtue of determination to transform darkness into light by the sheer alchemy of aspiration and felt need. But darkness *realized* is creative of a receptive theater for the drama of God's salvatory action in Christ; there is a *dynamics* of damnation, a process of perdition that may be used of the Spirit in such a way as to constitute of it a positive preparation for the Gospel.

> Brief glimpses have I had of Heaven
> Through the little holes in hell!

Sittler, Joseph, "A Theology for Earth," *Christian Scholar* 37 (Sept. 1954), pp. 369–374. Edited version.

II

Alongside of this dis-ease with neo-orthodoxy's almost proud repudiation of earth, and the feeling of some profound biblical promise distorted thereby, has gone another—a feeling that earth, fallen, cloven, and sinful—because given of God, capable in spite of all of becoming the cradle in which Christ is laid, is a transparency for the Holy. There is a meaning in the non-human world of nature: reason asserts it and all great art bears it witness. When the artist Cézanne paints a barrel of apples, he shows it bathed with a light which is more like a luminous nimbus than even the softest light of autumn sun. And when Willy Loman in Arthur Miller's play, *Death of a Salesman,* digs and manures and cares for a pathetic patch of sooty earth beside the door of his house in the Bronx, he is seeking for some green and fertile token of meaning in stubborn nature—something that will speak back to the brittle and sterile perdition of his soul. When theology does not acknowledge and soberly come to terms with the covert significance of the natural, the world of nature is not silenced. "Nature is never spent," cries Gerard Manley Hopkins in a famous poem, "There lives the dearest freshness deep-down things."

> The world is charged with the splendor of God
> It will flame out like shining from shock foil!

When Christian orthodoxy refuses to articulate a theology for earth, the clamant hurt of God's ancient creation is not thereby silenced. Earth's voices, recollective of her lost grace and her destined redemption, will speak through one or another form of naturalism. If the Church will not have a theology *for* nature, then irresponsible but sensitive men will act as midwives for nature's unsilenceable meaningfulness, and enunciate a theology of nature. For earth, not man's mother—which is a pagan notion—but, as St. Francis profoundly surmised, man's sister, sharer of his sorrow and scene and partial substance of his joys, unquenchably sings out her violated wholeness, and in groaning and travailing awaits with man the restoration of all things.

This theme—perilous if pursued outside Christian faith—when pursued within the context of the faith makes a man sensitive and restless under flashes of insight which have arisen within the uttered experience of our common life. While I cannot at the moment aspire to shape the systematic structure of Christian meaning out of these insights, I know that I shall as a son of earth know no rest until I have seen how they too can be gathered up into a deeper and fuller understanding of my faith. For these earthly protestations of earth's broken but insistent meaning have about them the shine of the holy, and a certain "theological guilt" pursues the mind that impatiently rejects them.

The inner pattern of this theological guilt is suggested by analogy with the young English poet of the early Nineteenth Century. In passionate pursuit of a proper poetic idiom for the communication of the crowding and impetuous stuff of his perceptions and feelings, the young John Keats played experimentally on the massive organ of his mighty predecessor, John Milton. He tried desperately to shape the inflammable stuff of his abounding genius to the grave and solemn cadences of the older man. The opening lines of *Hyperion* are an instance of how successfully he actually did contrive to make his muse speak Miltonically. But the poem is unfinished because Keats came gradually to know that what was natural to Milton was false to Keats!—that the sonorous measures of the elder poet were alien to the incandescent lyricism of his own inspiration. His moment of liberation and return is marked by the line, "The poetry of earth is never dead . . ."

A second analogy will serve not only to suggest again the claim of earth upon our Christian thought, but will provide a transition to what I want finally to suggest. In his *Goethe's Faust* (Princeton University Press, 1951) Professor Harold Jantz, discussing the Easter-Walk passage in the drama, declares of Faust as follows:

> "He has neglected the tangible and attainable of this earth for the intangible and unattainable. Had he pushed this tendency to the extreme he contemplated, with suicide on that critical night, his failure would have been complete, for the very reason that he failed with the Earth Spirit: he was attempting a direct approach without the necessary understanding which the full experience of life on earth would have given him. As he raises the cup to his lips to force the release of his heaven-tending soul from its earthly limitations so that it might soar up to its desired insights, he hears the first bells of Easter morning and the song, 'Christ is risen'. Christ's greatest triumph

comes with His resumption of His fleshly body; He will once more walk with it on earth, and then ascend with it to heaven, thus completing his victory over eternal death. With Faust's childhood memories and his deep-seated intuitive grasp of Christian symbol, he senses that a violent rejection of the earthly will not bring him the desired spiritual freedom. The Word itself was made flesh and dwelt among us. Man cannot fulfill his divine destiny on earth by a denial of the flesh. It is symbolical that Faust refrains from the folly of seeking to leave the material on the festival day of Christ's reunion with the material. He lowers the cup and says in simple, meaningful conclusion, 'the earth has me again'."

III

There are, in the large, two ways by which man has sought to do justice to the realm of meaning in the natural world; two forms of relationship by which he has sought to come to terms with what he cannot silence.

First, nature can be subsumed under man. Materially, that is, she is reduced to a resource for his needs; spiritually she is envisioned as only an unreplying theatre for his proud and pathetic life. Nature, that is to say, is divested of her own and proper life and is invested with the goods, the values and the ends of man. Her life, infinite in richness and variety, is made a symbolic companion of man's life; and all the moods and shadows, the pride and the pathos, the ambiguity and the sudden delight of man's life is read in her mobile face.

Another effort exists alongside this one and is its exact opposite: Man is subsumed under nature. This relationship gains in persuasiveness when man's spiritual powers, confused by their own perplexities, are conjoined with a fresh mastery of natural forces to serve his clamant lusts. In such a case man abdicates—and celebrates his shameful abdication by perverse delight in that which overcomes him.

Neither of these ways is adequate, and man knows it. For neither one does justice either to the amplitude and glory of man's spirit or to the felt meaningfulness of the world of nature. Christian theology, obedient to the biblical account of nature, has asserted a third possible relationship: that man ought properly stand alongside nature as her cherishing brother, for she too is God's creation and bears God's image.

When, for instance, one reads the 104th Psalm, one becomes conscious that this Psalm speaks of the relationship between man and nature in a quite new way. The poetical naivete of the images must not blind us to the majestic assertions of the song. In this Psalm nothing in the world of man and nothing in the world of nature is either independent or capable of solitary significance. Every upward-arching phenomenon, every smallest thing, is derived from the fountain of life. Light is a garment the deity wears and the heavens a curtain for his dwelling. The heavy voice of the thunder is his rebuke; the springs are his largess to every beast of the field. The trees and the birds, the grass and the cattle, the plump vine and wine that gladdens the heart of man are all bound together in a bundle of grace.

Yet this mighty structure of process and vitality, this complex of given creatureliness in which "the sun knows its time for setting"—all hangs by a slender thread. Natural and mortal life are incandescent with meaning because of their mutual dependence upon the will of the ultimate and Holy one. The Psalm says,

> These all look to thee,
> to give them their food in due season.
> When thou givest to them, they gather it up;
> when thou openest thy hand, they are filled with good things.
> When thou hidest thy face, they are dismayed;
> when thou takest away their breath, they die and return to their dust.
> When thou sendest forth thy Spirit, they are created;
> and thou renewest the face of the ground.

Here is a holy naturalism, a matrix of grace in which all things derive significance from their origin, and all things find fulfillment in praise. Man and nature live out their distinct but related lives in a complex that recalls the divine intentions as that intention is symbolically related on the first page of the Bible. Man is placed, you will recall, in the garden of earth. This garden he is to tend as God's other creation—not to use as a godless warehouse or to rape as a tyrant.

IV

Today, man is no longer related to nature in God's intended way. Nor can he from within himself find his way to the blasted garden of joy. That, fundamentally, is why he plunders what he ought to tend; why he finds in nature sardonic images of his own perversion, and at the same time cannot avert his eyes from his violated sister who is heard groaning "in pain and travail until now."

"By the Word of the Lord," so we read, "the heavens were made." But this Word ignored is not thenceforth silent; this Word repudiated is not therefore quiescent. Is it possible that the Creator-Word, by whom all things were made, should be driven from his field by us? The central assertion of the Bible is that he has not been so driven, but rather drives, loves and suffers his world toward restoration. It is of the heart of the Christian faith that this mighty, living, acting, restoring Word actually identified himself with his cloven and frustrated creation which groans in travail. "The Word became flesh and dwelt among us." To what end? That the whole cosmos in its brokenness—man broken from man, man in solitude and loneliness broken from Holy Communion with his soul's fountain and social communion with his brother—might be restored to wholeness, joy and lost love.

One finds nowhere in the Bible that strange assertion which one hears almost everywhere else—that God is concerned to save men's souls! How richly, rather, is restoration there presented in terms of men's material involvement in the world of nature. Real blindness is given sight, real hands of helplessness are restored, real death is overcome, real legs enable a paralytic to walk. God is the undeviating materialist. "He likes material; he invented it." I know no soul save an embodied soul, I have no body save this one born of other bodies, and there is no such thing as a man outside the created context of other men; therefore it is written that "God so loved the world."

God—man—nature! These three are meant for each other, and restlessness will stalk our hearts and ambiguity our world until their cleavage is redeemed. What a holy depth of meaning lies waiting for our understanding in that moment portrayed on the last evening of Christ's life: "And he took bread, and when he had given thanks he broke it and gave to them, saying, 'This is my body.' . . . Likewise also the wine . . . 'this cup is the new covenant in my blood.'"

Here in one huge symbol are God and man and nature together. Bread and wine, the common earthy stuff of our life when we have it, and of death when we've lost it. Both in the hands of the restoring God—man!

The problem of material is not a material problem, for man is in it, and he complicates every problem. The problem of enough to eat is not ultimately an economic problem. For as man confronts the marvelous richness of the earth he can use these riches or abuse them. Which of these he chooses is a matter not soluble by mere planning. For there will never be enough for both love and lust!

V

The largest, most insistent, and most delicate task awaiting Christian theology is to articulate such a theology for nature as shall do justice to the vitalities of earth and hence correct a current theological naturalism which succeeds in speaking meaningfully of earth only at the cost of repudiating specifically Christian categories. Christian Theology cannot advance this work along the line of an orthodoxy—neo or old—which celebrates the love of heaven in complete separation from man's loves in earth, abstracts commitment to Christ from relevancy to those loyalties of earth which are elemental to being. Any faith in God which shall be redemptive and regenerative in actuality dare not be alien to the felt ambiguities of earth or remain wordless in the resounding torments of history and culture. For the earth is not merely a negative illustration of the desirability of heaven!

Such positive theological work, it seems to me, must operate with the event of the Incarnation with a depth and amplitude at least as wide and far ranging and as grand as that of the New Testament. We may not be able to go beyond Ephesians, Colossians, and the eighth chapter of Romans; but we dare not stop short of the incomparable boldness of those utterances. For here heaven and earth are held together in the incarnate Christ; here the Scriptures sing both ends of the arc of the Christ-event in ontological footings.

The Incarnation has commonly received only that light which can be reflected backward upon it from Calvary. While to be sure, these events cannot be separated without the impoverishment of the majesty of the history of redemption, it is nevertheless proper to suggest that our theological tendency to declare them only in their concerted meaning *at the point of fusion* tends to disqualify us to listen to the ontological-revelational overtones of the Incarnation.

The Problem

SEYYED HOSSEIN NASR

OF LATE, NUMEROUS STUDIES HAVE BEEN made concerning the crisis brought about by modern science and its applications, but few have sought the profound intellectual and historical causes that are responsible for this state of affairs. When invited to deliver a series of lectures in this University on the meaning of war and struggle for the preservation of human dignity under conditions which threaten human existence itself, we felt that it would be more appropriate to deal with principles and causes rather than contingencies and effects, one of which is the problem of moral action on the social and human level, together with the possible consequence of war which modern technology and science have made total. We hope, therefore, to state the problem which has resulted from the encounter of man and nature today, then to seek the underlying causes that have brought this condition about and to cite the principles whose neglect have made the modern crisis so acute.

Today, almost everyone living in the urbanized centres of the Western world feels intuitively a lack of something in life. This is due directly to the creation of an artificial environment from which nature has been excluded to the greatest possible extent. Even the religious man in such circumstances has lost the sense of the spiritual significance of nature.[1] The domain of nature has become a 'thing' devoid of meaning, and at the same time the void created by the disappearance of this vital aspect of human existence continues to live within the souls of men and to manifest itself in many ways, sometimes violently and desperately. Furthermore, even this type of secularized and urbanized existence is itself threatened, through the very domination of nature that has made it possible, so that the crisis brought about through the encounter of man and nature and the application of the modern sciences of nature to technology has become a matter of common concern.[2]

Despite all the official clamour about the ever increasing domination over nature, and the so-called progress which is supposed to be its economic concomitant, many realize in their hearts that the castles they are building are on sand and that there is a disequilibrium between man and nature that threatens all man's apparent victory over nature.

The dangers brought about by man's domination over nature are too well known to need elucidation. Nature has become desacralized for modern man, although this process itself has been carried to its logical conclusion only in the case of a small minority.[3] Moreover, nature has come to be regarded as something to be used and enjoyed to the fullest extent possible. Rather than being like a married woman from whom a man benefits but also towards whom he is responsible, for modern man nature has become like a prostitute—to be benefited from without any sense of obligation and responsibility toward her. The difficulty is that the condition of prostituted nature is becoming such as to make any further enjoyment of it impossible. And, in fact, that is why many have begun to worry about its condition.

It is precisely the 'domination of nature' that has caused the problem of over-population, the lack of 'breathing space', the coagulation and congestion of city life, the exhaustion of natural resources of all kinds, the destruction of natural beauty, the marring of the living environment by means of the machine and its products, the abnormal rise in mental illnesses and a thousand and one other difficulties some of which appear completely insurmountable.[4] And finally, it is the same 'domination of nature', limited to external nature and coupled with giving complete freedom to the animal nature within man, that has made the problem of war so crucial, war which seems unavoidable, yet because of its total and almost 'cosmic' nature brought about by modern technology, must be avoided.

The sense of domination over nature and a mate-

Nasr, Seyyed Hossein, excerpts from "The Problem," in *Man and Nature: The Spiritual Crisis in Modern Man,* Chicago, IL: Kazi Publications, 1997, pp. 17–24, 31–38. Edited version. Reprinted by permission of the author.

rialistic conception of nature on the part of modern man are combined, moreover, with a lust and sense of greed which makes an ever greater demand upon the environment.[5] Incited by the elusive dream of economic progress, considered as an end in itself, a sense of the unlimited power of man and his possibilities is developed, together with the belief, particularly well developed in America, of boundless and illimitable possibilities within things, as if the world of forms were not finite and bound by the very limits of those forms.[6]

Man wants to dominate nature not only for economic motives but also for a 'mystique' which is a direct residue of a one-time spiritual relation *vis-à-vis* nature. Men no longer climb spiritual mountains—or at least rarely do so. They now want to conquer all mountain peaks.[7] They wish to deprive the mountain of all its majesty by overcoming it—preferably through the most difficult line of ascent. When the experience of flight to the heavens, symbolized in Christianity by the spiritual experience of the *Divine Comedy* and in Islam by the nocturnal ascension (*al-mi'râj*) of the Prophet Muhammad (upon whom be peace) is no longer available to men, there remains the urge to fly into space and conquer the heavens. There is everywhere the desire to conquer nature, but in the process the value of the conqueror himself, who is man, is destroyed and his very existence threatened.

Rather than man deciding the value of science and technology, these creations of man have become the criteria of man's worth and value.[8] Practically the only protest that is heard is that of the conservationists and other lovers of nature. Their voice, although of much value, is not fully heard because their arguments are often taken as being sentimental rather than intellectual. Well-known theologians and philosophers have for the most part remained silent or have bent backwards in order to avoid offending the prevailing scientific mood of the day. Only rarely has any voice been raised to show that the current belief in the domination of nature is the usurpation, from the religious point of view, of man's role as the custodian and guardian of nature.[9]

The sciences of nature themselves, which are in one sense the fruit, and in another the cause of the present crisis of man's encounter with nature, have themselves, through a gradual process which we shall examine later, become secularized. And this secularized knowledge of nature divorced from the vision of God in nature has become accepted as the sole legitimate form of science.[10] Moreover, due to the distance separating the scientist from the layman a major distortion and discrepancy has been created between scientific theories and their vulgarization upon which their supposed theological and philosophical implications are too often based.[11]

Altogether one can say that the problem concerns both the sciences and the means whereby they are understood, interpreted and applied. There are crises in the domains of both understanding and application. The power of reason given to man, his *ratio,* which is like the projection or subjective prolongation of the intellect or the *intellectus,* divorced from its principle, has become like an acid that burns its way through the fibre of cosmic order and threatens to destroy itself in the process. There is nearly total disequilibrium between modern man and nature as attested by nearly every expression of modern civilization which seeks to offer a challenge to nature rather than to co-operate with it.

That the harmony between man and nature has been destroyed, is a fact which most people admit. But not everyone realizes that this disequilibrium is due to the destruction of the harmony between man and God.[12] It involves a relationship which concerns all knowledge. And in fact the modern sciences themselves are the fruit of a set of factors which, far from being limited to the domain of nature, concern all Western man's intellectual and religious heritage. Because of this, or often as a reaction against it, the modern sciences have come into being. That is the reason why it is necessary to begin our analysis by turning firstly to the natural sciences and the views held concerning their philosophical and theological significance, and then to the limitations inherent within them which are responsible for the crisis that their application, and the acceptance of their world view, have brought about for modern man.

It must never be forgotten that for non-modern man—whether he be ancient or contemporary—the very stuff of the Universe has a sacred aspect. The cosmos speaks to man and all of its phenomena contain meaning. They are symbols of a higher degree of reality which the cosmic domain at once veils and reveals. The very structure of the cosmos contains a spiritual message for man and is thereby a revelation coming from the same source as religion itself.[13]

Both are the manifestations of the Universal Intellect, the Logos, and the cosmos itself is an integral part of that total Universe of meaning in which man lives and dies.[14]

In order for the modern sciences of nature to come into being, the substance of the cosmos had first to be emptied of its sacred character and become profane. The world view of modern science, especially as propagated through its vulgarization, itself contributed to this secularization of nature and of natural substances. The symbols in nature became facts, entities in themselves that are totally divorced from other orders of reality. The cosmos which had been transparent thus became opaque and spiritually meaningless—at least to those who were totally immersed in the scientific view of nature—even if individual scientists believed otherwise. The traditional sciences such as alchemy, which can be compared to the celebration of a cosmic mass, became reduced to a chemistry in which the substances had lost all their sacramental character. In the process, the sciences of nature lost their symbolic intelligibility, a fact that is most directly responsible for the crisis which the modern scientific world view and its applications have brought about.[15]

The quantitative character of modern science must be pointed out in particular because it exists as a general tendency which seeks as an ideal the reduction of all quality to quantity and all that is essential in the metaphysical sense to the material and substantial.[16] The suffocating material environment created by industrialization and mechanization, which is felt by all who live in large urban centres of today, is a consequence of the purely material and quantitative nature of the sciences whose applications have made industrialization possible. Moreover, due to the lack of a total world view of a metaphysical nature into which the modern sciences could be integrated, the symbolic aspect of number and quantity is itself forgotten. The Pythagorean-Platonic number theory has been made to appear, like so many other traditional sciences, as an old wives' tale.

The quantitative sciences of nature which, moreover, are a possible and in the appropriate circumstances legitimate science, come in fact to be the only valid and acceptable sciences of nature. All other knowledge of the natural and cosmic orders is deprived of the status of science and relegated to the rank of sentimentality or superstition. It seems as if modern science has made a condition of its acceptance the rejection of knowledge about the root of existence itself, although again many scientists as individuals may not share this view.[17] The total impact of modern science on the mentality of men has been to provide them with a knowledge of the accidents of things, provided they are willing to forgo a knowledge of the substance that underlies all things. And it is this limitation which threatens the most dire circumstances for man as an integral being.[18]

The very restrictive outlook connected with modern science makes the knowledge of cosmology in the true sense impossible in the matrix of the modern scientific world view. Cosmology is a science dealing with all orders of formal reality, of which the material order is but one aspect. It is a sacred science which is bound to be connected to revelation and metaphysical doctrine in whose bosom alone it becomes meaningful and efficacious. Today there is no modern cosmology, and the use of the word is really a usurpation of a term whose original meaning has been forgotten.[19] A cosmology which is based solely on the material and corporeal level of existence, however far it may extend into the galaxies, and which is moreover based on individual conjectures that change from day to day, is not real cosmology. It is a generalized view of a terrestrial physics and chemistry, and as has been pointed out by certain Christian theologians and philosophers, it is really devoid of any direct theological significance unless it be by accident.[20] Moreover, it is based on a material physics which tends to ever greater analysis and division of matter with the ideal of reaching the 'ultimate' matter at the basis of the world, an ideal however, which can never be attained because of the ambiguity and unintelligibility lying within the nature of matter and the border of chaos separating formal matter from that 'pure matter' which medieval philosophers called *materia prima*.[21]

The disappearance of a real cosmology in the West is due in general to the neglect of metaphysics, and more particularly to a failure to remember the hierarchies of being and of knowledge. The multiple levels of reality are reduced to a single psycho-physical domain, as if the third dimension were suddenly to be taken out of our vision of a landscape. As a result, not only has cosmology become reduced to the particular sciences of material substances, but in a more general sense the tendency of reducing the higher to the lower, and conversely trying to make the greater come into being out of the lesser, has become widely prevalent. With the destruction of all notion of hierarchy in reality, the rapport between degrees of knowledge and the correspondence between various levels of reality upon which the ancient and medieval sciences were based have disappeared, causing these sciences to appear as superstition (in the etymological sense of this word) and as something whose principle or basis has been destroyed or forgotten.

Metaphysics is similarly reduced to rationalistic philosophy, and this philosophy itself has become gradually the ancillary of the natural and mathematical sciences, to the extent that some modern schools consider the only role of philosophy to be to elucidate the methods and clarify the logical consistencies of the sciences. The independent critical function which reason should exercise *vis-à-vis* science, which is its own creation, has disappeared so that this child of the human mind has itself become the judge of human values and the criterion of truth. In this process of reduction in which the independent and critical role of philosophy has itself been surrendered to the edicts of modern science, it is often forgotten that the scientific revolution of the seventeenth century is itself based upon a particular philosophical position. It is not *the* science of nature but *a* science making certain assumptions as to the nature of reality, time space, matter, etc.[22] But once these assumptions were made and a science came into being based upon them, they have been comfortably forgotten and the results of this science made to be the determining factor as to the true nature of reality.[23] That is why it is necessary to turn, albeit briefly, to the view of modern scientists and philosophers of science as to the significance of modern science especially physics in determining the meaning of the total nature of things. Whether we like it or not, it is precisely such views that determine much of the modern conception of nature accepted by the general public, and they are thereby important elements in the general problem of the encounter of man and nature.

. . . In as much as we are concerned with the spiritual aspect of the crisis of the encounter between man and nature, it is also of importance to discuss briefly the views of Christian theologians and thinkers on this subject, in addition to those of the philosophers of science noted above. It must be said at the outset that there has been singular neglect of this domain among Christian theologians, particularly Protestants. Most of the leading theological trends have dealt with man and history, and have concentrated on the question of the redemption of man as an isolated individual rather than on the redemption of all things. The theology of P. Tillich is centred on the problem of ultimate concern with the ground of being that encompasses the sacred and the profane and turns more to the existential role of man in history and his position as an isolated being before God rather than as a part of creation and within the cosmos itself considered as a hierophany. Even more removed from this question are the theologians like K. Barth and E. Brunner, who have drawn an iron wall around the world of nature.[24] They believe that nature cannot teach man anything about God and is therefore of no theological and spiritual interest.[25] As for the de-mythologizers like R. Bultmann, rather than penetrate into the inner meaning of myth as symbol of a transcendent reality which concerns the relation between man and God in history as well as in the cosmos, they, too, neglect the spiritual significance of nature, and reduce it to the status of a meaningless artificial background for the life of modern man.

Nevertheless there are a few who have realized the importance of nature as a background for religious life, and a religious science of nature as a necessary element in the integral life of a Christian.[26] They have understood the need to believe that the creation displays the mark of the Creator in order to be able to have a firm faith in religion itself.[27]

The day has passed when it was believed that science, in its ever continuing onward march pushes back the walls of theology, whose immutable principles appear from the view of a sentimental dynamism as rigid and petrified dogma, at least in many leading academic circles.[28] There are scientists who realize and respect the importance of the discipline of theology, while certain Christian theologians have asserted that the modern scientific view, because of its break with the closed mechanistic conception of classical physics, is more congenial to the Christian point of view.[29] This argument has in fact been advanced in so many quarters that people have begun to forget that the secularized world-view of modern science, once taken out of the hand of the professional scientist and presented to the public, places a great obstacle before the religious understanding of things.

Although in a sense the very destruction of a monolithic, mechanistic conception of the world has given a certain 'breathing space' to other views, the popularization of scientific theories and technology today has deprived men even more of a direct contact with nature and a religious conception of the world. 'Our Father which art in heaven' becomes incomprehensible to a person deprived by industrialized society of the patriarchal authority of a father and for whom heaven has lost its religious significance and ceased to be any 'where', thanks to flights of cosmonauts. It is only with respect to the theoretical relation between science and religion that one can say in a way that the modern scientific view is less incompatible with Christianity than the scientific views of the eighteenth and nineteenth centuries.

Not forgetting the transient character of scientific theories, certain other Christian writers have warned against the facile and all too easy harmony between religion and science in which superficial comparisons are made between the two domains. All too often the principles and tenets of religion, which are transcendent and immutable, are presented as being in conformity with the latest findings of science, again following the well-known tendency of reducing the greater to the lesser.[30] Furthermore, by the time this process of conforming theology to current scientific theories is carried out and religion is made 'reasonable' by appearing as 'scientific', the scientific theories themselves have gone out of vogue. In this domain one can at least say that among a small but significant group there is a reaction against the simplistic attitude prevalent in certain quarters in the nineteenth century, although on the mass level there is much more retreat of religion before what appears as scientific than in any previous age.

Yet other writers have emphasized the close relation between Christianity and science by pointing out that many of the fundamental assumptions of science such as belief in the orderliness of the world, the intelligibility of the natural world and the reliability of human reason depend upon the religious and more particularly Christian view of a world created by God in which the Word has become incarnated.[31] Some have related the problem of unity and multiplicity in nature to the Trinity in Christianity[32] while others have insisted that only Christianity has, in a positive sense, made science possible.[33] But in all such cases one wonders at the total validity of this assertion if one takes into consideration the existence of sciences of nature in other civilizations (particularly Islam). These sciences insist on unity rather than trinity. Further, we must consider the havoc modern science and its applications have brought about within the world of Christianity itself.

More specifically, the relation between subject and object as held in modern science is said to derive from the relation between the spirit and the flesh in Christianity.[34] The order of the Universe is identified with the Divine Mind,[35] and the scientist is said to be discovering the mind of God in his scientific pursuits.[36] Scientific method itself has been called a Christian method of discovering God's mind.[37]

Of more central concern to our problem is the attempt of a few theologians, moving against the tide of the general modern trends of theology, to bring to life once again the sacramental character of all creation and to return to things the sacred nature of which recent modes of thought have deprived them. The importance of the created world as a sacrament revealing a dimension of religious life has been reasserted by this group,[38] and the forgotten truth that from the Christian point of view incarnation implies the sacramental nature of material things, without in any way destroying the causal nexus between things, has already been pointed out.[39] It has been reaffirmed that the only relation between the spiritual and the material which can in a deep sense be called Christian[40] is one in which the outward and material aspect of things acts as a vehicle for the inward, spiritual grace indwelling in all things, by virtue of their being created by God.[41] In order for God to be Creator and also eternally Himself, His Creation must be sacramental both to His creatures and to Himself.[42]

In the writings of this small group of theologians who have devoted some attention to the question of man's relation with nature, the revealed aspect of all the Universe has been brought out. If creation were not in some way revealed there would be no revelation possible.[43] Likewise, all creation must somehow share in the act of redemption in the same way as all creation is affected by the corruption and sin of man as asserted by St Paul in the *Epistle to the Romans* (Chapter VIII). The total salvation of man is possible when not only man himself but all creatures are redeemed.[44]

This point of view propounded above, which could have the profoundest significance in modern man's relation to nature, has however, rarely been understood and accepted. Even those who have devoted themselves most to a sacramental theology have, for the most part, failed to apply it to the world of nature. As a result, those who still feel and understand the meaning of the sacred, at least in religious rites, fail to extend it to the realm of nature. The sacramental or symbolic view of nature—if we understand symbol in its true sense—has not been in general propagated by modern schools of Christian theology. In fact the reverse holds true. In as much as the prevalent point of emphasis has been the redemption of the individual and disregard for the 'redemption of creation', most of modern religious thought has helped to secularize nature and has bent backwards to surrender to the dicta of science in the natural domain.

In discussing views of Christian authors on the sciences of nature, one cannot fail to mention the school of Neo-Thomism which has challenged the claim to totality and exclusiveness of scientific methods and has applied rigorous logical criteria to them.[45] The main tenet of the Neo-Thomist position has been to show that science is limited by its methods and cannot apply itself to a solution of metaphysical problems. It is not permissible to use the same methods and to proceed in the same manner in the domains of science and metaphysics. For, to quote St Thomas, 'It is a sin against intelligence to want to proceed in an identical manner in the typically different domains—physical, mathematical, and metaphysical—of speculative knowledge'.[46]

The knowledge of the whole Universe does not lie within the competence of science[47] but of metaphysics. Moreover, the principles of metaphysics remain independent of the sciences and cannot in any way be disproved by them.[48] One must realize the different forms of knowledge and place each within its own bounds. In fact the most important result of the Neo-Thomist view has not been so much to provide a new spiritual interpretation of nature and to return to it its sacred and symbolic character as to provide a philosophy of nature for science and to show through philosophical arguments the limitations existing within the scientific approach. It has been to safeguard the independence of theology and metaphysics from experimental sciences.[49] Whatever its shortcomings through being too rationalistic and not symbolic and metaphysical enough in the true sense, this school has at least affirmed and asserted a simple truth which is being forgotten more and more today, namely that the critical faculty of intelligence and of reason cannot be surrendered to the findings of an experimental science which that reason itself has made possible.

If one glances over the whole field of the relation between science, philosophy and theology, as we have done in a scanty and summary fashion, one becomes immediately aware of the lack of common ground between these three domains. Metaphysical doctrine, or that gnosis which alone can be the meeting ground of science and religion, has been forgotten, and as a result the hierarchy of knowledge has crumbled into a confused mass in which the segments are no longer organically united. Whereas philosophy has either recapitulated and surrendered itself to science or reacted totally against it, theology has either refused to consider the domain of nature and its sciences or has in turn adopted step by step the findings and methods of the sciences with the aim of creating a synthesis. This has often been as shallow as it has been transient. Moreover, a misunderstanding between the modern sciences of nature and a knowledge of the natural order which is of theological and spiritual significance has led to endless controversies and misunderstandings.[50]

For this very reason, and also despite all the activity in the natural sciences, there is today no philosophy of nature. While the medieval science of physics, which was indeed a natural philosophy, has become one science among other natural sciences, nothing has taken its place as the background of all the particular sciences of nature. Although the need for a philosophy of nature is felt even by some physicists (and many turn to the history of science precisely in order to receive inspiration for methods and philosophies which could be of aid in modern science), there still exists no generally accepted philosophy of nature, despite the philosophies proposed by several modern thinkers such as Whitehead and Maritain.[51]

One can say with even greater regret that there is also no theology of nature which could satisfactorily provide a spiritual bridge between man and nature. Some have realized the necessity of harmonizing Christian theology and natural philosophy to provide a theology of nature,[52] but such a task has not been accomplished, and cannot be so, until theology is understood in the intellectual light of the early

Church Fathers, the Christian metaphysicians of the Middle Age, such as Erigena and Eckhart, or in the sense of the theosophy of Jacob Böhme. As long as by theology is understood a rational defence of the tenets of the faith, there is no possibility of a real theology of nature, no way of penetrating into the inner meaning of natural phenomena and making them spiritually transparent. Only the intellect can penetrate inwardly; reason can only explain.

This lack of sense of the transparency of things, of intimacy with nature as a cosmos that conveys to man a meaning that concerns him, is of course due to the loss of the contemplative and symbolist spirit which sees symbols rather than facts. The near disappearance of gnosis, as understood in its true sense as a unitive and illuminative knowledge, and its replacement by sentimental mysticism and the gradual neglect of apophatic and metaphysical theology in favour of a rational theology, are all effects of the same event that has taken place within the souls of men. The symbolic view of things is for the most part forgotten in the West and survives only among peoples of far away regions,[53] while the majority of modern men live in a de-sacralized world of phenomena whose only meaning is either their quantitative relationships expressed in mathematical formulae that satisfy the scientific mind, or their material usefulness for man considered as a two legged animal with no destiny beyond his earthly existence. But for man as an immortal being they bear no direct message. Or rather it can be said that they still bear the message but there is no longer the appropriate faculty to decipher it.

There seems to be in this movement from the contemplative to the passionate, from the symbolist to the factual mentality, a fall in the spiritual sense corresponding to the original fall of man. In the same way that Adam's fall from Paradise implies that creation, which had until then been innocent and friendly and also inward, thus became hostile and also externalized, so does the change of attitude between pre-modern and modern man *vis-à-vis* nature imply a further stage in this alienation. The I-thou relation is destroyed to become the I-it and no amount of the pejorative use of such terms as 'primitive', 'animistic' or 'pantheistic' can make one forget the loss implied in this change of attitude. In this new fall man has lost a paradise as a compensation for which he has discovered a new earth full of apparent but illusory riches.[54] He has lost the paradise of a symbolic world of meaning to discover an earth of facts which he is able to observe and manipulate at his will. But in this new role of a 'deity upon earth' who no longer reflects his transcendent archetype, he is in dire danger of being devoured by this very earth over which he seems to wield complete dominion unless he is able to regain a vision of that paradise he has lost.

For meanwhile the totally quantitative conception of nature which thanks to technology has begun to dominate all of life is gradually displaying cracks in its walls. Some are joyous about this event and believe it is the occasion of a reassertion of the spiritual view of things. But as a matter of fact most often the cracks are filled by the most negative 'psychic residues' and the practices of the 'occult sciences' which, once cut off from the grace of a living spirituality, become the most insidious of influences and are much more dangerous than materialism.[55] They are the water that dissolves rather than the earth that solidifies. Yet, these are not the 'waters above' but the 'waters below', to use the very significant Biblical symbolism. It is far from accidental that in most pseudo-spiritualist circles much is made of the synthesis of science and religion into a 'new spiritual order' as if man could create a ladder to heaven by himself, or, to speak in Christian terms, as if man could unite with the Christ nature unless the Christ nature had itself become man.

What is needed is a filling of the cracks in the wall of science by the light from above not by the darkness from below. Science must be integrated into a metaphysics from above so that its undisputed facts could also gain a spiritual significance.[56] And because it is imperative, the need for such an integration is felt in many quarters[57] and many people with a degree of perspicacity look beyond the dangerous psycho-physical syntheses of today to which is usually added a spice of pseudo-Oriental 'wisdom'. A real synthesis would remain true to the deepest principles of the Christian revelation and the most rigorous demands of intelligence. This task can only be accomplished by re-discovering the spiritual meaning of nature. This discovery is itself dependent upon the remembrance of the most intellectual and metaphysical aspects of the Christian tradition which have been forgotten in so many circles today, along with awareness of the historical and intellectual causes that have brought about the present impasse. That is why we must first turn to consider certain phases in the history of science and philosophy in the West, as it is related to the Christian tradition, before turning to a discussion of metaphysical and cosmological principles in this tradition and in the traditions of the East—traditions which can act as an aid to recollection for those within the world view of Christianity.

NOTES

1. 'The cosmic liturgy, the mystery of nature's participation in the Christological drama, have become inaccessible to Christians living in a modern city. The religious experience is no longer open to the cosmos. In the last analysis, it is a strictly private experience; salvation is a problem that concerns man and his god; at most, man recognizes that he is responsible not only to God but also to history. But in these man-God-history relationships there is no place for the cosmos. From this it would appear that, even for a genuine Christian, the world is no longer felt as the work of God.' M. Eliade, *The Sacred and the Profane, the Nature of Religion,* New York, 1959, p. 179.

2. Many criticisms have appeared during the past two or three decades by naturalists, philosophers, social scientists, architects and men of other professions concerning the danger of domination over nature for man himself. The writings of Lewis Mumford and Joseph Wood Krutch represent two well known, but very different kinds of this type of literature which in a way echo in quite altered conditions the concerns of William Morris and John Ruskin a century ago.

3. 'Experience of a radically desacralized nature is a recent discovery; moreover, it is an experience accessible only to a minority in modern societies, especially to scientists. For others, nature still exhibits a charm, a mystery, a majesty in which it is possible to decipher traces of ancient religious values.' Eliade, *op. cit.,* p. 151.

4. 'In a certain, external sense it may be said that the great social and political evil of the West is mechanization, for it is the machine which most directly engenders the great evils from which the world today is suffering. The machine is, generally speaking, characterized by the use of iron, of fire and of invisible forces. To talk about a wise use of machines, of their serving the human spirit, is utterly chimerical. It is in the very nature of mechanization to reduce men to slavery and to devour them entirely, leaving them nothing human, nothing above the animal level, nothing above the collective level. The kingdom of the machine followed that of iron, or rather gave to it its most sinister expression. Man, who created the machine, ends by becoming its creature.' F. Schuon, *Spiritual Perspectives and Human Facts* (trans. D. M. Matheson), London, 1953, p. 21.

5. 'What needs to be understood, however, is that happiness depends on the preliminary acceptance of a number of unpalatable facts. Chief among those facts is the practical knowledge, as distinct from any theory, of what makes for happiness. This knowledge is especially hard to come by for us of the West, conditioned as we are to making large demands on our environment, and to entertain the illusion that to raise the standard of living is equivalent to nourishing the human spirit.' Dom A. Graham, *Zen Catholicism, a Suggestion,* New York, 1963, p. 38. The same applies today to all of those affected by the psychosis of progress on whatever continent they might live.

6. See J. Sittler, *The Ecology of Faith,* Philadelphia, 1961, p. 22. The same author writes (p. 23): 'The entire experience of the peoples of America has created and nurtured a world view which stands over against the world view of the Bible in sharpest contrast possible.'

7. On this question see the masterly analysis of M. Pallis in *The Way and the Mountain,* London, 1960, Chapter I.

8. '. . . no longer is it human intellect but machines—or physics, or chemistry or biology—which decide what man is, what intelligence is, what truth is. Under these conditions man's mind more and more depends on the "climate" produced by its own creations. . . . It is then science and machines which in their turn create man and if such an expression may be ventured, they also "create God" for the void thus left by dethroning God cannot remain empty, the reality of God and his imprint in human nature require a usurper of divinity, a false absolute which can fill the nothingness of an intelligence robbed of its substance.' F. Schuon, *Understanding Islam* (trans. D. M. Matheson), London, 1963, pp. 32–3.

'Values which we accept today as permanent and often as self-evident have grown out of the Renaissance and the Scientific Revolution. The arts and the sciences have changed the values of the Middle Ages. . . .' J. Bronowski, *Science and Human Values,* New York, 1965, p. 51.

9. 'Man has abused his trusteeship in God's world. He has employed his scientific knowledge to exploit nature rather than to use it wisely in accordance with God's Will.' G. D. Yarnold, *The Spiritual Crisis of the Scientific Age,* New York, 1959, p. 168.

10. 'Modern science is well equipped to provide certain kinds of information, but it denies itself the possibility of interpreting that information; the task of doing so is therefore left to the play of opinion, individual or collective, informed or ignorant. Its cardinal error therefore resides in its claim to be science itself, the only possible science, the only science there is.' Lord Northbourne, 'Pictures of the Universe', *Tomorrow,* Autumn, 1964, p. 275.

'. . . before the separation of science and the acceptance of it as the sole valid way of apprehending nature, the vision of God in nature seems to have been the normal way of viewing the world, nor could it have been marked as an exceptional experience.' F. Sherwood Taylor, *The Fourfold Vision*, London, 1945, p. 91.

11. This fact has been often affirmed by scientists themselves. For example, concerning the popular misunderstanding of the theory of relativity R. Oppenheimer writes: 'The philosophers and popularizers who have mistaken relativity for the doctrine of relativism have construed Einstein's great works as reducing the objectivity, firmness, and consonance to law of the physical world, whereas it is clear that Einstein has seen in his theories of relativity a further confirmation of Spinoza's view that it is man's highest function to know and understand the objective world and its laws.' R. Oppenheimer, *Science and the Common Understanding*, London, 1954, pp. 2–3.

12. *'L'équilibre du monde et des créatures dépend de l'équilibre entre l'homme et Dieu, donc de notre connaissance et notre volonté à l'égard de l'Absolu. Avant de demander ce qui doit faire l'homme, il faut savoir ce qu'il est.'* F. Schuon, 'Le commandment suprême', *Etudes Traditionnelles*, Sept.–Oct. 1965, p. 199.

13. 'It could be said that the very structure of the cosmos keeps memory of the celestial supreme being alive. It is as if the gods had created the world in such a way that it could not but reflect their existence; for no world is possible without verticality, and that dimension alone is enough to evoke transcendence.' M. Eliade, *op. cit.*, p. 129.

14. 'For religious man, nature is never only "natural"; it is always fraught with religious value. This is easy to understand, for the cosmos is a divine creation; coming from the hands of the gods, the world is impregnated with sacredness.' *Ibid.*, p. 116.

15. '. . . our knowledge (of cosmic phenomena) must be either symbolically true or physically adequate; in the second case it must retain for us a symbolic intelligibility, for without this all science is vain and harmful.' F. Schuon, *Light on the Ancient Worlds* (trans. Lord Northbourne), London, 1965, p. 105.

16. For a profound analysis of this question in all its aspects see R. Guénon, *The Reign of Quantity and the Signs of the Times* (trans. Lord Northbourne), London, 1953.

17. 'Modern science therefore asks us to sacrifice a good part of that which makes for us the reality of the world, and offers us in exchange mathematical schemes of which the only advantage is to help us to manipulate matter on its own plane, which is that of quantity.' T. Burckhardt, 'Cosmology and Modern Science', *Tomorrow*, Summer 1964, p. 186.

18. 'It could be demonstrated too that science, although in itself neutral—for facts are facts—is none the less a seed of corruption and annihilation in the hands of man, who in general has not enough knowledge of the underlying nature of Existence to be able to integrate—and thereby to neutralize—the facts of science in a total view of the world.' Schuon, *op. cit.*, p. 38.

19. '. . . all genuine cosmology is attached to a divine revelation, even if the object considered and the mode of its expression are situated apparently outside the message this revelation brings.

'Such is the case for instance, of Christian cosmology, the origin of which appears at first sight somewhat heterogeneous, since it refers on the one hand to the Biblical account of creation even while being based, on the other hand, on the heritage of the Greek cosmologists.' T. Burckhardt, "Cosmology and Modern Science', *Tomorrow*, Summer, 1964, p. 182.

20. See for example E. C. Mascall, *Christian Theology and Natural Science*, London, 1956, Chapter IV.

21. 'Modern science will never reach that matter which is at the basis of this world. But between the qualitatively differentiated world and undifferentiated matter there lies something like an intermediate zone: This is chaos. The sinister dangers attendant on atomic fission are but a pointer indicating the frontier of chaos and of dissolution.' T. Burckhardt, 'Cosmology and Modern Science', p. 190.

22. This fact has of course been realized by certain historians of science and philosophy such as E. A. Burtt in his *Metaphysical Foundations of Modern Physical Science*, London, 1925; and A. Koyré in his many masterly works on Renaissance and seventeenth-century science, but it is none the less too often forgotten by a large number of philosophers and historians of science.

23. 'Anyone familiar with contemporary writing and talking knows that people are readier to accept physics as true and to use it to construct a "philosophy" than to investigate the method of physics, its presuppositions and their philosophical basis.' E. F. Caldin, *The Power and Limits of Science, a Philosophical Study*, London, 1949, p. 42.

24. One of the followers of this school, K. Heim, has shown some interest in science as seen by his *Christian Faith and Natural Science*, New York, 1953. But the deepest problems involved have been hardly delved into especially as far as the question of the symbolic significance of natural phenomena and their religious meaning are concerned.

25. It might be pointed out in passing that surely it is not accidental that Barthian theology shows both a disregard for the study of nature and of comparative religion. Both the cosmos and other religions thus appear as a 'natural' domain cut off from the domain of grace with which Christian theology should be concerned.

26. See for example, J. Oman, *The Natural and the Supernatural*, Cambridge, 1936.

27. 'Only a thoroughgoing belief that "the things that are made" do, in spite of the Fall and its conse-

quences, manifest the true nature of their Maker can give any foundation for a reasonable faith.' C. E. Raven, *Natural Religion and Christian Theology*, Cambridge, 1953, p. 137.

28. We mean the point of view so characteristic of the writings of the turn of the century such as A. D. White, *A History of the Warfare of Science and Theology in Christendom*, 2 vols., New York, 1960.

29. 'But it is at once evident that the general outline of the structure of the universe, as presented by science today, is far more congenial to the theistic hypothesis, as we have been considering it, than were the scientific theories prevalent in the eighteenth and nineteenth centuries.' W. Temple, *Nature, Man and God*, New York, 1949, p. 474.

30. 'I can think of no greater disservice that could be done to the Christian religion than to tie it up with arguments based upon verbal confusions or with scientific views that are merely temporary.' Mascall, *Christian Theology and Natural Science*, p. 166.

31. See Smethurst, *Modern Science and Christian Belief*, pp. 17–18.

'Only the full catholic Christian faith can supply both the necessary theological and philosophical beliefs as to the nature of the universe which are required to justify studying it by scientific method, and also the impulse and inspiration which will impel men to undertake this study.' *Ibid.*, p. 20.

32. See for example R. G. Collingwood, *Essay on Metaphysics*, Oxford, 1940, p. 227.

33. 'I am convinced that Christianity alone made possible both positive science and technics.' N. Berdyaev, *The Meaning of History*, London, 1935, p. 113.

34. See W. Temple, *Nature, Man and God*, p. 478, where the author adds that Christianity is able to dominate over matter precisely because in contrast to other religions such as Hinduism it is 'the most avowedly materialist of all the great religions'.

'I believe that the distance which in the modern mind exists between the subject and the object is a direct legacy of the Christian distance from the world.' von Weizäcker, *The History of Nature*, p. 190.

35. This point of view is particularly developed by G. F. Stout in his *God and Nature*, Cambridge, 1952.

36. See for example Yarnold, *The Spiritual Crisis of the Scientific Age*, pp. 54 ff.

37. 'Thus, the scientific method should be regarded as one method which Christians employ to obtain a better understanding of the wisdom of God and the wonders of His Creation. . . .' Smethurst, *Modern Science and Christian Belief*, p. 71.

38. One is reminded of the saying of Oliver Chase, 'For mankind there are two unique sacraments which disclose the meaning and convey the experience of reality: They are the created Universe and the person of Jesus Christ' (quoted by Raven, *Natural Religion and Christian Theology*, p. 105). This is reminiscent of early American Protestant theologians like Jonathan Edwards who were concerned with the theological meaning of nature.

39. See A. N. Whitehead, *Science and the Modern World*, Chapter I.

40. 'It is not simply the relation of ground and consequent, nor of cause and effect, nor of thought and expression, nor of purpose and instrument, nor of end and means; but it is all of these at once. We need for it another name; and there is in some religious traditions an element which is, in the belief of adherents of those religions, so closely akin to what we want that we may most suitably call this conception of the relation of the eternal to history, of spirit to matter, the sacramental conception.' Temple, *Nature, Man and God*, pp. 481–2.

41. Through sacraments, 'The outward and visible sign is a necessary means for conveyance of the inward and spiritual grace'. *Ibid.*, p. 482.

42. 'His creation is sacramental of Himself to His creatures; but in effectually fulfilling that function it becomes sacramental of Him to Himself—the means whereby He is eternally that which eternally He is.' *Ibid.*, p. 495.

43. 'The world, which is the self-expressive utterance of the Divine Word, becomes itself a true revelation, in which what comes is not truth concerning God, but God Himself.' *Ibid.*, p. 493.

'Either all occurrences are in some degree revelations of God, or else there is no such revelation at all; for the conditions of the possibility of any revelation require that there should be nothing which is not revelation. Only if God is revealed in the rising of the sun in the sky can He be revealed in the rising of a son of man from the dead'; *ibid.*, p. 306.

44. 'The theatre of redemption is the theatre of creation.' J. Sittler, *The Ecology of Faith*, p. 25.

45. See for example the writings of J. Maritain, J. Weisheipl and A. G. Van Melsen, especially the latter's *The Philosophy of Nature*, Pittsburg, 1961; also V. E. Smith (ed.), *The Logic of Science*, New York, 1963, containing essays by M. Adler, J. A. Weisheipl and others on the neo-Thomistic philosophy of nature and science.

46. Quoted by J. Maritain in his essay, 'Science, Philosophy and Faith', in *Science, Philosophy and Religion, a Symposium*, p. 171.

47. 'But the depiction of the whole cosmos, in its complete complexity is a task that does not properly lie within the competence of Science.' F. R. S. Thompson, *Science and Common Sense*, London, 1937, p. 54.

48. '. . . in principle, theses of a genuinely metaphysical nature are not subject to verification by the senses, so that no amount of experimental research can ever dislodge them from their position.' H. J. Koren, *An Introduction to the Philosophy of Nature*, Pittsburgh, 1960, p. 181.

49. This can be seen particularly in the writings of a leading spokesman of this school, J. Maritain. See particularly his *Philosophy of Nature,* New York, 1947, and *The Degrees of Knowledge* (trans. B. Wall and M. Adamson), New York, 1938.

50. 'Indeed it is largely out of the misunderstanding between the order of nature and the field of science that our controversies have arisen.' Raven, *Natural Religion and Christian Theology, I, Science and Religion,* p. 6.

51. Putting Whitehead and his school aside and a few individual philosophers like Collingwood who have shown interest in nature, no other philosophical school has been as insistent on the necessity of a philosophy of nature and on trying to provide such a philosophy based on Thomism. Also phenomenology provides in itself a philosophy of nature but none of those schools have found wide or total acceptance.

52. See for example, Yarnold, *The Spiritual Crisis of the Scientific Age,* p. 23.

53. 'The feeling of the sanctity of nature survives today in Europe chiefly among rural populations, for it is among them that a Christianity lived as a cosmic liturgy still exists.' Eliade, *The Sacred and the Profane . . . ,* p. 178.

54. 'This transition from objectivism to subjectivism reflects and repeats in its own way the fall of Adam and the loss of Paradise; in losing a symbolist and contemplative perspective, founded both on impersonal intelligence and on the metaphysical transparency of things, man has gained the fallacious rich of the *ego;* the world of divine images has become a world of words. In all cases of this kind, heaven—or a heaven—is shut off from above us without our noticing the fact and we discover in compensation an earth long unappreciated, or so it seems to us, a homeland which opens its arms to welcome its children and wants to make us forget all lost Paradises. . . . ' Schuon, *Light on the Ancient Worlds,* p. 29. See also Eliade, *op. cit.,* p. 213.

55. Concerning this subject see Guénon, *The Reign of Quantity . . . , especially Chapter XXV, 'Fissures in the Great Wall'.*

56. 'I have suggested that scientific explanation, "from below", must be supplemented by something far wider and deeper, interpretation, from above. Until that is accomplished our hold upon essential Christian truth is weak and often ineffectual.' Yarnold, *The Spiritual Crisis of the Scientific Age,* p. 7.

57. 'The division of labor in acquiring knowledge, although it begets new sciences, is yet a recognition of the unity and integrity of all knowledge and a challenge to expose it. This is a much different undertaking than trying to piece together as parts of a whole the specific results of specific sciences or using the results of one of them to shape the concerns of the others. Nature, not the wit of man, gives to knowledge its integral character. This suggests a science of nature which is neither physics nor chemistry and the like nor the social sciences and their like. . . . ' F. J. E. Woodbridge, *An Essay on Nature,* New York, 1940, p. 58.

The Historical Roots of Our Ecologic Crisis

LYNN WHITE JR.

A CONVERSATION WITH ALDOUS HUXLEY NOT infrequently put one at the receiving end of an unforgettable monologue. About a year before his lamented death he was discoursing on a favorite topic: Man's unnatural treatment of nature and its sad results. To illustrate his point he told how, during the previous summer, he had returned to a little valley in England where he had spent many happy months as a child. Once it had been composed of delightful grassy glades; now it was becoming overgrown with unsightly brush because the rabbits that formerly kept such growth under control had largely succumbed to a disease, myxomatosis, that was deliberately introduced by the local farmers to reduce the rabbits' destruction of crops. Being something of a Philistine, I could be silent no longer, even in the interests of great rhetoric. I interrupted to point out that the rabbit itself had been brought as a domestic animal to England in 1176, presumably to improve the protein diet of the peasantry.

White, Lynn, Jr., "The Historical Roots of Our Ecologic Crisis." Reprinted with permission from *Science* 155 (March 10, 1967), pp. 1203–1207.

All forms of life modify their contexts. The most spectacular and benign instance is doubtless the coral polyp. By serving its own ends, it has created a vast undersea world favorable to thousands of other kinds of animals and plants. Ever since man became a numerous species he has affected his environment notably. The hypothesis that his fire-drive method of hunting created the world's great grasslands and helped to exterminate the monster mammals of the Pleistocene from much of the globe is plausible, if not proved. For 6 millennia at least, the banks of the lower Nile have been a human artifact rather than the swampy African jungle which nature, apart from man, would have made it. The Aswan Dam, flooding 5000 square miles, is only the latest stage in a long process. In many regions terracing or irrigation, overgrazing, the cutting of forests by Romans to build ships to fight Carthaginians or by Crusaders to solve the logistics problems of their expeditions, have profoundly changed some ecologies. Observation that the French landscape falls into two basic types, the open fields of the north and the *bocage* of the south and west, inspired Marc Bloch to undertake his classic study of medieval agricultural methods. Quite unintentionally, changes in human ways often affect nonhuman nature. It has been noted, for example, that the advent of the automobile eliminated huge flocks of sparrows that once fed on the horse manure littering every street.

The history of ecologic change is still so rudimentary that we know little about what really happened, or what the results were. The extinction of the European aurochs as late as 1627 would seem to have been a simple case of overenthusiastic hunting. On more intricate matters it often is impossible to find solid information. For a thousand years or more the Frisians and Hollanders have been pushing back the North Sea, and the process is culminating in our own time in the reclamation of the Zuider Zee. What, if any, species of animals, birds, fish, shore life, or plants have died out in the process? In their epic combat with Neptune have the Netherlanders overlooked ecological values in such a way that the quality of human life in the Netherlands has suffered? I cannot discover that the questions have ever been asked, much less answered.

People, then, have often been a dynamic element in their own environment, but in the present state of historical scholarship we usually do not know exactly when, where, or with what effects man-induced changes came. As we enter the last third of the 20th century, however, concern for the problem of ecologic backlash is mounting feverishly. Natural science, conceived as the effort to understand the nature of things, had flourished in several eras and among several peoples. Similarly there had been an age-old accumulation of technological skills, sometimes growing rapidly, sometimes slowly. But it was not until about four generations ago that Western Europe and North America arranged a marriage between science and technology, a union of the theoretical and the empirical approaches to our natural environment. The emergence in widespread practice of the Baconian creed that scientific knowledge means technological power over nature can scarcely be dated before about 1850, save in the chemical industries, where it is anticipated in the 18th century. Its acceptance as a normal pattern of action may mark the greatest event in human history since the invention of agriculture, and perhaps in nonhuman terrestrial history as well.

Almost at once the new situation forced the crystallization of the novel concept of ecology; indeed, the word *ecology* first appeared in the English language in 1873. Today, less than a century later, the impact of our race upon the environment has so increased in force that it has changed in essence. When the first cannons were fired, in the early 14th century, they affected ecology by sending workers scrambling to the forests and mountains for more potash, sulfur, iron ore, and charcoal, with some resulting erosion and deforestation. Hydrogen bombs are of a different order: a war fought with them might alter the genetics of all life on this planet. By 1285 London had a smog problem arising from the burning of soft coal, but our present combustion of fossil fuels threatens to change the chemistry of the globe's atmosphere as a whole, with consequences which we are only beginning to guess. With the population explosion, the carcinoma of planless urbanism, the now geological deposits of sewage and garbage, surely no creature other than man has ever managed to foul its nest in such short order.

There are many calls to action, but specific proposals, however worthy as individual items, seem too partial, palliative, negative: ban the bomb, tear down the billboards, give the Hindus contraceptives and tell them to eat their sacred cows. The simplest solution to any suspect change is, of course, to stop it, or, better yet, to revert to a romanticized past: make those ugly gasoline stations look like Anne Hathaway's cottage or (in the Far West) like ghost-town saloons. The "wilderness area" mentality invariably advocates deep-freezing an ecology, whether San Gimignano or the High Sierra, as it was before the first Kleenex was dropped. But neither atavism nor prettification will cope with the ecologic crisis of our time.

What shall we do? No one yet knows. Unless we think about fundamentals, our specific measures may produce new backlashes more serious than those they are designed to remedy.

As a beginning we should try to clarify our thinking by looking, in some historical depth, at the presuppositions that underlie modern technology and science. Science was traditionally aristocratic, speculative, intellectual in intent; technology was lower-class, empirical, action-oriented. The quite sudden fusion of these two, towards the middle of the 19th century, is surely related to the slightly prior and contemporary democratic revolutions which, by reducing social barriers, tended to assert a functional unity of brain and hand. Our ecologic crisis is the product of an emerging, entirely novel, democratic culture. The issue is whether a democratized world can survive its own implications. Presumably we cannot unless we rethink our axioms.

THE WESTERN TRADITIONS OF TECHNOLOGY AND SCIENCE

One thing is so certain that it seems stupid to verbalize it: both modern technology and modern science are distinctively *Occidental*. Our technology has absorbed elements from all over the world, notably from China; yet everywhere today, whether in Japan or in Nigeria, successful technology is Western. Our science is the heir to all the sciences of the past, especially perhaps to the work of the great Islamic scientists of the Middle Ages, who so often outdid the ancient Greeks in skill and perspicacity: al-Rāzī in medicine, for example; or ibn-al-Haytham in optics; or Omar Khayyám in mathematics. Indeed, not a few works of such geniuses seem to have vanished in the original Arabic and to survive only in medieval Latin translations that helped to lay the foundations for later Western developments. Today, around the globe, all significant science is Western in style and method, whatever the pigmentation or language of the scientists.

A second pair of facts is less well recognized because they result from quite recent historical scholarship. The leadership of the West, both in technology and in science, is far older than the so-called Scientific Revolution of the 17th century or the so-called Industrial Revolution of the 18th century. These terms are in fact out-moded and obscure the true nature of what they try to describe—significant stages in two long and separate developments. By A.D. 1000 at the latest—and perhaps, feebly, as much as 200 years earlier—the West began to apply water power to industrial processes other than milling grain. This was followed in the late 12th century by the harnessing of wind power. From simple beginnings, but with remarkable consistency of style, the West rapidly expanded its skills in the development of power machinery, labor-saving devices, and automation. Those who doubt should contemplate that most monumental achievement in the history of automation: the weight-driven mechanical clock, which appeared in two forms in the early 14th century. Not in craftsmanship but in basic technological capacity, the Latin West of the later Middle Ages far outstripped its elaborate, sophisticated, and esthetically magnificent sister cultures, Byzantium and Islam. In 1444 a great Greek ecclesiastic, Bessarion, who had gone to Italy, wrote a letter to a prince in Greece. He is amazed by the superiority of Western ships, arms, textiles, glass. But above all he is astonished by the spectacle of water-wheels sawing timbers and pumping the bellows of blast furnaces. Clearly, he had seen nothing of the sort in the Near East.

By the end of the 15th century the technological superiority of Europe was such that its small, mutually hostile nations could spill out over all the rest of the world, conquering, looting, and colonizing. The symbol of this technological superiority is the fact that Portugal, one of the weakest states of the Occident, was able to become, and to remain for a century, mistress of the East Indies. And we must remember that the technology of Vasco da Gama and Albuquerque was built by pure empiricism, drawing remarkably little support or inspiration from science.

In the present-day vernacular understanding, modern science is supposed to have begun in 1543, when both Copernicus and Vesalius published their great works. It is no derogation of their accomplishments, however, to point out that such structures as the *Fabrica* and the *De revolutionibus* do not appear overnight. The distinctive Western tradition of science, in fact, began in the late 11th century with a massive movement of translation of Arabic and Greek scientific works into Latin. A few notable books—Theophrastus, for example—escaped the West's avid new appetite for science, but within less than 200 years effectively the entire corpus of Greek and Muslim science was available in Latin, and was being eagerly read and criticized in the new European universities. Out of criticism arose new observation, speculation, and increasing distrust of ancient authorities. By the late 13th century Europe had seized global scientific leadership from the faltering hands of Islam. It would be as absurd to deny the profound originality of Newton, Galileo, or Copernicus as to deny that of the 14th century scholastic scientists like Buridan or Oresme on whose work they built. Before the 11th century, science scarcely existed in the Latin West, even in Roman times. From the 11th century onward, the scientific sector of Occidental culture has increased in a steady crescendo.

Since both our technological and our scientific movements got their start, acquired their character, and achieved world dominance in the Middle Ages, it would seem that we cannot understand their nature or their present impact upon ecology without examining fundamental medieval assumptions and developments.

MEDIEVAL VIEW OF MAN AND NATURE

Until recently, agriculture has been the chief occupation even in "advanced" societies; hence, any change in methods of tillage has much importance. Early plows, drawn by two oxen, did not normally turn the sod but merely scratched it. Thus, cross-plowing was needed and fields tended to be squarish. In the fairly light soils and semiarid climates of the Near East and Mediterranean, this worked well. But such a plow was inappropriate to the wet climate and often sticky soils of northern Europe. By the latter part of the 7th century after Christ, however, following obscure beginnings, certain northern peasants were using an entirely new kind of plow, equipped with a vertical knife to cut the line of the furrow, a horizontal share to slice under the sod, and a moldboard to turn it over. The friction of this plow with the soil was so great that it normally required not two but eight oxen. It attacked the land with such violence that cross-plowing was not needed, and fields tended to be shaped in long strips.

In the days of the scratch-plow, fields were distributed generally in units capable of supporting a single family. Subsistence farming was the presupposition. But no peasant owned eight oxen: to use the new and more efficient plow, peasants pooled their oxen to form large plow-teams, originally receiving (it would appear) plowed strips in proportion to their contribution. Thus, distribution of land was based no longer on the needs of a family but, rather, on the capacity of a power machine to till the earth. Man's relation to the soil was profoundly changed. Formerly man had been part of nature; now he was the exploiter of nature. Nowhere else in the world did farmers develop any analogous agricultural implement. Is it coincidence that modern technology, with its ruthlessness toward nature, has so largely been produced by descendants of these peasants of northern Europe?

This same exploitive attitude appears slightly before A.D. 830 in Western illustrated calendars. In older calendars the months were shown as passive personifications. The new Frankish calendars, which set the style for the Middle Ages, are very different: they show men coercing the world around them—plowing, harvesting, chopping trees, butchering pigs. Man and nature are two things, and man is master.

These novelties seem to be in harmony with larger intellectual patterns. What people do about their ecology depends on what they think about themselves in relation to things around them. Human ecology is deeply conditioned by beliefs about our nature and destiny—that is, by religion. To Western eyes this is very evident in, say, India or Ceylon. It is equally true of ourselves and of our medieval ancestors.

The victory of Christianity over paganism was the greatest psychic revolution in the history of our culture. It has become fashionable today to say that, for better or worse, we live in "the post-Christian age." Certainly the forms of our thinking and language have largely ceased to be Christian, but to my eye the substance often remains amazingly akin to that of the past. Our daily habits of action, for example, are dominated by an implicit faith in perpetual progress which was unknown either to Greco-Roman antiquity or to the Orient. It is rooted in, and is indefensible apart from, Judeo-Christian teleology. The fact that Communists share it merely helps to show what can be demonstrated on many other grounds: that Marxism, like Islam, is a Judeo-Christian heresy. We continue today to live, as we have lived for about 1700 years, very largely in a context of Christian axioms.

What did Christianity tell people about their relations with the environment?

While many of the world's mythologies provide stories of creation, Greco-Roman mythology was singularly incoherent in this respect. Like Aristotle, the intellectuals of the ancient West denied that the visible world had had a beginning. Indeed, the idea of a beginning was impossible in the framework of their cyclical notion of time. In sharp contrast, Christianity inherited from Judaism not only a concept of time as nonrepetitive and linear but also a striking story of creation. By gradual stages a loving and all-powerful God had created light and darkness, the heavenly bodies, the earth and all its plants, animals, birds, and fishes. Finally, God had created Adam and, as an afterthought, Eve to keep man from being lonely. Man named all the animals, thus establishing his dominance over them. God planned all of this explicitly for man's benefit and rule: no item in the physical creation had any purpose save to serve man's purposes. And, although man's body is made of clay, he is not simply part of nature: he is made in God's image.

Especially in its Western form, Christianity is the most anthropocentric religion the world has seen. As early as the 2nd century both Tertullian and Saint Irenaeus of Lyons were insisting that when God shaped Adam he was foreshadowing the image of the incarnate Christ, the Second Adam. Man shares, in great measure, God's transcendence of nature. Christianity, in absolute contrast to ancient paganism and Asia's religions (except, perhaps, Zoroastrianism), not only established a dualism of man and nature but also insisted that it is God's will that man exploit nature for his proper ends.

At the level of the common people this worked out in an interesting way. In Antiquity every tree, every spring, every stream, every hill had its own *genius loci,* its guardian spirit. These spirits were accessible to men, but were very unlike men; centaurs, fauns, and mermaids show their ambivalence. Before one cut a tree, mined a mountain, or dammed a brook, it was important to placate the spirit in charge of that particular situation, and to keep it placated. By destroying pagan animism, Christianity made it possible to exploit nature in a mood of indifference to the feelings of natural objects.

It is often said that for animism the Church substituted the cult of saints. True; but the cult of saints is functionally quite different from animism. The saint is not *in* natural objects; he may have special shrines, but his citizenship is in heaven. Moreover, a saint is entirely a man; he can be approached in human terms. In addition to saints, Christianity of course also had angels and demons inherited from Judaism and perhaps, at one remove, from Zoroastrianism. But these were all as mobile as the saints themselves. The spirits *in* natural objects, which formerly had protected nature from man, evaporated. Man's effective monopoly on spirit in this world was confirmed, and the old inhibitions to the exploitation of nature crumbled.

When one speaks in such sweeping terms, a note of caution is in order. Christianity is a complex faith, and its consequences differ in differing contexts. What I have said may well apply to the medieval West, where in fact technology made spectacular advances. But the Greek East, a highly civilized realm of equal Christian devotion, seems to have produced no marked technological innovation after the late 7th century, when Greek fire was invented. The key to the contrast may perhaps be found in a difference in the tonality of piety and thought which students of comparative theology find between the Greek and the Latin Churches. The Greeks believed that sin was intellectual blindness, and that salvation was found in illumination, orthodoxy—that is, clear thinking. The Latins, on the other hand, felt that sin was moral evil, and that salvation was to be found in right conduct. Eastern theology has been intellectualist. Western theology has been voluntarist. The Greek saint contemplates; the Western saint acts. The implications of Christianity for the conquest of nature would emerge more easily in the Western atmosphere.

The Christian dogma of creation, which is found in the first clause of all the Creeds, has another meaning for our comprehension of today's ecologic crisis.

By revelation, God had given man the Bible, the Book of Scripture. But since God had made nature, nature also must reveal the divine mentality. The religious study of nature for the better understanding of God was known as natural theology. In the early Church, and always in the Greek East, nature was conceived primarily as a symbolic system through which God speaks to men: the ant is a sermon to sluggards; rising flames are the symbol of the soul's aspiration. This view of nature was essentially artistic rather than scientific. While Byzantium preserved and copied great numbers of ancient Greek scientific texts, science as we conceive it could scarcely flourish in such an ambience.

However, in the Latin West by the early 13th century natural theology was following a very different bent. It was ceasing to be the decoding of the physical symbols of God's communication with man and was becoming the effort to understand God's mind by discovering how his creation operates. The rainbow was no longer simply a symbol of hope first sent to Noah after the Deluge: Robert Grosseteste, Friar Roger Bacon, and Theodoric of Freiberg produced startlingly sophisticated work on the optics of the rainbow, but they did it as a venture in religious understanding. From the 13th century onward, up to and including Leibnitz and Newton, every major scientist, in effect, explained his motivations in religious terms. Indeed, if Galileo had not been so expert an amateur theologian he would have got into far less trouble: the professionals resented his intrusion. And Newton seems to have regarded himself more as a theologian than as a scientist. It was not until the late 18th century that the hypothesis of God became unnecessary to many scientists.

It is often hard for the historian to judge, when men explain why they are doing what they want to do, whether they are offering real reasons or merely culturally acceptable reasons. The consistency with which scientists during the long formative centuries of Western science said that the task and the reward of the scientist was "to think God's thoughts after him" leads one to believe that this was their real motivation. If so, then modern Western science was cast in a matrix of Christian theology. The dynamism of religious devotion, shaped by the Judeo-Christian dogma of creation, gave it impetus.

AN ALTERNATIVE CHRISTIAN VIEW

We would seem to be headed toward conclusions unpalatable to many Christians. Since both *science* and *technology* are blessed words in our contemporary vocabulary, some may be happy at the notions, first, that, viewed historically, modern science is an extrapolation of natural theology and, second, that modern technology is at least partly to be explained as an Occidental, voluntarist realization of the Christian dogma of man's transcendence of, and rightful mastery over, nature. But, as we now recognize, somewhat over a century ago science and technology—hitherto quite separate activities—joined to give mankind powers which, to judge by many of the ecologic effects, are out of control. If so, Christianity bears a huge burden of guilt.

I personally doubt that disastrous ecologic backlash can be avoided simply by applying to our problems more science and more technology. Our science and technology have grown out of Christian attitudes toward man's relation to nature which are almost universally held not only by Christians and neo-Christians but also by those who fondly regard themselves as post-Christians. Despite Copernicus, all the cosmos rotates around our little globe. Despite Darwin, we are *not,* in our hearts, part of the natural process. We are superior to nature, contemptuous of it, willing to use it for our slightest whim. The newly elected Governor of California, like myself a churchman but less troubled than I, spoke for the Christian tradition when he said (as is alleged), "when you've seen one redwood tree, you've seen them all." To a Christian a tree can be no more than a physical fact. The whole concept of the sacred grove is alien to Christianity and to the ethos of the West. For nearly 2 millennia Christian missionaries have been chopping down sacred groves, which are idolatrous because they assume spirit in nature.

What we do about ecology depends on our ideas of the man-nature relationship. More science and more technology are not going to get us out of the present ecologic crisis until we find a new religion, or rethink our old one. The beatniks, who are the basic revolutionaries of our time, show a sound instinct in their affinity for Zen Buddhism, which conceives of the man-nature relationship as very nearly the mirror image of the Christian view. Zen, however, is as deeply conditioned by Asian history as Christianity is by the experience of the West, and I am dubious of its viability among us.

Possibly we should ponder the greatest radical in Christian history since Christ: Saint Francis of Assisi. The prime miracle of Saint Francis is the fact that he did not end at the stake, as many of his left-wing followers did. He was so clearly heretical that a General of the Franciscan Order, Saint Bonaventura, a great and perceptive Christian, tried to suppress the early accounts of Franciscanism. The key to an understanding of Francis is his belief in the virtue of humility—not merely for the individual but for man as a species. Francis tried to depose man from his monarchy over creation and set up a democracy of all God's creatures. With him the ant is no longer simply a homily for the lazy, flames a sign of the thrust of the soul toward union with God; now they are Brother Ant and Sister Fire, praising the Creator in their own ways as Brother Man does in his.

Later commentators have said that Francis preached to the birds as a rebuke to men who would not listen. The records do not read so: he urged the little birds to praise God, and in spiritual ecstasy they flapped their wings and chirped rejoicing. Legends of saints, especially the Irish saints, had long told of their dealings with animals but always, I believe, to show their human dominance over creatures. With Francis it is different. The land around Gubbio in the Apennines was being ravaged by a fierce wolf. Saint Francis, says the legend, talked to the wolf and persuaded him of the error of his ways. The wolf repented, died in the odor of sanctity, and was buried in consecrated ground.

What Sir Steven Ruciman calls "the Franciscan doctrine of the animal soul" was quickly stamped out. Quite possibly it was in part inspired, consciously or unconsciously, by the belief in reincarnation held by the Cathar heretics who at that time teemed in Italy and southern France, and who presumably had got it originally from India. It is significant that at just the same moment, about 1200, traces of metempsychosis are found also in western Judaism, in the Provençal *Cabbala*. But Francis held neither to transmigration of souls nor to pantheism. His view of nature and of man rested on a unique sort of pan-psychism of all things animate and inanimate, designed for the glorification of their transcendent Creator, who, in the ultimate gesture of cosmic humility, assumed flesh, lay helpless in a manager, and hung dying on a scaffold.

I am not suggesting that many contemporary Americans who are concerned about our ecologic crisis will be either able or willing to counsel with wolves or exhort birds. However, the present increasing disruption of the global environment is the product of a dynamic technology and science which were originating in the Western medieval world against which Saint Francis was rebelling in so original a way. Their growth cannot be understood historically apart from distinctive attitudes toward nature which are deeply grounded in Christian dogma. The fact that most people do not think of these attitudes as Christian is irrelevant. No new set of basic values has been accepted in our society to displace those of Christianity. Hence we shall continue to have a worsening ecologic crisis until we reject the Christian axiom that nature has no reason for existence save to serve man.

The greatest spiritual revolutionary in Western history, Saint Francis, proposed what he thought was an alternative Christian view of nature and man's relation to it: he tried to substitute the idea of the equality of all creatures, including man, for the idea of man's limitless rule of creation. He failed. Both our present science and our present technology are so tinctured with orthodox Christian arrogance toward nature that no solution for our ecologic crisis can be expected from them alone. Since the roots of our trouble are so largely religious, the remedy must also be essentially religious, whether we call it that or not. We must rethink and refeel our nature and destiny. The profoundly religious, but heretical, sense of the primitive Franciscans for the spiritual autonomy of all parts of nature may point a direction. I propose Francis as a patron saint for ecologists.

Discussion Questions

1. What is nature? What is *not* nature?
2. What is science? Is there only one science, or are there many? Is there such a thing as a value-neutral science?

3. Are humans fundamentally different from other species? What, if anything, is distinctive of humans?
4. Do Christian assumptions and values inform only the thought and behavior of Christians? Do Western assumptions and values inform only the thought and behavior of Westerners?
5. Is it possible to rethink religion? Are there examples of how this has been done?
6. What would it take to get modern humans to cease treating nature in an exploitative way?

Further Reading

Barbour, Ian, Ed., *Earth Might Be Fair: Reflections on Ethics, Religion, and Ecology,* Englewood Cliffs, N.J.: Prentice Hall, 1972.

Bonifazi, Conrad, *A Theology of Things: A Study of Man in His Physical Environment,* Philadelphia: Lippincott, 1967.

Carmody, John, *Ecology and Religion: Toward a New Christian Theology of Nature,* New York: Paulist Press, 1983.

Carson, Rachel, *Silent Spring,* Boston: Houghton Mifflin, 1994 [1962].

Cobb, John B., Jr., *Is It Too Late? A Theology of Ecology.* Rev. ed. Denton, Tex.: Environmental Ethics Books, 1995 [1972].

Nash, Roderick, *The Rights of Nature: A History of Environmental Ethics,* Madison: University of Wisconsin Press, 1989.

Nasr, Seyyed Hossein, *Man and Nature: The Spiritual Crisis in Modern Man.* Rev. ed. Chicago: Kazi, 1997 [1967].

Santmire, Paul, *The Travail of Nature: The Ambiguous Ecological Promise of Christian Theology,* Philadelphia: Fortress Press, 1985.

Spring, David, and Eileen Spring, Eds., *Ecology and Religion in History,* New York: Harper & Row, 1974.

Chapter 2

Humans, Nature, and Modernity

As the essays in the preceding chapter all pointed out, the prevailing ethic toward the natural environment within the post-Enlightenment Western worldview has been one of domination and control. Because these essays have also shown that domination represents only one possible interpretation of the inherited tradition, one may ask why and how this particular interpretation prevailed.

Many have sought an answer to this question in the blending of science and technology that began in Europe in the seventeenth century, a period known as the *Enlightenment.* Whereas previously Western science had been mainly speculative, many important thinkers of the Enlightenment increasingly sought to apply scientific knowledge to real-life situations. This approach is part of a broader developing worldview commonly known as *modernity.*

The modernist worldview arose in part from the thought of the European Renaissance, in particular the tendency to exalt human beings and their unique qualities, in some cases to the point of being nearly on a par with their creator. The mechanistic physics of Francis Bacon, René Descartes, and Isaac Newton portrayed the world not as something organic but as a machine—dead matter that could be taken apart, studied, and ultimately understood. Especially in the work of Bacon, Man's quest to master, comprehend, and use nature for his own ends is often expressed through the metaphor of violating a woman, forcing her to unveil her secrets and to do her master's will.

This aggressive and sexist imagery has made a deep impression on feminist critics such as historian Carolyn Merchant, who suggests that Bacon's intellectual agenda reflected the interests of "the middle-class male entrepreneur" at the expense of nature, women, and the lower classes. Merchant gives Bacon a large share of the credit (or blame) for the modern scientific approach to investigation, characterized by laboratory methods that involve manipulation, dissection, and scrutiny.

Implicit in Bacon's vision of mastery over nature is the modernist notion of *progress,* the idea that humanity is moving ever forward toward some lofty goal. Some have argued that the very idea of progress depends on a teleology such as that provided by Christianity; even today it is often difficult, at least for Westerners, to deconstruct the notion of progress and examine the assumptions it implies.

Contemporary modernist writers on the environment, who are often characterized as technological optimists, tend to take these assumptions for granted. For them, there is no question that humankind is capable of exercising ever greater dominance over nature, that it will inevitably continue to do so in the future, and that human beings are capable of determining whether the changes brought about by the use of new technologies will be beneficial or not. Their faith in technology and human progress is rooted in the humanistic positivism of the Enlightenment thinkers, as are their attitudes toward nature as primarily a supplier of resources for human use. In the latter respect, such views can be seen as a logical extension of the managerial approach advocated by Gifford Pinchot, a forester who became the first director of the United States Forest Service in the early part of the twentieth century.

The Renaissance theme of human uniqueness and faith in human abilities to meet all challenges is prominent in the writing of journalist Gregg Easterbrook, who presents himself as one who sees through the pessimism of much contemporary environmentalist rhetoric. Although his vision for a New Nature that is made better by humans seems very futuristic, its tone and underlying ethos almost exactly mirror those found in classic utopian works such as Francis Bacon's *The New Atlantis.*

Media critic Jerry Mander does not share the modernist optimism and faith in salvation through technology. He sees the technological worldview as being undemocratic, serving only the interests of those in power. Noting that the twentieth century has seen history's greatest and most rapid proliferation of new technologies being introduced in the virtual absence of any public debate, he calls for a more cautious approach in which the likely changes and possible dangers of new technologies would be weighed and considered by society at large before they are adopted.

Philosopher David R. Loy takes Mander's critique a step further. Whereas Mander sees a disappearance of the sacred in modern life, Loy feels rather that we have wrongly made sacred what does not deserve to be sacred. Echoing the diagnoses of White and Nasr, Loy characterizes the crisis of modern society as a crisis of misplaced values. Whereas overt references to religion are largely absent from the writings of Easterbrook and other advocates of modernity, Loy unveils and deconstructs the quasi-religious assumptions and value systems underlying the modern economistic worldview. In doing so, he shows the darker side of human progress and calls into question the assumption that modernity represents the highest achievement in human development.

Dominion over Nature

CAROLYN MERCHANT

DISORDERLY, ACTIVE NATURE WAS SOON forced to submit to the questions and experimental techniques of the new science. Francis Bacon (1561–1626), a celebrated "father of modern science," transformed tendencies already extant in his own society into a total program advocating the control of nature for human benefit. Melding together a new philosophy based on natural magic as a technique for manipulating nature, the technologies of mining and metallurgy, the emerging concept of progress and a patriarchal structure of family and state, Bacon fashioned a new ethic sanctioning the exploitation of nature.

Bacon has been eulogized as the originator of the concept of the modern research institute, a philosopher of industrial science, the inspiration behind the Royal Society (1660), and as the founder of the inductive method by which all people can verify for themselves the truths of science by the reading of nature's book.[1] But from the perspective of nature, women, and the lower orders of society emerges a less favorable image of Bacon and a critique of his program as ultimately benefiting the middle-class male entrepreneur. Bacon, of course, was not responsible for subsequent uses of his philosophy. But, because he was in an extremely influential social position and in touch with the important developments of his time, his language, style, nuance, and metaphor become a mirror reflecting his class perspective.

Sensitive to the same social transformations that had already begun to reduce women to psychic and reproductive resources, Bacon developed the power of language as political instrument in reducing female nature to a resource for economic production. Female imagery became a tool in adapting scientific knowledge and method to a new form of human power over nature. The "controversy over women" and the inquisition of witches—both present in Bacon's social milieu—permeated his description of nature and his metaphorical style and were instrumental in his transformation of the earth as a nurturing mother and womb of life into a source of secrets to be extracted for economic advance.

Bacon's roots can be found in middle-class economic development and its progressive interests and values. His father was a middle-class employee of the queen, his mother a Calvinist whose Protestant values permeated his early home life. Bacon took steps to gain the favor of James I soon after the latter's ascent to the throne in 1603. He moved from "learned counsel" in 1603 to attorney general in 1613, privy councillor in 1616, lord keeper in 1617, and, finally, lord chancellor and Baron Verulam in 1618. His political objectives were to gain support for his program of the advancement of science and human learning and to upgrade his own status through an ambitious public career.[2]

Bacon's mentor, James I, supported antifeminist and antiwitch-craft legislation. During the "controversy over women," females had challenged traditional modes of dress considered as appropriate to their place in society. In Holland, for example, young women were criticized for wearing men's hats with high crowns. In England, the title page of a work called *Hic-Mulier or The Man-Woman* (1620) showed a woman in a barber's chair having her hair clipped short, while her companion outfitted herself in a man's plumed hat.[3] In an attempt to keep women in their place in the world's order, King James in that same year enlisted the aid of the clergy in preventing females from looking and dressing in masculine fashions: "The Bishop of London had express commandment from the king to will [the clergy] to inveigh vehemently against the insolence of our women, and their wearing of broad-brimmed hats, pointed doublets, their hair cut short or shorn, and some of them [with] stilettos or poinards . . . *the truth is the world is very much out of order.*"[4] (Italics added.)

• • •

Bacon was also well aware of the witch trials taking place all over Europe and in particular in England during the early seventeenth century. His sovereign, while still James VI of Scotland, had written a book entitled *Daemonologie* (1597). In 1603, the first year of his English reign, James I replaced the milder witch laws of Elizabeth I, which evoked the death penalty only for killing by witchcraft, with a law that condemned to death all practitioners.[6]

It was in the 1612 trials of the Lancashire witches of the Pendle Forest that the sexual aspects of witch trials first appeared in England. The source of the women's confessions of fornication with the devil was a Roman Catholic priest who had emigrated from the Continent and planted the story in the mouths of accused women who had recently rejected Catholicism.

These social events influenced Bacon's philosophy and literary style. Much of the imagery he used in delineating his new scientific objectives and methods derives from the courtroom, and, because it treats nature as a female to be tortured through mechanical inventions, strongly suggests the interrogations of the witch trials and the mechanical devices used to torture witches. In a relevant passage, Bacon stated that the method by which nature's secrets might be discovered consisted in investigating the secrets of witchcraft by inquisition, referring to the example of James I:

> *For you have but to follow and as it were hound nature in her wanderings, and you will be able when you like to lead and drive her afterward to the same place again.* Neither am I of opinion in this history of marvels that superstitious narratives of *sorceries, witchcrafts, charms,* dreams, divinations, and the like, where there is an assurance and clear evidence of the fact, should be altogether ex-

> cluded. . . . howsoever the use and practice of such arts is to be condemned, yet from the speculation and consideration of them . . . a useful light may be gained, not only for a true judgment of the offenses of persons charged with such practices, *but likewise for the further disclosing of the secrets of nature. Neither ought a man to make scruple of entering and penetrating into these holes and corners, when the inquisition of truth is his whole object—as your majesty has shown in your own example.*[7] (Italics added.)

The strong sexual implications of the last sentence can be interpreted in the light of the investigation of the supposed sexual crimes and practices of witches. In another example, he compared the interrogation of courtroom witnesses to the inquisition of nature: "I mean (according to the practice in civil causes) in this great plea or suit granted by the divine favor and providence (whereby the human race seeks to recover its right over nature) *to examine nature herself* and the arts upon interrogatories."[8] Bacon pressed the idea further with an analogy to the torture chamber: "For like as a man's disposition is never well known or proved till he be crossed, nor Proteus ever changed shapes till he was *straitened* and *held fast,* so nature exhibits herself more clearly under the *trials* and *vexations* of art [mechanical devices] than when left to herself."[9]

The new man of science must not think that the "inquisition of nature is in any part interdicted or forbidden." Nature must be "bound into service" and made a "slave," put "in constraint" and "molded" by the mechanical arts. The "searchers and spies of nature" are to discover her plots and secrets.[10]

This method, so readily applicable when nature is denoted by the female gender, degraded and made possible the exploitation of the natural environment. As woman's womb had symbolically yielded to the forceps, so nature's womb harbored secrets that through technology could be wrested from her grasp for use in the improvement of the human condition:

> There is therefore much ground for hoping that there are still laid up in the womb of nature many secrets of excellent use having no affinity or parallelism with anything that is now known . . . only by the method which we are now treating can they be speedily and suddenly and simultaneously presented and anticipated.[11]

Bacon transformed the magical tradition by calling on the need to dominate nature not for the sole benefit of the individual magician but for the good of the entire human race. Through vivid metaphor, he transformed the magus from nature's servant to its exploiter, and nature from a teacher to a slave. Bacon argued that it was the magician's error to consider art (technology) a mere "assistant to nature having the power to finish what nature has begun" and therefore to despair of ever "changing, transmuting, or fundamentally altering nature."[12]

The natural magician saw himself as operating within the organic order of nature—he was a manipulator of parts within that system, bringing down the heavenly powers to the earthly shrine. Agrippa, however, had begun to explore the possibility of ascending the hierarchy to the point of cohabiting with God. Bacon extended this idea to include the recovery of the power over nature lost when Adam and Eve were expelled from paradise.

Due to the Fall from the Garden of Eden (caused by the temptation of a woman), the human race lost its "dominion over creation." Before the Fall, there was no need for power or dominion, because Adam and Eve had been made sovereign over all other creatures. In this state of dominion, mankind was "like unto God." While some, accepting God's punishment, had obeyed the medieval strictures against searching too deeply into God's secrets, Bacon turned the constraints into sanctions. Only by "digging further and further into the mine of natural knowledge" could mankind recover that lost dominion. In this way, "the narrow limits of man's dominion over the universe" could be stretched "to their promised bounds."[13]

Although a female's inquisitiveness may have caused man's fall from his God-given dominion, the relentless interrogation of another female, nature, could be used to regain it. As he argued in *The Masculine Birth of Time,* "I am come in very truth leading to you nature with all her children to bind her to your service and make her your slave." "We have no right," he asserted, "to expect nature to come to us." Instead, "Nature must be taken by the forelock, being bald behind." Delay and subtle argument "permit one only to clutch at nature, never to lay hold of her and capture her."[14]

Nature existed in three states—at liberty, in error, or in bondage:

> She is either free and follows her ordinary course of development as in the heavens, in the animal and vegetable creation, and in the general array of the universe; or she is driven out of her ordinary course by the perverseness, insolence, and forwardness of matter and violence of impediments, as in the case of monsters; or lastly, she is put in constraint, molded, and made as it were new by art and the hand of man; as in things artificial.[15]

The first instance was the view of nature as immanent self-development, the nature naturing herself of the Aristotelians. This was the organic view of nature as a living, growing, self-actualizing being. The second state was necessary to explain the malfunctions and monstrosities that frequently appeared and that could not have been caused by God or another higher power acting on his instruction. Since monstrosities could not be explained by the action of form or spirit, they had to be the result of matter acting perversely. Matter in Plato's *Timaeus* was recalcitrant and had to be forcefully shaped by the demiurge. Bacon frequently described matter in female imagery, as a "common harlot." "Matter is not devoid of an appetite and inclination to dissolve the world and fall back into the old Chaos." It therefore must be "restrained and kept in order by the prevailing concord of things." "The vexations of art are certainly as the bonds and handcuffs of Proteus, which betray the ultimate struggles and efforts of matter."[16]

The third instance was the case of art (techné)—man operating on nature to create something new and artificial. Here "nature takes orders from man and works under his authority." Miners and smiths should become the model for the new class of natural philosophers who would interrogate and alter nature. They had developed the two most important methods of wresting nature's secrets from her, "the one searching into the bowels of nature, the other shaping nature as on an anvil." "Why should we not divide natural philosophy into two parts, the mine and the furnace?" For "the truth of nature lies hid in certain deep mines and caves," within the earth's bosom. Bacon, like some of the practically minded alchemists, would "advise the studious to sell their books and build furnaces" and, "forsaking Minerva and the Muses as barren virgins, to rely upon Vulcan."[17]

The new method of interrogation was not through abstract notions, but through the instruction of the understanding "that it may in very truth dissect nature." The instruments of the mind supply suggestions, those of the hand give motion and aid the work. "By art and the hand of man," nature can then be "forced out of her natural state and squeezed and molded." In this way, "human knowledge and human power meet as one."[18]

Here, in bold sexual imagery, is the key feature of the modern experimental method—constraint of nature in the laboratory, dissection by hand and mind, and the penetration of hidden secrets—language still used today in praising a scientist's "hard facts," "penetrating mind," or the "thrust of his argument." The constraints against penetration in Natura's lament over her torn garments of modesty have been turned into sanctions in language that legitimates the exploitation and "rape" of nature for human good. The seventeenth-century experimenters of the Academia del Cimento of Florence (i.e., The Academy of Experiment, 1657–1667) and the Royal Society of London who placed mice and plants in the artificial vacuum of the barometer or bell jar were vexing nature and forcing her out of her natural state in true Baconian fashion.[19]

Scientific method, combined with mechanical technology, would create a "new organon," a new system of investigation, that unified knowledge with material power. The technological discoveries of printing, gunpowder, and the magnet in the fields of learning, warfare, and navigation "help us to think about the secrets still locked in nature's bosom." "They do not, like the old, merely exert a gentle guidance over nature's course; they have the power to conquer and subdue her, to shake her to her foundations." Under the mechanical arts, "nature betrays her secrets more fully . . . than when in enjoyment of her natural liberty."[20]

Mechanics, which gave man power over nature, consisted in motion; that is, in "the uniting or disuniting of natural bodies." Most useful were the arts that altered the materials of things—"agriculture, cookery, chemistry, dying, the manufacture of glass, enamel, sugar, gunpowder, artificial fires, paper, and the like." But in performing these operations, one was constrained to operate within the chain of causal connections; nature could "not be commanded except by being obeyed." Only by the study, interpretation, and observation of nature could these possibilities be uncovered; only by acting as the interpreter of nature could knowledge be turned into power. Of the three grades of human ambition, the most wholesome and noble was "to endeavor to establish and extend the power and dominion of the human race itself over the universe." In this way "the human race [could] recover that right over nature which belongs to it by divine bequest."[21]

The interrogation of witches as symbol for the interrogation of nature, the courtroom as model for its inquisition, and torture through mechanical devices as a tool for the subjugation of disorder were fundamental to the scientific method as power. For Bacon, as for Harvey, sexual politics helped to structure the nature of the empirical method that would produce a new form of knowledge and a new ideology of objectivity seemingly devoid of cultural and political assumptions.

• • •

MECHANISM AND THE NEW ATLANTIS

The scientific research institute designed to bring progress to Bensalem, the community of the *New Atlantis*, was called Salomon's House. The patriarchal character of this utopian society was reinforced by designating the scientists as the "Fathers of Salomon's House." In the *New Atlantis*, politics was replaced by scientific administration. No real political process existed in Bensalem. Decisions were made for the good of the whole by the scientists, whose judgment was to be trusted implicitly, for they alone possessed the secrets of nature.

Scientists decided which secrets were to be revealed to the state as a whole and which were to remain the private property of the institute rather than becoming public knowledge: "And this we do also, we have consultations, which of the inventions and experiences which we have discovered shall be published, and which not: and all take an oath of secrecy for the concealing of those which we think fit to keep secret, though some of those we do reveal sometimes to the state, and some not."[22]

The cause of the visit to the governor by a scientist from the distant Salomon's House, which resulted in a conference with the visitors to Bensalem, was shrouded in secrecy. No father of the institute had been seen in "this dozen years. His coming [was] in state, but the cause of his coming [was] secret."

The scientist father was portrayed much like the high priest of the occult arts, the Neoplatonic magus whose interest in control and power over nature had strongly influenced Bacon. He was clothed in all the majesty of a priest, complete with a "robe of fine black cloth with wide sleeves and a cape," an "undergarment . . . of excellent white linen," and a girdle and a clerical scarf, also of linen. His gloves were set with stone, his shoes were of peach-colored velvet, and he wore a Spanish helmet.

The worship to be accorded to the scientist was further enhanced by his vehicle, a "rich chariot" of cedar and gilt carried like a litter between four richly velveted horses and two blue-velveted footmen. The chariot was decorated with gold, sapphires, a golden sun, and a "small cherub of gold with wings outspread" and was followed by fifty richly dressed footmen. In front walked two bareheaded men carrying a pastoral staff and a bishop's crosier.

Bacon's scientist not only looked but behaved like a priest who had the power of absolving all human misery through science. He "had an aspect as if he pitied men"; "he held up his bare hand as he went, as blessing the people, but in silence." The street was lined with people who, it would seem, were happy, orderly, and completely passive: "The street was wonderfully well kept, so that there was never any army [which] had their men stand in better battle array than the people stood. The windows were not crowded, but everyone stood in them as if they had been placed."

Bacon's "man of science" would seem to be a harbinger of many modern research scientists. Critics of science today argue that scientists have become guardians of a body of scientific knowledge, shrouded in the mysteries of highly technical language that can be fully understood only by those who have had a dozen years of training. It is now possible for such scientists to reveal to the public only information they deem relevant. Depending on the scientist's ethics and political viewpoint, such information may or may not serve the public interest.

Salomon's House, long held to be the prototype of a modern research institute, was a forerunner of the mechanistic mode of scientific investigation. The mechanical method that evolved during the seventeenth century operated by breaking down a problem into its component parts, isolating it from its environment, and solving each portion independently. Bacon's research center maintained separate "laboratories" for the study of mining and metals, weather, fresh- and salt-water life, cultivated plants, insects, and so on.

The tasks of research were divided hierarchically among the various scientists, novices, and apprentices. Some abstracted patterns from other experiments, some did preliminary book research, some collected experiments from other arts and sciences; others tried out new experiments, or compiled results or looked for applications. The interpreters of nature raised the discoveries into greater observations, axioms, and aphorisms. This differentiation of labor followed the outlines of Bacon's inductive methodology.

In the laboratories of Salomon's House, one of the goals was to recreate the natural environment artificially through applied technology. Large, deep caves called the Lower Region were used for "the imitation of natural mines and the producing of new artificial metals by compositions and materials."[23] In another region were "a number of artificial wells and fountains, made in imitation of the natural sources and baths." Salt water could be made fresh, for "we have also pools, of which some do strain fresh water out of salt, and others by art do turn fresh water into salt."

Not only was the manipulation of the environment part of Bacon's program for the improvement of mankind, but the manipulation of organic life to create artificial species of plants and animals was specifically outlined. Bacon transformed the natural magician as "servant of nature" into a manipulator of nature and changed art from the aping of nature into techniques for forcing nature into new forms and controlling reproduction for the sake of production: "We make a number of kinds of serpents, worms, flies, fishes of putrefaction, where of some are advanced (in effect) to be perfect creatures like beasts or birds, and have sexes, and do propagate. Neither do we this by chance, but we know beforehand of what matter and commixture what kind of those creatures will arise."

These examples were taken directly from Della Porta's *Natural Magic* (1558), the second book of which dealt specifically with putrefaction and the generation of the living organisms mentioned by Bacon—worms, serpents, and fishes. The chapter dealing with putrefaction had discussed the generation of canker worms from mud, so that "we may also learn how to procreate new creatures."[24] "Serpents," wrote Della Porta, "may be generated of man's marrow, of the hairs of a monstrous woman, and of a horsetail, or mane," while "certain fishes," such as groundlings, carp, and shellfish, "are generated out of putrefaction." New beasts and birds could be generated through knowledge and carefully controlled coupling.

Della Porta also set down instructions as to how to produce a new organism in a series of trials. Such creatures "must be of equal pitch; they must have the same reproductive cycle, and one must be equally "as lustful as the other." Furthermore "if any creatures want appetite . . . we may make them eager in lust."

The *New Atlantis* had parks and enclosures for beasts and birds where just such experiments were performed: "By art likewise we make them greater or taller than their kind is, and contrariwise dwarf them, and stay their growth; we make them more fruitful and bearing than their kind is, and contrariwise barren and not generative. Also we make them differ in color, shape, activity, many ways."[25]

The scientists of Salomon's House not only produced new forms of birds and beasts, but they also altered and created new species of herbs and plants: "We have also means to make divers plants rise by mixtures of earths without seeds, and likewise to make divers new plants differing from the vulgar, and to make one tree or plant turn into another."

Rather than respecting the beauty of existing organisms, Bacon's *New Atlantis* advocated the creation of new ones:

> We have also large and various orchards and gardens, wherein we do not so much respect beauty as variety of ground and soil, proper for diverse trees and herbs. . . . And we make (by art) in the same orchards and gardens, trees and flowers to come earlier or later than their seasons, and to come up and bear more speedily than by their natural course they do. We make them by art greater much than their nature, and their fruit greater and sweeter and of differing taste, smell, color, and figure, from their nature.[26]

Della Porta had, again, given numerous examples of changing the colors and tastes of plants: a white vine could be turned into a black one, purple roses and violets could become white, and sweet almonds and pomegranates sour.

That such experimentation on animals and the creation of new species was ultimately directed toward human beings was intimated by Bacon: "We have also parks and enclosures of all sorts of beasts and birds, which we use not only for view or rareness but likewise for dissections and trials, that thereby we may take light [i.e., enlightenment] what may be wrought upon the body of man. . . . We also try all poisons and other medicines upon them as well of chirurgery as physic."[27]

Much of Bacon's strategy in the *New Atlantis* was directed at removing ethical strictures against manipulative magic, of the sort found in Agrippa's *Vanity of Arts and Science* (1530), a polemic probably written for Agrippa's own self-protection, containing important arguments against transforming and altering nature. Just as Agricola had been obliged to refute Agrippa's views on mining in order to liberate that activity from the ethical constraints imposed by ancient writers, so Bacon was obliged to refute the constraints against the manipulation of nature. Agrippa had argued against tampering with nature and maiming living organisms:

> Those exercises appurtenant to agriculture . . . might in some measure deserve commendation, could it have retained itself within moderate bounds and not shown us so many devices to make strange plants, so many portentous graftings and metamorphoses of trees; how to make horses copulate with asses, wolves with dogs, and so to engender many wondrous monsters contrary to nature: and those creatures to whom nature has given leave to range the air, the seas and earth so freely, to captivate and confine in aviaries, cages, warrens, parks, and fish ponds, and to fat them in coops, having first put out their eyes, and maimed their limbs.[28]

Agrippa had further inveighed against the manipulators of nature who had tried to discover "how to prevent storms, make . . . seed fruitful, kill weeds, scare wild beasts, stop the flight of beasts and birds, the swimming of fishes, to charm away all manner of diseases; of all which those wise men before named have written very seriously and very cruelly."

Much of Bacon's program in the *New Atlantis* was meant to sanction just such manipulations, his whole objective being to recover man's right over nature, lost in the Fall. Agrippa had observed that after the Fall nature, once kind and beneficent, had become wild and uncontrollable: "For now the earth produces nothing without our labor and our sweat, but deadly and venomous, . . . nor are the other elements less kind to us: many the seas destroy with raging tempests, and the horrid monsters devour: the air making war against us with thunder, lightning and storms; and with a crowd of pestilential diseases, the heavens conspire our ruin."

In order to control the ravages of wild tempestuous nature, Bacon set as one of the objectives of Salomon's House the artificial control of the weather and its concomitant monsters and pestilences: "We have also great and spacious houses, where we imitate and demonstrate meteors, as snow, hail, rain, some artificial rains of bodies and not of water, thunder, lightnings, also generation of bodies in air, as frogs, flies, and diverse others." Tempests (like that produced by Shakespeare's magician, Prospero), could also be created for study by using "engines for multiplying and enforcing of winds."[29]

The Baconian program, so important to the rise of Western science, contained within it a set of attitudes about nature and the scientist that reinforced the tendencies toward growth and progress inherent in early capitalism. While Bacon himself had no intimation as to where his goals might ultimately lead, nor was he responsible for modern attitudes, he was very sensitive to the trends and directions of his own time and voiced them eloquently. The expansive tendencies of his period have continued, and the possibility of their reversal is highly problematical.

Bacon's mechanistic utopia was fully compatible with the mechanical philosophy of nature that developed during the seventeenth century. Mechanism divided nature into atomic particles, which, like the civil citizens of Bensalem, were passive and inert. Motion and change were externally caused: in nature, the ultimate source was God, the seventeenth century's divine father, clockmaker, and engineer; in Bensalem, it was the patriarchal scientific administration of Salomon's House. The atomic parts of the mechanistic universe were ordered in a causal nexus such that by contact the motion of one part caused the motion of the next. The linear hierarchy of apprentices, novices, and scientists who passed along the observations, experimental results, and generalizations made the scientific method as mechanical as the operation of the universe itself. Although machine technology was relatively unadvanced in Bensalem, the model of nature and society in this utopia was consistent with the possibilities for increased technological and administrative growth.

In the *New Atlantis* lay the intellectual origins of

the modern planned environments initiated by the technocratic movement of the late 1920s and 1930s, which envisioned totally artificial environments created by and for humans. Too often these have been created by the mechanistic style of problem solving, which pays little regard to the whole ecosystem of which people are only one part. The antithesis of holistic thinking, mechanism neglects the environmental consequences of synthetic products and the human consequences of artificial environments. It would seem that the creation of artificial products was one result of the Baconian drive toward control and power over nature in which "The end of our foundation is the knowledge of causes and secret motions of things and the enlarging of the bounds of human empire, to the effecting of all things possible."[30] To this research program, modern genetic engineers have added new goals—the manipulation of genetic material to create human life in artificial wombs, the duplication of living organisms through cloning, and the breeding of new human beings adapted to highly technological environments.

THE BACONIAN PROGRAM

The development of science as a methodology for manipulating nature, and the interest of scientists in the mechanical arts, became a significant program during the latter half of the seventeenth century. Bacon's followers realized even more clearly than Bacon himself the connections between mechanics, the trades, middle-class commercial interests, and the domination of nature.

Lewis Roberts lamented the unexploited state of Mother Earth in his *Treasure of Traffike, or a Discourse of Foreign Trade* (1641):

> The earth, though notwithstanding it yieldeth thus naturally the richest and most precious commodities of all others, and is properly the fountain and mother of all the riches and abundance of the world, partly . . . bred within its bowels, and partly nourished upon the surface thereof, yet is it observable, and found true by daily experience in many countries, that the true search and inquisition thereof, in these our days, is by many too much neglected and omitted.[31]

John Dury and Samuel Hartlib, followers of Bacon and organizers of the Invisible College (ca. 1645), forerunner of the Royal Society, connected the study of the crafts and trades to increasing wealth. One of Dury's objectives was to make observations of the inventions and sciences "as may be profitable to the health of the body, to the preservation and increase of wealth by trades and mechanical industries, either by sea or land; either in peace or war."[32]

The avowedly Baconian utopia "The Kingdom of Macaria," (1641), attributed to Hartlib but probably written by Gabriel Plattes, an English writer on husbandry and mining, was dedicated not merely to the "knowledge of causes and secret motions of things," as was the *New Atlantis,* but to the total agricultural, commercial, and medical improvement of society.[33] In Macaria, the king has improved his forests, parks, and lands "to the utmost"—bringing in huge revenues. Owing to the efforts of the council of husbandry, "the whole kingdom is become like to a fruitful garden, the highways are paved, and are as fair as the streets of the city." Any man who held more land than he could develop and improve was admonished and penalized for each year during which he continued to leave it unimproved, until at last "his lands be forfeited and he banished out of the kingdom, as an enemy to the commonwealth." A council of fishing was to establish laws "whereby immense riches are yearly drawn out of the ocean," while the councils of trade by land and sea were to regulate the number of tradespeople and encourage all navigation that "may enrich the kingdom."

The health of the inhabitants was maintained by a "college of experience, where they deliver out yearly such medicines as they find out by experience." As members of the Society of Experimenters, all were required to defend any new ideas before a Great Council, which judged the truth or falsity of the discovery. "If any divine shall publish a new opinion to the common people, he shall be accounted a disturber of the public peace and shall suffer death for it."

Dissent, not only in science but also in religion, would be avoided "by invincible arguments as will abide the grand test of extreme dispute." Rational scientific judgment would thus overcome the passions and individualism of religious sects and promote health, welfare, and commercial growth in Macaria.

The virtuosi of the Royal Society were interested in carrying out Bacon's proposal to survey the history of trades and augment their usefulness. The English divine Thomas Sprat, whose *History of the Royal Society* (1667) defended it against its critics, desired to extract from the "operations of all trades," their "physical receipts or secrets," their "instruments, tools, engines, [and] manual operations." He extolled "our chief and most wealthy merchants and citizens" who had added their "industrious, punctual, and active genius" to the "quiet, sedentary, and reserved temper of men of learning."[34]

Human dominion over nature, an integral element of the Baconian program, was to be achieved through the experimental "disclosure of nature's secrets." Seventeenth-century scientists, reinforcing aggressive attitudes toward nature, spoke out in favor of "mastering" and "managing" the earth. Descartes wrote in his *Discourse on Method* (1636) that through knowing the crafts of the artisans and the forces of bodies we could "render ourselves the masters and possessors of nature."[35] Joseph Glanvill, the English philosopher who defended the Baconian program in his *Plus Ultra* of 1668, asserted that the objective of natural philosophy was to "enlarge knowledge by observation and experiment . . . so that nature being known, it may be mastered, managed, and used in the services of humane life." To achieve this objective, arts and instruments should be developed for "searching out the beginnings and depths of things and discovering the intrigues of remoter nature."[36] The most useful of the arts were chemistry, anatomy, and mathematics; the best instruments included the microscope, telescope, thermometer, barometer, and air pump.

The harshness of Bacon's language was captured in Glanvill's descriptions of the methods of studying nature. Bacon had advocated the dissection of nature in order to force it to reveal its secrets. For Glanvill, anatomy, "most useful in human life, . . . tend[ed] mightily to the eviscerating of nature, and disclosure of the springs of its motion." In searching out the secrets of nature, nothing was more helpful than the microscope for "the secrets of nature are not in the greater masses, but in those little threads and springs which are too subtle for the grossness of our unhelped senses."

According to Glanvill, Robert Boyle's experimental philosophy had advanced "the empire of man over inferior creatures" by taking seriously "those things which have been found out by illiterate tradesmen" and by developing the "dexterity of hand proper to artificers." Glanvill advocated chemistry as one of the most useful arts, for "by the violence of [its] artful fires it is made [to] confess those latent parts, which upon less provocation it would not disclose." By chemical techniques, "nature is unwound and resolved into the minute rudiments of its composition."

In his "Experimental Essays" (1661), Boyle distinguished between merely knowing as opposed to dominating nature in thinly veiled sexual metaphor: "I shall here briefly represent to you . . . that there are two very distinct ends that men may propound to themselves in studying natural philosophy. For some men care only to know nature, others desire to command her" and "to bring nature to be serviceable to their particular ends, whether of health, or riches, or sensual delight."[37]

The new image of nature as a female to be controlled and dissected through experiment legitimated the exploitation of natural resources. Although the image of the nurturing earth popular in the Renaissance did not vanish, it was superseded by new controlling imagery. The constraints against penetration associated with the earth-mother image were transformed into sanctions for denudation. After the Scientific Revolution, *Natura* no longer complains that her garments of modesty are being torn by the wrongful thrusts of man. She is portrayed in statues by the French sculptor Louis-Ernest Barrias (1841–1905) coyly removing her own veil and exposing herself to science. From an active teacher and parent, she has become a mindless, submissive body. Not only did this new image function as a sanction, but the new conceptual framework of the Scientific Revolution—mechanism—carried with it norms quite different from the norms of organicism.

NOTES

1. Treatments of Francis Bacon's contributions to science include Paolo Rossi, *Francis Bacon: From Magic To Science* (London: Routledge & Kegan Paul, 1968); Lisa Jardine, *Francis Bacon: Discovery and the Art of Discourse* (Cambridge, England: Cambridge University Press, 1974); Benjamin Farrington, *Francis Bacon: Philosopher of Industrial Science* (New York: Schumann, 1949); Margery Purver, *The Royal Society: Concept and Creation* (London: Routledge & Kegan Paul, 1967).

2. Farrington, *Francis Bacon,* p. 82. James Spedding,

The Letters and the Life of Francis Bacon, 7 vols. (London: Longmans, Green, Reader, and Dyer, 1869), vol. 3, pp. 56–66.

3. Louis Wright, "The Popular Controversy Over Women," in *Middle-Class Culture in Elizabethan England* (Chapel Hill: University of North Carolina Press, 1935), Chap. 13, pp. 493, 494; Anon., *Hic Mulier, or The Man-Woman, Being a Medicine to Cure the Coltish Disease of the Staggers in the Masculine-Feminines of Our Times* (London, 1620); Lucy Ingram Morgan, "The Renaissance Lady in England," unpublished doctoral dissertation, University of California at Berkeley, 1932.

4. "Letter of John Chamberlain," Jan. 25, 1620. Quoted in Wright, p. 493.

5. Thomas Overbury, *Miscellaneous Works,* ed. E. F. Rimbault (London: Smith, 1856), quotation on p. xxxvii; see also Spedding, *Letters and Life of Francis Bacon,* vol. 5, pp. 296–305, esp. 297, 298 n.; Violet A. Wilson, *Society Women of Shakespeare's Time* (London: Lane, Bodley Head, 1924), p. 205; Wright, p. 491.

6. James I, *Daemonologie* (New York: Barnes & Noble, 1966; first published 1597); Keith Thomas, *Religion and the Decline of Magic* (New York: Scribner's, 1971), p. 520; Wallace Notestein, *A History of Witchcraft in England from 1558 to 1718* (New York: Apollo Books, 1968), p. 101; Ronald Seth, *Stories of Great Witch Trials* (London: Baker, 1967), p. 83.

7. Bacon, "De Dignitate et Augmentis Scientiarum," (written 1623), *Works,* ed. James Spedding, Robert Leslie Ellis, Douglas Devon Heath, 14 vols. (London: Longmans Green, 1870), vol. 4, p. 296. The ensuing discussion was stimulated by William Leiss's *The Domination of Nature* (New York: Braziller, 1972), Chap. 3, pp. 45–71.

8. Bacon, "Preparative Towards a Natural and Experimental History," *Works,* vol. 4, p. 263. Italics added.

9. Bacon, "De Dignatate," *Works,* vol. 4, p. 298. Italics added.

10. Bacon, "The Great Instauration" (written 1620), *Works,* vol. 4, p. 20; "The Masculine Birth of Time," ed. and trans. Benjamin Farrington, in *The Philosophy of Francis Bacon* (Liverpool, England: Liverpool University Press, 1964), p. 62; "De Dignitate," *Works,* vol. 4, pp. 287, 294.

11. Quoted in Moody E. Prior, "Bacon's Man of Science," in Leonard M. Marsak, ed., *The Rise Of Modern Science in Relation to Society* (London: Collier-Macmillan, 1964), p. 45.

12. Rossi, p. 21; Leiss, p. 56; Bacon, *Works,* vol. 4, p. 294; Henry Cornelius Agrippa, *De Occulta Philosophia Libri Tres* (Antwerp, 1531): "No one has such powers but he who has cohabited with the elements, vanquished nature, mounted higher than the heavens, elevating himself above the angels to the archetype itself, with whom he then becomes cooperator and can do all things," as quoted in Frances A. Yates, *Giordano Bruno and the Hermetic Tradition* (New York: Vintage Books, 1964), p. 136.

13. Bacon, "Novum Organum," Part 2, in *Works,* vol. 4, p. 247; "Valerius Terminus," *Works,* vol. 3, pp. 217, 219; "The Masculine Birth of Time," trans. Farrington, p. 62.

14. Bacon, "The Masculine Birth of Time," and "The Refutation of Philosophies," trans. Farrington, pp. 62, 129, 130.

15. Bacon, "De Augmentis," *Works,* vol. 4, p. 294; see also Bacon, "Aphorisms," *Works,* vol. 4.

16. "De Augmentis," *Works,* vol. 4, pp. 320, 325; Plato, "The Timaeus," in *The Dialogues of Plato,* trans. B. Jowett (New York: Random House, 1937), vol. 2, p. 17; Bacon, "Parasceve," *Works,* vol. 4, p. 257.

17. Bacon, "De Augmentis," *Works,* vol. 4, pp. 343, 287, 343, 393.

18. Bacon, "Novum Organum," *Works,* vol. 4, p. 246; "The Great Instauration," *Works,* vol. 4, p. 29; "Novum Organum," Part 2, *Works,* vol. 4, p. 247.

19. Alain of Lille, *De Planctu Naturae,* in T. Wright, ed., *The Anglo-Latin Satirical Poets and Epigrammatists* (Wiesbaden: Kraus Reprint, 1964), vol. 2, pp. 441, 467; Thomas Kuhn, "Mathematical vs. Experimental Traditions in the Development of Physical Science," *Journal of Interdisciplinary History* 7, no. 1 (Summer 1976): 1–31, see p. 13. On the Accademia del Cimentio's experiments see Martha Ornstein [Bronfenbrenner], *The Role of Scientific Societies in the Seventeenth Century* (reprint ed., New York: Arno Press, 1975), p. 86.

20. Bacon, "Thoughts and Conclusions on the Interpretation of Nature or A Science of Productive Works," trans. Farrington, *The Philosophy of Francis Bacon,* pp. 96, 93, 99.

21. Bacon, "De Augmentis," *Works,* vol. 4, p. 294; "Parasceve," *Works,* vol. 4, p. 257; "Plan of the Work," vol. 4, p. 32; "Novum Organum," *Works,* vol. 4, pp. 114, 115.

22. Bacon, "The New Atlantis," *Works,* vol. 3, subsequent quotations on pp. 165, 154, 155. On politics and science in "The New Atlantis," see Joseph Haberer, *Politics and the Community of Science* (New York: Van Nostrand Reinhold, 1969), pp. 46, 47; see M. E. Prior, "Bacon's Man of Science," in L. M. Marsak, ed., pp. 41–53; P. Rossi, *Francis Bacon,* Chap. 1. On critiques of technology, see John McDermott, "Technology: The Opiate of the Intellectuals," *New York Review of Books,* July 31, 1969; Theodore Roszak, *Where the Wasteland Ends* (Garden City, N.Y.: Doubleday, 1963), Chap. 2.

23. Bacon, "The New Atlantis," *Works,* vol. 3, quotations on pp. 157, 158, 159.

24. G. della Porta, *Natural Magic,* ed. D. J. Price (facsimile of 1658 ed., New York: Basic Books, 1957; first published 1558), pp. 27, 29, 31–40.

25. Bacon, *Works,* vol. 3, quotations on pp. 159, 158. Cf. Della Porta, pp. 59, 61, 62.

26. Bacon, *Works,* vol. 3, p. 158; Cf. Della Porta, pp. 61–62, 73, 74–75, 81, 95–99.
27. Bacon, *Works,* vol. 3, p. 159.
28. Henry Cornelius Agrippa, *The Vanity of Arts and Sciences* (London, 1694; first published 1530), pp. 252–53.
29. Bacon, *Works,* vol. 3, pp. 157, 158.
30. *Ibid.,* p. 156.
31. Lewis Roberts, *The Treasure of Traffike, Or A Discourse of Foreign Trade* (London, 1641). Quoted in Charles Webster, *The Great Instauration: Science, Medicine and Reform, 1626–1660* (London: Duckworth, 1975), p. 356; for more details on the Baconian program in mid-seventeenth-century England, the reader is referred to Webster's thorough, scholarly study.
32. Quoted in Walter E. Houghton, "The History of Trades: Its Relation to Seventeenth Century Thought," in *Roots of Scientific Thought* p. 361.
33. [Attributed to Samuel Hartlib], *A Description of the Famous Kingdome of Macaria,* intro. by Richard H. Dillon (facsimile ed., Sausalito, Cal.: Elan, 1961; first published 1641), quotations on pp. 4, 5, 8, 5, 2. On Gabriel Plattes as the probable author, see Charles Webster, "The Authorship and Significance of Macaria," in C. Webster, ed., *The Intellectual Revolution of the Seventeenth Century* (London: Routledge & Kegan Paul), pp. 369–85. See also Houghton, p. 361, and Webster, *Great Instauration,* pp. 87, 368–69.
34. Thomas Sprat, *History of the Royal Society,* 4th ed. (London, 1734; first published 1667), pp. 129–30, 190; Houghton, pp. 370, 377. On the interest of the Royal Society in practical application and technology, see Robert K. Merton, *Science, Technology, and Society in Seventeenth Century England* (New York: Fertig, 1970; first published 1938).
35. Ren, Descartes, "Discourse on Method," Part 4, in E. S. Haldane and G. R. T. Ross, eds., *Philosophical Works of Descartes* (New York: Dover, 1955), vol. 1, p. 119.
36. Joseph Glanvill, *Plus Ultra* (Gainesville, Fla.: Scholar's Facsimile Reprints, 1958; first published 1668), quotations on pp. 9, 87, 13, 56, 104, 10.
37. Robert Boyle, *Works,* ed. Thomas Birch (Hildesheim, W. Germany: Olms, 1965; first published 1772), vol. 1, p. 310. On Boyle's mechanical philosophy, see Marie Boas, "The Establishment of the Mechanical Philosophy," *Osiris* 10 (1952): 412–541; Frederick O'Toole, "Qualities and Powers in the Corpuscular Philosophy of Robert Boyle," *Journal of the History of Philosophy* 12 (July 1974): 295–316; Margaret J. Osler, "John Locke and Some Philosophical Problems in the Science of Boyle and Newton," unpublished doctoral dissertation, Indiana University, 1968; Robert Kargon, "Walter Charleton, Robert Boyle, and the Acceptance of Epicurean Atomism in England," *Isis* 55 (1964): 184–92.

The New Nature

GREGG EASTERBROOK

In 1993 the Russian Space Agency Glavkosmos placed into orbit a large parafoil mirror designed to reflect sunlight toward the dark hemisphere of Earth, transforming night into a false twilight with about the luminescence of three full moons. Such mirrors, Russian engineers thought, might someday shine on cities, replacing street lights with zero-pollution, zero-fuel illumination. Or the mirrors might be held on station, available to train on the sites of nighttime natural disasters or search-and-rescue emergencies. In principle a large network of space mirrors might banish darkness from the face of the Earth altogether, maintaining the night hemisphere in perpetual half-light.

For technical reasons the experiment failed, though engineers remain convinced such mirrors could function. Environmental opposition to further research was emphatic. Bill McKibben declared that space-reflected illumination would "constitute the single most offensive form of pollution yet devised by man," here defining sunlight as pollution if that light arrives when the sun does not normally deliver it. "We should be screaming about this," McKibben suggested.

Needless to say, whether space mirrors would be desirable is open to dispute. Let's suppose for the sake of argument that someday space launches become inexpensive and people decide to ring the globe with orbital mirrors intended to end true darkness. This possibility offers a framework for pondering the sorts of global tampering of which genus *Homo* increasingly will become capable.

A space-mirror network would alter the ecology in significant ways. Like all human ecological meddling, such alterations might be good or bad. For instance having cities half-lit at night might cause crime and accidents to go down, but increase insomnia. Nocturnal life cycles would shift for many creatures. Plants might grow faster, aiding some at the expense of others. Biologists might petition to have the half-light switched off in areas where it seems to imperil a species. Parks and resorts might apply for exemptions, advertising the experience of true night. Going someplace with absolute darkness might become a lovers' holiday.

Yet within a few generations both people and living things would consider half-dark the normal condition, full dark unnerving and needlessly dangerous. Since the circumstances experienced in youth become through each person's nostalgia filter the image of what the world ought to be, women and men born to a world of half-dark night might consider full-dark night a violation of the presumed environmental Correct Reality. Nature might eventually be pleased by the adjustment, since once living things modified behaviorally and genetically for partial night, the net activity of the ecology might increase, the half-dark being able to sponsor more biological action than full-dark, in which few creatures function.

Whether the abolition of full darkness would on balance be good or bad will be a matter for some future century to settle. The only thing we can be sure of now is that the doctrinal environmental response—that such an idea should never be considered because artificial alteration of nature would be involved—is a dead end. A New Nature, modified by men and women, is coming. It cannot be stopped, nor should it. The issue that matters is how to make the New Nature good rather than bad.

NATURAL LIMITS

When environmental thinkers evince horror at the idea of people deliberately altering nature on a broad scale, what they evince is their human dislike of the consequences. Fair enough. But what might nature think about deliberate alteration of nature? Perhaps nature thinks, *It's about time.* Nature's accomplishments are legion and worthy of awe. Were nature to continue operating in purely spontaneous fashion, many further accomplishments would be recorded. But barriers would be reached as well. Nature has structural flaws and physical limitations. Genus *Homo* may be able to change that. People may be here because nature needs us—perhaps, needs us desperately.

Five fundamental barriers face the wholly spontaneous form of nature that many environmentalists extol.

First, nature cannot act by design. This is the most basic fault of the natural system. Action by design is far from perfect: plans go awry, good intentions have unwelcome consequences. Nevertheless action by design can accomplish ends that spontaneous forces cannot, perhaps helping nature surmount barriers it could not surmount on its own.

Second, nature can accumulate information only through genes. Adaptive intellect can store and make sense of information millions of times faster than genetic systems. Yes, adaptive intellect can also pursue evil ends. That fear aside, there is no reason in principle why nature ought to oppose the arrival of the high-speed analytical powers of the mind. Nature may have been dreaming of these very powers for 3.8 billion years.

Third, nature is limited by reliance on the sun. Most Earth organisms, including all the really interesting ones, rely on a food chain that begins with solar photons converted to chemical energy by photosynthesis. Most life depends on the sun to warm the climate. Reliance on the sun limits nature by restricting the amount of life in the high-northern and low-southern latitudes; by requiring life in the temperate latitudes to survive a taxing winter; by causing widespread ecological damage when the sun is blocked by dust from volcanos or asteroid strikes; and perhaps by foreclosing life on planets where sunlight is either too intense or too faint, such as all the planets in this solar system other than Earth. Worst, over the very long term in which nature thinks, the sun will become an enemy of the biosphere—first by growing hotter and making the oceans boil, then by fusing into metallic elements and eventually detonating.

And the sun is a profligate power source. Many environmental thinkers rightly note with disdain that the internal combustion engine converts a mere 20 percent of the energy value in petroleum to forward motion. Yet a gas-guzzling 1955 Chevy pushrod V-8 is a positive marvel of efficiency compared to nature's engines—stars—which waste energy on a phenomenal scale. Less than one-tenth of one percent of the sun's power output falls on Earth, where it becomes useful to life. So far as is known the 99 percent of solar energy that radiates off into deep space accomplishes nothing whatever, except perhaps providing career opportunities for astronomers on other worlds. A natural scheme based on an energy source that wastes nearly everything it generates, and that will fail in the long run, sounds like a scheme with flaws that might someday be corrected by adaptive intellect.

Fourth, nature is limited by the chance basis of DNA change. Evolution is not, as commonly said, a "random" process. By favoring some traits over others, natural selection guides the system in a better-than-random manner. But the gene changes that make for differing traits do have a chance basis, probably originating in copying errors during DNA replication. The chance basis of DNA change can cause individual species to be vulnerable, since the required mutation may not pop up during a period of ecological stress; can render it hard for the entire biosphere to gain from gene advances achieved in any particular species; and can tend to make the evolutionary process a conservative one, unlikely to stage grand departures from past forms. If something more is in store—perhaps a form of life based more on consciousness than biology—random evolutionary mutations may not be sufficient to reach that level.

Finally nature faces a fundamental restriction in that life requires planets. The universe may be rich with wondrous vitality arising in exotic locales. Based on what is known so far, the likelihood is that wholly spontaneous life can only evolve and exist on planets.

This restriction is deceptively significant. Only two (unnamed at this writing) planets have been discovered outside Earth's solar system, and they orbit a pulsar, a collapsed sun emitting radiation at such fantastic levels that life on these worlds defies imagination. Planets are much harder to spot than stars; the fact that astronomers have detected only two "extrasolar" planets hardly means there are not many faraway worlds. But some astrophysicists believe that of the many extrasolar planets presumed to exist, Earthlike worlds will turn out exceedingly rare. Even where Earthlike planets exist such bodies cannot secure life against cosmic forces like asteroid strikes and star detonations. Perhaps nature would like to break its reliance on planets, sequestering at least part of the living heritage beyond planetary vulnerabilities.

These fundamental restrictions of the environment—that nature cannot act by design, that natural accumulation of information is slow, that life is overdependent on suns, that natural selection is limited by random gene-copying accidents, and that life requires planets—are ones that might seem sufficiently elemental as to be knitted into the fabric of existence itself.

Yet restriction number one, the inability to act by design, is already being overthrown. Today human intellect may be riddled with flaws and used toward evil ends. But from the standpoint of nature, intellect is a project proceeding at remarkable speed with encouraging results, generating an entirely new aspect of life in a very short time by geologic standards. That makes it possible to imagine other basic restrictions of nature being overthrown, perhaps again quickly by nature's way of thinking.

THE NEW NATURE

Let's conduct a thought experiment into what a New Nature might be like.

First, the New Nature might include the end of predation by animals against animals. As detailed in part one, researchers such as the biologist Lynn Margulis increasingly believe that cooperation is the operating principle of most life. Ted Dawson, a plant ecologist at Cornell University, has discovered that tree roots do not, as previously assumed, draw all available water to the tree. Dawson found that at night the roots of the sugar maple pull up water from soils too deep for other plants to reach. In daytime maple roots discharge some of that water, helping smaller plants flourish. The closer plants such as goldenrod are to a sugar maple, the more likely their survival during dry seasons. Other biologists are finding similar water-sharing behavior in other trees. This is enlightened cooperation, not a bestial clash of all against all.

Obviously there are spectacular exceptions to the premise of cooperation among species. Yet is the destructive life-pattern of the predator a necessity of biology or a flaw of nature awaiting correction? Some very large, powerful creatures such as gorillas exist quite nicely as herbivores. It is possible at least in theory that through genetic intervention, present-day predators could become herbivores, continuing to live as wild bears or wolves or weasel, except leaving out the gruesome part. Nature might long for such a reform. Surely nature's prey species, a vast "silent majority" in biosphere demographics, would be pleased by an end of predation.

Next, the New Nature might include an end of predation against animals by people. Some advocate vegetarianism for reasons of ethics; some for the practical reason that Earth's agricultural output is today sufficient for the world to eat its fill of grains and fruits, but when a substantial amount of grain is fed to cattle and poultry to raise meat, malnutrition results among the impoverished. Both the ethical and pragmatic reasons for vegetarianism are sound, but the practice is unlikely to spread simply because most people like to eat meat and will continue to do so until either stopped by compulsion or given a desirable alternative. So let's give them a desirable alternative.

In theory it is not necessary to have animals in order to have meat. Carbohydrates and proteins, the basic stuff of nutrition, might be grown in plants to supply a sort of feedstock. This food-fuel might then be cultured into the cells of beef, chicken, or fish in genetic engineering production vats similar to those now employed to culture genetically engineered pharmaceuticals. The final product would be biological meat—just meat cells that skipped the stage of existing in an animal that suffered.

This idea is today being discussed in general terms by agronomists. Many environmentalists express disgust at the prospect of cultured meat, and not just because such techno-vegetarianism would be insufficiently punitive. Green doctrine is horrified by this prospect because genetic engineering would be required, and because people would consume a category of substance their romanticized hunter-gatherer ancestors never ate. Yet the confinement and slaughter of stock animals also would end; the dosing of stock with growth hormones and prophylactic antibiotics would end; methane emissions from beef herds would end; the content of meats could be manipulated to emphasize nutrition.

Of course if such products arrived in supermarkets today shoppers would turn away, insisting on "real" meat. But then today's consumers would turn away from the feathered carcass of a chicken whose neck had just been wrung—the form in which great-grandmother got her meat. Not far into the future, raising cattle in pens for slaughter in automated abattoirs will seem as primitive as wringing a chicken's neck in the kitchen seems today. Eventually the entire human species may be converted to de facto vegetarianism not through ethical philosophy but through the development of steak, chops, and sole that have nothing to do with animals.

Next, the New Nature may include the end of predation against people by people. In all of nature exist only a handful of creatures that kill their own. Unfortunately one is us.

The fact that most animals will not prey on others like themselves is not just some charming quirk: It must have a physical basis in the genetic inventories of living things. Suppose the DNA codes that prevent most species from killing their own can be isolated and moved into genus *Homo,* rendering men and women genetically averse to raising weapons against each other. An initiative to insert into the entire human DNA germ line a no-kill code would be complex and fraught with pitfalls. But if it worked perhaps the worst error of Earth history—the combination of intellect and predation—would be corrected. Would nature favor this entirely artificial development? One guess.

Next for the New Nature may be the end of extinctions. Nature has never been able to find a means to preserve species rendered extinct by the inevitability of ecological change. Perhaps woman [*sic*] and men can.

Next would be the end of disease. A few researchers have entertained the notion that diseases serve some undiscovered functional role in the natural scheme. But the likelihood is that disease is a defect of nature waiting to be corrected. The eradication of smallpox, declared extinct by the World Health Organization in 1977, shows that it is not utopian to imagine diseases being driven from the biosphere. And disease eradication need not be confined to the illnesses that afflict people but could extend to the diseases of the rest of the living world. Bear in mind that diseases cause far more suffering and death among animals than humans.

Next, the New Nature may be secure against killer rocks. Part one presented the increasingly uncomfortable evidence that devastating impacts of asteroids and comets were not confined to the primordial mists but are a global calamity the ecosystem has dodged as recently as this century. Millennia may pass before humankind is capable of a New Nature initiative as far-reaching as placing no-kill genes into DNA. Much sooner than that, women and men should be able to build a network of comet and asteroid detectors, linked to missiles or lasers that would push off course any dangerous objects headed toward Earth.

Such systems may be especially important in light of calculations published in 1994 in the *Quarterly of the Royal Astronomical Society* by the British scientist Robert Matthews. Our solar system travels within the galactic plane. Matthews believes that the next 46,000 years will be "rich in close encounters" between Sol, our star, and other suns, with at least six passing closer to the sun than the current closest star, Proxima Centauri. Matthews calculates these close encounters will cause gravitational effects that send monumental numbers of comets spiraling inward toward the Earth from the Oort cloud, a haze of comets believed to encircle the solar system.

Researchers suspect that gravitational consequences of the passage of the solar system through the galactic plane periodically perturbs the Oort cloud, explaining the barrages of celestial objects that now appear a persistent feature of natural history. Nature would long for this cosmic fusillade against the biosphere to end. Most chilling, Matthews calculates that it is possible one of the worst comet barrages in the 3.8 billion year living history of the Earth is about to commence, as in a few thousand years the solar system will pass unusually close to the binary star Alpha Centauri A-B, two suns whose combined mass may unleash a comet downfall of satanic proportions. However irksome human intellect may be, it may have arrived not a moment too soon to protect the living world from this devastation.

Next, in the New Nature there may be no more aging. Some physicians now believe that through improved nutrition, medicine, and exercise the normal human lifetime could be extended to around 125 years, without genetic engineering. A tantalizing hint of such a possibility comes from Michael Rose, a researcher at the University of California at Irvine, who has found that by selective breeding he could produce colonies of fruit flies that live twice as long as typical flies and are more hearty throughout their doubled lives.

Beyond that is the mystery of why living things age at all, since throughout life every creature maintains in every cell the DNA blueprint necessary to remake itself from scratch. Yet this knowledge is used only once: When cells begin to age, the blueprint is not reactivated. In the last decade some scientists have begun to ask whether the aging of living things is not some form of error that entered the DNA chain inadvertently. For instance Denham Harmon, the University of Nebraska researcher who in the 1950s first documented the presence in the body of "free radical" compounds that degrade cells, on making his discovery asked, If natural selection is so wise, why has it not produced genes for proteins to counter free radicals? A possible answer comes from Thomas Kirkwood, a biologist at the Medical Research Council in London, who has proposed that evolution never selected for longevity because almost all animals in the wild die young—killed by predators, disease, starvation, or accident long before they have the chance to age. Lack of resistance genes for cellular decline would be irrelevant to creatures fated to die young. All that would matter from the standpoint of evolutionary fitness would be the ability to reach sexual maturity, reproduce, and extend the gene line.

Pondering such notions some biologists have begun to toy with the idea that it will someday be possible to switch off the error genes that cause senescence, while perhaps inserting into DNA resistance genes for free radicals and other factors in aging. In principle this could be done for the entire biosphere, not just for people. Ageless people or animals would not be immortal, mortality continuing in accidents, from disease, through violence. But in an ageless biosphere, human death would not only be the moral loss it has always been; it would be still more poignant by virtue of rarity. As recently as two centuries ago, a third of children died before their first birthdays. Today, in the Western world, any death of a soft, breathing infant is considered a tragedy of high order. It is conceivable that someday, any death of anyone at any age will seem as tragic as a child's death seems today.

Next, the New Nature might end the waste of the Sun's output. Through the century to come men and women will get much better at using the energy that falls on Earth. But what about the vastly greater solar energies that stream off into the void? Some of that energy might be captured by space-solar generators that would beam electricity down to Earth. Some might be captured by reflectors that would concentrate sunlight into the atmosphere of Mars, warming that planet to the point of habitability. And in principle all solar energy might be captured. The physicist Freeman Dyson has proposed that someday humankind might detonate one of the presumably lifeless outer planets and use the debris to build a reflective sphere around the solar system. This sphere would be manipulated in such a way that Earth would remain at its current temperature while the rest of the very large area bounded by the outermost planets would be flooded by life-giving warmth and light.

Construction of a Dyson sphere would alter the spontaneous arrangements of nature on a planetary scale. Yet as every environment is born doomed, even the very planets are not exempt from alteration. Eventually all bodies of this solar system will be destroyed when the sun becomes a supernova. If, say, destroying lifeless Pluto a few billion years ahead of schedule led to a few billion years of life on Neptune, Uranus, and the moons of Saturn, would nature complain?

Finally the New Nature might offer the end of oblivion. At present human beings do not know whether upon death consciousness is lost or preserved in some higher form. For the sake of our own souls and those that have come before, we should hope an afterlife already exists. But if it does not, then people should make one.

Exactly what may constitute a soul is of course unknown, but it is not a shot in the dark to suppose the answer has something to do with consciousness. On a mechanical basis, consciousness appears to be mediated by electrical patterns in the brain. Today such patterns can be sustained only by a biological brain supported by a biological body. Perhaps someday those patterns could draw on some other form of support, one to which consciousness will move when the body of birth can no longer sustain itself. Perhaps someday some form of technology might even sustain patterns of consciousness in a noncorporeal manner. Lots of things could go wrong with such a premise. But here at least is the prospect that someday, in the New Nature, when the body dies the mind does not.

Today women and men look back on their forebears of distant centuries and view them with sadness as benighted creatures that lived out crude lives with constant material suffering and in ignorance of the most basic facts of the world around them. Someday our descendants may look back with greater sadness at us—we who view ourselves as so advanced—seeing us as the last benighted human generations that on physical death went to oblivion, rather than having their consciousness continue living, as for millennia people have supposed would be the fitting progression after temporal life.

ENVIRONMENTAL ECONOMICS

You may think that items on the above inventory of possible alterations for a New Nature represent progress and a gentle dawn. You may think they represent arrogance and foolhardy adventurism. Whichever may be the case men and women cannot reform nature unless they first reform themselves. Institutions of government must be improved to the point of being consistently benevolent, for example, before anyone in his or her right mind would endorse tinkering with the human gene line. Whether true benevolent government can be achieved is obviously an open question. As regards the environment, a necessary reform preceding a New Nature will be the fading of the materialist lifestyle. Here the odds of social progress may be more favorable.

Much of what manifests today as anger about the environment is really anger about the centrality of the materialist lifestyle. The treadmill of earn-and-spend, on which it is not possible to make progress, only exert oneself into exhaustion; the obsession with forgettable consumer acquisitions to the exclusion of appreciation of art, philosophy, and other things of lasting value; constant earnings anxiety even among the well-paid; and many similar problems inspire sentiments that express themselves as environmentalist fury against the corporations and government agencies promoting the materialist lifestyle. As the Age of Pollution ends, the sorts of gross ecological malfeasance that first animated the green movement will fall away. Environmentalism as the word is used today will no longer be necessary. But long after the fight against pollution ends the fight against materialism will continue. This struggle may become more important than it is today, as the achievement of a clean, sustainable form of economics will offer many benefits, yet will have the regrettable side effect of making it possible for the cycle of consumption to continue indefinitely. If the human soul is to be saved, the materialist urge must be overcome: Green thinking, now focused on opposition to industry and development, will eventually focus on the more subtle and telling question of the harm materialism does to humanity, not nature. To the extent environmental sentiment transforms into a critique of the materialist lifestyle it will serve a more important purpose than halting pollution, since it will help bring genus *Homo* not just clean air and safe water but something of greater value: inner peace.

Following the collapse of the Soviet monolith there is no doubt that capitalism has been shown dramatically superior to communism both in the production of necessities of life and in the enabling of human freedom. Defenders of capitalism now tout this line assiduously. But think what it is they tout: *We've proven that capitalism is better than communism.* We've proven our system is superior to the worst social organizing principle ever devised: Pop the corks! At best capitalism is a transitional phase between a feudal human past and some future social ordering that combines the productive efficiency of free markets with the equity and community capitalism lacks. And for capitalism to be modified, materialism must first decline.

Somehow the notion has arisen that the excesses of capitalism occurred in the Gilded Age. They continue today. Consider that in 1993 Michael Eisner, chair of the Disney Corporation, paid himself $203 million, or 8,465 times the average American annual income. The previous year Eisner paid himself $126 million, a mere 5,254 times the average wage. Such sums allow Eisner to live at a level of selfishness that would have embarrassed princes and dukes of previous centuries. Yet at the same time Disney's executive was conferring opulence on himself, he begrudged quarter-an-hour raises to thousands of low-wage personnel. Had Eisner paid himself just $10 million for 1993, still a spectacular sum, his company could have used the surplus to grant each of the 33,000 workers at its Disney World park an additional $5,848, which for working mothers and others poised on the boundary between success and dependence might have been the difference between a happy year and a stressful year on the edge. Eisner's windfall at the expense of his workers is at least as bad as anything that happened in the Gilded Age—worse in some ways, as the U.S. economic system is today supposedly well regulated. And his is not an isolated abuse. For instance, in 1992 Thomas Frist, Jr., chair of the Hospital Corporation of America, a company whose revenues are heavily tax-subsidized by Medicare, paid himself $127 million, or 5,297 times the average wage.

Consider another indictment of capitalism, the 1991 fire at a chicken processing plant in Hamlet, North Carolina, that killed 25 workers, most of them young parents. The dead were found huddled against fire exits bolted from the outside to prevent workers from sneaking chicken parts out under their gowns. Workers should not steal chicken parts. But most jobs in the Hamlet plant paid $5.75 hourly for hard, disgusting work. That wage equates to $11,500 per year, below the poverty line for a family of four. The workers were stealing chicken parts not from greed, there being no black market in gizzards, but to feed their families. These deaths of impoverished workers happened not in the coal mines of eighteenth-century Wales or the brick kilns of Rawalpindi during the Raj but in today's hip, high-tech United States, the richest society in history.

Don't care about wretched poultry hands in Southern backwaters? Only care, in the best capitalist tradition, about yourself? Then what has capitalism done for you lately?

The worldly unhappiness and apprehension that exist among the middle classes of the Western nations, a group that now counts several hundred million members, bear witness that the astonishing plenitude of capitalism does not confer satisfaction. Instead capitalism renders its chosen covetous, insecure, unfulfilled, constantly twitching—gives them everything anyone could ever want in a structure guaranteed to ensure they won't be happy about it. Materialist obsession has performed the amazing feat of making unprecedented abundance unsatisfactory to its beneficiaries.

There's nothing wrong with material things per se: What's wrong is when the quest for material things takes over life. By producing the necessities of life faster and cheaper, it once seemed capitalism could free human beings from subservience to material needs. Instead, snared in the cycle of earn-and-spend, today even well-to-do Westerners are more wrapped up in materialism than ever before. That is not a good outcome for society or for the soul. Environmentalism must steel itself with rationality to fight on against this outcome long after the last puff of pollution has been rinsed clean.

INDIAN REVIVAL AND THE ANTIMATERIALIST LIFE

Is the dream of movement away from materialism an idle one? No: Environmental and technical trends may conjoin to nudge society in that direction. This is among the most promising areas in which people, machines, and nature may learn to work together to each other's mutual benefit.

Per-capita consumption of most commercial materials—steel, concrete, aluminum, ammonia, phosphorus, even plastics—has already peaked and been in decline in the Western world for a decade or more. This conveys an important hint about the green future: that in addition to becoming steadily cleaner and more resource-efficient, technology may grow steadily less obtrusive.

Can you think of any important area in which consumer products are getting bigger rather than smaller? Cars have been downsizing for two decades; televisions have bigger screens, but the mechanicals are shrinking toward flat; vinyl records, famous consumers of space, are being replaced by little CDs; everything about computers continues to shrink. Newly built factories—I've been in several recently—tend to be smaller and less obtrusive than what they supplant, in addition to emitting little or nothing. This raises the intriguing prospect that future homes and towns will suggest pastoral country settings more than zoomy Jetsons spaceports. This would be especially true if advancing electronics could lend to pastoral homes and offices some of the benefits of cosmopolitan existence when required. Through recent decades people have crowded into dehumanizing high-rise corridors because economic and technical trends dictated such behavior. Once economic and technical trends point back toward a pastoral existence, many people will vote for that eagerly. Per-capita resource consumption will decline; the typical person will spend more of her or his time walking with nature. High tech will continue to be a central aspect of life but will reduce rather than advance resource requirements. American society will cycle back somewhat toward the texture of American Indian life.

Much romanticized nonsense has been churned out about indigenous America in recent years. I would never have wanted to live as a pre-Columbian Indian, shivering in the cold, starving when crops failed, watching my children die of infectious disease. Whatever mystic connections with the land Native Americans might once have felt seem to me entirely outweighed by the suffering they endured at the hand of nature.

But I might very well want to live as an Indian of the twenty-second century, and so might you. Suppose the best of Western technical culture—medical care, high-yield food production, security against the elements, electronics—could be combined with aspects of old American culture. A minor change might be one such as the recent trend, even among high-yield farmers, toward no-till planting, reverting to the Native American practice of not turning the earth each season. A major change might be eventual trends toward Native American concepts such as respect for the larger rhythms of the Earth, and judging the success or failure of a person's life based on deeds rather than on possession of stuff.

This raises the possibility that American Indian culture, an aspect of the environment once widely considered "destroyed," will in the future be more significant than it was in the past. When Europeans came to North America, the area now called the United States probably contained three to five million red people. By late in the nineteenth century that figure had fallen to less than 100,000; the Indian seemed fated for extinction. Today there are 1.8 million people of red ancestry in the United States. If current trends hold, sometime in the twenty-first century there will be as many Indians living in the U.S. as when the white man arrived here. By the twenty-second century the Indian population of the United States may exceed the pre-Columbian number. And society may turn to its red population for counsel on how to improve relations with the natural sphere.

That Indian thinking might someday expand anew through North America again places in perspective the resilience of the natural world. If the American Indian, persecuted without compunction for three centuries, nonetheless can bounce back—then you know the environment can, too.

THE REAL EDEN

An indicator both of the prospect of a return toward a more nature-oriented lifestyle, and of the blinders environmental dogma wears regarding the possibilities of a New Nature, is something called the Wildlands Project. Sponsored by the Society for Conservation Biology, this project envisions rearranging the United States with the needs of other species in mind. It calls for such momentous efforts as the relocation of ten million people away from the Oregon and California coastlines, tearing out most structures and roads there; the relocation of several million people out of the Blue Ridge corridor, tearing down most homes and resorts there; and restricting about half the United States to "minimal" use, roughly meaning that which can be done on foot. This would reestablish large blocks of wild land where nature would reassert itself. The Wildlands Project has won the backing of many well-known environmentalists and been the subject of international conferences attended by many ecologists.

Reed Noss, editor of the journal *Conservation Biology,* has said that the purpose of the project is to begin preparing for a time perhaps 200 years from now when the human population of the United States declines. Impossible? Projections from the United Nations show that if the entire world ultimately adapts the fertility rate that now prevails in Sweden—a Big If, surely—by the late twenty-second century the human population will fall considerably below its present level. Suppose then the global population does eventually decline. Suppose clean tech becomes the dominant economic form of life, and that the materialist impulse fades somewhat, as this book dearly hopes. Under such circumstances it would not be impossible to imagine restoring vast areas of the United States to wilderness status, including by the ripping out of roads.

After all by the twenty-second century roads may no longer be essential. Once Ronald Reagan got so carried away with movie worship that in a State of the Union address he declared, quoting the *Back to the Future* flicks, "Where we're going we won't need roads." What if it turns out that in fact where we're going we won't need roads? Mass transportation that does not require surface corridors may someday be a technical possibility, and would be a boon for nature. By the twenty-second century and perhaps sooner, something like the Wildlands Project could be in progress, with wilderness areas "destroyed forever" recovering with dizzying speed. But early thinking about the Wildlands Project is handicapped by the notion that its purpose should be a return to some imagined Environmentally Correct reality. Why not instead make the purpose of the project the establishment of a New Nature?

An important backer of the Wildlands Project is Michael Soule, a biologist at the University of California at Santa Cruz and a figure on the doomsday circuit. Soule has said that a goal of future environmentalism should be to restructure the United States so that the wilderness once again revolves around top-chain predators such as grizzly bears. Future large nature preserves, Soule has declared, should emphasize "a state of nature where danger is involved because of the amount of space and the presence of large animals. Being there [should] involve an increased possibility of dying or being hurt."

What a lovely vision: ripping out roads, bridges, and power plants at the cost of hundreds of billions of dollars in order to restore the sorts of frightening death enjoyed by settlers and Native Americans centuries ago. Perhaps orthodox enviros are fond of top-chain predators such as grizzlies because they are the sole animals capable of killing people. That makes them noble, provided the victim is SOMEBODY ELSE.

Another interpretation comes from Deborah Jensen, a scientist for the Nature Conservancy. She thinks adoration of the predator represents a "male fixation." Jensen says, "The male definition of nature is big, fierce things trying to kill you. My definition of nature is lots of diverse things trying to get along." Jensen's phrase might be a rallying cry for the New Nature movement that will someday come into being.

Nature might think it extremely odd if men and women, as they begin to restore the Earth, restore the environment's structural faults as well as its virtues. Why not instead a New Nature in which predators are converted to herbivores? In which no person fears any animal because no animal attacks to eat? In which no animal fears any person since no person exploits animals for food or fiber? In which no member of genus *Homo* fears another member because all carry naturally fashioned gene codes prohibiting them from killing?

In other words why not envision the realization of Eden? A genuine Eden in which all live in harmony, and none may hunger, and the lamb in truth lies down with the lion. Of course I do not know whether an edenic New Nature can be fashioned. I do know it is a more promising objective than restoration of the nature of the past.

In the Absence of the Sacred

JERRY MANDER

IN MAY 1990, THE *WASHINGTON POST* REported that the National Research Council, an arm of the National Academies of Sciences and Engineering, had thrown its support behind a technical scheme to battle the green-house effect, or global warming, caused by excessive carbon dioxide in the atmosphere.

Environmentalists have been arguing for over half a century that the solution to the problem was simple: drastically cut the use of fossil fuels and stop cutting down the earth's forests, which absorb carbon dioxide. But the environmentalists' solutions have been considered unfeasible, since they might interfere with industrial growth and profit, and would require changes in Western lifestyles. So the scientific community has been seeking technical fixes that can accommodate continued industrial activity.

The plan supported by the National Research Council, which advises Congress on behalf of the scientific establishment, proposes a massive "iron enrichment" of the oceans; that is, spraying hundreds of thousands of tons of iron powder onto the seas. This would in turn stimulate the growth of giant blooms of marine algae to soak up carbon dioxide, as the forests had previously done. The NRC called the plan "conceptually feasible" and suggested an expenditure of $50 to $150 million to begin research off the coasts of Alaska or Antarctica.

The scientific community became very excited by the idea. The *Post* quotes Roger Revelle, formerly of the Scripps Institution of Oceanography, as saying, "I see no reason why it shouldn't work. . . . I don't think there would be any negative consequences."

And Adam Heller, a chemical engineering professor at the University of Texas, said the plan would be cost-effective and he thought there was nothing "fundamentally stupid" about it.

A more cautious response was given by Anthony Michaels, a research scientist at the Bermuda Biological Station for Research. "It is an enticing idea that is being actively pursued," he said. But he added, "If you start playing God with the system, we don't understand it well enough to know what the outcome would be. The whole food web would be altered."

Michaels was reflecting on the fact that marine algae form the basic foundation of the ocean food chain. They feed the krill that are in turn eaten by fish, seals, penguins, and whales. Once human beings begin actively adjusting the balances, especially at the scale contemplated, there could be surprising ecological effects. According to *Washington Post* science writer William Booth, when the added iron nutrient is sprayed on the waters, "the marine plants should undergo tremendous growth, much like ordinary houseplants gorging themselves on plant food. . . . The researchers do not think their experi-

---

ment could run amok because the marine algae would grow only so long as other nutrients such as phosphorus and nitrogen held out."

The "iron enrichment" solution is only the most recently advocated technical fix contemplated by science. Here are some others the *New York Times* reported in August 1988:

- A plan to cover the oceans with polystyrene chips, while painting all the roofs of the houses on Earth bright white. This would cause sunlight to be reflected rather than absorbed on the earth's surface.
- A project to create orbiting satellites made of a very fine material, equal in size to about 2 percent of the earth's surface, that would block sunlight and cast a shadow on the planet, reducing temperature. (Such a scheme is also proposed to cool Venus, so that we might contemplate colonization there.)
- Last but not least, a proposal by Dr. Wallace Broecker, a professor of geochemistry at Colubia, to load several hundred jumbo jets with sulfur dioxide to be released at high altitudes. This would simulate the effect of a large volcanic explosion of the kind that has, from time to time, blocked the sun's rays, thereby cooling the earth's surface. The negative aspects of this plan, Broecker said, include an increase in acid rain, and a change in the color of the sky from blue to whitish. "This is not a big expense," he argued, "compared to the impact on industry if we give up reliance on fossil fuels."

• • •

A second contemporary atmospheric problem that science is attempting to correct is ozone layer depletion due to the excessive release of chlorofluorocarbons in the atmosphere. Again, environmentalists have offered a simple solution: Stop using CFCs for polystyrene, aerosols, and refrigeration. But again this would negatively affect industrial production. Science is seeking alternatives.

The *New York Times* quoted Princeton physicist Thomas H. Stix, who is promoting an idea called "atmospheric processing." He suggests aiming giant lasers at chlorofluorocarbons as they rise from the earth, shattering them before they get to the stratosphere. The only concern with this is whether it is possible to shoot the CFCs without also hitting other molecules, with unknown consequences.

Another suggestion was to shoot ozone bullets directly into the stratosphere, where they would melt and replenish the depleted ozone. Leon Y. Sadler, a chemical engineer at the University of Alabama, would load a fleet of jumbo jets—presumably a different fleet from Dr. Broecker's—with ozone manufactured by an earth-based industry, carry it as high as possible, and pump it back into the atmosphere.

This idea has great merit for industry. First of all, it places ozone into the category of "renewable resource," like a forest. (Of course, forest products, when cut down, are at least used for something, while ozone is destroyed for no purpose.) Dr. Sadler's plan would replace formerly unproductive atmospheric ozone with new ozone, produced in our factories on Earth, thereby creating jobs, profits, and economic growth.

The *Times* quotes some scientists as cautioning that these ideas are still on the drawing board and may not prove feasible. Nonetheless they felt that as such proposals are publicized, as the *Times* was doing (and as I am doing), scientific creativity is stimulated.

What neither the *Times* nor the scientists say is that this manner of approaching two planet-threatening problems—problems with very simple solutions (don't cut trees, don't use CFCs, reduce energy use, and apply an economic standard other than growth)—is perpetuating the very process that created the problem: more and bigger technological fixes for more and bigger technological problems. In my view, it is a form of obsessive insanity, rooted in our society's failure to grasp or respect the limits of the natural world.

MOLECULAR ENGINEERING

October 1988. My friend Mark Dowie telephones. He is the former editor of *Mother Jones* magazine and is now a freelance journalist focusing on the excesses of technology. His book *We Have a Donor* takes a blistering look at the organ-transplant industry. Dowie asks my opinion of the latest hot ticket on the technology frontier: nanotechnology. I tell him I've never heard of it.

"It's beyond genetics," Mark says. "Instead of merely redesigning the gene structures of living creatures, they're now into redesigning the molecular structure of absolutely everything. It's the new frontier, Jerry, working with the infinitely small. The guru for this movement was the physicist Richard Feynman [who died in 1988]. The idea is to zero down into the atomic structure of all materials and rearrange their molecules to get completely new forms, materials, and creatures. They barely make a distinction between what is an 'organic' material and an 'inorganic' material, since once you're down to the molecular level, it's all the same. I'm telling you, it's like the ultimate acid dream," says Dowie. "It's the 'new physics' all right, here and now. Once they can move the atoms around and redesign the molecular chains—and they're gaining on it—they will be able to redesign the whole world, molecule by molecule, and that's exactly what they intend. It's the technological fix to end them all. These nanotechnologists claim they will create new food, and end all famine. They have already designed tiny semi-organic engines called nanomachines that can enter your bloodstream and be programmed to destroy cancers or eat fat or make any cellular change you want. They're talking about other nanomachines called assemblers that will be superintelligent and will be able to build anything that's now made by workers in factories. These assemblers will just be thrown into a vat of specially chosen molecules and will rearrange them in such a way that they will interact with each other and cause an object to actually grow in that soup and emerge as a space capsule or laser weapon or hair dryer. If they're right, it's the end of the resource problem on Earth. We won't need resources anymore since the resources are the molecules themselves from which they can make anything: trees, houses, animals, weapons, people. Eventually, they promise to eliminate death. Jerry, nanotechnology will make the Industrial Revolution look like a hiccup."

By now I am sure that Mark is kidding me. He knows I'm skeptical about new technology. And this all sounds like science fiction. But he's not kidding. I tell him I don't know which would be worse, if they fail or they succeed. This much is for sure. They are fantasizing. They are living inside that best-case scenario frame of mind, although in the history of technology the best-case result has never once been achieved. I ask Mark who these people are.

"I've been all over the country interviewing them," says Mark. "I would say the main guy right now is a Stanford University lecturer named Eric Drexler, who wrote the bible of nanotechnology, *Engines of Creation*. He is hot. But Drexler is only one of them. There's another guy named Grant Fjermedal, who wrote *The Tomorrow Makers,* and a whole slew of them at IBM. They're all about forty and they're brilliant. They deeply believe they're doing something wonderful. It's like they're saying, 'Hey, this world is a mess. Technology has gotten out of control. We're heading for disaster. Let's wipe the slate clean and start all over. But this time, let's do it right, and let's not be limited by the way nature has chosen to organize things.'

"But Jerry, there's something missing from these people. I'm not sure what it is. These kids are the ultimate technology nerds. There's something cold and harsh in their perspective. Perhaps it's because they are the first generation of scientists born and raised in a world already totally overtaken by the high-tech vision. They really believe more in machines than people or nature. To them human beings are kind of out of date. The only thing really important is somehow finding a way to preserve their brains. They speak about *downloading* their consciousness into computers. I don't think they'd mind if their brains could be saved and the rest of their bodies—in fact, *all* human bodies—were thrown into the trash heap with the dinosaurs. They see their engines as an improvement over human brains, which have to be lugged around by clumsy bodies. It's the old sci-fi image of the disembodied brain. Or that old mad scientist flick where the scientist is ready to sacrifice all of humanity just to save some artificial creature he invented. At first I didn't think anyone would take them seriously, but unfortunately they are being taken seriously. Their work is being funded. The big universities are involved. They're making progress, Jerry; this is really important. We've got to write about them."

Dowie did. His article was called "Brave New Tiny World" and appeared in *California* magazine.

THE POSTBIOLOGICAL AGE

A few months after talking with Mark Dowie, I picked up a copy of Hans Moravec's *Mind Children*. Moravec is director of the Mobile Robot Laboratory of Carnegie Mellon University and his book was written to describe "the future of robot and human intelligence." To borrow Mark Dowie's phrase, it makes the Industrial Revolution *and* nanotechnology look like hiccups.

The author unashamedly presents a tightly reasoned, step-by-step argument in favor of a "post-biological" future: "It is a world in which the human race has been swept away by the tide of cultural change, usurped by its own artificial progeny."

Moravec calmly explains how within the next thirty years we will bypass the present limits upon artificial intelligence and robotic mobility, to the point where we will be able to "download" all of the content of our brains—which are now unfortunately stuck in decaying biological entities—into computers housed within mobile robots, thereby gaining "us" immortality, via these machines. The machines will "evolve" by their own design and, when given the collective knowledge of all the great thinkers on the planet, without the limitations and fragility of their flesh, will generate ideas and actions that will far exceed human achievement: "Such machines could carry on our cultural evolution, including their own construction and increasingly rapid self-improvement, without us, and without the genes that built us. When that happens, our DNA will find itself out of a job, having lost the evolutionary race to a new kind of competition. . . . The new genetic takeover will be complete. Our culture will then be able to evolve independently of human biology and its limitations, passing instead directly from generation to generation of ever more capable intelligent machinery."

Moravec bases his predictions on calculations that the human brain is capable of "performing 10 trillion (10^{13}) calculations per second." He continues, "This is about one million times faster than the medium-sized machines that now drive my robots, and 1,000 times faster than today's best supercomputers." So, according to Moravec, all that's required to match human calculating ability is a computer that operates at only 1,000 times the speed of today's supercomputers.

While acknowledging that his own calculations may be subject to criticism, Moravec predicts that a computer that can operate at the speed and capacity of the human brain, and that can include all elements of the brain (including the mechanistic equivalent of sense perceptions and emotions), can and should be achieved within the next thirty to fifty years. He reminds us that in only the last eighty years "there has been a *trillionfold* decline in the cost of calculation," so the changes he envisions are actually do-able, especially because of the burgeoning technologies of miniaturization, such as nanotechnology. "Atomic-scale machinery is a wonderful concept and would take us far beyond the humanlike point in computers, since it would allow many millions of processors to fit on a chip that today can hold but one. Just how fast could each individual nanocomputer be? . . . A single nanocomputer might have a processing speed of a trillion operations per second. With millions of such processors crammed onto a thumbnail-size chip, my human-equivalence criterion would be bested more than a millionfold!"

Moravec indicates that his work is driven by his fear that two other technologies—genetics and organ replacement—are simply insufficient to accomplish his futuristic vision. Genetics, which hold great promise for totally redesigning human beings to be more intelligent and efficient, if undifferentiated, is nonetheless limited by the flesh-and-blood factor; we can only live within climatic and atmospheric limits and eventually we die. As for organ transplants and artificial organs, Moravec has this to say:

> Many people are alive today because of a growing arsenal of artificial organs and other body parts. In time, especially as robotic techniques improve, such replacement parts will be better than any originals. So what about replacing everything, that is transplanting a human brain into a specially designed robot body? Unfortunately, while this solution might overcome most of our physical limitations, it would leave untouched our biggest handicap, the limited and fixed intelligence of the human brain. This transplant scenario gets our brain out of our body. Is there a way to get our mind out of our brain?*

That's where "downloading" comes in. Moravec goes into exquisite detail on various ways this can be achieved. To give you one idea of his thinking, I will quote one of his descriptions entirely. It involves the operating procedure for a voluntary "downloading" of consciousness into a computer:

*Reprinted by permission of the publisher from *Mind Children: The Future of Robot and Human Intelligence* by Hans Moravec, pp. 183–186, Cambridge, Mass.: Harvard University Press, copyright © 1988 by Hans Moravec.

You've just been wheeled into the operating room. A robot brain surgeon is in attendance. By your side is a computer waiting to become a human equivalent, lacking only a program to run. Your skull, but not your brain, is anesthetized. You are fully conscious. The robot surgeon opens your brain case and places a hand on the brain's surface. This unusual hand bristles with microscopic machinery, and a cable connects it to the mobile computer at your side. Instruments in the hand scan the first few millimeters of brain surface. High-resolution magnetic resonance measurements build a three-dimension chemical map, while arrays of magnetic and electric antennas collect signals that are rapidly unraveled to reveal, moment to moment, the pulses flashing among the neurons. These measurements, added to a comprehensive understanding of human neural architecture, allow the surgeon to write a program that models the behavior of the uppermost layer of the scanned brain tissue. This program is installed in a small portion of the waiting computer and activated. Measurements from the hand provide it with copies of the inputs that the original tissue is receiving. You and the surgeon check the accuracy of the simulation by comparing the signals it produces with the corresponding original ones. They flash by very fast, but any discrepancies are highlighted on a display screen. The surgeon fine-tunes the simulation until the correspondence is nearly perfect.

To further assure you of the simulation's correctness, you are given a pushbutton that allows you to momentarily "test drive" the simulation, to compare it with the functioning of the original tissue. When you press it, arrays of electrodes in the surgeon's hand are activated. By precise injections of current and electromagnetic pulses, electrodes can override the normal signaling activity of nearby neurons. They are programmed to inject the output of the simulation into those places where the simulated tissue signals other sites. As long as you press the button, a small part of your nervous system is being replaced by a computer simulation of itself. You press the button, release it, and press it again. You should experience no difference. As soon as you are satisfied, the simulation connection is established permanently. The brain tissue is now impotent—it receives inputs and reacts as before but its output is ignored. Microscopic manipulators on the hand's surface excise the cells in this superfluous tissue and pass them to an aspirator, where they are drawn away.

The surgeon's hand sinks a fraction of a millimeter deeper into your brain, instantly compensating its measurements and signals for the changed position. The process is repeated for the next layer, and soon a second simulation resides in the computer, communicating with the first and with the remaining original brain tissue. Layer after layer the brain is simulated, then excavated. Eventually your skull is empty, and the surgeon's hand rests deep in your brainstem. Though you have not lost consciousness, or even your train of thought, your mind has been removed from the brain and transferred to a machine. In a final, disorienting step the surgeon lifts out his hand. Your suddenly abandoned body goes into spasms and dies. For a moment you experience only quiet and dark. Then, once again, you can open your eyes. Your perspective has shifted. The computer simulation has been disconnected from the cable leading to the surgeon's hand and reconnected to a shiny new body of the style, color, and material of your choice. Your metamorphosis is complete.*

Moravec admits there may be some debate about whether *you* are merely your consciousness, which can be passed into the machine. He argues that our tendency to cling to our bodies, what he calls the "body-identity" position, is out-of-date thinking. He points out that the cells of our bodies are in a constant process of replacing themselves with new ones, and that within every seven years, *all* of our cells are new. He says it is absurd to believe that *you* have anything whatsoever to do with your body, your flesh. *You* are only your mind, or "your pattern," which, he argues, can be transmitted into a machine. In fact it can be transmitted into two or three or many machines simultaneously, not so much like a photocopy as a facsimile transmittal: teleportation, as in the "beam-down" machine in "Star Trek." In other words, the real *you* can be infinitely duplicated; so can the consciousnesses (the "patterns") of other intelligent creatures such as whales, dolphins, ele-

*Reprinted by permission of the publisher from *Mind Children: The Future of Robot and Human Intelligence* by Hans Moravec, pp. 183–186, Cambridge, Mass.: Harvard University Press, copyright © 1988 by Hans Moravec.

phants, and giant squids. Moravec wants all of these transferred into machines where they will "live" permanently, producing an unimaginably greater, richer new society that can literally reach to the entire universe, without the awful limits of the flesh. Meanwhile, organic life as we have known it can, at last, be abandoned forever. Our collective suicide will give birth to a new, higher species.

THE MADNESS OF THE ASTRONAUT

I am not sufficiently versed in science to tell you whether the ideas of Hans Moravec in robotics, or the work of Drexler in nanotechnology, or the ideas of Broecker, Stix, and Sadler for solving our atmospheric problems, or for that matter, the work of the genetic engineers, can possibly prove practical and achievable. But I do know this. The greatest universities in this country—Stanford, MIT, Harvard, Berkeley, Princeton—provide these projects funding and housing and a platform to speak from. The United States military—particularly the Navy—backs many of these researchers with multimillion-dollar grants. Giant corporations hunger to patent the concepts and exploit the finished products. Major publishers produce books extolling these ideas. Serious newspapers, journals, and magazines reverently review and report on the most recent advances.

All of these institutions can support these new modes of technological expression because the ideas are in every way consistent with the logic and the assumptions by which our society has operated for the past several centuries.

These were the same assumptions that were employed by the World's Fair planners of the 1930s, the ad agencies of the fifties and sixties, the Disney "imagineers" at EPCOT Center, and the people who envision utopian worlds of space colonies. Today's technological pioneers consider themselves original thinkers, but they are only the latest in a long line of advocates for the same set of propositions, the most prominent of which is that nature sets no limits on the degree to which humans may intervene in and alter the natural world. Manifesting the arrogance of Technological Man, the techno-pioneers assume they are authorized to go anywhere and rearrange anything, including alterations in the structure of human life, animal life, and now natural form itself.

In doing so, they are acting in service to the fundamental principle that has informed technical evolution in the modern era: *If it can be done, do it.* There are no boundaries, no rules, no sets of standards by which to moderate these activities. No sense of right or wrong, no taboos; there's only what will succeed in the marketplace. (Perhaps abandoning human biology will not *sell*—is that our only hope?)

The assumptions have been gaining strength for thousands of years, fed both by Judeo-Christian religious doctrines that have de-sanctified the earth and placed humans in domination over it; and by technologies that, by their apparent power, have led us to believe we are some kind of royalty over nature, exercising Divine will. We have lost the understanding that existed in all civilizations prior to ours, and that continues to exist on Earth today in societies that live side by side with our own; we have lost a sense of the sacredness of the natural world. The new technologists don't accept this notion; they live in a world that is removed from it; they themselves have lost touch with the source of that knowledge. They find it silly.

What is true for the new technologists has sadly become true for most people in the Western world. Having bought the idea that all problems can and should be solved by technology, never thinking back to any alternative knowledge that could provide a point of contrast, and not even knowing that alternative knowledge exists, we too have spun outward, away from the source, off into space, isolated from that knowledge by concrete and machines. Each new level of technical invention has taken us further away from the source. Each invention has spawned others, placing us ever deeper within technical consciousness and further away from organic reality, to the point where we can seriously consider abandoning the planet, abandoning nature, abandoning our bodies. These ideas are discussed and considered by intellectual leaders, as if such notions are sane.

Our entire society has begun to suffer the madness of the astronaut; uprooted, floating in space, encased in our metal worlds, with automated systems neatly at hand, communicating mainly with machines, following machine logic, disconnected from the earth and all organic reality, without contact with a multidimensional, biologically diverse world and with the nuances of world views entirely unlike our own, unable to view ourselves from another perspective, *we* are alienated to the nth degree. Like the astronaut, we don't know up from down, in from out. Our world and our thought processes are confined to technical boundaries. In such a state many insane ideas and solutions can seem logical because there are no standards by which to compare them. All invention, if achievable, becomes plausible, and even desirable, since it is part of the commitment we have already made, even if the commitment leads logically to reorganizing our genes, our trees, and our skies; and possibly abandoning the planet and life itself.

MEGATECHNOLOGY

Given the scale of the technologically caused environmental problems we now face; and given the scale of the technological fixes that have been proposed; and given the scale and implications of the new technological forms, one would assume these subjects would be hotly debated. As we have seen, they are not. Technology continues to be introduced and described by the people who stand to benefit most from its acceptance, and who deliver their visions in utopian form. The public is uninvolved; there are no forums for argument. No pros and cons. No referenda. Presidential candidates only mention the issues in passing references to solving the acid rain problem, or limiting oil drilling. By the time the body politic becomes aware of problems with technology, it is usually after they are well installed in the system and their effects are too late to reverse. Only now, four decades after the introduction of computers, are there any rumblings of discontent, any realizations of their full implications. By the time the alarm finally goes off, technologies have intertwined with one another to create yet another generation of machines, which makes unraveling them near to impossible, even if society had the will to do it.

As the interlocking and interweaving and spawning of new technologies take place, the weave of technology becomes ever tighter and more difficult to separate. For example, without computers, it would be impossible to have satellites, nuclear power, genetics, space technology, military lasers, information technologies, or nanotechnology. And because of computers, all of these technologies are intertwined with one another. We continue to view them as if they were separate, discrete systems, but they aren't. Computers are at the base of them all, and also plug them into one another and into central systems of management and institutional control, made larger than ever before possible. In fact, the whole complex web of systems ought properly to be thought of as *one* technology that effectively encircles the globe, and that can instantaneously communicate with all its parts. Rather than a biosphere, we have a technosphere. Call it megatechnology.

• • •

There is no conspiracy here, at least not in the usual sense. Human beings did not set out to create such a worldwide, interlocked technological entity. But at each stage human beings followed the logic of technical evolution, which seeks to expand its power over nature, and to employ other technologies to be reborn into ever newer, larger, more impactful forms; to strengthen the web of connection.

It is true that there are human beings who sit near the hub of the process, and who make deals with each other, and who advertise the process at such places as EPCOT, and who benefit financially if they can steer the process a certain way. But they are not really in charge. Technological evolution leads inevitably to its own next stages, which can be altered only slightly. The invention of the computer inevitably implied the invention of the supercomputer and its ability to spawn a thousand other high technologies, with their vast social and political consequences. It didn't matter who put the money down to further the process. The people and the machine were *inside* the technical project together; they were the same. If there was a conspiracy here, it is only one in the Ellulian sense; a *de facto* conspiracy; a conspiracy of technical form.

In any event, the result is a worldwide technical creature that includes us in its functioning: the way our minds operate, the way we perceive alternatives, what we imagine are good and bad ideas. We have entered into a universe that has been re-formed by machines; we are a species that lives its life within mechanistic creations; our environment is a product of our minds. Locked inside our cities and suburbs, working in our offices, controlling and conceptualizing nature as a raw material for our consumption, and now even including *ourselves* as raw material suitable for redevelopment, we are at one with the process.

If we have a worldwide technical creature, then computers are its nervous system. Television is the way human minds are made compatible with the system and identical with one another; it is the sales system, and the audiovisual training mechanism. Genetics has the role of reworking the biological structures to maximize economic potential. And nanotechnology and robotics make the leap beyond biology.

All of these technologies result from and are in service to the overall utopian conception: a technological vision of a single world-machine that looks and feels something like EPCOT Center or the bubble domes of space stations. Everything figured out. Everything planned. Everything created. The apparent purpose of this machine is to eliminate human ailments and human unhappiness (assuming we still have humans), to expand the human potential, and to create a world of abundance for human enjoyment. But the unstated purpose is to fulfill the inherent drive of technological society to feed its own evolutionary cravings, to expand its domination of both Earth and space, and to complete the utter conversion of nature into commodity form—even the part of nature that remains wild within human genes and molecular structures.

That's the bad news:

The good news is that even "perfect" technological systems are showing signs of leakage and fraud. Technological society, during the past half-century, has demonstrably not achieved the benefits it advertised for itself. Peace, security, public and planetary health, sanity, happiness, fulfillment are arguably less close at hand than they ever were in the past. And the awful sacrifices that the planet has made to satisfy the cravings of the technological thrust are now becoming visible in oil spills, global warming, ozone depletion, toxic pollution, and deforestation, all of which affect our sense of well-being in everyday life.

As a society we have been slow learners, but there is an emerging awareness that we may have been led down the garden path by false advertising toward a fantasy world, created by romantics who had an economic stake in our accepting their dream. The question now is: Will the new skeptics and advocates of alternative paths become prominent enough to be sufficiently heard, and to create a critical mass of public opinion? We'll see. At this moment the situation is not promising. We still have not developed an effective language with which to articulate our critiques. This, in turn, is because we ourselves are part of the machine and so we have difficulty defining its shape and its direction. But even if we have this difficulty, there are societies of people on this planet who do not.

STATEMENT TO THE MODERN WORLD

Millions of people still alive on this earth never wished to be part of this machine and, in many cases, are not. I am speaking of people who have lived on the fringes of the technical world. They have remained outside of our awareness, either because they live in obscure places, or their resources have not been coveted by technological society, or because many millions of them have been murdered or otherwise silenced. But *they* are still aware of certain fundamental truths, the most important of which require reverence for the earth—an idea that is subversive to Western society and the entire technological direction of the past century.

These are people whose ancestors and who themselves have said from the beginning of the technological age that our actions and attitudes are fatally flawed, since they are not grounded in a real understanding of how to live on the earth. Lacking a sense of the sacred we were doomed to a bad result. They said it over and over and they still say it now.

The following is an excerpt from *A Basic Call to Consciousness, the Hau de no sau nee* [Iroquois] *Address to the Western World,* delivered at the 1977 UN Conference on Indigenous Peoples, published by *Akwesasne Notes.*

> In the beginning we were told that the human beings who walk about on the Earth have been provided with all the things necessary for life. We were instructed to carry a love for one another, and to show a great respect for all the beings of this Earth. We were shown that our life exists with the tree life, that our well-being depends on the well-being of the Vegetable Life, that we are close relatives of the four-legged beings.
>
> The original instructions direct that we who walk about on Earth are to express a great respect, an affection and a gratitude toward all the spirits which create and support Life. . . . When people cease to respect and express gratitude for these many things, then all life will be destroyed, and human life on this planet will come to an end.
>
> . . . To this day the territories we still hold are filled with trees, animals, and the other gifts from

the Creation. In these places we still receive our nourishment from our Mother Earth. . . .

The Indo-European people who have colonized our lands have shown very little respect for the things that create and support Life. We believe that these people ceased their respect for the world a long time ago. Many thousands of years ago, all the people of the world believed in the same Way of Life, that of harmony with the Universe. All lived according to the Natural Ways.

Today the [human] species of Man is facing a question of [its] very survival. . . . The way of life known as Western Civilization is on a death path on which their own culture has no viable answers. When faced with the reality of their own destructiveness, they can only go forward into areas of more efficient destruction.

The air is foul, the waters poisoned, the trees dying, the animals are disappearing. We think even the systems of weather are changing. Our ancient teaching warned us that if Man interfered with the Natural laws, these things would come to be. When the last of the Natural Way of Life is gone, all hope for human survival will be gone with it. And our Way of Life is fast disappearing, a victim of the destructive processes.

The technologies and social systems which destroyed the animal and the plant life are destroying the Native people. . . . We know there are many people in the world who can quickly grasp the intent of our message. But our experience has taught us that there are few who are willing to seek out a method for moving toward any real change.

The majority of the world does not find its roots in Western culture or tradition. The majority of the world finds its roots in the Natural World, and it is the Natural World, and the traditions of the Natural World, which must prevail.

We must all consciously and continuously challenge every model, every program, and every process that the West tries to force upon us. . . . The people who are living on this planet need to break with the narrow concept of human liberation, and begin to see liberation as something that needs to be extended to the whole of the Natural World. What is needed is the liberation of all things that support Life—the air, the waters, the trees—all the things which support the sacred web of Life.

The Native people of the Western Hemisphere can contribute to the survival potential of the human species. The majority of our peoples still live in accordance with the traditions which find their roots in the Mother Earth. But the Native people have need of a forum in which our voice can be heard. And we need alliances with the other people of the world to assist in our struggle to regain and maintain our ancestral lands and to protect the Way of Life we follow.

The traditional Native people hold the key to the reversal of the processes in Western Civilization, which hold the promise of unimaginable future suffering and destruction. Spiritualism is the highest form of political consciousness. And we, the Native people of the Western Hemisphere, are among the world's surviving proprietors of that kind of consciousness. . . . Our culture is among the most ancient continuously existing cultures in the world. We are the spiritual guardians of this place. We are here to impart that message.

The Religion of the Market

DAVID R. LOY

RELIGION IS NOTORIOUSLY DIFFICULT TO DEFINE. If, however, we adopt a functionalist view and understand religion as what grounds us by teaching us what this world *is,* and what our *role* in that world is, then it becomes obvious that traditional religions are fulfilling this role less and less, because that func-

Loy, David R. "The Religion of the Market," in Harold Coward and Daniel Maguire, Eds., *Visions of a New Earth: Religious Perspectives on Population, Consumption, and Ecology,* pp. 15–27. Reprinted by permission of the State University of New York Press.

tion is being supplanted—or overwhelmed—by other belief systems and value systems. Today the most powerful alternative explanation of the world is science, and the most attractive value-system has become consumerism. Their academic offspring is economics, probably the most influential of the "social sciences." In response, this chapter will argue that our present economic system should also be understood as our religion, because it has come to fulfill a religious function for us. The discipline of economics is less a science than the theology of that religion, and its god, the Market, has become a vicious circle of ever-increasing production and consumption by pretending to offer a secular salvation. The collapse of communism makes it more apparent that the Market is becoming the first truly world religion, binding all corners of the globe into a worldview and set of values whose religious role we overlook only because we insist on seeing them as "secular."

So it is no coincidence that our time of ecological catastrophe also happens to be a time of extraordinary challenge to more traditional religions. Although it may offend our vanity, it is somewhat ludicrous to think of conventional religious institutions as we know them today serving a significant role in solving the environmental crisis. Their more immediate problem is whether they, like the rain forests we anxiously monitor, will survive in any recognizable form the onslaught of this new religion. The major religions are not yet moribund but, on those few occasions when they are not in bed with the economic and political powers that be, they tend to be so preoccupied with past problems and outmoded perspectives (e.g., pronatalism) that they are increasingly irrelevant (e.g., fundamentalism) or trivialized (e.g., television evangelism). The result is that up to now they have been unable to offer what is most needed—a meaningful challenge to the aggressive proselytizing of market capitalism, which has already become the most successful religion of all time, winning more converts more quickly than any previous belief system or value system in modern history.

This situation is becoming so critical that the environmental crisis may actually turn out to be a positive thing for religion, for ecological catastrophe is awakening us not only to the fact that we need a deeper source of values and meaning than market capitalism can provide, but to the realization that contemporary religion is not meeting this need either.

ECONOMICS AS THEOLOGY

> It is intolerable that the most important issues about human livelihood will be decided solely on the basis of profit for transnational corporations.
>
> —Herman E. Daly and John B. Cobb Jr., *For the Common Good*

In 1960 countries of the North were about twenty times richer than those of the South. In 1990—after vast amounts of aid, trade, loans, and catch-up industrialization by the South—countries of the North had become *fifty* times richer. The richest 20 percent of the world's population now have an income about 150 times that of the poorest 20 percent, a gap that continues to grow.[1] According to the UN Development Report for 1996, the world's 358 billionaires are wealthier than the combined annual income of countries with 45 percent of the world's people. As a result, a quarter million children die of malnutrition or infection every week, while hundreds of millions more survive in a limbo of hunger and deteriorating health. . . . Why do we acquiesce in this social injustice? What rationalization allows us to sleep peacefully at night?

> [T]he explanation lies largely in our embrace of a peculiarly European or Western [but now global] religion, an individualistic religion of economics and markets, which explains all of these outcomes as the inevitable results of an objective system in which . . . intervention is counterproductive. Employment is simply a cost of doing business, and Nature is merely a pool of resources for use in production. In this calculus, the world of business is so fundamental and so separate from the environment . . . that intervention in the ongoing economic system is a threat to the natural order of things, and hence to future human welfare. In this way of thinking, that outcome is just (or at least inevitable) which emerges from the natural workings of this economic system, and the "wisdom of the market" on which it is based. The hegemony achieved by this particular intellectual construct—a "European religion" or economic religion—is remarkable; it has become a dogma of almost universal application, the dominant religion of our time, shoring up and justifying what would appear to be a patently inequitable status quo. It has achieved an immense influence which dominates contemporary human activity.[2]

According to Dobell, this theology is based on two counterintuitive but widely accepted propositions: that *it is right and just* (which is why "the market made me do it" is acceptable as a defense of many morally questionable activities); and that *value can be adequately signaled by prices.* Since natural resources are unpriced, harvesting techniques such as drift nets and clearcuts are acceptable and often necessary in order to be competitive, despite the fact that "more or less everybody now knows that market systems are profoundly flawed, in the sense that, left on their own with present pricing and practices, they will lead inevitably to environmental damage and destruction of irreplaceable ecological systems."[3]

The basic assumption of both propositions is that such a system is "natural." If market capitalism does operate according to economic laws as natural as those of physics or chemistry—if economics were a genuine science—its consequences seem unavoidable, despite the fact that they are leading to extreme social inequity and environmental catastrophe. Yet there is nothing inevitable about our economic relationships. That misunderstanding is precisely what needs to be addressed—and this is also where religion comes in, since, with the increasing prostitution of the media and now universities to these same market forces, there seems to be no other moral perspective left from which to challenge them. Fortunately, the alternative worldviews that religions offer can still help us realize that the global victory of market capitalism is something other than the attainment of economic freedom: rather, it is the ascendancy of one particular way of understanding and valuing the world that need not be taken for granted. Far from being inevitable, our economic system is one historically conditioned way of organizing/reorganizing the world; it is a worldview, with an ontology and ethics, in competition with other understandings of what the world is and how we should live in it.

What is most impressive about market values, from a religious perspective, is not their "naturalness" but how extraordinarily persuasive their conversion techniques are. As a philosophy teacher I know that whatever I can do with my students a few hours during a week is practically useless against the proselytizing influences that assail them outside class—the attractive (often hypnotic) advertising messages on television and radio and in magazines and buses that constantly urge them to "buy *me* if you want to be happy." If we are not blinded by the distinction usually made between secular and sacred, we can see that this promises another kind of salvation, that is, another way to solve our unhappiness. Insofar as this strikes at the heart of the truly religious perspective—which offers an alternative explanation for our inability to be happy and a very different path to become happy—religions are not fulfilling their responsibility if they ignore this religious dimension of capitalism, if they do not emphasize that this seduction is deceptive because this solution to our unhappiness leads only to greater dissatisfaction.

Instead of demonstrating their inevitability, the history of economic systems reveals the contingency of the market relationships we now take for granted. Although we tend to view the profit motive as universal and rational (the benevolent "invisible hand" of Adam Smith), anthropologists have discovered that it is not traditional to traditional societies. Insofar as it is found among them it tends to play a very circumscribed role, viewed warily because of its tendency to disrupt social relations. Most premodern societies make no clear distinction between the economic sphere and the social sphere, subsuming economic roles into more general social relationships. Precapitalist man "does not act so as to safeguard his individual interest in the possession of material goods; he acts so as to safeguard his social standing, his social claims, his social assets. He values material goods only in so far as they serve this end." But in a capitalist society "instead of economy being embedded in social relations, social relations are embedded in the economic system."[4]

Tawney discovered the same perspective on market forces in the pre-Renaissance West: "There is no place in medieval theory for economic activity which is not related to a moral end, and to found a science of society upon the assumption that the appetite for economic gain is a constant and measurable force, to be accepted like other natural forces, as an inevitable and self-evident datum, would have appeared to the medieval thinker as hardly less irrational and less immoral than to make the premise of social philosophy the unrestrained operation of such necessary human attributes as pugnacity and the sexual instinct."[5]

The crucial transformation evidently began in the late Middle Ages—which, by no coincidence, is when the prevailing religious interpretation of the world began to lose its grip on people's lives. As profit gradually became the engine of the economic process, the tendency was for gradual reorganization of the entire social system and not just of the economic element, since *there is no natural distinction between them.*[6] "Capital had ceased to be a servant and had become a master. Assuming a separate and independent vitality it claimed the right of a predominant partner to dictate economic organization in accordance with its own exacting requirements."[7] It is another example of the technological paradox: we create complex systems to make our lives more comfortable, only to find ourselves trapped within the inexorable logic of their own development. The monster in Shelley's *Frankenstein* expresses it more brutally: "You are my creator, but I am your master."

The scholar who did the most to uncover the religious roots of market capitalism was Max Weber. His controversial theory not only locates the origins of capitalism in the "this-worldly asceticism" of Puritan ethics but suggests that capitalism remains essentially religious in its psychological structure. According to *The Protestant Ethic and the Spirit of Capitalism,* Calvinist belief in predestination encouraged what became an irresistible need to determine whether one was among the chosen; economic success in this world came to be accepted as demonstrating God's favor; this created the psychological and sociological conditions for importing ascetic values from the monastery into worldly vocations, as one labored to prove oneself saved by reinvesting any surplus rather than consuming it. Gradually this original goal became attenuated, yet inner-worldly asceticism did not disappear as God became more distant and heaven less relevant. In our modern world the original motivation has evaporated but our preoccupation with capital and profit has not disappeared with it; on the contrary, it has become our main obsession. Since we no longer have any other goal, there being no other final salvation to believe in, we allow the means to be, in effect, our end.

Weber's sociology of religion distinguishes more ritualistic and legalistic religions, which adapt themselves to the world, from salvation religions, more hostile to it. Salvation religions are often revolutionary due to the prophecies that motivate them, and missionary because they seek to inject a new message or promise into everyday life. Their efforts to ensure the perpetuation of grace in the world ultimately require a reordering of the economic system. Weber noticed that adherents of this type of religion usually "do not enjoy inner repose because they are in the grip of inner tensions."

This last point, which not only describes Puritan this-worldly ascetics but reminds us of our own situation, suggests that market capitalism began as, and may still be understood as, a form of salvation religion: dissatisfied with the world as it is and seeking to inject a new promise into it, motivated (and justifying itself) by faith in the grace of profit and concerned to perpetuate that grace, with a missionary zeal to expand and reorder (rationalize) the economic system. Weber's arguments imply that although we think of the modern world as secularized, its values (e.g., economic rationalization) are not only derived from religious ones (salvation by injecting a revolutionary new promise into daily life), they are largely the same values, although transformed by the loss of reference to an otherworldly dimension.

Our type of salvation still requires a future-orientation. "We no longer give our surplus to God; the process of producing an ever-expanding surplus is in itself our God."[8] In contrast to the cyclic time of premodern societies, with their seasonal rituals of atonement, our economic time is linear and future-directed, since it reaches for an atonement that can no longer be achieved because it has disappeared as a conscious motivation. As an unconscious incentive, however, it still functions, for we continue to reach for an end that is perpetually postponed. So our collective reaction has become the need for growth: the never-satisfied desire for an ever-higher "standard of living" (because once we define ourselves as consumers we can never have too much) and the gospel of sustained economic expansion (because corporations and the GNP are never big enough).

THE GREAT TRANSFORMATION

> Engels tells the story of remarking to a Manchester manufacturer that he had never seen so ill-built and filthy a city: "The man listened quietly to the end, and said at the corner where we parted: 'And yet there is a great deal of money made here; good morning, sir.'"
>
> —Kirkpatrick Sale, *Rebels against the Future*

The critical stage in the development of market capitalism occurred during the industrial revolution of the late eighteenth century, when new technology created an unprecedented improvement in the tools of production. This led to the "liberation" of a critical mass of land, labor, and capital, which most people experienced as an unprecedented catastrophe because it destroyed the community fabric—a catastrophe recurring today throughout much of the "developing" world. Karl Polanyi's *The Great Transformation* (1944) is an expression of outrage at these social consequences as well as an insightful explanation of the basis of this disfiguration: the way that the world became converted into exchangeable market commodities in order for market forces to interact freely and productively. Earlier the commercialization of English agriculture had led to enclosure of the common pasturage land that traditionally belonged to the community. The plague of industrial commodification proved to be much worse. The earth (our mother as well as our home) became commodified into a collection of resources to be exploited. Human life became commodified into labor, or work time, valued according to supply and demand. Social patrimony, the cherished inheritance laboriously accumulated and preserved for one's descendants, became commodified into fungible capital, a source of unearned income for the lucky few and a source of crushing debt for the rest.

The interaction among these commodifications led to an almost miraculous accumulation of capital and an equally amazing collapse of traditional community life, as villagers were driven off their land by these new economic forces. "To separate labor from other activities of life and to subject it to the laws of the market was to annihilate all organic forms of existence and to replace them by a different type of organization, an atomistic and individualistic one," emphasizes Polanyi. Such a system "could not exist for any length of time without annihilating the human and natural substance of society." The laissez-faire principle, that government should not interfere with the operations of the economic system, was applied quite selectively: although government was admonished not to get in the way of industry, its laws and policies were needed to help reduce labor to a commodity. What was called noninterference was actually interference to "destroy noncontractual relations between individuals and prevent their spontaneous re-formation."[9]

Is it a coincidence that the same doublespeak continues today? While so-called conservatives preach about liberating the free enterprise system from the restraining hand of government, federal subsidies are sought to support uneconomic industries (e.g., nuclear power) and underwrite economic failures (the Savings-and-Loan scandal), while international policies are designed to make the world safe for our multinational corporations (GATT, NAFTA, and the Gulf War). Until the last few centuries there has been little genuine distinction between church and state, between sacred authority and secular power, and that cozy relationship continues today: far from maintaining an effective regulatory or even neutral position, the U.S. government has become the most powerful proponent of the religion of market capitalism as the way to live, and indeed it may have little choice insofar as it is now a pimp dependent upon skimming the cream off market profits.

A direct line runs from the commodification of land, life, and patrimony during the eighteenth century to the ozone holes and global warming of today, and those commodifications have also led to another kind of environmental destruction that, in a different way, is just as problematic: the depletion of "moral capital," a horrible term that could only have been devised by economists, to describe another horrific social consequence of market forces. As Adam Smith emphasized in his *Theory of Moral Sentiments,* the market is a dangerous system because it corrodes the very shared community values it needs to restrain its excesses. "However much driven by self-interest, the market still depends absolutely on a community that shares such values as honesty, freedom, initiative, thrift, and other virtues whose authority will not long withstand the reduction to the level of personal tastes that is explicit in the positivistic, individualistic philosophy of value on which modern economic theory is based."[10] A basic contradiction of the market is that it requires character traits such as trust in order to work efficiently, but its own workings tend to erode such personal responsibility for others. This conflict tends toward a breakdown that is already quite advanced in many corporations. Massive "downsizing" and a shift to part-time workers demonstrate diminishing corporate concern for employees, while at the top astronomical salary increases (with lucrative stock options), and other unsavory practices such as management buy-outs reveal that the executives entrusted with managing corporations are becoming more adept at exploiting or cannibalizing them for their own personal benefit. Between 1980 and 1993 Fortune 500 firms increased their assets 2.3 times but shed 4.4 million jobs, while C.E.O. compensation increased more than sixfold, so that the average C.E.O. of a large corporation now receives a compensation package of more than $3.7 million a year.[11]

In such ways the market shows that it does not accumulate "moral capital"; it "depletes" it and therefore depends upon the community to regenerate it, in much the same way it depends upon the biosphere to regenerate natural capital. Unsurprisingly, long-range consequences have been much the same: even as we have reached the point where the ability of the biosphere to recover has been damaged, our collective moral capital has become so exhausted that our communities (or rather, our collections of now-atomized individuals each looking out for "number one") are less able to regenerate it, with disturbing social consequences apparent all around us. This point bears repetition because the economic support system that was created to correct the failures of capitalism is now blamed for the failures of capitalism. But the social rot affecting so many "developed" societies is not something that can be corrected by a more efficient application of market values (such as getting unmarried mothers off welfare so their work will contribute to society); rather, it is a direct consequence of those market values. The commodification that is destroying the biosphere, the value of human life, and the inheritance we should leave for future generations also continues to destroy the local communities that maintain the moral fiber of their members. The degradation of the earth and the degradation of our own societies must both be seen as results of the same market process of commodification—which continues to rationalize its operation as natural and inevitable.

The cumulative depletion of "moral capital" reminds us that a community is greater than the sum of its parts, that the well-being of the whole is necessary for the well-being of each member. This, however, is something that contemporary economic theory cannot factor into its equations. Why not? The answer brings us back to the origins of economic thought in the eighteenth century, origins embedded in the individualistic philosophy of utilitarianism prevalent at that time. Philosophy has developed considerably since then, yet economic theory remains in thrall to utilitarian values, all the more for being ignorant of its debt.[12] According to utilitarianism, society is composed of discrete individuals seeking their own personal ends. Human values are reduced to a calculus that maximizes pleasures (with no qualitative distinctions between them) and minimizes discomfort. Rationality is defined as the intelligent pursuit of one's private gain. In Adam Smith's understanding of this, "individuals are viewed as capable of relating themselves to others in diverse ways, basically either in benevolence or in self-love, but they are not constituted by these relationships or by any others. They exist in fundamental separation from one another, and from this position of separateness they relate. Their relations are external to their own identities."[13] Inasmuch as the discipline of economics seems to have attained priority among the social sciences, this view of our humanity has come to prevail at the same time that its presuppositions have been thoroughly discredited by contemporary philosophy, psychology, and sociology—not to mention religion, which has always offered a very different understanding of what it means to be a human being. Nonetheless, as market values lead to a decline in the quality of our social relationships, "[s]ociety becomes more like the aggregate of individuals that economic theory pictures it as being. The 'positive' model inevitably begins to function as a norm to which reality is made to conform by the very policies derived from the model."[14] We have learned to play the roles that fit the jobs we now have to do and the commercial images that constantly assail us.

Given the influence today of neo-Malthusian thinking about population, it is important to notice that Malthus stands within this tradition. His *Essay on the Principle of Population* (1798) argued for an iron law of wages: a subsistence wage is the just wage, because higher wages lead only to rapid population growth until that growth is checked by poverty. It follows that poverty is not a product of human institutions but the natural condition of life for most people. The influence of this way of thinking has been in inverse proportion to the (lack of) empirical evidence for it, for world demographic trends have provided little. The rapid population increase that occurred in nineteenth-century England, which occurred after many people had been driven off their land and into factory work, supports the contrary conclusion, that people are not poor because they have large families, but require large families because they are poor (there was a great demand for child labor). Morally, Malthusianism tends to gloss over the issue of who is actually consuming the earth's resources. Theoretically, its major propositions—that population grows geometrically while food increases arithmetically—arbitrarily isolate two causal variables from the complexity of historical factors, while assuming as constant perhaps the most important variables of all: the "naturalness" of an unfettered market and the competitive, self-seeking "rational" individual that neoclassical economics still presupposes.[15]

Our humanity reduced to a source of labor and a collection of insatiable desires, as our communities disintegrate into aggregates of individuals competing to attain private ends . . . the earth and all its creatures commodified into a pool of resources to be exploited to satisfy those desires . . . does this radical dualism leave any place for the sacred? for wonder and awe before the mysteries of creation? Whether or not we believe in God, we may suspect that something is missing. Here we are reminded of the crucial role that religions can serve: to raise fundamental questions about this diminished understanding of what the world is and what our life can be.

THE ENDLESS HUNGER . . . ARE WE HAPPY YET?

> It is not the proletariat today whose transformation of consciousness would liberate the world, but the consumer.
>
> —Daniel Miller, *Acknowledging Consumption*

From a religious perspective, the problem with market capitalism and its values is twofold: greed and delusion. On the one hand, the unrestrained market emphasizes and indeed requires greed in at least two ways. Desire for profit is necessary to fuel the engine of the economic system, and an insatiable desire to consume ever more must be generated to create markets for what can be produced. Within economic theory and the market it promotes, the moral dimension of greed is inevitably lost; today it seems left to religion to preserve what is problematic about a human trait that is unsavory at best and unambiguously evil at its worst. Religious understandings of the world have tended to perceive greed as natural to some extent, yet rather than liberate it they have seen a need to control it. The spiritual problem with greed—both the greed for profit and the greed to consume—is due not only to the consequent maldistribution of worldly goods (although a more equitable distribution is of course essential), or to its effect on the biosphere, but even more fundamentally because greed is based on a delusion: the delusion that happiness is to be found this way. Trying to find fulfillment through profit, or by making consumption the meaning of one's life, amounts to idolatry, that is, a demonic perversion of true religion; and any religious institution that makes its peace with the priority of such market values does not deserve the name of genuine religion.

In other words, greed is part of a defective value-system (the way to live in this world) based on an erroneous belief-system (what the world is). The atomistic individualism of utilitarianism, which "naturalizes" such greed, must be challenged and refuted intellectually and in the way we actually live our lives. The great sensitivity to social justice in the Semitic religions (for whom sin is a moral failure of *will*) needs to be supplemented by the emphasis that the Asian enlightenment traditions place upon seeing through and dispelling delusion (ignorance as a failure to *understand*). Moreover, I suspect that the former without the latter is doomed to be ineffective in our cynical age. We are unlikely ever to solve the problem of distributive social justice without also overcoming the value-delusion of happiness through individualistic accumulation and consumption, if only because of the ability of those who control the world's resources to manipulate things to their own perceived advantage. That is not to demonize such people, for we must recognize our own complicity in this system, not only through our own levels of consumption but also through the effects that our pension funds have upon the workings of the market.

According to the French historian Fernand Braudel, the industrial revolution was "in the end a revolution in demand"—or, more precisely, "a transformation of desires."[16] Since we have come to look upon our own insatiable desires as "natural," it is necessary to remember how much our present mode-of-desiring is also one particular, historically conditioned system of values—a set of habits as manufactured as the goods supplied to satisfy it. According to the trade journal *Advertising Age*, which should know, in 1994 the United States spent $147 billion for advertising—far more than on all higher education. This translated into a barrage of 21,000 television commercials, a million magazine advertising pages, 14 billion mail-order catalogs, 38 billion junk-mail ads, and another billion signs, posters, and billboards. That does not include related industries affecting consumer taste and spending, such as promotion, public relations, marketing, design, and most of all fashion, which amounted to another $100 billion a year.[17] Put together, this constitutes probably the greatest effort in mental manipulation that humanity has ever experienced—all of it to no other end than creating consumerist needs for the sake of corporate profit. No wonder a child in the developed countries has an environmental impact as much as thirty times that of a child in the Third World.

If the market is simply the most efficient way to meet our economic needs, why are such enormous industries necessary? Economic theory, like the market itself, makes no distinction between genuine needs and the most questionable manufactured desires. Both are treated as normative. It makes no difference why one wants something. The consequences of this approach, however, continue to make a great difference. The pattern of consumption that now seems natural to us provides a sobering context to the rapid deterioration of ecological systems over the last half-century: according to the Worldwatch Institute, more goods and services have been consumed by the people living between 1950 and 1990 (measured in constant dollars) than by all the previous generations in human history.[18]

If this is not disturbing enough, add to it the social consequences of our shift to consumption values, which, in the United States at least, has revolutionized the way we relate to each other. "With the breakdown of community at all levels, human beings have become more like what the traditional model of *Homo economicus* described. Shopping has become the great national pastime. . . . On the basis of massive borrowing and massive sales of national assets, Americans have been squandering their heritage and impoverishing their children."[19] So much for their patrimony. Our extraordinary wealth has not been enough for us, so we have supplemented it by accumulating extraordinary amounts of debt. How ingenious we have been to devise an economic system that allows us to steal from the assets of our descendants! Our commodifications have enabled us to achieve something usually believed impossible, time-travel: we now have ways to colonize and exploit even the future.

The final irony in this near-complete commodification of the world comes as little surprise to anyone familiar with what has become addictive behavior for so many millions of people in the United States. Comparisons that have been made over time and between societies detect little difference in self-reported happiness. The fact that we in the developed world are now consuming so much more does not seem to be having much effect on our level of contentment.[20]

This comes as no surprise to those with a more religious orientation to the world. The best critique of this greed for consumption continues to be provided by traditional religious teachings, which not only serve to ground us functionally but show us how our lives can be transformed. In Buddhism, to cite the example of my own religion, the insatiable desires of the ego-self are the source of the frustration and lack of peace that we experience in our daily lives. Overconsumption, which distracts and intoxicates us, is one of the main symptoms of this problem.

Later chapters in this book explore the ways Buddhism and other religions diagnose and attempt to resolve this problem. If we contrast their approaches with market indoctrination about the importance of acquisition and consumption—an indoctrination that is necessary for the market to thrive—the battle lines become clear. All genuine religions are natural allies against what amounts to an idolatry that undermines their most important teachings.

• • •

In conclusion, the market is not just an economic system but a religion—yet not a very good one, for it can thrive only by promising a secular salvation that it never quite supplies. Its academic discipline, the "social science" of economics, is better understood as a theology pretending to be a science.

This suggests that any solution to the problems they have created must also have a religious dimension. That is not a matter of turning from secular to sacred values, but the need to discover how our secular obsessions have become symptomatic of a spiritual need they cannot meet. As we have consciously or unconsciously turned away from a religious understanding of the world, we have come to pursue this-worldly goals with a religious zeal all the greater because they can never be fulfilled. The solution to the environmental catastrophe that has already begun, and to the social deterioration we are already suffering from, will occur when we redirect this repressed spiritual urge back into its true path. For the time being, that path includes struggling against the false religion of our age.

NOTES

1. David C. Korten, *When Corporations Rule the World* (West Hartford, Conn.: Kumarian Press, 1995), pp. 107–8.

2. A. Rodney Dobell, "Environmental Degradation and the Religion of the Market," in *Population, Consumption, and the Environment,* ed. Harold Coward (Albany: State University of New York Press, 1995), p. 232.

3. Ibid., p. 237.

4. Karl Polanyi, *The Great Transformation* (Boston: Beacon Press, 1944, 1957), pp. 46, 57.

5. R. H. Tawney, *Religion and the Rise of Capitalism* (New York: Harcourt, Brace, 1926), p. 31.

6. This implies that an alternative to our market religion would not require eliminating the market (and the failure of twentieth-century socialism suggests that it should not be eliminated), but restoring market forces to their proper delimited place within community social relations.

7. Tawney, *Religion and the Rise of Capitalism,* p. 86.

8. Norman O. Brown, *Life against Death* (New York: Vintage, 1961), p. 261. Since every God needs a Devil, and every religion a theory of evil, members of the market religion find evil in that which threatens their surplus: especially taxes, inflation, and (for corporations) governmental regulation, e.g., trade barriers.

9. Polanyi, *Great Transformation,* pp. 163, 3.

10. Herman E. Daly and John B. Cobb Jr., *For the Common Good,* 2nd ed. (Boston: Beacon Press, 1994), p. 50. I am much indebted to their highly recommended book, which presents a detailed critique of modern economic theory and demonstrates how our environmental and social problems can be solved if we have the will to do so.

11. Korten, *When Corporations Rule the World,* p. 218.

12. "Economics sprang at least half-grown from the head of Adam Smith, who may very properly be regarded as the founder of economics as a unified abstract realm of discourse, and it still, almost without knowing it, breathes a good deal of the air of the eighteenth-century rationalism and Deism." (Kenneth E. Boulding, *Beyond Economics* [Ann Arbor: University of Michigan Press, 1968], p. 187.)

13. Daly and Cobb, *For the Common Good,* p. 160.

14. Ibid., p. 162.

15. For an incisive critique of Malthusianism, see Mohan Rao, "An Imagined Reality: Malthusianism, Neo-Malthusianism and Population Myth," *Economic and Political Weekly,* 29 January 1994, pp. 40–52.

16. Fernand Braudel, *The Wheels of Commerce,* trans. Sian Reynolds (New York: Harper & Row, 1982), 183.

17. Alan Durning, *How Much Is Enough* (New York: Norton, 1992), p. 122.

18. Ibid., p. 38.

19. Daly and Cobb, *For the Common Good,* p. 373.

20. Durning, *How Much Is Enough,* pp. 38–40.

Discussion Questions

1. How is progress defined? Can it be quantified? Is progress necessary?
2. Is nature imperfect? Can humans improve on nature? Is "a well-tended garden better than a neglected woodlot"?
3. Is environmentalism incompatible with industrial development?
4. Would the New Nature have a place for spirituality or the divine? If so, what might it be, and what forms might they take?
5. Can market capitalism be considered a religion? What aspects of capitalist ideology could be considered religious? Does capitalism lack any features necessary to meet the definition of a religion?

Further Reading

Bacon, Francis, *The New Atlantis,* Arlington Heights, Ill.: Davidson, 1989.

Easterbrook, Gregg, *A Moment on the Earth,* New York: Viking, 1995.

Glendinning, Chellis, *When Technology Wounds,* New York: William Morrow, 1990.
Higgs, Eric, Andrew Light, and David Strong, Eds., *Technology and the Good Life?* Chicago: University of Chicago Press, 2000.
Mander, Jerry, *In the Absence of the Sacred: The Failure of Technology and the Survival of the Indian Nations,* San Francisco: Sierra Club Books, 1991.
McKibben, Bill, *The End of Nature,* New York: Anchor Books, 1989.
Merchant, Carolyn, *The Death of Nature: Women, Ecology, and the Scientific Revolution,* San Francisco: Harper, 1980.
Rifkin, Jeremy, *Biosphere Politics,* New York: Crown, 1990.
Thomas, Keith, *Man and the Natural World: Changing Attitudes in England 1500–1800,* Oxford: Oxford University Press, 1983.
Winner, Langdon, *The Whale and the Reactor,* Chicago: University of Chicago Press, 1986.

Part Two

Interpreting Tradition

Worldviews are shaped by the living context of the people that subscribe to them. As contexts evolve and change, so does people's understanding of the shared assumptions and norms that serve as the foundation of their culture. Successful systems of belief and practice, such as the world's major religions today, are those that have proven able to adapt themselves to different environments and circumstances throughout their histories. Often, as with the Hellenization (Greek influence) of Christianity or the Sinicization (Chinese influence) of Buddhism, the transformations are quite dramatic. Furthermore, worldviews are transformed by time and space so that, for example, among the Christians of the first century, the Middle Ages, and the present day as well as among contemporary Christians in Africa, Europe, and Latin America, one can detect considerable variations in priorities, concerns, doctrines, and rituals.

Indeed, culture is inseparable from its practitioners and shows many of the organic qualities and characteristics of a living entity. Typically, as in the natural world, cultural manifestations that do not adapt to changing realities do not survive. Theologian Paul Tillich has suggested that it is precisely in how successfully a religion addresses the emerging needs of any age that it continually reasserts and maintains its relevance and strength within a community of believers.

Environmental degradation is emerging today as the central crisis facing humanity. As more and more followers of various established religions come to acknowledge this, they are naturally turning to their own traditions to seek ways of dealing with the crisis. Although the results of this kind of inquiry vary enormously, one theme that emerges is that ecological values can be discovered within each and every one of the world's major existing religions.

Ever since Lynn White Jr. leveled his charge at Western Christianity in his well-known 1967 essay, many Christians have responded by demonstrating and articulating more ecological readings of their tradition than the one that White proposed. At the same time, others have taken up White's positive remarks regarding non-Western traditions and sought to explore ways in which Buddhism, Daoism, Hinduism, and various indigenous religions might appear to be more eco-friendly.

Both these approaches, of course, can be and have been challenged. As White himself pointed out, what is significant in the case of Christianity is not the eco-friendliness of its true form (whatever that might be), but rather the observation that it has often been *interpreted* in ecologically damaging ways. Likewise, some scholars of non-Western traditions, noting that environmental degradation is a worldwide and not a uniquely Western phenomenon, have challenged as overly simplistic the idea that non-Western cultures are inherently ecological. As with Christianity, it is becoming clear that *every* tradition can potentially lend itself to more and to less ecological readings.

To date, the academic forum has shown a marked preponderance of apologetic, ecological readings of the world's religious traditions, in contrast to the relatively smaller number of critical treatments; in many cases, the arguments have come from those writing within and, therefore, in support of a particular tradition. Some of the writers presented here fall into this category. Where possible, however, examples of critical views have also been included.

Chapter 3

First Peoples

WITH THE INCREASING acknowledgment that the modernist worldview has played a major role in allowing humans to destroy the life-support systems of their natural environment, there has been a growing interest in the various worldviews that the dominant modern culture has long sought to overcome. In such places as the Americas and Australia, for the past several centuries Western European immigrants and their descendants have imposed their worldview—sometimes through brute force, other times through more subtle pressures—on a wide variety of indigenous peoples whose ways of life were generally very closely tied to the land on which they lived. Since the 1960s, growing awareness of the ecological crisis has led many Americans and Australians of European descent to look anew to the traditions of native peoples whose knowledge of the land often reflects the experience of many thousands of years, as opposed to merely a few centuries. Whereas Europeans have sought to replicate in new surroundings the lifestyles and institutions of their own lands of origin, the cultural traditions of native peoples usually evolved over very long periods of time in response to the particular needs and demands of the lands in which they lived.

Indeed, one notion that seems to be common to indigenous worldviews around the world, from the Amazon to Siberia, is the native people's sense that they are an integral part of the land—that their identity is inseparable from it. This is reflected in the devastating experience that many of these peoples have shared over the past several centuries, namely the forcible alienation from their lands—whether through relocation or through degradation of their environment—that has led to a breakdown in their identity and ability to function as communities and as individuals.

Native societies from all over the world, or *first peoples* as they are sometimes called, are often categorized together, perhaps more for the sake of convenience than anything else. Admittedly, to speak of peoples as diverse as Siberian Yakut, Amazonian Yanomami, southern African Xhosa, and northern Scandinavian Saami in unitary terms is in some respects absurd. Yet, both in their worldviews and in their recent histories, many of these small-scale societies have themselves recognized common interests and perspectives, as attested by the various Fourth World and First Peoples movements that have grown prominent over the past decade or so.

Tragically, one issue that many if not most such groups face is the threat of their own cultural extinction. Traditional lifestyles everywhere are in jeopardy through a wide range of causes, some of which are explored in the essays in this chapter and in Chapter 13. Cultural diversity, like biological diversity, is threatened by the global trend toward economic and cultural homogenization. Another common theme in this chapter is that *development*, generally lauded as good and inevitable from a modernist perspective, is ambivalent at best when imposed on tribal societies, who often find themselves bearing a disproportionate share of the ecological and social costs of development and correspondingly reaping few of its benefits.

In indigenous societies, the kinds of beliefs and activities that modernists tend to categorize as religious are generally not easily separable from the daily life of the community. In other words, ritual and belief tend foremost to address communal rather than individual needs. Concepts of the supernatural or the divine are most often local and nonexclusive; the dogma and universalism characteristic of Christianity and Islam, for example, are rare.

A number of critics, most recently anthropologist Shepard Krech III in his book *The Ecological Indian* (1999), have challenged the popular stereotype of the "ecological primitive" by citing cases where indigenous groups historically engaged in practices that degraded their ecosystems, such as overhunting or overcultivation. Overall, however, the observation that in many areas throughout the world, such groups have successfully inhabited specific places for millennia suggests that they had developed lifestyles that were compatible with the ecologies of the particular environments in which they lived.

A number of scholars and activists now argue for giving a more prominent place to native knowledge alongside modern scientific knowledge. Around the world today, biologists and others are coming to recognize the detailed knowledge that indigenous peoples have of their native environments, sometimes referred to as *traditional ecological knowledge* (TEK). For example, ethnobotanists, as they are now called, are busy interviewing the shamans of the Amazon, New Guinea, and elsewhere in the hope of learning the medicinal properties of tropical plants before these plants are rendered extinct through rain forest destruction. Agricultural consultants are coming to advocate traditional farming practices that are more in tune with local conditions, instead of the one-size-fits-all industrial approach of the Green Revolution in the 1960s. In this and other fields, calls are increasing for appropriate technology, which in many cases turns out to be the sort of technology used by local peoples prior to the arrival of industrial civilization.

Vine Deloria Jr. is a Lakota Sioux activist, lawyer, and historian and one of the leading spokespersons for North American Indians since the 1960s. Deloria shows how issues of native rights to practice traditional religion have historically been tied to struggles with the U.S. government and other agencies about land. He draws a distinction between modernist and traditional notions of individual versus community priorities and of how land is perceived. Although Deloria admits that in some cases Whites are able to conceive of land as sacred, he points out that Indians, having lived in North America for many thousands of years longer than non-Indians, have a far greater number of sacred places. To deny Indians access to these places is, in a sense, to deny them their religion. Without the sense of the sacred that such places provide, Deloria cautions us, it is very hard to know our place in the world.

Two themes that are frequently associated with indigenous worldviews—namely, a people's connection to the land they inhabit, and their interconnectedness with the rest of the natural world—are taken up by Mary Graham in her essay. Herself an Australian Aboriginal elder, Graham takes issue with the common perception of her culture as backward and primitive. More than merely a survival strategy, she argues, the Aboriginal worldview allows for and facilitates the highest level of human development. Graham suggests specific ways in which Aboriginal and European worldviews can be combined to form a healthier Australian society.

Writing from an East African context, C. K. Omari also emphasizes the traditional concept of land. The African concept of land ownership differed markedly from the modern Western view in that land was seen as communal, not individual, property. When one considers the role that private property rights have played and continue to play in environmental debates in the United States, the implications of the more communitarian African model are great indeed. Implicit in the African requirement of collective consultation in land use issues is the awareness that what proprietors do with their land very often affects the entire community.

Omari also discusses traditional taboos that served to constrain the use of natural resources. Religious rituals served primarily communal as opposed to individual interests. Omari describes how the imposition of modernist values, particularly in the form of a monetary economy, has undermined and in places destroyed traditional African value systems in the interest of development.

Conservationist and scholar Gary Paul Nabhan describes the debate that has arisen about the ecological roles of indigenous North Americans in history. One aspect of this debate—whether humans are to be considered an integral part of an ecosystem or not—has important ramifications not only for defining *wilderness* for purposes of conservation legislation but also worldwide, because the U.S. conservation model has been applied throughout the developing world.

Sacred Places and Moral Responsibility

VINE DELORIA JR.

WHEN THE TRIBES WERE FORCED FROM THEIR aboriginal homelands and confined to small reservations, many of the tribal religious rituals were prohibited by the Bureau of Indian Affairs in the 1870s and 1880s because of an inordinately large number of Christian zealots as Indian agents. Traditional people had to adopt various subterfuges so that their religious life could be continued. Some tribes shifted their ceremonial year to coincide with the whites' holidays and conducted their most important rituals on national holidays and Christian feast days, explaining to curious whites that they were simply honoring George Washington and celebrating Christmas and Easter. Many shrines and holy places were located far away from the new reservation homelands, but because they were not being exploited economically or used by settlers, it was not difficult for small parties of people to go into the mountains or to remote lakes and buttes and conduct ceremonies without interference from non-Indians.

Since World War II, this situation has changed dramatically. We have seen a greatly expanding national population, the introduction of corporate farming practices that have placed formerly submarginal lands under cultivation, more extensive mining and timber industry activities, and a greatly expanded recreation industry—all of which have severely impacted the use of public lands in the United States. Few rural areas now enjoy the isolation of half a century ago, and as multiple use of lands increased, many of the sacred sites that were on public lands were threatened by visitors and subjected to new uses. Tribal religious leaders were often able to work out informal arrangements with federal and state agencies to allow them access to these places for religious purposes. But as the personnel changed in

Deloria, Vine, Jr., "Sacred Places and Moral Responsibility," in *God Is Red: A Native View of Religion*, Golden, Colo.: Fulcrum, 1994, pp. 267–282. Reprinted by permission.

state and federal agencies, a new generation of bureaucrats, catering to developers, recreation interest, and the well-established economic groups who have always used public lands for a pittance, began to restrict Indian access to sacred sites by establishing increasingly narrow rules and regulations for managing public lands.

In 1978, in a symbolic effort to clarify the status of traditional religious practices and practitioners, Congress passed a Joint Resolution entitled the American Indian Religious Freedom Act. This act declared that it was the policy of Congress to protect and preserve the inherent right of American Indians to believe, express, and practice their traditional religions. The resolution identified the problem as one of a "lack of knowledge or the insensitive and inflexible enforcement of Federal policies and regulations." Section 2 of the resolution directed the president to require the various federal departments to evaluate their policies and procedures, report back to Congress on the results of their survey, and make recommendations for legislative actions.[1]

Many people assumed that this resolution clarified the federal attitude toward traditional religions, and it began to be cited in litigation involving the construction of dams, roads, and the management of federal lands. Almost unanimously, however, the federal courts have since ruled that the resolution did not protect or preserve the right of Indians to practice their religion and conduct ceremonies at sacred sites on public lands.[2] Some courts even hinted darkly that any formal recognition of the existence of tribal practices would be tantamount to establishing a state religion,[3] an interpretation that, upon analysis, is a dreadful misreading of American history and the Constitution and may have been an effort to inflame anti-Indian feelings.

A good example for making this claim was the 1988 Supreme Court decision in the *Lyng v. Northwest Indian Cemetery Protective Association* case that involved protecting the visitation rights of the traditional religious leaders of three tribes to sacred sites in the Chimney Rock area of the Six Rivers National Forest in Northern California. The Forest Service proposed to build a 6-mile paved road that would have opened part of the area to commercial logging. This area, known by three Indian tribes as the "High Country," was the center of their religious and ceremonial life. The lower federal courts prohibited the construction of the road on the grounds that it would have made religious ceremonial use of the area impossible. Before the Supreme Court could hear the appeal, Congress passed the California Wilderness Act that made the question of constructing the road moot for all practical purposes. But the Supreme Court insisted on hearing the appeal of the Forest Service and deciding the religious issues. It turned the tribes down flat, ruling that the Free Exercise clause did not prevent the government from using its property in any way it saw fit and in effect rolling back the religious use of the area completely.

Most troubling about the Supreme Court's decision was the insistence on analyzing tribal religions within the same conceptual framework as western organized religions. Justice O'Connor observed,

> A broad range of government activities—from social welfare programs to foreign aid to conservation projects—will always be considered essential to the spiritual well-being of some citizens, often on the basis of sincerely held religious beliefs. Others will find the very same activity deeply offensive, and perhaps incompatible with their own search for spiritual fulfillment and with the tenets of their religion.[4]

Thus, ceremonies and rituals that had been performed for thousands of years were treated as if they were popular fads or simply matters of personal preference based upon the erroneous assumption that religion was only a matter of individual aesthetic choice.

Justice Brennan's dissent vigorously attacked this spurious line of reasoning, outlining with some precision the communal aspect of the tribal religions and their relationship to the mountains. But his argument failed to gather support within the Court. Most observers of the Supreme Court were simply confounded at the majority's conclusion that suggested that destroying a religion "did not unduly burden it" and that no constitutional protections were available to the Indians.[5]

When informed of the meaning of this decision, most people have shown great sympathy for the traditional religious people. At the same time, they have had great difficulty understanding why it is so important that these ceremonies be held, that they be conducted only at certain locations, and that they be held in secrecy and privacy. This lack of understanding highlights the great gulf that exists between traditional Western thinking about religion and the Indian perspective. It is the difference between individual conscience and commitment (Western) and communal tradition (Indian), these views can only be reconciled by examining them in a much broader historical and geographical context.

Justice Brennan attempted to make this difference clear when he observed, "Although few tribal members actually made medicine at the most powerful sites, the entire tribe's welfare hinges on the success of individual practitioner."[6] More than that, however, the "world renewal" ceremonies conducted by the tribes were done on behalf of the earth and all forms of life. To describe these ceremonies as if they were comparable to Oral Roberts seeking funds or Jimmy Swaggart begging forgiveness for his continuing sexual misconduct or Justice O'Connor's matters of community aesthetic preference is to miss the point entirely. In effect, the Court declared that Indians cannot pray for the planet or for other people and other forms of life in the manner required by their religion.

Two contradictory responses seem to characterize the non-Indian attitudes toward traditional tribal religions. Some people want the traditional healers to share their religious beliefs in the same manner that priests, rabbis, and ministers expound publicly the tenets of their denominations. Other people feel that Indian ceremonials are simply remnants of primitive life and should be abandoned. Neither perspective understands that Indian tribes are communities in ways that are fundamentally different than other American communities and organizations. Tribal communities are wholly defined by the family relationships; the non-Indian communities are defined primarily by residence, by an arbitrary establishment of political jurisdiction, or by agreement with generally applicable sets of intellectual beliefs. Ceremonial and ritual knowledge is possessed by everyone in the Indian community, although only a few people may actually be chosen to perform these acts. Authorization to perform ceremonies comes from higher spiritual powers and not by certification through an institution or any formal organization.

A belief in the sacredness of lands in the non-Indian context may become the preferred belief of an individual or group of people based on their experiences or on an intensive study of preselected evidence. But this belief becomes the subject of intense criticism and does not, except under unusual circumstances, become an operative principle in the life and behavior of the non-Indian group. The same belief, when seen in the Indian context, is an integral part of the experiences of the people—past, present, and future. The idea does not become a bone of contention among the people for even if someone does not have the experience or belief in the sacredness of lands, he or she accords tradition the respect that it deserves. Indians who have never visited certain sacred sites nevertheless know of these places from the community knowledge, and they intuit this knowing to be an essential part of their being.

Justice Brennan, in countering the arguments raised by Justice O'Connor that any recognition of the sacredness of certain sites would allow traditional Indian religions to define the use of all public lands, suggested that the burden of proof be placed on the traditional people to demonstrate why some sites are central to their practice and other sites, while invoking a sense of reverence, are not as important. This requirement is not unreasonable, but it requires a willingness on the part of non-Indians and the courts to entertain different ideas about the nature of religion—ideas which until the present have not been a part of their experience or understanding.

If we were to subject the topic of the sacredness of lands to a Western rational analysis, fully recognizing the such an analysis is merely for our convenience in discussion and does not represent the nature of reality, we would probably find four major categories of description. Some of these categories are overlapping because some groups might not agree with the description of certain sites in the categories in which other Indians would place them. Nevertheless, it is the principle of respect for the sacred that is important.

The first and most familiar kind of sacred lands are places to which we attribute sanctity because the location is a site where, within our own history, something of great importance has taken place. Unfortunately, many of these places are related to instances of human violence. Gettysburg National Cemetery is a good example of this kind of sacred land. Abraham Lincoln properly noted that we cannot hallow the Gettysburg battlefield because others, the men who fought there, had already consecrated it by giving "that last full measure of devotion." We generally hold these places sacred because people did there what we might one day be required to do—give our lives in a cause we hold dear. Wounded Knee, South Dakota, has become such a place for many Indians where a band of Sioux Indians were massacred. On the whole, however, the idea of regarding a battlefield as sacred was entirely foreign to most tribes because they did not see war as a holy enterprise. The Lincoln Memorial in Washington, D.C., might be an example of a nonmartial location, and, although Justice O'Connor felt that recognizing the sacredness of land and location might inspire an individual to have a special fondness for this memorial, it is important to recognize that we should have some sense of reverence in these places.

Every society needs these kinds of sacred places because they help to instill a sense of social cohesion in the people and remind them of the passage of generations that have brought them to the present. A society that cannot remember and honor its past is in peril of losing its soul. Indians, because of our considerably longer tenure on this continent, have many more sacred places than do non-Indians. Many different ceremonies can be and have been held at these locations; there is both an exclusivity and an inclusiveness, depending upon the occasion and the ceremony. In this classification the site is all important, but it is sanctified each time ceremonies are held and prayers offered.

A second category of sacred lands has a deeper, more profound sense of the sacred. It can be illustrated in Old Testament stories that have become the foundation of three world religions. After the death of Moses, Joshua led the Hebrews across the River Jordan into the Holy Land. On approaching the river with the Ark of the Covenant, the waters of the Jordan "rose up" or parted and the people, led by the Ark, crossed over on "dry ground," which is to say they crossed without difficulty. After crossing, Joshua selected one man from each of the Twelve Tribes and told him to find a large stone. The twelve stones were then placed together in a monument to mark the spot where the people had camped after having crossed the river successfully. When asked about this strange behavior, Joshua then replied, "That this may be a sign among you, that when your children ask their fathers in time to come, saying 'What mean ye by these stones?' Then you shall answer them: That the waters of Jordan were cut off before the Ark of the Covenant of the Lord, when it passed over Jordan."[7]

In comparing this site with Gettysburg, we must understand a fundamental difference. Gettysburg is made sacred by the actions of men. It can be described as exquisitely dear to us, but it is not a location where we have perceived that something specifically other than ourselves is present, something mysteriously religious in the proper meaning of those words has happened or been made manifest. In the crossing of the River Jordan, the sacred or higher powers have appeared in the lives of human beings. Indians would say something holy has appeared in an otherwise secular situation. No matter how we might attempt to explain this event in later historical, political, or economic terms, the essence of the event is that the sacred has become a part of our experience.

Some of the sites that traditional religious leaders visit are of this nature. Buffalo Gap at the southeastern edge of the Black Hills of South Dakota marks the location where the buffalo emerged each spring to begin the ceremonial year of the Plains Indians, and it has this aspect of sacred/secular status. It may indeed be the starting point of the Great Race that determined the primacy between two-legged and four-legged creatures at the beginning of the world. Several mountains in New Mexico and Arizona mark places where the Pueblo, Hopi, and Navajo peoples completed their migrations, were told to settle, or where they first established their spiritual relationships with bear, deer, eagle, and other peoples who participate in the ceremonials.

Every identifiable region has sacred places peculiar to its geography and as we extend the circle geographically from any point in North America, we begin to include an ever-increasing number of sacred sites. Beginning in the American Southwest we must include the Apache, Ute, Comanche, Kiowa, and other tribes as we move away from the Pueblo and Navajo lands. These lands would be sacred to some tribes but secular to the Pueblo, Hopi, and Navajo. The difference would be in the manner of revelation and what the people experienced. There is immense particularity in the sacred and it is not a blanket category to be applied indiscriminately. Even east of the Mississippi, though many places have been nearly obliterated, people retain knowledge of these sacred sites. Their sacredness does not depend on human occupancy but on the stories that describe the revelation that enabled human beings to experience the holiness there.

In the religious world of most tribes, birds, animals, and plants compose the "other peoples" of creation. Depending on the ceremony, various of these "peoples" participate in human activities. If Jews and Christians see the action of a deity at sacred places in the Holy Land and in churches and synagogues, traditional Indian people experience spiritual activity as the whole of creation becomes active participants in ceremonial life. Because the relationship with the "other peoples" is so fundamental to the human community, most traditional practitioners are reluctant to articulate the specific elements of either the ceremony or the locations. Because some rituals involve the continued prosperity of the "other peoples," discussing the nature of the ceremony would violate the integrity of these relationships. Thus, traditional people explain that these ceremonies are being held for "all our relatives" but are reluctant to offer any further explanations. It is these ceremonies in particular that are now to be denied protection under the Supreme Court rulings.

It is not likely that non-Indians have had many of these kinds of religious experiences, particularly because most churches and synagogues have special rituals that are designed to cleanse the buildings so that their services can be held there untainted by the natural world. Non-Indians have simply not been on this continent very long; their families have rarely settled in one place for any period of time so that no profound relationship with the environment has been possible. Additionally, non-Indians have engaged in the senseless killing of wildlife and utter destruction of plant life. It is unlikely that they would have understood efforts by other forms of life to communicate with humans. Although, some non-Indian families who have lived continuously in isolated rural areas tell stories about birds and animals similar to the traditions of many tribes indicating that lands and the "other peoples" do seek intimacy with our species.

The third kind of sacred lands are places of overwhelming holiness where the Higher Powers, on their own initiative, have revealed Themselves to human beings. Again, we can illustrate this in the Old Testament narrative. Prior to his journey to Egypt, Moses spent his time herding his father-in-law's sheep on or near Mount Horeb. One day he took the flock to the far side of the mountain and to his amazement saw a bush burning with fire but not being consumed by it. Approaching this spot with the usual curiosity of a person accustomed to the outdoor life, Moses was startled when the Lord spoke to him from the bush, warning, "Draw not hither; put off thy shoes from thy feet, for the place where on thou standest is holy ground."[8]

This tradition tells us that there are places of unquestionable, inherent sacredness on this earth, sites that are holy in and of themselves. Human societies come and go on this earth and any prolonged occupation of a geographical region will produce shrines and sacred sites discerned by the occupying people, but there will always be a few sites at which the highest spirits dwell. The stories that explain the sacred nature of these locations will frequently provide startling parallels to the account about the burning bush. One need only look at the shrines of present-day Europe. Long before Catholic or Protestant churches were built in certain places, other religions had established shrines and temples of that spot. These holy places are locations where people have always gone to communicate and commune with higher spiritual powers.

This phenomenon is worldwide and all religions find that these places regenerate people and fill them with spiritual powers. In the Western Hemisphere these places, with few exceptions, are known only by American Indians. Bear Butte, Blue Lake, and the High Places in the *Lyng* case are all well known locations that are sacred in and of themselves. People have been commanded to perform ceremonies at these holy places so that the earth and all its forms of life might survive and prosper. Evidence of this moral responsibility that sacred places command has come through the testimony of traditional people when they have tried to explain to non-Indians at various times in this century—in court, in conferences, and in conversations—that they must perform certain ceremonies at specific times and places in order that the sun may continue to shine, the earth prosper, and the stars remain in the heavens. Tragically, this attitude is interpreted by non-Indians as indicative of the traditional leader's personal code or philosophy and is not seen as a simple admission of a moral duty.

Skeptical non-Indians, and representatives of other religions seeking to discredit tribal religions, have sometimes deliberately violated some of these holy places with no ill effects. They have then come to believe that they have demonstrated the false nature of Indian beliefs. These violations reveal a strange non-Indian belief in a form of mechanical magic that is touchingly adolescent, a belief that an impious act would, or could trigger an immediate response from the higher spiritual powers. Surely these impious acts suggest a deity who jealously guards his or her prerogatives and wreaks immediate vengeance for minor transgressions—much as some Protestant sects have envisioned God and much as an ancient astronaut wanting to control lesser beings might act.

It would be impossible for the thoughtless or impious acts of one species to have an immediate drastic effort [*sic*] on the earth. The cumulative effect of continuous secularity, however, poses a different kind of danger. Long-standing prophecies tell us of the impious people who would come here, defy the creator, and cause the massive destruction of the planet. Many traditional people believe that we are now quite near that time. The cumulative evidence of global warming, acid rain, the disappearance of amphibians, overpopulation, and other products of civilized life certainly testify to the possibility of these prophecies being correct.

Of all the traditional ceremonies extant and actively practiced at the time of contact with non-Indians, ceremonies derived from or related to these holy places have the highest retention rate because of their extraordinary planetary importance. Ironically, traditional people have been forced to hold these ceremonies under various forms of subterfuge and have been abused and imprisoned for doing them. Yet the ceremonies have very little to do with individual or tribal prosperity. Their underlying theme is one of gratitude expressed by human beings on behalf of all forms of life. They act to complete and renew the entire and complete cycle of life, ultimately including the whole cosmos present in its specific realizations, so that in the last analysis one might describe ceremonials as the cosmos becoming thankfully aware of itself.

Having used Old Testament examples to show the objective presence of the holy places, we can draw additional conclusions about the nature of these holy places from the story of the Exodus. Moses did not demand that the particular location of the burning bush become a place of worship for his people, although there was every reason to suppose that he could have done so. Lacking information, we must conclude that the holiness of this place precluded its use as a shrine. If Moses had been told to perform annual ceremonies at that location during specific days or times of the year, world history would have been entirely different.

Each holy site contains its own revelation. This knowledge is not the ultimate in the sense that Near Eastern religions like to claim the universality of their ideas. Traditional religious leaders tell us that in many of the ceremonies new messages are communicated to them. The ceremonies enable humans to have continuing relationships with higher spiritual powers so that each bit of information is specific to the time, place, and circumstances of the people. No revelation can be regarded as universal because times and conditions change.

The second and third kinds of sacred lands result from two distinctly different forms of sacred revelations where the sacred is actively involved in secular human activities and where the sacred takes the initiative to chart out a new historical course for humans. Because there are higher spiritual powers who can communicate with people, there has to be a fourth category of sacred lands. People must always be ready to experience new revelations at new locations. If this possibility did not exist, all deities and spirits would be dead. Consequently, we always look forward to the revelation of new sacred places and ceremonies. Unfortunately, some federal courts irrationally and arbitrarily circumscribe this universal aspect of religion by insisting that traditional religious practitioners restrict their identification of sacred locations to places that were historically visited by Indians, implying that at least for the federal courts, God is dead.

In denying the possibility of the continuing revelation of the sacred in our lives, federal courts, scholars, and state and federal agencies refuse to accord credibility to the testimony of religious leaders. They demand evidence that a ceremony or location has *always* been central to the beliefs and practices of an Indian tribe and impose exceedingly rigorous standards of proof on Indians who appear before them. This practice allows the Supreme Court to command what should not to be done, it lets secular institutions rule on the substance of religious belief and practice. Thus, courts will protect a religion that shows every symptom of being dead but will create formidable barriers if it appears to be alive. Justice

Scalia made this posture perfectly clear when he announced in *Smith,* that it would be unconstitutional to ban the casting of "statues that are used for worship purposes" or to prohibit bowing down before a golden calf.

We live in time and space and receive most of our signals about proper behavior from each other and the environment around us. Under these circumstances, the individual and the group *must* both have some kind of sanctity if we are to have a social order at all. By recognizing the various aspects of the sacredness of lands as we have described, we place ourselves in a realistic context in which the individual and the group can cultivate and enhance the sacred experience. Recognizing the sacredness of lands on which previous generations have lived and died is the foundation of all other sentiment. Instead of denying this dimension of our emotional lives, we should be setting aside additional places that have transcendent meaning. Sacred sites that higher spiritual powers have chosen for manifestation enable us to focus our concerns on the specific form of our lives. These places remind us of our unique relationship with the spiritual forces that govern the universe and call us to fulfill our religious vocations. These kinds of religious experiences have shown us something of the nature of the universe by an affirmative manifestation of themselves and this knowledge illuminates everything else that we know.

The nature of tribal religion brings contemporary America a new kind of legal problem. Religious freedom has existed as a matter of course in America *only* when religion has been conceived as a set of objective beliefs. This condition is actually not freedom at all because it would be exceedingly difficult to read minds and determine what ideas were being entertained at the time. So far in American history religious freedom has not involved the consecration and setting aside of lands for religious purposes or allowing sincere but highly divergent behavior by individuals and groups. The issue of sacred lands, as we have seen was successfully raised in the case of the Taos Pueblo people. Nevertheless, a great deal more remains to be done to guarantee Indian people the right to practice their own religion.

A number of other tribes have sacred sanctuaries in lands that have been taken by the government for purposes other than religion. These lands must be returned to the respective Indian tribes for their ceremonial purposes. The greatest number of Indian shrines are located in New Mexico and here the tribal religions have remained comparatively strong. Cochiti Pueblo needs some 24,000 acres of land for access to and use of religious shrines in what is now Bandelier National Monument. The people also have shrines in the Tetilla Peak area. San Juan Pueblo has also been trying to get lands returned for religious purposes. Santa Clara Pueblo requested the Indian Claims Commission to set aside 30,000 acres of the lands that have religious and ceremonial importance to its people but are presently in the hands of the National Forest Service and Atomic Energy Commission.

In Arizona the Hopi people have a number of shrines that are of vital importance to their religion. Traditionals regard the Black Mesa area as sacred, but it is being leased to Peabody Coal by the more assimilative tribal council. The San Francisco Peaks within the Coconino National Forest are sacred because they are believed to be the homes of the Kachinas who play a major part in the Hopi ceremonial system. The Navajo have a number of sacred mountains now under federal ownership. Mount Taylor in the Cibola National Forest, Blanca Peak in southern Colorado, Hesperus Peak in the San Juan National Forest, Huerfano Mountain on public domain lands, and Oak Creek canyon in the Coconino National Forest are all sites integral to the Navajo tradition. Part of the Navajo religion involves the "mountain chant" that describes the seven sacred mountains and a sacred lake located within these mountains. The Navajo believe their ancestors arose from this region at the creation. Last, but certainly not least, is the valiant struggle now being waged by the Apache people to prevent the University of Arizona from building several telescopes on Mount Graham in southern Arizona.

In other states several sacred sites are under threat of exploitation. The Forest Service is proposing to construct a major parking lot and observation platform at the Medicine Wheel site near Powell, Wyoming, that is sacred to many tribes from Montana, the Dakotas, and Wyoming. Because the only value of this location is its relationship to traditional Indian religions that need isolation and privacy, it seems ludicrous to pretend that making it accessible to more tourists and subject to increasing environmental degradation is enhancing it. The Badger Two Medicine area of Montana, where oil drilling has been proposed, is a sacred area for traditional Blackfeet who live in the vicinity. The Pipestone Quarry in southwestern Minnesota was confiscated from the Yankton Sioux in the closing decades of the last century when some missionaries pressure the federal government to eliminate Indian access to this important spot.

Finally, there is the continuing struggle over the Black Hills of South Dakota. Many Americans are now aware of this state thanks to the success of the movie *Dances with Wolves* that not only depicted the culture of the Sioux Indians but also filled the screen with the magnificent landscape of the northern Great Plains. Nineteen ninety-one was a year of great schizophrenia and strange anomalies in South Dakota. Local whites shamelessly capitalized on the success of the movie at the same time they were frothing at the mouth over the continuing efforts of the Sioux people to get the federal lands in the Black Hills returned to them. Governor George Mickelson announced a "Year of Reconciliation" that simply became twelve months of symbolic maneuvering for publicity and renewal of political images. When some of the Sioux elders suggested that the return of Bear Butte near Sturgis would be a concrete step toward reconciliation, non-Indians were furious that reconciliation might require them to make good-faith effort to heal the wounds from a century of conflict.

The question that must be addressed in the issue of sacred lands is the extent to which the tribal religions can be maintained if sacred lands are restored. Would restoration of the sacred Pipestone Quarry result in more people seeking to follow the traditional religious life or would it result in continued use of the stone for tourism and commercial purposes? A small group of Sioux people have made a living during this century from making ashtrays and decorative carvings from this sacred rock; they refuse to stop their exploitation. A major shift in focus is needed by traditional Sioux people to prepare to reconsecrate the quarry and return to the old ways of reverence.

A very difficult task lies ahead for the people who continue to believe in the old tribal religions. In the past, these traditions have been ridiculed by disbelievers, primarily missionaries and social scientists. Today injuries nearly as grievous are visited on traditional religions by the multitude of non-Indians who seek entrance and participation in ceremonies and rituals. Many of these non-Indians blatantly steal symbols, prayers and teaching by laying claim to alleged offices in tribal religions. Most non-Indians see in tribal religions the experiences and reverence that are missing in their own heritage. No matter how hard they try, they always reduce the teachings and ceremonies to a complicated word game and ineffectual gestures. Lacking communities and extended families, they are unable to put the religion into practice.

Some major efforts must be made by the Indians of this generation to demonstrate the view of the world that their tradition teaches has an integrity of its own and represents a sensible and respectable perspective of the world and a valid means of interpreting experiences. There are many new studies that seem to confirm certain tribal practices as reasonable and sometimes even as sophisticated techniques for handling certain kinds of problems. It might be sufficient to show that these patterns of behavior are indicative of a consistent attitude toward the world and includes the knowledge that everything is alive and related.

Sacred places are the foundation of all other beliefs and practices because they represent the presence of the sacred in our lives. They properly inform us that we are not larger than nature and that we have responsibilities to the rest of the natural world that transcend our own personal desires and wishes. This lesson must be learned by each generation; unfortunately the technology of industrial society always leads us in the other direction. Yet it is certain that as we permanently foul our planetary nest, we shall have to learn a most bitter lesson. There probably is not sufficient time for the non-Indian population to understand the meaning of sacred lands and incorporate the idea into their lives and practices. We can but hope that some protection can be afforded these sacred places before the world becomes wholly secular and is destroyed.

NOTES

1. 92 Stat 469, 42 U.S.C. §1996.
2. See *Wilson v. Block,* 708 F2d. 735 (D.C. Cir 1983). Hopi and Navajo sacred sites and shrines on San Francisco peak were destroyed by the U.S. Forest Service to make room for a new ski lift. In *Fools Crow v. Gullet,* 706 F.2d 856 (8th Cir 1983) the court upheld intrusions by the U.S. Park Service on Sioux vision quest use of Bear Butte. In *Badoni v. Higginson,* 638 F.2d. 172 (10th Cir 1980) the court allowed the destruction of a Navajo sacred site at Rainbow Bridge in the Grand Canyon area.

3. The majority decision in *Lyng* even suggested that to recognize traditional Indian religious freedom would make it seem as if the Indians owned the federal lands.

> No disrespect for these practices is implied when one notes that such beliefs could easily require de facto beneficial ownership of some rather spacious tracts of public property. Even without anticipating future cases, the diminution of the government's property rights, and the concomitant subsidy of the Indian religion, would in this case be far from trivial. . . . 108 S. Ct 1319, 1327 (1988)

4. At 1327

5. Justice Brennan's dissent makes this point specifically,

> The Court today, however, ignores *Roy's* emphasis on the internal nature of the government practice at issue there, and instead construes that case as further support for the proposition that governmental action that does not coerce conduct inconsistent with religious faith simply does not implicate the concerns of the Free Exercise Clause. That such a reading is wholly untenable, however, is demonstrated by the cruelly surreal result it produces here: *governmental action that will virtually destroy a religion is nevertheless deemed not to 'burden' that religion.* (at 1337) (Emphasis added.)

6. At 1332

7. Joshua 4:6–7

8. Exodus 3:5

Some Thoughts about the Philosophical Underpinnings of Aboriginal Worldviews

MARY GRAHAM

> Western: What's the meaning of life?
> Aboriginal: What is it that wants to know?

> The white man's law is always changing, but Aboriginal Law never changes, and is valid for all people.
>
> (Mr. Bill Neidjie, 'Kakadu Man')

BASIC PRECEPTS OF THE ABORIGINAL WORLD VIEW

- The Land is the Law
- You are not alone in the world

Aboriginal people's culture is ancient, and certain observations have been made over many millennia about the nature of nature, spirit and being human. The most basic questions for any human group, despite advances in technology, have not changed much over time; they include:

- How do we live together (in a particular area, nation, or on earth), without killing each other off?
- How do we live without substantially damaging the environment?
- Why do we live? We need to find the answer to this question in a way that does not make people feel alienated, lonely or murderous.

A BRIEF DESCRIPTION OF THE TWO AXIOMS

The Land Is the Law

The land is a sacred entity, not property or real estate; it is the great mother of all humanity. The Dreaming is a combination of meaning (about life and all reality), and an action guide to living. The two most important kinds of relationship in life are, firstly, those between land and people and, secondly, those amongst people themselves, the second being always contingent upon the first. The land, and how we treat it, is what determines our human-ness. Because land is sacred and must be looked after, the relation between people and land becomes the tem-

Graham, Mary, "The Philosophical Underpinnings of Aboriginal Worldviews," *Worldviews: Environment, Culture, Religion* 3/2 (1999), pp. 105–117. Reprinted by permission of the author.

plate for society and social relations. Therefore all meaning comes from land.

You Are Not Alone in the World

Aboriginal people have a kinship system which extends into land; this system was and still is organised into clans. One's first loyalty is to one's own clan group. It does not matter how Western and urbanised Aboriginal people have become, this kinship system never changes. (It has been damaged by, for example, cultural genocide/Stolen Children/westernisation etc., but has not been altered substantially.) Every clan group has its own Dreaming or explanation of existence. We believe that a person finds their individuality within the group. To behave as if you are a discrete entity or a conscious isolate is to limit yourself to being an observer in an observed world.

LAND

Aboriginal People's Relationship to Land

Every different clan group has stories about their beginnings. Stories are like our archives, detailing how Creator Beings from under the earth arose to shape the land and to create the landscape. There are myriad variations of the story, but the theme stays the same.

The whole surface of the earth was like a moonscape, no features, no flora and fauna, just bare open plain. But there were Creator Beings sleeping in a state of potentiality just under the surface. At a certain time they were disturbed, whereupon their potentiality transformed into actuality and they arose out of the ground. When they finally emerged, they were very big and tall. These beings were spirit ancestors of many of the varieties of flora and fauna, especially large animals, in Australia. When this emergence was completed, the spirit ancestors started to interact with one another, fighting, dancing, running about, making love, killing. All of this activity shaped the Australian landscape as we know it today.

Throughout this period humans remained asleep in various embryonic forms, in a state like a kind of proto-humanity. They were awakened by all the activity above; the Creator Beings helped these proto-humans to become fully human, teaching them the Laws of custodianship of land, the Laws of kinship, of marriage, of correct ceremonies—they gave them every kind of knowledge they needed to look after the land and to have a stable society.

When this work was finished, the Creator Beings went back into the land, where they all still remain in the same eternal sleep from which they awakened at the beginning of time. The locations to which they returned have always been and are still today regarded as very important sacred sites.

Wherever the Creator Beings travelled, they left tracks or some kind of evidence of themselves. These traces determined the identity of the people. In other words, every Aboriginal person has a part of the essence of one of the original creative spirits who formed the Australian landscape. Therefore each person has a charter of custodianship empowering them and making them responsible for renewing that part of the flora and its fauna. The details of this metaphysics varied widely across the land with the physical environment, but the spiritual basis—the understanding that what separates humans from animals is the fact that each human bears a creative and spiritual identity which still resides in land itself—provided and still provides in many places the religious, social, political and economic force throughout Aboriginal Australia.

Land in Modern Australia: The Long-term View

Aboriginal society is accustomed to looking to the long term, and thinking strategically. A society which has a custodial ethic has to do this. From this perspective, short-term tactics are of less consequence: it is important to keep the big picture in mind.

Many White Australians are concerned to be involved in the maturation process of Australian society, through support for Aboriginal people/Reconciliation; they are searching for a new identity—politically or sociologically. The best way of achieving these ends is to start establishing very close ties with land, not necessarily via ownership of property but via locally-based, inclusive, non-political, strategy-based frameworks, with a very long term aim of simply looking after land.

How can such long-term views and goals be developed and maintained? Certainly not by having theoretical blueprints. From an Aboriginal perspective, *the goal must not be seen as a high moral ideal or 'holy grail'*. The custodial ethic is achieved through repetitive action, such that gradually, over time, the ethic becomes the 'norm'. For Aboriginal people, the land is *the* great teacher; it not only teaches us how to relate to it, but to each other; it suggests a notion of caring for something outside ourselves, something that is in and of nature and that will exist for all time. Every Aboriginal person had a place at some intersection within the kinship network which extended over the whole of Australia, and every intersection within that grid was anchored, eternally, to some point on the landscape by the relationship to Creator Being ancestors.

Outlined below are some ideas regarding how Australians might (together) manage the development of a collective spiritual identity, *one which is based in land—especially in the sacredness of land.*

STRATEGIES FOR ACHIEVING A COLLECTIVE SPIRITUAL IDENTITY[2]

(a) Accommodation within the education system of programs with activities through which this identity is grown in children, activities such as groups caring for particular chosen tracts of land, not only via gardening, but tending, having recreational and ceremonial activities there, creating stories about and artistic expressions of the relevant sites, protecting them from damage, and maintaining continuity with them throughout the formative years of childhood and on into adulthood.

(b) Teaching philosophy in schools—teaching children not so much what to think but how to think. This has never been more important than now with the growth of computer use in education and play, and the gradual 'removal' of children from the social landscape. Indigenous philosophies as well as general Western ideas should be taught, especially the notion of the 'reflective motive', which would help young people to be more contemplative.

The reflective motive is a group process of meditating upon our collective actions and experiential learning; it is not a matter of individuals reflecting in a random way but of the collectivity reflecting on why and how we as a group act and experience events. This process is encouraged, via acts of sharing and communal living, in as natural a way as possible ie not solely as an intellectual exercise. The result is that the process becomes habitual and, at the same time, non-egocentric.

The reflective and questing Aboriginal mind is always aligned with what everyone in the group wants, and what everyone wants is to understand ourselves in order to have and maintain harmonious relationships. The activity of philosophical speculation should not be engaged in alone, nor in a competitive, adversarial debate, but with others in a sharing environment, so that reflective thought is always associated with the 'other'.

(c) Two mutually opposing drives—one towards social stability and certainty, the other towards creativity and (especially technological) development—seem to be fundamental to the Western cultural psyche. Technological development creates ever more material goods to be acquired so that creativity itself now seems to be inextricably tied to consumerism, which in turn leads to increased tension and social alienation within and between classes and groups in many Western societies. Maybe 'smart' campaigns could be started by appropriate community groups to warn society about the dangers to health overall of incessant acquisition of unnecessary goods—campaigns like those of the anti-smoking, -drinking and -speeding lobbies. These campaigns would have to be conducted in a very clever, humorous way, without preaching.

(d) Identification of the metaphysical meaning of money (economics). Despite all the wonderful advances that science and economics have brought, it cannot be denied that a by-product has been a world devoid of value, meaning and spirit. Such a world is the inevitable outcome of any ontology which lacks a dimension of spirit or the sacred.

From an Aboriginal perspective, spirit or the sacred has been reified by Westerners as 'money': Western behaviour, as we have observed it over the last two hundred years, is consistent with that of a community for whom money is sacred. (In Aboriginal society, money has the same status as other useful resources, like food, clothing, transport and housing. These resources are there for the use and benefit of the family group firstly, and after that for the community. Money is therefore subject to the same sort of treatment as other resources—it is to be shared, not for idealistic or virtuous reasons, but for practical reasons and to prompt the reflective motive.)

Given the spiritual significance of money, there is almost an invisible contract for consumers to engage in what economists call a 'disutility', the pain necessary to earn the pleasures of money and leisure; the acceptance of the necessity of this disutility can do and has done serious damage to people's souls.

(e) Initiating a modern Rites of Passage program appropriate for modern, urban young people. This would include the following: physical challenges, artistic expression, self-defence, learning about sexuality, sports, cultural activities, the establishment and ritualisation of sacred relationship with land, community caring and celebration.

A View of the West from an Aboriginal Perspective

There never was and there never will be a paradise—neither an Indigenous one, a religious or moral one, a worker's, futuristic, technological or even a physical one. This is important to understand, because the hierarchical structure of many societies gives the impression that one is always on the way to some *destination,* to a better position, life or world. Although this is an illusion, Western people were (and still are) habituated to the notion of 'travelling', metaphorically, toward some great unknown where they hope that what might be waiting for them is, if not Heaven, then maybe, Happiness, Love, Security, a Theory Explaining Everything.

Throughout the whole historical period, from the birth of the state to the transformation of people into citizens of nations and members of ever-changing class systems, social relations became ever more disconnected, alienated and strained. This development was softened to some extent, and at the same time camouflaged, by economic materialism, which ensured that people sought spiritual and psychological security through an identity based on ownership. Throughout their history, the behaviour of Westerners has been consistent with that of a people who believe that they are quite alone in existence—that the individual is, metaphysically speaking, totally alone. This is also why the notion of spirit and the sacred gradually disappear from their intellectual discourse (though not from their writing and poetry).

If a society makes the sacred simply a matter of personal choice or private concern for individuals, then the next logical step is for these metaphysical isolates to extend themselves physically (which is in reality an unacknowledged search for meaning), and ownership is physical extension by accretion.

But what is the sacred, this domain of spirit that has been lost to Western society? What does it consist of? Where does it reside? From an Aboriginal perspective, it resides in the relationship between the human spirit and the natural life force. When there is a breach between the two, or rather, when the link between the two is weakened, then a human being becomes a totally individuated self, a discrete entity whirling in space, completely free. Its freedom is a fearful freedom however, because a sense of deepest spiritual loneliness and alienation envelopes the individual. The result is then that whatever form the environment or landscape takes, it becomes and remains a hostile place. The discrete individual then has to arm itself not just literally against other discrete individuals, but against its environment—which is why land is always something to be conquered and owned. Indeed the individual has to arm itself against loneliness and against nature itself—though not against ideas. It arms itself with materialism, ownership, possessiveness (not just vulgar materialism).

This is why economics generally has meant survival in Western society, not only in the practical sense, but in the moral, psychological and spiritual senses too. Enter economic rationalism, with its 'law of the jungle' approach to the market dictatorship of societies, which has compounded the already existing global sociopolitical crises. These crises, and the inadequacy of economism as a defense against meaninglessness, has ushered in a new search/struggle in the Western world for the true definition of identity or meaning—for the definition of *human* identity, that is, not political/nationalist identity. This raises again all those questions which many people thought had been answered: why are we here? why am I doing this job? where am I going? what does this global crisis mean? what can I do about anything?

These questions and many more are currently being asked by many Australians of themselves and of their own society. I firmly believe that the developments of the last decade with regard to Aboriginal land rights/Native Title have highlighted the ambivalent relationship Australians have with land in this country, and their uncomfortable relationship with Aboriginal people. Many Australians, however, have seen this period as a chance to understand themselves and their country and the kind of society they want in the future for their children.

Part of the problem for Aboriginal people in modern Australia is working out ways in which we can continue carrying out custodial responsibilities to land and, at the same time, try to obtain control over the economic development of our communities without falling prey to the seductions of individualism. At the same time we are trying to deal with issues of Native Title, Stolen Generations, Apologies and Reconciliation, or what's left of it.

SOCIETY

The Western question, 'what's the meaning of life?' is answered by the Aboriginal question, 'what is it that wants to know?'.

The Aboriginal cultural praxis maintains that one does not need work, money or possessions to justify one's existence; in fact there is no notion of having to justify one's existence at all.

There is an interesting story that illustrates this view. In NSW, during the 1800s, a Scottish farmer named Ogilvie found, after carrying out a survey comparing White Australian and Aboriginal work styles, that Aboriginals were quite different to White people: they hunted, they looked after their ancestral lands, they carried out their traditions, they observed their family obligations, and they attended to the sacred. They were, as he put it, gentlemen, and gentlemen do not work.

Over vast periods of time, Aboriginal people invested most of their creative energy in trying to understand what makes it possible for people to act purposively, or to put it another way, *what is it exactly that makes us human?* What Aboriginal people have done is to map the great repertoire of human feeling to such an extent that its continuities with the psychic life of the wider world become apparent; Aboriginal Law is grounded in the perception of a psychic level of natural behaviour, the behaviour of natural entities. Aboriginal people maintain that humans are not alone. They are connected and made by way of relationships with a wide range of beings, and it is thus of prime importance to maintain and strengthen these relationships.

Custodial Ethic toward Land

Although Indigenous people everywhere are westernised to different degrees, Aboriginal people's identity is essentially always embedded in land and defined by their relationships to it and to other people. The sacred web of connections includes not only kinship relations and relations to the land, but also relations to nature and all living things. When a controlling ethic, lacking such a collective spiritual basis prevails or is chosen, then the sacred becomes constrained by religious and political imperatives, and the voyage to societal and spiritual hierarchies begins. The logical end point of such a system is a narrow survivalist mentality and perspective on life and on existence itself. This is because such systems incorporate strong reward/punishment systems; they provide clear direction for people's fears, dreams, ambitions and ultimately status. In fact this mentality becomes both the reason and the impelling force for constant action, change and even belief without reflection. People become habituated to such systems if rewards are, not necessarily large or rich, but at least constant and established. Collective self knowledge is then seen as not very important; it could even be viewed as a chore or burden best avoided.

Old Aboriginal people have often stated that White Australians 'have no Dreaming', that is, they have no collective spiritual identity, together with no true understanding of having a correct or 'proper' relationship with land/reality. Many White Australians recognise this themselves and are working, planning and creating, quite often with Aboriginal people, to change this situation.

Reflective Motive

The non-ego based nature of Aboriginal society was grounded in an understanding of the human psyche. The Aboriginal understanding posits that the tendency to possess is more deeply embedded in the human psyche than is the tendency to share. In other words, possessiveness is a more 'primitive' mode of behaviour than sharing or altruism; possessiveness precedes altruism and it therefore takes a higher order of abilities to maintain 'sharing' behaviour than it takes to demonstrate possessive behaviour. Possessive behaviour is asserted or exhibited spontaneously and unreflectively. Sharing behaviour has to be inculcated in the first place and then 'maintained'. It involves such abstract concepts as 'reciprocity', 'strategy' and above all *'community.'*

When the Aboriginal child learns to share, he or she is given food and then invited to give it back; social obligations are pointed out and possessiveness gently discouraged, as in the following child's lullaby:

Give to me, Baby,
Give to her, Baby,
Give to him, Baby,
Give to one, Baby,
Give to all, Baby.

It must be said, however, that a collective responsibility to land is vital if people are even to attempt to transcend ego and possessiveness; the point is that land always comes before ego and possessions. These things tend to present a barrier to upholding obligations to look after land.

The effect of this transcendence of ego is to inculcate a sense of communal, rather than individuated, identity, and, most importantly, *to encourage reflective engagement in all activities.* Such a reflective effort, which in Western culture issued in science, resulted, in Aboriginal culture, in the thorough examination of what it means to be human. Therefore for Westerners, possessiveness—which emerges from within the smouldering ember of the *unreflective motive* found within the cult of individualism—is what makes modern Western economic activity possible and money valuable.

Logic

Aboriginal logic is very different to Western logic. Western logic rests on the division between the self and the not-self, the external and the internal. This means that it is the viewpoint of the human individual that is taken to be the window between the external world of fact and the internal world of beliefs. Within the terms of such a division, and the 'viewpoint' which it produces, things can only ever appear as either true or false if they are to appear to 'be' at all; this is the law of the Excluded Middle.

Aboriginal logic maintains that there is no division between the observing mind and anything else: there is no 'external world' to inhabit. There are distinctions between the physical and the spiritual, but these aspects of existence continually interpenetrate each other. All perspectives are thus valid and reasonable: there is no one way or meaning of life. There is never a barrier between the mind and the Creative; the whole repertoire of what is possible continually presents or is expressed as an infinite range of Dreamings. What is possible is the *transformative dynamic of growth.*

If one true way is posited, sooner or later individuals or groups are inclined to ideologise it; rigid thinking then follows (or vice versa), and the formation of groups of 'true believers', chosen people, sects, religions, parties etc., cannot be far behind.

Historically, different groups/individuals have assumed that there is only one *absolute answer to the question of existence,* usually their own. If this assumption is accepted, then logically there must be thousands, if not millions, of potential absolute answers to this age-old question. Aboriginal people however approached this dilemma differently: the only constant in the lives of human beings was, according to them, land/nature. Ideas are myriad and ever changing. This is why the custodial ethic, based on and expressed through Aboriginal Law, is so essential not only to Aboriginal society but to any society that intends to continue for millennia and wants to regard itself as mature.

Aboriginal law is valid for all people only in the sense that all people are placed on land wherever they happen to be, so that the custodial ethic, which is primarily an obligatory system, may be acted on by anyone who is interested in looking after or caring for land. It most certainly is not itself a 'true' way—there are no ideas surrounding it as to the right method, correct rules etc.; there are no small, powerful groups that are the 'only exponents'; there is no hard, soft, liberal, or orthodox approach to this ethic.

The custodial ethic/Aboriginal Law thus cannot be ideologised: it is a locus of identity for human beings, not a focus of identity: we can achieve the fullest expression of our human identity in a location in land. This identity emerges out of a place in the landscape with meaning intact. Ideology, in contrast, provides a sharp focus for ideas and a definition of the human individual, where this in turn places the individual, as human, against land, as mere backdrop. Meaning is then moulded to fit this framework (rather than emerging intact from a place in the landscape).

LAND AND ABORIGINAL LAW

Natural and Positive Law

Mr Neidjie's statement at the beginning of this paper is an observation that reveals one difference between positive and natural kinds of law. A system of natural law is one that is based on the way the real world is perceived to behave. For instance, the laws of physics describe how objects in the real world interact, so that physics can be seen to be a system of natural, physical law that never changes. If the laws of physical motion did change, we could expect to see the universe begin to fall apart before our eyes.

But just as it is possible to describe some of the ways in which the world seems to behave at a physical level, it may also be possible to describe some of the ways in which the world behaves at a non-physical, or 'spiritual', level. Aboriginal Law is grounded in a perception of this psychic level of natural behaviour. On that view, Aboriginal Law 'never changes and is valid for all people', because it implicitly describes the wider emotional, psychological and perhaps cognitive states of the world to which all human beings are subject, which means that Aboriginal Law is as natural (and as scientific) a system of law as physics. On this basis alone, Aboriginal Law is a very important system to understand.

Aboriginal Law refers to a complex relationship between humanity and land which extends to cover every aspect of life; to that extent it is what theorists call a 'complex system', in that it explains both the observer and the observed. In that sense the Law is both a science and a religion, in Western terms. It is a religion in that it explains both the origins and meaning of the cosmos (including the observer), and it is a science in that it does so rationally, and with empirical support. To this extent, Aboriginal Law differs from modern Western ideas of 'positive law'

Western philosophy of law can be divided into 'natural' and 'positive' categories. Historically, the Western definition of natural law is 'that which nature, that is God himself, taught all living things' (Bracton, 1968). By the 19th century Darwin had driven a wedge between humanity and the last vestiges of useful religion, and this seems to have triggered a wealth of theories about practically everything that moves. One of those theories (by John Austin) was the first positive theory of law.

According to Austin, law is not God-given but human-made, and it is effectively made by a legal sovereign, whoever or whatever that may turn out to be (Austin, 1954). The major differences between Austin's positive law and the old, natural theories of law is that positive law is capable of being legislated, amended and repealed by human agency, while natural law is not. In fact, legal positivists believe that there is no 'natural law' at all.

The Land Is the Law

On those Western theoretical criteria, Aboriginal Law is natural law, in that if it was legislated at all, this was done not by humans, but by the spiritual ancestors of the Dreaming, so that Aboriginal Law is incapable of being added to, amended or repealed by any human agency. What this means is that Aboriginal Law is like a cognitive science or applied psychology—it doesn't deal with the actions of humans or the events which befall them, but *with what makes it possible for people to act purposively, and experience 'events'*. That is to say, the perfectibility of human beings was never a concern for Aboriginal Law; rather this Law was/is always an attempt to understand what it is that makes us human. It was/is concerned with why and how it is that we act with purpose: where does this will come from? Why and how do we experience the events that occur in our lives? Why is the experience of one person different from that of another? Over millennia this understanding of the human experience in Australia has given rise to a form of law which Justice Blackburn, in a Northern Territory Land Rights case, described as

> . . . . a subtle and elaborate system highly adapted to the country in which the people lead their lives, which provided a stable order of society and was remarkably free from the vagaries of personal whim or influence. If ever a system could be called 'a government of laws, and not of men', it is that shown in the evidence before me. (Blackburn, 1970)

In this sense Aboriginal Law could be said to be both an action guide to living and a guide to understanding reality itself, especially in relation to land as the basis for all meaning.

At this level of conception, Aboriginal Law is comparable to Buddhism, which is also a psychology of life. There is however a major difference: Buddhism seeks an *escape* from normal, waking consciousness, on the grounds that no matter how richly endowed, waking existence is an endless wheel of birth, suffering and death. By contrast, Aboriginal Law, which is located in land, *celebrates* life in all its ups and downs, using the 'downs' to point to moral formulae.

Exemplars

People's level of knowledge was (and still is) judged by objectively observable canons of behavioural excellence. When a person's level of knowledge can be objectively gauged by his or her perceived behaviour, then this is sufficient for any community to determine whose opinion should be listened to and whose should not, and to what extent. In such a system, those whose opinions are backed by consistently wise public behaviour will end up being listened to, and this will determine much of what that community considers to be 'correct' or 'lawful'.

This could not happen if those who were knowledgeable started to tell others in advance what they should or should not do. To do that would be to embark on a voyage of monarchy, with all that that entails. This is why knowledgeable Aboriginal people let others find things out for themselves. It is also why Aboriginal child-rearing methods allow such freedom to children, why Aboriginal people everywhere insist upon personal autonomy, why they never enslaved each other or instituted class or caste systems, why the community never needed an institutionalised judiciary. And it is what 'custodianship' means. *To allow this natural wisdom to assert itself within the limits of accumulated community experience and knowledge is what custodianship consists in.* Custodianship is thus a philosophy, not just a green solution to environmental degradation. In a sense, Aboriginal Law is 'grown' not 'made'—and this is also what makes it a system of *natural* law. The outcome of this approach to knowledge is that absolutely everyone in the traditional Aboriginal community was acknowledged to have something unique to offer, because of his or her spiritual identity and personal experience of life. Essential to this system is the fact that Aboriginal personal identity extends directly into land itself; this helps to explain why knowledgeable members of the Aboriginal community continue to assert that, '*the land is the Law*'.

What Westerners seem to have been unable to do so far is to recognise Aboriginal Law as a system of natural moral law which establishes an extended, spiritual identity between land and person. One reason for this is that jurists lack reliable evidence to show that there can be a system of natural law which is grounded at a non-physical level, yet which is as valid, and as universally binding, as physical theory. Although considerable efforts have been made to resolve this problem (the Australian Law Reform Commission Report No 31), an answer cannot come from within the framework of legal positivism itself (see Appendix).

What is needed therefore is an on-going consensus involving White Australian and Aboriginal jurists, custodians, philosophers, theologians and others sitting down together in order to discover how each of these logically opposing systems can nonetheless accommodate each other.

CONCLUSION

The world is immediate, not external, and we are all its custodians, as well as its observers. A culture which holds the immediate world at bay by objectifying it as the Observed System, thereby leaving it to the blinkered forces of the market place, will also be blind to the effects of doing so until those effects become quantifiable as, for example, acid rain, holes in the ozone layer and global economic recession. All the social forces which have led to this planetary crisis could have been anticipated in principle, but this would have required a richer metaphysics.

Aboriginal people are not against money, economics or private ownership, but they ask that there be a recognition that *ownership is a social act and therefore a spiritual act.* As such, it produces effects in the immediate world which show up sooner or later in the 'external' world. What will eventually emerge in a natural, habituated way is the embryonic form of an intact, collective spiritual identity for all Australians, which will inform and support our daily lives, our aspirations and our creative genius.

NOTES

1. The overall perspectives of this paper are based on courses delivered by Mary Graham and Lilla Watson at University of Queensland during 1980s.

2. Some of these ideas are based on Graham et al. 1993.

REFERENCES

Austin, J. 1954. *The Province of Jurisprudence Determined.* London: Weidenfeld and Nicholson.

Blackburn, Justice 1970. *Milirrpum and others v. Nabalco Pty Ltd and the Commonwealth of Australia,* 17 Federal Law Report 267.

Bracton, Henry de, 1268. *On the Laws and Customs of England,* by Samuel E Thorne. Cambridge: published in association with the Seldon Society by the Belknap Press of Harvard University Press, 1968.

Graham, Mary; Bailey, Juanita and Morrow, Lin 1993. CrossCultural Training Modules, Adult and Community Education sector, Australian National Training Authority.

APPENDIX

Extract from Australian Law Reform Commission—Report No 31.

Report No 31 stated that Aboriginal customary laws did not reduce to a set of rules (p. 202), that there existed no systematic account of customary law (p. 99), and that Australian courts lacked organs with which to know and to deal with Aboriginal customary law (p. 631). The Commission issued a number of discussion papers during the course of its investigations and an extract from Discussion Paper No 17, issued in 1980, shows the direction already being taken by legal thinkers, concerning Aboriginal law:

> For traditional Aboriginals, the law had no separate identity but was woven into the whole social fabric. There was no legal system in the European sense of separately identifiable institutions. . . . Aboriginal law does not have a separate system of legal rules. The question is not so much 'what is Aboriginal customary law?' as 'how do Aboriginals maintain order in their community?' or 'by what means are quarrels dealt with in Aboriginal communities?'. (Summary of A.L.R.C. discussion paper No 17:2.)

Traditional African Land Ethics

C. K. OMARI

LAND AND NATURAL RESOURCES DIFFER considerably between traditional African and other societies. The differences are rooted in cultural and socio-economic relationships and in organizational development. They concern the value that is attached to land, the distribution of and access to land, and the right to use land for individual and community welfare. Such differences influence the human-to-land relation and the ethical issues that stem from it.

Most of the materials presented in this chapter were collected by the author, beginning with initial field work in the late 1960s and early 1970s among the societies of Tanzania.

OWNERSHIP RIGHTS VERSUS POSSESSION RIGHTS

Wherever in the world the capitalist mode of production is predominant, ownership of land and access to its natural resources is based on individual rights. These rights are usually stipulated in legal documents which may have resulted from a democratic process or may have been legislated by an elite who happened to control and influence community decisions. Land and its natural resources belong to someone and are commodities. Profit and exploitation of water, forests, minerals, and animals for the

Omari, C. K. "Traditional African Land Ethics," in J. Ronald Engel and Joan Gibb Engel, Eds., *Ethics of Environment and Development: Global Challenge, International Response,* Tucson: University of Arizona Press, 1990, pp. 167–175. Reprinted by permission.

benefit of the individual are explicit motives for land ownership. Once one has the right of occupancy, one usually has also the right of access to all the resources therein, although in some states and countries special permission must be obtained in order to exploit natural resources. Real estate and marketing systems are organized, and management skills are developed to enhance this system of economic development.

In Africa today, many states are governed by this mode of land use and management. This is one result of the impact of a money economy on African societies, which has altered considerably the traditional concepts of land use and attitudes towards natural resources. The ethical implications of this change are considerable.

In traditional African societies, there was a difference between 'ownership rights' and 'possession rights'. These two concepts constituted both a legal and social framework for individuals as well as social groups. One aspect could not exist without the other, since both concepts were interwoven in the fabric of the society.

With respect to ownership rights, it was the social group that was considered the owner of the land. This could be a clan, a kinship group, or a family. Every member of the social group had the right to ownership and had an obligation to see that this right was maintained and observed. To have the right of ownership meant a great responsibility for both the individual and the community, because the ultimate owner of the land was God, who is above all human beings. Thus, among the Kikuyu of Kenya, the land, *Githaka,* was owned by *mbari,* a social unit equivalent to a clan. The land was given to them by God.[1] Among the Chagga of northeastern Tanzania, the *kihamba,* a geographical area, was owned by the whole clan. The same was true of the Pare people of northeastern Tanzania with regard to the clan land, or *kithaka.*[2]

The important thing which united all African societies with regard to ownership of land was that land was considered a communal property belonging to both the living and the dead. Those ancestors who had lived on the land belonged to the same social unit which owned and controlled the land, and each individual who used the land felt a communal obligation for its care and administration before passing it to the next generation.

It was the duty of the head of the clan to oversee all matters related to land and its proper use and management. He was to assure that each member of the clan had access to the land. New members were assigned new areas of land where they could settle, build their houses, and raise the crops necessary for their subsistence. It was the responsibility of the new member to look after the farm plot since he had a 'possession right', but ultimate ownership rested with the social group or clan.

In some societies, individuals were allowed temporarily to transfer their piece of land to someone else who was in need. Such transfer was not in the manner of today's transfer of land and properties. No monetary transaction occurred between the owner and the new occupier. The individual was merely exercising his 'possession rights', while the 'ownership right', a community thing, continued to be preserved. Even within this practice, a consultation between the members of the family or clan had to take place before the piece of land was released to someone within or outside it. This was done in part to assure that every member of the group had enough land to cultivate. The obligation to see that each married male had access to the means of production, and that each individual had the right to exercise his freedom within the general structure of approved communal rights and obligations, were ethical considerations in land distribution and ownership.

In most cases a distinction prevailed between the family or clan and the larger community with respect to natural resources. Among the Pare of northeastern Tanzania, the individual family was allowed to exercise a limited authority in relation to ownership and control of farming land, but forests and water sources were controlled communally. Among semipastoral and pastoral people like the Maasai, grazing land and water for animals were also controlled communally. Everyone had access to these resources, but the ultimate control and ownership rested with the community. That is why transhumance and nomadism have been common phenomena among pastoralists. For them, grazing land is communal since it was given to the social group by God, who continued to exercise control through his ever-watching eye.[3] When sources of water were owned by the larger society, the village headman, or head of the clan, was in charge of the distribution process. This ensured that each family had access to water for irrigation, which was very important in a subsistence economy.

In the case of forests related to places of worship and initiation rite centres, control was left to the individual clan rather than the whole community. For example, among the Pare of northeastern Tanzania, each clan had its own forest in which its youth were trained and initiated into adulthood. Also, each clan, and sometimes even each lineage, had its own worshipping place which was considered sacred. No other person was allowed to worship in these places except the owners, since they were family- rather than community-based. People were united by their worship at these places, and individuals felt a sense of belonging and identity when they met. They also felt that they were using these places as trustees of a larger transgenerational family.[4] Later, religious centres of this nature became strong political institutions among certain clans, especially after the creation of a centrally-orientated authority among the Pare people.

These forests and shrubs were respected by the whole community. No one was supposed to cut the trees from these areas; it was considered morally wrong to do so. Firewood and building materials were fetched from places other than these sacred places.

REVERENCE FOR NATURAL RESOURCES

The reverence of Africans towards nature and natural places was a religious attitude and practice which, while it developed around the religious thought and history of a particular social group, indirectly served other social functions in the whole community. In the case of shrines and initiation rite centres, taboos developed around the destruction of trees, shrubs, and the sacred places themselves. The forests, certain kinds of trees, animals, and sources of water were preserved in the name of religion.

Perhaps people did not plan to practise such attitudes in the way a modern person would conserve the forests, but out of their religious beliefs and values and their reverence for sacred public places, an ecological and environmental concern was developed. As a result, in traditional African societies there was a balanced ecosystem; people and nature interacted in such a way that the harmony between them was maintained. These attitudes were stronger when they were attached to the ownership of land through myth. These may have been myths of the origin of the clan, of the place where the ancestors were given power, or of something with special historical meaning to the whole social group. In this way, belief in sacred places served as a common history which united all generations of the same social unit.[5]

In many instances, when people went to worship in sacred places, they were carrying out religious acts for the purpose of preserving harmony and tranquility in the community. They were fulfilling their obligation towards their God by an act of appeasing the ancestors or evil spirits, by praising and giving thanks to God, or by praying for peace and harmony in the community. For this reason, it is difficult for Africans to differentiate between religious and social action. There was always an interaction between the so-called 'religious' and 'secular' worlds, and both were interwoven in the same entity—the community.

The Africans anticipated no change in the future of their communities. The forests and shrubs of their worshipping places were preserved for both present and future generations. It was believed that if one destroyed the holy places, the ancestors would be angry, and as a result some misfortune might befall the community. It was also believed that future generations would face terrible misfortunes if God, who had entrusted these resources to them, was displeased by their misuse or destruction.

To dismiss these religious attitudes and values because they were suited to an underdeveloped, premodern world is not to appreciate the community function they served with respect to ecology and natural conservation.

For example, among the Luguru and Zaramo people of eastern Tanzania, there is a myth about Kolelo, a mythical hero believed to possess the power to bring rain. People from these areas worshipped near or in the direction of Morogoro where the Uluguru mountains are and where Kolelo was thought to live. As a result of this belief, the forests around this area and mountain were preserved. This made the area green and beautiful all the time.

Streams of water constantly ran down from the mountains. Such reverence, besides being a symbol of unity among the ethnic groups concerned, had an important function among them. Uluguru country is hilly. It enabled the peasants of the hilly Uluguru countryside to grow various types of vegetables and beans in sufficient quantities to feed not only the adjacent Morogoro town but even the city of Dar es Salaam about 125 miles away. Without this forest cover, their fields would have been washed away by soil erosion. Current lumbering practices are a threat to this and other areas.

In traditional African societies, religious taboos and restrictions took the place of aforestation campaigns which are now being waged by governments like that of Tanzania. People knew their responsibilities towards natural resources without being reminded through special campaigns. Positive values towards the use of natural resources were inculcated from generation to generation through songs, proverbs, and stories. Sometimes religious ceremonies or rituals, for example rituals for rain-making, strengthened natural resource values.

Each ethnic group developed its own taboos and restrictions towards animals according to its religious belief system and the values related to its historical development. Certain animals and birds, like the tortoise and python among the Pare people, were considered totems. It was believed that if these animals were killed, children would be caught up by rushes and wounded. Other species were killed only for special purposes. These may have been kinship or lineage totems, or may have been preserved for special purposes. Among the Pare, a kind of forest monkey with white spots (*mbega*) was not supposed to be killed. It was looked upon as a symbol of beauty and religious significance. Its skin was specifically used for the ceremonial caps worn by the chief at public ceremonies, or by the medicine man when performing rituals for the public interest. Since these monkeys were rare in the area, such religious restrictions kept them from being exterminated. Animals like leopards, whose skins were used by the traditional healers, were also protected. Only when such a skin was needed was anyone authorized to hunt and kill a leopard. The killing of certain animals, such as the owl, was believed to be a bad omen. Thus, animal species were preserved for generations as a result of the system of religious values and beliefs.

THE IMPACT OF A MONEY ECONOMY AND DEVELOPMENT

African societies are now undergoing great changes due to the impact of Western value systems, especially as they are embodied in Western economic systems.

A money economy has not only altered social relations among people, but it has also affected people's attitudes towards nature and natural resources. Because of the new values inculcated through Western education and religions like Christianity and Islam, people now see natural resources as objects for exploitation and profit-making. Resources are used for individual private gain and satisfaction. Furthermore, the Western concept of individual achievement through power relationships has undermined the communal decision-making processes which helped communities maintain a balance between available resources and their use by individuals. Instead, decisions about resource use are now based on a bureaucratic and legal system.

Many of the economic activities which seem to threaten the African ecology are done in the name of development. In many cases a foreign multinational company conducts the activities alone; sometimes, it collaborates with the local government or agents. Whether these local governments or agents are aware of the long-term environmental effects on their countries is not always clear. One thing is clear, however: they are lured by the profit they get out of such business, and on the basis of a bureaucratic decision procedure, they allow it. As a result, 'development' has acquired a negative meaning.

The mismanagement of the environment and the imbalance in the ecological system brought about by modern economic and value systems have led to 'environmental bankruptcy' in Africa.[6]

In the name of development—and with foreign investment—about 130,000 square kilometers of Africa's tropical rainforests are lost every year. In Tanzania precious ebony trees (*mpingo*) have been cut wildly and mercilessly, without any consideration for their future use and benefit to the society at large. In Kenya and Tanzania there is a scarcity of charcoal due to the lack of proper trees for making it. Mali, in West Africa, one of the countries worst hit by drought in the 1970s and early 1980s, is facing a critical shortage of fish due to low water levels in the Niger River. The Niger River used to produce 100,000 tons of fish for export annually. Now, major fish processing plants along the river banks have either suspended operations or closed down. The country has been left barren because of commercial deforestation. Climatologists have warned us that due to the environmental disturbance, especially to forests and water sources, rainfall in Africa will remain uncertain for the next ten to twenty years.

Yet, viewed in an ethical context, it is the human who has changed rather than the environment. Value systems which used to help keep balance between humans and the environment are no longer in place; instead, we have value systems controlled and motivated by the greedy accumulation of capital on an individual basis. As a result, even ethical decisions regarding the management of land and natural resources are guided by a production principle and the social principles that emerge from it.

Drought has been with the African people for a long time. What we have witnessed in the 1970s and 1980s is nothing new. In the past however, people knew how to deal with nature and the environment. They knew how to use dams and furrows for irrigation; they knew how to protect forests and water sources through belief systems and value systems attached to places. They acted as custodians of these resources for future generations within the kinship social group.

The introduction of a money economy with its capitalist mode of production, the introduction of religions like Christianity and Islam, and the introduction of state control of natural resources have destroyed the indigenous belief systems to the extent of altering production relations. This affects ethical decisions. The emphasis is no longer on how the community will benefit from the restoration or preservation of the forests and other natural resources, but on what the 'state class' or individual will get through the exploitation of these resources. People have been led to believe in 'modern' civilization and its destructive operations; they have been led to worship money, big business, or state institutions which have profit as their priority. People's loyalties and concern are for these institutions rather than for the community where ecological and environmental issues are of primary concern. Decisions are made at high levels of the state bureaucracy without prior consultation with the local people whose so-called development is at stake.

Thus, because of these new attitudes towards natural resources and their management, people have been persuaded to cut down trees for export to earn foreign exchange which is badly needed by many governments. But this has been done at the expense of the local environment and ecology, Furthermore, what is earned from the sale of these products rarely benefits the local people. An example from Tanzania illustrates this process.

In an effort to modernize agriculture and meet world market demands, the government of Tanzania, with the assistance of the World Bank, started tobacco production in the 1970s among the Nyamwezi people of western Tanzania. The project involved clearing bush areas for cultivation of the crop, which was a crucial feature in Tanzania's capital development and export programme. Since tobacco processing requires firewood, a great number of trees were harvested. This programme of tobacco production among the Nyamwezi was termed 'a success' by some scholars.[7] One wonders, a success on what terms? People from this area were forced to buy food crops as a result of this production system, a phenomenon which had not been observed among the Nyamwezi in the past. Moreover, due to extensive deforestation, the firewood shortage has been a problem in this area ever since.

THE IMPACT OF RELIGIOUS AND POLITICAL CHANGES

Perhaps we cannot return to the old religious belief systems. Few people in Tanzania profess to be followers of the traditional religious system which shaped their lives and values in the past. It is estimated, for example, that of 22 million people in Tanzania, 44 per cent are Christians, 32.5 per cent are Muslim, and 22.8 per cent are traditionalists. All of these religions influence individuals as well as communities. Moreover, state intervention through the policy of *ujamaa* development has also altered production relations among the people.

The impact of Christianity and Islam has been to shift considerably the attitudes among people of certain African communities away from traditional communal ownership of land and means of production. In Tanzania, in those communities where Islam has been predominant, as in Zanzibar, Pemba, the coast, and the central corridor of the mainland, a feudal mode of production has been admired and practised. The growth and expansion of a plantation economy in Zanzibar and Pemba could not have survived in the nineteenth and early twentieth centuries had it not been for slavery. To this day, on these islands, a successful person is one who has people who work for him or her. Such a person is called a *mwinyi,* a person who has properties and controls others. Along the coast, a successful person is one who has several hundred coconut trees and employs others to work on the coconut farm.

In Tanzania, where the Christian religion has dominated, capitalist tendencies are noticed. In areas like Kilimanjaro, Arusha, Pare, West Lake, and the southern Highlands, individual as well as small family-unit production farms have been emphasized, especially in coffee producing areas. Individual achievement and success, competition and profit making are stressed. People in these areas were buying and selling land before the state intervened in the 1960s.

Then came the state and its policy mechanism, especially the *Arusha Declaration* of 1967.[8] In this policy document, land and the major means of production were nationalized, and thus became the property of the state. No one was supposed to own a large tract of land or exploit laborers. It was also during this time that rural communities called *ujamaa* villages were organized to facilitate social development in the countryside. In 1975, the establishment of the Ujamaa and Village Act 1975 gave these rural social units the power to own and control land and all other natural resources within the village, except if such resources were under the ministry of the central government.

In both the 1967 Arusha Declaration and the 1975 Village Act, the aim was to reemphasize communal ownership of the means of production. Each village was to establish a governing council consisting of twenty-five members elected from among the villagers of the same unit, and from these members five different committees were to be established. One of these committees was to be responsible for the production and distribution of resources. In this way it was ensured that, besides the communal land and ownership of the means of production, every villager had personal access to land and its utilization. Other resources like water, forests, and some minerals were controlled communally. Minerals with foreign export value, like gold, diamonds, coal, and precious stones were controlled by the state.

I have cited Tanzania for examples of land and resource use, and thereby I have illustrated a trend throughout Africa. In the case of Tanzania, reorganization did not satisfactorily return communal control to the villagers. Control by the state *did* bring bureaucracy to the village level. Although the villagers have a measure of control over land and resources, the penetration of state machinery to the village level is obvious. Also, due to reorganization problems and food shortages, in 1983 the Tanzanian government reintroduced the large-scale farming which had been eliminated in 1967. This new direction in ownership and control of land has resulted in the following types of land tenure:

- large forests, national parks, and other designated areas belonging to the state;
- village communal areas—controlled by the villagers as communal social units;
- large-scale farms—individually owned and state-owned away from the village farms;
- individually owned farms—these may be family farms within the village communal land or outside.

In all these, however, the values that operate in relation to land use are more capitalist than communal. Interaction and the exchange of goods centre around profit and market value.

In Tanzania, as in many African countries, the development of land and resources has been guided by the principles of market demand at the village, national, or international level. Villagers no longer cultivate their land for subsistence. Through extension workers, marketing boards and other established economic institutions, the state directs the peasants in what to grow and what not to grow. Land must be used to the maximum so that it produces an export surplus which will bring in profits to help run the state apparatus. Thus, the peasants' traditional values of communal interest are undermined. This is true even at the village level where democratic procedures are supposedly in place. It is the state which decides what to plant and where to sell the products.

THE HOPE OF COMMUNAL SOLIDARITY

Sustainable development contradicts the present value system and practices. To take sustainable development seriously would involve programmes which enabled villagers to utilize land and land resources for their and the land's mutual benefit. It would involve local planning and decision-making processes, including decisions regarding what to plant and where to sell the produce. Furthermore, it would mean projects which boosted a community's self-reliance and self-esteem through the better utilization of land and resources for present and future generations.

It is on this level that I think governments and private non-governmental organizations should cooperate to initiate programmes on better land management which are supported by all the people at the village level. Communal solidarity, which is a part of the traditional African value system, should be utilized fully not only for the present generation, but for the future as well.

Traditional religions and Christian and Islamic belief systems ideally teach stewardship and responsibility towards land. Traditional religions and the Christian and Islamic religions include teachings which condemn greedy and selfish attitudes towards land use and management of resources. The concern for others, the concern that all of us are stewards for someone else, should guide us in this issue. For Africans, land belongs to all, living and dead. We will live in this land where our foreparents lived and where our great-great-grandchildren will live. To make sure that all benefit from this wealth, we have to take care of it properly now. This value system cuts across all ethnic groups in Africa.

Wherever we are, the land, its resources, and the environment contribute to our survival. If we destroy them, through bad policies or by sheer greed, we are responsible, and the present and future generations will suffer. We are responsible for what has happened in our society through 'development' and other forms of exploitation of land and resources in the name of the state or the market. We cannot go on without asking ethical questions about our relations to the land. We cannot remain silent without raising the question of who is responsible and what we can do to stop the present destruction.

NOTES

1. Jomo Kenyatta, *Facing Mount Kenya* (New York: Vintage Books, 1962).
2. C. K. Omari, *God and Worship among the Pare* (Dar es Salaam: University of East Africa, 1970).
3. Ibid.
4. I. N. Kimambo and C. K. Omari, 'The Development of Religious Thought and Centres among the Pare' in T. O. Ranger and I. N. Kimambo, eds, *Historical Study of African Religion* (London: Heinemann, 1972), 111–35.
5. B. C. Ray, *African Religions: Symbol, Ritual, and Community* (Englewood Cliffs, New Jersey: Prentice Hall, 1976).
6. C. K. Omari, 'The Churches and the Food Question in Africa', Keynote speech, Lutheran World Federation World Service Meeting, Bulawayo, Zimbabwe, 11–16 May, 1986.
7. J. Boesen and A. J. Mohale, *The 'Success Story' of Peasant Production in Tanzania* (Uppsala: Scandinavian Institute of African Studies, 1979).
8. Julius K. Nyerere, *Ujamaa: Essays on Socialism* (Dar es Salaam and Nairobi: Oxford University Press, 1968).

Cultural Parallax in Viewing North American Habitats

GARY PAUL NABHAN

A DEBATE IS RAGING WITH REGARD TO THE "nature" of the North American continent—in particular, the extent to which habitats have been managed, diversified, or degraded over the last ten thousand years of human occupation (Gomez-Pompa and Kaus 1992). This debate has at its heart three issues: whether the "natural condition of the land" by definition excludes human management; whether officially designated wilderness areas in the United States should be free of hunting, gathering, and vegetation management by Native Americans or other people; and whether traditional management by indigenous peoples is any more "benign" or "ecologically sensitive" than that imposed by resource managers trained in the use of modern Western scientific principles, methods, and technologies.

The debate, then, is not about the human mental "construction" of nature so much as it is about the physical "reconstructions" of habitats by humans and to what extent these are perceived as "natural" or "ecological." The debate is not merely an academic dispute. It involves hunters, gatherers, ranchers, farmers, and political activists from a variety of cultures, not just "Western scientists" versus "indigenous scientists." The outcome will no doubt shape the destiny of officially designated wilderness areas in national parks and forests throughout North America (Gomez-Pompa and Kaus 1992; Flores et al. 1990).

Consider, for example, the declaration of the 1963 Leopold Report to the U.S. Secretary of the Interior: that each large national park should maintain or recreate "a vignette of primitive America," seeking to restore "conditions as they prevailed when the area was first visited by the white man"—as if those conditions were synonymous with "pristine" or "untrammeled" wilderness (Anderson and Nabhan 1991:27). Such a declaration either implies that pre-Columbian Native Americans had no impact on the areas now found within the U.S. National Park System or that indigenous management of vegetation and wildlife as it was done in pre-Columbian times is compatible with and essential to "wilderness quality." For Native Americans with historic ties to land, water, and biota within parks, this latter interpretation provides them a platform for being *co-managers*, not merely harvesters of certain traditionally utilized resources, as currently sanctioned by the National Park Service (1987).

On one side of the debate are those who argue that Native Americans have had a negligible impact on their homelands and left large areas untouched. That is to say, these original human inhabitants did little to actively manage or influence wildlife populations one way or another. An early proponent of this view was John Muir: "Indians walked softly and hurt the landscape hardly more than the birds and squirrels, and their brush and bark huts last hardly longer than those of wood rats, while their enduring monuments, excepting those wrought on the forests by fires they made to improve their hunting grounds, vanish in a few centuries." Yet the Yosemite landscapes he knew so well are now known to have been dramatically shaped by Native American management practices (Anderson and Nabhan 1991:27).

Some proponents of this perspective even deny Muir's exception that controlled burns had a significant impact. Native Americans, they claim, would have no interest in managing the forests even if they were capable of it (Clar 1959:7): "It would be difficult to find a reason why the Indians [of California] should care one way or another if the forest burned. It is quite something else again to contend that the Indians used fire systematically to 'improve' the forest. Improve it for what purpose? . . . Yet this fantastic idea has been and still is put forth time and again."

A second stance on this side of the debate contends that Native American spirituality kept all members of indigenous communities from harming

Nabhan, Gary Paul, "Cultural Parallax in Viewing North American Habitats," in Michael E. Soulé and Gary Lease, Eds., *Reinventing Nature? Responses to Postmodern Deconstruction*, Washington, D.C.: Island Press, 1995, pp. 87–101. Reprinted by permission of the author.

habitats or the biota within them. Leslie Silko (1986:86), who is of Laguna Pueblo descent, has argued that "survival depended upon the harmony and cooperation, not only among human beings, but among all things—the animate and inanimate. . . . As long as good family relations [between all beings] are maintained . . . the Earth's children will survive." The implication is that Native Americans practiced a spirituality "earthly enough" to restrain any tendencies toward overharvesting or toward depletion of diversity through homogenizing habitat mosaics (Anderson 1993). As Max Oelschlaeger (1991:17) has assumed, "*harmony with* rather than *exploitation of* the natural world was a guiding principle for the Paleolithic mind and remains a cardinal commitment among modern aborigines."

The other side of this argument contends that Native Americans and other indigenous peoples have rapaciously exterminated wildlife within their reach and that their farming, hunting, and gathering techniques were often ecologically ill suited for the habitats in which they were practiced. Kent Redford (1985) and others have taken such a stance to play devil's advocate with the romantic notion of "the ecological noble savage." Award-winning science writer Jared Diamond (1993:268) has also tried to dispel what he sees as a myth of native peoples as "environmentally minded paragons of conservation, living in a Golden Age of harmony with nature, in which living things were revered, harvested only as needed, and carefully monitored to avoid depletion of breeding stocks."

Diamond (1993:263, 268) claims that in thirty years of visiting native peoples on the three islands of New Guinea, he has failed to come across a single example of indigenous New Guineans showing friendly responses to wild animals or consciously managing habitats to enhance wildlife populations: "New Guineans kill those animals that their technology permits them to kill," inevitably depleting or exterminating more susceptible species. His claim that all indigenous New Guinean cultures respond in the same manner to nature is astonishing when one considers that about one thousand of the world's remaining languages are spoken in New Guinea and that this cultural/linguistic diversity would presumably encode many distinctive cultural responses to the flora and fauna.

Yet to my knowledge, Diamond himself has never objectively field-tested his game depletion hypothesis as Vickers (1988) has done among Amazonian peoples, where it was demonstrated over several years that native hunters would switch to less desirable prey before locally extirpating rare game species. Redford and Robinson (1987) have also documented that indigenous South American hunters take a wider variety of game species than neighboring non-indigenous South American colonists, who are more likely to use degraded habitats near larger settlements, thereby further impoverishing the abundance and diversity of wildlife. Diamond has never demonstrated that he has systematically asked indigenous consultants about less obvious techniques by which hunters and gatherers may influence habitat quality and wildlife abundance, following research protocols such as those outlined by Blackburn and Anderson (1993:24). And yet, repeatedly, Diamond (1986, 1992, and elsewhere) has used the hypotheses of the Pleistocene overkill, and later selective cutting of fir and spruce in Chaco Canyon by Anasazi city-state dwellers, to indict all Native American hunters, gatherers, and farmers as exterminators of wildlife and aggravators of soil erosion.

This dismissal of enormous historic and cultural differences is at the heart of the problem inherent in most discussions of "the American Indian view of nature" and assessments of the pre-Columbian condition of North American habitats. To assume that even the Hopi and their Navajo neighbors think of, speak of, and treat nature in the same manner is simply wrong. Yet individuals from two hundred different language groups from three historically and culturally distinct colonizations of the continent are commonly lumped under the catchall terms "American Indian" or "Native American."

Even within one mutually intelligible language group, such as the Piman-speaking O'odham, there are considerable differences in what taboos they honor with respect to dangerous or symbolically powerful animals. While the River Pima do not allow themselves to eat badgers, bears, quail, or certain reptiles for fear of "staying sickness," these taboos are relaxed or even dismissed by other Piman groups who live in more marginal habitats where game is less abundant (Rea 1981; Nabhan and St. Antoine 1993). An animal such as the black bear—which is never eaten by one Piman community because it is still considered to be one of the "people"—is routinely hunted by another Piman-speaking group which prizes its skin and pit-roasts its meat—an act that would be regarded much like cannibalism in the former group (Rea 1981; personal communication). Moreover, contemporary Pima families do not necessarily adhere to all the taboos that were formerly paramount to all other cultural rules which granted someone Piman identity.

Despite such diversity within and between North American cultures, it is still quite common to read statements implying a uniform "American Indian view of nature"—as if all the diverse cultural relations with particular habitats on the continent can be swept under one all-encompassing rug. Whether one is prejudiced toward the notion of Native Americans as extirpators of species or assumes that most have been negligible or respectful harvesters, there is a shared assumption that all Native Americans have viewed and used the flora and fauna in the same ways. This assumption is both erroneous and counterproductive in that it undermines any respect for the realities of cultural diversity. And yet it continues to permeate land-use policies, environmental philosophies, and even park management plans. It does not grant *any* cultures—indigenous or otherwise—the capacity to evolve, to diverge from one another, or to learn about their local environments through time.

This distortion of the relationships between human cultures and the rest of the natural world is what I call "cultural parallax of the wilderness concept." If you remember your photography or astronomy lessons, *parallax* is the apparent displacement of an observed object due to the difference between two points of view. For example, consider the difference between the view of an object as seen through a camera lens and the view through a separate viewfinder. A cultural parallax, then, might be considered to be the difference in views between those who are actively participating in the dynamics of the habitats within their home range and those who view those habitats as "landscapes" from the outside. As Leslie Silko (1987:84) has suggested: "So long as human consciousness remains *within* the hills, canyons, cliffs, and the plants, clouds, and sky, the term *landscape,* as it has entered the English language, is misleading. 'A portion of territory the eye can comprehend in a single view' does not correctly describe the relationship between a human being and his or her surroundings."

Adherents of the romantic notion of landscape claim that the most pristine and therefore most favorable condition of the American continent worthy of reconstruction is that which prevailed at the moment of European colonization. As William Denevan (1992) has amply documented, the continent was perhaps most intensively managed by Native Americans for the several centuries prior to Columbus's arrival in the West Indies. Because European diseases decimated native populations through the Americas over the following hundred and fifty years, the early European colonists saw only vestiges of these managed habitats, if they recognized them as managed at all (Cronon 1983; Denevan 1992).

And yet, among many ecologists, including Daniel Botkin (1990:195), "the idea is to create natural areas that appear as they did when first viewed by European explorers. In the Americas, this world be the landscape of the seventeenth century. . . . If natural means simply *before human intervention,* then all these habitats could be claimed as natural." Thus Botkin equates the periods prior to European colonization with those prior to *human intervention* in the landscape and assumes that all habitats were equally pristine at that time. By this logic, either the pre-Columbian inhabitants of North America were not human or they did not significantly interact with the biota of the areas where they resided.

Human influences on North American habitats began at least 9,200 years prior to the period Botkin pinpoints—when newly arrived "colonists" came down from the Bering Strait into ice-free country (Janzen and Martin 1982; Martin 1986). Regardless of how major a role humans played in the Pleistocene extinctions, the loss of 73 percent of the North American genera of terrestrial mammals weighing one hundred pounds or more precipitated major changes in vegetation and wildlife abundance. By Paul Martin's (1986) criteria, North American wilderness areas have been lacking "completeness" for over ten millennia and would require the introduction of large herbivores from other continents to simulate the "natural conditions" comparable to those under which vegetation cover evolved over the hundreds of thousands of years prior to these extinctions.

It has always amazed me that many of the same scholars who are willing to grant pre-Columbian cultures of the Americas more ecological wisdom than recent European colonists still deny the possibility that these cultures could have played a role in these faunal extinctions, as if that wisdom did not take centuries to accumulate. Do they believe that the pre-Columbian cultures of North America became "instant natives" incapable of overtaxing any resources in their newfound homeland—an incapability that few European cultures have achieved since arriving in the Americas five centuries ago? As Michael Soulé (1991:746) has pointed out, "the most destructive cultures, environmentally, appear to be those that are colonizing uninhabited territory and those that are in a stage of rapid cultural (often technological) transition." My point is simply this: it may take time for any culture to become truly "native," if that term is to imply any sensitivity to the ecological constraints of its home ground.

I am not arguing that many indigenous American cultures did not develop increasing sensitivity to the plant and animal populations most vulnerable to depletion within their home ranges. To the contrary, I would like to suggest that all of pre-Columbian North America was not pristine wilderness for the very reason that many indigenous cultures actively managed habitats and plant populations within their home ranges as a response to earlier episodes of overexploitation. There is now abundant evidence that hundreds of thousands of acres in various bioregions of North America were actively managed by indigenous cultures (Anderson and Nabhan 1991; Denevan 1992; Fish et al. 1985). This does not mean that the entire continent was a Garden of Eden cultivated by Native Americans, as Hecht and Posey have erroneously implied for the Amazon (Parker 1992). Many large areas of the North American continent remained beyond the influence of human cultures, and should remain so. Nevertheless, it is clear that the degree to which North American plant populations were consciously managed—and conserved—by local cultural traditions has been routinely underestimated.

Hohokam farmers, for example, constructed over seventeen hundred miles of prehistoric irrigation canals along the Salt River in the Phoenix basin and intensively cultivated and irrigated floodplains along the Santa Cruz and Gila rivers, as well as on intermittent watercourses for one hundred and fifty miles south and west of these perennial streams (Nabhan 1989). At the same time, they cultivated agave relatives of the tequila plant over hundreds of square miles of upland slopes and terraces beyond where modern agricultural techniques allow crops to be cultivated today (Fish et al. 1985). Nevertheless, the discovery of native domesticated agaves being grown on a large scale in the Sonoran Desert has been made only within the last decade, despite more than a half century of intensive archaeological investigation in the region. Earlier archaeologists had simply never imagined that pre-Columbian cultures in North America could have cultivated perennial crops on such a scale away from riverine irrigation sources.

In the deserts of southern California, indigenous communities transplanted and managed palms for their fruits and fiber in artificial oases, some of them apparently beyond the "natural distribution" of the California fan palm. Control burns were part of their management of these habitats, and such deliberate use of fire created artificial savannas in regions as widely separated as the California Sierra and the Carolinas. In the Yosemite area, where John Muir claimed that "Indians walked softly and hurt the landscape hardly more than the birds and squirrels," Anderson's (1993) reconstructions of Miwok subsistence ecology demonstrate that the very habitat mosaic he attempted to preserve as wilderness was in fact the cumulative result of Miwok burning, pruning, and selective harvesting over the course of centuries.

So what Muir called wilderness, the Miwok called home; the parallax is apparent again. Is it not odd that after ten to fourteen thousand years of indigenous cultures making their homes in North America, Europeans moved in and hardly noticed that the place looked "lived-in"? There are perhaps two explanations for this failure. One response, as historians William Cronon (1983), William Denevan (1992), and Henry Dobyns (1983) have suggested, is that many previously managed landscapes had been left abandoned between the time when European-introduced diseases spread through the Americas and the time when Europeans actually set foot in second-growth forests, shrub-invaded savannas, or defaunated deserts. The second explanation is that Europeans were so intent on taking possession of these lands and developing them in their own manner that they hardly paid attention to signs that the land had already been managed on a different scale and level of intensity.

It was easier for Europeans to assume possession of a land they considered to be virgin or at least unworked and uninhabited by people of their equal. Columbus himself had set out to discover unspoiled lands where the seeds of Christianity—a faith that was being corrupted in Europe, he felt—could be transplanted. In 1502, well after his own men had unleashed European weeds, diseases, and weapons on the inhabitants of the Americas, Columbus wrote to Pope Alexander VI claiming that he had personally visited the Garden of Eden on his voyages to the New World.

Even those who have condemned Europeans for the effects of their ecological imperialism on indigenous American cultures too often frame their concern as "conquistadors raping a virgin land." As "subjects of rape," American lands and their resident human populations are simply reduced to the role of passive victims, incapable of any resilience or dynamic response to deal capably in any way with such invasions. And so we are often left hearing the truism, "Before the White Man came, North America was essentially a wilderness where the few Indian inhabitants lived in constant harmony with nature"—even though four to twelve million people speaking two hundred languages variously burned, pruned, hunted, hacked, cleared, irrigated, and planted in an astonishing diversity of habitats for centuries (Denevan 1992; Anderson and Nabhan 1991). And we are supposed to believe, as well, that they all lived in some static homeostasis with all the various plants and animals they encountered.

As Daniel Botkin (1990) has convincingly argued, few predator/prey or plant/animal relationships have maintained any long-term homeostasis even where humans are not present, let along where they are. Although there is little evidence to indicate that indigenous cultures regionally extirpated any rare plants or small vertebrate species, there are intriguing signs that certain prehistoric populations depleted local firewood sources and certain slow-growing fiber plants such as yuccas (Minnis 1978). Because different cultures used native species at different intensities, and each species has a different growth rate and relative abundance, it is impossible to generalize about the conservation of all resources in all places. Nevertheless, numerous localized efforts to sustain or enhance the abundance of certain useful plants have been well documented (Anderson 1993; Anderson and Nabhan 1991). It remains unclear whether by favoring certain useful plants over others, plant diversity increased or decreased in particular areas. To my knowledge, no study adequately addresses indigenous peoples' local effects on biological *diversity* (as opposed to their effects on the *abundance* of key resources).

It can no longer be denied that some cultures had specific conservation practices to sustain plant populations of economic or symbolic importance to their communities. In the case of my O'odham neighbors in southern Arizona, there have been efforts to protect rare plants from overharvesting near sacred sites, to transplant individuals to more protected sites, and to conserve caches of seeds in caves to ensure future supplies (Nabhan 1989). Landscape photographer Mark Klett (1990:73) has written that too often wilderness in the European American tradition is "an entity defined by our absence [as if] the landscape does best without our presence." I find in O'odham oral literature an interesting counterpoint to this notion. The O'odham term for wildness, *doajkam,* is etymologically tied to terms for health wholeness, and liveliness (Mathiot 1973). While it seems wildness is positively valued as an ideal by which to measure other conditions, the O'odham also feel that certain plants, animals, and habitats "degenerate" if not properly cared for. Thus their failure to take care of a horse or a crop may allow it to go feral, but this degenerated feral state is different from being truly wild. Similarly, their lack of attention to O'odham fields, watersheds, and associated ceremonies may keep the rains from providing sufficient moisture to sustain both wild and cultivated species. Many O'odham express humility in the face of unpredictable rains or game animals, but they still feel a measure of responsibility in making good use of what does come their way.

In short, the O'odham elders I know best still behave as active participants in the desert without assuming that they are ultimately "in control" of it. This, in essence, is the difference between participating in *untrammeled* wilderness (as defined by the U.S. Wilderness Act) and attempting to tame lands through manipulative management. (A *trammel* is a device which shackles, hobbles, cages, or confines an animal, breaking its spirit and capacity to roam.) What may look like uninhabited wilderness to outsiders is a habitat in which the O'odham actively participate. They do not define the desert as it was derived from the Old French *desertus,* "a place abandoned or left wasted." Their terms for the desert, *tohono,* can be etymologically understood as a "bright and shining place," and they have long called themselves the Tohono O'odham: the people belonging to that place. They share that place with a variety of plants and animals, a broad range of which still inhabit their oral literature (Nabhan and St. Antoine 1993).

Within their Sonoran Desert homeland, many O'odham people still learn certain traditional land management scripts encoded in their own Piman language, which they then put into practice in particular settings, each in their own peculiar way. What concerns me is that their indigenous language is now being replaced by English. Their indigenous science of desert is being eclipsed by more frequent exposure to Western science. And their internal or etic sense of what it is to be O'odham is being replaced by the mass media's presentation of what it is to be (generically) an American Indian. While I will be among the first to admit that change is presumably inherent to all natural and cultural phenomena, I am not convinced that these three changes are necessarily desirable. In virtually every culture I know of on this continent, similar changes are occurring with blinding speed. Both nature and culture are being rapidly redefined, not so much by what we learn from our immediate surroundings as by what we learn through the airwaves.

Let me highlight what Sara St. Antoine and I recently learned while interviewing fifty-two children from four different cultures, all of them living in the Sonoran Desert (Nabhan and St. Antoine 1993). Essentially we learned that with regard to knowledge about the natural world, intergenerational differences within cultures are becoming as great as the gaps between cultures. While showing a booklet of drawings of *common* desert plants and animals to O'odham children and their grandparents, for example, we realized that the children knew only a third of the names for these desert organisms in their native language that their grandparents knew. With the loss of those names, we wonder how much culturally encoded knowledge is lost as well. With over half the two hundred native languages on this continent falling out of use at an accelerating rate, a great diversity of perspectives on the structure and value of nature are surely being lost. And culture-specific land management practices are being lost as well.

One driving force in this loss of knowledge about the natural world is that children today spend more time in classrooms and in front of the television than they do directly interacting with their natural surroundings. The vast majority of the children we interviewed are now gaining most of their knowledge about other organisms vicariously; 77 percent of the Mexican children, 61 percent of the Anglo children, 60 percent of the Yaqui children, and 35 percent of the O'odham children told us they had seen more animals on television and in the movies than they had personally seen in the wild.

An even more telling measure of the lack of primary contact with their immediate nonhuman surroundings is this: a significant portion of kids today have never gone off alone, away from human habitations, to spend more than a half hour by themselves in a "natural" setting. None of the six Yaqui children responded that they had; nor had 58 percent of the O'odham, 53 percent of the Anglos, and 71 percent of the Mexican children. We also found that many children today have never been involved in collecting, carrying around, or playing with the feathers, bones, butterflies, or stones they find near their homes. Of those interviewed, 60 percent of the Yaqui children, 46 percent of the Anglos, 44 percent of the Mexicans, and 35 percent of the O'odham had never gathered such natural treasures. Such a paucity of contact with the natural world would have been unimaginable even a century ago, but it will become the norm as more than 38 percent of the children born after the year 2000 are destined to live in cities with more than a million other inhabitants. While few cities are entirely devoid of open spaces, manufactured toys and prefabricated electronic images have rapidly replaced natural objects as common playthings.

However varied the views of the natural world held by the myriad ethnic groups which have inhabited this continent, many of them are now converging on a new view—not so much one of experienced participants dynamically involved with their local environment as one in which they too may feel as though they are outside the frame looking in. Because only a small percentage of humankind has any direct, daily engagement with other species of animals and plants in their habitats, we have arrived at a new era in which ecological illiteracy is the norm. I cannot help concluding that we will soon be losing the many ways in which cultural diversity may have formerly enriched the biological diversity of various habitats of this continent. I can only hope that our children will pay more attention to this warning from Mary Midgley (1978:246) than we have:

> Man is not adapted to live in a mirror-lined box, generating his own electric light and sending for selected images from outside when he needs them. Darkness and bad smell are all that can come from that. We need a vast world, and it must be a world that does not need us; a world constantly capable of surprising us, a world we did not program, since only such a world is the proper object of wonder.

REFERENCES

Anderson, M. Kathleen. "The Experimental Approach to the Assessment of the Potential Ecological Effects of Horticultural Practices by Indigenous Peoples on California Wildlands." Ph.D. dissertation, University of California, Berkeley, 1993.

Anderson, Kat, and Gary Paul Nabhan. "Gardeners in Eden." *Wilderness* 55(194)(1991):27–30.

Blackburn, Thomas C., and Kat Anderson. "Introduction: Making the Domesticated Environment." In Thomas C. Blackburn and Kat Anderson (eds.), *Before the Wilderness: Environment Management by Native Californians.* Menlo Park: Ballena Press, 1993.

Botkin, Daniel. *Discordant Harmonies.* Oxford: Oxford University Press, 1990.

Clar, C. R. *California Government and Forestry from Spanish Days Until the Creation of the Department of Natural Resources in 1927.* Sacramento: California Division of Forestry, 1959.

Cronon, William. *Changes in the Land: Indians, Colonists, and the Ecology of New England.* New York: Hill & Wang, 1983.

Denevan, William M. "The Pristine Myth: The Landscape of the Americas in 1492." *Annals of the Association of American Geographers* 82(3) (1992):369–385.

Diamond, Jared. "The Environmentalist Myth: Archaeology." *Nature* 324(1986):19–20.

——. *The Third Chimpanzee.* New York: HarperCollins, 1992.

——. "New Guineans and Their Natural World." In Stephen Kellert and Edward O. Wilson (eds.), *The Biophilia Hypothesis.* Washington, D.C.: Island Press, 1993.

Dobyns, Henry F. *Their Numbers Become Thinned: Native American Population Dynamics in Eastern North America.* Knoxville: University of Tennessee Press, 1983.

Fish, Suzanne K., Paul R. Fish, Charles Miksicek, and John Madsen. "Prehistoric Agave Cultivation in Southern Arizona." *Desert Plants* 7(2) (1985): 107–112.

Flores, Mike, Fernando Valentine, and Gary Paul Nabhan. "Managing Cultural Resources in Sonoran Desert Biosphere Reserves." *Cultural Survival Quarterly* 14(4) (1990):26–30.

Gomez-Pompa, Arturo, and Andrea Kaus. "Taming the Wilderness Myth." *BioScience* 42 (1992):271–279.

Janzen, Daniel H., and Paul S. Martin. "Neotropical Anachronisms: Fruits the Gomphotheres Ate." *Science* 215 (1982):19–27.

Klett, Mark. "The Legacy of Ansel Adams." *Aperture* 120 (1990):72–73.

Martin, Paul S. "Refuting Late Pleistocene Extinction Models." In D. K. Eliot (ed.), *Dynamics of Extinction.* New York: Wiley, 1986.

Mathiot, Madeleine. *A Dictionary of Papago Usage.* Language Science Monograph 8(1). Bloomington: Indiana University Publications, 1973.

Midgley, Mary. *Beast and Man.* Ithaca: Cornell University Press, 1978.

Minnis, Paul S. "Economic and Organizational Responses to Food Stress by Non-stratified Societies: A Prehistoric Example." Ph.D. dissertation, University of Michigan, Ann Arbor, 1981.

Nabhan, Gary Paul. *Enduring Seeds.* San Francisco: North Point, 1989.

Nabhan, Gary Paul, and Sara St. Antoine. "The Loss of Floral and Faunal Story: The Extinction of Experience." In Stephen R. Kellert and Edward O. Wilson (eds.), *The Biophilia Hypothesis.* Washington, D.C.: Island Press, 1993.

National Park Service. "Revised Code of Federal Regulation for the National Park Service." *Federal Register* 52(14) (1987):2457–2458.

Oelschlaeger, Max. *The Idea of Wilderness.* New Haven: Yale University Press, 1991.

Parker, Eugene. "Forest Islands and Kayapo Resource Management in Amazonia: A Reappraisal of the *Apete.*" *American Anthropologist* 94 (1992):406–427.

Rea, Amadeo R. "Resource Utilization and Food Taboos of Sonoran Desert Peoples." *Journal of Ethnobiology* 2 (1981):69–83.

Redford, Kent H. "The Ecologically Noble Savage." *Orion* 9(3) (1985):24–29.

Redford, Kent H., and John G. Robinson. "The Game of Choice: Patterns of Indian and Colonist Hunting in the Neotropics." *American Anthropologist* 89(3) (1987):650–667.

Silko, Leslie M. "Landscape, History, and the Pueblo Imagination." In Daniel Halpern, ed., *On Nature.* San Francisco: North Point, 1987.

Soulé, Michael E. "Conservation: Tactics for a Constant Crisis." *Science* 253 (1991):744–750.

Discussion Questions

1. What are some characteristics that various first peoples often hold in common? Why are these features distinctive of first peoples and not of Westerners?
2. Is it possible for Westerners to feel a connection to the land? What conditions are necessary in order to feel such a connection?
3. Do you believe that first peoples are generally more ecologically aware than modernists? Can we learn from them and, if so, what?
4. Is it feasible to combine Western and indigenous knowledge systems to create a new, synthetic worldview? Which features of Western views would you retain, and which features of indigenous cultures would you adopt?
5. How should a native people's right of access to sacred sites be determined? How can conflicts with claims by other groups be resolved?
6. Are humans part of nature? Can human activities be unnatural? Should some natural areas be protected from all human activity?

Further Reading

Albanese, Catherine L., *Nature Religions in America: From the Algonkian Indians to the New Age,* Chicago: University of Chicago Press, 1990.

Chatwin, Bruce, *The Songlines,* New York: Penguin, 1987.

Deloria, Vine, Jr., *God Is Red: A Native View of Religion,* Golden, Colo.: Fulcrum, 1994.

———, *Red Earth, White Lies: Native Americans and the Myth of Scientific Fact,* Golden, Colo.: Fulcrum, 1997.

Durning, Alan, *Guardians of the Land: Indigenous Peoples and the Health of the Earth,* Washington, D.C.: Worldwatch, 1993.

Grim, John A., Ed., *Indigenous Traditions and Ecology: The Interbeing of Cosmology and Community,* Cambridge, Mass.: Harvard Center for the Study of World Religions, 2001.

Hughes, J. Donald, *American Indian Ecology,* 2nd ed., El Paso: Texas Western Press, 1996 [1983].

Johnson, Martha, Ed., *Capturing Traditional Environmental Knowledge,* Ottawa: Dene Cultural Institute and I.D.R.C., 1992.

Krech, Shepard, III, *The Ecological Indian: Myth and History,* New York: Norton, 1999.

Mander, Jerry, *In the Absence of the Sacred: The Failure of Technology and the Survival of the Indian Nations,* San Francisco: Sierra Club Books, 1991.

McLuhan, T. C., Ed., *Touch the Earth: A Self-Portrait of Indian Existence,* New York: Simon and Schuster, 1971.

Messer, Ellen, and Michael Lambek, Eds., *Ecology and the Sacred: Engaging the Anthropology of Roy A. Rappaport,* Ann Arbor: University of Michigan Press, 2001.

Nelson, Richard K., *Make Prayers to the Raven: A Koyukon View of the Northern Forest,* Chicago: University of Chicago Press, 1983.

Posey, Darrell Addison, Ed., *Cultural and Spiritual Values of Biodiversity: A Complementary Contribution to the Global Biodiversity Assessment,* London: Intermediate Technology Publications, 1999.

Rajotte, Freda, *First Nations Faith and Ecology,* London: Cassell, 1998.

Rappaport, Roy A., *Ecology, Meaning, and Religion,* Richmond, Calif.: North Atlantic Books, 1979.

Suzuki, David, and Peter Knudtson, *Wisdom of the Elders: Sacred Native Stories of Nature,* New York: Bantam, 1992.

Weatherford, Jack, *Indian Givers,* New York: Crown, 1988.

Chapter 4

South Asian Traditions

THE DIVERSITY OF WORLDVIEWS collectively referred to as Hinduism shares much with the worldviews of first peoples discussed in the previous chapter. In fact, the range of beliefs and practices that Hinduism subsumes probably preserves much of the worldview of South Asia's own first peoples. As a term, Hinduism (derived from the Persian word *hindu,* which originally simply meant *Indian*) came into use only in the nineteenth century in an attempt by the British colonizers of the Indian subcontinent to conceptualize the various native religious systems that they could not (as they could in the case of Indian Muslims, Zoroastrians, Christians, and Jews) otherwise categorize. Gradually, Indians themselves adopted the term, although even today one would be hard put to come up with anything that might serve as an adequate definition for a unified Hinduism.

The term Hinduism designates a broad array of beliefs and practices, in many though not in all cases finding their expression through a particular focus on one of three deities: Vishnu, often worshiped in his manifestations as Krishna or Rama; Shiva, who is associated especially with meditation and asceticism; or the Goddess frequently perceived in the form of Durga or Kali. Alongside these primary gods, Hindus recognize a large pantheon of other deities and supernatural beings, often local in nature. Many are associated with and worshiped in the context of particular phenomena, such as Ganesha, the elephant-headed god of obstacles and endeavors, or Lakshmi, the goddess of wealth. As in the case of first peoples, the tendency of Hinduism is toward nonexclusiveness. Indeed, although Hinduism's oldest textual traditions, the *Veda*s, most likely derive ultimately from Central Asian tribes known as Aryans, who migrated into South Asia during the second millennium BCE, many existing Hindu beliefs and practices probably trace back even earlier, to the original first peoples of South Asia. Among the core concepts shared by various South Asian worldviews, including Jainism, Hinduism, and Buddhism, are *dharma* (duty or necessity), *karma* (the weight of one's deeds), *ahimsa,* a cyclical though highly extended notion of time, and a belief in reincarnation.

Alongside—and, according to some views, within—the ancient pluralistic Hindu tradition exists an equally venerable tradition known as Jainism. Practiced by about 2 percent of the population of India today, Jainism is most prominently associated with the doctrine of ahimsa (nonviolence) popularized in the twentieth century by Mohandas K. Gandhi, but with a long history of influence in South Asian civilization. The ahimsa ideal is central to many expressions of Buddhism, which first arose in a South Asian context some twenty-five centuries ago. However, because with the exception of Sri Lanka, Buddhism today is practiced mainly outside of South Asia, it will be treated in a separate chapter.

In the first reading of this chapter, Christopher Chapple notes that notwithstanding the unworldly tendencies often associated with it, a potential for ecological awareness exists in

South Asian thought. In particular, Chapple notes the ethic of respect for life that is found in Jainism. Although explicit environmentalist activity among Jains may not be prominent at present, Chapple remarks that the simple lifestyle that their religion enjoins tends to minimize consumption, a major cause of environmental degradation. On the other hand, the involvement of Jains in some of India's major industries raises questions about how these ideals translate into practice.

O. P. Dwivedi's essay begins by emphasizing the severity of India's environmental crisis, pointing out the large role played by uncontrolled human population growth (India's population is likely to exceed China's by 2010, making it the most populous country in the world.). Against this ominous backdrop, Dwivedi proposes a number of Hindu concepts—mainly derived from textual sources—that he feels could help save and sustain India's threatened ecosystems.

Vasudha Narayanan reminds us in her essay that textual sources alone do not necessarily indicate the prevalent attitudes and behavior in a given society. She has us pose the question *which* texts and stories reflect and influence large numbers of people on a practical level. Narayanan also takes issue with those who would lay the blame for India's environmental crisis exclusively with Western influence, pointing out that many Indians have embraced destructive technologies and consumerism and have failed to control their own rate of population growth and that in some cases, their attitudes find support in Hindu texts.

In her article on the Gaṅgā (Ganges), one of India's most sacred yet most polluted rivers, Kelly D. Alley draws a distinction between scientific assessments of pollution and traditional notions of ritual impurity. The belief of many Hindus in the fundamental purity and purifying qualities of Mother Ganges creates a kind of cognitive dissonance, as modern Indians are faced with a scientific understanding of the effects of pollution on the river and on themselves. The Hindu priests attending the holy riverbank shrines at Banaras are less concerned for the physical deterioration of the sacred river than for the moral decay of human society.

Contemporary Jaina and Hindu Responses to the Ecological Crisis

CHRISTOPHER CHAPPLE

DURING A TRIP IN 1981 TO A SOUTH INDIAN industrial facility surrounded by denuded hills and dead trees due to factory pollution, I became intrigued and appalled by the obvious lack of sensitivity to environmental issues in India. How could the country of Gandhian justice, rich with religious perspectives that extol the beauty and value of life, be so oblivious to the harm incurred by unbridled industrialization? Three years later the Bhopal Union Carbide disaster catalyzed a new awareness amongst the Indian population regarding the dangers posed to both humans and the earth by the ravages of pollution.

Having written about the possible contributions that traditional Hindu religious values could make

Chapple, Christopher, "Contemporary Jaina and Hindu Responses to the Ecological Crisis," in Michael Barnes, Ed., *An Ecology of the Spirit: Religious Reflection and Environmental Consciousness,* Lanham, Md.: University Press of America, 1990, pp. 209–218. Reprinted by permission of the author.

to an indigenous environmental movement within India,[1] I travelled to India in 1989 to investigate organizations and resources on ecological issues that have developed recently. This journey revealed that although the outward appearances of the various institutions with which I established contact seemingly reflect the model for environmental action in the United States, in fact the movement in India is deeply influenced by indigenous perspectives. Ecological leaders of India highly value the transformation of the human psyche as the key to societal reform, placing less emphasis on legislative or governmental action. In what follows, I will begin with a brief survey of traditional Indian attitudes toward what in European terms is called the "natural world." I will then focus the discussion first on the Jaina tradition, due to its longstanding affirmation of respect for life, and then turn to various pan-Indian movements that advocate environmental protection. I will conclude with a discussion of some recurring themes within the Indian perspective.

The civilization of India, the beginnings of which have been dated as early as five thousand years ago, has produced a number of theologies and interrelated cosmologies that include human resources for dealing with the natural order. Quite often the traditions of India are associated with escapism and disregard for materiality. However, in my own experience of Indian traditions, several conceptual resources are present that can enhance respect for the environment.

In the Vedic hymns, for instance, we find an intimate relationship between persons and various personifications of the earth, water, thunderstorms, and so forth. The Vedic rituals, many of which are still performed today, serve as a matrix from which human prosperity and blessings may arise. In the somewhat later Samkhya tradition, the five great elements (*mahabhuta*) of earth, water, fire, air, and space, are reverenced as the essential building blocks of physical reality. From the Upanishads and later Vedantic formulations, all things with form (*saguna*) are seen to be essentially nondifferent from the universal consciousness or ultimate reality; any thing with form can be an occasion to remember that Brahman which is beyond form (*nirguna*). In this collective Hindu model, the human order can be seen as an extension of and utterly reliant upon the natural order. Meditation begins with concentration on external objects, a process that reveals that the world is not different from oneself. In the language of Vedanta, the Brahman is inseparable from its individual manifestations. As stated in the *Bhagavad Gita,* the person of knowledge "sees no difference between a learned Brahmin, a cow, an elephant, a dog, or an outcaste" (V:18). From the perspectives of Jainism and Hinduism, the killing of life forms is none other than the killing of our own kin. For an American, the loss of trees and lakes due to acid rain could be regarded with indifference. Aside from environmentalists and romantics, most Americans regard the natural world as an object for consumption or appreciation. To a classically trained Indian, the loss of a lake or a tree is the loss of that which composes oneself.

In addition to the Vedic and Vedantic worldview summarized above, the religious traditions of India have been profoundly influenced by the persistent and prophetic presence of the Sramanic or renouncer schools. Preeminent among these are the Jaina, Buddhist, and Yoga traditions. Whereas Yoga became closely associated with Vedic and Hindu forms (and somewhat preempted by Sankara's monism), and Buddhism departed from India with the advent of Islam (and likewise became somewhat subsumed into the larger Hindu tradition), Jainism retained its purity, both in terms of its world view and its community life. In Jainism, all elements have life: the earth, the water, plants, animals, and humans are all said to possess *jiva* or life force. This *jiva* takes repeated forms from beginningless time; each person in a prior existence might well have been a dog or a frog or even perhaps a clod of earth. Due to the continued accumulation of karma through acts of violence, *jivas* are reborn again and again. In order to stop this senseless, directionless reincarnation (a notion found also in Buddhism and later Hinduism), persons are encouraged to undertake an ethical life to mitigate existing karma and minimize future karma. The asceticism of India is designed explicitly so that in revering and respecting the life of another, one's own life is purified.

Rather like the movements of the radical reformation in the Christian milieu, Jainism has struggled to retain its traditional worldview despite the onslaught of competing social norms. Jainism has campaigned for the "vegetarianization" of Hindus and Muslims throughout Indian history, successfully convincing high caste Hindus to spurn consumption of meat and very nearly converting the Muslim Mughal emperor Akbar to a meatless diet. Using resources and arguments similar to the case made for vegetarianism, Jainism confronts modern issues like nuclear proliferation, ecological ravage, and various dilemmas related to the field of medical ethics, including the use of animals for research and production of medicines, and euthanasia.

The conceptual resources offered by Jainism for coping with the ecological dilemma would essentially be the same as for dealing with animals rights and medical ethics. Jainism holds as its fundamental tenet that all life is sacred, as exemplified in the Acaranga Sutra which states that "All beings desire to live." To harm living beings means that one violates this principle, resulting in the accretion of harmful karma that guarantees further violent action and certain rebirth. In order to extirpate these harmful influences, Jaina society advocates a quasi-ascetic lifestyle for its lay adherents and a rigorously ascetic lifestyle for its monks and nuns. No Jaina is allowed to eat nonvegetarian food or engage in professions that promote violent activity. Monastic Jainas adhere to a variety of vows, depending upon sect, which may include total nudity, total avoidance of bathing, sweeping one's path to avoid killing insects, and so forth.

The Jainas have campaigned against the production of nuclear weapons, the use of animals for product testing, and the unnecessary prolonging of life. On the nuclear issue, Anuvibha, an organization based in Jaipur and somewhat affiliated with the Terapanthi branch of the Svetambara Jainas, has forged links with various Western peace organizations and has conducted international conferences on peace issues.[2]

In an earlier study, I postulated that Jainas would disdain the killing of animals for the enhancement of medical research,[3] arguing that any harm to animals would be carefully avoided. However, I have subsequently discovered that the Jaina community controls the pharmaceutical industry in India and of course is required to adhere to safety and testing regulations. The compromise solution that the Jainas have put into effect combines modern exigency with a very traditional practice. Animals are used for testing but then are "rehabilitated" through shelters and recuperation facilities maintained by the laboratories. For instance, the pharmaceutical branch of India's Walchand Group of industries uses animals for the production of immunoglobulin but then releases them into the wild, as noted by Dr. Vinod Doctori.[4] This practice is not unlike the ages-old Jaina tradition of constructing animal shelter for infirm animals, allowing them to survive until their natural demise.[5]

In a tradition so highly concerned with the preservation of and respect for life, it is poignant that the manner of death receives a great deal of attention and has great importance. In the Jaina tradition animals are given shelter until death; human death is similarly ritualized. It is not an event to be avoided and postponed; if one knows that death is imminent, it is eagerly embraced.[6] A highly ritualized entry into death is practiced occasionally in Jainism through a fast unto death, in which one consciously "drops" the body as preliminary to reentry into the continuum of life. For highly advanced monastics, rebirth does not occur, but one dwells in an eternal state of energy, consciousness, and bliss unfettered by association with karma.

In some ways, given its *telos,* this religious tradition may seem utterly otherworldly and simply incapable of addressing the issue of environmental destruction. Many have criticized Indian forms of asceticism for the seeming disdain toward the material world. However, the nonviolent ethic of Jainism (*ahimsa*) as embodied by both monastic and lay practitioners, does indeed offer resources for a more ecologically balanced lifestyle. During a visit to Jain Vishva Bharati in Ladnun, a small desert town in Western Rajasthan, I visited with Acharya Tulsi, who has served as the head of the Terapanthi Svetambara sect since 1936.[7] I inquired as to whether the Jaina religion is responding to the current ecological crisis. His response was very much in the style of traditional Indian pedagogy. He spoke not of political or legislative action (though I did ask him about such matters) but rather referred to his own lifestyle. He showed me what he owns: his white robes, his eating utensils, and his personal collection of books. The latter can only be read with a magnifying glass: copies of the primary Jaina sutras and the original 250 year old document establishing his order have been rendered in tiny print, so as to allow easy transport. The life of a Jaina monk or nun is a life of homelessness. While in Ladnun, Acharya Tulsi occupies the corner of a classroom at Jaina Vishva Bharati; there is no place and very few things that he can call his own. In a very direct way, he was in fact showing me the most radical form of ecological lifestyle. He owns no automobile, no house, few clothes. *Aparigraha,* one of the five requirements for Jaina living, eschews attachment to any thing.

The work of Acharya Tulsi, in many ways akin to Gandhianism but largely free from an encumbered political agenda, has had a long history in India, and has been used for a variety of causes. On March 1, 1949, he instituted the Anuvrat movement, a series of twelve vows that he has urged persons to take, ranging from the vow of ahimsa: "I will not kill any innocent creature" to the twelfth, which states "I will do my best to avoid contributing to pollution."[8] The premise of this program is that the transformation of society must begin with transformation of the individual. S. Gopalan states that Acharya Tulsi insists "that the ills of society automatically get cured by means of the process of self-purification and self-control."[9] In support of the Anuvrat Movement, Sarvepalli Radhakrishnan, India's philosopher-president, has written:

> There is a general feeling in the country that while we are attending to the material progress and doing substantial work in that direction, we are neglecting the human side of true progress. A civilized human being must be free from greed, vanity, passion, anger. Civilizations decline if there is a coarsening of moral fibre, if there is callousness of heart. Man is tending to become a robot, a mechanical instrument caring for nothing except his material welfare, incapable of exercising his intelligence and responsibility. He seems to prefer comfort to liberty. . . . to remedy this growing indiscipline, lack of rectitude, egotism, the Anuvrat Movement was started on March 1, 1949. It requires strict adherence to the principles of good life.[10]

The goal of the Anuvrat movement, which has been active for over forty years, is to encourage persons to adapt their lifestyle to effect a more nonviolent world. Gandhi employed a similar technique in his Satyagraha campaigns. The current ecological drive towards bioregionalism, wherein people are encouraged to develop an intimate relationship with their immediate environment, is based on similar approaches. The essential message in both instances is that environmental ravage proceeds from over-consumption that arises from disregard. To minimize consumption is to minimize harm to one's environment.

However stark the life of Acharya Tulsi may be, it does not mandate that all Jainas follow the life of a monk. Jaina laypersons have long been challenged by the example of the monk to make their own lifestyles less violent, as indicated in the illustration of the pharmaceutical company's release of test animals back into the wild. The legendary frugality of the Jainas also underscores a concern to minimize the diminishment of one's resources. This careful lifestyle has ironically resulted in the accumulation of great wealth on the part of the Jainas. According to some sources, Jainas constitute only one percent of India's population, yet they pay approximately half of India's income tax.[11] Individual Jainas control the automobile, pharmaceutical, publishing, and other industries of India. And yet even the wealthiest of Jainas for the most part live simply.

As mentioned earlier, during a trip to India in 1981, I was struck with the damage to the environment incurred in India by its burgeoning industrialization. The level of awareness in this regard was close to nonexistent, much to my consternation and distress. However, when I returned this past winter, a noticeable change had taken place: virtually every newspaper included a daily story on the environment. Since the Bhopal Union Carbide disaster, two major centers have been established to serve as clearinghouses for environmental issues. In New Delhi the Center for Science and Environment, in addition to other activities, provides a news service that supplies India's many newspapers with stories of environmental and ecological interest. It clips those that appear in print and publishes them in a periodical entitled *Green File.* Although this may seem rather simple, it struck me as a resident of Los Angeles as particularly effective. In the *Los Angeles Times,* the Sierra Club is depicted as a dating service and the portrait painted of environmentalists in feature articles often borders on the absurd. California's "slow growth" movement has been maligned in the press, as well as outspent in referendum campaigns by developers seeking to protect their interests. At the *Newhall Signal,* an editor who suggested that a cluster of cancer deaths might be linked to chemical production in a Los Angeles suburb was dismissed from his post. Clearly, the editorial policies of our regional papers have been shaped by business interests; a parallel form of news control can be found in the *New York Times'* undying support for nuclear energy. One possible reason for the willingness of the Indian press to lend credibility to the environmental cause is that the head of the *Times of India,* the leading daily, Ashok Jain, is himself a member of the Jaina tradition.

While in the city of Ahmedabad, home to many Jainas and the residence of Mahatma Gandhi for two decades, I visited with Meena Rahunathan, special programmes officer of the Centre for Environment Education. The CEE was established in 1984 as part of the Nehru Foundation for Development. It conducts workshops and produces materials that reach over ten thousand teachers per year. It operates a "News and Features Service" similar to that of the Centre for Science and Environment. It has initiated rural education program [*sic*] to help stem the destruction of India's remaining forests. It conducts various urban programs, including the promotion of smokeless cooking fires through use of a chulha, a wood or dung burning stove with a damper system that captures smoke.[12] In 1986 it launched the Ganga Pollution Awareness Programme, which has been widely documented in the United States. In cooperation with the School of Forestry of the State University of New York, located in Syracuse, it produces a series of environmental films for children. It has developed interpretive materials for the National Zoological Park in Delhi and for Kanha National Park. Within the city of Ahmedabad, it has installed a permanent ecological exhibit at Gujerat University; maintains a bird sanctuary at Sundarvan, its fourteen acre campus; and has developed exhibits for the Gandhi Ashram.[13]

Another institution that has long been attuned to environmental concerns is Gandhi Peace Foundation in New Delhi. Gandhi's village-based economic model may be seen as an early paradigm for the bioregionalism that many ecoactivists promote today. Gandhi wrote:

> Industrialization on a mass scale will necessarily lead to passive or active exploitation of the villages as the problems of competition and marketing come in. Therefore, we have to concentrate on the village being self-contained.[14]

Gandhi also criticized industrial development in a style quite reminiscent of Thoreau's *Walden Pond:*

> This land of ours was once, we are told, the abode of the Gods. It is not possible to conceive Gods inhabiting a land which is made hideous by the smoke and din of mill chimneys and factories, and whose roadways are traversed by rushing engines, dragging numerous cars crowded with men who know not for the most part what they are after, who are often absent-minded and whose tempers do not improve by being uncomfortably packed like sardines in boxes and finding themselves in the midst of strangers who would oust them if they could and whom they would, in their turn, oust similarly. I refer to these things because they are held to symbolic [*sic*] of material progress. But they add not an atom to our happiness.[15]

Reflecting the influence of his Jaina neighbors and advisors, he proposed a solution to the twin problems of industrialization and alienation by advocating that every occupation work at the minimization of violence.

> Strictly speaking, no activity and no industry is possible without a certain amount of violence, no matter how little. Even the very process of living is impossible without a certain amount of violence. What we have to do is to minimize it to the greatest extent possible. Indeed the very word nonviolence, a negative word, means that it is an effort to abandon the violence that is inevitable in life. Therefore, whoever believes in Ahimsa will engage himself in occupations that involve the least possible violence.[16]

In addition to promoting and restating the works of Gandhi, the Gandhi Peace Foundation has engaged in various projects to promote village-based economies. It has encouraged farmers to grow food for themselves in addition to cultivating the usual cash crop. In cooperation with the Centre for Rural Development and Appropriate Technology of the Indian Institute of Technology, the Gandhi Peace Foundation has promoted the implementation of organic farming according to the model of Masanobu Fukuoka, who advocates no tilling or weeding, and no use of fertilizers or herbicides.[17] Although this project is in a rudimentary phase, T. S. Ananthu, a research associate, spoke of the foundation promoting this program elsewhere in India.

Two movements in India have taken direct action in an effort to bring attention to environmental concerns. The Chipko Movement in Uttar Pradesh involves local women saving trees by embracing them, staving off bulldozers.[18] Baba Amte, winner of the 1990 Templeton Prize for progress in religion, has focused resistance to the Narmada River Valley dam project by conducting a vigil unto death in protest of the planned destruction by flooding of over 325,000 acres of forest and agricultural land in western India. The first Asian to win the United Nations Human Rights Award, Baba Amte is best known for his pioneering work on behalf of India's lepers. Following the Bhopal disaster of 1984 that claimed over 3,800 lives, he began an environmental campaign, stating that "It is this invisible leprosy of greed and ambition that is turning our world into a wasteland."[19] His style on behalf of environmental causes has taken him to villages directly affected by the Narmada River Valley and other super dam projects, somewhat reminiscent of Gandhian grassroots movements.

We have surveyed three Indian approaches aimed at correcting the current ecological assault: changing one's own lifestyle, as advocated by the example of Acharya Tulsi; efforts at general education, as seen with the Centre for Science and Environment and the Centre for Environment Education; and the direct action of the Chipko movement and Baba Amte. The Gandhi Peace Foundation seemingly combines all three approaches. Each of these movements is rooted in a uniquely Indian orientation and each has demonstrated a degree of success, though perhaps not easily discernable by Euro-American standards. The purest of models is perhaps the first, held forth by Jaina monastics, who own virtually nothing, who will not even as much as touch a leaf, who tend to stay in the desert so that natural life forms will not be disturbed. The second model and third models, focusing on education and direct action, are perhaps more "Western" in approach, at least on the surface. One notable cultural difference, however, is that there seems to be less concern for legislative lobbying in India. When queried, neither the Gandhi Peace Foundation nor the Centre for Environment Education nor Anuvibha knew of environmental lobbying groups comparable to Greenpeace in India. When pressed on this issue, the standard response was that "In India, people do no pay attention to laws; the consciousness must be changed." This basic orientation has not strayed far from Gandhian and traditional religious models.

In many ways the current lifestyle of India contains elements that support the environmental perspective. Most persons live within a short scooter ride or walking distance to work. Foodstuffs consumed by Indians are comprised of grains purchased in bulk from the market and cooked with vegetables procured from travelling greengrocers who push their carts through virtually every neighborhood all day long. Waste is collected and used for fertilizer.

Yet all of this may soon change. In Delhi, I was served yogurt in a disposable plastic container. Private automobiles have begun to proliferate. The advent of a consumer economy seems to be eroding the possibility for an ecologically sound form of development. Although industrialization and technologization of the subcontinent are modest by American standards, the sheer numbers of people entering into the middle class make it difficult for the same mistakes of Western development to be avoided. One small example is the automobile: India now produces its own small cars, and increasingly they are owned by individuals. By some accounts (and verified by personal experience) the Delhi area has perhaps the most polluted air in the world.

• • •

And yet as the general awareness of environmental ravage increases, even here in the United States, the best and most cutting-edge solutions seem to follow the model proposed by Acharya Tulsi in India. It is only when each individual makes a change in his or her lifestyle that a societal leap forward can occur. In America, the seeds of this transformation have been sown; over 80% of the populace define themselves as "environmentalists," indicating that concern for ecological harmony has been widely accepted. Americans now are educating themselves on how to minimize the use of the fabulous technology available to us, from household chemicals to nuclear weapons.

In India, people traditionally have not been divorced from the earth: to think of themselves as separate from the ongoing and all pervasive cycle of life and death would be inconceivable. And yet now India and its religious traditions face the challenges of modernity, technology, consumptionism, and technological ravage; in short, buying into the American dream where the world and one's relationship to it become estranged and objectified. Part of the solution to ecological ravage requires the hard work of scientists, technocrats, and educators, those responsible for inventing and inculcating the values of consumer society. However, we need also to look off the wheel, so to speak; we need to get out of the car to fix it. For this, the example set by the renouncers of India who advocate minimal consumption continues to offer a solution for myriad problems. By attacking the source of human misery through uprooting human attachment itself, a true type of peace that automatically extends to others can be fostered.

NOTES

1. Christopher Chapple, "Ecological Nonviolence and the Hindu Tradition," in *Perspectives on Nonviolence,* edited by V.K. Kool (New York: Springer-Verlag, 1990), pp. 168–177.

2. S.L. Gandhi, International Secretary of Anuvibha, has been a valuable resource for my research on Jainism. The address of his organization is A-12, Anita Colony, Bajaj Nagar, Jaipur, Rajasthan 302015, India.

3. Christopher Chapple, "Noninjury to Animals: Jaina and Buddhist Perspectives" in Tom Regan, editor, *Animal Sacrifices: Religious Perspectives on the Use of Animals in Science* (Philadelphia: Temple University Press, 1986), 213–236.

4. *Ahimsa: Nonviolence,* Michael Tobias, executive producer, writer, and director, Public Broadcasting Service, 1986.

5. For a graphic depiction of an animal shelter in Ahmedabad, see the film *Frontiers of Peace: Jainism in India,* directed by Paul Kuepferle and Barry Lynch.

6. For details on this practice, see my forthcoming article "The Fast Unto Death in Jaina Tradition."

7. For a complete biography of Acharya Tulsi, see *Acharya Tulsi: Fifty Years of Selfless Dedication,* edited by R. P. Bhatnagar, S.L. Gandhi, Rajul Bhargava, and Ashok K. Jha (Ladnun, India: Jain Vishva Bharati, 1985).

8. See S.L. Gandhi, ed., *Anuvrat Movement: A Constructive Endeavor Towards a Nonviolent Multicultural Society* (Rajasmand, India: Anuvrat Vishva Bharati, 1987).

9. Gandhi, *Anuvrat Movement* 33.

10. Gandhi, *Anuvrat Movement*; as quoted from S. Radhakrishnan, *Living With a Purpose* (Glastonbury, CT: Ind-US, Inc., 1983), a profile of fourteen distinguished personalities.

11. *Ahimsa: Nonviolence.*

12. One of the greatest sources of airborne pollutants in India is particulants given off by the burning of cow dung, the prime fuel used for cooking fires. This simple device, if universally applied, would greatly reduce air pollution, particularly in urban areas.

13. "Centre for Environment Education Annual Report, 1987–88," Nehru Foundation for Development, Ahmedabad.

14. M.K. Gandhi, *The Village Reconstruction* (Bombay: Bhatatiya Vidya Bhavan, 1966) 43.

15. M.K. Gandhi, *My Socialism* (Ahmedabad: Navajivan Publishing House, 1959) 34.

16. Gandhi, *My Socialism* 35.

17. "The Mohanpur Experiment in Natural Farming: Second Interim Report, June 1988," Gandhi Peace Foundation and IIT, Delhi.

18. Information on this movement is included in the periodical publication *Worldwide Women in the Environment,* P.O. Box 40885, Washington, D.C. 20016.

19. Mark Fineman, "A River, A Dam, and an Old Man's Last Battle" *Los Angeles Times* (May 1, 1990, Section H, World Report) 1.

Dharmic Ecology

O. P. DWIVEDI

THE MANY ENVIRONMENTAL PROBLEMS INDIA faces may be summarized as follows: 1) continuous degradation, in varying degrees, of productive land (due to increased salinity and alkalinity, desertification, water-logging, and deforestation); 2) shortage of wood fuel and fodder for rural needs, which jeopardizes existing forests; 3) depletion of the forest cover, which in turn threatens the survival of indigenous biodiversity and affects wildlife habitat; 4) excessive and unwise use of pesticides and fertilizers

Dwivedi, O. P., "Dharmic Ecology," in Christopher Key Chapple and Mary Evelyn Tucker, Eds., *Hinduism and Ecology: The Intersection of Earth, Sky and Water,* Cambridge, Mass.: Harvard University Press, 2000, pp. 3–22. Reprinted by permission of the Center for the Study of World Religions, Harvard Divinity School.

and ill-advised agricultural practices (including monoculture), which further stresses the fragile environment; and 5) poorly monitored and inadequately enforced environmental regulations for various natural resource extraction activities (such as mining, metallurgy, aggregate production, and other manufacturing industries).

A cursory glance at the extent of some of these major environmental problems reveals that all India's environmental issues are interconnected and together constitute an increasingly deteriorating environment and rapid depletion of natural resources—whether the issue in question is health hazards caused by water and air pollution, such as the use of fuel wood or dung for cooking purposes; population pressure and urbanization straining the resources of local governments that have to provide various civic amenities, the dearth of which imperils the quality of life of people living in urban areas; myopic land management policies that are severely straining the ecosystem in order to meet people's requirements of food and other agricultural products; long-term degradation of land and increasing desertification which is jeopardizing people's futures; the use of hazardous chemicals to meet today's short-term needs without an eye to future costs; or the rapid shrinkage of natural resources such as grazing land and the lack of fodder, firewood, and timber due to deforestation. India faces yet another major challenge to its environmental well-being: continuing poverty coupled with growing population and the attendant side effects of enhanced industrial activities (including human settlement patterns and movements). The existence of poverty affects the meager natural resources that India wishes to protect and conserve: people are so desperate to improve their families' living conditions that they do not hesitate to damage the environment if the short-term gains ensure fulfillment of their family's daily basic needs.[1]

India's population of 844 million in 1991 is increasing at the rate of 2.11 percent annually, which means about 17 million people are added each year. Furthermore, India has probably the largest cattle population on the earth—about 500 million domesticated animals—with only 13 million hectares of grazing land. The multiplying population of both human beings and animals is putting tremendous pressure on India's environment. In the race for survival, both animals and human beings suffer. In addition, over 250 million children, women, and men suffer from malnutrition. The prospects for the future are alarming indeed.

Needless to say, India faces a double jeopardy in attempting to industrialize quickly while confronting poverty and a growing population. India's environmental problems are complex and the choices available are difficult. Vision and "environmentally sound" foresight based on a holistic approach to problem-solving are required and entail bringing the secular, socioeconomic, cultural, religious, and traditional domains together. In this essay, I will examine India's ecospirituality against the context of dharmic ecology from four interrelated perspectives. These are 1) *Vāsudeva sarvam,* the Supreme Being resides in all beings; 2) *Vasudhaiva kuṭumbakam,* the family of Mother Earth; 3) *Sarva-bhūta-hitā,* the welfare of all beings; and 4) Dharmic ecology as a strategy toward putting into practice the Hindu concept of ecocare.

VĀSUDEVA SARVAM, THE SUPREME BEING RESIDES IN ALL THINGS

One of the main postulations of the *Bhagavadgītā* is that the Supreme Being resides in all. Chapter 7, verse 19, states:

> Only after taking many births is a wise person able to comprehend the basic philosophy of the creation; which is: whatever is, is Vāsudeva. If anyone understands this fundamental, such a person is indeed a Mahatma.[2]

Later, in chapter 13, verse 13, the Lord Kṛṣṇa says: "He resides in everywhere" (*sarvam āvṛtya tiṣṭhati*). As explained in the *Śrīmad Bhāgavata Mahāpurāṇa* (book 2, discourse 2, verse 41), "ether, air, fire, water, earth, planets, all creatures, directions, trees and plants, rivers, and seas, they all are organs of God's body; remembering this, a devotee respects all species." Further, the definition of a pundit is one who treats a cow, an elephant, a dog, and an outcaste with the same respect shown to the Brahman endowed with great learning and yet humble (*Gītā* 5.18). Thus, the basic concept is: seeing the presence of God in all, and treating the creation with respect without harming and exploiting others (*vāsudevaḥ sarvam iti*). The *Śrīmad Bhāgavata Mahāpurāṇa* (2.2.45) confirms this fundamental principle: a good devotee is the one who sees in all creation the presence of God (*sarva bhūteṣu yaḥ paśyed bhagvadbhāvamātmanaḥ*).

Such veneration, respect, and acceptance of the presence of God in nature is required of Hindus in order to maintain and protect the natural harmonious relationship between human beings and nature.[3] In the *Mahābhārata*, it is claimed that all living beings have soul, and God resides as their inner soul: *Sarvabhūtātmbhūtastho* (Mokṣadharma Parva, chapter 182, verse 20). It also means that all this universe and every object in it has been created as an abode of the Supreme God; it is meant for the benefit of all; individual species must therefore learn to enjoy its benefits by existing as part of the system, in close relationship with other species and without permitting any one species to encroach upon the others' rights. This stipulation is later endorsed in the *Mahābhārata*, where it is stated:

> The Father of all creatures, Lord God, made the sky. From sky he made water, and from water made fire (*agni*) and air (*vāyu*). From fire and air, the earth (*pṛthivī*) came into existence. Actually, mountains are his bones, earth is the flesh, sea is the blood, and sky is his abdomen. The sun and moon are his eyes. The upper part of the sky is his head, the earth is his feet, and directions are his hands. (*Mahābhārata*, Mokṣadharma Parva, 182.14–19).

Thus, at least for the Hindus of the ancient period, God and nature were one and the same. While Prajapati (the "Lord of Creatures" of the Rgveda) is the creator of the sky, the earth, the oceans, and all the species, he is also their protector and eventual destroyer. He is the only Lord of Creation. Human beings have no special privilege or authority over other creatures; on the other hand, they do have more obligations and duties.[4]

Hindu scriptures attest to the belief that the creation, maintenance, and annihilation of the cosmos is completely up to the Supreme Will. In the *Gītā*, Lord Kṛṣṇa says to Arjuna: "Of all that is material and all that is spiritual in this world, know for certain that I am both its origin and dissolution" (*Gītā* 10.8). "By my will it is manifested again and again and by my will it is annihilated at the end" (*Gītā* 9.8). Furthermore, the Lord says: "I am the origin, the end, existence, and the maintainer (of all)" (*Gītā* 10.32). Thus, for Hindus, God and *prakṛti* (nature) are interrelated.

Furthermore, the Hindu belief in the cycle of birth and rebirth, wherein a person may come back as an animal or a bird, means that Hindus are called to give other species not only respect, but reverence. This reverence finds expression in the doctrine of *ahiṃsā*, nonviolence (or non-injury) against other species and human beings alike. It should be noted that the doctrine of *ahiṃsā* presupposes the doctrines of *karma* and rebirth (*punarjanma*). The soul continues to take birth in different life-forms, such as birds, fish, animals, and humans. Based on this belief, there is a profound opposition in the Hindu religion (and in Buddhist and Jaina religions) to the institutionalized breeding and killing of animals, birds, and fish for human consumption. From the perspective of Hindu religion, the abuse and exploitation of nature for selfish gain is considered unjust and sacrilegious.

God Reincarnates in the Form of Animals and Humans

One of the central tenets of Hinduism is the doctrine of reincarnation, when the Supreme Being was himself incarnated in the forms of various species. The Lord says: "This form is the source and indestructible seed of multifarious incarnations within the universe, and from the particle and portion of this form, different living entities, like demigods, animals, human beings and others, are created" (*Śrīmad Bhāgavata Mahāpurāṇa* 1.3.5). Among the various incarnations of God are a fish, a tortoise, a boar, and a dwarf. His fifth incarnation was as a man-lion. As Rāma, God was closely associated with monkeys, and, as Kṛṣṇa, he was surrounded by cattle. These are some examples where different species are accorded reverence.

Almost all the Hindu scriptures place a strong emphasis on the notion that God's grace cannot be received by killing animals or harming other creatures. That is why *not* eating meat is considered both appropriate conduct and one's *dharma*. For example, as mentioned in the *Viṣṇu Purāṇa:* "God, Keśava, is pleased with a person who does not harm or destroy other nonspeaking creatures or animals" (*Viṣṇu Purāṇa* 3.8.15). Further, the pain a human being causes other living beings to suffer will eventually be suffered by that same person, either in this life or in a later rebirth. It is through the transmigration of the soul that a link has been provided between the lowliest forms of life and human beings. In the *Manusmṛti,* the laws of Manu, a warning is given: "A person who kills an animal for meat will die of a violent death as many times as there are hairs of that killed animal" (*Manusmṛti* 5.38). The *Yājñavalkyasmṛti* warns those who kill domesticated and protected animals of hellfire (*ghora naraka*): "The wicked person who kills animals which are protected has to live in hellfire for the days equal to the number of hairs on the body of that animal" (*Yājñavalkyasmṛti,* Acaradhyayah, verse 180). And, the *Narasiṃha Purāṇa* states that a person who roasts a bird for eating will surely be a sinner:

> O Wicked person! what is the use of you taking a bath in sacred rivers, doing pilgrimage, worshiping, and performing *yajñas* if you roast a bird for your meals.[5]

The *Mahābhārata* describes an event in which the *ṛṣis* and gods debated the merits of offering grain or the lamb (goat) as the sacrifice, *yajña.* The *ṛṣis* insisted that, according to the Vedas, the sacrificial material ought to be the grain only, and thus no animal should be killed for the purpose of *yajña:*

> The *ṛṣis* told the Gods that according to the Vedas and *śrutis,* the sacrificial offering should be of grain. The term "Aj" does not mean animal or goat as you denote, the term means only grain or seed. Thus, an animal must not be sacrificed. Further, that which sanctions the killing of any animal cannot be a true Dharma of a moral people.[6]

Thus, it would seem that the practice of grain sacrifice may have started from that time.

Ecological Unity in Hindu Mythological Diversity

How to protect and conserve the biological diversity is exemplified by the family and habitat of the god Śiva, his consort Pārvatī, and his two sons Kārttikeya and Gaṇeśa. His habitat is Mount Kailāsa, with snowy peaks representing the cosmic heavens. The nascent moon on his forehead denotes tranquillity; the constant stream of Gaṅgā's water from the interplaited lock of hair on his head indicates the purity and preeminence of water; Nandi, the bull, as his mount, represents livestock; serpents signify the presence of toxicity in nature; the lion used by his consort Pārvatī represents wildlife; the peacock, the mount of Kārttikeya, one of the most colorful birds, represents the avian species; and the mouse, the mount of Gaṇeśa, represents pests. Thus, various forms of animate and inanimate life are represented in the household and habitat of Lord Śiva. However, another important significance of the family of Lord Śiva is the harmonious relationship between natural enemies. In Lord Śiva's household, various natural enemies live in harmony with each other. The carnivorous lion's food is the vegetarian bull, the peacock is the enemy of the serpent, and the mouse is the serpent's food; nevertheless, all live together. Thus, when a devotee worships the family of Lord Śiva, he or she observes this co-existence and is influenced by what in contemporary times might be seen as analogous to the concept of ecological harmony and respect for biological diversity.

A story from Hindu scriptures illustrates this coexistence between good and evil. Cursed by the *mahārṣi* Dūrbhaṣa, the *devas* (demigods) were deprived of their divine vigor and strength. Soon, they were defeated by the *asuras* (demons) and dislodged from their heavenly abode. They then prayed to Lord Viṣṇu to seek his intervention. Lord Viṣṇu suggested that the only course open to them lay in securing the Nectar of Immortality, which would make them invincible. In order to obtain this nectar, they had to put every herb in the cosmic sea of milk and churn the sea by using the mountain of Mandarachal as a pestle and the snake king, Vāsuki, as the noose. To churn the sea, they needed the assistance of the demons to hold one end of the rope. The demons agreed to assist on the condition that the nectar received from the churning would be shared equally. From their churning, the most sought after nectar was obtained, along with many precious stones, wealth, and worldly riches. But, along with these priceless and rare items, a most venomous poison was produced. If that poison was not immediately disposed of, *sarvanāśa* (total annihilation) of the entire universe could result; however, no one, god or demon, was willing to touch this most fatal toxic waste. Finally, all went to Lord Śiva agreed to take help in stopping the obliteration of the universe. Śiva agreed to take care of the toxic waste by drinking it, and thus the impending disaster was averted. Later, with the assistance of Lord Viṣṇu, the demigods were able to trick the demons out of their share of the nectar, so that only the gods became immortal. This story instructs us that the consequences of an activity can be both beneficial and disastrous. Both nectar and poison result from the same activity, and one cannot be acquired without the other. In contemporary terms, an ecological balance has to be maintained between the nectar of riches and the side effects (poisons) of technology and industrialization. As we live on the same planet, we suffer or benefit together.

Based on a metaphorical interpretation of the above stories, one can suggest the premise that every entity and living organism is part of one large extended family system (*kutumba*) presided over by the eternal Mother Earth, Devī Vasundharā. The development of humanity from creation until now has taken place nowhere else but on Earth. Our relationship with Earth, from birth to death, is like that of children and their mother. The mother, in this case Earth, not only bears her children but also is the main source of fulfillment of their unending desires. It is Earth which provides energy for the sustenance of all species. And, just as one ought not insult, exploit, or violate one's mother, but be kind and respectful to her, so should one behave toward Mother Earth. We are enjoined to take care of God's creation by engaging in ecostewardship.

VASUDHAIVA KUṬUMBAKAM, THE FAMILY OF MOTHER EARTH

In the *Atharva Veda*, an entire hymn, the Pṛthivī Sūkta, has been devoted to praise of Mother Earth. The hymn's sixty-three verses integrate many of the thoughts of Hindu seers concerning the concept of nature, the dependence of human beings on Earth, and the resultant respect required.[7] These verses are addressed to Devī Vasundharā, Mother Earth. Earth is seen as the abode of a family of all beings (humans and others alike). *Vasudhā* means "this earth," while *kuṭumba* means "extended family"—including human beings, animals, and all living beings. Every entity and organism is a part of one large extended family system presided over by the eternal Mother Earth. It is she who supports us with her abundant endowments and riches; it is she who nourishes us; it is she who provides us with a sustainable environment; and it is she who, when angered by the misdeeds of her children, punishes them with disasters:

> O Mother Earth! Sacred are thy hills, snowy mountains, and deep forests. Be kind to us and bestow upon us happiness. May you be fertile, arable, and nourisher of all. May you continue supporting people of all races and nations. May you protect us from your anger (natural disasters). And may no one exploit and subjugate your children.[8]

The hymn's composer, the Atharva *ṛṣi*, envisions Mother Earth in her pristine nature, not denuded of her natural cover. The Pṛthivī Sūkta also exemplifies the relevance of environmental sustenance, agriculture, and biodiversity to human beings.[9] The three main segments of our physical environment—water, air, and soil—are highlighted and their usefulness detailed. The various water resources, such as seas, rivers, and waterfalls, flow on Earth (*Atharva Veda* 12.3). Verse 2 of this hymn depicts the majesty of mountains and rivers, the beauty of small springs, and the invaluable tiny medicinal plants which save the lives of humans. But all these elements are treated equally by Mother Earth, who does not discriminate between the high and mighty (*uddhataḥ*), such as mountains and oceans, and the low (*prayataḥ*). For Mother Earth, all species are of equal value; she has not accorded any one species special authority over other species. Thus, humans do not have the authority to destroy the environment at the expense of others, including their own species, in nature.

The Pṛthivī Sūkta maintains that attributes of the earth (such as its firmness, purity, and fertility) are for everyone, and that no one group or nation has special authority over it. That is why the welfare of all and hatred toward none constitute the core values for which people on this planet ought to strive (verse 18). For example, there is a prayer for the preservation of the original fragrance of the earth (verses 23 and 25) so that its natural legacy is sustained for future generations. There is also a prayer which says that even when people dig the earth, either for agricultural purposes or for extracting minerals, they should do so in such a way that her vitals are not hurt and that no serious damage is done to her body and appearance (verse 35).

The Pṛthivī Sūkta enunciates the unity of all races and among all beliefs; further religious, linguistic, and cultural harmony is urged, with a prayer that

Mother Earth bestow upon all the people living in any part of the world the same prosperity for which the *ṛṣi* Atharva of India has pleaded:

> Mother Earth, where people belong to different races, follow separate faiths and religions and speak numerous languages, cares for them in many ways. May that Mother Earth, like a Cosmic Cow, give us the thousandfold prosperity without any hesitation, without being outraged by our destructive actions.[10]

In verse 63 of this hymn, a prayer is offered to Mother Earth and her blessings are sought for all:

> O, our Mother Earth! May we possess the intellect and wisdom which enable us to speak in concord with heavenly beings, may we continue to enjoy your blessing of hidden riches, glory, and realization of material and spiritual well-beings.[11]

In summary, it can be said that the Pṛthivī Sūkta, whose sixty-three verses have been dedicated to Mother Earth, is the foremost ancient spiritual text from India, enjoining all human beings to protect, preserve, and care for the environment. This is beautifully illustrated in verse 16, which says that it is up to us, the progeny of Mother Earth, to live in peace and harmony with all others:

> O Mother Earth! You are the world for us and we are your children; let us speak in one accord, let us come together so that we live in peace and harmony, and let us be cordial and gracious in our relationship with other human beings.[12]

These sentiments denote the deep bond between the earth and human beings and exemplify the true relationship between the earth and all living beings, as well as between humans and other forms of life. The Sūkta guides us to behave in an appropriate manner toward nature and defines our duty toward the environment.

SARVA BHŪTA HITĀ, THE WELFARE OF ALL BEINGS

How is the welfare of all beings related to the Hindu view of life? As mentioned earlier, the prerequisite for understanding this concept in Hindu thinking is to accept the view that Brahman (the Supreme Being) is the ultimate source and cause of the universal common good, not only of humans but of all beings in creation. That common good, for Hindus, is the concept of *sarva-bhūta-hitā*, the highest ethical standard that Hindus ought to apply, according to their *dharma*. Further, the Hindu tradition requires that a common good (such as protection of the environment, welfare of the poor and needy, or the well-being of other living beings) takes precedence over a private good (including individual material and personal well-being). Under such a system, a dharmic citizen should act for *sarva-hitā:* enhancing the common good of all together. In other words, the term "common good" can be related to the concept of *sarva-kalyāṇkarī-karma,* which denotes a deed resulting in the common good of all. This also relates to the concept of "caring for others," meaning a deed (*karma*), which results in universal welfare based on mutual cooperation and respect. To reiterate, the question of *sarva-bhūta-hitā* care and taking care of the others or serving others, is entirely intertwined with the concept of dharmic ecology. It is an obligation that human beings owe, not only to each other, but also to all of nature and the entire cosmos.

The requisite duties and mode of conduct to perform *sarva-bhūta-hitā,* and to protect and sustain the common good, has been provided in Hindu scriptures. For example, this advice is given by Lord Kṛṣṇa in the *Gītā:*

> One ought to understand what is duty, and what is forbidden in the commands laid down by the scriptures [*śāstras*]. Knowing such rules and regulations, one should behave as ordained by scriptures.[13]

Lord Kṛṣṇa later says:

> O Partha! that understanding by which one knows what ought to be done and what ought not to be done, what is to be feared and what is not, what is obligatory and what is permitted, leads to the righteous path [*Sattvika Pravṛtti*].[14]

That righteous path in the Hindu religion is called *dharma*.

Dharma is one of the most intractable and unyielding terms in Hindu, Buddhist, and Jaina religions and philosophies. Instead of discussing the root and theological or philosophical definitions of the term, the author of the *Mahābhārata* goes directly to the common usage of the term:

> Dharma exists for the general welfare (*abhyudaya*) of all living beings; hence, that by which the *welfare* of all living creatures IS sustained, that for sure is *Dharma*.[15]

Thus, *dharma* can be considered an ethos, a set of duties, that holds the social and moral fabric together by maintaining order in society, building individual and group character, and giving rise to harmony and understanding in our relationships with all of God's creation.

Duty toward humanity and God's creation is an integral part of Hindu ecology and *dharma*. While all other species conduct themselves according to the *dharma* of their kind, only human beings, because of free will, think that they are very powerful and act in an adharmic manner. Such acts are to be avoided, as *ṛṣi* Markandeya says in the *Mahābhārata* during a conversation with the Pandavas:

> O king, all creatures act according to the laws of their specific species as laid down by the Creator. Therefore, none should act unrighteously (*adharma*), thinking, "It is I who is powerful."[16]

Dharma requires that one consider the entire universe an extended family, with all living beings in this universe members of the same household. This is also known as the concept of *vasudhaiv kuṭumbakam,* discussed above. Only by considering the entire universe as a part of one's extended family can one develop the necessary maturity and respect for all other living beings. The welfare and caring of all (*sarva-kalyānkarī-hitā*) is realized through the golden thread of spiritual understanding and cooperation.

Dharma can help us master our baser characteristics, such as our greed and our exploitation, abuse, mistreatment, and defilement of nature. Before we can hope to change the exploitative tendencies of society, it is absolutely essential that we discipline our own inner thoughts. This is where the role of *dharma* comes into play. It is important to appreciate that the concept of *dharma* can be used in any culture (although the term has become synonymous with the practices and rituals of Hinduism, Buddhism, and Jainism). *Dharma* in its pure form can be the mechanism that creates respect for nature, since it transcends institutional structures, bureaucratic impediments, and rituals associated with organized religions; it enables people to center their values upon the notion that there is a cosmic ordinance and a natural or divine law that must be maintained. *Dharma* thereby provides a code of conduct as well as a vision. It serves both as a model and an operative strategy for the transformation of human character. And, if the goal of transformation is to achieve an environmentally conscious and sustainable world, then *dharma's* precept that reward after death can be attained through actions in this world may provide the incentive for humanity to seek peace with nature.[17] The manifestation of *dharma* necessitates, however, the acceptance of the concept of *karma*.

Karma and the Environment

The term *karma* comes from the root *kṛ,* meaning "to do," and thus has a general connotation of "action," but in its broadest sense it applies also to the effects of such actions. People often confuse the law of *karma* with the law of destiny. This misunderstanding needs to be rectified because an appropriate understanding is essential to appreciate the use of this precept in Hindu and Buddhist ways of life. A brief definition of the law of *karma* is that each act, willfully performed, leaves a consequence in its wake. These consequences, also called *karma-phala* (fruits, or effects, or action), will always be with us, although their impact may not be felt immediately. Thus, the law related to *karma* tells us that every action performed creates its own chain of reactions and events, some of which are immediately visible, while others take time to surface. Environmental pollution is but one example of the *karma* of those people who thought that they could continue polluting the environment without realizing the consequences of their actions for future generations. For example, those who buried the toxic waste in Love Canal (near Niagara Falls, in New York State) thought that by concealing their actions, the problem would go away; instead it surfaced a few years later. Every action creates its own reaction. What is important to know is that a right action, that is a dharmic action, generates beneficial results, while an adharmic action results in harmful effects. It is not always easy to foresee the consequences of one's actions, but one should be ready either to overcome obstacles that arise or suffer the repercussions of one's actions.

Once *karma* has started, it continues without a break; even though a person may be dead, his or her *karma* survives in the form of a memory and carries over into the next life. This is stated in the *Mahābhārata:*

> An action, which has been committed by a human-being in this life, follows him again and again (whether he wishes it or not).[18]

Furthermore, it is stated in the *Brahmavaivarta Purāṇa* that whatever action, good or bad, is knowingly performed by a person, he or she must face its consequences.[19] Sometimes karmic justice is indecipherable to individuals, when an individual's family and later descendants are forced to pay for the past crimes and mistakes of that person. Bhīṣma acknowledges this to King Yudhiṣṭhira in the *Mahābhārata:*

> O king, although a particular person may not be seen suffering the results of his evil actions, yet his children and grandchildren as well as great-grandchildren will have to suffer them.[20]

Such suffering may continue to visit humanity unless we realize that the destruction we are inflicting on our natural surroundings will result in dire consequences for current and future generations. Only if we recognize and act on this philosophy of life will people start paying due respect to nature and taking active responsibility for the care of the environment. Understanding this is the key to the point being made here, and it draws on the concept that people living in any part of the world are our brothers and sisters. All of our actions are interrelated with and interconnected to what eventually happens in this world. Although we may not face the consequences individually, someone is going to be burdened by or benefit from our actions. It is in this context that the concepts of *dharma* and *karma* become meaningful.

Once our *dharma* and *karma* to the environment are appropriately understood, their precepts recognized, and their relevance to environmental protection and conservation accepted, then a common strategy for ecospirituality and stewardship can be developed. Such a strategy will depend much upon how different people together 1) perceive a common future for society; 2) act both individually and as a group toward that end; and 3) realize that each individual has a moral obligation to support his society's goal, since his acts will have repercussions on the future of society and on his own destiny.

TOWARD A DHARMIC ECOLOGY AND ENVIRONMENTAL STEWARDSHIP

Since the late 1980s, there has been a steadily growing awareness among the people of India about the ecological challenges facing their society. There has also been an impressive growth of regulatory and administrative institutions to deal with the problems of pollution and environmental conservation, at both national and state levels. At the same time the mounting pressures of population, expanding urbanization, and growing poverty have led to the ecologically unsustainable exploitation of natural resources that is threatening the fragile balance in India. The nation would do well to draw on its ecospirituality and rich cultural heritage as well as on traditional conservation practices, such as those preserved by the Bishnois.

A Hindu Strategy for Dharmic Ecology?

The effectiveness of any religion in protecting the environment depends upon how much faith its believers have in its precepts and injunctions. Its value also depends upon how those precepts are transmitted and adapted in everyday social interactions. In the case of the Hindu religion, some of its precepts became ingrained in the daily life and social institutions of a certain segment of the population. Two such examples illustrate this point.

The Bishnois, Defenders of the Environment: The Bishnois, a small community in the state of Rajasthan, practice environmental conservation as a part of their daily religious duty. They believe that cutting a tree or killing an animal or bird is sacrilege. Their religion, an offshoot of Hinduism, was founded by Guru Maharaj Jambaji, who was born in 1451 C.E. in the Marwar area. When he was young, he witnessed how, during a severe drought, people cut down trees to feed animals; when the drought continued, nothing was left to feed the animals, which resulted in their deaths. Jambaji thought that if trees were protected, animal life would be sustained, and his community would survive. So he formulated twenty-nine injunctions. Principal among them was a ban on the cutting of any green tree and killing of any animal or bird. His community accepted these injunctions. Over time, their geographic area developed into a lush dense forest with substantial trees. About three hundred years later, when the king of Jodhpur wanted to build a new palace, he sent his soldiers to the Bishnoi area to secure timber for it. Villagers protested, and when soldiers would not pay any attention to the protest, the Bishnois, led by a woman, encircled the trees in order to protect them with their bodies. The soldiers had orders to bring timber, so they began killing the villagers. As the soldiers continued, more and more of the Bishnois came forward to honor the religious injunction of their guru. Finally, when the king heard about this human sacrifice, he ordered his soldiers back to Jodhpur and gave the Bishnois state protection for their beliefs. Even today, the Bishnoi community continues to protect trees and animals in their area with the same zeal. Their dedication became the inspiration for the Chipko movement of 1973.

The Chipko Movement: In March 1973, in the town of Gopeshwar in Chamoli district, Uttar Pradesh, villagers formed a human chain and encircled earmarked trees to keep them from being felled for a nearby factory producing sports equipment. The same situation later occurred in another village, when forest contractors wanted to cut trees under license from the Government Department of Forests. Again, in 1974, women from the village of Reṇi, near Joshimath in the Himalayas, protested logging by hugging trees and forced the contractors to leave. Since then, the Chipko Andolan (movement) has continued to grow from a grassroots ecodevelopment movement.[21]

The genesis of the Chipko movement has its background not only in religious belief, but also in ecological or economic concerns. Villagers have noted how industrial and commercial demands have denuded their forests, how they cannot sustain their livelihood in a deforested area, and how floods continually play havoc with their small agricultural communities. Women, specifically, have seen how men tend not to mind destroying nature in order to get money, while they themselves have to walk miles in search of firewood and fodder or other suitable grazing. In a sense, the Chipko movement is a feminist movement to protect nature from the greed of men. In the Himalayan areas, the pivot of the family is the woman. It is the woman who worries most about nature and its conservation in order that its resources are available for her family's sustenance. On the other hand, men often go away to distant places in search of jobs, leaving the women, children, and elders behind.

These two examples are illustrative of the practical impact of Hinduism on environmental conservation, or dharmic ecology in action. The Bishnoi and Chipko experiences demonstrate that when appeals to secular norms fail, one can draw on cultural and religious sources for environmental conservation.

There is no doubt that Hindu religion and culture, in ancient and medieval times, has provided a system of moral guidelines for environmental preservation and conservation. Environmental ethics, as propounded by the ancient Hindu scriptures and seers, was practiced not only by common persons, but by rulers and kings. They observed these fundamentals, sometimes as religious duties, often as rules of administration or obligations for law and order, but always as principles properly entwined with the Hindu way of life. That way of life did enable Hindus as well as other religious groups residing in India to use natural resources but to have no divine powers of control and dominion over nature and its elements. The Hindu belief [*sic*] that so long as Mother Earth is able to sustain magnificent mountains, lush forests, streams and rivers, and related endowments, she will be able to nourish all, particularly the human race and its progeny. This is expressed in the following prayer to the goddess Durgā:

> So long as the earth is able to maintain mountains, forests, trees, etc., until then the human race and its progeny will be able to survive.[22]

If such has been the tradition, philosophy, and ideology of Hinduism, what then are the reasons behind the present environmental crisis facing India? As we have seen, Hindu ethical beliefs and religious values do influence people's behavior toward others, including our relationship with all creatures and plant life. If, for some reason, those noble values become displaced by other beliefs that are either thrust upon the society or transplanted from another culture through invasion, then the faith of the masses in the earlier cultural tradition is shaken. As appropriate answers and leadership are not provided by the religious leaders and priests, the masses become ritualistic, caste-ridden, and inward-looking. However, besides the influence of alien cultures and values, what has really damaged India's environment are the forces of materialism, consumerism, individualism, and corporate greed, the blind race to industrialize the nation immediately after achieving independence, and the capriciousness and corruption among forest contractors and ineffective enforcement by forest officials.[23] All these acted against the maintenance, or resurgence, of respect for nature in India. Under such circumstances, religious values that had acted as sanctions against environmental destruction were sidelined as insidious forces worked to inhibit the transmission of ancient values that encouraged respect and due regard for God's creation.

How can those ancient values and wisdom be transmitted into practice? Can there be a practical dharmic ecology? It is not sufficient to examine and extol the ancient wisdom of Hindu seers, to dwell on the Vedic heritage, and then simply hope that a self-correcting process for environmental problems will set in. What is more important is how to put into practice that ecocare vision and make it relevant to modern times. I would propose the following strategy. The Hindu religion and its followers should become effective advocates and practitioners of the concept of ecocare and dharmic ecology, rather than staying on the sidelines. Hindu religious leaders should: 1) take the initiative and help secular institutions by providing timely and appropriate advice to encourage greater integration of ecocare heritage into educational curricula; 2) strengthen the capability of secular institutions to meet their goals of sustainable development and environmental conservation; 3) promote the concept of *sarva-bhūta-hite ratāḥ* (to serve all beings equally); 4) take the lead in promoting the concept of *vasudhaiv kuṭumbakam,* the family of Mother Earth, and the obligation of humanity to accept a world of material limits; 5) protect and restore places of ecological, cultural, aesthetic, and spiritual significance; and 6) build partnerships across social, economic, political, and environmental sectors, including dialogue with other religions and spiritual traditions.[24] The choice before the Hindu religion (as well as before all other religions) is either to care for the environment or be a silent participant in the destruction of planetary resources. Partnership with secular institutions must be forged and cooperation fostered at local, regional, national, and international levels. An environmental and sustainable development strategy, based on the lines suggested above, could offer a way of bridging the gap and making the essential link between secular, scientific, and spiritual forces.

An environmental stewardship that draws upon the Hindu concept of *dharma* and *karma* to the environment can provide new ways of valuing and acting. It can promote policies for sustainable development and introduce environmental protection initiatives. *Dharma,* if globally manifested, will provide the values necessary for an environmentally caring world and will not advance economic growth at the cost of greed, poverty, inequality, and environmental degradation. There is an urgent need to instill in all people a respect for nature and to strengthen decision-making processes in favor of environmental protection. This must be the focal point for a new global consciousness in an environmentally caring world.

In summary, a new universal consciousness must be developed that believes in at least two dictums: "what we sow is what we reap" and "everything is connected to everything else"; and our inherent *dharma,* or obligation, is toward the environment. These two concepts are intertwined with a third: *sarva-bhūta-hite ratāḥ,* serve all beings equally. The Hindu religion, like other religions and spiritual traditions, has the capacity to move the individual toward the divine because of its belief in divinity in nature; thus, it is imperative that such an inherent capacity is strengthened to its ultimate end. To achieve this, we need a new paradigm of thought, a dharmic ecology, perhaps. By developing such a paradigm, drawing upon the concept of *dharma* and *karma,* and based on the notions of *vasudeva sarvam, vasudhaiv kuṭumbakam,* and *sarva-bhūta-hitā,* we may be able not only to sustain the present generation, but also to leave a healthy legacy for future generations. Can the Hindu religion take up this challenge and act upon it as an integral part of its conscious strategy and vision for a sustainable future?

NOTES

1. O. P. Dwivedi, *India's Environmental Policies, Programmes and Stewardship* (London: Macmillan, 1997), 21.

2. Bahūnāṃ janmanām ante jñanvān māṃ prapadyate,
Vāsudevaḥ sarvam iti sa mahātmā sudurlabhaḥ.
(*Bhagavadgītā* 7.19)

All translations are my own.

3. O. P. Dwivedi, "Vedic Heritage for Environmental Stewardship," *Worldviews: Environment, Culture and Religion* 1, no. 1 (April 1997): 25–36.

4. O. P. Dwivedi, B. N. Tiwari, and R. N. Tripathi, "Hindu Concept of Ecology and the Environmental Crisis," *Indian Journal of Public Administration* 30, no. 4 (January–March 1984): 33–67. We first presented this paper at the annual conference of the Canadian Asian Studies Association, University of British Columbia, Vancouver, 4 June 1983. When it appeared in the *Indian Journal of Public Administration,* it may have been the first such research paper to be published.

5. Pakṣi dagdhaḥ sudurbudhhe pāpātman sāmpratam vṛthā,
Vṛthā snānam vṛthā tirthaṃ vṛthā japtaṃ vṛthā hutaṃ.
(*Narasiṃha Purāṇa,* 13.44)

6. Bijaiyarjñesu yaṣṭyyamiti vai vadikī śruti
Aj sanjñani bijani cchāgan no hantumarhatha
Naiṣadharmaḥsatāmdevāyatravadhyetavaipasuḥ
Idaṃ kṛtayugaṃ śreṣṭhaṃ kathaṃ vadhyeta vai pasuḥ.
(*Mahābhārata,* Santiparva, Moksadharma, 337.4–5)

7. O. P. Dwivedi, *Vasudhaiv Kutumbakam: A Commentary on Atharvediya Prithivi Sukta,* 2d ed. (Jaipur: Institute for Research and Advanced Studies, 1998).

8. Giryaste parvatā hima vanto raṇyaṃ te pṛthivī syonamastu
Babhrum kṛushṇaṃ rohīṇīm vishvarūpāṃ dhruvaṃ bhūmiṃ pṛithivī mindraguptāṃ
Ajītohato akṣhatoadhyathāṃ pṛithivīmaham.
(*Atharva Veda,* Kanda 12, hymn 1, verse 11)

9. Dwivedi, *Vasudhaiv Kutumbakam.*

10. Janaṃ bibhratī bahudhā vivācasaṃ nāndharmāṇaṃ pṛithivī yathaukasaṃ
Shastraṃ dhārāḥ draviṇasya me duhāṃ dhruveva dhenurana pasphurantī.
(*Atharva Veda,* Kanda 12, hymn 1, verse 45)

11. Bhūme mātarni dhehi bhadrayā supratisthitam
Saṃvidana divā kave shṛiyā mā dhehi bhūtyām.
(*Atharva Veda,* Kanda 12, hymn 1, verse 63)

12. Tā naḥ prajāḥ saṃ duhatāṃ samagrā vacho madhu pṛithivi dhehi mahyaṃ.
(*Atharva Veda,* Kanda 12, hymn 1, verse 16)

13. Tasmāc chāstraṃ pramāṇaṃ te kāryākāryavyavasthitau
Jñatvā shāstra vidhānoktaṃ karma kartum ihārhasi.
(*Gītā* 16.24)

14. Pravṛttiṃ ca nivṛttim ca kāryākārye bhayābhaye
Bandhaṃ mokṣaṃ ca yā vetti buddhiḥ sā Pārtha sāttvikī.
(*Gītā* 18.30)

15. Prabhavārthaya bhūtānām dharma pravacanaṃ kṛtaṃ
Yahasyāt prabhav saṁyuktaṃ sa dharma iti niścayaḥ.
(*Mahābhārata,* Shanti Parva, chapter 109, verse 10)

16. Sarvāni bhūāni Narendra paśya tatha yathāvad vihitaṃ vidhātra
Svayonitaḥ karma sadā caranti neśe balasyeti cared dharmaṃ.
(*Mahābhārata,* Vanaparva, chapter 25, verse 16)

17. O. P. Dwivedi, "Our Karma and Dharma to the Environment," in *Environmental Stewardship: History, Theory, and Practice,* ed. Mary Ann Beavis, 59–74 (Winnipeg: Institute of Urban Studies, University of Winnipeg, 1994).

18. Yesāṃ ye yāni karmāṇi prak sṛiṣṭyam pratipedire
Tāny eva pratipādyante sṛigyamānāḥ punaḥ punaḥ.
(*Mahābhārata,* Shanti Parva, chapter 232, verse 16)

19. Na Bhuktam Kṣīyate Karma Kalpa koṭiṣtairapi
Avaśyamaiva bhoktavyam kṛtam karma śubha ā subhaṃ.
(*Brahmavaivarta Purāṇa,* Prakṛti. 37.16)

20. Pāpaṃ karma kṛtam kiṃcid yadi ṭasmin na dṛśyate
Nṛpate tasya putreṣu pautreṣu api ca naptriṣu.
(*Mahābhārata,* Shanti Parva, chapter 139, verse 22)

21. Chandi Prasad Bhatt, "Chipko Movement: The Hug That Saves," in *The Hindu Survey of the Environment, 1991* (Madras: The Hindu, National Press, 1991), 17.

22. Yāvadbhūmaṇḍalaṃ dhatte sāsailvavana kānanaṃ,
Tāvat tiṣṭhati medinyaṃ śāntātiḥ putrapautrikī.
(*Durgā Saptaśati,* Devi kavacham, verse 54)

23. Ashish Kothari, "Forest Bill: Old Wine in a New Bottle," in *The Hindu Survey of the Environment, 1995* (Madras: The Hindu, National Press, 1995), 51–54.

24. Dwivedi, *India's Environmental Policies, Programmes and Stewardship.*

Water, Wood, and Wisdom
Ecological Perspectives from the Hindu Traditions

VASUDHA NARAYANAN

From the cradle that is a baby's first bed to the cremation pyre that is the last resting place for the body in many Hindu traditions, wood is an integral part of Hindu lives. From home hearths to religious sacraments, wood and fire are conspicuously present. Hindu weddings take place in front of a sacred fire that is considered to be an eternal witness; at death, the bodies are consigned to the fire.

The ashes of the cremated body are immersed in holy waters—the same rivers that feed and irrigate paddy fields; the same water that cooks the rice and bathes the dead before cremation. From cradle to cremation, Hindus have long had a palpable, organic connection with nature. But today they must also face the reality of environmental disaster. With the population hovering around a billion in India (with eight hundred million Hindus), the use, abuse, and misuse of resources is placing India on the fast track to disaster. What, if anything, can Hindu tradition say about this looming environmental crisis? Are there any resources in the Hindu religious and cultural traditions that can inspire and motivate Hindus to take action?[1]

While in the Western world one has to argue for the significance and relevance of religion in everyday life, in India the interest and involvement in religion is tangible; religious symbols are ubiquitous. The traditional mantra heard among Hindus, "Hinduism is more than a religion; it is a way of life," is more than a trite saying. There is a deep relationship between religion and ingrained social structures and behavioral patterns. The characters featured in the various Puranas, or ancient texts about the Hindu deities, are known and loved by the masses. People never seem to tire of these stories. Only vernacular cinema seems to rival the epic and Puranic narratives in popular influence.

But do the many Hindu philosophies and communities value nature and privilege the existence of plants, trees, and water? Although the short answer is "yes," Hindus have answered this question in many different ways that have been documented in excellent texts.[2] Plants and trees are valued so highly in Hindu sacred texts that their destruction is connected with doomsday scenarios. The Puranas and epics such as the *Ramayana* and the *Mahabharata* give detailed narratives of the periodic and cyclic destruction of the world. There are four aeons in each cycle, and by the beginning of the third aeon, things are perceptibly going awry. As the *Kurma Purana* puts it, "then greed and passion arose again everywhere, inevitably, due to the predestined purpose of the Treta [Third] Age. And people seized the rivers, fields, mountains, clumps of trees and herbs, overcoming them by strength." [3] The epic *Mahabharata* (c. 500–200 B.C.E.) graphically depicts the events at the end of the fourth—and worst—aeon, and what happens after a thousand such aeons:

> At the end of the Eon the population increases . . . and odor becomes stench, and flavors putrid. . . . When the close of the thousand Aeons has come and life has been spent, there befalls a drought of many years that drives most of the creatures, of *dwindling reserves* and starving to their death. . . . The Fire of Annihilation then invades . . . [and] burns down all that is found on earth. . . . Wondrous looking huge clouds rise up in the sky. . . . At the end of time all men—there is no doubt—will be omnivorous barbarians. . . . All people will be naturally cruel. . . . Without concern *they will destroy parks and trees* and the lives of living will be ruined in the world. Slaves of greed they will roam this earth. . . . All countries will equally suffer from drought. . . . [It] will

Narayanan, Vasudha, "Water, Wood and Wisdom: Ecological Perspectives from the Hindu Traditions," *Daedalus* 130/4 (2001), pp. 179–206. Reprinted by permission of *Daedalus*, Journal of the American Academy of Arts and Sciences, from the issue titled, "Religion and Ecology: Can the Climate Change?"

> not rain in season, and the crops will not grow, when the end of the Eon is at hand.[4]

What we note almost immediately is that these destructions are portrayed as cyclical and periodic. The first quotation about the third aeon evokes the inevitable, predestined nature of such events. One wonders if human beings are powerless against such cosmic configurations. But even if we were to take these epics seriously, we have quite a while to wait. According to very conservative Hindu almanacs and reckoning, the end of *this* aeon—the fourth—is not expected before 428,898 C.E.

We also notice in the Hindu texts a close correlation between *dharma* (righteousness, duty, justice; from *dhr*, or that which sustains) and the ravaging of Earth. When *dharma* declines, human beings despoil nature. There is, however, no Hindu text focusing on *dharma* that advises us to be passive and accept the end of the world with a life-negating philosophy. Many Hindu texts are firm in their view that human beings must enhance the quality of life. A popular blessing uttered in many Hindu temples and homes focuses on human happiness in this life, on this earth: "May everyone be happy, may everyone be free of diseases! / May everyone see what is noble / May no one suffer from misery!"

Despite this unequivocal ratification of the pursuit of happiness, Hindus of every stripe have participated in polluting the environment. In this essay, we will look at the resources and limitations within the many Hindu traditions to see how the problem of ecology has been addressed. Before we look at these resources, a few caveats and qualifications are in order.

The first important issue to be aware of is that there are many Hindu traditions, and there is no single book that all Hindus would agree on as authoritative. In this essay, I will cite many texts from a spectrum of sources. The second point to note is that the many texts within Hindu traditions have played a limited role in the *history* of the religion. Although works like the *Ramayana*, the *Mahabharata*, and the many Puranas have been generally influential, philosophical works like the Upanishads are not well known by the masses. The texts on right behavior (*dharma shastras*) have been only selectively followed, and popular practice or custom has had as much weight as religious law. All these texts, along with Puranic and epic narratives, have been the carriers and transmitters of *dharma* and devotion (*bhakti*).

Dharma is all-important in Hindu communities, but the texts that define and discuss *dharma* were known only by a handful of Brahman men. Instead, notions of *dharma* were communicated through stories from the epics and Puranas, and such moral tales were routinely retold by family or village elders. Like Aesop's fables—or MTV today—these narratives shaped notions of morality and acceptable behavior. The exaggerated reliance on texts of law is a later development and can be traced to the period of colonization by the British.[5] With the intellectual colonization by the West and the advent of mass media, Hindus today, especially in the diaspora, think of texts alone—rather than oral tradition or community customs—as authoritative. Many Hindu temples in India now hold classes and study circles on the *Bhagavadgita* ("the Song of the Lord"; a text composed circa second century B.C.E. that is part of the epic *Mahabharata*). The Ramakrishna and Chinmaya missions publish theological books and tapes with translations and commentaries to explain their canonic texts to an educated middle-class public.

Finally, I do not speak about these resources for anyone except those who in some manner belong to one of the Hindu traditions. Gerald Larson has alerted us to the dangers of indiscriminate use of philosophical texts as a generic resource for environmental philosophy, and one has to be mindful of these warnings.[6] Still, given the increasing popularity of sacred texts among many sectors of Hindu society in the late twentieth century, I feel comfortable in using many Hindu texts as resources in this essay. We will see shortly that some Hindu institutions are citing esoteric passages on *dharma* from sacred texts in order to raise the consciousness of people about contemporary social issues. The regulation of *dharma* with a dual emphasis on text and practice has given it a flexibility that we can use to our advantage today.

The resources from which the Hindu traditions can draw in approaching environmental problems are several and diverse: there are texts, of course, but also temples and teachers. Hindu sacred texts starting with the Vedas (c. 1750–600 B.C.E.) speak extensively about the sanctity of the earth, the rivers, and the mountains. The texts on *dharma* earnestly exhort people to practice nonviolence toward all beings; other texts speak of the joys of a harmonious relationship with nature. Temples are large economic centers with endowments of millions. Many have had clout for over a millennium; devotees, pilgrims, and politicians (especially after an election) donate liberally to these centers. Finally, there are gurus. Teachers like Sathya Sai Baba can influence millions of devotees around the world and divert enormous resources to various projects.

These vast and varied religious resources can undoubtedly be used to raise people's consciousness about environmental problems. In this essay, I will explore some of the resources in the Hindu traditions that may be relevant to the environmental crisis, discuss a few cases of environmental mobilization that have sprung from religious sensibilities, and finally assess some of the other strands in the Hindu traditions that often impede the translation of philosophies into action.

THE NARRATIVE, RITUAL, AND PHILOSOPHICAL TRADITIONS

In most Hindu traditions, Earth is to be revered, for she is our mother. Mother Earth, known by one of her several names (Bhu, Bhumi, Prithvi, Vasudha, Vasundhara, Avni) is considered to be a *devi,* or a goddess. She is seen in many temples together with Lord Vishnu ("all-pervasive") in South India and is worshiped as his consort. She is to be honored and respected; classical dancers, after pounding on the ground during a concert, touch the earth reverentially to express their esteem for the earth. The earliest sacred texts, the Vedas, have inspiring hymns addressed to Earth.[7]

The ethical texts have many injunctions that are directly relevant to environmental problems. Many of them stress the importance of nonviolence toward *all* creatures. Nonviolence in thought, word, and deed is considered to be the highest of all forms of righteousness, or *dharma.*[8] Normative nonviolence, if followed, would inevitably promote biodiversity.

Nor are other, more specific, ethical injunctions lacking in Hindu traditions. Manu, the law giver, said around the beginning of the Common Era, "Impure objects like urine, feces, spit; or anything which has these elements, blood, or poison should not be cast into water."[9]

Ritual and devotional resources that privilege the natural environment abound in the Hindu tradition. The protection of groves and gardens, as well as pilgrimage to sacred and pure places, is recommended by some Hindu communities and mandated by others. The Puranas and the epics mention specific places in India as holy and charged with power. Many Hindu texts say that if one lives or dies in the holy precincts of a sacred place, one is automatically granted supreme liberation. There are lists of such cities and villages. Many lists are regional, but some are pan-Indian and span the subcontinent, creating networks of sacred spaces and consolidating the various Hindu communities.

In the time of the *dharma shastras* around the beginning of the Common Era, the description of the sacrality of the land was confined to the northern part of India. Manu says:

> That land, created by the gods, which lies between the two divine rivers Sarasvati and Drishadvati [is] . . . Brahmavarta. . . .
>
> . . . the tract between those two mountains which extends between the eastern and western oceans, the wise call Aryavarta (the country of the noble ones).
>
> The land where the black antelope naturally roams, one must know to be fit for the performance of sacrifices; [this land] is different from the country of the barbarians.[10]

Later, the sacred lands were extended beyond the land between the Himalaya and Vindhya mountains to cover the whole subcontinent.

More recently, India personified as the mother (Bharata Mata) has been important in political thinking. Mayuram Viswanatha Sastri (1893–1958), a musician who participated in the struggle to free India from colonial rule, composed a song popular among all South Indian classical singers, called "Victory, Victory to Mother India" (*jayati jayati bharata mata*). In this and many such songs, India is personified and extolled as a compassionate mother-goddess filled with forests, filled with sanctity that should not be violated.

While India is personified as a mother and considered holy, most Hindus localize the sanctity and go regularly to the regional temple or a sacred place that has been important to their families for generations. The whole town surrounding any temple is said to be sacred. Every tree, every stream near the precincts of the temple exudes this sense of sacredness. Bathing in the sea, river, stream, or pond of water near the temple is said to grant salvation. Hindus are beginning to use these notions of sacrality and rituals of pilgrimage as one inspiration for ecological cleanups.[11]

The philosophical visions of the various Hindu traditions portray the earth, the universe, and nature in many exalted ways. Nature is sacred; for some schools, this Prakriti ("nature," sometimes translated as "cosmic matter") is divine immanence and has potential power. These links have been explored in a quest for indigenous paths to solving the environmental crisis.[12] In a related way, the five elements of nature—earth, water, fire ether/space, and air—are sacred. Rivers are particularly revered.[13] The philosophical images of Prakriti are often awe-inspiring. Consider just one of these images: central to the *Bhagavadgita* is the vision of the universe as the body of Krishna, an incarnation of Vishnu. While the first consequence of this vision in its narrative context is to convince the warrior Arjuna of the supremacy of God, many theologians, including Ramanuja (traditional dates 1017–1137), have understood these passages, as well as several in the Upanishads, as depicting the correct relationship between the Supreme Being and creation. Ramanuja and his followers equally emphasize the immanence and the transcendence of the Supreme Being. The elaboration of this philosophy is found in the many texts of Ramanuja's disciples, the members of the Sri-Vaishnava community.[14]

According to Ramanuja, the universe, composed of sentient matter (*chit*) and nonsentient matter (*achit*), forms the body (*sarira*) of the Vishnu. Just as a human soul (*chit*) pervades a nonsentient body (*achit*), so, too, does Vishnu pervade all souls, the material universe, and time. The name Vishnu, in fact, means "all pervasive." Vishnu-Narayana is inseparable from Sri-Lakshmi, the Goddess. According to the Sri Vaishnava theologian Vedanta Desika (1268–1368), both Vishnu and Sri pervade the universe together; the universe is their body. It is important to note that in this philosophy, it is *not* the case that the material universe is female and the transcendent god is male; together, the male and female deities create and pervade the universe, and yet transcend it. We—as part of the universe—are the body of Vishnu and Sri; we are owned by them and are supported by them. Vishnu is the personal name given to the Supreme Being, or Brahman; the two are identical. In his famous work *Summary of the Teachings of the Veda (Vedartha Sangraha),* Ramanuja says that Brahman is purity, bliss, and knowledge. The sentient and nonsentient beings form the body of Brahman. Before creation, they are undifferentiated in name and form from Brahman. By the will of the Supreme Being it becomes manifest as the limitless and diversified world of moving and nonmoving beings. At any given time, therefore, the universe is one with this Brahman, both before and after creation.[15]

All of creation has the Supreme Being as its soul, its inner controller and support. All physical forms have Brahman or the Supreme Being as their ultimate Self or soul. Ramanuja makes this identification clear through a process of "signification," or pointing:

> Therefore all terms like gods, men, yaksa [a celestial being], demon, beast, bird, tree, creeper, wood, stone, grass, jar and cloth, which have denotative power, formed of roots and suffixes, signify the objects which they name in ordinary parlance and through them they signify the individual selves embodied in them and through this second signification, their significance develops further till it culminates in Brahman, the highest Self dwelling as the inner controller of all individual selves. Thus all terms are denotative of this totality.[16]

While Ramanuja's argument is based on language and grammar in this passage, he argues for the reality of all of creation and its divinity based on scriptural passages. The reality of all of creation is pulsating with divinity. This vision of organic connection between the Supreme Being and all other created beings invites us to look at the world with wonder and respect. If the entire universe is divine, how can we bring ourselves to pollute it? Ramanuja's is only one of the many philosophical visions of the universe that has bearing on the ecological enterprise.

ONE TREE IS EQUAL TO TEN SONS: *DHARMA* AND *ARTHA* TEXTS AND PRACTICES AS RESOURCES FOR ECOLOGY

The many texts that focus explicitly on *dharma,* or righteous behavior, were composed in the first few centuries of the Common Era. In addition to these, many sections of the epics *Ramayana* and *Mahabharata* and the Puranas are also focused on *dharma*. Other scriptures have encouraged the planting of trees, condemned the destruction of plants and forests, and said that trees are like children.

In this context, a passage from the *Matsya Puranam* is instructive. The goddess Parvati planted a sapling of the Asoka tree and took good care of it. She watered it, and it grew well. The divine beings and sages came and told her: "O [Goddess] . . . almost everyone wants children. When people see their children and grandchildren, they feel they have been successful. What do you achieve by creating and rearing trees like sons . . . ? Parvati replied: "One who digs a well where there is little water lives in heaven for as many years as there are drops of water in it. One large reservoir of water is worth ten wells. One son is like ten reservoirs and one tree is equal to ten sons (*dasa putra samo druma*). This is my standard and I will protect the universe to safeguard it. . . ."[17]

The words of Parvati are relevant today. Trees offer more than aesthetic pleasure, shade, and fruit. They are vital to maintain our ecosystem, our planet, our well-being, and Parvati extols them by saying they are comparable to ten sons. The main Puranas, texts of myth and lore, composed approximately between the fifth and tenth century C.E., have wonderful passages on trees. The *Varaha Purana* says that one who plants five mango trees does not go to hell, and the *Vishnu Dharmottara* (3.297.13) claims that one who plants a tree will never fall into hell.[18] The *Puranas* differ in the number and description of hells in the universe, and one may perhaps take the liberty of interpreting "hell" as symbolic of various levels of suffering, including a steamy planet where we keep poking holes in the ozone layer. The *Matsya Purana* also describes a celebration for planting trees and calls it the "festival of trees."[19]

Just as the planting of trees was recommended and celebrated, cutting them was condemned by almost all the *dharma shastras*. Kautilya's *Arthashastra* (c. fourth century B.C.E.) prescribes varying levels of fines for those who destroy trees, groves, and forests. Kautilya says:

> For cutting off the tender sprouts of fruit trees, flower trees or shady trees in the parks near a city, a fine of 6 panas shall be imposed; for cutting off the minor branches of the same trees, 12 panas, and for cutting off the big branches, 24 panas shall be levied. Cutting off the trunks of the same shall be punished [with a fine between 48–96 panas]; and felling of the same shall be punished with [a fine between 200–500 panas]. . . . For similar offenses committed in connection with the trees which mark boundaries, or which are worshipped . . . double the above fines shall be levied.[20]

Despite these exhortations, the twentieth century has seen a massive destruction of trees. In the deforestation that has occurred in the Himalayas and in the Narmada basin, there has been a tragic transgression of *dharma*. Temples are now in the forefront of reforestation movements, urging devotees to plant saplings.

We have looked at some of the narrative, ritual, philosophical, and ethical resources in the Hindu traditions that could help us fashion a respectful and reciprocal relationship with the natural world. We know that the environmental problems facing India are tremendous, but there is also no doubt that religion is a potential resource for raising people's consciousness about these problems. Of course, Hindus, like people of other faiths, have been delightfully selective in the ways in which they have used scripture, practices, and modern technology. Pointing out the scriptural resources does not mean they will be incorporated into an effective worldview. In what follows, I will therefore examine more closely how specific Hindu groups have successfully used particular Hindu beliefs and texts to encourage eco-friendly actions.

"Trees, When Protected, Protect Us"

Many of the stories and narratives in Hindu texts focus on the value of trees and plants. One of the most successful attempts at reforestation in recent years has been through the initiative of the large temple at Tirumala-Tirupati. Billboards with statements like "A tree protects: Let us protect it" or "Trees, when protected, protect us" greet visitors to the sacred pilgrimage town of Tirumala-Tirupati, in Andhra Pradesh, South India. The statement is obviously adapted from the Laws of Manu, which say that *dharma*, or righteousness, when protected, protects us.

In response to the ecological crisis in India, the Venkateswara ("Lord of Venkata Hills," a manifestation of Lord Vishnu) temple at Tirumala-Tirupati began what is called the *Vriksha* ("tree") *Prasada* ("favor") scheme. Whenever a pilgrim visits a temple in India, he or she is given a piece of blessed fruit or food to take home. This is called a *prasada* or "favor" of the deity. Some temples in India are known for their preparation of sweets; the Tirupati temple, for instance, is well known for making and selling *laddus,* a confection the shape and size of a tennis ball. Although small quantities of *prasada* in most temples are free, *laddus* are also sold for a small fee. Approximately 80,000 to 125,000 are sold daily by the temple kitchens.[21] Ingesting *prasada* is a devotional and mandatory ritual; by eating what is favored and blessed by the deity, divine grace is said to course through one's body. The Tirumala-Tirupati temple, which is located at an elevation of 3,000 feet, was once surrounded by heavy forests. In an effort to honor the beauty of its original setting, the temple has established a large nursery and encourages pilgrims to take home tree saplings as *prasada*. This temple is the richest shrine in India and carries with it a great deal of *dharmic* and financial clout, both in India and with the "NRI" ("non-Resident-Indian") temples of Hindus in the diaspora. The wealth of the temple is legendary; in 1996, the reported annual income was upward of U.S. $35.6 million a year. This does not include the gold and silver contributions (around 300 kgs of gold and 1,880 kgs of silver in 1996) or the income from investments. This temple has about 12 major temples under its care, and its initiatives are emulated elsewhere.

The plants sold as *prasada* are inexpensive; they cost about the equivalent of five cents each. The saplings cultivated are suitable for the soil in various parts of India, and by planting them at home one can have a piece of the sacred place of Tirumala wherever one lives. At the same time, officials at the temple have since 1981 run a "bioaesthetic" program under the name of Sri Venkateswara Vanabhivriddhi. In this program, a devotee donates money for the purchase and planting of trees and plants. The donor is honored by being granted special *darshan* (viewing of the deity in the inner shrine), accommodations on Tirumala (normally very hard to get), and public acknowledgment of the gift (strategically placed boards list the names of donors and the amount of their donations). This initiative has apparently been successful: over 2,500,000 indigenous trees are said to have been planted on India's hills and plains.[22]

Sacred Trees in Temples

Almost every temple in South India dedicated to the gods Shiva or Vishnu, or to a manifestation of the goddess, has a *sthala vriksha,* a special tree regarded as sacred to that area. This "official" tree is usually a grand old specimen, surrounded by a path used for circumambulation by pilgrims and devotees. The *sthala vriksha* symbolizes all trees and reminds pilgrims that all trees are worthy of respect.

The Trees of Badrinath. Badrinath, a major pilgrimage center in the Himalayas, was a victim of overuse. A handful of pilgrims would go to the temple, high in the forested mountains. Located at 3,130 meters, it used to be surrounded by heavy forests. Now, with new roads, over 400,000 pilgrims visit the temple every year. Through the joint efforts of the director of the G. B. Pant Institute of India's Himalayan Environment and Development, the chief priest of the temple, and the residents of the town, thousands of trees were planted in 1993. The Institute supplied the plants; the priest blessed them and urged the pilgrims to plant the trees as a sign of religious devotion. The priest told the story of how the Goddess Ganga (the river) would not come to Earth until Lord Shiva promised to break her fall. Shiva's matted hair contained her and she did not flood the plains. The priest likened the forests to the matted hair of Shiva. The trees are now cut; in summer the Ganga floods the land and landslides destroy the local villages. The priest urged the pilgrims: "Plant these seedlings for Lord Shiva; you will restore his hair and protect the land." The religious leader who supervised the planting efforts said that "We all have a duty to plant trees: they give shade and inspire meditation." And the village headman remarked, "These are sacred trees that we will do our best to protect."

Many of the plants died during the winter that followed. In response, the G. B. Pant Institute established a nursery at Hanumanchatti to acclimatize seedlings. It also designed special metal covers to prevent snow from breaking the soft tips of the plants. Scientists determined the most promising native trees for planting and preserving biodiversity—Himalayan birch, oak, maple, spruce, and juniper, as well as other species. As a consequence, survival rates improved dramatically, and some plants have reached a height of two meters.[23]

The Paradise of Vrindavana. Vrindavan, the pastoral home of Lord Krishna in the Puranas, is the site of major environmental initiatives.[24] The International Society of Krishna Consciousness (ISKCON) is working with the World Wide Fund for Nature (WWF), Eco-corps, and Environ, a U.K.-based agency, to plant trees, clean the holy Yamuna River, and stop the dumping of toxic waste in the area. The World Vaisnava Association is actively involved in this project. The "patron saint," as it were, is Balarama, the elder brother of Krishna. Many of the unemployed young people now work with BAL (Balaram Eco Sena, or the Ecological Army of Balaram). Organizers have urged the local population to join the movement, telling them the Lord Balaram "is calling every one of us for Dham Seva (service to the holy land)."[25] As we see in the story of Vrindavana, it is not just trees and groves but also the mighty rivers of India that are considered to be sacred.

Rivers: Physically Polluted Moral Purifiers

By bathing in the great rivers of India, one is said to be morally cleansed of sins *and* to acquire merit or auspiciousness. A story popular in oral tradition makes the point: A king goes to sleep on the banks of the River Ganga. When he wakes up in the middle of the night, he sees some women covered in filth taking a dip in the holy river. They emerge from the river cleansed and then disappear. The king returns on several nights and sees the same thing. Eventually he asks them who they are; they reply that they are the embodiments of the rivers of India. Every day, they tell him, human beings bathe in the rivers and their sins are absolved by that act. The rivers—embodied as women—absorb the moral dirt and then come to the Ganga, the grand purifier, to purify themselves. Variations on the story describe where the Ganga goes to get herself purified, although it is generally assumed that she needs no purification.[26]

The generic version of the story distinguishes between two kinds of dirt. Moral dirt or sin, known as *papa* in Sanskrit, is perceptible as physical dirt in the bodies of the river. The story, therefore, makes a direct connection between morality and physical pollution. In addition to moral purity and physical purity, one may also note that in other Hindu contexts there is a third kind of purity: ritual purity.[27] Bathing in rivers and other bodies of water ritually purifies the pilgrim and his or her clothes. Ritual purity encompasses physical purity, but all that is physically clean is not ritually pure.[28] Even if a person is physically and ritually clean, the mere association with people and garb deemed ritually unclean or impure may be contagious enough to "pollute" him or her.

Given the pollution of India's rivers, the traditional story about the River Ganga and the need of other rivers to purify themselves in its waters is particularly poignant. Rapid industrialization has produced dangerous levels of toxic waste in many of India's rivers. The sacred rivers are often being used as latrines, despite the injunctions in the *dharma* texts against such a practice. The rivers that are to supposed to purify stand stagnant, reflecting the rancid countenance of *adharma,* unrighteous behavior.

Veer Bhadra Mishra, a priest and engineer, works to keep his "Mother Ganga" free from more pollution. A *mahant* (spiritual and administrative head) of the second-largest temple in Varanasi, he educates people on why and how the holy River Ganges should be kept free of bacterial pollution. He notes that corpses, not quite burnt from the funeral pyre, are dropped into the Ganga. "These people," says Mishra bitterly, "are trying to kill my Mother."[29] Mishra avers that there is a saying that Ganges grants us salvation; he added: "this culture will end if the people stop going to the river, and if the culture dies, the tradition dies, and the faith dies." It has been observed that "Mishra's blend of culture tradition and faith with science and technology could be what ultimately saves the Ganges."[30]

Devotion and law have also come together in the saving of the Yamuna River. The Yamuna River is one of the most sacred in India, beloved for its close association with the life of Krishna. When Krishna was born, his father carried him across the river to a place of safety; growing up on the banks of this river, Krishna played with the cowherd girls and stole their clothes while they were bathing in the river. It was on the banks of the Yamuna that he played his magic flute and danced through the moonlit nights. And yet this is today one of the most polluted rivers in India, with tons of industrial dyes, sewage, and other pollutants being dumped into the sacred waters. Gopishwar Nath Chaturvedi, a traditional ritual leader for pilgrims and a resident of Mathura (the birthplace of Lord Krishna), has taken the lead in trying to save the river. Leading a group of pilgrims to the river for a ritual bath in 1985, he saw the water colored red and green from industrial dyes that had been dumped from the nearby mills. Dead fish covered the ground, and birds were picking at their flesh. This scene struck him as a desecration of his mother, the river Yamuna. Since then, Chaturvedi has been working to "save his mother" by filing several "Public Interest Litigation" (PIL) briefs in the Allahabad High Court. The legal counsel in these cases was M. C. Mehta, an attorney who has been at the forefront of cases dealing with the environment. After the court found in Sri Chaturvedi's favor, an Additional District Magistrate was appointed in Mathura to implement the court decision.[31]

One may also reflect briefly on the gender of the rivers. Though there are some exceptions, most of the rivers of India are considered to be female, while mountains are generally male. Rivers are perceived to be nurturing (and sometimes judgmental) mothers, feeding, nourishing, quenching, and when angered flooding the earth. Rivers are also personified as deities; Ganga is sometimes portrayed as a consort of Lord Shiva. In the plains of Tamilnadu, Kaveri Amman (Mother Kaveri) is seen as a devotee and sometimes the consort of Lord Vishnu, and several temples (like Terazhundur, near Kumbakonam) have a striking image of this personified river in the innermost shrine. In the pre-eighth-century Vishnu temple at Tirucherai, a small village near Kumbakonam, the River Kaveri is seen as in a maternal posture with a child on her lap. When the Kaveri is swollen after the early monsoon rains, I have heard the residents of Srirangam (a large temple town on an island in the middle of the river) say she was pregnant. This is a wonderful celebration of her life-giving potential: the surging river, rich with the monsoon waters, sweeps into the plains, watering the newly planted crops in the Thanjavur delta, and giving birth to the food that will nourish the population. On the feast of *patinettam perukku,* the eighteenth day in the Tamil month of *Adi* (July 15–August 14), all those who live on the banks of Kaveri in the Tamilnadu celebrate the river's "pregnancy food cravings." They take a picnic to the banks of the river and eat there; Kaveri Amman is the guest at every picnic. Just as the food cravings of pregnant women are indulged by the family, Kaveri Amman's extended family celebrates her life-giving potential by picnicking with her. In some families, the oldest woman of the family "[leads] the festival and [throws] a handful of colored rices to satisfy the *macakkai* [food cravings during pregnancy] of the swiftly flowing Kaveri . . . as she hastened to the Lord's house."[32] According to oral tradition and local *sthala puranams* (pamphlets that glorify a sacred place), bathing in the river Kaveri during a specific month of the year (generally held to be the Tamil month of *Aippasi,* October 15–November 14) washes away one's sins and gives a human being supreme liberation. Thus, according to some Hindu traditions, only Lord Vishnu or Mother Kaveri can give one both nourishment and salvation.

Women and Ecology

The despoliation of rivers in recent years is sometimes compared to the denigration of women at various times in many civilizations. In India, the situation is complicated; there have been powerful women whose names are known as poets, patrons, performers, and philosophers; on the other hand, there have also been some androcentric texts and practices in which the lot of women has not been good. Although one cannot make a general statement that women have been dominated by men in the history of the Hindu tradition and that this corresponds to man's domination of nature (as is seen in many ecofeminist studies), it is hard not to draw a comparison between the rivers and the plight of women who are the target of crimes of greed and power.

At the same time, a number of Indian women have become active around ecological issues. In many parts of India, women are involved in the Chipko movement, which promotes the protection of trees.[33] Women are also involved in communicating the tragedy of ecological disasters, sometimes using such art forms as Bharata Natyam, a traditional Indian dance. The theory and practice of classical dance in India (*natya shastra*) is seen as a religious activity. In other words, dance—indeed, most performing arts—is a path to salvation within some Hindu traditions. Mallika Sarabhai, a noted dancer and feminist communicator, presents the story of the Chipko (or "tree-hugging") movement in her dances entitled *Shakti: The Power of Women.*

Sujatha Vijayaraghavan's compositions on ecological themes are choreographed by Rhadha, a well-known dance teacher in Channai, and regularly performed by Suchitra Nitin and Sunanda Narayanan. One of Vijayaraghavan's pieces is particularly striking in this context. The song refers to a myth in which the God Shiva drank poison to save the universe. When the gods and the demons were churning the ocean of milk, using the serpent Vasuki as a rope, the snake spit out poisonous fumes, which overwhelmed the participants. Shiva saved them by consuming the poison and his neck turned blue. He is known as Nilakantha—the blue-throated one. The following song is set in the pattern of Karnatic music in the raga *Begada:*

> O Nilakantha, lord, come here!
> You have your work cut out for you;
> I understand you consumed poison that day,
> but will it do just to sip
> a tiny bit of poison in your palm?
>
> We have spread potent poison
> all over this earth,
> the waters of the sea, the air, everywhere.
> O Shiva, be a sport, O Shiva, be a sport
> —if you suck this poison out
> you too will turn blue all over like Vishnu! [34]

Notice that the references here are not to philosophical texts, but to a story from the Puranas that many Hindus would know. The tone of the song is teasing—a mood adopted in many classical Bharata Natyam songs, in which the young girl flirts with a god, frequently in a romantic situation. Here, Shiva is told that the sipping of a little poison at the time that the cosmic ocean of milk was churned is not enough; he is to suck out the poison from the whole world. The traditional context is preserved, but the message has been modified to draw attention to the poison that we have spread through our earth, water, and air. The mythic context enables the writer to use the strong word "poison," rather than a more muted word like "pollution."

The audience for these ecologically aware dance recitals is diverse. It includes the very government workers, industrialists, and management executives who are responsible, either directly or indirectly, for regulating pollution. Mallika Sarabhai dances in urban and rural areas where she is able to get the attention of multiple audiences. A particular strength of dance as a medium is its subtlety: without being strident, the songs and expressions convey a message that lingers long after the performance is over. To a large extent, I would argue, the performance does the work that theological texts once did: that of reshaping and transforming attitudes and perspectives in the Hindu context.

Sathya Sai Baba and Clean Water Supply

Sathya Sai Baba is one of the most influential gurus in modern India. After he became aware that some parts of Rayalseema in Andhra Pradesh, India, had suffered drought conditions for years, the guru announced in 1994 that a "Water Supply Project" would be undertaken by his Sathya Sai Central Trust. He drew the attention of the people and the prime minister to the forty-five-year-old water problem. Sai Baba clearly draws connections between the rivers, religion, and morality. He is quoted as saying: "Rivers are the gift of God. In rivers like the Krishna, the Godavari, a lot of water is allowed to flow into the sea. . . . If there is constraint of finance, I am prepared to meet the cost even if it is 100 or 200 crores for fulfilling this dire need of the Rayalaseema people. The devotees are prepared to make any sacrifice but I have not stretched my hands to anyone." [35]

In attributing the lack of water to the decline of morality, Sai Baba also stated: "Water is getting scarcer every day. What is the reason? Because of the decline of morality among men, water is getting scarce in the world. For human life morality is the life breath. Morality makes humanness blossom. Because morals have been lost, water is getting scarce." [36]

The Water Project covers 20,000 square kilometers and includes 750 villages without water. Mobilizing his devotees and financial resources, Sai Baba has allegedly been able to increase the region's supply of safe drinking water. His devotees regard the project as a gesture of Sai Baba's "love and compassion"—as well as an implicit indictment of the government. Although the ecological impact of Sai Baba's activities can be debated, the power of the teacher is undisputable. Gurus like Sai Baba may ultimately have in their hands the power to change the behavior of devotees.

Limitations and Constraints

Some environmental philosophers have argued that Western religious traditions encourage dominion and control over nature, and thus bear a special burden of responsibility for the tragic state of our natural environment today. Such environmental philosophers sometimes turn to Eastern traditions to seek spiritual resources to help Westerners abjure and embrace eco-friendly policies. But if Eastern traditions, including Hinduism, are so eco-friendly, why do the countries in which these religions have been practiced have such a lamentable record of ecological disasters and rampant industrialization?

The answers are, obviously, complex. Rich as the devotional and *dharmic* resources have proven in India, Hinduism can be a source of complacency as well. Some Hindu values may impede ecological activism. Moreover, for Hindus, some texts are more effective than others in inspiring action. Articles on environmental philosophy furthermore often assume that there is a direct link between Hindu worldviews and practice. But in fact, there are competing forces that determine behavior within the Hindu tradition. Recent academic scholarship tends to blame Western thought and actions for the devastation of land in Third World countries. J. Baird Callicott and Roger T. Ames have suggested that Western intellectual colonization is responsible for the failures we see in eastern and southern Asia.[37] This view is also held by some Indian authors, like Vandana Shiva, an important figure in India's environmental movement. In evaluating her position, however, Lance Nelson notes that she "focuses almost entirely on the West, and the Third World's experience of colonialism, modernization, modernist developmentalism, and so on, as the root of her country's environmental devastation. She thus tends to ignore the precolonial aspects of the problem. . . . She also tends to give idealized readings of the environmental implications of certain aspects of Hindu thought."[38]

The responsibility and blame, I believe, has to be spread around. There are passages and texts within the Hindu religious traditions that encourage the acquisition of wealth in certain contexts. One must keep in mind that in the Hindu hierarchy, Bhu-Devi/Prithvi (the Earth Goddess) is of less importance than Sri/Lakshmi, the goddess of wealth and good fortune. Lakshmi has traditionally had a far greater hold on people's faith and aspirations than the Earth Goddess, and the quest for wealth seems to be more intense than reverence for the earth. In a world where good fortune seems to depend on consumer spending and industrial growth, the Earth Goddess faces some very stiff competition.

There are other strands in Hindu religious traditions that have helped contribute to the current ecological crisis. One is the Hindu conviction that rivers like Ganga are so inherently pure that nothing can pollute them.[39] Others have quite correctly pointed to the notion of sacred space as contributing to pollution. If certain spots like Vrindavana are inherently sacred and ought to be kept clean, one may pollute the "profane earth which is not sacred, which is not attached to Puranic or devotional narratives."[40]

And then there is the focus on "individuality" in some of the Hindu traditions. Anil Agarwal notes: "Hinduism's primary focus lies on the self, one's immediate family, and one's caste niche, to the neglect of the larger society and community. . . . Whereas the private sphere is carefully scripted in Hindu tradition, public life in India borders on and often descends into chaos. . . . A Hindu may go down to the Ganges River to purify himself or herself. The next moment, the same person will flush the toilet and discharge effluent into the very same sacred river. . . ."[41] While this is more true in some Hindu communities than others, the emphasis on the "self" has to be noted, at least in some traditions.

TEXTS ON *DHARMA* AND TEXTS ON THEOLOGY: BIMORPHIC WORLDVIEWS

Classical Hindu texts in the beginning of the Common Era enumerate the goals—or matters of value—of a human being. These are *dharma, artha* (wealth, power), *kama* (sensual pleasure), and *moksha* (liberation from the circle of life and death).[42] While *dharma,* wealth, and sensual pleasure are usually seen as this-worldly, *moksha* is liberation from this world and the repeated rebirths of a soul. There are texts that deal with *dharma,* wealth, sensual pleasure, and liberation. The multiple Hindu traditions do differ from other world religions in having this variety of goals and the array of texts that accompany them. This means that Hinduism presents adherents with several competing conceptual systems, intersecting but distinct.

The texts that deal with *moksha,* or liberation, are generally concerned with three issues: the nature of reality, including the supreme being and the human soul; the way to the supreme goal; and the nature of the supreme goal. Generally the nature of reality is called *tattva* (truth) and corresponds with the term "theology." These texts do not focus much on ethics or righteous behavior in this world; that is the province of *dharma* texts.

The theological texts or sections that deal with *tattva* focus on weaning a human being from the earthly pursuit of happiness to what they consider to be the supreme goal of liberation (*moksha*) from this life. It is important to keep this taxonomy in mind, because theological doctrines that are oriented to liberation do not necessarily trickle down into *dharmic* or ethical injunctions; in many Hindu traditions, in fact, there is a disjunction between *dharma* and *moksha.*

Indeed, J. A. B. van Buitenen says that there is a fundamental opposition between them: "*Mokṣa,* 're-lease,' is release from the entire realm which is governed by *dharma.* . . . It stands, therefore, in opposition to *dharma.* . . . Mokṣa, however, is the abandonment of the established order, not in favor of anarchy, but in favor of a self-realization which is precluded in the realm of *dharma.*"[43] While Daniel Ingalls disagrees on the sharp nature of the cleavage described by van Buitenen, he does acknowledge that "[a]lways there were some men, and a few of them among India's greatest religious leaders, who insisted on the contradiction between *dharma* and *moksha.*"[44] *Dharma* texts promote righteous behavior on Earth, and *moksha* texts encourage one to be detached from such concerns. A few texts like the *Bhagavadgita* have tried to bridge *dharma* and *moksha* paradigms.

Thus, a theology that emphasizes the world as a body of God, a pervasive pan-Indian belief that Goddess Earth (Prithvi, Vasundhara, Bhu Devi) is also a consort of Vishnu, or the notion that the Mother Goddess (Amba, Durga) is synonymous with Nature (*prakriti*) does not necessarily translate to eco-friendly behavior. Likewise, renunciation, celibacy, and detachment are laudable virtues for one who seeks liberation from the cycle of life and death, but the texts on *dharma* say that begetting children is necessary for salvation. These bimorphic worldviews have to be kept in mind if we are to see the relevance for the Hindu traditions of Western viewpoints such as deep ecology. On another front, the dissonance between *dharma* and *tattva/moksha* texts also accounts in part for the fact that while some Hindu traditions hold the Goddess to be supreme, women may not necessarily hold a high position in society.

It is quite correct to say that some theological/*tattva* texts speak of certain kinds of "oneness" of the universe and, in some cases, the "oneness" of all creation. Some, though not most, *tattva* texts speak of the absolute identity between the supreme being and the human soul (*atman*)—an identity that in fact transcends the concept of equality of many distinct souls. This philosophical system of nonduality is discussed by Western philosophers as an important resource in ecology. Eliot Deutsch writes, ". . . what does it mean to affirm continuity between man and the rest of life? Vedanta would maintain that this means the recognition that fundamentally all life is one, that in essence everything is reality, and that this oneness finds its natural expression in a reverence for all things."[45] The main thrust of the arguments made by Deutsch, Callicott, and others is to show that Hindu philosophy emphasizes that all creation is ultimately Brahman, or the supreme being, and therefore, if we hurt someone we hurt ourselves.

While the "oneness" doctrine and its ecological implications are underscored by Callicott, Lance Nelson has recently argued that the *advaita* ("non-dualism") conceptual system does *not* promote eco-friendly behavior.[46] Nelson shows how the doctrine developed by the Hindu philosopher Shankara (c. seventh century) actually *devalues* nature. He concludes that non-dualistic Vedanta philosophy "is not the kind of non-dualism that those searching for ecologically supportive modes of thought might wish it to be."[47]

The philosophies of Shankara and Ramanuja are relevant to those who seek liberation, but not to those seeking moral rules to govern everyday behavior. Hindu communities and customs are established not on the sense of oneness or equality found in *moksha,* but on many differences and hierarchies based on gender, caste, age, economic class, and so on.

With all their limitations and richness, therefore, we have had to deal with the texts, narratives, and traditions of *dharma* rather than the rule of *moksha* for actions leading to prosperity of the earth.

What I am urging is a shift in our perspective from the *tattva/moksha* texts to the resources that have a more direct relevance to worldly behavior. These are the popular practices embodied in the *dharmic* tradition and in the *bhakti*/devotional rituals. *Dharma* texts and narratives are in some ways like law codes in other countries: sometimes followed, sometimes flouted, sometimes ignored, sometimes evaded—and sometimes taken to heart as the right thing to do to maintain social stability. In addition to *dharma* texts, devotional (*bhakti*) exercises seem to be the greatest potential resource for ecological activists in India. As we have seen, devotion to Krishna or to Mother Ganga or Yamuna has impelled some people to take action to supply safe drinking water, plant and protect trees, and clean up rivers.

What can we learn from such success stories? Clearly, some Hindu texts, traditions, and rituals can inspire eco-friendly behavior. Narratives like the story of Shiva and Ganga, Parvati and the saplings seem to have more impact than talking about the universe as the body of God. The sanctity of rivers as Mother Goddesses has evoked great passion and inspired the cleaning up of the Ganga and Yamuna rivers; other rivers, one hopes, will be taken care of soon. Gurus and teachers can mobilize awareness and organize action, and these teachers may hold the key to avoiding ecological tragedy. It is when leaders, whether they are from the priestly families like Chaturvedi and Mishra, or gurus, or heads of environmental institutions like Dr. Purohit, team up with temples, scientists, and lawyers that Hindu ecological activists have the greatest potential for success.

Stories, gurus and goddesses, hagiographic literature, and *dharmic* models will all have to be pressed into service before we can make further progress. Prithvi Devi, or Mother Earth, can protect us if we protect her. If she is abused, she can transform herself from a nourishing mother into a wrathful deity.

One of the goals of the Hindu texts is to encourage human beings to seek enlightenment. Vairamuthu, a composer and poet popular in South India, recently wrote a song on the beauty of a tree. In the last line, he urges us to have the right attitude toward the tree. Every tree, he says, is a Bodhi tree. The Buddha was enlightened under the Bodhi tree: now every tree in the world can enlighten us about the burden on Mother Earth.

NOTES

1. Some paragraphs in this essay appeared in an earlier paper of mine, "'One Tree is Equal to Ten Sons': Some Hindu Responses to the Problems of Ecology, Population and Consumption," *Journal of the American Academy of Religion* 65 (2) (June 1997): 291–332.

2. Two of the most important books that have highlighted the many answers to this question are Lance Nelson, ed., *Purifying the Earthly Body of God: Religion and Ecology in Hindu India* (Albany, N.Y.: State University of New York Press, 1998) and Christopher Key Chapple and Mary Evelyn Tucker, eds., *Hinduism and Ecology: The Intersection of Earth, Sky and Water* (Cambridge: Center for the Study of World Religions, Harvard Divinity School, 2000). For an overview of early Indian literature, see Purushottama Bilimoria, "Environmental Ethics of Indian Religious Traditions," at <http://www.emory.edu/COLLEGE/RELIGION/faculty/bilimoria/paper.htm>.

3. *Kurma Purana,* 1.27.16–57. Cornelia Dimmitt and J. A. B. van Buitenen, *Classical Hindu Mythology: A Reader in the Sanskrit Puranas* (Philadelphia: Temple University Press, 1978), 39.

4. J. A. .B. van Buitenen, trans., *The Mahabharata: The Book of the Forest* (Chicago: The University of Chicago Press, 1978), 586–589, 595–596; emphasis added.

5. Richard Lariviere, "Justices and *Paṇḍitas:* Some Ironies in Contemporary Readings of the Hindu Legal Past," *Journal of Asian Studies* 48 (4) (1989): 757–769.

6. Gerald J. Larson, "Conceptual Resources in South Asia for 'Environmental Ethics,'" in *Nature in Asian Traditions of Thought: Essays in Environmental Philosophy,* ed. J. Baird Callicott and Roger T. Ames (Albany, N.Y.: State University of New York Press, 1989), 267–277.

7. For a typical hymn of this genre and its connection to environmental ethics, see O. P. Dwivedi, "Dharmic Ecology," in Chapple and Tucker, eds., *Hinduism and Ecology,* 10–11. Christopher Key Chapple summarizes the literature on ecology and the Vedas in his article "Towards an Indigenous Indian Environmentalism," in Nelson, ed., *Purifying the Earthly Body of God.*

8. "Ahimsa paramo dharma" ("Nonviolence is the highest form of *dharma*"), *Mahabharata,* Anusasana Parva 115.1. "Lack of malice to all beings in thought, word, and deed; this is the essence of the eternal faith." *Mahabharata,* Shanti Parva, quoted in Pandurang Vaman Kane, *History of Dharmaśāstra (Ancient and*

Mediaeval Religious and Civil Law) (Poona, India: Bhandarkar Oriental Research Institute, 1958).

9. *Manu Smriti,* 4:56.

10. *Manu Smriti,* 2:17–23; adapted from Georg Buhler, *The Laws of Manu* (New Delhi: Motilal Banarsidass, 1964), 32–33.

11. See David Kinsley, "Learning the Story of the Land: Reflections on the Liberating Power of Geography and Pilgrimage in the Hindu Tradition," in Nelson, ed., *Purifying the Earthly Body of God,* 225–246.

12. See, for instance, Vandana Shiva, *Staying Alive: Women, Ecology and Survival in India* (New Delhi: Kali for Women), 1988, and Kapila Vatsyayan, *Prakriti: The Integral Vision,* 5 vols. (New Delhi: Indira Gandhi National Center for the Arts), 1995. For a revisionistic Tantric view, see Rita DasGupta Sherma, "Sacred Immanence: Reflections of Ecofeminism in Hindu Tantra," in Nelson, ed., *Purifying the Earthly Body of God,* 89–132.

13. K. Seshagiri Rao, "The Five Great Elements (*Pañcamahābhūta*): An Ecological Perspective," in Chapple and Tucker, eds., *Hinduism and Ecology,* 23–38.

14. John Carman, *The Theology of Ramanuja* (New Haven, Conn.: Yale University Press, 1974), 124–133.

15. S. S. Raghavachar, trans., *Vedārtha Saṅgraha of Sri Rāmānujācārya* (Mysore: Sri Ramakrishna Ashram, 1968), 11, 13.

16. Ibid., 14.

17. *Matsya Puranam,* chap. 154, 506–512. Adapted from "A Taluqdar of Oudh," *Matsya Puranam,* pt. 2 (Allahabad: Surendra Natha Vasu of Bhuvaneswari Asrama, Bahadurganj, 1917).

18. Kane, *History of Dharmaśāstra (Ancient and Mediaeval Religious and Civil Law),* vol. V, pt. 1, 415–416.

19. Ibid., 415.

20. Shamasastry, trans., Kautilya's *Arthasastra* (Mysore: Mysore Printing and Publishing House, 1967), 225.

21. Choodie Shivaram, "Court Decree Retires Tirupati Temple's Hereditary Priests," *Hinduism Today* 18(6) (1996): 1.

22. Pamphlet of T. T. Devasthanam, n.d., available in the information office of T. T. Devasthanam. For general information see <http://www/tirumala.org/vana_schemes_p7htm>.

23. Edwin Bernbaum, "Badrinath's Trees: Local Forests Being Restored as Pilgrims Now Plant Trees as Offering to God," *Hinduism Today,* May 1999, and at <http://www.hinduismtoday.com/1995/5/#gen382>. G. B. Pant Institute of Himalayan Environment and Development is located at Kosi-Kat Armal, Almora, Uttar Pradesh, India.

24. For discussion on the involvement of the International Society of Krishna Consciousness with ecological schemes and the philosophical background, see Ranchor Prime, *Hinduism and Ecology: Seeds of Truth* (Delhi: Motilal Banarsidass, 1994), and Michael A. Cremo and Mukunda Goswami, *Divine Nature: A Spiritual Perspective on the Environmental Crisis* (Los Angeles: Bhaktivedanta Book Trust, 1995). The ecological efforts in Vrindavana and the textual sources that inspire such activities are also discussed in Bruce M. Sullivan's detailed article "Theology and Ecology at the Birthplace of Krsna," in Nelson, ed., *Purifying the Earthly Body of God,* 247–267.

25. Swami B. V. Parivrajak, "Where is 'That' Vrindavan?" (15 January 1999) in VINA (Vaishnava Internet News Agency) at <http://www.vina.org/articles/where_is_that_vrindavan.html>.

26. Professor Diana Eck, Harvard University, personal communication.

27. Vasudha Narayanan, "The Two Levels of Auspiciousness in Srivaisnava Ritual and Literature," *Journal of Developing Societies* 1 (1) (1985): 57.

28. Kelly D. Alley, "Idioms of Degeneracy: Assessing Ganga's Purity and Pollution," in Nelson, ed., *Purifying the Earthly Body of God.*

29. Meenakshi Ganguly, "Veer Bhadra Mishra: Holy War for 'My Mother,'" *Time Magazine,* 2 August 1999, 81.

30. Robert Sanders, "Saving the 'Mother of India': Berkeley Technology May Clean Up Ganges River," <http://www.berkeley.edu/news/berkeleyan/1998/1118/India.html>.

31. I am indebted to David Haberman for this information. Professor Haberman's work on the Yamuna River will be published in his forthcoming book, *Yamuna: River of Love in an Age of Pollution.*

32. V. Sadagopan, personal communication.

33. Vandana Shiva, *Staying Alive: Women, Ecology, and Development* (London: Zed Books, 1988); J. Baird Callicott, *Earth's Insights: A Survey of Ecological Ethics from the Mediterranean Basin to the Australian Outback* (Berkeley, Calif.: University of California Press, 1994), 220–221; Bart Gruzalski, "The Chipko Movement: A Gandhian Approach to Ecological Sustainability and Liberation from Economic Colonisation," in *Ethical and Political Dilemmas of Modern India,* ed. Ninian Smart and Shivesh Thakur (New York: St. Martin's Press, 1993), 100–125. See also Mark Shepard, "'Hug the Trees!': Chandi Prasad Bhatt and the Chipko Movement," at <http://www.markshep.com/nonviolence/GT_Chipko.html>.

34. Sujatha Vijayaraghavan, "Neelakanthare Varum Ayya," song in *Begada* raga, unpublished, personal communication.

35. *Sanathana Sarathi,* December 1994, 323; quoted in "The Sathya Sai Water Project: The Acute Need for Water," at <http://members.aol.com/introsai/works/water.htm>.

36. "The Sathya Sai Water Project," as above.

37. J. Baird Callicott and Roger T. Ames, *Nature in*

Asian Traditions of Thought: Essays in Environmental Philosophy (Albany, N.Y.: State University of New York Press, 1989), 281.

38. Nelson, "The Dualism of Non-Dualism," in *Purifying the Earthly Body,* 82–83, n. 16.

39. See the excellent article by Kelly Alley, "Idioms of Degeneracy: Assesing Ganga's Purity and Pollution," in Nelson, ed., *Purifying the Earthly Body of God,* 297–330.

40. David Kinsley, "Learning the Story of the Land: Reflections on the Liberating Power of Geography and Pilgrimage in the Hindu Tradition," in Nelson, ed., *Purifying the Earthly Body of God,* 242.

41. Anil Agarwal, "Can Hindu Beliefs and Values Help India Meet its Ecological Crisis?" in Chapple and Tucker, eds., *Hinduism and Ecology,* 174.

42. Kane, *History of Dharmaśāstra (Ancient and Mediaeval Religious and Civil Law),* vol. II, pt. 1, 2d ed. (Poona, India: Bhandarkar Oriental Research Institute, 1974), 8–9.

43. J. A. B. van Buitenen, "Dharma and Mokṣa," *Philosophy East and West: A Journal of Oriental and Comparative Thought* 7 (1) (1957): 33–40; 7 (2) (1957): 37.

44. Ingalls, "Dharma and Mokṣa," in ibid., 48.

45. Eliot Deutsch, quoted in J. Baird Callicott, *Earth's Insights: A Survey of Ecological Ethics from the Mediterranean Basin to the Australian Outback* (Berkeley: University of California Press, 1994), 49.

46. Callicott, *Earth's Insights,* 50; Nelson, "The Dualism of Non-Dualism."

47. Nelson, "The Dualism of Non-Dualism," 65.

Idioms of Degeneracy
Assessing Gaṅgā's Purity and Pollution

KELLY D. ALLEY

INTRODUCTION: ASSESSMENTS AND WORLDVIEWS

Scientists, government workers, and religious leaders in India hold differing conceptions of the purity and pollution of the natural world. Their conflicting assessments reflect a larger debate between worldviews and the divergent ways worldviews define the sacred and the profane. Especially in discussions about the river Gaṅgā (or Ganges), the sacred river that flows across northern India, we find marked disagreement between arguments defending the Gaṅgā's sacred purity and warnings about river pollution. These arguments point to a conflict of worldviews holding different assumptions about human existence. The various assessments of the river draw logical and moral or ethical legitimacy from theology, scientific discourse, and the secular policies of the state and, therefore, are windows into the ways Indian citizens use wider networks of knowledge. In this paper, I examine the most recent assessments of the condition of this river and demonstrate how specific groups of Indian citizens and state officials use these assessments to articulate their worldview differences in public debates.

Theological discourses, more than scientific and secular ones, establish various connections between moral and ecological values through sacred texts, drama, and iconography (see, for example, Hargrove 1986, Spring and Spring 1974, Suzuki and Knudtson 1992). Several contemporary social scientists have attempted to find common threads in these diverse renderings of the universe, seeking the means to create a universally plausible environmental ethic.[1] But this goal assumes far too much. The ways that people define nature cannot be idealized solely in terms of ethical and rational notions of sustainable, equitable resource use. Portrayals of Banaras in the Hindu sacred texts (*śāstras*), for example, depict this famous pilgrimage place on the bank of the sacred river

Alley, Kelly D., "Idioms of Degeneracy: Assessing Ganga's Purity and Pollution," in Lance E. Nelson, Ed., *Purifying the Earthly Body of God: Religion and Ecology in Hindu India*, pp. 297–331. Reprinted by permission of the State University of New York Press.

Gaṅgā as a conch shell, or the trident of Lord Śiva. These religious images have no parallel in materialist interpretations of space and create symbolic dissonance with spatial meanings constructed by scientific and official governmental worldviews. Hindu representations such as these underscore, as Singh (1993b, 113) has noted, a vision that integrates matter, mind, and spirit. Symbolic representations of space in Hindu sacred texts and the ancient concepts associated with them call for an approach to ecological understanding that moves beyond secular notions of "environment." To understand this we need to examine, in a particular locale such as Banaras, the cognitive categories and symbolic processes giving religious meaning to "natural resources" such as the Gaṅgā. This will allow us to analyze how residents respond to or resist the environmental ideologies more familiar to secular thinking.

Banaras is an important pilgrimage place and urban center bordering the sacred river. Residents and pilgrims regard Banaras as the center of Śiva's universe, as well as the beginning and end point of human civilization. Eck (1982, 23) notes that local residents claim that Kāśī, the ancient name for Banaras, contains the whole world and everything on earth that is powerful and auspicious. The Mahāśmāśāna, the great cremation ground of Banaras, survives the cyclic dissolution of the cosmos brought about by Śiva's ascetic power (see Parry 1980, 89; 1981, 339). On a more secular note, Banaras is the site of the largest combined pilgrim/tourist trade in India today. It is therefore an important locale for witnessing transformations taking transformations taking place in the politics of pilgrimage.

Not sharing the ideology of the typical Hindu world-renouncer (*saṃnyāsin,*) pilgrims who visit Banaras and residents who live in neighborhoods along the riverbank do not denigrate or seek detachment from the physical or natural world. Rather, pilgrims and residents alike believe that rivers and mountains are sacred and powerful. This is why many sacred places in India are located aside rivers or on top of mountains (see Feldhaus 1995). The river Gaṅgā, in the Hindu religious vision, takes the form of a goddess who possesses the power to purify all sorts of human and worldly impurities. Hindu residents and pilgrims invoke the purifying power of "Mā Gaṅgā" (Mother Gaṅgā) through ritual ablution, meditation, and worship (*snān, dhyān,* and *pūjā*). Even as officials in state and central government offices espouse scientific theories of river pollution to undermine what they dub a "traditional" religious relationship with the river, devout Hindus of Banaras reject these alienating claims. This is because, as we shall see, many residents of this pilgrimage place see science and the state as powers which bring on ecological degeneracy in the name of preventing it.

In what follows, I explore assessments of the state of the river Gaṅgā and the larger worldview issues that contextualize them by presenting the perspectives of three groups of people. These are: (1) *paṇḍās* or pirgrim priests working on southern Daśāśvamedha in Banaras, (2) members of the Clean Ganga Campaign or CGC (Swatcha Ganga Abhiyan), who also live in Banaras, and (3) officials working in projects under the Ganga Project Directorate or GPD. Some government officials in the third group are Banaras residents while others reside in Delhi and other major Indian cities. Despite their varied orientations toward the sacred and secular, members of these groups have one thing in common: they consider the present period a degenerate one. The ways that each group locates spheres of degeneracy are connected to their assessments of the river's condition.

Scientific assessments made by government officials and members of the Clean Ganga Campaign locate degeneracy in ecological systems. From their point of view, human processes of population growth, urbanization, and industrial and technological development have brought on the decline in ecological balance. In contrast, residents of southern Daśāśvamedha, a neighborhood of the city which flanks the river, envision themselves at the end of a cosmic cycle. In this context, they interpret immoral behavior and abuses of the Gaṅgā as signs of diminished virtue and moral degeneracy. Scientific theories use terms such as Biological Oxygen Demand (BOD) and Fecal Coliform Count (FCC) to indicate a decline in the quality of river water. Residents of Daśāśvamedha explain that marketplace competition, cheating, and corruption are signs of the moral degeneracy of the current age. These factors, they believe, create an atmosphere in which people disrespect Gaṅgā. The former group measures how polluted the Gaṅgā has become, while the latter ponders how Gaṅgā herself might help reset the degenerate moral and cosmic order.

THE GAṄGĀ AT DAŚĀŚVAMEDHA

The pilgrim priests residing and working on the southern half of Daśāśvamedha express a theory of degeneracy based on their understanding of the immediate surroundings. They link degeneracy to the religious significance of their neighborhood and the Gaṅgā at that spot. Daśāśvamedha is a sacred place (*tīrth*) as well as a residential neighborhood. Its border with the river is fortified by a series of stone steps called *ghāṭs* which give pilgrims access to the Gaṅgā. The *ghāṭ* at Daśāśvamedha is a meritorious site for ritual ablution and is ranked in sacred importance with the other important *ghāṭs* of Asi, Varaṇā, Maṇikarṇikā, Kedār, and Pañcagaṅgā.[2] The *ghāṭ* marks the place where Lord Brahmā performed a ten horse sacrifice (*daśa-aśva-medha*) to gain power over the reigning King Divodāsa. Pilgrims visit the temples of Śulataṅkeśvara, Brahmeśvara, Vārāheśvara, Abhaya Vināyaka, Gaṅgā Devī, and Bandī Devī on this *ghāṭ* (Singh 1993a, 82).

The physical features of the *ghāṭ* tell another story. In its present form, the *ghāṭ* is divided into southern and northern sections (the Gaṅgā flows northward at Banaras). The sections were once divided by the Godāvarī, a tributary that drained into the Gaṅgā. In 1740, the southern section of the *ghāṭ* was fortified by Bajirao Pesava I. Ahilyabhai Holkar of Indore then extended the *ghāṭ* in 1775 (Singh 1993a, 82). At the turn of the twentieth century, Havell (1905, 106) wrote that Daśāśvamedha was the *ghāṭ* toward which the principal roads of the city converged. It was also an important point for boats bringing stone from the Chunar quarries upstream. In 1904, Maharani Puthia of the former state of Digpatia in North Bengal constructed another *ghāṭ*. She laid the foundation on the island created where the Godāvarī separated into a fork before reaching the Gaṅgā. This become Prayāg Ghāṭ. Urban construction eventually covered over the Godāvarī and residents changed the name of the area to Godaulia (Singh 1993a, 39, 84). The area lying between Prayāg Ghāṭ and Rājendra Prasād Ghāṭ (formerly Ghoḍā Ghāṭ) is the northern part of ancient Daśāśvamedha. On the southern section, we find the Śītalā Temple, which still contains the ancient *liṅga* of Daśāśvamedheśvara Mahādev, Śiva as Lord of Daśāśvamedha (see also Vidyarthi et al., 29). Behind this temple, the shrine of Prayāgeśvara lies buried beneath the house of a powerful pilgrim priest *(paṇḍā)*. The *Kāśī Khaṇḍa (KKh)*, a sacred text describing Banaras from the eighth to thirteenth century, refers to this *liṅga* and shrine (see Havell 1905, 110; *KKh* 44.16–47, *KKh* 61.36–38; Singh 1993a, 48, 82–85). On a more profane note, the *ghāṭ* at Daśāśvamedha is also known for its "mafia-like" businesses fed by the reverence of pilgrims (see also Parry 1994, van der Veer 1988).

Most residents of Banaras, whether they work in government service or private business, emphasize the sacred purity of the Gaṅgā. They do this by calling upon her divine power in worship rituals (*pūjā*). They understand Gaṅgā's deep symbolic history and cite eulogies to her developed in the sacred texts. In the *Rāmāyaṇa, Mahābhārata,* the *purāṇas,* and the *māhātmyas*—and in temple sculpture and art—she is worshiped as a purifier, mother, sustainer, and daughter or co-wife of Śiva.[3] A popular narrative, drawn from a chapter of the *Rāmāyaṇa,* describes how she descended from heaven on to the locks of Lord Śiva. (see Vatstyayan 1992). Her motherly character is praised in the *Mahābhārata,* and the *purāṇas* extoll her powers to purify. Several places of healing and sacred power for Hindus are located along her 2,525 kilometer traverse across northern India (Vidyarthi et al. 1979). In these sacred complexes, pilgrims and residents perform ablutions and undertake the ritual of *āratī* to revere her. Devotees perform *āratī* by waving an oil lamp in front of Gaṅgā while standing on the riverbank. The sounds of bells, gongs, drums, and conch shells play a prominent role in the ritual. The festivals of Gaṅgā Daśaharā and Gaṅgā Saptamī celebrate her purifying power. But while they can please Gaṅgā, these rituals and festivals cannot purify her. Purity is part of a more holistic process of cosmic order and balance, within which humans should strive to live harmoniously (see also Fuller 1979, 460; 1992, 76). Still, when Gaṅgā is pleased she blesses the faithful and purifies their minds and souls. She may also grant a devotee's wishes if they are requested through worship with pure faith.

When asked how the sacred texts (*śāstras*) guide their relationships with Gaṅgā, many residents of Daśāśvamedha point to rituals of *snān* and *pūjā* and the importance of *gaṅgā jal* (sacred Gaṅgā water) in Hindu life. When pilgrims perform *snān* or ritual ablution, Gaṅgā absolves religious impurities and, with her flow, carries away physical uncleanness. This creates, at one level, an interlocking relationship between ritual, spiritual purity, and physical cleanness. As one merchant on Daśāśvamedha put it, "People who bathe and do meditation and ritual worship of gods and goddesses understand that this is our history (*itihās*) and knowledge (*jñān*)." Dumont and Pocock (1959, 30) point out that one must be spiritually pure to approach gods and goddesses. Even though humans may not reach the purity of the divine, there is some expectation that purity is a condition for contact with deities to be beneficial.

There are two views in current popular discourse at Daśāśvamedha about whether Gaṅgā can purify an impure person. In one view, an impure person cannot become pure simply by bathing in a sacred place. Rather, one must engage in the more holistic process of committing one's soul to Śiva. The other, more lenient view holds that one who merely recites the name of Gaṅgā gains mastery over "sin" (*pāp*). One who takes auspicious sight (*darśan*) of her achieves well-being (*kalyāṇ*) and one who performs *snān* purifies seventy generations.[4] The *Gaṅgā Stuti*, a hymn to Gaṅgā sung in Hindi by a *paṇḍā* of Daśāśvamedha, carries this theme. One *paṇḍā* sings this eulogy in Hindi during Ganga *āratī:*

> From the place where the lotus foot of the Lord, where Bhagīrath did great *tapasyā* (ritual austerities),
> Gaṅgā flowed out from Brahmā's jug into the locks of Śiv-Śaṅkar.
> She then descended to earth on earth on a mountain of countless sins.
> Tulsī Dās says, Open your two eyes and see how naturally she flows as a stream of nectar.
> Those who take her name in memory will get *mukti* (liberation);
> Those who do *praṇām* (salutation) will arrive at God's place.
> Those who come to the banks of Gaṅgā will find heaven;
> Those who see the waves of emotion will get *mokṣa* (liberation).
> O Taraṅginī [Gaṅgā], this is the nature God has given to you.
> O Bhāgīrathī [Gaṅgā], though I am full of sin and dirtiness,
> I believe you will give me *mukti* and a place at your feet.[5]

IDIOMS OF DEGENERACY: *GANDAGĪ* AND DIRTY BUSINESS

Pilgrims who visit Daśāśvamedha relate moral values to the Gaṅgā through rituals of ablution and worship. Therefore, ritual specialists become important players in the relationships pilgrims forge with the Gaṅgā. This makes the perspective of pilgrim priests especially significant and central to the exchanges conducted on an everyday basis with the river. Much of the scholarly literature on Hinduism has treated pilgrim priests as if they were members of a common caste (*jāti*) association. But *paṇḍās* explain that the *paṇḍā* profession (*paṇḍāgīrī*) is not a *jāt* (caste group) but a *peśā* (occupation).[6] This *peśā* is concerned with serving specific groups of pilgrims. *Paṇḍās* in this occupation establish hereditary title to identified groups of pilgrims and then defend their hereditary rights to serve those pilgrims against shifting claims made by individuals with "man and money power."

A pilgrim priest maintains his position and gains power vis-à-vis other priests by controlling access to clients. Rights to act as head priest for specified groups of pilgrims may pass through male and female lines. Affinal bequests, however, are less prestigious, so *paṇḍās* often disguise them as gifts from the patrilineage. As local accounts go, many priests are unable to keep these rights within the family without struggle. As one informant explained it, inserting an English phrase into his Hindi dialogue, members of the community with more "man and money power" wrestle away these titles from those who inherited them. Curiously enough, this informant chose to use the English phrase "man and money power" whenever referring to this form of influence.

Paṇḍās say that a good moral order exists when hereditary titles are honored. This allows the occupation to retain the family pride and honor that has surrounded it for generations. A corrupt (*gandā*) moral order, on the other hand, emerges when this family honor is threatened by members representing other family lines or outsiders with "man and money power." Outsiders use "man and money power" to usurp hereditary rights. By "man and money power," *paṇḍās* mean power exercised by physical coercion and violence. Individuals using this power manipulate others by controlling their labor and selling them protection. A powerful individual of this nature has many men to do his work for him (to divert pilgrims to the location he controls and to perform the rituals they request) and the coercive might to make sure that at the end of the day these men turn over part of their earnings to him. When this kind of power succeeds in Banaras, the *paṇḍās* of Daśāśvamedha say, cheating and corruption rear their ugly heads and create a dirty social condition.

These Banaras residents, like many others, express degeneracy through the notion of *gandagī*. *Gandagī* is the Hindi term for filth and dirtiness. It refers to material waste and some forms of human excretion. In the Hindu worldview expressed by Banaras residents, *gandagī* is also a metaphor for corrupt religious, social, and political relations and, generally, for the undesirable conditions of existence. To focus the discussion on how *gandagī* impacts the river Gaṅgā, we must understand the concept in relation to the more complicated term *purity* and its opposite *impurity,* and the related but not synonymous term *pollution*.

Mary Douglas (1966) explained the concept of pollution as referring to that which is not included in the conceptual category of purity and is therefore powerful by virtue of its marginality. Dumont, in *Homo Hierarchicus* (1970), saw impurity as the conceptual opposite of purity, and argued that the two were inextricably bound up with social status (see also Dumont and Pocock 1959). After that, studies of Hindu caste and ritual began to use the English terms impurity and pollution interchangeably to code status and variables such as sin and evil, other aspects of morality, and the relations between gods and human beings (Das 1977; Fuller 1977, 473; O'Flaherty 1976). Later studies highlighting the centrality of the concepts of auspiciousness and inauspiciousness in Hindu ritual and caste relations expanded the understanding of the Hindu worldview.[7] But the term pollution remained confused in these accounts, clouding the Hindu distinction between ritual impurity and material dirtiness. Use of the word pollution becomes even more problematic when attempting to differentiate the meanings of environmental pollution and ritual impurity when they occur in the same context.

The notion of environmental pollution is an important term in the modern scientific worldview, crucial to a vision that seeks to expand human control of natural processes and forces. Residents of Daśāśvamedha, however, give little credence to the notion espoused in scientific and official circles. To understand how they think about physical dirtiness, it would be helpful to abandon use of the term *pollution* in its religious sense of ritual pollution. Instead I will use the term *ritual impurity* when speaking of the conceptual opposite of ritual purity. This way we will avoid any confusion between ritual impurity and the very different notion of environmental pollution.

In this chapter, the term *pollution* will denote the form of environmental degeneracy that is the subject of scientific and official government worldviews. The terms *purity* and *impurity,* on the other hand, will stand for the moral, bodily, and cosmic states proper to the religious concerns of Banaras residents. This attempt at conceptual clarification is not, however, intended to obscure the fact that Hindus recognize material waste. The notion of waste or dirtiness is an important part of the Hindu view as well. But the local understanding of material waste, encompassed by the term *gandagī,* must be understood in its own terms, as something somewhat different from the scientific/official notion of environmental pollution.

This allows us to move into a discussion of the distinction between physical cleanness and religious purity (and their antonyms) as they are elaborated in the Hindi language. As the discussion will show, at times the distinction appears blurred. But it becomes strikingly clear when *paṇḍās* explain the impact of waste on the Gaṅgā. The Clean Ganga Campaign also relies upon this distinction to articulate its focus. Understanding how residents articulate these concepts is a difficult task because the sets of terms I will describe are sometimes used interchangeably. Nevertheless, the distinction remains an important element of the Hindu worldview and Hindu assessments of the Gaṅgā.

The social scientific literature has had little to say about this distinction. The few exceptions are found in references made by Srinivas in 1952 and, more recently, by Alter in his account of the wrestling ground. Srinivas (1952, 105) argued that ritual purity cannot be simply associated with cleanliness. This is because one may find a ritually pure robe that is very dirty or snow-white clothes that are ritually impure.

In his discussion of the Mīnākṣī Temple in Madurai, Fuller (1979, 473) hinted that these categories function independently in this way. He pointed out that the physical cleanness of the temple is a precondition for its spiritual purity. Alter (1990) has contributed the most thus far in his elaboration of the spatial dimensions that mark off the pure from the unclean at the *akhāṛā* grounds in Bananas. I will return to Alter's account in a moment.

The ways that *paṇḍās* of Daśāśvamedha distinguish between physical cleanness and ritual purity are central to how they define *gandagī* and assess its impact on the river. Again, their concept of *gandagī* is altogether different, conceptually, from the notion of environmental pollution espoused by science and government. *Paṇḍās* use eight Hindi terms to explain the impact of *gandagī*. Operating as four sets of binary oppositions, they are: *sāf* and *gandā, svaccha* and *asvaccha, śuddha* and *aśuddha,* and *pavitra* and *apavitra*. The first two pairs—*sāf/gandā* and *svaccha/asvaccha*—refer to material or external cleanness and uncleanness. The other two—*śuddha/aśuddha* and *pavitra/apavitra*—refer to purity and impurity of cosmos, soul, and heart. Although residents treat them as sets of binary oppositions, they do not necessarily exclude one set when using the other to signify an event or condition. This is because residents demonstrate considerable flexibility when using these terms to define their world. For example, a Banaras resident might say that Gaṅgā water is *śuddha* as if he or she means both good to drink in the sense of cleanness and good to worship in the sense of possessing eternal power. This means that *sāf/svaccha* and *śuddha/pavitra* can signify similar conditions. In many ritual contexts, cleanness and purity are closely linked. Likewise, terms designating physical uncleanness and ritual impurity may signify the same condition. *But this is not always the case.* This interchangeability demonstrates how the use of these terms is complicated. But when we focus on discussions of the river Gaṅgā, the importance of these terminological distinctions becomes more apparent.

Most informants on Daśāśvamedha define the following elements that enter the Gaṅgā as materially unclean (*gandā* or *asvaccha*): dirty water from drains (*nālās*), industrial waste, household trash, soap from bathing and washing clothes, human excrement from "doing latrine" on the riverbank, and betelnut (*pān*) spit. Many believe that material dirtiness and bodily wastes have a similar impact on Gaṅgā. Residents do not say that such *gandagī* is dangerous for the Gaṅgā, but they do value the rule for keeping dirtiness away from Gaṅgā and other places of worship. Sacred texts and popular manuals on pilgrimage, spiritual life, and good conduct communicate ideas about distancing unclean bodily functions from bodies of pure water. The *Śiva Purāṇa (ŚP),* for example, makes numerous references to proper conduct near bodies of water, and particularly next to rivers and tanks. About morning defecation and other routine activities, it teaches as follows:

> [For defecation,] he must never sit in front of water, fire, a brahmin or the idol of any god. He must screen the penis with the left hand and the mouth with the right. After evacuating the bowels, the feces should not be looked at. Water drawn out in a vessel should not be used for cleaning (i.e. no one should sit inside the tank or river-water for cleaning purposes). No one shall enter the holy tanks and rivers dedicated to deities, manes, etc. and frequented by the sages. The rectum must be cleaned with mud seven, five or three times. . . .
>
> For gargling, the water can be taken in any vessel or a wooden cup; but water shall be spit outside (not in the river or tank). Washing of the teeth with any leaf or twig must be without using the index finger and outside the water. . . . In all sacred rites the upper cloth should also be used while taking bath in the holy river or tank; the cloth worn shall not be rinsed or beaten. The sensible man shall take it to a separate tank or well or to the house itself and beat it on a rock or on a plank to the gratification of the manes, O brahmins. (*ŚP* 13.10–13, 15–18)

These passages direct people to distance some everyday human processes such as defecation, brushing teeth, spitting, and washing clothes from the riverbank. This principle of distancing, also mentioned in a favorite text of one *paṇḍā,* the *Paramśānti Kā Mārg* ("Path to Great Peace"), appears to serve as a well-understood spatial benchmark for keeping uncleanness away from the Gaṅgā.

Alter's description of the *akhāṛā* (wrestling) ground reflects this spatial ordering. He outlines (1990, 33) how Banaras residents distance uncleanness and human dirtiness from the center of the *akhāṛā* ground. In the center lies a deep well of pure water which draws its strength from the soil of the *akhāṛā* (considered a tonic of sorts), the trees, and its proximity to the Gaṅgā. Swampy ponds encircle the clean area of the compound. Wrestlers use these ponds for cleaning after defecation. The swampy area is the unclean periphery, where the dirtiness accrued to the body through everyday life is washed away. Alter finds that a system of hydraulic classification structures *akhāṛā* space and the residents' movement through it. Wrestlers distinguish between swampy water used to clean one's anus, water from a peripheral well used to dampen the ground, water from another tank used to wash one's self and one's clothes, and water from the well in the center of the *akhāṛā*, which is for drinking. In this case, the pure well lies closest to the *akhāṛā* ground, and both together constitute the center of the arena. This hydraulic classification shows that physical cleanness and ritual purity alike are distanced from physical and bodily uncleanness.

On Daśāśvamedha, this rule is recognized as the ideal, even when it is breached. Unfortunately, residents claim, this spatial order is exactly what cannot be enforced on the *ghāṭ*. For many, the rule of distancing seems impossibly difficult to follow. On Daśāśvamedha *ghāṭ*, while pilgrims perform ablutions, others wash clothes with soap, a *paṇḍā* spits, an old woman "does latrine" on a corner of the *ghāṭ* (for lack of public facilities), and urban sewage flows into the river under the *ghāṭ* floor. *Gandagī* surrounds the people seeking purification.

The collapse of the spatial ideal of separating what is unclean from what is pure disturbs most residents. However, they claim they cannot do much to change the situation. In fact, apathy about control of public behavior runs high on Daśāśvamedha. Most argue that the public nature of the *ghāṭ* at this spot makes regulation virtually impossible. Banaras, some point out, does not have a strong centralized religious authority, like that in the city of Hardwar, to enforce rules strictly.

Many residents point out the rise in dead bodies immersed in wholly uncremated form in the Gaṅgā. Local residents complain that the police are often responsible for the problem because they dispose of unclaimed dead bodies in the river to avoid the costs of electric cremation, which their department has to bear. Along with unclaimed bodies, corpses are brought to the river by families who are unable to afford proper cremation. According to Hindu trial, corpses are carriers of ritual impurity. The Hindu practice of cremation along the banks of the river, at the two auspicious *ghāṭs* of Maṇikarṇikā and Hariścandra, aims to reduce the corpse into the five basic elements of existence: fire, air, water, ether, and earth. Hindus use the words *aśuddha* or *apavitra* to describe the ritual impurity of the corpse as well as the ritual impurity of the surviving family members in charge of performing the cremation rituals. After cremation, the ashes and any remaining bones are immersed in the Gaṅgā and purified by her. The impurity associated with the surviving family members is absolved after they perform rituals of *śrāddha* (rites in honor of the spirits of the deceased) over a prescribed period of time. According to the sacred texts, some individuals are not allowed to be cremated, namely holy men (*sādhus*), children, lepers, and smallpox victims (see Das 1982, 123; Parry 1994, 184–5). In the religious view, therefore, dead bodies, per se, are not problematic for Gaṅgā, because she can ritually purify them. However, cremation does constitute a good sacrificial death for corpses (other than those specified above) and absolves the impurity of the physical body. The *paṇḍās* of Daśāśvamedha point out that most of the fully uncremated corpses found floating down the Gaṅgā should have been cremated according to rules set out in the *śāstras* (because they were neither *sādhus*, children, lepers, nor smallpox victims). To the priests, this indicates a lapse in the public respect for ritual order. The practice of partially cremating corpses in the wood or electric crematorium, and then dumping the partially burned remains in the Gaṅgā, is more excusable because the ritual procedure, although short circuited due to financial constraints, has been respected.

The *paṇḍās'* views about corpses, however, are more complicated because, when they make references to fully uncremated dead bodies in the Gaṅgā, they sometimes conflate notions of ritual impurity and physical uncleanness. That is, they also refer to these corpses as signs of *gandagī*. The fact that residents of Daśāśvamedha refer to dead bodies as *gandagī* is the result of more than a decade of media reports on river pollution, which have defined corpses as secular bodies.

Since the 1980s, media and official reports have claimed that the number of dead bodies immersed in the Gaṅgā in uncremated or partially cremated form has visibly increased. Officials have attributed this to the rising cost of cremation, which is making it difficult for some families to cremate their deceased kin. Media reports began to publicize this phenomenon toward the end of the decade. From 1985 through 1990, reporters from Delhi and abroad published descriptions and photos of floating corpses in reports of "Ganga pollution."[8]

Although they were meant to shock the citizenry into a concern for ecological degeneracy, these media reports did little to convince Daśāśvamedha residents of Gaṅgā's impending demise. On the contrary, residents continue to believe that Gaṅgā purifies the ashes of cremated individuals and, if need be, carries away the partially cremated—or even fully uncremated—bodies without being adversely affected. What residents of Daśāśvamedha argue is that fully uncremated bodies in the Gaṅgā are less dangerous than the social conditions they reflect. These bodies represent, to them, a decline in the practice of cremation and therefore mark the moral degeneracy of contemporary society.

Paṇḍās tend to refer to corpses as *gandagī* when speaking with others who appear to embrace a scientific or ecological view of the river. Although, in these discussions, they tend to consider corpses in a secular sense, they also mock the very argument put forth by media and official reports that dead bodies, as *gandagī*, are harmful for the river. They often pointed out dead bodies to me in phrases such as, "Look Madam, dead body!" and then laughed at my disgust. Such mocking exclamations made me realize that they were not as alarmed about the uncleanness of Gaṅgā caused by corpses as scientists and officials claimed to be. In fact, they generally tended to steer the discussion about fully uncremated dead bodies back to the societal ills that the bodies reflected, which they believed were far more disturbing to their values and occupational existence.

Some residents blame pollution prevention projects for the rise in cases of partially cremated and fully uncremated corpses. Under the Ganga Action Plan, the government constructed an electric crematorium on Hariścandra Ghāṭ to ease the pollution load on the river. In addition, this was to provide a viable solution to the increasing cost of wood for cremation. When it began, pilgrim priests involved with cremation rituals opposed the project because it threatened to disturb traditional Hindu practices of wood cremation (see Parry 1994, 67–68). Today, the increasing use of the electric crematorium still disturbs them, especially those priests whose services are tied up with wood cremation. The fully uncremated dead bodies floating down the Gaṅgā today do not come from the electric crematorium. Still, in the minds of the *paṇḍās*, the facility is implicated. They are a result, the *paṇḍās* say, of the further decline in respect for traditional practices set in motion when the government established an alternate form of cremation.

Residents often complain that government projects rarely serve the best interests of the public. In 1987, Ganga Action Plan authorities created a turtle breeding farm to raise and release turtles into the river to eat the flesh of floating corpses. Most residents consider this project a complete failure because they never see the turtles consuming corpses. A bicycle rickshaw pedaler I have used for many years often finds the turtles swimming up the Varaṇā river. They tend to make life difficult for residents taking their morning bath in that tributary. The turtle breeding farm at Sarnath outside the city limits of Banaras showed signs of downsizing in 1993. By 1995, the project had been eliminated from Phase II of the Ganga Action Plan.

As indicated above, *paṇḍās* firmly believe that partially cremated or fully uncremated dead bodies dumped in the river do not threaten Gaṅgā's spiritual integrity. But they seem to fear that industrial waste, or more generally "dirty water" from drains, may have a harmful impact over time, by making the Gaṅgā *asvaccha* or physically unclean. Still residents insist that *gandagī* cannot alter Gaṅgā's power to give liberation (*mukti* or *mokṣa*) and purify the ashes of the deceased. This power is eternal and not subject to fluctuations in material reality. They add that as long as humans demonstrate their reverence through ritual ablution, *āratī*, and other forms of worship, Gaṅgā will remain happy. As long as she is happy, she will purify the cosmos, soul, body, and heart. But even if, in theory, Gaṅgā's purificatory power remains infinite, residents do express concern about their personal health and appear disturbed by *gandagī*. Two of the three dominant *paṇḍās* of Daśāśvamedha rarely bathe at their *ghāṭ*. They recommend cleaner locations! The most powerful boatman in the area complains that his doctor suggested he also avoid bathing at Daśāśvamedha—to prevent skin disease.

In *Water and Womanhood,* Feldhaus (1995) describes how residents of Maharashtra associate the river with feminine imagery. She argues that they stress a river's female attributes over its purificatory power. Banaras residents also conceive of the river in feminine terms, but they link femininity with motherliness, house-keeping and clean-up, and forgiveness. Many Daśāśvamedha residents and pilgrims remark that Gaṅgā, like a good mother, cleans up the messes her children make and forgives them lovingly. In this way, she cleans up other kinds of dirtiness people bring to her and excuses dirty behavior with maternal kindness.[9] Gaṅgā is forgiving rather than angry about human dirtiness.

Residents of Banaras, therefore, differ quite markedly from residents of the village of Ghatiyali in Rajasthan. Residents of Ghatiyali claim that God is angered by deforestation and, in retaliation, withholds rain. The forgiving nature of Gaṅgā that Banaras residents describe is problematic for the environmental activists in the Clean Ganga Campaign, who hope to raise awareness about pollution prevention. Environmental activists in Banaras argue that this view of sacred purity and loving tolerance leads to a passive acceptance of polluting behavior. However, these very activists understand that revising this deep religious association between water and long-suffering womanhood, so as to include human responsibility for Gaṅgā's well-being, will be difficult indeed. The villagers Gold describes may be in a better position to accept the message of environmental activism because they understand that the environment participates in the fruits of human sin. Residents of Daśāśvamedha, on the other hand, link morality to *gandagī* but do not find that the Gaṅgā participates in the sin-game (*pāp-līlā*) of humans. This means that she is, by extension, unaffected by the sins of humans and not motivated toward retaliation. She did, after all, descend to earth to wash away those very misdeeds.

Environmental activists are frustrated by the fact that residents of Daśāśvamedha passively accept the conditions of *gandagī* by pointing to Gaṅgā's own power to solve the problem. To understand the broader context of this apparent complacency, however, we must trace how pilgrim priests connect Gaṅgā's purity (and purificatory power) to their own occupational interests. *Paṇḍās* consistently defend their conviction that human-created *gandagī* does not alter Gaṅgā's purity. But they do not deny the presence of *gandagī* in the river. This position is most noticeable when they argue that Gaṅgā may be materially unclean (*gandā* or *asvaccha*)—that is, affected by *gandagī*—but not impure (*aśuddha* or *apavitra*). In their discussions about how waste impacts the Gaṅgā, the distinction between physical cleanness and sacred purity is most salient. Their comments allow us to see that the blurring of the distinction in the spatial dimensions of the *akhāṛā* does not mean that, because purity and cleanness are closely connected, they mean the same thing all the time. Impurity and uncleanness are also intimately linked in references to the fully uncremated dead bodies floating in the Gaṅgā. But when residents attempt to logically explain how uncleanness and sacred purity coexist in the Gaṅgā, they allow the conceptual categories to work independently. Gaṅgā, while she can be dirty, cannot be impure. Therefore, like the robe Srinivas found, she is both dirty and pure. However, if she is dirty (*gandā/asvaccha*), it is because people have made her that way (see Alley 1994, 130).

The idea that Gaṅgā's purity overrides human *gandagī* is a self-serving one for *paṇḍās*. Pilgrim service is lucrative and *paṇḍās* want it to remain that way. As one *paṇḍā* put it, "From sunrise to sunset, it is just earning, earning, earning." Many scholarly accounts have estimated that over the past four decades the number of pilgrims visiting Banaras daily to see the divine (take *darśan*) has steadily increased (see Fuller 1992, 205; Parry 1994, 108; Veer 1994, 122). Local gossip puts the *paṇḍās'* earnings at well above average for Banaras. *Paṇḍās* do in fact own substantial homes on southern Daśāśvamedha. In them sacred icons are enshrined. One mansion towers above the Rām temple on Prayāg Ghāṭ. Another home contains the Prayāgeśvara shrine, and a third shelters a goddess, reputedly made of gold. From look-out points on their property, these *paṇḍās* watch over the activities on the *ghāṭ* and oversee the exchanges that the lower-ranked pilgrim priests, *tīrth purohits* and *ghāṭiyas,* undertake with pilgrims. For over three generations, the *paṇḍās* of southern Daśāśvamedha have retained their rights to serve pilgrims coming from the former princely states of Palamu, Singrauli, and Sonbhadhra. Even as the district names have changed over time, many pilgrims continue to identify—when looking for the Banaras priest who serves clients from their region—with the former princely states within whose old borders they still live.

These princely states were located in regions which now extend across the north Indian states of Uttar Pradesh and Bihar. They mark the historical homelands of several tribal groups in India. These tribal groups now comprise the agricultural or small land-holding class in these states. Pilgrims pay fees (*dakṣiṇā*) and offer donations (*dān*) to *paṇḍās* in exchange for shelter, offerings blessed by deities (*prasād*), and ritual services. *Paṇḍās* also receive commissions from the income of the other priests who rent spaces on the *ghāṭ* from them. On their wooden platforms, the lower-ranked priests preside over pilgrims' offerings throughout the morning, assisting them also by watching over their personal possessions.

Like the villagers of Ghatiyali, *paṇḍās* feel caught up in a moral and cosmic degeneracy which sets the context for their social concerns. In their account of the present degenerate state of the world, *paṇḍās* deflect blame from human agency by pointing toward a cosmic design in which truth turns against humankind. The cosmos passes through many aeons in its cyclical passage; the Kali Yuga is the last of four declining ages that form one such aeon. The Kali Yuga, or "Dark Age," began on February 18, 3102 B.C.E. and will continue for another 426,904 years (Fuller 1992, 266). This time spells diminished virtue, moral degeneracy, and sin for all living souls. As Madan (1987, 128) put it, in this age people do not engage in severe penance to gain the favor of gods and goddesses, and therefore very few individuals receive divine blessing. The *Śiva Purāṇa* describes the Kali Age as follows:

> At the advent of the terrible age of *Kali* men have become devoid of merits. They are engaged in evil ways of life. They have turned their faces from truthful avocations. They are engaged in calumniating others. They covet other men's wealth. Their attention is diverted to other men's wives. Injuring others has become their chief aim. (*ŚP* 1.12–13)

For *paṇḍās,* the Kali Yuga forms the cosmic backdrop to their current predicament. *Paṇḍās* argue that "man and money power" has succeeded in dominating the pilgrim services and businesses in Banaras. Because of this, the *paṇḍā* profession has been dirtied. In discussions of power, *paṇḍās* extend the metaphor of *gandagī* to signify immoral and ritually imbalanced social conditions. *Paṇḍās* argue that because they are forced to defend their hereditary right rather than remain divinely entitled to it, their moral authority wanes. This instability contributes to the lax ritual atmosphere in which respect for Gaṅgā is diminishing. But the degenerate pull of the Kali Yuga does not overpower her. She staves off the collapse, retains her purity, and continues to wash away human dirtiness. The *Bhāgavata Purāṇa* powerfully expresses this theme in the myth of Gaṅgā's descent from heaven. Gaṅgā flowed over the foot of Viṣṇu into Brahmā's water jug (*kamaṇḍal*) and "washed away the dirt, in the form of the sins of the whole of the world, by her touch, and yet, remained pure" (*BhP* 5.17.1).

Given Gaṅgā's transcendent power, people can aim to please her and thereby assist in partially rejuvenating the moral order. *Paṇḍās* believe that pilgrims can please Gaṅgā by worshiping her, even if they cannot purify her. Purificatory power can be achieved only by the few. The rare individuals who have purified themselves through *yoga* and become saints, channels of divine blessing, do have powers to repurify Gaṅgā. As Vatsyayan (1993, 167) writes, the respect paid to Gaṅgā by saints is especially important, as the transfer of their ascetic power (*tapas*) to Gaṅgā can re-purify the cosmos. But ordinary pilgrims and residents cannot emulate saints. *Paṇḍās* know their spiritual power is limited, because they have not renounced the material world and live amidst human *gandagī*. Nevertheless, they know they can at least please Gaṅgā by performing *āratī* on auspicious occasions.

At the time of my field study, I suggested to the *paṇḍās* that they make speeches in their forthcoming *āratī* celebration to raise awareness about the problems *gandagī* creates for Gaṅgā. This was not an entirely unusual proposition. In February of 1994, they performed their first big *āratī* (*mahāratī*) on the auspicious occasion of Māgha Pūrṇimā. Māgha Pūrṇimā is the full moon day in Māgh (January–February), a day when Gaṅgā *snān* is especially meritorious. The group claimed a concern for cleanness then, and media reports praised them for their efforts to clean the *ghāṭs* before the worship ceremony.

They performed their second public *āratī* alongside a music festival organized by the Clean Ganga Campaign on Tulsī Ghāṭ. The third performance fell on Kārtik Pūrṇimā, the full moon day in the auspicious month of Kārtik.

While *āratī* evokes public praise for Gaṅgā and affirms her purifying power, *paṇḍās* also expect the ceremony to generate donations. They often complained to me that *āratī* was expensive for them. They had imported the silver lamps and whisks (*cavār*) from Bengal and had the "gents and ladies" costumes made with fine cloth. *Paṇḍās* claim that it is difficult to bear the cost of *āratī* on a monthly basis. They continue to conclude, however, that *āratī* is the only method they can use to encourage reverence for Gaṅgā.[10] The relationship that people establish with Ganga through *āratī* is meant to be morally uplifting. Proper morality is reflected in the respect worshipers give to powerful cosmic forces (such as Gaṅgā's purificatory power). Efforts to please the gods and goddesses that control these forces are meritorious moral acts that can help to bring the population out of the current state of degeneracy.

This assessment, that Gaṅgā's purity is the primary force staving off moral and cosmic degeneracy as well as physical pollution, puts the *paṇḍās* outside policy discourses on pollution prevention carried out by government agencies and non-governmental citizen-action groups. The *Paṇḍās* do not act as city advisors or assume positions in organizations such as the Rotary Club, the Lions Club, or the Clean Ganga Campaign. Their own organization is called the Ganga Seva Sangh, which means "Association for [Religious] Service to Gaṅgā." It is focused exclusively on the religious concerns of Hindu pilgrims.

DEGENERACY AND THE GENEALOGY OF ENVIRONMENTAL POLLUTION

Government officials and scientists articulate idioms of degeneracy markedly different from those expressed by the *paṇḍās* of southern Daśāśvamedha. Unlike the *paṇḍās*, they locate degeneracy in the physical river Gaṅgā and in the ecological system within which the river is an integral water supplier. Ecological degeneracy is, for them, a consequence of human activities associated with industrialization, urban growth, and the overpopulation of the river basin.

Discussions of ecological degeneracy go back no more than fifteen years in Indian scientific and secular discourses. Three professors who teach engineering at Banaras Hindu University were the first to focus public attention on problems of river pollution. In 1982, they formed an organization called the Clean Ganga Campaign (Swatcha Ganga Abhiyan) and listed it under a religious institution run by one of its principal members. They find that the distinction between physical cleanness and sacred purity is crucial to their environmental message, and they evoke it as a way to form a syncretism of Hinduism and science. The importance of this distinction is at first evident in their organization's name. They use the word *svaccha* (which they spell *swatcha*) to show that they are an organization concerned with physical cleanness rather than sacred purity. But CGC members are not removed from religious concerns. The leading member of the group is also the head priest of a religious institution, the Sankat Mochan Foundation. This organization manages the Saṅkaṭ Mocan Temple, an important Hindu temple where the saint-poet Tulsī Dās received his vision of Hanumān, the monkey-god of the *Rāmāyaṇa*. The leaders explain that their concern is with the impact of waste on the physical Gaṅgā. They do not contest or seek to denigrate her eternal sacred purity.[11] While they revere Gaṅgā through worship rituals in their private lives, they do not claim to promote a revitalization of such rituals through their own organization work.

The Clean Ganga Campaign's agitation in the early 1980s focused Indira Gandhi's attention on issues of river pollution. They asked her to consider establishing sewage management programs in cities bordering the river. After Mrs. Gandhi's death and the passage of power to her son Rajiv, the first official policies addressing sewage management and pollution prevention were drawn up. In 1986, Rajiv Gandhi established an agency called the Ganga Project Directorate to oversee the Ganga Action Plan. The Ganga Action Plan or GAP was set up to create pollution prevention programs and sewage treatment infrastructure in five Class I cities (those with populations over 100,000) bordering the Gaṅgā. Well before sufficient data had been collected to understand the waste complex, decisions were made on sewage treatment and management. The many contracts for treatment plants, funded by foreign lenders, were modeled on energy-intensive methods more suitable for climates in Western countries. In Kanpur and Mirzapur, for example, the Indo-Dutch Cooperation Programme established treatment plants according to the process called the Upflow Anaerobic Sludge Blanket (UASB). Using a different method in Banaras, the government built one activated sludge treatment plant to treat eighty million liters of urban sewage per day (mld). They made other renovations to sewage lines and pumping stations under the first phase of the Plan. In June of 1993, the Ministry of Environment and Forests announced that under Phase I of the Ganga Action Plan they had commissioned fifteen treatment plants. All the plants combined are able to treat 300 million liters of sewage per day.[12]

In official and scientific reports, the parameters of Biological Oxygen Demand (BOD) and Fecal Coliform Count (FCC) have been used to measure levels of river pollution. Under the first phase of the Plan, several universities in the Gangetic plain received grants to establish water monitoring programs in four cities—Hardwar, Allahabad, Banaras, and Patna (Murti et al. 1991). Until 1992, data were forwarded to the Ganga Project Directorate, which then published results selectively. Since that time, however, the CGC members have considered the data passed to the Directorate by academic departments and government water monitoring agencies invalid (see Sankat Mochan Foundation 1990, 1992, 1994). The CGC has, in fact, used the issue of validity to challenge government monitoring programs in a more comprehensive way. To do this, in 1992 they established their own water monitoring laboratory with domestic and foreign financial assistance. But their aim was not simply to generate alternate data. They pressed the GPD to expand its own monitoring program. While official monitoring used the parameter of BOD—along with others such as dissolved oxygen, conductivity, pH and temperature—it did not include the parameter of fecal coliform count (FCC) (see Alley 1994, 134–36). Clean Ganga Campaign members argued that fecal coliform, an important indicator of human sewage levels, ought to be a required component of monitoring. Furthermore, the FCC data could be used to evaluate the effectiveness of the sewage management system. After the CGC made this argument in many meetings, the government agreed to include this parameter and began testing for it in 1994. The Clean Ganga Campaign, on the other hand, began monitoring water quality with the FCC parameter in 1992.

In their June 1993 report, the GPD announced that pollution levels in the Gaṅgā were declining because of infrastructural improvements in sewage management and treatment. They reported a decline in BOD levels in Banaras from ten mg/liter in 1986 to between one and two mg/liter in 1992 (Ministry of Environment and Forests 1993). Members of the Clean Ganga Campaign charged that these declines were exaggerated. According to CGC reports published in 1994, BOD levels just downstream from Daśāśvamedha Ghāṭ were much more variable. In May, BOD varied from 1.11 mg/liter to 26.50, depending on the time of day monitoring occurred. Higher figures tended to reflect times when the sewage lines leading to the Gaṅgā under the *ghāṭs* were open (see Sankat Mochan Foundation 1994). FCC levels were as high as 440,000 colonies per 100 ml in March and exceeded 320,000 in April of 1994.[13]

ASSESSING POLLUTION IN ORDER TO TREAT IT

After the treatment plant in Banaras was completed in the spring of 1993, the Clean Ganga Campaign began to notice various operational problems. For example, the plant's collection chamber proved too small to hold incoming discharge from the city during the monsoon. Consequently, the sewage backed up through the main trunk line after heavy rains. During previous monsoons, officials had diverted the city's discharge into the Gaṅgā through the outlet point lying downstream from Rāj Ghāṭ (see Alley 1992, 126–27; Alley 1994, 132–34). In early 1994, the Clean Ganga Campaign members demanded that government officials close the outlet drain to the Gaṅgā. They asked them to comply with the stated objectives of the project and divert all sewage to the plant. Consequently, the sewage backed up, creating what they called a "surcharge" in the main trunk line. The CGC pointed to this as proof of the inappropriate design of the collection chamber. After many requests from the CGC, the Ganga Project Directorate convened a meeting of technical experts in the field of sewage treatment to discuss the problems at the Banaras plant. This occurred in August of 1994. The CGC was invited to attend, and I followed along as a foreign member. At the forum, CGC members charged that monitoring officials had not conducted a thorough study of city waste discharge before designing the plant. Consequently, they constructed the collection chamber improperly. They added that discharge rates put out by the Ganga Project Directorate in 1994 were also dubious. Pointing out that the data from their research contradicted official reports, they demanded a role as an outside witness in future discharge measurement and monitoring.

Additionally, the Clean Ganga Campaign members presented a proposal for oxidation ponds as an alternate method of sewage treatment. This proposal had the support of their cadre of foreign experts, which included researchers at the University of California at Berkeley and the University of Stockholm. More suited to India's hot climate, it uses only a fraction of the energy consumed by the activated sludge process. This alternative, they submitted, would avoid the high energy costs incurred by the activated sludge plant. This is crucial because the electric board of the state of Uttar Pradesh has not consistently supplied the required energy to the plant since its commissioning.

Alongside its role as a watchdog of official policy, the Clean Ganga Campaign also considers itself the local vanguard for raising awareness about pollution prevention. Since 1982, it has organized many educational programs to bring this issue to public attention. In late 1994, they hosted a "Public Forum" with Dr. Karan Singh, the chairman of the People's Commission on Environment and Development and former Indian Ambassador to the United States. They organized this event to hear residents' opinions on waste problems affecting their sacred river. During my fieldwork, I passed on to the *paṇḍās* of Daśāśvamedha invitations to the event. They attended under the banner of their organization, the Ganga Seva Sangh, and had their first formal meeting with Clean Ganga Campaign members.

The CGC maintains respect for religious notions of Gaṅgā's purificatory power, while pleading for measures to reduce the material waste load on the river. They do not state that Gaṅgā is impure in a sacred sense, for they do not believe this and science provides no proof for it. Instead, they maintain the distinction between physical cleanness and purity to argue that despite her purificatory power, she is becoming *asvaccha* and needs to be *svaccha*. At the same time, in official circles using scientific language, they publish their water quality data to argue for accountability in sewage management and treatment. The individuals who debate about measurement and data, however, constitute a small circle. This circle does not include any residents of Daśāśvamedha. While discourse on water quality data does not alienate other Banaras residents, it has not achieved the effect of increasing local membership in environmental groups such as the CGC. This is precisely because residents do not understand the scientific ideas within their assessments.

There are no other organized groups which challenge government projects in Banaras. There are a few smaller clubs which claim concern for the environment and several professors, journalists, and playwrights who are, in passing, critical of current sewage management. But they do not regularly contest the official view. Therefore, the gradual increase in government attention to waste management projects has not coincided with the emergence of an environmental movement. Terms such as BOD and FCC mean nothing to most residents of Banaras. Moreover, citizens interpret the tendencies of officials to package their environmental goals with instrumental-scientific rationality as attempts to forward the material interests of the elite. For them, this means that everything, in the final analysis, is reduced to money. Both governmental and nongovernmental organizations tend to talk in a scientific language that assumes a position of superiority. At the same time, the government's assessments imply the inferiority of religious modes of discourse. Defensively, the *paṇḍās* of Daśāśvamedha argue that their knowledge, informed by sacred texts, is more authoritative. *Paṇḍās* admit, however, that sacred (*śāstrik*) knowledge is weak in material power and explanation, and therefore threatened in the Kali Yuga by science and the "man and money power" behind it. Thus, according to *paṇḍās,* not only does science negate divine power, but it is associated, through money, with the moral degeneracy of the Kali Yuga.

IN THE NAME OF GAṄGĀ

While there is no sociologically recognizable environmental movement in Banaras today (see, for example, Buttel 1987, 1992; Buttel and Taylor 1992), residents engage in constant verbal resistance to the government's ineffectual campaign to combat pollution. The CGC does engage in direct confrontation with government officials in the Ganga Project Directorate, but their activities involve only a small minority of the local population. The GPD, the CGC, and residents of Daśāśvamedha are for the most part aware of each other's claims about sacred purity and environmental pollution. However, while all claim to be acting out of genuine concern for her welfare, each group is skeptical of the others' desire to respect the Gaṅgā's purity or prevent her being polluted. In other words, each group accuses the other of acting "in the name of Gaṅgā" (*gaṅgā ke nām par*), not in true service to her. There is a sense on all sides that concern for the Gaṅgā is more often than not rhetorically staged to obfuscate other, more self-interested motives. *Paṇḍās* see sewage treatment plants and projects as vehicles for state moneymaking. Quite often, they complain that pollution prevention work is merely "on paper" and does not produce any productive results. Many residents of Daśāśvamedha insist that officials have not adequately capped the drains feeding dirty water (*gandā pānī*) into the Gaṅgā. *Paṇḍās* are also suspicious about the activities of the Clean Ganga Campaign, since they remain outside that circle as well. They charge that most of the CGC's work includes foreigners, who are contributing money and material supplies. Moreover, *paṇḍās* argue that all the money allocated for sewage management has been "eaten." They often express this with the phrase, "They've eaten it all up" (*sab khā liyā*) The efforts of both are vitiated, in the *paṇḍās*' eyes, by the money-grabbing ethos of the Kali Yuga.

The CGC agrees that the Government of India has not used public funds properly to build effective sewage treatment plants and to renovate existing infrastructure. In response, the Ganga Project Directorate charges that the CGC is offering exaggerated criticisms and fanciful proposals for alternatives. Government officials also blame pilgrims and residents of Banaras for their adherence to a tradition that encourages an intensive use of the river for religious purposes. Furthermore, government officials point out that *paṇḍās* uphold the ideology of purity to support their own economic interests. Finally, all groups are suspicious that the anthropologist, with her curious concern for Gaṅgā, is studying pollution also to make money.

CONCLUSIONS

Both *paṇḍās* and the scientific-official camp agree that degeneracy exists, but they locate its core in different spheres. For *paṇḍās,* marketplace competition, cheating, and corruption are signs of moral degeneracy and reflect a cosmic cycle. Although to some extent, they believe they are caught in this cosmic cycle, *paṇḍās* suggest that the moral order can be reset by Gaṅgā's power to purify. A conviction among people to follow principles in sacred texts through adherence to ritual, they maintain, could also bring back a popular respect for Hindu beliefs. Religious beliefs do not provide a disincentive for cleaning the river, per se, because they affirm a high value for Gaṅgā and are based upon a deep spiritual understanding of the river. However, that ablution (*snān*) and worship (*pūjā*) continue to occur, even in a context of *gandagī,* reassures Hindu believers that the integrity of *Gaṅgā's* sacred purity is protected. Moreover, *paṇḍās* make sacred purity a much more complicated issue because they use this conviction to support their occupational activities. The belief in sacred purity in this case makes acceptance of immoral or corrupt behavior possible even when that very behavior is denounced.

I have shown that residents of Daśāśvamedha and the sacred texts they read advocate the distancing principle to deal with the problems of human uncleanness and *gandagī.* Religious attitudes would not, therefore, necessarily bode ill for the ecological future of the river if residents and pilgrims could enforce the distancing principle while worshiping Gaṅgā's sacred purity. The urban predicament, however, is complicated, and even *paṇḍās* know that waste drainage and treatment systems are essential to keeping Daśāśvamedha livable. Residents seem to want better enforcement of both religious and secular laws to regulate public behavior on the *ghāṭs.* Unfortunately, current scientific-official projects do not, in many residents' eyes, meet this need. *Āratī* may please Gaṅgā and help to rejuvenate the moral order, but *paṇḍās* know the ceremony alone cannot enforce the ancient ideal of distancing uncleanness from the river bank.

Academics and officials, even while respecting religious ideas about Gaṅgā's power to provide for human well-being, locate degeneracy in the ecological balance of the river. There is no common agreement between academics, officials, and residents of Daśāśvamedha about how to approach the problem of *gandagī* and its impact on the Gaṅgā. *Paṇḍās* and Clean Ganga Campaign members evoke the distinction between physical cleanness and sacred purity and therefore share some common ground in their assessments. However, the scientific knowledge of the latter group is meaningless to the former. All players do acknowledge that sewage treatment and public activity on the riverbank fall well short of keeping human uncleanness away from the river. But when residents face what they consider are the vacant meanings of scientific concepts and witness the blunders in official cleaning and sewage treatment projects, the divide between the concerned parties is heightened and communication is blocked.

A local journalist recently remarked that I would not find the seeds for a mass revolution (against *gandagī* and dirty business) on Daśāśvamedha. On the other hand, efforts to clean up pollution are tied to infrastructural and monetary assistance at the national and global levels. Therefore, we can expect to find more pollution prevention schemes developed by officials and scientists in the coming years. Indeed, *gandagī* is everywhere, and to everyone a burden. Whatever environmental activists and government officials may think, they need to be aware that the worldview of the local people must be an important factor in any solution. Since environmental activists find that the belief in sacred purity ultimately allows residents to reject or opt out of projects to tackle the problems of *gandagī*, they should try to interact with local religious leaders to sort out how occupational interests linked to ritual purity can become more connected with the need for physical cleanness. Greater communication between environmental activists and residents of Daśāśvamedha and other neighborhoods could also heighten the public awareness needed to force government agencies to be accountable for the municipal cleaning and waste management projects they undertake.

On one occasion, when I pleaded that *paṇḍās* take a greater interest in cleaning their *ghāṭ* and enforcing rules of distancing uncleanness from Gaṅgā, one *paṇḍā* insisted that it was the government's duty to clean the area, through the local municipality. If they do not do their work, he argued, then our only alternative is to turn to Gaṅgā. Reminding me about a passage from the *Gaṅgā Stuti,* he then began to sing, "O Bhāgīrathī [Gaṅgā], though we are full of sin, give us a place at your feet, give us *mukti.*"

NOTES

1. See, for example, Callicott 1994, Capra 1991, Fox 1990, India International Centre 1993, Lovelock 1988 and Singh 1993b.

2. See Eck 1993, 13–14; 1982; Havell 1990 (1905), 109–10; Motichandra 1985; Singh 1993a; *KKh* 52.1–10; and Vidyarthi et al. 1979 for discussions of the sacred importance of Daśāśvamedha.

3. See Alley 1994, 130–31 for other references to Gaṅgā's forms and meanings.

4. This account comes from a *paṇḍā*'s favorite text: *PM,* p. 39. In Hindi, the passage is as follows: Gaṅgā apnā nām uccāraṇ karnewāle ke papo kā nāś karti hai, darśan karnewāle kā kalyāṇ karti hai, aur snānpān karnewāle kī sat pīṛiyo tak ko pavitra karti hai.

5. This *stuti* was written by Kavi Kesav. One *paṇḍā* had the *stuti* hand-written on a single sheet of paper and helped me in translating it. It is sung in their *ārati* ceremonies.

6. See Veer 1988 and Parry 1980, 1981, 1994 for other characterizations of this occupational group. The term *paṇḍā,* however, is a designation that these pilgrim priests do not particularly like, though they use it to refer to each other in local discourse. When I informed them that I use this term in my description of their occupation, they requested that I use a more respectable term to describe their work. They suggested that I use the title *rāj purohit* (the king's priest) or *paṇḍit* (learned Brahmin). These are terms which in their mind do not carry a negative connotation. This discontent with the title *paṇḍā* reflects their feeling that outsiders and brokers have spoiled the image of the *paṇḍāgīrī* by cheating pilgrims and corrupting the service occupation.

7. see Carman and Marglin 1985; Gold 1988; Madan 1985, 1987; and Raheja 1988.

8. English-medium newspapers in India and other countries have tended to sensationalize the issue of dead bodies in the Gaṅgā more than the Indian papers written in the Hindi medium have. An article from the *Washington Post* entitled "Devout Hindus Resist Efforts to Clean Up the Sacred Ganges" (Claiborne 1983) and a report in the *Patriot Magazine* entitled "Save the Ganga" (Singh 1984) are the earliest media reports to highlight dead bodies as signs of Gaṅgā pollution. They predate the formation of GAP. The *Patriot Magazine* opens its article with the following description:

> At the edge of the steps on the Dashasmedh [*sic*] *ghat* a bare bodied man sits cross legged getting ready for his "aachman." A few feet to his right bobs the decayed carcass of a cow in the river, a crow hovering over it. I turn away in disgust, but a more grisly sight awaits me: two dead bodies floating near the edge of a *ghat* and a group of pilgrims having bath completely oblivious to them.

Along with this, the caption for a photograph of a corpse washed up on the riverbank reads: "A *Ghat:* As mysterious as the dead bodies floating." Later reports in the *Star Tribune* (Tempest 1987) and the *Smithsonian* (Ward 1985), among others, also consider dead bodies an environmental problem. The Hindi newspapers have been less inclined to highlight dead bodies, and have tended to focus more on the activities of the Clean Ganga Campaign and on reports of water quality. One of only a few exceptions to this is found in an article in *India Today* entitled "No Bhagirath Came" (Sharma 1987). The article opens with the following passage: "Ganga—one clean [*svaccha*], pure [*śuddha*] and benign [*mṛdu*] Ganga. But there is one dream that burdens the Hindu heart. In Varanasi today half-burnt corpses are seen swimming in this river." In most Hindi reports published from 1987 through 1994, the term *svaccha* is frequently used in calls for a clean Gaṅgā. In a few reports, the word *śuddha* is used interchangeably with *svaccha*. These Hindi reports also use the terms pollution (*pradūṣaṇ*) and polluted (*pradūṣit* or *dūṣit*) when describing the condition of the river. Many reports refer to cleaning projects as methods that will "free Gaṅgā of pollution" (*gaṅgā pradūṣaṇ se mukt hogī*).

9. Curiously, unlike other gods or goddesses who may become angry if defiled by humans (see Dumong and Pocock 1959, 31; Fuller 1979, 469; 1992, 76; Harper 1964, 183–86; Sharma 1970, 1819; Srinivas 1952, 41–42, 78), Gaṅgā does not lash back at this human abuse and defilement.

10. This reminded me of a story that a devotee of Anandamayi Ma, a highly regarded female saint, told me in 1994:

> Śiva and Pārvatī were talking, and Pārvatī asked him a question. She said, "If so many people are taking bath (*snān*) and absolving their sins, why does the same kind of life persist?" Śiva took Pārvatī to the riverbank to demonstrate his response. Śiva disguised himself as an old man with leprosy and stood near the bathing area. As people were leaving, he asked them, "Whoever has been purified and is not without sin, bless me with Gaṅgā water (*gaṅgā jal*) so I may be saved." Despite his requests, no one stopped for him. Finally one man agreed to bless him because he said he had just performed ablutions. He purified the old man and walked on. Then Śiva said, as he turned to Pārvatī, "Because not enough people have faith, they carry their sin and do ablutions as a mere routine. You cannot simply do it," he concluded, "you must believe it."

11. See Alley 1994, 135 for one leader's formula for reconciling the contradictions between scientific and Hindu worldviews.

12. See Ministry of Environment and Forests pamphlet entitled "Ganga Action Plan Achievements" issued by Project Director, Central Ganga Authority, Ministry of Environment and Forests, 5 June, 1993.

13. Biological Oxygen Demand (BOD) indicates whether there is enough oxygen in the water to sustain aquatic life. Acceptable BOD levels for bathing are set at 1–3 mg/liter and for drinking, at less than 1 mg/liter. Fecal Coliform Count (FCC) is the most probable number of bacterial colonies in a water sample. Acceptable levels for bathing are less than 500 per 100 ml.

REFERENCES

Primary Sources, with Abbreviations

BhP *Bhāgavata Purāṇa*. Translated and annotated by G. V. Tagare. Part 2 (*Skandhas* 4–6). Delhi: Motilal Banarsidass, 1976.

KKh *Kāśī Khaṇḍa*. Edited by A. S. K. Tripathi. 2 parts. Varanasi: Sampurnanand Sanskrit University, 1991. (All translations cited are from Singh 1993a.)

PM *Paramśānti Kā Mārg*. Shri Jaidayaal Goyandka. Varanasi, n.d. (All translations are my own.)

ŚP *Śiva Purāṇa*. Translated by a board of scholars and edited by J. L. Shastri. Vol. 1. Delhi: Motilal Banarsidass, 1990.

Secondary Sources

Alley, Kelly D. 1992. "On the Banks of the Ganga." *Annals of Tourism Research* 19 (Winter): 125–27.

———. 1994. "Ganga and *Gandagi:* Interpretations of Pollution and Waste in Benaras." *Ethnology* 33 (Spring): 127–45.

Buttel, Frederick H. 1987. "New Directions in Environmental Sociology." *Annual Review of Sociology* 13: 465–88.

———. 1992. "Environmentalization: Origins, Processes, and Implications for Rural Social Change." *Rural Sociology* 57 (Spring): 1–27.

Buttel, Frederick, and Peter Taylor. 1992. "Environmental Sociology and Global Environmental Change: A Critical Assessment." *Society and Natural Resources* 5 (July–September): 211–30.

Callicott, J. Baird. 1994. *Earth's Insights: A Survey of Ecological Ethics from the Mediterranean Basin to the Australian Outback.* Berkeley: University of California Press.

Capra, F. 1991. *Belonging to the Universe: Explorations on the Frontiers of Science and Spirituality.* San Francisco: Harper San Francisco.

Carman, J. B., and F. A. Marglin. 1985. *Purity and Auspiciousness in Indian Society.* Leiden: E. J. Brill.

Claiborne, William. 1983. "Devout Hindus Resist Efforts to Clean Up the Sacred Ganges." *The Washington Post,* 8 May, 18–19 (A).

Das, Veena. 1982. *Structure and Cognition: Aspects of Hindu Caste and Ritual.* 2d ed. Delhi: Oxford University Press.

Dimmit, C., and J. A. B. van Buitenen. 1978. *Classical Hindu Mythology.* Philadelphia: University of Pennsylvania Press.

Dumont, L. 1970. *Homo Hierarchicus.* Chicago: University of Chicago Press.

Dumont, L., and D. F. Pocock. 1959. "Pure and Impure." *Contributions to Indian Sociology* 3: 9–34.

Eck, D. 1982. *Banaras: City of Light.* New York: Alfred Knopf.

———. 1993. "A Survey of Sanskrit Sources for the Study of Varanasi." In *Banaras (Varanasi): Cosmic Order, Sacred City, Hindu Traditions,* ed. R. P. B. Singh, 9–19. Varanasi: Tara Book Agency.

Feldhaus, Anne. 1995. *Water and Womanhood: Religious Meanings of Rivers in Maharashtra.* New York: Oxford University Press.

Fuller, C. J. 1979. "Gods, Priests and Purity: On the Relation Between Hinduism and the Caste System." *Man (N.S.)* 14 (September): 459–76.

———. 1992. *The Camphor Flame.* Princeton: Princeton University Press.

Gold, Ann. 1988. *Fruitful Journeys: The Ways of Rajasthani Pilgrims.* Berkeley: University of California Press.

Hargrove, Eugene. 1986. *Religion and Environmental Crisis.* Athens: University of Georgia Press.

Havell, E. B. 1990 (1905). *Benares: The Sacred City.* Varanasi: Vishwavidyalaya Prakashan.

India International Centre. 1993. *Indigenous Vision: Peoples of India, Attitudes to the Environment.* India International Centre Quarterly. Delhi: India International Centre.

Kane, P. V. 1973. *History of Dharmasastra.* 2d ed. 4 vols. Government Oriental Series Class B, No. 6. Poona: Bhandarkar Oriental Research Institute.

Kinsley, D. 1987. *Hindu Goddesses: Visions of the Divine Feminine in the Hindu Religious Tradition.* Delhi: Motilal Banarsidass.

Lovelock, J. 1988. *The Ages of Gaia: A Biography of Our Living Earth.* New York: Norton.

Madan, T. N. 1985. "Concerning the Categories Subha and Suddha in Hindu Culture: An Exploratory Essay." In *Purity and Auspiciousness in Indian Society,* ed. J. B. Carman and F. A. Marglin, 11–29. Leiden: E. J. Brill.

———. 1987. *Non-Renunciation: Themes and Interpretations of Hindu Culture.* Delhi: Oxford University Press.

Moti Chandra, D. 1985. *Kashi Ka Itihas* 2d ed. Varanasi: Vishwavidyalaya Prakashan.

Murti, C. R. K., K. S. Bilgrami, T. M. Das, and R. P. Mathur, eds. 1991. *The Ganga: A Scientific Study.* New Delhi: Ganga Project Directorate.

O'Flaherty, W. D. 1976. *The Origins of Evil in Hindu Mythology.* Berkeley: University of California Press.

———. 1981. *The Rig Veda: An Anthology.* London: Penguin Press.

Parry, J. 1980. "Ghosts, Greed and Sin: the Occupational Identity of the Benaras Funeral Priests." *Man (N.S.)* 15 (March): 88–111.

———. 1994. *Death in Banaras.* Cambridge: Cambridge University Press.

Raheja, G. 1988. *The Poison in the Gift: Ritual, Prestation and the Dominant Caste in a North Indian Village.* Chicago: University of Chicago Press.

Sankat Mochan Foundation. 1990. *Swatcha Ganga Campaign Annual Report 1988–1990.* Varanasi: Swatcha Ganga Campaign.

———. 1992. *A Seminar on Pollution Control of River Cities in India: A Case Study of Varanasi.* Varanasi: Swatcha Ganga Campaign.

———. 1994. *Proposal for GAP Phase II at Varanasi.* Varanasi: Swatcha Ganga Campaign.

Sharma, B. K. 1987. "No Bhagirath Came" (*Koī Bhagīrath Nahī Āyā*). *India Today,* 15 July, 80.

Singh, B. R. S. 1984. "Save the Ganga." *Patriot Magazine,* 5 August, 1.

Singh, R. P. B., ed. 1993a. *Banaras (Varanasi): Cosmic Order, Sacred City, Hindu Traditions.* Varanasi: Tara Book Agency.

———. 1993b. *Environmental Ethics.* Varanasi: National Geographic Society.

Sivaramamurti, C. 1976. *Ganga.* Delhi: Orient Longman.

Spring, David, and Eileen Spring, eds. 1974. *Ecology and Religion in History.* New York: Harper and Row.

Srinivas, M. N. 1952. *Religion and Society Among the Coorgs of South India.* Bombay: Asia.

Suzuki, David, and Peter Knudtson. 1992. *Wisdom of the Elders.* New York: Bantam Books.

Tempest, Rone. 1987. "Holy River." *Star Tribune,* 25 October, 25–26(A).
van Buitenen, J. A. B. 1973. *The Mahabharata.* Chicago: University of Chicago Press.
Vatsyayan, Kapila. 1993. "Ecology and Indian Myth." In *Indigenous Vision: Peoples of India, Attitudes to the Environment,* ed. India International Centre, 157–80. Delhi: India International Centre.

Discussion Questions

1. What are the ecological implications of the doctrine of nonviolence (*ahimsa*)?
2. Do asceticism and world renunciation lead to an indifference toward the state of the environment?
3. How greatly do textual sources affect popular attitudes and behaviors toward the environment? What other factors have an effect?
4. Is the distinction between ritual and actual pollution in Hindu thought an obstacle to ecological awareness?

Further Reading

Callicott, J. Baird, and Roger Ames, Eds., *Nature in Asian Traditions of Thought,* Albany, N.Y.: SUNY Press, 1989.
Chapple, Christopher Key, Ed., *Jainism and Ecology,* Cambridge, Mass.: Harvard Center for the Study of World Religions, 2002.
Chapple, Christopher Key, and Mary Evelyn Tucker, Eds., *Hinduism and Ecology: The Intersection of Earth, Sky, and Water,* Cambridge, Mass.: Harvard University Press, 2000.
Cremo, Michael, and Mukunda Goswami, *Divine Nature: A Spiritual Perspective on the Environmental Crisis,* Los Angeles: Bhaktivedanta Book Trust, 1995.
Feldhaus, Anne, *Water and Womanhood. Religious Meanings of Rivers in Maharashtra,* New York: Oxford University Press, 1995.
Gosling, David, *Religion and Ecology in India and Southeast Asia,* New York: Routledge, 2001.
James, George A., Ed., *Ethical Perspectives on Environmental Issues in India,* New Delhi: A. P. H. Publishing Corporation, 1999.
Nelson, Lance E., Ed., *Purifying the Earthly Body of God: Religion and Ecology in Hindu India,* Albany, N.Y.: SUNY Press, 1998.
Prime, Ranchor, *Hinduism and Ecology: Seeds of Truth,* London: Cassell, 1992.

Chapter 5

Buddhism

HAVING ARISEN IN NORTHEASTERN India some 2,500 years ago, Buddhism holds claim to being the world's first *universal* philosophy. That is, in contrast to the previously discussed worldviews of first peoples and Hinduism, which were traditionally nonexclusive expressions of local communities, the teachings of the Buddha are understood by Buddhists to be valid and applicable to *all* peoples, regardless of their differing historical and social contexts.

Buddhism has developed quite differently within its various historical–cultural contexts (for example, in India, China, Tibet, Japan, and the United States) and in every case has been greatly influenced by pre-existing local worldviews. Buddhism's adaptability and capacity to absorb diverse beliefs and practices into itself, which has also been characteristic of Christianity and Islam, no doubt enables it (and other universalist systems) to persist and thrive in vastly different cultural environments.

The Buddha, or "enlightened one," whose given name was Siddhartha Gautama, probably lived sometime in the fifth century BCE (Differences in ancient calendars make precise dating difficult.). The essence of his teaching is contained in the Four Noble Truths, outlined in his first public sermon near modern-day Banaras, following many years of meditation that had resulted in his enlightenment. The first noble truth is the Buddha's diagnosis of the human condition, namely, that life consists of suffering (*dukkha*). The second is his observation that suffering is caused by desires (*tṛṣṇa*—literally, "thirst"). The third noble truth is that there is a way out of suffering, and the fourth states that the way is through following the Eightfold Path of right opinions, right thought, right speech, right conduct, right livelihood, right effort, right mindfulness, and right concentration.

Out of these basic teachings arose a very complex worldview, which was informed by the philosophies of the Buddha's native India and, over time, by the philosophies of the Central and East Asian civilizations to which his ideas were spread by Buddhist missionaries. As a result of Buddhism's historical movement across Asia, today one can find an enormous variety of beliefs and practices among the many diverse societies that consider themselves Buddhist.

Even so, some themes loom large in Buddhist thought across many of its different expressions. One is the ancient Indian concept of nonviolence. Especially the Mahayana branch of Buddhism, to which most Buddhists belong, adds the component of compassion toward all creatures. Another central tenet of Buddhism—which echoes a belief found in the cosmologies of many first peoples—is the belief in the interconnectedness of all phenomena in the universe. Buddhism teaches that our notions of self are illusory: There is nothing in us that exists as a discrete entity that we could identify as uniquely ourselves. Rather, we and all things exist as *processes* through the interactions of phenomena in flux.

(Interestingly, contemporary physicists, having for the most part abandoned the mechanistic worldview of the Western Enlightenment, are coming increasingly to see the universe in the same terms of processes and interactions that Buddhist ontology articulated more than two millennia ago!) The Buddhist concepts of nonviolence/compassion and interconnectedness have significant potential ecological implications, as several of the selections in this chapter demonstrate.

Within the recent search for ecological teachings in established religious traditions, the interpretations of American Buddhists have been the most visible. Rita Gross, who is a scholar of Buddhism and a practicing Buddhist, notes in her essay how dramatically lifestyles have changed in only the last generation or two. She suggests that we have confused luxuries with necessities and that it is largely our addiction to inessentials that has brought on the environmental crisis. Gross concedes that historically, Buddhism has not explicitly articulated what she would call an environmental ethic (as opposed to a simple reverence for nature), but she argues that Buddhist tradition does provide a basis for discouraging the excessive consumption and reproduction that she sees as environmentally destructive.

Ian Harris, a scholar more concerned with what the tradition has actually said than with what it might potentially say, raises doubts about whether Buddhism possesses any inherent ecological qualities. He points out that because environmentalism as such is a recent phenomenon, one would not expect to find environmentalist views explicitly articulated in premodern sources. Harris fails to detect anything resembling environmentalist attitudes in actual Buddhist traditions and, furthermore, indicates some features of Buddhist thought that might actually work against such attitudes.

Donald Swearer responds to the challenges posed by Harris through an analysis of the environmentalist thought of two twentieth-century Thai monks. On the basis of these contemporary examples, Swearer suggests that Harris's normative approach to Buddhist tradition is too narrow.

Poet, educator, and practicing Buddhist, Stephanie Kaza is one of the more prominent voices in contemporary American Buddhism. In her essay, Kaza takes a comparative look at how ecological principles are being applied in various North American contexts. Although many American Buddhists today are showing a strong environmental commitment, Kaza opens the debate on the relative influences of North American environmentalism and Buddhist tradition and poses questions about how this relationship might develop in the future.

Toward a Buddhist Environmental Ethic

RITA M. GROSS

WHENEVER I THINK ABOUT ISSUES OF CONSUMPTION and population, I think about the way I lived early in my life. For eighteen years I lived without central heating, indoor plumbing, pesticides, processed foods, packaging, or neighbors that could be seen from our home. We carried water from a spring, cut our own firewood, grew much of our own food, and used an outhouse, even in subzero temperatures. Dragonflies, butterflies, fireflies, and many other beautiful creatures that I never see in my city lot abounded. Traffic noise was a novelty. At night one could see a million stars in the black sky. Major environmental problems were nonexistent because we were few people (a family of three) living simply. Because we were so few living in a sparsely populated rural area, we could use simple technologies and renewable resources for heat and waste management without harming the land, water, or air, even though those same technologies become extremely problematic when people live in crowded conditions. This is one of many reasons why population growth is so environmentally devastating.

Though many would evaluate such a lifestyle as unacceptably primitive and uncomfortable, it was not particularly a deprivation. Even now when I return to my cabin for meditation retreats and writing time, I do not mind that lifestyle. Electricity for lights, the laptop computer, and a boombox that plays classical music is completely sufficient for a satisfying lifestyle with low environmental impact. Environmentally sensitive lifestyles and scaling back to live such lifestyles do not really deprive people once it becomes clear that the levels of reproduction and consumption indulged in by most people are not necessary to well-being.

But what does my religion of choice—Buddhism—say about this vision? In this chapter, I shall be writing as both a scholar trained in comparative studies in religion and as a practicing Buddhist. My own Buddhist affiliation is with Tibetan Vajrayana Buddhism as taught by the late Chogyam Trungpa, but I will write about Buddhism in generic terms that could be accepted by most or all Buddhists.

BUDDHISM AND ECOLOGY

Currently, there is some debate about whether Buddhism can support an environmental ethic or the worldview of deep ecology and some Western scholar-observers are very skeptical of Buddhist efforts to derive an ecological ethic. As a scholar of religion familiar with both historical and constructive methods, I find that question somewhat beside the point. Historically, we know that all living religions have gone through major changes to remain relevant in altered circumstances. There is no reason that the same thing cannot happen in response to the ecological crisis. As a Buddhist feminist "theologian," I am more than familiar with the process of working within a traditional symbol system and worldview while doing reconstructive work to eliminate certain problematic conventions. The question is not what *has* Buddhism said about ecology and the environment, but what *could* Buddhism say about these subjects.

At the outset, I would suggest that Buddhism has not been especially oriented to an environmental ethic historically. In my view, other religious traditions, including the indigenous traditions so often praised for their reverence for nature have not historically focused on an environmental ethic either. I make this somewhat controversial statement because of a claim that I will make many times in this chapter. An *environmental* ethic must discourage excessive consumption and reproduction, even when such levels of consumption and reproduction are common in the culture and seem unproblematic to many people. By itself, a rhetoric of reverence for nature is insufficient as an environmental ethic. Too often a

Gross, Rita, "Toward a Buddhist Environmental Ethic," in Harold Coward and Daniel Maguire, Eds., pp. 147–160. Reprinted by permission of the State University of New York Press.

rhetoric of reverence for nature is combined with primitive technologies that limit human ability to destroy the environment, but when more sophisticated and destructive technology becomes available, it is readily adopted. To qualify as genuinely ecological, religious teachings and practices must entail *a choice* against excessive reproduction and consumption.

Environmental concerns are now so grave because humans have the technologies to consume and reproduce in ways that seem likely to destroy the ecological basis for human life. Therefore, the key question is what values and practices would convince people to consume and reproduce less when they have the technological ability to consume and reproduce more. The world's religions have not previously faced this situation, which explains why ecological ethics have not been in the forefront of religious thinking in any tradition. What we must do then, as constructive thinkers in our various traditions, is to place the inherited values and insights of our traditions in the light of the current ecological crisis to see what resources the tradition affords us and where we need to extrapolate new visions. The "religion of the market" has stepped up to supply what the classical religions are not supplying, a definition of what is truly sacred. The corporations are the primary teachers of values in this new arrangement and they are extraordinarily effective. Religions that ignore this are doomed to irrelevance.

When I am faced with a major intellectual puzzle, I usually contemplate it using a strategy that I learned from the oral traditions of Tibetan Buddhism—threefold logic. This strategy suggests that most problems can be fruitfully analyzed by locating a starting point, a process of change and development, and an end product. The task of articulating a Buddhist ethical response to the environmental crisis is daunting enough that I spent many hours going back to the basics of using a traditional threefold logic with which to think about what Buddhism might have to offer. The traditional system of threefold logic that offered the most insight is a system called "view, practice, and result." This particular system focuses first on the theoretical analysis appropriate to a specific issue—the view. Then, with the view well in hand, we turn to the question of what practices or spiritual disciplines will enable one to realize or internalize the view, so that it is no longer merely an intellectual theory. Finally, understanding the view and having practiced the appropriate contemplative and meditative exercises, what actions will one take when the view is fully internalized? In this chapter, I will apply the threefold logic of view, practice, and result to Buddhist teachings as they might be relevant to the ecological crisis.

My approach to developing a Buddhist environmental ethic will emphasize two things. First, I will appeal to simple pan-Buddhist teachings and practices for the most part, rather than to the doctrines of advanced Buddhist philosophy or the practices of esoteric forms of Buddhism. I do this so that Buddhists everywhere could find a Buddhist environmental ethic that is accessible and relevant. Second, I will emphasize practice over view. One of the reasons for working with the specific system of threefold logic that I chose is because the view—the theoretical analysis—is only the beginning of the discussion. I have been somewhat disappointed with the current small body of literature on Buddhist environmental ethics because most authors have focused on view or theory and have not sufficiently discussed practices promoting environmentally sound lifestyles.

In my view, Buddhism has many intellectual and spiritual resources that can easily support an environmental ethic. At the simplest level, because nonharming is so fundamental to Buddhism ethics, once one realizes that excessive consumption and reproduction are harmful, one is obliged to limit such activities. Such advice is also in accord with the most fundamental of all Buddhist guidelines—the Middle Path between extremes. This guideline is always applied to all questions, from questions about how much effort to put into one's meditation practice to how much luxury is appropriate to metaphysical questions about existence and nonexistence. It could perhaps be argued that these simple basics—nonharming and the Middle Way—which would automatically come to mind for any Buddhist could be a sufficient basis for an environmental ethic that would encourage limited consumption and reproduction.

THE VIEW ACCORDING TO BUDDHISM: INTERDEPENDENCE

When one brings the vast collection of Buddhist teachings into conversation with environmental concerns, one basic teaching stands out above all others.

That is the Buddhist teaching of interdependence, which is also one of the most basic aspects of the Buddhist worldview. This law of interdependence is said to have been discovered by the historical Buddha on the night of his enlightenment experience during the third watch of the night, the same time period during which the Four Noble Truths were discovered. Mythically, this story indicates how basic the teaching of interdependence is to Buddhism.

Simply put, interdependence means that nothing stands alone apart from the matrix of all else. Nothing is independent and everything is interdependent with everything else. Logically, the proof of interdependence is that nothing can exist apart from the causes and conditions that give rise to it. But those causes and conditions are also dependent on other causes and conditions. Therefore, linear causality and isolating a single cause for an event gives way to a more weblike understanding of causality in which everything affects everything else in some way because everything is interconnected.

Given interdependence, our very identity as isolated, separate entities is called into serious question and we are invited to forge a more inclusive and extensive identity. We do not simply stop at the borders of our skin if we are truly interdependent with our world. When we know ourselves to be fundamentally interdependent with everything else, rather than independent entities existing in our own right, our self-centered behaviors will be altered in very basic ways. Nothing that we do is irrelevant, without impact on the rest of our matrix.

The implications of this profound, thoroughgoing interdependence for ecology have already been articulated in a moving fashion by Joanna Macy and others.[1] In fact, interdependence is the most commonly invoked concept in Buddhist environmental ethics to date. Most often, it is celebrated as a view of our relationships with our world that invites and requires ecological concern and a view that is much more emotionally satisfying and realistic than the Western emphasis on the individual as the ultimately real and ultimately important entity. Western Buddhists especially seem to find immense relief in their discovery of what Harold Coward calls the "we-self." This joy is quite understandable, given the emotional burdens concomitant with modern Western individualism.

However, rather than emphasizing the lyrical beauty of interconnectedness, as others have already done very well, I wish to emphasize its more somber implications. First, given interdependence, we cannot intervene in or rearrange the ecosystem without affecting everything to some extent. Therefore, human interference in the ecosystem cannot be a glib pursuit of "progress" and "growth," two things that many view as ideals. The effects of growth and technological progress on the whole interconnected system are much more important and these effects are often not anticipated. For example, lowering the death rate, especially the infant mortality rate, through modern medicine seems like clear progress. But failure to see the link between the death rate and the birth rate, which sanctions the continuation of reproductive practices appropriate when the death rate is high, is an important factor in the current population explosion. Even when people have some awareness of the effects of human intervention into the ecosystem, stopping such intervention can be difficult. Even though many are thoroughly alarmed at the global consequences of destroying the Amazon rain forest, its destruction continues because of the overwhelming power of consumerism. The reality of interdependence is sobering, as well as poetic. Each of us feels the effects of actions taken far away by people whom we do not know and whom we cannot influence directly.

If pervasive interconnectedness is an accurate view, then nothing can be delinked from anything else. Taking interdependence seriously urges us to apply "both-and" solutions, rather that "either-or" arguments to knotty problems. This applies particularly to consumption and population. When discussing environmental ethics, one of the most important, but largely unrecognized, moral agendas is the need to establish the fundamental similarity of the urge to consume more and the urge to reproduce more, rather than being lured into superficial arguments about whether excessive consumption or overpopulation is *the* major environmental problem, as so often happens in "North" versus "South" debates.

Not only are excessive consumption and excessive reproduction similar in their negative impact on the environment but also in the self-centered motivations from which they spring. The former similarity is somewhat recognized but the similarity of self-centered motivation has been completely overlooked. This is the case even for Buddhist environmental ethics, where, given Buddhism's especially developed critic [*sic*] of ego, one would expect to find such insights. This literature contains many denunciations, on Buddhist grounds, of personal, corporate, and national greed concerning consumable goods and many discussions of how such greed damages the interdependent ecosystem. But there are almost no discussions of the fact that excessive population growth is at least equally devastating environmentally and would make impossible the vision articulated in many Buddhist environmental writings of the value of the ecosystem, of wilderness, and of nonhuman sentient beings. More important, Buddhist ecological literature includes almost no discussions of the fact that much reproductive behavior is fueled by individual or communal greed and ego, and, therefore, on Buddhist grounds is just as suspect as greed for assets. Buddhist ecological literature ignores the reality that most frequently, physiological reproduction results because patrilineages or individuals desire physical immortality, or because of the many ways in which birth control fails, not because of altruistic, non-ego-based motives.

In this regard Buddhist ecological ethics follows a tendency common in religious or moral discussions—a predisposition to regard individual greed and excessive consumption as a moral failing, while excessive reproduction is not similarly regarded as a moral failing. In fact, reproduction is idealized and romanticized. Religions often promote large families, both through their discouragement of fertility control and their patriarchal tendency to view women primarily as reproducers, while governments implement pronatalist tax and social policies in an overpopulated world. Thus, to keep population and consumption properly linked, in religious discourse we may need to focus more on population issues. Because we can assume a moral condemnation of excessive consumption in religious ethics, such a focus will actually bring our attention to consumption and population into balance with each other.

Furthermore, if one accepts interdependence, then we must realize that many things that people regard as private individual choices, most especially choices regarding how much to consume and whether or how many children to bear, actually are not private matters because of their profound implications for all sentient beings. The "we-self," in Harold Coward's terminology, has very strong interest in individual practices regarding reproduction and consumption and its perspective needs to be taken seriously. Very strong ethical arguments that everyone must limit their consumption and reproduction follow. These arguments can be made both in terms of rights—the rights of other beings not to be infringed upon by our excessive reproduction and consumption—and in terms of responsibilities—our own responsibility not to harm other beings unnecessarily through our reproduction and consumption.

THE CORE PRACTICE: BUDDHIST MEDITATIONS AND CONTEMPLATIONS ON INDIVIDUAL DESIRE IN AN INTERDEPENDENT WORLD

An ecological ethic has been defined as a value system and set of practices through which people come to appreciate the entire matrix of life enough to limit their own consumption and reproduction for the well-being of that matrix. These limits are adopted despite technologies and economies that, by ignoring the big picture and the long run, foster the illusion that having more children and consuming more material goods are unproblematic. Buddhism, in my view, has some important, perhaps unique, insights to offer toward developing such an ethic.

Buddhism suggests that we look into our own desires when confronted with problems and misery and I believe such practices are quite relevant for developing the kind of environmental ethic defined above. The Four Noble Truths, often characterized as the Buddha's verbalization of his enlightenment experience, provide the basis for developing an ethic of adopting limits for the sake of the matrix of life. The First and Second Noble Truths foster especially fruitful contemplations relevant to ecological ethics. The First Noble Truth states that conventional lifestyles inevitably result in suffering; the Second Noble Truth states that suffering stems from desire rooted in ignorance. Translated into more ecological language, a conventional lifestyle of indulging in desired levels of consumption and reproduction results in the misery of an environmentally degraded and overpopulated planet.

The Second Noble Truth, with its emphasis on desire as the cause of suffering, is the key to a Buddhist environmental ethic. But before we can develop the implications of the Second Noble Truth for environmental ethics, it is necessary to clarify the meaning of the term "desire," since that term is widely misunderstood, with the result that Buddhism is often caricatured as a pessimistic, world-denying religion. The usually-chosen English word "desire" translates the Pali *tanha* and the Sanskrit *trishna,* but the connotations of the term "desire" are not strong enough to carry the meaning of Second Noble Truth. Most English-speaking people regard desire as inevitable and only a problem if it gets out of hand. But, in Buddhist psychology, *trishna* is always out of hand, inevitably out of control. Therefore, I believe more accurate connotative translations of *trishna* would be "addiction" or "compulsion," which more adequately convey its insatiable demands and counterproductivity. "Grasping," "attachment," "clinging," "craving," and "fixation" are also possible, more accurate translations; and the way the term "greed" is now used when discussing some multinationals also could translate *trishna*. All of these terms suggest that the object of desire is actually more powerful, more in control, than the desiring subject, which is precisely why *trishna* causes *duhkha*—misery.

Trishna is not about having lightly held plans or about preferring an adequate diet to malnourishment, as many people think when they try to refute Buddhism by saying that life without attachment is impossible. *Trishna* is about the extra weight we bring to our plans and preferences when they so control us that any change throws us into uncontrollable, heedless emotional turmoil. That is how *trishna* causes *duhkha. Trishna* is also about the mistaken view that getting something—wealth or a male child, for example—will bring happiness and satisfaction. Because of this view, such goals are pursued compulsively and, therefore, suffering results. Thus, it is clear that from a Buddhist point of view, *trishna* is at the root of both excessive consumption and overpopulation. Neither would occur if people did not think that more wealth or more children would satisfy an existential itch that only is cooled by equanimity. "I want . . ." are the two words that fuel the suffering of excessive consumption and overpopulation.

Because it is so counterintuitive to suggest that attachment is the cause of human miseries, let us perform a mental exercise. Buddhists, contrary to popular Western stereotypes about them, regard happiness as favorably as any other people. The First Noble Truth is not about preferring misery to happiness but about noting that conventional ways of pursuing happiness produce sorrow instead. Most people think that happiness results from getting what we crave, whereas Buddhists would say that happiness happens when *trishna* is renounced. Thus, craving and happiness are incompatible. Some reflection on one's last experience of unrelieved, intense longing will quickly confirm that it was not a pleasant experience. One endures the longing because of the pleasure that comes when cravings are satisfied. But the satisfaction is shortlived, quickly replaced by yet another longing. The satisfaction of our cravings is virtually impossible because of the insatiable, addictive nature of *trishna,* which always wants more. Since craving and happiness are incompatible, which one should be renounced?

The good news of Buddhism is that the mental attitude of grasping and fixation is not the only alternative. "I want . . ." can be replaced with simply noting what is. The enlightened alternative to *trishna* is detachment—equanimity and even-mindedness beyond the opposites of hope and fear, pleasure and pain. It is the unconditional joy that cannot be produced by the satisfaction of cravings, but that arises spontaneously when we truly experience unfabricated mind. Equanimity has nothing to do with getting what we want and everything to do with developing contentment with things as they are. It is the hard-won ability to be at least somewhat even-minded whether one gets one's heart-desire, or is denied it. It is the hard-won ability to put space around every experience, to realize that nothing lasts forever without feeling cheated, and to be at least somewhat cheerful no matter what is happening. Therefore, fundamentally, *trishna* and equanimity are states of mind; they have little to do with what we have or do not have. According to Buddhism, external factors, whether other people or material objects, are not the source of joy or suffering; rather *attitudes* toward people and things determine which we experience. Both rich and poor can be ridden by *trishna* and both can cultivate equanimity, though extreme poverty is not especially conducive to developing it. Those in poverty are often too consumed with survival to develop equanimity and enlightenment—

strong arguments to work toward a small population living well, rather than a large population living in dire circumstances or the current extreme inequities between rich and poor.

On the other hand, greed is normal in people who live conventional lives, which is why it seems so counterintuitive to suggest that longings, such as those for more wealth or more children, are the cause of suffering. According to Buddhism, greed is normal in conventional people because of a pervasive and deep-seated erroneous view of the self. Craving for *more,* whether children or things, is rooted in ignorance. Ignorance of what? Classically, craving is rooted in ignorance and denial of our fundamental nature, which is the lack of a permanent individual self—*anatman*. But *anatman* is simply another name for interdependence. Because we are interdependent with everything else in the matrix of existence, we do not exist in the way we conventionally believe that we do—as self-existing, self-contained bundles of wants and needs that end with our skin, or, if we feel generous, with our immediate families. That imagined independent self that greedily consumes and reproduces itself is a fiction. It has never really existed and so giving up on it is not a loss but a homecoming. This is the aspect of Buddhism that has been so inspiring to deep ecologists, who have claimed that Asian worldviews are more conducive to ecological vision than Western emphases on the unique, independently existing, eternal individual.

Furthermore, when Buddhists discuss *trishna* as the cause of suffering, all compulsions are equally problematic because craving is incompatible with equanimity. Therefore, on other grounds than interdependence, one cannot delink population from consumption, or either from the environment. Frequently outsiders will ask whether it is not permissible to have "good" longings. The negative answer to this question is especially important in this context because it puts desire for too many things and desire for too many children on exactly the same footing. Both are equally problematic and destructive. The environmental crisis is not solved by arguing about whether overpopulation or excessive consumption is more serious but by "both-and" linkages between them.

These contemplations on individual longing in an interdependent world are rather steep, but they have many virtues in promoting a more radical way of linking consumption, reproduction, and the environment. The most important is that, while in terms of absolute truth individuals do not exist as independent entities, in terms of relative truth, a profound reorientation of consciousness to that fact, individual by individual, is necessary if the root causes of excessive consumption and reproduction are to be overcome. While I certainly favor governmental, economic, and social programs and policies that discourage excessive consumption and reproduction, I also think that, by themselves, such interventions at the macrolevel will be insufficient. Nor does Buddhism have a great deal to say about such policies. But, in addition to such policies, individual people need to realize and experience that their happiness does not require or depend on *more* of anything, and Buddhist practices have a great deal to offer in promoting such personal transformation. So long as limits, whether to consumption or fertility, are regarded as a dreary duty imposed from above and a personal loss, people will resent and try to evade them. But if one experiences such limits, not as personal loss but as normal, natural, and pleasant in an interdependent matrix, then they are not a problem.

WALKING THE MIDDLE PATH: RESULTS OF BUDDHIST PRACTICE

A frequent complaint against religion in general and Buddhism in particular is that the profound ethical insights of the tradition have little practical impact on the world. In popular stereotypes, Buddhism, with its emphasis on silent, motionless meditation practices, is accused of being otherworldly. But this widespread evaluation is based on a serious misunderstanding of Buddhist ethics. Buddhism generally teaches that the first moral agenda is to develop clarity and equanimity oneself, before trying to intervene in or influence society at large. Thus, Buddhism's emphasis on practices promoting individual transformation is not antisocial or otherworldly in any way, but instead is aimed at avoiding the self-righteous excesses so common in religions that promote activism for all. According to Buddhist understandings of moral development, the meditative and contemplative practices discussed above result in the development of genuine compassion, said to be the only basis for a helpful program of social action.

Furthermore, stereotypes aside, the Buddhist

record of personal transformation leading to social benefit is impressive. It must be remembered that Buddhism has been the dominant religion in very few societies; those societies, such as Tibet and Southeast Asia, are not especially overpopulated and have not been markedly aggressive since their conversion to Buddhism. Two of the most respected and effective recent winners of the Nobel Peace Prize, the Dalai Lama and Aung San Suu Kyi, are Buddhists and base their social activism directly on Buddhist principles and their meditative discipline. The Dalai Lama has publicly advocated both population regulation and environmental protection as vital to the survival and well-being of the planet. Nor are these isolated examples. Twentieth-century Buddhism has developed a global movement called Engaged Buddhism, which some see as the Buddhist equivalent of liberation theology.

As already noted, thus far contemporary Buddhist ethical thought has not brought together the interrelated issues of population, consumption, and the environment. But certain conclusions regarding appropriate actions follow inevitably from the view of interdependence and the practice of replacing compulsion with equanimity. Within a finite matrix, it is not possible to have both all the material goods and all the fertility that people conventionally want. Some choices must be made. We could continue the current obscene distribution patterns, with a few people consuming most of the earth's resources and the majority of people pushing the margins of existence. If consumer goods are the ultimate concern, we could have a world in which most people have their personal automobile, though only with a significantly reduced population if breathing oxygen continues to be necessary for humans. If fertility and reproduction are the ultimate concern, we could reproduce until the entire earth is as crowded and impoverished as today's most crowded places, though I think the traditional controllers of population—violence, epidemic, and famine—would intervene well before such an apocalypse could occur. Or we could chart a middle course, balancing consumption and reproduction in ways that result in a world in which there are few enough people consuming moderately enough that all can be adequately cared for materially, emotionally, and spiritually.

I will conclude this chapter exploring the ways in which some traditional Buddhist ethical teachings might be applied to take action regarding issues of population, consumption, and the environment. I will work with Buddhist teachings that are specifically devoted to providing guidelines for compassionate action—the *paramita*-s ("transcendent virtues") discussed as part of the *bodhisattva* path in Mahayana Buddhism. I will also link my discussion of *paramita* practice with some Western ethical concepts relevant to issues of population and consumption, namely the language of rights and responsibilities. For Western Buddhists in particular, such linkages and cross-cultural conceptual translations are important, both for our understanding of Buddhism and for making Buddhist contributions to our Western cultural milieu.

In this context, it is helpful to focus on the first two *paramita*-s, generosity and discipline. Generosity is highly valued in Buddhism. Wealth is not inappropriate for a Buddhist, but wealth should be circulated rather than hoarded. Generosity is evaluated as the primary virtue of the *bodhisattva,* without which the other *paramita*-s cannot develop or will develop improperly. On the other hand, generosity by itself is meaningless and may well be counterproductive. It needs to be balanced and informed by the *paramita* immediately following generosity—discipline. If it is not so balanced and informed, generosity may well lead to what my teacher called "idiot compassion"—giving people things that are not helpful to them because one lacks disciple and *prajna* (discriminating awareness wisdom) in being generous. Instead, he often said, the *paramita* of discipline involves uttering "the giant NO" when the situation called for it. One could even talk of the gift of the "giant NO." (It should be pointed out that, ideally *paramita* practice is based on enough understanding of interdependence that the practice is nondualistic. Therefore, the question of giver and receiver of generosity or discipline does not arise, There is simply one spontaneous field of action.)

I suggest that it might be helpful to link this discussion of generosity and discipline to Western language about rights and responsibilities. Regarding such language, I agree with the widespread observation that it is a product of the European Enlightenment and individualism, and does not fit easily onto most Asian systems of thought, including Mahayana discussions of the *paramita*-s. This lack of fit is due to the fact that language of rights and responsibilities is extremely dualistic, based on assumptions of independently existing individuals who have rights and responsibilities vis-à-vis each other. I would also argue that in much contemporary Western discourse, rights and responsibilities have become dangerously delinked from one another. Claims for multiple rights abound, but very few wish to discuss the corresponding responsibilities, which often lends a tone of childish demand to claims about rights.

Nevertheless, despite lack of a perfect fit between the *paramita*-s of generosity and discipline with Western concepts of rights and responsibilities, some comparisons may be instructive. The example of the way generosity and discipline are linked in Mahayana thought may well prove a useful model for how to link rights and responsibilities in Western discussions. One could see generosity as roughly analogous to rights and discipline as analogous to responsibility. Those in need have rights to the generosity of those with more wealth but, to merit continued generosity, they have responsibilities to be disciplined in their own lives. Likewise, those with relative wealth have a responsibility to be generous with their consumables, but they also have both a right and a responsibility to exercise discipline in giving and to avoid "idiot compassion." Because generosity and discipline so balance and inform each other, the sharp line between rights and responsibilities is diminished. Those with wealth have something beyond responsibility to share it; sharing is a spontaneous discipline beyond rights and responsibility. Likewise, discipline undercuts the question of rights and responsibilities; whatever rights one may think one has, discipline is more integral to self-esteem and well-being. When discipline is well established, responsible and generous action is spontaneous and joyful, rather than onerous.

The way in which generosity and discipline balance and inform each other in this discussion suggests how to balance and link rights and responsibilities in Western discussions of population, consumption, and the environment. One frequently hears claims of rights to an adequate standard of living, as well as rights to reproduce as much as an individual chooses. But corresponding discussions of the effects of unlimited exercise of these "rights" on the ecosystem, corresponding discussions of the need for responsibility when exercising these rights is not always heard. The net effect is that these two rights are on a collision course with each other. Rather than discussing such rights as if they could be independent of each other, it is important to realize that the more seriously we take the claim of a right to a universal minimum standard of living, the more critical universal fertility regulation becomes. Only if we don't really think it is possible to divide the world's resources equitably can we afford to be casual about universal fertility regulations. And the more unrestricted fertility earth experiences, the more difficult it will become ever to achieve equitable distribution. Conversely, if unregulated wasteful consumption continues unabated, inequities of wealth and poverty can only grow; then the poor, whose only resource is their children, cannot possibly do without enough of them to put minimal food on the table and to provide minimal old-age care. The more that destructive patterns of growth and consumption increase, the more difficult it becomes to avoid excessive population growth. Only if it is thought that the wealthy can somehow insulate themselves from the negative environmental consequences of such growth can we afford to be casual about the need to forbid excessive and wasteful consumption. Like generosity and discipline, rights exist only in interdependence with responsibilities. Those who refuse to meet their responsibilities lose their rights, which is why involuntary fertility regulation and involuntary limits to consumption are not always inappropriate. No one's rights to their consumables or their fertility are so absolute that they include destroying or damaging the environment in which we all live.

While writing this essay, I returned to my childhood home, noting with sadness the negative effects of more people than ever before consuming at greater levels than ever before. The spring, the outhouse, and the woods to provide firewood are still there and all are still used. But traffic noise from long-distance eighteen-wheel trucks hauling consumables often interrupts the silence unpleasantly. My cabin is now on the first open land from town, and a nearby lake, wild and unsettled in my childhood, is now surrounded by houses as crowded together as if they were in a city. Year by year increased population increases the pressure to subdivide and sell my land; before I die, higher taxes due to these population pressures may force me to sell. One can still see more stars in the black sky than in a city, but those to the north are whited out by light pollution from the nearest town. Now I comment on dragonflies, butterflies, and fireflies because they are not as common as they once were.

To trade in this sacred, pristine environment to support more people consuming at unprecedented levels seems a poor bargain. I can see no way in which all this "more"—more people, more stuff—has improved the quality of life, except perhaps that I can now buy Chinese spices at the local grocery store! But surely we can figure out ways to increase quality without increasing quantity, and if not, I'd rather do without Chinese spices than without the spacious, untrammeled environment. More is not better, whether it is more people or more consumables. "Growth," the god we worship, is a false idol, needing to be replaced by "no growth," if not by "negative growth." "Growth" and "more" represent the unbridled reign of *trishna,* not appreciation and reverence for the interdependent matrix of the environment in which we live and upon which we depend unconditionally. But to be consumed by *trishna* is not human nature, not our inevitable lot or inescapable original sin. With enough meditation and contemplation of interdependence, *trishna* will give way to equanimity. Would that *trishna* give way to contentment and equanimity—speedily and in our time!

NOTE

1. Joanna Macy, *World as Lover, World as Self* (Berkeley, Calif.: Parallax Press, 1991).

Ecological Buddhism?

IAN HARRIS

ECOLOGICAL THINKING HAS COME TO THE fore in the late twentieth century. If this view is accepted, then one will be hard pressed to discover more than the odd resonance of environmentalism in the literature of the ancient world. This fact is recognised by many influential representatives of the ecological movement today. Thus, Eugene C. Hargrove (1989), in his examination of the thought of ancient Greece, concludes that it was impossible for Greek philosophy to think ecologically. The metaphysical assumptions underpinning much of the thought current at that time were clearly at variance with those operating today; therefore a concern for the natural world is highly problematic in the Greek context.

It may seem rather strange to begin a discussion on the attitude of Buddhism to the environment by reference to Greek thought, but there is method in my madness. In an influential and, in terms of recent interest in environmental ethics, early piece of work, John Passmore (1980) concludes that western philosophy is incompatible with a concern for nature. Passmore is particularly scornful of the negative role played by Christianity. For him the doctrine of human dominion over nature, found in the writings of Augustine, Aquinas, Calvin, etc., has done much to alienate the modern industrialised world from its natural environment. More recent commentators on the impact of Christianity on environmental ethics have shown that Passmore tends to overstate his case. Robin Attfield (1983) is a good case in point. While it is true that some remarkably negative statements on our relations with nature are to be found in the writings of major theologians, another more positive tradition of stewardship and care for the environment runs side by side with the negative throughout most of the history of Christianity. This attitude is exemplified in the traditions of Francis of Assisi, and in the works of some Orthodox theologians. Christianity, then, appears to contain an essentially negative official attitude to the environment, underpinned by an influential but minority position far more favourable to an environmentalist ethic. Some writ-

Harris, Ian, "Buddhism," in Jean Holm and John Bowker, Eds., *Attitudes to Nature,* London: Pinter Publishers, 1994, pp. 8–26. Reproduced with permission from the publisher.

ers, most notably Lynn White Jnr (1967), have claimed that eastern religions, and Buddhism in particular, are more explicitly positive in their concern for the natural world. I find this attitude difficult to square with any actually occurring Buddhist tradition and shall argue that the Christian situation is more or less precisely mirrored in Buddhism.

BUDDHISM AND THE NATURAL WORLD

In its earliest phases Buddhism was essentially a world-denying religion. Existence was conceived of as having the characteristics of suffering (*dukkha*), impermanence (*anicca*) and insubstantiality (*anattā*) and thus the goal of the monk (i.e. *nirvāṇa*) was thought of as outside this world. In other words, the best thing that one could do was to turn one's back on the world—to escape from it. The essence of this way of thinking is contained in the Buddha's celebrated first sermon in which he outlines the Four Noble Truths. In this sermon we hear of the inherent unsatisfactoriness of conditioned things (i.e. the idea that all causally produced entities are impermanent and, as such, fail to confer happiness), and of the path which leads away from the suffering associated with the world. It is not surprising, given this rather sombre vision, that the early Buddhist texts fail, in any systematic way, to develop a coherent world picture. Beyond the occasional snippet of information, the Pāli canon of Theravāda Buddhism, the earliest collection of Buddhist scriptures available, is notable in its lack of cosmological lore. It seems, almost studiously, to avoid any discussion of cosmic and human origins. This is probably connected to the character of early Buddhism which denies the existence of one divine creator, though Buddhists have always accepted the existence of a plurality of gods who have the capacity to bring about real effects in the human realm. The recognition and appeasement of these divine beings is enormously important in the lives of rural lay Buddhists today, but, having said this, it is clear that Buddhism is unique in the religions of the world for its disinclination to offer a prominent theory of creation. It is difficult to know precisely why, but this situation was not allowed to continue in the Buddhist tradition down to the present day.

Approximately 1,000 years after the death of the Buddha a number of prominent Buddhist commentators appeared on the scene, and they seemed to recognise the need for a more fully worked out cosmology than that present in the canon itself. Perhaps this shift in position was felt to be necessary in order to get into effective dialogue with, and demonstrate superiority over, members of other religious traditions, most notably the Hindus. Certainly at this stage in their history the Hindus had a fairly complex and elegant world picture, which possessed the advantage that it could be used to predict certain simple natural phenomena, such as the distinction between night and day. One assumes that their Buddhist opponents may have felt at a bit of a disadvantage. In time, then, the Hindu world picture was adopted by the rival religious tradition and revised to bring it into line with fundamental Buddhist axioms. The two most prominent Buddhists in this connection are Vasubandhu, a fourth-century writer from northern India, and Buddhaghosa, a very exceptional commentator on the Pāli canon, who lived approximately a century after Vasubandhu. This being the case, the relatively late *Abhidharmakośa* of Vasubandhu, and the *Visuddhimagga* of Buddhaghosa, provide us with the most comprehensive descriptions of the world as seen from a Buddhist point of view. They are remarkably consistent with each other and I shall draw on both for the following description.

In line with Hindu thought, Buddhists hold that the world is periodically brought into being and, at a later stage, many millions of years in the future, it is destroyed. This process has no beginning and no end. In this sense, the Indian religions differ from Judaism, Christianity and Islam. Unlike the latter traditions, which hold an essentially linear idea of history based on a definite starting point and an equally definite conclusion to the world process, Indian thought prefers to deal in enormously long cycles of history, one following the other for all eternity. In other words, the cosmos persists for a lengthy period, is dissolved, and at some stage in the future is again brought forth out of the void until it meets the same fate, and so on, and on. Now this fact alone provides us with a useful means by which we may contrast the Buddhist understanding of existence with that more familiar to us from the Christian tradition, in which creation is brought into being by a benign and purposeful creator.

The purpose or meaning of the Buddhist world

order is more difficult to establish. For one thing it does not come into being as the result of the activities of a Supreme Being. In the second place, there is no indication that it is moving towards any condition of fulfilment. It simply runs on, from one cycle to another, *ad infinitum*. Rather than being a purposeful process leading inevitably to an unknown but meaningful conclusion, the Buddhist vision of the world is more pessimistic. The world is endless, meaningless and purposeless. This does not mean that the Buddhist must be seized by despair, for after all the Buddha has taught the means to escape from conditioned existence. As such, the Buddha's teaching (*dharma*) is regarded as a very remarkable thing, the greatest of all gifts. Nevertheless, the world is viewed, particularly in the earliest phase of Buddhism, as a vicious circle (*saṃsāra*). Knowledge that this is so leads to the inevitable desire to find the means of escape from such an unsatisfactory state. Since desires for worldly things are considered to bind us even more strongly to existence and increase our suffering, Buddhism extols the virtues of the world-renouncer. For Buddhism, the renouncer *par excellence* is the monk (*bhikkhu*). Membership of the monastic community (*saṅgha*) is considered to be the most effective means of hastening one's spiritual liberation.

The traditions preserved in the Pāli canon give the strong impression that during the Buddha's lifetime a considerable number of persons experienced liberation. On the attainment of enlightenment (*nirvāṇa*), a person is referred to as an *arhat*. Study of the relevant early texts seems to suggest that arhatship could be brought about in two basic ways. For some individuals, presumably already far advanced on the path as a result of their own efforts, merely hearing the word of the Buddha was sufficient. However, the majority of *arhats* were required to put the teachings they received from the Buddha into practice for some finite period in order to achieve *nirvāṇa*. In effect, the methods recommended in the teachings fairly rapidly brought the practitioner to a state in which all desires were uprooted. Now it seems as though the death of the Buddha brought these spectacular and sudden transformations in spiritual status pretty much to an end.

As time went on, the time required for a monk to achieve liberation increased. The canon tells us that the Buddha predicted such a state of affairs. He taught that, from the time of his death, the teachings (*dharma*) would go slowly and inexorably into decline until the stage was reached when they would disappear altogether. Perhaps the increased time that a monk appears to have needed in order to attain his goal was a function of this decline in the *dharma*. Another explanation is simply that the fervour of the early period, in which the founder was still present and ministering to his disciples, was replaced by a more relaxed attitude to the possibility of liberation. Whatever the explanation, a new attitude towards the world and the beings it contains began to develop. The spiritual path began to take on a more gradual character. The possibility of sudden enlightenment began to seem less realistic. As a result, the likelihood of a monastic career spanning a good many lives (perhaps many millions of lives) became the norm. In this way the career of the monk began to share some of the characteristics of the lay path, which had been seen as an enormously lengthy process from the earliest period of Buddhist history. Not surprisingly, the radical other-worldliness of the early period is pushed out of the foreground in the thinking of the *saṅgha*, and a slightly more positive vision of the world begins to form. It should be noted that the Buddhist laity probably always regarded the natural world in a more concerned manner than the largely urban members of the *saṅgha*. It is a pity that we do not possess any substantial account of their views on the subject, though this is not surprising, given the fact that learning and literacy were almost entirely the preserve of the monks. Nevertheless, as the tradition develops and becomes more realistic, even the outlook of its community of renouncers starts to see the natural world in a new light.

The description of the world contained in the writings of Vasubandhu and Buddhaghosa has come down to the Buddhists of the present day virtually unchanged. In this respect Buddhism differs from Christianity. In the Christian tradition a radical redrawing of the cosmos was occasioned by the crisis caused by the rise of science in the early modern period. The findings of Galileo and Copernicus, despite initial condemnation by the church, were ultimately to win the day. However, the essentially alien nature of western scientific thinking has had a marginal impact on the traditional systems of thought of Asia, perhaps because, at least in part, the status of myth and story has been higher in the East than in the West (cf. Bowker, 1990). Nevertheless, recent evidence suggests that in some regions of the Buddhist world, most notably in Thailand and Sri Lanka, the situation is changing, and Buddhist doctrine is, in educated circles, coming to align itself with the findings of science.

For traditional Buddhism the world in which we live is a golden disk floating on a mighty cosmic ocean. This ocean is in turn supported by a circle of wind which itself rests on space. In one of the few cosmological fragments of the Pāli canon, the Buddha explains that earthquakes may be caused by turbulence in the circle of wind which causes a similar effect in the ocean. This is communicated to the golden earth which then shakes. Many contemporary Buddhists, particularly in Sri Lanka, regard this as a surprisingly modern view of the origin of earthquakes, but when read in context, we discover that this is only one special category of earthquake discussed in the text. By far the most prominent of the explanations given for these apparently natural occurrences is based on non-naturalistic principles. Most earthquakes are ascribed to the activities of a *buddha*. Decisive moments in the life of one destined to obtain enlightenment, such as his birth, renouncing of home, moment of enlightenment, death, etc., are said to be accompanied by earthquakes.

An enormous mountain, Mount Meru, some 84,000 *yojanas* high (one *yojana* = c. nine miles) is said to be situated at the centre of our golden earth. It is surrounded by seven concentric rings of mountains, each one half the height of the former as one moves outwards to the perimeter of the disc. All of the mountains are golden. At the extreme rim of the disc is a circle of iron mountains. Between the last range of golden mountains and circles of iron (*cakravāla*) we find an ocean. Four island continents are located at the four cardinal points within this ocean. Humans live on the most southerly of the islands, which, because of the nature of its vegetation, is called the Rose-Apple land (*Jambudvīpa*). We are said to share this land with the animals and the hungry ghosts (*pretas*). Animals also flourish in the ocean surrounding our continent. On terraces cut into the slopes of Mount Meru live the gods (*devas*), their status in the divine hierarchy determined by their position on the mountain. At the summit is the palace of Indra, the chief deity in vedic times. Other gods with more subtle bodies are held to exist in realms above the summit. At a distance as far below the earth as Indra's palace is above it, we find the abodes of the denizens of hell. There are a range of hellish existences, each one characterised by a different form of suffering for its inhabitants. In the Buddhist cosmos, then, five distinct kinds of being are to be found, i.e. humans, animals, ghosts, gods and denizens of hell. Some texts add a sixth group, the demi-gods (*asuras*), who spend their time locked in conflict with the gods themselves.

These six discrete destinies (*gati*) are interrelated. As beings eternally process around the circle of birth and deaths (*saṃsāra*) they are destined to spend innumerable lives in each of the *gatis*. As a consequence, we are intimately related to a very wide range of beings. A horse in the field may, for instance, have been our brother in a previous existence. This state of affairs clearly leads to a strong feeling of solidarity and fellow feeling with all beings. We are all in the same boat together. We are all circulating through various forms of suffering (even the divine destinies involve suffering, though on a more subtle level than we experience as humans), and are all, in our own way, destined to obtain eventual release.

A visually striking representation of the six destinies is found in the Buddhist wheel of life (*bhavacakra*). These complex and symbolic works of art are found particularly in the Tibetan tradition, and consist of a six-spoked wheel in which the gaps between the spokes contain scenes depicting the life-styles of beings in each of the six *gatis*. At the hub of the wheel one generally finds three animals in a circle attempting to devour the tail of the creature in front. These are the pig, the cockerel and the snake, which respectively represent greed, hatred and delusion, the three aspects of ignorance (*avidyā*) which is the destructive principle at the root of all forms of existence. The message of this image is straightforward. No perfection is possible within the realm of conditioned things. Everything, no matter how attractive it appears on the surface, is marked by suffering (*dukkha*), impermanence (*anicca*) and insubstantiality (*anattā*). Without going into enormous detail, it might be worth examining one further feature of the wheel of life (*bhavacakra*). The outer rim of the wheel contains a series of twelve images which, when put together, depict the progress of beings from one life to another. The strength of the series is that it explains the inevitability of the causal process at work in the world. Our desires are shown to bind us ever more closely to the world, with the consequence that on death the force of our desire impels us on into a new life. This life, even if it reaches its natural span, must inevitably close with old age, sickness and death. Yet still our desires force us ever onward into fresh forms of existence. The principle of causation which imparts the sense of inevitability to things was the fundamental discovery of the Buddha on attaining enlightenment. It is referred to as dependent origination (*pratītyasamutpāda*) and the series of twelve images on the rim of the wheel represent an attempt to give this principle visual form.

Some recent scholars have claimed that the Sanskrit word *pratītyasamutpāda* is the nearest equivalent in Buddhist sources to our term 'nature'. They go on to argue that since this is so, it is self-evidently the case that Buddhism, from its inception, has had a concern for nature. We now need to examine this view in more depth. The doctrine of dependent origination (*pratītyasamutpāda*) highlights the Buddhist notion that all apparently substantial entities within the world are in fact wrongly perceived. We live under the illusion that terms such as 'I', self, mountain, tree, etc., denote permanent and stable things. The doctrine teaches that this is not so. What appears to be permanent is, in fact, in a state of perpetual flux. The Theravadin position is that the ordinary objects of consciousness may actually be resolved into a stream of momentary and mutually conditioning entities called *dharmas*. Someone skilled in meditation may observe the rise and fall of these *dharmas*. For them the illusion of permanence and substantiality is undermined at a more fundamental level by the flux of radical change. The world is like a raging torrent which never remains the same from one moment to the next. Now, modern environmentalist thinking makes much of the interdependence of things in the natural world, and it is certainly true that the doctrine of *pratītyasamutpāda* is in tune with a world view which accepts complex, interdependent relationships. However, there is a problem associated with making a comparison between Buddhism and environmentalist thinking which the scholars mentioned above fail to acknowledge. The Buddhist analysis of things, be they animate or inanimate, is far more radical than that adopted by western ecology.

Let us take the example of an endangered species such as the black rhino. For the environmentalist the potential demise of these noble creatures is a matter of sadness and concern. To counteract this possibility, measures will be taken to protect the species by mitigating the destructive forces at work in the rhino's habitat, be they human-made or essentially independent of humanity. In this sense, environmentalism represents a 'fight against pollution and resource depletion'. A Buddhist is unlikely to view things in this way. I am not suggesting for one moment that Buddhists would rejoice at the extinction of the black rhino—very far from it—but, as we have previously noted, change, dissolution, suffering and death are the hallmarks of all conditioned things. At the deepest level, what we take to be a rhino is nothing more than a complex series of momentary *dharmas* which have come together in a certain pattern. To the eye of ignorance this patterning appears as a bulky, African quadruped. Looked at from a different perspective, the rise and fall of things, whether they be mountains or animals is part of the inexorable process Buddhists call *saṃsāra*. In a sense, contemplation of this fact brings home to us our own lack of substance and permanence. It may have a positive impact on the development of the spiritual life. The recognition of this deep impermanence may prompt us to investigate the teachings of the Buddha and opt to follow the Buddhist path which leads to *nirvāṇa*.

If we take stock of the argument to this point, it becomes clear that Buddhism does not provide the kind of doctrinal foundation from which environmental concerns can be easily developed in the way that some other religions, notably the semitic religions of Judaism, Christianity and Islam, do. In these traditions the natural world is the creation of a loving and Supreme Being. The natural world, since it is part of the created order, must have a distinct purpose in the divine scheme of things, and it can be coherently argued that humans must get their relations with this order right for the final purpose of existence to be realised. As we have already noted, Buddhism repudiates that kind of theism and the theistic response to the world. Purpose and meaning as such are missing from the equation, but we should be on our guard against misinterpreting the Buddhist outlook on the world. Far from being cold-hearted or nihilistic, Buddhism places great stress on loving-kindness and compassion to all beings. After all, we are all in the same boat. Let us now examine this strand of the tradition in more detail.

NON-INJURY IN THE BUDDHIST TRADITION

The principle of non-injury is one of the characteristic features of many ancient Indian religious traditions. There is some evidence to suggest that the avoidance of harming living things pre-dates the arrival of the Aryans in the subcontinent some 4,500 years ago. The religion of the Aryans, preserved as it is in the vedic writings, is an essentially sacrificial religion and, as such, was dependent from time to time on the sacrifice of animals. In contrast, we find no evidence of such practices in the classical system of Yoga or in the religion of the Jainas. The same may be said for Buddhism. It is noteworthy that these three traditions were essentially traditions of renunciants. Since renunciation is not easily reconciled with the martial and life-affirming world view of the Aryans, there may be some substance to the view that both renunciation and the practice of non-injury were indigenous Indian modes of behaviour. Certainly non-injury (*ahiṃsā*) is stressed quite frequently in the early texts of Buddhism.

The frequency of occurrence of this doctrine is at least partly explained by Buddhist adherence to the idea of rebirth. As we have already noted, our very large number of previous lives means that we have already established intimate relations with virtually the whole of the animal kingdom. We are in some, unconscious, sense part of an enormous family of fellow sufferers. To contribute to the further suffering of any individual member of this family would be as serious an offence as harming one's mother or father. Anthropologists and psychoanalysts tell us that offences of this kind are treated with particular opprobrium in the majority of cultures. However, in the Buddhist context the emphasis on non-harming may have another dimension. A number of texts teach that this practice may lead to a favourable future birth. The implication is clearly that harming results in rebirth in an unfavourable destiny (*gati*). Perhaps someone who has committed acts of cruelty to animals will become an animal, ghost or even a denizen of hell. In this sense, an act of cruelty contaminates the person who commits the deed—as a result he or she becomes impure. This impurity is viewed as a physical contaminant which drags the person down to a lower level of existence after death. If this interpretation is accepted, then there is something to be said for the view that non-injury (*ahiṃsā*) was regarded in a positive light as much for its purificatory role in a person's spiritual development as it was for its effects on animal and human welfare.

The case of vegetarianism brings this contrast to prominence. It is often assumed that the Buddha taught vegetarianism. This certainly seems to follow logically from the doctrine of non-injury. In fact, examination of the relevant sources reveals a rather more complicated situation. The Pāli canon reveals that the Buddha was himself occasionally to be found eating meat. Not only that, but, under certain conditions, he gave members of the *saṅgha* permission to eat meat. The only requirement for a monk is that the meat should be properly cooked and pure. In other words, the monk should neither see, hear nor suspect that the meat has been prepared specifically for him. A final proviso is that the monk should refrain from eating ten kinds of meat, e.g., the flesh of the snake, lion, elephant, dog, etc. It has been convincingly argued, by Ruegg (1980) and others, that strict vegetarianism only became a coherent position in Mahāyāna Buddhism, at a pretty late stage in the history of the tradition. We should bear two factors in mind here. In the first place, vegetarianism is not a necessary condition for concern for the environment. In the second, compassion for the fate of individual members of the animal kingdom is not the same as the more general concern for the destiny of species characteristic of much environmentalist literature.

In order to expand on the foregoing discussion, let us now turn to an aspect of Buddhist meditational practice. This is the cultivation of lovingkindness (*mettā*). A frequently recommended series of meditational subjects are the four divine abidings (*bramavihāras*). Concentration on the *bramavihāras* (i.e., loving kindness, *mettā;* compassion, *karuṇā;* sympathetic joy, *muditā;* and equanimity, *upekkhā*) is believed to form an important preliminary in the Buddhist system of mental cultivation. Of the four, the meditation on lovingkindness is perhaps the most widely practised. By extending *mettā* towards others, goodwill is promoted and the heart becomes filled with love. However, in a discussion of this practice in his influential work on meditation, called the Path of Purification (*Visuddhimagga*), Buddhaghosa mentions eleven advantages which accrue to the practitioners themselves. Strangely, no advantages are listed for the recipient of the *mettā*. At another point in the discussion, we are told to avoid the directing of *mettā* towards animals. It is thought to be better, certainly in the early stages of the practice, to confine one's attention to a human object, and preferably a human towards whom one harbours no strong feelings, whether they be positive or negative.

In the Pāli texts, the Buddha is occasionally described as extending *mettā* towards animals. However, when the context of these occurrences is examined, it is clear that the Buddha does this for a very specific purpose. It is done to calm an enraged animal. A good example of this is the occasion when an attempt was made on the Buddha's life. A mad elephant is set loose to trample him and his entourage, but, through the Buddha's defensive use of *mettā*, this dangerous situation is diffused. Clearly *mettā* practice is an important feature of the Buddhist path, but when we look into its rationale we are forced to draw surprising conclusions. In general, the advantages of the practice are felt by the practitioner not by the living being to whom it is directed. In particular, successful practice is believed to result in rebirth in one of the divine realms. Non-human focuses of *mettā* are only infrequently met with in the scriptures, and even when they are, the objective of the practitioner is to render a potential threat harmless. A good example of this is to be found in the chanting of a portion of one of the Buddha's sermons (A.ii.72 *Khandha Paritta*) as a charm to ward off dangerous snakes.

I have argued (Harris, 1991) that, when seen in this light, the Buddhist attitude towards animals is essentially instrumental. Its essential function is to aid the practitioner in his search for spiritual perfection, and any good done to the being to whom *mettā* is extended is merely a happy side-effect. This fact is actually recognised by the tradition itself, for the scriptures accept that the cultivation of the *brahmavihāras* does not lead directly to *nirvāṇa*. Since the practice is directed towards beings within the world, the results are held to be basically mundane (*lokiya*). In effect, the attitudes of mind reflected by the practice express our highest ethical ideals, and these ideals can be applied only within the realm of conditioned things. It is important to emphasise the fact that these ideals in themselves do not bring about any supramundane achievement. They are not essentially Buddhist ideals. They simply refer to actions which are viewed in a positive light by society as a whole. Actually the scriptures acknowledge that *brahmavihāra* practice does not originate within the Buddhist tradition. It was employed by the sages of old and merely preserved by the Buddha. The Buddha was quite prepared to accept these ideals, particularly since they perform a clear role in the maintenance of civilised values, but he stressed that one must accept their fundamentally provisional nature. Ultimately they bind us more tightly to the world, when the goal must be release.

In view of what has been said above, it seems clear that kindness and the avoidance of cruelty are civilised forms of behaviour endorsed by the Buddhist tradition. In accordance with this principle, the Buddha recommended that his lay followers should take the welfare of their domestic animals seriously. For instance, cowherds are warned not to milk their herds dry. It is a common custom in Buddhist regions of South and Southeast Asia, even today, to release animals, and particularly birds, from captivity. This practice probably derives from the Buddha's command that monks should free animals caught in hunters' traps.

However, there is little doubt that, for Buddhism, animals belong some way down the hierarchy of beings. They occupy one of the three unfavourable destinies (*gatis*). They are less wise than humans and cannot make effective progress on the Buddhist path. They cannot, therefore, be admitted as members of the *saṅgha*, for their presence within the monastic community would be deleterious. In the literature of monastic discipline, the Buddha regularly lists animals alongside hermaphrodites, thieves, parent-killers and, most significantly, those guilty of the most heinous of all crimes, murderers of a *buddha*.

There are plenty of incidents within the canon in which animals behave impeccably, and in many respects better than the average human, but nevertheless the animal realm is in general something to be wary of. Animals are thought to be more vicious than humans. The forest-dwelling monk is particularly prone to the dangers represented by wild animals. He may be attacked by tigers or snakes. Hence the importance of the practice of *mettā* as a protective mechanism. Looked at from another perspective, he is subject to the depredations of many small creatures. Their cumulative effect is to make his existence in the forest distinctly uncomfortable. Insects, rats and the like are continually attacking his limited range of possessions. Now, though this may be inconvenient on one level, the monk can turn this to his advantage. The activity of the animal kingdom is an example, on the grand scale, of the process of decay which affects all conditioned things. Meditation on this fact can develop a deeper understanding of the impermanence, insubstantiality and suffering associated with the world. As a result, the monk's desires for worldly things diminish. In fact, the perception of danger may itself be utilised on the spiritual quest. Fear is a particularly strong emotional state. Its strength and associated physical effects may become meditational objects. Investigation of fear in this manner may lead to important insights into the functioning of the mental processes, and this in turn may lead to greater insight into the *dharma*. Certainly this practice is recommended by some meditation teachers in Thailand today. It is said to have a powerful therapeutic value.

Before moving on, let us summarise the conclusions of this section. Kindness towards animals is encouraged by Buddhism. Such kindness is in accordance with worldly conventions. On this level the Buddha has no argument with the ethics of his day. However, Buddhism ultimately expects to transcend such considerations, for the tradition ideally represents an attempt to escape from the restrictions imposed on us by our position as beings within the world. Concern for the animal kingdom is compatible with Buddhism but does not arise naturally from its central insights into the nature of reality. It can happily be taken along as baggage on the path to perfection, but at some stage it must be abandoned. In actual fact, many of the practices which seem, at one level, to be targeted at the welfare of animals, have as their ultimate aim the spiritual development of the practitioner. The Buddhist ethic in this area is essentially instrumental.

THE NATURAL ENVIRONMENT AND BUDDHISM

If Max Weber was correct, and there is some evidence to suggest that he was, then it looks likely that Buddhism has its origins in the growing urban centres of northern India some 500 years before Christ. Tradition holds that the Buddha's favourite residing places were parks and pleasure groves which came into the possession of the early *Saṅgha* as gifts from wealthy lay followers. These were clearly convenient places for the reception of alms from surrounding residents, and from such suburban locations the Buddha was well poised to extend his influence. A life spent in the heart of the jungle would hardly have been as useful in this respect. The Pāli canon indicates that the laying out of such areas was thought to be a highly meritorious action, but it is important to note that these locations are essentially artificial. They are made by humans.

In the *Cakkavatisihānadasutta,* an early Pāli text, a description of the far future, in which conditions have improved greatly on the present, is given. At that time, humans can expect a life span of approximately 80,000 years. However, cities then will have grown to such an extent that the countryside will have all but disappeared. Surprisingly, the text gives no hint that this will be an undesirable state of affairs. On the contrary, the wilderness will have been tamed, and this is portrayed as a positive advance for humanity. The text might be interpreted as evidence for the great confidence felt by early Buddhists in the superiority of urban over rural culture.

It is an acknowledged fact that Buddhist sources are rather light on glowing descriptions of the natural world. One or two passages can be identified in which the author appears to be delighting in the glories of nature, but these are few and far between. There is a good reason for this. The doctrinal content of the Buddha's teaching paints the world in a rather sombre light. It is subject to corruption and intrinsically unsatisfactory. It is possible that one may be instantaneously struck with aesthetic pleasure on viewing a natural scene, but for the Buddhist this can never be more than a fleeting perception. There is no value attached to holding on to such experiences. In such a doctrinal environment it is difficult for natural mysticism to take a firm hold. This is clearly in great contrast to Christianity. For the latter tradition, the world can be read as a text revealing evidence of the divine creator's purpose. The perception of beauty can draw one closer to an appreciation of the author of such beauty. In short, nature reveals God. This is impossible with Buddhism. I do not mean by this that Buddhists themselves may not rejoice in the astonishing profusion of the natural world; there is no intentional dourness in Buddhism. But they cannot be led on from such reflections to any ultimate end. Delight in the world can too easily be a stage on the way towards increased desire for more such delights, and this must eventually lead to further suffering.

Buddhism shares many of the characteristics of the ancient traditions of Indian renunciation. So, despite its possible urban roots, the ideal of forest-dwelling had an impact on at least a proportion of the Buddha's followers. The forest is the antithesis of the cultivated and cultured environment of the town. It is the home of a variety of wild beasts and for this reason alone it induces fear. But there is another attendant problem associated with the forest—it may also be a haven for any number of malicious spirits. As such it is a place of ill-will and wickedness. It is an alien land. As a consequence, nuns are prevented from taking up abode here; they may be seduced by unwholesome influences. Some forests are referred to by name in the Pāli texts, and we are told that they were once cleared for cultivation but became reforested as a result of the ill-will of certain sages. Lack of cultivation, then, has a certain connection with negative emotions and outright wickedness. Cultivation on the other hand is equated with righteousness.

However, the forest can be employed as a meditational device. A number of prominent Buddhist writers recommend mindfulness of the forest as a means of gaining insight into impermanence. Buddhaghosa, for instance, extols the positive consequences of attention to falling leaves, and in the Mahāyāna the forest is sometimes seen as a metaphor for *saṃsāra* itself. It is not surprising, then, to find that Buddhist literature is full of natural imagery to describe the course of spiritual progress. For instance, one is said to move from a state in which the path is not cultivated to one in which it is. One sows the seeds of merit in the field of the Buddha. One takes the middle path to enlightenment. Paths which wander through uncharted territory must be avoided.

Buddhist scriptures contain rather little to indicate how the vegetable kingdom should be treated. However, a few snippets of information may be gleaned from a reading of the texts of monastic discipline. Monks must avoid damage to plant life. Incurring such damage is an offence which requires expiation on the part of the monk. This seems a clear-cut matter, but on closer investigation it appears that the texts are primarily concerned with damage to crops. If this is so, then one wonders about the intention underlying the rule. Is it wrong to damage any form of plant life, or is there an offence only when cultivated produce is concerned? It is difficult to give a precise answer, but we know that monks are prohibited from engaging in agricultural activity. This ruling presumably arose for a variety of reasons. In the first place, farming is a full-time occupation and leaves little spare time for the cultivation of the spiritual life. On the other hand, agricultural activities, such as ploughing, digging, etc., lead inevitably to the accidental death of soil organisms. Perhaps the avoidance of damage to crops is a simple extension of this principle. Monks will naturally damage crops in the harvesting process, therefore, they should avoid agriculture entirely. Now this is a fairly specific regulation, and some evidence exists to suggest a more wide-ranging ethic. The Buddha is certainly said to have avoided all damage to seed and plant life. This may be interpreted as an extension of the principle of non-injury (*ahiṃsā*) to the vegetable kingdom. However, while monastic conduct may be regulated along such lines, the life of the lay Buddhist must necessarily be less exacting.

The vast majority of Buddhist populations, at all phases of the history of the tradition, have been tied to the land as a matter of life and death. The laity must ensure that adequate foodstuffs are available for their families, but they have an added responsibility: they must provide alms for members of the *saṅgha*. Under such conditions monks would be ill-advised to demand unrealistic levels of behaviour among the ordinary people. There is a gulf, then, between the expectations imposed on monks and those thought appropriate for the laity. Monks must avoid all activities which result in harm to flora and fauna. Failure to observe these measures will lead to failure on the path to *nirvāṇa*. The laity, on the other hand, is compelled, by circumstance, to inflict a moderate level of harm on the natural environment. Agriculture cannot take place without some damage. However, the undesirable consequences of agricultural activity are diminished by lay alms-giving. By making regular offering of food to the *saṅgha*, the lay person is ensured rebirth in a favourable destiny (*gati*) after death. Weber refers to this less restrictive code practised by the Buddhist laity as an 'insufficiency ethic'. The term implies that lay activity, while it may be determined by certain moral criteria, is not sufficient in itself to bring about the ultimate goal of the tradition, i.e. *nirvāṇa*.

Before leaving this section, it is necessary for us to investigate the status of plants in the Buddhist scheme of things. They are certainly not conceived of as inanimate objects. They are thought to possess the single sense of touch, though none of the other faculties is present, e.g. the hearing, taste, mind, etc., which characterise higher organisms. They can nevertheless experience pain. It is apparent from our earlier discussion that the world of plants is not one of the six destinies—we can never be reborn as a tree or piece of grass. This is noteworthy because some Hindu *dharma* texts do accept this as a possibility. For Buddhism, though, the realm of vegetable life stands apart from the sphere of beings ultimately destined for enlightenment. It is part of the stage on which salvation is played, but does not itself possess the capacity for perfection. From the perspective of enlightenment, plant life shares in the purposelessness and meaninglessness of the entire realm of conditioned things. This does not mean that Buddhists may treat the vegetable kingdom with contempt. An individual's role as lay person or monk will be a crucial factor in determining the precise manner in which responsibilities are exercised, but the principle of non-injury must always be present as the background to behaviour. The major difference is that the *saṅgha* member works with a hard interpretation of the principle, while the lay person adopts a softer approach.

CONCLUSION

It is obvious that Buddhism starts with a very different set of priorities from those encountered in the religions of the ancient Near East. Its lack of a supreme creator, plus an insistence on the eternity of the world process, stand in stark contrast to the Judaeo-Christian tradition. In its origin Buddhism is a religion of world-weariness, though this situation clearly underwent significant modification as the centuries progressed. Nevertheless, the Buddha's prime importance as a religious teacher was his identification of the world as a domain devoid of substantiality. Recognition of this fact results in non-reliance on the things of the world. In consequence, the typical follower of the Buddha in the early period is a renouncer.

In essence and theory, then, Buddhism cannot uphold an environmentalist ethic. The reason for this is straightforward. There is nothing within the sphere of nature which can be said to possess any meaning or purpose. There can be no Buddhist justification for the fight to preserve habitats and environments. Everything, without exception, is subject to decay. It is not at all clear that change, within the natural world, can be positively affected by human interventions.

In practice, however, the situation is a little different. Since its inception Buddhism has been a missionary religion. In order to increase its influence in Asia, missionary monks have seen the sense in preserving local traditions as long as they do not come into conflict with central doctrinal concerns. The result of this activity has been that in many regions of the Buddhist world the renunciatory concerns of the early period have rested lightly on the lay population. We also know that the Buddha himself adopted an ethical outlook which drew substantially from pre-Buddhist systems of thought. From our perspective, his most important borrowing was the insistence on non-injury (*ahiṃsā*). Buddhists are expected to apply this principle in their dealings with all beings. All actions—be they bodily, verbal or mental—are to be referred back to this ideal. This is the essence of right action, one of the members of the noble eightfold path.

A consequence of this insistence is that animals and plants are to be respected and such respect arises naturally from the insight, provided by Buddhist cosmology, that all sentient beings are intimately interrelated. The level at which the principle of non-injury may be practised is effectively determined by a person's status in the Buddhist community. Agriculturalists must attempt to protect animal life but some injury is unavoidable, owing to the nature of the work. Monks are prevented from working on the land, for the negative consequences entailed by such tasks would be harmful to the spread of the *dharma*.

We should not imagine that the doctrine of *ahiṃsā* was imported into Buddhism without modification. On the contrary, it had to be incorporated into a coherent vision of things. The justification for non-injury is essentially instrumental. By behaving in a loving and compassionate fashion, one is ensured a favourable rebirth as a god (*deva*). This does not mean that the beings to whom love is directed will not benefit. In fact they will have their unfortunate lives enhanced, particularly if they are animals, and may in time come to a fuller understanding of the *dharma*.

In short, Buddhism endorses a spirit of toleration and cooperation with the natural world. It does so because this traditional mode of behaviour is given a specific sense by the tradition, and in the final analysis does not come into conflict with the ultimate goal, which is escape. From the perspective of enlightenment nothing may have a final purpose or essential value, but, at least in the early stages of the spiritual path, Buddhism acts as though it does. Here then is one of the many paradoxes encountered in the study of this unique religious system of thought.

FURTHER READING

Attfield, R. (1983) 'Western Traditions and Environmental Ethics,' in Eliot, R. and Gane, A. (eds), *Environmental Philosophy,* Milton Keynes, Open University Press.
Bowker, J. W. (1990) 'Cosmology, Religion and Society,' *Zygon,* 25: 7–23.
Hargrove, E. C. (1989) *Foundations of Environmental Ethics,* Englewood Cliffs, New Jersey, Prentice-Hall.
Harris, I. C. (1991) 'How Environmentalist is Buddhism?', *Religion,* 21: 101–14.
Passmore, J. (1980) *Man's Responsibility for Nature,* London, Duckworth.
Ruegg, D. S. (1980) 'Ahimsa and Vegetarianism in the History of Buddhism,' in Balasooriya, S. *et al.* (eds), *Buddhist Studies in Honour of Walpola Rahula,* London, Gordon Fraser.
White, L. Jnr (1967) 'The historical roots of our ecological crisis,' *Science,* 155: 1204 ff.

The Hermeneutics of Buddhist Ecology in Contemporary Thailand

Buddhadāsa and Dhammapitaka[1]

DONALD K. SWEARER

The world's environmental crisis has prompted religiously committed, socially concerned people throughout the world to search their traditions for resources to address its root causes and its symptoms. Buddhists are no exception. The compatibility between the Buddhist worldview of interdependence and an "environmentally friendly" way of living in the world, the values of compassion and nonviolence, and the example of the Buddha's lifestyle and the early *saṅgha* are cited as important contributions to the dialogue on ways to live in an increasingly threatened world. This essay seeks to interject a particular insight into this discussion through an examination of selected writings of Buddhadāsa Bhikkhu and Phra Prayudh Payutto (current monastic title, Dhammapiṭaka), the Thai *Saṅgha*'s most highly regarded interpreters of the *buddhadhamma*.[2] In particular, I propose to explore their distinctive ecological hermeneutics, that is to say, the particular environmental lessons each draws from the texts and traditions of Thai Buddhism. In conclusion, I shall briefly assess the recent critical evaluation of Buddhist environmentalism by Ian Harris[3] from the perspective of my construction of the ecological hermeneutics of Buddhadāsa Bhikkhu and Phra Prayudh.

Swearer, Donald K., "The Hermeneutics of Buddhist Ecology in Contemporary Thailand: Buddhadasa and Dhammapitaka," in Mary Evelyn Tucker and Duncan Ryuken Williams, Eds., *Buddhism and Ecology: The Interconnection of Dharma and Deeds,* Cambridge, Mass.: Harvard University Press, 1997, pp. 21–44. Reprinted by permission of the Center for the Study of World Religions, Harvard Divinity School.

INTRODUCTION

During the past half century, economic and social configurations have changed dramatically throughout the world as a consequence of population increases, urbanization, industrialization, and technical achievement. These changes have, to a certain extent, created a common economic culture determined by the necessities of the modern nation-state and the business interests of multinational corporations. This economic culture is primarily "materialistic" in nature in the sense that human well-being tends to be defined in terms of the production and consumption of goods. It is commonplace, for example, to measure the wealth of a nation in terms of its GNP (gross national product).

The consequences of the development of an economically defined modern culture are manifold. For example, it has led to a general increase in life expectancy among most populations of the world as a consequence of improved health services, more adequate housing, and so forth. In short, in respect to material aspects of life more people share in the benefits of the increased production and use of various kinds of goods. Yet even from an economic perspective, the increase in the production and use of goods has been a mixed blessing. In general, even though by GNP measurements the world has seen a significant increase in the amount of material wealth, critics are quick to point out the gross disparity between the rich and the poor, not only in "developing" countries, such as Thailand, but also in "developed" countries, such as the United States. For instance, in Thailand conflicts that began in 1988 over water use between the wealthier industrial/urban sector and the poorer agricultural/rural sector have prompted numerous farmer protests over low water supplies that came to a head in the drought year 1993.[4] Internationally, it can also be pointed out that despite improvements in agricultural technology hunger has emerged as a persistent and pervasive worldwide problem. The capital-intensive green revolution, with its dependence on chemical fertilizers and pesticides, has produced more systemic, long-range problems than it has solved, and biotechnology may raise even more questions about the consequences of genetic engineering.[5]

Developments in many different kinds of technologies have led to dramatic breakthroughs in everything from space exploration to microscopic laser surgery. At the same time, however, technological advancement has contributed to the sense of hopelessness and prevalent violence experienced by modern society, as evidenced by the plague of drug addiction, increasing levels of armed violence, or the seemingly insurmountable problem of waste disposal, especially the threat of the widespread nuclear waste contamination and the toxic contamination of water and food supplies.

Our modern economic culture has also had a generally deleterious effect on classical moral values and religious worldviews and on traditional ways of understanding human existence and what constitutes the good or happy life. In the face of a perceived threat to traditional ways of being by modern economic culture, some seek a return to the verities of a simpler era believed to be embodied in an earlier historical age or represented by an idealized, mythic time of primal beginnings. Religious fundamentalisms, whether Christian, Jewish, Muslim, Hindu, or Buddhist, may be interpreted as a retreat from the confusions and threats of the modern world to the truths and values of an earlier age. But there are other, more creative and constructive religious responses to modernity than today's various fundamentalisms. Thoughtful religious adherents throughout the world are seeking to understand and interpret their traditions in ways that preserve the lasting insights and values of their faith, while at the same time engaging the realities of existence in today's world rather than retreating from them.

In the past several years the media in Thailand has devoted considerable attention to the conflicts between the goals of national and commercial development, the well-being of the majority of the Thai people (especially the rural, farming populations), and the health of the environment. In particular, the Seventh National Development Plan has been criticized for following in the footsteps of its predecessors by emphasizing material growth at the expense of a more balanced development and an equitable distribution of wealth. Dr. Ananda Kanchanapan of the Faculty of the Social Sciences at Chiang Mai University observes that development in Thailand has emphasized the GNP and in doing so has undermined the moral and spiritual integration between the social and natural environment.[6] An article in the *Matichon* newspaper representative of this point of view charges that development in Thailand has benefited the elites at the expense of the environment and proposes a reformist Buddhist perspective that would challenge selfishness and greed and the excessive lifestyle that has resulted from "too much wealth, too much power, too much to eat and drink, too many cars and mistresses."[7]

BUDDHADĀSA BHIKKHU: NATURE AS DHAMMA

Like Thomas Merton, the late American Trappist monk and peace activist, Buddhadāsa exemplifies the truth that thoughtful spiritual engagement with the world requires a degree of contemplative distance.[8] In much the same way as Merton, Buddhadāsa spent most of his active career living and teaching in a forest hermitage (Wat Suan Mokkhabalārāma [Thai, Mōkh], Chaiya, south Thailand). Like Merton, he was also extraordinarily responsive to the issues of his time. Although known in Thailand primarily as a teacher or a "monk of wisdom" (Thai, *phra paññā*), Buddhadāsa used the doctrinal tenets of non-attachment, dependent co-arising, and emptiness as the bases for addressing an exceptionally broad range of issues, problems, and concerns, from meditation, monastic discipline, and ritual observances to world politics, women in Buddhism, and the environment.

The core of Buddhadāsa's ecological hermeneutic is found in his identification of the *dhamma* with nature (Thai, *thamachāt;* Pali, *dhammajāti*). It was his sense of the liberating power of nature-as-*dhamma* that inspired Buddhadāsa in 1932 to found Wat Suan Mōkh as a center for both teaching and practice in a forest near the small town of Chaiya in Surat Thani Province, rather than pursue a monastic career in Bangkok. For Buddhadāsa the natural surroundings of his forest monastery were nothing less than a medium for personal transformation.[9]

> Trees, rocks, sand, even dirt and insects can speak. This doesn't mean, as some people believe, that they are spirits [Thai, *phī*] or gods [Pali, *devatā*]. Rather, if we reside in nature near trees and rocks we'll discover feelings and thoughts arising that are truly out of the ordinary. At first we'll feel a sense of peace and quiet [Thai, *sangopyen* = quiet-cool] which may eventually move beyond that feeling to a transcendence of self. The deep sense of calm that nature provides through separation [Pali, *viveka*] from the troubles and anxieties that plague us in the day-to-day world functions to protect heart and mind. Indeed, the lessons nature teaches us lead to a new birth beyond the suffering [Pali, *dukkha*] that results from attachment to self. Trees and rocks, then, can talk to us. They help us understand what it means to cool down from the heat of our confusion, despair, anxiety, and suffering.[10]

Buddhadāsa's identification of nature and *dhamma* prompts him to read nature as a text. Indeed, because experiencing nature involves not just the mind but all of the bodily senses, to listen to the "shouts of nature" is potentially more liberating (read *nibbāna*) than studying the Pali scriptures. Buddhadāsa, moreover, makes the extraordinarily strong claim that nature is a much more appropriate context or environment in which to pursue liberation than sitting at a desk: "If we don't spend time in places like this [Wat Suan Mōkh], it will be virtually impossible for us to experience peace and quiet. It is only by being in nature that the trees, rocks, earth, sand, animals, birds, and insects can teach us the lesson of self-forgetting."[11] In Buddhadāsa's spiritual biocentric view, being attuned to the lessons of nature is tantamount to at-one-ment with the *dhamma*. By inference, the destruction of nature implies the destruction of the *dhamma*.

Cynics could argue that Buddhadāsa's ecological hermeneutic is self-serving. After all, his essay *Shouts from Nature* (*Siang Takọn Jāk Thamachāt*) was a Visākhā Pūja sermon at Wat Suan Mōkh, so could not his teaching be interpreted as a clever strategy to promote interest in and support of his forest ashram? Such an argument can be summarily dismissed in the face of Buddhadāsa's exemplary integrity over a monastic career of sixty-five years. Two additional, more serious criticisms might be made, however: 1) while his message is not gauged to promote Wat Suan Mōnk, it might be argued that it constructs Buddhist practice as a retreat to the forest rather than engagement with the world; 2) from a deep ecology perspective Buddhadāsa appears to be more anthropocentric than biocentric; that is to say, the forest is valued simply as a place for spiritual practice rather than for its inherent value. Although both criticisms are not without merit, I propose to challenge these two views.

Toward the end of his life the destruction of the natural environment became a matter of great concern for Buddhadāsa. One of his informal talks at Wat Suan Mōkh in 1990, three years before his death, was titled "Buddhists and the Care of Nature" (*Buddhasāsanik Kap Kān Anurak Thamachāt*). This essay provides insight into both the biocentric and ethical dimensions of Buddhadāsa's ecological hermeneutic.[12] Let us begin by exploring the essay's two central terms—"care" (Thai, *anurak;* Pali, *anurakkhā*) and "nature" (Thai, *thamachāt;* Pali, *dhammajāti*).[13]

Within the context of the worldwide concern for environmental destruction, the Thai term *anurak* is often translated into English as "conservation." In fact, the dozens of Thai monks involved in efforts to stop the exploitation of forests in their districts and provinces have been labeled *phra kānanurak pā*, or "forest conservation monks." *Anurak,* as embodied in the life and work of Buddhadāsa, however, conveys a richer, more nuanced meaning closer to its Pali roots, namely, to be imbued with the quality of protecting, sheltering, or caring for. By the term *anurak,* Buddhadāsa intends this deeper, dhammic sense of *anurakkhā*, an intrinsic, active "caring for" that issues forth from the very nature of our being. In this sense, to care for nature is linked with a pervasive feeling of human empathy (Pali, *anukampā*)[14] for all of our surroundings. If you will, caring is the active expression of empathy.

One cares for the forest because one empathizes with the forest just as one cares for people, including oneself, because one has become empathetic. *Anurak,* the active expression of a state of empathy, is fundamentally linked to non-attachment or liberation from preoccupation with self, which is at the very core of Buddhadāsa's thought. He develops this theme using various Thai and Pali terms, including *mai hen kae tua* (not being selfish),[15] *cit wāng* (non-attachment or having a liberated heart-mind), *anattā* (not-self), *suññatā* (emptiness). In a talk to the Dhamma Study Group at Sirirāt Hospital in Bangkok in 1961, he stated unequivocally the centrality of non-attachment to Buddhist spirituality: "This is the heart of the Buddhist Teachings, of all Dhamma: nothing whatsoever should be clung to."[16] It is just such non-attachment or self-forgetting—the heart of the *dhamma*—that we learn from nature.

We truly care for our total environment, including our fellow human beings, only when we have overcome selfishness and those qualities which empower it: desire, greed, hatred. Buddhadāsa's profound commitment to this truth can be seen in "Overcoming Selfishness Is Essential to a Political System" (*Khwām Mai Hen Kae Tua Jampen Samrap Rabop Kanmuang Khong Lōk* [1989]); "Serving Others Makes the World Peaceful" (*Kān Rapchai Phūœn Tham Hai Lōk Santi* [1960]); "Working with a Liberated Heart and Mind for the Good of Society" (*Kān Tham Ngān Duœ Cit Wāng Phū'a Sangkhom* [1975]). Note the persistent linkage between non-attachment, selflessness, and the capacity to be truly other-regarding. Caring in Buddhadāsa's dhammic sense, therefore, is the active expression of our empathetic identification with all life-forms: sentient and nonsentient, human beings and nature.

Caring in this deeper sense of the meaning of *anurak* goes beyond the well-publicized strategies to protect and conserve the forest, such as ordaining trees, implemented by the conservation monks, as important as these strategies have become in Thailand. This is where the second term, *thamachāt,* enters the picture. The Thai term *thamachāt* is usually translated as "nature." Its Pali root, however, denotes everything that is linked to *dhamma* or that is dhamma originated (*jāti*). That is to say, *thamachāt* includes all things in their true, natural state, a condition that Buddhadāsa refers to as "norm-al" or "norm-ative" (*pakati*), that is, the way things are in the true, dhammic condition. To conserve (*anurak*) nature (*thamachāt*), therefore, translates as having at the core of one's very being the quality of empathetic caring for all things in the world in their natural conditions; that is to say, to care for them as they really are rather than as I might benefit from them or as I might like them to be. Indeed, *anurak thamachāt* implies that the "I" is not over against nature but interactively co-dependent with it. In other words, the moral/spiritual quality of non-attachment or self-forgetfulness necessarily implies the ontological realization of interdependent co-arising.

From an ethical perspective this means that our care for nature derives from an ingrained selfless, empathetic response. It is not motivated by a need to satisfy our own pleasures as, say, in the maintenance of a beautiful garden or even by the admirable goal of conserving nature for our own physical and spiritual well-being or for the benefit of future generations. To care for nature in these pragmatic, functional terms has immense value, to be sure. I think that Buddhadāsa would not dispute this fact. A carefully tended garden is both meaningful to the gardener and inspirational to the viewer; furthermore, human survival may depend on whether or not we are able to conserve our dwindling natural resources and solve the problems of our increasingly polluted natural environment. Laudable as these two senses of conserving nature are, they lack the profound transformational or spiritual sense of what Buddhadāsa means by *anurak thamachāt.* I propose that Buddhadāsa's identification of nature and *dhamma* makes his view inherently biocentric. That is, listening to nature and caring for nature are both forms of dhammic self-forgetting, not merely instrumental to human flourishing.

The concept of active caring for other human beings needs little explication.[17] The word itself evokes numerous examples from our own experience: the parent who cares for a child, the mutual caring among friends, the responsible caring of citizens for the well-being of the state. But what does Buddhadāsa mean by caring for nature, *thamachāt*? By *thamachāt* Buddhadāsa does not have in mind either a metaphysical or a romantic concept of nature. Quite the contrary. For Buddhadāsa, things in their natural, true state are characterized by their dynamic, interdependent nature (*idappaccayatā, paticca samuppāda*). Everything is linked in a process of interdependent co-arising, or as Buddhadāsa often says, "We are mutual friends inextricably bound together in the same process of birth, old age, suffering, and death."[18] In other words, the world is a conjoint, interdynamic, cooperative whole (Thai, *sahakorn;* Pali, *saha* + *karaṇa*), not a collection of disparate, oppositional parts.[19] In the deepest sense, therefore, to care for nature means participation in this state of inter-becoming, not just human beings preserving nature for the sake of human beings.

While human linkages are self-evident to us, as in our relationships with family and friends, the interdependence of human beings and nature has been less self-evident. Only in recent years has it been commonly understood that the destruction of the Brazilian rain forest or the ocean dumping of toxic waste affects the entire world ecosystem; or, in more immediate and personal terms, that whether I personally conserve water, electricity, gasoline, and so on affects not only my utility bills but the health of the entire cosmos. To care for (*anurak*) nature (*thamachāt*), therefore, stems from a realization that I do not and cannot exist independently of my total environment. I am not "an island unto myself"; or, in Buddhadāsa's terminology, I do not and cannot exist unto myself (Pali, *atta;* Thai, *tua kū khong kū*) because to do so contravenes the very laws of nature (*dhammajāti* = *idappaccayatā*).

Buddhadāsa's sense of a cooperative society (*sahakorn*), therefore, extends to the broadest reaches of the cosmos.

> The entire cosmos is a cooperative. The sun, the moon, and the stars live together as a cooperative. The same is true for humans and animals, trees and the earth. Our bodily parts function as a cooperative. When we realize that the world is a mutual, interdependent, cooperative enterprise, that human beings are all mutual friends in the process of birth, old age, suffering, and death, then we can build a noble, even a heavenly environment. If our lives are not based on this truth then we'll all perish.[20]

My own personal well-being is inextricably dependent on the well-being of everything and everyone else, and vice versa. In Buddhadāsa's view this is an incontrovertible, absolute truth (*saccadhamma*). To go against this truth is to suffer the consequences. Today, we are suffering the consequences. As Buddhadāsa expressed it in terms approaching an apocalyptic vision:

> The greedy and selfish are destroying nature. . . . Our whole environment has been poisoned—prisons everywhere, hospitals filled with the physically ill, and we can't build enough facilities to take care of all the mentally ill. This is the consequence of utter selfishness [Thai, *khwām hen kae tua*]. . . . And in the face of all of this our greed and selfishness continues to increase. Is there no end to this madness?[21]

In Buddhadāsa's view, caring for *thamachāt* necessarily means not only that we care for other human beings and for nature, but also that we care for ourselves. Outwardly, *thamachāt* means physical nature. But the inner truth of nature is *dhammadhātu,* the essential or fundamental nature of *dhamma,* namely, the interdependent co-arising nature of things (*paticca samuppāda, idappaccayatā*). "When we realize this truth, the truth of *dhammadhātu,* when this law of the very nature of things is firmly in our hearts and minds, then we will overcome selfishness and greed. By caring for this inner truth we are then able to truly care for nature."[22]

Buddhadāsa's environmental philosophy can be characterized as a spiritual biocentrism based on the identification of nature and *dhamma.* The simplicity of his life-style amidst the natural surroundings of Suan Mōkh, furthermore, provides a compelling testimony to the possibility of putting these teachings into practice. By basing his ecological hermeneutic on the identification of nature and *dhamma,* Buddhadāsa challenges the criticisms that his environmental philosophy is either too otherworldly or too anthropocentric. Another kind of criticism, that Buddhadāsa fails to take sufficient account of Theravāda historical traditions to justify his ecological hermeneutic, brings us to a consideration of Phra Prayudh Payutto.

DHAMMAPIṬAKA: NATURE AND THE PURSUIT OF ENLIGHTENMENT

Grant A. Olson's introduction to Dhammapiṭaka's (Phra Prayudh Payutto) *Buddhadhamma* provides a sketch of his life. Phra Prayudh was born in 1939, seven years after Buddhadāsa founded Suan Mōkh. His monastic career has followed a very different trajectory from that of Buddhadāsa. He passed the ninth and highest level of Pali studies in Thailand on the way to being acknowledged as the finest Pali scholar in the Thai *saṅgha.* His scholarly work includes two Pali dictionaries, editorial leadership in the newest edition of the Thai Pali *tipiṭaka* and the Mahidol University CD-ROM Pali canon, as well as his magnum opus of doctrinal interpretation, *Buddhadhamma: Natural Laws and Values for Life.*[23] Although in recent years Phra Prayudh has dedicated himself to scholarly work, from the mid-1960s to the mid-1970s he was actively involved in institutional leadership roles as the abbot of Phra Phirain Monastery in Bangkok and the deputy secretary-general of Mahāchulalongkorn University for Buddhist monks. He has also been awarded several honorary doctorates and in 1994 received the UNESCO Prize for Peace Education.

While Buddhadāsa's fame rests largely on his innovative, creative interpretation of the *dhamma,* Phra Prayudh's teachings are more systematic in nature and more consistently grounded in Pali texts and Theravāda historical traditions. These differences reflect, in part, their distinctive career patterns. Whereas Buddhadāsa built a monastic life-style essentially outside the normal structures and regimes of the Thai *saṅgha,* Phra Prayudh has chosen to work within them as educator and scholar. Perhaps even more importantly, he wrote *Buddhadhamma* as an objective presentation of the teachings of the Buddha free from subjective bias.[24] Buddhadāsa's teachings, in contrast, are grounded in certain fundamental themes—non-attachment, not-self, interdependent co-arising—which he orchestrates around various contextual issues with little concern for textual or "objective" historical reference. Buddhadāsa does not ignore the Pali canon, especially the *suttas;* however, scriptural references are not definitive for his philosophical musings.

Buddhadāsa and Phra Prayudh use the resources of both Pali text and tradition to address environmental problems, but they do so employing distinctive hermeneutical techniques which reflect their differing histories, backgrounds, and relationships to the Thai *saṅgha.* In his recent monograph *Khon Thai Kap Pā* (Thais and the forest), Phra Prayudh delineates several doctrinal principles relevant to a Buddhist environmental ethic. Although these principles resonate with Buddhadāsa's interpretation, Phra Prayudh's hermeneutical strategy differs from Buddhadāsa's in several ways, in particular by extensive references to Pali texts, a topical use of Pali terms rather than Thai, and a more systematic organization and development. In other words, Phra Prayudh's writings, including those about the environment, reflect the concerns of a textual scholar and a systematically organized writer. Buddhadāsa, by contrast, is primarily a philosopher oriented more to an oral rather than a written medium.[25]

Phra Prayudh organizes *Thais and the Forest* around three chronological perspectives: past, present, and future. In regard to the present, he attributes environmental destruction to a Western worldview flawed by three erroneous beliefs: that humankind is separated from nature, that human beings are masters of nature, and that happiness results from the acquisition of material goods.[26] In his essay prepared for the 1993 World Parliament of Religions, Phra Prayudh develops the same position but from a more general, less polemical perspective. He identifies the three erroneous beliefs as wrong attitudes toward nature, fellow human beings, and personal life objective.[27] All three constitute a wrong view (*micchadiṭṭhi*) that must be transformed if environmentally destructive attitudes and actions are to be curbed. Phra Prayudh holds the conventional Theravāda position that right views lead to right action.[28] In agreement with Buddhadāsa and other environmental philosophers, he argues that until the right view prevails and human beings are seen as part of nature, the worldwide trend toward environmental devastation will continue unchecked.

In contrast to Buddhadāsa's dhammic biocentrism grounded in the identification of nature and *dhamma*, Phra Prayudh stresses the centrality of Buddhist ethical values for an environmental philosophy. He emphasizes three Buddhist moral values that promote a positive, beneficial attitude toward the environment, including plants, animals, and fellow human beings: *kataññū* (gratitude), *mettā* (loving-kindness), and *sukha* (happiness). His discussion of gratitude begins with a passage from the *Khuddaka Nikāya* (Collection of minor dialogues): "A person who sits or sleeps in the shade of a tree should not cut off a tree branch. One who injures such a friend is evil."[29] Phra Prayudh observes:

> This maxim reminds us that the shade of a tree we enjoy is enjoyed by others as well. A tree is like a friend which we have no reason to injure. To injure a tree is like hurting a friend. Such a virtuous inner attitude toward nature will prevent us from destructive behavior, on the one hand, and will prompt helpful actions, on the other.[30]

Phra Prayudh links together the moral values of gratitude and loving-kindness (*mettā*). The latter arises from the recognition that according to the law of nature (Thai, *kottamachāt*) humans and all other sentient beings are bound together in a universal process of birth, old age, suffering, and death. This sense of mutuality, Phra Prayudh argues, promotes cooperative and helpful feelings and actions toward everything around us rather than competitive and hostile ones.[31] He suggests that the recognition of a common enemy, the King of Death (*maccurāja*) or Māra, serves to engender *mettā*. From this recognition he draws the causally framed ecological lesson that "Our use of plants and animals must be thought out carefully and rationally and not carelessly without contemplating the consequences of our actions,"[32] the implication being that with right understanding we will not willfully add to the balance of suffering in the natural and human world. In contrast to Buddhadāsa's more intuitive, ontologically oriented perspective, Phra Prayudh's approach to the environment is seen as rational and ethical. He emphasizes the karmic side of the mutual interdependence of all life-forms, noting that we need to weigh carefully the *consequences* of our actions so that we do not willingly increase the suffering of sentient and nonsentient beings.

For the third ecologically relevant moral value, Phra Prayudh looks to the Buddhist teaching that human happiness (*sukha*) is dependent on our natural surroundings in two ways: 1) simply living within a natural setting engenders a greater sense of happiness and well-being; and 2) nature serves as a teacher of both mind and spirit. Nature trains us not only in moral virtue but also in mental concentration and attentiveness. He argues that for this reason the forest was the context in which Buddhism arose. Monks pursued their vocation in the forest. The forest is the ideal location for training the body and mind to overcome defilements (*kilesa*) that hinder the attainment of mental freedom.[33] Here again Phra Prayudh's approach to nature, that is, to the forest, contrasts with Buddhadāsa's. Wild nature—the forest, mountains, caves—is the best context in which to overcome the defilements that hinder the attainment of *nibbāna*. This view is more anthropocentric and instrumentalist than Buddhadāsa's view of the intrinsic dhammic value of nature.

Phra Prayudh's ecological hermeneutic focuses on the life of the Buddha and the *saṅgha* as exemplifications of the Buddhist attitude toward nature, in particular toward the forest: "The history of Buddhism as found in various Pali texts clearly indicates that monks saw the forest as a place to practice the *dhamma* and to achieve a feeling of well-being, a happy state of mind, and eventually higher states of mental consciousness."[34] Specifically in regard to the life of the Buddha, Phra Prayudh, in concert with other Thai voices of "green Buddhism," such as Chatsumarn Kabilsingh,[35] observes:

> From the time the Buddha left his palace Buddhism has been associated with forests. The Buddha's quest for the truth (*saccadhamma*) took place in the forest. It was in the forest that for six years he sought to overcome suffering and it was under the Bodhi tree that he attained enlightenment. Throughout his life the Lord Buddha was involved with forests, from his birth in the forest garden of Lumbini under the shade of a Sāl tree to his *parinibbāna* under the same kind of tree. Thus, Buddhism has been associated with the forest from the time of the life of its founder.[36]

Beyond general references to the example of the Buddha and the early *saṅgha*, however, Phra Prayudh cites specific passages from the Pali *suttas* to justify his views. For example, he notes that the Buddha spoke of nature as the best environment in which to seek enlightenment (*bodhiñāṇa*): "O monks, in search of the good (*kusala*), the best place is a rural area such as Uruvelā. There you will find a refreshing environment of trees and fields, a cool flowing river, pleasant landings with homes to go for alms (*gocaragāma*). Such delightful surroundings are suitable for monks to pursue their religious practice."[37] Phra Prayudh also cites stories of forest-dwelling disciples of the Buddha, such as Vanavaccha Thera, Citta Thera, and Cūla Thera, who praised mountains, birds, and insects as well as forests. He also mentions the Venerable Mahākassapa, who advised monks to dwell in caves and mountains situated in beautiful natural surroundings with forests, animals, and birds.[38]

Phra Prayudh grounds his argument for the value of nature for religious practice in stories of the Buddha and the early disciplines found in Pali texts. Buddhadāsa also links nature and religious practice to spiritual realization but does so by using Suan Mōkh as his primary illustration rather than citing specific passages in canon and commentary. Phra Prayudh, furthermore, makes a strong appeal to reason. Unlike some Thai Buddhist environmentalists who encourage such practices as ordaining trees or the promotion of a tree deity cult to preserve a stand of trees, Phra Prayudh believes that modern Buddhists need to go beyond appealing to Buddhist values, such as gratitude and loving-kindness, and citing scripturally grounded stories of the Buddha and the early *saṅgha* and should utilize scientific evidence to address global problems, such as pollution and environmental preservation.

Phra Prayudh's response to the case of Phra Prajak Kuttajitto, a much publicized activist monk from Buriram Province in northeast Thailand, is instructive. Phra Prajak, who has returned to lay life, was twice arrested in 1991 for his efforts in forest conservation, first, for trespassing on National Forest Reserve land and establishing a meditation center there and, second, for organizing villagers in Korat Province. In both cases, he led a protest opposing the government's program to remove villagers from National Forest Reserves. Phra Prajak questioned the legality of the removal of villagers from the lands and also objected to the proposed replacement of natural, diversified forests with trees, principally eucalyptus, grown for commercial purposes.

In response to Phra Prajak's controversial activities Phra Prayudh delivered a talk on 2 October 1991, later printed under the title *Phra kap Pā: Mī Panhā Arai?* (Monks and the forest: Is there a problem?). He began his remarks with the comment that he did not intend to speak to the Phra Prajak case per se, in particular whether or not he had acted correctly or had broken the law. Rather, his concern was for the possible detrimental impact on Thai Buddhism:

> We need to look at the case from the Buddhist perspective. For example, there's a rumor that the government may enact a law forbidding monks to enter forests. I don't know if this is true or false, but if such a law were to be enacted then we would need to examine it carefully from the perspective of Buddhism, especially the relationship between the *saṅgha* and the forest. If we understand the principles of this relationship then we'll act appropriately.[39]

Rather than taking sides on this politically sensitive issue, Phra Prayudh advocates a rational approach grounded in the texts and traditions of Theravāda Buddhism.

After observing that the Buddha's birth, enlightenment, and death all took place under trees, Phra Prayudh notes that many of the major monasteries donated to the *saṅgha* were in forest groves: Veluvana (donated by Bimbisāra), Jetavana (donated by Lord Jetam), Jīvakamphavana (given by the physician

Jīvaka), and many others, such as the Mahāvana monastery where the Buddha resided when he visited Kapilavattu, the capital of the Sakyas. Although the Buddha advised monks to dwell in forests—"O, Ānanda, when a *bhikkhu* enters the Order he should be encouraged to practice the *dhamma,* to follow the *pātimokkha,* to limit conversation, and to live in a tranquil place, *if possible a forest*" [40]—and extolled the forest as a good environment to practice the *dhamma,* Phra Prayudh argues against a naïve, simplistic identification of Buddhism with nature. The *principle* behind the Buddha's advocacy of a forest as a monastic retreat was its appropriateness as a place for the pursuit of monastic training, not that forest dwelling was a necessary and sufficient condition of the monastic life. On the contrary, because a monk's responsibility extends not only to the pursuit of enlightenment but also to other members of the *saṅgha* and to lay society, the Buddha stipulated that monasteries were to be located not too far from or too near a town. This is the second principle that needs to be kept in mind. The monastery "should be a quiet place, appropriately isolated, not disorderly and noisy. Too close a proximity to a town tends to make a monastery too busy and noisy but being too far away may jeopardize the work of the monks."[41]

Monks have a responsibility toward one another. They are required to assemble twice monthly for formal business meetings (*sanghakamma*). Furthermore, monks are forbidden by *vinaya* rules to support themselves. Because monks depend on the laity for food, they cannot live in isolation from society. The first of these rules joins monks or nuns together as a community; the second links them to laypeople. Therefore, even though the Buddha praised forest dwelling, this did not suggest following the withdrawn, isolated life of an ascetic. Indeed, one finds in early Buddhism ambivalent feelings toward forest-dwelling ascetics, as suggested by the following five-fold classification of *dhutaṅga* monks: those who are thickheaded and stupid, those who seek fame and praise, those who are deranged, those who follow the praiseworthy example of the Buddha, and those who seek solitude and quiet in order to practice the *dhamma.*[42] Thus, although Phra Prayudh notes the importance of the forest in the experience of the Buddha and the early *saṅgha* as the best environment in which to pursue spiritual practice, he also suggests that early Buddhism considered the forest with some misgivings. Furthermore, he suggests that wild nature at a far remove from human habitation is problematic for monastic practice because monks are dependent upon the laity for food and other material necessities.

Phra Prayudh bases his ecological hermeneutic on a close reading of the life of the Buddha and the early *saṅgha* in the Pali scriptures and the primary intentionality of the *dhamma* to overcome suffering and realize personal liberation. He finds within the Buddhist worldview of mutual cooperation an alternative to Western dualism and materialism, which he holds responsible for many forms of global exploitation. Phra Prayudh, however, does not construct a theory of Buddhist *gaia* or biocentric ecology, nor does he identify nature and *dhamma* in the manner of Buddhadāsa or paint a romantic portrait of the Buddha and his disciples holding forth in shaded glens. He warns:

> The Buddha shouldn't be revered because he lived near trees or because he taught that one should eat only enough food to get by for one day. Rather, he should be respected as one who realized the *dhamma* and then taught it. The Buddha advocated a life of simplicity and sufficiency not as an end in itself but as the context for the development of knowledge of the cause and effect of all actions. The Buddha praised monks who lived in the forest such as Mahākassapa . . . [but he] said that whether or not one lived in the forest was a matter of individual intent.[43]

Buddhadāsa Bhikkhu and Phra Prayudh represent two distinctive, complementary approaches to the environment within the context of contemporary Thai Buddhism. Buddhadāsa's intuitive, ontologically oriented view of nature as *dhamma* and the ethic of caring-for-nature (*anurak thamachāt*) that flows from it finds a greater commonality with what Ian Harris terms "ecoBuddhism" than does the ethical approach of Phra Prayudh, which is grounded primarily in reason, texts, and historical tradition. Buddhism—as well as the other great world religions—is complex, variegated, and dynamic and defies general, facile characterizations. As these two examples from Thai Buddhism illustrate, even within a single contemporary cultural tradition there is no univocal Buddhist ecological hermeneutic.

COUNTERPOINT: BUDDHIST ENVIRONMENTALISM—CRITICS IN THE FOREST

The effort of Buddhists and students of Buddhism to construct a Buddhist environmental ethic has encountered several disclaimers. Among the strongest critics of the ecoBuddhism project are Noriaki Hakamaya, Lambert Schmithausen, and Ian Harris.[44] This brief postscript cannot examine these criticisms in depth; rather, it is intended only to suggest the nature of this critical assessment in the light of this study of Buddhadāsa and Dhammapiṭaka.

In the view of Ian Harris, recent writings in the area of Buddhism and environmental ethics can be divided into four broad categories: (1) a full endorsement of Buddhist environmental ethics by traditional guardians of doxic truth, for example, His Holiness, the Dalai Lama; (2) a similar literature by Japanese and North American scholar-activists that seeks to identify the doctrinal bases for an environmental ethic, represented by Joanna Macy; (3) critical studies which nonetheless argue for an authentic Buddhist response to environmental problems, such as those by Lambert Schmithausen; and (4) an outright rejection of the possibility of Buddhist environmental ethics on the grounds of its otherworldliness, as put forth by Noriaki Hakamaya.[45] Harris identifies himself with the fourth position, although he admits that he is more sympathetic toward the third. This makes him a particularly strong critic of what he terms ecoBuddhism and also causes him to be suspicious of attempts to ground Buddhist environmental ethics in classical doctrines such as causality. Harris develops his critique in a series of articles published in *Religion* and the new electronic *Journal of Buddhist Ethics*. It is not my intent to give Harris's analysis the attention it deserves but rather to suggest the direction of his interpretation.

In his initial foray into this field, Harris established the critical stance he has continued to develop in subsequent articles. In contrast to the "ecospirituality," "ecojustice," and "ecotraditionalists" he cites,[46] Harris argues that the primacy of the spiritual quest in the Buddhist tradition privileges humans over the realms of animals and of nature. He points out, for example, that although the interconnected destinies of human beings and animals might suggest that humans should feel some solidarity with animals, in fact animals are regarded as particularly unfortunate. They cannot grow in the *dhamma* and *vinaya* nor can they be ordained as monks.[47] Furthermore, while animals may appear to be beings destined for final enlightenment, they have no intrinsic value in their animal form. Indeed, claims Harris, "The texts leave one with the impression that the animal kingdom was viewed. . . with a mixture of fear and bewilderment."[48] The plant world does not fare much better in Harris's analysis. He summarizes the canonical view of nature as being either something to be improved or cultivated or something to be confronted in a therapeutic encounter.[49]

In his study of ecoBuddhism as a contemporary American attempt to articulate an authentically Buddhist response to present environmental problems, he argues that this movement represents a teleological transformation of traditional Buddhist cosmogony.[50] In an earlier article which surveys Pali, Sarvāstivāda, Sautrāntika, Mādhyamika, and Yogācāra positions, Harris focuses his critique even more substantially on what he characterizes as the teleological transformation of Buddhist causality. There he argues, first, that a Buddhist action guide in regard to the natural world should be "specifically authorized by the Buddha," and, second, that the dysteleological nature of Buddhist thought does not lend itself to an environmental ethic in regard to such broadly contested issues as global warming or biodiversity.[51]

For the purposes of this essay, Harris's view of the problematic of a Buddhist environmental ethic serves primarily as a counterpoint to the views of Buddhadāsa and Phra Prayudh and to the general tenor of the essays on Buddhism and ecology in this volume. Although the ecological hermeneutics of Buddhadāsa and Phra Prayudh differ in some significant respects, both are at odds with Harris's critique of Buddhist eco-apologetics. Buddhadāsa and Phra Prayudh would, I believe, object to Harris's view on at least three general grounds: (1) His position is founded on too narrow a construction of the Buddhist view of nature and animals based on a selective reading of particular texts and traditions. Harris might have nuanced his claims about the Buddhist attitude toward animals had he included an analysis of selected Jātaka narratives, for example. (2) It is debatable whether or not a theory of causality (or conditionality) must be teleological in order to be environmentally viable. For instance, Buddhadāsa's biocentric ontology can be interpreted deontologically, or, as Buddhadāsa phrases it, nature implies certain moral maxims or duties. (3) Although the *buddhavacanaṃ* is authoritative in the Theravāda tradition, moral action guides do not need to be authorized by the Buddha in a literal sense.

Although Phra Prayudh seems to agree with Harris that the primary positive view of nature in Buddhism is a context for spiritual development, that is, primarily for its therapeutic value, Buddhadāsa's more biocentric perspective goes beyond such an instrumental understanding of nature as the ideal context for the pursuit of the ultimate goal of human flourishing. For Buddhadāsa nature has an inherent, dhammic value, not one merely instrumental to the monastic pursuit of spiritual transformation. In reacting against what he understands to be a well-intended but problematical interpretation of Buddhist thought by eco-apologists, Harris's normative standard of Buddhist orthodoxy judges Buddhadāsa's ecological hermeneutic to be inauthentically Buddhist or merely "accorded authenticity" by virtue of the fact that Buddhadāsa is a "high profile Buddhist" associated with "reformist circles" in Thai Buddhism.[52]

Harris's critical typology of Buddhist environmental ethics would evaluate Phra Prayudh's ecological hermeneutic more favorably than Buddhadāsa's because Phra Prayudh adheres more closely to Theravāda doctrinal orthodoxy. Phra Prayudh's position would be closest to Harris's type three, namely, an environmental ethic based on a critical reading of the tradition by a Buddhist monk. Buddhadāsa, in Harris's assessment, would be included in type one as an ecoBuddhist apologist of doxic truth. Buddhadāsa would probably not object to being associated with the Dalai Lama as a type one ecoBuddhist, although it is doubtful that he would consider himself to be a guardian of doxic Theravāda truth.

NOTES

1. Dhammapiṭaka is the ecclesiastical title conferred in 1993 on Phra Prayudh Payutto, whose previous titles were Sivisuddhimoli, Rājavaramunī, and Debvedī. Published works by Phra Prayudh Payutto appear under all of these names. Here I use Dhammapiṭaka in the article title but in the text I use Phra Prayudh, following the convention established by Grant A. Olson in his translation of *Buddhadhamma*.

2. For introductions to the thought of Buddhadāsa Bhikkhu and Phra Prayudh Payutto, see Buddhadāsa Bhikkhu, *Me and Mine: Selected Essays of Bhikkhu Buddhadāsa,* ed. and with an introduction by Donald K. Swearer (Albany: State University of New York Press, 1989); and Phra Prayudh Payutto, *Buddhadhamma: Natural Laws and Values for Life,* trans. and with an introduction by Grant A. Olson (Albany: State University of New York Press, 1995). See also Grant A. Olson, "From Buddhadasa Bhikkhu to Phra Debvedi: Two Monks of Wisdom." in *Radical Conservatism: Buddhism in the Contemporary World* (Bangkok: Sathirakoses-Nagapradipa Foundation, 1990); and Santikaro Bhikkhu, "Buddhadasa Bhikkhu: Life and Society through the Natural Eyes of Voidness," in *Engaged Buddhism: Buddhist Liberation Movements in Asia,* ed. Christopher S. Queen and Sallie B. King (Albany: State University of New York Press, 1996). Essays in Thai consulted for this essay include Buddhadāsa, *Buddhạsāsanik Kap Kān Anurak Thamachāt* (Buddhists and the care of nature) (Bangkok: Kōmol Khīmthọng Foundation, 1990); Buddhadāsa, *Siang Takọn Jāk Thamachāt* (Shouts from nature) (Bangkok: Sublime Life Mission, 1971); Debvedī (Phra Prayudh Payutto), *Phra Kap Pā: Mī Panhā Arai?* (Monks and the forest: Is there a problem?) (Bangkok: Vanāphidak Project, 1992); Dhammapiṭaka (Phra Prayudh Payutto), *Khon Thai Kap Pā* (Thais and the forest)(Bangkok: Association for Agriculture and Biology, 1994). For general essays in English on Thai culture and the natural environment, see *Culture and Environment in Thailand: A Symposium of the Siam Society* (Bangkok: Siam Society, 1989), *Man and Nature: A Cross-Cultural Perspective* (Bangkok: Chulalongkorn University Press, 1993).

Transliteration of Thai terms follows the Library of Congress with some modifications, in particular "j" rather than "čh."

3. Ian Harris, "How Environmentalist Is Buddhism?" *Religion* 21 (April 1991): 101–14; Harris, "Buddhist Environmental Ethics and Detraditionalization: The Case of EcoBuddhism," *Religion* 25, no. 3 (July 1995): 199–211; Harris, "Causation and 'Telos': The Problem of Buddhist Environmental Ethics," *Journal of Buddhist Ethics* 1 (1994):45–57; Harris, "Getting to Grips with Buddhist Environmentalism: A Provisional Typology," *Journal of Buddhist Ethics* 2 (1995): 173–90: and Harris's contribution in this volume.

4. "EGAT Warns of Low Water Level in Dams," *Bangkok Post,* Monday, 13 November 1989, pp. 1 and 3.

5. For example, see Francesca Bray, "Agriculture for Developing Nations," *Scientific American,* July 1994, 30–37; D. Pimentel et al., "Benefits and Risks of Genetic Engineering in Agriculture," *Bioscience* 39, no. 10 (1989):606–14.

6. Paraphrased from a lecture delivered at the McGilvary Theological Faculty of Payap University on

27 October 1989, entitled "Quam Khawjai Kiewkap Sangkhom Thai: Khabuankan Chai Amnāt lae Kanyaek Chīwit Ok Pen Suan" (Understanding Thai society: Violence and alienation).

7. It is interesting to observe that the first issue of *Generation* (October 1989). an expensive, elitist magazine, contained a lead article, "Namtatthakhot: Anicca Buddhasāsana nai Muang Thai" (The Buddha's tears: The decline of Buddhism in Thailand), 39–55. In the article some of the more important voices for reform of the Thai *saṅgha* and Thai society are mentioned, including Buddhadāsa Bhikkhu and Sulak Sivaraksa.

8. Buddhadāsa died 3 July 1993.

9. Buddhadāsa, *Siang Takọn Jāk Thamachāt.* For essays on the relationship between ecoBuddhism and deep ecology, see *Dharma Gaia: A Harvest of Essays in Buddhism and Ecology,* ed. Allan Hunt Badiner (Berkeley: Parallax Press, 1990).

10. Buddhadāsa, *Siang Takọn Jāk Thamachāt,* 5–7; translation mine.

11. Ibid., 7.

12. For an ethical critique of biocentrism, see Luc Ferry, *The New Ecological Order,* trans. Carol Volk (Chicago and London: University of Chicago Press, 1995).

13. Selections of my discussion of *Buddhasāsanik Kap Kān Anurak Thamachāt;* appeared in "Buddhadāsa on Caring for Nature," *Seeds of Peace* 10, no. 2 (September-December 1994): 36–38.

14. Western students of Buddhism often translate *anukampā* as "sympathy." In my view "empathy" is a more apt translation. I have in mind the image or metaphor of a tuning fork that resonates empathetically with its environment. See Harvey B. Aronson, *Love and Sympathy in Theravāda Buddhism* (Delhi: Motilal Banarsidass, 1980).

15. One of nine booklets published by the Dhamma Saphā, a group formed to disseminate Buddhadāsa's teaching, is *Kan Tham Lāi Khwām Hen Kae Tua* (Rooting out selfishness) (Bangkok: Dhamma Saphā, n.d.).

16. Buddhadāsa Bhikkhu, *Heartwood from the Bo Tree* (Bangkok: United States Overseas Mission Foundation, 1985), 13. Those who criticize Buddhadāsa for being a modernist, eclectic thinker should keep in mind that he never relinquished the centrality of the concept of nonattachment. While this notion is certainly pan-Buddhist and figures prominently in the ethical emphasis of modern Buddhist apologists, the concept of nonattachment is also fundamental to classical Theravāda *sīla-dhamma.*

17. For example, see Nel Noddings, *Caring: A Feminine Approach to Ethics and Moral Education* (Berkeley: University of California Press, 1984).

18. Buddhadāsa frequently used this phrase in his talks. See, for example, *Buddhasāsanik Kap Kān Anurak Thamachāt,* 34.

19. Buddhadāsa, *Buddhasāsanik Kap Kān Anurak Thamachāt,* 34–35.

20. Ibid., 35; translation mine. The similarity between Buddhadāsa's vision and comparable ecological visions in other religious traditions is striking. For example, see Ernesto Cardenal, "To Live Is to Love," in *Silent Fire: An Invitation to Western Mysticism,* ed. Walter Holden Capps and Wendy M. Wright (New York: Harper and Row, 1978).

21. Buddhadāsa, *Buddhasāsanik Kap Kān Anurak Thamachāt,* 15–16. I have given a free rendering of the Thai in order to convey my understanding of Buddhadāsa's meaning.

22. Ibid., 12–13.

23. Grant A. Olson translated the first edition (*Phutatham: Kotthamachāt læ Kham Samrup Chīwit* [Buddhadhamma: Natural laws and values for life] [Bangkok: Samnakphim Sukhaphāp, 1971]). The second edition is being translated in Thailand by Bruce G. Evans. Currently, Phra Prayudh's English monographs include a wide range of topics, e.g., *Thai Buddhism in the Buddhist World* (Bangkok: Amarin, 1984); *Looking to America to Solve Thailand's Problems* (Bangkok: Sathirakoses-Nagapradipa Foundation, 1987); *Toward a Sustainable Science* (Bangkok: Buddhadhamma Foundation, 1993); *Good, Evil, and Beyond: Kamma in the Buddha's Teaching* (Bangkok: Buddhadhamma Foundation, 1993); *A Buddhist Solution for the Twenty-First Century,* 2nd ed. (Bangkok: Sahathammik 1993); *Buddhist Economics: A Middle Way for the Market Place,* 2nd ed. (Bangkok: Buddhadhamma Foundation 1994).

24. Olson, introduction to Phra Prayudh Payutto, *Buddhadhamma,* 26–27.

25. This distinction between written and oral/aural mediums should not be drawn too sharply. Phra Prayudh gives many lectures; however, in contrast to Buddhadāsa, whose fame stems largely from his transcribed, published talks, Prayudh continues to be more oriented to the written word and is steeped in Pali canon and commentary.

26. Dhammapiṭaka (Phra Prayudh Payutto), *Khon Thai Kap Pā,* especially 43–68.

27. Phra Debvedī (Phra Prayudh Payutto), *A Buddhist Solution for the Twenty-First Century,* 7.

28. See Phra Prayudh Payutto, *Buddhadhamma,* pt. 2. This claim does not address the philosophical debate within Buddhism between those who argue for "no view" over "right view."

29. Dhammapiṭaka (Phra Prayudh Payutto), *Khon Thai Kap Pā,* 22: translation mine.

30. Ibid., 22–23.

31. Ibid., 24

32. Ibid., translation mine.

33. Ibid., 26.

34. Ibid., 27; translation mine.

35. For example, see Chatsumarn Kabilsingh, "Bud-

dhist Monks and Forest Conservation," In *Radical Conservatism: Buddhism in the Contemporary World* (Bangkok: Sathirakoses-Nagapradipa Foundation, 1990), 301–11.

36. Debvedī (Phra Prayudh Payutto), *Phra Kap Pā* 4; translation mine.

37. Dhammapiṭaka (Phra Prayudh Payutto), *Khon Thai Kap Pā,* 28; translation mine.

38. Ibid., 29–33.

39. Debvedī (Phra Prayudh Payutto), *Phra Kap Pā,* 3.

40. Ibid., 10; translation and italics mine.

41. Ibid., 11; translation mine.

42. Ibid., 15.

43. Ibid., 17.

44. Lambert Schmithausen, *Buddhism and Nature,* Studia Philologica Buddhica, Occasional Paper Series 7 (Tokyo: International Institute for Buddhist Studies, 1990); *The Problem of the Sentience of Plants,* Studia Philologica Buddhica, Occasional Paper Series 8 (Tokyo: International Institute for Buddhist Studies, 1991); and "The Early Buddhist Tradition and Ecological Ethics," *Journal of Buddhist Ethics* 4 (1997):1–42; and Noriaki Hakamaya, "Shizen-hihan to-shite no Bukkyo" (Buddhism as a criticism of physis/natura), *Komazawa Daigaku Bukkhogakubu Ronshu* (1990): 380–403.

45. Harris, "Getting to Grips with Buddhist Environmentalism," 177. I have omitted Harris's category of engaged Buddhist activists. Doctrinally, they can be linked to his first type.

46. Ibid. In one sense Harris's typology represents forms of what he labels "eco-apologetics."

47. Harris, "How Environmentalist Is Buddhism?" 105.

48. Ibid., 107.

49. Ibid., 108.

50. Harris, "Buddhist Environmental Ethics and Detraditionalization." Harris focuses his critique on the transformation of the theory of causality in "Causation and 'Telos.'"

51. Harris, "Causation and 'Telos,'" 54.

52. Harris, "Getting to Grips with Buddhist Environmentalism," 177.

To Save All Beings
Buddhist Environmental Activism

STEPHANIE KAZA

MEDITATORS FORM A CIRCLE AT THE BASE camp of the Headwaters Forest. All are invited to join the Buddhists sitting still in the flurry of activity. While others drum, talk, dance, and discuss strategy, the small group of ecosattvas—Buddhist environmental activists—focus on their breathing and intention amidst the towering trees. They chant the *Metta Sutta* to generate a field of loving-kindness. Here in volatile timber country they renew their pledges to the most challenging task of Buddhist practice—to save all beings.

In this action, old-growth redwoods are the beings at risk, slated for harvest on the Maxxam company property in northern California. Until recently the sixty-thousand-acre ecosystem was logged slowly and sustainably by a small family company. Then in 1985 logging accelerated dramatically following a hostile corporate buyout. Alarmed by the loss of irreplaceable giants, forest defenders have fought tirelessly to halt clear-cutting and preserve these ancient stands of redwoods. They have been joined by Hollywood stars, rock singers, and Jewish rabbis, many willing to practice civil disobedience in protest. How is it that Buddhists have become involved with this effort?

Motivated by ecological concerns, the ecosattvas formed as an affinity group at Green Gulch Zen Center in Marin County, California. As part of their practice they began exploring the relationship between Zen training and environmental activism.

Kaza, Stephanie, "To Save All Beings: Buddhist Environmental Activism," in Christopher S. Queen, Ed., *Engaged Buddhism in the West,* pp. 159–179.

They wanted to know: What does it mean to take the bodhisattva vow as a call to save endangered species, decimated forests, and polluted rivers? What does it mean to engage in environmental activism from a Buddhist perspective?[1] The ecosattvas are part of an emerging movement of ecospiritual activism, backed by a parallel academic development which has become the field of Religion and Ecology.[2] Christian scholars, Jewish social justice groups, Hindu tree-planting projects, and Islamic resistance to usurious capitalism are all part of this movement. Buddhist efforts in the United States like those of the ecosattvas are matched by monks in Thailand protesting the oil pipeline from Burma and Tibetans teaching environmental education in Dharamsala.[3]

Activist scholar Joanna Macy suggests these actions are all part of the "third turning of the wheel [of Dharma]," her sense that Buddhism is undergoing a major evolutionary shift at the turn of the millennium.[4] In today's context, one of the oldest teachings of the Buddha—*paticca samuppada* or dependent co-arising—is finding new form in the ecology movement. If ecosystem relationships are the manifestation of interdependence, then protecting ecosystems is a way to protect the Dharma: "with the Third Turning of the Wheel, we see that everything we do impinges on all beings."[5] Acting with compassion in response to the rapidly accelerating environmental crisis can be seen as a natural fruit of Buddhist practice.

Is there a Buddhist ecospiritual movement in North America? Not in any obvious sense, at least not yet. No organizations have been formed to promote Buddhist environmentalism; no clearly defined environmental agenda has been agreed upon by a group of self-identified American Buddhists. However, teachers are emerging, and Buddhist students of all ages are drawn to their writings and ideas. Writers Joanna Macy and Gary Snyder have made ecological concerns the center of their Buddhist practice. Teachers Thich Nhat Hanh and His Holiness the Dalai Lama have frequently urged mindful action on behalf of the environment. Activists John Seed, Nanao Sakaki, and others are beginning to define a Buddhist approach to environmental activism. There is a strong conversation developing among Western and Eastern Buddhists, asking both practical and philosophical questions from this emerging perspective. With environmental issues a mounting global concern, Buddhists of many traditions are creatively adapting their religious heritage to confront these difficult issues.

In this chapter I begin the preliminary work of documenting the scope of Buddhist environmentalism in the late 1990s, gathering together the historical and philosophical dimensions of what has been called "green Buddhism." This study will be necessarily limited to Western Buddhism, in keeping with the focus of this volume. However, it is important to note the strong relationship with other global initiatives. Buddhist tree-ordaining in Thailand, for example, has inspired similar ceremonies in California.[6] Environmental destruction by logging and uranium mining in Tibet has prompted the formation of the U.S.-based Eco-Tibet group.[7] Environmental issues in Buddhist countries have been a natural magnet for Buddhist activists in the West. But Western Buddhists have taken other initiatives locally, bringing their Buddhist and environmental sensibilities to bear on nuclear waste, consumerism, animal rights, and forest defense.[8] Out of these impulses Buddhist environmental activism is taking shape, based on distinct principles and practices.

One of the most challenging aspects of documenting these developments is finding the hidden stories. In the United States today, environmentalism has grown so strong as a political and cultural force that it is suffering the impact of "brownlash," as biologists Raul and Anne Ehrlich call it. Christian fundamentalism is often allied with the wing of the conservative right that promulgates anti-environmental views. Taking a strong environmental position as a self-proclaimed Buddhist can be doubly threatening. My personal experience is that the environmental arena is a place to act as a small "b" Buddhist. This means concentrating on the message of the Buddha by cultivating awareness, tolerance, and understanding, and acting from a loving presence. "In Buddhism, we say that the presence of one mindful person can have great influence on society and is thus very important."[9] Mindful Buddhist practitioners engaging difficult environmental issues may not proclaim their Buddhism to help solve the problem at hand. Yet they can bring inner strength and moral courage to the task at hand, drawing on the teachings of the Buddha as a basic framework for effective action.

LOOKING BACK

When Buddhism arrived in the West in the mid-1800s, there was little that could be called an environmental movement. Although Henry David Thoreau had written *Walden* in 1854, it was not until the end of the century that a serious land conservation movement coalesced. Advocates recognizing the unique heritage of such landforms as Yellowstone, Yosemite, and the Grand Canyon pressed for the establishment of the National Park system. Conservationists alert to the ravaging of eastern forests and the rush to cut the West spurred the formation of the National Forest Service. But serious concern about overpopulation, air and water pollution, and endangered species did not ignite until the 1960s. Since then the list of dangerous threats has only increased—toxic wastes, ozone depletion, global climate change, genetic engineering, endocrine disrupters—fires are burning on all fronts.

The most recent Western wave of interest in Buddhism coincides almost exactly with the expansion of the environmental movement.[10] Young people breaking out of the constrictions of the 1950s took their curiosity and spiritual seeking to India, Southeast Asia, and Japan; some discovered Buddhist meditation and brought it back to the United States.[11] During this period, Gary Snyder was probably the most vocal in spelling out the links between Buddhist practice and ecological activism. His books of poetry, *Turtle Island* (1974) and *Axe Handles* (1983), expressed a strong feeling for the land, influenced by his seven years of Zen training in Japan. His 1974 essay "Four Changes" laid out the current conditions of the world in terms of population, pollution, consumption, and the need for social transformation. Core to his analysis was the Buddhist perspective "that we are interdependent energy fields of great potential wisdom and compassion."[12] Snyder's ideas were adopted by the counterculture through his affiliation with beat writers Jack Kerouac and Allen Ginsberg and then further refined in his landmark collection of essays, *The Practice of the Wild*.[13]

Interest in Buddhism increased steadily through the 1970s along with the swelling environmental, civil rights, and women's movements. While Congress passed such landmark environmental laws as the Marine Mammal Protection Act, the Endangered Species Act, and the National Environmental Protection Act, Buddhist centers and teachers were becoming established on both coasts. San Francisco Zen Center, for example, expanded to two additional sites—a wilderness monastery at Tassajara, Big Sur, and a rural farm and garden temple in Marin County. By the 1980s the Buddhist Peace Fellowship was well along in its activist agenda and a number of Buddhist teachers were beginning to address the environmental crisis in their talks. In his 1989 Nobel Peace Prize acceptance speech His Holiness the Dalai Lama proposed making Tibet an international ecological reserve.[14] Thich Nhat Hanh, the influential Buddhist peace activist and Vietnamese Zen monk, referred often to ecological principles in his writings and talks on "interbeing," the Buddhist teaching of interdependence.[15]

The theme was picked up by Buddhist publications, conferences, and retreat centers. Buddhist Peace Fellowship featured the environment in *Turning Wheel* and produced a substantial packet and poster for Earth Day 1990.[16] The first popular anthology of Buddhism and ecology writings, *Dharma Gaia*, was published by Parallax Press that same year, following the more scholarly collection, *Nature in Asian Traditions of Thought*.[17] World Wide Fund for Nature brought out a series of books on five world religions, including *Buddhism and Ecology*.[18] *Tricycle* magazine examined green Buddhism and vegetarianism in 1994;[19] *Shambhala Sun* interviewed Gary Snyder and Japanese anti-nuclear poet-activist Nanao Sakaki.[20] The Vipassana newsletter *Inquiring Mind* produced an issue on "coming home"; *Ten Directions* of Zen Center Los Angeles, *Mountain Record* of Zen Mountain Monastery, and *Blind Donkey* of Honolulu Diamond Sangha also took up the question of environmental practice.

Some retreat centers confronted ecological issues head on. Green Gulch Zen Center in northern California had to work out water use agreements with its farming neighbors and the Golden Gate National Recreation Area. Zen Mountain Monastery in New York faced off with the Department of Environmental Conservation over a beaver dam and forestry issues. In earlier days when vegetarianism was not such a popular and commercially viable choice, most Buddhist centers went against the social grain by refraining from meat-eating, often with an awareness of the associated environmental problems. Several Buddhist centers made some effort to grow their own organic food.[21] Outdoor walking meditation gained new stature through backpacking and canoeing retreats on both coasts.

By the 1990s, spirituality and the environment had become a hot topic. The first "Earth and Spirit" Conference was held in Seattle in 1990, and Buddhist workshops were part of the program. Middlebury College in Vermont hosted a "Spirit and Nature" conference that same year with the Dalai Lama as keynote speaker, sharing his Buddhist message for protection of the environment.[22] More interfaith conferences followed and Buddhism was always represented at the table. By 1993, human rights, social justice, and the environment were top agenda items at the Parliament of the World's Religions in Chicago. Buddhists from all over the world gathered with Christians, Hindus, pagans, Jews, Jains, and Muslims to consider the role of religion in responding to the environmental crisis.

Parallel sparks of interest were ignited in the academic community. Though both environmental studies and religious studies programs were well established in the academy, very few addressed the overlap between the two fields. In 1992 religion and ecology scholars formed a new group in the American Academy of Religion and began soliciting papers on environmental philosophy, animal rights, Gaian cosmology, and other environmental topics. Out of this initiative, colleagues generated campus interreligious dialogues and new religion and ecology courses. In the spring of 1997, Mary Evelyn Tucker and John Grimm of Bucknell University convened the first of a series of academic conferences with the aim of defining the field of religion and ecology.[23] The first of these addressed Buddhism and Ecology; the volume of collected papers was the first publication in the series.[24] The spring 1998 meeting of the International Buddhist-Christian Theological Encounter also focused on the environment, looking deeply at the impacts of consumerism.[25]

For the most part, the academic community did not address the *practice* of Buddhist environmentalism. This was explored more by socially engaged Buddhist teachers such as Thich Nhat Hanh, Bernie Glassman, the Dalai Lama, Sulak Sivaraksa, Christopher Titmuss, John Daido Loori, and Philip Kapleau.[26] One leader in developing a Buddhist ecological perspective for activists was Joanna Macy. Her doctoral research explored the significant parallels and distinctions between Western general systems theory and Buddhist philosophy.[27] In her sought-after classes and workshops, Macy developed a transformative model of experiential teaching designed to cultivate motivation, presence, and authenticity.[28] Her methods were strongly based in Buddhist meditation techniques and the Buddhist law of dependent co-arising. She called this "deep ecology work," challenging participants to take their insights into direct action. Working with John Seed, a Buddhist Australian rainforest activist, she developed a ritual "Council of All Beings" and other guided meditations to engage the attention and imagination on behalf of all beings.[29] Thousands of councils have now taken place in Australia, New Zealand, the United States, Germany, Russia, and other parts of the Western world.

Following in the footsteps of these visionary thinkers, a number of Buddhist activists organized groups to address specific issues—nuclear guardianship, factory farming, and forest protection. Each initiative has had its own history of start-up, strategizing, attracting interest, and, in some cases, fading enthusiasm. When these groups work with well-established environmental groups, they seem to be more successful in accomplishing their goals. Some Buddhist environmental activists have been effective in helping shape the orientation of an existing environmental group. The Institute for Deep Ecology, for example, which offers summer training for activists, has had many Buddhists among its faculty, especially on the West Coast.

Though the history of Buddhist environmentalism is short, it has substance: bright minds suggesting new ways to look at things, teachers and writers inspiring others to address the challenges, and fledgling attempts to practice ecospiritual activism based in Buddhist principles. As Western interest in Buddhism grows, it affects wider social and political circles. As other Buddhist activists take up the task of defining the principles and practices of socially engaged Buddhism, environmental Buddhism can play a vital role. As Buddhist teachers come to see the "ecosattva" possibilities in the bodhisattva vows, they can encourage such practice-based engagement. The seeds for all this are well planted; the next ten years of environmental disasters and activist responses will indicate whether Buddhist environmental activism will take its place among other parallel initiatives.

PHILOSOPHICAL GROUND

During its two-thousand-year-old history, Buddhism has evolved across a wide range of physical and cultural geographies. From the Theravada traditions in tropical South and Southeast Asia, to the Mahayana Schools in temperate and climatically diverse China and Japan, to the Vajrayana lineages in mountainous Tibet—Buddhist teachings have been received, modified, and elaborated in many ecological contexts. Across this history the range of Buddhist understandings about nature and human-nature relations has been based on different teachings, texts, and cultural views. These have not been consistent by any means; in fact, some views directly contradict each other.

Malcolm David Eckel, for example, contrasts the Indian view with the Japanese view of nature.[30] Indian Buddhist literature shows relatively little respect for wild nature, preferring tamed nature instead; Japanese Buddhism reveres the wild but engages it symbolically through highly developed art forms. Tellenbach and Kimura take this up in their investigation of the Japanese concept of nature, "what-is-so-of-itself"; Ian Harris discusses the difficulties in comparing the meaning of the word "nature" in different Asian languages.[31] When Harris reviews traditional Buddhist texts, he does not find any consistent philosophical orientation toward environmental ethics. He also challenges claims that Buddhist philosophies of nature led to any recognizable ecological awareness among early Buddhist societies, citing some evidence to the contrary. Lambert Schmithausen points out that according to early Buddhist sources, most members of Buddhist societies, including many monks, preferred the comforts of village life over the threats of the wild.[32] Images of Buddhist paradises are generally quite tame, not at all untrammeled wilderness. Only forest ascetics chose the hermitage path with its immersion in wild nature.

Even with these distinctions, Buddhist texts do contain many references to the natural world, both as inspiration for teachings and as source for ethical behavior. For Westerners tasting the Dharma in the context of the environmental crisis, all the Buddhist traditions are potential sources for philosophical and behavioral guidelines toward nature. The newest cultural form of Buddhism in the West will be different from what evolved in India, Thailand, China, and Japan. In seeking wisdom to address the world as it is now, Westerners are eagerly, if sometimes clumsily, looking for whatever may be helpful. From the earliest guidelines for forest monks to the hermitage songs of Milarepa, from the Jataka tales of compassion to Zen teachings on mountains and rivers, the inheritance is rich and diverse.[33] In this section, I lay out the principal teachings identified by leading Buddhist environmental thinkers in the late twentieth century as most relevant to addressing the current environmental situation.

Interdependence

In the canonical story of the Buddha's enlightenment, the culminating insight comes in the last hours of his long night of deep meditation. According to the story, he first perceived his previous lives in a continuous cycle of birth and death, then saw the vast universe of birth and death for all beings, gaining understanding of the workings of karma. Finally he realized the driving force behind birth and death, and the path to release from it. Each piece of the Buddha's experience added to a progressive unfolding of a single truth about existence—the law of mutual causality or dependent origination (in Sanskrit *pratityasamutpada,* in Pali *paticca samuppada*). According to this law, all phenomena, that is, all of nature, arise from complex sets of causes and conditions, each set unique to the specific situations. Thus, the simple but penetrating Pali verse:

> This being, that becomes;
> from the arising of this, that arises;
> this not being, that becomes not;
> from the ceasing of this, that ceases.[34]

Ecological understanding of natural systems fits very well within the Buddhist description of interdependence. This law has been the subject of much attention in the Buddhism and Ecology literature because of its overlapping with ecological principles.[35] Throughout all cultural forms of Buddhism, nature is perceived as relational, each phenomenon dependent on a multitude of causes and conditions. From a Buddhist perspective these causes include not only physical and biological factors but also historical and cultural factors, that is, human thought forms and values.

The Hua-Yen School of Buddhism, developed in seventh-century China, placed particular emphasis on this principle, using the jewel net of Indra as a teaching metaphor. This cosmic net contains a multifaceted jewel at each of its nodes. "Because the jewels are clear, they reflect each other's images, appearing in each other's reflections upon reflections, ad infinitum, all appearing at once in one jewel."[36] To extend the metaphor, if you tug on any one of the lines of the net—for example, through loss of species or habitat—it affects all the other lines. Or, if any of the jewels become cloudy (toxic or polluted), they reflect the others less clearly. Likewise, if clouded jewels are cleared up (rivers cleaned, wetlands restored), life across the web is enhanced. Because the web of interdependence includes not only the actions of all beings but also their thoughts, the intention of the actor becomes a critical factor in determining what happens. This, then, provides a principle of both explanation for the way things are, and a path for positive action.

Modern eco-Buddhists working with this principle have taken various paths. Using the term "interbeing," Thich Nhat Hanh emphasizes nonduality of view, encouraging students to "look at reality as a whole rather than to cut it into separate entities."[37] Gary Snyder takes up the interdependence of eater and eaten, acknowledging the "simultaneous path of pain and beauty of this complexly interrelated world."[38] Feminist theologian Rita Gross looks at the darker implications of cause and effect in the growing human population crisis.[39] Activist Joanna Macy leads people through their environmental despair by steadily reinforcing ways to work together and build more functional and healing relationships with the natural world.[40]

The law of interdependence suggests a powerful corollary, sometimes noted as "emptiness of separate self." If all phenomena are dependent on interacting causes and conditions, nothing exists by itself, autonomous and self-supporting. This Buddhist understanding (and experience) of self directly contradicts the traditional Western sense of self as a discrete individual. Alan Watts called this assumption of separateness the "skin-encapsulated ego"—the very delusion that Buddhist practices seek to cut through. Based on the work of Gregory Bateson and other systems theorists, Macy describes a more ecological view of the self as part of a larger flow-through.[41] She ties this to Arne Naess's deep ecology philosophy, derived from a felt shift of identification to a wider, more inclusive view of self. Buddhist rainforest activist John Seed described his experience of no-self in an interview with *Inquiring Mind:* "All of a sudden, the forest was inside me and was calling to me, and it was the most powerful thing I have ever felt."[42] Gary Snyder suggests this emptiness of self provides a link to "wild mind," or access to the energetic forces that determine wilderness. These forces act outside of human influence, setting the historical, ecological, and even cosmological context for all life. Thus "emptiness" is dynamic, shape-shifting, energy in motion—"wild" and beyond human imagination.[43]

The Path of Liberation

The Buddhist image of the Wheel of Life contains various realms of beings; at the center are three figures representing greed, hate, and delusion. They chase each other around, generating endless suffering, perpetrating a false sense of self or ego. Liberation from attachment to this false self is the central goal in Buddhist practice. The first and second of the four noble truths describe the very nature of existence as suffering, due to our instincts to protect our own individual lives and views. The third and fourth noble truths lay out a path to liberation from this suffering of self-attachment, the eight-fold path of morality, awareness, and wisdom.

Buddhist scholar Alan Sponberg argues that green Buddhism has overemphasized interdependence or the relational dimension almost to the exclusion of the developmental aspect of practice.[44] By working to overcome ego-based attachments and socially conditioned desires, students cultivate the capacity for insight and compassion. This effort, he says, is crucial to displacing the hierarchy of oppression that undermines the vision of an ecologically healthy world. Sponberg suggests that a Buddhist environmental ethic is a virtue ethic, based fundamentally on development of consciousness and a sense of responsibility to act compassionately for the benefit of all forms of life. This is the basis for the Mahayana archetype of the bodhisattva, committed to serving others until suffering is extinguished. Macy argues that this responsibility need not be some morally imposed self-righteous action (often characteristic of environmentalists) but rather an action that "springs naturally from the ground of being."[45]

The path of liberation includes the practice of physical, emotional, and mental awareness. Such practice can increase one's appreciation for the natural world; it can also reveal hidden cultural assumptions about privilege, comfort, consumption, and the abuse of nature. When one sees one's self as part of a mutually causal web, it becomes obvious that there is no such thing as an action without effect. Through the practice of green virtue ethics, students are encouraged to be accountable for all of their actions, from eating food to using a car to buying new clothes. Likewise, they can investigate the reigning economic paradigm and see how deeply it determines their choices. Through following the fundamental precepts, environmentally oriented Buddhists can practice moderation and restraint, simplifying needs and desires to reduce suffering for others. For Westerners this may mean withdrawal from consumer addictions to products with large ecological impacts, such as coffee, cotton, computers, and cars.

Practice in Action

Buddhist environmental teachers and writers point to three primary arenas of practice that can serve the environment: compassion, mindfulness, and non-harming. In the Theravada tradition, one practices loving-kindness, wishing that all beings be free from harm and blessed by physical and mental well-being. In the Mahayana tradition one takes up the bodhisattva path, vowing to return again and again to relieve the suffering of all sentient beings—the life work of an environmentalist! Both practices are impossible challenges if interpreted literally; the environmental implications of these prayers or vows can be overwhelming. Yet the strength of intention offers a substantial foundation for Buddhist environmental activism. Budding eco-Buddhists struggle with the application of these spiritual vows in the very real contexts of factory farms, pesticide abuse, genetic engineering, and loss of endangered species habitat.

Mindfulness practice, a natural support to Buddhist environmentalism, can take a range of forms. Thich Nhat Hanh teaches the basic principles of the *Satipatthana Sutta* or the mindfulness text, practicing awareness of breath, body, feelings, and mind. Walking and sitting meditation generate a sense of grounded presence and alertness to where one actually is. Environmental educators stress mindfulness through nature appreciation exercises and rules of respect toward the natural world. Environmental strategists use promotional campaigns to generate awareness of threatened species and places. These efforts take mindfulness practice off the cushion and out into the world where alarming situations of great suffering require strong attention.

The practice of *ahimsa* or non-harming derives naturally from a true experience of compassion. All the Buddhist precepts are based fundamentally on non-harming or reducing the suffering of others. Practicing the first precept, not killing, raises ethical dilemmas around food, land use, pesticides, pollution, and cultural economic invasion. The second precept, not stealing, suggests considering the implications of global trade and corporate exploitation of resources. Not lying brings up issues in advertising and consumerism. Not engaging in abusive relations covers a broad realm of cruelty and disrespect for nonhuman others. As Gary Snyder says, "The whole planet groans under the massive disregard of ahimsa by the highly organized societies and corporate economies of the world."[46] Thich Nhat Hanh interprets the precept prohibiting drugs and alcohol to include the toxic addictions of television, video games, and junk magazines.[47] Practicing restraint and non-harming is a way to make Buddhist philosophy manifest in the context of rapidly deteriorating global ecosystems. Zen teacher Robert Aitken offers this vow:

> With resources scarcer and scarcer, I vow with all beings—
> To reduce my gear in proportion even to candles and carts.[48]

BUDDHIST ENVIRONMENTAL ACTIVISM

How is green Buddhism being practiced? What is the evidence of green Buddhism on the front lines? Macy suggests three types of activism that characterize environmentalism today: 1) holding-actions of resistance, 2) analysis of social structures and creation of new alternatives, and 3) cultural transformation.[49] Some of the best examples of Buddhist environmentalism come from outside the West, but here I report only on local efforts in North America.

Holding-actions aim primarily to stop or reduce destructive activity, buying time for more effective long-term strategies. The small group of ecosattvas protesting the logging of old growth redwood groves is part of the holding-actions in northern California.

They draw on local support from Buddhist deep ecologist Bill Devall and his eco-sangha in Humboldt County as well as support from the Green Gulch Zen community and the Buddhist Peace Fellowship. For the big 1997 demonstration, the ecosattvas invited others to join them in creating a large prayer flag covered with human handprints of mud. This then served as visual testimony of solidarity for all those participating in Headwaters actions. Six months after the protest, several ecosattvas made a special pilgrimage deep into the heart of the Headwaters, carrying a Tibetan treasure vase. Activists used the vase to bring attention to the threatened trees at various Bay Area sangha meetings. People were invited to offer their gifts and prayers on behalf of the redwoods. On a rainy winter's day, the vase was ceremonially buried beneath one of the giants to strengthen spiritual protection for the trees.[50]

Resistance actions by Buddhists Concerned for Animals were initiated by Brad Miller and Vanya Palmers, two Zen students in the San Francisco area. Moved by the suffering of animals in cages, on factory farms, and in export houses, they joined the animal rights movement, educating other Buddhists about the plight of monkeys, beef cattle, and endangered parrots. Vanya has continued this work in Europe, where he now lives, focusing on the cruelty in large-scale hog farming.[51]

When the federal government proposed burial of nuclear waste deep under Yucca Mountain, a group of Buddhists and others gathered together under Joanna Macy's leadership and met as a study group for several years. They took the position that nuclear waste was safer above ground where it could be monitored, and they developed an alternate vision of nuclear guardianship based in Buddhist spiritual practices.[52] At about the same time, Japan arranged for several shipments of plutonium to be reprocessed in France and then shipped back to Japan. Zen student and artist Mayumi Oda helped to organize Plutonium-Free Future and the Rainbow Serpents to stop these shipments of deadly nuclear material. One ship was temporarily stopped, and although shipments resumed, the actions raised awareness in Japan and the United States, affecting Japanese government policies.[53]

The second type of activism, undertaking structural analysis and creating alternative green visions, has also engaged twentieth-century Buddhists. Small "b" Buddhist Rick Klugston directs the Washington, D.C.-based Center for Respect of Life and the Environment, an affiliate of the Humane Society of the United States. He and his staff work on sustainability criteria for humane farming, basing their work in religious principles of nonharming. In 1997 the Soka Gakkai-affiliated group, Boston Research Center for the 21st Century, held a series of workshops addressing the people's earth charter, an international negotiated list of ethical guidelines for human-earth relations. The center published a booklet of Buddhist views on the charter's principles for us [*sic*] in discussions leading up to United Nations adoption.[54] A subgroup of the International Network of Engaged Buddhists and the Buddhist Peace Fellowship, called the "Think Sangha," is engaged in structural analysis of global consumerism. Collaborating between the United States and Southeast Asia, they have held conferences in Thailand on alternatives to consumerism, pressing for moderation and lifestyle simplification.[55] One of the boldest visions is the Dalai Lama's proposal that the entire province of Tibet be declared an ecological reserve. Sadly, this vision, put forth in his Nobel Peace Prize acceptance speech, is nowhere close to actualization.[56]

Scholars have offered structural analyses using Buddhist principles to shed light on environmental problems. Rita Gross, Buddhist feminist scholar, has laid out a Buddhist framework for considering global population issues.[57] I have compared eco-feminist principles of activism with Buddhist philosophy, showing a strong compatibility between the two.[58] Through Buddhist-Christian dialogue, process theologian and meditator Jay McDaniel has developed spiritual arguments for compassionate treatment of animals as a serious human responsibility.[59] Sociologist Bill Devall integrated Buddhist principles into his elaboration of Arne Naess's Deep Ecology philosophy urging simplification of needs and wants.[60] Joanna Macy likewise draws on Buddhist philosophy and practices to analyze the paralyzing states of grief, despair, and fear that prevent people from acting on behalf of the environment.

As for the third type of activism, transforming culture, these projects are very much in progress and sometimes met with resistance. Two Buddhist centers in rural northern California, Green Gulch Zen Center and Spirit Rock, already demonstrate a serious commitment to the environment through vegetarian dining, land and water stewardship efforts, an organic farm and garden at Green Gulch, and ceremonies that include the natural world.[61] On Earth Day 1990, the abbot led a tree-ordaining precepts ceremony and an animal memorial service. Other environmental rituals include special dedications at the solstices and equinoxes, a Buddha's birthday celebration of local wildflowers, Thanksgiving altars from the farm harvest, and participation in the United Nations Environmental Sabbath in June. The ecosattvas meet regularly to plan restoration projects that are now part of daily work practice. When people visit Green Gulch, they can see ecological action as part of a Buddhist way of life. Similar initiatives have been undertaken at Spirit Rock Meditation Center, also in the San Francisco Bay area.

In the Sierra foothills, Gary Snyder has been a leader in establishing the Yuba River Institute, a bioregional watershed organization working in cooperation with the Bureau of Land Management. They have done ground survey work, controlled burns, and creek restoration projects, engaging the local community in the process. "To restore the land one must live and work in a place. To work in a place is to work with others. People who work together in a place become a community, and a community, in time, grows a culture."[62] Snyder models the level of commitment necessary to reinhabit a place and build community that might eventually span generations. Zen Mountain Center in Southern California is beginning similar work, carrying out resource management practices such as thinning for fire breaks, restoring degraded forest, and limiting human access to some preserve areas.[63] Applying Buddhist principles in an urban setting, Zen teacher Bernard Glassman has developed environmentally oriented small businesses that employ local street people, sending products to socially responsible companies such as Ben and Jerry's.[64]

As the educational element of cultural transformation, several Buddhist centers have developed lecture series, classes, and retreats based on environmental themes. Zen Mountain Monastery in the Catskills of New York offers "Mountains and Rivers" retreats based on the center's commitment to environmental conservation. These feature backpacking, canoeing, nature photography, and haiku as gateways to Buddhist insight. Ring of Bone Zendo at Kitkitdizze, Gary Snyder's community, has offered backpacking *sesshins* in the Sierra Mountains since its inception. Green Gulch Zen Center co-hosts a "Voice of the Watershed" series each year with Muir Woods National Monument, including talks and walks across the landscape of the two valleys. At Manzanita Village in southern California, Caitriona Reed and Michele Benzamin-Masuda include deep ecology practices, gardening, and nature observation as part of their Thich Nhat Hanh-style mindfulness retreats.

Most of these examples represent social change agents working within Buddhist or non-Buddhist institutions to promote environmental interests. But what about isolated practitioners, struggling to consider the implications of their lifestyles in consumer America and other parts of the West? Independent of established groups, a number of Buddhists are taking small steps of activism as they try to align their actions with their Buddhist practice. One growing area of interest is ethical choices in food consumption, prompted both by health and environmental concerns. Many people, Buddhists included, are turning to vegetarianism and veganism as more compassionate choices for animals and ecosystems. Others are committing to eat only organically grown food, in order to support pesticide-free soil and healthy farming. Thich Nhat Hanh has strongly encouraged his students to examine their consumption habits, not only around food and alcohol, but also television, music, books, and magazines. His radical stance is echoed by Sulak Sivaraksa in Thailand, who insists the Western standard of consumption is untenable if extended throughout the world. Some Buddhists have participated in "International Buy Nothing" Day, targeted for the busiest shopping day right after Thanksgiving. Others have joined support groups for reducing credit card debt, giving up car dependence, and creating work cooperatives. Because Buddhism is still so new in the Western world, the extent of Buddhist lifestyle activism is very hard to gauge. But for many students, environmental awareness and personal change flow naturally from a Buddhist practice commitment.

ELEMENTS OF GREEN BUDDHIST ACTIVISM

What makes Buddhist environmentalism different from other environmental activism or from other eco-religious activism? The answer in both cases lies in the distinctive orientation of Buddhist philosophy and practice. Buddhist environmentalists turn to principles of nonharming, compassion, and interdependence as core ethics in choosing activism strategies. They aim to serve all beings through equanimity and loving-kindness. Though activists may not fulfill the highest ideals of their Buddhist training, they at least struggle to place their actions in a spiritual context. This reflects an underlying premise that good environmental work should also be good spiritual work, restoring both place and person to wholeness.

To be sure, there are significant challenges. Engaged Buddhist scholar Kenneth Kraft outlines four dilemmas a generic American Buddhist environmentalist ("Gabe") might encounter.[65] First, he or she would likely encounter some gaps between the traditional teachings and current political realities. Most of the Buddha's advice to students deals with individual morality and action; but today's environmental problems require *collective* action and a conscious sense of group responsibility. It is not so easy to find guidelines for global structural change within these ancient teachings. Second, Gabe must make some tough decisions about how to use his or her time. Meditate or organize a protest? When political decisions are moving at a rapid rate, activists must respond very quickly for effective holding action. Yet cultivating equanimity, patience, and loving-kindness requires regular hours of practice on the cushion. The yearning for time dedicated to Buddhist retreats can compete with time needed for soul-renewing wilderness. Third, Gabe may question the effectiveness of identifying his or her efforts as specifically Buddhist. It may be easier just to "blend in" with others working on the same issue. Fourth, Gabe may also begin to wonder about the effectiveness of some forms of practice forms [*sic*] in combatting environmental destruction. How can meditation or ceremony stop clear-cut logging? Can spiritually oriented activists make a difference in the high pressure political world? Given these and other challenges, green Buddhists nonetheless try to carry out their work in a manner consistent with Buddhist practice and philosophy.

Characteristic ideals for green Buddhism can be described in terms of the Three Jewels: the Buddha, Dharma, and Sangha. The Buddha exemplified a way of life based on spiritual practice, including meditation, study, questioning and debate, ceremony and ritual. Each Buddhist lineage has its own highly evolved traditional practice forms that encourage the student to "act like Buddha." At the heart of the Buddha's path is reflective inquiry into the nature of reality. Applying this practice in today's environmental context, eco-activists undertake rigorous examination of conditioned beliefs and thought patterns regarding the natural world. This may include deconstructing the objectification of plants and animals, the stereotyping of environmentalists, dualistic thinking of enemy-ism, the impacts of materialism, and environmental racism.

In addition, the green Buddhist would keep his or her activist work grounded in regular engagement with practice forms—for example, saying the precepts with other activists, as Thich Nhat Hanh has encouraged, or reciting sutras that inspire courage and loving-kindness (that is, the *Metta Sutta* for example, or the Zen chant to Kanzeon). Ring of Bone Zen students chant Dogen's "Mountains and Rivers" treatise on their backpacking retreats. Mindfulness practice with the breath can help sustain an activist under pressure, during direct political action or in the workplace. Green Buddhist ceremonies are evolving, often as variations on standard rituals—for example, the Earth Day precepts at Green Gulch, and the earth relief ceremony at Rochester Zen Center.[66] If the Buddha's path is foundational to Buddhist environmental activism, it means each engaged person undertakes some form of spiritual journey toward insight and awakening. Activism is the context in which this happens, but the Buddha's way serves as the model.

Of the Buddha's teachings, or Dharma, several core principles contribute to a green Buddhist approach. First, it is based on a relational understanding of interdependence and no-self. This may mean, for example, assessing the relationships of the players in an environmental conflict from a context of historical and geographical cause and conditions. It may also mean acknowledging the distribution of power across the human political relationships, as well as learning about the ecological relationships that are under siege. Second, green Buddhist activism could reflect the teachings of ahimsa, non-harming, with compassion for the suffering of others. For the Buddhist environmentalist this may extend to oppression based on race, class, or gender discrimination as well as to environmental oppression of plants, animals, rivers, rocks, and mountains. This recognition of suffering in the non-human world is rarely acknowledged by the capitalist economy. Voicing it as a religious point of view may open some doors to more humane policies. This green Buddhist teaching is congruent with many schools of ecophilosophy that respect the intrinsic value and capacity for experience of each being.

A third Buddhist teaching applicable to activism is the *nondualistic* view of reality. Most political battles play out as confrontations between sworn enemies: loggers vs. spotted owl defenders, housewives vs. toxic polluters, birdlovers vs. pesticide producers. From a Buddhist perspective, this kind of hatred destroys spiritual equanimity; thus, it is much better to work from an inclusive perspective, offering kindness to all parties involved, even while setting firm moral boundaries against harmful actions. This approach is quite rare among struggling, discouraged, battle-weary environmentalists who, in fact, are being attacked by government officials, sheriffs, or the media. A Buddhist commitment to nondualism can help to stabilize a volatile situation and establish new grounds for negotiation.

A fourth Buddhist teaching reinforces the role of *intention*. Buddhist texts emphasize a strong relationship between intention, action, and karmic effects of an action. If a campaign is undertaken out of spite, revenge, or rage, that emotional tone will carry forth into all the ripening of the fruits of that action (and likely cause a similar reaction in response). However, if an action is grounded in understanding that the other party is also part of Indra's jewel net, then things unfold with a little less shoving and pushing.

Perhaps the most significant teaching of the Dharma relevant to Buddhist activism is the practice of detachment from the ego-generating self. Thus, a green Buddhist approach is not motivated primarily by the need for ego identity or satisfaction. Strong intention with less orientation to the self relieves the activist from focusing so strongly on results.[67] One does what is necessary in the situation, not bound by the need for it to reinforce one's ideas or to turn out a certain way. By leaning into the creative energies moving through the wider web but holding to a strong intention, surprising collaborative actions take place. Small 'b' Buddhists have been able to act as bridge-builders in hostile or reactive situations by toning down the need for personal recognition.

Sangha, the third of the Three Jewels, is often the least recognized or appreciated by American Buddhists. As newcomers to the practice in a speedy, product-driven society, most students are drawn to the calming effects of meditation practice and the personal depth of student-teacher relationships. Practicing with community can be difficult for students living away from Buddhist centers. Building community among environmental Buddhists is even harder, since they are even more isolated geographically from each other and sometimes marginalized even by their own peers in Buddhist centers. From a green Buddhist perspective, sangha work presents not only the challenges of personal and institutional relations, but also ecological relations. Some of the leading green Buddhist thinkers have suggested ways to move toward this work in an integrated way.

Gary Snyder brings his sangha work home through the framework of bioregional thinking and organizing. His foundation for this is more than ecological; it is aesthetic, economic, and practice-based. He suggests that "by being in place, we get the largest sense of community." The bioregional community "does not end at the human boundaries; we are in a community with certain trees, plants, birds, animals. The conversation is with the whole thing."[68] He models and encourages others to take up the practice of *reinhabitation,* learning to live on the land with the same respect and understanding as the original indigenous people. He expects this will take a number of generations, so the wisdom gathered now must be passed along to the young ones. Spiritual community on the land offers one place to do this.

Others can participate in eco-sangha through supporting and lobbying for ecological practices at their local Buddhist centers. The hundreds of people who come to Green Gulch Zen Center or Spirit Rock Meditation Center, for example, follow the centers' customs regarding water conservation, recycling, vegetarianism, and land protection. With each step toward greater ecological sustainability, local community culture takes on a greener cast. These actions need not be only a painful commitment to restraint, rather they can become a celebration of environmental awareness. Printed materials such as the booklet on environmental practices at Green Gulch can help to educate visitors about institutional commitments.

Joanna Macy recommends sangha-building as cen-tral to deep ecology work. Through trust-building exercises, brainstorming, and contract-making, Macy helps people find ways to support each other in their activist efforts. Learning networks of Buddhists and non-Buddhists often stay together after her workshops for mutual support and prevention of activist burnout. Macy helps people taste the power of *kalyana mitta,* or spiritual friendship—acting together in the web to help others practice the Dharma and take care of this world.

CONCLUSION

How might Buddhist environmentalism affect the larger environmental movement and how might it influence Western Buddhism in general? Will Buddhist environmentalism turn out to be more environmental than Buddhist?[69] The answers to these questions must be largely speculative at this time, since green Buddhism is just finding its voice. It is possible that this fledgling voice will be drowned in the brownlash against environmentalists, or in the Western resistance to engaged Buddhism. Environmental disasters of survival proportions may overwhelm anyone's capacity to act effectively. The synergistic combination of millennialism and economic collapse may flatten green Buddhism as well as many other constructive social forces.

But if one takes a more hopeful view, it seems possible to imagine that green Buddhism will grow and take hold in the minds and hearts of young people who are creating the future. Perhaps some day there will be ecosattva chapters across the world affiliated with various practice centers. Perhaps Buddhist eco-activists will be sought out for their spiritual stability and compassion in the face of extremely destructive forces. Buddhist centers might become models of ecological sustainability, showing other religious institutions ways to encourage ecological culture. More Buddhist teachers may become informed about environmental issues and raise these concerns in their teachings, calling for moderation and restraint. Perhaps the next century will see Buddhist practice centers forming around specific ecological commitments.

Making an educated guess from the perspective of the late 1990s, I predict that the influence of green Buddhism may be small in numbers, but great in impact. Gary Snyder, for example, is now widely read by college students in both literature and environmental studies classes. Joanna Macy has led workshops for staff at the White House and the Hanford nuclear reactor in Washington State. Thich Nhat Hanh has shared his commentaries on the interbeing of paper, clouds, trees, and farmers with thousands of listeners on lecture tours throughout the West. Some practicing Buddhists already hold influential positions in major environmental groups such as the Natural Resources Defense Council, Rainforest Action Network, and Greenpeace. Perhaps in the near future they will also hold cabinet positions or Congressional committee chairs or serve as staff for environmental think tanks.

Buddhist centers and thinkers will not drive the religious conversation in the West for quite some time, if ever. The Judeo-Christian heritage of the West is still a prominent force in Western thinking, laws, and religious customs. However, Buddhists are already significant participants in interfaith dialogue regarding the environment. This could have an increasing impact on public conversations by raising ethical questions in a serious way. Right now, decisions that affect the health and well-being of the environment are often made behind closed doors. To challenge these in a public way from a religious perspective could shed some much needed light on ecologically unethical ways of doing business.

What happens next lies in the hands of those who are nurturing this wave of enthusiasm for green Buddhism and those who will follow. It may be religious leaders, writers, teachers, or elders; it may be the younger generations, full of energy and passion for protecting the home they love. Because the rate of destruction is so great now, with major life systems threatened, any and all green activism is sorely needed. Buddhists have much to offer the assaulted world. It is my hope that many more step forward boldly into the melee of environmental conflict. Side by side with other bodhisattvas, may they join the global effort to stop the cruelty and help create a more respectful and compassionate future for all beings.

NOTES

1. For information on ecosattva activity, see "Universal Chainsaw, Universal Forest," *Turning Wheel* (winter 1998): 31–33.

2. See, for example, such recent volumes as Steven C. Rockefeller and John C. Elder, *Spirit and Nature: Why the Environment Is a Religious Issue* (Boston: Beacon Press, 1992); Mary Evelyn Tucker and John A. Grim, eds., *Worldviews and Ecology* (Lewisburg, PA: Bucknell University Press, 1993); Fritz Hull, ed., *Earth and Spirit: The Spiritual Dimensions of the Environmental Crisis* (New York: Continuum, 1993); David Kinsley, *Ecology and Religion: Ecological Spirituality in Cross-Cultural Perspective* (Englewood Cliffs, NJ: Prentice Hall, 1995); Dieter T. Hessel, ed., *Theology for Earth Community: A Field Guide* (Maryknoll, NY: Orbis Books, 1996); Roger Gottlieb, ed., *This Sacred Earth: Religion, Nature, and Environment* (New York: Routledge, 1996).

3. Parvel Gmuzdek, "Kalayanamitra's Action on the Yadana Pipeline," *Seeds of Peace* 13.3 (September–December 1997): 23–26.

4. Joanna Macy, "The Third Turning of the Wheel," *Inquiring Mind* 5.2 (winter 1989): 10–12.

5. Ibid., p.11.

6. Wendy Johnson and Stephanie Kaza, "Earth Day at Green Gulch," *Journal of the Buddhist Peace Fellowship* (summer 1990): 30–33.

7. See reports on their activities in Bay Area Friends of Tibet newsletters.

8. Stephanie Kaza and Kenneth Kraft, eds., *Dharma Rain: Sources of Buddhist Environmentalism* (Boston: Shambhala Publications, 1999).

9. Sulak Sivaraksa, "Buddhism with a Small 'b,'" *Seeds of Peace* (Berkeley, CA: Parallax Press, 1992), p. 69.

10. Peter Timmerman, "It Is Dark Outside: Western Buddhism from the Enlightenment to the Global Crisis," in Martine Batchelor and Kerry Brown, eds., *Buddhism and Ecology* (London: Cassell, 1992), pp. 65–76.

11. See Rick Fields, *How the Swans Came to the Lake: A Narrative History of Buddhism in America* (Boston: Shambhala Publications, 1986), for a thorough history of these and earlier forays to the East by Westerners.

12. Gary Snyder, *A Place in Space* (Washington, D.C.: Counterpoint Press, 1995), p. 41.

13. Gary Snyder, *The Practice of the Wild* (San Francisco: North Point Press, 1990).

14. "The Nobel Peace Prize Lecture," in Sidney Piburn, ed., *The Dalai Lama: A Policy of Kindness* (Ithaca, New York: Snow Lion Publications, 1990), pp. 15–27.

15. Thich Nhat Hanh, *Love in Action* (Berkeley, CA: Parallax Press, 1993).

16. Issues on the theme of environmental activism were published in spring 1990, spring 1994, and spring 1997.

17. Alan Hunt-Badiner, ed., *Dharma Gaia* (Berkeley, CA: Parallax Press, 1990); J. Baird Callicott and Roger T. Ames, eds., *Nature in Asian Traditions of Thought* (Albany: State University of New York Press, 1989).

18. The other four books in the series address Christianity, Hinduism, Islam, Judaism, and Ecology.

19. See *Tricycle* 4.2 (winter 1994): 2, 49–63.

20. For Gary Snyder interviews, see "Not Here Yet" 2.4 (March 1994): 19–25; "The Mind of Gary Snyder" 4.5 (May 1996): 19–26; for Nanao Sakaki, see "Somewhere on the Water Planet" 4.2 (November 1995): 45–47.

21. For a detailed study of two Buddhist centers see Stephanie Kaza, "American Buddhist Response to the Land: Ecological Practice at Two West Coast Retreat Centers," in Mary Evelyn Tucker and Duncan Ryuken Williams, eds., *Buddhism and Ecology: The Interconnectedness of Dharma and Deeds* (Cambridge: Harvard University Press, 1997), pp. 219–48.

22. See conference talks in Rockefeller and Elder, eds., *Spirit and Nature*.

23. Mary Evelyn Tucker, "The Emerging Alliance of Ecology and Religion," *Worldviews: Environment, Culture, and Religion* 1.1 (1997): 3–24.

24. Tucker and Williams, eds., *Buddhism and Ecology*.

25. See one of the lead papers from the meeting: Stephanie Kaza, "Overcoming the Grip of Consumerism," forthcoming in *Journal of Buddhist-Christian Studies*.

26. See, for example, such works as Thich Nhat Hanh, "The Individual, Society, and Nature," in Fred Eppsteiner, ed., *The Path of Compassion* (Berkeley, CA: Parallax Press, 1988), pp. 40–46; Dalai Lama, "The Ethical Approach to Environmental Protection," in Piburn, ed., *The Dalai Lama: A Policy of Kindness* (Ithaca, NY: Snow Lion Publications, 1990), pp. 118–28; Sulak Sivaraksa, *Seeds of Peace* (Berkeley, CA: Parallax Press, 1992); Christopher Titmuss, "A Passion for the Dharma," *Turning Wheel* (fall 1991): 19–20; John Daido Loori, "River Seeing River," in *Mountain Record* 14.3 (spring 1996): 2–10; and Philip Kapleau, *To Cherish All Life: A Buddhist Case for Becoming Vegetarian* (San Francisco: Harper and Row, 1982).

27. Joanna Macy, *Mutual Causality in Buddhism and General Systems Theory: The Dharma of Natural Systems* (Albany: State University of New York Press, 1991).

28. Joanna Macy, *Despair and Personal Power in the*

Nuclear Age (Philadelphia: New Society Publishers, 1983).

29. John Seed, Joanna Macy, Pat Fleming, and Arne Naess, *Thinking Like a Mountain: Towards a Council of All Beings* (Philadelphia: New Society Publishers, 1988).

30. Malcolm David Eckel, "Is There a Buddhist Philosophy of Nature?" in Tucker and Williams, eds., *Buddhism and Ecology,* pp. 327–50.

31. Ian Harris, "Buddhism and the Discourse of Environmental Concern: Some Methodological Problems Considered," in Tucker and Williams, eds., *Buddhism and Ecology,* pp. 377–402; and Hubertus Tellenbach and Bin Kimura, "The Japanese Concept of 'Nature,'" in *Nature in Asian Traditions of Thought,* ed. J. Baird Callicott and Roger T. Ames (Albany: State University of New York Press, 1989).

32. Lambert Schmidthausen, "The Early Buddhist Tradition and Ecological Ethics," *Journal of Buddhist Ethics* 4 (1997): 1–42.

33. Represented in Stephanie Kaza and Kenneth Kraft, eds., *Dharma Rain.*

34. *Samyutta Nikaya* II.28,65; *Majjhima Nikaya* II.32.

35. See, for example, Francis H. Cook, "The Jewel Net of Indra," in Callicott and Ames, eds., *Nature in Asian Traditions of Thought,* pp. 213–30; Bill Devall, "Ecocentric Sangha," in Hunt-Badiner, ed., *Dharma Gaia,* pp. 155–64; Paul O. Ingram, "Nature's Jeweled Net: Kukai's Ecological Buddhism," *The Pacific World* 6 (1990): 50–64; Joanna Macy, *Mutual Causality in Buddhism;* and Gary Snyder, *A Place in Space.*

36. Tu Shun, in Thomas Cleary, *Entry into the Inconceivable: An Introduction to Hua-Yen Buddhism* (Honolulu: University of Hawaii Press, 1983), p. 66.

37. Thich Nhat Hanh, "The Individual, Society, and Nature," in Eppsteiner, ed., *The Path of Compassion,* p. 40.

38. Snyder, *A Place in Space,* p. 70.

39. Rita Gross, "Buddhist Resources for Issues of Population, Consumption, and the Environment," in Tucker and Williams, eds., *Buddhism and Ecology,* pp. 291–312.

40. Joanna Macy and Molly Young Brown, *Coming Back to Life: Practices to Reconnect Our Lives, Our World* (Gabriola Island, British Columbia: New Society Publishers, 1998).

41. Macy, *Mutual Causality in Buddhism.*

42. Interview with John Seed, "The Rain Forest as Teacher," *Inquiring Mind* 8.2 (spring 1992): 1.

43. Gary Snyder, "The Etiquette of Freedom," in *The Practice of the Wild,* p. 10.

44. Alan Sponberg, "Green Buddhism and the Hierarchy of Compassion," in Tucker and Williams, eds., *Buddhism and Ecology,* pp. 351–76.

45. Joanna Macy, "Third Turning of the Wheel," *Inquiring Mind* 5.2 (winter 1989): 10–12.

46. Snyder, *A Place in Space,* p. 73.

47. See his discussion of the fifth precept in Thich Nhat Hanh, *For a Future to Be Possible* (Berkeley, CA: Parallax Press, 1993).

48. Robert Aitken, *The Dragon Who Never Sleeps* (Berkeley CA: Parallax Press, 1992), p. 62.

49. Macy and Brown, *Coming Back to Life.*

50. Wendy Johnson, "A Prayer for the Forest," *Tricycle* 8.1 (fall 1998): 84–85.

51. Vanya Palmers, "What Can I Do," *Turning Wheel* (winter 1993): 15–17.

52. Joanna Macy, "Guarding the Earth," *Inquiring Mind* 7.2 (spring 1991): 1, 4–5, 12.

53. Kenneth Kraft, "Nuclear Ecology and Engaged Buddhism," in Tucker and Williams, eds., *Buddhism and Ecology,* pp. 269–90.

54. Amy Morgante, ed., *Buddhist Perspectives on the Earth Charter* (Cambridge, MA: Buddhist Research Center for the 21st Century, November 1997).

55. See 1998–1999 issues of *Seeds of Peace* for reports and announcements of these events.

56. Tenzin Gyatso, "The Nobel Peace Prize Lecture," in Piburn, ed., *The Dalai Lama: A Policy of Kindness,* pp. 15–27.

57. Gross, "Buddhist Resources for Issues of Population, Consumption, and the Environment," in Tucker and Williams, eds., *Buddhism and Ecology,* pp. 291–312.

58. Stephanie Kaza, "Acting with Compassion: Buddhism, Feminism, and the Environmental Crisis," in Carol Adams, ed., *Ecofeminism and the Sacred* (New York: Continuum, 1993).

59. Jay B. McDaniel, *Earth, Sky, Gods, and Mortals: Developing an Ecological Spirituality* (Mystic, CT: Twenty-Third Publications, 1990).

60. Bill Devall, *Simple in Means, Rich in Ends: Practicing Deep Ecology* (Salt Lake City: Peregrine Smith Books, 1988).

61. Stephanie Kaza, "American Buddhist Response to the Land: Ecological Practice at Two West Coast Retreat Centers," in Tucker and Williams, eds., *Buddhism and Ecology,* pp. 219–48.

62. Snyder, *A Place in Space,* p. 250. See also David Barnhill, "Great Earth Sangha: Gary Snyder's View of Nature as Community," in Tucker and Williams, *Buddhism and Ecology,* pp. 187–217.

63. Jeff Yamauchi, "The Greening of Zen Mountain Center: A Case Study," in Tucker and Williams, eds., *Buddhism and Ecology,* pp. 249–65.

64. Interviewed by Alan Senauke and Sue Moon, "Monastery in the Streets: A Talk with Tetsugen Glassman," *Turning Wheel* (fall 1996): 22–25.

65. Kenneth Kraft, "Nuclear Ecology and Engaged Buddhism," in Tucker and Williams, eds., *Buddhism and Ecology,* pp. 280–83.

66. A selection of such evolving practice forms is presented in the forthcoming anthology by Kaza and Kraft, *Dharma Rain.*

67. See Christopher Titmuss, "A Passion for the Dharma," *Turning Wheel* (fall 1991): 19–20; also Chogyam Trungpa, *Shambhala: The Sacred Path of the Warrior* (Boston: Shambhala Publications, 1988).

68. David Barnhill, "Great Earth Sangha: Gary Snyder's View of Nature as Community," in Tucker and Williams, *Buddhism and Ecology,* p. 192.

69. As Ian Harris suggests in "Buddhism and the Discourse of Environmental Concern: Some Methodological Problems Considered," in Tucker and Williams, eds., *Buddhism and Ecology,* pp. 377–402.

Discussion Questions

1. What are some specific examples of how applying Buddhist principles might lead to a more ecological way of life?
2. What aspects of the Buddhist worldview might work against a concern for the environment?
3. How does one reconcile engaged Buddhism with the ideal of nonattachment? If the world is an illusion, why bother to protect it?
4. How will the growing popularity of Buddhism in the West shape and perhaps alter the tradition? Is the emergence of Green Buddhism likely to play a role in transforming it?

Further Reading

Badiner, Allan Hunt, Ed., *Dharma Gaia: A Harvest of Essays in Buddhism and Ecology,* Berkeley, Calif.: Parallax Press, 1990.

Batchelor, Martine, and Kerry Brown, Eds., *Buddhism and Ecology,* London: Cassell, 1992.

Callicott, J. Baird, and Roger Ames, Eds., *Nature in Asian Traditions of Thought,* Albany, N.Y.: SUNY Press, 1989.

De Silva, Padmasiri, *Environmental Philosophy and Ethics in Buddhism,* New York: St. Martin's Press, 1998.

Kaza, Stephanie, *The Attentive Heart: Conversations with Trees,* Boston: Shambhala, 1996.

Kaza, Stephanie, and Kenneth Kraft, Eds., *Dharma Rain: Sources of Buddhist Environmentalism,* Boston: Shambhala, 2000.

Macy, Joanna, *World as Lover, World as Self,* Berkeley, Calif.: Parallax Press, 1991.

Queen, Christopher S., Ed., *Engaged Buddhism in the West,* Boston: Wisdom Publications, 2000.

Queen, Christopher S., and Sallie B. King, Eds., *Engaged Buddhism: Buddhist Liberation Movements in Asia,* Albany, N.Y.: SUNY Press, 1996.

Sandell, Klas, Ed., *Buddhist Perspectives on the Ecocrisis,* Kandy, Sri Lanka: Buddhist Publication Society, 1987.

Sivaraksa, Sulak, and Chandra Muzaffar, *Alternative Politics for Asia: A Buddhist Muslim Dialogue,* New York: Lantern Books, 2000.

Tucker, Mary Evelyn, and Duncan Ryuken Williams, Eds., *Buddhism and Ecology: The Interconnection of Dharma and Deeds,* Cambridge, Mass.: Harvard University Press, 1998.

Chapter 6

Chinese Traditions

CHINESE CIVILIZATION IS ONE of the oldest in the world, stretching back more than 4,000 years. Like the term Hinduism in the South Asian context, the term Daoism (also written Taoism) in the Chinese setting refers more to an often diffuse set of traditional beliefs and practices than to any kind of uniform or normative religious system in the Western sense.

As in the case of Indian civilization, the Chinese worldview tends toward inclusiveness; although Daoism, Confucianism, and Chinese Buddhism have their own histories and have sometimes been in tension with each other, for the most part they have coexisted as schools of thought and ways of life. Together and separately, these three expressions of the Chinese worldview draw on many ideas, concepts, symbols, and practices that have very ancient roots in Chinese culture.

Among the notions central to the Chinese worldview is that of order and harmony in the universe. Heaven, Earth, and humans are seen as coexisting, interdependent, and interconnected through their ongoing relationships with each other. The dynamics of these relationships, conceptualized as the flow of vital energy or *ch'i,* determine how the balance and harmony of the cosmos is maintained. This worldview suggests constant flux and change, envisioned through the symbol of the *yin* and the *yang,* the positive–negative, male–female, light–dark, hot–cold polarities that are in constant and harmonious interaction.

Each of the three major Chinese religions incorporates these basic elements in its own way. Daoism emphasizes living in accordance with the *dao,* the natural course of things, as opposed to striving against it. Confucianism focuses more on maintaining harmony within society, as a reflection of the cosmic harmony. Buddhism, coming to China some 2,000 years ago via the Central Asian trade routes, initially represented a very different, foreign set of ideas that had to be adapted and reinterpreted according to the Chinese worldview. Thus, for example, early Buddhist missionaries to China equated the *dao* with the *dharma* or reality as conceptualized in the Four Noble Truths. On the other hand, the Chinese worldview has had an enormous impact on Korean, Japanese, and Southeast Asian civilizations, especially in the form of Confucian social ethics.

In his essay, Confucian scholar Tu Weiming emphasizes the centrality in Chinese thought and cosmology of interconnectedness, what in Chinese terms is known as the *continuity of being.* Furthermore, Tu notes, in Chinese thought the cosmos consists not primarily either of spirit or of matter, but rather of *ch'i* which is both at once. Thus, *ch'i* infuses modes of being as diverse as rocks and heaven itself, which are all parts of a continuum. Thus, humans form one holistic body with the entire universe, and the subject–object dichotomy characteristic of Western thought does not apply.

Mary Evelyn Tucker presents the indigenous Chinese traditions of Taoism and Confucianism as two complementary forces, consistent with the Chinese view of dynamic polarity. She finds the Taoist goals of harmony and noninterference with nature to be basic ecological values that could make an important contribution to contemporary environmentalism. Whereas Confucianism, by contrast, focuses primarily on the internal stability of human society, Tucker suggests that as a form of social ecology, it could have a beneficial impact on human dealings with nature, especially if the Confucian concept of filial piety is extended to the cosmic realm.

Philosopher Chung-Ying Cheng discusses five axioms by which a Taoist environmental ethic can be established. They are the axioms of total interpenetration, self-transformation, creative spontaneity, the will not to will, and nonattaching attachment. Cheng explains each axiom in terms of its traditional interpretation and in terms of its potential application to contemporary environmental discourse.

Finally, Ole Bruun looks at the ancient practice of Chinese geomancy, *fengshui*, in the context of human–nature relationships. A basic premise of *fengshui* is that there are good and bad ways of channeling *chi*. The ecological dimension of this principle is obvious: "When the landscape is rich and healthy, humans may prosper; when the landscape deteriorates, people suffer." However, as Bruun points out, assessments of these states are themselves value judgments that tend to reflect the interests and priorities of particular groups of humans.

The Continuity of Being
Chinese Visions of Nature

TU WEIMING

THE CHINESE BELIEF IN THE CONTINUITY OF being, a basic motif in Chinese ontology, has far-reaching implications in Chinese philosophy, religion, epistemology, aesthetics, and ethics. F. W. Mote comments that

> the basic point which outsiders have found so hard to detect is that the Chinese, among all peoples ancient and recent, primitive and modern, are apparently unique in having no creation myth; that is, they have regarded the world and man as uncreated, as constituting the central features of a spontaneously self-generating cosmos having no creator, god, ultimate cause, or will external to itself.[1]

This strong assertion has understandably generated controversy among Sinologists. Mote has identified a distinctive feature of the Chinese mode of thought. In his words, "the genuine Chinese cosmogony is that of organismic process, meaning that all of the parts of the entire cosmos belong to one organic whole and that they all interact as participants in one spontaneously self-generating life process."[2]

However, despite Mote's insightfulness in singling out this particular dimension of Chinese cosmogony for focused investigation, his characterization of its uniqueness is problematic. For one thing, the apparent lack of a creation myth in Chinese cultural history is predicated on a more fundamental assumption about reality; namely, that all modalities of being are organically connected. Ancient Chinese thinkers were intensely interested in the creation of the world. Some of them, notably the Taoists, even

Tu Weiming, "The Continuity of Being: Chinese Visions of Nature," in Leroy S. Roumer, Ed., *On Nature*, South Bend, Ind.: University of Notre Dame Press, 1984, pp. 113–127. Reprinted by permission of the author.

speculated on the creator (*tsao-wu che*) and the process by which the universe came into being.[3] Presumably, indigenous creation myths existed, although the written records transmitted by even the most culturally sophisticated historians do not contain enough information to reconstruct them.[4] The real issue is not the presence or absence of creation myths but the underlying assumption of the cosmos: whether it is continuous or discontinuous with its creator. Suppose the cosmos as we know it was created by a Big Bang; the ancient Chinese thinkers would have no problem with this theory. What they would not have accepted was a further claim that there was an external intelligence, beyond human comprehension, who willed that it be so. Of course, the Chinese are not unique in this regard. Many peoples, ancient and recent, primitive and modern, would feel uncomfortable with the idea of a willful God who created the world out of nothing. It was not a creation myth as such but the Judeo-Christian version of it that is absent in Chinese mythology. But the Chinese, like numerous peoples throughout human history, subscribe to the continuity of being as self-evidently true.[5]

An obvious consequence of this basic belief is the all-embracing nature of the so-called spontaneously self-generating life process. Strictly speaking, it is not because the Chinese have no idea of God external to the created cosmos that they have no choice but to accept the cosmogony as an organismic process. Rather, it is precisely because they perceive the cosmos as the unfolding of continuous creativity that it cannot entertain "conceptions of creation *ex nihilo* by the hand of God, or through the will of God, and all other such mechanistic, teleological, and theistic cosmologies."[6] The Chinese commitment to the continuity of being, rather than the absence of a creation myth, prompts them to see nature as "the all-enfolding harmony of impersonal cosmic functions."[7]

The Chinese model of the world, "a decidedly psychophysical structure" in the Jungian sense,[8] is characterized by Joseph Needham as "an ordered harmony of wills without an ordainer."[9] What Needham describes as the organismic Chinese cosmos consists of dynamic energy fields rather than static matter-like entities. Indeed, the dichotomy of spirit and matter is not at all applicable to this psychophysical structure. The most basic stuff that makes the cosmos is neither solely spiritual nor material but both. It is a vital force. This vital force must not be conceived of either as disembodied spirit or as pure matter.[10] Wing-tsit Chan, in his influential *Source Book in Chinese Philosophy,* notes that the distinction between energy and matter is not made in Chinese philosophy. He further notes that H. H. Dubs's rendering of the indigenous term for this basic stuff, *ch'i,* as "matter-energy" is "essentially sound but awkward and lacks an adjective form."[11] Although Chan translates *ch'i* as "material force," he cautions that since *ch'i,* before the advent of Neo-Confucianism in the eleventh century, originally "denotes the psychophysiological power associated with blood and breath," it should be rendered as "vital force" or "vital power."[12]

The unusual difficulty in making *ch'i* intelligible in modern Western philosophy suggests that the underlying Chinese metaphysical assumption is significantly different from the Cartesian dichotomy between spirit and matter. However, it would be misleading to categorize the Chinese mode of thinking as a sort of pre-Cartesian naïveté lacking differentiation between mind and body and, by implication, between subject and object. Analytically, Chinese thinkers have clearly distinguished spirit from matter. They fully recognize that spirit is not reducible to matter, that spirit is of more enduring value than matter. There are, of course, notable exceptions. But these so-called materialist thinkers are not only rare but also too few and far between to constitute a noticeable tradition in Chinese philosophy. Recent attempts to reconstruct the genealogy of materialist thinkers in China have been painful and, in some cases, far-fetched.[13] Indeed, to characterize the two great Confucian thinkers, Chang Tsai (1020–1077) and Wang Fu-chih (1619–1692), as paradigmatic examples of Chinese materialism is predicated on the false assumption that *ch'i* is materialistic. Both of them did subscribe to what may be called philosophy of *ch'i* as a critique of speculative thought, but, to them, *ch'i* was not simply matter but vital force endowed with all-pervasive spirituality.[14]

The continuous presence in Chinese philosophy of the idea of *ch'i* as a way of conceptualizing the basic structure and function of the cosmos, despite the availability of symbolic resources to make an analytical distinction between spirit and matter, signifies a conscious refusal to abandon a mode of thought that synthesizes spirit and matter as an undifferentiated whole. The loss of analytical clarity is compensated by the reward of imaginative richness. The fruitful ambiguity of *ch'i* allows philosophers to explore realms of being which are inconceivable to people constricted by a Cartesian dichotomy. To be sure, the theory of the different modalities of *ch'i* cannot engender ideas such as the naked object, raw data, or the value-free fact, and this cannot create a world out there, naked, raw, and value-free, for the disinterested scientist to study, analyze, manipulate, and control. *Ch'i,* in short, seems inadequate to provide a philosophical background for the development of empirical science as understood in the positivistic sense. What it does provide, however, is a metaphorical mode of knowing, an epistemological attempt to address the multidimensional nature of reality by comparison, allusion, and suggestion.

Whether it is the metaphorical mode of knowing that directs the Chinese to perceive the cosmos as an organismic process or it is the ontological vision of the continuity of being that informs Chinese epistemology is a highly intriguing question. Our main concern here, however, is to understand how the idea of the undifferentiated *ch'i* serves as a basis for a unified cosmological theory. We want to know in what sense the least intelligent being, such as a rock, and the highest manifestation of spirituality, such as Heaven, both consist of *ch'i.* The way the Chinese perceive reality and the sense of reality which defines the Chinese way of seeing the world are equally important in our inquiry, even though we do not intend to specify any causal relationship between them.

The organismic process as a spontaneously self-generating life process exhibits three basic motifs: continuity, wholeness, and dynamism.[15] All modalities of being, from a rock to Heaven, are integral parts of a continuum which is often referred to as the "great transformation" (*ta-hua*).[16] Since nothing is outside of this continuum, the chain of being is never broken. A linkage will always be found between any given pair of things in the universe. We may have to probe deeply to find some of the linkages, but they are there to be discovered. These are not figments of our imagination but solid foundations upon which the cosmos and our lived world therein are constructed. *Ch'i,* the psychophysiological stuff, is everywhere. It suffuses even the "great void" (*t'ai-hsü*) which is the source of all beings in Chang Tsai's philosophy.[17] The continuous presence of *ch'i* in all modalities of being makes everything flow together as the unfolding of a single process. Nothing, not even an almighty creator, is external to this process.

This motif of wholeness is directly derived from the idea of continuity as all-encompassing. If the world were created by an intelligence higher than and external to the great transformation, it would, by definition, fall short of a manifestation of holism. Similarly, if the world were merely a partial or distorted manifestation of the Platonic Idea, it would never achieve the perfection of the original reality. On the contrary, if genuine creativity is not the creation of something out of nothing, but a continuous transformation of that which is already there, the world as it now exists is the authentic manifestation of the cosmic process in its all-embracing fullness. Indeed, if the Idea for its own completion entails that it realize itself through the organismic process, the world is in every sense the concrete embodiment of the Idea. Traditional Chinese thinkers, of course, did not philosophize in those terms. They used different conceptual apparatuses to convey their thought. To them, the appropriate metaphor for understanding the universe was biology rather than physics. At issue was not the eternal, static structure but the dynamic process of growth and transformation. To say that the cosmos is a continuum and that all of its components are internally connected is also to say that it is an organismic unity, holistically integrated at each level of complexity.

It is important to note that continuity and wholeness in Chinese cosmological thinking must be accompanied in the third motif, dynamism, lest the idea of organismic unity imply a closed system. While Chinese thinkers are critically aware of the inertia in human culture which may eventually lead to stagnation, they perceive the "course of Heaven" (*t'ien-hsing*) as "vigorous" (*chien*) and instruct people to model themselves on the ceaseless vitality of the cosmic process.[18] What they envision in the spontaneously self-generating life process is not only inner connectedness and interdependence but also infinite potential for development. Many historians have remarked that the traditional Chinese notion of cyclic change, like the recurrence of the seasonal pattern, is incompatible with the modern Western idea of progress. To be sure, the traditional Chinese conception of history lacks the idea of unilinear development, such as Marxian modes of production depicting a form of historical inevitability. It is misleading, however, to describe Chinese history as chronicling a number of related events happening in a regularly repeated order.[19] Chinese historiography is not a reflection of a cyclic worldview. The Chinese worldview is neither cyclic nor spiral. It is transformational. The specific curve around which it transforms at a given period of time is indeterminate, however, for numerous human and nonhuman factors are involved in shaping its form and direction.

The organismic life process, which Mote contends is the genuine Chinese cosmogony, is an open system. As there is no temporal beginning to specify, no closure is ever contemplated. The cosmos is forever expanding; the great transformation is unceasing. The idea of unilinear development, in this perspective, is one-sided because it fails to account for the whole range of possibility in which progress constitutes but one of several dominant configurations. By analogy, neither cyclic nor spiral movements can fully depict the varieties of cosmic transformation. Since it is open rather than closed and dynamic rather than static, no geometric design can do justice to its complex morphology.

Earlier, I followed Mote in characterizing the Chinese vision of nature as the "all-enfolding harmony of impersonal cosmic function" and remarked that this particular vision was prompted by the Chinese commitment to the continuity of being. Having discussed the three basic motifs of Chinese cosmology—wholeness, dynamism, and continuity—I can elaborate on Mote's characterization by discussing some of its implications. The idea of all-enfolding harmony involves two interrelated meanings. It means that nature is all-inclusive, the spontaneously self-generating life process which excludes nothing. The Taoist idea of *tzu-jan* ("self-so"),[20] which is used in modern Chinese to translate the English word *nature,* aptly captures this spirit. To say that *self-so* is all-inclusive is to posit a nondiscriminatory and nonjudgmental position, to allow all modalities of being to display themselves as they are. This is possible, however, only if competitiveness, domination, and aggression are thoroughly transformed. Thus, all-enfolding harmony also means that internal resonance underlies the order of things in the universe. Despite conflict and tension, which are like waves of the ocean, the deep structure of nature is always tranquil. The great transformation of which nature is the concrete manifestation is the result of concord rather than discord and convergence rather than divergence.

This vision of nature may suggest an unbridled romantic assertion about peace and love, the opposite of what Charles Darwin realistically portrayed as the rules of nature. Chinese thinkers, however, did not take the all-enfolding harmony to be the original naïveté of the innocent. Nor did they take it to be an idealist utopia attainable in a distant future. They were acutely aware that the world we live in, far from being the "great unity" (*ta-t'ung*) recommended in the *Evolution of the Rites,*[21] is laden with disruptive forces, including humanly caused calamities and natural catastrophes. They also knew well that history is littered with internecine warfare, oppression, injustice, and numerous other forms of cruelty. It was not naïve romanticism that prompted them to assert that harmony is a defining characteristic of the organismic process. They believed that it is an accurate description of what the cosmos really is and how it actually works.

One advantage of rendering *ch'i* as "vital force," bearing in mind its original association with blood and breath, is its emphasis on the life process. To Chinese thinkers, nature is vital force in display. It is continuous, holistic, and dynamic. Yet, in an attempt to understand the blood and breath of nature's vitality, Chinese thinkers discovered that its enduring pattern is union rather than disunion, integration rather than disintegration, and synthesis rather than separation. The eternal flow of nature is characterized by the concord and convergence of numerous streams of vital force. It is in this sense that the organismic process is considered harmonious.

Chang Tsai, in his celebrated metaphysical treatise, "Correcting Youthful Ignorance," defines the cosmos as the "Great Harmony":

> The Great Harmony is called the Way (Tao, Moral Law). It embraces the nature which underlies all counter processes of floating and sinking, rising and falling, and motion and rest. It is the origin of the process of fusion and intermingling, of overcoming and being overcome, and of expansion and contraction. At the commencement, these processes are incipient, subtle, obscure, easy, and simple, but at the end they are extensive, great, strong and firm. It is *ch'ien* (Heaven) that begins with the knowledge of Change, and *k'un* (Earth) that models after simplicity. That

> which is dispersed, differentiated, and capable of assuming form becomes material force (*ch'i*), and that which is pure, penetrating, and not capable of assuming form becomes spirit. Unless the whole universe is in the process of fusion and intermingling like fleeting forces moving in all directions, it may not be called Great Harmony.[22]

In his vision, nature is the result of the fusion and intermingling of the vital forces that assume tangible forms. Mountains, rivers, rocks, trees, animals, and human beings are all modalities of energy-matter, symbolizing that the creative transformation of the Tao is forever present. Needham's idea of the Chinese cosmos as an ordered harmony of wills without an ordainer is, however, not entirely appropriate. Wills, no matter how broadly defined, do not feature prominently here. The idea that Heaven and Earth complete the transformation with no mind of their own clearly indicates that the harmonious state of the organismic process is not achieved by ordering divergent wills.[23] Harmony will be attained through spontaneity. In what sense is this what Mote calls "impersonal cosmic function"? Let us return to Chang Tsai's metaphysical treatise:

> [*Ch'i*] moves and flows in all directions and in all manners. Its two elements [yin and yang] unite and give rise to the concrete. Thus the multiplicity of things and human beings is produced. In their ceaseless successions the two elements of yin and yang constitute the great principles of the universe.[24]

This inner logic of *ch'i,* which is singularly responsible for the production of the myriad things, leads to a naturalistic description of the impersonal cosmic function. Wang Fu-chih, who developed Chang Tsai's metaphysics of *ch'i* with great persuasive power, continues with this line of thinking:

> The fact that the things of the world, whether rivers or mountains, plants or animals, those with or without intelligence, and those yielding blossoms or bearing fruits, provide beneficial support for all things is the result of the natural influence of the moving power of [*ch'i*]. It fills the universe. And as it completely provides for the flourish and transformation of all things, it is all the more spatially unrestricted. As it is not spatially restricted, it operates in time and proceeds with time. From morning to evening, from spring to summer, and from the present tracing back to the past, there is no time at which it does not operate, and there is no time at which it does not produce. Consequently, as one sprout bursts forth it becomes a tree with a thousand big branches, and as one egg evolves, it progressively becomes a fish capable of swallowing a ship. . . .[25]

The underlying message, however, is not the impersonality of the cosmic function, even though the idea of the moving power of *ch'i* indicates that no anthropomorphic god, animal, or object is really behind the great transformation. The naturalness of the cosmic function, despite human wishes and desires, is impersonal but not inhuman. It is impartial to all modalities of being and not merely anthropocentric. We humans, therefore, do not find the impersonal cosmic function cold, alien, or distant, although we know that it is, by and large, indifferent to and disinterested in our private thoughts and whims. Actually, we are an integral part of this function; we are ourselves the result of this moving power of *ch'i.* Like mountains and rivers, we are legitimate beings in this great transformation. The opening lines in Chang Tsai's *Western Inscription* are not only his article of faith but also his ontological view of the human.

> Heaven is my father and Earth is my mother, and even such a small creature as I find an intimate place in their midst.
>
> Therefore that which fills the universe I regard as my body and that which directs the universe I consider as my nature.
>
> All people are my brothers and sisters, and all things are my companions.[26]

The sense of intimacy with which Chang Tsai, as a single person, relates himself to the universe as a whole reflects his profound awareness of moral ecology. Humanity is the respectful son or daughter of the cosmic process. This humanistic vision is distinctively Confucian in character. It contrasts sharply with the Taoist idea of noninterference on the one hand and the Buddhist concept of detachment on the other. Yet the notion of humanity as forming one body with the universe has been so widely accepted by the Chinese, in popular as well as elite culture, that it can very well be characterized as a general Chinese worldview.

Forming one body with the universe can literally mean that since all modalities of being are made of *ch'i,* human life is part of a continuous flow of the blood and breath that constitutes the cosmic process. Human beings are thus organically connected with rocks, trees, and animals. Understandably, the interplay and interchange between discrete species feature prominently in Chinese literature, notably popular novels. The monkey in the *Journey to the West* came into being by metamorphosis from an agate;[27] the hero in the *Dream of the Red Chamber* or the *Story of the Stone,* Pao Yü, is said to have been transformed from a piece of precious jade;[28] and the heroine of the *Romance of the White Snake* has not completely succeeded in transfiguring herself into a beautiful woman.[29] These are well-known stories. They have evoked strong sympathetic responses from Chinese audiences young and old for centuries, not merely as fantasies but as great human drama. It is not at all difficult for the Chinese to imagine that an agate or a piece of jade can have enough potential spirituality to transform itself into a human being. Part of the pathos of the White Snake lies in her inability to fight against the spell cast by a ruthless monk so that she can retain her human form and be united with her lover. The fascinating element in this romance is that she manages to acquire the power to transfigure herself into a woman through several hundred years of self-cultivation.

Presumably, from the cosmic vantage point, nothing is totally fixed. It need not be forever the identity it now assumes. In the perceptive eye of the Chinese painter Tao Chi (1641–1717), mountains flow like rivers. The proper way of looking at mountains, for him, is to see them as ocean waves frozen in time.[30] By the same token, rocks are not static objects but dynamic processes with their particular configuration of the energy-matter. It may not be far-fetched to suggest that, with this vision of nature, we can actually talk about the different degrees of spirituality of rocks. Agate is certainly more spiritual than an ordinary hard stone and perhaps jade is more spiritual than agate. Jade is honored as the "finest essence of mountain and river" (*shan-ch'uan ching-ying*).[31] By analogy, we can also talk about degrees of spirituality in the entire chain of being. Rocks, trees, animals, humans, and gods represent different levels of spirituality based on the varying compositions of *ch'i.* However, despite the principle of differentiation, all modalities of being are organically connected. They are integral parts of a continuous process of cosmic transformation. It is in this metaphysical sense that "all things are my companions."

The uniqueness of being human cannot be explained in terms of a preconceived design by a creator. Human beings, like all other beings, are the results of the integration of the two basic vital forces of yin and yang. Chou Tun-i (1017–1073) says, "the interaction of these two *ch'i* engenders and transforms the myriad things. The myriad things produce and reproduce, resulting in an unending transformation."[32] In a strict sense, then, human beings are not the rulers of creation; if they intend to become guardians of the universe, they must earn this distinction through self-cultivation. There is no preordained reason for them to think otherwise. Nevertheless, the human being—in the Chinese sense of *jen,* which is gender neutral—is unique. Chou Tun-i offers the following explanation:

> It is human beings alone who receive [the Five Agents] in their highest excellence, and therefore they are most intelligent. Their physical form appears, and their spirit develops consciousness. The five moral principles of their nature (humanity or *jen,* righteousness, propriety, wisdom, and faithfulness) are aroused by, and react to, the external world and engage in activity; good and evil are distinguished; and human affairs take place.[33]

The theory of the Five Agents or the Five Phases (*wu-hsing*) need not concern us here. Since Chou makes it clear that "by the transformation of yang and its union with yin, the Five Agents of Water, Fire, Wood, Metal, and Earth arise" and that since "the Five Agents constitute one system of yin and yang,"[34] they can be conceived as specific forms of *ch'i.*

That humankind receives *ch'i* in its highest excellence is not only manifested in intelligence but also in sensitivity. The idea that humans are the most sentient beings in the universe features prominently in Chinese thought. A vivid description of human sensitivity is found in the "recorded sayings" (*yü-lu*) Ch'eng Hao (1032–1085):

> A book on medicine describes paralysis of the four limbs as absence of [humanity (*pu-jen*)]. This is an excellent description. The person of [humanity] regards Heaven and Earth and all things as one body. To him there is nothing that is not himself. Since he has recognized all things as himself, can there be any limit to his humanity? If things are not part of the self, naturally they

> have nothing to do with it. As in the case of paralysis of the four limbs, the vital force [ch'i] no longer penetrates them, and therefore they are no longer parts of the self.[35]

This idea of forming one body with the universe is predicated on the assumption that since all modalities of being are made of *ch'i,* all things cosmologically share the same consanguinity with us and are thus our companions. This vision enabled an original thinker of the Ming dynasty, Wang Ken (1483–1540), to remark that if we came into being through transformation (*hua-sheng*), then heaven and earth are our father and mother to us; if we came into being through reproduction (*hsing-sheng*), then our father and mother are Heaven and Earth to us.[36] The image of the human that emerges here, far from being the lord of creation, is the filial son and daughter of the universe. Filial piety connotes a profound feeling, an all-pervasive care for the world around us.

This literal meaning of forming one body with the universe must be augmented by a metaphorical reading of the same text. It is true that the body clearly conveys the sense of *ch'i* as the blood and breath of the vital force that underlies all beings. The uniqueness of being human, however, is not simply that we are made of the same psychophysiological stuff that rocks, trees, and animals are also made of. It is our consciousness of being human that enables and impels us to probe the transcendental anchorage of our nature. Surely the motif of the continuity of being prevents us from positing a creator totally external to the cosmic organismic process, but what is the relationship between human nature and Heaven which serves as the source of all things? Indeed, how are we to understand the ontological assertion in the first chapter of the *Doctrine of the Mean* that our nature is decreed by Heaven?[37] Is the Mandate of Heaven a one-time operation or a continuous presence? Wang Fu-chih's general response to these questions is suggestive.

> By nature is meant the principle of growth. As one daily grows, one daily achieves completion. Thus by the Mandate of Heaven is not meant that Heaven gives the decree (*ming,* mandate) only at the moment of one's birth. . . . In the production of things by Heaven, the process of transformation never ceases.[38]

In the metaphorical sense, then, forming one body with the universe requires continuous effort to grow and to refine oneself. We can embody the whole universe in our sensitivity because we have enlarged and deepened our feeling and care to the fullest extent. However, there is no guarantee at the symbolic or at the experiential level that the universe is automatically embodied in us. Unless we see to it that the Mandate of Heaven is fully realized in our nature, we may not live up to the expectation that "all things are complete in us."[39] Wang Fu-chih's refusal to follow a purely naturalistic line of thinking on this is evident in the following observation: "The [profound person] acts naturally as if nothing happens, but . . . he acts so as to make the best choices and remain firm in holding to the Mean."[40] To act naturally without letting things take their own course means, in Neo-Confucian terminology, to follow the "heavenly principle" (*t'ien-li*) without being overcome by "selfish desires" (*ssu-yü*).[41] Selfish desires are forms of self-centeredness that belittle the authentic human capacity to take part in the transformative process of Heaven and Earth. In commenting on the *Book of Changes,* Ch'eng Hao observes:

> The most impressive aspect of things is their spirit of life. This is what is meant by origination being the chief quality of goodness. . . . Humans and Heaven and Earth are one thing. Why should man purposely belittle himself?[42]

Forming a trinity with Heaven and Earth, which is tantamount to forming one body with the myriad things, enjoins us from applying the subject-object dichotomy to nature. To see nature as an external object out there is to create an artificial barrier which obstructs our true vision and undermines our human capacity to experience nature from within. The internal resonance of the vital forces is such that the mind, as the most refined and subtle *ch'i* of the human body, is constantly in sympathetic accord with the myriad things in nature. The function of "affect and response" (*kan-ying*) characterizes nature as a great harmony and so informs the mind.[43] The mind forms a union with nature by extending itself metonymically. Its aesthetic appreciation of nature is neither an appropriation of the object by the subject nor an imposition of the subject on the object, but the merging of the self into an expanded reality through transformation and participation. This creative process, in Roman Jakobson's terminology, is "contiguous," because rupture between us and nature never occurs.[44]

Chuang Tzu recommends that we listen with our minds rather than with our ears; with *ch'i* rather than with our minds.[45] If listening with our minds involves consciousness unaffected by sensory perceptions, what does listening to *ch'i* entail? Could it mean that we are so much a part of the internal resonance of the vital forces themselves that we can listen to the sound of nature or, in Chuang Tzu's expression, the "music of Heaven" (*t'ien-lai*)[46] as our inner voice? Or could it mean that the all-embracing *ch'i* enables the total transposition of humankind and nature? As a result, the aesthetic delight that one experiences is no longer the private sensation of the individual but the "harmonious blending of inner feelings and outer scenes,"[47] as the traditional Chinese artist would have it. It seems that in either case we do not detach ourselves from nature and study it in a disinterested manner. What we do is to suspend not only our sensory perceptions but also our conceptual apparatus so that we can embody nature in our sensitivity and allow nature to embrace us in its affinity.

I must caution, however, that the aesthetic experience of mutuality and immediacy with nature is often the result of strenuous and continual effort at self-cultivation. Despite our superior intelligence, we do not have privileged access to the great harmony. As social and cultural beings, we can never get outside ourselves to study nature from neutral ground. The process of returning to nature involves unlearning and forgetting as well as remembering. The precondition for us to participate in the internal resonance of the vital forces in nature is our own inner transformation. Unless we can first harmonize our own feelings and thoughts, we are not prepared for nature, let alone for an "interflow with the spirit of Heaven and Earth."[48] It is true that we are consanguineous with nature. But as humans, we must make ourselves worthy of such a relationship.

NOTES

1. Frederick W. Mote, *Intellectual Foundations of China* (New York: Alfred A. Knopf, 1971), 17–18.
2. Ibid., 19.
3. For a thought-provoking discussion on this issue, see N. J. Girardot, *Myth and Meaning in Early Taoism* (Berkeley: University of California Press, 1983), 275–310.
4. For a suggestive methodological essay, see William G. Boltz, "Kung Kung and the Flood: Reverse Euphemism in the *Yao Tien*," *T'oung Pao* 67 (1981): 141–53. Professor Boltz's effort to reconstruct the Kung Kung myth indicates the possibility of an indigenous creation myth.
5. Tu Wei-ming, "Shih-t'an Chung-kuo che-hsüeh chung te san-ko chi-tiao" (A preliminary discussion on the three basic motifs in Chinese philosophy), *Chung-kuo che-hsüeh shih yen-chiu* (Studies on the history of Chinese philosophy) (Peking: Society for the Study of the History of Chinese Philosophy) 2 (March 1981): 19–21.
6. Mote, *Intellectual Foundations of China*, 20.
7. Ibid.
8. See Jung's foreword to the *I ching (Book of Changes)*, translated into English by Cary F. Baynes from the German translation of Richard Wilhelm, Bollingen Series, 19 (Princeton: Princeton University Press, 1967), xxiv.
9. Needham's full statement reads as follows: "It was an ordered harmony of wills without an ordainer; it was like the spontaneous yet ordered, in the sense of patterned, movements of dancers in a country dance of figures, none of whom are bound by law to do what they do, nor yet pushed by others coming behind, but cooperate in a voluntary harmony of wills." See Joseph Needham and Wang Ling, *Science and Civilisation in China*, 2 (Cambridge: Cambridge University Press, 1969), 287.
10. Actually, the dichotomy of spirit and matter does not feature prominently in Chinese thought; see Tu, "Shih-t'an Chung-kuo che-hsüeh," 21–22.
11. *A Source Book in Chinese Philosophy*, trans. and comp. Wing-tsit Chan (Princeton: Princeton University Press, 1963), 784.
12. Ibid.
13. For a notable exception to this general interpretive situation in the People's Republic of China, see Chang Tai-nien, *Chung-kuo che-hsüeh fa-wei* (Exploring some of the delicate issues in Chinese philosophy) (T'ai-yuan, Shansi: People's Publishing Co., 1981), 11–38, 275–306.
14. For a general discussion on this vital issue from a medical viewpoint, see Manfred Porkert, *The Theoretical Foundations of Chinese Medicine: Systems of Correspondence* (Cambridge, Mass.: MIT Press, 1974).
15. Tu, "Shih-t'an Chung-kuo che-hsüeh," 19–24.
16. A paradigmatic discussion on this is to be found in the *Commentaries on the Book of Changes*. See Chan, *Source Book in Chinese Philosophy*, 264.
17. See Chang Tsai's "Correcting Youthful Ignorance," in Chan, *Source Book in Chinese Philosophy*, 501–14.
18. For this reference in the *Chou i*, see *A Concordance to Yi Ching*, Harvard-Yenching Institute Sinological Index Series, Supplement no. 10 (reprint; Tapei: Chinese Materials and Research Aids Service Center, Inc., 1966), 1/1.
19. The idea of the "dynastic cycle" may give one the impression that Chinese history is nondevelopmental.

See Edwin O. Reischauer and John K. Fairbank, *East Asia: The Great Tradition* (Boston: Houghton Mifflin Co., 1960), 114–18.

20. *Chuang tzu,* chap. 7. See the Harvard-Yenching Index on the *Chuang tzu,* 20/7/11.

21. See *Sources of Chinese Tradition,* comp. Wm. Theodore de Bary, Wing-tsit Chan, and Burton Watson (New York: Columbia University Press, 1960), 191–92.

22. Chan, *Source Book in Chinese Philosophy,* 500–501.

23. Ibid., 262–66. This idea underlies the philosophy of change.

24. Ibid., 505, §14. In this translation, *ch'i* is rendered "material force." The words *yin* and *yang* in brackets are my additions.

25. Ibid., 698–99.

26. Ibid., 497.

27. Wu Ch'eng-en, *Hsi-yu chi,* trans. and ed. Anthony C. Yü as *Journey to the West,* 4 vols. (Chicago: University of Chicago Press, 1977–83), 1:67–78.

28. Ts'ao Hsüeh-ch'in (Cao Xuequin), *Hung-lou meng* (Dream of the Red Chamber), trans. David Hawkes as *The Story of the Stone,* 5 vols. (Harmondsworth, England: Penguin Books, 1973–86), 1:47–49.

29. For two useful discussions on the story, see Fu Hsi-hua, *Pai-she-chuan chi* (An anthology of the White Snake story) (Shanghai: Shanghai Publishing Co., 1955), and P'an Chiang-tung, *Pai-she ku-shih yen-chiu* (A study of the White Snake story) (Tapei: Students' Publishers, 1981).

30. P. Ryckmans, "Les propos sur la peinture de Shi Tao traduction et commentaire," *Arts Asiatique* 14 (1966): 123–24.

31. Teng Shu-p'in, "Shang-ch'uan ching-ying-yü te i-shu" (The finest essence of mountain and river—the art of jade), in *Chung-kuo wen-hua hsin-lun* (New views on Chinese culture) (Taipei: Lien-ching, 1983), section on arts, 253–304.

32. Chan, *Source Book in Chinese Philosophy,* 463. Again, this translation renders *ch'i* as "material force."

33. Ibid.

34. Ibid.

35. Ibid., 530, §11.

36. Wang Ken, "Yü Nan-tu chu-yu" (Letter to friends of Nan-tu), in *Wang Hsin-chai hsien-sheng ch'üan-chi* (The complete works of Wang Ken) (1507 edition, Harvard-Yenching Library), 4.16b.

37. Chan, *Source Book in Chinese Philosophy,* 98.

38. Ibid., 699.

39. *Mencius,* 7A.4.

40. Chan, *Source Book in Chinese Philosophy,* 699–700.

41. For example, in Chu Hsi's discussion of moral cultivation, the Heavenly Principle is clearly contrasted with selfish desires. See Chan, *Source Book in Chinese Philosophy,* 605–6.

42. Ibid., 539.

43. For a suggestive essay on this, see R. G. H. Siu, *Ch'i: A Neo-Taoist Approach to Life* (Cambridge, Mass.: MIT Press, 1974).

44. Roman Jakobson, "Two Aspects of Language and Two Types of Aphasic Disturbances," in Roman Jakobson and Morris Halle, *Fundamentals of Language* ('s-Gravenhage: Mouton, 1956), 55–82. I am grateful to Professor Yu-kung Kao for this reference.

45. *Chuang tzu,* chap. 4. The precise quotation can be found in *Chuang tzu ying-te* (Peking: Harvard-Yenching Institute, 1947), 9/4/27.

46. *Chuang tzu,* chap. 2, *Chuang tzu ying-te,* 3/2/8.

47. For a systematic discussion of this, see Yu-kung Kao and Kang-i Sun Chang, "Chinese 'Lyric Criticism' in the Six Dynasties," American Council of Learned Societies Conference on Theories of the Arts in China (June 1979), published as *Theories of the Arts in China,* ed. Susan Bush and Christian Murck (Princeton: Princeton University Press, 1983).

48. See *Mencius,* 7A.13.

Ecological Themes in Taoism and Confucianism

MARY EVELYN TUCKER

> Humans do not oppose Earth and therefore can comfort all things, for their standard is the Earth. Earth does not oppose Heaven and therefore can sustain all things, for its standard is Heaven. Heaven does not oppose Tao and therefore can cover all things, for its standard is Tao. Tao does

Tucker, Mary Evelyn, "Ecological Themes in Taoism and Confucianism," in Mary Evelyn Tucker and John Grim, Eds., *Worldviews and Ecology: Religion, Philosophy and the Environment,* Maryknoll, NY: Orbis, 1994, pp. 150-159. Originally published in Bucknell Reviews, Vol. 37, No. 2, 1993, published by Bucknell University Press. Reprinted by permission.

> not oppose Nature and therefore it attains its character of being. (A Taoist commentary from Wang Pi, 226–249 C.E.)[1]

> Mencius answered [King Hui], "If your majesty can practice a humane government to the people, reduce punishments and fines, lower taxes and levies, make it possible for the fields to be plowed deep and the weeding well done, men of strong body, in their days of leisure may cultivate their filial piety, brotherly respect, loyalty, and faithfulness, thereby serving their fathers and elder brothers at home and their elders and superiors abroad." (A Confucian text from Mencius, 372–289 B.C.E.)[2]

NEARLY TWO DECADES AGO THOMAS BERRY called for "creating a new consciousness of the multiform religious traditions of humankind" as a means toward renewal of the human spirit in addressing the urgent problems of contemporary society.[3] More recently Tu Wei-ming has written of the need to go "beyond the Enlightenment mentality" in exploring the spiritual resources of the global community to meet the challenge of the ecological crisis.[4]

In drawing upon the great religious traditions of the past for a new ecological orientation in the present, it is clear that the traditions of East Asia have much to offer. My method in this essay is to examine some of the principal texts of Taoism and Confucianism for a phenomenological description of ecological worldviews embedded in these traditions. I risk the inevitable distortions of reducing complex teachings from 2500-year-old traditions to generalizations that need qualification and development. I am also relying primarily on the philosophical and religious ideas of these traditions as evident in their texts and am not discussing their varied religious practices which arose in different periods of Chinese history. Nor am I making claims for a historical consciousness in China of the issues of ecology as we are beginning to understand them in the late twentieth century. Furthermore, I am aware of the ever-present gap between theoretical positions and practical applications in dealing with the environment throughout history.[5] I am also conscious of the dark side of each religious tradition as it developed in particular historical contexts. Nonetheless, in seeking guidance from the past it is becoming increasingly important to examine the perspectives of earlier civilizations and their attitudes toward nature as we seek new and more comprehensive worldviews and environmental ethics in the present.[6] There is not sufficient time or space to work out all of these methodological issues here. However, I would suggest that this project is an important step in creating a new ecumenism of the multiform religious traditions of the human community in dialogue with pressing contemporary problems such as the environment and social justice.[7]

GENERAL COMMENTS ON TAOISM AND CONFUCIANISM

The two indigenous traditions of China, Taoism and Confucianism, arose in the so-called Axial Age in the first millennium before the birth of Christ. As Karl Jaspers noted, this was approximately the same time as the philosophers in Greece, the prophets in Israel, Zoroaster in Persia, and Buddha in India.[8] In China this period in the Chou dynasty was a time of great intellectual creativity known as the age of the 100 philosophers.

Although there are many historical uncertainties and ongoing scholarly debates about the life and the writings of Lao Tzu and Confucius, it is indisputable that these two figures are of primary importance in Chinese religion and philosophy. Indeed, some writers on Chinese thought see these traditions as complementary to each other and in a kind of creative tension. While Taoism and Confucianism are quite different in their specific teachings, they share a worldview that might be described as organic, vitalistic, and holistic. They see the universe as a dynamic, ongoing process of continual transformation.[9] The creativity and unity of the cosmos are constant themes which appear in the Taoist and Confucian texts. The human has a special role in this vitalistic universe. This is viewed in a more passive manner by the Taoists and a more active mode by the Confucians.

It is, however, this organic, vitalistic worldview which has special relevance for developing a contemporary ecological perspective. Indeed, it can be said that within this holistic view Taoist and Confucian thought might provide an important balance of passive and active models for ecological theory and practice.[10] Like a yin-yang circle of complementary opposites, Taoist and Confucian thinkers have evoked important considerations from each other and may still do the same for us today.

In very general terms we can compare and contrast these two traditions as follows. Taoism emphasizes primary causality as resting in the Tao, while Confucianism stresses the importance of secondary causality in the activities of human beings. Thus the principal concern in Taoism is for harmony with the Tao, the nameless Way which is the source of all existence. In Confucianism the stress is on how humans can live together and create a just society with a benevolent government. For both the Taoists and the Confucians harmony with nature is important. The Taoists emphasize the primacy of unmediated closeness to nature to encourage simplicity and spontaneity in individuals and in human relations. For the Taoists, developing techniques of meditation is critical. The Confucians, especially the Neo-Confucians, stress harmonizing with the changing patterns in nature so as to adapt human action and human society appropriately to nature's deeper rhythms. For them the *Book of Changes* is an important means of establishing balance with nature and with other humans.

For the Taoists, in order to be in consonance with the Tao in nature one must withdraw from active involvement in social and political affairs and learn how to preserve and nourish nature and human life. For the Confucians, social and political commitment was an indispensable part of human responsibility to create an orderly society in harmony with nature. Indeed, for the Confucians cultivating oneself morally and intellectually was a means of establishing a peaceful and productive society. The ideal for the Taoist, then, was the hermit in a mountain retreat, while for the Confucian it was the sage, the teacher, and the civil servant in the midst of affairs of government and education. Taoism did provide a model of an ideal ruler, but one who led without overt involvement but rather by subtle indirection and detachment. The Confucians, on the other hand, called for a moral ruler who would be like a pole star for the people, practicing humane government for the benefit of all. The Taoists stressed the principle of non-egocentric action (*wu wei*) in harmony with nature for both ruler and followers. The Confucians, on the other hand, underscored the importance of human action for the betterment of society by the ruler, ministers, teachers, and ordinary citizens. A pristine innocence and spontaneity was valued by the Taoists, while the Confucians continually emphasized humanistic education and ethical practice for the improvement of individuals and society as a whole.

It is perhaps some combination of these two perspectives which may be fruitful for our own thinking today. In order to understand and respect natural processes, we need a greater Taoist attention to the subtle unfolding of the principles and processes of nature. As the deep ecologists constantly remind us, without this fine attunement to the complexities of nature and to ourselves as one species among many others, we may continue to contribute unwittingly to destructive environmental practices. Yet without the Confucian understanding of the importance of moral leadership, an emphasis on education, and a sense of human responsibility to a larger community of life, we may lose the opportunity to change the current pattern of assault on the natural world. Taoism challenges us to radically reexamine human-earth relations, while Confucianism calls us to rethink the profound interconnection of individual-society-nature. Let us turn to examine the worldview of each of these traditions and their potential contributions to a newly emerging environmental ethics.

TAOISM AND ECOLOGY: COSMOLOGY AND ETHICS

The principal text of Taoism is the *Tao te Ching (The Way and Its Power)*, also known by the title *Lao Tzu*, its author. There have been numerous translations of this text into many languages and perhaps no other Chinese work compares to it in terms of international popularity.[11] The *Tao te Ching* contains a cosmology and an ethics which may have some relevance in our contemporary discussions on ecology.

In terms of cosmology the Tao refers to the unmanifest source of all life which is eternal and ineffable yet fecund and creative. "The Nameless [the Tao] is the origin of Heaven and Earth; / The named is the mother of all things."[12] The Tao, then, is the self-existent source of all things, namely, a primary cause. It is both a power which generates and a process which sustains. It is the unity behind the multiplicity of the manifest world. It is beyond distinction or name and can only be approached through image, paradox, or intuition. In its manifest form in the phenomenal world it is said to have no particular characteristics and thus be empty. As such it is full of potentiality. Indeed, the "Tao is empty (like a bowl), / It may be used but its capacity is never exhausted" (4). It can be described, however, with images such as valley, womb, and vessel, suggestive of receptivity and productivity.

The implications of this holistic cosmology for an environmental ethic should be somewhat self-evident. There is a distinct emphasis in Taoist thought on valuing nature for its own sake, not for utilitarian ends. The natural world is not a resource to exploit but a complex of dynamic life processes to appreciate and respect. Harmony with nature rather than control is the ultimate Taoist goal. This tradition has certain affinities with contemporary movements in deep ecology which decry an overly anthropocentric position of human dominance over nature.[13] Indeed, the Taoists, like the deep ecologists, would say that manipulation of nature will only lead to counterproductive results.[14]

To achieve harmony with nature the Taoists value simplicity and spontaneity. They distrust education and the imposition of moral standards as interfering with true naturalness. Intuitive knowledge and a pristine innocence are highly regarded.[15] A direct, unmediated encounter with nature is far better than book knowledge or hypocritical morality. As Lao Tzu urges, one should: "Abandon sageliness and discard wisdom; Then the people will benefit a hundredfold. . . . Manifest plainness, embrace simplicity, reduce selfishness, have few desires" (19).

Moreover, in terms of human action that which is understated, not forceful or directive, is considered optimal. Excess, extravagance, and arrogance are to be avoided. Nonegocentric action (*wu wei*) which is free from desire and attachments is essential.[16] In short, "By acting without action, all things will be in order" (3). In light of this, the *Tao te Ching* celebrates the paradox that yielding brings strength, passivity creates power, death creates new life.

These ideas are illustrated in the text with feminine images of fecundity and strength springing from openness and receptivity such as in motherhood, in an empty vessel, or in a valley. They also underlie images such as water wearing away at solid rock or the idea of an uncarved block waiting to reveal its form at the hands of a skilled sculptor. These demonstrate the potentiality and generative power which exist in unexpected and hidden places.[17]

> He who knows the male (active force) and keeps
>   to the female (the passive force or receptive
>   element)
> Becomes the ravine of the world.
> . . . .
> He will never part from eternal virtue.
> He who knows glory but keeps to humility,
> Becomes the valley of the world.
> . . . .
> He will be proficient in eternal virtue,
> And returns to the state of simplicity (uncarved
>   wood).
>
> (28)

In short, the *Tao te Ching* demonstrates the ultimate paradox of the coincidence of opposites, namely, that yielding is a form of strength. (This is clearly illustrated in the martial art of judo, which means the "way of yielding.") Indeed, the lesson of Taoism is that reversal is the movement of the Tao, for things easily turn into their opposites. "Reversion is the action of Tao. Weakness is the function of Tao. All things in the world come from being. And being comes from non-being" (40).

Thus both personally and politically Taoism calls for noninterfering action. A Taoist government would be one of conscious detachment and the ideal leader would be one who governs least. While this seems antithetical to the Confucian notion of active political involvement, the wisdom of the Taoist ideal of noninterference was not lost in the highest quarters of Chinese Confucian government. Over one of the thrones in the imperial palace in Beijing are the characters for *wu wei* (nonegocentric action), perhaps serving as a reminder of the importance of a detached attitude in political affairs.

All of this has enormous implications for our interactions with nature, namely that humans cannot arrogantly or blindly force nature into our mold.[18] To cooperate with nature in a Taoist manner requires a better understanding of and appreciation for nature's processes. While an extreme Taoist position might advocate complete noninterference with nature, a more moderate Taoist approach would call for interaction with nature, a more moderate Taoist approach would call for interaction with nature in a far less exploitive manner. Such cooperation with nature would sanction the use of appropriate or intermediate technology when necessary and would favor the use of organic fertilizers and natural farming methods. In terms of economic policy it would foster limited growth within a steady state economy that could support sustainable not exploitive development. Clearly, a Taoist ecological position is one with significant potential in the contemporary world.

CONFUCIANISM AND ECOLOGY: COSMOLOGY AND ETHICS

Let us turn to the early classical texts of the *Analects* and the *Mencius* to explore the ecological dimensions of Confucian thought.[19] These works have had an enormous impact on Chinese society, education, and government for over two millennia. Along with two shorter texts, the *Great Learning* and the *Doctrine of the Mean,* these became known as the Four Books and were the basis of the civil service examination system from the fourteenth century until the twentieth.

Cosmologically, early Confuciansm, like Taoism, understood the world to be part of a changing, dynamic, and unfolding universe.[20] The ongoing and unfolding process of nature was affirmed by the Confucians and seasonal harmony was highly valued. There is no common creation myth per se for the Confucians or Taoists.[21] Rather, the universe is seen as self-generating, guided by the unfolding of the Tao, a term the Confucians shared with the Taoists although with variations on its meaning in different contexts and periods. There is no personification of evil; instead, there is a balance of opposite forces in the concept of the yin and the yang.

Indeed, there is no radical split between transcendence and immanence such as occurs in the Western religions. In fact, it has become widely accepted that the sense of immanence rather than transcendence dominates both Taoist and Confucian thought. Although this needs qualification, it is true that the notion of "the secular as the sacred" was critical in Chinese philosophy and religion.[22] The significance of this view is that a balance of the natural and the human worlds was essential in both Taoist and Confucian thought. While the Taoists emphasized harmony with nature and downplayed human action, the Confucians stressed the importance of human action and the critical role of social and political institutions.

Within this cosmology certain ethical patterns emerged in Confucianism which are distinct from Taoism. Examining these patterns may be helpful for our understanding of the ecological dimensions of Confucian thought. While Taoism can be characterized as a naturalistic ecology having certain affinities with contemporary deep ecology, Confucianism might be seen as a form of social ecology having some similarities with the contemporary movement of the same name.[23] Taoism is clearly nature centered, while Confucianism tends to be more human centered. Neither tradition, however, succumbs to the problem of egocentric anthropocentrism or radical individualism such as has been characteristic of certain movements in the modern West. Both have a profound sense of the importance of nature as primary. For the Taoists nature is the basis of nourishing individual life and for the Confucians it is indispensable for sustaining communal life.

A Confucian ethic might be described as a form of social ecology because a key component is relationality in the human order against the background of the natural order. A profound sense of the interconnectedness of the human with one another and with nature is central to Confucian thinking. The individual is never seen as an isolated entity but always as a person in relation to another and to the cosmos. A useful image for describing the Confucian ethical system is a series of concentric circles with the person in the center. In the circle closest to the individual is one's family, then one's teachers, one's friends, the government, and in the outer circle is the universe itself. In the Confucian system relationality extends from the individual in the family outward to the cosmos. This worldview has been described as an anthropocosmic one, embracing heaven, earth, and human as an interactive whole.[24] In Confucianism from the time of the early classical text of the *Book of History,* heaven and earth have been called the great parents who have provided life and sustenance.[25] Just as parents in the family deserve filial respect, so do heaven and earth.[26] Indeed, we are told they should not be exploited wantonly by humans.

In Confucianism, then, the individual is both supported by and supportive of those in the other circles which surround him or her. The exchange of mutual obligations and responsibilities between the individual, others in these circles, and the cosmos itself constitute the relational basis of Confucian societies. Like a social glue, the give and take of these relationships help to give shape and character to these societies. Many of these patterns of social and cosmological exchanges become embedded in rituals which constitute the means of expressing reciprocal relations between people and with nature. Thus the value of mutual reciprocity and of belonging to a series of groups is fostered in Confucian societies. In all of this, education was critical. As the *Great Learning (Ta Hsueh)* so clearly demonstrates, to establish peace under heaven we must begin with the cultivation of the mind-and-heart of the person.[27] Education for the Confucians embraced the moral and intellectual dimensions of a person and was intended to prepare them to be a fully contributing citizen to the larger society.

In addition to these ethical patterns of social ecology for the individual in relation to others and to the cosmos itself, Confucianism developed an elaborate theory of government which might be described as a political ecology. Taking the same model of the individual embedded in a series of concentric circles, the Confucians situated the emperor at the center and suggested that his moral example would have a rippling effect outward like a pebble dropped into a pond. The influence of this morality would be felt by all the people and humane government would be possible when the emperor had compassion on the people and established appropriate economic, social, and ecological policies.

Thus while both Confucianism and Taoism are relational in their overall orientation, Confucianism is clearly more activist, especially with regard to moral leadership and practical policies. Many of the principles of humane government such as those advocated by Mencius and other Confucians include policies such as an ecological sensitivity to land and other resources, equitable distribution of goods and services, fair taxation, and allowing the people to enjoy nature and cultivate human relations.[28] The recognition that humane government rests on sustainable agriculture and maintaining a balance with nature is key to all Confucian political thought.

Thus both in terms of individuals and society as a whole there was a concern for larger relationships that would lead toward harmony of people with one another and with nature, which supported them. This social and political ecology within an anthropocosmic worldview has something to offer in our own period of rampant individualism, self-interested government, and exploitation of natural resources. The continuation of cooperative group effort to achieve common goals that are for the benefit of the whole society is an important model for a new form of social ecology. At the same time the ideal of humane government which develops and distributes resources equitably is central to a political ecology so much needed at the present.

CONCLUSION

This essay only begins to suggest some of the rich resources available in the traditions of Taoism and Confucianism for formulating an ecological cosmology and an environmental ethics in our time. As we seek a new balance in human-earth relations, it is clear that the perspectives from other religious and philosophical traditions may be instrumental in formulating new ways of thinking and acting more appropriate to both the vast rhythms and the inevitable limitations of nature. As our worldview in relation to nature is more clearly defined, we can hope that our actions will reflect both a Taoist appreciation for natural ecology and a Confucian commitment to social and political ecology.

NOTES

1. *Commentary on the Lao Tzu*, trans. Wing-tsit Chan, in *A Source Book in Chinese Philosophy* (Princeton: Princeton University Press, 1963), 321.

2. *Mencius* 1A:5, trans. Wing-tsit Chan, *A Source Book in Chinese Philosophy*, 61.

3. Thomas Berry wrote: "The religious traditions must not only become acclimated to the new scientific and technological environment, they must undergo a breathtaking expansion of their own horizons as they become universalized, mutually present to each other, and begin creation of the multiform global religious tradition of humankind, a tradition that is already further advanced in the realities of human history than in the books we write." From "Future Forms of Religious Experience," in Berry's Riverdale Papers (an unpublished collection of essays).

4. Tu Wei-ming, "Beyond the Enlightenment Mentality: An Exploration of Spiritual Resources in the Global Community," a paper presented at the Fourth Conference on World Spirituality, East-West Center, Honolulu, June 15–19, 1992, and adapted for publication in this volume of *Bucknell Review*.

5. The Chinese have not had a strong environmental

record in the modern period as demonstrated by Vaclay Smil, *The Bad Earth* (Armonk, N.Y.: Sharpe, 1984) and Lester Ross, *Environmental Policy in China* (Bloomington: Indiana University Press, 1988).

6. Charlene Spretnak has attempted such an examination in her comprehensive book *States of Grace* (San Francisco: Harper San Francisco, 1991). Another significant contribution is J. Baird Callicott and Roger T. Ames, eds., *Nature in Asian Traditions of Thought* (Albany: State University of New York Press, 1989).

7. This was also one of the aims of the Parliament of World Religions held in Chicago in September 1993.

8. Karl Jaspers describes the Axial period in his book *The Origin and Goal of History* (New Haven: Yale University Press, 1953).

9. For a more detailed account of this see Frederick Mote, *Intellectual Foundations of China* (New York: Knopf, 1971), chap. 2, and Tu Wei-ming's essays in *Confucian Thought: Selfhood as Creative Transformation* (Albany: State University of New York Press, 1985), esp. "The Continuity of Being: Chinese Visions of Nature," 35–50.

10. Indeed, just as Rene Dubos noted the need for both a "passive" Franciscan model of reverence for nature along with the more "active" model of Benedictine stewardship in the West, so too can Taoism and Confucianism provide this complementary model. See Rene Dubos, "Franciscan Conservation versus Benedictine Stewardship" in *A God Within* (New York: Scribner's, 1972).

11. There are many editions of this text in English, including the James Legge translation (first published in 1891 and reissued by Dover in 1962), the Witter Bynner translation (published by Capricorn in 1944), the D. C. Lau translation (published by Penguin in 1963). See also Wing-tsit Chan's translation in *A Source Book in Chinese Philosophy.*

12. The *Tao te Ching,* chap. 1. Unless otherwise noted, the translations here are Wing-tsit Chan's; subsequent references will be cited by chapter number in the text.

13. The term "deep ecology" implies that the human is deeply embedded in nature and not set apart from it. This term was coined by Arne Naess and is developed by Bill Devall and George Sessions in their book *Deep Ecology* (Salt Lake City, Utah: Peregrine Smith, 1985).

14. Witter Bynner translates the opening of chapter 29 of the *Tao te Ching:* "Those who would take over the earth / and shape it to their will / Never, I notice, succeed." (Chan and Lau translate "earth" as "empire.")

15. See the *Tao te Ching,* chaps. 18, 19, 20, and 38 for examples of this.

16. See the *Tao te Ching,* chaps. 29, 37, 43, 48, 63 and 64.

17. See the *Tao te Ching,* chaps. 6, 10, 20, 25, 28, 32, 52, 55, 59, 78.

18. The degree of our contemporary hubris toward nature is revealed in an editorial essay in *Time,* 17 June 1991: "Nature is our ward. It is not our master. It is to be respected and even cultivated. But it is man's world. And when man has to choose between his well-being and that of nature, nature will have to accommodate."

19. See Arthur Waley's translation of the *Analects* (New York: Vintage Books, 1938) and D. C. Lau's translation of *Mencius* (Harmondsworth: Penguin Books, 1970).

20. See Tu Wei-ming's essays in *Confucian Thought,* esp. "The Continuity of Being"; also see Mote, *Intellectual Foundations of China,* chap. 2.

21. See Mote, *Intellectual Foundations of China,* 17–18.

22. See Herbert Fingarette, *Confucius—The Secular as Sacred* (New York: Harper Torchbooks, 1972).

23. Social ecology has been developed by such theorists as Murray Bookchin. See his book *The Ecology of Freedom: The Emergence and Dissolution of Hierarchy* (Palo Alto, Calif.: Chesire Books, 1982). However, in contrast to Bookchin's position, which chooses to ignore the spiritual dimensions of ecology in the interest of establishing social justice in the human order, Confucianism tends to see the individual as embedded in a spiritual universe infused with *ch'i* (matter-energy). Harmonizing with the *ch'i* in the universe is essential for humans in a Confucian framework.

24. See Tu Wei-ming's use of this term in *Centrality and Commonality* (Albany: State University of New York Press, 1989) and in *Confucian Thought.*

25. See Book of Chou, The Great Declaration, *The Chinese Classics,* vol. 3, *Book of History,* trans. James Legge (Oxford: Clarendon Press, 1865), 283.

26. See Kaibara Ekken's *Yamato Zokkun,* translated in my book *Moral and Spiritual Cultivation in Japanese Neo-Confucianism* (Albany: State University of New York Press, 1989) 54–55, 136–42.

27. See the *Great Learning,* trans. Wing-tsit Chan, *Source Book in Chinese Philosophy,* 84–94.

28. See examples of humane government in book 1 of *Mencius.*

On the Environmental Ethics of the *Tao* and the *Ch'i*

CHUNG-YING CHENG

How the *Tao* applies to the ecological understanding of the human environment for the purpose of human well-being as well as for the harmony of nature is an interesting and crucial issue for both environmentalists and philosophers of the *Tao*. I formulate five basic axioms for an environmental ethic of the *Tao:* (1) the axiom of total interpenetration; (2) the axiom of self-transformation; (3) the axiom of creative spontaneity; (4) the axiom of a will not to will; and (5) the axiom of non-attaching attachment. I show that each axiom generates important consequences for environmental ethics and that together they provide a necessary foundation for environmental ethics.

I. METHODOLOGICAL CONSIDERATIONS

Although environmental ethics is one of the applied ethics arising from contemporary interest in applying and exploring certain ethical concepts and positions in relation to a set of concrete situations which human persons confront in their life world,[1] a close reflection on this applied ethics leads to a metaphysical critique of certain basic ethical positions concerning relationships of human beings to nature, to other human beings, and to themselves. The fact is that ethics cannot be applied until we have a clear understanding of the underlying concepts of the human person and his/her end-values as well as a clear understanding of the objects or situations to which the applications pertain. Both understandings require a disclosure of presupposed reality and, therefore, a resolution on the order or scheme of things in which human persons find themselves.

Methodologically speaking, we could treat problems of applied ethics at three levels: the metaethical level, where meanings of ethical terms are clarified; the metaphysical level, where the fundamental premises of the nature of reality are examined; and finally, the normative level, where ethical norms of actions and attitudes are formulated. Environmental ethics apparently cannot be clearly understood until we come to grips with these three levels of understanding. This approach is particularly appropriate in consideration of the fact that environmental ethics is not a well-formed system of ethical concepts, and that no system of norms for this ethical concern has been fully formulated and agreed upon. The openness of this field is a feature not to be deplored, but to be commended, because inquiry into identifying its problems, not even to say resolving its problems, is a worthy methodological and metaphysical exercise and will be rewarding in terms of possible creative insights, not only into environmental-ethical issues, but also into a deeper foundation for ethics in general. We may indeed consider the three levels of understanding mentioned above as pertaining to the analytics of ethics, the teleology of ethics, and the deontology of ethics. In dealing with environmental ethics we must be concerned with its analytical, its teleological, as well as its deontological dimensions.[2]

II. ANALYTICAL CONSIDERATIONS

One central question for environmental ethics which must be raised before any other questions is what the term *environment* means or stands for. *Environment* is derived from *environs,* meaning "in circuit" or "turning around in" in Old French.[3] It is apparently a prepositional word, indicating an external relation without a context, also certainly devoid of a rela-

Cheng, Chung-ying, "On the Environmental Ethics of the *Tao* and the *Ch'i*," *Environmental Ethics* 8 (1986), pp. 351–370. Reprinted by permission of the author.

tionship of organic interdependence. Yet when we reflect on the experience of environment, we encounter many different things and different processes in the context of organic interdependence. We might say what we experience presupposes the existence of life and the living processes of many forms. This experience of environment is better expressed by the Chinese philosophical paradigm, *sheng-sheng-pu-yi* ("incessant activity of life creativity").[4] We must, therefore, make a distinction between a surface meaning and a depth meaning for environment. Without understanding life and the living process of life, we cannot understand the depth meaning of environment. On the other hand, without understanding the constituents and conditions of life, we cannot understand life and the living process of life. Hence, the very essence of environment requires an understanding of reality and the true identity of life in both its state and process aspects. This means we have to understand the *Tao* content and the *Tao* process in the environment, whereas Tao indicates the way of life-creativity in ceaseless movements and in a multitude of forms.

With the above analysis of the meaning of environment, it is clear that the essential depth meaning of environment was lost in modern man's conception of environment. The modern man's conception of environment is founded on the surface meaning of environment, which is typified by technology and science; with its underlying philosophy of modern-day materialism, Cartesian dualism, and mechanistic naturalism, the concept of environment of modern man was very much objectified, mechanized, rigidified, dehumanized, and possibly even de-enlivened, and so de-environmentalized.[5] Environment is no longer an environment at all; environment becomes simply "the surroundings," the physical periphery, the material conditions and the transient circumstances. The environment is conceived as a passive deadwood, and very often as only visible and tangible externalia. In fact, as the depth meaning of environment suggested above, environment is active life; it is not necessarily visible or tangible, and certainly it cannot be simply a matter of externality. Hence, it cannot be treated as an object, the material conditions, a machine tool, or a transient feature. Environment is more than the visible, more than the tangible, more than the external, more than a matter of quantified period of time or a spread of space. It has a deep structure as well as a deep process, as the concept of *Tao* indicates.

The distinction between the surface meaning and the depth meaning of environment also suggests a distinction between the Western and the Chinese approach to environment. Whereas the West focuses on the external relation of man to his surroundings based upon a qualitative separation and confrontation between the human and nonhuman worlds, the Chinese focus on the internal relation of man to his surroundings based upon an integrative interdependence and a harmony between man and the world. For modern Western man after Descartes, the nonhuman world is to be rationally studied, researched, and then scientifically manipulated and exploited for the maximum utility of serving man. This will to conquer and dominate nature is, of course, premised on the externality of nature to man, but there are two other rational principles or assumptions involved in exercising this will to conquer and dominate.

First, it is assumed that nature is a completed work of mechanical forces with one-dimensional natural laws controlling its workings. The one-dimensional natural laws are revealed in the physical sciences and the reductionistic methodology of physicalism. Hence, biological laws are very often reduced to laws of physics and chemistry; no other laws are permitted to stand on their own. Yet the relationship between various forms of life in the totality of nature cannot be said to be fully captured by physicalistic laws; nor can the relationship between man and the world of things be said to be regulated by these laws. The very fact of the breakdown of the environment in industrialized societies, as reflected, for example, in the problems of water-air-noise pollution, precisely points to the lack of understanding of the relationship between various forms of life and man and his environment by way of modern science and technology.

There is a second assumption of the modern mechanical sciences: everything in the world forms an entity on its own as a closed system, and therefore can be individually and separately dealt with. This isolationist and atomistic assumption in the problem-solving methodology of modern science is strongly reflected in Western medical diagnostics and treatments. It was not until recent times that modern medical and health care researchers became aware of the potential limitations of this isolationist and atomistic approach, and became awakened to a holistic approach.

In contrast with the Western externalistic point of view on environment, the Chinese tradition, as represented by both Confucianism (with the *I Ching* as its metaphysical philosophy) and Taoism (with Chuang Tzu and Lao Tzu as its content), has developed an internalistic point of view on the environment. The internalistic point of view on the environment in Chinese philosophy focuses on man as the *consummator* of nature rather than man as the conqueror of nature, as a participant in nature rather than as a predator of nature. Man as the consummator of nature expresses continuously the beauty, truth, and goodness of nature; and articulates them in a moral or a natural cultivation of human life or human nature. This is paradigmatically well expressed in Confucius' saying, "Man can enlarge the Way (*Tao*) rather than the Way enlarging man."[6] It is also expressed in Chuang Tzu's saying, "The *Tao* penetrates and forms a Unity."[7] As part and parcel of nature, man does not stand opposite nature in a hostile way. On the contrary, man has profound concern and care for nature at large, as befitting his own nature. For his own growth and well-being, man has to cultivate the internal link in him between himself and Mother Nature. To conquer nature and exploit it is a form of self-destruction and self-abasement for man. The material consequence of the conquest and exploitation must be forestalled by an awakening to what man really is or in what his nature really consists.

In contrast with the two Western assumptions about the environment, Chinese philosophy clearly asserts that nature, and therefore man's environment, is not a complete work of production by a transcendent God, but rather is a process of continuous production and reproduction of life. In Bruno's words, nature is *Natura naturans,* not merely *Natura naturata*. In other words, nature is an organism of continuous growth and decay, but never devoid of internal life. With this understanding men cannot treat nature as an isolated and atomic part without regard for the totality involving a past and a future. This leads to the second understanding contrary to the Western methodology of atomism: man has to interact with nature in a totalistic manner, realizing that there is no single linear chain of causality. There is always a many-to-many relationship between cause and effect. Hence, man has to consider a many-to-many level approach to relate the potential needs of man to nature. Man has to naturalize man as well as to humanize nature, treating nature as his equal and as a member within the family of the *Tao*. This approach to nature is reflected in the holistic approach of Chinese medicine in both its diagnostic and medical/health care aspects.

The modern mandarin translation for *environment* is *huan-chin,* meaning "world of surroundings." This translation apparently reflects the surface meaning of *environment* correctly. But when embedded in the contexts of Chinese philosophy and Chinese cultural consciousness the "world of surroundings" does not simply denote individual things as entities in a microscopic structure; it also connotes a many-layered reality such as heaven and earth in a macroscopic enfoldment. This "world of surroundings" is generally conceived as something not static but dynamic, something not simply visible but invisible. It is in this sense of environment that we can speak of the *tao* as the true environment of man: the true environment of man is also the true environment of nature or everything else in nature.

When asked about the presence of the *tao,* Chuang Tzu had this to say: "(The *tao* is) nowhere not present." Pressed as to where exactly the *tao* lies, Chuang Tzu replied that the *tao* is in the ants, in the weeds, in the ruins, and in the dungs.[8] The import of Chuang Tzu's message is that the *tao* embraces everything, large or small, in the universe and imparts a unity of relationships in our environment, and that the *tao* is a totality as well as a part of the totality pervading everything beyond our perception so that we cannot ignore what is hidden in our understanding of the environment. If understanding is the basis for action, this understanding of the environment in terms of the *tao* is very essential for formulating an ethic of the environment, namely for articulating what human persons should do or attitudinize toward their world of surroundings. Two more observations have to be made in order to explicate the philosophy of the *tao* for the purpose of the formulating an environmental ethics of the *tao* or an ethics of the environment based on an understanding of the *tao*.

The first observation concerns the *Tao* as the *tzu-jan. Tzu-jan* means "doing-something-on-its-own-accord," or natural spontaneity. In the *Tao Te Ching* it is said that "Man follows earth; earth follows heaven; heaven follows the *Tao* and the *Tao* follows *tzu-jan*."[9] But *tzu-jan* is not something beyond and above the *Tao*. It is the movement of the *Tao* as the *Tao*, namely as the underlying unity of all things as well as the underlying source of the life of all things. One important aspect of *tzu-jan* is that the movement of things must come from the *internal life* of things and never results from engineering or conditioning by an external power. That is why the life-creativity nature of the *Tao* is the only proper way of describing the nature of the movement of the *Tao*. However, to say this is not to say that only the *Tao* can have the movement of *tzu-jan*. In fact, all things can follow *tzu-jan* insofar as they follow the *Tao*, or in other words, act and move in the manner of the *Tao* and in unison and in accordance with the *Tao*. Perhaps a better way of expressing this is: things will move of their own accord (*tzu-jan*) insofar as they move by way of the *Tao* and the *Tao* moves by way of them. One has to distinguish between, on the one hand, *Tao*-oriented or *Tao*-founded movement and, on the other hand, thing-oriented or thing-founded movement. Only when the movement of a thing comes from the deep source of the thing—the *Tao* and its harmony with the totality of the movements of all other things—will the movement of things be genuinely of its own accord and, therefore, be spontaneous. Spontaneity (*tzu-jan*) is a matter of infinite depth and infinite breadth in an onto-cosmological sense.

One can, of course, speak of different degrees of *tzu-jan* in view of the different degrees of depth and breadth in harmonious relating and self-assertion among things. Just things have their own histories [*sic*] and defining characteristics in form and substance, things also have their relative freedom of self-movement and life-creativity. Things, in fact, can be considered as conditions or preconditions of various forms of *tzu-jan* (spontaneity): insofar as things preserve their identity without destroying the identities of other things, and insofar as things change and transform without interfering with the process of change and transformation of other things, there is *tzu-jan*. This explains the mutual movement, rise and decline, ebb and flow, in things of nature.

For human beings, *tzu-jan* finds its rationale not only in the internal movement and life-creativity of human activity, but in the principle of least effort with maximum effect. Whatever produces maximum effect by minimum effort in human activity manifests natural spontaneity. One may, therefore, suggest that only in following natural spontaneity is there least effort and maximum effect. This can be called the *ecological principle of nature*.[10] Using this principle we can correctly interpret the most important point ever made about the nature of the *Tao*: "The *Tao* constantly does nothing and yet everything is being done" (*Tao-chang-wu-wei erh wu-pu-wei*).[11] That the *Tao* constantly does nothing means that the *Tao* does not impose itself on things: the *Tao* only moves of its own accord. This also means that all things come into being on their own accord. The constant nonaction of the *Tao* is the ultimate cosmological principle of life-creativity and the only foundation for the evolution of the variety of life and the multitude of things. The nonaction of the *Tao* in this sense is an intrinsic principle of ultimate creativity; this intrinsic principle of ultimate creativity consists in an unlimitedness and an unlimitation of expression of life forms and life processes in a state of universal harmony and in a process of universal transformation.[12] In this ultimate sense of creativity, there is no effort made by the *Tao*, and yet there is an infinite effect, achieving life-creativity. The ecological principle reaches its ultimate limit in the principle of *chang-wu-wei*. Hence, we can conceive of the principle of least effort with maximum effect as an approximation to the *tzu-jan* of the *Tao* on the human plane.

With this principle correctly understood, we can resolve the dilemma and predicament arising from civilization and knowledge. The Taoist questions the value of knowledge and civilization, since they lead to greed, lust, and evil (tricks and treachery) in human society. In the same spirit, we can question the value of science and technology. In resolving many problems of man, do science and technology create more problems for man? Do science and technology seem to lead man to a purely pessimistic future? The Taoistic criticism here is that without an understanding of the *Tao* it is indeed possible and necessary that knowledge and civilization, science and technology, will doom man to self-slavery and self-destruction. Man simply falls into the bondage of his own conceptual prison and becomes a victim of his own desires. The Taoistic criticism of *wu-wei* is supposed to awaken man to self-examination and self-doubt; in this way man is awakened to a quest for self-surpassing and self-overcoming in an understanding of the totality of reality and its secret of creativity through *wu-wei* and reversion (*fan*).[13] With this awakening, man can still proceed with his knowledge and civilization, science and technology, if he is able to neutralize and temper his intellectual and intellectualistic efforts with a sense of the *Tao*. This means that man has to develop knowledge and civilization, science and technology, not out of pace with his efforts to relate to things, other humans and himself. His knowledge and civilization, science and technology, have to contribute to his relating to and integrating with the world of his surroundings. To do this he has to keep pace with his own growth as a sentient moral being, having regard and respect for his own identity and dignity as well as the identity and dignity of other beings, including his fellow man. Furthermore, he has to use his knowledge and, hence, science and technology, in keeping with the order of things, with his best interests conceived and deferred in harmony with life and in preservation or promotion of universal creativity. He also has to closely follow the principle of least effort, if not the principle of no effort, with maximum effect, if not infinite effect in terms of life and creativity—preservation and promotion—for his intellectual/scientific/technological/organizational activities.

As man is part and parcel of the *Tao,* it is only when man loses the sense of the *Tao* and respect for the *Tao* in his actual life that man becomes alienated from the *Tao* and his activities become a means of self-alienation which will inevitably result in losing the true identity of man by way of self-destruction. This is the natural and spontaneous reaction of the *Tao* to the self-alienation of man in his intellectual/scientific/exploitative engrossment and obsession with himself. Hence, the remedy for knowledge and civilization, or for science and technology, is not more knowledge and more civilization, or more science and more technology, but a constant relating and integrating of these with the *Tao*. To do so is to naturalize as well as humanize knowledge and civilization, science and technology. It is to make these a part of the *Tao*. Although knowledge and civilization, science and technology, are man's forms for the appropriation of nature (the *Tao*), these forms should not remain apart: man should also let nature reappropriate them by integrating them into nature (the *Tao*). This is the essential point of an ethics of man's relation to the environment. To understand the *Tao* and to follow the *Tao* is the essence of the ethics of the environment; it is also the way to transform the artificiality and unnaturalness of knowledge and civilization, science and technology, into the spontaneity and naturalness of the *Tao*.

In light of this understanding, the conflict between the *Tao* and knowledge/civilization/science/technology can be resolved; the true ecology and life-creativity of nature can be restored with knowledge/civilization/science/technology. They can be seen as enhancing rather than obstructing, complementing rather than opposing, the actual spontaneity and harmony of the creativity of the *Tao*. This is the true wisdom of the Taoist critique of knowledge and civilization, science and technology. It is called *hsi-ming,* "hidden light," by Lao Tzu, and *liang-hsing,* "parallel understanding," by Chuang Tzu.[14] In this wisdom lies the most profound principle of both the ecology of nature and the ethics of the environment.

My second observation concerns the *Tao* as a process of the ramification and differentiation of the *ch'i*. Before I explain the meaning and reality of *ch'i* in Chinese philosophy, it is important to appreciate the significance of bringing in *ch'i* as an explanation of the depth structure and depth process of the environment. We have seen that the depth structure and depth process of the environment has been explained in terms of the *Tao* and its life-creativity (*sheng-sheng*). Even though this explanation is necessary in pinpointing the ontological being and becoming of the environment, it is not sufficient, on the one hand, to illuminate the dynamics and dialectics of the differentiation and ramifications of the *Tao* and, on the other hand, to manifest those dynamics and dialectics of the unification and integration of the *Tao*. In other words, there is a gap between the ontology of the *Tao* and the cosmology of the *Tao* which must be bridged.

It is when the *Tao* is seen in the form and activity of *ch'i* that this bridging takes place. It might be suggested that the *Tao* expresses itself in terms of three perspectives which result in three characterizations in the history of Chinese philosophy. The first perspective is derived from understanding the quality of the activity: it is the perspective of life-creativity as clearly formulated in the texts of the *I Ching*. This perspective has already been discussed above. The second perspective is derived from understanding the patterns of the activity: it is the perspective of the movement of internal spontaneity, reversion and return, as clearly formulated in the texts of the *Tao Te Ching* as well as those of the *Chuang Tzu*. In fact, a concentration on the patterns of the movement of the *Tao* may lead one to see the *Tao* in terms of principles and reasons. The Neo-Confucianist metaphysics of *li* ("principle") is a logical result of this development. This development also leads to an epistemology of the *Tao*. In both the ontology of the *Tao* (life-creativity) and epistemology of the *Tao* (principles of nonaction, etc.), the *Tao* is always conceived as a totality and a unity; the nature of the unity and totality of the *Tao* is stressed above all. In fact, the very concept of the *Tao* carries with it a reference to its unity and totality. Yet the *Tao* is as much a distribution and diversification of being and becoming as a unity and totality of being and becoming. Hence, we need another explanation of this former aspect of the *Tao* which will also serve the purpose of cosmologizing the ontology and epistemology of the *Tao*. This is how the *Tao*-as-the-*ch'i* paradigm comes in. This is also how the concept of *ch'i* based on experience of the *Tao* as *ch'i* develops. We might therefore suggest that to understand environment in its depth meaning, one has to focus on both the totalistic and distributive aspects of the environment. Hence, one must focus on both the *Tao* as *tzu-jan* and the *Tao* as *ch'i*.

Another consideration with regard to the importance of the *Tao* as the *ch'i* is that whereas the *Tao* focuses on reality as a passage of dynamic processes, the *ch'i* focuses on reality as a presence of material—stuff which leads to an actualization of things and the concretization of events. Hence, for understanding the formation and transformation of the environment in its substantive structure, one has to understand *ch'i*. It is in understanding *ch'i* that one can see and grasp the subtleties of the environment *vis-à-vis* human beings. It is only on this basis (i.e., understanding the *Tao* as *ch'i*) that one is capable of formulating an ethics of the environment or an ethics of the *Tao* toward the environment.[15] For this reason, we may consider the discussion of the nature of *ch'i* as constituting a metaphysical inquiry into the depth structure and depth process of the environment. As the goal of an ethics of the environment is to understand how human beings should relate to the environment *via* a true understanding of environment, we may see how a metaphysical inquiry into the structure and process of the environment also constitutes a teleological inquiry into the nature of the environment in relation to man. It is only when we are able to understand the nature of the environment in its true identity that we are able to see what the end-values of our thinking about and acting toward the environment are. The end-values are provided by our understanding of reality: to act in accordance with reality and our true nature will be our end and ultimately will be the criterion of value. Hence, the metaphysics of the environment becomes a teleology of the environment, because that is where environmental ethics is grounded. With this foundation we can then rightly speak of an environmental ethics of the *Tao* which is the deontology of the *Tao*.

III. METAPHYSICAL TELEOLOGICAL CONSIDERATIONS

There are several passages in the *Tao Te Ching* which justify our attempt to explain the *Tao* in terms of the *ch'i*. In chapter fourteen of the *Tao Te Ching*, the *Tao* is described as something invisible, inaudible, and ingraspable.

> Being invisible is called the Great (*yi*); being inaudible is called the Silent (*hsi*); being ingraspable is called the Subtle (*wei*). The source of these three cannot be fully disclosed. They merge to form Oneness. The Above of this Oneness is not bright, and the Below of this Oneness is not dark. As a continuum it cannot be named, and it again vanishes no-thing-ness. It is therefore the form of no-form, the image of no object. It is called "Seeming-To-Be" (*fu-huang*).[16]

This description of the *Tao* is no doubt applicable to *ch'i* as the primary source of being and becoming. Hence, the *Tao* is *Tao*-as-*ch'i*, and the *ch'i* is *ch'i*-as-*Tao*. In chapter twenty-one of the *Tao Te Ching*, the *Tao* is again described as being constantly indeterminate and unformed (*fu-huang*), and obscure and dark (*yao-min*), and yet containing and yielding concrete things.

> The *Tao* is something indeterminate and unformed. Being indeterminate and unformed, there emerges the forms; being unformed and indeterminate, there emerges the things. Being

> obscure and dark, there emerges the essences (*chin*); these essences are very real, wherein the truth (*hsin*) exists.[16]

The essences (*chin*) are generally explained by commentators as the *chin-ch'i*, or the quintessential *ch'i*, which is the primary or elementary *ch'i*.[17] In this way, it is possible to state how the *Tao* is related to the *ch'i*: *Tao* in its actual movements becomes the *ch'i*. Or alternatively speaking, the movement of the *ch'i* is the *Tao*. In fact, chapter twenty-five of the *Tao Te Ching* gives an even more vivid characterization of the *Tao* as *ch'i*, i.e., as something which is the primary substance for all things.

> There is something which comes into being before heaven and earth. It is silent and formless. It exists without depending on anything else. It moves in circles ceaselessly. I do not know its name, so I just call it the Tao. I also try to call it the Great. The Great is passing; the Passing is distant; the Distant returns to its own.[18]

Although Lao Tzu does not speak straightforwardly about the *Tao* as *ch'i*, it remains clear that the *Tao* must present itself as the *ch'i* for the purpose of cosmos making and thing making. In other words, to speak of the *Tao* as *ch'i* is necessary insofar as there is a need for explaining the constitution of the world of things. Similarly, in order to satisfy the need to explain the totalistic and transformational nature of things, one has to speak of the *ch'i* as *Tao*. It is only when one understands the *Tao* in the form of *ch'i* and *ch'i* in the form of *Tao* that we are able to understand thoroughly the nature of reality which forms our environment, and which defines a teleology of end-values for our ethical demands on our behavior toward the environment.[19] In the following, I give a characterization of *Tao* as *ch'i* by answering the question, "What is *ch'i*?" I follow the classical literature on *ch'i* in *Lao Tzu*, *Chuang Tzu*, *Kuan Tzu*, and the *I Ching*, and even more importantly, in the classic of Chinese medicine, the *Nei Ching*.

What is ch'i? Ch'i is the most fundamental concept in Chinese philosophy as well as in Chinese common sense. *Ch'i* has been variously translated into English as "material force," "vital force," and "energy." Like many fundamental Chinese philosophical terms, no translation captures its full meaning. In fact, all existing translations conceal and obscure the rich experiential structure of meaning in the concept of *ch'i*. It is important to recognize that the concept of *ch'i* already contains a metaphysical theory, an epistemological theory, and a scientific theory. It also contains a structure of levels and implies a process of stages. *Ch'i*, on the natural level, is simply the vapor in the form of steam over the rice paddies and the cloud/mists in the sky. On the human level, with regard to human daily experience, *ch'i* is simply breath. As breath is linked to air, so *ch'i* covers organic life-energy and the energy in nature in various forms. Hence, nothing in human body is not *ch'i* and nothing in nature is not *ch'i*. There are two important conditions involved in understanding *ch'i*: (1) *ch'i* is the vital energy of no form. It moves, rests, goes and comes, condenses and stretches. In other words, it transforms; (2) *ch'i*, nevertheless, forms all things in the universe: it can change into various forms depending on how it moves and rests and how it relates to things formed from *ch'i*. By itself *ch'i* does not have any determinate form (indeed, no form at all). But it is precisely because of its indeterminateness and inner capacity of creativity that *ch'i* can creatively form into things, and this in turn is the reason why things have no permanent form and substance. Ultimately the life and death of man and other species have to be explained on the basis of the impermanence of the form of *ch'i*.

The onto-cosmology of *ch'i* has been developed to the extent that to think of *ch'i* one also has to recognize three other characteristics of *ch'i*. (1) *Ch'i* is universally present; it is not confined to a single region, just as it is not confined to a simple form. Hence, there exists a universal sympathy and consanguinity among things in the universe. Yet, the difference in kind, structure, and level of things makes a difference of degrees of sympathy and consanguinity among things. To discover which things are in sympathetic resonance and which things are not are two important efforts in both traditional applied environmental analysis (*feng-shui*) and diagnosis/heading therapy in Chinese medicine.

(2) In the pre-Chin philosophy of *ch'i*, the order, structure, and form exhibited by *ch'i* are inherent in and internal to the *ch'i* itself. As to how different things are formed, the apparent randomness of *ch'i* actually conceals an ordering force of balance, control, cohesion, sustenance, and qualitative elevation or evolution. Hence, *ch'i* is not to be conceived as an arbitrary chaotic existence: it is to be conceived as

leading to seasoned and proportionate evolution and sustenance of life. In fact, reason and principle (*li*) can be explained as the essence of *ch'i*, i.e., as that which constitutes the nature of *ch'i* insofar as *ch'i* behaves in accordance with them. Hence, one should not speak of *li* apart from or external to *ch'i*. *Li* belongs to *ch'i*. This explains why there are orderly principles in the formation of the natural world and human physiology, and similarly why nature in itself exhibits regularity and produces *laws* and *patterns* open to human understanding. The possibility of human understanding can indeed be explained as the sympathetic activities of *ch'i* inside one person in resonance with *ch'i* externally in the world.

(3) The basic order inherent in *ch'i* is exhibited in the distinction between *yin* and *yang*. *Yin* and *yang* refer to two aspects of *ch'i* as a whole; yet in the process of change and transformation one aspect could become dominant. As such the dominant aspect of *ch'i* becomes perceptible and is experienced. Yet, at the same time, the other aspect continues to exist or subsist, although it takes a subtle mind to experience it, and it takes a period of time to see its functioning. *Yin* and *yang* originally referred respectively to the shady and the lighted (the bright) under the sun. Both the shady and the bright have light as their central subject. Similarly, the *yin* and *yang* have *ch'i* as their central subject.

In terms of the *yin/yang* distinction we can speak of two polarities of *ch'i*. In doing this, we must remember that the *yin/yang* concepts have primary experiential roots. They are not arbitrary inventions of man, but instead reflect deep features of the nature of *ch'i*. Thus, we can speak of *yin-ch'i* and *yang-ch'i*. In light of the primary experience of *ch'i*, one can immediately see how *yang-ch'i* can be interpreted and perceived in motion, brightness, and firmness (*kang*), and *yin-ch'i* in rest, darkness, and softness (*jou*). The reason for this interpretation is experiential: *yang-ch'i* or *yin-ch'i* is not experienced as a definite single quality, but rather is experienced as an indefinite mass phenomenon, the nature of which reveals itself in different ways under different circumstances. Hence, in terms of the *yin/yang* distinction, an indefinite subcategorization for either *yin* or *yang* can be introduced by way of sympathetic understanding and in spontaneous revelation. In addition to the *yang* natures of motion/light/firmness and the *yin* natures of rest/shade/softness, a long list of other qualities or states of things can also be divided naturally into *yin/yang* groups. In each of these divisions, an identification of the *yin* and the *yang* will enrich and make more definitive the *yin/yang* experiences and their corresponding concepts. Yet no complete distinction and exhaustion of the *yin/yang* totality can be given. Perhaps, we can speak of an inductive and implicit definition of the *yin/yang*: *yin/yang* are those natures or qualities compatible with and strengthening those natures or qualities already known as *yin/yang*.

Philosophically speaking, both the *I Ching* and Lao Tzu's *Tao Te Ching* have conveyed a general criterion for distinguishing between *yin/yang*. *Yin* is passive, receptive, close-in, downward, soft, resting, and background-like, whereas *yang* is active, creative, open-ended, upward, firm, moving, and foreground-like. *Yin/yang* become more clearly described when we look at them relative to concrete things on different levels. Therefore, we can speak of heaven/earth as *yin/yang*, man/woman as *yin/yang*, life/death as *yin/yang*, etc. In each case, of course, the substantive reference to *ch'i* is presupposed, for apart from *ch'i* how can the *yin/yang* become discovered or revealed? In reference to *ch'i*, we can establish the following list of *yin/yang* distinctions:

> For *yin:* shade/rest/softness/cold/the weak/closure;
> For *yang:* light/motion/firmness/hot/the strong/openness.

There are five principles governing *yin/yang* distinctions:

(1) *The principle of universality. Yin/yang* exist in all things and for all things on different levels. Indeed, it is because of the *yin/yang* distinction that things come to exist in different kinds and on different levels. This is related to the principle of creativity established by the *I Ching*.

(2) *The principle of relationality.* The *yin* and the *yang* always exist in close relation to each other, which should explain how things are always related in *yin/yang*. Insofar as there are relations, there are *yin/yang* distinctions and unities underlying all things. The relationships are established in accordance with the next principle.

(3) *The principle of opposite complementarity. Yin/yang* form a unity in which *yin* and *yang* are opposite to each other, and yet depend on each

other, and therefore complement each other for their being distinguished as opposites. What makes opposite complementarity possible is the pervading unity I spoke of earlier. The opposite complementarity is opposite because of difference, and complementary because of unity. Unity and difference exist at the same time as internal natures of the *ch'i* or as internal dynamical tendencies in the *ch'i.* As such, we can speak of the unifying and differentiating aspects of *ch'i* which give rise to *yin/yang* and their natural bond of oneness in difference and opposition. This is again made very clear in the *I Ching.* In light of this principle, we may indeed speak of *yin/yang* as polarities of *ch'i.*

(4) *The principle of relativity.* All states of *ch'i* and hence all things, can be both *yin* and *yang* relative to different states of *ch'i* or things. As individual things *ch'i* reveals a manifold of contexts in which things are related. Hence, no single *yin/yang* distinction is sufficient to characterize things in their relation to many other things. A wife who is an employer can be *yin* relative to her husband, but can be *yang* relative to her employees. In fact, she can be both *yin* and *yang* to the same object, depending on the contexts of relationships which give rise to differences of activities and positions. A network of *yin/yang* develops for a single state of *ch'i* or an individual thing. One can see how complex the human body or the whole universe can be presented in terms of a network of the *yin/yang.*

(5) *The principle of creativity.* With the polarity of *yin/yang* aspects inherent in *ch'i,* activities involving the disturbance of the balance or harmony in *yin/yang,* the development of a new level of balance or harmony, or the restoration of a given balance and harmony are possible. In fact, all things in the universe are results of the creative activities of *yin/yang;* and all these creative activities are actual results of *yin/yang* movements of opposition and unity. By *yin* alone or by *yang* alone there can be no continuation of life and creativity. Since there are life and creativity in the evolution of new entities or new generation of things, *yin/yang* can be perceived as ever present among all things. In regard to this creative capacity, the *yin/yang* unity of differences is specifically called the *ta'i-chi* (the great ultimate). It is clear that the *ta'i-chi* is *ch'i* in its totality, the ever-renewing activities of producing and maintaining the order of things in the environment of man.

Given these principles, it is easy to see how the Chinese notion of the natural environment, insofar as it is developed on the basis of *ch'i*-philosophy, and hence in terms of the *yin/yang* distinction, is totalistic, phenomenalistic, and organismic. The reason is simple. *Ch'i* with its internal *yin/yang* activities is totalistic, phenomenalistic, and organismic, since *ch'i* is a totality, dynamically presenting itself on different levels of reality, and yet well-related with reference to all its parts. These characteristics of *ch'i* not only lead to the development of a conception of the natural environment as a *ch'i* differentiation without loss of its unity, but also as a process, on the one hand, constantly involving the internal interaction of its parts and circulation within the *ch'i,* and, on the other, constantly involving the human *ch'i* with external things in the world. The purpose of environmental care is to maintain both the internal and external harmony of the dynamical interaction of *ch'i,* just as the purpose of medical care is to restore balance and harmony to either the disrupted internal state of *ch'i* or to the disrupted state of *ch'i* in reference to the external world. Chinese traditional environmental studies is precisely and intimately founded and developed on the basis of the *ch'i* philosophy.

With *ch'i* as the basic substance-process of all things in the world, we have the *yin/yang* activities of *ch'i* providing both a structure and a process of creative transformation among all things in the world. With regard to concrete things in the context of the *yin/yang* interchange, we have to introduce another structural distinction, the concretizing activities of the *ch'i* based on *yin/yang.* This is the distinction of *wu-hsing* (five powers). The "five powers" theory dates back to ancient times when people started to wonder about how things were constituted and related. Because *ch'i* philosophy recognizes *ch'i* as a dynamical power, the "five powers" are conceived as agencies rather than as elements, as processes rather than as states. Hence, the *wu-hsing* can be seen as five agencies or even five functions of *ch'i* realized in the concrete processes of things. The *wu-hsing* are powers of metal, wood, water, fire, and earth. The basic characteristics of these five powers are as follows: metal is sharp and cutting; wood is firm and growing; water is soft and penetrating; fire is bright and burning; and earth is solid, yet adjustable. In light of these basic characteristics, two orders of relationships can be established between them:

the generative order and the destructive order. These two orders can be described as follows: the generative order consists of wood generating fire, fire generating earth, earth generating metal, metal generating water, and water generating wood again; the destructive order consists of wood destructing earth, earth destructing water, water destructing fire, fire destructing metal, and metal destructing wood.

At the level of the five powers, *yin/yang* are still the background force, and indeed they can be considered the motivating force of the *wu-hsing*. Although each power can be analyzed into *yin/yang* components or aspects, they cannot be described as exclusively *yin* or exclusively *yang*. Thus, water is more *yin* than *yang*, fire more *yang* than *yin*, wood can be either more *yin* (*yin* wood) than yang or more yang (*yang* wood) than *yin;* similarly metal can be either more *yin* (*yin* metal) than *yang* or more *yang* (*yang* metal) than *yin*. Similarly, one can speak of a *yin* earth (more *yin* than *yang*) or *yang* earth (more *yang* than *yin*). This analysis is possible in terms of the light trigrams (*pa-kua*) of the *I Ching*, a generative-empirical (*hou-t'ien*/late heaven) arrangement, which precisely produces a generative order of the *wu-hsing* with more detailed *yin/yang* identification of the *wu-hsing*.

The significance of the *yin/yang* analysis of the *wu-hsing* theory for the Chinese conception of environment is that we can consider the opposite and complementary relations among *ch'i* structures, in the human being or between the human being and the external environment, not only in the second-order relations of generation/destruction of *wu-hsing*, but also in the primary-order relations of differentiation, unification, balancing, and harmonization of *yin/yang*. This means that the *I Ching* philosophy of the unity of difference and identity and its dialectics of transformation based on "one-dividing-into-two" and "two-unifying-into-one" are always in the background of the formation of views on human life, the environment, and their relationship in the Chinese tradition.[20]

IV. DEONTOLOGICAL/TRANS-DEONTOLOGICAL CONSIDERATIONS

What I have said above constitutes a metaphysical picture of reality on the basis of which our conception of the environment can be built. As reality is conceived in terms of *sheng-sheng* (life-creativity), *Tao* (the way of transformation), and *ch'i* (vital force), so environment can also be understood under these three categories, and thus can be seen as being intimately related to human beings in a relationship of part and whole: man is part of the environment; the environment is a part of man; and they both are a part of the same whole. It is evident that these propositions are meaningful in light of the *Tao* and *ch'i* metaphysics of reality as developed in the Chinese philosophical tradition. Although man and his environment may form different orders of their own, they also belong to the same totality, which is the universal process of transformation which is called the *Tao*. Within this totality of transformation, man and his environment are interdependent, interacting as well as interpenetrating elements. Hence, man cannot treat his environment as a mere object for knowing, controlling, and exploitation. The environment consists of many processes, involved with and related to the process exemplified and embodied in the *Tao*, life-creativity, and the *ch'i* properties. Hence, the environment should always preserve a unity, a harmony, and a balance inherent in the relationship of things and processes on an appropriate level. Man is part of this unity, harmony, and balance, and should contribute to their continuous sustenance and growth. This is the supreme categorical imperative for man's behavior toward the environment.

With the environment understood as *Tao* and *ch'i*, we can also deduce important conclusions regarding the misuse or abuse of the environment. The environment can react in a harmful way if it is itself harmed. This is a natural consequence of the intrinsic movement of reversal in the *Tao*. On the other hand, the environment can preserve life and enhance health, if life-preserving and health-enhancing measures are adopted by man in relation to the environment. The environment is a perfect mirror of man. Man's benevolence, justice, and integrity are reflected in the life-generating and health enhancing powers of the environment, just as human selfishness, inconsiderations, and cruelty are reflected in catastrophes and disasters in the environment. From this point of view, benevolence, justice, and integrity are not just simply human virtues toward one's fellow man and the human community, but are also virtues toward things and nature in general, since they can be conceived as life-preserving and health-enhancing powers of nature. On the basis of a metaphysical understanding of the environment, human ethics can be transformed into environmental ethics.

The environmental ethics of the *Tao* begins with an understanding of the *Tao*. After the *Tao* is understood, the *Tao* becomes the supreme end for man. Man has to treat nature as if there is an intrinsic end in nature. But the proper way of treating nature in this sense is to share and embody the *Tao* in nature; in other words, to achieve the supreme end of the *Tao* is to be with the *Tao*, in the *Tao*, and of the *Tao*. The environmental ethics of the *Tao* becomes an art of harmonizing with the *Tao*, as well as the art of self-realization in nature by way of the *Tao*. Here we may indeed say that our deontological duties toward nature or the environment come from nature or the environment itself. It may appear to be an imposition of nature on man independent of his understanding of nature. But when man comes to understand nature, the deontological considerations in the environmental ethics are no longer deontological. This is because the deontological becomes part of the teleology of nature; they represent what nature really is. It is in this sense that the environmental ethics of the *Tao* is not only founded on the basis of the environmental metaphysics of the Tao, but becomes one with it. Of course, we still can recognize that the metaphysics of the environment can produce a true picture of the nature of reality as an end.

We can now formulate four axioms of a metaphysics of the environment on the basis of our understanding of the reality as *Tao* process and *ch'i* structure. Then we can establish four corresponding principles of the deontology of environmental ethics on the basis of these four metaphysical axioms.

(1) *The axiom of Self-Transformation.* The *Tao*, or reality as the *Tao*, presents itself in a process of temporal, spatial, material, immaterial, and relational transformations. There is no simple linear relation of cause and effect, but a manifold of levels and dimensions in organic relation.

(2) *The axiom of Creative Spontaneity.* The creativity of reality consists in a natural process toward the emergence of life. Even though proper physical conditions for emergence of life are required, the emergence of life and its nourishing have to be conceived as inherent in a self-transforming movement of the *Tao* and *ch'i*. Life is not only part of the whole nature of *ch'i*, but it is vested in every particle and wave of the *ch'i*.

(3) *The axiom of Interpenetration.* All elements in nature are interdependent, interacting, and interpenetrating. There can be no real separation among them. Hence, there is the effect of the whole on the part and the effect of the part on the whole. No life process or creative effort can be achieved without taking into consideration the interpenetrating relationships of things.

(4) *The axiom of Harmonization.* All elements in nature can maintain a relationship of harmony and balance on relevant levels of being and becoming. There is always an inherent harmony pertinent to a given level of relationship. But to achieve a proper harmony on the proper level, one has to relate to all elements in a proper way on that level and also to relate to all elements in a proper way on lower levels. Otherwise, a natural return to a lower level of harmony would appear as an ecological breakdown of harmony on a higher level.

Corresponding to these four axioms of nature there are four corresponding deontological principles in man's relationship to nature or his environment.

(1) *The Principle of Harmonization.* Man has to preserve a sense of harmony with regard to nature. This sense of harmony should be articulated in his conscious efforts to love life and to appreciate what is good in life. This sense of harmony should not only be expressed in a sound conservationist position on the ecology of nature, but also in man's well coordinated strategies for cultural development. This is because nature and culture can enhance each other's value, and thus together enhance the value of life.

(2) *The Principle of Interpenetration.* Man has to develop science and design technology with a totalistic sense of reality. Man must recognize that there are visible and invisible elements of nature, and that there are many concentric circles of *ch'i* structures which all can act and react on the well-being of man. Man has to incorporate his understanding of the interpenetration among things in his technological exploration of nature. This is essential for making technology not only humanized, but naturalized as well.

(3) *The Principle of Creative Spontaneity.* Man has to learn to seek creativity in a spontaneous way so that he can contribute to the richness of life and harmony among things while fulfilling his own needs. In

becoming creative, following the *Tao* will help insure that man's research and invention do not issue from a desire to dominate or result in a will to control. Many things that men have done in history have been a waste of life and energy. This can be avoided by following the creative spontaneity of the *Tao*.

(4) *The Principle of Self-Transformation.* Man eventually has to learn to transform himself in accordance with the totality of reality. He has to see himself as embodying the *Tao,* and acting with a will not to will. It is only with this understanding that he is able to resolve conflicts within himself and conflicts between himself and the environment. His self-transformation consists in constantly interacting with nature so that he can be said to be part of nature and nature can be said to be a part of himself. It is in nature and the *Tao* that man should find his true self.

Whereas the four axioms of the environmental metaphysics of the *Tao* and the *ch'i* exhibit an order of ontogenesis, the corresponding deontological principles of the environmental ethics of the *Tao* and *ch'i* exhibit an order which returns to the source and embraces the totality. It is in this order of going back to the source and embracing the totality that the environmental ethics of the *Tao* and the *ch'i* transforms the metaphysics of the *Tao* and the *ch'i* not only into a teleology, but also into a deontology. The integration and unification of the teleological and the deontological in the metaphysics of the *Tao* and *ch'i* will eventually lead to a maturity of the environmental ethics of the *Tao* and *ch'i,* and it is in terms of this mature form of the environmental ethics of the *Tao* and *ch'i* that we will be able to speak of the embodiment of a new reason in the mind of man.

NOTES

1. J. Baird Callicott has traced the beginning of the origin of environmental ethics in some of his papers. See "Conceptual Resources for Environmental Ethics in Asian Traditions of Thought: A Propaedeutic," *Philosophy East and West* 37. no. 2 (1987) and "The Metaphysical Implications of Ecology," *Environmental Ethics* 8 (1986).

2. By *teleology* I actually mean the study of the metaphysics or ontology of ends or values for a given ethical concern. Therefore, the teleological corresponds to the metaphysical level of consideration. Similarly, the analytical corresponds to the metaethical level of consideration, whereas the deontological corresponds to the normative level of consideration.

3. Cf. Ernest Weekley, *An Etymological Dictionary of Modern English* (New York: Dover, 1967), p. 516 (*environ*), p. 1583 (*veer*).

4. *Sheng-sheng* is derived from the Great Appendix of the *I Ching,* sec. 5, where it is said that "*Sheng-sheng* is called the change." "*Pu-yi*" is derived from the *Book Of Poetry* in "Chou Sung," where it is said that "The mandate of Heaven is indeed profound and incessant (*pu-yi*)." This stanza is quoted in *Chung Yung* to describe the depth and width of the reality of Heaven and Earth. It is quite clear that the incessant activity of life-creativity is precisely what the *Tao* is. As a life-experience based concept of reality, *Tao* was universally conceived by ancient philosophers as a universal process of change and transformation as well as the fountainhead of all forms of life in the world. Therefore, *Tao* can be said to be the in-depth foundation, background, and context of the so-called environment for any sentient being. We shall see a more metaphysical consideration of the *Tao* in the writings of Lao Tzu.

5. When I use the word *objectified,* I mean "being treated as an object"; when I use the word *mechanized,* I mean "being used merely as a machine"; when I use the word *rigidified,* I mean "being placed in the state of *rigor mortis;* and when I use the word *de-enlivened,* I mean "being depleted of life and the living process"; when I use the word *dehumanized,* I mean "being given no consideration of human feeling and care"; finally, when I use the word *de-environmentalized,* I mean "being devalued as environment."

6. *Analects,* 15: 28.

7. *Chuang Tzu,* Chi Wu Lun.

8. See the Chih Pei Yu chapter of *Chuang Tzu.*

9. *Tao Te Ching,* 25.

10. *Ecology* originally meant the economy of nature; when nature acts, it acts ecologically. The production of life and all things in nature can be said to come from the ecological movement of nature. In understanding the ecology of nature, one would naturally understand the *Tao;* but only when one independently sees the universality, unity, and life-creativity of the *Tao,* will one truly understand the ecology of nature. Hence, the *Tao* can be said to be the metaphysical foundation of the ecology of nature, whereas the ecology of nature is one principle of movement manifesting the *Tao,* corresponding to its spontaneity.

11. Cf. *Tao Te Ching,* 37.

12. This principle can be indeed expressed as the following equivalence: *cheng-wu-wei* = *tzu-jan* = *sheng-sheng* = *wu-pu-wei,* i.e., the constant self-restraining of externality = spontaneity = life-creativity = the natural harmony of all things.

13. *Jan* ("reversion") refers to the fact that the *Tao* re-

verses what is done against the nature of things. But *jan* is also *fu* ("return"). If things are done according to their nature and of their own accord, things will return to their origin and their identity will be recurrently assured. See the distinction in the context of the *Tao Te Ching*, 40. "Reversion is the movement of the *Tao*," 25. "The distant is the reversion," and 16, "All ten thousand things take place concurrently. I observe their recurrence (*fu*) (*via* their origin)."

14. Cf. *Tao Te Ching*, 2: *Chuang Tzu*, Chi Wu Lun.

15. *Tao Te Ching*, 14.

16. *Tao Te Ching*, 21.

17. Cf. Ren Zhi-Yu, *Lao Ze Jin Yi* (Hong Kong; 1955). See also *Zhong Guo Zhe Xue Shi Ze Liao Suan Zhi, Xian Chin Zhi Bu Zhong* (Beijing; 1959), p. 451.

18. *Tao Te Ching*, 25.

19. In the *Tao Te Ching* there are two direct references to the term *ch'i*. Chapter 10 speaks of "concentrating on *ch'i* to reach softness," and in chapter 55 we find: "when heart-mind controls the *ch'i* it is called strength." It is clear that *ch'i* is the primary substance for the concretion of life, mental effort, and things. In the case of *Chuang Tzu*, although no full theory of *ch'i* was developed, Chuang Tzu has implicitly referred to *ch'i* in describing the piping sound of wind and nature in the Chi Wu Lun chapter. He even speaks of nature as "the great mass breathing the *ch'i*" (*ta k'uai yi ch'i*). It is again quite clear that *ch'i* is assumed to be the primary substance of things and the force of all movements in the totality of the reality identified as the *Tao*. The *Tao* and the *ch'i* can be said to refer to the same reality in different aspects: the macroscopic and the microscopic.

20. Cf. my unpublished paper, "On Transformation and Harmony: Paradigms from the Philosophy of the *I Ching*." Also see my paper. "Model of Causality in Chinese Philosophy: A Comparative Study," *Philosophy East and West* 26 (1976): 1–20.

Fengshui and the Chinese Perception of Nature

OLE BRUUN

THE INTENTION IN THIS ESSAY IS NOT TO GO into great detail about the techniques involved in *fengshui*,[1] the Chinese art of placement, which in lack of more precise terms we translate as 'geomancy.' Many similar techniques are practised across East and Southeast Asia. Instead, I shall focus on *fengshui* as a system of statements on the man–nature relationship in an environment of holistic thought. Of particular interest is the use of natural metaphors: how the *fengshui* idiom provides common people in China with a means of paraphrasing relations in the social world, explaining not only hierarchy, social competition and personal success and failure, but also allowing strong anti-authoritarian political statements to be dressed up in a metaphorical language.

There are, nevertheless, good reasons for investigating *fengshui* as a key element in the Chinese approach to nature. Developed from a diffuse vitalism, *fengshui* has a long continuous history dating back several centuries BC,[2] and it was already in the fourth century AD divided into two main schools of thought, Fujian and Jiangxi, emphasizing 'orientations' and 'shapes' respectively (March 1968:261; Needham 1962:242). It bridges classical literary works and public uses, and it seems to have been utilized by all strata of Chinese society (Freedman 1968:8) and taken seriously by many eminent Chinese thinkers (March 1968:1), although Confucianism has repeatedly opposed it as overblown magic. It is spread geographically all over the Chinese world (Needham 1962:240),[3] it has been used continuously in Hong Kong, Taiwan and Singapore, and it is currently being seen to increase its influence dramatically on the mainland, despite its strong suppression there since the revolution in 1949.

PREMISES

Any social scientist who has been working in China knows that the written tradition and the ordinary so-

Bruun, Ole, "*Fengshui* and the Chinese Perception of Nature," in Ole Bruun and Arne Kalland, Eds., *Asian Perceptions of Nature: A Critical Approach*, Richmond, Surrey, U.K.: Curzon Press, 1995, pp. 173–187. Reprinted by permission of the author.

cial life of the Chinese are often far apart. They may even represent separate realities—not in the sense that one is true and the other false, but by both being indispensable to the Chinese social ethos, since the Chinese have continuously preferred to depict their world by means of such contradictions. When we investigate the Chinese perception of nature (*ziran*), these problems are further amplified. The Chinese have a long literary tradition emphasizing the veneration of nature, but we have few means of investigating how this was applied in practice.[4] We should keep in mind that in this field a profound discrepancy may also have prevailed between word and practice, with philosophy being a moralizing agency stressing ideal culture rather than observed reality. A tension between natural philosophy and concrete human interaction with nature must have been felt, for instance between Confucianism maintaining that 'wealth and honour are from Heaven' and common ancestor beliefs and burial rituals indicating how men may alter Heaven's doom.

When dealing with comparisons between literary expressions of nature in China and the West, we run the risk of comparing dissimilar classificatory, or cognitive, spaces for which highly different terminologies are used. In such cross-cultural comparison a basic consideration should be semantics, syntax and noun typology of the languages concerned.[5]

The Chinese are known for anthropocentrism in their philosophy and extreme sociocentrism in basic orientations—meaning that by far the greater part of the 'world that matters' is made up by humans and human society. Yet I shall not argue that the Chinese perception of what belongs to 'nature' is totally different from our own. China has a long history of reflections on nature, and many of the concepts derived from 'nature' compare with western terms. We may also speak in Chinese of the 'natural world' (*ziranjie*), 'natural environment' (*ziran huanjing*), 'nature preserve' (*ziran baohuqu*), 'natural resources' (*ziran ziyuan*), 'natural behaviour' (*ziran xingwei*), and even 'naturalism' (*ziran zhuyi*). The term signifying nature, *ziran,* indicates spontaneity, while the natural sciences (*bowu*) refer to the study of the 'abundant matter'.

Nature in a pure, material sense—like untouched ground and landscape, wild animals and life hidden in the depth of the ocean—is probably understood and signified in terms comparable with the West. However, the closer we get to the zone where nature and culture blend, the sharper the differences are in a cross-cultural perspective.

Fengshui

Fengshui operates exactly on the borderline between society and nature. *Fengshui,* meaning wind-water,[6] interprets the influence of natural forces on human constructions, primarily houses and graves. The shape of the landscape and the flow of rivers and canals are of prime importance, since these are the products of the creative forces of the 'winds and waters'. *Fengshui* traces human success and failure, not so much to individual acts, but to the mysterious workings of earthly forces, of which wind and water are only their physical aspects. Such forces are believed to be responsible for determining health, prosperity, position and fortune in general (Rossbach 1983:1).

According to *fengshui,* man and landscape are linked together in a system of immanent order. Nature, consisting of balanced forces, reacts to any interference imposed on it, and this reaction immediately resounds in man. As in a large organism, everything is interdependent and pulsating with energy, penetrating and embracing every single part. In this thinking, the environment should be utilized thoughtfully, since harmful interference hits back like a boomerang. It raises the wrath of the Green Dragon, or the White Tiger—universal figures to be detected by configurations in the landscape. China's strong attachment to agriculture is evident: nature contains forces, which have both creative and destructive potential, and thus must be turned to the benefit of the agriculturalist. Winds carry hot or cold weather and bring rain. Mild winds are beneficial to the crops, but strong winds are damaging. Water determines the growth of crops; it should be led to the fields and water power can be harnessed.

The basic logic of *fengshui* is straightforward—when the landscape is rich and healthy, humans may prosper; when the landscape deteriorates, people suffer. *Fengshui* states that people are affected by their immediate surroundings, of which, however, some are better, more auspicious or more blessed than others. Every mountain, hill, river, cluster of trees, even buildings and other human constructions such as roads and railways have an effect. But *fengshui* is far from deterministic. It is an active endeavour, concluding that if you change your surroundings, you may change your life (Rossbach 1983:2).[7] The aim of *fengshui* can be said to change and harmonize the environment to improve fortunes.

Fengshui is an art of placement, of selecting the best possible ground and to carefully orientate human constructions according to the flow of natural forces at that particular site. Of utmost importance is catching and balancing the flow of *qi*, the cosmic current. The Chinese term *qi* denotes a fundamental life-giving force, often described as the beginning of everything, and the continuous creative force in shaping the earth and breathing life into its inhabitants. The cosmic *qi* and the human *qi* are not exactly the same: the cosmic *qi* is weather, air, gas, invisible forces. The human *qi* includes breath, energy, aura, life-force and manner. *Fengshui* intends to direct the cosmic *qi* in order to stimulate the flow of human *qi*, flowing in a microcosm analogous to the macrocosm of the outside. By contrast to other types of divination, *fengshui* does not involve interaction with gods or spirits (Ahern 1981:50), and its practitioner is not reporting from a world beyond (Feuchtwang 1974:201).

Fengshui has its roots in all corners of Chinese thought. It uses ancient classics such as the *I Ching (Yijing)*—'Book of Changes', it spans a whole range of philosophical thought from Taoism to Buddhism, and incorporates various aspects of rural divination and magic. It applies the theories of *yin-yang*, Five Elements/Phases, the Chinese calendar and astrology. It stands out as a pragmatic constellation of elements in belief systems in the Chinese world that may have a bearing on human fortune. However, its structural position is at an intermediate level between higher learning and popular beliefs. If the higher learning of late Imperial China encompassed the science of the calendar and the exclusive knowledge of cosmology, and thus was tied to the principles of government, then the application and arts of divination belonged to the lower learning, although used by all. It has been suggested that 'it was through these arts of divination that the cosmology of higher learning was shared throughout the empire' (Feuchtwang 1992:37). The *fengshui* practitioner held a corresponding social position; he was the dubious member of the elite, perhaps only a 'half-educated man from a farmer's family' (Eberhard 1962:230), whose services may be acquired by commoners, and therefore a mediator between two strata (Freedman 1968:9–10).

Thus *fengshui* is essentially public, expressing the collective adherence to a number of complementary belief systems so typical to ordinary Chinese religion and thought: if something has a grain of truth in it, it should not be rejected. And people will make sure that if it has an effect, they will not miss it, according to the Chinese device: 'never slip an opportunity, it may not come again' (*ji bu ke shi, shi bu zai lai*).

Fengshui simultaneously defines the ideal place for habitation and sets up remedies for improving a location that is not optimal, since Chinese society passed the level of unrestrained resources long ago—presumably due to a strong centre-orientation as much as lack of geographical space.[8] Within these shared cultural preferences, choices of habitation are exceedingly limited. *Fengshui* compensates for this: it is pragmatic and positive by making the utmost of one's actual place—it attempts to bring the entire universe to this particular house or grave to exploit its forces. As a science, *fengshui* bridges ends and means: it manipulates the given by turning it into the selected, or at least, places one's location within a hierarchy of possibilities, where it could be more auspicious, but certainly also much worse. It grants recognition to a site for people to settle down peacefully.

It is put to use in a corporate practice, which in our terms covers such diverse areas as practical concern for shelter from the winds and access to water and basic resources, proto-scientific concern for orientations and natural forces, aesthetic concern for a harmony-inspiring environment, religious concern for blocking the influence of evil spirits, astrological concern, and psychological concern for stable, uncontested conditions of life. But in spite of our ability to dissect *fengshui* into a number of components to fit its description within a western rationale,[9] it should not be understood in this way. It is thought of and practised as a corporate whole, by use of elastic concepts covering its entire range of meanings rather than signifying them one by one.

THINKING IN IMAGES

As a corporate system, *fengshui* operates by use of images. When a *fengshui* specialist investigates a site he reads the environment. He intends to interpret and decode the totality of forces in action at a given place; he may say he employs 'a hundred senses', that he brings 'a hundred phenomena to one' ('hundred' itself symbolizing totality). Over the unity of impressions from a site, he establishes a configuration, a judgement, over its total impact on its inhabitants: good or bad, causing good health or disease, bringing happy or unhappy family life.

The judgement of a site is held against an established frame of reference, like placing a matrix over it to check how it fits. This frame of reference tends to be narrowly aligned with an ideal image: the picture of the successful, the powerful, the accomplished within the high Chinese ideal—almost invariably the balanced combination of wealth and social standing.[10]

Although *fengshui* is a corporate body of beliefs, which in our terms range from magical religion to abstract metaphysics, its aim is well-defined and concrete: boundless, inexplicable luck—seen as high position, booming business, quick fortune, money pouring in, the family prospering, sons to continue the line—this is harmony. There are no limits to the forces in the invisible world that may be employed to further one's interests in the visible world, or to the spiritual powers used in the pursuit of material aims.

Since the image of the good may change with new social values, new circumstances, or new experience, so may the ideal *fengshui* in the human environment. If someone living under supposedly bad *fengshui* influence nevertheless gets rich, it is not an anomaly, an exception from the rule. The forces reckoned with are the same, only they have been misunderstood, or misinterpreted at this particular site. Or if a man defies the rules of *fengshui,* like for instance living in a house or a room that anyone knows has bad *fengshui,* but nevertheless becomes successful, the image of that house or room changes with his success. It suddenly becomes a place of beneficial *fengshui,* its image incorporates this new life story, which is an example to follow. It is interpreted in terms of the good *fengshui* being hidden to earlier occupants, who were either unaware of it or unable to exploit it, or ascribed to changes in the environment accounting for the improved *fengshui*—graves being built or moved, new buildings being erected, pagodas, poles, lampposts and mirrors reflecting *fengshui* and the like.

Through extreme flexibility and pragmatism, *fengshui* may remain intact under almost any set of circumstances. It has a high adaptability to a new environment, for instance the modern city. In Hong Kong or Singapore it has developed into a religion of wealth. Anything from private persons to large companies will employ *fengshui* specialists, and incredible amounts of money change hands for advice on the best places for houses, graves, shops, restaurants, banks, hotels and factories. Similarly, in the interior design of private dwellings and offices, no efforts are spared by the wealthy to make full use of *fengshui.* In fact, in the modern city, where people have little influence on the layout of streets, buildings and apartment blocks, *fengshui* concerns tend to change from exterior to interior design. Increased attention is paid to the layout of rooms, placement of kitchens, living rooms and bedrooms in relation to directions, and the shapes or groundplans of the houses, which by their similarity to for instance boats, boots, axes or knives may be attributed symbolic powers. Also the neighbouring buildings that can be seen from one's windows, and the positive or negative influence of one's neighbours become important to the *fengshui* situation in the modern city. In Hong Kong mirrors are a common means to reflect bad *fengshui* from unhealthy influences in the surroundings.

New economic activities are easily incorporated into the *fengshui* thinking. The long, straight streets of the city are seen to increase the flow of *qi,* and too strong a flow should be avoided (Rossbach 1983:87). Thus corner positions are often better than the middle of a block, and positions slightly set back from the street are preferred since *qi* can rest there. Parallels to the flow of customers and to outstanding positions catching the eyes of customers are of course part of the symbolism. The flow of water is a frequent metaphor for the flow of money, so large companies and factories may benefit from adjacent rivers since their flow of *qi* will stimulate the flow of wares and money. Premises overlooking rivers or the seaside are also ideal for homes.

Success in life is invariably ascribed to beneficial *fengshui,* provided, of course, that you work for it in the highly competitive Chinese universe. However, if someone neglects his duties to work for an improved position for himself and his household, this may also be interpreted in terms of *fengshui.* Bad or missing *qi* may be held responsible for the insufficient human *qi,* counting for laziness, lack of energy or sickness. What strikes the western observer is that having a simple life as an aim in itself, without seeking material improvement, is exceedingly difficult to fit into the *fengshui* thought as it appears today.

The judgement of the *fengshui* configuration in a given place is intuitively composed by use of multiple sources of information, held against a complex range of beliefs. Various impressions of a place are interpreted, translated, manipulated, or even reversed to fit the demands of the moment. Dominance of either *yin* or *yang* in the surroundings should be counterbalanced, the flow of *qi* stimulated or modified, high and low brought into harmony. The judgement is holistic in the strongest sense of the word, amassing impressions and information to a degree that is at odds with any strict classification of nature. Nature and society represent a continuum of influences, when seen entirely from the perspective of the individual. That *fengshui* is anthropocentric is seen from the various means of compensation that are possible for improving a bad site. The nineteenth-century colonial powers quickly learned that the damage done by building roads that for instance cut across what the local inhabitants saw as a dragon's tail, could be made good by monetary payments. Thus, to the people affected, worsened *fengshui* in the long run was counterbalanced by improved *fengshui* in the present. The Hong Kong and Singapore authorities still pay out considerable sums as compensation for violating people's environment when constructing housing, roads, railway lines and harbours.

However, if it is correct that the ideal *fengshui* situation of a given place can be tried against a ready-made image of the ultimate good, it follows that this image of the good is a communal one. This common image, or picture of the good, is in fact one of the most important aspects of *fengshui*, and maybe an important quality of the Chinese perception of nature, too.

There is a classical story about a man who employed a *fengshui* specialist to determine where he should place his father's grave for maximum benefit to his own career. He employed the best specialist of all. The old master investigated the whole area closely, and when he was ready for his judgement, he took out bow and arrow, and shot an arrow into the air. Then he told the man to build the grave where the arrow fell, whereupon he went away. To make sure that he did the right thing, the man employed another *fengshui* specialist, the second best, who happened to be the son of the old master. The procedure repeated itself. After investigating the site the old master's son also shot an arrow into the air, stating that it would indicate the correct position. The arrow eventually hit the arrow shot by the old master, cleaving it end to end. The man build the grave on this auspicious spot, and eventually became the next emperor.

Such old stories intend to demonstrate the masterly skills of the *fengshui* specialists; that what they were practising was science, which unambiguously points to the one and only correct location for the grave. Eventually, the story says more. It tells us perhaps that if there is only one optimal position for the grave among the countless forces and influences of nature, then there apparently is only one path for the son of the deceased. If *fengshui* is correctly handled, two *fengshui* specialists would not disagree about the grave, the judgement, the impact on the living, and the correct path for this man. His aim was to attain the one ultimate and final position—that of the emperor.

Moreover, in spite of the basic assumption of *fengshui* that the environment bears on human fate, it is not to any significant degree assumed that this environment has a different bearing on different people, or that differing personalities may have different needs with regard to the forces of their environment. There are certainly varying *fengshui* situations prescribed for various types of constructions—graves being *yin* dwellings must have maximum harmony, houses being *yang* dwellings have more practical considerations, and businesses should be placed so that the flow of people and money is optimal. Considerations are for types of constructions, integrated into types of environments—to a lesser extent for types of people. *Fengshui* apparently assumes that human values are known and uniform, and that the natural environment is used for specific ends according to shared values.

When social values change it is assumed that it is not the values of individual people that change, but a common model, an image, that flows and has be to taken into account by the *fengshui* specialist. Thus, in this interpretation, *fengshui* implicitly denotes a profoundly competitive society, with little variation in basic life-aim orientations.

THE SOCIAL DISCOURSE

A writer on *fengshui* in Korea, where identical techniques are used, lists the five (the sacred number) most important factors for choosing an auspicious location for a house:

> a. Selecting a favorable house location.
>
> b. Choosing the direction the house should face.
>
> c. Determining the spatial organization or form of a house.
>
> d. Completing a surrounding fence.
>
> e. Deciding what kind of person should live there.
>
> From the above five considerations, we can infer that all are about ways to achieve a perfect harmony between man and his environment (Yoon:76–7).

Venerating wealth as much as nature, *fengshui* obviously fits badly into the policy of the communist regime of the People's Republic, just as it is at odds with the Chinese collective identity emphasizing modesty and a simple life.[11] Discourse on morality and principles for social regulation have penetrated Chinese writings over the centuries. While the Chinese literary traditions such as Confucianism, the historical records, or Chinese Marxism have stressed ideal culture, *fengshui* is different: It is a raw and unclothed expression of the values of everyday life, but the means of obtaining them is ritualised and 'cooked' (Lévi-Strauss 1969).

As the common Chinese see it, no man is equal to another. He is older or younger than the other, higher or lower placed in the state hierarchy, having his native home in a better or worse location in relation to the centre, and, being himself a man, he is superior to a woman. Likewise with the Earth: no two positions on it rank equal, although their relative rank may be disputed.

Countless incidents are recorded of *fengshui* accusations being raised: against villagers building their houses a bit higher than others', one village accusing another for increasing its tapping from common water canals, one market town against another for attracting too much trade, one port against another for catching all the ships etc. Remedies are always possible—since *fengshui* is a boundless aggregation of 'things that matter'. Much of the flexibility, or plasticity, in *fengshui* stems from the social discourse contained in it. Individual people living in a village will take care not to depart from common rules—a whole range of reprisals are possible, drawing on the *fengshui* idiom: a defiant villager may see his ancestors' graves demolished, his fields and crops hit by accidents, his household experience bad luck. Small wars have been fought between families or between villages on matters relating to 'stolen *fengshui*.'

Although *fengshui* is an instrument of competition, there may also be a muting of competition involved (e.g. Freedman 1968:14). *Fengshui* emphasizes the common fortune of a household as related to the influence of its surroundings. By establishing concepts like the common *fengshui* of a village, it may strengthen a communal identity (e.g. Frazer 1913:170). It clearly follows the pattern of the Chinese identity in stressing own household, own local area, own region, even own nation in a serial conception, and always with a clear inside-outside distinction. But even among relatives it may come to open conflict over *fengshui* matters. Writers tell of brothers competing endlessly in building the most attractive grave for their deceased father (e.g. Giles 1908:447), and such rivalry may even be a built-in tendency in the kinship system (Freedom 1970:178).

A clear symbolism is written into the *fengshui* idiom, under the disguise of which keen social competition is expressed. Its techniques aim at attracting to one's own household the largest possible share of limited and clearly defined values, by means of careful management of own resources and manipulation of common resources. In relation to the highly formalized Chinese public morality and public virtue, *fengshui* is the complementary component. It provides an institutionalized outlet for the expression of village characteristics, for familiarism, for individualism, and even egotism in a society that demands all voices in public to confirm the 'common will' of all and revolve around the theme of the 'common good' (Bruun 1993:221). Moreover, *fengshui* should be analyzed against the background of a culture that inhibits open con-frontation [*sic*], suppresses expressions of sexuality, cultivates dignity and the observance of 'face'. Similarly, Chinese expressions of nature should be held against the prevalent style of communication in the context of culture.

China has a long tradition of producing nature-related symbols and writing symbols into nature, for instance by infusing social content into landscape painting. A rich 'vocabulary' of symbols, of which many apparently had erotic content (Eberhard 1983:10c), was used in art by means of interpreting natural forms, forces and constellations. A great number of word compounds such as mountain-water (*shan-shui*), mountain-spirit (*shan-jing*) and the Emperor's court-wilderness (*chao-ye*), which all build on extensions of the *yang-yin* pair (antithesis where the first word denotes masculinity and the second femininity), constitute a huge and rather uninvestigated semantic field (ibid.:14). Also in *fengshui* the sexual connotations of *yang-yin* often becomes explicit, when the feeling of liveliness and diversity in the landscape is represented as the coupling of male and female elements (March 1968:258).

If the Chinese literary tradition has a strong moralizing tone, beliefs such as *fengshui* are profoundly anti-authoritarian by defying the social 'Will of Heaven'. They provide commoners with a symbolism to express resistance against exploitation and subjugation, perennial aspects of Chinese civilization. Also, forces of nature could become a symbolism of power. When westerners were met with *fengshui* charges in pre-revolution China (e.g. Eitel 1873:1–2) it may have been due to the fact that their presence was fostering images of inferiority and subjugation among Chinese officials and commoners alike. *Fengshui* charges and social mobilization to support them are the weapons of all. By a pragmatic constellation of anything that matters, *fengshui* expresses the interests of those inside against those outside.

It is an old theme in anthropology that classifications of culture and nature run parallel, fostering discussions as to what came first. Chinese society has been used as an example of such classificatory unity by for instance Durkheim and Mauss, Lévi-Strauss, Foucault and a number of others. And that 'nature' may be drawn in to legitimize, give authority to, or emphasize aspects of social affairs is of course a universal aspect of myths, medicine, religion, cosmology and so on. 'Nature' is frequently used as a metaphor for the inevitable, or what may not be manipulated.

In China, nature is consistently employed as a source of metaphors, a parallel idiom allowing for themes such as 'individual fate', 'individual success and prosperity', 'one's own way' (as in Taoism) and so forth to be played out in public. Since egocentric concepts are unacceptable without the natural metaphor, techniques like *fengshui* frame in nature a social discourse that runs counter to established ideals of social considerations, the will of the collective, the common good of the family, the masses, and the nation.

COMMENTS

It was mentioned in the beginning how in the cross-cultural comparison 'distant nature' may be classified similarly, whereas the classification of the 'immediate nature', being closer to human enterprise, shows profoundly more variation. *Fengshui* is a borderline science, dealing with borderline phenomena between nature and culture. Instead of maintaining a demarcation between the two, it investigates their interaction, and does so for specific purposes. *Fengshui* expresses great concern for the immediate nature, how to bring it to bear positively on human fortune—whereas the distant, the unimportant, the invisible, or just other people's nature are not included in *fengshui* concerns. By implication, *fengshui,* and perhaps with it Chinese cosmology in general, says little about nature as an independent category (but here we must tread cautiously as westerners, seeing an independent nature as our spiritual frame of reference).

China's long tradition of natural philosophy, emphasizing cosmic harmony, has inspired philosophers, scientists, politicians, ecologists, environmentalists and so on all over the world. It has repeatedly been mentioned as a source of conceptual renewal in the western environmental philosophy and in popular literature. Yet contemporary China boasts some of the world's most polluted rivers, heavy air pollution, some of the worst working conditions in her mining and chemical industry, the laying waste of huge tracts of land, not only affecting her own territories, but also the lands of other cultures in her periphery.[12] This is of course an irony. What is the Chinese view of nature anyway—or what is Chinese history, classical tradition, or present public practice—except for being concepts of eternal contra-diction [*sic*] when translated to the world outside? On Chinese beliefs such as *fengshui* precarious assertions have been made, concerning an inherent Chinese capacity for nature conservation and environmental harmony.

If we favour comparisons between China and the West, and if such comparison sees control and domination as key concepts in the West, we should certainly find exploitation a key concept in China. Chinese culture optimizes the use of natural powers, even to a degree where the *qi*—universal energy—is regarded as a limited resource subject to human competition. The very life space of humans is limited. An important conception in the Chinese discourse on nature is 'the world that matters' contrary to 'the world beyond', mostly left unexplored and unnamed.

In summarizing these notes on *fengshui,* I may come close to suggesting that in the Chinese view, 'nature' not only contains essential resources, it is resources *per se.* The world that matters embraces that untouched nature which has an aesthetic function. Beyond the narrowly visible, where nature is dressed to fit into a picturesque scenery, nature only consists of potential resources to be drawn in as culture expands.

The 'credence' that westerners give to 'nature' is apparently unique. We seem to believe, along with our cosmological transcendence, that nature exists as an entity separate from society and independent of the human mind, and that nature has a right to exist without human interference. We suppose that if mankind was extinguished, maybe animals or insects would survive, and certainly that nature as a category would continue to exist. The Chinese prefer not to engage in such speculations, since they have always operated with human life as belonging to the spontaneously self-generating life processes of nature (Tu 1989:68), without beginning or end.

Fengshui is a holism, linked to cosmological immanence. However, all 'holisms' tend to be narrowly oriented towards the aspects of the cosmos that are of immediate interest to man. In one way or another, closed tautological belief systems—such as *fengshui* or Marxism—appeal to the Chinese since they lessen the conflicts with the experienced world and thereby permit human resources to remain intact and unchallenged. They induce only minimum disturbance to human devotion and energy, classified among the basic forces shaping the world.

NOTES

1. The Chinese encyclopedia *cihai* accounts of *fengshui* as follows: 'Fengshui, also called *kan yu.* A superstition of the old China. Considers wind directions, water streams and other topographical features in the surroundings of a house or a grave site in order to indicate the inhabitants' disaster or good fortune. Also way of directing residences and graves'.

2. For a discussion of several theories on the origin of 'Chinese geomancy', see Yoon (1976:245–59).

3. Needham, occupied with the Chinese contribution to 'world science', has only treated *fengshui* principles sporadically: 'Purely superstitious though in many respects they sometimes became, the system of ideas as a whole undoubtedly contributed to the exceptional beauty of positioning of farmhouses, manors, villages and cities throughout the realm of Chinese culture' (1962:240).

4. Several writers, for instance John B. Cobb (1972), stress that the Chinese natural philosophy has not prevented deforestation and destruction of the environment in history.

5. The implications of the Chinese exclusive use of mass-nouns (as compared to count-nouns) on the perception of nature are treated by Chad Hansen 1983, although his interpretation is radical.

6. In Chinese the term may be seen to denote 'that which cannot be seen and that which cannot be grasped' (Giles 1908:447). Western writers have, according to argument and attitude, labelled *fengshui* as for instance a science (ibid.), as the rudiments of natural science (Eitel 1873), as pseudo-science (Needham 1956:346), as superstition and 'a ridiculous caricature of science' (de Groot 1897:938), and as a cosmological model (Feuchtwang 1974:14).

7. Building on experience from Hong Kong and writing for an American audience, Rossbach evidently emphasizes the active aspect of *fengshui.* Further emphasis is on its alternative potential, for instance by supporting modern ideas of ecology and harmonizing with nature (1983:9, 19, 40).

8. Yoon (1976:259) has suggested that 'The idea that deficiences in the auspicious place in geomancy can be remedied (artificially by man) is a later development in geomancy.'

9. According to March (1968:1) *fengshui* is likely to impress us as a 'silly mish-mash of things better sorted out as physical science, religion, aesthetics, psychology, philosophy, and sociology'.

10. For the importance of this combination in another context see, for instance, Bruun 1993, chapter 8.

11. For an interpretation of *fengshui* as a medium of expression opposed to the morality and rationalism of Chinese high culture, see Bruun 1994.

12. For reports on environmental problems and strategies in China see 'The Ruined Earth' (FEER 1991:39); 'Human Population, Modernization, and the Changing Face of China's Eastern Pacific Lowlands (CEN 1990:3) and 'Urgent Action Needed on East Asia's Environment' (WBN 1993).

REFERENCES

Ahern, Emily. 1981. *Chinese Ritual and Politics.* Cambridge: Cambridge University Press.

Bruun, Ole. 1993. *Business and Bureaucracy in a Chinese City. The Ethnography of Individual Business Households in Contemporary China.* Berkeley: Institute of East Asian Studies, University of California.

——— 1994. (Forthcoming). 'Fengshui and the Chinese Nature. The Revival of Organic Symbolism in the People's Republic'.

CEN (*China Exchange News*). 1990(3): 'Human Population, Modernization, and the Changing Face of China's Eastern Pacific Lowlands'. Washington.

Cobb, John B. 1972. *Is is Too Late? A Theology of Ecology.* Beverly Hills, Calif.: Faith and Life Series.

de Groot, J. J. M. 1897. *The Religious System of China,* Vol. 3 (Reprint 1964). Taipei: Literature House Ltd.

Eberhard, Wolfram. 1962. *Social Mobility in Traditional China.* Leiden: E. J. Brill.

——— 1983. *Chinese Symbols. Hidden Symbols in Chinese Life and Thought.* London: Routledge and Kegan Paul.

Eitel, E. J. 1873. *Feng-shui, or, the Rudiments of Natural Science in China.* (Reprint 1973.) Taipei: Ch'eng Wen.

FEER (*Far Eastern Economic Review*). 1991. '"The ruined Earth". Focus on Environment in Asia'. 19 September, p.39.

Feuchtwang, Stephan. 1974. *An Anthropoloical Analysis of Chinese Geomancy.* Vientiane: Vithagna.

——— 1992. *The Imperial Metaphor.* London: Routledge.

Frazer, J. G. 1913. *The Golden Bough,* Vol. 1. London.

Freedman, Maurice. 1968. *Geomancy.* Presidential Address 1968. Proceedings of the Royal Anthropological Institute of Great Britain and Ireland, 1968–70. London.

——— 1970. *Family and Kinship in Chinese Society.* Stanford: Stanford University Press.

Giles, Herbert A. 1908. *Strange Stories from a Chinese Studio.* Reprint 1968. Hong Kong: Kelly and Walsh.

Hansen, Chad. 1983. *Language and Logic in Ancient China.* Ann Arbor: University of Michigan Press.

Lévi-Strauss, Claude. 1969. *The Raw and the Cooked.* New York: Harper & Row.

March, Andrew L. 1968. An Appreciation of Chinese Geomancy. *Journal of Asian Studies,* 27(2):253–67.

Needham, Joseph. 1956. *Science and Civilization in China,* Vol. 2. Cambridge: Cambridge University Press.

——— 1962. *Science and Civilization in China,* Vol. 4, part 1. Cambridge: Cambridge University Press.

Rossbach, Sarah. 1983. *Feng Shui. The Chinese Art of Placement.* New York: E. P. Dutton.

Tu, Wei-Ming. 1989. 'The Continuity of Being: Chinese Visions of Nature'. In Callicott, J. B. and R. T. Ames (eds), *Nature in Asian Traditions of Thought: Essays in Environmental Philosophy.* Albany: State University of New York Press.

WBN (*World Bank News*). 1993. 'Urgent Action Needed on East Asia's Environment'. October 14.

Yoon, Hong-key. 1976. *Geomantic Relations between Culture and Nature in Korea.* Taipei: Chinese Association for Folklore.

Discussion Questions

1. What are the implications of seeing reality as a continuum as opposed to being composed of discrete forces?
2. Which of the two indigenous Chinese philosophies, Taoism or Confucianism, lends itself more readily to ecological readings? How so?
3. Do the traditional axioms of Taoism enjoin an ecologically oriented lifestyle? Could such a lifestyle be practiced on a wide scale in the contemporary world?
4. If traditional Chinese thought conceives of humans as being interconnected with all other forms of being, how does one account for the severity of China's environmental crisis today?
5. If the practice of *fengshui* is directed essentially toward human ends, can it have a positive ecological impact? What are the constraints, if any?

Further Reading

Allan, Sarah, *The Way of Water and Sprouts of Virtue,* Albany, N.Y.: SUNY Press, 1997.

Black, Alison Harley, *Man and Nature in the Philosophical Thought of Wang Fu-chih,* Seattle: University of Washington Press, 1989.

Bruun, Ole, and Arne Kalland, Eds., *Asian Perceptions of Nature: A Critical Approach,* Richmond, Surrey: Curzon, 1995.

Callicott, J. Baird, and Roger Ames, Eds., *Nature in Asian Traditions of Thought,* Albany, N.Y.: SUNY Press, 1989.

Chen Congzhou, *On Chinese Gardens,* Shanghai: Tongji University Press, 1984.

Elvin, Mark, and Liu Ts'ui-Jung, Eds., *Sediments of Time: Environment and Society in Chinese History,* Cambridge: Cambridge University Press, 1998.

Girardot, N. J., James Miller, and Liu Xiaogan, Eds., *Daoism and Ecology: Ways Within a Cosmic Landscape,* Cambridge, Mass.: Harvard Center for the Study of World Religions, 2001.

Henderson, John B., *The Development and Decline of Chinese Cosmology,* New York: Columbia University Press, 1984.

Major, John S., *Heaven and Earth in Early Han Thought,* Albany, N.Y.: SUNY Press, 1993.

Smil, Vaclav, *China's Environmental Crisis: An Inquiry into the Limits of National Development,* Armonk, N.Y.: Sharpe, 1993.

Tuan Yi-Fu, *Topophilia: A Study of Environmental Perception, Attitudes, and Values,* Englewood Cliffs, N.J.: Prentice Hall, 1974.

Tucker, Mary Evelyn, and John Berthrong, Eds., *Confucianism and Ecology: The Interrelation of Heaven, Earth and Humans,* Cambridge, Mass.: Harvard University Press, 1998.

Yencken, David, John Fien, and Helen Sykes, Eds., *Environment, Education and Society in the Asia-Pacific,* New York: Routledge, 2000.

Chapter 7

Japanese Traditions

THE INDIGENOUS JAPANESE religion is known as Shinto, the way of the *kami* (spirits), a nature-centered tradition that is similar in many respects to traditions of indigenous peoples around the world. Since about the sixth century, however, Japan has undergone continuous cultural influence from China, both directly and via Korea. Thus, Confucian ethics and Chinese Buddhism have been central to the development of the Japanese worldview.

In Shinto, the *kami* spirits are perceived as inhabiting everything: mountains and rocks, trees, water, weather, and human ancestors. They are neither inherently malevolent nor inherently beneficent, but they should be respected and honored. Shinto shrines tend to be set in areas of natural beauty. Even in the midst of a bustling modern metropolis like Tokyo, one can find refuge and serenity in shrine gardens. The Japanese garden, in fact, represents a highly developed art form, reflecting a nature aesthetic also found in landscape paintings, tea ceremonies, and haiku poetry. But do these cultural expressions demonstrate a love for nature as such, or do they rather show a desire to control it?

Brian Bocking suggests a number of features that define the Japanese worldview, contrasting them in many cases with Western attitudes. The primary distinction Bocking makes is that Western attitudes toward nature derive from values that are posited to be universal, whereas Japanese culture focuses more on the context of the *uchi* or "inside" world of one's own group (which includes the nonhuman components of one's environment) and rejects responsibility for that which is *soto* or "outside." Thus, Bocking posits, the Japanese worldview will generally fail to recognize environmental issues that do not directly impinge on the welfare of Japan.

Noting that the Japanese aesthetic of nature is expressed in realms as diverse as seasonal rituals, textile design, gardening, architecture, folk arts, and cooking, landscape scholar Yuriko Saito looks at the different ways in which the Japanese have traditionally identified with nature. Saito suggests that the Japanese sensitivity to nature's transience (*mono no aware*), especially in literature, mirrors a pathos for the transience of human beings, leaving open the question whether this sensitivity has genuine ecological implications or not.

Norwegian anthropologist Arne Kalland confronts the issue of the Japanese love of nature head on, arguing that this is a long-standing misperception. Rather, Kalland claims, the overriding Japanese attitude toward nature is one of control, albeit without conceptually distinguishing oneself from it, as is typical of the West. Kalland draws the conclusion that given the severity of Japan's environmental crisis, a cultural ethic of embeddedness in nature is not adequate insurance against ecological despoliation.

Joy Hendry looks more closely at the nature–culture dichotomy in terms of the specific example of Japanese gardening. She sees the Japanese garden as an attempt to "wrap" nature so as to bring it from the *soto* realm into that of the *uchi*. In this context, the Western distinction between nature and culture becomes irrelevant, to be replaced by the Japanese dichotomy of "outside" or "not us" versus "inside" or "us." Taming nature, for the Japanese, simply means bringing it into the internal realm, which can constitute a process of control.

Japanese Religions

BRIAN BOCKING

A STUDY OF JAPANESE ATTITUDES TO NATURE must begin with a few words about our current attitudes to Japan and Japanese people. Images of Japan probably include ideas about martial arts, and an impression that the Japanese follow Buddhism and Shinto, two religions which teach peaceful co-existence with nature. At the same time, the Japanese are known worldwide for their advanced technology and business success, and some claim the Japanese are 'eco-terrorists' because they eat whales and are accused of deforesting Southeast Asia. Whales have become a symbol of the beauty, grandeur and fragility of the natural world, and in the battle to save the whale, the Japanese seem to have become the enemy. Our image of the Japanese, therefore, contains at least two contradictory pictures: a rather positive image of a disciplined and religious people living in harmony with nature, and a negative image of a business army prepared to plunder the earth's natural resources in pursuit of economic growth. In the context of these mixed perceptions, it is not surprising that in 1991 the Japanese Government set up a four-year research project involving over a hundred historians, archaeologists and specialists in economics, sociology and ecology, to establish what exactly are the differences between Japanese and western attitudes to nature (Ishi 1992: 2).

ARE THERE 'EASTERN' AND 'WESTERN' ATTITUDES TO NATURE?

According to Hiroyuki Ishi, a Japanese environmentalist and member of the research project on attitudes to nature, western and eastern attitudes developed out of two different patterns of agriculture, summed up as 'wheat and meat' in the West, and 'rice and fish' in the East. For example, in the West forests were always looked upon, in Ishi's words, as 'targets for development'. As land used for crops or grazing gradually became infertile, huge areas of forest were felled to provide new farmland. This led eventually to deforestation on a massive scale, especially in Mediterranean areas where western agriculture first began and where forests and topsoil have almost completely disappeared.

In Southeast Asia, by contrast, rice cultivation in paddy fields (artificial swamps) became the dominant mode of food production. Paddies are mainly constructed on flat or gently sloping land, so rice-growing is less likely to destroy hillside forests. Rice cultivation, moreover, relies on forests to soak up the rainwater flooding down from the mountains, and rice paddies can remain fertile for thousands of years. According to Ishi (1992: 3), 'great care was taken to ensure the availability of water, and forests, which acted as "green dams", were carefully protected. The protection of forests as a means of securing water resources has been a major concern in Japan throughout its history'. In Japan's Edo period (1600–1868) severe penalties were prescribed for people caught damaging trees—a finger was cut off for stealing a twig, an arm for a branch, and beheading for cutting down a tree. 'Records from the time show that large numbers of people suffered the ultimate penalty for stealing trees' (Ishi, 1992: 2–3).

On the controversial subject of whaling, Ishi observes that whales, though technically mammals,

Bocking, Brian, "Japanese Religions," in Jean Holm and John Bowker, Eds., *Attitudes to Nature*, London: Pinter Publishers, 1994, pp. 160–168. Reproduced with permission from the publisher.

were traditionally thought of as fish by the Japanese, and fish were (and are) an important element in the Japanese diet. By contrast, the slaughtering of land animals such as cows and sheep, an accepted feature of traditional western societies, was frowned upon in Japan by both Buddhism (which tends to vegetarianism) and Shinto (which regards blood and death as polluting). Meat production in Japan was surrounded by taboos, and restricted to outcaste social groups (which have traditionally existed in Japan, as in India). Following the western example, introduced in the late nineteenth century, meat is now commonly eaten in Japan, and the flat northern island of Hokkaido, opened up to Japanese agriculture a century ago, is cattle-rearing country. Inhibitions about meat-eating have virtually disappeared now that meat is widely available.

Much more recently, the attitude of Japanese people towards whales has changed quite dramatically. A survey in 1991 showed that sixty-three per cent of Japanese respondents now regarded whales as wild animals deserving of protection, while thirty-three per cent thought whales were a source of food that could be hunted. The Japanese pro-whaling lobby had called for Japan to withdraw from the International Whaling Commission (the body which banned commercial whaling in 1982) but seventy-one per cent of Japanese people in the survey disagreed with this stance, although twenty-two per cent supported it. 'Whale watching' is now catching on as a leisure activity in Japan, so there has been a clear shift in attitudes to whales in Japan, as part of a general and worldwide change in consciousness of 'environmental' issues.[1]

These very recent changes in attitude, however, seem to show up the extent to which Japanese attitudes to nature seem to be *similar* to, rather than different from, 'western' attitudes. Japanese forests were protected, not because the Japanese had a particular reverence for trees as such, but because forests were necessary to the success of crops. As rice cultivation in Japan has decreased in recent years, disused paddy fields and associated forests have fallen into decay. In addition, concern for the preservation of forests has not extended to Japanese operations in other countries in Southeast Asia, where massive and unsustainable logging operations are providing wood for the Japanese construction industry and other purposes. Westerners have preserved forests when they wanted to (e.g. for hunting), and westerners too used to catch and process whales without any special affection for them or any regard for the eventual environmental impact of high-tech whaling. Like the Japanese, people in the West conventionally class whales as fish because they swim in the sea, and westerners have had inhibitions about eating some land animals, as well-known dietary laws in Islam and Judaism, and customary taboos on eating dogs or, in the UK, horses, demonstrate. Westerners were using whale products until very recently when the whale became, first an endangered species, and then a symbol of the ecosystem. Can we really accept that there is a difference between western 'wheat and meat' and eastern 'rice and fish' attitudes to nature?

Differences between 'western' and 'Japanese' attitudes to nature might not lie so much in different forms of food production, as in different understandings of what 'nature' means, and hence of what our responsibilities towards 'nature' are. Modern western attitudes to nature derive from the religious traditions of Judaism, Christianity and Islam, which share, broadly speaking, the same model of the relationship between humans and the natural world. On this model, God created the world for human beings. Nature is fundamentally different from the human world—for example, animals do not have souls—and nature is there mainly to feed, clothe and shelter human beings, who have a responsibility to manage it well. A 'responsible' attitude here implies one which puts the interests of all human beings in the world first.

Modern environmental consciousness can be seen as a new, quasi-religious doctrine of the western type. The 'religion' of environmentalism emphasises the wonder of the creation, contrasts this with the alienation and folly of humans which need urgently to be replaced by reconciliation and wisdom, and looks forward either to a 'saved' (ecologically balanced) world or to the hell of an environmental armageddon if we do not repent of our ways. Within this 'religion', the whale has become a central symbol of the faith, an icon to distinguish the believer from the unbeliever, the responsibly minded from the irresponsible.

JAPANESE RELIGION

How does this western-style 'religion of environmentalism', with its emphasis on our responsibility to nature and warnings about the future, fit, if at all, with

Japanese attitudes to nature? Japanese attitudes and patterns of thinking are not derived from Judaism, Islam or Christianity, though there are, of course, Japanese adherents of these faiths today. The Japanese world view was formed over 1500 years by the interaction of Taoism, Confucianism, Buddhism and Shinto. Taoism and Confucianism came from China; Buddhism originated in India and entered Japan from China through Korea; Shinto (originally a collective term for innumerable local religions) originated in Japan. These religions form in the Japanese mind a variegated single tradition which we can call 'Japanese religion', whose chief characteristics are as follows:

1. Japanese religion is local, not universal. The Japanese do not feel responsible for the salvation of the whole world. They do feel a very strong responsibility for others in their own social group, such as their own family, community, or sometimes nation.
2. Humans can live happily in the world. Japanese religion does not consider human beings to be intrinsically sinful, as 'cast out' into the world. Problems occur in the world but they are not a punishment or consequence of original sin. Problems are just problems, and have to be dealt with in a matter-of-fact way.
3. The world comprises different kinds of beings, such as spirits, gods, humans, ancestors, animals, fish, trees and rocks. Human beings are part of the flow of things (the *tao*) and have no particular responsibilities over and above other kinds of beings.
4. Japanese religion does not expect the end of the world, when those who are right will be saved and the rest destroyed. The future will probably be very much like the present in all important respects. Nothing that humans do is going to bring about the end of the world.
5. Religious practice is a private affair. It is accepted that different groups within society will develop a relationship with different symbols and objects of faith (as in Hinduism). There are no religious symbols which everyone ought to revere, and no single 'right' religion.
6. Japanese life has always been, and still is, permeated by the Confucian ethic, which puts social harmony and the well-being of the group (rather than individual rights) at the heart of morality. This means that a 'responsible' attitude is one which conforms to the views and values of one's immediate social group (e.g., the family, or one's company). A person who thinks or acts in ways which undermine the group consensus is seen as weak and unreliable. A 'group ethic' approach is not unique to Japan; it is found in many traditional societies and in sub-groups within advanced industrial nations (such as the Freemasons in the UK, or the Mafia in the USA). However, Japan is an advanced industrialised society with a great deal of economic influence in the world, and mainstream Japanese society is based on a group-centred morality. This kind of morality disturbs those who claim to hold 'universal' moral values. However, in practice the more 'universal' a value-system is, the more likely it is that informal sub-systems will develop within it to give priority to the interests of certain groups, such as nations.

In the light of these six characteristics of the traditional Japanese world view, what can we expect Japanese attitudes to nature and the environment to look like?

Japanese Religion Is Local, Not Universal

For the ordinary Japanese person, 'nature' means the local, rather than the world, environment. Japanese people, as the whaling survey mentioned at the beginning of this chapter showed, are well able to think globally on issues such as whaling, but they are unlikely to do so unless (a) global matters are shown to have local implications, and (b) attention to global issues does not divert attention from local concerns, which are automatically seen as more important than distant matters. Once an issue is accepted as belonging to the local community (which may often these days be 'Japan'), the Japanese can move with extraordinary speed to remedy the situation, and will strive to achieve a consensus in order to make radical changes if necessary. On the other hand, environmental destruction happening abroad tends to be regarded as 'not our problem' until a connection with Japan is established.

Humans Can Live Happily in the World

The Japanese have a strong sense of belonging within a natural world which can be a comfortable, beautiful and enjoyable place. According to Japanese thinking, human perfection is possible, though occasionally things go out of balance. When things go well, one can just enjoy life. When things go badly, one does one's best to set things straight. Floods, earthquakes and typhoons are regular occurrences in Japan, but nature also sustains us and instructs us. Most Japanese are not impressed by the claim that we need to be saved from this world, and consequently are not easily persuaded that the world needs to be saved from us! To the Japanese mind, human beings and nature are equally at home with each other. This affinity is expressed in the Shinto notion of *kami,* and in Zen Buddhism, which has strong affinities with Chinese Taoism.

The World Comprises Different Kinds of Beings

It is a conceit, to the Japanese mind, to think that humans have superior rights over other kinds of beings. Ancestors are a case in point. Traditional Japanese attitudes to ancestral spirits suggest that life is seen as a 'repayment' to ancestors (parents, grandparents, et al.) for bringing us into the world and giving us education, sustenance and opportunities. This should be repaid with care and reverential treatment. In the same way, human beings are indebted to nature (often personified in the notion of *kami,* sacred energies or spirits who inhere in natural phenomena) for the nourishment and shelter nature provides. Dore (1967) asked a hundred Japanese city dwellers the question: 'People say that we are the recipients of *on* [favours which require repayment] from the moment that we come into this world. What do you think?' Among the varied replies was one from a man who said, 'I can't say directly, but, for instance, when the weather clears after a long spell of rain, somehow you feel as if you want to thank somebody'.[2]

The model is one of reciprocity between different sorts of being, rather than stewardship of a resource. There are some disgruntled ancestors and spirits, who can be dealt with if necessary through religious practice, but there are also helpful spirits and benign ancestors. There is no Prince of Darkness sowing evil in the world, and the Japanese feel that human nature, far from being innately sinful and corrupt, is a perfectly adequate measure of right and wrong.

Japanese Religion Does Not Expect the End of the World

In keeping with its broadly optimistic view of human nature and the world, Japanese religion does not anticipate a cataclysm. On the contrary, Japanese religion tends to be rather nostalgic—looking back to a time when things were in balance and reciprocal relationships between humans, gods and nature were untroubled, and seeking to restore that balance. The idea that, if we get it wrong now, a final judgement will fall upon us, is simply alien to Japanese consciousness; it is not found in any of the religions which have contributed to the Japanese world view. The threat of global environmental disaster, therefore, seems far more familiar and convincing to those who are influenced by western religious thought-patterns than it does to the ordinary Japanese.

Religious Beliefs Are a Private Affair

Despite the emphasis on behavioural conformity in Japanese society, the influence of Buddhism, which teaches that there are many paths to the goal of enlightenment, and the example of Shinto, which celebrates the presence and power of the *kami* in an astonishing variety of local ways, have meant that the Japanese are used to living with a multiplicity of religious beliefs and practices, including different religious symbols and objects of devotion. Such objects of devotion (for example, a particular named *buddha* or *kami*) do not have the same universal meaning in Japan as an image of Jesus, say, might have in the West.

In the case of 'environmental religion', Japanese people can readily understand that some people wish to refrain from killing any whales at all, for quasi-religious reasons (namely, that the whale symbolises for those people fragile nature). Most find it difficult to grasp why those who are not devotees of the 'way of the whale' should also be expected to refrain from killing or eating a few whales. Religious tolerance, which has been greatly valued in Japan when governments have allowed it (as at present), implies a 'live and let live' attitude to various truth-claims. This is frustrating to missionaries of any universalist gospel.

The Confucian Ethic Puts Social Harmony and the Well-Being of the Group (Rather Than Individual Rights) at the Heart of Morality

Finally, the Japanese attitude to nature must be put into context as part of a Confucian world view. Confucianism evaluates things according to their effect on the social group. A person, animal, field or forest is either *uchi* (ours—literally 'inside') or *soto* (not ours—literally 'outside'). Nature, in the sense of wild life and uncultivated tracts of land, is not, in traditional Japanese thought, *uchi*. Remote forests and mountains in Japan are dangerous, 'other' places, the haunt of strange beings such as the half-human, half-bird *tengu*,[3] and suitable only for Buddhist or Shinto ascetic practices.

To the Japanese way of thinking, any humans, animals, crops and forests which are 'inside' (*uchi*), in the sense of belonging to 'my' social world, have an absolute claim to my protection and support. However, that part of the human and natural world which falls 'outside' (*soto*) 'my' social world or group is, emphatically, not my responsibility. Thus a 'responsible' person in Japanese terms is one who fulfils all obligations within the group—the *uchi* context—but also recognises the precise limits of responsibility and does not seek to interfere in 'outside' areas.

CONCLUSION

In summary, contemporary western attitudes to nature derive from 'universal' values, which are really values applying to the group of all human beings in the world. In order to safeguard the interests of the group of human beings, 'nature', which is defined as anything outside the human realm, must be properly managed. If not, the mismanagement of nature will bring about the well-deserved destruction of humankind (which those in the West are conditioned by their religious heritage to expect).

Japanese attitudes to 'nature' define nature in different way, to mean 'the world enjoyably inhabited by our social group.' Within this world, there are natural, human and supernatural elements. These interact, and get out of balance when proper reciprocity is not observed. Imbalance can be corrected by recognising that something we are doing is having an adverse effect on 'our' group, and then acting decisively, using our group's wisdom, to remedy it. This may involve redefining 'our' group to include elements previously thought not to be part of 'us' (such as activities done on our behalf in other countries). The world is not going to come to a cataclysmic end—that would damage our group—so we will assess the situation, reach a consensus and then take the necessary steps to avoid a cataclysm.

NOTES

1. The survey is discussed by Ishi, H. (1992) pp. 7, 11. Ishi notes that when respondents in the USA, the (former) USSR and Japan were recently asked to list the issues that concerned them most, the Japanese chose the environment first, while environment came third in the other countries. Ishi concludes (p. 11) that 'public opinion [in Japan] is changing ahead of government policy'.

2. Dore R. (1967), p. 371.

3. For a description of the *tengu* (and an encounter with one) see Carmen Blacker (1975) pp. 182–5.

FURTHER READING

Blacker, C. (1975) *The Catalpa Bow; a Study of Shamanistic Practices in Japan*, London, George Allen and Unwin.

Bocking, B. (1987) 'The Japanese Religious Traditions in Today's World', in Whaling, F. (ed.), *Religion in Today's World*, Edinburgh, T & T Clark.

Davis, W. (1992) *Japanese Religion and Society*, Albany, State University of New York Press.

Dore, R. (1967) *City Life in Japan*, Berkeley and Los Angeles, University of California Press.

Earhart, H. B. (1974) *Religion in the Japanese Experience: Sources and Interpretations*, Encino, California, Dickenson Publishing Company.

Hori, I. (ed.) (1981) *Japanese Religion*, Tokyo, Kodansha.

Ishi, H. (1992) 'Attitudes Toward the Natural World and the Whaling Issue', *The Japan Foundation Newsletter*, Vol. XIX, No. 4: 1–7, 11.

Ono, S. (1962) *Shinto: the Kami Way*, Rutland Vermont, Tuttle.

Reader, I. (1991) *Religion in Contemporary Japan*, London, Macmillan.

Reid, D. (1984) 'Japanese Religions', in Hinnells, J. R. (ed.) *Handbook of Living Religions*, Harmondsworth, Penguin.

The Japanese Appreciation of Nature

YURIKO SAITO

ONE OF THE CHARACTERISTICS OF JAPANESE culture is often said to be the close and harmonious relationship between man and nature. Accordingly, the Japanese attitude towards nature is described as 'man in harmony with nature' or 'man in nature' while the Japanese appreciation of nature invokes such phrases as 'the Japanese traditional love of nature' or 'the great Japanese love of nature and sense of closeness to it'.[1]

Commentators on Japanese culture point to phenomena principally taken from the aesthetic realm as evidence for this unique attitude towards and appreciation of nature in Japan. There are important seasonal festivals that celebrate the beauty of nature (such as cherry blossom-viewing, moon-viewing, snow-viewing festivals); the Japanese often attempt to bring nature into the proximity of their daily lives by designing patterns in kimono fabric after natural objects and phenomena; they construct gardens even in confined spaces, or reduce nature into miniaturized presentations by arranging flowers in an alcove, cultivating a dwarfed pine tree (*bonsai*) or creating a miniature landscape on a tray (*bonkei*). Traditional Japanese architecture is designed to harmonize with, rather than dominate, its natural surroundings. The Japanese gardens are designed without references to the kind of abstract geometrical forms employed in European formal gardens. Various Japanese folk arts, crafts and even packaging often express the respect for the qualities inherent in the natural materials. Similarly, Japanese cooking is noted for preserving as much as possible the natural qualities (not only taste, but flavour, texture, colour, and shape) of the material. Perhaps most importantly, the subject-matter of Japanese art and literature is predominantly taken from natural objects and phenomena.[2]

Such a predominance of natural themes in art, cooking, literature and architecture appears to imply that the Japanese have a very intimate relationship with and a special love for nature. However, a precise analysis of the Japanese aesthetic appreciation of nature is needed to examine the ways in which the Japanese relationship between man and nature is considered to be harmonious, since there are several possible ways in which this is rendered harmonious. Man can conceive of nature as a contrasting force and still consider the relationship to be harmonious and unified through a balance of conflicting elements. Or man can consider nature as essentially identical with man and the relationship between the two to be harmonious because of their identity. In this essay, I shall show that the traditional Japanese love of nature is based upon the conceived identity between man and nature and this conception of nature forms an important basis for their aesthetic appreciation of nature.

I. THE LACK OF SUBLIME OBJECTS IN JAPANESE APPRECIATION OF NATURE

Many commentators have noted that the Japanese appreciation of nature is directed exclusively towards those objects and phenomena which are small, charming and tame. This characteristic becomes conspicuous especially when we compare it with the Western and other Oriental (such as Chinese and Korean) traditions which appreciate not only those small, tame objects of nature but also gigantic or frightful aspects of nature.

Citing various short ancient poems which are perhaps the best record of the traditional Japanese appreciation of nature, Hajime Nakamura points out that 'the love of nature, in the case of the Japanese, is tied up with their tendencies to cherish minute things and treasure delicate things'.[3] Even when a grand landscape is appreciated, it is not the grandeur or awesome scale of the scene but rather its composition compressed into a compact design that is praised.

Consider, for example, how mountains are de-

Saito, Yuriko, "The Japanese Appreciation of Nature," *British Journal of Aesthetics* 25/3 (1985), pp. 239–249. Reprinted by permission.

scribed and appreciated by the Japanese. The following well-known poem from the eighth century illustrates that the poet's appreciation of Mount Fuji is due to its graphic, compositional aspect rather than its soaring height or voluminous mass.

> When going forth I look far from the Shore of Tago,
> How white and glittering is
> The lofty Peak of Fuji,
> Crowned with snow![4]

We do not find, in this kind of appreciation, the Chinese taste for the grandiose, 'a broad prospect from the top of a tall-peak . . . craggy mountains and the dim vastness of waters'.[5] Neither do we detect a sense of fright, mystery or darkness exuded by the mountain.

A graphic illustration of the Japanese appreciation of mountains as friendly and warm rather than hostile and formidable can be found in some of the wood block prints of the Edo period. Consider, for example, Andō Hiroshige's depiction of Mount Hakone from the *Fifty-Three Sceneries of Tōkaidō*. While successfully conveying the difficulty of passing this steep mountain by fantastically exaggerating its profile, this print does not give the viewer an impression that the mountain is hostile, or that it challenges us to conquer it. Moreover, despite its steep shape, the size of the mountain relative to the size of men in procession is rather reduced, avoiding the impression that the mountain is overbearing. In addition, the colour used for the men in procession and the mountain are almost in indistinguishable, again avoiding a stark contrast between the two.

The same observation can made of the Japanese depiction of the sea. When the Japanese appreciate the ocean, it is never 'great oceans' but 'bays where boats passed to and fro between islands'; never 'the mighty ocean over which the great ships to T'ang China sailed', but rather 'the sea . . . somewhere small used by tiny boats and pleasure craft'.[6] The following poems are representative of such appreciation of the ocean.

> As the tide flows into Waka Bay,
> The cranes, with the lagoons lost in flood,
> Go crying towards the reedy shore.

> As we row round the jutting beaches,
> Cranes call in flocks at every inlet
> Of the many-harboured lake of Omi.[7]

Even when a rough sea is depicted in visual art (which is not frequent), it never gives the impression of ferociousness. Take, for example, the famous wood block print by Katsushika Hokusai of a gigantic wave almost swallowing boats, with Mount Fuji seen at a distance. While the represented state of affairs might be horrifying, the work does not convey such a feeling at all. Although highly evocative of dynamic movement, because of a fairly contrived and calculated composition with a distant Mount Fuji as a static focal point, this print gives us a feeling which is neither insecure nor dreadful.

Likewise, creatures depicted by the Japanese are often small, harmless ones such as butterflies, warblers, copper pheasants, cuckoos. On the other hand, ferocious, life-endangering animals such as tigers are frequently objects of appreciation in other traditions. Indeed, in the Japanese tradition we do not find a praise for 'forests filled with wild beasts'; instead there is a constant appreciation of things which are 'small, gentle and intimate'.[8]

Some thinkers ascribe this conspicuous absence of the sublime in the Japanese appreciation of nature wholly to Japan's relatively tame landscape and mild climate.[9] Tall cliffs, unbounded landscapes and soaring mountains may indeed be lacking in Japanese topography. However, the lack of appreciation of the sublime in the Japanese tradition cannot be wholly accounted for by reference to this factor. The fierce and awful aspects of nature such as annual autumn typhoons, earthquakes and rough seas are fully experienced by the Japanese, perhaps most eloquently documented by a mediaeval Buddhist recluse, Kamo no Chōmei, in his *An Account of My Hut* (1212).

In spite of the frequent occurrences of devastating typhoons, however, it is noteworthy that the morning *after* a typhoon, not the typhoon itself, is praised for its aesthetic appeal in three major classics in the Japanese tradition, *The Pillow Book* (c. 1002), *The Tale of Genji* (c. 1004) and *Essays in Idleness* (c. 1340). For example, in *The Pillow Book,* a series of anecdotes and essays concerning the Heian period court life, Sei Shōnagon praises the beauty of the morning after the storm without describing her experience of the storm itself during the previous night. The only reference made to the storm is her amazement at recognizing the arrangement of leaves 'one by one through the chinks of the lattice-window' is the work of 'the same wind which yesterday raged so violently'.[10]

How do we then account for the fact that the grand and fearful aspects of nature, while experienced by the Japanese, are not acknowledged as objects of aesthetic appreciation in their tradition? It may be helpful here first to examine, as a point of comparison, the Western notion regarding the appreciation of the sublime. Perhaps the most theoretical discussion of man's appreciation of the sublime in the West can be found in Kant's aesthetic theory. In his theory of the sublime, Kant proposes that man's appreciation of the sublime in nature (either vast or powerful parts of nature) is based upon the fundamental contrast between nature and man. The contrast is twofold. First, man is contrasted with nature because of his apparent inadequacy to grasp the magnitude of a vast part of nature or to have dominion over its powerful part. However, second, man is also contrasted with nature because of his ultimate dominion and superiority over nature. That is, in experiencing the vast parts of nature, the feeling of pleasure is generated because we recognize that our rational faculty is capable of *thinking of* infinity in spite of the inability of our sensible faculty to grasp it. Our appreciation of the powerful aspects of nature is brought about by a similar recognition. While the power of nature may have dominion over our physical being we have ultimate dominion over nature due to our super-sensible faculty of reason which is free from those causal laws governing the phenomenal world. Indeed, Kant describes the play of mental faculties (imagination and reason) involved in our experience of the sublime to be 'harmonious *through their very contrast*'.[11]

The lack of appreciation of the sublime in the Japanese appreciation of nature, then, is explained by the Japanese view of nature in its relation to man. Rather than conceiving the relationship between man and nature as contrasting, I shall argue that the Japanese appreciate nature primarily for its identity with man. As Masaharu Anesaki observes:

> Both Buddhism and Shintoism teach that the things of nature are not essentially unlike mankind, and that they are endowed with spirits similar to those of men. Accordingly awe and sublimity are almost unknown in Japanese painting and poetry, but beauty and grace and gentleness are visible in every work of art.[12]

In what way then is nature considered to be essentially the same as man in the Japanese tradition? There are two ways in which the Japanese have traditionally identified with nature. One may be called emotional identification and the other is identification based upon the transience of both man and nature.

2. EMOTIVE IDENTIFICATION WITH NATURE

There is a long tradition in Japanese literature of emotional expression in terms of natural objects or phenomena. Lament and love, two strong emotions which constitute the major subject-matters of Japanese literature, are often expressed not directly but in terms of or by reference to nature. This tradition goes as far back as the oldest anthology of Japanese poems, *Manyōshū*, compiled in the eighth century. Shūichi Katō explains that this anthology indicates 'the court poets of the *Manyōshū* expressed their profound feelings in terms of their daily natural surroundings'.[13]

Perhaps the most explicit expression of this tradition in Japanese literature is found in Ki no Tsurayuki's preface to *Kokinshū*, another anthology of poetry, compiled in 905. In this preface Tsurayuki explicitly defines the nature of poetry as expression of emotion *in terms of* nature. Its opening paragraph states:

> Japanese poetry has the hearts of men for its seeds, which grow into numerous leaves of words. People, as they experience various events in life, speak out their hearts *in terms of* what they see and hear. On hearing a warbler chirp in plum blossoms or a kajika frog sing on the water, what living thing is not moved to sing out a poem?[14]

This identification of man and nature through emotive affinity is developed into an important aesthetic concept by an Edo-period philologist and literary critic, Motoori Norinaga (1730–1801) in his theory of *mono no aware*. Variously translated as 'pathos of things' or 'sensitivity of things', and sometimes compared to the Latin notion of '*lacrimae rerum*' ('tears of things'), *mono no aware* refers to the essential experience of sympathetic identification with natural objects or situations.

The experience and appreciation of the identification with natural objects or situations occur in two ways. Sometimes we intuit the *kokoro* (essence, spirit) of the object or situation and sympathize with it: this results in an aesthetic experience of the object based upon *mono no aware*. Hence, with respect to situations (*koto*), Norinaga claims,

> What does it mean for one to be moved by knowing *mono no aware*? It is, for example, when one is confronted by some situation which is supposed to be happy, one feels happy. One feels happy because one apprehends the *koto no kokoro* which is happiness in this case. By the same token, one feels sad when confronted with what is supposed to be sad; because one apprehends its *koto no kokoro*. Therefore, to know *mono no aware* is to apprehend the *koto no kokoro*, which is sometimes happy and sometimes sad, depending upon the situation in question.[15]

Regarding natural objects (*mono*), he makes a similar point:

> To see cherry blossoms in full bloom and to see them as beautiful flowers is to know *mono no kokoro*. To recognize their beauty and to be moved by feeling that they are deeply beautiful is to know *mono no aware*.[16]

Some other times, when we are possessed with a strong emotion, we experience an identification with natural objects and events by colouring these objects with our emotion. Norinaga claims that the aesthetic appeal of many classical Japanese literary works is derived from descriptions of this kind of emotional identification with nature. He agrees with Ki no Tsurayuki that '*mono no aware*, which is so intense that any verbal expression seems inadequate, can be expressed in a profound manner if one expresses it by what one sees or hears' such as 'the sound of wind or crickets, . . . the colour of flowers or snow'.[17] Indeed, according to Norinaga, the most important aesthetic appeal of *The Tale of Genji*, the work he praises for its expression of *mono no aware*, is its description of nature which has affinity with the characters' emotive states.

Some natural objects and phenomena are associated with certain emotive content in Japanese literature so frequently that they have been established as symbols for expressing particular emotions. For example, cherry blossoms (especially when they are falling) are often associated with sorrow in classical Japanese literature because they epitomize the transience of beauty. The autumn evening is a favourite symbol among mediaeval poets for expressing desolation and loneliness.

Whether the emotive identification between man and nature is rendered primarily as a result of man's intuitive grasp of the essence of a natural object or as a result of the imposition of feeling onto the outward reality, this appreciation of nature for being emotionally charged constitutes an important aspect of the Japanese aesthetic appreciation of nature: the appreciation of nature for its expressive quality.

While the notion of expression relevant in the aesthetic sense has become a point of dispute, I believe that George Santayana's 'two-term' account of expression is generally correct. According to him, the aesthetic expression takes place when the following 'two terms' are united or fused together: 'the first is the object actually presented, the work, the image, the expressive thing; the second is the object suggested, the further thought, emotion, or image evoked, the thing expressed'.[18] Only when these two terms are 'fused' or 'confounded' in our experience is the object said to be expressive of the idea or emotion. Many instances of our aesthetic appreciation of nature are based upon this 'fusion' between the object's sensuous surface and various associated facts such as scientific facts, historical or literary associations, or practical values. For example, we may appreciate the tremendous geological age *manifested* by the weathered surface and many layers of a geological formation; the way in which the fierceness of a battle is *reflected* in a disfigured landscape with poor vegetation; or the manner in which the danger of an animal is perceptibly *realized* in its fierce appearance. The above are all *aesthetic* appreciation of these respective objects, distinct from mere appreciation of *the fact* that the landscape is aged, the battle took place on the site, or the animal is dangerous to us.

Emotion is also often associated with a natural object or phenomenon. Emotion can be said to be aesthetically expressed by a natural object when we can *see* the landscape as emotionally charged. If the emotive content remains distinct from the object and the viewer's experience is dominated by the emotion he experiences, then the aesthetic component in the appreciation diminishes. In other words, if the appreciation is directed merely towards the feeling of loneliness, the appreciation does not seem to be aesthetic; but if it is directed towards the way in which the feeling of loneliness is embodied by the actual landscape, then the appreciation is aesthetic. While this mode of appreciating nature as a mirror of one's emotion is not limited to the Japanese tradition, it constitutes an important aspect of the Japanese aesthetic appreciation of nature.

3. THE JAPANESE APPRECIATION OF THE TRANSIENCE OF NATURE

The Japanese appreciation of nature for its affinity rather than contrast with man has another basis. In addition to appreciating the relatively small and gentle objects and phenomena of nature, the Japanese are also known for their appreciation of the transitory aspects of nature. This fact is most significantly reflected in the traditional phrase by which the Japanese refer to nature as an object of appreciation—*kachōfūgetsu,* flower, bird, wind and moon. Flowers (most notably cherry blossoms) do not stay in bloom forever; the bird song is always changing and passing; wind is literally passing and transitory by definition; and the moon is constantly changing its appearance and location. Indeed these natural objects and phenomena form the favourite subjects for Japanese art. Other natural objects and phenomena frequently referred to in Japanese art are also short-lived: rain, dew, fog, insects, and various seasonal flowers.[19]

The Japanese preoccupation with the change of seasons should be understood in this regard. In many instances of appreciation of nature from the earliest record, the Japanese have been most sensitive to the characteristics of each season and the transition from one to the other. Consider the following examples. *The Pillow Book* begins with the famous description of the best of each season; the first six volumes of *Kokinshū* is organized according to the four seasons;[20] a famous passage in *Essays in Idleness* (a well-known series of essays by a fourteenth-century retired Buddhist monk, Yoshida Kenkō) also is directed towards appreciating the transition of seasons.[21]

The Japanese sensitivity towards seasonal change is even today manifested in the following aesthetic phenomena. Some natural objects or phenomena are celebrated for their symbolic presentation of their respective seasons. This symbolic import has been established throughout the long tradition of the required use of the season word, *kigo,* in haiku poetry and the celebration of the seasonal festivals mentioned at the beginning of this paper.[22]

The importance of seasons in the Japanese appreciation of nature is not limited to the symbolic import vested in various individual objects and phenomena. Just as emotion often organizes various components of nature into a unified expressive whole, seasons are also used as an aesthetic organizing principle. In other words, sometimes a composition made up of various natural objects and phenomena is praised for the 'fittingness' of the objects which creates a unified whole suggestive of a particular season. For example, one of the norms of flower arrangement is to suggest the mood of a season. Master Sennō advises: 'when there comes the season for autumn flowers like chrysanthemums and gentians, your work must suggest the desolation of a withered winter moor'.[23] Japanese cooking also reflects the Japanese appreciation of seasonal changes by its emphasis on seasonable dishes and the incorporation of appropriate materials for garnish and decoration. Accordingly, many contemporary Japanese cookbooks are arranged by season.

What is the basis for this Japanese appreciation of the transitory nature of natural objects and phenomena? There is an immediate aesthetic appeal of something which does not last for long. Psychologically we tend to cherish and appreciate objects or events more if we know that they will never be the same. Hence, commentators discussing the notion of Japanese wisdom point out that the Japanese appreciation of the flower, moon and snow is based upon 'regret for the transience of phenomena' which compels them to cherish 'those rare occurrences fitting to each season and time'.[24]

A contemporary Japanese painter, Higashiyama Kaii, indicates that his experience of viewing the full moon in the spring against the foreground of drooping cherry blossoms in full bloom in the Maruyama district of Kyoto is intensified by the recognition of the transitory and non-recurring nature of the phenomenon.

> Flowers look up at the moon. The moon looks at the flowers . . . This must be what is called an encounter. Flowers stay in their fullest bloom only for a short period of time and it is very difficult

> for them to encounter the moon. Moreover, the full moon is only for this one night. If cloudy or rainy, this view cannot be seen. Furthermore, I must be there to watch it . . .
>
> If flowers are in full bloom all the time and if we exist forever, we won't be moved by this encounter. Flowers exhibit their glow of life by falling to the ground.[25]

Higashiyama, therefore, recommends that we 'think of the encounter with a particular landscape occurring only once'.[26] Such advice would have us avoid the fatigue factor which is detrimental to the aesthetic experience of any object. It is not yet clear whether transitoriness itself directly contributes to the aesthetic quality of the object, but it is aesthetically relevant in the sense that it predisposes the viewer to attend very carefully to the object and fully savour whatever the object has to offer at the moment.

Another appeal of the transitoriness of natural objects and phenomena is also aesthetic. It is based upon the pleasure we derive from imagining the condition of the object before or after the present stage and comparing them. This aspect of the appeal of the transitory and changeable nature of natural objects and phenomena is discussed by Yoshida Kenkō. In a well-known passage in *Essays in Idleness* he claims that natural objects such as flowers or the moon are best appreciated before or after their full stage.[27] 'Branches about to blossom or gardens strewn with faded flowers are worthier of our admiration' than blossoms in full bloom. As in a love affair between a man and a woman, 'in all things, it is the beginnings and ends that are interesting' because such stages of the phenomena are more stimulating to one's imagination. In particular, we appreciate the exquisite contrast between the present condition and the imagined condition of the previous or following stage. Even when an object or phenomenon is at the peak of its beauty, the appreciation is deepened by pathos based upon the apparent contrast between its present appearance and what will become of it later on.

The Japanese taste for such natural objects as cherry blossoms and moon, therefore, can be explained from the aesthetic point of view: these objects most eloquently exhibit to one's senses the transience of nature in general. Cherry blossoms are more effective than other flowers for symbolizing transience because they look most fragile and delicate, they stay in full bloom for only a short period of time, and they drift down slowly petal by petal, giving an impression that they regret falling.[28] But why is such sensuous manifestation of transience so cherished and appreciated? Why not appreciate the (apparent) permanence and stability of a rock, for example? After all, isn't transience of everything, including ourselves, considered a primary source of man's suffering?

The Japanese traditional appreciation of the transient aspect of nature stems from a further metaphysical consideration. One of the most important ideas spread by the introduction of Buddhism in the sixth century was the impermanence of everything. Everything, both nature and man, will sooner or later change through modification, destruction or death. Transience of human life was often considered a source of people's suffering and an object of lament. Youth and beauty pass. Wealth and power do not last. And, of course, no one avoids death.

Lament over these facts is the subject-matter of major literary pieces in Japan. *An Account of My Hut*, for example, presents in the first chapter the following observation on the human condition.

> It might be imagined that the houses, great and small, which vie roof against proud roof in the capital remain unchanged from one generation to the next, but when we examine whether this is true, how few are the houses that were there of old. Some were burnt last year and only since rebuilt; great houses have crumbled into hovels and those who dwell in them have fallen no less. The city is the same, the people are as numerous as ever, but of those I used to know, a bare one or two in twenty remain. They die in the morning, they are born in the evening, like foam on the water. (197)

The same theme is expressed in the beginning paragraph of perhaps the most famous tale from the Japanese mediaeval period, *The Tale of the Heike:*

> Yes, pride must have its fall, for it is as unsubstantial as a dream on a spring night. The brave and violent man—he too must die away in the end, like a whirl of dust in the wind . . .[29]

What interests us here in these two passages is not merely their rather pessimistic outlook on man's life.

What is noteworthy is that the description of the transience of human life is compared to the transience of natural phenomena. Kamo no Chōmei's passage is preceded by: 'The flow of the river is ceaseless and its water is never the same. The bubbles that float in the pools, now vanishing, now forming, are not of long duration: so in the world are man and his dwellings' (197). The passage from *The Tale of Heike* is also preceded by the famous beginning: 'The bell of the Gion Temple tolls into every man's heart to warn him that all is vanity and evanescence. The faded flowers of the sala trees by the Buddha's deathbed bear witness to the truth that all who flourish are destined to decay'.

This practice of comparing the transience of human life to the transience of natural phenomena abounds in Japanese literature. Consider, for example, a well-known poem by Ono no Komachi, a ninth-century poetess renowned for her beauty, in which she laments the passing of her youth and beauty by comparing them to the passing of flowers:

> The flowers withered,
> Their colour faded away,
> While meaninglessly
> I spent my days in the world
> And the long rains were falling.[30]

This frequent association between transience of nature and transience of human life stems from the conviction that nature and man are essentially the same, rooted in the same principle of existence. As Higashiyama remarks, referring to his discussion of viewing the full moon against the cherry blossoms at Maruyama,

> Nature is alive and always changing. At the same time, we ourselves, watching nature change, are also changing day by day. Both nature and ourselves are rooted in the same fated, ever-changing cycle of birth, growth, decline and death.[31]

This belief concerning the co-identity of man and nature is the ground of the Japanese appreciation of the evanescent aspects of nature. Grief experienced at the transience of human life is transformed to aesthetic pathos when it is compared to the transience of nature. By identifying human life with nature, the Japanese find a way to justify the transience of life. That is, since *everything* is in constant flux there is no escaping change and this recognition leads to resignation and finally to an acceptance of the sorrow of human existence.[32]

As a psychologist, Hiroshi Minami, commenting on Japanese psychological characteristics, suggests, this preoccupation with the co-identity of man and nature and the appreciation of the transient are based upon 'the perception of nature and life as one and the same, and the ascription of unhappiness and misfortune to the transiency and evanescence of nature and things impermanent'.[33] This identity between man and nature leads to resignation before the facts of life and then to acceptance of life, with all its sorrow and suffering. 'Unhappiness in life is expressed through the guise of nature; because of the evanescence of nature, man realizes that it is senseless to grieve and should become reconciled to fate'.[34]

Many contemporary thinkers, in particular those concerned with ecological matters, often praise the Japanese attitude of 'man in harmony with nature' for being ethically more desirable than the Western tradition of 'man over nature' or 'man against nature'. I believe that a further critical study is needed to determine whether their praise of the Japanese attitude towards nature for its ecological implication is justified. However, the preceding discussion does suggest that the Japanese regard man and nature as fundamentally identical and appreciate nature for its unity with man. The content of this unity and co-identity between man and nature should be understood in the sense that both man and nature share the most important principle of existence in common: transience.[35] The Japanese appreciation of the evanescent aspects of nature is rooted in the psychological benefit the Japanese derive from them: justification of the impermanence of human existence.

NOTES

1. For discussion of the Japanese harmonious relationship to nature, see Ian McHarg, *Design with Nature* (New York: Doubleday/Natural History Press, 1971), pp. 27–8; Ian McHarg, 'The Place of Nature in the City of Man', in *Western Man and Environmental Ethics* (Reading: Addison-Wesley Publishing Company, 1973); Ian Barbour, 'Environment and Man: Western Thought', in *Encyclopedia of Bioethics,* ed. Warren Reich (New York: The Free Press, 1978), I: 336–73; Lynn White, 'The Historical Roots of Our Ecological Crisis', *Science,* 155 (March 1967): 1203–7; 'Towards an Ecolog-

ical Ethic', Editorial, *New Scientist,* 48 (December 1970): 575. As for the Japanese appreciation of nature, the first phrase comes from Hajime Nakamura, *Ways of Thinking of Eastern People* (Honolulu: The University Press of Hawaii, 1981), p. 355. The second phrase comes from Edwin O. Reischauer, *The Japanese* (Cambridge, Mass.: Harvard University Press, 1982), p. 148.

2. In addition to various sources which discuss each specific item (such as Japanese architecture, kimono, or Japanese cooking), the above observation is presented in the following writings on the general characteristics of Japanese culture. Masaharu Anesaki, *Art, Life, and Nature in Japan* (Tokyo: Charles E. Tuttle, 1973), Chapter I; Tatsusaburō Hayashiya, Tadao Umesao, Michitarō Tada and Hidetoshi Katō, *Nihonjin no Chie* (*The Japanese Wisdom*) (Tokyo: Chūōkōronsha, 1977); Hajime Nakamura, 'Environment and Man: Eastern Thought', in *Encyclopedia of Bioethics;* Hajime Nakamura, *Ways of Thinking,* Chapter 34; Masao Watanabe, 'The Conception of Nature in Japanese Culture', *Science,* 183 (January, 1974): 279–82.

3. Nakamura, *Ways of Thinking,* p. 356.

4. By Yamabe no Akahito, included in *Manyōshū.* Translation is taken from Nakamura, *Ways of Thinking,* p. 356.

5. Sōkichi Tsuda, *An Inquiry into the Japanese Mind as Mirrored in Literature,* trans. Fukumatsu Matsuda (Tokyo: Japanese Society for the Promotion of Science, 1970), p. 282.

6. Shūichi Katō, *A History of Japanese Literature,* trans. David Chibbett (New York: Kodansha International, 1979), I; pp. 65–6.

7. The translation of the first poem is taken from Nakamura, *Ways of Thinking,* p. 356. The second poem is taken from Katō, *History,* p. 65.

8. Katō, *History,* p. 66. And Kamo no Chōmei explains that his appreciation of the mountain life with the hooting of the owl and various other elements is dependent upon the fact that 'it is not an awesome mountain' (209). *An Account of My Hut,* trans. Donald Keene, included in *Anthology of Japanese Literature,* ed. Donald Keene (New York: Grove Press, 1960). The page reference from this work will be indicated within parentheses.

9. Anesaki, *Art, Life, and Nature,* pp. 7–8.

10. *The Pillow Book of Sei Shōnagon,* trans. and ed. Ivan Morris (Harmondsworth: Penguin Books, 1982), p. 194. Another famous passage on the typhoon in *The Tale of Genji,* while describing the storm itself, does not express a sense of awe felt by being wholly overpowered by nature's brutal force. This is partly because the experience during the storm is narrated from a house, looking out to a small enclosed garden rather than in the midst of a vast moor or a thick forest where the effect of the storm is felt to the utmost degree. See the chapter entitled 'Typhoon' in *A Wreath of Cloud: Being the Third Part of 'The Tale of Genji',* Trans. Arthur Waley (Boston: Houghton Mifflin Company, 1927). See also section 19 of *Essays in Idleness,* trans. Donald Keene (New York: Columbia University Press, 1967).

11. Kant, *Critique of Judgment,* trans. J. H. Bernard (New York: Hafner Press, 1974), section 27, p. 97, emphasis added.

12. Anesaki, *Art, Life, and Nature,* p. 10.

13. Katō, *History,* p. 66 (my translation). Chibbett's translation reads rather inaccurately: 'the court poets of the *Manyōshū* were profoundly influenced by nature and both their love poems and their elegies reflect this'.

14. Translation is taken from Makoto Ueda in *Literary and Art Theories in Japan* (Cleveland: The Press of Western Reserve University, 1967), p. 3. This practice of expressing one's emotion by reference to nature gives rise to the important aesthetic effects of 'constraint' and 'suggestion' in Japanese literature. See Donald Keene's discussion of these effects in *Japanese Literature: An Introduction for Western Readers* (New York: Grove Press, 1955), Chapter I 'Introduction'.

15. Motoori Norinaga, *Isonokami Sasamegoto* (*My Personal View of Poetry*) in *Complete Works* (Tokyo: Chikuma Shobō, 1968), II, pp. 99–100, my translation.

16. Motoori Norinaga, *Shibun Yōryō* (*The Essence of The Tale of Genji*) in *Complete Works,* IV, p. 57, my translation.

17. Norinaga, *Isonokami,* pp. 110–11.

18. George Santayana, *The Sense of Beauty* (New York: Dover Publications, 1955), p. 121.

19. Barbara Sandrisser points out that rain is often an aesthetically celebrated phenomenon in Japanese literature and visual art. She correctly attributes the Japanese finding attraction in rain to their preoccupation with impermanence: 'Rain is inspiring. Perhaps its impermanence encourages this feeling . . . Rain appears and disappears. The experience of rain, although similar, is never the same'. 'Fine Weather—the Japanese View of Rain', *Landscape,* 26 (1982), p. 47.

20. Volumes I and II of *Kokinshū* are devoted to spring poems, volume III to summer poems, volumes IV and V to autumn poems, and volume VI to winter poems. The rest (volumes VII–XX) is devoted to poems concerning love, travel, farewell, etc., but it is commonly regarded that the best poems are found in the first six volumes.

21. Sei Shōnagon further observes in section 245 that 'things which pass quickly' are 'boat with a hoisted sail, people's age, spring, summer, fall and winter'. Also see *Essays in Idleness,* section 19.

22. The bond between cherry blossoms and spring is so firm and entrenched in the Japanese mind that an Edo-period thinker felt it necessary to remind people that cherry blossoms blooming after the spring is over are also appreciable. (Referred to by Tsuda, *Inquiry,* p. 265.)

23. Translation is by Ueda in his *Literary and Art Theories,* p. 81.
24. Hayashiya, *et. al., Nihonjin,* pp. 60–1, my translation.
25. *Nihon no Bi o Motomete* (*In Search of Japanese Beauty*) (Tokyo: Kodansha, 1977), pp. 26–7, my translation. The same point is made by Yoshida Kenkō in *Essays in Idleness* in which he claims that 'if man were never to fade away like the dews of Adashino, never to vanish like the smoke over Toribeyama, but lingered on forever in the world, how things would lose their power to move us!', p. 7.
26. Ibid., p. 27.
27. Yoshida Kenkō, *Essays,* pp. 115–18.
28. This aspect of cherry blossoms can be contrasted with camellia flowers, for example, which Natsume Sōseki describes 'will live in perfect serenity for hundreds of years far from the eyes of man in the shadow of the mountains, flaring into blossom and falling to earth with equal suddenness'; they 'never drift down petal by petal, but drop from the branch intact'. *Kusamakura* (*Grass Pillow*) in *Complete Works* (Tokyo: Chikuma Shobō, 1971), II, p. 188, my translation.
29. *The Tale of Heike,* trans. Hiroshi Kitagawa and Bruce T. Tsuchida (Tokyo: University of Tokyo Press, 1975).
30. Translated by Donald Keene, included in Keene, *Anthology,* p. 81. Yoshida Kenkō similarly describes the changeableness of this world 'as unstable as the pools and shallows of Asuka River' (25) and transitoriness of people's affection 'like cherry blossoms scattering even before a wind blew' (27). Kenkō, *Essays.*
31. Higashiyama, *Nihon no Bi,* p. 27.
32. The Japanese tendency towards the absolute acceptance of the phenomenal world is thoroughly discussed by Nakamura in *Ways of Thinking,* Chapter 34.
33. Minami, *Psychology of the Japanese People,* trans. Albert R. Ikoma (Toronto: University of Toronto Press, 1971), p. 63.
34. Ibid., p. 60. I changed Ikoma's translation here because he translates the passage incorrectly as: 'because of the evanescence of nature, man should realize that it is senseless to grieve and should become reconciled to fate'.
35. I thank the editor for his helpful comments and advice on this paper.

Culture in Japanese Nature

ARNE KALLAND

A GROWING AWARENESS OF A WORLDWIDE ENvironmental crisis has given rise to a new discourse on the connectedness between world-views and management of natural resources. In particular, the present dominant world-view—which has variably been attributed to Judaeo-Christian influences, the development of the market economy, the rise of capitalism, patriarchal societies (Devall and Sessions 1985:45) or the Scientific Revolution (Merchant 1980)—is seen as the root of the problem facing us today. A dichotomy between nature and culture is seen as fundamental to this world-view, with people separated from, and in command of, nature. Therefore new paradigms in which human beings are seen as part of, and in harmony with, nature are called for.

Inspiration for formulating new concepts and perceptions of man's relation to nature comes from a wide variety of sources, such as native North American cultures and eastern traditions, not least from Chinese and Japanese philosophies. In this regard it will be especially rewarding to analyse the Japanese attitudes to nature because Zen—particularly through the writings of the thirteenth century Japanese master Dōgen—has profoundly influenced the *Deep Ecology* movement (Devall and Sessions 1985:100–101). Zen is said to pervade Japanese attitudes and is given credit for their alleged love of nature (Suzuki 1988).

This paper will offer an alternative interpretation of Japanese relations to nature. An attempt will be made to show that the 'nature-loving Japanese' is to a great extent a misconception, which is created by

Kalland, Arne, "Culture in Japanese Nature," in Ole Bruun and Arne Kalland, Eds., *Asian Perceptions of Nature: A Critical Approach,* Richmond, Surrey, U.K.: Curzon Press, 1995, pp. 243–255. Reprinted by permission of the author.

taking Japanese praise of nature—as expressed in literature and the visual arts—at face value and not as metaphors for something else. It will be argued that the Japanese try to control nature, or 'conquer' it, by processes of taming but without resorting to the nature-culture dichotomy, which Lévi-Strauss (1973) claims is a basic distinction made in all cultures. On the contrary, nature and culture are not always exclusive categories in Japanese. Nevertheless, Japan has faced more severe environmental disruptions than most countries. World-views where humans beings are firmly integrated in nature might be a precondition for an enlightened resource management regime, but it is certainly not a sufficient condition.

DO THE JAPANESE LOVE NATURE?

Much has been said and written about Japanese attitudes toward nature (*shizen, tennen*),[1] It has been taken more or less as an established fact that they love it. Taking poems, paintings, sculptures, gardens and other artefacts as proofs of this alleged love, scholars and others have been preoccupied with trying to explain *why* the Japanese love nature rather than with testing the validity of this widely-held notion as such. Among the popular explanations is the one suggested by the late Daisetz Suzuki, the scholar who has done more than anyone else to introduce the ideas of Zen to the western world. In his celebrated *Zen and Japanese Culture,* he writes that the 'Japanese love of Nature, I often think, owes much to the presence of Mount Fuji in the middle part of the main island of Japan' (1988:331). Others have echoed this view and claimed that the beauty and perfect shape of the mountain are proofs of the divine character of the Japanese islands (e.g. Idemitsu 1971). Such a view falls within the *nihonjinron* ('Japanese uniqueness') genre of analysis and has little explanatory value as it presupposes the existence of an objective—and thus not culturally acquired—standard of beauty. Such an assumption is, in my view, not warranted.

Closely related to this notion of love is the equally widely-held notion that the Japanese live in harmony with nature, which frequently is contrasted with the quest to 'conquer nature' allegedly found among westerners. 'The Japanese lives too close to nature for him to antagonize her, the benign mother of mankind', writes another authority on the subject (Anesaki 1973:6). Generalising for the whole of the Orient, Suzuki writes that in 'the East . . . this idea of subjecting Nature to the commands or service of man according to his selfish desires has never been cherished . . . Nature has been our constant friend and companion, who is to be absolutely trusted . . .' (1988:334).

But if these two notions are true, how can we then account for air and water pollution caused by Japanese companies both at home and abroad? How can we explain their reckless stripping of rain forests in Southeast Asia? And why is Mount Fuji—and other national parks—covered with litter after the tourist season? At the more subtle level, why are the trees in a Japanese garden not allowed to grow 'naturally', e.g. without being trimmed by humans? Or is it perhaps the case that the Japanese *used to* love nature and *used to* live in harmony with it, before the original ways of thought—perhaps embedded in Shintō and Buddhist sentiments—were destroyed by bad influences from the West?

Not so. There have been many serious cases of environmental destruction in premodern Japan. Marine resources have been depleted (Kalland 1994) and forests have been stripped (Totman 1989). Writing about forest recoveries in preindustrial Japan, Conrad Totman has the following important point to make:

> Foreigners, and some Japanese as well, often speak fondly of a special Japanese 'love of nature' that can be credited with this early modern forest recovery. To so argue, however, invites the tart query: did they love nature so much less during the ancient and early modern predations? More seriously, to advance this 'love of nature' as an explanation would be to misconstrue terms. The 'nature' of this sensibility is an aesthetic abstraction that has little relationship to the 'nature' of a real ecosystem. The sensibility associated with raising *bonsai,* viewing cherry blossoms, nurturing disciplined ornamental gardens, treasuring painted landscapes, and admiring chrysanthemums is an entirely different order of things from the concerns and feelings involved in policing woodlands and planting trees (Totman 1989:179).

In our attempts to contrast Japan—and the rest of Asia—with the western world we have looked for dissimilarities and ignored similarities. We have overlooked the fact that for millennia the Japanese have tried to conquer nature as much as westerners have done. At the technological level, rice fields have been carved out of steep hills, breakwaters have been built to make safe harbours, bays have been filled in to give additional farm land, animals have been domesticated and fishermen and sailors have obtained more seaworthy boats better able to stand against the wrath of the sea. At the cosmological level, rituals have been performed in order to come to terms with spirits that influence natural forces. In these matters, the Japanese hardly stand out from the rest of mankind.

The Japanese have, like most other people, an ambivalent attitude toward nature, in which their love of nature is only one dimension. But they also fear nature. They have learnt to cope with natural disasters caused by earthquakes, erupting volcanoes, typhoons and floods. But the threat of nature goes beyond this. Many Japanese seem to feel an abhorrence toward 'nature in the raw' (*nama no shizen,* Buruma 1985:65), and only by idealization or 'taming' (*narasu*)—e.g. 'cooking', through literature and fine arts, for example — does nature become palatable and even lovable. In other words, nature can be both raw and cooked, wild and tamed. Torn by destructive and creative forces, nature oscillates between its raw and cooked forms,[2] and in its cooked form nature and culture merge. It is in this latter state, as idealized nature, that nature is loved by most Japanese (cf. Saito 1985).

TAMING NATURE

There is a common belief in Japan that people, animals, plants and even inorganic objects have 'souls', or some inert power. In Buddhist doctrine one takes a holistic view and talks about 'Buddha-nature' in all things,[3] while in Shintō one talks about *kami,* e.g. a supernatural power that resides in anything which gives a person a feeling of awe. But to infuse animals and plants with Buddha-nature or *kami* does not mean that they are elevated to the status of some high-ranking deities, as claimed by Hajime Nakamura (1985:149). On the contrary, as *everything* has Buddha-nature or has the potential of harbouring supernatural powers, all living creatures are on the same level. There is thus not a sharp line, as in much of Judaeo-Christian thinking, between people and the rest.

This has, of course, far-reaching implications for Japanese attitudes but has not induced the Japanese to take a 'no-touch' approach to nature, as is the case with much of the recent ecological movement in the West. It is recognized that it is the nature of things that one organism feeds upon another, creating relations of indebtedness in the process. Although the Japanese do not talk about 'animal rights' (Totman 1989:180), human beings are considered to become indebted to nature when exploiting it. A whale which has been killed is regarded as having given itself up to mankind so that we can live, and in return the whalers have to perform memorial rites (*kuyō*) so that the whale can reach enlightenment, in much the same way as whalers do for their own ancestors (Kalland and Moeran 1992:150–155).[4]

Although there is no sharp distinction between deity, man and beast in Japanese cosmology, there is a clear dichotomy between 'inside' (*uchi*) and 'outside' (*soto*). The inside covers one's social universe. Through extensive flows of gifts and services, people are linked to one another through mutual obligations (*giri*). The inside world is predictable; one knows what to expect from one's relatives, neighbours and friends. The outside world is, on the other hand, threatening. This applies to one's social world as well as to nature.

One interesting Japanese concept in this connection is *yama,* usually translated as 'mountain'. But *yama* can also mean the 'wild' as opposed to the cultivated, particularly in connection with plants and animals, as when people refer to the completely flat pine grove (*matsubara*) along the beach as *yama. Yama-neko* is the term both for a wild cat and a lynx, and *yama-dashi* means a countryman. The notion of the wild is also apparent in the term *yama-ke/yama-ki* (lit. 'mountain spirit, mind or heart'), which can be translated as 'speculative disposition' or 'a gambling spirit'.[5] Finally, in Buddhist context *yama* has come to mean the temple.

What then do mountains, forests, 'the wild', and temples have in common? They can all be said to be bridges between the inside and the outside (e.g. between heaven and earth, or between this and the spiritual world). *Yama* denotes a zone of transition and is therefore potentially dangerous. It is precisely where most of the malevolent spirits are to be found, as mountains and trees are ideal abodes (*himorogi*) for spirits.[6] The *yama* therefore makes the ideal site for pilgrimages and other religious exercises. But *yama* is not only a bridge between human and divine worlds, it also denotes the outside in opposition to human society, which is inside.

Yama is thus both outside (in relation to society) and the border between inside and outside (in relation to the human and divine worlds), and for this reason—and also probably because of the physical discomfort of penetrating dense Japanese forests—most Japanese do not like to hike through forests and mountains, and if they occasionally do they take great precautions. The trip is turned into a ritual. Whether it is the lone pilgrim or a women's club going on a picnic, the paraphernalia must be proper. The pilgrim should preferably be dressed in white, carry a staff symbolizing the bonze Kōbō Daishi (774–835) and wear a straw hat symbolizing a coffin (Reader 1991:113–114; Statler 1984). By shaking rattles and chanting sutras, pilgrims try to ward off dangerous spirits. The women's club on an outing will most likely dress up in boots, rucksacks and hats, and their noisy chattering and laughter will be just as efficient to warn the spirits as the pilgrim's rattling and chanting.

The borders between the inside and the outside are not absolute but contextual and must be defined from case to case. Frequently the passage from one to the other is punctuated by rituals. When leaving the civilized world and entering forests, pilgrims may toss some dried fish (*iriko*) or salt so as to feed hungry ghosts and thus keep them busy eating. The entering and leaving of houses is also ritualized, and the entrance, being neither completely inside nor outside, is an anomalous zone (Ohnuki-Tierney 1984; Hendry 1987). In Shingū in the Fukuoka prefecture, most of the houses have an altar for the hearth deity Kōjin at the entrance in order to protect the house and its residents. The borders between the village and the outside world are also clearly marked by a series of powerful stones and other religious objects. The village shrine protects the community from bad influences originating in the dangerous northeast direction, and the temple and the graveyard protect Shingū from the almost equally dangerous southwest (Kalland, forthcoming).

By infusing spirits into nature, the Japanese also obtain the means of coming to terms with nature by establishing a working relationship with the spirits. This is done by performing rituals in which purification and offerings are a central part. In return, the spirits offer their protection. Harmony and happiness are seen as a 'natural', or original, states of affairs—the Japanese term for healthy, *genki,* literally means the original spirit—but this bliss can easily be destroyed if the balanced reciprocity between man and spirit is lost. Illness and accidents are often interpreted as an attempt by spirits—whether *kami,* ancestors or Buddhas—to communicate their misgivings and sufferings (Kalland 1991). By establishing a relationship of mutual dependency with the spirit world through rituals, the Japanese metaphorically come to terms with nature.

It has been argued that when nature is seen as immanently divine, as it allegedly is in Japan, this leads to a 'love of nature' relationship (Hjort and Svedin 1985:162). But such a world-view can also imply a danger to the environment, at least if nature is preserved because of the spirits residing therein. This can prevent the development of a true concern for nature as such. One may try to adjust to the spiritual forces, as when forces of geomancy (*kasō*) are taken into account in connection with building houses, but it is always possible to remove spirits through powerful rituals from one area of nature in order to utilize the area in question. Before the construction of a house can commence, for instance, a groundbreaking ceremony (*jichinsai*) is invariably performed. Spirits can be enticed to move into shrines so that their old abodes, in nature, can be appropriated. A divine nature is, therefore, by no means a guarantor against environmental degradation (see also Boomgaard, this volume).

There are other means of taming (*narasu*) or controlling nature than working through spirits. One way is to violate nature, as is done when forests are felled, mountains levelled or bays filled in order to create living space. Less destructive to the environment is taming, through making models of nature, such as can be seen in the Japanese gardens and miniature *bonsai* trees, where nothing is allowed to grow according to its programmed genes. Like a witch who tries to control and inflict harm upon a person by attacking a doll substitute, the Japanese gardener or *bonsai* enthusiast can control nature by violating its model.

In these examples the outcome is clearly a cultural product. But unlike the Versaille park, which with its strict symmetry is not intended to be anything but culture, the Japanese garden and miniature tree are meant to give an impression of being natural. They become idealized models of nature, as does fish when eaten in a Japanese meal. Pretending to be raw (e.g. 'uncooked'), it has gone through a highly ritualized process, which in fact can be said to have turned the fish into 'cooked' food (Lévi-Strauss 1969).[7] The Japanese garden, the miniature tree and the raw fish are all used as metonyms for both nature and culture, making nature and culture into overlapping rather than exclusive categories.

NATURE AS METAPHOR

With this rather negative approach to nature in the raw, to 'what is of itself', one might wonder why so many Japanese write poems about it. There are several possible answers to this seeming puzzle. First of all, writing about nature is a taming process in itself. Through literature, as well as through the visual arts, people become acquainted with nature, albeit in an idealized form. The Japanese verb *narasu,* which I have translated as 'to tame' can also mean 'to become accustomed to something'. The known is in Japan, as elsewhere, less threatening than the unknown.

Secondly, writing poems is a kind of spiritual training (*shugyō*), on a par with fencing, standing under waterfalls, meditating and other austerities. Thus, when the war lord Date Masamune (1565–1636) could find 'room in his brain to appreciate Nature and write poems on it' (Suzuki 1988:333), this is not—as claimed by Suzuki—necessarily an indication of 'how innate the love of Nature is in the Japanese heart' (ibid.), but must rather be seen as spiritual preparation for war. It is a method of reaching a higher level of awareness. Masamune could equally well have meditated or drunk a cup of tea. Probably he did both as parts of his spiritual training.

Finally, we have to understand much of the writing about nature as metaphors. It is hardly novel to claim that nature can be used metaphorically. Durkheim and Mauss pointed this out almost a century ago in their *Primitive Classification* (Durkheim and Mauss 1903), arguing that we use elements from nature in order to say something about the social (cf. also Hastrup 1989). And as pointed out by Ian Buruma:

> In art and daily life Japanese like to use natural images to express human emotions. Japanese novelists are masters at weaving natural metaphors and images into the fabric of their stories. And letters and postcards written by a Japanese always begin with a short description of the season (1984:64).

Through metaphors we understand the abstract in terms of the concrete (Lakoff and Johnson 1980:112). We try to say something about human emotions—like sadness, happiness, love, anger, frustration and so on—as well as about life—birth, ageing and death—through metaphors taken from a more concrete world. In Japanese culture the natural environment plays a prominent role as a repertoire for metaphors. Although they can be creative and highlight similarities hitherto hidden, metaphors are frequently conventional in that they play on already established similarities, as is usually the case when animals and plants are used metaphorically by the Japanese.[8]

Usually, if not always, animals and plants are stereotyped and given a standardized interpretation. Foxes are smart and badgers are tricksters, while turtles are hardworking, rabbits are easygoing, and carps are intelligent, strong and have—like turtles, elephants and cranes—long lives. Elements from nature are thus introduced in order to underscore a special point; the story-teller uses nature as metaphors for something else.

The same can be found in literature. In *haiku* poetry as well as in *enka* songs special meanings are conveyed by referring to the moon, cherry blossom, mountains, pines, rain and so forth. These all appear in a predictable, or conventional, way and even authors who have hardly been outside the main cities have become renowned for their sensitive praise of nature. The full moon is frequently used as a metaphor for the approaching degeneration ultimately leading to death but the moon also symbolizes the transient world; birth is followed by death in an endless cycle. The short transient life is also symbolized by the cherry blossom and even more so by the short blossom of the morning glory. The mountain bridges earth and heaven and the pine tree, with its long life and being an evergreen, might symbolize life's victory over death. Falling rain makes the ideal setting for farewells—as can be seen from the countless number of *enka* texts—and thus serves as a perfect metaphor for tears.

Beautiful landscapes are—like Japanese gardens—ranked in a hierarchy with the three places of Itsukushima, Amanohashidate, and Matsushima recognized as the most beautiful ones. The single most important factor for how many Japanese experience landscapes is whether they have beforehand been told that the landscape is of particular beauty. It might be argued that a landscape only becomes beautiful to the Japanese if something like a tourist board, a national committee or a film manufacturing company, has classified the spot as such, or if it has been praised by some famous poet or painter.[9] Only then, or when it has been designated as a national park, are people attracted to the site, and construction companies move in to build sky-line highways and hotels so that as many people as possible can enjoy the beauty from their car or bus windows and become 'one with nature'.[10] Moreover, experiencing nature in specific ways becomes institutionalized, as when the 'ecotourist' is told how to appreciate these beautiful spots in the best way—as to view Amanohashidate by bending down and looking between one's legs or to view the cherry blossom while drinking and singing with friends and colleagues, for example. A landscape is thus a catalyst, or a means to evoke certain emotions, and travelling to a famous scenic spot enables the Japanese to partake in a national tradition and to feel a member of the Japanese tribe.

Nature also structures time, and it does so at several levels. Buddhism stresses the impermanence of things, and this has certainly influenced the Japanese and made them more sensitive to seasonal changes in nature. The Japanese take great care to do everything at a proper time. Flower decorations (*ikebana*) and hanging scrolls (*kakejiku*) are adjusted to the season, and nobody climbs Mt. Fuji or goes swimming before the season is properly opened through Shintō rituals (*yama-biraki* and *umi-biraki*, respectively) in which spirits are requested to protect the climbers and swimmers. And the full moon is only worth seeing in September, when moon-viewing turns into a ritual. Other full moons are hardly worth appreciating.

Nature structures time and there are natural symbols for practically all annual celebrations, in *rite de passages* and in separating ceremonial time from ordinary time. I will not make an exhaustive list of plants and animals used in these ways but limit myself to mentioning the plants which are most closely associated with the 'Five Festivals' (*gosekku*) (Casal 1967). New Year decorations make liberal use of pines and we have already alluded to the symbolic meaning of this tree in Japanese culture.[11] Peaches and dolls are symbols for Girls' Day celebrated on 3 March and irises and flying carps are symbols for Boys' Day on 5 May. Besides blooming at the proper time, the peach and iris symbolize the female and male genitals, respectively. Bamboo plays a central role in the Star Festival (*Tanabata*) on 7 July, when bamboo poles adorned with colourful pieces of paper are on display. Bamboo is rich in symbolic meanings and is extensively used in Shintō rituals. In the autumn carefully grown chrysanthemums are exhibited throughout Japan, and this is the remnants of the fifth of the *gosekku* festivals, the Chrysanthemum Festival (originally held on the ninth day of the ninth lunar month). Blooming late in autumn, the chrysanthemum signals the coming of winter, and death, but it is also a metaphor for the sun (Casal 1967:102).[12]

CONCLUSION

The Japanese sensitivity to nature has been taken by many as 'love of nature' but, as has been argued in this chapter, this is nature in its idealized form. Matching this 'love' is their abhorrence towards nature in the raw. One therefore seeks to tame, or to come to terms with, nature in various ways, such as through rituals, literature and visual arts. Through such processes, nature appears in a cultivated form (e.g. gardens, miniature trees, raw fish), which then can be used metonymically for both nature as a whole and for culture. Hence nature and culture fail to become exclusive categories in Japan, like in many other societies (see, for example, Goody 1977; MacCormack 1980; Strathern 1980).

But above all nature is used as a reservoir for metaphors. The Japanese like to express themselves in metaphors and a great number of these metaphors are taken from their natural environments. This and the Buddhist concept of the impermanence of all things have certainly caused some Japanese to be sensitive to nature and to changes therein. For those socialized into a certain culture, references to animals, stones, landscapes or natural phenomena might set off a series of associations. Through standardized usages in literature and folktales, metaphors evoke a given feeling in the listener or reader (Berque

1986:105). It is thus possible to transmit a message rich in content by a short *haiku*, as in the following written by Ryōta in the eighteenth century, in which rain, the moon, pines and the season are all important images:

In the June rains,
One night, as if by stealth
The moon, through the pines

(Suzuki 1988:387)

To take this sensitivity to nature for love masks important points, however. For it matters little to most Japanese whether they observe these changes in a small flower in the backyard or in a vaste nature reserve. The quantity of nature, if I can put it that way, is of no great importance, and nature invisible to an actor—as one located in faraway places—is of little general interest. Many scholars have stressed the particularistic character of Japanese norms and this applies equally well to the environment. It is just as difficult to get Japanese to fight against environmental destruction *per se*, as it is to get them to fight for human rights in distant countries. Only when nature is brought into the realm of the known, e.g. tamed, and there are some immediate personal gains, do most Japanese become interested in protecting nature (McKean 1981; Mouer and Sugimoto 1986:336–337). The persons who are most likely to protect the environment are those with vested economic interests in it, like fishermen, farmers and loggers—or the tourist industry if nature is turned into a commodity for their use. One important lesson we can learn from this is that there is hardly any direct relationship between the Japanese sensitivity to nature and their environmental behaviour.

NOTES

1. There are a number of Japanese terms for 'nature', the most common are probably *shizen* (lit. 'by the way of itself') and *tennen* ('by the way of heaven'). There is a slight difference in nuance between the two concepts. There is a tendency for *tennen* to refer more to concrete objects, as in *tennen shigen* (natural resources), while *shizen* refers more to the abstract, as in *shizenhō* (natural law) and *shizen no chikara* (forces of nature). Both appear as adjectives (natural; *shizen no* and *tennen no*) and as adverbs (naturally; *shizen ni* and *tennen ni*). For a recent discussion of the concept *shizen*, see Tellenbach and Kimura (1989).

2. The oscillation between nature in the raw and cooked forms appears in Japanese myths, as in the struggle between the Sun Goddess Amaterasu and her unruly brother, Susano-o, who destroys her rice-fields. The contest between creative and destructive forces is, of course, a central theme in most religions.

3. Nishitani sees 'nature' as a process (1982:149): 'Each thing is itself in not being itself, and is not itself in being itself. Its being is illusion in its truth and truth in its illusion. This may sound strange the first time one hears it, but in fact it enables us for the first time to conceive of a *force* by virtue of which all things are gathered together and brought into relationship with one another, a force which, since ancient times, has gone by the name of "nature" (*physis*).'

4. *Kuyō* are also performed for inorganic objects, as for example old needles. It should also be stressed that nature, e.g. plants and animals, might be indebted to benevolent human beings.

5. *Yama-ke* is written in two characters which alternatively can be read *san-ki*, in which case it means 'mountain air'.

6. For this reason trees are often venerated in Japan, as are mountains. Most shrines are situated in a grove of trees, and sacred Shintō paraphernalia—such as the sprig offered to the deities (*tamagushi*) and the sacred staff *gohei* which both symbolize the presence of deities—symbolize trees.

7. Something similar is at work when the Japanese paint an ugly concrete wall green to allude to nature, or when the Umeda underground station in Osaka plays singing birds over the loudspeaker system. The Japanese are quite at ease with this kind of 'synthetic nature'.

8. In an essay discussing the occurrence of animals and plants in Japanese folktales, Mayer (1981) has analysed 3,000 folktales from the Niigata prefecture, featuring 22 kinds of four-legged animals, 35 kinds of birds, 18 kinds of fish, 19 kinds of other animals (including snakes), 17 kinds of insects, 37 kinds of trees and 64 kinds of other plants.

9. Recognized beauty spots are celebrated in an unending stream of novels, poetry, paintings and gardens. Mt. Fuji, for example, has been painted from all conceivable, and most inconceivable, angles by all kinds of artists and it is praised in literature. Models of the mountains are also important features in gardens, as for example at Kumamoto's Suizenji.

10. This is indeed very different from the attitude in many other countries where any building activity, as well as motor transport, in a national park is prohibited.

11. A bitter orange *daidai*, which written in other characters also means 'generation after generation', is frequently used together with twigs of pine for such decorations, thus underlining the request for a long life and prosperity of the house.

12. Casal (1967:102–103) sees the chrysanthemum as a symbol of the sun, with the flower's petals as rays, which

might explain why the descendants of the Sun Goddess have a stylized chrysanthemum on their crest. It should, perhaps, be added here that Japanese culture is, like most others, a totemic society in that natural objects, such as animals and plants, are used to classify people. Clans and lineages often have plants on their crests, and each prefecture has a prefectural flower and animal, for example. (See also Moeran and Skov, this volume.)

REFERENCES

Anesaki, Masaharu. 1973. *Art, Life, and Nature in Japan*. Tokyo: Charles E. Tuttle.

Berque, Augustin. 1986. 'The sense of nature and its relation to space in Japan'. In Hendry, J. and J. Webber (eds), *Interpreting Japanese Society: Anthropological Approaches*. Oxford: JASO.

Boomgaard, Peter. 1995. 'Sacred trees and haunted forests in Indonesia—particularly Java, nineteenth and twentieth centuries'. In Bruun, O. and A. Kalland (eds), *Asian Perceptions of Nature: A Critical Approach*. Richmond, Surrey, U.K.: Curzon Press.

Buruma, Ian. 1985. *A Japanese Mirror: Heroes and Villains in Japanese Culture*. Harmondsworth: Penguin Books.

Casal, U. A. 1967. *The Five Sacred Festivals of Japan—Their Symbolism & Historical Development*. Tokyo: Sophia University/Charles E. Tuttle.

Devall, Bill and George Sessions. 1985. *Deep Ecology—Living as if nature mattered*. Salt Lake City: Gibbs Smith, Publ.

Durkheim, Emile and Marcel Mauss. 1903. *Primitive Classification*. (English edition 1963, translated by R. Needham). London: Cohen-West.

Goody, Jack R. 1977. *The Domestication of the Savage Mind*. Cambridge: Cambridge University Press.

Hastrup, Kirsten. 1989. 'Nature as historical space'. *Folk* 31:5–20.

Hendry, Joy. 1987. *Understanding Japanese Society*. London: Croom Helm.

Hjort, Anders and Uno Svedin (eds), 1985. *Jord—Människa—Himmel*. Stockholm: Liber Förlag.

Idemitsu, Sazō. 1971. *Be A True Japanese*. Tokyo: Idemitsu Kosan Co., Ltd.

Kalland, Arne. 1991. 'Facing the spirits: Illness and healing in a Japanese Community'. *NIAS Report*, 1991–2. Copenhagen: Nordic Institute of Asian Studies.

——— 1994. *Fishing Villages in Tokugawa Japan*. London: Curzon Press/Honolulu: University of Hawaii Press.

——— forthcoming. 'Geomancy in a Japanese Community'. In Asquith, P. and A. Kalland (eds), *The Culture of Japanese Nature*. London: Curzon Press.

Kalland, Arne and Brian Moeran. 1992. *Japanese Whaling—End of an Era?* London: Curzon Press.

Lakoff, George and Mark Johnson. 1980. *Metaphors We Live By*. Chicago: The University of Chicago Press.

Lévi-Strauss, Claude. 1969. *The Raw and the Cooked*. New York: Harper & Row.

——— 1973. *Structural Anthropology*. Harmondsworth: Penguin Books.

MacCormack, Carol P. 1980. 'Nature, culture and gender: a critique'. In MacCormack, C. and M. Strathern (eds), *Nature, Culture and Gender*. Cambridge: Cambridge University Press.

McKean, Margaret A. 1981. *Environmental Protest and Citizen Politics in Japan*. Berkeley: University of California Press.

Mayer, Fanny Hagin. 1981. 'Fauna and flora in Japanese folktales'. *Asian Folklore Studies* 40(1):23–32.

Merchant, Carolyn. 1980. *The Death of Nature—Women, Ecology and the Scientific Revolution*. New York: Harper & Row.

Moeran, Brian and Lise Skov. 1994. 'Japanese advertising nature: Ecology, women, fashion and art'. In Bruun, O. and A. Kalland (eds), *Asian Perceptions of Nature: A Critical Approach*. London: Curzon Press.

Mouer, Ross and Yoshio Sugimoto. 1986. *Images of Japanese Society*. London: KPI.

Nakamura Hajime. 1985. 'Japansk kultursfär'. In Hjort, Anders and Uno Svedin (eds), *Jord—Människa—Himmel*. Stockholm: Liber Förlag.

Nishitani, Keiji. 1982. *Religion and Nothingness*. Berkeley: University of California Press.

Ohnuki-Tierney, Emiko. 1984. *Illness and Culture in Contemporary Japan—An Anthropological View*. Cambridge: Cambridge University Press.

Reader, Ian. 1991. *Religion in Contemporary Japan*. London: Macmillan.

Saito, Yuriko. 1985. 'The Japanese appreciation of nature'. *The British Journal of Aesthetics* 25(3):239–251.

Statler, Oliver. 1984. *Japanese Pilgrimage*. London: Pan Books.

Strathern, Marilyn. 1980. 'No nature, no culture: the Hagen case'. In MacCormack, C. and M. Strathern (eds), *Nature, Culture and Gender*. Cambridge: Cambridge University Press.

Suzuki, Daisetz. 1988. *Zen and Japanese Culture*. Tokyo: Charles E. Tuttle.

Tellenbach, Hubertus and Bin Kimura. 1989. 'The Japanese concept of "nature"'. In Callicott, J. B. and R. T. Ames (eds), *Nature in Asian Traditions of Thought: Essays in Environmental Philosophy*. Albany: State University of New York Press.

Totman, Conrad. 1989. *The Green Archipelago: Forestry in Preindustrial Japan*. Berkeley: University of California Press.

Nature Tamed

Gardens as a Microcosm of Japan's View of the World

JOY HENDRY

INTRODUCTION

Gardens all over the world represent the efforts of human beings to create cultural versions of their natural surroundings, whether it be for purely functional reasons such as the production of food and shelter, or for more spiritual and/or aesthetic purposes.[1] They display local ideas about how the natural world is perceived, how it is constructed by that particular culture, how it relates to ideas about the supernatural, and how things in it are or should be ordered in a domesticated form. Attention to gardens, then, in Japan or elsewhere, provides a useful way of approaching the theme of this book and investigating the extent to which categories of culture and nature can be identified and discussed in a particular local context.

Kalland has argued that nature and culture fail to make exclusive categories in Japan, as in many other societies, and he sees the act of creating gardens as one of the processes through which nature is cultivated into a form which 'can be used metonymically for both nature as a whole and for culture' (Kalland 1995: 254). He argues that the Japanese 'love of nature' is for nature in an idealized form, such as a garden, and this may be contrasted with the Japanese 'abhorrence towards nature in the raw' which necessitates a seeking 'to tame, or to come to terms with' nature (ibid.). One way to 'tame' nature is to control it by making models of it, he argues.

In contrast, Japanese writers emphasize that they live in harmony with nature, unlike the Westerner, who is concerned with controlling or conquering nature (e.g. Stewart-Smith 1987: 108). Kalland notes this emphasis, but he argues that the Japanese have for millennia tried to conquer nature just as Westerners have done. They have carved rice-fields out of steep hillsides, built breakwaters to make safe harbours, and they have learned to cope with disasters caused by earthquakes, erupting volcanoes, typhoons and floods. They fear 'nature in the raw', and the nature they love is 'cooked' nature, made palatable through culture such as literature and fine arts, through religious ritual, and through cultivation. A garden may be seen as a prime example of this 'cooked nature'.

According to Kalland's argument, it is through this 'cooking' process that a garden provides a means of bringing the beautiful but unpredictable and dangerous wild into a manageable, cultural context. In terms familiar to students of Japanese society, building a garden is a way of mediating between the threatening, fearful aspects of the 'outside', of nature in the raw, and the safety and security of the 'inside' world of social and cultural life. The garden is within a house or temple compound, very often totally hidden from the outside world, but it represents the world outside. By this means the Japanese can 'love' a nature which is also seen as dangerous, and which, as Kalland and others point out forcibly, is frequently exploited in its untamed form (e.g. Stewart-Smith 1987).

In this chapter, some of the characteristics of Japanese gardens will be examined in the context of this model. If gardens are a means of taming or cooking nature, then they should reveal a wealth of information about the complicated relationship between culture and nature in that particular context. As it happens, they also reveal ideas about how the wild outside nature may be approached. In any society, a garden is an expression of a system of ideas, a system of classification and order, and in this chapter the Japanese version will be scrutinized, both in its present form and its historical development.

My own interest in gardens arose from a longer-term interest in 'wrapping' (Hendry 1989, 1993), and

Hendry, Joy, "Nature Tamed: Gardens as a Microcosm of Japan's View of the World," in Pamela J. Asquith and Arne Kalland, Eds., *Japanese Images of Nature: Cultural Perspectives,* Richmond, Surrey, U.K.: Curzon Press, 1997, pp. 83–103. Reprinted by permission of the author.

I have tentatively discussed gardens as an example of the wrapping of space. Various writers have used notions of layering, folding, creasing, and even wrapping itself, to describe the way Japanese gardens are arranged (Bognar 1985: 51–54, 61; Duff-Cooper 1991: 14; Maki 1978, 1979), but there seemed to be a lack of anything significant which could be described as the 'wrapped'. This is a problem which I have addressed in another paper (Hendry 1994), but the concept of wrapping in the way I have used it would seem to describe a process of cultural refinement very similar to the 'cooking' or 'taming' process discussed above.

Actually, the idea of 'wrapping' is more appropriate for describing Japanese gardens than the idea of 'cooking', because the term more easily embodies the aesthetic aspects of creating a garden. In English, neither term does justice to the Japanese concern with aesthetics in both wrapping and cooking, but the former is closer and it makes possible a comparison with the wrapping of the body and the wrapping of space as well as the wrapping of objects (Hendry 1993). In the latter case, the aesthetics of preparing food are not necessarily associated with cooking, rather with cutting and shaping, but the term does carry more anthropological content to represent the complicated cultural process of mediating between 'raw' and 'cooked' nature.

Either way, the garden can be read as an expression of the perception of nature held by its creators at the time when it was created, and both metaphors will be employed in the pages that follow. The material to be presented covers different periods in Japanese history, and views of nature have clearly undergone many influences and modifications which can be detected in different garden styles. In the earliest examples, there is a much stronger supernatural element than in the later ones, for example, and it will be seen that influences from further and further afield have affected the perception of the relationship between the natural and the supernatural, and its cultural manifestation.

A benefit of this approach is that it allows the identification of an underlying form for the garden in its role as a mediator between culture/nature, and this form, once realized, can be detected in other human modifications of the apparently natural world. The first section of this chapter introduces some of the most basic elements of this form, as they appear in contemporary Japanese gardens; and they are then examined and refined in the two historical sections that follow. In the last section, it is argued that the resultant new form of the garden may be identified in human encounters with a wilder version of nature so that the principles of 'wrapping' again allow a socially acceptable version of the mediation process.

ENCLOSURE, *OKU* AND 'BORROWED SCENERY'

The distinction between inside (*uchi*) and outside (*soto*) is an important one at various levels in Japanese society, as has often been discussed (Hendry 1995; Kalland 1995). Its application is as clear in defining the physical boundaries of a house and garden as it is in identifying a group of relatives to entertain at a rite of passage. In the first case, a porch between the inside and outside worlds provides a place for shoes to be left: their removal marks the transition from one world to the other. In the second case, a seating plan will reflect the relationships of the guests to the principal characters of the occasion, whether it be for birth, marriage or death.

Children in Japan grow up gradually increasing their circles of inside acquaintances, drawing into their social world neighbours, classmates, friends and colleagues to supplement the inner family core, and extending the physical boundaries of known space within which they may operate relatively safely. The home is the first inside space, then the neighbourhood, the kindergarten, school, the workplace and so on. The social world has multiple layers, just like a formal gift. The notion eventually becomes a conceptual one, and it is relative to the situation a little like a segmentary system, but it is a firm and clear idea, even at the level of Japan and the outside world.

Within this system of classification, a Japanese garden is usually conceptually 'inside', though it is probably physically outside. It may be inside a family home; indeed one of the words commonly used for home, *katei,* includes the character for garden in combination with the character for house. It is not like gardens in Britain and America, however, which are very often at least in part on view to passers-by, situated between the house and the main road. In Japan the gardens of a house are generally hidden from the public gaze, glimpsed instead from the inner rooms, and usually best viewed from the guest's seat in the reception room for special occasions. They are a piece of the outside enclosed or 'wrapped up' by layers of inside.

Other gardens are located inside temples, or shrines, and there is usually little hint from the outside world of the beauty that can be found within the layers that surround it. Even when a garden is built to surround a building such as a palace, a hotel or a skyscraper, it is important that there be some kind of enclosure around that (e.g. Cave 1993: 72), and the nature of this enclosure may be an integral part of the construction of the garden. Very often it will be a bamboo fence or a hedge, but it may also be a white-washed wall, perhaps with a tiled roof on top of it. In any event the garden is *enclosed* and this is one of the most persistent characteristic features of its form.

The conception of the garden as associated with 'inside' can be developed further. A word often used in describing features of Japanese gardens is *oku,* a complex notion which stands for the interior or inner recesses of a building, wood or mountain; for the wife of a household whose place is thereby expressed as inside; and for an inner depth which has esoteric connotations. It is imbued with a kind of sacredness which 'implies something abstract and profound', according to the architect, Maki Fumihiko (1979: 53). Within the garden, one of the aims is to create an illusion of space and distance in a relatively confined space in order to give a sense of depth and mystery. This may in turn be expected to invoke a kind of communion with nature, or, with the help and symbolism of the enclosure, to focus the mind on a spiritual or transcendental experience.[2]

The garden is enclosed, then, but the enclosure by no means ignores and seals off the world outside itself. Indeed, another phenomenon which is often found in Japanese gardens is an element of *shakkei,* which literally means 'borrowed scenery'. The garden may be purposely planned to incorporate features of the distant landscape into its overall design, so that it allows a part of the surrounding, very often a 'wild' mountain to be safely viewed from within its walls. Although *shakkei* is a relatively recent word to describe this element of garden construction,[3] the practice of incorporating some distant view into the design of a garden is much older (e.g. Higuchi 1983: 20). According to one source, it dates back to the middle of the fourteenth century when the garden of the Tenryūji temple became the place to view the cherry blossom and the colours of maple created on the slopes of Arashiyama by the *shogun* Ashikaga Takauji (Itō 1973: 26–27). The practice became known in Kyoto as *ikedori*—'capturing alive' some distant view as a feature of a specific garden.[4]

According to Itō Teiji's book about *shakkei* and its prototype *ikedori* (Itō 1973), neither notion is expressed by a mere garden with a view, however. There is much more to the phenomenon than this. His study identifies four essential features which the gardens share. The first two are the given elements: the garden and the view. The third is a device known as *mikiri,* whereby the view is 'trimmed' to capture only certain desired parts of it,[5] by means of a wall, a thick, pruned hedge, or perhaps by the use of a low hill or embankment within the garden itself. The fourth essential feature is a means of linking the distant scenery with the foreground of the garden through intermediary objects such as an arrangement of stones (in the case of Tenryūji), some tall trees, a wood, a stone lantern, or by careful use of the sky as an 'empty' area in the scene created.

The garden is not exclusively 'inside', then, for it literally draws on a part of the 'outside', illustrating Kalland's argument perfectly. The garden may be enclosed, even expressing a human concern to look inside more deeply, but in 'capturing alive' a distant scene, it clearly still expresses an open interest in the raw nature beyond. This raw nature is 'captured', if not entirely 'tamed', and the garden designer focuses attention on the effect created in the garden. He trims it for his own purposes; he adjusts the middle ground successfully to link it into his own creation; he 'cooks' or 'wraps' the scene so that the garden successfully mediates between the house and the wild.

GARDENS AS SACRED SPACES

The notion of *shakkei* is an illustration of the way in which an 'inside' garden nevertheless draws clearly on the 'outside' world. It is simply an example, and there are others that will emerge, but it is interesting at this point to look for pre-existing classificatory principles which it may have manifested in an adapted form. Although *shakkei* itself is said to be a relatively new concept, with an earlier version in the Heian period, the principles it expresses go back even further. An examination of these sets the stage for describing the way the development of other features of Japanese gardens fall into place in the classificatory system being established.

The prototype for the garden (*niwa*) in Japan is said to have been a cleared space, bounded with a straw rope or bamboo fence, and very often covered in small pebbles, or moss.[6] The area was sacred, cleared and purified for the purpose of summoning deities, a point of contact and communication with the spiritual world (Bring and Wayembergh 1981: 145; Hayakawa 1973: 27). A particularly fine extant example is to be found at the Kamowake-Ikazuchi Shrine, at Kamigamo in Kyoto, which, according to local publicity, was originally constructed in the seventh century for the worship of the nearby Mount Kōya. Although there is no mention of the idea of *shakkei* here, the mountain was evidently the focus of attention when it was built and there had previously been another shrine on top of it.

The elements of a garden discussed above are clearly present in this example. The area is enclosed, if only in a symbolic fashion, with a length of twisted straw rope, and there is an outside feature which is being drawn in. A sacred space of this sort may be described as a *yorishiro,* a 'landing place' for the gods, thus providing a means of communication with the spiritual world. In this case, the object of attention was Mount Kōya, and the example clearly illustrates the way Japanese views of nature must inevitably include the spiritual presence that natural phenomena are held to embody. This early 'garden' mediates the human/spiritual divide in a form that clearly represents the culture/nature distinction being discussed.

Other sacred spaces focus their attention on other 'natural' phenomena, perhaps trees or large stones and rocks, and sometimes these can be enclosed and worshipped as they stand. A shrine compound may be built around them and they become part of the controlled 'inside' world. Within the Kamigamo Shrine in Kyoto, there are several bounded trees and rocks, and these provide other examples of *yorishiro.* They are within the shrine compound, but again they represent the spiritual presence they are said to embody. This is a point of contact, bounded by the shrine compound—a physical attempt literally to capture and tame the spiritual force, but the force is of course much larger. It is part of the great 'natural' world outside.

The Kamigamo Shrine illustrated another common pattern in Japan of situating a shrine at the entrance to a sacred site which is itself the location of another shrine further away. The distant inner shrine in these cases is known as the *okumiya,* where *oku* (inside, or innermost recess) is as discussed above, and *miya* is simply a word for shrine. The *oku* in this case has a physical location which is represented in the second shrine, and may provide a paradigm for the later use of a conceptual *oku* in garden design. Indeed, Maki traces the development of the directional and sacred attributes of the notion of *oku* from the way villages would nestle against a sacred mountain, whose often forbidden depths provide the site of their *okumiya* (Maki 1979: 54–55). The physical protection of the 'natural' mountain was thereby reflected in ideas about the supernatural force it was held to embody.

An alternative theory Maki cites about the origin of the word *oku* traces it from *oki,* meaning 'offshore', which relates the notion to an idea that gods originated from over the sea (ibid.: 56). This idea is supported by the next major influence in Japanese gardens which did literally come from over the sea, where Chinese legends seem to have given rise to the widespread form of islands in water as key features composing a garden. This was apparently originally due to efforts of the Han Emperor Wu (140–89 B.C.), who tried to lure the Immortals to his palace by constructing representations of the mythical isles where they were reported to live (Keswick 1986: 35–40; Kuck 1968: 39–43).

These isles must again have been associated with the periphery of known territory for they were reported to float in and out of view, and to disappear if one tried to approach them, hence the Emperor's novel idea to attract the Immortals to him. One tale reports that the Immortals grew tired of floating around so the Supreme Being sent enormous tortoises to carry them on their backs, although two of the islands were lost altogether when a passing grant scooped up the animals in a net (Kuck 1968: 40–43). The Immortals were also said to ride around on the backs of cranes (ibid.: 40), and some of the later depictions of these islands, termed Hōrai in Japanese, include arrangements which are said to represent the tortoise and the crane, together now known as symbols of longevity.

Certainly the characteristic features mentioned in early reference to a garden in the seventh-century book of Japanese poetry known as the *Manyōshu* are a pond and an island (Ota 1972: 106). The first is said to have been built by Sōga Umako, who was also an early supporter of Buddhism, introduced from south-west Korea, so Ota surmises that the art of garden-making may have been introduced from this source too (ibid.). He also notes that in another of these early gardens the pond was bordered by rocks 'arranged to give the impression of a rocky seashore' (ibid.: 107), appropriate he feels since 'from ancient times rocks like this were worshipped as they were thought to be places where the Gods descended' (ibid.).

The precise origin and port of entry of this type of garden, and the reasons for its success, remain open to discussion, but the pond with an island or islands is a feature which has persisted through to the present day in many Japanese gardens. Again, its early prototype would seem to have been an attempt at mediation between the cultural world of humans and the supernatural world which was held to populate the 'natural' world beyond. From the perspective of Japan, I suggest that the form of wrapping or taming nature in this early version expresses an area of conceptual overlap between the world of gods and the world of strangers over the sea, which has been much discussed in the anthropological literature on Japan (e.g. Hendry 1988; Yoshida 1981).[7]

During the Heian period, from the ninth to the twelfth centuries, Japanese culture developed its own version of the Chinese models for government and architecture it had imported more or less wholesale for the first capital city of Nara, after which the preceding era was named. According to the paintings and literature of the period, it was common for nobles in Japan, as in China, to construct a large lake in the grounds of their palaces and boat amongst the islands as an expression of their love of nature. They would also go fishing, but although both these practices continue on the lakes of Chinese gardens, Japanese ponds are now usually only stocked with ornamental fish which are viewed from the banks or a nearby building.

The gardens of this type which still exist in Japan were modified to a more specific kind of sacred space, associated directly with Buddhism. A good example is preserved at Byōdoin in Uji, just outside Kyoto.[8] Originally the site of the villa of a member of the powerful Fujiwara family, Michinaga, it was converted into a Buddhist temple by his son Yorimichi in 1052. Like later gardens of the twelfth and thirteenth centuries, it aimed to reconstruct the Jōdō Buddhist paradise on earth (Ota 1972: 113; cf. Buisson 1981: 218), which, according to Hayakawa, spells a tale of disenchantment with the government of the period and an expression of hope for salvation after death (Hayakawa 1973: 36). The sacred space has taken on a new dimension, then, but the garden continues to concern itself with the 'cooking' or 'wrapping' of nature.

THE RECONSTRUCTION OF NATURE AND ZEN GARDENS

It was during the Heian period, in the eleventh century, that the first extant document explicitly about gardening in Japan was written. Unsigned, and known simply as the *Sakuteiki* ('Manual of Garden Construction'), it is usually attributed to the son of Yorimichi, mentioned above, one Tachibana-no-Toshitsuna. Three overall principles, laid out on the first page, make a very clear connection between observing nature and creating gardens (Tachibana 1976: 1). The first exhorts the garden designer 'to design each part of the garden tastefully, recalling your memories of how nature presented itself for each feature' (ibid.). The second advises study of the work of past masters, and the third reads: 'Think over the famous places of scenic beauty throughout the land, and . . . design your garden with the mood of harmony, modelling after the general air of such places' (ibid.).

A whole section is devoted to taboos on the placement of stones, and there is much reference to Taoist and Buddhist ideas, so the supernatural is still a concern, as are the foreign influences, but the overall thrust of the advice is about the representation of the 'natural' physical environment. The word used for 'landscape' (*sansui*) is taken directly from the Chinese, a combination of the characters for mountain and water, and a great deal of space is devoted to types of water and island design. The latter may be made to depict hills, fields, forests, rocky shores, clouds and mist, among other things, and nine different manners of falling are discussed for waterfalls. The placement of stones is of substantial importance throughout the document, and there is a section on the planting of trees.

This manuscript also briefly introduces the idea of a 'dry landscape' (*kare-sansui*) of stones, where various impressions, including that of a waterfall, may be created through the use of stones. Such arrangements were developed over the succeeding centuries and have since become well known as the contemplative gardens of Zen Buddhism. They were built to represent much more than the features of a real landscape: intended, on the one hand, to recall an ink painting of the real mountain/water landscape, after the Chinese fashion, but also to carry deeper meaning in the way the stones were arranged. Their transcendental aspect, said to invoke profound understanding inexpressible in other forms, provides a good illustration of the complexity of the relationship between culture and nature in the Japanese case.

The garden of Daisen'in, in the Daitokuji complex in Kyoto, is a well-known example where a written explanation is available (Daisen'in n.d.). Built in 1509, it has one group of stones which represents a giant tortoise, said to symbolize the depths to which the human spirit can sink, since it seeks the bottom of the ocean. Another group is arranged like a crane with extended wings since the crane in flight symbolizes the heights to which the human spirit can soar. Mount Hōrai, in the middle, thus represents a union of heaven and earth, joy and disappointment, which are said to comprise the human experience. White gravel represents water, flowing around the islands in various moods, each depicting a stage in the course of life: the impulsiveness of youth; the confrontation with the 'why' of existence; a great wall of doubt and contradiction as the flow comes up against a corridor crossing the garden. This flows on into the broader stream of human understanding around a ship laden with the treasures of experience, and finally, into the purifying ocean of eternity (ibid.).

Another good example is the dry stone waterfall in the upper part of the famous moss garden (Kokedera) at Saihōji, designed by Musō Sōseki, the priest who gave the gardens their present character in the early fourteenth century. This collection of stones still inspires debate 600 years later. According to Hayakawa Masao, who describes them as suggesting 'immovable resistance against the pounding of a mighty waterfall and the frantically dashing currents at its base' (Hayakawa 1973: 62), they also 'express the passion that raged in the heart of a great man who . . . lived in a Japan torn by civil strife . . . and filled with suffering and insecurity' (ibid.: 64).

Hayakawa questions the suggestion of another commentator, the architect Horiguchi Sutemi, who traces the appeal of this stone garden 'to the sacred precincts and the stone-and-gravel arrangements of Shintō shrines' (ibid.: 66). He recognizes that in both cases there is 'a sympathy between stones and the inner world of human emotions' (ibid.), but he argues that there is a difference. The emotions inspired by the stones in shrine gardens 'are those of reverence before something created by nature', whereas those awakened by Musō's garden 'center upon respect for the results of human creativity' (ibid.: 67). An apparently clear differentiation between nature and culture is then immediately modified, however, for Hayakawa goes on to concede that in each case there are mutual reverberations between the human heart and the physical form—it is merely the point of departure which is different (ibid.).

In both cases, the stones provide a representation of 'raw' natural phenomena in a 'cooked' form, but the cooking process has changed. The stones which were worshipped in Shintō shrines were seen as a means of communicating with the deities they were thought to embody, as explained above, and the enclosure was part of a process of mediation between the inside and the outside world of nature. In the Zen Buddhist garden, the mediation is through elements of nature, enclosed into a work of art which represents the outside world to be sure, but the direction of attention is inward. The gardens are expected to inspire an understanding of the inner self, a clearing of the worldly distractions to be found outside.

The next stage in the development of gardens in Japan pursues this aim even further, but also draws on the Shintō idea of purification by introducing water basins. The prototype for these was a natural pool by a waterfall, to be seen at Ginkakuji in Kyoto, but a variety of stone and bamboo arrangements are now to be found in the tea garden. Sometimes known as the *rōji,* or dewy path, this kind of garden was designed to help participants in the tea ceremony to prepare themselves psychologically as they approached the tea house (Itō 1973: 69). There is an outer and an inner garden and a physical move from one to the other is seen as parallel to the symbolic journey 'from the mundane to the ritual', according to the anthropologist Dorinne Kondo, whose structural analysis of the tea ceremony also describes it as a 'path to Enlightenment' which in a Zen context is supposed to lead to a state of 'emptiness' (Kondo 1985: 291–294).

Here in the tea garden is perhaps the best representation of the communion between culture and nature, for the tea house itself is supposed to be as simple and unpretentious as possible, as are the utensils employed in the ceremony. The house is designed to resemble a hut in the mountains, with an entrance that human beings must almost crawl through it, and the cups and serving utensils are plain and rugged. Yet the ceremony represents the height of Japanese culture. It requires years of practice to be able to perform it to perfection, and days of preparation to create exactly the right atmosphere for the guests. Much attention is given to the garden, which should be simple and unadorned, giving the artless impression of a path in the hills (Kuck 1968: 195), but it should be scrupulously clean and freshly watered.

It is here that the wrapping metaphor becomes more useful than the cooking and taming ones again, for it is clear that the cultural version of nature is now heavily influenced by the raw (wild) version so that, as Kalland has noted, 'in its cooked form nature and culture merge' (Kalland 1995: 246). If we posit wrapping as a cultural activity which expresses ideas through its particular variety, though building on an existing form, we can now talk of the importance to Japanese culture of the period, and indeed, to this day, of the elements of uncluttered nature, though neatly bounded within an entirely cultural context. Moreover, the *idea* of nature itself is being used to express a high level of cultural refinement.[9]

We have shown in this section that the human relationship with that cultural version of nature can be abstract and profound, that elements of nature, suitably arranged (or wrapped) in an artistic form, can be read as expressions of the deepest human concerns. In the previous section, the garden expressed a relationship with a 'natural' world full of supernatural beings, not clearly distinguished from the strange people who lived over the sea. In the final section, we turn to a more secular expression of the relationship between nature and culture, and we take the principles of classification of the Japanese garden out into the wider world.

GARDENS AS A MODEL FOR JAPAN'S VIEW OF THE WORLD

While early Japanese gardens aimed to commune with and later reproduce mythological worlds, or represent life in a transcendental form, some gardens built during the Tokugawa period were concerned with reconstructing natural sites and scenes for different reasons. The garden became a place to stroll around, with various 'viewing spots', and these were often designed to evoke images. The oldest garden in Tokyo (then called Edo)—the Koishikawa Kōrakuen, first laid out in 1629 by Tokugawa Yorifusa—reproduces scenic spots such as the Lushan (mountain) in China, the Oikawa (river) and the Togetsukyō (bridge) in Kyoto. Waterfalls and bridges were designed to allow lords from the country to evoke their homeland without making an arduous journey away from the capital.

Something of the same spirit may have inspired Baron Iwasaki Yatarō, a founder of the Mitsubishi firm, who reconstructed in the early twentieth century another Edo garden now known as Kiyosumi Teien, and delivered huge stones brought from all over the country as ballast in his ships, to be laid out and named as special features of the garden. The same man acquired another beautiful Edo garden, Rikugien, but this one was restored to its original arrangement of providing spots of literary significance—eighty-eight in all—the idea of its founder, Yanagisawa Yoshiyasu, of who was known for his literary accomplishments. Even in 1958, the designer of the garden of the Ueno Arts Museum, Yoshida Isoya, reproduced images of Kyoto gardens—Katsura, Shūgakuin and Ryoanji—in his 'modern' design.

Since Japan's official opening to the outside world in the mid-nineteenth century after a two-hundred-year period of seclusion, gardens have been constructed which reflect influences from the West. Lawns were introduced for the first time at Shinjuku Park, for example, and an English architect and landscape artist by the name of Josiah Condor, who introduced a number of Western buildings to Tokyo, left an interesting legacy at Kyūfurukawa Teien, where a very English house is now surrounded by a heavily Japanized version of a garden modelled after Versailles. Part of it is a rose garden, where the roses are marked individually with their names and countries of origin. Roses from France, Belgium, Germany, the United States and Japan are included, but there is not a single English one!

The introduction of trains and other rapid systems of transport during the period of Westernization has opened up much wider spaces for 'strolling', however, and it is possible to consider other representations of Western life as constructed in the same vein as the earlier replicas of the Japanese (and formerly Chinese) landscape. There have for long been *bokujo,* for example, literally meadows for cattle in Europe but sites to visit for a day-out in Japan. More recently, an abundance of 'villages' have appeared, each representing a particular foreign country—from Holland-village in Kyūshū to Canada-village in Hokkaido. There is apparently an English model for a new park being constructed in Mito, also the site of one of Japan's three most famous and first public garden, Kairakuen, designed in the mid-nineteenth century by Tokugawa Nariaki.

These parks and 'villages' are like gardens writ large. They use the principles of garden design—of drawing part of the outside world into Japan, of miniaturizing it, and creating an enclosure around it and thereby mediating between the wild (or foreign) and the tame (inside of Japan). They are associated with the supernatural only in the sense that all foreigners are marked off as to some extent different from the way the Japanese see themselves as natural, but this has been a recurrent theme. Gardens help people come to terms with outsiders, spiritual or corporal, and these representations of the West offer an opportunity for just that.

The whole idea of a national park, introduced to Japan in 1931,[10] could be seen as an extension of the 'garden', at least in form. They are known as *kōen* (public *en*), where *en* is one of the components of *teien* (garden), which incorporates the idea of enclosure, and it was now not a new idea to open gardens for public pleasure. A designated portion of 'natural' landscape is marked off, if not physically entirely enclosed, and it is even provided with viewing spots or photo opportunities, seats, and welcoming bars and cafés. The English word 'garden' has also been used to designate an area of land set aside for tourists to hunt deer, which furthers the association, although gardens are now not usually hunting grounds.[11]

In this way some of the principles of a bounded reconstruction of nature have been taken out into 'nature' itself, where boundaries are created for the preservation of nature (Kokuritsu Kōen Kyōkai 1981: 5), but also to designate portions of nature for public enjoyment. From the turn of the century, mountaineering has been enjoyed in Japan, so the previously forbidden sacred mountains were drawn into the 'strolling' route, and rest-houses and restaurants came to complement the shrines and sacred sites which had previously drawn pilgrims into the hills. More recently, ski resorts allow visitors in droves to enjoy 'communing with nature', this time even more tamed than in Europe, with loudspeakers on the lift to keep the human component in touch with their cultural base.

This feature of Japanese ski resorts distinguishes them from many of the European ones that inspired them, despite the persistent use of German words for elements of the activity, and the viewing spots, as well as restaurants, bars and shops distinguish Japanese national parks from their prototypes in the United States and elsewhere. Just as Chinese and Western features of gardens in Japan have been modified in accordance with local systems of classification (or wrapping), the strolling path, with fixed viewing spots, characterizes Japanese approaches to enjoying the wider world even beyond her shores.

A 'tour' is an appropriate way to travel for most Japanese, and like the gardens of the Edo period, this is usually built around a series of famous sites, each to be captured in photographic form with the tour party placed in front. It may also involve a visit to sites associated with a favourite author, whether Japanese or Western,[12] just like the spots of literary significance in Rikuguen. The outside world is tamed then, as are the national parks, with viewing spots like those of Japanese gardens; and the location of enclosed representations of the outside world within Japan may be compared with the location of a garden within the compound of a house or shrine.

It may seem strange to classify foreign culture along with nature in this way, but if we are to take seriously the Japanese idea that they live in harmony with, or at one with, nature, we must take on board the inevitable implication that human activities are to be included in the wider view of the natural world. Bruno Taut made an insightful observation when he questioned the idea that a Japanese garden should be considered as a miniature landscape, so strongly did he feel that Japanese see it as created to harmonize with the house (Taut 1958: 89). During Japan's first encounter with Europeans in the sixteenth century, the outsiders were literally known as 'wild' barbarians (*yabanjin*), and their inevitable association with the outside *vis-à-vis* Japan implies a need to tame or wrap them for local consumption, just as the supernatural and the Chinese Immortals had to be wrapped in the earlier gardens.

Thus Western 'villages' can be discussed in the same context as national parks, and the whole of the rest of the world may be seen as one great natural resource, to be captured as an example of *shakkei* to Japan, or to be strolled around as part of a tour. It is also clearly an economic resource for the purposes of the inside Japanese, just as the wild parts of Japan are, and the argument thus comes full circle to explain how Japan can speak positively about the rest of the world while at the same time exploiting her. She loves the world, just as she loves nature, but it is a world/nature wrapped up for cultural appreciation. In its naked form, it is simply 'outside'.

The Japanese perception of nature may seem stretched beyond all recognition to a Western reader, but the aim is to break down a neat nature/culture distinction which we find so hard to relinquish. Nature in Japan is supernatural beings; it is mythology and it is art. It is also a means to achieve a deep understanding of the human condition, and it is the culture of humans outside Japan's shores. It is of course the culture of Japan too, because, as we are so often told, the Japanese people live at one with nature, and nowhere do they express this better than in their splendid gardens.

NOTES

1. The coral gardens described by Malinowski (1935) were largely for growing food, but an examination of the magic practised in association with them is most revealing of Trobriand ideas about their environment, natural and supernatural. Elsewhere, too, ideas are found about communing with the spiritual or transcendental through gardens, or of using them to represent a world long lost, like the Garden of Eden, or an imaginary paradise to come (e.g. Comito 1978: xi; King 1979). Chinese gardens are built according to intricate rules of *yin* and *yang* (Feuchtwang 1974; Hu 1991) which express the way they fit into a wider view of the natural and supernatural surroundings in which the Chinese perceive themselves to reside.

2. An explicit example is the way the *rōji*, or 'dewy path', of the tea ceremony garden is designed gradually to bring guests into a ritual frame of mind before they partake of the ceremony (Kondo 1985: 293). See below.

3. The word *shakkei* has apparently been used only since the Edo period, following ideas discussed in a seventeenth-century Chinese gardening manual known in Japanese as *En'ya* (Itō 1973: 15).

4. The notion of 'capturing' in the creation of gardens is certainly not confined to discussions of Japanese gardens, but there is a distinction between capturing 'some of the universal beauty' within a garden and 'capturing alive' something from without for the purposes of the garden.

5. Itō uses the word 'trimming' to translate *mikiri*, but another useful English notion would be 'framing'.

6. Hayakawa Masao asserts that the word *niwa* first appears in Japanese literature in the *Nihon Shoki* 'where it is used to refer to a place purified for the worship of gods' (Hayakawa 1973: 27).

7. The association between gods and strangers in a Japanese view is a theme which has been held to explain some of the same ambiguity which may be noted in Japanese treatment of foreigners as is found in the treatment of nature.

8. This site is well known in Japan for the distinctive Phoenix Hall to be found there, a popular site for tourist visits and school party outings. It is also depicted on the 10-yen coin.

9. It is important to explain for the general reader that at the level of gifts and foodstuffs, a choice of materials for wrapping them up allows a sophisticated system of communication too. This includes an apparently artless fold of rough paper or a single fresh leaf, perhaps expressing a kind of intimacy or a love of nature, respectively. In the construction of rooms, the inner space is thought to be beautiful if enclosed in unpainted wooden posts, a floor made of woven rush, and sliding screens of that rough paper again. Gardens may now be of a great variety, but they are almost invariably said to represent a Japanese love of nature.

10. The National Parks Law in Japan was first promulgated in 1931, and in 1934 the first three national parks were designated after the model of the Yellowstone Park in the United States (Kokuritsu Kōen Kyōkai 1981: 7). In 1981 Japan was reported to have 27 national parks, 51 'quasi' national parks and more than 200 prefectural parks, as well as a number of nature conservation areas and nature trails (ibid.: 9).

11. At least two existing gardens in Japan include areas that were used for attracting and hunting ducks in the past, however. These are the Hamarikyu Teien in Tokyo and the Ritsurin Teien in Takamatsu (Shikoku).

12. A biographer of the Brontës wrote to me recently, perplexed to know why their home and village at Haworth has become so popular with Japanese tourists.

REFERENCES

Bognar, Botond. 1985. *Contemporary Japanese Architecture.* New York: Van Nostrand Reinhold Company.

Bring, Mitchell and J. Wayembergh. 1981. *Japanese Gardens: Design and Meaning.* New York: McGraw-Hill.

Buisson, Dominique. 1981. *Temples et sanctuaires au Japon.* Paris: Editions du Moniteur.

Cave, Philip. 1993. *Creating Japanese Gardens.* London: Aurum Press.

Comito, Terry. 1978. *The Idea of the Garden in the Renaissance.* New Brunswick, NJ: Rutgers University Press.

Daisen'in. n.d. created by Sōbisha to commemorate the 450th anniversary of Daisen'in. Kyoto: Daisen'in.

Duff-Cooper, Andrew. 1991. 'Three Essays on Japanese Ideology', Occasional Publication of Seitoku University, Department of Humanities, Tokyo.

Feuchtwang, Stephen. 1974. An *Anthropological Analysis of Chinese Geomancy.* Vientiane: Edition Vithagna.

Hayakawa, Masao. 1973. *The Garden Art of Japan.* New York: Weatherhill and Tokyo: Heibonsha.

Hendry, Joy. 1988. 'Sutorenja toshite no minzokushigakusha: Nihon no tsutsumi bunka wo megutte' [The Ethnographer as Stranger: Wrapping Culture in Japan]. In T. Yoshida Teigo and H. Miyake (eds), *Kosumosu to Shakai* [Cosmos and Society], pp. 407–425. Tokyo: Keio Tsushin.

——— 1989. 'To Wrap or Not to Wrap: Politeness and Penetration in Ethnographic Inquiry'. *Man* (N.S) 24: 620–635.

——— 1993. *Wrapping Culture: Politeness, Presentation and Power in Japan and Other Societies.* Oxford: Oxford University Press.

——— 1994. 'Gardens and the Wrapping of Space in Japan: Some Benefits of a Balinese Insight'. *Journal of the Anthropological Society of Oxford* XXV(1): 11–19.

——— 1995. *Understanding Japanese Society.* London and NY: Croom Helm, 2nd edition.

Higuchi, Tadahiko. 1983. *The Visual and Spatial Structure of Landscapes* (trans. Charles Terry). Cambridge, Mass: Massachusetts Institute of Technology Press.

Hu, Dongchu. 1991. *The Way of the Virtuous: the Influence of Art and Philosophy on Chinese Garden Design.* Beijing: New World Press.

Itō, Teiji. 1973. *Space and Illusion in the Japanese Garden* (trans. R. Friedrich and M. Shimamura). New York, Tokyo and Kyoto: Weatherhill/Tankosha.

Kalland, Arne. 1995. 'Culture in Japanese Nature'. In O. Bruun and A. Kalland (eds), *Asian Perceptions of Nature: a Critical Approach.* London: Curzon Press, pp. 243–257.

Keswick, Maggie. 1986. *The Chinese Garden.* London: Academy Editions.

King, Ronald. 1979. *The Quest for Paradise.* Weybridge: Whittet/Windward.

Kokuritsu Kōen Kyōkai. 1981. *Nihon no Fukei* [Japanese Landscape] (*Shizen Kōen 50 shūnen kinen*). Tokyo: Gyosei Ltd.

Kondo, Dorinne. 1985. 'The Way of Tea: a Symbolic Analysis', *Man* (N.S.) 20:287–306.

Kuck, Loraine. 1968. *The World of the Japanese Garden: from Chinese Origins to Modern Landscape Art.* New York and Tokyo: Walker/Weatherhill.

Maki, Fumihiko. 1978. 'Nihon no Toshi-kukan to Oku' [Japanese City Spaces and *Oku*]. *Sekai* [World] (Dec.), pp. 146–162.

——— 1979. 'Japanese City Spaces and the Concept of *oku*'. *Japan Architect* 264: 50–62.

Malinowski, Bronislaw. 1935. *Coral Gardens and their Magic.* London: Allen & Unwin.

Ota, Hirotaru. 1972. *Traditional Japanese Architecture and Gardens.* Tokyo: Kokusai Bunka Shinkokai.

Stewart-Smith, Jo. 1987. *In the Shadow of Fujisan: Japan and its Wildlife.* Harmondsworth: Viking/Rainbird.

Tachibana-no-Toshitsuna. 1976. *Sakuteiki* (trans. of an eleventh-century manuscript by Shimoyama Shigemaru). Tokyo: Toshikeikaku Kenkyūjo.

Taut, Bruno. 1958. *Houses and People of Japan.* Tokyo: Sanseido.

Yoshida, Teigo. 1981. 'The Stranger as God: The Place of the Outsider in Japanese Folk Religion', *Ethnology* XX(2): 87–99.

Discussion Questions

1. How do Japanese conceptions of responsibility differ from those in Western societies?
2. What does it mean to empathize with nature in the Japanese context?
3. Is it a mistake to take the Japanese love of nature at face value, and not as a metaphor for something else? Can such a metaphor have positive implications for the treatment of ecosystems?
4. Is the Japanese garden a natural space?

Further Reading

Anesaki, Masaharu, *Art, Life and Nature in Japan,* Tokyo: Charles E. Tuttle, 1973.

Asquith, Pamela J., and Arne Kalland, Eds., *Japanese Images of Nature: Cultural Perspectives,* Richmond, Surrey, U.K.: Curzon, 1997.

Bernard, Rosemarie, Ed., *Shinto and Ecology,* Cambridge, Mass.: Harvard Center for the Study of World Religions, 2002.

Bruun, Ole, and Arne Kalland, Eds., *Asian Perceptions of Nature: A Critical Approach,* Richmond, Surrey, U.K.: Curzon, 1995.

Buruma, Ian, *A Japanese Mirror: Heroes and Villains in Japanese Culture,* Harmondsworth, U.K.: Penguin Books, 1985.

Callicott, J. Baird, and Roger Ames, Eds., *Nature in Asian Traditions of Thought,* Albany, N.Y.: SUNY Press, 1989.

Colligan-Taylor, Karen, *The Emergence of Environmental Literature in Japan,* New York: Garland Press, 1990.

Earhart, H. Byron, *A Religious Study of the Mounta Haguro Sect of Shugendo: An Example of Japanese Mountain Religion,* Tokyo: Sophia University Press, 1970.

Huddle, Norie, M. Reich, and N. Stiskin, *Island of Dreams: Environmental Crisis in Japan,* New York: Autumn Press, 1975.

Ito, Teiji, *The Japanese Garden: An Approach to Nature,* New Haven, Conn.: Yale University Press, 1972.

Matsuhara, Iwao, *On Life and Nature in Japan,* Tokyo: Hokuseido Press, 1964.

Reader, Ian, *Religion in Contemporary Japan,* London: Macmillan, 1991.

Suzuki, Daisetz, *Zen and Japanese Culture,* Tokyo: Charles E. Tuttle, 1988.

Totman, Conrad, *The Green Archipelago: Forestry in Preindustrial Japan,* Berkeley: University of California Press, 1989.

Wong, Anny, *The Roots of Japan's Environmental Policies,* New York: Routledge, 2000.

Chapter 8

Judaism

MUCH OF THE CONTEMPORARY critique of Western Christianity's role in potentially fostering the destruction of the environment focuses on some passages in the Hebrew Bible, most notoriously on the "subdue the earth" commandment in Genesis 1:28. It is sometimes difficult, however, for Christians (or for critics of Christianity, for that matter) to recognize that Jews and Christians read the Bible in very different ways. The tendency to conflate biblical interpretation into a putative Judeo-Christian tradition, therefore, is bound to be misleading.

In particular, it is often noted that Judaism is a distinctly this-worldly religion, as opposed to Christianity, which is held to place a greater emphasis on the hereafter. In the wake of Lynn White Jr.'s critique of more than thirty years ago, many Jews have sought to provide ecological and particularly Jewish readings of scriptural tradition. Talmudic commentary offers a further, distinctively Jewish source of attitudes toward the natural environment.

These commentaries notwithstanding, Jewish tradition does present some problematic issues when dealing with nature. Adam, the first Jewish man, is created from the soil (*adamah*). One of the earliest biblical commands is "*Bal tashchit*"—"Do not destroy." On the other hand, much of the early history of the Israelites takes place against the tense and sometimes violent backdrop of their failure to abandon the practices of nature paganism and to abide by their covenant to worship only the transcendent Yahweh. Later, following the dispersions of the Assyrian, Babylonian, and Roman periods, the majority of Jews suffered a disconnection from the land of Israel with which they identified, substituting instead the portable homeland of the Torah. The re-establishment of the state of Israel in 1948 has brought its own challenges, as urbanization, industrial agriculture, and overpopulation take their toll on the ecology of the promised land. In recent years, a growing number of Jewish environmentalists, mainly in the United States but increasingly also in Israel, have sought to find new meaning in the medieval kabbalistic notion of *tikkun olam*, "repair of the world," in light of the contemporary ecological crisis.

Aloys Hüttermann directly addresses the well-known passage in Genesis 1:28 that many have seen as constituting a divine directive for humans to master the earth for their own purposes. Arguing that this passage is "the most misunderstood part of the Bible," Hüttermann sets the verse in the context of others and concludes that although the Bible accords humans a special rank in nature, their use of it is restricted. He then looks at medieval rabbinic commentaries to discover how earlier Jewish interpretations differed from modern Jewish and Christian ones.

Tikva Frymer-Kensky looks more broadly not only at the biblical tradition itself but at the ancient Near Eastern context from which it emerged. She contrasts the biblical view of the relationship between God and the Earth with that in the older Babylonian creation story. In the latter, Frymer-Kensky finds a distinct hierarchy, in which the Earth exists to serve humans so that humans may serve the gods. But whereas in the Babylonian story ecological destruction comes about because of the gods, in Genesis this happens through the degeneracy of humans. Ecological integrity is thus directly tied to human morality.

Steven S. Schwarzschild emphasizes this theme of human morality as an overriding concern in Judaism, though without the linkage to ecology proposed by Frymer-Kensky. Although he admits that the Bible does not permit humans to wantonly destroy nature, Schwarzschild holds that its purpose is a practical one; he rejects the notion that nature is sacred. For at least the past 2,000 years, argues Schwarzschild, Jews have been people of culture, not nature.

Arthur Waskow challenges this contention by looking further back in history to the time of the early Israelites. The original relationship of the Israelites to nature *was* a sacred one, expressed through a variety of rituals tied to the Earth's seasonal cycles. Waskow also re-envisions the traditional Jewish concept of *kashrut* (the kosher code) as applying not only to food but to all we consume, not only as individuals but as a society. Suggesting that our consumption of substances like petroleum and plutonium is not "eco-kosher," Waskow calls on us to re-examine the impact of all our consumption patterns, to slow ourselves down in the restful spirit of the Sabbath, and to "catch our Breath"—that is, the breath of life that we all breathe.

Genesis 1—The Most Misunderstood Part of the Bible

ALOYS HÜTTERMAN

1 In the beginning, God created the heavens and the
earth. 2 The earth was without form and void, and
darkness was upon the face of the deep; and the
Spirit of God was moving over the face of the waters.

. . .

11 And God said, "Let the earth put forth vege-
tation, plants yielding seeds, and fruit trees bear-
ing fruit in which is their seed, each according to its
own kind upon the earth." And it was so. 12 The
earth brought forth vegetation, plants yielding seed
according to their own kinds, and trees bearing
fruit in which is their seed, each according to its
kind.

. . .

20 And God said, "Let the waters bring forth
swarms of living creatures, and let birds fly above
the earth across the firmament of the heavens."
21 So God created the great sea monsters and every
living creature that moves, with which the waters
swarm, according to their kinds, . . . And God saw
that it was good. 22 And God blessed them, saying,
"Be fruitful and multiply and fill the waters in
the sea and let the birds multiply on the earth."
23 And there was evening and there was morning,
a fifth day.

24 And God said, "Let the earth bring forth liv-
ing creatures according to their kinds: cattle and
creeping things and beasts of the earth according to
their kinds." And it was so. 25 And God made the
beasts of the earth according to their kinds and the
cattle according to their kinds, and everything that
creeps on the earth according to their kinds. And

Hüttermann, Aloys, excerpts from *The Ecological Message of the Torah: Knowledge, Concepts, and Laws Which Made Survival in a Land of "Milk and Honey" Possible*, Atlanta: Scholars Press, 1999, pp. 11–22. Reprinted by permission.

God saw that it was good. 26 Then God said, "Let us make man in our image, after our likeness; and let them have dominion over the fish of the sea, and over the birds of the air, and over the cattle, and over all the earth, and over every creeping thing that creeps upon the earth." 27 So God created man in his own image, in the image of God he created him; male and female he created them. 28 And God blessed them, and God said to them, "Be fruitful and multiply, and fill the earth, and subdue it: and have dominion over the fish of the sea, and over the birds of the air and over every living thing that moves upon the earth." 29 And God said, "Behold, I have given you every plant yielding seed, which is upon the face of all the earth, and every tree with seeds in his fruit, you shall have them for food. 30 And to every beast of the earth, and to every bird in the air, and to every thing that creeps on the earth, everything that has the breath of life, I have given every green plant for food." And it was so. 31 And God saw everything that he had made, and behold, it was very good. And there was evening and there was morning, a sixth day. (Gen. I)

GENESIS I AS THE INTELLECTUAL BASIS FOR THE DEVELOPMENT OF MODERN SCIENCE

Genesis 1 begins with a very important statement: "In the beginning God created . . ." and then continues with a list of the items which he created. Thus the first crucial point of this text is that it describes the *creatio ex nihilo,* the creation from nothing (c.f. Eichrodt, 1984). The second important feature of the text is that the Scriptures, a large volume of holy texts, begin with God, then nature, and finally, rather late, man. This is unique to religious texts, especially when compared to its counterparts in this geographic region. Neither the Hellenistic, Egyptian, nor Mesopotamian religious texts begin with god and continue in this order (c.f. Keel and Küchler, 1983; anon, 1996). In addition, the text is timeless, unlike its Babylonian counterparts (Zenger, 1995), it does not make any attempt to legitimate the power of an existing ruler.

Genesis 1 shows the paramount importance that the Hebrew Bible gives to nature. Its uniqueness can be seen when this origin myth is compared with the mythology of the Vedes, the holy Hinduistic scriptures from India (c.f. Frese, 1973), the creation myths from China (Chen and Yang, 1995), or the origin myths of the various tribes of the American Indians (Taylor, 1995; c.f. Radin, 1973). Unlike the Book of Genesis, all these texts lack a precise and definite statement about the origin of creation. The Germanic mythology completely lacks a creation myth: the world was already created when the first gods came into the picture (Meyer, 1903). According to Meyer (1903), this absence of statements about creation was an important and quite convincing argument for the early Christian missionaries trying to convert the Germanic tribes through their discussions with Germanic leaders.

The listing of the many things which God created leaves absolutely no doubt about one fact: all items which are to be found in the universe are made by God and cannot be gods themselves. This is strongly emphasized in the Book of Wisdom, which was written during the last century B.C.E.:

> 1 But all men are vain, in whom there is not the knowledge of God: and who by these good things that are seen, could not understand him that is, neither by attending to the works have acknowledged who was the workman: 2 But have imagined either the fire, or the wind, of the swift air, or the circle of the stars, or the great water, or the sun and moon, to be the gods that rule the world. 3 With whose beauty, if they, being delighted, took them to be gods: let them know how much the Lord of them is more beautiful than they: for the first author of beauty made all those things. 4 Or if they admired their power and their effects, let them understand by them, that he that made them, is mightier than they: 5 For by the greatness of the beauty, and of the creature, the creator of them may be seen, so as to be known thereby. (Book of Wisdom 13:1–5)

This is of extreme importance to the development of Western science. Since it excluded even the slightest possibility of anything present in nature being a god or like God, it cleared the mind and set up the conditions for a rational study of nature. Max Weber calls this process the "disenchantment of nature", the beginning of a rationalization concerning the conception of the world and the philosophical structures of life (Weber, 1920).

The feeling that there was a difference between the Jewish view of the world and the neighboring countries was present among the Jews in ancient times (c.f. the Book of Wisdom 7:15–23). The intellectual frame which was created by such an environment is also outlined in the same book:

> 15 And God hath given to me to speak as I would, and to conceive thoughts worthy of those things that are given me: because he is the guide of wisdom, and the director of the wise: 16 For in his hand are both we, and our words, and all wisdom, and the knowledge and skill of works. 17 For he hath given me the true knowledge of the things that are: to know the disposition of the whole world, and the virtues of the elements, 18 The beginning, and ending, and midst of the times, the alterations of their courses, and the changes of seasons, 19 The revolutions of the year, and the dispositions of the stars, 20 The natures of living creatures, and rage of wild beasts, the force of winds, and reasonings of men, the diversities of plants, and the virtues of roots, 21 And all such things as are hid and not foreseen, I have learned: for wisdom, which is the worker of all things, taught me. 22 For in her is the spirit of understanding: holy, one, manifold, subtle, eloquent, active, undefiled, sure, sweet, loving that which is good, quick, which nothing hindereth, beneficent, 23 Gentle, kind, steadfast, assured, secure, having all power, overseeing all things, and containing all spirits, intelligible, pure, subtle. (Book of Wisdom 7:15–23)

This is the *Magna Charta* of the intellectual approach, which a scientist takes, regardless of his faith, and whether or not he believes in God. A scientist needs to be curious and open. He also has to have the intellectual capacity to understand facts and the power to put these facts together into cogent theories. . . .

For the early scientists, at the beginning of modern times, the research of nature was a legitimate way demonstrating [*sic*] the greatness of the Creator ("To show the greatness of the creator in the anatomy of a louse") (c.f. Ruderman, 1995; Patai, 1994; Noack, 1979; Hübner, 1979). Rudermann (1995) describes the complicated intellectual situation of Medieval Jewish scientists, which in my opinion—apart from the special Jewish situation—more or less also applied to the Christian scientists of that time, in the following way:

> Most of all, certain rabbis, interpreting and embellishing key biblical passages assigned religious meaning to the quest to understand nature, both celestial and earthly, as a direct means of understanding God and of fulfilling his revealed commandments.
>
> The Jewish encounter with the dynamic intellectual life of medieval Islam in such centers as Baghdad, Cairo, and Cordova, and later in stimulating Christian territories such as Spain, Sicily, Italy, and Provence, provided an impetus for perpetuating the rabbinic approaches to nature while deepening their religious and intellectual significance. With the translation of the philosophical and scientific corpus of classical antiquity into Arabic, several influential Jewish figures in the Muslim world recast the Jewish Tradition into a philosophic key, elevating the quest for an understanding of God and his natural creation to the ultimate ideal of Jewish religiosity. Hand in hand with this newly articulated religious aspiration went an intellectual appreciation of the intrinsic worth of understanding the cosmos, as well as an awareness of the pragmatic value such knowledge could yield in terms of social and economic status. In the relatively open intellectual and social setting of medieval Islamic cities, Jews consumed the classic texts of philosophy and science, studied the contemporary Islamic modifications and elaborations, and produced a philosophical and scientific literature of their own in Arabic and Hebrew.

For instance, Hildegard von Bingen, a famous woman scientist of the twelfth century, wrote a book with the title: *Physica aut liber simplis medicinae secundum creationem* (Physics or Book of Simple Medical Drugs in the Order of the History of Creation). Not only many founders of our modern science, such as Kepler and Newton, took their motivation to do scientific research from their religion (DiTrocchio, 1998), the same spirit can be found with leading scientists of our century also (Noble, 1998).

THE MOST MISUNDERSTOOD PART OF THE HEBREW BIBLE: GENESIS 1:28—OR WHAT DOES *DOMINATIO TERRAE* REALLY MEAN?

In my view Gen. 1:28 is the most misunderstood part of the Hebrew Bible. In numerous incidents this passage has apparently been taken as a permit for the destruction of our environment by the Western (i.e. Christian) civilization to such an extent that in 1970, at a conference on "Theology of Survival", a group of Protestant theologians went so far as to assert "that any solution to the current environmental crisis would require major modifications of current religious values" (quoted from the New York Times of May 1, 1970; c.f. Freudenstein, 1970). A similar statement is given by Jossuttis (1989).

On the other hand, this is also the basis for a recently developing Eco-anti-Semitism that ascribes the global crisis to "the Judeo-Christian Tradition" (Hayutman, 1992). The discussion started in the late sixties in the United States (White, 1967; Barbour, 1973; Bateson, 1972). Carl Amery (1974) wrote a book entitled *"Das Ende der Vorsehung, von den gnadenlosen Folgen des Christentums"* (The End of Providence, the Merciless Consequences of Christianity). His Royal Highness Prince Charles (1991), Drewermann (1991), and Passmore (1995) took up this line as well.

Although this passage of the Bible has been thoroughly misunderstood for centuries, the truth is that the basis for a proper use of natural resources has been laid down in the first chapter of the first book of the Torah.

We should bear in mind that this is a text which has been phrased with extreme care, much like a juridical text, in which every word is important and has its own special meaning. In addition, this text was not written in order to impress the reader with its biological wisdom. It was written to convey a theological message and to uplift the spirits of the readers, who were in exile in Babylon. It is the beginning of the founding document of the normative Judaism of the Second Temple Times (c.f. Neusner, 1987, p. 34 f). Just as with any other text of this kind, we must also look at the relevant context and consult the important commentaries for a real and complete understanding of their meaning.

However, if we read the passage about the creation of man and how he was entrusted with the domination of the world, we come inevitably to the astonishing conclusion that this is rather limited.

- — The command "be fruitful and multiply" had earlier also been given to the animals, which means that man has to populate the earth in the same manner as the animals.
- — Man rules over the animals, but he is not allowed to feed on them. Plants are excluded from the general dominion.
- — The use of plants is restricted to the use of their fruits as food. This concession is the same that was given to the animals.

Translated into the language of ecology, this means that man has a special rank in the order of nature. He is indeed allowed to use nature properly. This usage, however, is rather restricted. He is not permitted to kill animals or touch plants in their basic existence.

BIBLICAL PASSAGES REFERRING TO THE "DOMINION OF THE WORLD"

There are a few very indicative passages from the Scripture which indicate that the *dominatio terrae* is perhaps not what it appears to be.

The first example is the story of Noah. He is not simply allowed to rescue his own life and that of his family from the coming flood, but he has to build a huge ark so that he can save the whole animal life of the world; even including the unpleasant "creeping things" (which include rats, mice, and snakes). After the ark is again on safe ground, God makes a covenant with him:

> *8 Then God said to Noah and to his sons with him, 9 "Behold, I establish my covenant with you and your descendants after you, 10 and with every living creature that is with you, the birds, the cattle, and every beast of the earth with you, as many as came out of the ark. 11 I establish my covenant with you, that never again shall all flesh be cut off by the waters of a flood, and never again shall there be a flood to destroy the earth." 12 And God said, "This is the sign of the covenant which I make between me and you and every living creature that is with you, for all future generations: 13 I set my bow in the cloud, and it shall be a sign of the covenant between me and the earth. 14 When I bring clouds over the earth and the bow is seen in the clouds, 15 I will remember my covenant which is between me and you and every living creature of all flesh; and the waters shall never again become a flood to destroy all flesh. 16 When the bow is in the clouds, I will look upon it and remember the everlasting covenant between God and every living creature of all flesh that*

is upon the earth." 17 God said to Noah, "This is the sign of the covenant which I have established between me and all flesh that is upon the earth." (Gen. 9:8–17)

From this pericope it is very clear that the creation is not a legal *nullum,* but that it is also a part of the covenant which God has established with man. God had laid down his weapon, hung up his bow in the sky and converted it to a symbol of peace between him and the whole creation (Zenger, 1983). This action of converting weapons to instruments of peace was taken up later by the prophets Isaiah (Is. 2) and Micah (Mic. 4), who used the picture of wielding swords into ploughshares to symbolize the peace which is given by God.

The notion that creation is not at the merciless disposal of mankind is also present in the covenant pericope of Hoseah:

18 And I will make for you a covenant on that day with the beasts of the field, the birds of the air, and the creeping things of the ground; and I will abolish the bow, the sword, and war from the land; and I will make you lie down in safety. 19 And I will betroth you to me for ever; I will betroth you to me in righteousness and in justice, in steadfast love, and in mercy. 20 I will betroth you to me in faithfulness; and you shall know the LORD. (Hos. 2:18–20)

This peace with and among the creation is accompanied by political peace (Ebach, 1989). This motif is brought up again by Ezekiel:

25 I will make with them a covenant of peace and banish wild beasts from the land, so that they may dwell securely in the wilderness and sleep in the woods. 26 And I will make them and the places round about my hill a blessing; and I will send down the showers in their season; they shall be showers of blessing. 27 And the trees of the field shall yield their fruit, and the earth shall yield its increase, and they shall be secure in their land; and they shall know that I am the LORD, when I break the bars of their yoke, and deliver them from the hand of those who enslaved them . . . 29 And I will provide for them prosperous plantations so that they shall no more be consumed with hunger in the land, and no longer suffer the reproach of the nations. (Ez. 34:25–27, 29)

All these quotations point into the same direction: the covenant between God and humans is not exclusive, the whole creation is included. In addition, the whole affair is a peaceful one, no violence is allowed on either side.

JEWISH MIDRASHIC COMMENTARIES

Genesis Rabbah

With regard to the general topic of this section, quotations from two Parasha are of importance. The first reference deals with the status of the Torah and is taken from Parasha One on Genesis 1:1.:

I:I.2:

D. In the accepted practice of the world when a mortal king builds a palace, he does not build it out of his own head, but he follows a work-plan.
E. And [the one who supplies] the work-plan does not build out of his own head, but he has designs and diagrams, so as to know how to situate the rooms and the doorways.
F. Thus the Holy One, blessed be he, consulted the Torah when he created the world.

These quotations make perfectly clear that the Torah is not only the paramount document of Judaism, but that it was actually the master plan for God's creation.

With regard to the question of human domination over the world, Genesis Rabbah makes two short but remarkable statements (Parasha Eight, Genesis 1:26–28):

VIII:XII.

1. A. "And rule over the fish of the sea" (Gen. 1:28):
B: "If [man] merits, 'Rule' (RD), and if not, 'Go down' (YRD)."
4. A. What is written is "And conquer her" (Gen. 1:28) bearing the implication that a man must subjugate his wife so that she not go out to the market place.

[. . .]

Pirqe Aboth:

V.1

By ten sayings the world was created. And what is learned therefrom? For could it not have been created by one saying? But it was that vengeance might be taken on the wicked, who destroy the world that was created by ten sayings; and to give a goodly reward to the righteous, who maintain the world that was created by ten sayings.

According to Taylor (1897), "The point of view in the text is that the grandeur of creation is more impressively portrayed in the outcome of repeated acts of power, than as the immediate result of a single fiat of omnipotence". The "ten sayings" also demonstrate the paramount guilt of the sinners who destroy the creation and the greatness of the task to keep and preserve it.

Kohelet Rabbah

This statement in the ancient midrash, which was also incorporated into the corpus of Jewish legends (bin Gorion, 1997, p. 69), illustrates the attitude which, according to Scripture, man should have towards nature.

> "In the hour when God created the first person, He took him and let him pass before all the trees of the Garden of Eden and said to him: 'See my works, how fine and excellent they are! Now all that I have created, for you have I created. Think upon this and do not corrupt and desolate My World, for if you corrupt it, there is no one to set it right after you.'" (Kohelet Rabbah 7:28)

It has become relevant in our times.

From all theses ancient texts it is quite obvious that the interpretation of the *dominatio terrae*, especially as it has developed during the last centuries, has nothing in common with the interpretation given by Scripture itself.

JEWISH EXEGETES

Rashi

Deeper insight is obtained by studying the pertinent commentaries. Among these I will concentrate on Rashi's Commentary, since Rashi is highly authoritative among the Jewish theologians and especially concentrates on the very meaning of the exact vocabulary used in the scripture (c.f. Noveck, 1972; Wigoder, 1989; Schoeps, 1992). Since I have the impression that Rashi's work is not very well known to the majority of Non-Jewish authors, at least for those who work and publish in the field of bioethics and exegesis of the Hebrew bible, I feel that it is very important to devote a few lines to Rashi's interpretation of the pericope which received so much blame.

The most important point in Genesis 1:26–28 is the exact meaning of the words which are used to describe the relationship between man and the creation. The most notable words in this connection are the two verbs: וירדו "to have dominion" and וכבשה "to subdue".

The first of these is usually translated as "to have dominion". For Rashi, this verb cannot be as simply defined as it appears to be in the English translation:

> The expression וירדו may imply dominion as well as declining—if he is worthy, he dominates over the beasts and cattle, if he is not worthy, he will sink lower than them, and the beasts will rule over him. (Rashi, ed. 1934, p. 7)

This interpretation is really breathtaking. Rashi actually leaves open the option that man, if he does not dominate the world properly, will lose his supremacy and, in the end, will be dominated by the "beasts". Rashi came to this interpretation by a very careful semiotic analysis of the text.

One wonders whether he knew how revolutionary this analysis was in the context of the contemporary concept of the world. He first states that the same philosophy of conditional ruling applies to the mandate of man to rule over the Creation as it is found in the Germanic concept of the kingship. A king obtains his mandate, the *Königsheil,* from heaven on the condition that he is worthy of it. As long as it seems obvious that the king has this mandate, his rule is sacrosanct because it is from heaven. However, as soon as it becomes evident that he has lost his *Königsheil,* a person who is able to prove that the *Königsheil* has been transferred to him, may rise up and take the kingship for himself. Through this ruling, the Karolingian dynasty overthrew the Merowingians and took the rule of the Kingdom of the Franks. Rashi thus simply assumes that the same rules which govern the relations between a Germanic king and his subjects are also relevant to the relations between man and nature.

In doing so, he reveals a very modern concept of nature. Up to the time of Darwin, i.e. the middle of the last century, the prevalent view of the world was that of a static system, which was basically unchanged since the beginning of creation and would not undergo any basic changes in the future. Mayr (1991) shows very clearly that one of the four pillars of the so-called Christian *Weltanschauung* of that time, which made Darwin's theory so difficult to accept, was in fact the dogma of a completely static world. According to his interpretation Rashi had a completely different view. On the basis of pure semiotic analysis, he could indeed envision a world which undergoes evolution. This may even evolve to such an extent that the situation is reversed, in that man loses his supremacy (perhaps even his means of physical survival) and that other animals, perhaps insects, as is nowadays speculated among biologists, will be the rulers of the world.

The next word which is important is וכבשה "to subdue". Here Rashi states:

> The word lacks a ו after the ש, so that it may be read as meaning: and subdue her (i.e. the woman), thereby teaching you that the male controls the female in order that she may not become a gad-about; . . . (Rashi, ed. 1934, p. 7)

For Rashi it is self-evident that nature has its own right to develop in harmony. This is so basic for him that he states the relationship between humans and nature as a model of the partnership between man and woman in marriage. Since man has to allow nature to develop in harmony, a husband has to treat his wife in such a way that she does not develop into a gad-about (every psychologist knows that such a habit develops only in women who have not had the chance to develop in harmony).

The last expression that is important in the context of our considerations, is the ending of the sixth day: יום הששי. Here Rashi states:

> The letter ה, the numerical value of which is five, is added to the word ששי when the work of creation was complete, to imply that He made a stipulation with them *that it endures only* (special attention was made by Rashi) upon the condition that Israel should accept the five books of the Torah. (bShabb. 88a) (Rashi, ed. 1934, p. 8)

The part of the Talmud which Rashi is referring to is the following:

> It is written: *"And it was evening and it was morning, day the sixth."* For what then is the superfluous ה necessary? This teaches that the Holy, praised be He, made an agreement with his work of creation and said to him: If the Israelites accept the Torah, than you (the creation) will flourish, if not, I will turn you back into desert and emptiness. (bShabb. 88a)

The pericope *expressis verbis,* which is referred to and explained in the Talmud in two places (the Talmudic text quoted above is repeated almost *verbatim* in bAb. Zarah 3a), states that nature can only survive if mankind keeps the Torah. So for the Talmud, and of course for Rashi also, the Torah is not just a book which gives instructions about human relationships and the relationship between man and God, but also gives advice on how to treat His Creation. If this advice is not followed, God will turn the Creation into desert and emptiness.

A second interpretation given by Rashi for the term יום הששי "the sixth day" is:

> The whole creation (the universe) stood at a state of suspense (moral imperfection) until the sixth day—that is the sixth day of Sivan which was to be destined to be the day when the Torah would be given to Israel (bAb. Zarah 3a).

According to this explanation, the words "the sixth day" must be read together with the opening words of the next verse: *Thus the heavens and the earth were finished (Gen. 2:1).* According to this view, the text should be read: "On the sixth day of Sivan the heavens and the earth were perfected". This way of reading is actually followed in the introductory verses of the Jewish Friday evening prayer at the start of the Sabbath celebration.

Thus, three very interesting facts can be learned from Rashi about the very meaning of Genesis 1: 28–31:

i. Man has indeed a mandate to dominate over the world, but this mandate is given only on the condition that he shows himself to be worthy of it, otherwise he himself will be dominated by the beasts.

ii. From the true meaning of the verb "subdue" Rashi deduces that a man has to treat his wife in a way that will allow her to develop as a full, mature, and harmonic person. So his freedom to dominate the creation is rather limited.

iii. Creation was only completed when the Torah was given to man and it can only survive if man keeps the Torah.

It is a great pity that these interpretations, which shed a completely new light on one of the most critical pericopes of the Bible, have not really been considered by modern exegetes, both Jewish and Christian.

A second important aspect can be deduced from the interpretation of the report on the sixth day of creation which was given in the Talmud and outlined further by Rashi: The verbs "dominate" and "subdue" describe a general ethical behavior towards nature which has to be dealt with in a benevolent way. These general rules indicated by these verbs, however, become concrete when the connection with the Torah is established. With this step, the general ethical commandments given in the two verbs quoted above are filled with precise rules on how to treat nature.

Other Jewish Exegetes

An important non-biblical Jewish text that deals with the story of creation is the work of Flavius Josephus, who was first a Jewish Priest and a member of the Sanhedrin in Jerusalem—in the Jewish War he was an Army Commander in the Northern region. During the war, after the fall of the city of Jotapata, he changed sides and became a follower of the Emperor Vespasian, who later supported Josephus' life materially. Josephus wrote two books with the aim of convincing the Roman upper class of the values of Judaism: *Antiquitatea Judaicae* and *Contra Apionem*. In *Antiquitatae Judaicae,* he starts with a report on the creation, following the Hebrew Bible quite closely. In this report, he completely omits the "critical passage" on human domination and exploitation of the world: "On the sixth day God created the quadrupeds, male and female, and afterwards man. On the seventh day, God took a rest" (AJ I, 1). Obviously the *dominatio terrae* was not an issue in his eyes. In *Contra Apionem,* he does not even treat this topic.

Maimonides, the other great medieval interpreter of the Torah and the Talmud besides Rashi, who in his "Guide for the Perplexed" had the ambition to explain the Torah on a rational basis, attempted to deal with creation on a philosophical basis against the background of Aristotelian philosophy. In doing so, Maimonides found himself at odds with Aristotle on the problem of creation, which he had to repudiate, because Maimonides held the view that the world was an act of creation by God and there was nothing in existence before God started his creation. The case of *dominatio terrae* was not of real importance to Maimonides. He approaches this verse stating:

> For no part of the creation is described as being in existence for the sake of another part, but each part is declared to be the product of God's will and to satisfy by its existence the intention [of the Creator]. This is expressed by the phrase, "And God saw that it was good" (Gen. 1:4, etc.). You know our interpretation of the saying of our Sages, "Scripture speaks the same language as is spoken by man". But we call "good" that which is in accordance with the object we seek. When therefore Scripture relates in reference to the whole creation (Gen. 1:31): "And God saw all that He had made, and behold it was exceedingly good," it declares thereby that everything created was well fitted for its object, and would never cease to act, and never be annihilated. . . . You must not be misled by what is stated of the stars [that God put them in the firmament of the heavens] to give light upon the earth, and to rule by day and by night. You might perhaps think that here the purpose of their creation is described. This is not the case; we are only informed of the nature of the stars, which God desired to create with such properties that they should be able to give light and to rule. In a similar manner we must understand the passage: "And have dominion over the fish of the sea" (ibid. 1:28). Here it is not meant to say that man was created for this purpose, but only that this was the nature which God gave man. But as to the statement in Scripture that God gave the plants to man and other living beings, it agrees with the opinion of Aristotle and other philosophers. (Maimonides, Guide for the Perplexed, p. 275)

From this passage, it is not possible to derive that a strong mandate was given to humans to rule the world in a suppressive way. Maimonides first states that all objects of creation have their own right and purpose, before he turns to Gen. 1:28. Near the end of this chapter he comes to the matter of ruling again: "Thus some citizen may imagine that it was for the purpose of protecting his house by night from thieves that the king was chosen". Therefore when Maimonides speaks of Gen. 1:28, he does not see any absolute ruling, without any conditions, for man.

In modern times, i.e. the present and last century, the view of Rashi on the ecological aspects of the first chapter of the Hebrew Bible is more or less completely neglected in leading general commentaries (such as that by Hirsch (1867) or those on the weekly reading pericopes of the Torah (parasha) (c.f. Jacobson, 1987)). Cohen (1919) quotes Rashi only in connection with his commentaries on Isaiah, Psalms, and the laws of the sabbath. He develops his theology of creation mainly on the basis of Greek Philosophy and Maimonides. Guttmann (1933) does not quote Rashi at all. More recently, commentaries written in English on this pericope of the Torah follow the example of the ones quoted above. Although Chill (1990), for instance, introduces Rashi as the "leading commentator on the Bible and Talmud", he does not mention him in his commentary on Gen 1:28. Solomon (1992) deals explicitly with Gen. 1:28 in his article "Judaism and the environment". The introduction of the book mentions Rashi as the leading commentator. Solomon calls the term "and rule over it" perverse, but the commentary of Rashi, who stated as early as 800 years ago that this interpretation is entirely wrong, is not mentioned at all. In Rosner's book on Jewish Bioethics (Rosner, 1977), ecology does not have any place at all. Carmell (1976), in his article "Judaism and the quality of the environment", does not cite Gen. 1:28. In the Part on "Justice for the Environment" in his book "Master plan—Judaism: its program, meanings, goals" (Carmell, 1991), to which 71 pages are allotted, Gen. 1:28 is also carefully avoided. For Aviezer, a professor of Physics at the Bar-Ilan University, the blessing "fill the land and subdue it", is fulfilled during the Neolithic Revolution (Aviezer, 1990, p. 101), and for him there is not the slightest doubt "that man is the pinnacle of creation, and that everything in the universe was formed for his benefit," even the distant stars of the universe (Aviezer, 1990, p. 109). Marcus (1991) starts his exegesis to this passage by quoting Rashi's commentary to Gen. 1:1 "What is the reason that it (the Torah) commences with the account of the Creation?". . . in order to teach that "All the earth belongs to the Holy One, blessed be He". However, he does not cite Rashi's translation of the crucial, misunderstood verbs "dominate" and "subdue". Loevinger (1998) refers to Maimonides in his statement on how this passage is misread and concentrates on the idea of a biocentric "Deep Ecology Position".

This list is not made to ridicule my Jewish colleagues and to challenge their sincerity and depth of knowledge on the Torah and its commentators which definitely surpasses my own. I think that the reason for the omission of this pericope and the Rashi commentary on it is the following: on the one hand, they are very much aware of the sensitivity of this pericope in the way the Western World sees it. Therefore, they either avoid it or simply state that what is apparently written there is not really meant. Then they outline why they think that this is true. On the other hand, they apparently do not expect Rashi to provide any enlightenment in a relevant exegesis of this pericope. For this reason they did not read the relevant parts of Rashi's commentary and consequently do not quote him.

REFERENCES

Amery, C. (1974) Das Ende der Vorsehung. Die gnadenlosen Folgen des Christentums. p. 15 ff., Rowohlt, Reinbek.

Anonymous. (1966) Schöpfungserzählungen der Alten Welt, Welt und Umwelt der Bibel. 20 p., Kath. Bibelwerk, Stuttgart.

Aviezer, N. (1990) In the Beginning—Biblical Creation and Science. 138 p., KTAV Publ. House, Hoboken.

Barbour, I. G. (ed.) (1973) Western man and environmental ethics. 276 p., Reading, Addison Wesley.

Bateson, G. (1972) Steps to an ecology of mind. 545 p., Chandler Publ., San Francisco.

bin Gorion, M. J. (1997) Die Sagen der Juden. 1174 p., Parkland Verlag, Köln.

Carmen, A. (1976) Judaism and the quality of the environment. In: A. Carmell and C. Domb (eds.) Challenge—Torah views on science and its problems. p. 500–525, Association of Orthodox Jewish Scientists, London.

——— (1991) Masterplan—Judaism its program, meanings, goals. 397 p., Jerusalem Academy Publ., Jerusalem.

Chen, J.-n and Yang, Y. (1995) The world of Chinese myths. 210 p., Beijing Language and Culture University Press, Beijing.

Chill, A. (1990) The Mitzvaot. 508 p., Keter Books, Jerusalem.

Cohen, H. (1919) Religion der Vernunft aus den Quellen des Judentums. 629 p., Kaufmann, Frankfurt (new English edition: Scholars Press, Atlanta, 1995).

DiTrocchio, F. (1998) Newtons Koffer—Geniale Außenseiter, die die wissenschaft blamierten. 285 p., Campus, Frankfurt.

Ebach, J. (1989) Schöpfung in der hebräischen Bibel. In: Altner, G. (ed.) Ökologische Theologie. Perspektiven zur Orientierung, p. 98–128, Kreuz Verlag, Stuttgart.

Eichrodt, W. (1984) In the beginning: A contribution to the interpretation of the first word of the bible. In: B. W. Anderson (ed.) Creation in the Old Testament, pp. 65–73, Fortress Press, Philadelphia.

Frese, W. (1973) Die Sache mit der Schöpfung. Eine Geschichte der Kosmologie—von der Mythologie zur Astrophysik. pp. 15 ff., BLV Verlagsgesellschaft, München.

Freudenstein, E. G. (1970) Ecology and the Jewish tradition. Judaism, 19, 408–414.

Guttmann, J. (1933) Die Philosophie des Judentums (modern edition 1985). 412 p., Fournier Verlag, Wiesbaden.

Hayutman, Y. I. (1992) Eco-antisemitism, eco-paganism and hebrew-biblical eco-logics. Abstr. 5th Conf. Israel. Associat. Ecology and Environmental Quality. 8 p.

Hirsch, S. R. (1867–1878) Der Pentateuch, modern English edition 1986: The Pentateuch. 1058 p., The Judaica Press, New York.

Hübner, J. (1979) Die Sprache evangelischer Naturtrommigkeit als praktische Theologie der Natur. In: K. M. Meyer-Abich (ed.) Frieden mit der Natr. p. 75–90, Herder, Freiburg.

Jacobson, B. S. (1987) Bina Bamikra, Gedanken zur Tora. 406 p., publ. by W. Z. O. Morascha, Zürich.

Jossuttis, M. (1989) Lebenskampf und Ehrfurcht vor dem Leben. in: Herrmann, B., and Budde, A. (eds.) Naturwissenschaftliche und historische Beiträge zu einer ökologischen Grundbildung, p. 14–19, Das Niedersächsische Umweltministerium, Hannover.

Keel, O., and Küchler, M. (1983) Synoptische Texte aus der Genesis. Teil. I. 60 p., Die Texte. Schweizerisches Katholisches Bibelwerk, Fribourg.

Loevinger, N. J. (1998): (Mis)reading of Genesis: A response to environmentalist critiques of Judaism. In: E. Bernstein (ed.) Ecology and the Jewish spirit. Where nature and the sacred meet, p. 32–40, Jewish Lights Publ., Woodstock, Vermont.

Maimonides, M. (1904) (reprinted 1956). The guide for the Perplexed. Translated by M. Friedländer. 414 p., Dover, New York.

Radin, P. (1973) The Winnebago Tribe. (Originally published as part of the Thirty-Seventh Report of the Bureau of American Ethnology, Smithsonian Institution, Washington 1923). p. 302 ff., University of Nebraska Press, Lincoln.

Rashi (1934) Chumash with Targum Onkelos, Haphtaroth and Rashis Commentary, Rabbi A. M. Silbermann and Rev. M. Rosenbaum eds. 5 vols. The Silbermann Family, Jerusalem.

Rosner, F. (ed.) (1977) Medicine in the Bible and Talmud. 247 p., KTAV Publ. House, New York.

Ruderman, D. B. (1995) Jewish Thought and Scientific Discovery in Early Modern Europe. 424 p., Yale University Press, New Haven.

Schoeps, J. H. (1992) Neues Lexikon des Judentums. 496 p. Bertelsmann, Gütersloh.

Solomon, N. (1992) Judaism and the environment. In: Rose, A. (ed.) Judaism and Ecology. p. 19–53, Cassel Publ., London.

Taylor, C. (1897) Sayings of the Jewish Fathers comprising Pirqe Aboth. 183 p., Cambridge University Press, new Printing 1969 KTAV Publ. House, New York.

——— (1995) Myths of the North American Indians. 176 p., Laurence King Publ., London.

Weber, M. (1920) Die Protestantische Ethik under der „Geist" des Kapitalismus. New edition: K. Lichtblau and J. Weiß (eds.) 203 p., Beltz Athenäum, Weinheim, 1996.

White, L. (1967) The historical roots of our ecologic crisis. Science 155, 1203–1207.

Wigoder, G. (1989) The Enzyclopedia of Judaism. The Jerusalem Publ. House, Jerusalem.

Zenger, E. (1983) Gottes Bogen in den Wolken, Untersuchungen zu Komposition und Theologie der priesterlichen Urgeschichte. 121 p., Kath. Bibelwerk, Stuttgart.

——— (1995) Politische Aufgabe der Schöpfungsmythen. Christ in der Gegenwart 47 (9), 71.

Ecology in a Biblical Perspective

TIKVA FRYMER-KENSKY

WE HAVE BECOME ACCUSTOMED, IN BOTH Judaism and Christianity, to attribute to the Bible the origin of everything good and everything evil. Needless to say, such an attitude has no basis in fact: the world was not a barren wasteland before the writing of the Bible. Nevertheless, it has become the conceit of the Western religious tradition to imagine that the Bible came to bring light to those in utter darkness and to write God's word on the *tabula rasa* of humankind.

It should therefore not be surprising that ever since Lynn White, Jr.'s, seminal article,[1] the Bible, in particular the Hebrew Bible, has stood accused of teaching us to kill the earth. White's article has been refuted hundreds of times on many different grounds, not the least of which are the many articles showing that the Bible simply doesn't support the "conquest of nature" theology that was imposed upon it a few hundred years ago.[2] Despite all the refutation, it remains constantly cited whenever people once again discover that there is an earth and that the Bible has given us some problems with it.

THE BABYLONIAN CREATION STORY

I would like to take a different path, and tell a story from pre-biblical ancient Babylonia that gives us a good indication of what a pre-biblical Near Eastern view of the relationship of God and the earth was like. The story has a long history. Our copy was written around 1550 BCE. This copy is probably not the original composition, for the copyist tells us that he is a junior scribe.[3] The story had at least a thousand-year history and we find tablets from a thousand years later that contain parts or all of this text, which we call the *Atrahasis Epic,* and they called, "When the gods as humans."

The story begins when there was an earth, but before the creation of humankind. It is a primordial history of humankind, and tells us of the defining characteristics of that pre-human world: the gods had to work. They had to work because they had to eat, and since this text was written in Iraq, the work that they engaged in was digging irrigation ditches. Seven gods seized power and became the administrators, and everybody else worked backbreaking labor for a very long time. They were, of course, gods: the irrigation ditches that they produced were the Tigris and Euphrates Rivers, and the dirt from the excavation piled up as the mountains of Iran. But even for gods, this was a lot of work, and they got very tired of it.

One day, one of the gods (whose name is not given)[4] instigates the others and calls them to strike, and the gods decide they do not want to work anymore; they are going to create a disturbance. In the middle of the night, they set fire to their pickaxes and their spades, and they march to surround the palace of the chief administrator, the god Enlil. The watchman sees them and rouses the vizier; the vizier rouses Enlil, and he immediately wants to set the defense and defeat these rabble-rousers. The vizier halts him, reminding him that "these are your sons." They call a council of the seven power wielders. Anu, the god of heaven, comes down and the god of the subterranean world, the wise god Enki, comes up, and they decide that they need to find out what is happening and why the gods are doing this.

One can imagine this story as an early D. W. Griffith movie, or, better, a Pete Seeger song, because when the council tells Enlil to find out what is happening, he directs his servant to find out who started it. But when the servant goes and asks who proclaimed this rebellion, who started this revolt, then (to the strains of "Solidarity Forever") all the gods answer, "We all did, every one of us declared rebellion." When this word is brought back, Enlil, the very personification of power, says, in effect, "Well, we gotta break the strike, let's just go in and mash a few heads and set an example of our power." The heaven god, Anu, admonishes that the council has been hearing the worker gods groaning and muttering in the pits for a long time and that they should find a solution to the workers' hard labor.

At this point the wisest of all the gods, the friend of humanity, the god Enki (or Ea, depending on whether you name him in Sumerian or Akkadian) has a brilliant idea: that the gods need a substitute work force, a permanent underclass. Enki proposes a procedure: the gods should purify themselves in a ritual immersion, should moisten the clay that Enki provides with their spittle, and the mother goddess should create a worker person.

The mother goddess, Mami, mixes the clay with the blood of a god slain for this purpose,[5] a god whose name has never been heard of before, in this text or any other myth. His name is We-ilum, which is a play on the word for humankind, *awilum*. Moreover, We-ilum is said to be a god *sa-isu temu,* a god who has sense. Once again, this is a wordplay on the word *etimmu,* the ghost that we have when our body is dead.[6] By infusing the clay of the earth with this god's blood, they give this new creature rationality and create a being who can remember that it has been created. Mami creates seven pairs of this *lullu,* the primitive worker-human, and they create seven pairs of men and women.

The gods then load upon this creature the tasks of the gods. A break on the tablet obscures a long speech about the duties of humankind and when the text picks up again, we hear about an unexpected problem: "twelve hundred years had not yet passed when the lands extended and the earth multiplied, the land was roaring like a bull." The god Enlil cannot sleep from the noise, calls his council, and they send a plague on humankind.

This devastating plague continues until the god Enki, our friend the wisest of all the gods, tells his human devotee, Atrahasis (literally "supersage" or "megabrain") that all human beings should stop worshipping any gods or goddesses except Nambar, the god of the plague. They should devote themselves to him, build him a temple, and bribe him into lifting the plague. Once they do so and the plague stops, then the text continues: "twelve hundred years had not yet passed when the earth extended and the land multiplied, the earth was bellowing like a bull."

Once again, the god Enlil cannot sleep. The problem has recurred, and this time Enlil gets the gods to agree to send a drought. When the drought comes and decimates humankind, once again Enki tells Atrahasis that people should worship only Adad the god of rain, once again humans respond and the drought lifts. But the problem recurs yet again: the text is broken, but it is clear that the gods now pollute the earth and make the soil saline. Once again, Enki saves humankind. The gods then gather to try to find a final solution to the problem, an ending, a *gamirtam*. They decide to bring a flood, and they bind Enki by an oath that he will not inform humankind of this flood. They are determined to end the problem that humans pose.

Needless to say, Enki is not so dumb, and neither is Megabrain—Atrahasis. The next time Atrahasis comes to the Temple on a vision quest, he overhears Enki talking to the walls, saying "Wall, listen to me: reed, but attend my words. Break down your house, build a boat, leave your possessions and save your life." Atrahasis, realizing that this message might have something to do with him, builds a boat, and loads animals and humans on it. The flood comes and destroys all of the earth except for this one boat in which Atrahasis and his family and animals survive.

The gods soon realize what they have done in destroying humanity. To quote the text, "Their hearts were broken and they thirsted for beer." Nobody is feeding them—and their hunger brings them to a realization of the enormous consequences of their actions. Ishtar gets up and articulates the issue, lamenting that they have destroyed their own creation, and the gods turn angry at Enlil who moved them to take such an action.

Once they are truly upset that humanity has been destroyed, Enki has Atrahasis come out of the ark and offer a sacrifice from his animals. The gods are so hungry that they swarm over the sacrifice "like flies." While they are eating, Enlil, the god who instigated the flood, comes and is dismayed that humanity has been saved. But the gods will no longer listen, and wise Enki presents a permanent solution to the problem:

Let there be a third class among people,
the women who bear and women who do not bear;
Let there be a pashittu-demon to snatch babies away
from the women who bear them;

Let there be Entu, Ugbabtu and Igisitu women
who are taboo, and thus stop childbirth, . . .

Here, still in the middle of Enki's solution to the human problem, the text gets very broken, but clearly another innovation is death, or timely death. No longer, after the flood, do people live for thousands of years.[7] After this broken speech comes the poet's summation, "I shall sing of the flood to all people; listen!"

The Atrahasis story is a primeval history that seeks to tell us that the great danger in creation is overpopulation, that the gods try "nature's" methods of controlling population (drought, pestilence, famine), and that when none of these prove anything more than temporary solutions, they are ready to destroy the whole world. In nonmythological language: if overpopulation is not controlled, then the world will be destroyed.

The story then depicts a new order in which the universe is changed so as to contain built-in population safeguards that should prevent a recurrence of overpopulation. These safeguards are perinatal death, barrenness (natural and social), and a shortened lifespan of at most 120 years.[8] The myth thus provides a framework for viewing personal tragedies as cosmic necessities. It also contains a reassuring note about humanity's place in the cosmos, for it turns out that the gods, who are able to destroy humankind, ultimately discover how much they need humanity. To be the workers of the god may imply subservience and dependence on the gods' good will, but it also makes humans indispensable and assures our continued existence. The world of gods and humans is thus interdependent.

The myth does not have such a happy message for the earth itself. The gods are willing to sacrifice the soil and the environment. They send droughts and pollution on the earth in order to decimate humankind. Of course, from our nonmythological perspective, droughts, famine and pestilence are a direct consequence of overpopulation, but the myth does not see it that way. Instead, the mutilation of the earth is the weapon that the gods use against humanity.

The myth does not present an integrated view of nature, humanity, and the gods; on the contrary, the purpose of the soil is to nourish humans, and the purpose of humans is to nourish the gods. This tale presents a clearly defined hierarchical order gods–humans–earth in a mythological setting of a definitely nonmonotheist religion.

THE GENESIS CREATION STORY

When we look at biblical mythology, the situation is much more complicated. I will concentrate on the much-discussed creation story in Genesis, Chapter 1, in order to point out one facet that has been overlooked.

In this chapter, the priestly celebration of creation, God creates by introducing distinctions, divisions, and hierarchies: the very essence of creation is the bringing of order to the formless mass of chaos, depicted as the featureless deep. On the first day, God creates light and declares it good. On the second day God creates the firmament and declares it good. On both days there has been a one-step process and one thing has been created, making one distinction: light/dark, waters above/below, and pronouncing this new creation good. On the third day God creates the division between the seas and the dry land and pronounces it good, but the third day doesn't end with the creation of earth. On that very same day, God has the earth bring forth vegetation, which is self-perpetuating and seed-bearing and will maintain its own distinct varieties. Only then does the third day end.

This compositional strategy has a significant implication: there is not one moment in cosmic time that the earth exists barren. The earth is created as a fertile, self-sustaining unit. In Genesis 1, there is no need for fertility rituals and no need for humanity to produce a fertile earth: this is the way that earth was created and this is the way it remains if it is not interfered with.[9] By doubling the creations of the third day, Genesis 1 conveys an important theological point. The cult neither has to produce fertility nor even to offer thanksgiving for the fertility because a good universe is fertile, and God created a well-ordered universe.

Genesis 1 uses a similar technique on the sixth day. Both humans and animals are created on the sixth day. The earth did not have animals without humans; the two are interconnected, and humans administrate. The essential position of humankind in the cosmos is not the farmer, but the executive. This is spelled out: humans are to be the *tzelem elohim,* the image of God. *Salmu* (cognate of *tzelem*) is a term we know from Mesopotamian inscriptions, where the king is the "image" of the god. It means the avatar of God on earth, the one who keeps everything going properly. This is humanity's proper human role in the cosmos.

The following chapters, the primeval history of Genesis 2–11, show (among other things) a progressive diminution in the fertility of the world; the world is created fertile, say the priests, but Chapters 2–11 show us that every time humans do something, the world becomes that much less fertile. From the garden that at most has to be tended, humans go out to the world, which has to be tilled by difficult agriculture. After the murder of Abel, that land is no longer fertile and can no longer be successfully planted: the blood of a murdered victim has ended the life of that soil and Cain is told that if he tills it, it will not answer. By the time of the birth of Noah, Noah is named Noah because, the text says, "this one will give us consolation"[10] "from the ground which God had cursed" (Genesis 5:29). The world has become a very infertile place.

In Chapter 6, God looks at the world and sees that it has become contaminated, *nishatah*. *Nishatah* is also used to describe the rotten cloth that Jeremiah first buries and then digs up (Jeremiah 13:7–9). God sees that this earth, which was created fertile and beautiful (Chapter 1) or which humans were supposed to guard and cultivate (Chapter 2), this earth has instead become rotten and full of stains. In this context, the flood comes as a response to this problem. Unlike in Mesopotamia, the problem is not too many people and the post-flood solution is not to build in population safeguards. In Israel the problem is the undirected and lawless activity of humankind and the pollution that results, and the post-flood solution is the giving of law.[11]

After the flood collapsed the old creation by undoing the separation of the waters, then God reasons that God no longer wants to curse the earth because of the deeds of humans. God creates a regular order of nature: summer and winter, cold and heat, so that nature will not constantly fluctuate according to human acts. God also seeks to bring order to human activity; in Chapter 9, by declaring that humans must guard and avenge human life. A clear hierarchy is made very explicit—humans are in control of nature, and their authority reaches over all the animals. Moreover, both animals or humans will forfeit their lives if they kill a human. Humans can kill animals for their own use (without eating the blood), but no one can kill a human being, the avatar of God.

There are three specific regulations in Chapter 9. In the first, humans are told to be fruitful and multiply and fill the earth, probably the only command of God that we've ever fully obeyed. Next, they are told to refrain from eating blood because that is the life: hierarchy does not imply total domination. The third regulation emphasizes that no one (human or animal) can kill human beings, those responsible for the earth, and demands the death penalty for that terrible crime. These laws do not eliminate violence, indeed they include violence, the violence of the law. Violence is ordered and sanctioned as the antidote to violence: "whoever sheds the blood of a human, by a human his blood will be shed" (Genesis 9:6). The blood of the murder is not expurgated except with the blood of the murderer.

These laws do not prevent violence. However, they do protect the earth from being polluted by lawless behavior. The laws are meant to protect the earth. God makes it very clear that God no longer wants to have the earth cursed because of human deeds. Why God wants an earth, we have no idea; for God has no need to eat food. Chapter 2 links the creation of humans with the earth: they are to tend it; but it never tells us why God wants an earth. Chapter 9, a priestly text, explains that God gives the whole legal structure of the world to protect the earth from suffering, but once again it doesn't tell us why God wants the earth. The entire creation is an act of absolute divine desire ("grace"); we don't know what motivates it.

BIBLICAL PROPHECY: THE LAND AND PEOPLE OF ISRAEL

After Genesis 1–11, the biblical discourse of the Pentateuch and the Prophets is not about humanity and the cosmos, but specifically about the people and the land of Israel. These books talk about the resonsibility of Israel and the protection of the sacred land of Israel. As modern readers, we extrapolate and restore a universalist sense to the text. The universalism may have always been there, but the text expresses itself in the immediate terms of its audience, the people of Israel.

In the Pentateuch, the sense that human behavior is responsible for the condition of the earth is very strong. Moral misdeeds pollute the earth: Israel is told to refrain from murder because it will contaminate the land; to refrain from allowing killers to go free because it will contaminate the land (Numbers 35); to refrain from acts of sexual abomination in order to keep the land pure (Leviticus 18, 20).

The book of Deuteronomy, produced by the teachers, makes this explicit. Deuteronomy 11 states the responsibility of humanity starkly: if you do good, God brings rain and abundance and you live a long time on the land; if you do wrong, then skies dry up, the earth will not produce, and you lose the land.

In such a text, we get a strong sense that humans are the intermediary between God and nature, and that God's behavior towards the earth is very reactive to human deeds. In this tradition, unlike in the priestly tradition of Numbers 35 and Leviticus 18, God does not show any more allegiance to the earth than did the gods of Mesopotamia who were prepared to send a drought to decimate humanity. Not only do human misdeeds immediately pollute the earth, but God adds to the earth's suffering by stopping up the skies.

In Israel's prophetic books, particularly Hosea, Jeremiah, and Ezekiel, the contamination of the land of Israel will lead to disaster. The most extreme formulation of this idea is found in Jeremiah's vision in Chapter 4: here, because of the deeds of Israel, Jeremiah sees the entire collapse of creation. The skies go dark, and no Adam can be found. So, too, Isaiah sees the very earth broken and falling apart (Isaiah 24:19–23).

In all these passages, the Bible presents a very strong statement of human responsibility. The centrality of humanity means that human beings are the intermediaries who influence the condition of the earth both directly, by the immediate polluting impact of their misdeeds, and indirectly by causing a divine reaction that ends the rain and further pollutes the earth.[12] Humanity has long run away from facing this responsibility, but it has become hard to ignore now that technology increasingly gives us the power to impact on the environment and really create destruction by our social misdeeds. At this point a statement that what humans do determines whether the earth continues or not is a simple statement of fact.

Of course, a statement that human actions determine whether the world continues is only a statement of fact if our definition of the world includes humanity. However, even if (horrors to contemplate) we thoroughly pollute the soil or deplete the ozone; even if we bring a nuclear disaster (God and humanity forbid), it may be that the earth will stand and the cockroaches will still survive as they have survived since the age of the dinosaurs, and so in a sense the world will still continue. We will not have destroyed it utterly: we will only have eradicated it as a habitable place for humanity. The earth, Gaia, the ecosystem, existed before us and will continue after us. Somehow, such thinking, characteristic of the Gaia-thinkers, is supposed to make us feel better.

We should note that this approach is almost totally unbiblical. The late biblical prophetic tradition does consider the question. The prophet Zephaniah's terrible prediction of doom might envision earth remaining even though life has gone: "I will utterly sweep away everything from the face of the earth, I will sweep away humans and beasts, I will sweep away the birds of the air and the fish of the sea. . . . I will cut off humankind from the face of the earth" (Zephaniah 1:2–3). But this is not a prophecy that Zephaniah utters with any consolation. Deutero-Isaiah constantly emphasizes the importance of human life in the creation scheme: "[God] who creates heavens and stretches them out, who hammers out the sky and its teeming life, who gives breath to humankind and life-spirit to those who walk upon it" (Isaiah 42:5). Isaiah further tells us that when God created the world, God didn't create it to be unformed (*tohu*) but to be inhabited and inhabitable (*la-shevet*) (Isaiah 45:18). God's ultimate purpose for the earth, whatever it may be, includes a functioning human and animal community.

THE PRIESTLY VOICE: AN AWESOME EARTH

I would also like to praise another voice in the Bible, one which is very often maligned in all contexts, including the ecological discussion: P, the priestly tradition of ancient Israel. It is in priestly writings and in temple writings that we find a profound sense of the awesomeness of nature, of the revelation of God through the beauty of nature, and of the place of humanity as a creature within nature. This love of nature is explicit in such Psalms as 104 and 98. It also underlies priestly legislation, where it is concerned with the land of Israel.

To these priests, the land of Israel is sacred and primary. Leviticus 18 and 20 explain that when the peoples before Israel pollute the earth, the land vomited out these people. This land belongs to God, and God will protect it. Israel's tenure includes a mandate to protect the land of Israel from becoming polluted by the performance of abominable acts. In this priestly sense of the sacredness of the very soil of Israel, no less than in the prophetic tradition of Hosea, Jeremiah, and Ezekiel, Israel loses its right to the land if it doesn't protect it; the forced exile of the people separates the land from this contaminating force. This exile does not mean that God abandons Israel: the priests hold that God has great allegiance to Israel that goes beyond the land, and present the covenant of circumcision as the sign that land or no land, the relationship with Israel continues forever.

But the land itself is holy, and Israel may be separated from the land and sent far off to a land unknown. In priestly theology, two elements, the land of Israel and the people of Israel, are both extremely vital to God, and neither will be sacrificed for the other.

Interestingly enough, with all the priestly purification rituals, there is no ritual to purify the land.[13] Pollution must be prevented; once it settles in, it cannot be remedied by religious action or petition. The cult helps purify the people and the temple, not the land itself. But the priestly cult did not ignore the land; in fact, the *tamid* sacrifices, offered according to the calendar, were directed towards the whole cosmos to help keep the entire system going.

As we apply the priestly concept of the two independent foci to our current understanding, we must hold both elements, humanity and the ecosystem, in equilibrium. For whatever reason God created the cosmos, God has great allegiance to it. Humanity cannot continue to damage the earth for its own benefit. But, in the biblical viewpoints, humanity also has independent and equal importance.

In biblical theology, the earth must be a place where human ideals of harmony can be fulfilled, a place where humans behave well towards each other, so that the earth is both fertile and inhabited. Forms of deep ecology that place the earth above humanity are not biblical theologies, for the biblical ideal of *shalom* includes the presence of humanity.

This ancient language does not tell us whether, if humans continue on their current disharmonious path, the whole world will be destroyed, or just the people removed and the land preserved for the cockroaches. But it does bring home the recognition that we cannot escape the consequences of the human impact on the world. It further insists that today, now that we have technology that greatly magnifies our powers of destruction, if we do not make and obey rules of harmony and equity, then our connection with the earth will somehow be broken, and whether the cockroaches survive or not, the end of human history will have come, and with it the end of the divine plan.

NOTES

1. Lynn White, Jr., "The Historical Roots of Our Ecologic Crisis," *Science* 155 (1967).
2. See, e.g., Jeanne Kay, "Concepts of Nature in the Hebrew Bible," *Environmental Ethics* 10:4 (1988): 309–27, and recently J. Baird Callicott, "Genesis Revisited: Murian Musings on Lynn White, Jr. Debate," *Environmental History Review* 14:1–2 (1990): 65–90.
3. This copy of the *Atrahasis Epic* was published by Lambert and Millard, Cuneiform *Texts from Babylonian Tablets in the British Museum,* XLVII, 2965. Lambert and Millard published the edition and English translation in *Atrahasis: the Babylonian Story of the Flood* (Oxford, 1969).
4. Moran constructed the text differently, understanding the "one god" in the tablet who instigates the rebellion not as "a god," but as a specific god, whose name may have been in a break, and who is identical to the god We-ilum, who was killed in the creation of humankind. See William Moran "The Creation of Man in Atrahasis I, 192–248" BASOR 200 (1970): 48–56.
5. For Moran, it is not "a god" but "the god"; instead of "one who has sense" he translates "the one who had the plan."
6. For a study of these wordplays, see Steven Geller, "Some Sound and Word Plays in the First Tablet of the Old Babylonian *Atrahasis Epic,*" in *The Frank Talmage Memorial Volume I,* ed. Barry Wahlfish (Haifa University Press, 1993), pp. 137–44.
7. In the Sumerian King List (ed. Thorkild Jacobsen, *Assyriological Studies II*), the kings before the flood had reigns into the thousands of years; after the flood, their reigns were more normal.
8. Jacob Klein, "The 'Bane' of Humanity: A Lifespan of One Hundred Twenty Years," *Acta Sumerologica 12* (1990): 57–70.
9. This is not the view of Genesis 2, where the earth

is barren until humanity is created. Genesis 2 is a farmers' myth, Genesis 1 is not.

10. Or "this one will give us rest," reading the Hebrew word as *yenihemenu*, which would conform to the Greek, as the standard *yenahamenu*, "will comfort us," also matches the Greek, for the technical use of the word *nhm* means to have release from work-bondage. However, since Noah's name is not Nahum, "give us rest" fits his name better.

11. See Tikva Frymer-Kensky, "The Atrahasis Epic and its Significance for Our Understanding Genesis 1–9," *Biblical Archaeologist* 40 (1977): 147–55.

12. For a further discussion of the nature of human responsibility, see Tikva Frymer-Kensky, *In the Wake of the Goddesses* (Macmillan, 1992), pp.83–107 and 243–49.

13. The closest rite is the ritual of the decapitated heifer, performed when a corpse is discovered and the murderer cannot be found. This ritual seeks to prevent the pollution from settling in; once it does, nothing can remove it and it builds up until it reaches a critical mass. For further understanding of this concept of pollution, see Tikva Frymer-Kensky, "Pollution, Purification and Purgation in Biblical Israel," in *The Word of the Lord Shall Go Forth: Essays in Honor of David Noel Freedman*, ed. Carol Meyers and Michael O'Connor (Winona Lake, Ind.: Eisenbrauns, 1983), pp. 399–414.

The Unnatural Jew

STEVEN S. SCHWARZSCHILD

I argue that Judaism and Jewish culture have paradigmatically and throughout history operated with a fundamental dichotomy between nature ("what is") and ethics (i.e., God and man—"what ought to be"). Pagan ontologism, on the other hand, and the Christian synthesis of biblical transcendentalism and Greek incarnationism result in human and historical submission to what are acclaimed as "natural forces." Although in the history of Jewish culture such a heretical, quasi-pantheistic tendency asserted itself, first in mediaeval kabbalism and then in modern Zionism, from a traditional Jewish standpoint nature remains subject to humanly enacted ends. Evidence for this general thesis can be found in biblical. Talmudic, medieval philosophic, and mystical literature, in modern religious, poetic, and Zionist literature, and in the history of general philosophy.

I. INTRODUCTION

IN MY PHILOSOPHY DEPARTMENT THE GRADUATE students organize an annual picnic. For some time past quasi-formal invitations have explicitly excluded me on the ground that I am known to be at odds with nature. So I am. My dislike of nature goes deep: nonhuman nature, mountain ranges, wildernesses, tundra, even beautiful but unsettled landscapes strike me as opponents, which, as the Bible commands (Gen. 1:28–30), I am to fill and conquer. I really do not like the world, and I think it foolish to tell me that I had better. Like Dryden, "I contemn the world when I think on it." One explanation of my attitude is historical. My paternal family lived in Frankfurt-on-the-Main, where I was born, since before 1500. We have been urban for well over half a millennium.

Here I want to analyze whether this is only an idiosyncratic or mainly historical attitude or whether more important, even philosophical, factors are significantly involved. Might it be that Judaism and nature are at odds? Richard Popkin once put this Zen

Schwarzschild, Steven S., "The Unnatural Jew," *Environmental Ethics* 6/4 (1984), pp. 347–362. Reprinted by permission.

problem to me: who was the last famous Jewish mountain climber? Indeed, most Jews in remembered history are unnatural persons.

II. JEWISH LITERATURE: CELAN

Paul Celan (1920–1970) is among the most important poets of this century, especially *qua* Jew. Among his few narrative works is "Conversation in the Mountains."[1] The story moves on many levels and, despite its typical compactness, carries a lot of freight. In the following summary, I concentrate on one important theme, probably the central one.

The Jew went into the mountains, away from "where he belongs, in the valleys." There he ran into an older cousin. On the narrative level the two are cousins; on another level both of them are Celan himself—on his way away from Judaism, when he was small, "Mr. Klein," and on his way back, when he was grown, "Mr. Gross."[2] There is never silence very long between Jews, not even in the mountains, "for the Jew and nature, they are two different things, still now, also today, also here." The cousins pay no attention to the natural beauties that surround them. They have veils behind their eyes, so that in their perception any object that strikes the eye becomes a mixture of the image and the veil. "Tongue are they and mouth." They realize that nature, too, has a language, a visual language, but they say that it is "not for you and not for me . . . a language without I or you, all he, all it, all sir *[Sie]*."[3] God does not communicate with Jews through nature. Nature as such does not communicate, "because no one hears it"; it merely speaks.

Let me take up one more aspect of "Conversation in the Mountains," an aspect of its "inter-textuality," in the sense of contemporary literary and philosophical theory. Twice in the six pages of the story the Jew went "*wie Lenz*" through the mountains. *Lenz* is the old poetic German for "spring" (compare *Lent*) and also the hero of Georg Buechner's "Lenz" (1835),[4] a quasi-historical story about a German poet who retired into the mountains. Buechner's "Lenz" begins with the words: "On the 20th [of January 1778] Lenz went into the mountains."[5] Celan wants to "compare" his two Jews, who went into the mountains, with (because they are "like") the Protestant Lenz, whose experiences Buechner, basing himself on historical evidence,[6] powerfully describes.

I can describe Buechner's story of Lenz here only very selectively, with an eye toward the purpose at hand. It contains lengthy romantic descriptions of nature and of extreme psychological states suffused with mysticism, Protestant Germanic theology, and a strong dose of pantheism. This is a relationship to nature completely different from Celan's; yet, there are important features that Lenz and "the Jew" have in common.

As Lenz walked through the mountains, "he was not concerned with the path," and "he found nothing." And as of "the Jew, you know, what does he have that really belongs to him," also of Lenz it is said that "he had nothing." Celan's story begins with the words, "One evening, the sun, and not only the sun, had gone down." Lenz, too, "would have wanted to run after the sun." On the other hand, the Jew "walked in the shadow," whereas "when Lenz descended the mountain, he saw that a rainbow of rays surrounded his shadow." And quoting a church hymn, although Lenz "has no friend in this world, I have my treasure, and he is far." When he learns that a child has died in a neighboring village, Lenz puts on sackcloth and ashes, goes to the village, and tries to resurrect her. He fails. "He had to laugh aloud, and together with the laughter atheism took hold of him. . . . 'I am the Wandering Jew. . . . But, were I omnipotent, I would save.'"

Celan's very Jewish Jews and the two very German Protestants Lenz and Buechner are in general worlds apart, and yet there are some important characteristics they share. It is far from accidental that the Rumanian Jew Celan, whose entire life, work, and death are totally formed by the Nazi experience, became the most important poet of his century in German-language culture. Lenz, too, eventually went insane. There is an aura of unfinishedness, perhaps intentional, about Buechner and his work. Celan's life also was left tragically unfinished when he walked not into the mountains but into the Seine.

Celan's Jew, too, is then an unnatural Jew. But this could be an accidental result of Jewish history—the explanation routinely given. That is, Celan's Jew is the end product of two-thousand years of exile from "the Land." Some Jews contemporary with Celan did return to Zion, and their relationship to nature is very different from that of Jews of the exile, like Celan, whose suicide came right after his only visit to the State of Israel.

What happened to the two cousins/one person in the mountains after the end of Celan's story? We know that the historical Lenz left the mountains and returned to the densely inhabited world; did they/he, too, return to the valleys, or did he/they perhaps die in the wilderness? The exiled Jew is "alienated" from nature, as his historically characteristic "unhealthy" vocational demography illustrates, but the prevailing view has it that this is due not to the fact that he is a Jew nor to Judaism, but to his exile.

III. JEWISH PHILOSOPHY

The main line of Jewish philosophy (in the exilic age) has paradigmatically defined Jewishness as alienation from and confrontation with nature. As text I use an essay by Hans Jonas, "Jewish and Christian Elements in Philosophy: Their Share in the Emergence of the Modern Mind," to develop my argument.[7]

Jonas, following Hegel, isolates the Christian component in Western culture as what is not shared with Judaism, the doctrine of the incarnation. According to this doctrine God becomes man, and as such he enters the world, enters nature. I believe Jonas can be shown to be wrong in holding that "it was not before Hegel's theory of the absolute Spirit, its alienation and self-consummation through history, that the theme of incarnation found major expression in philosophy—and then only by the boldest transmutation."[8] This belief can be shown to have played a major role in Western philosophy long before Hegel.[9] The doctrine of the incarnation is, among other things, a re-paganization of Biblical religion in the limited but crucial sense that nature is re-sanctified. God not only is, was, and can be nature, but also nature was and can be God. The closing thought of Jonas's essay is, therefore, the more true: "[T]he ultimate secularization of theology, the idea of history as a self-operative vehicle of redemption is much more of Christian than of Jewish provenance. One may see in it a transmuted form of the Holy Spirit doing his work through man in the interval between incarnation and the second coming,"[10] because, once God has become nature, thereafter he works through and like nature, by natural law, until it is no longer a limited God = nature identity but a total one—that is, the second coming when God will again have become "all in all" (1 Cor. 15:28).

Hegel is penetrating but as usual wrongheaded here. For Hegel, Judaism is what is invariably rendered in English as "the religion of sublimity." The German word for *sublimity (Erhabenheit)* is a form of *Un-aufgehobenheit,* i.e., "unsublatedness." The Jewish God is absolutely transcendent to man and the world, "elevated above naturalness."[11] He is the "absolute alien," *der Fremde.*[12] The Jew is, therefore, in turn, totally alienated from God and his world.[13] Hegel contrasts this with the spiritually emancipated Greek and his Christian heirs who have risen to understand that man and the world are God and God is one with them—"sublated."[14]

Hegel is right factually and wrong in his evaluation. The biblical and Jewish God is, indeed, absolutely transcendent. Nature is never in any way identical with him. It can serve him, as it can serve human beings made in the "image of God." What makes humans "images of God" is that they share with him the "will," the rational and the ethical. Jonas here rightly cites Maimonides and Kant,[15] although the vast bulk of Jewish philosophy would serve equally well,[16] and he even cites Kant as in the Jewish current: "In this connection one must also remember Kant's majestic effort to synthesize voluntarism and rationalism. The synthesis appears in the categorical imperative (surely of Hebrew vintage)."[17] In such a rationalistic, volitionalistic, and transcendental context, nature possesses no value in itself. Its value lies in its serviceability to man and God, although, to be sure, it must be protected and even improved for precisely this purpose. "The Lord God took man and placed him in the garden of Eden to work it and to guard it."[18] To quote a quasi-legal, quasi-authoritative, and less exegesis-ridden text, *Sefer Chinuch* (a popularization of Maimonides' *Book of the Commandments*), "nature is that which works well and effectively for human beings."[19] This is anthropocentrism, or theocentrism, or ratiocentrism long before Kant. "The understanding obtains its laws [a priori] not from nature but prescribes them to it."[20] Helmut Holzhey correctly summarizes the Kantian conception of nature in his essay about Kantian ecology by saying that "nature is the lawfully determined object of cognition, and its legislator is the human understanding."[21]

Jewish philosophers and theologians in the nineteenth century, primarily in Germany, were then torn between Kant and Hegel, but even those strongly attracted to Hegel had to reassert the primacy of freedom and ethics over the innate dialectic of the world and therewith the ultimacy of Judaism. At the end of the century the battle was decisively won in favor of Kant by Hermann Cohen.

In the High Middle Ages one shoot branched off of Jewish thought which was destined to overshadow its mother-tree. Salomon ibn Gabirol (Avicebron), the neo-Platonist philosopher and poet, tried to solve in one fell swoop two fundamental problems: the origin of matter and the derivation of the manifold from the one. His solution was the daring doctrine that *matter* emerges from the *essence* of God and *form* emerges from his *spirit*.[22] Even most specialized scholars have not seen how this doctrine implies at least logically the materiality of God.[23] Gershom Scholem makes no bones about the perennial stream of the pantheistic temptation, to put it mildly, in Kabbalah throughout his classic *The Major Trends of Jewish Mysticism*. For example, he relates the twelfth-century German-Jewish pietists to Scotus,[24] and to bring things down to approximately the period of the Renaissance where we left them philosophically above, he speaks of Cordovero's "formula—a century before Spinoza and Malebranche—that 'God is all reality, but not all reality is God.'"[25]

In subsequent European intellectual history, this strange amalgam of scientific rationalism and near-pantheistic mysticism became the scientific revolution of the seventeenth and eighteenth centuries. In Judaism, chassidism and other quasi-modernizing movements perpetuated and developed these themes. Martin Buber tries too hard in his "Spinoza, Sabbatai Zvi, and the Baal-Shem"[26] to represent chassidism and Spinoza as opponents. Even he cannot close his eyes completely to the pantheistic temptation in chassidism. In any case, when you eliminate the exclusiveness of the rational/ethical connection between God and man, pantheism is only one of several possible results; the temptation of acosmism, that nothing is all there is, also arose in chassidism.[27] This entire complex was renewed by the Spinoza revival in the age of Hegel and his successors in German "philosophy of nature."

This is, then, in broad outline the history of a Jewish heretical tendency. Scholem puts it this way: "[A]uthoritative Jewish theology . . . like Saadia, Maimonides and Hermann Cohen . . . formulated an antithesis to pantheism."[28] In an earlier analysis I conclude that "it is, perhaps, worth noting the Jewish origin of the three great 'immanentists' in Western culture, Paul of Tarsus, Spinoza, and Marx. Like Christianity itself, immanentism would seem to be a specifically Jewish heresy."[29]

Hans Jonas is insufficiently sensitive to the heretical character of this development, because he himself is philosophically somewhere between immanentism and transcendentalism. He advocates a partial, but only a partial, "re-Judaization" of Western, naturalistic, Christian, quasi-pantheistic incarnationism. On the one hand, he follows R. Bultmann.[30] On the other hand, he rightly argues that language *(logos)* is "pure signification . . . free from the bonds of likeness" (that is, sensuousness, in Kantian terms), and that, therefore, especially mathematics and ethics are humanly imposed on nature ("some prophets of Israel saw only injustice about them").[31] These two sides are synthesized by Jonas in his philosophy of biology, which results in a doctrine of "emergent evolution." Inorganic nature contains within itself, (as Spinoza and Teilhard de Chardin say) hylozoistically and panpsychically, the potentiality of higher organic and even rational developments.[32] In *The Phenomenon of Life* Jonas sees the historical connection that I have made here.[33] Dualism killed the vitalism of the Renaissance, but the mechanistic and rationalistic outlook of dualism can now no longer do justice either to the needs of biological science or to the spiritual needs of human society.[34] As a result, Jonas can still speak of "the Jewish-Christian separation of God and world" and of "Western voluntarism."[35]

Jewish philosophy and culture followed a more "unnatural" path. God and man are totally distinct from and superior to nature. The universe is not even *in potentia* structured as it ought to be by spontaneous natural forces, and, therefore, reason and morality ought to whip things into shape.

IV. ECOSOPHY

I started in a personal vein and then presented some solid evidence using Celan's view as a paradigmatically Jewish contemporary literary source. I have also presented some philosophical underpinnings of that view. I now deal with the question at issue, the Jewish relationship to nature itself.

Nature has in this century become a matter of major concern, partly as a result of the modern naturalization of philosophy. Add to this the recent anxieties of ecologists and of society about shrinking natural resources. No reasonable person will fail to share these concerns. Anthropocentric ethicists will obviously worry about shrinking natural resources. They will want to husband nature as carefully, intelligently, productively, and economically as possible. As Richard A. Watson puts it: "Preserve . . . ecology: human survival depends on it."[36] But note that this argument is based on the view that nature serves man, not man nature. The biblical theorem that man is the master of nature is fully preserved. As Maimonides interprets Genesis 1:26–28: "Act ye according to your will . . . to build and to uproot the planted and to dig out of the mountains copper and so forth." As Descartes put it: *"nous rendre comme maîtres et possesseurs de la nature."*[37]

"Humanistic ecology" should not be defined in a narrowly utilitarian fashion. It gives no license to damage or destroy any part of nature whose immediate human usefulness is not obvious or at least possible. Human enjoyment is also to be valued past utility and as long as it does not conflict with moral values. Moral values may sometimes be enshrined by analogy in nonhuman nature: for example, we judge suffering to be offensive not only in humans, but also in nonhuman sentient animals.[38] Unabashed anthropocentrist that I am, I gladly admit that my pacifism and vegetarianism comprise an element of ecologism.[39]

There is, on the other hand, a wild-eyed "ecosophy" whose proponents argue that precisely the Western, Jewish-Christian ethos of lordship over nature has produced the ecological crisis. They assert the contrary ethos, that man is part of nature, nature is sacred, and man, therefore, ought to serve nature, rather than *vice versa.* "We belong to earth and not earth to us."[40] Lynn White, Jr., perhaps the most influential ideologist of this sort in this country, even advocates an "advance" into paganism or Far Eastern quasi-pantheistic religion in order to safeguard the sanctity of nature.[41] White alleges that for historic biblical religion, rape is the only form of engagement with nature. (The claim is White's; the words are those of the Protestant "death-of-God" theologian, William Hamilton.[42])

As part of their political Leftism, the thinkers of "the Frankfurt school" also insist that capitalist domination, exploitation, and alienation of human beings are the result of the attitude of lordship toward an "alienated, thingified" nature. In the wake of Hegel and Heidegger they propose a "dialectical," rather than a Kantian dualistic, relationship between nature and reason. Man is to be naturalized and nature humanized in the ultimate synthesis. T. W. Adorno complains that Schoenberg (whom he otherwise admires) dominates nature rather than works in and out of it.[43] In his music, therefore, Schoenberg loses "the instinctual life of the sounds."[44]

Ernst Bloch, in his optimistic way, falls into a sort of pantheistic mysticism with a strong dose of Marxism. He holds that *natura naturans* is a "natural Subject," which, like rational men, assures the reconciliation of man and nature.[45] Herbert Marcuse wagers on "erotic desire"[46] and a "naturalistic foundation for reason."[47] Further, the pessimistic Adorno is reduced to hylozoism: his *reductio hominis* is accompanied, as it has to be, by the ascription of anthropomorphic individuality to objects and by "a love of things."[48]

The re-sacralization of nature can be defended by three philosophical explanations. One is that nature is sacred in, of, and by itself *(an-sich).* But surely Kant made mincemeat of such a view. It is only from the human perspective that nature is important or sacred. To ask what nature is according to any nonhuman perspective, or "to itself," is clearly a nonsensical question by definition.[49] But it is not nonsensical enough to keep Christopher Stone from answering the question of his title *Should Trees Have Standing?*[50] in the affirmative. This "standing" is supported by panpsychic, Spinozistic reasons.

Left to her own devices, nature is a fickle mother anyway. She kills many of her own children. Most species were produced and destroyed long before humans arrived. The sentimental notion of nature as omnibenevolent has rightly been ridiculed by philosophers. The Christian Isaac Watt composed a stomach-turning ditty about "the busy little bee" that gives "for everyday some good account at last." Lewis Carroll thought otherwise: "How doth the little crocodile / improve his shining tail, /. . . How cheerfully he seems to grin, / How neatly spreads his claws / and welcomes little fishes in, / With gently smiling jaws!"[51] As Celan's Jew said in the mountains: nature speaks "not for you and not for me." We can, therefore, quite peremptorily dismiss the notion that nature is sacred.

A second defense of the re-sacralization of nature is to admit, on the one hand, as critics of the Frankfurt School do, that the "sanctity" of nature is not intrinsic but relational. It arises in a "dialectical" relationship to the human spirit. But then, on the other hand, one can assume an absolutely aesthetic, contemplative, posture toward it, a "pure" relation as distinguished from Kant's "practical" one. The practical view is Habermas's "humanly interested," *logos*-determined, ideally linguistic posture. In the pure relationship, you have "the preponderance of the object."[52] In the aesthetic attitude nature is regarded not only as noumenal but also as numinous.[53]

This is the quintessence of paganism. Maimonides accordingly defines idolatry as "the love of a form, because it functions so beautifully."[54] Cynthia Ozick calls art "the religion of the Gentile nations."[55] Here nature is man's lord. Greece has triumphed over Jerusalem. Kant's and Hermann Cohen's ethicization of art, in which sublimity is envisioned as rational infinity, beauty as rational and real morality, and humor as the infinite gap between reality and ideality, is here retracted (as though "the Copernican revolution" had not also occurred in aesthetics!). The neo-Kantian Cohen rejected emphatically what he called "the absolute identity of nature and spirit, this pantheistic vehicle of Romantic metaphysics,"[56] and when he, too, like Bloch, needed to advance a postulate of the ultimate, infinite reconciliation of nature with ethical reason, he did it in the wake of Kant's infinite, regulative, ethical ideal and in terms of the Jewish/biblical metaphor of the rainbow,[57] that is, in terms of regulatives of universal human, social morality.

The third argument for the re-sacralization of nature returns us to Jonas, paralleled in the writings of S. Langer and T. de Chardin, who tend here to converge with the original Frankfurt school. Holzhey discusses a current European school of "evolutionary epistemology" (e.g., G. Vollmer, Lorenz, Riedl, etc.): "What Kant differentiated as an accomplishment of the understanding here becomes a function of the organism."[58] Darwinism is interpreted so that human reason is itself a product of nature. What Holzhey refers to as "evolutionary epistemology" Braun calls "naturalistic evolutionism."[59] Adorno then draws the consistent but unacceptable conclusion: "If human identity is totally repressive, then nature must be liberating,"[60] and in this he discovers the following lessons: (a) "end the compulsion to have an identity," and (b) "try to live such that you can believe that you were a good animal."[61] The radical critique of this approach by neo-Kantians in the immediate wake of Darwin is still cogent today: "evolutionary epistemology" confuses causality with validity. Hermann Cohen anticipated even Gilbert Ryle's critique of "the ghost in the machine" by mocking "the ghost of a soul."[62] (What is a good animal, anyway—Isaac Watt's "busy little bee" or Lewis Carroll's "little crocodile"?)

V. JUDAISM

I can finally return to the basic sources of the Jewish relationship to nature. Christians and Jews have so combed the Bible for a proper understanding of nature that I do not need to go into details here. Nature is precious, because God is its *koneh* ("maker"-"owner"). Man is God's perpetual partner in perfecting the world toward and by means of the kingdom of God. He is the steward, the responsible caretaker, and husbandman of nature. Only with this in mind do "the heavens tell of the glory of God and the firmament [bespeak] his handiwork" (Ps. 19), for "when I see your heavens, the work of your fingers, the moon and the stars that you established—what is man? . . . You have set him as ruler of the work of your hands. You have laid all under his feet" (Ps. 8:4f., 7f.). Even what may look like an occasional biblical, quasi-Rousseauite "return to nature," e.g., the Nazirites or Rechabites who live a desert-like existence without houses, wives, wine, or haircuts, is really just a few ethical athletes (at that not favorably countenanced by authoritative Judaism), who want to abstain from material accumulations, concupiscence, mindlessness, and fashion.

My favorite text is the *mishnah,* "Chapters of the Fathers," 3:9: "Rabbi Jacob said: 'One who walks by the road, studying, and interrupts his study and says: 'How lovely is that tree!' or 'How lovely is that furrow!'—Scripture imputes it to him as if he had forfeited his soul!'" This classic Jewish text has attracted the usual commentaries. Recently, Cynthia Ozick returned to the ethos of the *mishnah* in her title story "The Pagan Rabbi," using this Talmudic text as its motto.[63] The hero of the story is a schizophrenic, who, on the one hand, is "a dusty old man trudging . . . he reads as he goes . . . a Tractate of the Mishnah . . . , who passes indifferently through the beauty of the field . . . and won't heed the cricket spitting in the field," and, on the other hand, is "the pagan rabbi" himself, who "insisted on picnics" and who proclaims: "there is nothing that is Dead. . . . Great Pan lives."[64]

Susan Handelman[65] makes clear how contemporary "deconstructionist" literary theory (Lacan, Derrida, Harold Bloom)[66] resumes the struggle of Jewish bookishness ("textuality") against pagan/Christian nature and metaphysics—the Book of Books *versus* "the Book of Nature." A quotation from Derrida shows conveniently how deconstructionism drinks from the Jewish sources that I have here traced: "For the Jew—and the poet—the book becomes folded and bound to itself, infinitely self-reflective, its own subject and its own representation. The home of the Jew and the poet is the text: they are wanderers born only of the book . . . Between the fragments of the Broken Tablets the poem grows and the right to Speech takes root. Once more begins the adventure of text as weed, as outlaw far from the 'fatherland of the Jews,' which is a 'sacred text surrounded by commentaries'."[67] This reads like a conflation of Celan's "Conversation in the Mountains" and *Aboth* 3:9.

In Jewish modern, post-traditional literature our *mishnah* was treated by Achad Ha'am and H. N. Bialik, the founding fathers of the Hebrew Renaissance, in a *locus classicus,* "Halakhah and Aggadah."[68] On the one hand, the man walking by the road, studying, is "the people 'walking by the road' that possesses nothing but a book and whose spiritual bond to any of the lands in which it dwells is only spiritual."[69] On the other hand, there is condemnation: "[I]t is a pathetic *mishnah*"and arouses among our "aesthetic and sensitive people" a great desire to break out into the natural world. Micah Joseph Berdichevsky, a pagan, Nietzschean writer of the Hebrew Renaissance, goes further. Commenting on his *mishnah,* he says: "But I assert that then alone will Judah and Israel be saved when another teaching is given unto us, namely: Whoever walks by the way and sees a fine tree and a fine field and a fine sky and leaves them to think on other thoughts—that man is like one who forfeits his life! Give us back our fine trees and fine fields! Give us back the Universe. . . . We with our thoughts and feelings . . . and all we have and are, are the drippings of the bucket, the dust in the scales . . . for Nature is the father of all life."[70] Berdichevsky draws the Nietzschean, Zionist, programmatically pagan conclusion: "[T]he blade and the bow, by whose force Israel fared so nobly," must be restored in the place of the book in Israel's renaissance.[71] (In his book *Sinai and Gerisim,* Berdichevsky advocated a Jewish return to pre-Mosaic paganism, as Oskar Goldberg did in Germany after World War I.[72])

The connection between such early Zionist ideology and much later "Canaanism" is obvious.[73] But there is more to it than this. The truth is that a back-to-nature thrust inheres in the Zionist enterprise. In the earlier quotation from Bialik/Ahad Ha'am, the back-to-nature push is only less radical than Berdichevsky's, and A. Hertzberg rightly recognizes the Nietzschean inspiration even in the founding-father ideologists of Zionism.[74] Also, among the later and genuine saints of Zionism, the resumed love affair with nature appealed to the widest conceivable circles.[75] The workers' prophet A. D. Gordon proclaimed: "And when, oh man, you will return to Nature . . . you will know that you have returned to yourself, . . . when you hid from nature you hid from yourself," whereas in the past "the Jewish people has been completely cut off from nature and imprisoned within city walls these 2,000 years."[76] "Nature itself has created the people . . . [which] is like a funnel that receives the infinity of the cosmos."[77] Saul Tchernikovsky, another pagan Nietzschean, the Hebrew poet of that generation, raised Berdichevsky's conception to even higher literary levels. On the religious end of the Zionist spectrum, chief-rabbi Kook incorporated nature mysticism into his panentheistic Zionism.[78] Also the quasi-mystic Martin Buber undergirded his utopian-socialist program with a renewed appreciation of the soil and nature. In short, the Jewish philosophical heretical trend, which originated in the Middle Ages, developed in the diaspora and continues in Zionism.

There is nothing "wrong" with trees. To the contrary, God (*Eccl. R.* 7:28) pointed them out to Adam in the garden of Eden, but immediately added the normative purpose for doing so: "Think about this, and do not corrupt or desolate my world, for if you do corrupt it there will be none to set it aright after you." The Jew is obligated to recite the following benediction when he sees a blooming tree: "Praised be you, oh Lord, our God, king of the world, who has not left a thing lacking in his world and created in it good creatures and good trees, so that human beings can benefit from them."[79] But when a tree is not blooming, that is, when it is not immediately useful to man, the benediction is much more nonchalant: "Praised be you . . . whose world is like this."[80] Even the sun itself was created so as to serve mankind.[81] In short, the rabbis wanted to enthrone "the beauty of Japhet [Greece] in the tents of Shem [Israel]."[82]

The thought of J. B. Soloveitchik is relevant here. In "The Lonely Man of Faith,"[83] he takes the two texts from Genesis 1 and Genesis 3, which we have had occasion to use a good deal, and develops an entire typology of man: "Adam, the First," who is practical, and "Adam, the Second," who is aesthetic. In many ways Soloveitchik treats the aesthetic Adam as more akin to *homo religiosus*—at least as more akin to the religious man's mystic, God-intoxicated, dimension. Despite this, and undoubtedly due to his self-evident commitment to the centrality of *halakhah* ("praxis"), he eventually subordinates the aesthetic Adam to the practical: nature is conceived as existing for halachic purposes; man is God's partner in making the world; "the man of *halakhah* is a ruler in the kingdom of reason and spirit,"[84]—"the subject rules the object, the person the thing."[85] The practical use of nature rules.

In sum, the culture of beauty is prized but subordinated to the culture of morality by Judaism (as Matthew Arnold also understood in *Culture and Anarchy*).

VI. CONCLUSION

I began by calling myself an urban man for more than half a millennium. It turns out, unsurprisingly, that as a Jew I have been an unnatural man much longer. Well before the rise of towns and cities, Jews were not supposed to reside where there are no synagogues, physicians, artisans toilets, water supplies, schoolteachers, scribes, organized charities, or courts.[86] An "ignoramus" or *'am-ha' aretz* (literally, a "man of the land," "peasant") is frowned upon by "civilized," pious people.[87] Irving Agus, in his historical studies summarizes: "The Jews were the first self-ruling town-dwellers of Western Europe in the early Middle Ages."[88] Was it only a pun when the Talmudic rabbis warned against the use of the Torah as a spade (*Aboth* 4:7)? Or were they warning against subordinating intellectual and moral pursuits to material ends?

NOTES

1. *Ausgewaehlte Gedichte,* ed. Klaus Reichert (Frankfurt: Suhrkamp, 1970), pp. 181–86.
2. Cf. Celan's acceptance speech of the Buechner Prize, "The Meridian," in *Ausgewaehlte Gedichte,* almost all of which deals with this story, pp. 142, 146ff. Cf. also Jerry Glenn, *Paul Celan* (New York: Twayne, 1973), pp. 43–46 about this story—which is generally an unsatisfactory introduction.
3. Compare also Martin Buber's *I and Thou,* 2nd ed. (New York: Charles Scribner's Sons, 1958) and the famous Yiddish, Chassidic folk song "The Dudele."
4. G. Buechner, *Wozzek-Lenz* (Frankfurt: Insel-Buecherei, n.d.).
5. Cf. Werner R. Lehmann, ed., Georg Büchner, *Sämtliche Werke und Briefe* (Hamburg: Wegner, 1967), 1:436.
6. Ibid., pp. 436–83 for a comparison of Buechner's text with the eyewitness account of Jean Frédéric Oberlin (1740–1826), the pastor after whom Oberlin College is named.
7. In Hans Jonas, *Philosophical Essays—From Ancient Creed to Technological Man* (Chicago: University of Chicago Press, 1974).
8. Ibid., p. 25.
9. Cf., e.g., H. A. Wolfson, *The Philosophy of the Church Fathers* (Cambridge: Harvard University Press, 1964), pp. 223–32: "'Eternal Generation,' 'by Will' and 'by nature'," and chap. 16/3: "Orthodox Use of the Analogies of Physical Union." All of Susan A. Handelman's *The Slayers of Moses—The Emergence of Rabbinic Interpretation in Modern Literary Theory* (Albany: State University of New York Press, 1982) turns on the classical and modern opposition between Christian incarnationism and Jewish textuality. It is an important, though far from faultless, book (cf. sec. 5 below).
10. Jonas, *Philosophical Essays,* p. 44.
11. G. W. F. Hegel, *Vorlesungen über die Philosophie der Religion, Werke,* vol. 17, ed. Moldenhauer and Michel (Frankfurt: Suhrkamp, 1969). pp. 47, 83.
12. Ibid., p. 92.
13. Ibid., pp. 67, 77, 84.
14. Compare, e.g., the section on "Judea" in Hegel's *Philosophy of History,* and his early essay "Athens and Judea—Should Judea be the Teutons' Fatherland?" (1795), in *On Christianity.* . . . trans. T. M. Knox (New York: Harper Torchbook, 1961), pp. 145ff.

15. Jonas, *Philosophical Essays,* pp. 29, 31, 33.

16. Cf. Steven Schwarzschild, "The Lure of Immanence—The Crisis in Contemporary Religious Thought," *Tradition* 9, nos. 1–2 (1967): 72–78, esp. 81f.

17. Jonas, *Philosophical Essays,* p. 43.

18. Compare *Aboth de R. Nathan,* 11. In the pursuit of relevance, a good deal of mid-brow literature has recently been produced to demonstrate the ecological morality of historic Judaism. The best technical example of such a compilation is N. Rakower, ed., *The Protection of the Environment* [Hebrew], Series of Studies and Analyses in Hebrew Law, no. 26 (Jerusalem: Justice Ministry, 1972); compare also P. J. Bentley, "Rabbinic Sources on Environmental Issues," Justice and Peace Committee of the Central Conference of American Rabbis, mimeographed, n.d., and T. Weiss-Rosmarin, "Relevance and the Jewish Heritage." *The Jewish Spectator,* Summer 1980, pp. 3–7.

19. Commandment 62. Compare M. B. Margolies, *Samuel David Luzzatto: Traditionalist Scholar* (New York: Ktav, 1979), pp. 108f., for an example of ecological concern for human ends.

20. Kant, *Prolegomena,* sec. 36, last sentence, in italics in the original (compare 1st *Critique,* B159f., 163f.). It has often been noted that "Copernican revolution" is a paradoxical term for it: Kant put man, or, anyway, reason, back in the center of the universe, from which Copernicus had expelled him. (Cf. N. Hanson, "Copernicus' Role in Kant's Revolution." *Journal of the History of Ideas* 20 [1979]: 274–81.)

21. Helmut Holzhey, "Kritik und Natur," *Neue Zürcher Zeitung,* 4–5 July 1981, p., 60. Compare also the same author's more substantive treatment in "Evolutionäre Erkenntnistheorie und ökologische Kritik," in *Schweizer Monatshefte* 63, no. 3 (March 1983): 215–27. Unfortunately the conclusions in both articles remain somewhat up in the air (and he misinterprets the biblical view in the latter article, n. 5).

22. Jonas, *Philosophical Essays,* p. 36, n. 14. Compare also Jacques Schlanger, *La Philosophie de Salomon ibn Gabirol—Etude d'un Néoplatonisme* (Leiden: Brill, 1968), pp. 20–22: J. Guttmann, *Die Philosophie des Judentums* (Munich: Reinhardt, 1933), pp. 102f.; and J. Bobik, *Aquinas on Being and Essence* (Notre Dame: University of Notre Dame Press, 1965), chap.5.

23. E.g., H. A. Wolfson, *The Philosophy of Spinoza* (New York: Meridan Books, 1958), p. 223.

24. Cf. G. Scholem, *Major Trends in Jewish Mysticism* (New York: Schocken, 1946), p. 109.

25. Ibid., p. 252; compare also p. 402, n. 64, on kabbalistic pantheism, and J. ben-Shlomoh, "The Problem of Pantheism in Theistic Mysticism—R. Moses Cordovero and Meister Eckhart," in *Revelation Faith Reason, A Collection of Papers* [Hebrew], M. Hallamish, M. Schwarz (Ramat-Gan: Bar-Ilan University, 1976), pp. 71–81.

26. *The Origin and Meaning of Hasidism* (New York: Harper Torchbook, 1966), pp. 89ff.

27. Cf. Scholem's attack on "M. Buber's Interpretation of Hasidism," in *The Messianic Idea in Judaism. . . .* (New York: Schocken, 1971), esp. pp. 240–44, where he summarizes the acosmic aspect of chassidism in these words: "It is necessary to reduce things to their nothingness in order to restore them to their true nature" (p. 242). This conception emerges especially in the *Tanya.* Compare the acosmic and, indeed, nihilistic ending of the Spinozist Isaac B. Singer's *The Family Moskat* (New York: Knopf, 1950).

28. Scholem, *Major Trends,* p. 38.

29. S. Schwarzschild, "The Lure of Immanence," p. 97, n. 12.

30. Cf. Jonas, "The Abyss of the Will: Philosophical Meditations on the Seventh Chapter of Paul's 'Epistle to the Romans,'" *Philosophical Essays,* loyally dedicated to Bultmann, but see also Hans Jonas, "Heidegger and Theology," chap. 10, in *The Phenomenon of Life—Toward a Philosophical Anthropology* (New York: Harper and Row, 1966).

31. Jonas, "Sight and Thought: A Review of Visual Thinking," *Philosophical Essays,* pp. 231, 233, 235.

32. Ibid., p. 222.

33. Jonas, *Phenomenon of Life,* pp. 12ff.

34. Ibid., p. 61.

35. Jonas, *Philosophical Essays,* pp. 29, 39; see Emanuel Levinas, *Autrement qu'être ou au-delà de l'essence* (The Hague: Nijhoff, 1974), pp. 34, 123, 140, 145, 168, 199, 214, 223, etc. on Jewish, philosophical, ethicist anti- ("occidentalism" = ontologism).

36. The last sentence of Richard A. Watson's "A Critique of Anti-Anthropocentric Biocentrism," *Environmental Ethics* 5 (1983): 256.

37. Descartes, *Philosophical Works* (New York: Dover Publications, 1955), 1: 119. Cf. also Holzhey, "Evolutionäre Erkenntnistheorie," p. 219 and his accurate derivation of Descartes' posture from the Renaissance spirit in Pico della Mirandola's and (his Jewish associate) Leone Hebreo's *De Dignitate Hominis,* ibid., pp. 217–19 (via E. Cassirer).

38. Peter Singer demonstrates how one can make rational decisions in this field by arguing in favor of "animal liberation," on the one hand (in *Moral Problems—A Collection of Philosophical Essays,* ed. James Rachels [New York: Harper and Row, 1979], pp. 83ff.), and yet countenancing "Fetal Research" (pp. 197ff.) within proper ethical limits.

39. For a survey of Judaism on animals cf. Noah J. Cohen. *Tza'ar Ba'aley Chayim* [English] (Washington: Catholic University of America, 1959).

40. Quoted by Watson, "Critique," p. 247.

41. Cf. Lynn White, Jr., *Machina ex Deo: Essays in the Dynamism of Western Culture* (Cambridge: M.I.T. Press, 1968), chap. 5: "The Historical Roots of Our

Ecologic Crisis." White apparently knows nothing of the incarnationist abyss between Christianity and Judaism (cf. Jonas), and he contradicts himself in acknowledging, on the one hand, the special "dynamism of Western culture," only to turn around and advocate the elimination of the very factor to which that dynamism is attributed. Wendell Berry's "The Gift of the Good Land," *Sierra* 64, no. 6 (November/December 1979): 20–26, is a moderate, but also modest, reply to White.

42. Cf. S. Schwarzschild, "The Lure of Immanence," n. 26.

43. T. W. Adorno, *Philosophy of Modern Music* (Frankfurt: Europäische Verlaganstalt. 1958), pp. 61–65.

44. Ibid., pp. 78, 61–65, 106–16.

45. Cf. P. Brenner, "Aspekte und Probleme der neueren Utopiediskussion in der Philosophie," in *Utopie-Forschung—Interdisziplinaere Studien zur neuzeitlichen Utopie,* ed. W. Vosskamp (Stuttgart: Metzler, 1982); see also J. Habermas, *Toward a Rational Society* (Boston: Beacon Press, 1970) pp. 86–90, on Bloch's peculiar "naturism."

46. H. Marcuse, *An Essay on Liberation* (Boston: Beacon Press, 1969), p. 10.

47. Cf. the Marcuse-Habermas interview in *Telos,* no. 38 (Winter 1978–79): 136, and compare H. van der Linden's "The Idea of a Repressive *vs.* a Liberated Domination of Nature in the Work of H. Marcuse" [Dutch], M.A. thesis, Groningen, 1978.

48. Carl Braun, *Kritische Theorie versus Kritizismus—Zur Kant-Kritik T. W. Adornos,* Kantstudien, Ergänzungshefte, no. 115 (Berlin: de Gruyter, 1983) p. 53; compare also his discussion, p. 176, of Adorno's "reason [developed] genetically from instinctual energy."

49. Watson, "Critique," pp. 250ff., crystallizes other logical incoherences in "ecosophy."

50. Christopher D. Stone, *Should Trees Have Standing?—Toward Legal Rights for Natural Objects.* (Los Altos: William Kaufmann, 1974). Compare Watson's counterarguments: "Self-Consciousness and the Rights of Nonhuman Animals and Nature," *Environmental Ethics* I: (1979): esp. 120ff. (I am indebted to Hamner Hill for bringing me up to date on this debate.)

51. Lewis Carroll, The *Annotated Alice,* ed. Martin Gardner (New York: New American Library, 1960), pp. 38f. Carroll was even more correct than he, perhaps, knew: Spinoza's famous passage about might = right, in the *Theologico-Politico Tractate, Chief Works of Spinoza,* trans. Elwes (New York: Dover, 1951), p. 200, and the passage in *Ethics,* pt. 4, prop. 37, n. 1 about "the womanish superstition" of worrying about the feelings of animals, are couched precisely in the metaphor of the big and the little fishes. Compare with regard to the fish metaphor, *'Avodah Zarah,* 3f., Rashi to *Betzah,* 23b, "and not," and Seneca, *Moral Epistles,* 103:3.

52. Cf. Braun, *Kritische Theorie,* pp. 240ff., 284.

53. Cf. Watson, "Critique," on the Heidegger and Huxley "aesthetic" connections.

54. Maimonides, *Mishneh Torah,* "Laws of Idolatry," 3:6.

55. Cynthia Ozick, "Toward a New Yiddish," in *Art and Ardor—Essays* (New York: A. Knopf, 1983), p. 157ff.

56. Hermann Cohen, *Kant's Begründung der Aesthetik,* (Berlin: Dummler, 1889), pp. 339, 348.

57. Cf. S. Schwarzschild, "Introduction," in Hermann Cohen, *Ethik des reinen Willen, Werke,* vol. 7 (Hildesheim/New York: Olms, 1981), pp. xxiiiff.

58. Holzhey, "Evolutionäre Erkenntnistheorie," pp. 222ff. (N.b. that Jonas converges with Riedl in the former's *Macht oder Ohnmacht der Subjektivität? Das Leib-Seele-Problem im Vorfeld des Prinzips Verantwortung* (Frankfurt: Insel, 1981), p. 116. Compare F. M. Wuketits, ed., *Concepts and Approaches in Evolutionary Epistemology* (Hingham, Mass.: Reidel, 1983).

59. Braun, *Kritishe Theorie,* p. 245.

60. Ibid., p. 271.

61. Ibid., p. 282.

62. Cf. S. Schwarzschild, "The Tenability of H. Cohen's Construction of the Self," *Journal of the History of Philosophy* 8 (1975): 363.

63. Cynthia Ozick, *The Pagan Rabbi and Other Stories* (New York: A. Knopf, 1971). (Handelman, *Slayers of Moses,* pp. 64f., also refers to this *mishnah.*)

64. It is clever and Derridaesque on the part of Ozick to have her hero study the book that invented him. We have by now encountered schizophrenia as the enactment of man's relationship to nature, especially but not exclusively the Jew's, in the mishnaic man, Lenz, Celan, and now Ozick! As Harold Bloom says, *Kabbalah and Mysticism* (New York: Seabury, 1975), p. 111: "Schizophrenia is disaster in life, and success in poetry."

65. Handelman, *Slayers of Moses.*

66. Compare S. Schwarzschild, "Authority and Reason," in *Reason and Revelation as Authority in Judaism,* Academy for Jewish Philosophy, vol. 2, pp. 53f. But see Cynthia Ozick, "Judaism & Harold Bloom," *Commentary* 67, no. 1 (January 1979): 43–51.

67. Handelman, *Slayers of Moses,* pp. 175f.

68. *Kol Kitvē H. N. Bialik* [Hebrew] (Tel Aviv: Dvir, 1951), p. 210.

69. This is reminiscent of Heine's famous description of the Bible as the Jews' portable fatherland. In fact, I could not find this phrase when I looked for it. The closest I could come is "the written fatherland": cf. *Sämtliche Werke,* ed. H. Kaufman (Munich: Aufbau, 1964), 7: 99.

70. A. Hertzberg, *The Zionist Idea—A Historical Analysis and Reader* (New York: Meridian, 1960), p. 296.

71. Ibid. (James Diamond and Sam Fishman have helped me track down the details of this essay by Berdichevsky. It was first published in the American He-

brew weekly *HaPisgah,* 19 August 1898, entitled "The Janus-Face"; compare *Ma'amarim,* Tel-Aviv, 1942, p. 45.)

72. *The Reality of the Hebrews—Introduction to the System of the Pentateuch* [German] (Berlin: David, 1925); Erich Unger, *The Problem of Mythic Reality* [German] (Berlin: David, 1926); compare J. Taubes, "From Cult to Culture," *Partisan Review* 21, no. 4 (1954): 387–400. (Thomas Mann was transfixed by these kooky Jews.)

73. Cf. Gerson Shaked, "First Person Plural—Literature of the 1948 Generation," *The Jerusalem Quarterly,* no. 22 (1982), and the Cannanite journal *Aleph;* B. Kurzweil, "The New 'Canaanites' in Israel," *Judaism* 21, no. 1 (1953): 2–15, and its Hebrew original; and E. b. Ezer, ed., "The New Hebrew Nation (the 'Canaanite' outlook)," in *Unease in Zion* (New York: Quadrangle, 1974), pp. 201–34.

74. Hertzberg, *The Zionist Idea,* pp. 55f., 66.

75. Ibid., pp. 118f. On Berdichevsky (= Bin-Gorion), compare D. Jacobson, "Fiction and History in the Writings of . . . ," *Prooftexts,* vol. 3, no. 2 (May 1983): 205–10.

76. Ibid., pp. 371f., 381. Compare S. H. Bergman, *Faith and Reason—An Introduction to Modern Jewish Thought* (Washington, D.C.: B'nai B'rith, 1961): "Men are but organic parts of the cosmos" (p. 103). After the (intellectual) Fall, "through religion man begins to feel once again that he is an inseparable and organic part of creation."

77. Bergman, *Faith and Reason,* p. 113.

78. Ibid., pp. 124, 128, 137.

79. t. *Ber.* 43b, *R.H.* 11.

80. t. *Ber.* 58b. Bialik realized the connection between our *mishnah* and these benedictions: cf. *Kol Kitvē.*

81. *Lev. R.* 20:2: "Resh Lakish said in the name of R. Simon b. Menasya: 'The first man was created for God's use and the disk of the sun for human use.'"

82. t. *Meg.* 96 *ad Gen.* 9:27, about the beauty of the Greek language in the Septuagint.

83. J. B. Soloveitchik, "The Lonely Man of Faith," *Tradition* (Summer 1965), pp. 5–67.

84. "The Man of the Law," in *Ish haHalakhah-Galuy veNisstar* [Hebrew] (Jerusalem: Zionist Organization of America, 1979), p. 72.

85. Ibid., p. 120. Compare also D. Singer and M. Sokol, "Joseph Soloveitchik: Lonely Man of Faith," *Modern Judaism,* vol. 2 (1982), esp. pp. 251f.; and "Man of Faith," *Tradition,* p. 15, and "But if you Search There," p. 4.

86. Tract. *Sanh.* 17; Maimonides, *Code,* "Laws of Belief," 4:23.

87. *Aboth,* 2:5; compare Maimonides *Code,* 3:14; *Sotah* 22a. Compare Heidegger's Nazi cult of the peasant.

88. Irving Agus, *The Heroic Age of Franco-German Jewry—The Jews of Germany and France of the 10th and 11th Centuries, the Pioneers and Builders of Town-life, Town-government and Institutions* (New York: Yeshiva University Press, 1969), p. 187; compare also the very title of his *Urban Civilization in Pre-Crusade Europe,* 2 vols. (New York: Yeshiva University Press, 1965).

And the Earth Is Filled with the Breath of Life

ARTHUR WASKOW

THE WISDOM OF THE JEWISH PEOPLE ALONE cannot heal the earth, but there are unique wisdoms and unique energies that we can bring to this healing. In doing so, we can renew the deepest and most powerful energy of Judaism, energy that has been embanked and hidden so long that we have forgotten it's there. In the ensuing coolness we have ourselves cooled to large areas of Torah that can reawaken to us if we can dis-cover them, get the coverings off.

In the deepest origins of Jewish life, the most sacred relationship was the relationship with the earth. Ancient Israel got in touch with God by bringing food to the Holy Temple. We use an abstract term to describe this, the "sacrificial system," but it was food—all the foods of the Land of Israel. And so we affirmed, not in words but with our bodies, "We didn't invent this food; it came from a Unity of which we are a part. The earth, the rain, the sun, the seeds, and our work—together, *adam* and *adamah,* the earth and human earthlings, grew this food. It came from the Unity of Life; so we give back some of it to that great Unity."

Through food and with the earth, not through words, was how biblical Jews got in touch with God. And in turn there was a way of relating to the earth that was not working the earth, or making the earth work, but resting with the earth. The tradition affirmed the earth's restfulness and the restfulness of human beings in relation to the earth. Not only the seventh-day Shabbat but the *shmitah* year, the sabbatical year. Every seventh year the earth was entitled to rest and the human community that worked the earth was obligated to rest as well.

Shabbat—not only the Sabbath day but also the sabbatical year—was one of the most powerful ways in which the community affirmed the Unity of all. That rhythm of work and rest, and that affirmation of what connects *adam* and *adamah,* the humans and the humus, the earth and the earthlings, affirmed that we live in a world of All, a world of joyfulness, spiritually together. There really was a down-to-earth Judaism.

The question is, What does it mean to us, who have lived through the Diaspora experience? It is not that we have lived only in cities—there were Jewish farmers—but that we have had a limited share of the responsibility for dealing with the earth, because we were usually not in a position of power to shape the economic or environmental policy of the communities we lived in.

What does it mean for us living in the Diaspora now? We live in a modernity in which the human race has created technology and a work system that is the most brilliant act of work in all of human history—new forms of controlling the earth, dominating the earth, making, doing, inventing. We have already affected the planet in ways no human beings ever have before. We have changed the biology and chemistry of the planet. The last commensurate level of change came from a great meteor strike 65 million years ago. Now one of the earth's own species, one that evolved with the technological ability, the intellectual ability, and the consciousness to review and improve its own work, has taken so much power into its own hands as to affect the entire planet.

We must strive to understand what this means for us. We must open ourselves to the larger meaning of this event: Why is this happening to us? And we must also seek to invoke the wisdom of the landed people—shepherds, farmers, and tree-keepers—that we were a couple of thousand years ago.

First, my own thoughts on how to think Jewishly about why this is happening to us. Some Kabbalists have taught that an Infinite and Utterly unfettered God, One Who encompassed all that was and wasn't, is and isn't, contracted inward in order to leave space for a universe to emerge. But in that empty space, what was the seed of the world? It was the "left-overs" of God, the thin film, as it were, of olive oil that is left within a vessel when one pours the oil out. It was this thin film of God that grew and grew, appearing as the universe—itself indeed the universe, God disguised by folds of God into seeming something other than God. And this aspect of God grows toward revealing Itself, toward mirroring the Infinite Beyond.

This growth, this process of self-revelation and self-mirroring of the God Whose Name is Ehyeh Asher Ehyeh, "I Will Be Who I Will Be," makes up all that we may see of evolution and history. This growth appears to us as a double spiral.

In one spiral, growing self-awareness is used in the service of greater efficiency at controlling the surrounding universe—greater power.

In the other spiral, growing self-awareness is turned toward creating deeper love, broader connection.

In one spiral, my I eyes what I have just done, to do it more effectively.

In the other spiral, my I eyes the face of an Other and sees within it my own face, sees within its differentness my own uniqueness, and so can love my neighbor as deeply as my Self.

These two spirals were rooted in the living universe long before there emerged what we call life, or humankind. What we call life, and then what we call humankind, are themselves leaps forward in both spirals—the one that is more efficient, and the one that is more loving.

The two spirals are not independent of each other. They are intertwined. What Martin Buber called I–It intertwined with I–Thou. One spiral of more Doing intertwined with one of deeper Being.

Each of these comes into the world as a step in the journey of the world to become more and more a Mirror for God, more and more a fully aware being, ever more fully aware of its own Unity.

What makes each of them a spiral is the other. As each moves forward in what might have been a straight line, it reaches a point of impending self-destruction that calls forth the other into vigor. Each curve forward in the one spiral calls for a curve forward in the other. An increase in efficiency unaccompanied by any increase in a sense of connection threatens that the more efficient being will gobble up its own nurturing environment—and ultimately find itself without nourishment—unless it learns to become part of a larger whole, a deeper, fuller comununity. Whether the being is a proto-protein hmmming in a sweet and early sea, or an amoeba devouring all the sugar-water in the neighborhood, or a global human civilization using up all the space in which other species can survive, the discipline of learning to love, to connect—or to die—is very strict.

And the creation of a new level of community—a multi-celled creature at one level of this double spiral; at another level, a society that understands it is part of a larger, richer habitat in which grow other species—the achievement of this new level creates the context for another leap forward in efficiency and power.

One of these spirals—the one in which self-awareness gives a being the ability to "look" at its techniques for acquisition, see its shortcomings, imagine a more effective solution, and make it happen—is the "competitive natural selection" aspect of evolution. The mistake of social Darwinists is to see this as the only aspect of evolution, ignoring the I–Thou spiral.

The emergence of life was one enormous leap forward in the ability of aspects of the universe to understand and control, and then of these same aspects to pause, reflect, love, and be self-aware.

The emergence of the human race was another such great step. For the universe to continue on this journey toward self-awareness, there needs to be a species capable of self-awareness—made up of individuals who can reflect upon their own selves, and also able as a species to reflect upon itself and to see itself as part of the Unity of the universe—on which it is also capable of reflecting. That is what it means to live in the Image of God—to reflect upon the Unity, and thus to mirror God's Own Self. Among the species on this planet, the human race so far bears this Image of God—the self-awareness of Unity—most fully. That does not mean that other beings have no share in this Image, nor does it mean that the unfolding of the Image stops with us.

And within human history, the pastoral and agricultural revolutions were further leaps forward in accessing the Divine attributes of power. Each meant that human beings were able to hold and use powers that previously had been held only by Divine "outsiders"—gods, spirits, God. Each meant that some aspect of Divine power became more available to human hands. And in response to each, human beings created new forms of connective community, intended to cradle the new energy of doing in new forms of loving.

And so the thin film of God that became the universe revealed Itself more and more fully, as the universe grew toward mirroring the Infinite.

And on each of these occasions, a leap forward in power and control had to be followed by a broadening of love and a deepening of self-aware reflection. Otherwise the new intensity of power would have swallowed up the world. And each growth of broader community gave the context and the impetus for another leap forward on the Doing, Making, I–It spiral. Thus the double spiral continues.

The agricultural revolution was one such turn on the Doing, I–It spiral—and it required the emergence of biblical Israel, Buddhism, and the other great ancient traditions on the Being, I–Thou spiral. From this perspective, some scholars have suggested that what we know as Torah was the response of a community that had been gatherers and shepherds to an encroaching agricultural empire, Babylonia, and the attempt of Israelites to absorb and limit the new imperial agriculture. Thus the Garden of Eden and the tale of Cain and Abel are seen as a mythic portrayal of this leap in knowledge and its tragic aspects of alienation from the earth and from each other—a leap repeated again and again in human history since.

From this perspective, the Sabbath and the sabbatical year are ways of limiting the engulfment of the new agriculture: limiting its imperial destructiveness of Doing by pausing to become gatherers and shepherds again, pausing to love and to Be.

Another great turn on the Doing, I–It spiral came when Hellenism brought a more powerful form of economics, science, politics, and war to the Mediterranean Basin. This leap shattered biblical Judaism as well as other traditional cultural and religious forms. The I–Thou response was the creation of Rabbinic Judaism, Christianity, and Islam.

In the last several hundred years, we have been living through another such leap forward in the I–It powers of the human race. This leap is what we call modernity. It is by far the greatest of these leaps, for it brings the human race into the arena in which it is transforming the very web of planetary life from which it sprang.

That we would reach this point was probably inevitable. For to be capable of self-aware life inevitably also means to be capable of creating the technology that can wreck the planet. Human social history is simply incomparably swifter than biological evolution at applying self-awareness to technological improvement—so swift that it reaches the asymptote of possible self-destruction.

That swiftness, to some extent throughout human history but with utter urgency today, gives the human race a mandate unique among all species: to act as if it were a steward for the planet. If we fail in this task, the planet's ruination will take us with it. In that sense, we are strange stewards and the "steward" model is not fully adequate, for we remain partially embedded in the earth we steward.

Today, what is the alternative to ruination? It is another curve forward on the spiral of Being, Loving, I–Thouing. It is the renewal and transformation of Judaism, Christianity, Islam, Buddhism, Hinduism, the spiritual traditions of all indigenous peoples—a renewal and transformation that can deepen each tradition in its own uniqueness while broadening the circle of love it can encompass. It is the bringing of restfulness and reflectiveness to a deeper level, just as work has been brought by modernity to a higher level. It is extending our love to the whole of the earth of which we are a part, without denying our uniqueness in its web of life.

Now that we live in the era of high-tech industrialism, and are not shepherds or farmers or orchardists in the ordinary sense, we must learn to be shepherds, or farmers or tree-keepers again in a different sense. For shepherds, farmers, and orchardists know you must not exhaust the earth you live on. If you're a shepherd and you let the sheep eat all the grass in one year, the sheep may be fatter and the wool thicker, but you're finished off. And farmers, vintners, and tree-keepers learn the same thing.

What does this mean for us who have forgotten it, in the wild rush of making, doing, inventing, producing over the last couple of hundred years? What does it mean for us to renew that shepherds' wisdom, the wisdom which knew that consuming what comes from the earth is a central sacred act, is a way of being in touch with God? What would it mean for us to renew that wisdom?

I want to imagine a new version of the Jewish people—a new way of understanding and shaping ourselves. Imagine that we were to decide to see ourselves as having a mission, a purpose on the earth. A purpose to heal the earth—one that is not brand new but is described in the Torah as one of the great purposes of the Jewish people.

What does it mean that Shabbat is a symbol, a sign between the God of the universe and "His" once whole people? The Shabbat of Sinai comes in two different guises. In Exodus, we hear it as the moment when our restfulness connects us with the cosmic resting that imbues all of creation. In Deuteronomy, Shabbat renews the liberation of human beings and the earth. And there is also the Shabbat that comes before Sinai—the Shabbat that comes with the manna in the Wilderness, betokening our free and unlabored reconnection with the earth. This Shabbat betokens the peace agreement ending the primordial war between ourselves and earth which began as we left Eden—which came from a misdeed of eating and brought us painful toil and turmoil in our eating.

What would it mean for us to renew the sense that deep in our very covenant, deep in our covenant-sign Shabbat, is the call to be healers of the earth?

Imagine the Jewish people as a kind of transgenerational transnational "movement," committed for seven generations, from one generation to the next and beyond, to transmit the wisdom and the practice that can heal the earth. Imagine a people that can reach out to others and can encourage others, work with others, to do that.

I want to suggest four dimensions of a Jewish people through which we could be pursuing that mission to heal the earth. These four dimensions correspond to the four worlds through which our Kabbalists, our mystics, saw Creation.

One dimension is the explicit celebration of the Spirit through the rituals, the ceremonies, the symbols of celebration that we use to get in touch with the One. Look, for example, at the second paragraph of the *Sh'ma,* the one that says, "And if you act on Torah then the rain will fall, the rivers will run, and the earth will be fruitful and you will live well. And if you don't act on Torah, if you reject it, if you cut yourself off from this great harmony of earth, then the great harmony will cease to be harmony and will cut itself off from you, and the rains won't fall [or, I would say, they will turn to acid] and the rivers won't run [or they and the oceans will flood], and the sky itself will become your enemy [as in the shattering of the ozone layer or the fouling of the atmosphere with too much carbon dioxide], and you will perish from all this good *adamah* that you grew up with."

Today we can see this as a searing truth. Yet in many of our synagogues and havurot this passage is said in an undertone or even omitted. What would it mean for us to elevate it to a central place in our liturgy, and perhaps every four weeks or so, perhaps on the Shabbat before the new moon or the Shabbat before the full moon, to read it with a fanfare: to remind ourselves that we are part of the web of life, its most conscious part, the part most aware of the Wholeness of which we and all the rest are part—but still a part of the web, endangered whenever we bring danger on the web?

We need to focus on the second paragraph of the *Sh'ma*. By racing through it, we race through a central place of our celebration and a central place in our lives; we blind ourselves to the world around us, racing through a wonderful ecosystem without pausing to see its rich intertwining.

Let me take another example. I wrote a piece that appeared in several American Jewish newspapers in the early 1990s. It began with a fantasy.

One day in the fall, all over North America, tens of thousands of Native Americans show up at the edge of rivers everywhere. They are carrying a sacred object of their own tradition, and they are also carrying willow branches. They dance seven times around their sacred symbol; they beat the willow branches on the earth; and they invoke the Holy Spirit and ask for help to heal the planet from plague and disaster and drought.

It would be on the front pages of every American newspaper and on the evening news of every television network. Everywhere students on college campuses would be demanding courses on Native American spirituality. And members of Congress and presidents of corporations would be bombarded by letters. "Something's wrong with the rivers, what are you doing about it?"

Now imagine a different fantasy—that it wasn't tens of thousands of Native Americans, but tens of thousands of American Jews who showed up on this day in the fall. Their sacred object was the Torah, and they danced around it seven times and they beat willow branches on the earth, and they prayed in English and Hebrew for the YHWH, the Breath of Life, to help them heal the earth. They too appeared on television, and they too led demands that Congress and the corporations heal the earth.

What would many of our present Jewish leaders say?—Probably, I thought, "This is primitive, this is pagan, this is radical, this is un-Jewish!"

Yet what I have just described is at the end of most traditional Jewish prayer books, because it's a description of the seventh day of Sukkot, Hoshanah Rabbah. But we don't do it anymore, we certainly don't do it that way. A few people in some traditional synagogues will gather in a small chapel and beat willow branches on the rug. Nobody ever hears about it. And they say the words of prayer to heal the earth, but they don't connect the words with any act that might be done.

Look at the prayer books, however. Look up Hoshanah Rabbah, the seventh day of the festival of Sukkot, and look at the words of "Hosha na." "Hosha na" got transliterated into the rather meaningless English word "hosanna"—it actually means "Please save us." Right there: "Save the earth, save us!" And read the words of these prayers, for many of them name the dangers that face the earth and plead with the Breath of all Life to save the earth from plague and drought. One of them ends, "Save the earth—suspended in space."

In 1998, The Shalom Center gathered about 250 Jews and 50 people from other spiritual traditions—a leader of the Lakota Nation, Catholic nuns, Pete Seeger—at the banks of the Hudson River in Beacon, New York. And on the seventh day of Sukkot, we celebrated Hoshanah Rabbah. We danced the seven dances with great bright banners, each in one of the colors of the rainbow, keyed to the seven days of Creation. We chanted "Hosha na," some in ancient Hebrew and some in English, newly written. One of the prayers we broke into, verse by verse, with shouted headlines about the pollution of the Hudson by the General Electric Corporation. Broken world, broken prayer. And as part of the liturgy, we signed petitions demanding that GE clean up the damage it had done. Ancient form, made profoundly new. Its deepest meaning, unchanged.

Those are just two examples; the tradition is rich with possibilities.

Our whole festival cycle, after all, is attuned to the rhythms of the earth. Let us imagine it alive with earth again:

- On Tu B'Shvat, the festive New Year of the Trees that comes at the full moon of deep winter, we can plant the trees that together make up the Tree of Life. (One year in the Headwaters redwood forest of California, two hundred Jews actually trespassed on the land of a corporation that was threatening to log those grand and sacred groves, so old they were living when the Temple fell. It was Tu B'Shvat; we planted redwood seedlings.)
- At Pesach we can eliminate the swollen *chameytz* ("leavening") that makes our lives swell up, and embrace instead a week of simple living. And at Pesach we can identify the pharaonic institutions that are bringing upon us the plagues that turn our seas and rivers to "red tide," that fill our cattle with disease, that infest one or another ecosystem of the earth with swarms of invasive species that destroy a habitat. We can call on these corporate pharaohs to open their hearts instead of hardening them, and to save the land they are destroying.
- And not only can we face the dark side of Pesach, the *chameytz* and the plagues, but we can also read together the Song of Songs, that lovely evocation of a spring in which humanity at last learns how to live in loving, playful peace with all of earth as well as with each other.

For us to celebrate our ancient festivals in such ways, however, to pray such "Hosha na"s, we would have to be convinced of their wisdom and their truth, of our own authenticity in so invoking them. We would have to believe that our prayerful pleas do not fall into emptiness but into a Place that hears and can respond.

In short, we would have to understand God in such a way that such prayers could be addressed not only to a distant disembodied Mystery but also to an embodiment of holiness on earth. We would have to believe, really believe, that the great Unity includes the processes of the earth.

One of the great Hasidic rebbes, the Rebbe of Chernobyl, about two hundred years ago said, "What is the world? The world is God, wrapped in robes of God so as to appear to be material. And who are we? We are God wrapped in robes of God and our task is to unwrap the robes and to dis-cover, uncover, that we are God."

So, think of the earth as one aspect of God, and think what it would mean for us to pray those prayers with that Hasidic understanding. We pray them, can we act on them? As Rabbenu Heschel, our teacher Abraham Joshua Heschel, said when he came back from the civil rights march in Selma, Alabama, "I felt my legs were praying."

What would it mean for us to pray not only with our mouths but also with our arms and legs?

Or, to put it another way: if earth is Spirit, then politics may be the deepest prayer, and prayer the deepest politics. We may realize that we are always choosing between a politics that may be prayers to idols, mere carved-out pieces of the Whole, things of partial value that we elevate to ultimates, and a politics that we may shape with such deep caring that it becomes prayer to the One.

The Kabbalists taught us that the process of Creation involved a great outpouring of Divine energy so intense that this river of Divinity crashed through each vessel intended to contain it, swept over four great waterfalls, Four Worlds of the Divine Flow, shattering Itself until it came to a shattered calmness in our world.

Each of these Four Worlds holds all four within it, like a set of Chinese boxes. In our own world, the world that from God's perspective is the world of *Asiyah,* Doing and Acting, we are able to experience and in our own lives replicate all four of the

Four Worlds. When we reach toward experiencing the First World, *Atzilut,* Being, the world of Spirit, we do this by entering ritual, prayer, and celebration. That is the world we have just been exploring.

Just below *Atzilut,* on the next water-level of the Divine river, is the second of the Four Worlds, another dimension of what it would mean to shape from Jewish peoplehood a transgenerational movement to heal the earth. This Second World is *Briyyah,* Creative Intellect, Knowing, Learning. This involves learning Torah, learning science, and learning public policy, and especially learning how all these intertwine.

Suppose we learn Torah simply because it was written down once upon a time, a matter of "religion" that teaches only about prayer and ceremonial. And suppose we learn science by going to a university department and politics and public policy from yet another university department or from the mass media. Then what do these three have to do with each other? Nothing, or very little.

But that's not in fact what Torah was. It was a celebration of the great Unity; therefore it was politics, and it was also science, the best science available to every generation of Jews who were encoded into the process. So, when the Jubilee chapter of Leviticus (Lev. 25) says, "Hey, some guy with a master's degree in Business Administration is going to say to you, 'If you let the fields lie fallow on the seventh year, what do you think we are going to eat?'" the Torah says, "Hang on! You will have more to eat, I promise you, if you let the earth rest every seventh year than if you try to work it to death."

Of course, this is a call to faith. It is "religion."

It is also "science," the science that knows the fields are more fruitful if they have a chance to lie fallow. Torah is not something separate from science. It affirms what is holy in the world, and what is holy includes knowledgeable science.

And this process did not stop with the Torah, or the biblical period. The Rabbis of the Talmud proclaimed that no one should herd "small cattle"—that is, goats and sheep—in the Land of Israel. Why? because they destroy trees and grass. The Rabbis say this even though they know perfectly well that our forebears were shepherds and goat herders. Why do they make such an amazing departure from tradition?

Because their experience, and their science, have taught them something new. Their deep sense that our relationship with the earth is sacred causes them to oppose what was normal for the early Torah period. The basic values continue; how to affirm them changes in accord with new scientific information.

Today, we might imagine saying to ourselves: "Our Torah forbids us to cut down fruit trees, even in time of war. Today we know that every tree gives oxygen to the web of life, and great forests are crucial to the life of the entire planet. Does that mean that we may cut down any tree only if it is possible to replace its fruitful supply of oxygen? That we may not cut down great forests at all? That this is now Torah because we understand the science of trees in ways our forebears did not (though they certainly knew trees were important to their lives), and we uphold the values that they held?"

We can think such thoughts and ask such questions only if we begin to interweave the knowledge that in the modern age has been separated into religion, science, and politics. What would it mean for us to take the lines of Torah in Leviticus 26, which are incredibly powerful as both a sacred and a scientific statement, not two separate things, the lines that ask, "'And what happens if you don't let the earth make its Shabbos year?'" and answer, "'The earth gets to rest anyway—on your head. The earth gets to rest through exile, disaster, desolation. The earth gets to rest, that is the law of gravity. The only question is whether you are going to rest with it and celebrate the rest and take new life, or if the earth is going to expel you from its midst into a painful exile, so that it can rest.'"

This understanding was both sacred and scientific three thousand years ago, and it still is. Today, when ecologists say, "If you insist on pouring carbon dioxide into the atmosphere and never letting the atmosphere rest from that overdose, there is going to be global warming and your civilization is going to be knocked awry if not shattered;" they are simply saying what Leviticus 26 said.

What would it mean for us, both children and adults, to intertwine that learning, to shape our Torah study so that it always includes those knowledges about the web of life? What would it mean for us to reshape every Jewish curriculum and study group as if the web of life in which we live were the most important sacred fact about our lives?

The Fourth World, the fourth dimension of our

imagined sacred people—I will come back to the Third World in a moment—is the world of Doing, Action, Physicality. The world of eco-kosher. It was Rabbi Zalman Schachter-Shalomi who coined the word "eco-kosher." That word almost teaches its lesson in the word itself, if you let it reverberate in your head a little while. But let me unfold it just a tiny bit.

For people who were shepherds and farmers, celebrating food was the way of celebrating the crucial relationship between *adam* and *adamah,* because food was the crucial connection between them. And so our people generated the elaborate celebrations of that sacred nexus not only through the offerings of food at the Holy Temple but also through an elaborate pattern of what food to eat, and in what way: the kosher code. When the elaborate Temple offerings were no longer possible, the Rabbis of the Talmud compensated by making the rules of *kashrut* even more elaborate.

In the society we live in, while food is obviously important, it is not the biggest piece of our economic relationship with the earth. It's not all we eat anymore. We eat coal. We eat oil. We eat electric power, we eat the radiation that keeps some of that electric power going, and we eat the chemicals that we turn into plastic. What does it mean to eat them in a sacred way? What does it mean to say that we're eco-kosher? What does it mean to apply more broadly the basic sense of *kashrut* that what you eat and how you eat it matters?

Today our most dangerous addictive substances are not heroin or nicotine or alcohol. They are plutonium and petroleum. These are social addictions, not individual ones. I do not mainline oil or gasoline into my own body's veins, but the United States mainlines gasoline into our society's veins.

What is addiction? It is feeling unable to control or limit a behavior, especially using a substance—even one that in some limited uses may be beneficial—in such a way as to receive immediate pleasure at the high risk of long-run disease and death. And that describes the American relationship to gasoline.

Addictions are to a great extent a spiritual problem—what in ancient Jewish language was called idolatry. Carving out a small part of the great Flow of Life and worshipping that small part. Letting it take over our lives. A serious Jewish community today should see these social addictions as idolatries; we must work out ways of infusing our use of oil, coal, paper, and all the rest with holiness. We must eat them in an eco-kosher way.

Is it eco-kosher to eat vegetables and fruit that have been grown by drenching the soil with insecticides?

Is it eco-kosher to drink the wine of the Shabbat *kiddush* from throw-away nonbiodegradable plastic cups? Or would it be eco-kosher to share ceramic cups; to begin each *kiddush* with the *kavvanah,* the intentional focus, that we are using these cups to heal the earth; and to end each meal with the sacred act of washing these cups so as to heal the earth?

Is it eco-kosher to use electricity generated by nuclear power plants that create waste products that will remain poisonous for fifty thousand years?

Is it eco-kosher to ignore the insulation or lack of it in our homes, synagogues, community centers, and nursing homes, so that we burn far more fuel than necessary and drunkenly pour carbon dioxide into the atmosphere, thereby accelerating the heating of our globe?

Is it eco-kosher to use unrecycled office paper and newsprint in our homes, our synagogues, our community newspapers? Might it be eco-kosher to insist on 10 percent recycled paper this year, and 30 percent in two years, and 80 percent in five years?

I want to suggest that what makes a life-practice eco-kosher may not be a single standard, a black-and-white barricade like "pork is *treyf* (not kosher)," but rather a constantly moving standard in which the test is, Are we doing what is more respectful, less damaging to the earth than what we did last year?

What would it mean to evolve a code of daily Jewish practice for how we consume, how we eat all these things that come from *adamah*? What would it mean for each Hillel House, each congregation, each Jewish community center and nursing home to review what kind of paper, what kind of energy it uses? Do we invest money in industries that destroy the earth or in industries that heal the earth?

Most of the Jewish community is not asking those questions yet. What must we do, then, to begin the creation of eco-*kashrut*?

Let us turn back to the third dimension, the third of the Four Worlds, the world of *Yetzirah,* Relationship. For indeed the Jewish community, acting on its own, cannot heal the world. I could say to myself all day, "Hey, every time you drive the car you are polluting the planet and bringing on global warming," and yet if my society is set up so that the only way I can get from where I live to where I work is to drive, and there are no bike paths, and mass transit is rare, run-down, and expensive, then I am going to feel guilty but I am going to drive the car.

It does not help the planet if I feel guilty.

In other words, we have to act with other peoples and other communities to shape a society where we can walk from where we work to where we sleep, or we can bike, or we can take mass transit that is far more efficient and less wasteful and less likely to damage the atmosphere.

And we have to draw on the energy and clout of the Jewish people, our new ability in the Diaspora to make a difference in the societies we are a part of.

One of the notions that has arisen in American society in the last twenty years is that acting to heal the earth means acting to damage ordinary people, that there is, for example, a war between owls and timber workers, so that any action to protect the owls hurts the timber workers.

Recent American politics, however, has shown that the enemies of the owls and of the timber workers are the same—they are the institutions that see it as their task to gobble up the planet. To gobble it up biologically, to gobble it up culturally by destroying small communities which just don't fit, and to gobble up local and regional economies that just don't fit into the global market economy. To gobble up the kinds of enterprises where owners and workers felt responsible to each other, where even in the midst of struggles management and labor unions felt some kind of responsibility, a sense of limits of what profits could be, a sense of limits on whether you can fire tens of thousands of people in a prosperous, profitable company. The new corporations of Modernity Amok destroy such companies: their profits could be bigger; in this way regional and local economies are shattered along with local cultures and local bioregions, ecosystems.

Gobbling the globe means chewing up living creatures, thousands of species. It means chewing up small, odd cultures: the Jews of Eastern Europe, the natives of the Amazon Valley, the Shoshone. It means chewing up the local factory neighborhoods in Philadelphia, even the IBM towns of upstate New York. It means chewing up the family in all its forms.

The institution of Global Gobble is the global corporation, and its *torah* says that producing is what human life is all about. Producing, and of course consuming, which is not the opposite of producing, but only the other side of the coin (and I do mean coin). In the *torah* of the global corporation, resting, celebrating, reflecting, loving, being there, are all a waste of time, literally. Shabbat, a waste of time!! Think what you could be making if you were not resting!

That attitude toward the earth becomes also an attitude toward human beings. It creates a technology which pushes people in two directions: either being disemployed because the technology is better, more efficient, or keeping their jobs, but being forced to match their lives to the speed of the machine.

The result is that more and more people who keep their jobs don't work eight-hour days, but ten-, twelve-, or even fourteen-hour days. And people who lose their jobs scrabble together two, three, even four jobs in order barely to hold on by their fingertips.

In the process community is dying, divided between the disemployed and the overworked. The overworked have no time for family or neighborhood or religious life or grass-roots politics. Some of the disemployed—those who end up on the streets with no work at all or in prison because they get desperate, crazy, drugged, or alcoholic—get a perverse form of leisure, but they cannot use it for family, neighborhood, religious life, or politics. Some of the disemployed end up in ill-paid dead-end jobs with no access to health insurance, and turn themselves into the overworked—two jobs, or three—in order barely to pay their bills for rent and food.

Neither the overworked nor the disemployed can get their lives together to help shape a decent society. Neither the desperate disemployed nor the exhausted overworked can shape a loving family. In their neighborhoods, the only thing you have the energy to do after a twelve-hour day is to sit in front of the television set, which takes your depressed and exhausted self and reawakens it with jolts of your own adrenaline. And then since you are feeling jangled from being awakened that way, it calms you down with "Hey, here's something wonderful to buy." So if you're exhausted or desperate you don't create PTA's, neighborhoods, synagogues, churches, or political parties.

There is a wonderful study by Robert Putnam called "Bowling Alone." The bowling leagues are disappearing; people still bowl but they bowl alone, because they don't have the energy anymore even to organize a bowling league. If this seems so unimportant as to be ridiculous even to mention, the point is that the seedbed of democracy, as De Tocqueville taught, is all those networks of local organizations.

We need to be serious about addressing both the issues of what we call the economy and what we call the environment. They are deeply intertwined. An economy is the way in which earthlings and the earth fit together. Economy and ecology: it is no accident that they both begin with the Greek word for household; they are both about the same processes of the human relationship with the earth. And those who want to heal the earth must also understand the institutional structures that are damaging the earth and also damaging our society. To act on either, we must act on both.

What does it mean to "act" where global corporations are concerned? Using the categories I have suggested, we can see the global corporation as another leap forward in the I–It spiral. It is a tool for Doing: efficient, effective, powerful. It carries both the virtues and the dangers of I–It. Our task may be not to destroy it, but to make of it an instrument in the service of broader community. To make it socially and ethically responsible, to humankind and to the planet. To teach it to love, and even to Be.

To do this, we need to deepen and broaden our sense of loving community by acting in all four dimensions of reality. First, the Spirit: what we call ritual, ceremony, prayer, meditation, celebration, the direct ways of getting in touch with that sense of unity, of allness in the world. Second, Knowledge: the kind of education that intertwines our ancient tradition with the constantly growing edges of tradition, with knowledge in all the spheres of relationship between human beings and the earth. Third, Relationship: reaching out to other communities and societies everywhere to join with us to heal the wounded earth. And fourth, Doing: the daily eco-kosher practice of our own self, of our households, and our community organizations.

These four need to be treated not as four separate parts but as aspects of the One. When they are split apart, very little happens. In most synagogues today, if issues of the earth are dealt with at all, they are broken up in separate spheres. Issues of the earth and ritual are discussed within the ritual committee; issues of the earth and knowledge are discussed within the education committee; issues of the earth in everyday practice are dealt with in the house committee that decides what paper is bought or who comes in to check the insulation; issues of society are dealt with by the social action committee. In each of those committees, however, the issue of how to deal with the relationship to the earth is probably third or fourth or fifth on the list of priorities. Perhaps on one committee the issue of the earth will come forward, but on the next front where the issue must be addressed, the specific committee is not interested, and the question molders.

We should not let this happen. The issue of the earth is such that in a unique way, all these in fact are intertwined. So I think perhaps the crucial strategic switch in any Jewish community, congregation, or organization comes when that community decides to create an *adam*-and-*adamah* committee, even if it has to be called the Committee on the Environment.

(The words "*adam*-and-*adamah*" say, "Hey, we ain't identical but we sure are closely intertwined." You can't say *adam* without hearing *adamah*, you can't say *adamah* without hearing *adam*. "Environment" is a word that means "in the environs, out there, something else, somewhere else. For sure, not intertwined." So even if we use the conventional English word, we should keep the sense of the Hebrew alive within us.)

But whatever we name the committee, I think the crucial change in any Jewish community or organization may be when a single *adam*-and-*adamah* body is created that has responsibility for all of those four dimensions, to report on them to the community as a whole.

From then on, judging from the places where this has already happened, things are different. The community begins to imagine itself as a piece of a broader movement to heal the earth, to imagine that that is a major aspect of what Judaism is all about.

Reframing Judaism in this way can evoke passionate commitment from the next generation of Jews in ways that few other things can. Much of what the human race is doing to the planet will have its worst effects on the planet thirty, forty, fifty years from now. Our children will have to live in what we have created. Judaism which addresses the future of the earth will evoke their passion, energy, intelligence, commitment, and spirit. Conversely, a Judaism which says, "Hey, what's this earth stuff got to do with us?" won't fly.

The passionate engagement which comes from a sense that we fit into the great Unity is profoundly necessary if the human race is to decide to stop gobbling up the earth. Those who are spiritually starving will need to fill their bellies with something—and they will try to fill themselves by gobbling the earth. Intense song, dance, Torah study, drushodrama, the engagement of the whole body, the full involvement of both women and men in shaping spiritual practice—all this spiritual intensity is crucial to a recovering addict. Spiritual vitality is necessary if we are to heal the planet.

I would encourage any of you who talk with people who talk of Jewish continuity to say, "Continuity? What is its content? Because if its content is a real, alive, down-to-earth Judaism, then I'm ready to put my passion into this. And if not, I will put my passion elsewhere, or perhaps I will cynically give up, and put my passion nowhere. For this is a question of life and death to me, a question of the life and death of my children who are not yet in this world. If you're not interested in my life or death, then I am not interested whether the empty Judaism you speak for lives or dies. Its continuity means nothing."

It does not have to be that way. Together we can create a Judaism that has a purpose for its continuity, a Judaism that answers the question, "What for?"

In this way, a renewed and renewing Judaism would become one of the elements of a great new spiral of I–Thouing in the world. We would help create the new sense of planetary community that must respond to the new fact of globalizing I–It. Not by giving up our unique symbols, languages, metaphors, ceremonies, practices, but by deepening them and connecting them to the spiritual lives of other communities.

What for? For the Breath of Life Who fills the universe. For the web of life that is the universe. And here is where we share in our depth the Breath that all peoples breathe—by whatever Name they name the One Who is always becoming.

We do the breathing, and we are the Breath. All of us. Not only do the trees breathe in what we breathe out, and we breathe in what the trees breathe out, but so do all the species, all the peoples.

Shabbat did not come to us because we were "the Jews"; we became "the Jews" because we heard the silence of Shabbat. We should be welcoming others into that hearing, even as we ourselves—some of us—have had to relearn it from the breathing of yoga and the sitting of Zen and the meditating of Buddhists and the whirling of Sufis and the chanting of those who still live on Turtle Island.

It is now the restful task of all the spiritual traditions, Buddhism and Hinduism, Christianity and Islam, Judaism and Wicce, to learn from each other how to rest. To catch our Breath. To dance another turn in the great spiral of I–Thou. Together.

Discussion Questions

1. Does reverence for nature pose a danger to monotheism? What is the difference between reverence and worship?
2. What does it mean to be stewards of the Earth? Can we be stewards of the Earth while remaining embedded in it?
3. Can nature be seen as sacred in Judaism?
4. What are the ecological implications of the Sabbath or the sabbatical year? What about other Jewish practices?
5. What is eco-kosher? Can it have meaning for non-Jews?

Further Reading

Bernstein, Ellen, Ed., *Ecology and the Jewish Spirit,* Woodstock, Vt.: Jewish Lights, 1998.

CCAR Journal: A Reform Jewish Quarterly, special issue on Judaism and Ecology, 48/1 (Winter 2001).

Cone, Molly, *Listen to the Trees: Jews and the Earth,* New York: UAHC Press, 1995.

Elon, Ari, Naomi M. Hyman, and Arthur Waskow, Eds., *Trees, Earth, and Torah: A Tu B'shvat Anthology,* Philadelphia: Jewish Publication Society, 1999.

Gerstenfeld, Manfred, *Judaism, Environmentalism and the Environment : Mapping and Analysis,* Jerusalem: Rubin Mass, 1998.

Hadassah and Shomrei Adamah, *Judaism and Ecology,* New York: Hadassah, 1993.

Hiebert, Theodore, *The Yahwist's Landscape: Nature and Religion in Early Israel,* New York: Oxford University Press, 1996.

Hüttermann, Aloys, *The Ecological Message of the Torah: Knowledge, Concepts, and Laws Which Made Survival in a Land of "Milk and Honey" Possible,* Atlanta: Scholars Press, 1999.

Issacs, Ronald H., *The Jewish Sourcebook on the Environment and Ecology,* Northvale, N.J.: Jason Aronson, 1998.

Jacobs, Mark X., *Caring for the Cycle of Life: Creating Environmentally Sound Life-Cycle Celebrations,* New York: Coalition on the Environment and Jewish Life.

Rose, Aubrey, Ed., *Judaism and Ecology,* New York: Cassell, 1992.

Tirosh-Samuelson, Hava, Ed., *Judaism and Ecology,* Cambridge, Mass.: Harvard Center for the Study of World Religions, 2002.

Waskow, Arthur, Ed., *Torah of the Earth,* 2 vols., Woodstock, Vt.: Jewish Lights, 2000.

Yaffe, Martin, *Judaism and Environmental Ethics: A Reader,* Lanham, MD: Lexington Books, 2001.

Chapter 9

Christianity

Due in large part, perhaps, to its being the particular focus of Lynn White Jr.'s widely circulated essay, "The Historical Roots of Our Ecologic Crisis," Christianity has become something of a lightning rod for subsequent discussions on religion and the environment. Many Christians have rallied to the defense of their tradition, whereas others have taken White's critiques even further. Some, like Christian theologian Paul Santmire, have accepted the ambiguous promise of Christianity in meeting contemporary environmental challenges, admitting the tradition's historical shortcomings but emphasizing how it might be read more ecologically today.

Since the 1980s, virtually every major Christian denomination has issued some kind of formal declaration on environmental stewardship. In a belated response to Lynn White Jr.'s suggestion, in 1979 Pope John Paul II declared St. Francis of Assisi to be the patron saint of ecologists. In his 1990 statement on the World Day of Peace, the pope called the environmental crisis "a moral issue" and "a common responsibility for everyone." The American Baptist Churches (U.S.A.) have issued a document entitled "Creation and the Covenant of Caring," which includes a policy statement on ecology. The position of the Evangelical Lutheran Church in America is outlined in the publication *Caring for Creation: Vision, Hope, and Justice.* Likewise, the World Council of Churches has produced a report called "Liberating Life." Other denominations have produced similar statements, although ecological teaching remains marginal or nonexistent at the level of most local parishes.

To date, the strongest high-level rhetoric by far has come from the Ecumenical Orthodox Patriarch Bartholomew, who has declared environmental degradation to be a sin. Since the early 1990s, the patriarchate, which is based in Istanbul, Turkey, and oversees Orthodox churches not only in Greece and Eastern Europe but all over the world, has organized numerous conferences on the environment, although the message does not appear to have trickled down to most Orthodox congregations, who remain mired in other issues such as nationalism.

Anna Peterson's essay focuses on the particular tensions that have arisen within Western Christianity about the issue of how humans ought to view the world and their place in it. She suggests that these questions can be addressed in terms of what she calls Christianity's "theological anthropology." By exploring the diverse ways in which Christians have understood their place in the world throughout history, Peterson provides a broad historical overview of Christian ideas about nature.

Theologian Sallie McFague places Christology at the center of the debate on Christianity and the environment. Arguing that Christ must be understood differently in every age, McFague suggests that at the present time, the environmental crisis is an appropriate context for such a reinterpretation. Looking in turn at Christologies she categorizes as prophetic, wisdom, sacramental, eschatological, process, and liberation, McFague articulates the ecological potential of each. She concludes by offering an ecological Christology of her own, compatible with what she terms a "Christian nature praxis," or practice (as opposed to theory) of loving nature, which McFague finds has been lacking. She admits that such a practice will be "painful" but argues that it offers a richer kind of abundance than that promised by materialism.

The first thing one notices on entering any Eastern Orthodox church is a preponderance of icons—idealized images of Jesus, Mary, and the saints. Greek Orthodox theologian John Chryssavgis focuses on the symbol of the icon as a gateway to the divine mysteries of creation. He contrasts Orthodoxy with Western Christianity, stating that the eastern traditions have never separated humans from nature or glorified the rationality of the individual, as was done in the West (just as Lynn White Jr. concedes in his essay). Chryssavgis cites John of Pergamon's teaching that humans have a "priestly" role to play in the transformation of nature into something sacred (This presupposes, of course, that nature is not sacred in its original state.). The art of the icon is a means for transforming humans and nature, effacing the boundary between this world and the next.

Writing from an Evangelical Protestant perspective, Calvin DeWitt proposes that in order for Christianity to provide effective answers to the environmental crisis, Christians must ask the right questions. For DeWitt, the crucial questions are (1) Is Jesus Christ Lord of Creation? (2) Is creation a lost cause? and (3) Whom are we following when we follow Jesus Christ? The answers to these questions, according to DeWitt, enjoin Christians to exercise a dominion not of domination, as they have done up to now, but of stewardship.

In and of the World?
Christian Theological Anthropology and Environmental Ethics

ANNA PETERSON

OVER THIRTY YEARS AGO, THE HISTORIAN Lynn White Jr. wrote, "Especially in its Western form, Christianity is the most anthropocentric religion the world has seen" (White, 1967: 1206). Since White's influential essay was published, a number of Christian theologians and ethicists, as well as many non-Christians, have debated his claims. Some have supported and even extended his critique. Others have argued that White's claims were too sweeping and that Christianity has, or at least can have, an ecologically positive message. A number have pointed to an ambivalence within the tradition itself, which White himself suggested with his tribute to St Francis as the "patron saint of ecology" (1967: 1207). Others have sought to defend Christianity not as a mixed bag but as powerfully, perhaps uniquely, able to generate a compelling environmental ethic in the modern West.

In this essay, I seek, first, to assess some of the reasons why White and other critics have objected to

Journal of Agricultural and Environmental Ethics, 12/3, (2000), pp. 237–261, "In and of the World" by Anna Peterson. Reprinted with kind permission of Kluwer Academic Publishers.

Christianity. Here I am interested in what David Laitin, following Max Weber, has termed "practical religion": "The interaction between the original doctrine and the social, political, and economic conditions of the time." As Laitin noted, practical religion "can have an independent effect on political life, often quite different from the political or economic intentions of the original propagating group" (Laitin, 1978: 571). It is, in fact, misleading to refer to "practical religion" in the singular, since it takes many forms according to different historical and geographic locations. In this essay, I am interested in a particular aspect of Christianity's "original doctrine"—its teachings on humanity's character and place in the world, i.e., its theological anthropology. It is an important theological task to reflect on what Jesus, Paul, or Augustine might have meant or intended, but it is not my task here. In other words, I am concerned with the ways these doctrines have been interpreted in and through their interactions with social conditions. More specifically, I examine the ways Christian doctrines about humanness have shaped—or been perceived to shape, by critics and apologists alike—attitudes and behavior towards nature.

In the second and third sections of this article, I look at the ways some contemporary thinkers re-present and/or redefine Christian understandings of humanity's place in nature. Many of these theologians claim that Christianity's charismatic founders—Jesus, Paul, Augustine, Aquinas, among others—did not intend to instrumentalize or exploit nature, and that readings of their ideas in ecologically damaging terms are in fact misreadings. My interest, again, lies not in the historical accuracy or sacred truth of any reading—past or present, "green" or not. Rather, I hope to shed light on some of the reasons that so many traditional readings (or misreadings) of Christianity have helped legitimize environmental harm and on the issues that are most important for current efforts to redirect the practical consequences of Christian thought. I argue that among these issues, one of the most crucial is theological anthropology. In other words, any attempt at a Christian environmental ethic must come to grips with the ways that claims about God shape claims about humans, and the ways that claims about humans in turn shape understandings of nature.

Before I proceed, several further caveats are in order. First, this is not a comprehensive evaluation of the Christian tradition regarding the natural environment, a task better covered by a range of recent books (see Northcott, 1996; Santmire, 1985; Hessel, 1992, among others). In addition, when I speak of a "mainstream" Christian tradition, I am not suggesting that the tradition as a whole is either unanimous or static. Such a view, in fact, is explicitly rejected by the understanding of practical religion that I adopt. What counts as "mainstream" has changed substantially over the past two millennia. For example, in Christianity's formative period (roughly, the three centuries prior to the conversion of Constantine in 313 C.E.) and in the Middle Ages, prevailing Christian interpretations of human and non-human nature—and of many other issues—diverged widely from modern approaches. Further, throughout Christian history certain longstanding currents, notably mysticism, have challenged dominant interpretations of non-human nature. This is all to say that Christianity is a diverse, changing, and complex tradition, and I do not make any claims here to cover (or to condemn or redeem) the whole of it.

HUMAN SEPARATION FROM NATURE IN CHRISTIAN TRADITION

In one of his most important writings, Paul told the Christians of Rome: "Do not be conformed to this world" (Romans 12:2). In the almost 2000 years since, Christian theologians have continually struggled with the question of humans' place in the world. What "this world" means is ambiguous both for Paul and for later theologians. Some take it to mean only the particular social structures and institutions of their time, while others interpret it to encompass earthly life, the physical realm, and embodiment in general. A number of Christian thinkers, from Paul's time to our own, have interpreted human separation from "this world" to imply human separateness from the natural world. While this is not the only possible reading of Paul (and many theologians insist that it is not the truest or best one), the notion that humans are not ultimately at home in the natural world has undeniably shaped Christianity and, through the tradition, influenced Western culture in general.

Christian claims about human uniqueness usually rest on the assertion that humans alone possess an eternal spirit or soul, what Augustine, in *City of God,* termed the image of God and thus of the trinity within them. The soul definitively separates humans from the "non-spiritual" part of creation. It links humans in their origins, capacities, and ultimate destiny to God and, thus, forever divides them from the rest of creation. The soul is not just an added piece of equipment but a dimension that transforms the meaning of humanness. (In this sense, the soul in Christianity performs the same function that qualities such as conceptual thought and language fulfill for secular thinkers, especially those in the Cartesian lineage. In other senses, of course, the Christian notion of the soul differs significantly from these philosophical categories, especially insofar as the soul establishes humans in relationship to the sacred.)

The pre-eminent source for Christian claims about the soul, of course, is the Bible, especially creation stories. The Hebrew Bible offers two accounts of God's creation of the world and humanity. The best known and most influential, found in Genesis 1:26–28, clearly distinguishes humans from the rest of God's creatures. Humans alone are created in God's likeness and, not incidentally, given dominion over the rest of creation. According to this version, creation proceeded thus:

> 26 And God said, "Let us make man in our image, after our likeness, and let them have dominion over the fish of the sea, and over the birds of the air, and over the cattle, and over all the earth, and over every creeping thing that creeps upon the earth."
>
> 27 So God created man in His own image, in the image of God he created him; male and female he created them.
>
> 28 And God blessed them, and God said to them, "Be fruitful, and multiply, and fill the earth and subdue it; and have dominion over the fish of the sea and over the birds of the air and over every living thing that moves upon the earth."

"Having dominion" and "subduing," some Christian and Jewish thinkers argue, need not be interpreted in this context as unqualified exploitation. Interpreted in terms of stewardship, as I discuss later, human power over nature is oriented and constrained by God's ultimate authority over humans. Dominant popular and academic readings, however, take Genesis 1 as legitimating human domination over and utilization of the natural world.

In any of these interpretations of Genesis 1, it is clear that the assertion of humanity's uniqueness—its creation in the image of God—is inextricably tied to human power over the earth and other animals.[1] The soul that all other animals lack both defines humans and gives them transcendent value. The human soul also joins creation and salvation in Christian theological anthropology. In the end, the image of God implanted in the human creature returns to God. This means, crucially, that humanity's real home does not lie among the rest of creation but rather with God in heaven. It also means that humans' most important relationship is the vertical stretch to the divine rather than—or at least before—horizontal ties to other people or creatures. Thus humanity is defined first and foremost not by relations among persons, by physical embodiedness, or by embeddedness in the natural world, but by an invisible tie to an invisible God.

Ambivalent Embodiment

Ambivalence about or even hostility to nature has been more or less prominent in different periods and movements within Christianity. It is especially strong in those dimensions of Christian thought most influenced by Greek thought, especially the Platonic idea that the essences of things or beings are more real than physical bodies. In this tradition, as Gordon Kaufman summarizes, "both man [sic] and that which was taken to be ultimately real were understood in terms of those features of man's being which most sharply distinguish us from other creatures" (1972: 352). The Hellenistic tendency to devalue the bodily and look to the transcendent has emerged in different points throughout Christian history. Perhaps the most extreme version is Gnosticism, which thrived in the first few centuries C.E. and peaked with the Manicheans, followers of the third-century prophet Mani. Manicheans defined Jesus as pure spirit and salvation as knowledge (*gnosis*) of the divine. Like a number of other early Christian movements, they rejected the notion that Jesus was fully human and died a physical death. Their Christology reflected their anthropology: what was important about Jesus and every human being was the soul, which was trapped in earth but oriented towards its true home in heaven. In heaven resided the true God, who neither created nor governed the material world. Earth, in fact, was a segment of the Divine that fell into the created world. Humans, as carriers of this divine spark, exist, like God, in radical opposition to the created world. Gnostics awaited a savior who would descend to earth to give them knowledge that would enable individual souls to leave the physical world and the body behind and reunite with the divine substance in Heaven.

The extreme dualism of Gnosticism highlights the close ties between visions of nature and human nature in Christian theology. Gnosticism, especially its Manichean form, defined what is distinctively and positively human as what transcends the material body and earth. In this perspective, just as God is radically other to the created world, so humans—as carriers of the divine spark—are other, not just more, than their bodies. On earth, humans are lost travelers, imprisoned in nature and ruled by capricious powers that enslave them, especially through the physical body. Body and soul are not just different but actively hostile to each other. In this vision, the human condition involves, first, a fundamental alienation from all that ties us to the earth and, second, a ceaseless longing for what might enable us to transcend the material realm. Humans, or at least Christians, are "strangers and pilgrims" wandering through the world, never at home in it (Santmire, 1985: 13).

While Manicheanism represented an extreme, the dualism it reflects has resurfaced again and again in Christian history, in popular movements as well as ratified theologies. In thirteenth-century France, for example, the Cathari (or Albigenses) revived the extreme division between spirit and body. They saw the body as entirely negative and the spirit as wholly good, despite its imprisonment in physicality. Like the Manicheans, the Cathari embedded their theological vision in a narrative that began with a flawed creation and ended, at least for true believers, with a return to their true home with God in heaven. The Cathari so despised physical life that they condemned having children as a sin, since it trapped more souls. The official church condemned the Albigensians as heretical, just as Augustine had condemned Manicheanism. In both cases, the extreme positions pushed mainstream theology to a fuller endorsement of physical life, reproduction, and the created world generally, as seen in various councils and doctrinal statements of both the first few centuries C.E. and the medieval period. Throughout Christian history, however, tendencies to body-spirit dualism have struggled continually with more positive valuations of human embodiment. Official Christianity has in most cases condemned extremely dualistic positions, but ambivalence about the body and nature generally has remained a strong current in both popular and academic theologies.

The Kingdom of the World

Christian uneasiness about physical bodies has been closely tied to ambivalence about the created world generally. Body and world are physical and transitory in contrast to the spiritual and eternal nature of the soul and of heaven. Christian orthodoxy, however, insists that a benevolent God created both physical bodies and the cosmos itself, which means that material creation cannot simply constitute a trap for spirit. Christian thinkers' efforts to understand the relationship between soul and body reflect the tradition's larger struggle to make sense of the relationship between the spiritual and the physical, between the things of God and the things of the world. These questions raise a number of ethical questions: What is the value of "this world"? How does God will humans to act in relation to the material creation? Underlying these questions is a central concern of theological anthropology: what is the place of humans, as both physical and spiritual creatures, in the created world?

Paul inaugurated the enduring Christian effort to resolve these tensions by positing a vision of humans, or at least Christians, as "in but not of" the world. In contrast to Gnosticism and other dualistic movements, Paul saw the material world and the physical body as creations of a benevolent God. Perhaps more important, given Paul's emphasis on salvation, the world is the locus of redemption by an embodied savior. Thus humans must be in the world, and not grudgingly—but also not fully. Although Paul did not define the world and the body in their present form as evil, neither did he declare them Christians' true or final home. His primary concern was the salvific meaning of Jesus's death and resurrection and the consequences of these events for human life and history. For Paul, human redemption through Christ creates the "new man," not through the transcendence of the material world but via its actual recreation: a new earth to go with the new vision of heaven that is made possible by the crucifixion and resurrection (see, for example, Romans 8). In this context, creation serves essentially as a background for the drama of redemption. While the old earth is not evil, neither is it of permanent importance for human salvation, which alone gives meaning to human life.

Several centuries after Paul, Augustine continued to engage the dualistic tendencies in Christianity's view of nature and human nature. Like Paul, Augustine sought a balance between the conviction that the highest good lay in heaven, on the one hand, and a positive valuation of creation, on the other. Augustine was a Manichean prior to his conversion to Christianity, and his ongoing ambivalence about the body and nature reflect his—and his religion's—struggles with the seductive appeal of dualism. Augustine explicitly rejected the Gnostic notion that the earth and the body are essentially fallen. The Manichaeans are wrong to despise earthly bodies as evil, in his view. He devotes large sections of *City of God* (e.g., most of Book XIII) to arguing that not the fact of embodiment but the wrong use of the will leads to sin. The fact that the body is corruptible and (as a result of original sin) mortal, not "the body itself, is heavy to the soul" (1945a: 12). All creation, including the human body, is a revelation of God's goodness, he wrote in his *Confessions,* because God created "the earth which I walk on" as well as the human body—the "earth which I carry" (*Confessions* 12.2., cited in Santmire, 1985: 66). Thus the body cannot be the prison of the soul but rather is its partner.

Although soul and body may belong together, they are far from equal partners. Augustine views both the created world and the physical body as the good works of a benevolent God, but he insists that ultimate value lies only with spiritual things. While the body is not innately evil, it is ephemeral and therefore subordinate to the eternal soul. More generally, all earthly goods are trivial in comparison to the supreme good of eternal life with God in heaven. On earth, Augustine insists, the believer remains "a heavenly pilgrim" (1945b: 252). A pilgrim, of course, is looking for something better. The end of the journey, the true fulfillment of the divinely-ordained narrative in which human life unfolds, is for Augustine the transcendence of physical existence through eternal life. Because only the fate of the soul is of ultimate importance, the non-spiritual created world lacks deep significance, and whatever significance and value it does have comes from its relation to God and eternal life. Despite his conditional valuation of creation against Gnosticism, Augustine reinforces the idea that our relations to material creation lack ultimate meaning in comparison to our relations to God and heaven.

The Augustinian tension between the things of God and the things of the world continues to mark Christianity. This is particularly evident in the Protestant tradition, beginning with Luther's reworking of Augustine's two cities metaphor. For Luther, as for Augustine and Paul, humans must live in the "kingdom of man" and strive to improve it and obey its rules. However, they must also never forget that their true home and destiny lie in the reign of God. This dual citizenship, with its sometimes-contradictory demands, stems from a deep anthropological dualism. In Luther's words, "Man has a twofold nature, a spiritual and a bodily one" (Luther, 1961: 53). The former comes from and owes its allegiance to God alone, while the latter, subordinate, nature results from the temporary human condition of embodiment in a flawed material world. Humanity's two natures, as Luther sees them, never harmonize completely, within individuals or in society more generally, and when they conflict openly, the believer's duty to God and the heavenly kingdom must always come first. For Luther and for Calvin, as Michael Northcott writes, "it is not the relations between selves, and between humans and created order, which are salvifically and morally significant but the choosing of particular individual selves by the will of God to be objects of his eternal love and goodness" (Northcott, 1996: 220). The ethical demands of living in the world ultimately neither lead to nor modify the all-important goal of personal salvation and eternal life with God in heaven. Christians' spiritual citizenship ought to make them better residents of the material world, but their earthly social lives should not affect their understandings of or path to final redemption.

The Reformation ambivalence about "the world" resurfaces in the writings of neo-Orthodox theologians in the twentieth century. Reinhold Niebuhr, for example, asserts that human existence is distinguished from animal life by humans' "qualified participation in creation. Within limits it breaks the forms of nature and creates new configurations of vitality" (Niebuhr, 1964: 26). Humans, in other words, are not entirely subject to their "creatureliness" as are other animals; we alone share something of God's creativity (1964: 55). However, Niebuhr believes that people are rarely inclined to live up to their transcendent potential, because the inclination to sin is so powerful. Thus he is far from offering an unqualified celebration of human goodness and rationality. His approach to ethics rests on a conviction that the selfishness that usually drives human behavior requires social (as well as rational and religious) constraints on this inclination (Niebuhr, 1960). Still, at their core, humans have an ethical potential, grounded in their unique participation in God's creative and transforming power, which all other creatures lack. Human nature is defined by the tension, within each person, between the divine spark and the limitations of fallible, selfish embodiment.

Niebuhr does not simply reproduce the Lutheran dualism between the world and God, nor does he consider the material realm irrelevant to Christian theology. To the contrary, Niebuhr took life in the world very seriously and brought his theological concerns to bear on concrete social projects. Still, his ethics were shaped by a vision of human nature as divided between reason, on the one hand, and emotion and self-interest, on the other. Morality involved dominating what Niebuhr understood, literally, as the baser instincts, through the combined efforts of rationality, religion, and social control. This approach refines the ambivalence evident in Augustinian and Lutheran theology: the world cannot simply be rejected as evil but must be confronted and improved to the extent possible. Like Augustine and Luther, however, Niebuhr viewed the things of the world, including the "baser" part of human nature, as separate from and ultimately detrimental to reason, transcendence, and efforts to realize humans' intrinsic connection to God.

Niebuhr's ambivalence about world reflects the deeply rooted Protestant assumption that human nature is divided between spirit and body. The spirit, the link to the divine, which provides both what is important and what is unique in human life, exists in constant tension with the physical existence shared with other creatures. Following Luther, Protestant thinkers including Niebuhr reject a simple identification between human sinfulness and the body or the created world, while remaining uneasy about the moral and spiritual status of physical creation. This ambivalence, which sometimes becomes open hostility, toward "the world" is evident in many, though not all, variants of Pentecostal Protestant theology. Latin American Pentecostal leaders, for example, frequently warn against the dangers of the things of the world (*las cosas del mundo*), which they see as radically opposed to the things of God.

The Roman Catholic tradition, in contrast, views the created world in much more positive terms. While Protestantism has mostly seen human life on earth as radically separated from the spiritual realm or the reign of God, Catholicism has perceived greater continuity between the human and the divine and therefore between the material and the spiritual, creature and creator. This Catholic position was systematized in Thomas Aquinas's "medieval synthesis." Thomas wrote in the context of a revived interest, in the Middle Ages, in the notion of a "Great Chain of Being," which joined all creatures in a harmonious hierarchy. The medieval appropriation of the Great Chain of Being was tied both to growing confidence in humanity's mastery over nature, on the one hand, and to a grand vision of the hierarchy of being, on the other. Linking these two themes was the idea of the human creature as microcosm. Nature, as an ordered structure, reflected the human self and vice-versa (Santmire, 1985: 81–82).

Thomas summarized the harmonious relationship between God and creation and among different aspects—human and non-human—of that creation in his notion of natural law. "The whole community of the universe," as Thomas proclaimed in the *Summa Theologica,* "is governed by the divine reason" (1948: 616). Thus the first key aspect of Thomas's thought, in relation to understandings of nature, is his insistence that "everything that in any way is, is from God" (1948: 234), and that all aspects of creation are linked together because "all things partake in some way in the eternal law" (1948: 618). Rational creatures, meaning (male) humans and angels, partake in the eternal law through the imprint of eternal law upon them (or their participation in the eternal law), which is what Thomas terms specifically natural law (in distinction from eternal and human law). Natural law frames human nature in optimistic terms, emphasizing human rationality and humans' capacity and inclination to act in harmony with God's will.

More generally, natural law refers to the entire system that links humans to God and also to the other levels of creation. A second crucial aspect of Thomistic thought is that these linkages are not only harmonious but also hierarchical. "In natural things," Thomas explains, "species seem to be arranged in a hierarchy: as the mixed things are more perfect than the elements, and plants than minerals, and animals than plants, and men more than other animals" (1948: 263). God has not only created and distinguished the creatures but also made them unequal. Humanity's place in this hierarchy is a little below the angels but clearly above the other animals. This elevation stems from humans' possession of an eternal soul, which all other animals, as well as the inanimate features of creation, lack.

Subsequent Roman Catholic thought, about nature as about so much else, builds on Thomistic foundations. Rather than opposed kingdoms or cities, Catholicism perceives creation in terms of an unbroken ascent from lowest to highest levels. God is not opposed to any part of creation, and no part of creation can be termed evil. What is crucial is understanding the nature and proper place of every element. While God creates and rules all of creation, God is not equally near to all of creation. Lower creatures can approach divine goodness only through their relationship to higher ones, and humans, as rational creatures, are superior to other animals and to all of inanimate creation. Their greater closeness to the divine makes humans not only more perfect than but also dominant over other creatures. Thus, Thomas writes, "the subjection of other animals to man is natural" (1948: 918).

Statements like these, along with later interpretations of natural law as justifying human domination, lead many environmental ethicists to conclude that Thomism inevitably reinforces human-centered and exploitative attitudes towards nature. As I discuss in the next section, however, some contemporary Roman Catholic and Anglican thinkers have argued that natural law can provide a strong basis for a positive environmental ethic. The Thomistic tradition, like most other currents within Christianity, generates ambiguous ecological consequences. This has provided ample fruit for eco-theologians and ethicists seeking to redeem Christian attitudes towa human nature.

CHRISTIAN RE-EVALUATIONS OF NATURE

In recent years, a number of Christian theologians and ethicists—Protestant, Catholic, and Orthodox—have sought to revise or reread some core doctrines in light of contemporary environmental problems. Central to many of these eco-theologies are revised understandings of what it means to be human in both ecological and theological terms.

Christian environmental reflections on the human often begin with efforts to rethink the physical body. Many theologians have drawn on feminist theory for this task. Embodiment is a central issue for feminism because of the longstanding Western tendency to associate women with the body and nature and men with the mind and culture. This mind-body dualism, Adrienne Rich argues, has made the body "so problematic for women that it has often seemed easier to shrug it off and travel as a disembodied spirit" (Rich, 1976: 22). Acquiescence to dualism and to the degradation of the body, however, ultimately harms women, since "the struggle of women to become self-determining is rooted in our bodies" (Rich, 1979: 272). "Shrugging off" our bodies means relinquishing the possibility of an integral liberation for women, which would allow women to determine the shape of their lives and to embrace their identity as a whole rather than a fragmented polarity. Instead of adopting the mind-body dualism of the dominant culture, feminist thought needs to integrate body and mind, to "think through the body" (Rich, 1976: 290).

Influenced by feminist approaches, Protestant theologian Sallie McFague seeks to help Christians "think and act as if bodies matter. They are not all that matters but they do, and if we believed they mattered and understood in detail what that belief entailed, how might that change our way of being in the world?" (McFague, 1993: viii). McFague contends that "thinking through the body" would change our ideas about a range of issues. First, it would change our thinking about the human person or self, discarding dualism for a holistic view. In this perspective, McFague writes, "The body is not a discardable garment cloaking the real self or essence of a person (or a pine tree or a chimpanzee); rather, it is the shape or form of who we are. It is how each of us is recognized, responded to, loved, touched, and cared for—as well as oppressed, beaten, raped, mutilated, discarded, and killed. The body is not a minor matter; rather, it is the main attraction" (1993: 16).[2] McFague thus rejects the "docetic" view of humans as accidentally encased in bodies that do not shape their "true" identities and argues instead for a fully incarnational model, in which all dimensions of human being are embodied.[3] Nothing we do or are, nothing we hope to be, exists in isolation from the fact that we are embodied creatures living alongside, and dependent on, other bodies. Focusing on the body, McFague writes, provides "a way, a lens, a glass, by which we might see ourselves more clearly, see where we belong in the scheme of things—not as a spirit among bodies, but as a spirited body among other spirited bodies on our planet" (1993: 19).

Further, taking embodiment seriously transforms ways of thinking about God. McFague proposes understanding the earth as "the body of God." This model, she argues, takes incarnation seriously, in a way that the docetic tendency in mainstream theology has not. Seeing the universe as God's body, writes McFague, radicalizes the incarnation "beyond Jesus of Nazareth to include all matter" (1993: xi). If the world is God's body, she continues, then everything that happens to the world also happens to God (1993: 176). This redirects Christian attention away from its dominant, even exclusive focus on relations with God and personal salvation and towards the "carnal," human and nonhuman bodies, the embodied earth itself.

McFague emphasizes that we need not only to affirm our embodiment but also to think differently about it (1993: 25). Thinking differently about bodies requires a transformation of theological anthropology, away from the doceticism of mainstream Christianity, the common notion that there is some separate human essence (reason, soul) that "has" a body. This view sees embodiment as either irrelevant to what humans "really" are or as an obstacle to full self-expression. In contrast, McFague argues that humans are not just spirits who happen to be in bodies but "inspirited bodies within the larger body" (1993: 22). Having a body, in this light, constitutes not a dilemma but rather the condition that makes a good and truly human life possible.

Conformed to the World

Defining humans as fully, not just provisionally and ambivalently, embodied would transform humans' relationship to the physical world. A fully incarnational theological anthropology, in other words, implies an end to what McFague calls the "sojourner sensibility" of mainstream Christianity (1993: 102). If we are not just spirits accidentally housed in bodies that have nothing to do with our true selves, then neither are we merely "passing through" this earthly life. We do not always have one foot in heaven but instead are both *of* and *in* this world. This claim, however, in turn demands further revisions in theological anthropology. As the title of a recent volume (Brown et al., 1998) asks, what happens to the soul? How can a fully embodied, this-worldly ethic retain a Christian understanding of human origins, the meaning of life, and salvation?

Efforts to answer this question struggle to retain a notion of human distinctiveness that does not entail alienation from and domination over the natural world. These approaches emphasize the need, as Protestant theologian Shannon Jung puts it, to be "at home" on earth, *of* the world. Jung rejects the "fiction that human beings [are] not constitutionally part of the world of nature" (Jung, 1993: 31). This erroneous belief has generated many of current environmental problems, Jung notes, and is closely tied to consumerism and other economic factors. To improve both environmental conditions and the quality of human life more generally, we need to understand that "The earth is not an external home; we are part of the home. We are part of the earth. The whole web of life that is the earth cannot be externalized from us. We are all part of God's home; we constitute nature. *We are not at home; we are home!*" (1993: 69). This echoes the claim that we are not just *in* bodies but we *are* bodies.

Jung takes a new look, through an ecological lens, at Augustine's idea of the body as the "earth we carry." "Each of us," Jung writes, "is an environment. Our local environment is our body. It is a body connected with other bodies—animal, human, celestial. . . . We have a connection to every other environment; the environment moves through us; we modify the environment. All of us are part of the environment" (1993: 5). These claims draw support from contemporary science, including evolutionary theory and postmodern physics as well as ecology. The sciences tell us, as Sallie McFague summarizes, "that the universe is a whole and that all things, living and nonliving, are interrelated and interdependent." This "organic model" predominated for most of human history, but modern science and philosophies (including much of Christian thought) have replaced it with a mechanistic model. Environmental ethics gains from a reconsideration of the organic model. This model invites Christians in particular, "who have been made to feel that we do not, in a fundamental sense, *belong* on the earth (for our home is in another world)," to be at home on earth (McFague, 1993: 31).

McFague ties the sense of being at home to a particular model of the earth and its history, rooted in the "common creation story" of evolution. This emphasis on evolution is important for contemporary understandings of human belonging on earth, because it emphasizes both human continuity with the rest of nature and our adaptiveness to particular environments and ecological relationships. This point is also central to the work of Catholic ecotheologians such as Rosemary Radford Ruether and Thomas Berry. "We have no home outside the earth," Ruether writes, "And so our destruction of this home is the permanent destruction of ourselves as well" (1992: 86). Echoing Ruether's critique of the otherworldliness of mainstream Christianity, Thomas Berry argues that the tradition has taught that "we somehow did not belong to the community of earth. We were not an integral component of the natural world. Our destiny was not here. We deserved a better world, although we had not even begun to appreciate the beauty and grandeur of this world or the full measure of its entrancing qualities" (Berry, 1990: 205). This failure of appreciation, Berry claims, stems in part from the historical legacy of forms of Christianity that have been concerned less with the natural world than with "redemption out of the world through a personal savior relationship that transcends all such concerns" (1990: 129).

While criticizing Christianity's otherworldly tendencies, Berry and Ruether do not dismiss its redemptive possibilities for nature. Ruether makes two arguments: first, that despite its problems, Christianity also has value for ecological concerns, and second, that the search for environmental solutions ought to begin with one's own tradition, if only because "the vast majority of the more than one billion Christians of the world can be lured into an ecological consciousness only if they see that it grows in some ways from the soil in which they are planted" (Ruether, 1992: 207).

Berry also recognizes the potential (however muted) of Christianity to contribute to ecological solutions. However, he strives to integrate Christian cosmologies with those of science, especially evolutionary biology, to generate an integrated narrative that can both ground sustaining values and resolve social problems. Religion is a crucial aspect of this solution, he writes, but "existing religious traditions are too distant from our new sense of the universe to be adequate to the task that is before us. We cannot do without the traditional religions, but they cannot do what needs to be done. We need a new type of religious orientation. This must . . . emerge from our new story of the universe. This constitutes . . . a new revelatory experience that can be understood as soon as we recognize that the evolutionary process is from the beginning a spiritual as well as a physical process" (1990: 87).

Berry's focus on the spiritual dimensions of evolution echo, in some ways, the thought of the French Jesuit thinker Pierre Teilhard de Chardin, who perceives evolution as not only increasing organizational complexity but also as a teleological process of moral and spiritual improvement and "psychical concentration." This process culminates in the "Omega point," "a *distinct Centre radiating at the core of a system of centres;* a grouping in which the personalisation of the All and personalisations of the elements reach their maximum" (Teilhard de Chardin, 1959: 262–63; emphasis in original). The ultimate end of evolution, then, is "the expectation of perfect unity, steeped in which each element will reach its consummation at the same time as the universe. . . . fulfilling itself in a synthesis of centres in perfect conformity with the laws of union. God, the Centre of centres" (1959: 294).

Teilhard's vision is idiosyncratic and very far from Berry's in many ways. What the two share, however, is an effort to join the natural law understanding of an ordered, harmonious, and ultimately meaningful universe with a commitment to evolutionary accounts of the origin of life. In this view, evolution is a process with not only biological but also spiritual significance. Like Teilhard, Berry seeks "to remythologize the new creation story from a Christian perspective. . . . to reimagine Christian doctrine in terms of twentieth-century science and to see the new scientific story in Christian terms" (McFague, 1993: 82). With a greater ecological emphasis than Teilhard, Berry hopes to construct a new, compelling story that combines scientific accounts of how the world came to be with spiritual and ethical conclusions about humans' place on earth and what we ought to do. The right origin story, in other words, will tell us "how the future can be given some satisfying direction" (Berry, 1990: 124).

Berry (and Teilhard) draw on a longstanding Roman Catholic vision of the created world as harmoniously and inextricably linked to God's intentions for humankind. The natural world, even the planet itself, is full of meaning, as is the ongoing process of evolutionary change.[4] In this process, humans have a particular place—for Berry as for Teilhard and Thomas before him. Berry explains: humans are "genetically coded toward a further transgenetic cultural coding whereby we invent ourselves in the human expression of our being" (Berry, 1990: 200). This capacity for self-formation is both a privilege and a responsibility. Berry thus substantially dilutes and also redirects the anthropocentrism of the Christian, and particularly Roman Catholic, tradition, so that human uniqueness calls forth obligations rather than triumphalism.

THEOLOGICAL ANTHROPOLOGY AND STEWARDSHIP ETHICS

A coherent Christian environmental ethic must account for core elements of doctrine at the same time it affirms ecological responsibility. Among many possible versions of Christian environmental ethics, one of the most influential and widespread models is that of "stewardship," which affirms that God has made people caretakers and protectors of the rest of creation. Many variants of Christian stewardship ethics exist, including some that are largely utilitarian and human-centered as well as more radical or demanding versions. In all of these ethics, theological anthropology plays a central role. Stewardship ethics seek, in short, to allow for human distinctiveness and a special relationship between humans and God while also placing limits on human freedom and dominion over the rest of nature. In rethinking what it means to be stewards, this approach emphasizes human subjection to God as much as human power over nature.

Lutheran theologian Philip Hefner highlights the importance of definitions of humanness in his approach to stewardship. Hefner defines humans as God's "created co-creators" and humans' purpose as being "the agency, acting in freedom, to birth the future that is most wholesome for the nature that has birthed us—the nature that is not only our own genetic heritage, but also the entire human community and the evolutionary and ecological reality in which and to which we belong. Exercising this agency is said to be God's will for humans" (Hefner, 1993: 27). Hefner's approach underlines the effort of contemporary stewardship ethics to retain a privileged place for humans while placing human power in the context of both responsibility (to seek a more "wholesome" future) and dependence (upon ecological and evolutionary processes as well as God). In this model, humans possess special features, including a unique degree of freedom, but we cannot employ these qualities for arbitrarily chosen ends. Rather, we have been granted freedom by God to enable us "to participate in the intentional fulfillment of God's purposes" (McFague, 1993: 54). This is a theocentric, not an anthropocentric, ethic. Humans may be superior to the rest of creation in certain respects, but in equally profound ways we remain dependent upon God and nature. We are God's vice-regents, as the Muslim form of stewardship terms it, always subordinate to divine power (Nasr, 1992).

Stewardship ethics confront Christianity's traditional ambivalence about human nature and the created world. Like Paul and Augustine, contemporary stewardship approaches hope to affirm the goodness of creation without limiting the meaning of human life only to the physical realm. This means they must seek a balance between human continuities with and dependence on the natural world, on the one hand, and human distinctiveness and power, on the other. McFague, for example, describes humans as particular kinds of beings with special gifts and also distinctive limitations. In light of evolution as the common creation story, she writes, humans are "*decentered* as the point and goal of creation and *recentered* as God's partners in helping creation to grow and prosper in our tiny part of God's body" (McFague, 1993:

197, 108). We are distinguished from the rest of creation not by our superiority but by our "peculiar form of individuality *and* interdependence," she continues. "We are the responsible ones, responsible for all the rest upon which we are so profoundly dependent" (1993: 109). Shannon Jung frames the question of human distinctiveness in explicitly teleological terms: "what are people for?" Our purpose, he replies, is linked to our capacity for responsibility (Jung, 1993: 86).

Many theologians tie this responsibility to our greater degree of consciousness, as a key element of the qualitative difference between humans and the rest of creation. McFague describes this difference as the fact that "we are, to our knowledge, the only creatures on our planet who not only participate in it but *know* that they do:" We possess information about who we are in the scheme of things and how much we depend on the rest of nature. This knowledge gives us a choice: "we can choose to be at home on our planet, learn to follow its house rules, value its fragility and beauty, share in its limited resources with other human beings and other life-forms. We may decide not to do so, but we will not be able to say 'If only we had known.' We *do* know" (McFague, 1993: 60). Our knowledge, further, is complemented by a capacity for intentional action. We have the option of deciding differently, of changing intentionally, through culture, and not exclusively through biological evolution. Stewardship ethics provide guidelines for these decisions, which must be based on awareness of our distinctive features, including technological power and scientific knowledge, and also of the limitations placed on us by nature and by God's will for the world.

These models challenge more conservative understandings of stewardship that advocate "responsible" management of resources while emphasizing human lordship and relegating divine power over humans to a distant background. In contrast, many contemporary eco-theologies emphasize the limitations upon human stewardship. Land, for example, is a gift of God and is always ultimately referred back to God. In this perspective, as Holmes Rolston points out, "In legal terms, land ownership is imperfect and does not carry the right irreplaceably to destroy. In theological terms, land ownership is stewardship" (Rolston, 1992: 140). This echoes the Roman Catholic insistence on the common purpose of created things. Catholic social thought has long asserted, as the Second Vatican Council reaffirmed in *Gaudium et Spes,* that "God intended the earth and all that it contains for the use of every human being and people." Thus *Gaudium et Spes* declares that "by its very nature private property has a social quality deriving from the law of the communal purpose of created goods" (Second Vatican Council, 1991: 203, 204). God and the community have prior claims to all forms of property. Individuals may use property only as long as they serve the common good and do not deny the basic needs of others. Christian eco-theologians add to this social quality an ecological quality, so that not only human needs but also environmental concerns place constraints on the ownership and use of property.

We face limits not only in our right to control nature but also in our capacity to do so. We are powerful and thus responsible, but we are neither all-powerful nor all-responsible. Interpreted in theological terms, this means, as Jung writes, "No single individual is responsible for the state of the natural world. Only God sustains, oversees, and renews the world. God has chosen to work through individuals and communities to do this. *I am* responsible for my contribution to the health of the environment individually and through my communities" (Jung, 1993: 21).[5] This puts stewardship within a theocentric model that challenges what Sharon Welch (1990) terms the "ethic of control," the notion that individuals can achieve unilateral, total solutions to problems. Theocentric revisions of stewardship ethics aim to avoid both arrogance and fatalism, two dangers of thinking in terms of an ethic of control.

Natural Law

Protestant theology has been much more concerned with human sin, and particularly the sin of arrogance, than Roman Catholic or Orthodox theologies. The emphasis on human fallibility tends to reinforce a pessimistic view of human nature and, often, of "the world" in general. Some thinkers have turned to other streams within the Christian tradition to ground an environmental ethic that values the natural world without reservation. One important resource, in this light, is the natural law tradition, dominant in Roman Catholic and many Anglican theologies. Natural law, as noted earlier, views all elements of the universe as harmoniously ordered and related to God's ultimate design. In this context, humans are basically good and capable of co-operation with God. In place of the gap between the human (created) and the divine emphasized by Luther and Calvin, natural law affirms that plants, animals, and humans are all linked in a harmonious, albeit hierarchical, chain of being. This approach is helpful for environmental ethics insofar as it affirms the goodness of creation generally and also the intrinsic worth of non-human nature as a part of creation with its own ends and value (LeBlanc, 1999: 295).

Natural law can be seen as a variant of stewardship ethics, at least insofar as it balances this positive valuation of non-human nature with an insistence on the distinctive place of humans in creation. *Gaudium et Spes* summarizes the Catholic position with its assertion that "man is the only creature on earth that God willed for itself," i.e., the only creature that is an end in itself rather than a means for others (Second Vatican Council, 1991: 174). Here we see again Thomas's hierarchical vision, expressed in the claim that humans alone, of all creation, share the divine capacity to be an end for itself and for others. Thus, the Council declares, God made man "master of all earthly creatures that he might subdue them and use them to Christ's glory" (167). These themes are echoed in Pope John Paul II's 1980 encyclical *Redemptor Hominis,* which celebrates the "unrepeatable reality" of each person, chosen by God for "grace and glory" and also given the earth to subdue and dominate (John Paul II, 1991: 332). Modern Catholic humanism envisions this dominion, however, in the larger context of a cosmic hierarchy that assigns a purpose and value, however limited or subordinate, to all the elements of creation. A number of Catholic eco-theologies revise this model to elevate the meaning and value of nature, on the one hand, and to downplay (without completely denying) human uniqueness, on the other.

Natural law not only values both the natural world and human embodiment but also takes a more relational view of human nature than many Protestant approaches, which tend to emphasize the individual in relationship to God alone. As Michael Northcott points out, natural law asserts that relationships among persons and among levels of creation, along with the human relationship to God, are necessary both to define and to fulfill human existence (Northcott, 1996: 229). This builds on the social view of human nature in the Jewish tradition, in contrast with what some interpreters view as the Hellenistic and Reformation tendency to focus on the vertical tie between the individual and the absolute as the only relationship that is constitutive for human life. The natural law, and especially Roman Catholic, emphasis on human sociability stresses the importance of responsibilities and constraints generated by ties to other persons and even to non-human nature. In all these ways, the natural law tradition can offer important resources for environmental ethics and particularly for the anthropology underlying it.

Is Stewardship Enough?

The insistence in stewardship ethics upon human dominion (though not necessarily domination; see LeBlanc, 1999: 297) has led some Christian eco-theologians to argue that they necessarily fall short. Critics of stewardship models contend that increasingly severe global ecological crises demand a more radical ethic, which does not allot a special place or power to humanity. George Kehm contends, for example, that a stewardship ethic "inevitably falls into some form of utilitarianism with respect to extra-human creation" (Kehm, 1992: 89). In other words, stewardship persists in seeing nature as a resource subject to human interests. Paul Santmire concludes that the theme of human dominion over the earth, central to stewardship models (especially in the Protestant tradition, he suggests), cannot encompass the radical revisions that ecological crises require. Dominion reinterpreted as stewardship may suggest how humans might manage the productivity of the earth wisely, but this model still fails to see nature as "a world with its own life and its own value . . . its own history with God" (Santmire, 1992: 60). Santmire argues that Christian eco-theology must find a way of showing that "God has a history with nature that is independent of God's history with humanity, although the two, nature and humanity, are also intimately interrelated and interdependent" (1992: 75).

To replace the stewardship notion of special responsibility, Santmire proposes cooperation as the best model for human interaction with and use of nature (1992: 77). This model accords more closely with the biocentric or ecocentric models advocated by many secular environmental philosophers. The strength of such approaches is their attribution of intrinsic value to non-human nature and their insistence that humans are simply "plain members and citizens" of the biosphere, as Aldo Leopold, father of ecocentric ethics, put it (Leopold, 1966: 240). Such egalitarian environmental ethics, however, also have drawbacks. As Baird Callicott notes, environmental ethics requires some objective source of intrinsic value to counter the danger of seeing nature in terms either of subjective human preferences or of economistic "resource value." While the source of intrinsic value need not be theistic, the injunction to value what God values is especially powerful. In stewardship ethics, as Callicott puts it, God steps in as a "disinterested valuer" to fill an "axiological void" (Callicott, 1994: 21). Belief in God also helps environmental ethics resolve the dilemma of moral reciprocity posed by ecological holism or egalitarianism. If people are "plain members and citizens" of the biotic community, then why do other members not have the same responsibilities as humans? Why should we not hold elephants responsible for deforestation, cats for endangering songbird species? In stewardship and natural law ethics, human uniqueness provides a "moral asymmetry" that solves the problem. Other species have value, but not the same ultimate value or, crucially, the same responsibilities as humans (Callicott, 1994: 22).

From a practical perspective, stewardship models also provide a helpful understanding of humanity's real power and capacity for harm. Secular environmental ethics often emphasize human continuity with and dependence upon other life forms, which may be realistic in light of evolutionary theory but fail to take account of humans' real capacity for destruction. As Callicott argues, a stewardship ethic "powerfully speaks to the present condition of the relationships of human beings to nature" (Callicott, 1994: 23). Christian eco-theologians have made the same point: "Human power has assumed a frighteningly new responsibility," Ruether writes. "The capacity to be the agents of destruction of the earth also means that we must learn how to be its co-creators *before* such destruction becomes terminal" (Ruether, 1992: 86). Ruether draws on the traditional Roman Catholic optimism about human capacity to be God's co-creators but also emphasizes, along the lines of stewardship ethics, that our special powers and privileges must be restrained.

Other eco-theologians, including Berry and McFague, also strive to retain a special place for humans while insisting that power carries responsibility and that we must redefine human rights and duties in the light of ecological and theological dependencies. These approaches emphasize the centrality of theological anthropology to the appeal of stewardship models. Not only do they acknowledge human distinctiveness, but they also admit human weakness and ambivalence. Stewardship models acknowledge, first, that human beings have needs that require us to use and consume nature. They do not ask people to become completely innocent in their dealings with nature. Second, stewardship provides not only guidelines for using nature but also a reason for following these guidelines: the demands of a personal relationship with God. Failure to follow these guidelines requires repentance and humility, enforced by the divine will that is the ultimate source of value for both humans and the nonhuman world.

The main practical difficulty with stewardship ethics, as Callicott puts it, is that they require belief in a transcendent God. Clearly this diminishes their credibility for those who do not believe in the Bible and/or Christian (or Jewish or Muslim) doctrine. Callicott tries to resolve the practical problem by eliminating God, or, as he puts it, "purging" Jewish and Christian stewardship ethics of their "literal elements" (Callicott, 1994: 23). Callicott appreciates the practical efficacy of stewardship ethics, in other words, but wants them without their associated theology. However, purging God from a theological ethic is neither simple nor inconsequential. The purged ethic will neither look the same nor, crucially, act the same—i.e., it may not provide convincing motivation to non-believers. Like any religious ethic, stewardship works to the extent that it does precisely because of its "literal" elements. Without these elements, especially without God, we are left with an "axiological void," as Callicott himself acknowledges.

Callicott's dilemma reflects the problematic relationship that many philosophers have with religious ethics, insofar as they seek to understand them as a subset of philosophical ethics. This approach makes literal elements, such as belief in God or convictions about salvation, accidental to the system of beliefs and values. Religious ethics, however, do not constitute "isolated systems of moral reasoning," as Robin Lovin and Frank Reynolds write. Rather, they are "integrated into a complex cultural whole that includes both moral beliefs and beliefs about reality."

We cannot, therefore, "isolate moral propositions for analysis apart from propositions about how things are in the world and how they came to be that way" (Lovin and Reynolds, 1985: 3, 4). Ideas about God are crucial to theistic models of the world. This is true especially for models of nature, which depend heavily on accounts of divine intention in creation. Thus one of the key strengths of stewardship models also emerges as an obstacle to generalizing them to a secular audience.

CONCLUSION

Lynn White's 1967 essay is often read as an unqualified attack upon Christianity. In fact, however, White argues that at the same time the roots of our ecological crisis are religious, so the solution must also, in some sense, be religious. In other words, White saw Christianity as a powerful and unavoidable influence on environmental attitudes, which in the past has had largely negative consequences but which also holds the possibility—embodied for him in St. Francis—of a positive response to ecological crisis. The value of Francis as an environmentalist role model lies in his respect for the "spiritual autonomy" of all aspects of nature (1967: 1207). Contemporary Christian eco-theologians strive to affirm this autonomy—what philosophers term the intrinsic value of non-human nature—while also maintaining the Christian insistence upon human distinctiveness.

Stewardship and natural law ethics seek to hold these values in tension by granting a special place to humans while also limiting human power in response to God's ultimate lordship over all of creation, human and other. These models retain a degree of human-centeredness that make them unacceptable to many biocentric and ecocentric environmental philosophers and activists. However, as even some secular thinkers have argued, stewardship and other moderate, religiously based ethics may be more practicable and compelling to many people than other approaches (Callicott, 1994; see also Oelschlaeger, 1994). Many people, even in the contemporary West, continue to understand themselves and their place in the world on the basis of religious, and especially Christian, ideas and values. Thus Christian environmental ethicists need to illuminate resources in their tradition that can help us, as White put it, "to rethink and refeel our nature and destiny" (White, 1967: 1207). The distinctive task facing Christian eco-theology points, further, to a more general challenge for environmental ethics: to theorize the ways that understandings of humans' "nature and destiny" shape attitudes to and behavior in the natural world.

NOTES

1. The second ("Jahwist") creation account in Genesis (beginning at 2:18) does not celebrate human lordship so clearly. Callicott argues that in this account, "man is neither essentially different from other animals nor separated from them by a metaphysical gulf" (Callicott, 1994: 17). This version of creation is both less well known and less influential, at least within Christianity, than Genesis 1.

2. It is worth noting that Christianity never confuses the body of a chimp or tree with a mere outside cover. It does not see non-humans seen as spirits trapped in physical shells but rather "reduces" them to their bodies, as it also does to women. The problem, as McFague recognizes despite her confusing parenthetical clause, lies in seeing bodiliness as a "reduction" in the first place.

3. Doceticism was an early Christian movement that played a central role in the Christological controversies of the first few centuries. Doceticism insisted that Jesus was not fully human; rather, God "adopted" a human body merely as a shell or covering. Eventually another Christological model—which saw Jesus as "fully God, fully human"—won and was enshrined by ecumenical councils and official theologies.

4. This approach has affinities with an "organic" vision of the world as active, changing, perhaps even conscious that has influenced a number of Protestant thinkers, including Sallie McFague and many process theologians. Some of these authors are also influenced by the "Gaia" hypothesis, first proposed by James Lovelock and Lynn Margulis, which views the Earth itself as a conscious organism.

5. More concisely, Jung quotes a note he has posted in his bathroom: "You are not absolutely, irrevocably, personally responsible for everything. That's my job. Love, God" (19).

REFERENCES

Augustine, *City of God, Volume I* (J. M. Dent & Sons, London, 1945a).

Augustine, *City of God, Volume II* (J. M. Dent & Sons, London, 1945b).

Berry, Thomas, *The Dream of the Earth* (Sierra Club Books, San Francisco, CA, 1990).

Brown, Warren, Nancey Murphy, and H. Newton Malony (eds.), *Whatever Happened to the Soul? Scientific and Theological Portraits of Human Nature* (Fortress Press, Minneapolis, MN, 1998).

Callicott, J. Baird, *Earth's Insights: Multicultural Environmental Ethics from the Mediterranean Basin to the Australian Outback*. (University of California Press, Berkeley, CA, 1994).

Hefner, Philip, *The Human Factor: Evolution, Culture, and Religion* (Fortress Press, Minneapolis, MN, 1993).

Hessel, Dieter, 1992. *Nature's Revolt: Eco-Justice and Theology* (Fortress Press, Minneapolis, MN, 1992).

John Paul II, "Redemptor Hominis," in Michael Walsh and Brian Davies (eds.), *Proclaiming Justice and Peace: Papal Documents from* Rerum Novarum *through* Centesimus Annus (Twenty-Third Publications, Mystic, CT, 1991 [1980]).

Jung, L. Shannon, *We Are Home* (Paulist Press, New York, 1993).

Kaufman, Gordon, "The Concept of Nature: A Problem for Theology," *Harvard Theological Review* 65 (1972), 337–366.

Kehm, George H., "The New Story: Redemption as Fulfillment of Creation," in Dieter Hessel (ed.), *After Nature's Revolt: Eco-Justice and Theology* (Fortress Press, Minneapolis, MN, 1992).

Laitin, David D., "Religion, Political Culture, and the Weberian Tradition," *World Politics* 30(4) (July 1978), 563–592.

LeBlanc, Jill, "Eco-Thomism," *Environmental Ethics* 21(3) (Fall 1999), 293–306.

Leopold, Aldo, *A Sand County Almanac, With Essays on Conservation from Round River* (Oxford University Press, Oxford, 1966).

Lovin, Robin and Frank Reynolds (eds.), *Cosmogony and Ethical Order* (University of Chicago Press, Chicago, IL, 1985).

Luther, Martin, *Martin Luther: Selections from his Writings*. Edited by John Dillenberger (Anchor Books, New York, 1961).

McFague, Sallie, *God's Body: An Ecological Theology* (Fortress Press, Minneapolis, MN, 1993).

Nasr, Seyyed Hossein, "Islam and the Environmental Crisis," in Steven C. Rockefeller and John C. Elder (eds.), *Spirit and Nature: Why the Environment is a Religious Issue*. (Beacon Press, Boston, MA, 1992).

Niebuhr, Reinhold, *Moral Man and Immoral Society* (Charles Scribner's Sons, New York, 1960).

Niebuhr, Reinhold, *The Nature and Destiny of Man: A Christian Interpretation. Volume I: Human Nature* (Charles Scribner's Sons, New York, 1964).

Northcott, Michael, *The Environment and Christian Ethics* (Cambridge University Press, Cambridge, 1996).

Oelschlaeger, Max, *Caring for Creation: An Ecumenical Approach to the Environmental Crisis* (Yale University Press, New Haven, CT).

Rich, Adrienne, *Of Woman Born: Motherhood as Experience and Institution* (Bantam, New York, 1976).

Rich, Adrienne, *On Lies, Secrets, and Silence: Selected Prose, 1966–1978* (Norton, New York, 1979).

Rolston, Holmes III, "Wildlife and Wildlands: A Christian Perspective," in Dieter Hessel (ed.), *After Nature's Revolt: Eco-Justice and Theology* (Fortress Press, Minneapolis, MN, 1992).

Ruether, Rosemary Radford, *Gaia & God: An Ecofeminist Theology of Earth Healing* (Harper Collins, New York, 1992).

Santmire, Paul, *The Travail of Nature: The Ambiguous Ecological Promise of Christian Theology* (Fortress Press, Minneapolis, MN, 1985).

Santmire, Paul, "Healing the Protestant Mind: Beyond the Theology of Human Dominion," in Dieter Hessel (ed.), *After Nature's Revolt: Eco-Justice and Theology* (Fortress Press, Minneapolis, 1992).

Second Vatican Council, "Gaudium et Spes," in Michael Walsh and Brian Davies (eds.), *Proclaiming Justice and Peace: Papal Documents from* Rerum Novarum *through* Centesimus Annus (Twenty-Third Publications, Mystic, CT, 1991 [1965]).

Teilhard de Chardin, Pierre, *The Phenomenon of Man* (Harper & Row, New York, 1959).

Thomas Aquinas, *Introduction to St. Thomas Aquinas: The Summa Theologica, The Summa Contra Gentiles* (Edited by Anton C. Pegis) (Modern Library, New York, 1948).

Welch, Sharon, *A Feminist Ethic of Risk* (Fortress Press, Minneapolis, MN, 1991).

White, Lynn Jr., "The Historic Roots of Our Ecologic Crisis," *Science* 155 (10 March 1967), 1203–1207.

An Ecological Christology
Does Christianity Have It?

SALLIE MCFAGUE

ECOLOGICAL CHRISTOLOGIES

THIRTY YEARS AGO WHEN LYNN WHITE, IN A now-famous essay, accused Christianity of being ecologically bankrupt, he revealed an ignorance of theological history.[1] To be sure, for the last few centuries Christianity's celebrated "turn to the self" has meant a neglect of nature and, as liberation theologians have pointed out, millions of oppressed human beings as well. But it was not always so. From the earliest days of Christianity, the cosmological context was a major interpretive category along with the psychological and the political.[2]

The renewal of creation, the salvation of the individual, and the liberation of the people were all seen as necessary components of the work of God in Christ. The cosmological context—the assertion that the Redeemer is the Creator—is deeply rooted in Hebrew faith and surfaces in John's incarnational Christology, Paul's cosmic Christ, Irenaeus's notion of Christ recapitulating all of creation, as well as in sacramental motifs in Augustine and Thomas. Christianity is not entirely anthropocentric, although it was substantially so from the Enlightenment until recently and therein lies the justification for White's indictment.

Since Christology is the heart of Christianity, we must ask whether Christology can be ecological. This question cannot be answered simply by citing Christianity's cosmological roots. What creation meant in the first or third or twelfth century cannot serve as an answer to the question, how can Christians act responsibly toward nature in the twenty-first century?

Jesus' enigmatic question to Peter, "Who do you say that I am?" must be answered differently in every age. Is there an ecological answer? This is not a frivolous question; in fact, it is one of the central questions that recent theologians have tried to answer, and it is one that cannot be avoided. To be a Christian is to deal with Jesus; Jesus is, for Christians, Emmanuel, God with us. Hence, current issues of oppression needing God's saving grace provide the contexts for christological interpretation. In our time ecology is one such important context. Christologies written since White's essay appeared thirty years ago acknowledge this context and reveal a wealth of ecological potential.

A typology of some of these Christologies includes the following motifs: prophetic, wisdom, sacramental, eschatological, process, and liberation. While a theologian's Christology might embrace several motifs, a typology can only lift up the ecological assets and limitations of each. Thus, like all typologies, it will be artificial, but it can at least suggest the rich ecological potential of contemporary Christologies.

Prophetic or covenantal Christologies focus on Jesus' ministry to the oppressed—his inheritance of Hebraic concerns with justice, evident in his parables overturning conventional hierarchies, in his healings to the suffering, and in his practice of eating with outcasts. Jesus is paradigmatic of a way of life that ends on the cross, since the rights of the oppressed will usually be opposed by the powerful. For the disciples who practice this way, life will be cruciform, characterized by justice for the oppressed and limitations on the oppressor.

This Christology is easily extended to nature: nature is the "new poor"; nature deserves justice; other life-forms have rights that must be acknowledged; human beings are in a covenantal relationship with God to protect nature even as they should care for other human beings.[3] The ecological value of

McFague, Sallie, "An Ecological Christology: Does Christianity Have It?" in Dieter T. Hessel and Rosemary Radford Ruether, Eds., *Christianity and Ecology: Seeking the Well-Being of the Earth and Humans*, Cambridge, Mass.: Harvard University Press, 2000, pp. 29–45. Reprinted by permission of the Center for the Study of World Religions, Harvard Divinity School.

prophetic Christologies is the insistence that Jesus' message of justice is relevant to nature: other life-forms are not means to our ends, but like human subjects, have intrinsic worth and should be considered as deserving ethical consideration. Prophetic Christologies provide a firm base for extending *rights* to other life-forms, countering the supposition that sentimental attachment to nature is sufficient. A limitation of this position is its possible deformation toward individualism; for example, emphasis on the rights of particular animals rather than focus on the well-being of an entire ecosystem.

Wisdom Christologies understand Jesus as the embodiment of *Sophia*, God's creative and ordering energy in both the human and natural worlds.[4] Untying Jesus from the Logos tradition, which feminists see as both patriarchal and anthropocentric, and attaching him to the Hebraic Wisdom trajectory allows his work to include nature. As Elizabeth Johnson writes, "As the embodiment of *Sophia* who is fashioner of all that exists, Jesus' redeeming care extends to the flourishing of all creatures and the whole earth itself."[5] A form of incarnationalism, Wisdom Christologies understand the Divine in Jesus (and in his followers) in a natural, everyday way—wherever justice, care, and respect for others, including nature, occur—rather than focusing on "once-for-all sacred deeds in history."[6] The ecological value of this Christology is its turn to the earth, a turn that contemporary Christians profoundly need. The rich textual resources of the Hebrew scriptures for reinterpreting Jesus' work and person in Wisdom rather than Logos imagery has ecological potential for both liturgy and ethics. The considerable assets of this tradition in supporting everyday life point to a limitation: it says little about the cross, a feature of Christology which many of us would rather avoid; but dealing with it, I believe, is integral to Christian faith.

Sacramental Christologies are characterized by divine immanentalism, the incarnation of God in Jesus (and often in the world at large).[7] Whether the form of divine incarnation is the Logos, Wisdom, or the Spirit, the direction of these Christologies is toward immanentalism, overcoming the traditional emphasis in Christianity on divine transcendence—often God-world dualism. These Christologies can see Jesus as the explicit expression of what is implicit everywhere: divine presence. As Gerard Manley Hopkins expresses the sacramental perspective, "The world is charged with the grandeur of God."[8] While a narrow incarnational Christology—Jesus alone as embodying divine presence—is anthropocentric, a wider incarnational interpretation is very hospitable to ecological concerns: God is in nature as well as in Jesus. And all of nature, human beings included, is knit together organically. This wider view was the basis for the oldest Christian affirmation of nature, seen preeminently in Augustine and his love of "light and melody and fragrance and food and embrace" as ways to God.[9]

Incarnationalism affirms the flesh, the body, and hence, by implication, nature. But as we are all well aware, Christianity's extraordinary verbal affirmation of the body—bread and wine as the body and blood of Christ, the resurrection of the body, the church as the body of Christ—has not resulted in appreciation for bodies (especially the female body) or, until recently, great concern for starving, tortured, or raped human bodies. And it certainly has not resulted in a love of nature. Hence, while sacramental Christologies find God in nature, do they respect nature itself? Do they pay attention to the other or do they use it, however subtly, as a way to God?

The three other types of Christology—eschatological, process, and liberation—can be dealt with more briefly, for in significant ways they overlap with prophetic, Wisdom, and sacramental Christologies. However, each of them offers one or more significant notes for an ecological Christology.

Eschatological Christologies, such as those of Jürgen Moltmann and Catherine Keller, underscore renewal and hope: God's Spirit working in Christ recreates, transforms, the entire universe toward reconciliation and peace. As the firstborn of the new creation, the resurrected Christ symbolizes the power of life over death. Nothing, no scrap of creation, will be excluded from this new life: "the body of Christ is the whole cosmos."[10] Eschatological Christologies speak to one of the most difficult issues in ecological praxis: despair. The slow unraveling of the earth's living networks permits human beings to be in a state of denial concerning the seriousness of the deterioration. Those who wake up to reality often experience hopelessness: Can anything be done? The eschatological images of a resurrected creation speak to this despair.

Process Christologies also provide ecological motifs; specifically, those of nature's intrinsic worth and its interrelationship and interdependence.[11] Similar in some respects to sacramental Christologies in their stress on organic unity, process Christologies differentiate the subjects in this unified body more adequately. Process ontology, in which everything, from an atom to God, is both subject and object, understands the intrinsic worth of all beings, including those in the natural world. The process view of the one and the many, of unity and differentiation, is close to the ecological view: unity is characterized by radical individuation in networks of profound interrelationship and interdependence. Process thinking offers a contemporary way to speak of the subjecthood or intrinsic worth of *all* life-forms.

Finally, a word about the contributions to an ecological Christology from the very broad and diverse category called liberation theologies.[12] To a significant degree, most liberation Christologies fall under the prophetic type, focusing as they do on Jesus' ministry to the oppressed and his death as a consequence of this solidarity. Initially, most liberation Christologies were not cosmological; in fact, they were militantly political, concerned with the liberation of oppressed people and often only of people with a particular oppression. But increasingly, liberation theologies have recognized the intrinsic connections between human oppression and nature's oppression.

Leonardo Boff speaks of social ecology as "the study [of] social systems in interaction with ecosystems," acknowledging the way human well-being and nature's well-being are mutually dependent.[13] Or, Chung Hyun Kyung invokes the Spirit through the spirits of all the oppressed, from the murdered "spirit of the Amazon rainforest" to the spirits of exploited women and indigenous peoples, victims of the Holocaust and of Hiroshima, as well as Hagar, Jephthah's daughter, Malcolm X, Oscar Romero, and all other life-forms, human and non-human, that, like "the Liberator, our brother Jesus," have been tortured and killed for greed and through hate.[14] Thus, recent liberation theologies make an essential contribution to an ecological Christology: the intrinsic connection between all forms of oppression, and especially between that of poor people and degraded nature.

From our brief overview of recent Christologies, we can appreciate the ecological potential they offer. Specifically, the following points emerge as needed dimensions of an ecological Christology: the insistence on justice to the oppressed, including nature, and the realization that solidarity with the oppressed will result in cruciform living for the affluent; the need to turn to the earth, respecting it and caring for it in local, ordinary, mundane ways; the recognition that God is with us, embodied not only in Jesus of Nazareth but in all of nature, thus uniting all creation and sanctifying bodily life; the promise that includes the entire cosmos and speaks to our ecological despair; the appreciation of the intrinsic worth of all life-forms, not just of human beings; and, finally, acknowledgment that human salvation or well-being and nature's health are intrinsically connected.

AN ECOLOGICAL CHRISTOLOGY: PROPHETIC AND SACRAMENTAL PRAXIS

Can these various motifs be united into an ecological Christology? I am sure there are many ways they might be; I will attempt just one. Needless to say, my attempt will be from my own context as a white, North American, middle-class feminist. Its limitations and partiality will be obvious.

Before turning to this Christology, we need to ask about the urgency of answering the christological question from an ecological perspective. Edward Schillebeeckx helps us with this issue when he suggests that the way to pose the christological question today is not "Who do you say that I am?" but "How have you been committed to the reign of God?" [15] Most contemporary Christians do not know what it means to be committed to the reign of God when it comes to nature. Nature has not been a central Christian concern for several hundred years. In order to have a Christian praxis toward nature—a nature-oriented commitment to the reign of God—we will need to look at Jesus, at Christology, but also at contemporary knowledges about nature. If Christian nature praxis is the goal of the christological question, then we need guidance from both Christology and ecological science. The rest of this essay will be concerned with these matters: we will see how Christology might guide our praxis and we will then turn to "a hole in the center," our lack of acquaintance with how nature works.

My attempt at an ecological Christology can be summarized by the phrase "God with us." I will try to unpack this phrase in several stages of increasing detail. An ecological Christology means that *God* is with us—we are dealing with the power and love of the universe; it means that God is *with* us—on our side, desiring justice and health and fulfillment for us; it means that God is with *us*—all of us, all people and all other life-forms, but especially those who do not have justice, health, or fulfillment. The ecological Christology would then be very "high" and very "low": it will acknowledge that in Jesus we see the presence of God, and that God's presence is embodied, paradigmatically, in a mere human being. However, such a Christology, centered as it is on God's presence with all of us, is not Jesusolatry: Jesus is the finger pointing to the moon.

An ecological Christology summarized by the phrase "God with us" focuses on the ministry of Jesus of Nazareth for the *content* of our praxis toward nature and on the incarnation and resurrection for its *range* and *promise*. What is a Christian nature praxis? How inclusive is it? Can we practice it without despair?

Prophetic Christology

The first question is answered in the prophetic ministry of Jesus and his death on a cross. While there is little in Jesus' teachings about nature (and it is futile to rummage about with fig trees and hens, trying to make Jesus into a nature-lover), his ministry to the oppressed can be extended to nature. His parables, which overturn conventional human hierarchies, should include the hierarchy of humans over nature; his healing stories can be extended to the deteriorating ecosystems of our planet; his practice of eating with outcasts is pertinent to the extinction of species and loss of habitats due to human overdevelopment and consumption.

Who are the oppressed to whom Jesus' message of hope and renewal is preached? The answer has changed over the centuries. The circle has widened to include among the poor those suffering because of their gender, race, sexual orientation, or physical and mental challenges. The inclusion of nature as the "new poor" may seem sentimental or even ludicrous from an anthropocentric perspective, but it does not seem so from either a theocentric or a cosmocentric point of view. If the Redeemer is the Creator, then surely God cares also for the other 99 percent of creation, not just for the 1 percent (actually, less than 1 percent) that humans constitute.

Hence, I am suggesting that all the language about justice, rights, care, and concern that Christians believe the human neighbor, especially the oppressed neighbor, deserves should be extended to the natural world. What this will mean in practice is complex, varied, and costly, just as love for the needy neighbor is. But the *principle* that Jesus' ministry is focused on God's oppressed creatures must, in our day, include the deteriorating planet.

To say that Jesus' ministry to the oppressed should be extended to nature suggests a similar extension of the Great Commandments. We are told to love God and neighbor as "subjects," as valuable in and for themselves, as ends rather than means, but we are given no instructions concerning nature. Should we not extend that model—the model of loving others as having intrinsic worth and hence deserving of justice and care—to the natural world?

Jesus' ministry to the oppressed resulted in his death on a cross. Solidarity with the oppressed is likely to end this way, as many of his loyal disciples over the centuries have discovered. This suggests a theology of the cross: reality has a cruciform shape. Jesus did not invent the idea that from death comes new life. We see it in nature; for instance, in the "nurse" logs on the ground in old-growth forests which, in their decaying state, provide warmth and nutrients for new saplings. Some must give that others might live. Raising the cruciform shape of reality as the central principle for human living is Jesus' contribution.

But it is not easy to live this way, especially for the well-to-do. Cruciform living has particular relevance to today's affluent Christians, whether of the first or third worlds, in regard to their praxis toward nature. Our consumer culture defines the "abundant life" as one in which "natural resources" are sacrificed for human profit and pleasure and "human resources" are the employees who will work for the lowest wages. Both nature and poor people are means to the end of consumerism. The World Council of Churches in several of its recent publications has stated that it is crucial to redefine the abundant life in terms that recognize the limits of our planet, that encourage sustainable communities, that embrace a philosophy of "enoughness."[16] For affluent Christians this should mean a different understanding of abundance, one which embraces the contradiction of the cross: giving up one's life to find it, limitation and diminishment, sharing and giving—indeed, sacrifice. This sacrifice is summed up in Charles Birch's pithy statement: "The rich must live more simply that the poor may simply live."[17]

Sacramental Christology

"God with us" also suggests the range and promise of divine concern. In the discussion of prophetic Christology we considered what it meant ecologically to say God with us; now we consider the inclusivity of justice for and care of nature, as well as the possibility of such inclusion. In sacramental Christology we move from the anthropological to the metaphysical: from the human Jesus and his distinctive ministry and death to issues of divine scope and power. This metaphysical move is necessary because Christology is not just about a prophet, even a unique prophet, but about *God*. This move avoids Jesusolatry and anti-Judaism. It means salvation is not just for me or for humans, but for all of creation; it gives hope for the well-being of all. In other words, sacramental Christology underscores that it is God who we are dealing with (and who is dealing with us) and that this God cares for the entire creation. And since God is with us, we need not despair of the outcome. We are, then, concerned here with the incarnation and the resurrection, with the embodiment of God in creation as well as the hope of a new creation.

The incarnation is a crucial feature of an ecological Christology for two reasons: inclusion and embodiment. By bringing God into the realm of the body, of matter, nature is included within the divine reach. This inclusion, however, is possible only if incarnation is understood in a broad, not a narrow, fashion; that is, if Jesus as the incarnate Logos, Wisdom, or Spirit of God is paradigmatic of what is evident everywhere else as well.[18] In other words, nature, not just Jesus, is the sacrament of God; the entire creation is *imago Dei,* as Thomas Aquinas suggests when he claims that the whole panorama of creation is needed to reflect the divine glory.[19] The scope of God's power and love is cosmological. It must include every scrap of creation: atoms and newts, black holes and elephants, giant redwoods and dinosaurs. Otherwise, God would not be God. The logic of divinity pushes to the limits; a God of history is a lesser God than the God of nature, since human history is embraced within nature. Christianity has expressed this inclusivity with the phrase "the cosmic Christ."

In addition to inclusivity, incarnational Christology underscores embodiment. The tradition has expressed this in John's phrase "the Word became flesh." But often, Logos Christologies are narrow, validating only Jesus' flesh. Recent Spirit and Wisdom Christologies widen the range: both can include other life-forms—the Spirit of God can dwell in spirits other than human ones, and Wisdom makes her home in creation.[20] Incarnational Christology valorizes matter; moreover, it focuses the justice and care of the prophetic dimension of Christology on physical needs and well-being.

Incarnational Christology means that salvation is neither solely human nor spiritual. It must be for the entire creation, and it must address what makes different creatures and ecosystems flourish. Incarnational Christology says that God wants all of nature, human beings and all other entities, to enjoy well-being in body and spirit. Incarnational Christology, then, expands the ministry and death of Jesus, the model for Christians of "God with us," to envelop the entire universe. The metaphysical dimension of Christology is its big bang, exploding that gram of matter to the limits to the universe.

Sacramental Christology adds one more crucial note to an ecological Christology: hope. There are few contemporary issues that engender more despair than ecological deterioration: climate change, the extinction of species and habitats, clear-cutting of old-growth forests, the pollution of streams and lakes—the problems are overwhelming, seemingly infinite, and deeply saddening. To be sure, many people deny that there is ecological decay because they fear the costly personal and commercial changes that are necessary to reverse it. But others, even those who feel ready to live in a cruciform way so that other people and creatures can survive, feel despair over the immensity and complexity of environmental issues. Needless to say, the resurrection will not solve our ecological crisis; it will not tell us what to do with regard to either small or large problems.

But it can give us hope. Whatever else the resurrection might mean, it certainly symbolizes the triumph of life over death. As Dante knew a long time ago when he wrote *The Divine Comedy,* Christianity is not a tragic vision. The resurrection claims, as a woman in labor knows, that new life is hard. It is usually preceded by diminishment and pain; it sometimes involves death. But it is a sign of hope. Christians see the resurrection of Christ as the first day of the new creation. His resurrection is emblematic of the power of God on the side of life and its fulfillment. We are not alone as we struggle for the planet's well-being: God is on our side.

In summary, an ecological Christology, characterized by the prophetic and the sacramental, claims that "God is with us." This Christology looks Godward through Jesus: Jesus is the model for Christians of what "God with us" means. God is with us in Jesus' particular ministry of justice and care as well as in his death, which gives us a pattern for cruciform living. God is also with us through inclusive divine embodiment, valorizing physical well-being as well as divine victory over the powers of death and despair. Both of these dimensions—the prophetic and the sacramental—are necessary in an ecological Christology. The one tells us how to live with nature; the other informs us that all of nature and nature's renewal is within divine love and power.[21] Together, they suggest an ecological Christology summarized by "God with us." The focus of this Christology is not on Jesus except as the lens through whom we see God. Hope for our world lies not only in what Jesus tells us to do, but also, and more deeply, in Christian belief that God is with us as we attempt to do it.

A HOLE IN THE CENTER: IS CHRISTOLOGY ENOUGH?

For the past several hundred years, Christians have not had a practice of loving nature; we have not practiced justice toward nature, nor cared for it. We have lacked a well-informed, respectful, unsentimental concern for nature similar to that which we have tried to develop toward other human beings. There is a hole in the center of Christianity's environmental ethic, and it is not a theological or christological hole. It is a hole created by centuries of indifference, ignorance, and destruction of nature. Christians need to become reacquainted with nature at all levels: local, regional, planetary. We need to learn about the natural world by taking care of houseplants; working to create city parks; fighting environmental racism; and informing ourselves about climate change, soil degradation, deforestation, and sustainability.

The task now is to embody in praxis the ecological Christologies that have been developing over the last several decades. Further refining Christology is less critical than putting Christology into practice. The problem is not that we need to know more Christology; rather, we need to know more about nature and how to live out these Christologies in relation to nature.

The benchmark draft of the Earth Charter, which is presently being hammered out as nature's "civil rights," makes this point repeatedly in its list of principles: Respect Earth and all life; Care for Earth, protecting and restoring it; Live sustainably; Share equitably between rich and poor, and so on.[22] In order to follow these principles, we must know what helps different life-forms flourish, how the health of human beings and nature's health are interrelated, what sustainability involves in different bioregions, how economics interfaces with ecology, what limits and reductions are required of wealthy individuals and nations so that poorer ones can have a fair share. In other words, Christians need to become "ecologically literate" in order to embody an ecological Christology appropriately and justly.

Ecological literacy means learning how our planet works. "Ecology," or words about the *oikos,* the house called Earth, is the study of how living things are related to one another and to their environment. This study results in some "house rules," a few of which are so essential that they ought to be stuck on everyone's refrigerator.

The first and most essential rule is "There is no free lunch," or, more eloquently, the second law of thermodynamics. This law says that whenever anything changes (moves, heats up, cools down), it uses energy and this energy dissipates in quality, through the quantity remains the same. For instance, when wood is burned to cook meals or heat homes, it dissipates into the atmosphere as carbon dioxide. This gas is a less usable form of energy than wood; it cannot be recycled; and in order for human beings to have the benefit of this energy, something must pay for it—in this case, trees.

The implications of the second law are self-evident: in order for the elites of the world to have the abundant life, consumer-style, which depends on burning vast amounts of fossil fuels, nature must pay, and it pays dearly. As one commentator puts it, "The device by which an organism maintains itself at a fairly high level of orderliness really consists in continually sucking orderliness from its environment."[23] If that "organism" is over five billion human beings, most of whom yearn for a high-energy-use life-style, the house rule becomes alarmingly important: No free lunch.

Nature is not the only one that pays; the poor also do. Since energy resources on the planet are limited, those with power will be able to steer a disproportionate percentage of the resources their own way. Thus, nature and the poor will tend to suffer at similar rates. If we want a barometer of how nature and the poor are faring on our planet, we should look at the representative human being of the twenty-first century: a poor, third world woman of color who lives at the juncture of human poverty and nature's poverty, often reduced to gathering the few remaining sticks of wood to cook her family's meal. The elites of the world mask both ecological and social injustice, for they (we) have the power to suck large amounts of energy out of nature as well as deprive poorer human beings of their fair share of energy.

The second law of thermodynamics, then, is an illustration of one necessary bit of knowledge Christians need in order to put an ecological Christology into practice. It tells us that we live on a planet with finite energy sources; if we use these finite resources in nonsustainable ways, we will destroy nature as well as deal unjustly with other human beings. The second law raises ecological, economic, and justice issues: Who benefits? Who pays?

These issues can be illustrated using the example of climate change—a hot topic in every sense of the word. Ecological and economic knowledge, the consumer life-style, corporate profits, the degradation of nature, injustice to poor people: all come together in this complex, highly contentious, and potentially devastating problem. In order to respond justly and with care to the changing climate, and to understand the full reality of the problem, Christians need to study the 1995 Report of the Intergovernmental Panel on Climate Change. In the report, twenty-five hundred of the world's top weather experts state that human influence on the world's warming trend is now discernible, that temperatures will rise significantly over the next century, and that the effects, especially on third world and low-lying countries, will be devastating.[24]

Big business and others who do not want to control rampant consumerism question the report, claiming that "some scientists" disagree. Yet, the IPCC report was passed by the twenty-five hundred scientists with no dissenting or minority report. And, the findings of the IPCC are based on greater scientific certitude than were the Montreal Protocols, which the world's nations adopted in order to reduce ozone depletion. While scientific predictions of a matter as complex as weather can never be absolute, the "precautionary principle" advises us, as it did with the ozone issue, to act now. Climate change challenges the fossil fuel industry, as well as America's love affair with the car. Hence, denial and resistance are high.

The climate change case calls Christology into immediate practice. For affluent Christians, it demands a different view of the abundant life, one that includes cruciform living, the practice of restraint, diminishment, the death of unlimited desire, and control of ecological selfishness.[25] Ecological Christology defines sin as the refusal to share the necessities of life with others, both other humans and other life-forms. Sin is insatiable greed, wanting to have it all. Acting justly toward nature and other human beings demands sacrifices from Christian elites. Sustainable living involves acceptance of finite limits, such as how we drive our cars, emissions controls, and carbon taxes on industry. It includes "free trade," the policies of the World Bank, and stock market investments as they affect the natural world and poor people. When we see where Christology, economics, and ecology intersect on an issue such as climate change, the need for different practices at personal, professional, national, and global levels becomes apparent.

The incarnate Christ joins the prophetic Jesus in underscoring this point. The God who is with *all* of creation, especially the poor, has a word of judgment about climate change, unlike President Clinton's painless policy, which will "create a wealth of new opportunities for entrepreneurs. . . ."[26] As an editorial in the *New York Times* summed it up, "innovation, incentives and the free market can get the job done without serious economic turmoil."[27] An incarnational Christology takes a dimmer view: too little and too late for a country with 5 percent of the world's population, 22 percent of its wealth, and 25 percent of its emissions. The impact on other people, especially third world populations, and on nature itself is not considered by Clinton's statement or the *Times's* editorial. An incarnational Christology announces divine concern as planet-wide and judges harshly those who have contributed most to its present deterioration. Christians need to respond from a christological position that will indeed be painful to practice.

Finally, Christology also provides a word of hope in dismal times. Christians believe not only in the prophetic and incarnate God, but also in divine renewal, in the possibility of a new creation. Belief in the resurrection helps Christians overcome denial and despair on an issue such as climate change. Denial comes not only from ecological selfishness, but also from ignorance over what to do and feelings of hopelessness about results. Becoming ecologically literate overcomes ignorance, but not despair. How can we keep from burning out on an issue such as climate change, when the government, Wall Street, and consumer-oriented citizens want to do as little as possible?

Ezekiel's valley of the dry bones, one of scriptures's most haunting and lovely resurrection texts, makes a suggestion. When God leads Ezekiel to the valley and asks him, "Mortal, can these bones live?" Ezekiel answers (with, one imagines, a bit of despair), "O Lord God, you know." God then undertakes a second creation story, forming sinews, flesh, and skin onto dry bones, bringing life out of death, but God does not do it alone, as in the first creation story. Now God has two helpers: a human being and nature. Ezekiel is the mediator of God's word, told by God to prophesy to the bones, which he does and they come together, bone to bone, forming a whole being. The body, however, is still dead—there is no breath in it. So God calls on a second helper, nature, the "four winds," to supply the breath. Then the new beings become alive and stand up. The power of life can override the reality of death with the help of God's partners, human beings and nature itself. The passage says that with God all things are possible, even the reconstitution of dry bones.

In my mind's eye I see huge mounds of elephant bones, remnants of the ivory trade; the spindly remains of an old-growth forest after a clear-cutting; and the visible skeleton of a starving child. Can they also live? Those who trust in the God of creation and re-creation, the God of the resurrection, answer, Yes—even these dry bones can live. But, remembering the cruciform reality of Christian life, we must add, only if we, as partners of God, turn from ecological selfishness and live a *different* abundant life.

NOTES

1. Lynn White, Jr., "The Historical Roots of Our Ecologic Crisis," *Science* 155 (10 March 1967): 1203–7.

2. For a brief treatment of these categories, see George S. Hendry, *Theology of Nature* (Philadelphia: Westminster Press, 1980), chap. 1.

3. Christologies with prophetic motifs include those of Rosemary Radford Ruether, H. Paul Santmire, James A. Nash, and Larry L. Rasmussen.

4. Outstanding work on Wisdom Christologies has been done by Elisabeth Schüssler Fiorenza and Elizabeth A. Johnson.

5. Elizabeth A. Johnson, "Wisdom Was Made Flesh and Pitched Her Tent among Us," in *Reconstructing the Christ Symbol,* ed. Mary Anne Stevens (New York: Paulist Press, 1993), 113.

6. Ibid., 97.

7. The wide range of sacramental Christologies includes the disparate ones of Pierre Teilhard de Chardin, Karl Rahner, Matthew Fox, Carter Heyward, Brian Swimme and Thomas Berry, and Eastern Orthodoxy.

8. *A Gerard Manley Hopkins Reader,* ed. John Hick (New York: Oxford University Press, 1953), 13.

9. Augustine, *The Confessions of St. Augustine,* bks. 1–10, trans. F. J. Sheed (New York: Sheed and Ward, 1942), 10.6.

10. Jürgen Moltmann, *The Way of Jesus Christ: Christology in Messianic Dimensions,* trans. Margaret Kohl (San Francisco: HarperCollins, 1990), 275. Elsewhere he writes: "Christology can only arrive at its completion at all in a cosmic Christology" (278).

11. Among others, see the Christologies of John Cobb, Jr., Rita Nakashima Brock, Jay McDaniel, and Charles Birch.

12. Even a partial listing of ecologically significant liberation Christologies is not possible. I will simply mention a few theologians whose work in this regard I have found helpful: Leonardo Boff, Dorothee Soelle, Chung Hyun Kyung, Delores Williams, Gustav Gutierres, Ada Maria Isasi-Diaz, Mercy Amba Oduyoye.

13. Leonardo Boff, *Ecology and Liberation: A New Paradigm,* trans. John Cumming (Maryknoll, N.Y.: Orbis Books, 1995), 26.

14. Chung Hyun Kyung, "Welcome the Spirit; Hear

Her Cries: The Holy Spirit, Creation, and the Culture of Life," *Christianity and Crisis* 51 (15 July 1991): 223.

15. As quoted by Elizabeth A. Johnson, *Consider Jesus: Waves of Renewal in Christology* (New York: Crossroad Press, 1991), 62.

16. See, for instance, *Sustainable Growth: A Contradiction in Terms?* (Geneva: Visser 't Hooft Endowment Fund, 1993).

17. In his address to the World Council of Churches' fifth assembly (Nairobi 1975), "Creation, Technology, and Human Survival," reprinted in *Ecumenical Review* 28 (January 1976): 70.

18. Sarah Coakley gives six definitions of incarnation; her first two definitions suggest incarnation as I am using the term. The first definition says that it is characteristic of God to reveal the divine self to humanity; the second definition, that in Jesus God takes a special initiative for the sake of humankind (*Christ without Absolutes: A Study of the Christology of Ernest Troeltsch* [Oxford: Clarendon Press, 1988], 104). I would, however, modify Coakley's object of divine incarnation from humanity to include as well the natural world.

19. "But creatures cannot attain to any perfect likeness of God so long as they are confined to one species of creatures; because, since the cause exceeds the effect in a composite and manifold way. . . . Multiplicity, therefore, and variety, was needful in the creation, to the end that the perfect likeness of God might be found in things according to their measure" (as quoted in Arthor O. Lovejoy, *The Great Chain of Being: A Study of the History of an Idea* [Cambridge, Mass.: Harvard University Press, 1936], 76).

20. As Moltmann says, "Logos Christology is originally Wisdom Christology and is as such cosmic Christology" (*The Way of Jesus,* 282). For Spirit, see chap. 5 of my book, *The Body of God: An Ecological Theology* (Minneapolis: Fortress Press, 1993).

21. The prophetic and the sacramental as critical to environmental ethics are mentioned in different ways by both Rosemary Radford Ruether and Elizabeth A. Johnson. Ruether's treatment occurs as "The Covenantal Tradition" and "The Sacramental Tradition" in *Gaia and God: An Ecofeminist Theology of Earth Healing* (San Francisco: HarperSanFrancisco, 1992). Johnson compares covenantal and sacramental ecological ethics to orthodox Christologies in *Consider Jesus,* 70: the ascending, historical, salvation history, from below (covenantal) and the descending, metaphysical, incarnational, from above (sacramental).

22. "The Earth Charter: Benchmark Draft," *Earth Ethics* 8 (winter/spring 1997): 1–3. These principles carry through into Benchmark Draft II of the Earth Charter, April 1999.

23. As quoted in lan Barbour, *Issues in Science and Religion* (Englewood Cliffs, N.J.: Prentice-Hall, 1966), 319.

24. IPCC, Second Assessment Report of the Intergovernmental Panel on Climate Change, Geneva, 1995.

25. Fore more information on climate change and a Christian analysis of it, see the new booklet from the World Council of Churches, "Climate Change and the Quest for Sustainable Societies" (Geneva: WCC, 1988). Fax: +41-22 791 0361; E-Mail: mpt@wcc-coe.org.

26. *New York Times,* 23 October 1997, sec. A14.

27. Ibid., sec. A20.

The World of the Icon and Creation

An Orthodox Perspective on Ecology and Pneumatology

JOHN CHRYSSAVGIS

THEOLOGY AND MYSTERY

ANY DISCUSSION OF THE BEAUTY OR SACREDNESS of the world, at least from an Orthodox perspective, necessarily involves an exploration into the theology and mystery of the icon, that is to say, into the doctrine behind and the vision beyond icons. For the world of the icon not only presupposes a way of thinking and demands a way of living, but it also offers new insights into our worldview, new perceptions of the world around us, and something of the eternal in everything we see. Our generation is char-

Chryssavgis, John, "The World of the Icon and Creation: An Orthodox Perspective on Ecology and Pneumatology" in Dieter T. Hessel and Rosemary Radford Ruether, Eds., *Christianity and Ecology: Seeking the Well-Being of Earth and Humans,* Cambridge, Mass.: Harvard University Press, 2000, pp. 83–96. Reprinted by permission of the Center for the Study of World Religions, Harvard Divinity School.

acterized by behavior that results from an autism with regard to the natural cosmos: a certain lack of awareness, or recognition, causes us to use, even waste, the beauty of the world. And so we are locked inside the confines of our own concerns, with no access to the outside world. We have disestablished a continuity between ourselves and the outside, with no possibility for intimate communion and mutual enhancement. The world of the icon restores this relationship by reminding us what is outside and beyond, what ultimately gives value and vitality.

The iconographer aspires to achieve the inner vision of the world, an image of the world as intended by God. The "iconic" world, however, is not an unreal world; rather, it is the real world which is called to ingress upon, and to spill over into, this world. Orthodox iconography seeks to discover and then to disclose the reality of the experience of the heavenly kingdom in this world. In fact, the icon articulates with theological conviction the faith in this kingdom and its activity in the earthly realm. Unfortunately, we have desacralized, or denaturalized, this world by disconnecting it from "heaven." The icon reverses perspective as we know it and does away with the "objective" distance between this world and the next. There is no double order in creation. There is no sharp line of demarcation between "material" and "spiritual." The icon constitutes the epiphany of God in the world and the existence of the world in the presence of God. It is neither idealism nor idolatry. Like the unborn child in the womb of its mother, the icon presents to us the visible seeds of the divinity in the world. Its art and beauty represent God's art and beauty in the creation. The icon speaks in this world, yet in the language of the age to come.

The icon is an integral part of Orthodox spirituality, a central aspect of the celebration of creation. Like the Incarnation and the Creation, the icon is meant to be the piercing of space and time, that is, matter is met by God's eternal nature. The entire church building—with its architecture, frescoes, and mosaics—accomplishes through space and matter what the liturgy does through time and praise: the anticipation of the heavenly kingdom and the participation of the divine presence. The seeming contradiction of an inaccessible God and a crucified Christ constitutes the ultimate measure of God's measureless love for the world. For it is God's freedom that makes God's limitless love so powerful that it breaks all barriers and all limitations. The God who created out of love, who was incarnated out of love, now saturates the whole world with divine energies.

The icon reveals all the tensions, conflicts, and contradictions through which one is called to transparency; every fall is inscribed on it. But there is ultimately resurrection through communion, for to encounter Christ in the icon is to encounter an image beyond suffering, solitude, and hell, an image that will never die. Therefore, the basis of the icon is christological, allowing the wholly inaccessible to be shared entirely. With the event of the Incarnation, as with the epiphany of the icon, the cycle of the non-representation of the Old Testament God (cf. Exod. 20:4–5 and John 1:18) is completed.

"God became human that humanity might be deified," wrote the Christian fathers.[1] The saints are those who emanate the light of deified humanity, while icons indicate the participation of humanity and the entire created world in divine life and light. As a result, faces of saints in icons are always frontal, "all eyes" (Bessarion), transparent, susceptive of divine energy.[2] I see someone also means I am seen, and therefore I am in communion.

CREATOR AND CREATION

Since the doctrine of the divine Incarnation is at the heart of iconography, what is being represented is God's affirmation and assumption of the world. In color and on wood, the icon proclaims "God was made flesh" (John 1:14). In his work entitled *On Divine Images,* John of Damascus, the eighth-century champion of icons, claims, "I do not adore creation in place of the creator, but I worship the One who became a creature."[3] And since it is through matter that "God has worked out our salvation,"[4] there is an appropriate honor due to material things. I would argue that it is this sense of the salvific power of matter that we have lost today and which we need to rediscover. As John of Damascus writes: "Because of the Incarnation, I salute all remaining matter with reverence."

In the Western High Middle Ages, the "image of God" in the human person was identified with rational nature, deemed superior to the rest of creation. Such an individualistic view of humanity has contributed greatly to the rise of our ecological problems. In the Greek fathers' view, however, the "image of God" in humanity lay in its specific value of freedom. The human person must be associated with, and not dissociated from, the created world, for it is through the human person that the created world must be transformed and offered to God. And so the world is freed from its natural limitations and becomes a bearer of life. In the words of Metropolitan John (Zizioulas) of Pergamon:

> We believe that in doing this "in Christ" we, like Christ, act as priests of creation. When we receive these elements back, after having referred them to God, we believe that because of this reference to God we can take them back and consume them no longer as death but as life. Creation acquires for us in this way a sacredness which is not inherent in its nature but "acquired" in and through Man's free exercise of his *imago Dei,* i.e. his personhood. This distinguishes our attitude from all forms of paganism, and attaches to the human being an awesome responsibility for the survival of God's creation.[5]

This view of the priestly or parapriestly character of the human person was in earlier times acknowledged by Leontius of Cyprus (seventh century):

> Through heaven and earth and sea, through wood and stone, through relics and Church buildings and the Cross, through angels and people, through all creation visible and invisible, I offer veneration and honor to the Creator and Master and Maker of all things, and to him alone. For the creation does not venerate the Maker directly and by itself, but it is through me that the heavens declare the glory of God, through me the moon worships God, through me the stars glorify him, through me the waters and showers of rain, the dew and all creation, venerate God and give him glory.[6]

Thus, an entire anthropology and cosmology are given artistic shape and utterance in the icon. This is why the two main events for Orthodox iconography are the Incarnation and the Transfiguration. The first reforms what was "originally" deformed through sin and grants to the world the possibility of sanctification. The second realizes the consequences of divinization and grants to the world a foretaste even now of the beauty and light of the last times. We are, in this world, placed at a point of intersection between the present age and the future age, uniting the two as one. In his perceptive book, *The Sacred in Life and Art,* Philip Sherrard claims that the art of the icon presents holy personages

> ready to convert the beholder from his restricted and limited point of view to the full view of their spiritual vision. For the art of the icon is ultimately so to transform the person who moves towards it that he no longer opposes the worlds of eternity and time, of spirit and matter, of the Divine and the human, but sees them united in one Reality, in that ageless image-bearing light in which all things live, move, and have their being.[7]

THE LIGHT THAT KNOWS NO EVENING

The light of an icon is an uncreated, sanctifying light, a light that is not of this world and knows no evening. Perspective is abolished, history is telescoped, and proportion is altered. The icon bears witness to a "different way of life."[8] This life and light are shed from the Risen body of Christ and reveal the joy of the Resurrection.

The value of the icon is not pedagogical or aesthetic, but mystical or "sacramental." It surpasses any opposition between this world and the next, uniting the two in an act of communion. It also transcends any opposition between figurative or nonfigurative art and appears instead as transfigurative. The icon presupposes and even proposes another means of communication, beyond the conceptual, written, or spoken word. It is the articulation of what cannot be expressed in theology.

"IN THE IMAGE AND LIKENESS OF GOD"

The human person, too, is an icon. Created in the image of God, humanity is also a living image of the created universe. The church fathers see humanity as existing on two levels simultaneously—on the level of the spiritual and on the level of material creation. The human person is characterized by paradoxical dualities: humanity is limited yet free, animal yet personal, individual yet social, created yet creative. To attempt escaping this fundamental tension within humanity would be to undermine the Christian doctrine of humanity created "in the image and likeness of God" (Gen. 1:26) and as the image of Jesus Christ who is at once human and divine. A human being, says Gregory the Theologian (fourth century), is like "another universe,"[9] standing at the center of creation, midway between strength and frailty, greatness and lowliness. Humanity is the meeting point of all the created order. The idea of the human person as a bridge, a point of contact and union, is developed as early as the seventh century by the lay monk Maximus Confessor.[10] As an image of the world, the human person constitutes a microcosm. Another monastic writer, Nilus of Ancyra (fifth century), makes this point very clearly:

> You are a world within a world. . . . Look within yourself and there you will see the entire world.[11]

The world in its entirety forms part of the liturgy of heaven. Or, as we have already seen, the world constitutes a cosmic liturgy. God is praised by the trees and the birds, glorified by the stars and the moon (see Ps. 18:2), worshiped by the sea and the sand. There is a dimension of art, music, and beauty in the world. And the very existence of material creation constitutes a revelation of God (Eph. 4:6), awaiting its liberation through the children of God (Rom. 8:19). The world, then, becomes the clearest, albeit the most silent and inconspicuous, sermon declaring the word of God, a sign of the kingdom of heaven, the bridal chamber (Ps. 18), where God can touch the work of creation in the most intimate manner.

When Orthodox Christians enter a church, they bow down before the altar, reverence the holy icons, bow to the minister, and lower their heads at certain points of the liturgy. After receiving the Sacrament of the Eucharist, however, they depart bowing to none, for their conviction is that the life of the world and the heart of the Church are at that moment seeded and seated deeply inside their own heart. When one is initiated into the mystery of the Resurrection and transformed by the light of the Transfiguration, then one understands the purpose for which God has created all things.[12] The world is rendered as a gift—a gift received from, and returned to, God. The climax of the Orthodox Liturgy is found in the words: "Your own from your own we offer to you, in all and through all."

Someone who sees the whole world as an icon experiences from this world the realities of the future and final resurrection. That person has already entered the life of resurrection and eternity. John Climacus, the abbot at St. Catherine's Monastery on Mt. Sinai, was convinced that, in the very beauty and beyond the shattered image of this world:

> such a person always perceives everything in the light of the Creator God, and has therefore acquired immortality before the ultimate resurrection.[13]

There is a sense in which this person is indicating and anticipating here and now the transfiguration of the world. The result is a prefiguration of the restored image of the world, a configuration in this world of uncreated and created elements.

THE ICON AS COMMUNION

When the Russian monk St. Andrei Rublev (ca. 1360–1430) painted his masterpiece *The Holy Trinity*—which depicts the Old Testament narrative of the three angels who visited Abraham and Sarah (Gen. 18:1–33), sometimes also known as "the hospitality of Abraham"—he was in fact representing the open communion of the triune Godhead, a love that is showered upon the face of the earth and in the hearts of people. The Rublev icon is an image of what the Trinity is: a celebration and communication of life. This is why there is an empty or open place at the table of communion. The three persons of the Trinity are seated on three of the four sides of the rectangular table, allowing for, or rather inviting, the world to communion. Indeed, the very contours of their bodies create and reproduce in macro-image the communion chalice about which these angels are seated.[14] The potential sacredness of the world is more than a mere possibility; it is a vocation.

THE IMAGE OF CHRIST

There is no thing, no place, no time, and no person that escapes, or is excluded from, the comprehensive love of Christ (John 1:9). For Christ is God's categorical affirmation and assumption of the whole world. And there is, as a result, no condition, no tragedy, no experience outside the embrace of Christ. To be an imitator of Christ is to be assimilated to him. One can then walk on Earth as Christ and in the authority of Christ: "For it is not I who lives but Christ lives in me" (Gal. 2:20).

The Christ dimension is also suggested in Orthodox icons of the enthroned Jesus, particularly in the truly magnificent mosaic of the late thirteenth century which still survives in the Constantinopolitan monastery of Chora (later known as the Kariye Cami). The icon of Christ over the door to the nave is entitled "The land [χώρα] of the living." The same notion of the resurrection of the dead or newness of life is envisaged in our personal spiritual life through the dynamic stage of for-give-ness (συγ-χώρη-σις), which implies a death to self and "allowing room for others," making space (χώρα) for the rest of the world, giving up of the self, and opening up in communion and acts of giving and givenness. Nothing and no one is excluded. Symeon the New Theologian poetically describes this cohabitation, or co-indwelling, of Christ in the world:

> You make of all Your home and dwelling-place;
> You become a home to all, and we dwell in You.[15]

Everything therefore assumes a Christ dimension; everything is in some way sacramental. All depends on the receptiveness and openness of our hearts. By the same token, everything is rendered unique, inasmuch as it has its particular place and meaning. Nothing is secular or profane; nothing is pagan or foreign.[16] Indeed, if God were not visibly present in the material creation, then we could not properly worship him as invisible. Were God not tangibly accessible in the very earthliness of this world, then he would not be the loving, albeit transcendent author of the universe. This is surely the implication of the basis of the Christian faith, namely, that "the Word assumed [or became] flesh" (John 1:16), which we all too often, in a reductionist manner, take to mean "became human." Yet, the early Christian writers categorically stated that "what God did not assume, God did not heal."[17] What God did not reach out and touch, did not come down and sanctify, cannot possibly be related to or loved by God. And unless Christ may be discovered "in the least of his brethren" (Matt. 25:40) and in the least particle of matter, then he is too distant to matter. There is a wonderful saying attributed to Jesus, which expresses the reality of his presence everywhere:

> Lift up the stone, and there you will find me;
> cleave the wood, and I am there.[18]

Matter is not merely an object for our possession and exploitation. The earth has not only economic but also moral and sacramental value. For "the earth and all its fullness" (Ps. 23:1) is a bearer of God, a place of encounter with Christ, the very center of our salvation. In the words of Leonardo Boff:

> All things are sacraments when viewed in God's perspective and light. The word, human beings, and things are signs and symbols of the transcendent.[19]

THEOLOGY IN COLOR

The theological statement made by the icon is, therefore, threefold:

1. that the world was created good and therefore needs to be loved;
2. that at the Incarnation, Christ assumed a human body, thereby affirming the intrinsic value of the whole created world; and
3. that salvation embraces all of created matter, as well as human body and soul.

The entire world is an icon. The whole of creation constitutes an icon painted before all ages, an image eternally engraved by the unique iconographer of the Word of God, namely, the Holy Spirit. This image is never totally destroyed, never fully effaced. Our aim is simply to reveal this image in the heart and to reflect it in the world. Yet, the image itself, the icon, is indelible, for the world has been forever "sealed with the gift of the Holy Spirit."[20] In our age, green is perhaps most fittingly the color of the Holy Spirit, recalling as it does Greek patristic thought[21] and indicating the renewal of life itself and the revival of all things.

PNEUMATOLOGY AND ECOLOGY

This brings me to emphasize the close connection of pneumatology and ecology. Nature speaks a truth scarcely heard among theologians: the world relates in very tangible terms the spiritual connection between the uncreated and the creation.

Just as the Spirit is the "air" that the whole world breathes, so too the earth is the "ground" which we all share. Were God not present in the density of a city, or in the beauty of a forest, or in the sand of a desert, then God would not be present in heaven either. So if, indeed, there exists today a vision that is able to transcend—perhaps transform—all national and denominational tensions, it may well be that of our environment understood as sacrament of the Spirit. The breath of the Spirit brings out the sacramentality of nature and bestows on it the fragrance of resurrection.

Eastern theological thought has been concerned with the meta-historical or the spiritual dimensions of this world seen in the light of the kingdom of heaven and the liturgical nature of time. Facts and figures are considered in terms of the Holy Spirit; power is understood from the perspective of the Sacrament of the Eucharist; the world around is appreciated in relation to the heavens above. The understanding is that eschatology is not an apocalyptic teaching, the last chapter of the New Testament, or perhaps an unnecessary chapter of a Christian manual of doctrine. Rather, it is the teaching about the "last-ness" and "lasting-ness" of all things.

ASCETIC THEOLOGY

A second characteristic of Orthodox spirituality is the ascetic tradition. The discipline of ascesis is the necessary and critical corrective for the excess of our consumption. We have learned all too well and only too painfully that the ecological crisis both presupposes and builds upon the economic injustice in the world. Ascesis is a reality of the spiritual life because it is the reassurance of our difficult and painful struggle to relate our theology to the world, our justice and our economy to the poor.

Ascesis is not primarily an achievement, but an attitude of attendance to and expectation of the Spirit. Hence, once again, the liturgical aspect of ascesis is a continual invocation (epiclesis) of the Paraclete. As one Orthodox theologian puts it: "we are called not just to do something, but simply to stand there." Ascesis is not another or a better way of acting; it is, in fact, a way of inaction, of stillness, of vigilance. We are called to remember that the present ecological crisis is a result precisely of our action—of considerable human effort and success to "change" or "better" the world—and not only of our greed or covetousness. The primary cause of our devastation and destruction is the relentless pursuit of what many people consider a good or desirable thing—namely, the modern, industrial-technological model of development. Yet, this "developmental" ideology has not created a sustainable world for everyone; it has encouraged exploitation and an unsustainable world.

Ascesis means allowing room for the Spirit, for an action beyond our action. It means "leaving space" (lit., "for-give-ness" or *syn-chore-sis*). The patristic term *peri-chore-sis* has the same root etymologically as *syn-choresis: synchoresis* includes the aspect of reconciliation, while *perichoresis* includes the dimension of joy and celebration toward nature for the sake of future generations. When we reduce the spiritual or religious life to ourselves (to *our* concerns, to *our* needs, and to *our* interests), then we forget the calling of the Church to implore God—always and everywhere—for the salvation of the whole polluted cosmos, to the least of our brothers and sisters, and to the last speck of dust in the universe.

It is always alarming to see how easily the term "spirituality" is used without reference to the Spirit which is the giver of all gifts. The Greek patristic tradition does not even have an equivalent term for spirituality, preferring rather to speak about the action of the Holy Spirit in the world. It is not always clear in contemporary theological writings if the Spirit is anything more than just certain abstract nouns—love, justice, peace, or perhaps green peace—with capital letters. The Spirit, of course, "blows where it wills" (John 3:8), as Christ confided to one of his friends on a rooftop. We only know of the Spirit what we may experience on a rooftop on a hot summer's day with a cool breeze blowing: we know that we are touched, that we are refreshed, and that our clothes move a little. The Spirit is only known in contact and in communion with our environment.

The distinction between the "Spirit of God" and the "Spirit of Creation" was one that early Christian ascetics experienced in their very bodies, in their intense struggle to maintain the interdependence of body and soul. The Spirit is indeed the "giver of life" and of all forms of life. It penetrates and permeates the world and cannot be conceived apart from this world. Yet, if the Spirit and the earth are *conformed*, or confused, then the Church is no longer called to *transform* the world; then the Spirit itself ceases to be something that is promised, and becomes something that is compromised. This is why the patristic tradition underlined that the divine Spirit is at once known and unknown, both seen and unseen, revealed and veiled alike. Such is the conviction of Symeon the New Theologian and of Gregory Palamas. Such is the depth of the distinction between divine essence and divine energy. In his treatise *On Divine Names,* Dionysius the Areopagite describes the divinity as *en-cosmic,* as *peri-cosmic,* and as *hyper-cosmic.*[22]

APOPHATIC THEOLOGY

This brings me to a third characteristic of Orthodox theology, the close connection between theology and poetry, between "ascetics" and "aesthetics." Often, our theology does not have sufficient poetry. There has undoubtedly occurred an unfortunate shift in emphasis: from God to man, from body to soul, from theological symbolism to mathematical analysis. Yet, in the tradition of the Orthodox, certainly the greatest and most acclaimed of theologians were also poets: John the Divine, Gregory of Nazianzus, and Symeon the New Theologian. There is always much more to be said than can ever be expressed. This is why the emphasis in the East is on the apophatic dimension of all theological talk and thought. I believe that this apophatic dimension is wonderfully, indeed "naturally," fostered in creation. The breadth and beauty of this earth is a reflection of the boundlessness and splendor of divine grace; and our respect toward the environment results in a parallel allowance for the surprising abyss of God. Our admiration for creation reflects our adoration of the absolute, a vocation to the beyond, an invitation to transfiguration.

Apophasis is an element of *askesis;* the silence of poetry is a form of surrender to the living God; it is like dying to the flesh in order to live fully in the Spirit. Silence and death go hand in hand; to be utterly silent can feel like death. Silence and ascesis issue in resurrection and new life through the Spirit.

CONCLUSION

If, indeed, there is a Spirit of God, and it is the very Spirit of Creation; if this world is the Body of God, the actual flesh of the divine Word; if, in fact, the Spirit of God reveals the Image of God in creation, beyond the brokenness and shatteredness of this world; then there is a sense in which this earth is not merely a reflection,[23] but even a perfection of heaven. Just as we are incomplete without the rest of the animal and the material creation, so, too, the kingdom of God remains incomplete without the world around us.

NOTES

1. See Athanasius *On the Divine Incarnation* 54.

2. Bessarion, saying 11, in *Sayings of the Desert Fathers,* trans. Benedicta Ward (London: A. R. Mowbray, 1975), 35. Reference to "all eyes" is also found in Barsanuphius *Letters* 120 and 241.

3. John of Damascus *On Divine Images* 1.4.

4. Ibid., 16.

5. "Preserving God's Creation," *King's Theological Review* (London) 13, no. 1 (1990): 5. See also the first two parts of this illuminating article in vol. 12, no. 1–2 (1989): 1–5 and 41–45. These articles have, with additional material and editorial changes, appeared in a book published in Greek, entitled *The Creation as Eucharist* (Athens: Akritas, 1992).

6. See *Apologetic Sermon 3 . . . on the Holy Icons* (Migne *PG* 93.1604ab).

7. Philip Sherrard, *The Sacred in Life and Art* (Ipswich, England: Golgonooza Press, 1990), 84.

8. From the Resurrection Canon chanted at Easter Matins.

9. Gregory the Theologian *Homily* 38.11 (Migne *PG* 36.321–24).

10. Maximus Confessor *De Ambiguis* 91. See also his *Mystagogia* 7 (Migne *PG* 91.672).

11. Nilus of Ancyra *Epistles* 2.119 (Migne *PG* 79:252b). See also Origen *Homily on Leviticus* 5.2 (Migne *PG* 12.448–50). See also D. S. Wallace-Hadrill, *The Greek Patristic View of Nature* (Manchester: Manchester University Press, 1968), especially 66–79.

12. See Maximus Confessor *Gnostic Chapters* 1.66 (Migne *PG* 90.1108ab). On the priestly character of humanity, see Kallistos Ware, "The Value of the Material Creation," *Sobornost* (London) 6, no. 3 (1971): 154–65.

13. John Climacus *The Ladder of Divine Ascent, Step 4,* 58 (Migne *PG* 88.892d–893a).

14. For a detailed description of selected icons, including that by Rublev of the Trinity, see Paul Evdokimov, *The Art of the Icon: A Theology of Beauty,* trans. Fr. Steven Bigham (Redondo Beach, Calif.: Oakwood Publications, 1990). About the icon of Rublev, Pavel Florensky once exclaimed: "there is Rublev's *Trinity,* therefore there is God." See V. V. Bychkov, *The Aesthetic Face of Being* (Crestwood, N.Y.: St. Vladimir's Seminary Press, 1993), 42.

15. Symeon the New Theologian *Hymn* 15.132–33. As with the concept of "sophia," so also the notion of "chora" may equally be applied to the Virgin Mary (cf. the Akathistos Hymn, Stasis 1: She "contained [*choresasa*] the One who contains [*chorei*] the universe"). On

the relationship between liturgy, iconography, and creation, see the articles in *Orthodoxy and Ecology: Resource Book* (Bialystok: Syndesmos, 1996), 72–81.

16. See Leonardo Boff, *Sacraments of Life—Life of Sacraments* (Washington, D.C.: Pastoral Press, 1987), 49–51.

17. Gregory Nazianzus *Letter 101 to Cleidonius* (Migne *PG* 37.181c).

18. In Joachim Jeremias, *Unknown Sayings of Jesus*, trans. Reginald H. Fuller (London: SPCK, 1957), 95.

19. Boff, *Sacraments*, 38. Pierre Teilhard de Chardin wrote in similar fashion echoing Maximus Confessor's image of the "cosmic liturgy." See Teilhard, *Mass on the World*, in *Hymn of the Universe*, trans. G. Vann (New York: Harper and Row, 1972), 16: "Once again the fire has penetrated the earth . . . the flame has lit up the whole world from within."

20. From the Service of the Sacrament of Baptism in the Orthodox Church.

21. See Dionysius the Areopagite *Celestial Hierarchy* 15.7 (Migne *PG* 3.336bc).

22. Dionysius the Areopagite *On Divine Names* 1.6 (Migne *PG* 3.596) and 13.1–2 (Migne *PG* 3.977); translation mine. For the works of Dionysius, see *Pseudo-Dionysius: The Complete Works*, trans. Colm Luibheid, the Classics of Western Spirituality (New York: Paulist Press, 1987).

23. This is a significant point of divergence between Christian theology and Platonist philosophy. The Hellenistic conception of the created world as a "mirror," or "image," of the eternal realm is a privilege as well as a problem in terms of the value and sacredness of creation. Perhaps this is also the reason for the "ambivalence" of the patristic texts themselves, which will sometimes underline the creation of this world by a loving God while at other times undermine the intimate connection between the Creator and the creation. The result is an apparent paradox between a "monarchical" theology and its consequential "dualistic" anthropology and cosmology to which Sallie McFague and others rightly react.

The Three Big Questions

CALVIN DEWITT

CAN CHRISTIANITY PROVIDE AN EFFECTIVE response to the need for human care of creation? It depends on the answers we give to the big questions. These are the three big questions we must ask in this global crisis if we confess that Christ is the Creator and the Great Integrator and Reconciler of all things.

1. Is Jesus Christ Lord of Creation?
2. Is creation a lost cause?
3. Whom are we following when we follow Jesus Christ?

QUESTION 1: IS JESUS CHRIST LORD OF CREATION?

Through Jesus Christ, God created the world, holds everything together, and reconciles all things (Col. 1:15–20). Followers of Jesus Christ have known this remarkable teaching of Colossians from the beginning. The depth and significance of this passage are there for all to see.

> [Christ] is the image of the invisible God, the firstborn over all creation. For by him all things were created: things in heaven and on earth, visible and invisible, . . . all things were created by him and for him. He is before all things, and in him all things hold together. And he is the head of the body, the church; he is the beginning and the firstborn from among the dead, so that in everything he might have the supremacy. For God was pleased to have all his fullness dwell in him, and through him to reconcile to himself all things, whether things on earth or things in heaven, by making peace through his blood, shed on the cross.

DeWitt, Calvin B., "The Three Big Questions" in *Caring for Creation: Responsible Stewardship of God's Handiwork*, (Grand Rapids, Mich.: Baker Books, 1998), pp. 35–47. Reprinted by permission. "The Three Big Questions" was the 1996 Kuyper Lecture sponsored by The Center for Public Justice.

We observe three things about this passage of Scripture. First, Christ is the Creator of all things (*ta panta*), the Author of all things. Not only did he create all things but all things were created for him. Second, in Christ all things (*ta panta*) hold together. Everything derives its integrity from Christ, and without him things would fall apart. Christ is Sustainer and Integrator of all things. Third, God reconciles all things (*ta panta*) to himself through Christ by making peace through his blood, shed on the cross. So Christ is Reconciler and Harmonizer of all things.

The Scriptures make it clear that the claims of Jesus Christ on the world are comprehensive. It is the claim made by the one who made the world, holds the world together, and reconciles the world. The comprehensive claims of Jesus Christ on the world derive from his being its Author, Integrator, and Harmonizer.

Second Corinthians 5:15 takes us further in our understanding of the consequences of this claim of Jesus Christ on the world. There it states that "he died for all, that those who live should no longer live for themselves but for him who died for them and was raised again." This has a remarkable consequence: namely, that living in Christ, we no longer regard Christ or anyone else from a worldly point of view. In Christ we are a new creation and live as his ambassadors, committed to the message of reconciliation (2 Cor. 5:16–20).

What, then, does it mean to be Christ's ambassadors? It is inconceivable that those who are in Christ and who themselves have been made new creatures should find themselves in opposition to Christ's work of creation, integration, and reconciliation. Can we honor our Creator without respecting his creation? Can we honor our Creator and despise his magnificent works? Can we thank God for loving the world and not care about it?

My purpose in all of this is to help enlarge our understanding of the lordship of Jesus Christ so we appreciate that Jesus Christ is Creator, Sustainer, and Reconciler. My conclusion is this: Jesus Christ *is* Beautiful Savior, but more than that, Jesus Christ *is* King of Creation. Have we dismembered our Creator into Savior on the one hand and Maker of the material world on the other? Have we separated the spiritual from the material? Are we treating the great gallery of our Creator in a way that expresses our love and respect for our Triune God?

QUESTION 2: IS CREATION A LOST CAUSE?

Because of the degradation human beings have brought across the face of the earth, we are *tempted* to ask whether creation is a lost cause. I use the word *tempted* here deliberately, for it is in fact a temptation to consider giving up on creation altogether, and many have done so. The temptation that entices us is this: that we should live as best we can for now and pin our hopes on the life to come. Yielding to this temptation may bring us to a position where we do not care about the material world at all. We would profess not only that matter does not matter but that matter in the material world is ugly, perhaps even evil.

It is devastating to ourselves and to God's world when we yield to this temptation. We should be put on guard by the warning of Revelation 11:18, where in the last judgment, following the sounding of the seventh trumpet, the proclamation is made that "the time has come for . . . destroying those who destroy the earth." On the positive side, there is God's love for the world, God's love for the cosmos, a love so great that God takes on material flesh. There is also the powerful taking on again of the flesh in Christ's resurrection. So we must not yield to this temptation, since to God incarnate, matter matters!

Abraham Kuyper has a contribution to make here. It comes by way of an exposition he gave in 1903 of John 3:16 ("For God so loved the world") over half a century before our recognition of a crisis, even before any popular understanding of ecology or "the environment."

> So God loved the world, that He gave it His Only-begotten Son . . . . God loves *the world*. Of course not in its sinful strivings and unholy motions. . . . But God loves the world for the sake of its origin; because God has thought it out; because God has created it; because God has *maintained* it and *maintains* it to this day. We have not made the world, and thus in our sin we have not maltreated an art product of our own. No, the world was the contrivance, the work and the creation *of the Lord our God*. It was and is His world, which belonged to Him, which He had created for His glory, and for which we with that world were by Him appointed. It did not belong to us, but to Him. It was His. And it is *His* divine world that we have spoiled and corrupted.

> And herein roots the love of God, that He will repair and renew this world, His own creation, His own work of wisdom, His own work of art, which we have upset and broken, and polish it again to new luster. And it *shall* come to this. God's plan does not miscarry, and with divine certainty He carries out the counsel of His thoughts. Once that world in a new earth and a new heaven shall stand before God in full glory.
>
> But the children of men meanwhile can fall out of that world. If they will not cease to corrupt His world, God can declare them unworthy of having any longer part in that world, and as once He banished them *from Paradise,* so at the last judgment He will banish them *from this world. . . .*
>
> And therefore whoever would be saved with that world, as God loves it, let him accept the Son, Whom God has given to that world in order to save the world. Let him not continue standing afar off, let him not hesitate.[1]

Clearly, then, creation is not a lost cause. God expresses his eternal love for the world by giving us his Son. Reflecting on this gift in the context of what we have learned from Colossians 1:15–20, we are struck by the fact that God's gift to the world pre-exists the world. God's gift to the world, Jesus Christ, is before all things. Yet he comes in the flesh. The Creator takes on created matter as part of himself. The material creation matters to God.

Beyond the incarnation is the resurrection of Jesus Christ. In it we have the conclusive answer to the question of whether creation is a lost cause. It is through the resurrection in particular that creation is vindicated. Evangelical ethicist Oliver O'Donovan puts it this way:

> We are driven to concentrate on the resurrection as our starting-point because it tells us of God's vindication of his creation, and so of our created life. . . .
>
> The meaning of the resurrection, as Saint Paul presents it, is that it is God's final and decisive word on the life of his creature, Adam. . . . It might have been possible, we could say, before Christ rose from the dead, for someone to wonder whether creation was a lost cause. If the creature consistently acted to uncreate itself, and with itself to uncreate the rest of creation, did this not mean that God's handiwork was flawed beyond hope of repair? It might have been possible before Christ rose from the dead to answer in good faith, Yes. Before God raised Jesus from the dead, the hope that we call "gnostic," the hope for redemption *from* creation rather than for the redemption *of* creation, might have appeared to be the only possible hope. "But in fact Christ has been raised from the dead . . ." (15:20). That fact rules out those other possibilities, for in the second Adam the first is rescued. The deviance of his will, its fateful leaning towards death, has not been allowed to uncreate what God created.[2]

The resurrection of Jesus Christ means that the creation is not a lost cause. Creation is affirmed by its Creator.

We continually confront in the church the devilish temptation to reduce the Lord of Creation to one who merely saves. Under the continuing influence of the Gnosticism that infected the early church, some have reduced God to the one who saves us out of creation. This separation of Savior from Creator goes so far that belief in the Creator is reduced to empty words. As art critics might somehow find it acceptable to trample Rembrandt's paintings while honoring Rembrandt's name, some people praise the Creator while trampling on his creation. Regrettably, some God-praising people have comfortably neglected creation's evangelical testimony[3] and even assist in bringing about creation's degradation.

Saving people "out of creation" is not a biblical idea, of course. Instead, it is rooted in the Platonic notion that physical nature is a source of ignorance and evil and a snare to the soul. When joined with the idea of human transcendence, this resulted in a theology that "laid most stress on the salvation of the *soul,* and which tended to dismiss as insignificant the body and the creation of which it was a part."[4]

QUESTION 3: WHOM ARE WE FOLLOWING WHEN WE FOLLOW JESUS CHRIST?

We sometimes sing, "Christ shall have dominion, over land and sea." Jesus Christ, the Lord of Creation, is our model for dominion, but what is that model? The apostle Paul puts it this way in his letter to the Philippians, 2:5–8: "Your attitude should be the same as that of Christ Jesus, who, being in very nature God, did not consider equality with God something to be grasped, but made himself nothing, taking the very nature of a servant, being made in human likeness. And being found in appearance as a man, he humbled himself and became obedient to death—even death on a cross!"

Jesus Christ, the Son of God, did not consider equality with God something to be grasped. Even more so we, the followers of Jesus Christ, should not view ourselves equal to God or Jesus Christ. Far from being equal with God, we must confess our total dependence upon God in every aspect of our lives and vocations. The example of Jesus Christ, our model of dominion, helps interpret for us the dominion material in Genesis 1:26–28. Taken in the context of the example of Jesus Christ, this passage helps us understand our responsibility toward the Lord's creation. The passage reads as follows (KJV, emphasis mine):

> And God said, Let us make man in our *image,* after our likeness: and let them have *dominion* over the fish of the sea, and over the fowl of the air, and over the cattle, and over all the earth, and over every creeping thing that creepeth upon the earth.
>
> So God created man in his own *image,* in the *image* of God created he him; male and female created he them.
>
> And God blessed them, and God said unto them, Be fruitful, and multiply, and replenish the earth, and *subdue* it: and have *dominion* over the fish of the sea, and over the fowl of the air, and over every living thing that moveth upon the earth.

In this passage, the Hebrew word *radah* is translated "have dominion" (KJV) or "rule" (NIV). An even more forceful word is "subdue," a translation of the Hebrew *kabash.* Without the example of Jesus Christ, one might conclude that this passage suggests "anything goes."[5] However, Jesus Christ brings us to see this dominion as service rather than as a license for ungodly behavior.

It also is clear from the requirements for kings in Deuteronomy 17:18–20 that those to whom God gives dominion must fully reflect God's will in their rule. They must reflect God in the way they relate to their subjects—mirroring, representing, reflecting, and imaging God's will and God's relationship to creation.[6] Thus, God's proclamation through Ezekiel, "Woe to the shepherds of Israel who only take care of themselves! Should not shepherds take care of the flock? You eat the curds . . . but you do not take care of the flock. . . . You have ruled [*radah*] them harshly and brutally" (Ezek. 34:2–4).

The Lord shows by divine example what should be done: "I myself will search for my sheep and look after them. . . . I will pasture them on the mountains of Israel, in the ravines and in all the settlements in the land. . . . I myself will tend my sheep and have them lie down, declares the Sovereign LORD. I will search for the lost and bring back the strays. I will bind up the injured and strengthen the weak, but the sleek and the strong I will destroy. I will shepherd the flock with justice" (Ezek. 34:11, 13, 15–16).

Lest people take the mandate to subdue the earth as a license to serve self rather than God and creation, God judges between those who use creation with care and those who abuse it. "Is it not enough for you to feed on the good pasture? Must you also trample the rest of your pasture with your feet? Is it not enough for you to drink clear water? Must you also muddy the rest with your feet? Must my flock feed on what you have trampled and drink what you have muddied with your feet?" (Ezek. 34: 18–19).

What, then, is dominion in biblical and Christian terms? What does it mean to subdue the earth? It is serving God and creation. It is reflecting God's love for the world, God's law for creation, and God's justice for the land and creatures. Without this responsibility we might have little reason other than pragmatic and utilitarian ones for keeping creation. We might work to save and nurture only what is useful or attractive to us. But as Noah in his obedience to God's will worked to perpetuate the fruitfulness of endangered species, so we must think not only of the animals that Noah kept but of the other creatures as well.

TWO KINDS OF DOMINION

Dominion as domination is forbidden. Dominion as stewardship is required as a God-given responsibility for all people. Human dominion, however, is exercised across a broad spectrum, one end of which is dominion exercised in behalf of self and the other dominion in behalf of creation. Dominion at the first extreme can be called domination; dominion at the other extreme can be called stewardship. More specifically, in relation to creation, domination is service in behalf of self at the expense of creation; stewardship is service to creation in behalf of the Creator. Thus, we can distinguish between two kinds of dominion: domination and stewardship.[7]

Much of Genesis 1–11 is addressed to the wrongness of domination. The scriptural view is that seeking first one's own selfish interests at the expense of creation and its creatures is sinful domination worthy of punishment, even death. Thus, Adam and Eve's pressing into service the forbidden fruit to know good and evil is domination; its consequence is their own death and degradation of the ground. The murdersome domination of Cain over Abel results in Cain being cursed by God, made restless, driven from the land, and the ground no longer yielding crops for him. The corrupting of creation by human society brings with it the deluvian destruction.[8] The rebellious event at Babel, where people "undertook a united and godless effort" to make for themselves "by a titanic human enterprise," a worldwide reputation and renown through which they "would dominate God's creation," results in their scattering across the earth.[9] In scriptural language, domination, defined as seeking first ourselves at the expense of creation, is "missing the mark," it is failing to meet the Creator's expectations for us, it is sin.

The scriptural view is that seeking first to do the will of God with respect to creation is the right exercise of dominion. We have seen from Genesis 1–11 what stewardship is not; from Genesis 2:15 we can learn something of what it is. Here we learn that Adam and his descendants are expected to *serve* and *keep* the garden. The word keep is a translation of the Hebrew word *shamar,* which is also used in the Aaronic blessing given in Numbers 6:24 (emphasis mine): "The LORD bless you and *keep* you," a blessing very widely used in Jewish and Christian congregations to this day.[10]

When we invoke God's blessings to keep the assembled people, we are not praying merely that God would keep them in a kind of preserved, inactive, uninteresting state, like one might keep a museum piece, a preserved specimen, or pickles in a jar, but rather that God would keep them in all their vitality, with all their energy and beauty. This keeping is one that would nurture all life-sustaining and life-fulfilling relationships—with family, spouse, and children, with neighbors and friends, with the land that sustains human life and the living creatures, with the air and water, and with God. *Shamar* is an extremely rich word with a deeply penetrating meaning that evokes a loving, caring, sustaining keeping.

This is also the thrust of Genesis 2:15. When we act on God's will and charge to keep the garden, we make sure that the creatures under our care are maintained with all their proper connections with members of the same species, with the many other species with which they interact, and with the soil and air and water upon which they depend. The rich and full *keeping* that we invoke with the Aaronic blessing is the kind of rich and full keeping that we should bring to the garden of God, to God's creatures, and to all creation. As God keeps those who invoke divine keeping, so those whom God keeps keep creation. Human beings should be engaged in the care and keeping of creation, with all the richness and fullness this implies.[11]

In addition to recognizing the fullness of the meaning of *shamar* in Genesis 2:15, it is also helpful to our understanding of stewardship to attend to the preceding word, *abad.* In *Young's Literal Translation of the Holy Bible* the passage is rendered, "And Jehovah God taketh the man and causeth him to rest in the garden of Eden, to *serve* it and to keep it." Here *serve* is a translation of the word *abad.* For those who have heard this translated "cultivate," "till," or "dress," this may come as a surprise. The word *abad* is also used in another famous passage: "Choose for yourselves this day whom you will serve. . . . But as for me and my household, we will serve the LORD" (Josh. 24:15). A search of the use of *abad* will show that it is translated "serve," as in Joshua 24:15, except when it is applied to agriculture. No matter how one deals with the proper translation of the text, however, whether as translated with agricultural language or literally as "serve," the idea of service comes through clearly.

While serving the garden or serving creation might sound peculiar to modern ears, we might consider what the Garden of Eden consisted of. The Scriptures say that it was planted by God (Gen. 2:8), which makes us wonder how God plants things in creation. In God's garden, hoe, shovel, and plow might simply have been out of place, especially if it was more like the gardens of some tropical peoples, where interplanting and high diversity are the rule. Perhaps it was a tropical garden not amenable to turning over the ground but still open to service. Whatever the case, to understand the meaning of stewardship, one must ponder the meaning of service.

The biblical expectation that human beings will "serve the garden" means that our dressing, tilling, and tending are done as acts of service. With the prefix *con,* this can be applied to indicate "service with," as with the word con-serve. We may take this to mean that as the garden serves us, so we should provide reciprocal service. The biblical expectation, I believe, is con-service. As stewards of a creation, whether our stewardship is over a small garden or the whole biosphere, we are expected to be about the business of con-servancy. Conversely, when human beings fail to serve and instead abuse the garden or creation, they should expect payment back in kind. Intended abuse of creation can have severe consequences, as we know full well. Unintended abuse of the garden can also have severe consequences, but if we are committed to tending the garden, the repercussions of such abuse can be part of our stewardship education. The key to proper service always is to consider our service as Christ's service. Our service should reflect God's love for the world.

When dominion is taken as license to do whatever meets one's self-interest, it is a misappropriation of the image of God, and a failure to follow the example of Jesus Christ. Responsible appropriation of this image is to seek first not self but the kingdom of God. To image God is to image God's love and law. To be made in the image of God is to be endowed with dignified responsibility to reflect God's goodness, righteousness, and holiness. It is to use our intellectual powers, natural affections, and moral freedom to reflect the wisdom, love, and justice of God. It is to commune prayerfully with God through Jesus Christ and to anticipate the ultimate fulfillment of all things in the way we live our lives.

We conclude from all this that human beings are distinct with respect to other species in their exercise of dominion over creation. To the extent that being made in the image of God confers upon human beings what is distinctive with respect to other species, the exercise of dominion is part of the consequence of humans being made in the image of God. Failure to seek God's purposes in creation leads to a perverted and sinful dominion, a domination whose goal is serving self rather than the Creator or creation. The proper exercise of dominion by human beings who seek truly and fully to mirror God's wisdom, love, and justice is stewardship. So human beings should make every attempt to overcome the forces that would compel them to dominate creation, and by diligently seeking creation's integrity, vigorously and prayerfully pursue a life of stewardship with God's kingdom as its goal.

Resorting to the idea of stewardship does not eliminate the symptoms, but rather addresses problems at their roots. People can mislead themselves and each other—through selfish intent, ignorance, or denial—by confusing symptoms with the underlying causes of environmental problems. A sound understanding of the idea of stewardship will help us appreciate the difference.

The biblical imperative, then, is for stewardship in behalf of God's creation no matter what its condition. Christian environmental stewardship is not crisis management but a way of life. God's call to serve and keep the garden is our calling no matter whether it is our vegetable garden or the whole of creation, and no matter if it is being degraded, staying the same, or improving. Caring for creation is much like caring for families—in sickness or health, in riches or poverty, in crisis or harmony. And this caring must be done wisely. Caretakers must be ever aware, alert, and vigilant in a sinful world, alert even to our own sinfulness (Rom. 3:23). We must face squarely the human predicament (Rom. 7:7–25) and also be ready to give a response in word and deed for the faith that is within us (1 Peter 3:15). We need not have all the data, but we must be dedicated to imaging God's love for the world in our lives and landscapes. Responsible stewardship is not an option but a continuing privilege and responsibility.[12]

NOTES

1. Kuyper, "So God Loved the World!" 70–71.

2. Oliver O'Donovan, *Resurrection and Moral Order: An Outline for Evangelical Ethics* (Leicester, England: InterVarsity Press; Grand Rapids: Eerdmans, 1986), 13–14.

3. See Psalm 19:1, Acts 14:17, and Romans 1:20 for passages describing creation's testimony to God. Consider too that creation's telling of God's glory and love is echoed by Scripture. God lovingly provides rains, cyclings of water, and food for the creatures, fills people's hearts with joy, and satisfies the earth (Ps. 104:10–18;

Acts 14:17). It is through this manifest love and wisdom that creation declares God's glory and proclaims the work of the Creator's hands (Ps. 19:1). Creation's evangelical testimony is so powerful that it leaves everyone without excuse (Rom. 1:20).

4. Quote from Loren Wilkinson, ed., *Earthkeeping in the Nineties: Stewardship of Creation* (Grand Rapids: Eerdmans, 1991), 299. For evidence that all Christian thought does not make this unbiblical distinction between the physical and the spiritual and does not espouse a salvation that turns people away from creation, see Wilkinson. *Earthkeeping,* 202–306. For a theological study of the importance of matter and of creation, and of the unbiblical hatred of creation by Marcion and Greek and Gnostic leaders, see Raymond C. Van Leeuwen, "Christ's Resurrection and the Creation's Vindication," in C. B. DeWitt, ed., *The Environment and the Christian: What Can We Learn from the New Testament?* (Grand Rapids: Eerdmans, 1991), 57–71.

5. See "Theology, Science, and Creation: Extending the Horizon of Science and the Christian Faith," *Faculty Dialogue* 1995, no. 24, http://www.idnet.org/pub/facdialogue/24/dewitt24, for other reasons why it cannot be interpreted as "anything goes."

6. Creation here, as elsewhere, must be understood in the biblical sense of comprising all things created, including human beings.

7. For a more detailed treatment, see "Theology, Science, and Creation."

8. For a description of Noah's faithfulness in relation to this, see C. B. DeWitt, "The Price of Gopher Wood," *Faculty Dialogue,* no. 12 (1989): 59–62.

9. This paragraph is based on "Theology, Science, and Creation."

10. This paragraph is based on "Theology, Science, and Creation" and the next two paragraphs are taken from it directly.

11. That "care and keeping" were recognized before our time is evident in a prayer published in 1566: "Finally, O Lord, wilt Thou take us and our dear ones and all that concern us into Thy care and keeping" (from "A Prayer for All the Needs of Christendom," from the *Psalter* by Petrus Dathenus published in translation in the *Psalter Hymnal* [Grand Rapids: Board of Publications of the Christian Reformed Church, 1976], 183). That the connection is made in this prayer with Numbers 6:24 is indicated in its conclusion, which is a recitation of the Aaronic Blessing: "Jehovah bless thee, and keep thee; Jehovah make his face to shine upon thee, and be gracious unto thee; Jehovah lift up his countenance upon thee, and give thee peace. Amen."

12. This paragraph is taken from my piece to be published in the winter 1997 issue of the *Christian Research Journal.*

Discussion Questions

1. What aspects of the Christian tradition best lend themselves to ecological interpretations?
2. Do people reinterpret the meaning of Christ in different times and places? Is constant reinterpretation consistent with an unchanging truth?
3. How can the painting of an icon transform people and nature? Do people and nature need to be transformed?
4. What does it mean for humans to have dominion over the rest of creation?
5. How do beliefs about a separation between spirit and matter affect or inform environmental values?
6. Is Christianity too otherworldly to be ecological? Is a worldly spirituality possible?

Further Reading

Austin, Richard Cartwright, *Hope for the Land: Nature in the Bible,* Atlanta: John Knox Press, 1988.

Barbour, Ian G., Ed., *Earth Might Be Fair: Reflections on Ethics, Religion, and Ecology,* Englewood Cliffs, N.J.: Prentice Hall, 1982.

Birch, Charles, and John B. Cobb Jr., The Liberation of Life: From the Cell to the Community, Cambridge, U.K.: Cambridge University Press, 1981.

Birch, Charles, William Eakin, and Jay McDaniel, Eds., *Liberating Life: Contemporary Approaches to Ecological Theology,* Maryknoll, N.Y.: Orbis Books, 1991.

Breuilly, Elizabeth, and Martin Palmer, Eds., *Christianity and Ecology,* London: Cassell, 1992.

Carmody, John, *Ecology and Religion: Toward a Christian Theology of Nature,* New York: Paulist Press, 1983.

DeWitt, Calvin B., *Caring for Creation: Responsible Stewardship of God's Handiwork,* Grand Rapids, Mich.: Baker Books, 1998.

Elsdon, Ron, *Bent World: A Christian Response to the Environmental Crisis,* Downers Grove, Ill.: InterVarsity Press, 1981.

Fox, Matthew, *The Coming of the Cosmic Christ: The Healing of Mother Earth and the Birth of a Global Renaissance,* San Francisco: Harper, 1988.

Gibson, William E., *Keeping and Healing the Creation,* Louisville, Ky.: Presbyterian Church [U.S.A.], 1989.

Granberg-Michaelson, Wesley, *A Worldly Spirituality: The Call to Take Care of the Earth,* San Francisco: Harper & Row, 1984.

Hall, Douglas John, *The Steward: A Biblical Symbol Come of Age,* rev. ed., Grand Rapids, Mich.: Eerdmans, 1990.

Hargrove, Eugene, Ed., *Religion and Environmental Crisis,* Athens: University of Georgia Press, 1986.

Hart, John, *The Spirit of the Earth: A Theology of the Land,* New York: Paulist Press, 1984.

Haught, John F., *The Promise of Nature: Ecology and Cosmic Purpose,* Mahwah, N.J.: Paulist Press, 1994.

Joransen, Philip N., and Ken Butigan, Eds., *Cry of the Environment: Rebuilding the Christian Creation Tradition,* Santa Fe, N.Mex.: Bear, 1984.

McDaniel, Jay B., *Of God and Pelicans: A Theology of Reverence for Life,* Louisville, Ky.: Westminster/John Knox Press, 1989.

———, *Earth, Sky, Gods, and Mortals: Developing an Ecological Spirituality,* Mystic, Conn.: 23rd Publications, 1990.

Murphy, Charles M., *At Home on Earth: Foundations for a Catholic Ethic of the Environment,* New York: Crossroad, 1989.

Nash, J. A., *Loving Nature: Ecological Integrity and Christian Responsibility,* Nashville, Tenn.: Abingdon Press, 1991.

Northcott, M. S., *The Environment and Christian Ethics.* Cambridge, U.K.: Cambridge University Press, 1996.

Oelschlaeger, Max, *Caring for Creation: An Ecumenical Approach to the Environmental Crisis,* New Haven, Conn.: Yale University Press, 1996.

Ruether, Rosemary Radford, and Dieter Hessel, Eds., *Christianity and Ecology: Seeking the Well-Being of Earth and Humans,* Cambridge, Mass.: Harvard University Press, 2000.

Santmire, H. Paul, *The Travail of Nature: The Ambiguous Ecological Promise of Christian Theology,* Philadelphia: Fortress, 1985.

———, *Nature Reborn: The Ecological and Cosmic Promise of Christian Theology,* Minneapolis: Fortress, 2000.

Skolimowski, Henryk, *A Sacred Place to Dwell: Living With Reverence Upon the Earth,* Rockport, Mass.: Element, 1993.

Squiers, Edwin, Ed., *The Environmental Crisis: The Ethical Dilemma,* Mancelona, Mich.: AuSable Trails Institute of Environmental Studies, 1982.

Wilkinson, Loren, Ed., *Earthkeeping: Christian Stewardship of Natural Resources,* Grand Rapids, Mich.: Eerdmans, 1980.

Chapter 10

Islam

As the third and most recent major Abrahamic tradition, Islam has much in common with Judaism and Christianity. In terms of cosmology, all three traditions situate humans in a privileged position vis-à-vis the rest of creation. Unlike Christianity, however, Islam does not see creation as fallen or in need of redemption. Although nature is to be used for the benefit of humankind, it should not be ruthlessly exploited but rather cultivated through conscientious stewardship. Having originally arisen in a desert environment, Islam has tended to place a high value on "bringing dead lands (as they are erroneously referred to in the literature) to life."

Although historically Islam has focused primarily on the relationship between humans and God, in today's world the environmental crisis affects most Muslims very directly. The overwhelming majority of Muslims live in developing countries, and a large proportion of them are poor. Problems of water supply and quality are widespread, as are the issues of desertification and public health. Most Muslim societies have very high birthrates, and population control has been a very sensitive issue.

The Qur'an carries a strong message of social justice, and Muslims most often see environmental problems as a symptom of social problems rather than as central concerns in their own right. Islam's tradition of social engagement is perhaps its most promising contribution to meeting contemporary environmental challenges, and local grassroots movements are now widespread throughout the Muslim world.

The articulation of an explicitly Islamic environmental ethic, on the other hand, is quite recent and has arisen largely in response to the critique of Christianity launched by Lynn White Jr. several decades ago. It has also been a discussion held primarily among Muslim intellectuals in the industrialized world, although recently this has been changing. At present, it remains to be seen what role, if any, Islamic values will play in addressing the environmental problems faced by more than a billion Muslims in diverse societies throughout the world.

In my own essay, I summarize the themes that contemporary Islamic environmental ethicists have drawn from the Qur'an and *hadith* (reports about the Prophet Muhammad, which are the most extensive source of Islamic norms) traditions. I then ask to what extent these values appear to be present in the lives of Muslims today and to what extent they affect how Muslims treat their environment. I note several areas in which Islamic tradition may actually present obstacles to ecological practice, such as pronatalism, fatalism, and anthropocentrism. Finally, I consider the role of Islamic values in the environmental legislation of several Islamic countries.

Iranian scholar Kaveh L. Afrasiabi, writing from the perspective of the Shi'ite minority (about 20% of the world's Muslims, although in Iran they are the majority), expresses further doubts about the ecological viability of traditional Islam. Afrasiabi points to contradictions in the reasoning of several contemporary Islamic environmental thinkers, focusing especially on the problem of Islamic anthropocentrism. He proposes that a radically new Islamic theology, in which the anthropocentric element is dramatically reduced, will be required if Muslims are to adequately address the environmental crisis we face today.

Muslim feminist Nawal H. Ammar makes the point that Muslims are inclined to frame any discussion of environmental problems in terms of the social justice paradigm that characterizes traditional Islamic thought. Specifically, environmental problems are regarded as the direct result of human injustices. The remedy, from such a perspective, is to establish a just society, from which other benefits (such as a healthy environment) will result. The Islamic feminist critique adds that the establishment of a just society requires the empowerment of women.

Fazlun M. Khalid, director of the Islamic Foundation for Ecology and Environmental Science, evokes the reality that Muslims constitute a disproportionately high percentage of the world's poor and dispossessed. Khalid compares the experiences of two Muslims from very different societies: Ali, a tribesman from the Malaysian island of Borneo, and Maryam, a Tuareg nomad from the African Sahara. Both are representative of communities that have been losers in the game of economic globalization and have been especially hard hit by the ecological degradation of their homelands.

Khalid concludes by relating a number of Qur'anic passages to the current social, economic, and ecological crisis. Within the present context, Khalid suggests, the traditional lifestyles of Ali and Maryam are more ecologically sustainable and more Islamic than those of the dominant world culture that has placed their very existence in jeopardy.

Islamic Environmentalism in Theory and Practice

RICHARD C. FOLTZ

The world is frozen; its name is inanimate, which means "frozen," O master.

Wait till the rising sun of Resurrection that thou mayest see the movement of the world's body.

Since God hath made Man from dust, it behooves thee to recognize the real nature of every particle of the universe,

That while from this aspect they are dead, from that aspect they are living; silent here, but speaking yonder . . .

They all cry, "We are hearing and seeing and responsive, though to you, the uninitiated, we are mute."

Jalal al-Din Rumi (1207–1273)

THE ARABIC TERM *TABI'A*, TYPICALLY RENdered in English as *nature,* was used by medieval Muslim philosophers in the sense of the Greek *physis.* Avicenna wrote that "*tabi'a* is an essential first principle for the essential movement of that in which it is present"; a clearly Aristotelian definition. Another medieval Muslim philosopher, pseudo-Majriti, gives the definition of the physicians: "They apply the term *tabi'a* to humor, natural heat, aspects of

Foltz, Richard C., "Islamic Environmentalism in Theory and Practice." By permission of the author.

the bodily organs, movements, and the vegetative soul."[1] The definition given in the *Treatise* of the Pure Brethren, on the other hand, reflects Neoplatonic notions of emanation: ". . . *tabi'a* is only one of the potentialities of the Universal Soul, a potentiality spreading through all sublunar bodies, flowing through each of their parts."[2] Within the Neoplatonic hierarchy of creation as appropriated by many Muslim philosophers, only humans possessed all three attributes of *tabi'a*, intellect, and desire.[3]

Yet for Muslims, an important qualification is given in the divine revelation of the Holy Qur'an, where one reads, "In whose hand is the dominion of all things" (23:88). In the words of Hossein Nasr, this makes clear that the natural order "is not an independent domain of reality, but that its principle resides in another realm of reality, which is Divine."[4] The Andalusian Muslim Ibn 'Arabi (1165–1240) writes that "there is no property in the cosmos without a divine support and lordly attribute."[5] Ibn 'Arabi found support for his concept of *wahdat al-wujud* or "unity of being" in the Qur'anic verse (2:115) that states, "Whithersoever you turn, there is the Face of God." Although Ibn 'Arabi's monist metaphysics have been enormously influential on the thought of Sufi mystics in particular—especially in South Asia even to the present day—orthodox Islam has tended to reject the doctrine of *wahdat al-wujud* as verging dangerously close to pantheism. In the seventeenth century, Ibn 'Arabi's popularity in India gave rise to a response by the conservative Sufi teacher Shah Waliullah, who attempted to substitute a concept he called *wahdat al-shuhud* or "unity of witness" through which the boundary lines between the Creator and the Creation could be firmly maintained.

The ecological aspects embedded in the treatise entitled *The Case of the Animals versus Man* by a group of tenth-century Muslim philosophers who called themselves the *Ikhwan al-Safa*, or Pure Brethren, were explored by Lenn Evan Goodman more than twenty years ago in a study that remains little noticed but ought to be of considerable interest to environmental philosophers. Goodman points out that this treatise introduces into medieval Islamic philosophy "two of the central notions of the science of ecology, that of the eco-niche and that of succession. Species are adapted each to a particular sector of the environment not by natural selection but by the adjustment of their specific organs and behaviors to the resources and hazards of the environments they inhabit . . . these adjustments are accomplished in the organisms' behalf by divine design. Moreover, the organisms, species by species and kind by kind, form a system in which no organism exists solely for its own sake . . . There is not merely a food chain but a food circle or food circles. The interconnectedness of all the links in this system of cycles creates an ecosystem—a third central concept of ecology."[6] The Pure Brethren's view of the natural world is all the more striking for its exceptionality in the context of tenth-century Muslim society. They were a radical group, as indicated by their choice to remain anonymous; in subsequent centuries, only the heterodox Sevener-Shi'i or Isma'ili sect, identified today with the Aga Khan, adopted their writings as authoritative.

CONTEMPORARY ISLAMIC ENVIRONMENTAL ETHICS

In recent years, a number of Muslim writers, mainly living in the West, have published essays claiming that based on the scriptural sources of the tradition, Islam is an ecologically oriented religion.[7] Whereas the medieval Islamic philosophers, when they addressed issues of the natural world, were concerned primarily with constructing theoretical arguments about justice, contemporary writers tend to articulate Islamic environmental ethics in more practical terms, often by way of response to Lynn White Jr.'s 1967 critique of Western Christianity. Iqtidar Zaidi, for example, is clearly paraphrasing White when he states that the ecological crisis is "a crisis rooted in moral deprivation."[8] Hossein Nasr, in fact, claims to have anticipated White's critique in his own earlier lectures given at the University of Chicago.[9]

It may be useful to restrict the use of the term *Islamic* to what can be derived from the canonical sources of Islam, as opposed to the activities or attitudes of Muslims, which may or may not be directly motivated by those sources. In other words, there is a distinction to be made between *Islamic* environmentalism—that is, an environmentalism that can be demonstrably enjoined by the textual sources of Islam—and *Muslim* environmentalism, which may draw its inspiration from a variety of sources including but not limited to religion.[10] Around the world today, one can find increasing examples of both.

Muslims have always been culturally diverse, and never more so than today, when they number a billion or more and inhabit every corner of the globe. Historically, the one indisputable source of authority that all Muslims have agreed on is the will of Allah as expressed in the revealed scripture of the Qur'an. In addition, the Sunni majority (perhaps 80 percent of all Muslims) accept six collections of reports about the deeds and words of the Prophet Muhammad, called *hadith,* as supplementary sources of authority. Shi'ites agree with some but not all of these reports and have compiled collections of their own.

Islamic environmentalists today have therefore attempted to derive an environmental ethic based on the Qur'an and the *hadith,* giving comparatively little attention to possible cultural contributions from the various societies in which Muslims live. This is because local or regional attitudes cannot form a basis for any kind of universal Islamic ethic, because they are almost invariably perceived by Islamists as accretions, and therefore un-Islamic. For example, at the Harvard conference on Islam and Ecology in May 1998, an anthropologist's presentation depicting the survival of an age-old river festival in Bangladesh as a positive sign of the rural Bengali Muslims' continuing sense of connectedness with the river, elicited angry accusations from Muslims in the audience of polytheism (*shirk*)—the worst sin in Islam.[11]

The politics of environmental activism among Muslims, where present, have tended to be region-specific. For example, when Palestinians seek to assert territorial claims by planting olive groves,[12] one cannot say that this is an Islamic issue, because many Palestinians are not Muslims. From an Islamist perspective, the mere involvement of Muslims does not make an activity or ideology Islamic; only its basis in the Qur'an and the *hadith* does. This is not to suggest that broader cultural contributions by Muslims living in diverse societies around the world may not be significant in addressing the environmental crisis.

THE SCRIPTURAL BASIS FOR ISLAMIC ENVIRONMENTALISM

For an idea to achieve anything approaching universal acceptance by Muslims as Islamic, it must be convincingly demonstrated that it derives from the Qur'an, or failing that, from the example of the Prophet Muhammad. Recognizing this, contemporary Islamic environmentalists have defined environmentalism as a facet of the Qur'anic concept of stewardship, expressed by the Arabic term *khilafa.* The following verses are cited: "I am setting on the Earth a vice-regent (*khalifa*)" (2:30), and "It is He who has made you his vice-regent on Earth" (6:165). Citing a *hadith* that states, "Verily, this world is sweet and appealing, and Allah placed you as vice-regents therein; He will see what you do," one contemporary scholar has gone so far as to suggest that "vice-regency forms a test which includes how human beings relate to the environment."[13]

The Qur'anic concept of *tawhid* (unity) has historically been interpreted by Muslim writers mainly in terms of the oneness of God (in contradistinction to polytheism), but contemporary Islamic environmentalists have preferred to see *tawhid* as meaning "all-inclusive." Some suggest that the idea of *wahdat al-wujud* or unity of being, associated with the medieval philosopher Ibn 'Arabi, can be understood in environmentalist terms. Ibn 'Arabi, however, has always been a highly controversial figure for Muslims, as many have accused him of holding pantheist or monist views incompatible with Islam's radical monotheism.

In support of the more inclusive interpretation of *tawhid,* a Qur'anic verse (17:44) is often cited that states that all creation praises God, even if this praise is not expressed in human language. Another verse (6:38) states that "There is not an animal in the earth, nor a flying creature on two wings, but they are peoples like unto you." This would seem to be a basis for tempering the hierarchical notion of stewardship implied in the concept of *khilafa.* The Qur'an also describes Islam as the religion of *fitrah,* "the very nature of things." By extension, some contemporary thinkers have reasoned that a genuinely Islamic lifestyle will naturally be environmentally sensitive.[14]

Traditional accounts of the deeds and sayings of the Prophet Muhammad, which together with the Qur'an have formed the basis for Islamic law, emphasize compassion toward animals. The Prophet is believed to have said, "If you kill, kill well, and if you slaughter, slaughter well. Let each of you sharpen his blade and let him spare suffering to the animal he slaughters"; also, "For [charity shown to] each creature which has a wet heart [that is, is alive], there is a reward." Muslims are urged to respect plant life as well, as in the Prophet's saying, "Some trees are as blessed as the Muslim himself, especially the palm."

The Qur'an contains judgment against those who despoil the Earth (2:205): "And when he turns away [from Thee] his effort in the land is to make mischief therein and to destroy the crops and the cattle; and Allah loveth not mischief"; and (7:85) "Do no mischief on the Earth after it has been set in order." Wastefulness and excess consumption are likewise condemned (7:31): "O children of Adam! Look to your adornment at every place of worship, and eat and drink, but be not wasteful. Lo! He [Allah] loveth not the wasteful". The Qur'an repeatedly calls for maintaining balance in all things (13:8, 15:21, 25:2, and elsewhere). Certain sayings of the Prophet seem particularly relevant to contemporary issues of sustainability: "Live in this world as if you will live in it forever, and live for the next world as if you will die tomorrow", and, "When doomsday comes, if someone has a palm shoot in his hand, then he should plant it."[15]

Direct application of these injunctions to contemporary environmental problems is a matter for interpretation by analogy (*qiyas*). Mustafa Abu-Sway has argued that *hadith* reports that enjoin Muslims from relieving themselves on public pathways or into water sources can be understood "to prevent pollution in the language of today." Because we now know that discharging toxic chemicals and waste into the water supply is harmful to human health, Abu-Sway reasons that "by analogy, from the perspective of the Shari'ah, this is prohibited."[16]

FROM THEORY TO REALITY

Are the ecological applications of these sources by Islamic environmentalists—the most prominent of whom live in the West and write for western audiences—in any way representative of the attitudes of most Muslims worldwide, or even of a significant number of them? Strong environmentalist interpretations have recently been derived from traditions such as Buddhism and Hinduism as well as from indigenous local traditions. A growing number of Jewish and Christian theologians and laypersons have been actively seeking to reinterpret the sources of their faith in environmentally sensitive ways. By contrast, Islam has not figured prominently in discussions on religion and the environment; rather, the same articles keep appearing in anthologies and the same faces at meetings, little more than tokens of Islamic representation.

For the most part, contemporary Muslim writers on the environment have characterized environmental degradation as merely a symptom of social injustice. The problem, they argue, is not that humans as a species are destroying the balance of nature, but rather that *some* humans are taking more than their share. If, in accordance with the Qur'anic prohibition of interest taking (*riba*), the interest-based global banking system is eliminated, then there will be no more environmentally destructive development projects and there will be plenty of resources for all. Overpopulation is usually dismissed as a non-issue. The problem is stated to be the restriction of movement; if visa restrictions are eliminated, then people will simply migrate from overpopulated areas to underpopulated ones.

In recent times, global initiatives on birth control and women's reproductive rights have been most strongly opposed in Muslim countries. Such efforts are frequently met with accusations that "the West is trying to limit the number of Muslims." Warnings of starvation and deprivation from overpopulation generally elicit the response that "God will provide," which draws its support from the Qur'anic verse (11:6) that reads, "There is no beast upon the Earth for which Allah does not provide."

Yet, unlike Roman Catholicism, Islam has no inherent barriers to practicing contraception. The medieval theologian Abu Hamid Muhammad Ghazali (1058–1111), who has been called "the second greatest Muslim after Muhammad" and whose writings remain highly influential throughout the Muslim world today, argues in his book *The Proper Conduct of Marriage (Kitab adab al-nikah)* that birth control in the form of coitus interruptus (*'azl*) is permitted in Islam. He suggests, furthermore, that "the fear of great hardship as a result of having too many children . . . is also not forbidden, since freedom from hardship is an aid to religious devotion." In response to the Qur'anic verse cited earlier, Ghazali comments that "to examine consequences . . . while perhaps at odds with the attitude of trust in Providence, cannot be called forbidden."[17]

In fact, the founder of the Family Planning Society of Kenya, Dr. Yusuf Ali Eraj, is a Muslim. "Using birth control does not mean following the West," he says. "Muslims can practice family planning, following Islamic principles. It is a *myth* that Islamic doctrine opposes it! All methods are approved, even sterilization."[18]

Despite these arguments, many Muslims still see arguments against having more children than one can afford as being symptomatic of unbelief (*kufr*), which to Muslims is quite a serious charge. Today, Iran is the only Muslim country where an official policy of birth control and reduction of birthrate is backed up with Islamic rhetoric.

The traditional Muslim response to doomsday scenarios is that of *tawakkul* or trust in God (Qur'an 5:23, 14:11–12, 65:3, 25:58, 26:217–218). This tendency, which is often perceived by Westerners as fatalism, reminds one of the *hadith* in which a companion of the Prophet neglected to tie up his camel, and the camel wandered off and was lost. The owner complained of his loss to the Prophet, saying, "I trusted in God, but my camel is gone." The Prophet replied, "First tie up your camel, then trust in God." There is ample evidence today that human growth—reproductive as well as economic—is creating a dangerous imbalance within the biosphere. One wonders, are Muslims who refuse to acknowledge this perhaps leaving their camels untied? In counterbalance to the familiar refrain of *tawakkul,* an Islamic environmentalist might in the spirit of Ghazali posit the concept of *'aql* or rational intelligence, which according to Islam is a gift from God, given for a purpose (Qur'an 39:9).[19] There would appear to be nothing un-Islamic about suggesting that the gift of *'aql* has applications in recognizing a crisis and finding ways to avert impending disaster.

Nevertheless, among Muslim ethicists today there is far more interest in human-centered issues of justice than in the biosphere as an integral whole. This view would seem to bear some similarity to attitudes in the West, which is not surprising given Islam's common heritage with Judaism and Christianity. Islam holds that the world is a passing phenomenon, created to serve God's purpose, and will cease to be once that purpose has been fulfilled. Islam likewise emphasizes the relationship between humans and God above all else and has by comparison little to say about the importance of our myriad fellow creatures. Whether the true essence of Islam is pro-environment or not, in practice, throughout most of its history Muslim theologians, philosophers, and laypersons have focused almost exclusively on the relationship between Allah and humanity. Islam, like Christianity and Judaism, has for the most part been manifestly *theanthropocentric,* to use Karl Barth's somewhat unwieldy term. Iqtidar Zaidi implicitly confirms this when he states that "we are seeking a religious matrix which maintains man's position as an ecologically dominant being."[20] Indeed, one Muslim writer has recently concluded that "Islamic anthropocentrism negates the claims of Islamic ecology."[21]

Keith Thomas has remarked that whether Christianity is inherently environmentally destructive or not, the reality is that its proponents often *have* been.[22] The same observation may apply to Muslims. Given the importance of the petroleum industry and the widespread pursuit of materialistic, consumption-oriented lifestyles in numerous countries with a Muslim majority, it would appear that Muslims must now share with Christians some of the blame for the present, rapidly deteriorating state of environmental crisis.

Some of the most severe environmental problems in the world today are found in countries where the majority of inhabitants are Muslim. Even if we allow a degree of outside responsibility, these problems would clearly be less pronounced if large numbers of Muslims were shaping their lifestyles according to an interpretation of Islam that strongly emphasizes *khilafa* as applied to the natural environment. The reality is that most Muslims are not, and this includes governments for whom development and economic growth are the top priority.

ISLAMIC ENVIRONMENTALISM IN PRACTICE

If Islamic sources do offer models for increased environmental responsibility among Muslims, the urgency of the environmental crisis implies a need to assess whether and to what degree the latent potential for Islamic models of stewardship (*khilafa*) is currently being realized anywhere in the Muslim world.

A possible starting point for this inquiry would be to analyze current environmental policy in countries where Islam is claimed as a basis for legislation by the government in power. The Kingdom of Saudi Arabia, The Islamic Republic of Pakistan, and the

Islamic Republic of Iran are three countries that currently make this claim.[23]

In 1983, the government of Saudi Arabia commissioned a group of Islamic scholars at the University of Jeddah to formulate an Islamic policy on the environment. A short paper was prepared and published in English, French, and Arabic by the IUCN in Switzerland, but unfortunately this paper has not been widely circulated.[24] Nevertheless, according to two non-Saudi Muslims who have worked for the Saudi government, Mawil Izzi Dien (an Iraqi) and 'Uthman Llewelyn (an American), the ideological basis for the Meteorology and Environmental Protection Administration of Saudi Arabia is one of Islamic environmentalism.[25]

The government of Pakistan, which began to adopt an Islamist platform in 1978, created a National Conservation Strategy Unit (NCS) in 1992 within the Ministry of Environment, Local Government, and Rural Development. There are also several environmentalist NGOs active in Pakistan that have been striving to influence government policy toward the environment. These include the Sustainable Development Policy Institute (SDPI) and a national branch of the IUCN, which together formulated the Pakistan Environment Programme (PEP) in 1994.[26]

These organizations have achieved some successes in bringing about environmental legislation in Pakistan, such as the Environmental Protection Act of 1997. However, specifically Islamic rhetoric has not thus far been part of their approach. Only as recently as 1998 did the government of Northwest Frontier Province begin to envision an ulema project as part of the Sarhad Provincial Conservation Strategy (SPCS), in an effort to bring Islamic discourse into the discussion on the environment; it is therefore too early to determine whether this initiative will bear fruit or not.

Developments in the Islamic Republic of Iran may offer the strongest evidence of an applied Islamic environmental ethic in the world today.[27] The revolutionary government has gone so far to assert its ideological commitment to environmental protection as to include it in the nation's constitution. Article 50 reads,

> In the Islamic Republic, protection of the natural environment, in which the present and future generations must lead an ever-improving community life, is a public obligation. Therefore all activities, economic or otherwise, which may cause irreversible damage to the environment are forbidden.

The Iranian president, Mohammad Khatami, stated recently before a meeting of environmental ministers from neighboring Persian Gulf countries that pollution poses an even greater threat than war and suggested that the fight to preserve the environment might be the most positive issue for bringing the Gulf nations together.[28]

The current Iranian vice president for environmental affairs is the former revolutionary spokeswoman Massumeh Ebtekar. Thus far, her role in shaping her government's environmental policy has skirted the intriguing questions of the potential relationship of environmentalist Islam to feminist Islam as well as the broader discussion that links the historical subjugation of the Earth by patriarchal society with the subjugation of women.

There has been some evidence of a rising feminist voice in certain aspects of Iranian policy, in particular concerning population control. Iran's Department of the Environment has set the remarkably ambitious goal of reducing the country's rate of population growth, which was nearly 4% in the 1980s, from 2.82% in 1993 to 1% within 20 years. A government report on population control concludes with the observation that

> Although these changes will not happen overnight, the economic pressures of contemporary life along with education provided by political, religious and scientific leaders should convince the people that family planning and population control is not mere propaganda, but [rather] it is to their own benefit to have fewer children, *inshallah!*[29]

Iran's revolution in 1978–1979 demonstrated that the most effective means for disseminating ideas and motivating change in a traditional Muslim society is through local mosques. In a paper submitted by Iran's Department of the Environment to the Third Session of the Committee on Environment and Sustainable Development at Bangkok in 1996, it was suggested that mosques, which have served as community education centers throughout Muslim history, are perfectly appropriate locations for conducting informational sessions and community discussions on environmental issues. This paper, which reflects the official position of the Iranian government, states that "it is now the duty of environmentalists to encourage the Friday Prayer speakers to convey environmental messages to the public."[30]

Iran now counts 149 environmental NGOs. One of the most visible is the Green Front of Iran (*Jabheh ye Sabz-e Iran*). Among their many activities and projects, they have put together a committee that seeks out references to environmental stewardship in the Qur'an and the *hadith* and sends them to religious leaders and organizations.[31]

In Iran, official and public attitudes toward the natural environment appear to be unique in the Muslim world. The fact that Iran's official voice is expressing some unusually progressive perspectives vis-à-vis other Muslim countries may be related to the fact that Islamists are in power in Iran and must therefore face certain hard realities that accompany the responsibility for directing their country's future policies.

Because the Iranian government is in a position to actually implement unconventional policies regarding the environment, it would not be surprising to see Iran play a future role in shaping the development and application of an Islamic environmental ethic elsewhere in the Muslim world. Particularly around the oil-rich Caspian Sea, where most of the newly independent states are Muslim, an avowedly Islamist Iran may be more likely to succeed in exerting ethical restraints on the careless and short-sighted exploitation of the region's resources than are any of the various Western governments or corporations now operating there.

CONCLUSION

For Muslims and non-Muslims alike, the practical and active relationship between religion and the environmental crisis is often not immediately obvious. Even so, some Muslims, believing with Lynn White Jr. that the environmental crisis is at root a spiritual crisis, have been attempting to illuminate that connection through writing, activism, and policy making.

Muslim reformers throughout history have claimed that the problems facing society resulted from the fact that an Islamic lifestyle based on the Qur'an and *sunna* was absent in their age. Islamic reform movements have thus typically aimed to encourage Muslims to rediscover how the sources of the faith instruct one to live. This process of rediscovery is referred to as *islah,* a cleansing of the tradition in order to return Islam to the original, pristine state that these sources are believed to evoke. There are indications that Islamic environmentalism will increasingly be expressed in these terms. One may cite the example of Turkey, where soon after taking power in 1994, the new Islamist mayor of Istanbul had the cobblestones surrounding the city hall painted green, declaring that this symbolized the environmentalist aspect of his party's policy.[32]

There has been a tendency in recent years, especially among scholars of religion, to study the sources of various cultural traditions in order to find support for claims that this or that tradition is originally *eco-friendly;* a corollary argument is often made that the environmental crisis can be remedied through a rediscovery of ecological principles that have supposedly been lost. These arguments may be somewhat misguided. Assertions about what constitutes the original or proper interpretation of a tradition, or that true Christianity, Buddhism, Islam, or whatever, is eco-friendly, beg the counterargument that the proponent has falsely construed the pristine form of the worldview in question.

It might be more productive instead to adopt the correlational method proposed by Paul Tillich, which assumes that it is precisely through a tradition's success in drawing on its own internal resources to confront an ever-changing array of historical crises and concerns that a tradition reinvigorates itself and demonstrates its ongoing vitality and relevance.[33] According to this approach, it matters little whether the original essence of Islam is eco-friendly or not; the point is that an eco-friendly Islam is urgently needed in the world today, and as more and more Muslims come to realize this and to work toward its articulation and practice, Islamic environmental philosophy in its contemporary form is likely to play a major role in reshaping and revitalizing Islam as a guiding force and principle in Muslim communities around the globe.

Air, earth, water, and fire are God's servants
To us they seem lifeless, but to God living

Rumi

NOTES

1. David Pingree and S. Nomanul Haq, *"Tabi'a," Encyclopedia of Islam,* 2nd ed., Leiden, The Netherlands: Brill.

2. Lenn Evan Goodman, Tr., *The Case of the Animals versus Man,* Boston: Twayne, 1978.

3. Pingree and Haq, *op. cit.*

4. S. Hossein Nasr, *Religion and the Order of Nature,* New York: Oxford University Press, 1996, p. 61.

5. William Chittick, *The Sufi Path of Knowledge,* Albany, N.Y.: SUNY press, 1989, p. 38.

6. Lenn Evan Goodman, Tr., *The Case of the Animals versus Man,* Boston: Twayne, 1978, pp. 5–6.

7. See for example Mawil Izzi Dien, *The Environmental Dimensions of Islam,* Cambridge, U.K.: Lutterworth, 2000; Akhtaruddin Ahmad, *Islam and the Environmental Crisis,* London: Ta-ha Publishers, 1997; Abou Bakr Ahmed Ba Kader, et al., Eds., *Islamic Principles for the Conservation of the Natural Environment,* Gland, Switzerland: International Union for the Conservation of the Natural Environment, 1983; S. Hossein Nasr, *Man and Nature: The Spiritual Crisis of Modern Man,* Chicago: Kazi, 1997 [1967]; Iqtidar H. Zaidi, "On the Ethics of Man's Interaction with the Environment: An Islamic Approach," *Environmental Ethics* 3 (1981), pp. 35–47; and the essays in Harfiya Abdel Haleem, Ed., *Islam and the Environment,* London: Ta-ha Publishers, 1998, and Fazlun Khalid and Joanne O'Brien, Eds., *Islam and Ecology,* New York: Cassell, 1992.

8. Zaidi, "On the Ethics of Man's Interaction with the Environment," p. 35.

9. S. H. Nasr, *Religion and the Order of Nature,* New York: Oxford University Press, 1996, p. 225, note 12.

10. Safei El-Deen Hamed, "Seeing the Environment through Islamic Eyes: Application of Shariah to Natural Resources Planning and Management," *Journal of Agricultural and Environmental Ethics* 6/2 (1993), p. 146.

11. Shakeel Hossain, "Between Sinful Innovation and the Ethos of the Land: Sacred Traditions and Ritual Art of the Indian Muslims," paper presented at the conference on Islam and Ecology, Harvard Center for World Religions, 7–10 May 1998.

12. I am grateful to an anonymous reviewer for suggesting this example.

13. Mustafa Abu-Sway, "Towards an Islamic Jurisprudence of the Environment" [Fiqh al-Bi'ah f'il-Islam], lecture given at Belfast mosque, February 1998. http://homepages.iol.ie/~afifi/Articles/environment.htm

14. Sadia Khawar Khan Chishti, "Islam, Environment, and Sustainable Development", paper presented at the conference on Islam and Ecology, Harvard Center for World Religions, 7–10 May 1998.

15. A nearly identical saying exists in Jewish Mishnah: "Rabbi Yochanan ben Zakkai used to say, 'If you happen to be standing with a sapling in your hand and someone says to you, "Behold, the Messiah has come!", first plant the tree and then go out to greet the Messiah.'" (*The Fathers according to Rabbi Nathan,* Tr. Judah Goldin, New Haven: Yale University Press, 1955, p. 12.)

16. Abu Sway, "Towards an Islamic Jurisprudence."

17. Abu Hamid Muhammad Ghazali, *The Proper Conduct of Marriage in Islam* [*Adab an-Nikah*], Tr. Muhtar Holland, Hollywood, Fla.: Al-Baz Publishing, 1998, p. 79.

18. Marjorie Hope and James Young, *Voices of Hope in the Struggle to Save the Planet,* New York: Apex Press, 2000, p. 173.

19. See Zaidi, "On the Ethics of Man's Interaction with the Environment," p. 41. For a fuller discussion of the Islamic terms *tawakkul* and *'aql,* see the relevant articles in *Encyclopedia of Islam,* 2nd ed.

20. Zaidi, "On the Ethics of Man's Interaction with the Environment," p. 36.

21. Oguz Erdur, "Reappropriating the 'Green': Islamist Environmentalism," *New Perspectives on Turkey* 17 (Fall 1997), p. 160.

22. Keith Thomas, *Man and the Natural World,* New York: Oxford University Press, 1984, p. 24.

23. The Green Party of Egypt was granted official status in 1990, but Islamic rhetoric plays only a small part in its activities.

24. Ba Kader et al., 1983.

25. Izzi Dien, *op. cit.*

26. Aban Kabraji, IUCN Pakistan office, Karachi, personal communication, 7 April 2000.

27. See my "Environmental Initiatives in Contemporary Iran," *Central Asian Survey* 20/2 (2001), pp. 155–165.

28. "Pollution More Fatal than War," *Iran Times,* 27.12.1376 (Feb. 1998), p. 1.

29. Islamic Republic of Iran Country Paper, Third Session of the Committee on Environment and Sustainable Development, Bangkok, 7–11 October, 1996, Tehran: Department of the Environment, 1996, p. 36.

30. Iran Country Paper, p. 27.

31. Shadi Mokhtari, "The Green Front of Iran," *Iran News,* 17 May 1998, p. 3.

32. Erdur, "Reappropriating the 'Green'," p. 151. Green is traditionally the color associated with the Prophet Muhammad, hence its prominence in the flags of Saudi Arabia and Pakistan.

33. Paul Tillich, *Systematic Theology,* Vol. 1, Chicago: University of Chicago Press, 1951, pp. 59–66.

Toward an Islamic Ecotheology

K. L. AFRASIABI

INTRODUCTION

THE AWAKENING OF ECOLOGICAL CONSCIOUSness since the 1960s has had an immediate effect on Islamic theology: the basic tenets of Islam have come under the heavy fire of ecologists, and it is perhaps not an overstatement to describe these criticisms as devastating. The criticism begins from the argument that Islam, much like other monotheistic religions, is anthropocentric, and concludes that the pursuit of an ecologically-minded theology must necessarily transcend these religions in search of alternative traditions and belief systems.[1] According to this line of criticism, Islam is anthropocentric because it takes human value and importance as its starting point: man is given dominion over nature and its other creatures and these have value only in their use to human beings who are bestowed with stewardship (*khalīfat*) by the Almighty.[2] What is criticized here are the Qur'ānic ideas of nature as a tool, resource, favor, or even a trust (*amānat*), and its doctrine of creation which mandates the human subduing of the earth.[3] Deemed as entirely utilitarianist, these ideas are traced to the theological dualism of man and nature, and to the corollary axiom that nature as God's artifact has no purpose save to serve man.

These criticisms raise many difficulties. For one thing, they point to an Islamic basis for what ecologists and philosophers have come to deplore about the so-called technical rationality. The nub of technical rationality is a means-ends view of man's relations with nature that permits the objectification and exploitation of outer nature on an unlimited basis often in the name of human progress.[4] Closely identified with the productivist paradigm of modern capitalism, technical rationality is sometimes considered to be the real evil behind the plethora of ecological problems facing us today. The pertinent question is, of course, if there is an Islamic foundation for the evolution of technical rationality that has led to the wanton exploitation of nature in the name of human progress?

Islamic Responses to the Ecological Criticism

The Islamic response to the ecological criticism(s) has taken two forms: a) a defense of Islam based on an alternate reading of Islam and Islamic history; and b) moves toward the construction of a viable Islamic conception of nature.[5] Although somewhat different in scope and focus from the parallel attempts in Christianity and other religions, the volume and quality of Islamic literature devoted to the nature-and-religion problematic has begun to increase recently.

For the most part, this growing literature reflects strong objections to the ecological criticisms aforementioned. A number of authors, including Nasr, Sardar, Manzoor, and others have sought to dispel the criticism—that Islam lacks an ecological dimension—by appealing to the Qur'ān, *ḥadīth,* as well as to the history of Islamic theological, philosophical, and scientific thought. Disputing the ecological criticism as a tissue of erroneous interpretation of Islam, these authors have presented an alternative view of Islam as a comprehensive religion that contains all the essential ingredients of "environmentalism." Essential to their argument are the notions of *amr bi al-ma'rūf wa nahī al-munkir* (practising good and prohibiting evil), ethical responsibility of "vicegerent" man toward his earthly environment, and the tradition of nature-conscious science in Muslim civilization.[6]

Concerning the latter, Nasr has cogently argued that medieval Muslim scientists, unlike their counterparts in the West, were keenly aware of the potential hazard of their work with respect to nature.[7] For Nasr in particular, the charge of technical rationality laid at the door of Islam represents an unfounded criticism that overlooks the difference of Islam and, say Christianity, vis-a-vis their respective views of the

Afrasiabi, K. L., "Toward an Islamic Ecotheology," *Hamdard Islamicus* 18/1 (1995), pp. 33–44. Reprinted by permission.

relation of man and nature. Behind Nasr's and other like-minded authors' call on Muslims to rediscover their authentic faith is a confident assertion that Islam proper is a self-contained religion that roughly corresponds with the ecological perspective which forms the core of these erroneous interpretations of Islam as unecological; their argument that there is no need to redress the wrongful neglect of nature has led these authors to question the key implication of the ecological criticism, namely, that there is a need to rethink the Islamic theology in radically new ways. But does this response really stand the weight of critical scrutiny? Have these authors satisfactorily addressed the question of ecology from their Islamic perspective?

Interestingly, Nasr himself reinforces the anthropocentric image of Islam when writing that within Islam's doctrine of creation "the causes for animals are the same (as man-KLA) except that their final cause is their use by man."[8] Likewise, Izutsu has written, "Man, his nature, conduct, psychology, duties, and destiny are, in fact, as much a central preoccupation of the Qu'ānic thought as the problem of God himself."[9] This interpretation follows closely the interpretation of Islam offered by Qutb, Rahman, and others.[10] The common thread running through their work is an anthropocentric portrayal of life and, in some cases, of afterlife; the tendency to present an anthropocentric image of afterlife is rooted in the Qur'ānic conception of heaven.[11]

The anthropocentric interpretation may, arguably, be based on a faithful reading of aspects of the Qur'ān and *ḥadīth,* but it hardly confirms the non-utilitarian, ecological wisdom of Islam alluded to by Nasr and others mentioned above. This interpretation corresponds roughly with what we may define as Islamic humanism, i.e., as an expression of a religious perspective which places man at the centre of history and makes him the privileged creator on earth. Various authors have traced the genesis of Islamic humanism to the metaphysical notion of man as God-like, which has held sway among Muslim thinkers for generations.[12]

A central feature of the contemporary debate on Islam and ecology is whether or not the religious humanism of Islam can be reconciled with the ethical concerns of ecology. On a broader level, one might ask if this "Eastern" humanism can withstand the pressure of recent anti-humanist, anti-historicist attacks on various anthropocentric philosophies. Both Foucault and Derrida have given us ample ammunition to deconstruct Islamic humanism, by virtue of the fact that this humanism and the secular humanism of the West have the anthropocentric core in common; consequently, Foucault's denunciation, in the *Archaeology of Knowledge,* of the "sovereignty of the subject and the twin figures of anthropology and humanism" in the Western thought applies, *mutatis mutandis,* to the humanist tradition in Islam.[13]

Following Derrida, we can, hypothetically, extend the provenance of Foucault's critique by arguing that the Islamic tendency to construe the anthropocentric view of man in terms of origins (i.e., Adamic man) is the inevitable counterpart of the teleological concept of the highest man as a perfect and divine presence (*insān-i-kāmil*). This criticism particularly applies to the modernist thinkers such as Shariati and Muttahari. Between the two, Shariati has been more explicitly forthcoming with his elaboration of *insān-i-kamīl:* "This is an ideal human being (who) passes through nature and understands God and reaches God . . . In nature he is God's successor . . . is a God-like in the exile of earth . . . (who) reaches the end of history and the borders of nature."[14]

It can be shown that the embrace of the idea of *insān-i-kāmil* has definite anthropocentric implications. Even though Shariati and others have enveloped this idea in modernist language, in essence they have reinforced the traditional Islamic denial of the non-reductionist role of nature and the resultant lack of progress towards a theological doctrine of nature in contemporary Islam.

Furthermore, the question of whether such views of perfect man inadvertently carry atheistic connotations can be posed from a Fuerbach-Blochian angle which maintains that since the aim of all religion is the attainment of human perfection, it is in the final analysis based on an implicit elimination of God: "The utopia of Kingdom destroys the fictions of God the creator and the hypothesis of God in heaven."[15] This is not to necessarily endorse this point of view, rather to emphasize that the recent theorization(s) of *insān-i-kāmil* have lent it an air of validity. As in the case of Shariati, in the custody of many modernist Muslims, "nature" has been denatured and interpreted deterministically and mechanically, bereft of its ethical value and autonomy. We may take this point one step further and make a sweeping claim: That the deconstruction of the Islamic humanism as it stands today is the essential prerequisite for the objective of arriving at the door of an alternative Islamic theology that would be capable of integrating within its horizon the fundamental ecological precepts. Amplifying a thesis recently debated in the ecological, religious, and philosophical literature, the force of this claim makes the culpability of the Islamic humanism in the neglect of nature a central issue; it shows that from an ecological critique of Islam to a critique of the Islamic humanism is but a small step, that the two types of critique are in fact highly intertwined; it also calls for an integral theology that meets the conditions for focusing on viable themes of nature and ecology. Contrary to Manzoor, Sardar, Agwan and others, it is not enough to show that pro-ecology insights can be found in Islam. Before the ecological criticism can be dismissed what is needed is a convincing presentation of ecological parameters *sui generis* to Islam, if there is any. There remains, at the outset of our work, an inconclusive if and but about the discovery of ecologically-relevant facets of Islam, first of all, due to the broad deconstructionist implications of the ecological criticism: Will there be any thing retrievable for a viable Islamic theology once we apply the (hermeneutic and) deconstructionist method? Or will this lead us to give up on this project altogether?

Indeed, the jury is still out on this question and the related question of the nature of relationship between Islam and ecology; short of lapsing into dogmatic and emotional defense of Islam, I am afraid the intellectual debate over Islam and ecology, is yet to be won in principle. What we know for sure is that the ecological perspective has unleashed a serious challenge to the Islamic thought and values, and that the attempts to deny any trace of anthropocentrism and technical rationality in Islam have often ended in the snares of their own contradictions. Given the force of ecological criticisms and the various shortcomings of the Islamic responses, such as evading the core criticisms as in the case of Sardar,[16] Islam has become resignative; its concept of "corruption on earth" (*mufsid fi al-arḍ*) can at most unmask the unreason at the heart of what has passed for reason, without account of its own, in a word, has reached a dead end.

This unhappy situation is basically the product of a double, concurrent crisis, that is, on the one hand the crisis of Islamic humanism and, on the other hand, the crisis of theoretical attempts to rethink the viability of Islam along ecological lines, the fact that these attempts have had to defend Islam against the ecological criticism in vain. These (largely modernist) attempts have suffered from a conspicuous absence of a past tradition to build upon; their crisis stems partially from the relative void of "ecological parameter" in the contemporary, twentieth century discourses on Islam: From Abduh to Iqbal to Shariati, and so on, a common thread of the various so-called reconstructive projects in Islam has been a near complete obliviousness to the need to infuse a credible ecological dimension.[17] Thus, whereas Iqbal's pioneering "reconstruction of Islamic thought" was for the most part except at the most abstract theological level, closed to ecological insights, Shariati on the other hand invoked the anti-ecological view of nature as the "objectified other" by describing nature as a "prison."[18] This deplorable lacuna in the reconstructive project has had vast ecological and even cultural implications; unintentionally, at least, it skewed the course of the modernistic Islamic thought in the direction of humanism and anthropocentrism, without achieving any major progress in Islamic theology of nature, and, consequently, without addressing the limitations of the pre-existing views of nature—as a prison or as the metaphoric "place of forgetfulness" (Ibn al-'Arabī) or as "dream of a sleeper" (Rumi).[19] Besides the absence of critical reflection on pre-modern Islamic interpretations of nature where nature was often downgraded as the antithesis of spirit, the reconstructive project has increasingly focused on sociological and cultural issues at the cost of neglecting the cosmological and theological implications. The "modernist" Islam in its main manifestation has lost credibility by its explicit and wilful choice of priorities that has bracketed the large vision of the place of humanity in the cosmos; many of its pundits have stressed harmony with religion, but their flirtation with nature has rarely, if ever, led them in the direction of a new theology.

For the past couple of decades, the development of Islamic thought in the Muslim World has been dominated by the so-called fundamentalism and or "revivalism", a phenomenon of such magnitude and force that has set the tone and agenda for many

Muslim theologians, some of whom are self-styled "liberation theologists" not unlike their Christian counterparts. The vast vagaries and differentiated attitudes of this movement notwithstanding, it is not far-fetched to charge its proponents with a relative neglect of nature as a result of their prioritization of politico-economic and cultural issues. A survey of the recent revivalist works shows that concern for nature and the related ecological issues has never been a top priority. Even among the more academically-inclined advocates of "Islamization of knowledge", we have yet to see attempts to address this deficiency and to propose a new theological approach that reintegrates the theme of nature.[20]

The very idea of Islamization of ecological knowledge, though it sounds appealing, nonetheless has the fault of carrying the seeds of an inseparable romanticism that romanticizes Islam's capability to address the various ecological themes and issues. Prompted in large measure by a catching-up new agenda to address ecological concerns from an authentic Islamic perspective, the proponents of this idea have assumed, a priori, both the self-contained quality of the Islamic view of nature and the unproblematic process of application of the Islamic insights to contemporary ecological issues. But in hindsight, both these positions may prove to be unwarranted, for neither the adequacy of Islamic theology of nature can be taken for granted, nor can we presume that the problematic of Islam and ecology is a simple one of drawing from the arsenal of Islamic insights to tackle the thematic and practical issues of ecology.

Furthermore, a related criticism of the "Islamization of knowledge" and "revivalist" projects is that, regardless of their points of dissimilarities, they evince a latent (and at times manifest) common tendency toward dogmatic self-enclosure vis-a-vis relevant insights from other cultures and traditions. Coupled with this tendency is another tendency, namely, the tendency to exaggerate the clashing views and interests between Islam and the West and, thereby, lose sight of the global issues and the globalization of ecological concerns in today's "globalized context."[21]

The phenomenon of global interdependence has created the drive to a new uniformity of concerns over such issues as global warming, air and water pollution, population explosion, depletion of natural resources on a planetary scale, and the like, and this runs against the temptation (among some Muslim thinkers and activists) to shun any meaningful dialogue with the non-Muslim West, which they regard from their prism of "hermeneutic of suspicion" as a dangerous prelude for a new "mental colonization", whose goals would be to obliterate the autonomy of their culture and impose conformity to the Western standards. Seeking to nullify these dangers, these Muslims have adopted a strategy of resistance that often invokes the crusade-type image of "fortress Islam", as if by ex-communicating the radically other (i.e., the West) at the discursive and knowledge levels it is possible to rehabilitate the *ummah.* Still, it must be recognized that this is to some extent a defensive strategy imposed from the without, i.e., by the Western cultural and ideological impositions that have recently taken on new guises such as the "end of ideology" and world historical "triumph of liberalism" that carry totalitarian connotations and either directly or indirectly question the validity of cultural polycentrism on a world scale.[22] In other words, the prejudices, the overt signs of hostility, the economically superior position of the West and its cultural "invasion" have directly dictated the defensive Islamic strategy (of survival) which has manufactured its own shields of protection laden with meanings and prejudices.[23] Acknowledging the merits of this strategy and its emancipatory potential is at the same time an acknowledgment of the difficulty of establishing the possibility of an undistorted communicative interaction, to borrow a term from Habermas, in a situation of asymmetry and conflict of interests.[24] What has so far blocked this possibility is a variety of factors emerging from the hermeneutical (mutual) lack of recognition of the other, ranging from ignorance of the other's tradition, to intolerance to outright repugnance. Thus, while the fear of "green threat" runs rampant in the West, the Islamic revivalists and populists often succumb to the image of the West as a hostile other that embodies only the evil.[25] For these Muslims, entering into a conversation with the West becomes like entering into a zero-sum game where the validity claims of each side is at stake; their strategy of self-insulating from the Western influences has, as stated above, a rational basis connected to the striving of Muslims for cultural autonomy and emancipation in the light of onslaught of Western values and norms.

But the difficulty with the rational side is that it coexists, and one might say is even buried, under an irrational side that comes from the dogmatic religious belief that places an antimodern emphasis on the autonomy of the *ummah,* as if Islamic civilization is land-locked in a closed horizon. Inadequately cognizant of the common global problems that bind the human inhabitants of the planet together in an unprecedented way, the Muslim revivalists have, conceivably, overemphasized sociopolitical and cultural issues and underemphasized theological and ecological issues; the two types of issues are of course interrelated and cannot be divorced from each other, except through the fiat of pragmatic revivalist movements guided by a burning desire to change the Muslim society from various forms and manifestations of corruption on earth, without fully addressing the ecological aspect of this corruption and its doctrinal roots in Islam itself. As a result, the recently surfaced ideas of the environmental *Jihād,* an Islamic green movement, and the like, have yet to take hold of imagination of worthy Muslim theologians and jurisprudents, most of whom appear to have confined themselves to rhetorical recycling of pre-modern norms and are hitherto unaffected by the ecologically-imposed needs for rethinking their conceptions of nature, man, and the cosmos. Thus, for instance, there is a conspicuous absence of a credible Islamic notion of limit, one that could, theologically speaking, define and elaborate upon limits in the Islamically sanctioned usage and exploitation of nature. Sadly lacking is even a minimal theological discourse that would exhibit a keen awareness of the inadequacy of Islamic theology when it comes to human self-limitation vis-a-vis nature and animals.

To substantiate this latter criticism, we may glance at the Shi'ite jurisprudence (*fiqh*) in this century and the previous centuries. Such a scrutiny shows a remarkable uniformity of views in terms of a common obliviousness, on the part of the leading Shi'ite jurisprudents, to ecological insights.

Concretely, various *ayatollahs* (*āyat Allah*) such as Golpayegani, Khoi, Brujerdi, Montazeri, and Khomeini, each has explicated as precisely as possible the meanings and limits of the vast issue of *dakhl wa taṣṣarruf dar ṭabīʿat* (drawing from and possession of nature) yet, not only is the attention placed one-sidedly on *taṣṣarruf* and *dakhl* has been relatively neglected, the added problem with the exegisis of the *Sharīʿah* by these *ayatollahs* is their shared inability to go beyond vague references to Islamic limits of human *dakhl* in nature and to include ecologically-relevant conditions. More specifically, all these *ayatollahs* have spelled out in great detail the Islamic law pertaining to animal hunting, yet none has grappled with the issue of endangered species. To give an example, Ayatollah Montazeri writes in his *Tawḍīḥ al-Masā'il* about the categories of birds whose meat is forbidden to Muslims, e.g., vultures and eagles, since they are "rapacious and have claws."[26] However, no mention is made of the endangered birds and the role of the *Sharīʿah* in protecting them. Far from representing an exception, Montazeri's serious omissions are in fact shared by all the other leading *ayatollahs* aforementioned; the ecological shortcomings of their *Tawdīh al-Masā'il* points at a major lacuna in the Shīʿīte jurisprudence, which is unfortunately not limited to Shi'ism and engulfs other Muslim sects and denominations as well; this lacuna points at what is urgently needed at the present time: an up-to-date, ecologically conscious *Tawdih al-Masā'il.* From within Shi'ism, this would imply a new articulation of the issue of *dakhl wa taṣṣarruf dar ṭabīʿat* which, with the help of more refined concepts and understandings of limits, would be able to present moral and ethical solutions for the growing ecological problems. Yet, a satisfactory articulation of this issue cannot possibly be realized without occurring as part and parcel of a wider theological agenda and, perhaps, a theological detour.

The reason a theological detour may be necessary has to do with the need to remove the fundamental theological roadblocks that have obliterated the space for a new articulation of the Islamic *Sharīʿah;* in a word what is needed is an alternative Islamic theology which has Qur'ān and *ḥadīth* on its side, that seeks to telescope this theology to the need for spiritual deepening and a renewed sense of hope among the Muslims, the young generation especially.

Indeed, the young Muslims everywhere are in dire need of a new religious "manifesto", a dynamic, genuinely Islamic perspective that is thoroughly contemporary and dynamic, theoretically appealing and action-oriented, idealistic and yet non-utopian and non-dogmatic, a perspective based on a systematic theology that would be deemed satisfactory by what Iqbal has identified to be a criterion of the modern

Islamic mind, i.e., "a concrete living experience of God."[27]

Integrating Ecology and Islamic Theology: The Tasks Ahead

The challenge to the Muslims of articulating and developing a sound ecological theology, which we may call ecotheology for purely heuristic purposes, are quite enormous. First of all, this is the challenge of establishing that, contra Tillich, a theology of inorganic is potentially present in Islam.[28] Second, this is the challenge of proving that within Islam, utilitarianism does not reign supreme; and that creation outside human beings has more than just utilitarian values and, third, that the earth as a whole is thought of as a living, even an intelligent being. Fourth, the challenge is that of spelling out in a coherent fashion the fundamentals of an Islamic theology of "reverence for life" directed to man, nature and animals as a whole, and, fifth, applying the parameters of this theology to such practical ecological issues such as clashing interests between human beings and animals: Given that the preservation of endangered species often involves some cost to human interests the question of 'how does Islamic ecotheology view this issue and what solutions it presents' is of special importance. This is so because the theological concerns with the mundane global issues and their various moral and ethical questions form a central preoccupation of Islamic ecotheology; of course, this interpretation runs contrary to a popular misunderstanding of what theology is all about, that is, the notion that theology belongs exclusively to the realm of higher grounds, i.e., metaphysics and eschatology. This points, sixth, to another challenge of ecotheology, that of establishing a series of mediating concepts to bridge the gap between theology and ecology.

Seventh, in the process of developing these mediating concepts, Islamic theology can and should translate itself into a fashionable language attractive to the modern mind of the present and future generations. As a responsible service to the *bildung* of Muslims, ecotheology's main task is to self-present as the repository of a future-oriented practical theology that is centered on hope in close proximity to preexisting values and interpretations. Certain discontinuities of language are nested in this project which must remain in a healthy state of hybridity vis-a-vis the elements of continuity. Surely, the Islamic ecotheology will rise or fall by its ability to provide a delicate balance between continuity and discontinuity. Relatedly, eighth, the Islamic ecotheology must walk the tight rope of, simultaneously, satisfying the requirement of addressing the concerns of (the Muslim and non-Muslim) ecological critics of Islam and, on the other hand, quieting the concerns of the Islamic conservatives and traditionalists, who may question it as heretical. Thus, unless the double tests of authenticity and innovation are passed successfully, which is no mean task by any measure of imagination, the Islamic theology will inevitably start down the road of identity crisis where the wolves of history prowl. Put in other words, the challenge before the self-declared Islamic ecotheologists is that, besides avoiding the ethnocentric temptation of self-imprisoning within the confines of the primordial tradition as perfect and complete, they must also prove that they can constructively and critically appropriate the wisdom of the non-Muslim world on ecology without succumbing to either unprincipled eclecticism or "Westoxication."[29] Following Ibn Khaldūn's footsteps, it can be safely assumed that without an open mind capable of absorbing the wisdom of others, the Islamic thought will inevitably ghettoize itself on ruinous grounds.[30] To prevent this unwanted outcome, and to lift the heavy chain of dogmatism that shuns the rest of the world as unessential to the development of its thought (perhaps except as negative points of reference), the Islamic ecotheology draws its inspiration—to borrow foreign ideas and infuse them into its repository—based on the inviolability of its communicative theological ethics that touches on universal human progress across visible and invisible frontiers; undoubtedly, such a progress means in today's shrinking world a process of forging partnership and collective action on the part of different peoples around the world.

Launched by a new sense of realism about the shared global problems and the welter of interdependencies that characterize today's world society, this communicative theology is bound to jailbreak from the twin hazards of Western and Eastern self-centrism. Responding to the enthusiasm generated by the impact of greater and greater intrafaith communication, this "school" of theology is potentially readied for substantial learning from without. And at the same time, its openness to interfaith communication implies that the Islamic ecotheology's requirement is not necessarily an epistemological *courpure* pure and simple, that in fact the parameters of this theology can perhaps be best described as neo-conservative. The neo aspect of its conservatism comes from its particular view of what it takes to have an Islamic renaissance in the late twentieth century?

If we start from the view that the aim of the Islamic ecotheology is to present an authentic interpretation of Islam intimately in tune with the need for renewal in the historically changed circumstances, then it is easier to proceed with confidence towards the stated project of Islamic renaissance. Though this means taking Islam in a new direction, the course of the Islamic ecotheology still retains the threads of continuity in many respects: it concurs with the prevalent view among the Muslim scholars that the refinement of theological method is the *sine qua non* of Islamic knowledge, that without theological beliefs the harmony of man and nature is difficult if not impossible to achieve, and that any attempt to rethink the unity of man and nature must by necessity travel through metaphysics as a viable, and not a self-defeating, solution.[31]

Henceforth, the Islamic ecotheology has cut for itself a huge job. It must articulate a defensible non-anthropocentric conception of Islam; it must provide a non-objectivating view of nature, and a dialectical view of man that is not overlaid with the stereotypical monarchical connotation of vicegerency; it must be an integrated theology which views all life as sacred and deals with man's relation with His Deity, man's relation with man, and man's relation with nature; it would open new inquiries about all these relations. Concerning the latter, it would seek deeper views than the conventional one according to which living beings are at the disposal of man, it would favor a more complex theological discourse to cast in new lights the religious interpretation of man-nature dualism; it would seek all these by and through a critical self-reflection that would amount to (a) a reconstruction of meaning of key Islamic terms and their interrelationships, e.g., *tawḥīd* (divine unity), *khalqiyat* (creation), *'ahd* (covenant), *amānat* (trust), *qiyamat* (apocalypse), and *ummah* (community), and (b) a deconstruction of those Islamic cosmological, theological, and ethical perspectives deemed untenable either wholly or in parts. In pursuing these objectives, the Islamic ecotheology would contribute to the ongoing debates on ecology and ethics, showing the exalted place of Islam in the planetary struggle for survival and evolution. Should the Islamic ecotheology succeed in raising to the occasion of challenges aforementioned, in that case its proponents will have very little difficulty proving that Islam and care for the earth and its creatures are one and the same, that where there is an Islamic theological vision there is no scarcity of ethics of responsibility toward the environment, and that Islamic attempts to conceive of nature as a moral category potentially give rise to a human species capable of self-limiting from undue exploitation, and who communicates with nature as part of a moral order. The shift to an Islamic ecotheology might well have consequences for the Muslims' sense of obligation to nature and for the norms governing their interaction with nature that they regard as justifiable. A final introductory note and that is, the Islamic ecotheology is less concerned about the newness of its approach, as a new "paradigm", and more with the self-prescribed criterion of consistency vis-a-vis its theological route. This route is paved to a considerable degree with extractions from *kalām* and *falsafah* backgrounds. Transgressing the time-honored distinctions, the Islamic ecotheology's newness derives from its novel combination of manifestly hostile subviews within Islam, and from the addition of elements of novelty inspired by advances in human knowledge.

In bringing this introductory writing to a close, if we were to ask instead, whether or not the Islamic ecotheology promises more than it delivers, and whether its potential to distort surpasses its potential to illuminate, then we have a legitimate excuse to pause for a healthy moment of self-doubt, followed by a conscientious effort to delineate the specifics of the Islamic ecotheology.

NOTES

1. See, Lynn White, "The Historical Roots of the Ecological Crisis", *Science* 156, March 1967, pp. 1203–7. Prior to White, Arnold Toynbee articulated the ecological attack on monotheistic religions. See, "The Religious Background of the Present Environmental Crisis", in *Ecology and Religion in History,* edited by David and Eileen Spring, New York, 1974.

2. Al-Qur'ān: "Then We made you heirs in the land

after them, to see how ye would behave", Al-Qur'ān, Eng. tr. by A. Y. Ali, Qatar ed., X:14. See also *ibid.*, XXVII:62, XXXV:39 and LXVII:14.

3. "Seest thou not that God has made subject to you (men) all that is an the earth?" *Ibid.*, XXII:65. "It is He Who hath made you (His) agents, inheritors of earth: He hath raised you in ranks, some above others: that He may try you in the gifts He hath given you." *Ibid.*, VI:165.

4. For a critique of technical rationality see, Jurgen Habermas, *The Theory of Communicative Action, l: Reason and Rationalization of Society,* Boston, 1984; *Zur Rekonstruktion des Historischen Materialismus,* Frankfurt, 1976. Also Max Weber, *The Methodology of the Social Sciences,* New York, 1949.

5. See, Seyyed Hussein Nasr, *The Encounter of Man and Nature,* London, 1968; Ziauddin Sardar, *The Future of Muslim Civilization,* London, 1979; S. Parvez Manzoor, "Environment and Values: the Islamic Perspective", in *The Touch of Midas: Science, Values and Environment in Islam and the West,* edited by Ziauddin Sardar, Manchester, 1984, pp. 150–170; A.R. Agwan, *The Environmental Concern of Islam,* New Delhi, 1992.

6. See, Fazlun Khalid and Joanne O'Brien, eds., *Islam and Ecology,* London, 1992.

7. Seyyed Hussein Nasr, *Science and Civilization in Islam,* Cambridge, 1987.

8. Seyyed Hussein Nasr, *Islamic Life and Thought,* New York, 1981.

9. Toshihiko Izutsu, *God and Man in the Koran,* Tokyo, 1964, p. 75.

10. Fazlur Rahman, *Major Themes of the Qur'an,* Chicago, 1980; Seyyed Qutb, *This Religion of Islam,* al-Manar Press, 1967; also, Wan Mohd Nor Wan Daud, "God in the Quran: An Objective and Functional Existent", in *Islam and the Modern Age,* vol. XIX, No. 3 (1988), pp. 155–165.

11. "But those who believe and work deeds of righteousness—to them We shall give a Home in Heaven,—lofty mansions, beneath which flow rivers,—to dwell therein for aye;—an excellent reward for those who do (good)! (Al-Qur'ān, XXIX:58). For more on this issue see, Colleen McDonnel and Bernard Lang, *Heaven: A History,* New Haven, 1988. Also, Juan Eduardo Campo, *The Other Sides of Paradise,* South Carolina, 1991.

12. For example, see, Murteza Muttahari, *Fundamentals of Islamic Thought: God, Man and the Universe,* translated by Hamid Algar, Berkeley, 1985.

13. Michel Foucault, *The Archaeology of Knowledge,* London, 1970. For a greater elaboration on postmodern anti-humanism see, K. Soper, *Humanism and Anti-Humanism,* Hutchinson, 1986. Derrida's view can be found in his book *Margins of Philosophy,* Chicago, 1983.

14. Ali Shariati, *Islamology* (in Fārsī), Tehran, 1981, p. 100.

15. Ernst Bloch, *Danz Prinzip Hoffnung,* Frankfurt, 1981, p. 1412.

16. The problem with Sardar's defense of Islam is that he does not grapple with those passages in the Qur'ān and *hadīth* which, according to the ecological critics, are anthropocentric. See Sardar's introduction in the *Touch of Midas, op.cit.,* p. 8.

17. See, Shaikh Muhammad Abduh, *al-Islam wan-Nasraniya,* Cairo, 1954; Muhammad Iqbal, *The Reconstruction of Religious Thought in Islam,* Oxford, 1932; Ali Shariati, *On the Sociology of Islam,* Berkeley, 1979.

18. Shariati, *ibid.*

19. Ibn 'Arabi writes about "the confines of nature . . . the place of forgetfulness." See, W.C. Chittick, *The Sufi Path of Knowledge,* New York, 1989, p. 165. For Rumi's view, see, *Discourses of Rumi,* translated by A. J. Arbery, London, 1961, p. 60. Similar views can be found in the Asha'ari school. See, Richard J. McCarthy, *The Theology of* al-Ash'ari, Beirut, 1953.

20. *Towards Islamization of Disciplines,* Washington, 1989; *Islamization of Knowledge,* Washington, 1991; also, Seyyed Hussein Nasr, "Islam and the Environmental Crisis", *Journal of Islamic Science,* 6, No. 2 (July-December, 1990).

21. See, Max L. Stackhouse, *Apologia: Contextualization, Globalization, and Mission in Theological Education,* Grand Rapids, 1988. Also, Hans Kung, *Global Responsibility: In Search of a New World Ethic,* New York, 1991.

22. For example, see, Francis Fukuyama, *The End of History and the Last Man,* New York, 1992, p. 217. In this book, Fukuyama portrays Islam as an "illiberal ideology" that is "very hard to reconcile with liberalism and the recognition of universal rights, particularly freedom of conscience or religion."

23. See, Mona Abul-Fadl, *Where East Meets West: Agenda of Islamic Revival,* Washington, 1992. Also, John L. Esposito, *The Islamic Threat,* Oxford, 1992.

24. Jurgen Habermas, *The Theory of Communicative Action,* vol. II (Boston, 1987). For critical evaluations of Habermas see, Axel Honneth and Hans Joas, eds., *Communicative Action,* Cambridge, MA, 1991.

25. David C. Gordon, *Images of the West,* Lanham, MD, 1989.

26. Hussein Ali Montazeri, *Tawzih al-Masail,* Tehran, 1984, p. 516.

27. Iqbal, *The Reconstruction of Religious Thought in Islam, op. cit.,* p. 183.

28. "A theology of the inorganic is lacking." Paul Tillich, *Systematic Theology,* vol. III, Chicago, 1963, p. 18. Similarly, Albert Schweitzer has written, "The greatest fault of ethics hitherto has been to deal only with man's relation with man." *Ethics and Civilization,* London, 1929, p. 133. In this book, Schweitzer writes that no man is fully ethical unless all of life is sacred to

him "that of plants and animals as that of his fellowman." Page 216. For contemporary attempts in Christianity and other religions to address the ecological issues see, among others, John B. Cobb, Jr., *Sustainability,* Orbis, 1992; Jay B. McDaniel, *Of God and Pelican: A Theology of Reverence for Life,* Westminister, 1989; Conrad Cherry, *Nature and Religious Imagination,* Albany, NY, 1980; Dieter T. Hessel, *For Creation's Sake: Preaching, Ecology and Justice,* Geneva, 1985; Warwick Fox, *Toward a Transpersonal Ecology: Developing New Foundations for Environmentalism,* Boston, 1990; Judith Plant, ed., *Healing Wounds: The Promise of Ecofeminism,* Philadelphia, 1989; Robert Disch, *The Ecological Conscience,* New York, 1971; M. Sethna, "Zoroastrianism and the Protection of Nature", in *Religion, Nature and Survival;* New Delhi, 1992.

29. On the concept of Westoxication see, Jala Al-e Ahmad, *Westoxication,* in Farsi, Tehran, 1981.

30. In the beginning of his book, Ibn Khaldun admonishes his contemporary Muslims for their failure to imitate the Western visitors who learnt what they could from the East. See, *Mughaddimah,* translated by Franz Rosenthal, New York, 1958.

31. Habermas has argued that attempts to re-establish the unity of reason "would have to lead back to metaphysics, and thus behind the levels of learning reached in the modern age into a re-enchanted world." Jurgen Habermas, "Reply to My Critics", in James Thompson and David Held, eds., *Habermas: Critical Debates,* Cambridge, MA, 1982, p. 245. The question left unanswered by Habermas is how his own theory of communication can restore the autonomy of nature against the assault of technical rationality short of, at a minimum, falling back on the "quasi-transcendental" notion of human interests (which Habermas has bracketed since taking the linguistic turn in his philosophy)?

SELECTED BIBLIOGRAPHY

Avicenna, *On Theology,* trans. by A. J. Arbery, Hyerion Press, 1957.

A. R. Agwan, *The Environmental Concern of Islam,* New Delhi: Institute of Objective Studies, 1992.

———, "Towards an Ecological Consciousness", *The American Journal of Islamic Social Sciences,* 10, no. 2 (Summer 1993).

William Lane Craig, *The Kalam Cosmological Argument,* McMillan, 1979.

Oliver Leaman, *An Introduction to Medieval Islamic Philosophy,* Cambridge Univ. Press, 1985.

Herbert A. Davidson, *Alfarabi, Avicenna, and Averroes, on Intellect,* Oxford, 1992.

Michael Walzer, *Greeks into Arabic: Essay on Islamic Philosophy,* Oxford, 1962.

S. M. Stern, A. Hourani, and U. Brown, *Islamic Philosophy and the Classical Tradition,* Univ. of South Carolina, 1972.

H. A. R. Gibb, *Modern Trends in Islam,* Octagon Books, 1978.

Richard J. McCarthy, *The Theology of al-Ashari,* Beirut: Imprimerie Catholique, 1953.

Juan Eduardo Campo, *The Other Side of Paradise,* Univ. of South Carolina, 1991.

Ignaz Goldziher, *Introduction to Islamic Theology and Law,* trans. A. R. Homar, Princeton, 1981.

Colleen McDonnell and Bernard Lang, *Heaven: A History,* Yale, 1988.

George Makdissi, *Religion, Law and Learning in Classical Islam,* London: Variorum, 1991.

A. S. Tritton, *Muslim Theology,* London: Luzac, 1947.

Pervez Hoodbhoy, *Islam and Science,* ZED, 1991.

———, *Towards Islamization of Disciplines* (IIIT, 1989).

———, *Islamization of Knowledge* (IIIT, 1991).

Mona Abul-Fadl, *Where East Meets West: Agenda of Islamic Revival* (IIIT, 1992).

S. Waqar Ahmad Hussaini, *Islamic Environmental Systems Engineering,* McMillan Press, 1980.

Ziauddin Sardar, ed., "The Touch of Midas: Science, Values and Environment," in *Islam and the West,* Manchester Univ. Press, 1984.

Seyyed Qutb, *This Religion of Islam,* Al-Manar Press, 1967.

Toshihiko Izutsu, *God and Man in the Quran,* Tokyo: Keio Institute of Cultural and Linguistic Studies, 1964.

Fazlur Rahman, *Major Themes of the Quran,* Chicago: Bibliotheca Islamica, 1980.

Ali Shariati, *The Sociology of Islam,* Mizan Press, 1984.

Riazal-Hassan Gilani, *The Reconstruction of Legal Thought in Islam,* Delhi, 1982.

A. J. Arbery, *The Discourses of Rumi,* London, John Murray, 1961.

Al-Ash'arī, *Al-Ibna an Uṣūl al-Diyāna,* trans. by Walter C. Klein, American Oriental Society, 1940.

Reza Mutahhari, *Fundamentals of Islamic Theology,* Mizan Press, 1985.

W. C. Chittick, *The Sufi Path of Knowledge,* Sunny, 1989.

Seyyed Hossein Nasr, *Islamic Science: An Illustrated Study,* World of Islam Publishing Company, 1976.

———, *The Encounter of Man and Nature,* Allen and Unwin, 1978.

———, *Science and Civilization in Islam,* Islamic Text Society, 1987.

———, "Islam and the Environmental Crisis," *Journal of Islamic Science,* 6, no. 2, July–December, 1990.

Dieter T. Hessel, *For Creation's Sake: Preaching, Ecology and Justice,* Geneva Press, 1985.

William Ophuls, *Ecology and the Politics of Scarcity,* W. H. Freman and Co., 1977.

Robert Disch, *The Ecological Conscience,* Prentice Hall, 1971.

A. M. Sethna, "Zoroastrianism and the Protection of Nature", in *Religion, Nature and Survival,* New Delhi: Inter-Religious Forum for Communal Harmony, 1992.

Johann Baptist Metz and Edmund Schillebeeckx, *No Heaven Without Earth,* SCM Press, 1991.

Paul Tillich, *Systematic Theology,* Chicago University Press, 1963.

Conrad Cherry, *Nature and Religious Imagination,* Fortress Press, 1980.

Alistair MacIntyre, *After Virtue,* Notre Dame Univ., 1984.

Immanuel Kant, "Duties to Animals and Spirits", in *Lectures On Ethics,* Harper & Row, 1963.

Jay B. McDaniel, *Of God and Pelican: A Theology of Reverence for Life,* Westminister/John Knox Press, 1989.

David C. Thomasma, *Human Life in the Balance,* Westminister/John Knox Press, 1990.

Wesley Granberg-Michaelson, *Redeeming the Creation: The Rio Earth Summit: Challenges for the Churches,* WCC Publication, 1992.

John B. Cobb, Jr., *Sustainability,* Orbis, 1992.

———, *Is It Too Late? A Theology of Ecology,* Bruce, 1972.

Yam Kim Hao, *Doing Theology in A Pluralist World,* Kin Keong Printing, 1990.

Harold H. Oliver, *Relatedness: Essays in Metaphysics and Theology,* Mercer, 1984.

Claude Y. Stewart, Jr., *Nature in Grace: A Study in the Theology of Nature,* Mercer, 1983.

Frederick Ferre, ed., *Concepts of Nature and God,* Univ. of Georgia, 1989.

N. Max Wildiers, *The Theologian and His Universe: Theology and Cosmology From the Middle Ages to the Present,* Seabury, 1982.

Gordon Kaufman, *The Theological Imagination: Constructing the Concept of God,* Westminister, 1981.

Michel Foucault, *The Archaeology of Knowledge,* Pantheon, 1969.

Jacque Derrida, *Of Grammatology,* Johns Hopkins Univ. Press, 1967.

———, *Writing and Difference,* Chicago Univ. Press, 1978.

Jurgen Habermas, *The Theory of Communicative Action,* two Volumes, Beacon Press, 1988.

———, *The Philosophical Discourse of Modernity,* MIT Press, 1988.

David Harvey, *The Condition of Postmodernity,* Basil Blackwell, 1989.

Francoise Lyotard, *The Postmodern Condition,* Univ. of Minneapolis Press, 1984.

David C. Gordon, *Images of the West: Third World Perspectives,* Rowman and Littlefield Publishers, 1989.

Akbar S. Ahmed, *Postmodernism and Islam,* Routledge, 1992.

David Ehrenfeld, *The Arrogance of Humanism,* Oxford, 1978.

R. Kerry Turner, David Pearce and Ian Bateman, *Environmental Economics,* Johns Hopkins Univ. Press, 1993.

Lynton Keith Caldwell, *International Environmental Policy,* Duke Univ. Press, 1990.

Carloyine Thomas, *Environment in International Relations,* Royal Institute of International Affairs, 1992.

Donald Scherer and Thomas Attig, eds, *Ethics and the Environment,* Prentice Hall, 1983.

John Passmore, *Man's Responsibility for Nature,* John Screibner's Sons, 1974.

R. F. Dasman, *Environmental Conservation,* John Wiley, 1984.

Tom Regan, *The Case for Animal Rights,* Univ. of California, 1984.

Eugene C. Hargrove, *Foundations of Environmental Ethics,* Prentice-Hall, 1989.

Warwick Fox, *Toward a Transpersonal Ecology: Developing New Foundations for Environmentalism,* Shambhala, 1990.

Carolyn Merchant, *Death of Nature: Women, Ecology and the Scientific Revolution,* Harper and Row, 1980.

Judith Plant, ed., *Healing Wound: The Promise of Ecofeminism,* Philadelphia: New Society Publishers, 1989.

Anna Bramewell, *Ecology in the Twentieth Century: A History,* Yale University, 1989.

Arne Naess, "The Arrogance of Antihumanism?" *Ecophilosophy,* 6 (1984).

Robyn Eckersley, *Environmentalism and Political Theory: Toward an Ecocentric Approach,* Sunny, 1992.

Bill Devall and George Sessions, *Deep Ecology: Living as if Nature Mattered,* Peregrine Smith, 1985.

M. J. Roads, *Talking with Nature,* H. I. Kramer, 1987.

Peter S. Wenz, *Environmental Justice,* Sunny, 1988.

Paul and Anne Ehrlich, *Extinction,* Ballantine, 1981.

Richard Rarre, *Nature and Culture in Western Discourses,* Routledge and Kegan Paul, 1988.

An Islamic Response to the Manifest Ecological Crisis
Issues of Justice

NAWAL H. AMMAR

INTRODUCTION

THE CRISIS OF AN EARTH BLEEDING AND burning to accommodate a fivefold economic expansion in just the last forty years is, by definition, global, and not specific to Muslims per se. Nonetheless, the manifestations of the crisis in Muslim communities and countries are as alarming as anywhere else in the world and illustrate some of the problems that afflict other religions. Some argue that the ecological crisis is the divine will of God as revealed by the Qur'an denoting the nearing of the end of life on earth. As such all this discussion about avoiding an ecological crisis is futile since it is predestined. The collective human disapproval of the crisis is of no consequence and it is actually discredited as a standard of value by some in Islam.[1] This view of predestination in Islam is not, however, maintained by all believers, although it dominates today. Islam also includes a progressive view wherein humans impact and change the world in ways that are not predestined. This debate between predestination and human free will in Islam is known as the *naql* (knowledge transmitted from revelation and tradition) versus *aqal* (knowledge transmitted from independent reason) debate. The proponents of *naql* see morality and values as not subject to human free will because only God can know what is good and what is bad.[2] The *aqal* view proponents, on the other hand, maintain that reason, guided by revelation, can provide the basis for a progressive Islamic vision of human action. Evidence supporting this progressive view can be found as early as the seventh century. The party of Unity and Justice, or the *Mu'tazilites,* insisted that God gave humans intellect to "choose conduct to decide and even to create their own acts free from predestination."[3] Reason guides in accordance with general principles and revelation gives particular parables of such principles.[4] The Qur'an emphasizes rationalism for example "Say (unto them Muhammad): Are those who know equal to those who know not? It is those who are endued with understanding that receive admonition."[5] Hence, humans, according to this school, when punished in the hereafter will be punished for sins they could have avoided. This [essay] will be framed by arguments proposed by *ahl al-aqal* (the rationalists) with revelation guiding the general principles of reason.

A MUSLIM RESPONSE TO THE ECOLOGICAL CRISIS

Framing the Issues

It is not difficult to understand the ecological crisis in its apparent manifestations as polluted air, radiation, contamination of water, and the eradication of entire species of animals and plants. It is, however, more difficult to ascertain that the processes that lead to environmental depletion and thus an ecological crisis of the magnitude we are experiencing on our earth today are the result of human injustices and greed. This type of correlation between behavior and the resulting ecological crisis is particularly difficult for a group of people, such as the Muslims in the world, who view themselves as victims of post-colonialism, racism, poverty, enslavement, and an unfair demonization. In this [essay], I am proposing, based on a rational basis, a retrieval of an Islamic response to the ecological crisis that has been long forgotten. This response assumes a confident and responsible world community of Muslims that sees itself engaged in the problems on this earth as active contributors to a global solution. This response

Ammar, Nawal H., "The Ecological Crisis and Islamic Social Justice," in Harold Coward and Daniel Maguire, Eds., *Visions of a New Earth: Religious Perspectives on Population, Consumption, and Ecology,* pp. 131–144. Reprinted by permission of the State University of New York Press.

views the reasons underlying human crisis (including the ecological one) to be behaviors of greed, lack of moderation, inequity, and disrespect (or, . . . believing in the religion of the market). Islamic history is full of examples of how such behavior has lead to losing battles against the pagans, making bad judgements, and losing the Islamic empire and hence, the Islamic identity altogether in the nineteenth century. Contemporary behavior of Muslims is also full of examples of greed, lack of moderation, and hence nonreverence to God's creation. In recent years Muslims have extracted eightfold their level of consumption of oil for export to the United States, Western Europe, and Japan.[6] The extraction of oil and its by-products is undertaken with minimal controls on toxic emissions and hazards. The Muslim world owns 800 billion barrels of oil in future reserves.[7] To keep the price of oil at a competitive level for global consumption, stringent pollution controls are not likely to be introduced. Muslims must join other world religions in recovering the sense of the sacred, which, as Daniel Maguire says, is at the heart of all religion. The false sacreds of the market religion are invading and pervading all cultures and are the modern idols challenging all world religions today.

The polluting effect of oil reaches far beyond its production. We were all reminded of this in 1990 by the "Desert Shield/Desert Storm" war. The Iraqi invasion of Kuwait meant a loss of 25 percent of world oil reserves and a future threat to 54 percent of the world's oil reserves held by Saudi Arabia and the Emirates (Tanzer 1991, 271–72). In a war that the British press dubbed "the real estate war," 93 percent of the "precision" bombs dropped were misguided and 75 percent missed their target. At least two hundred thousand people were killed and injured. More than ten thousand Kurds were displaced. Today, a large number of U.S. Desert Storm veterans suffer from what is feared to be the consequences of a germ warfare.[8]

The setting ablaze of over six hundred oil wells on 22 February 1991 exemplifies the environmental impact of war. Toukani and Barnaby, two British scientists, summarized the global environmental effects by stating "Close to Kuwait, the plume could cause a considerable reduction in daylight; the obstruction of sunlight might significantly reduce the surface temperature locally. This in turn could reduce the rainfall over parts of South East Asia during the period of summer monsoon. If the smoke reaches the ozone layer, the smoke could lead to small reductions in ozone concentrations within the northern hemisphere."[9] Once again, the maldistribution of resources and the desire to maintain or extend access to them is directly implicated in this "real estate" war.

More than thirty Muslim nations were directly involved in this war that environmentalists are calling the "Nuclear Winter," because the effects of the oil burning has reduced sunlight and temperatures throughout the region. The future does not look any brighter for Muslims. In the last world Arms Proliferation Treaty (1995), two among the countries that refused to sign the treaty were Muslim, Pakistan and Turkey.

War, however, is not the only polluting factor in Muslim countries and communities. Water is also polluted in Muslim countries. Waste dumping into rivers, seas, or nearest streams is common and the state apparatus cannot control it. Explosives are also used to fish, thus eradicating the symbiotic environment in the habitat. Air pollution results from unregulated industrial waste disposal, the use of leaded gasoline, and the overcrowding in cities. A recent study conducted by the U.S. Agency of International Development (AID) in Egypt shows that air in Cairo is ten times more polluted than a city equal to its size in the United States. Industries discharge 1,350 tons of lead yearly into the air in Egypt. Drinking water has at its lowest estimate 9.3 milligrams more lead than the average acceptable rate globally.[10]

The behaviors illustrated above that lead to human crisis can be understood through the Arabic word *hay'a*. The word is virtually untranslatable to English. It actually denotes behaviors that reflect shyness out of respect and reverence rather than out of fear. It is behavior that reflects balance, honorable manners, and protection of God's glory including his creatures and other creation. For the purpose of this [essay] I will translate the word as "dignified reserve." I am proposing that we revive this conceptual framework of *hay'a* as a guiding theological principle that could avert an ecological crisis. I suggest that the absence of *hay'a* has contributed to a livelihood among Muslims that is causing the ecological crisis. This is reflected in the disparity between the poor and the rich, a production system that is entirely dependent on the monopolies and big corporations, which in turn leads to maldistribution of resources and overconsumption, authoritarian leadership, wars, disrespect of human diversity, and finally a way of life that depletes natural and human resources. In this livelihood that lacks dignified reserve Muslims have also dehumanized women, which in turn has contributed to reducing their status to reproductive apparatuses only, hence causing the overpopulation that Muslim communities experience today. This overpopulation in turn has led to the manifest results of environmental depletion in the forms of pollution, disease, infant mortality, and crime.

In the balance of this [essay] I will look at how the behaviors that lack *hay'a* in production and consumption, and toward women have contributed to the manifestations of ecological depletion. I will suggest throughout some ethical responses that are Islamic in principle and hope that their retrieval provides a solid response to averting the doomsday approach that some Muslims believe is beyond human free will and reason.

The Issues in Detail: Muslims' Economic and Political Livelihood and the Ecological Crisis

Islamic teachings from the Qur'an, Hadith, Sunna, and history all emphasize the need for moderation and modesty in a Muslim's life. The integration of Muslim countries and communities into the larger market economy as a consequence of national modernization, development, and desegregation have left them with maldeveloped patterns of production and consumption that do not function by moderation principles. Although Muslim countries and communities are considered as peripheral in terms of their production capacity—that is, they are marginal contributors to manufacturing markets—the way Muslim countries produce and consume creates glaring disparities between the poor and the rich, makes them dependent on monopolies, leads to authoritarian leadership, and creates an elite class that overconsumes and overproduces and, hence, contributes to depleting the environment. By and large the forty-six Muslim countries mainly extract raw materials, oil being the most important (56 percent of the world's oil export). Although Muslim countries have some manufacturing industries such as cement, textile, and light armaments, it is not at a level to move them into a competitive advantage within the global market.[11] Hence, most of the trade (95 percent) that occurs is with non-Muslim countries. The oil industry, although nationalized, is heavily dependent on foreign technology, expertise, and security (as the Gulf War lately showed), and the maintenance of an elite group with which foreign heads of state can interact.

Robert Reich notes this structure of elites benefitting from the global economies wherever they are by stating, "the economic globalization . . . has served to delink the interests of the wealthy classes from a sense of a national interest and thereby from a sense of concern for an obligation to their less fortunate neighbors. . . . It is no longer meaningful to speak about this delinking in terms of a North-South divide. . . . It is class."[12]

For Muslim countries, the problem involves the uneven development in the global capitalist system that has led to extreme disparities between the elites and nonelites both among and within nations. Understood in terms of disparity between the poor and the rich, Islam has a very clear response to how Muslims should produce and consume. Hourani, a famous scholar of Islam writes "Islam could also be a basis of economic life . . . and if accepted that will ensure social justice and liberate humans from servitude."[13] The Islamic economic system has been set forth as a "third way" that differs from both "laissez-faire capitalism and Marxist socialism."[14] The basis of the system is set out in general terms in the Qur'an, but the details have been worked out by legal scholars. The system, ideally, creates a society of private ownership and enterprise without the vast accumulation and concentration of wealth. Two principles summarize the Islamic economic system. The first sees that income, exchange, and trade should be based on just transaction and not claims on natural or market resources. The second . . . sees that the community has an overriding priority over individuals. Adherence to these principles would serve to constrain the unequal distribution of resources and, hence, the overconsumption and overproduction of resources among the few. The following outlines these principles.

Principle One: Income, exchange, and trade should be based on just transaction and not claims on natural or market resources. Just interaction in the Islamic perspective should not be confused with the Buddhist concept of eliminating desire. . . . Actually Islam sees desire as a source of happiness, but what is problematic with desire is its attainment. In Islam individual desires should be attained in ways that permit everyone in the community to fulfill his/her individual desires and individual desires take a lower priority over community desires. Hence, there are conditions that regulate individual and communal fulfillment of desire.

Work is one of the conditions of just interaction. The Qur'an is very clear about issues of reward and revenues. For example it states "Humans shall have nothing but what they strive for."[15] People who work are not equal to those who do not in Islam.[16] Work in the Islamic tradition includes more than a "job," and the word would translate as "labor."

Equal, exact, and honest exchange is another condition of the just transaction in Islam. The Qur'an emphasizes "O my people give full measure and full weight with equity, and wrong not people in respect of their things, and act not corruptly in the land making mischief."[17] This concept becomes clearer to many of us living in the West when we consider the madness of Christmastime and the desire to buy toys for children during this time. In 1996 in the United States, a toy called 'Tickle Me Elmo' from the *Sesame Street* children's show that sells normally for $26 became so rare in the market that some people were auctioning it for over $1,500. This kind of exchange that is based on creating an artificial need and crazed desire is not permitted in the Islamic system. All exchange in the Islamic system ought to be of *use value*—that is, a good, or service for another equivalent in value. Exchange should never be of *surplus value*—i.e., a commodity with a value altered for some humanly imposed reason. Surplus-value exchanges (i.e., values determined not by the real use value of the good or service, but by the value imposed by supply/demand forces of the market) are considered usury.

Usury, *riba*, is forbidden in Islam. The rule governing *riba* in Islam states that any profit or interest accrued without working for it, or without being a full partner in the risks of gain and loss makes the transaction unjust. *Riba*, thus, is defined as "asking something for nothing in an interaction . . . it is not equal for equal."[18] As such the Qur'an warns "that they used usury though it was forbidden and that they usurped human wealth with falsehood."[19]

Interest accrued from Western-style banking is considered *riba*. The client in Western-style banking, according to Islamic interpretation, is at a disadvantage. As a depositor his/her money is used to create more money under false guarantees of delivery. As a borrower, she/he pays interest on imaginary assets that the banks do not have. The imaginary money that banks have creates artificial wealth by exploiting the hard-working depositor and the needy borrower. In addition this artificial wealth is not redistributed equitably, but remains concentrated in the hands of a small minority of financiers. The Qur'an refers to such practices by saying "That which you lay out for increase through the property of [other] people, will have no increase with God: but that which you lay out for charity seeking the countenance of God, [will increase], it is these who will get a recompense multiplied."[20]

Cummings, Askari, and Mustafa note that the Islamic banking system operates on the principle of equity ownership not interest.[21] Money invested in a bank as though it were a business venture without guarantees of profit or loss would be Islamic. Hence, the investor gains interest only if the business produces profit. This kind of investment guarantees more conservative risk-taking ventures and thereby reduces creation of vast sums of artificial wealth and its concentration in few hands.

Principle Two: The right of the community over individuals. Islam emphasizes the concept of communal good and duties to the community. . . . This community of believers has a collective ethos of goodness: "let there arise out of you a band of people inviting to all that is good, enjoining what is right and forbidding what is wrong."[22] It is a community where Muslims protect each other, hold together tightly, and cooperate on generosity and righteousness.[23] Islam's emphasis on the right of the community over the individual is demonstrated through its position on issues of distributive justice in general. The particularities of this position can be best illustrated in Islam's treatment of the three issues of: (*a*) taxation, (*b*) community leadership, and (*c*) its vision of the "other" in the community.

a. Taxation. Islam outlines three tax structures: one for Muslims, one for non-Muslims, and one that is universal and applies to all regardless of religion. All taxes aim to redistribute the wealth and power of the rich to the poor. *Zakat* is a tax that all Muslims should pay. It is a tax that has become a religious obligation and it is particularly intended for the rich to fulfill the needs of the poor in the community. This fulfillment is not charity in the Western sense but a community obligation. The state, *dar al-Islam,* oversees the collection of *zakat.* The exact levy of the *zakat* varies in accordance with different legal schools of thought. Generally, a 2.5 percent tax on one's wealth is applied. Some Islamic jurists include taxation on mines as part of the *zakat,* others assess it as a separate tax. Regardless all Muslims must pay a tax for extracting the land's wealth. Some jurists also argue that if *zakat* is inadequate to meet the demands of the needy, then the state can impose additional taxes.

Muslims also pay taxes on agricultural land, *ushur.* The levy on land is applied to the gross production before deduction of production costs.[24] The Qur'anic injunction recommending this tax states: "O you who have attained to faith spend on theirs out of the good things which you may have acquired and out of that which we bring forth for you from the earth."[25] Non-Muslims living in an Islamic state pay a poll tax (*jiziyah*). This tax is paid as compensation for being defended by and included in the state. The tax rate is based on a community consensus (*ijma'*) and should be assessed on the ability to pay.[26] Finally, all citizens of the Islamic state must pay a land tax (*kharaj*). The tax is levied on two bases. The first is assessed on a fixed rate regardless of the output, and the second is paid only if there is output from the land.

Islam's prescriptions on taxation offer an economic mechanism for limiting the disparities in access to resources the economic system otherwise generates. Nonetheless, two noneconomic prescriptions concerning community leadership and respect for human diversity are also critically important for an Islamic economic system and further serve to diminish inequities in the Islamic community.

b. Distributive Justice beyond Utilitarian Economies: Leadership Qualities. The Imam, Caliph, or Sultan is the person who leads the Islamic community and who would be responsible to facilitate and promote distribution within it. The quality of the leader is a very important element in securing a just community. Mernissi writes: "It is difficult to imagine a weaker political leader than a Muslim one. The ideal leader is modest, trembling with fear before his God and terrified before those he/she governs for making an unjust decision will lead him directly to hell."[27] The legitimacy of the Muslim leader is based on the will of the community (*ummah*) according to Islamic jurisprudence.[28] In Islam the leader has no divine powers.[29] The leader of the Islamic state ought to guarantee freedom for the subjects.[30] The leader ought to treat subjects equitably, and consult the community on the affairs of the state. The Qur'an states clearly the issue of justice as the working ideology of the leader in many verses.[31] Ibn Taymiya, a famous Muslim thinker who based his interpretations on reason, stated that "people have never disagreed on the negative consequences of injustice and the positive impact of justice. As such God will render a just nation victorious even if its citizens were non-believers, while the unjust state will be defeated even if its citizens were believers."[32]

The above-mentioned characteristics of the Islamic leader have disappeared in our modern day. Most leaders today in the Islamic world exercise some kind of authoritarianism. According to Mernissi: "The vulnerability has disappeared from the scene through the combined effect of the separation of Muslim memory from the rationalist tradition and the modern media that have created an unchallenged leader."[33] As such the issue of disparity between the poor and the rich in Islamic countries that are the result of maldevelopment requires the restoration of a just leader who is accountable to the community he/she rules. Once the leaders are ruling under Islamic precepts—justice, equality, and humility—rather than manipulating them, economic policies aimed at distributive justice could work and the ecological crisis resulting from the lack of distributive justice could be checked.

The above response, however, partially disregards the fact that Muslims do not live alone in this world. The relationship between Muslims and non-Muslims is very important to ensure equitable distribution of resources. Since I am writing an Islamic response I will focus on Islam's position toward non-Muslims.

c. Distributive Justice beyond Utilitarian Economies: The Vision Of the "Other" in Islam. In addition to the need of having a just leader, Islam enjoins Muslims to treat others peacefully and kindly if distributive justice is to be a characteristic of their community. There is some confusion about what Islam says concerning the relationship of Muslims to non-Muslims. Visions of the "other" are often tainted by three verses of Surah 9, Al Tawbah in the Qur'an.[34] The three verses enjoin Muslims to fight those who do not believe in Allah. Chapter 9 of the Qur'an is among the last that was revealed to the Prophet Muhammad. Sayed Qutb, a well-known Egyptian Islamist and a prominent thinker among the Muslim Brotherhood, argues that this chapter provides a final and absolute injunction. He argues that all other verses enjoining mercy, justice, tolerance toward non-Muslims were voided by this revelation.[35] This interpretation leads a number of Muslims to believe that Islam is the religion of the sword in its relationship to the non-Muslims. Numerous Muslim scholars (Abdu, Rida, Shaltout), however, disagree strongly with Qutb's interpretation. They argue that this chapter was revealed to address one specific historic instance. Al-Ghazzali notes that the Qur'an contains 120 verses related to respecting the non-Muslims including pagans, and that three verses cannot void so many injunctions.[36]

Difference and diversity in Islam must be understood as God's will.[37] This will of God for diversity among humans has to be respected: "We have indeed created humans in the best mold."

The Prophet's tradition and Islamic history are also full of stories about respect for non-Muslims. "Upon the passing of a funeral procession near where the Prophet gathered with some of his friends, he stood up in respect and so did the rest of the gathered. After the procession passed, one person in the crowd said: O Messenger of God did you know that this was the funeral of a Jew? The Prophet replied: Wasn't he human and had a human soul? Was he not a human created and made by God? Wasn't he a being with dignity?"[38] Another well-known story in Islamic history about the fourth Orthodox Caliph Ali is indicative of respect of the "other." Ali told the ruler he sent to Egypt, Malik al-Ashtar: "fill your heart with mercy and love to your subjects since they are two kinds: A sibling in belief or a human created by God the same way you were."

Islam not only prescribes respect of the "other," but urges cooperation with all peoples and nations.[39] Muslims are very clearly ordered to befriend the "other." The Qur'an states: "If one amongst the pagans sought asylum or refuge grant it to him."[40]

To summarize, the maldevelopment in the economic systems of Muslim communities that led to maldistribution of resources, overconsumption, disparity between the rich and the poor, dependency, authoritarianism among leaders, and disrespect of human diversity are at the basis of the ecological crisis. Islam prescribes an economic system that constrains the extent of the maldistribution of resources through its principles of taxation and distributive justice. Once Muslims practice these principles of equity in distribution of resources and treatment of others, which are at the heart of Islamic teachings, we will be moving one more step toward averting the ecological crisis.

The economic and political principle of *hay'a* (dignified reserve) has implications for other social and cultural relationships that pertain to the ecological crisis, namely the relationship between men and women. It is to this that I now turn.

Absence of Hay'a toward Women and the Ecological Crisis

Scientists have ascertained that overpopulation is a major contributing factor in the ecological crisis. The population growth rate in Muslim countries is among the highest in the world. The crude birth rate of the forty-six Muslim countries is 1 percent higher than that of the developing world as a whole.[41] In the mid-1980s even countries that adopted family planning programs (with the exception of Indonesia) in the early 1960s had very high natural increase rates of the population. For example, Pakistan's rate of increase was 2.8%, Egypt's rate was 2.6%, while the rate of increase in non-Muslim countries such as India and Colombia was 2.3% and 2.1%.[42]

Islam is indisputably a pronatal religion.[43] Nonetheless, family planning programs have also used Islamic teachings to convince people to use contraception. Various verses from the Qur'an that favor family planning outcomes were stressed. These included injunctions concerned with leaving heirs in good conditions, educating children to be useful, the quality and not the quantity of children, and how children are an enormous responsibility for parents.[44] Other interpretations based on reason were reiterated. For instance, in the Arab Muslim world distinctions between lifetime family planning (*Tah-*

did al-nasl) versus family planning as the spacing of children (*Tanzim al-nasl*) were made to sanction the use of contraception.

Although Islam sanctions the use of various methods of family planning and many Muslim countries and communities have adopted family planning as a state policy, only one country, Indonesia, has succeeded in curtailing its population increase significantly. What accounts for the limited success of these attempts to reduce population growth through the adoption of family planning programs and hence reduce the pressure on environmental resources?

The root of the reproductive problems for most Muslim women lies in the fact that they live either in the less developed world or the less affluent parts of the developed world. As such their social and material conditions inhibit following family planning programs successfully. While women are the target of most family planning programs, seldom do they participate directly in their design and implementation (i.e., they remain "invisible"). The human context of women in the programs ought to be emphasized and brought to the forefront. Data has shown that the empowerment of women through higher education, active involvement in the labor force, legislative policies, and increased access to health services often serve to delay marriage, reduce the number of offspring, and diminish the incidence of polygamy.[45] In Egypt, for example, 60% of women who cannot read and write had at least one co-wife, while the incidence of polygamy was reduced to 0.01% among women who had university degrees.[46] In most Muslim countries the patriarchal, misogynist local cultures favor interpretations of the Qur'an that debase women. Islam, however, sees women as equal to men and deserving of the same treatment; and both men and women will be judged on equal grounds before God.[47]

The equity that Islam grants women is not reflected in popular culture, economic opportunities, or formal substantive law. For instance, popular culture, as reflected in some Arabic proverbs, encourages violence against women ("if you break a girl's rib, twenty-four other ribs will grow"), glorifies male offspring ("those who bear boys never die"), and encourages women's dependence on men ("a straw husband is better than none").

Women's participation in the paid labor force still remains marginal in most Muslim countries and the jobs they do take typically offer little power, prestige, or income. According to statistics from the 1990 UN report on the Situation of Women, women constituted only 6% of the labor force in the United Arab Emirates (one of the wealthiest Muslim countries) and 62% of women above the age of fifteen were illiterate. Similarly, women made up only 10% of the labor force in Egypt (one of the poorest Muslim countries), and of these 20% worked in agriculture (a low-paying job) and 41 percent were self-employed (a less secure job).

Legal codes in Muslim countries, whether totally dependent on divine law (Shari'a) or partially dependent at the level of personal status codes, very clearly debase women. In all these countries, codes are legislated to favor men over women even if the punishment was un-Islamic. For example, in fornication cases, women are punished more severely than men, a practice that goes against the letter of the Qur'an. In cases where the texts are silent, the codes derived from the spirit of the text also favor men. Hence, a Muslim woman from an Islamic country cannot give her citizenship to her children if she is married to a foreign man. A man from a Muslim country, however, can give his children his citizenship even if his wife is foreign and he does not live in his native country. Women cannot divorce their husbands except in court, while men can declare a wife divorced by verbally uttering the words "I divorce you" three times. In many Muslim countries a Muslim man can divorce his wife or take a co-wife without any legal requirements to inform the concerned wife.

The empowerment of Muslim women as humans is central to the discussion about population increase and its impact on the ecology. Unless we improve the conditions of Muslim women according to Islamic teachings, the discussion of family planning would be as relevant as talking to an incubator. This means including women as active participants in family, economic, and political decision making. This can only be made possible by improving the conditions under which they live and bringing equity and dignity to women.

The improvement of Muslim women's status applies to both the rich and the poor. Islam has its own share of powerful women both in its history and in the contemporary world. Consequently, a return to Islamic teachings about women is essential to make family planning successful. Muslims, hence, need to remember how the Qur'an emphasizes the dignity of women by stating "Never will I suffer to be lost the work of any of you be he male or female ye are members of one of another" and behave with hay'a toward them.[48]

In sum, Islam offers much in response to the manifest ecological crisis of population growth. This response, however, focuses on a behavior toward women as humans rather than simply permitting a technological fix such as family planning. While Islam leaves open several avenues for family planning, traditional approaches using education about contraception have achieved limited success in most Muslim countries. This suggests that the population problem runs deeper than merely extending the knowledge about and availability of contraceptive devices. Rather, the empowerment of women (or lack thereof) lies at the core of the population problem, and hence, the ecological crisis. Islam views women and men as equal participants in the Muslim community, even if, in most Muslim (and, I might add, non-Muslim) countries this equity has not been realized. The population problem, then, appears to stem from un-Islamic behaviors and attitudes that lead to inequity between men and women. I am thus suggesting a revival of the Islamic behaviors of dignified respect toward women as mentioned in the Qur'an and Hadith.

CONCLUSION

Progressive Islam has several effective responses toward the ecological crisis. These responses have action-oriented components toward averting evil and promoting the good. Hence, the Qur'an emphasizes: "Verily never will Allah change the condition of a people until they change themselves."[49] The orientation of action in progressive Islam toward averting the ecological doom is one of dignified reserve: *hay'a*.

In relation to distributive justice between the poor and the rich that creates an elite that overconsumes and overproduces, and hence contributes to the ecological crisis by depleting the environment *hay'a* is reflected in the ethic of hard work. *Hay'a* is also reflected in the economic system of exchange that is based solely on use value versus surplus value of a good. Such an exchange value would bring equity among community members, reduce concentration of wealth and diminish the maldistribution of resources. The leader's humility and consultative duties with the community also bring forth the issue of respect of the leader to his/her subjects, which would eventually promote distributive justice. Further, Islam advises the respect for human diversity, something that is necessary for averting wars and for ensuring distributive justice within and outside the community.

In relation to population increase that also puts pressure on the ecology, *hay'a* requires action toward empowering women to have family planning programs, which would contribute to a reduction in natural growth rates in population.

Islam has a very clear and unequivocal response to the depletion and destruction of the environment and nature. Nature was created by God in an orderly fashion.[50] This nature is given to humans as a trust (*ammanah*). Thus, the Qur'anic injunction says "I am setting on earth a vice-regent."[51]

This vice-regent is a manager of the trust and not an owner. Depending on how humans manage this trust, they will be judged in the hereafter. Hence, there is a direct relationship between the utilization of nature and rewards on the day of judgment. The relationship not only emphasizes a "no-harm" principle to nature, but insists on the doing of good. The Prophet, for example, said: "anyone who witnesses evil should remonstrate upon it by hand, mouth or heart, the last is the weakest of faith."

Islam counsels Muslims to use of environmental resources in accordance with five rules:

1. The use of nature and its resources in a balanced, not excessive manner;
2. Treat nature and its resources with kindness;
3. Do not damage, abuse or distort nature in any way;
4. Share natural resources with others living in the habitat; and
5. Conserve.

These rules are set forth by jurors to ensure that nature and its resources are managed well by humans who are the executors of God's trust. Balance, admonitions against excess, justice, and the sharing of resources are, once more, found at the core of the Islamic attitude toward the environment. *Hay'a* of

God's creation requires that Muslims use earth's resources in moderation and conserve it.

The dignified reserve prescribed by Islam toward life on earth is not only the responsibility of some people, but it is every Muslim's duty. Muslim jurists have set forth a rule stating that "the executor is a guarantor even if the act is not deliberate or intentional." On account of this rule, every Muslim and every community claiming the faith ought to listen. Regardless of one's ethical preference to human free will or predestination, given the state of the earth's warming climate, increasing pollution, rates of deforestation, state of war, and disease due to the ecological imbalance, Muslims will be and are responsible on the day of judgment for this crisis.

NOTES

1. The following format will be utilized to denote reference to Qur'anic chapters and verses: Fatir: 8.
2. Al Ra'd: 17
3. G. F. Hourani, 1985, *Reason and Tradition in Islamic Ethics* (Cambridge, England: Cambridge University Press) p. 7.
4. M. Khadduri, 1984, *The Islamic Conception of Peace* (Baltimore, MD: Johns Hopkins University Press), p. 41–48.
5. Al Zumar: 9.
6. BP Statistical Review of World Energy, 1990, (London: British Petroleum Educational Service).
7. BP Statistical Review of World Energy, 1990.
8. The Presidential Gulf War Illnesses Commission Report has shown that a large number of U.S. Desert Storm Veterans have been exposed to germ warfare during combat.
9. Penny Kemp, 1991, "For Generations to Come: The Environmental Catastrophe", in: *Beyond the Storm: A Gulf Crisis Reader,* ed. P. Bennis and M. Moushabeck (New York: Olive Branch Press), p. 331.
10. "Al-Qahira Akhthar Mudin al'Alam Talwitha" (Cairo is the most polluted city in the world), *Al-Akhbar Daily News,* 6 June 1995, p. 8.
11. Quoted in Pervez Houdbhoy, 1991, *Islam and Science* (London: Zed Books Ltd), p. 30.
12. Quoted in David Korten, 1994, "Sustainability and the Global Economy: Beyond Bretton Woods" (Opening Plenary Presentation to Fall Retreat, 13–15 October 1994, The Environmental Grantmakers Association, Mount Washington Hotel & Resort, Bretton Woods, New Hampshire), p. 7.
13. Hourani, *Reason and Tradition in Islamic Ethics,* p. 372.
14. J. T. Cummings, H. Askari, and A. Mustafa, 1980, "Islam and Modern Economic Change", in *Islam and Development: Religion and Sociopolitical Change,* ed. John Espisito (Syracuse, NY: Syracuse University Press, pp. 25–48), p. 44.
15. Al Najm: 39.
16. Al Nisa': 95.
17. Hud: 85.
18. Umar Vadillo and Fazlun Khalid, 1992, "Trade and Commerce in Islam", in: *Islam and Ecology,* ed. Fazlun Khalid and Joanne O'Brien (New York, NY: Cassell) p. 73.
19. Al Baqarah: 161.
20. Al Rum: 39.
21. Cummings, Askari, and Mustafa, "Islam and Modern Economic Change".
22. Ali Imaran: 104.
23. Tawbah: 71; Ali Imran: 103; Al Mai'dah: 2.
24. Cummings, Askar, and Mustafa, "Islam and Modern Economic Change", p. 27–29.
25. Al Baqarah: 267.
26. Cummings, Askar, and Mustafa, "Islam and Modern Economic Change", p. 30.
27. Fatima Mernissi, 1992, *Islam and Democracy: Fear of the Modern World* (translated by Mary Jo Lakeland, New York: Addison-Wesley Publishing Co), p. 27.
28. Fahmi Houidi, *Al-Islam wa al-Democratiah* (Islam and democracy, Cairo: Markaz al-Ahram Llitargamah wa al-Nashr), p. 124.
29. Al Ghashiyah: 21–23.
30. Al Kahf: 29.
31. Al Nisa: 58; Al Mai'dah: 8; Al Nahl: 90; Al Shura: 15, 38; Al Hujurat: 9, 13.
32. Houidi, *Al-Islam wa al-Democratiah,* p. 122.
33. Mernissi, *Islam and Democracy,* p. 22–22.
34. Verses 5, 29, 36.
35. Houidi, *Al-Islam wa al-Democratiah,* p. 33–35.
36. Houidi, p. 24.
37. Yunus: 99; Hud: 18.
38. Houidi, p. 27.
39. Al Nahl: 92; Al Qasas: 18, 38.
40. Al Tawbah: 6.
41. I use the word *countries* because I can only obtain statistics from such geopolitical designations. It is essential to remember that Islam sees its adherents and those who live with them as a community (*ummah*).
42. Indonesia has had the most successful family planning programs in the developing world. See Hayim Adid, 1987, "Islamic Leaders' Attitudes Towards Family Planning in Indonesia 1950s–1980s," a master's thesis, Australian National University, Canberra.
43. Al Nahl: 72; Al Kahf: 46.
44. Al Nisa: 9; Al Tur: 21; Al Anfal: 28.
45. Hamed Abu Gamrah, 1980, "Fertility and Childhood Mortality by Mother's and Father's Education in Cairo", in *Population Bulletin of the Economic Commission of Western Asia* (Beirut, Lebanon), p. 81.

46. "Aqed al-Jawaz al-Jadid" (The new marriage contract), in *Nisf al-Dunia* (a weekly magazine), 15 June 1995, pp. 21–26.
47. Al Nisa: 1, 32.
48. Ali Imran: 195.
49. Al Ra'd: 11.
50. Al Ra'd: 8; Al Sajdah: 4; Al Mulk: 3, 4.
51. Al Baqarah: 30.

The Disconnected People

FAZLUN M. KHALID

A TALE OF TWO PLACES

THE RAIN WAS HEAVY AND INCESSANT, AS rains usually are in Sarawak on the island of Borneo. The river was swollen but not unusually so. Ali, the Dyak tribesman, watched in dismay as his small patch of cultivated land crumbled into the river and was washed downstream.[1] He had to cross this same river to get to the logging company hut. His people practised shifting agriculture and his needs were immediate. But later, Ali will reflect on the fact that the river has swallowed not only his living but the ancient lifestyle of his people in one monsoon. His people lived in the forest of Sarawak for generations. They took from it what they needed and produced very little waste. What waste they produced went back into the soil, soon to become part of it as it decayed. The air was clean and it was quiet in this part of the forest except for the natural sounds of the people and animals, the wind, the rain and the river.

Now, all of that has changed since the arrival of the chain saws and tractors. There were profits to be made from the forest and the government needed revenue for its development programme. The forests were a resource, coveted by distant, voracious industrial countries, that could be used in the construction of shopping centres, recreation centres and other amenities. In order to meet these demands the logging companies continue to be given licences to fell the trees and export the logs, resulting in the clearance of massive tracts of land. As a consequence, the top soil is washed away into the river, the rivers silt up and the fish die. The animals that Ali and his community used to hunt are not to be found either since they have sought sanctuary deeper in the forest.

Ali does not know where to turn for help. His ancestral lands, his patch of cultivation and his home have all disappeared. His family and his community have scattered. He did not invite these strangers here and they did not bother to ask him if they could come. Someone from the government had come to his village to inform him that this was for the development and progress of his nation. But no one had ever come to speak to him about the good of the nation before, so why was it so necessary now? Decisions that affected his future were being taken in distant 'advanced countries' and their desire to improve their lifestyle resulted in the destruction of his. One day soon the land on which the forest stood will be covered with endless hectares of cash crops such as cocoa, coffee, palm oil, bananas, pineapple for consumers in the 'advanced countries'. Ali and his people will use very little or nothing of this themselves. They will be invaded by giant multinational companies and may be given no choice but to work for them in return for low wages and long hours. They will probably be told that what has happened will improve their standard of living. They will be bombarded by advertisements for things they never knew existed and had so far managed very well without. They will become consumers of very interesting and useless things made in faraway places and many will run up large debts in order to buy these things. They will become producers and consumers in the mega-markets of the world in less than a lifetime.

As yet, Ali knows nothing of this as with difficulty

Khalid, Fazlun, " The Disconnected People," in Fazlun Khalid and Joanne O'Brien, Eds., *Islam and Ecology,* New York: Cassell, 1992, pp. 99–110. Reprinted by permission.

he crosses the swollen river and scrambles over the opposite bank into the company camp. He stumbles over dead tree stumps and squelches his way ankle deep in mud to the manager's hut. He calls the manager to the door, points to the gaping hole in the river bank opposite and complains bitterly.

'You have destroyed our lives. You are responsible.'

The logging camp manager, a minor cog in a big machine, was a kindly man. He had seen and heard this before and was well used to dealing with the situation. He listened sympathetically and then gave Ali 1,000 Malaysian dollars (about £220). The money came from what the company call the 'suspense account' that was provided to deal with these cases. Ali, his way of life and the traditions of his people were bought in a brief moment for a pittance.

There were other things Ali did not know. The trees that protected him would be transported and processed many times and a great deal of money would be made by other people in the process. The largest amount of money will be made by the people living furthest away from where the trees grew. The trees will go to Japan and other Pacific Basin countries. They will go to the West, to places like Britain and the rest of Europe. In Japan, it is likely that his trees, now turned into panels, would be used just once as casing for concrete on building sites and then discarded. In Britain, it is likely that Ali's trees will be turned into beautiful kitchens to adorn the houses in one of its many cities. The chances of Japanese construction workers and British housewives sparing a thought for the plight of Ali and his people are as remote as their houses are from the patch of land that Ali once tilled and which is now no more than silt in the sea.

Maryam lives a few thousand miles to the west of Ali's country. She is a Tuareg and her home once moved to and fro across the sands of the Sahara and the Sahel.[2] Her particular community are now settled as farmers in northern Nigeria. They are contemptuous of their present way of life but were driven there by the disastrous drought of the early 1970s.

The Tuareg are a nomadic people. They were and still are like a bridge across the Sahara. They cover the expanse of west central Sahara and the Sahel. That is an area roughly covered by what is today southern Algeria, south-west Libya, Niger and northern Mali. A generation ago they were almost wholly nomadic stock breeders. They were also caravan traders with their routes criss-crossing the Sahara in many directions. They exchanged their livestock, African gold and ivory for food, salt and Arabian and European goods. When the Europeans, particularly the French, came to this area things rapidly began to change. Lines began to appear on the map where no lines were before, cutting across ancient lifestyles and relations. The Tuareg were subjected to the influences of political boundaries determined by faraway people and were no longer free to graze their stocks and trade as before. Other people wanted to settle them down when the majority of the Tuareg had no desire for this. Governments in the area wanted to include them in the national systems of the country; they wanted to educate them and bring them into an economy based on cash and tax.

As pastoral nomads the Tuareg have maintained a balance with their environment since ultimately they depend on it for sustenance. It is the combined effects of drought, increased desertification (which meant that the wells and other resources were overused), and governmental pressure that restrict the movement of the Tuareg. The extreme climatic conditions that the Tuareg are suffering is thought by many scientists to be linked to the burning of fossil fuels in industrialized countries. This has contributed to what has been termed the 'greenhouse' effect and caused the earth's temperature to rise by an average 0.5 degrees Centigrade in the past century. We are told that of all the energy consumed in the past 2,000 years, over half has been consumed in this century. Of this over 80 per cent has been consumed by countries in the Northern hemisphere. The effect of this has been to push rainfall towards the poles and allow drier weather to spread towards the equator.[3] These temperature changes may seem small but the earth and biosphere are in such fine balance that they can cause massive and irreversible changes to people's lifestyles. Nature makes a mockery of national boundaries. For example, it has been known for the wind to drop tons of Saharan topsoil on vast areas of Europe as red rain.

But this is not the end of the story for Maryam and her people. Multinational companies will persuade them to use this or that fertilizer, this or that pesticide, this or that tractor. They will inevitably become consumers in a world market just like Ali and his people on the opposite side of the earth. Before all this happens somebody should remember to tell Maryam and her people that, according to the United Nations Environment Programme, one-third of the world's farmland will be desert by the year 2000.[4] By developing methods of agriculture and irrigation that can be sustained without importing expensive technology, and by balanced use of natural resources, parts of the desert can be farmed and can support local communities, but a large proportion of the marginal land that the Tuareg are now farming is better suited to their traditional nomadic lifestyle. Many of the Tuareg find that they have been pulled out of the desert only to be pushed back into it.

GOING NOWHERE FAST

The differences between Ali's and Maryam's lives are obvious, but what are the similarities? Firstly, they each belonged to a traditional people who had evolved a lifestyle unique to the environment in which they lived. Secondly, they lived in balance with their environment and thirdly, within the space of a generation or two, their lifestyles underwent sudden and drastic disruption. Now they lack control over their lives and are part of political structures and institutions which are not of their choosing. They have been deprived of their independent self-sustaining lifestyle and are forced into a global cash economy. They are now subject to the changes of commodity markets and interest rates which have more to do with the ups and downs of powerful industrial countries and nothing at all to do with their lives. Finally, they are Muslims, living in Muslim countries, although it must be said that traditional people living the world over have experienced similar tragic disruption to their lives.

In terms of the vast time scales of our Creator what happened to Ali and Maryam was sudden and violent. The life span of our planet is estimated at about 4.5 billion years and the human species has been on this earth for about 1/10,000th of the earth's life span. The major civilizations emerged in the latest 1 per cent of human existence. The age of atomic power and high technology only came about in the last half of the twentieth century at about 1/1,000,000,000th of the earth's life span. Our lives and our times may seem important to us and they obviously are, but compared to cosmic time our lives are very small fractions of seconds. Another matter that clouds our vision about the suddenness of these changes is the fact that our recent forebears have themselves lived through a period of change and upheaval. Permanence and familiarity have been traded for change and insecurity. We are born into a society that has already changed and we continue to live in it experiencing change all the time. Change is now a way of life for us and only recently have we begun to acknowledge that this is leading us to environmental catastrophe and social collapse. The Qur'an says this about time:

> By (the token of) time through the ages
> Verily man is in loss
> Except such as have faith, and do righteous deeds,
> and (join together) in the mutual teaching of
> truth, and of patience and constancy.
> (Qur'an 103:1–3)

Ali and Maryam have been defrauded of their very different but equally valid ways, which took centuries to evolve, in less than one lifetime. Their loss is a consequence of other people's greed and their futures are uncertain.

What we notice about all this, is that after centuries of gradual movement, the process we call history has suddenly accelerated.[5] To an independent observer in geo-stationary orbit over the mid-Atlantic for the past 500 years, which as we have seen is a comparatively short time, our actions might have looked frantic. As for the last 100 years this same observer will most probably conclude that our conduct verges on madness. Many analysts from widely differing backgrounds have come to the conclusion that history is accelerating and continues to do so at an ever increasing rate. What does this mean? We have seen how fuel consumption has accelerated. This kind of very rapid increase is described as exponential growth and in the context of this discussion it would not be far-fetched to call it explosive or frightening growth. There are enough examples around us to sustain this point which is that all areas of production, consumption, progress and development have grown exponentially in the past 500 years and are continuing to do so.

So the questions remain. Do we know that we are

accelerating ourselves into oblivion? Do we know in what direction we as a species are moving?

THE NATURAL STATE

The earth is Allah's creation, a very small part of the rest of His creation which is an infinitely vast universe. We are at a stage in history when we have enough information at our disposal to lead us uniquely to the conclusion that everything is connected. We are part of a vast galaxy of stars that makes our solar system look tiny. Yet the sun that gives us life is 93 million miles away. The earth's companion, the moon, is a quarter of a million miles away, yet it controls our tides and has an influence over our weather systems. The protective atmospheric shell around the earth which is held to it by gravity, is proportionately no thicker than the skin of a potato. We are in fact being carried along in a sea of space, in a very finely engineered, self-regulating, space ship. Not very long ago, people who knew nothing at all about these things lived with an intuitive knowledge that recognized the earth for what it was and protected it in the way they went about their business. We now claim to be infinitely superior in knowledge to the ancients, but the savagery with which we treat the environment exceeds all bounds. We claim to belong to the high point of civilization. Yet, we are in the middle of a process that will destroy our life-support systems and consequently existence as we know it.

We say the earth has shrunk, it is getting to be an ever smaller place. By this we mean we know more about distant people and places and can get to them more quickly. Fifty years ago it would have taken us six to eight weeks to get to Ali's river. Today we can do this in a day or two. Ali is now a neighbour and we cannot go on uprooting his trees forever. We know Ali does not like it because it affects him immediately and directly. But we now know that Ali's trees must stay where they are, because if they do not it will affect us too. If the effect is not immediate it will sooner or later be direct. Similarly, our lifestyle with its excessive use of fossil fuels did not affect Maryam and her people immediately but, when it did, the effect was direct and as we have seen drastic. We have lost the art of living in the *fitra* state, that is the natural state, in balance and in harmony with creation. Recognizing that our every action affects other people, other species and other places both near and far, the Qur'an says:

> (God) most gracious
> It is He who has taught the Qur'an
> He has created man
> He has taught him speech (and intelligence)
> The sun and the moon follow courses (exactly) computed
> and the herbs and the trees both (alike) bow in adoration
> and the firmament has He raised high, and He has set up the balance (of justice)
> In order that ye may not transgress (due) balance
> So establish weight with justice and fall not short in the balance
> It is He who has spread out the earth for (his) creatures
> Therein is fruit and date palms, producing spathes (enclosing dates)
> Also corn with (its) leaves, and stalk for fodder and sweet smelling plants
> Then which of the favours of our Lord will ye deny?
>
> (Qur'an 55:1–13)

Everything is connected with each other and each with the whole. Evaporation from the sea rises as moist clouds, falls as rain, flows as rivers and returns to the sea again. Many things happen during this cycle. The seeds and roots wait for the rain in the soil surrounded by natural nutrients. The sun combines with the rain to produce food for people, fodder for animals, wood for fuel and for building shelters and useful artefacts, waste for turning into organic matter that returns to the soil as nutrients to await the next cycle. The water having done its work on the surface flows down into the water table and replenishes it until the rains return again. The rest flows into rivers providing sustenance for other communities further downstream. Stocks of fish are replenished providing protein for people. This was how it was not very long ago. But now? Rain contaminated with industrial smog falls as acid rain and destroys forests and corrodes mountains and buildings. Rivers are no longer clean and many thousands of miles of water are poisoned, contaminated by industrial and agricultural waste products. The fish have lost their habitat, the people their protein. Some rivers are dammed and others diverted, as part of national development programmes supported by the World

Bank and the International Monetary Fund, disrupting lives and flooding villages, obliterating cultures in the name of progress. Local and international disputes occur over the control and distribution of water. The seas around the estuaries of rivers flowing through industrial countries receive increasing doses of heavy metal poison. The fish are contaminated. Disease is introduced into the food chain. The Qur'an says:

> See ye the seed that ye sow in the ground?
> Is it ye that cause it to grow or are We the cause?
> Were it our will, We could crumble it to dry powder and ye would be left in wonderment
> (Saying) 'We are indeed left with debts for (nothing)
> Indeed we are shut out (of the fruits of our labour)'
> See ye that the water which ye drink?
> Do ye bring it down (in rain) from the cloud or do We?
> Were it our will We could make it salt (and unpalatable) then why do ye not give thanks?
>
> (Qur'an 56:63–70)

The human species is connected to Allah's creation too, because we are part of it. This needs to be repeated because we have been behaving as a species apart, arrogant and selfish, taking diabolical liberties with the rest of creation. We are rampaging through the delicate balance of nature. Savaging other species to extinction. Robbing future generations of their inheritance. We have become so trapped in our self-indulgence we are not even aware of it.

Two basic kinds of decisions confront us in life. One is about how we relate to other people and the other about how we relate to the environment. However, most of our relations with other people sooner or later affect the environment. Purely person-to-person transactions are very small in number. The baby cries for attention and finds comfort in the mother's embrace. But when the baby cries for food and the mother feeds it, the nature of that transaction is different from the first, because on this occasion they both draw from the environment where the food originates. We can safely conclude from this that very nearly all our decisions have something to do with the environment—taking from it, putting things back into it, shaping it, changing it, modifying it. The process of making decisions presents us with a range of choices and in order to be able to exercise choice Allah has given us the gift of free will and the ability to reason. This is unique to the human species. With this comes the twin concepts of guardianship and responsibility which place mankind, the supreme exploiter of resources, in a central and sensitive position. The Qur'an says, on guardianship:

> It is He (Allah) who has made you his viceregent on earth.
>
> (Qur'an 6:165)

On responsibility:

> . . . for us is the (responsibility for) our deeds, and for you for your deeds. . . .
>
> (Qur'an 42:15)

The mandate from the Creator enables us to take from His creation enough to satisfy need and thus continue to maintain the fine balance He has established. That is to be aware of the limits. But those of us who are living in the richer countries have now grossly exceeded our limits. We have created a large number of wants that are without limits. The borderline between needs and wants can be recognized. The borderline between wants and greed is always unclear. Whilst needs can be defined wants cannot. This is why the idea of 'standards of living' means different things to different people. Ali and Maryam are hostages to our standards of living.

There is another range of decisions we make which moves beyond the person-to-person. They are the decisions we make collectively as a group, a community, a country. These decisions are political by nature and it will be difficult, if not impossible, to find political decisions that sooner or later do not involve the environment. This is why Islam does not make a distinction between politics and religion. Life is one whole. Our attitudes and behaviour in one area affect other areas. Everything is connected, which inevitably means that all economic activity is connected with the environment. This is why, in order for the environment to function in balance as it should, we should not cheat it and plunder it under the guise of improving our living standards. But, the economic institutions we have set up and function under do precisely that. The banks, the practice of charging interest, the stock markets, the commodity markets, are all part of a massive fraud and we are defrauding nobody but ourselves. . . .

There is one inevitable conclusion to all this: each one of us is responsible for what is happening to our environment today. The effect of what we do is not confined to our own homes, neighbourhoods and countries. It is far-reaching and tragic as we have seen in the cases of Ali and Maryam. If the communities of these people still seem far away and remote then there is one disturbing and worrying event that connects us with them directly and that is the hole we have managed to make in the ozone layer above us. The shield that protects all of us is now weakening through the effects of our actions and the radiation that seeps through the cracks does not discriminate between people living in Asia, Africa, America and Europe.

Whilst being individuals and individualistic is important, how we have come to interpret this must change. Self-indulgence or selfishness is clumsily hidden in the idea of improving oneself. It is connected with the idea of 'the quality of life' which, like 'standards of living', is misleading. This has led us to compete with each other as consumers, as individuals and as countries sucking things out of the earth at an ever-increasing rate and discharging a level of waste which the earth cannot recycle, thus contributing to the rapid destruction of the habitats and lifestyles of the weakest amongst us.

There are now a few things we can say in summary about ourselves that may give us an understanding of how we have reached a situation where we have put our home, the earth, under severe strain. As we have just seen, our attitude as individuals has not helped. We are invited to compete feverishly with each other to get the most out of the finite resources on earth. This means that we constantly exceed our limits. We all want more, to be and look better, to be bigger, to be faster, to be grander, to be richer. We have also lost the ability to distinguish between need and greed, or we are simply not interested in the difference. We have lost the intuitive knowledge of relating to each other, to nature and to the environment. And as a result of this we have lost a sense of proportion and balance. All these are symptoms of a disconnected people. We have an image about what we need and what we want and we obscure the truth about ourselves. We are people on the wrong side of the great divide who cannot distinguish between stability and familiarity on the one hand and perpetual change and alienation on the other. We have discarded the fitra way of living for a lifestyle that is illusory and artificial. To relearn how all things in Allah's creation are interrelated and to realize that we are part of the same, we could do no better than to go to people like Ali and Maryam and absorb what they have to give before it is too late. The Qur'an says:

> Do no mischief on the
> Earth after it has been
> set in order . . .
> (Qur'an 7:85)

The role model for us is the Prophet of Islam (S). The model of generosity, compassion and moderation. When he was asked by a companion about the most virtuous act of giving he said:

> Give away what you have while you are in good health, and while you have a keen desire to amass wealth, and while you are afraid of adversity and while you are longing for money. Do not wait to give your wealth away until you are dying . . .
> (*Riyadh as Salihin*)

For us the first step towards this is to think about the way we take and the effect this has on other people, other species and other places.

REFERENCES

1. For further information on the Dyak see *The Atlas of Man,* Marshall Cavendish, London, 1981.
2. Ibid., for further information on the Tuareg.
3. *The Gaia Atlas of Planet Management,* Pan Books, London, 1985.
4. André Singer, *Battle for the Planet,* Channel Four Books, 1987.
5. Gerard Piel, 'The acceleration of history' in Ritchie Calder (ed.), *The Future of a Troubled World,* Heinemann, London, 1983.

Discussion Questions

1. How does the Qur'anic concept of stewardship (*khilafa*) compare with the biblical version in Genesis?
2. Does Islam present any obstacles to ecological practice?

3. Is a less anthropocentric Islam possible?
4. How does Islam see environmental degradation as connected to issues of social justice? Are these issues separable?
5. What aspects of traditional Islamic values, if applied in the world today, might have a positive ecological impact?

Further Reading

Agwan, A. R., *The Environmental Concern of Islam,* New Delhi: Institute of Objective Studies, 1992.

Ahmad, Akhtaruddin, *Islam and the Environmental Crisis,* London: Ta-Ha Publishers, 1997.

Ba Kader, Abou Bakr Ahmed, et al., *Islamic Principles for the Conservation of the Natural Environment,* Gland, Switzerland: IUCN, 1983.

Haleem, Harfiyah Abdel, Ed., *Islam and the Environment,* London: Ta-Ha Publishers, 1998.

Izzi Dien, Mawil Y., *The Environmental Dimensions of Islam,* Cambridge, U.K.: Lutterworth, 2000.

Khalid, Fazlun, and Joanne O'Brien, Eds., *Islam and Ecology,* New York: Cassell, 1992.

Masri, Al-Hafiz, *Islamic Concern for Animals,* Petersfield, Hants., U.K.: Athene Trust, 1987.

Nanji, Azim, Frederick Denny, and Azizan Baharuddin, Eds., *Islam and Ecology,* Cambridge, Mass.: Harvard Center for the Study of World Religions, forthcoming 2003.

Nasr, Seyyed Hossein, *Man and Nature: The Spiritual Crisis in Modern Man,* rev. ed., Chicago: Kazi, 1997 [1967].

Sardar, Ziauddin, Ed., *Touch of Midas: Scientific Values and the Environment in Islam and the West,* Manchester, U.K.: Manchester University Press, 1984.

Sivaraksa, Sulak, and Chandra Muzaffar, *Alternative Politics for Asia: A Buddhist Muslim Dialogue,* New York: Lantern Books, 2000.

Chapter 11

Emerging Religions

RELIGIOUS MOVEMENTS ARISE in history. Some succeed in winning large followings; others don't and remain marginal or disappear altogether. Christianity and Buddhism once appeared as tiny sects following a radical, charismatic teacher; today, they count billions of followers. Who is to say how some of today's smaller religious communities of recent foundation (sometimes referred to as "new religions," although the term is potentially misleading) may fare in the future?

With the immense range of recently emerged religious movements, it is somewhat problematic to present only four here. The selections that follow can scarcely begin to suggest, much less exhaust, the potential for ecological thought in this area. Some religions, such as Mormonism and Baha'i, call for representation by sheer force of their millions of adherents. Others, such as Paganism and ISKCON, have made such explicit environmental statements that it seems appropriate to include them here.

The Baha'i faith, which currently counts upwards of 10 million adherents worldwide, began in the middle of the 19th century. It arose originally in Iran as an offshoot of Shi'ite Islam. A universal faith, Baha'i regards all established religions as facets of one truth and sees history's great religious figures as prophets appropriate to their own times and places. The core of Baha'i teaching, however, is found in the writings of its own founders, particularly Mirza Husayn Ali Nuri Baha'u'llah (1817–1892). Violently persecuted in Iran throughout the mid-1800s, Baha'i spread to Europe, North America, and elsewhere and now constitutes communities in most parts of the world.

The origins of the Church of Jesus Christ of Latter-day Saints (LDS), which first arose in the context of Protestant Christianity, were contemporaneous with those of Baha'i and equally troubled. Joseph Smith, the Church's prophet and founder, was murdered by vigilantes in 1844 in Carthage, Illinois. The main body of his followers migrated West under the leadership of Brigham Young, finally settling in what is now the state of Utah, where they currently make up about 70 percent of the population. Like the Baha'i, Mormons (as the members of the LDS Church are known) currently number somewhat over ten million worldwide.

Another growing contemporary religious movement, the International Society for Krishna Consciousness (ISKCON; the Hare Krishnas), comes out of a Hindu context. Unlike mainstream Hinduism, which does not have a strong proselytizing tradition, it has won many followers in North America, Europe, and elsewhere. ISKCON is a devotional movement, ostensibly based on the ancient Sanskrit Vedic texts but in practice focused on the figure of Krishna. Whereas mainstream Vaishnava Hindus in India see Krishna as an incarnation (*avatar*) of the god Vishnu, Hare Krishnas affirm him as the supreme godhead rather than simply an avatar. The movement was founded in the United States in 1965 by an Indian immigrant, A. C. Bhaktivedanta Swami Prabhupada (1896–1977), but it now has centers worldwide.

Among all emerging traditions, the Neopagan movement of Europe and North America most explicitly addresses the discussion on environmental values. In fact, Neopaganism (or, as it is now increasingly called, contemporary Paganism) could almost by definition be characterized as a religion of nature. Most Neopagans see themselves as practicing a revival of the most ancient forms of human spirituality and religiosity, and they would likely characterize theirs as a re-emerging rather than an emerging religion. Neopaganism, which subsumes the revived practice of Wicca or witchcraft, tends to base its rituals on the seasonal cycles of the Earth and locates sacrality in the living, experienced world, as opposed to seeking it in transcendence or in a disembodied afterlife. In all of these respects, Neopaganism resembles the worldviews and some of the practices of first peoples, although it is often articulated in very contemporary terms.

Robert A. White ties the dominant Baha'i theme of universalism to the environmental crisis by arguing that the emerging environmental consciousness is part of a broader evolution in human culture. Echoing the Buddhist notion of interconnectedness, Baha'i teaches that all of nature (including humankind) constitutes a unified whole. On the other hand, like the Semitic traditions, the Baha'i view places humans at the highest level of creation and attributes a special spirituality to our species as being closest to God.

Land use and private property rights, which have long been highly contentious issues in the American Southwest, have rarely been discussed in terms of religious values. In my own essay, however, I note that a large portion of this region—specifically, the state of Utah and adjacent parts of all the states that border it—is populated by Mormons, a people whose worldview is distinctive in many ways. I argue that this fact needs to be taken into account by those seeking to understand popular attitudes toward the environment in the lands where Mormons form a majority of the population. I further seek to demonstrate that the Mormon tradition contains abundant teaching on the subject of environmental stewardship, although such teachings are often not emphasized today.

Bruce M. Sullivan describes the work of ISKCON in preserving the sacred lands of Braj in north central India, which are associated with the life of the Hindu god Krishna. Although these lands are held sacred by all Vaishnava Hindus, the region has not escaped the ravages of industrial pollution and overdevelopment that have plagued much of the rest of India. It is perhaps somewhat ironic that the impetus for saving this sacred territory has come largely from non-Indian Hare Krishna devotees such as the Englishman Ranchor Prime (also known as Ranchor Dasa).

Graham Harvey is a leading scholar of contemporary Paganism. In his article, Harvey emphasizes the centrality of nature in Paganism, characterizing it as "fundamentally 'Green.'" At the same time, he highlights the diversity within Paganism, a tradition that lacks formal institutions or theology. Rather than speak of connections or harmony with nature, Harvey suggests that the notion of "mutuality" best illustrates the contemporary Pagan understanding of humans' relationship to nature.

A Baha'i Perspective on an Ecologically Sustainable Society

ROBERT A. WHITE

THIS ESSAY TAKES A BROAD MACROEVOLUTIONARY approach to our changing relationship to nature in light of the teachings of the Baha'i Faith. It suggests that humanity is in a process of evolving consciousness that is leading to the development of a new planetary culture which will be based on a mature cooperative relationship between humanity and the ecosphere that gave it birth. This paper first explores the basic attitudes to nature that are contained within the Baha'i writings and then examines how the emergence of an ecologically sustainable social order is linked to some of the principles of the Baha'i Faith. Implicit throughout is the Baha'i view of the balance and cohesion of material and spiritual realities. While references are made to Baha'i texts, the interpretation presented is a personal one.

RELATIONSHIP WITH NATURE IN REVISION

The cumulative breakdown of the relationship between the human species and the ecosphere has reached a point at which mere technical and social adjustments to prevailing models of development are inadequate to ensure planetary sustainability. The call for a "radically new metaphysic"[1] that recognizes the reciprocal relationship between humanity and nature has spawned various schools of thought such as "deep ecology," "ecophilosophy," and "ecofeminism." With an even more comprehensive vision Thomas Berry eloquently describes the essential dimensions of an "Ecological Age" into which we are now moving.[2] All of these schools of thought call, in one form or another, for a transformation of consciousness away from seeing the earth as a collection of resources to be exploited and consumed to one of humanity living as an integral, cocreative part of the ecosphere. This fundamental change involves an appreciation of the spiritual dimension as a necessary element of our relationship to nature both individually and collectively.

It is within this context that the teachings of the Baha'i Faith make a significant contribution. In their emphasis on unity and evolutionary thinking, the Baha'i teachings offer a view of nature that embraces both animistic wisdom and contemporary ecological understanding. At the same time, these teachings affirm divine transcendence and the essential unity of religious expression throughout history. Furthermore, they present a challenging interpretation of what religion is and its role in transforming the current world order. In addition, many of the tenets and principles for an alternative society based on ecological wisdom are found within the writings and institutions of the Baha'i Faith.

RELATIONSHIP WITH NATURE: A BAHA'I PERSPECTIVE

In an examination of the principles of the Baha'i Faith as they apply to agriculture, Paul Hanley articulates a threefold relationship between humanity and nature involving principles of unity, detachment, and humility.[3] These same principles will be explored in depth here.

Unity with Nature

'Abdu'l-Bahá asserts that "all parts of the creational world are of one whole. . . . All the parts are subordinate and obedient to the whole. The contingent beings are the branches of the tree of life while the Messenger of God is the root of that tree."[4] He illustrates this essential unity in the following analogy:

> Liken the world of existence of the temple of man. All the limbs and organs of the human body assist one another; therefore life continues. . . . Likewise, among the parts of existence there is a

White, Robert A., "A Baha'i Perspective on an Ecologically Sustainable Society," in Mary Evelyn Tucker and John Grim, Eds., *Worldviews and Ecology: Religion, Philosophy and the Environment,* Maryknoll, N.Y.: Orbis, 1994, pp. 96–111. Originally published in *Bucknell Reviews,* Vol. 37, No. 2, 1993, published by Bucknell University Press. Reprinted by permission.

> wonderful connection and interchange of forces, which is the cause of the life of the world and the continuation of these countless phenomena. . . . From this illustration one can see the base of life is this mutual aid and helpfulness.[5]

According to 'Abdu'l-Bahá, the cooperative interrelations of creation are a manifestation of love, which is "the secret of God's holy Dispensation." Through God's love the world of being receives life:

> Love is the cause of God's revelation unto man, the vital bond inherent, in accordance with the divine creation, in the realities of things . . . Love is the most great law that ruleth this mighty and heavenly cycle, the unique power that bindeth together the divers elements of this material world, the supreme magnetic force that directeth the movements of the spheres in the celestial realms.[6]

Further, the mineral, plant, and animal are seen to possess various grades and stations of spirit. 'Abdu'l-Bahá wrote in 1921:

> it is indubitable that minerals are endowed with a spirit and life according to the requirements of that stage. . . .
>
> In the vegetable world, too, there is the power of growth, and that power of growth is the spirit. In the animal world there is the sense of feeling, but in the human world there is an all-embracing power . . . the reasoning power of the mind. . . .
>
> In like manner the mind proveth the existence of an unseen Reality that embraceth all beings, and that existeth and revealeth itself in all stages.[7]

There is a cohesiveness within life's ever-increasing differentiation—an underlying spirit that animates all of existence. The prevailing view of nature as "environment" made up of material components of air, water, soil, and organisms is therefore inadequate. The very word "environment" implies that which is external and peripheral to what is assumed to be the central object of concern, human beings. This human self-preoccupation ignores the reality that life and spirit are properties of the whole and its reciprocal interactions.

Spiritual Detachment from Nature

Humanity is part of the whole of creation which in turn reflects, in its harmony and unity, a divine and unseen reality. At the same time, paradoxically, human beings occupy a unique station that can be consciously realized only through detachment from nature. 'Abdu'l-Bahá states that the human being "is in the highest degree of materiality, and at the beginning of spirituality."[8]

Creation is seen as a progression of increasingly complex orders from the mineral kingdom to vegetable and animal life to human beings. Humanity, however, has the capability and the power of spiritual advancement, our very purpose being to advance toward God. As stated by 'Abdu'l-Bahá:

> God has created all earthly things under a law of progression in material degrees, but He has created man and endowed him with powers of advancement toward spiritual and transcendental kingdoms.[9]

All other created things are "captives of nature and the sense world," but human beings, created in the "image of God," occupy a unique station in creation. We have evolved through all the physical kingdoms and contain all of their capacities plus the distinguishing capacity for rational and self-reflective thought. The development of this unique capacity of the mind that allows us to mediate between the material and spiritual dimensions has required us to separate ourselves from nature both externally and internally. Through this separation humanity has gained the capacity to know nature from the outside and to unravel its secrets. In an internal sense we have partially removed ourselves from the physical and instinctual responses that guide all other life forms and have developed conscious faculties of judgment and volition.

The freedom these capacities give us involves a commensurate responsibility to recognize the "unseen Reality that embraceth all beings" (*BR*, 222). Our spiritual evolution depends on the degree of our attunement to that greater reality, which is described by Bahá'u'lláh and all the great prophets as limitless and eternal. Thus, to truly develop a conscious spirituality and to awaken to our full potential we are called to sever our immediate identification with the physical dimension of nature. 'Abdu'l-Bahá discusses this concept:

> And among the teachings of His Holiness Bahá'u'lláh is man's freedom, that through the ideal Power he should be free and emancipated from the captivity of the world of nature. . . . Un-

til man is born again from the world of nature, that is to say, becomes detached from the world of nature, he is essentially an animal, and it is the teachings of God which converts this animal into a human soul. (*BWF*, 288–90)

What is problematic is an absorption in the material, as an end in itself. Detachment from the physical world is a means of gaining conscious access to the spiritual realities that lie behind and beyond the physical. Paradoxically, this detachment allows us to see that the physical world perfectly and fully reflects the spiritual world. This is demonstrated, as John Hatcher points out, in our growing awareness of ecology.[10] As we begin to understand the ecological principle that everything is connected to everything else in the physical world, we are learning the essential truth of the spiritual law of unity that pervades and animates all of creation.

The paradox between our unity and our detachment can be seen on deeper reflection as representing the multidimensionality of our humanness. The recognition of our unity with the earth, which in a very real sense gestated us, reflects both animistic wisdom and contemporary ecological understanding. At the same time, as earlier religious revelations emphasized, we must reach beyond the material world to discover our spiritual potential and to fulfill our destiny as conscious beings. That potential and destiny, which has been reflected to us by a progression of divine messengers, is an unfolding one in an ongoing process of creation. Faith in and vision of our perfectibility gives us the strength to progress toward fulfillment of all our potential and to participate in spiritualizing our social existence.

While the Baha'i Faith is not the first belief system to recognize this tension between the material and spiritual dimensions, it brings a fuller appreciation of the balance in this relationship. Matthew Fox seeks just such a balance in his call for "panentheism."[11] Like pantheism, panentheism sees the spirit of God as present in all things; at the same time, God is an independent Being above and beyond all things. Similarly, Bahá'u'lláh has written:

> The whole universe reflecteth His glory, while he is Himself independent of, and transcendeth His creatures. This is the true meaning of Divine unity. He Who is the Eternal Truth is the one Power Who exerciseth undisputed sovereignty over the world of being, Whose image is reflected in the mirror of the entire creation."[12]

Humility

In this delicate balance between unity and detachment, we are called on to honor creation, to recognize its sacredness, and to humble ourselves before it. In the miracle of life's evolution, God has acted through nature in an "emergent" way. Creation is intrinsically endowed with meaning and purpose, and reflects the unity, beauty, and ultimate mystery of God. The earth itself reveals the attributes of God as Bahá'u'lláh affirms:

> How all-encompassing are the wonders of His boundless grace! Behold how they have pervaded the whole of creation. Such is their virtue that not a single atom in the entire universe can be found which doth not declare the evidences of His might, which doth not glorify His holy Name, or is not expressive of the effulgent light of His unity. So perfect and comprehensive is His creation that no mind nor heart, however keen or pure, can ever grasp the nature of the most insignificant of His creatures; much less fathom the mystery of Him Who is the Day Star of Truth, Who is the invisible and unknowable Essence. (*G*, 62)

'Abdu'l-Bahá describes creation as one of the "two Books" of God. "The Book of Creation is in accord with the written Book"—the sacred revelations of all the prophets of God. Like the written book, "The Book of Creation is the command of God and the repository of divine mysteries."[13]

The spirituality of the world's aboriginal cultures is based on understanding the primary "scripture" of the "Book of Creation"; and in the revealed religions, symbols of nature such as trees, water, and mountains also carry spiritual meaning. Both by direct contact and through symbolic reflection, the human soul is nourished by connection with the beauty, mystery, and grandeur of nature.

An attitude of awe and gratitude toward the earth is part of attaining spiritual humility. Humility means literally of the ground or humus. Bahá'u'lláh describes this relationship:

> Every man of discernment, while walking upon the earth, feeleth indeed abashed, inasmuch as he is fully aware that the thing which is the source of

> his prosperity, his wealth, his might, his exaltation, his advancement and power is, as ordained by God, the very earth which is trodden beneath the feet of all men. There can be no doubt that whoever is cognizant of this truth, is cleansed and sanctified from all pride, arrogance, and vainglory.[14]

A NEW VISION OF WHOLENESS IN OUR RELATIONSHIP TO NATURE

Developing new attitudes of respect for and cooperation with nature requires, first of all, a vision of wholeness in our relationship to nature. This requires a perspective of human evolution and human purpose that unifies material and spiritual realities. The focus on transcending nature, which has characterized Western civilization in particular, is reflected in the current species' self-centeredness of the human race. The divorce of human destiny from the reality of physical life on earth now requires a reconciliation. However, this cannot be achieved through the replacement of our anthropocentrism by a biocentrism. Rather, our separation and detachment from nature and our unity with it must be understood as a creative dialectic in the development of human consciousness.

The process of becoming conscious beings has required us to break away from our unconscious roots in nature and to identify with a vision of our potential that transcends the physical. This separation has left us with no secure grounding for who we are and no clear vision of our wholeness. We retain only a dim memory of our unconscious unity with nature and a vague hope for the restoration of peace and wholeness in an abstract heaven or a future kingdom of God. The negative self-concept we hold as fallen creatures itself breeds guilt, despair, and abasement of both ourselves and creation. However, the Baha'i writings make it clear that we came into being in a perfect creation and that our station in it is a noble one. We are the "fruit of creation," conscious beings given the responsibility of fulfilling creation by reflecting its perfections. 'Abdu'l-Bahá addresses this situation as follows:

> One of the things which has appeared in the world of existence, and which is one of the requirements of Nature, is human life. Considered from this point of view man is the branch; nature is the root. Then can the will and the intelligence, and the perfections which exist in the branch be absent in the root? (*SAQ*, 4)

He further states that humanity "in the body of the world is like the brain and mind in man . . . man is the greatest member of this world, and if the body was without this chief member, surely it would be imperfect. We consider man as the greatest member, because, among the creatures, he is the sum of all existing perfections" (*SAQ*, 178). Bahá'u'lláh addresses the same theme:

> To a supreme degree is this true of man, who, among all created things, hath been invested with the robe of such gifts, and hath been singled out for the glory of such distinction. For in him are potentially revealed all the attributes and names of God to a degree that no other created being hath excelled or surpassed. (*G*, 177)

We are, in other words, nature becoming conscious of itself, but the gift of that consciousness lifts us into another dimension. Nature is perfect in itself because it is governed by laws and rules ordained by God. This perfection is reflected in all the metaphors of nature used in the writings of Bahá'u'lláh and earlier prophets. The perfection of human beings, however, are unrealized. We must choose to realize them through the development of our latent spiritual capacities. These capacities to reveal the "attributes and names of God" are always evolving and are reflected to us by a series of divine messengers and their revelations. In the evolution of humanity toward conscious wholeness and completion, the messenger of God is the key to the union of material and spiritual realities. Thus the center of existence is neither humanity nor nature (neither anthropocentrism nor biocentrism). It is God through his manifestation that is the "root" of the "tree of life" (*BWF*, 364). In this era, Baha'is believe, the unification manifested by Bahá'u'lláh has released the potential for us to transform ourselves toward a more complete reflection of the perfections of God and the wholeness of creation.

In this light, the deepening crises of planetary destruction must be seen not as the inevitable failure of fallen humanity but as a crucial stage in the evolution of human consciousness toward greater wholeness. These crises impel us to reflect on the incompleteness of our current vision and respond with urgency to the forces of transformation. The second part of this paper will explore the social dimensions of this spiritual process of transformation.

TOWARD A GLOBAL CIVILIZATION: THE EVOLUTION OF AN ECOLOGICALLY SUSTAINABLE SOCIETY

Understanding creation as sacred and whole and seeing the role of human beings to be conscious, compassionate, and creative participants in the evolution of life is the ultimate requirement for an ecologically sustainable society. However, developing this society will require not only a transformation in our individual attitudes and values but also a complete reordering of our social structures. Most of the socioeconomic institutions of modern industrial societies are based on the pursuit of material progress through separation from and conquest over nature. This separation denies a meaningful relatedness to the whole of creation and thereby denies sacredness to life. This loss of meaning and the ensuing emptiness fuel, in turn, the search for fulfillment through consumption, competition, and other addictive behaviors. The separation from nature underlying modernism corresponds to a division between mind and heart.

Incorporating a new vision of wholeness in our relationship to the earth requires a reincorporation of the spiritual dimension. Yet we cling, says Henryk Skolimowski, to our ideals of "secular salvation" because the successes of science and humanism seem too hard won to betray.[15] Despite this resistance, the prevailing worldview of secular materialism is being undermined both by the proliferation of its problems and contradictions and by the emergence of more inclusive cosmologies that provide new organizing principles. The unity of the material and spiritual dimensions is just such a principle that provides a foundation for a vision of humanity in relation to the whole of creation. Discoveries on the new frontiers of science point to this kind of integration and provide analogies such as in physics where light is understood as both a wave and a particle. The emerging world vision must similarly account for human beings as both biological and spiritual beings. Skolimowski asserts that humans

> are the custodians of the whole of evolution, and at the same time only the point on the arrow of evolution. . . . The sacredness of man is the uniqueness of his biological constitution which is endowed with such refined potentials that it can attain spirituality. (*E-P*, 74–75)

The Baha'i Faith is based on such an evolutionary perspective. As has been discussed earlier, it views our spiritual origin and destiny as part of the whole evolution of life on the planet. Spirit is expressed in all the stages and processes of existence and is realized consciously through the distinctive capacities of human awareness. The development of civilization itself is seen as a progressive organic process of maturation in which all the great religious revelations and scientific advancements are integral components. This dynamic and holistic perspective can help us pierce the socially constructed dichotomy of humanity versus planet and overcome the destructive divisions of the human race. In this larger evolutionary movement our current situation can be understood as a crucial stage in the birth of a new world order appropriate to humanity's spiritual and intellectual maturity. The teachings of the Baha'i Faith not only delineate the past and future dimensions of this process, they also offer values, principles, and new institutional forms that can guide us through this transition to maturity and the development of a global civilization.

Evolutionary Perspective

In the Baha'i writings the evolution of humanity is viewed as a purposeful organic process. Natural images, such as the earth developing in "the matrix of the universe" and the human species growing and developing in the "womb of the earth," are used to describe the nature of this process (*SAQ*, 182–83). The evolution of civilization is also viewed organically using the analogy of human developmental stages.[16]

Within this framework of maturation it is possible to sketch out humanity's changing relationship to the earth. In the earliest phases of the human journey, human dependence on the earth was embodied in myths and cultural forms. Symbols of the life-giving earth as "mother" signified the bonding typical of childhood. By association, the role of the "feminine" in its generative and nurturing aspects was generally accorded greater recognition.

In the emergence of the axial civilizations there was greater emphasis on rationality, independence, and order, representing a shift to the primacy of the "masculine." As a result, nature was gradually demythologized and spiritual and intellectual pursuits separated and abstracted from the instinctive primal energies of the body and the earth.

Western science developed in this context and took as its basic operating assumption the radical separation of subject and object, humanity and nature. The earth ceased to be a community to which humanity belonged and increasingly became a commodity for use and possession. As a result, our original dependence on the natural world has been replaced by alienation from nature and power over a meaningless material world.[17]

As destructive as this alienation has been in terms of the domination of nature, this mindset can be understood in the larger evolutionary context as a necessary phase of humanity's maturing consciousness. Just as in adolescence, when individuation requires the fragile ego to emerge and assert itself, so too the human race has had to break away from the primordial natural unity. However, to continue to assert an extreme degree of independence and "false sense of omnipotence" is no longer viable.[18]

Our evolutionary imperative is to leave this adolescent phase and progress to a mature understanding of our true interdependence with nature. This relationship will involve the integration of religious and scientific dimensions. Religion expresses the sense of being encompassed by something greater with which harmony is sought, while science expresses the urge to encompass and to know ("Science," 15–16). Maturity in our relationship to the earth implies a genuine humility about our dependent position in the ecosphere, while at the same time meeting human needs through applying skills and technologies based on ecological principles.

Science has itself become the means by which the truth of life's profound interdependence has come to light. The emergent paradigms in ecology, quantum physics, neurology, and psychology all point to the fundamental unity of life and to the interpenetration of matter and spirit. The fact that science is now confirming this dynamic interconnectedness of life does not by itself restore a subjective relatedness or sense of wholeness. Restoration of that wholeness on a conscious level is a process related to the root meaning of religion—to reconnect, or bind back. However, in this era of expanding human knowledge this healing reconnection requires a religious understanding that is complementary to the scientific principle that truth is relative and progressive.

In the nineteenth century, Bahá'u'lláh stated that the revelation of religious truth is an ongoing, open-ended process that has animated humanity's development toward greater unity and consciousness. Within this context, Bahá'u'lláh claimed that the role of his revelation was to initiate a process of conscious unification on a planetary scale—a process appropriate to humanity's maturation and growing technological capacities. The pivotal expression of this process is the recognition and acceptance of the unity of the human family. Planetary unity is the necessary and inevitable fruition of humanity's collective spiritual and material development—"the consummation of human evolution."[19]

The Unity Paradigm: Precondition for an Ecologically Sustainable Society

The oneness of humanity as enunciated by Bahá'u'lláh is not simply "an expression of vague and pious hope" or a renewal of traditional calls for solidarity. "It implies an organic change in the structure of present-day society, a change such as the world has not yet experienced" (*WOB*, 42–43). It calls for a reflection in the world of humanity of the fundamental law of oneness in the whole of creation. The Baha'i Faith, therefore, presents a unity paradigm which reflects an altered understanding of the relationship of parts to each other and to the whole. This new degree of integration is part of humanity's maturing consciousness following upon its entire developmental process and its increasing levels of interaction and interdependence.

This coming of age requires not just a perceptual shift; it requires institutional arrangements which acknowledge the primacy of the whole. Foremost among these is some form of world federal system guided by universally agreed upon values and laws, which can reflect the reality of humanity's oneness and its integral dependence on the encompassing ecosphere, which is itself a unified whole. Systems of thought and governance appropriate to humanity's adolescence must give way to new patterns and new institutions necessary to manage cooperatively an increasingly interdependent world.

Recognition of the consequences of disunity and the necessity of unity is a crucial component of this transition. The costs of nationalism, racism, and other forms of disunity can be tallied in the social and ecological effects of war, inequality, and grossly irresponsible military expenditure. The global military budget continues to run in excess of nine hundred billion dollars annually despite prospects of de-escalation due to the end of the cold war. Less than five percent of this amount (forty-five billion annually) would fund the most urgent global environmental requirements—preventing soil erosion, protecting and replanting forests, protecting the ozone layer, cleaning up hazardous wastes, developing renewable sources of energy, and stabilizing population.[20]

Current global issues, especially ecological concerns that transcend national boundaries, are, in effect, "forcing functions" requiring the community of nations to move beyond ad hoc and reactionary approaches to solving problems. The call for an integrated global ethic and policy of sustainable development raised in *Our Common Future,* and further amplified throughout the Earth Summit process, represents a growing acceptance of the need for unity in solving global problems. With this acceptance, there is a growing search for ways to bring about the changes in attitude and motivation required for unified global action. The creation of a Sustainable Development Commission by the United Nations, as part of the implementation of the Earth Summit's "Agenda 21," is one small but significant step in the recognition of the need for global goals and principles that anticipate and guide future development.[21]

While all such steps are important and necessary, political and social reorganization can only become effective to the degree that the consciousness of the oneness of humanity is the operating premise. This spiritual and organic truth, once accepted, can release the constructive energy that will be needed to make the far-reaching structural changes required for fostering sustainable patterns of development. The principle of unity must be the foundation for building and mandating institutions that can responsibly address environment and development issues on a global scale. It is for this reason that a major emphasis of the Baha'i International Community is on developing a consultative and institutional framework that demonstrates the viability of operating as a unified global community.

Globalism and Decentralism

The call by deep ecologists and other social theorists for decentralized, small-scale, community-based technologies and economies, at first glance, seems to represent the opposite extreme of the global thinking introduced above. "Ecological consciousness," it is reasoned, has mostly developed within a "minority tradition" that includes tribal cultures, utopian communities, and many monastic and religious communities.[22] There is a concern that a "global" society would become just a more effective superstate for the conquest of the ecosphere. What is needed, decentralists suggest, is to develop communities on an ecosystem-specific basis (bioregionalism) with people committed to "reinhabiting" and restoring that ecosystem and developing a renewed "sense of place."

There are several aspects of the Baha'i approach that relate to these decentralist concepts. First and foremost, the Baha'i concept of globalism is highly cognizant of the importance of traditional cultures and religions, while recognizing the need for global order and regulation. The Baha'i concept of globalism "repudiates excessive centralization on one hand, and disclaims all attempts at uniformity on the other. Its watchword is unity in diversity" (*WOB,* 42).

The present structure of the Baha'i International Community offers a pattern for constructing a worldwide society whose vision is world-embracing but whose members and activities are exceedingly diverse. It comprises over 116,000 local communities in some 210 countries and dependent territories operating under the guidance of a single, elected, global body, the Universal House of Justice. While following common goals and principles for spiritual and social development, each community must adapt itself to the exigencies of its cultural and ecological context. This adaptation is fostered through local, elected, consultative institutions which can develop community resources as well as draw on the national and international resources of the larger community. Each community perceives itself as a "cell" in a "global organism," which itself is a prototype for a future world community.

This relationship between global integration and local adaptation and differentiation is not unlike the relationship between the ecosphere and its component ecosystems.[23] Ecosystems vary greatly according to their locale, but all operate by similar ecological principles and are organically interwoven in the larger encompassing ecosphere. The Baha'i model of an organically structured social order also illustrates how, in general, spiritual and natural principles are correlative.

Aside from the structural arrangements for coordinating global and local concerns, there are several principles outlined in the Baha'i writings that suggest a land and community-based orientation. Agriculture is described as a "fundamental principle" and "village reconstruction" as the initial stage of economic development. Blueprints for the establishment of central community institutions to facilitate community self-reliance and development are also outlined in the Baha'i writings. A key principle is that development should support and benefit whole communities rather than allow individuals or elites to monopolize wealth. Thus the Baha'i view of a global society is one based on individual, family, and local self-reliance, integrated with sophisticated interdependence on the national and global levels.

Male and Female: Equality and Balance

Our prevailing social order is the symbolic expression of the male ego and its tendencies toward rationality and competitiveness. However, qualities of nurturance, intuition, and emotional sensitivity, which many believe to be more associated with the feminine principle, are the qualities most needed in healing our relationship to nature. The emergence of environmental awareness and the equality of women show parallel development.

For Baha'is, the equality of women is seen as an essential objective and a precondition for the establishment of a just and peaceful world. While a full discussion of this important principle is beyond the scope of this paper, the Baha'i writings emphasize that as long as women are prevented from reaching their full potential, society will be unbalanced. In 1912, 'Abdu'l-Bahá advanced the following proposition on this important theme:

> man has dominated over woman by reason of his more forceful and aggressive qualities both of body and mind. But the scales are already shifting—force is losing its weight and mental alertness, intuition, and the spiritual qualities of love and service, in which woman is strong, are gaining ascendancy. Hence the new age will be an age less masculine, and more permeated with the feminine ideals.[24]

SUMMARY

The writings of the Baha'i Faith offer a vision of fundamental global transformation that embodies a new set of principles for understanding and guiding humanity's relationship to nature. The religious impulse they contain is a comprehensive source of spiritual, social, and intellectual resources. They affirm that the realization of a spiritualized world order which has been the promise of the sacred scriptures of all ages is now the potential and requirement of our time.

Elements of this transformative vision include an affirmation of the divine within creation and an elucidation of the essential unity of the material and spiritual dimensions throughout the whole evolutionary process. Humanity, as part of this communion of life, has gone through a progressive developmental process. The prevailing social order represents an adolescent stage of this development. Having passed from the dependence of childhood through the impetuous autonomy-seeking stage of adolescence, humanity is now at the point of transition to conscious maturity. The long historical journey to becoming conscious beings through separation from nature is culminating in a mature understanding of life's profound interrelatedness.

The Baha'i writings suggest that this process of maturation requires an expanded religious consciousness complementing and integral to our scientific advancement. It is only in this context that the latent capacities of the human spirit can be fully quickened and released. These capacities, such as spirituality, creativity, and altruism, can encourage selfless action on behalf of the planet, its peoples, and future generations. They are an infinite resource in the face of depleting material resources. The development of spiritual qualities is the requirement of this age and a fruition of human purpose within the whole evolution of life.

In order to help foster the release of individual spiritual potential and focus it as a force for cultural transformation and moral regeneration, institutions founded on a comprehensive vision of unity need to be established. The Baha'i International Community is itself an embryonic model for such a process of ordered social transformation.

This process of transformation is neither idealistic nor utopian: in the face of the disastrous ecological and human consequences that face us if we continue with "business as usual," this is the new realism. This transformation is possible because the forces that propelled life's evolution from the beginning are still operating within human society. There is reason to believe that the mysterious forces that have "shaped the planet under our feet" and "guided life through its bewildering variety of expression" in natural ecosystems and human cultures "have not suddenly collapsed under the great volume of human affairs in this late twentieth century."[25]

In conclusion, the Baha'i writings offer a vision of wholeness in our relationship to nature and of spiritual purpose in the whole evolution of life that gives a basis for creating a life-affirming culture and empowers individuals to become agents of transformation in developing a sustainable global civilization.

NOTES

1. John Livingston, "Ethics as Prosthetics," in *Environmental Ethics: Philosophical and Policy Perspectives,* ed. Philip P. Hanson (Burnaby: Institute for the Humanities, Simon Fraser University, 1986), 67–81.

2. Thomas Berry, *The Dream of the Earth* (San Francisco: Sierra Club Books, 1988), 36–49.

3. Paul Hanley, "Agriculture: A Fundamental Principle," *Journal of Baha'i Studies* 3, no. 1 (1990): 11–12.

4. Bahá'u'lláh and 'Abdu'l-Bahá, *Baha'i World Faith: Selected Writings of Bahá'u'lláh and 'Abdu'l-Bahá,* rev. ed. (Wilmette, Ill.: Baha'i Publishing Trust, 1956), 364; hereafter, *BWF,* with page references cited in the text.

5. See *Star of the West* 8, no. 11 (27 September 1917): 138.

6. 'Abdu'l-Bahá, *Selections from the Writings of 'Abdu'l-Bahá* (Haifa: Baha'i World Centre, 1978), 27.

7. 'Abdu'l-Bahá, "Tablet to Dr. August Forel," in *The Baha'i Revelation* (London: Baha'i Publishing Trust, 1955), 221–22; hereafter, *BR,* with page references cited in the text.

8. 'Abdu'l-Bahá, *Some Answered Questions,* trans. Laura Clifford Barney, rev. ed. (Wilmette, Ill.: Baha'i Publishing Trust, 1981), 235; hereafter, *SAQ,* with page references cited in the text.

9. 'Abdu'l-Bahá, *Promulgation of Universal Peace,* comp. Howard MacNutt, 2d ed. (Wilmette, Ill.: Baha'i Publishing Trust, 1982), 302.

10. John Hatcher, *The Purpose of Physical Reality* (Wilmette, Ill.: Baha'i Publishing Trust, 1987), 69.

11. Matthew Fox, *Original Blessing: A Primer in Creation Spirituality* (Santa Fe, N.M.: Bear and Co., 1983), 90.

12. Bahá'u'lláh, *Gleanings from the Writings of Bahá'u'lláh,* trans. Shoghi Effendi, 2d ed. (Wilmette, Ill.: Baha'i Publishing Trust, 1976), 166; hereafter, *G,* with page references cited in the text.

13. 'Abdu'l-Bahá, *Makátíb,* 1:436–37. This quote from the Persian book *Makátíb* (unpublished in English) was cited by Bahiyyíh Nakhjavání in her book *Response* (Oxford: Ronald, 1981), 13.

14. Bahá'u'lláh, *Epistle to the Son of the Wolf,* trans. Shoghi Effendi, new ed. (Wilmette, Ill.: Baha'i Publishing Trust, 1988), 44.

15. Henryk Skolimowski, *Eco-Philosophy: Designing New Tactics for Living* (London: Boyars, 1981), 71; hereafter, *E-P,* with page references cited in the text.

16. Though a developmental sequence is suggested, there is no indication of cultural superiority. Different cultural streams have explored and developed different capacities that are all integral to the current period of reconciliation.

17. Nature devoid of spirit became matter, with all sense of its mystery and numinosity lost. Yet the word *matter* has evolved from our original understanding of the earth as "mother." The word for mother in Greek is spelled *meter;* in Latin, *mater* and in Sanskrit, *matr.*

18. William Hatcher, "The Science of Religion," *Baha'i Studies* 2 (1980): 16; hereafter, "Science," with page references cited in the text.

19. Shoghi Effendi, *The World Order of Bahá'u'lláh,* 2d ed. (Wilmette, Ill.: Baha'i Publishing Trust, 1982), 43; hereafter, *WOB,* with page references cited in the text.

20. R. L. Sivard, *World Military and Social Expenditures* (Washington, D.C.: World Priorities, Inc., 1991), 43, and 42.

21. International Institute for Sustainable Development, "Earth Summit Bulletin," no. 2 (1992), 13. Also see World Commission on Environment and Development, *Our Common Future* (Oxford: Oxford University Press, 1987) and "Rio Declaration on Environment and Development" (an Earth Summit press release by the United Nations Department of Public Information, 1992).

22. Bill Devall and George Sessions, *Deep Ecology: Living as if Nature Mattered* (Salt Lake City, Utah: Peregrine Smith Books, 1985), 18.

23. Arthur Lyon Dahl, *Unless and Until: A Baha'i Focus on the Environment* (London: Baha'i Publishing Trust, 1990), 81–82.

24. See *Star of the West* 3, no. 3 (28 April 1912): 4.

25. Berry, *Dream of Earth,* 47.

Mormon Values and the Utah Environment

RICHARD C. FOLTZ

Abstract

Although there has been little if any discussion of Mormon environmentalism outside the tradition, it is increasingly apparent that such an ethic does exist though whether this ethic is with or against the current of formal LDS teaching is less clear. This article provides an overview of contemporary Mormon ecological thought and its roots within the LDS tradition, and highlights some of the tensions connected with environmental issues within the Mormon community today in Utah and elsewhere.

keywords: environmentalism, Latter-day Saints, Utah, land use, Mormon

> *And it came to pass that Enoch looked upon the earth; and he heard a voice from the bowels thereof saying: Wo, wo is me, the mother of men; I am pained, I am weary, because of the wickedness of my children. When shall I rest, and be cleansed from the filthiness which is gone forth out of me? When will my Creator sanctify me, that I may rest, and righteousness for a season abide upon my face?*
>
> *And when Enoch heard the earth mourn, he wept, and cried unto the Lord, saying: O Lord, wilt thou not have compassion upon the earth?*
>
> *The Pearl of Great Price*, Moses 7:48–49.

ON JULY 24, 1999, A DAY MORMONS CELEBRATE as 'Pioneer Day' commemorating the arrival of Brigham Young and his followers in the Salt Lake valley in 1847, the annual parade in the town of Escalante, Utah featured a float in which a dummy environmentalist was pinned to the front of the vehicle as if it had been hit. Amidst the day's festivities, the home of two local environmentalists was vandalized. In an interview shortly after the event, the local Mormon bishop, Wade Barney, stated that the couple had 'asked for it' and were 'lucky' not to have suffered worse.

Less than three weeks earlier, addressing a rally on July 5, Bishop Barney had called for a 'religious war' against environmentalists. Though Barney claimed to be speaking as a citizen and not in his capacity as church official, it was quickly pointed out by one local resident that since well over eighty percent of Escalante's population is Mormon, 'What he says has a big influence around here' (Kennedy 1999). In a letter to *The Salt Lake Tribune*, a Mormon writer expressed his concern that 'clearly [Barney] is using his church calling for leverage for his views' (Robison 1999).

In the following weeks other Utah Mormons sent in letters expressing the view that the Bishop's activities were not in the true spirit of the faith. One self-proclaimed Mormon environmentalist wrote that he was 'disgusted by such statements and the implications that such words are backed by the LDS Church' (S. Owens 1999). Another Mormon writer, noting that 'Brigham Young once stated, "The soil, the air, the water, are all pure and healthy. Do not suffer them to become polluted in the wilderness"', wrote that 'There is no excuse for [the vandalism] or for the comments made by Barney when he declared war on environmentalists' (Eurick 1999).

The political influence of Mormonism—which leads some Utahns to remark, only half-jokingly, that they live in a theocracy—is indeed little known and inadequately acknowledged by most environmentalists. The fact that wilderness designation vs. 'private property' rights and 'wise use' debates are currently

Foltz, Richard C., "Mormon Values and the Utah Environment," *Worldviews: Environment, Culture, Religion* 4/1 (2000), pp. 1–19. Reprinted by permission of the author.

reaching a fevered pitch over the Clinton administration's sometimes undemocratic actions to protect vast tracts of Utah wilderness make the state a particularly relevant focus today.

Utah is known for conservative politics. All five of the state's federal legislators—Senators Robert Bennett and Orrin Hatch and Representatives Christopher Cannon, Merrill Cook, and James Hansen—are Mormon and Republican. (Of the sixteen Mormons currently holding seats in Congress, only two, Senator Harry Reid of Nevada and Representative Tom Udall of New Mexico, are Democrats.)

Like conservatives elsewhere in the country, Utahns tend to see environmental protection legislation as outside interference and a threat to private property rights. Across the state developers rule the day, seemingly bent on plastering every last hillside with rabbit-hutch condominiums and tract houses, not to mention cashing in on the building boom currently taking place in anticipation of the 2002 Olympics.[1] Car culture is largely unquestioned, despite increasingly long commutes, traffic jams, and smog; an ongoing battle against improved mass transit in Salt Lake City is led by a citizens' group called 'Utahns Against Light Rail'. Utah is also home to an organization which calls itself the 'Anti-Wilderness Society'. It was reported in early 1999 that mothers in southeastern Utah were keeping their children home from school on field-trip days, fearing they would be taught 'environmental extremism'.[2]

Since many of these observations about public attitudes can be made about other Western states where Mormons are but a small minority, one might question the connection between Utah's religious and political cultures. Yet both the politics and the economy of Utah have their own distinct histories in contrast to surrounding regions of the American West. Mormon history has been characterized by tensions with 'mainstream' America since the very beginning, and relations with the federal government during Utah's period of territorial status throughout the second half of the nineteenth century created a legacy of distrust.[3] While, paradoxically perhaps, throughout the twentieth century Mormons tended to be devoutly patriotic Americans, their sense of distinct community and obsession with retaining control over their own affairs have always been powerful forces.

Utah's political culture has been since pre-statehood times and remains today intensely pro-business even by broader American standards. Amidst the growing public awareness of how corporate globalization threatens the environment (Korten 1995, Mander and Goldsmith 1996), it is not irrelevant to note that the LDS Church today controls assets amounting to as much as thirty billion dollars. It has interests in stocks and bonds, communications, mining, railroads, banks, lumber, and other industries, and owns over 150 farms and ranches (including Florida's 312,000-acre Deseret Ranch, the largest cattle ranch in the United States); the Church's one million acres in holdings make it one of the country's largest landowners and a major player in agribusiness.[4]

A number of large transnational corporations, the Marriott hotel chain being one of the more visible, are Mormon-owned.[5] Utahn Jon Huntsman, who owns the patent for styrofoam, is one of the richest men in the United States with a net worth of around $2.2 billion. The Kennecott mining company operates massive mines at enormous environmental cost within sight of Salt Lake City. Perhaps not surprisingly for a politician representing such a pro-corporate culture, former Utah Senator Jake Garn has said that people should learn to live with industrial pollution rather than endanger the profits of corporations.

Environmental voting scores published by the League of Conservation Voters regularly rank most Mormon legislators near the bottom of the list. Utah's two Republican Senators, Robert Bennett and Orrin Hatch, each scored 7 out of a possible 100 during the 105th Congress in 1997–98, up from 0 for each during the 104th. Representative Jim Hansen (R), a vigorous opponent of the Endangered Species Act (ESA) who has openly called for a number of 'undesirable' endangered species simply to be eradicated for good, scored a 10 in the 105th Congress, as did Representative Chris Cannon (R). Utah's third U.S. Representative, Merrill Cook (R), was little better at 24. The records of Mormon legislators from other states show a similar pattern (LCV 1999).

Beyond their voting records, Mormon politicians have been personally outspoken anti-environmentalists. Several years ago the ESA Task Force in Washington received a complaint from a California schoolteacher that Mormon Congressman Wally Herger (R-CA) had verbally abused her and her fourth and fifth-grade students when they attempted to tell an ESA hearing about a class project in which they worked with ranchers to protect endangered fairy shrimp (ESA 1995). In 1998 Utah Senator Hatch helped produce a pamphlet which listed 'preoccupation with environmental issues' as a sign by which parents could tell their children are abusing drugs (Rauber 1999).

With LDS-affiliated elected officials being among the most visible and audible proponents of anti-environmental views, many outsiders find it hard to imagine that there could even be a Mormon environmentalism. Yet the words and actions of ecologically-minded Mormons increasingly demonstrate that such an ethic does exist—though whether this ethic is with or against the current of formal LDS teaching is less clear.

MORMONISM: A BRIEF OVERVIEW

The Church of Jesus Christ of Latter-day Saints, or LDS Church, is a nominally Christian denomination but with its own distinct history and sense of community.[6] The Church was founded in 1830 in upstate New York by Joseph Smith, who, according to Mormon belief, had discovered a set of plates upon which was engraved 'the Book of Mormon'—an account of Israelites who had migrated to the western hemisphere in ancient times. Considered heretical by many of their contemporaries, Smith and his followers were frequent victims of persecution, often in the form of mob attacks. Smith himself, along with his brother Hyrum, was murdered in 1844 in Carthage, Illinois. In 1846 the main body of the Church migrated westward under the leadership of Brigham Young in search of land where they could practice their faith and way of life in peace. Arriving in the Salt Lake valley in the summer of 1847, Young declared, 'This is the right place', and the Mormon community established itself in what it has since referred to as the promised land, or Zion. After nearly half a century of troubled relations with the U.S. government, the Utah territory (of which Brigham Young had been governor during the last four decades of his life) was incorporated into the United States in 1896.

The LDS Church espouses numerous doctrines which do not exist in mainstream Christianity. Among the beliefs unique to Mormonism are the divine nature of *The Book of Mormon, The Doctrine and Covenants* (revelations given to Joseph Smith and other contemporary prophets), and *The Pearl of Great Price* ('supplementary' texts of the Hebrew prophets); the possibility of ongoing revelation to all believers; the eternal nature of marriage and family ties; baptism on behalf of the dead; the priesthood available to all worthy male believers over the age of twelve; and that the faithful can become gods.

The Mormon belief most obviously relevant to the environmental crisis is that there exist large numbers of souls, or 'spirit children', who are waiting to be born into this world; it is therefore the duty of married couples to bring these souls to earth. As a result Mormons tend to have large families, and to oppose birth control. While the Church appears recently to have broadened its teaching on family size to make some allowance for choice and personal capacity (Ellsworth 1992), the prevailing cultural norm favors having many children.[7] Among Mormon women, especially, the 'bringing down' of as many souls as possible continues to be a great source of pride and achievement.

At present, the Church maintains the official position that human overpopulation is not an issue. In a 1995 instructional essay in *The Ensign*, an official organ of the LDS Church, Second Counselor President James E. Faust approvingly quotes articles by publisher Malcolm Forbes in *Forbes* magazine and journalist Stephen Budiansky in *U.S. News and World Report* to the effect that human population growth is a good and not a danger (Faust 1995). His chosen citation from the Forbes editorial echoes the mantra of former University of Maryland economist Julian Simon: 'Free people don't exhaust resources. They create them' (Forbes 1994). Faust goes on to cite Budiansky's argument (roundly dismissed by current scientific consensus) that the earth is capable of supporting a human population of eighty billion (Budiansky 1994). President Faust concludes by instructing Mormons that "Those who argue for sustainable growth lack vision and faith. The Lord said, "For the Earth is full, and there is enough to spare [D & C 104:17]." That settles the issue for me. It should settle the issue for all of us. The Lord has spoken' (Faust 1995: 5).

All young Mormon men are strongly encouraged to spend two years of their lives (usually after their first year of college) serving as missionaries. Retired couples often serve on missions as well. As a result, the LDS Church is one of the world's fastest-growing religious denominations, with a membership that has grown from less than three million to over ten million within the past thirty years.[8] Supported through the obligatory tithing of its members, the Church is the wealthiest in the United States for its size, with worldwide assets of 25 to 30 billion dollars and five to six billion dollars annual income (Ostling and Ostling 1999: xvi). In the state of Utah and adjacent areas of neighboring states, Mormons form a strong majority and therefore tend to dominate local politics. Although the official position of the Church has historically been to abstain from political involvement, members are now encouraged to be politically active especially at the local level. In any event, given that Mormons make up nearly three-quarters of the population of the state of Utah, it would seem difficult to imagine that Church teachings could fail to affect the political process there.

Mormons have long tended to see the internal dynamics of their community as being nobody's business but their own. Yet today, as historian of religion Jan Shipps has commented, 'What occurs within Mormonism is no longer merely an internal matter, and what Mormonism does is becoming vitally important to the larger culture' (Shipps 1998). Given the undeniable political influence of Mormon society in Utah and beyond, one has the sense that contemporary debate over the politics of wilderness and conservation—especially as carried out in Washington and elsewhere in the northeastern United States—is not adequately cognizant that a distinct worldview is operating within the dominant culture of a region where so much of this debate is focused, and that it would benefit those involved to take this worldview into account.

THE STRUGGLE OVER LAND USE IN UTAH

As elsewhere, conservationists in Utah have long been at odds over mining, ranching, and other interests. William B. Smart, former editor of the Mormon-owned Salt Lake newspaper *Deseret News,* has remarked that 'In the past half century, no issue has torn apart my state as the use of the land that once seemed so limitless' (Smart 1998: 1).

The construction of the Glen Canyon dam on the Colorado River in 1963 and subsequent flooding of the canyon to form Lake Powell generated a flurry of protest which has not abated to this day. Indeed, nearly forty years later, calls for the dismantling of the dam and draining of the lake are stronger than ever, buttressed by increasing scientific understanding of how the processes of salinization, silting, and water loss through surface evaporation from reservoirs outweigh the benefits for irrigation and other purposes (Reisner 1993: 470–476).[9]

Roughly one-third of Utah land is publicly-owned, most of it administered by the federal Bureau of Land Management (BLM). Beginning in late 1995, the Republican-led Congress began a campaign to weaken the Wilderness Act of 1964 so as to open up pristine areas to development. These 'reforms' failed to pass through either the House or the Senate, however. Meanwhile, in the hope of protecting as much of the remaining Utah wilderness as possible, members of the Utah wilderness Coalition—a group that includes the Sierra Club, the Southern Utah Wilderness Alliance, and other organizations—were seeking to have millions of acres of public lands classified as eligible for wilderness protection. The spring and summer of 1996 saw furious debates in Washington over the wilderness issue, culminating in a Republican filibuster which threatened to preclude any settlement.

On 17 September 1996, President Bill Clinton announced before a crowd assembled on the south rim of the Grand Canyon that he was drawing on the 1906 Antiquities Act (through which President Theodore Roosevelt had set aside the land which would become Grand Canyon National Park) to designate 1.7 million acres of southern Utah lands as the new Grand Staircase-Escalante National Monument. Of this, 1.2 million acres was designated as wilderness. The President's act was hailed as a bold move by environmentalists, while elected officials and others especially in southern Utah condemned it as a cynical and undemocratic power play. Local governments in southern Utah defiantly responded by accelerating their efforts to build roads into protected areas (SUWA 1996).

Conservationist groups, who had been lobbying for 5.7 million acres of Utah wilderness, have claimed more recently that as much as 8.8 million acres qualifies for such protection (Watkins 1998). Whatever the outcome, it seems certain that the tensions and animosity between competing visions of how Utah land is to be used will only intensify in the future.

MORMON ENVIRONMENTALISTS

A 1991 report on the environmental policies of the thirty largest Christian denominations in the United States placed the LDS Church in its fifth and lowest category, 'Policies of Inaction'—that is, denominations formally committed to inaction (Massey 1991). The editors of a recent collection of essays by Mormon writers on the environment (Terry Tempest Williams, William B. Smart, and Gibbs M. Smith, eds., *New Genesis: A Mormon Reader on Land and Community,* Salt Lake City: Gibbs Smith Publisher, 1998) tacitly validate this unflattering assessment, enjoining their target audience of fellow Mormons to 'change our behavior of inactivity toward the earth, personally and collectively, by first recognizing our past relationship to place as holy, tied to our religious sovereignty, and by honoring the Creator through his creation' (Williams et al. 1998: ix).

Wayne Owens, a former U.S. Congressman from Utah whose pro-environment stand makes him a rare exception among Mormon politicians, remarks that, 'Our doctrine is enormously progressive as it relates to the environment, but our cultural interpretation has not followed suit. Our theology has not translated politically into a powerful environmental ethic' (W. Owens 1998: 224). In the view of William Smart, "The challenge for Utahns is to awaken to the value of what is all around them, the priceless resource of unspoiled land, and find creative ways not only to keep it unspoiled but to prosper in and from it' (Smart 1998: 4).

A common theme of many of the essays in *New Genesis* is that Mormons today have lost sight of the ecological wisdom that originally characterized their culture. According to the editors, Brigham Young 'preached sustainable agriculture and dreamed a United Order while allotting time in LDS general conference for talks on appropriate farming practices and community vitality in harmony with the land' (Williams et al. 1998: ix). The 'United Order' refers to an experimental approach to property practiced in some early Mormon communities, where 'all local lands and possessions were held in common and meted out as stewardships according to individual need . . . But the idea never caught hold' (Smith 1998: 78). Mormon villages were once self-sufficient, but this model of social organization did not survive the transition from agrarian to industrial society. Utah's main agricultural product now is hay, and most of the state's food is imported from elsewhere.

Another theme upon which Mormon environmentalists, like nature spiritualists from other traditions, often draw, is the nourishment and revitalization that can come from spending time in the wilderness. Joseph Smith's First Vision came to him in 1820 at age fourteen at a 'Sacred Grove' in Palmyra, New York. William Smart points out that 'Abraham, Moses, Elijah, Joseph Smith, the Savior himself all went to the wilderness to hear God's voice. Repeatedly, Book of Mormon peoples fled there for succor and redemption' (Smart 1998: 6). Marilyn Arnold, a former Professor of English at Brigham Young University in Provo, Utah (hereafter BYU), writes that 'The longer I am acquainted with wilderness, the more I understand the need of Jesus, of Enos, of Joseph Smith, and others to leave the distractions of the workaday world in order to pray lengthily, to meditate, to seek guidance and resolve—or pardon—without interruption. Whether in the desert, woods, or waterside, human beings—and even Christ himself—have communed with the Spirit and been blessed with instruction, commitment, and renewal' (Arnold 1998: 29). Further on she explains that 'just as I discover Eudora Welty by living with her eloquent words, and Georgia O'Keeffe by examining her extraordinary paintings, so do I move toward understanding the Lord by contemplating the natural world he created as well as the words he spoke' (Arnold 1998: 31).

Mormonism, which includes the Hebrew Bible among its sacred scriptures—and with it the injunction in Genesis 1:28 '. . . Be fruitful and multiply, and fill the earth and subdue it . . .' which environmentalists have made so infamous—sees Creation as having been made for the use and benefit of human beings. The reverse side of this divine command, which is the responsibility that comes with stewardship, is quite explicit in Mormon scripture, however. In the *Doctrine and Covenants* one reads, 'For it is expedient that I, the Lord, should make every man accountable, as a steward over earthly blessings, which I have made and prepared for my creatures. I, the Lord, stretched out the heavens, and built the earth, my very handiwork; and all things therein are mine' (D & C 104:13–14). Another passage reads, 'Thou shalt be diligent in preserving what thou hast, that thou mayest be a wise steward; for it is the free gift of the Lord thy God, and thou art his steward' (D & C 136:27). Profligacy is likewise forbidden: 'And it pleaseth God that he hath given all these things unto man; for unto this end were they made to be used, with judgment, not to excess, neither by extortion' (D & C 59:20).

To many living in Utah today, it is apparent that these commands are being neglected.

More than twenty years ago, then Church President Spencer W. Kimball said in his bicentennial address: '. . . when I review the performance of this people in comparison with what is expected, I am appalled and frightened . . . I have the feeling that the good earth can hardly bear our presence upon it . . . The Brethren constantly cry out against that which is intolerable in the sight of the Lord: against pollution of mind, body, and our surroundings' (Kimball 1976: 4). In a similar vein, Mormon essayist and university professor Hugh Nibley wrote that 'We have taught our children by precept and example that every living thing exists to be converted into cash, and that whatever would not yield a return should be quickly exterminated to make way for creatures that do' (Nibley 1978).

The LDS scriptures seem both to anticipate this state of affairs, and to warn of its results. A passage from the *Doctrine and Covenants* reads: '. . . I have promised . . . their restoration to the land of Zion . . . Nevertheless, if they pollute their inheritances, they shall be thrown down; for I will not spare them if they pollute their inheritances' (D & C 103:13–14). Mormon pioneer Orson Pratt likewise cautioned the early community, 'If we shall be unwise in the disposition of this trust, then it will be very doubtful, whether we get an inheritance in this world or in the world to come' (*Journal of Discourses* 21: 151).

Although a stated aim of the pioneers was improve and redeem the land in preparation for the Kingdom of God (Kay and Brown 1985: 257), in actuality their farming and ranching practices brought about rapid environmental deterioration across the Utah territory from the very beginning (Ball and Brotherson 1999: 69–76). Thomas G. Alexander observes that '. . . many Utah Mormons *acted* as if ecclesiastical pronouncements regarding the environment were, in fact, little more than rhetoric . . .' (Alexander 1994: 344).

Similar observations are made of Mormon behavior today. Donald L. Gibbon writes, 'The natural world seems to have very little place in the panoply of things most Mormons worry or even think about. This isn't so different from most Americans . . . but aren't we supposed to be a peculiar people, different in important ways?' (Gibbon 1998: 130). To some Mormons, even the sense of sacred place, which has been so much a part of their historical identity, is being lost. 'Zion has become like any other place in America', laments William Smart (Smart 1998: ix).

Architect Ron Molen, noting that Utah is the sixth most urbanized state in the country, observes that 'Gridlocked traffic on the freeways, pollution alerts, crime, drugs, violence, and political corruption are constant reminders that Utah suffers from the same problems as other highly urbanized states . . . A drive through the urban sprawl along I-15 [the north-south freeway which bisects the Salt Lake valley] shows development not at peace with the land. It shouts greed and hostility, not cooperation and community.' Molen believes that 'We have yet to earn the right to live in this exquisite mountain setting. Yes, we have made the desert blossom, but we have paved more of it, and worse, we seem to have no idea where we are going' (Molen 1998: 43).

Shawn Skabelund of Northern Arizona University has taken up this theme as well, suggesting that 'Just as the Israelites were left in their wilderness for forty years to try and find themselves . . . I see Mormons going off to the Great Basin to be left alone to worship how they may, but in the years since have lost their way—meaning they really don't know who they are anymore. They have lost the meaning of trying to forget oneself for the good of the whole, the community, the holy, the creation. Somewhere, sometime Mormonism got caught up in the individualism we see in the American West—private property rights versus public or common ones' (Skabelund 1999).

Do these assessments indicate that contemporary Mormon society lacks an explicit environmental ethic which can guide them into a sustainable future? Ardean Watts, former conductor of the Utah Symphony and Professor of Music at the University of Utah, offers the following remarks:

> In light of the importance Mormons place on the LDS Church being guided by living prophets, it is natural for them to look to their prophets, seers, and revelators for direction on important

> social issues. Although general public interest in environmental matters has risen dramatically during the past generation, there appears to be little sustained focus on them coming from church leadership. Positive references to environmental concerns in conference addresses and publications are offset, for example, by public denial that there is a global population problem (Watts 1998: 49).

Current LDS President Gordon B. Hinckley has stated that 'This earth is [God's] creation. When we make it ugly, we offend Him' (Rogers 1990: 16). In a 1998 address to the Chamber of Commerce of St. George, Utah (an increasingly overbuilt and characterless resort town of 47,000 in southern Utah which has been described as 'basically a strip mall next to a golf course'), Hinckley may have been calling for restraint when he said, 'it may be foolish to say to any member of a chamber of commerce—and particularly to realtors—that I hope you won't continue to grow. If you do, then the culture, the spirit, and the ambiance of the community will change as it already has done so in a measure (Williams et al. 1998: xii).

A more explicit environmentalist teaching is evident in the July 1991 issue of *The Ensign*, a monthly magazine published by the Church for its members. In an article entitled, 'Earth: A Gift of Gladness', G. Michael Alder states that 'God has made us responsible for the earth and all living things', and asks, 'How well are we doing?' Alder acknowledges 'the environmental damage caused by such man-made problems as acid rain, excessive carbon dioxide and other chemicals in the atmosphere, deforestation, and the pollution of our oceans, lakes, and streams.' He observes that humans now have 'the power to radically alter the global environment' and that '[t]hese changes outstrip our present ability to cope with them, largely because the world's financial, social, and political systems are out of step with natural processes.' Alder then provides an outline of the kinds of environmental damage being wrought by humans, and suggests some ways in which Mormons might practice greater mindfullness. He concludes his essay by encouraging the readers of *Ensign* to reduce consumption, avoid using environmentally destructive products, recycle, and learn more about natural processes through gardening, composting and the like (Alder 1991: 27–28).

Articles such as Alder's are still quite rare in mainstream Mormon literature, however.[10] Notwithstanding a few sporadic (and, as pointed out by Ardean Watts above, somewhat less than forceful) signals from the Church leadership, the environmental crisis does not appear to be a major preoccupation within the LDS hierarchy. Emphasizing the important role Church leadership plays in shaping the worldview of Mormons, Shawn Skabelund comments that 'without their leaders' guidance in a compassion for creation, I see little hope' (Skabelund 1999).

In the absence of more widespread instruction or guidance from the Church leadership on environmental issues, Mormon environmentalists are indeed developing an ecological reading of the tradition on their own. A jumping off point for some is the passage in the *Doctrine and Covenants* (59:18–19), which reads: 'Yea, all things which come of the earth, in the season thereof, are made for the benefit and the use of man, both to please the eye and to gladden the heart; Yea, for food and for raiment, for taste and for smell, to strengthen the body and enliven the soul.' Commenting on this passage, William Smart remarks, 'I like his [God's] priorities—that pleasing the eye and gladdening the heart and enlivening the soul are as important as food and raiment. If the fulness of the earth [a reference to D & C 59:16; cf. Psalms 24:1 and Isaiah 6:3] is to benefit the eye and the heart and the soul, surely it is to include unpolluted skies and water and landscapes' (Smart 1998: 6). Referring to the same passage, Marilyn Arnold surmises that 'The concept of "benefit" and "use", when applied to the natural world, is as much spiritual as temporal' (Arnold 1998: 32). In his *Ensign* article cited above, Michael Alder notes that a subsequent verse adds the qualification of responsibility to human stewardship of these gifts, which are to be used 'with judgment, not to excess' (D & C 59:20).

Another passage from *Doctrine and Covenants* forms the basis of the Mormon belief that not only humans, but all life forms have eternal souls: '. . . that which is spiritual being in the likeness of that which is temporal; and that which is temporal in the likeness of that which is spiritual; the spirit of man in the likeness of his person as also the spirit of beast and every other creature which God has created' (D & C 77:2). Thomas G. Alexander, a professor of American History at BYU, observes that this belief has more in common with the Native American and even the emergent Gaian worldviews than with that of nineteenth-century Christianity (Alexander 1998: 209). In a similar vein, BYU English professor Eugene England writes of his hope that he will be able one day to explain to his granddaughter 'the unusual Mormon concept that all God's creations—animals, plants, even, it seems, the rocks themselves—have a spiritual existence and identity that can be loved and must be respected . . .' (England 1998: 89).

It may be noted that the LDS Church does not as a rule take kindly to private theologies, and has been known to censure members for publicly expressing too personal interpretations of Mormon scripture. In one such case in 1996, BYU English professor Gail Turley Houston was denied tenure for suggesting Mormons pray to Mother in Heaven—a notion, given the recent emergence of eco-feminist discourse, with possible ecological ramifications for Mormon believers (AAUP 1997: 52–71).[11] Though according to Mormon belief God is married, LDS President Gordon Hinckley had stated in 1991 that 'I consider it inappropriate for anyone in the Church to pray to our Mother in Heaven' (Ostling and Ostling 1998: 235). Given such limitations on individual interpretation, the boldness with which some Mormon environmentalists have expressed their views is all the more striking.

One Mormon intellectual who has ventured to challenge his society's prevailing views on human population control is University of Utah Political Science professor James B. Mayfield. He writes, 'If it is accepted that God wants us to multiply and replenish the earth, there is still the question of whether this is true in all cases and in all situations . . . while it is physically possible for a couple to have 15 to 20 children, any careful reading of the brethren would not conclude that all couples must have all the children that they physically are capable of having, nor that there is no choice in the matter' (Mayfield 1998: 59). Taking into account the Mormon doctrine that there are countless children in pre-existence waiting to be born, Mayfield advances the notion that since 'God has created "worlds without number" [*Pearl of Great Price,* Moses 1:33] . . . there is plenty of space for an infinite number of spirit children in the larger scheme of things.' Though clearly choosing his words carefully, Mayfield would appear to be tacitly acknowledging that the human population has now exceeded the earth's carrying capacity, and suggesting as a solution that excess children might henceforth be born elsewhere in the universe. He concludes by stating his belief that 'God wants people to make good choices, to use wisdom in determining how many children they will have, and that in the long run as systems of education and literacy are implemented throughout the world, the problem of overpopulation will take care of itself (Mayfield 1998: 62).

The editors of *New Genesis* offer an even more sweeping proposal. 'The highest and truest progress in Zion,' they write, 'would be the recognition that saving souls and saving the planet are the same thing—testaments of divine creation (Williams et al. 1998: xii).

CONCLUSIONS

The validity of Lynn White's assertion that the environmental crisis reflects an underlying spiritual crisis (White 1967) is still not apparent to many people, Mormons being no exception. As one Mormon academic puts it, 'The environmental issue is not a religious one. Problems of open land, wildlife, and particularly water are western issues, not church issues. These are carpet-bagger matters . . . problems between locals and outlivers'.[12] The essays collected in *New Genesis,* nearly all of which are written by Utah Mormons, belie this claim. They should likewise lay to rest any doubt as to whether a meaningful and practical environmental ethic can be derived from the LDS tradition, or that there exist today Mormons who are both devout in their faith and deeply committed to discovering—or rediscovering—a healthier sense of place in the natural world. Nevertheless, it is hard to escape the sensation that these are somewhat lonely voices within a tradition that by and large continues to avoid facing issues of maldevelopment, irresponsible use of land and resources and uncontrolled human population growth.

One need not be Mormon to detect a prophetic quality in the words Joseph Smith spoke over 150 years ago: 'The great failure of many of our modern ways—for some day we shall see how mistaken and vain our ambitions have been—is that we substitute man's ways for God's ways . . . We were created to inhabit, beautify, and replenish the earth' (Published in *Juvenile Instructor,* 15 December 1905; quoted in Arnold 1998: 31).

Echoing John Muir, former Salt Lake City mayor Ted Wilson suggests one way in which this might be accomplished. 'Shouldn't we view God's handicraft as temples?' he asks. 'Shouldn't we respect the few remaining places upon Earth that are wild, uninterrupted, and unblemished?' Observing that 'the forces of development on an increasingly overcrowded planet threaten to tear down our temples of nature,' Wilson proposes, 'Shouldn't we offer a tithe to save God's natural handicraft on Earth?' (Wilson 1998: 7).

The editors of *New Genesis* go still further to suggest, 'Perhaps it is not too much to dream that The Church of Jesus Christ of Latter-day Saints will exercise its organizational genius from the ground up on behalf of the earth, that we might return to our root nature of both pragmatism and vision, with an eye toward both heaven and earth (Williams et al. 1998: xii).

For all who have known and loved Utah's wilderness, as for all those who have been touched by the ecological renaissance taking place within many of the world's religious traditions over the past several decades, it should be of the greatest interest and importance to see if the LDS Church is able to incorporate in any formal sense the enormous, revitalizing energy which is being generated by ecologically-minded Mormons in Utah and elsewhere today.

NOTES

I am grateful to Claudia Bushman, Alexandra Carpino, Edwin ('Phil') Pister, Aaron, Lee, Shawn and Todd Skabelund for their comments on earlier drafts of this paper.

1. Church-owned businesses contributed $211,000 to the committee which secured the Olympics bid for Salt Lake City (Ostling and Ostling 1999: xvii).

2. This followed an incident where students reportedly had been instructed by a teacher to 'hug a tree' (SUWA 1999).

3. The classic history of the early community by a Mormon scholar is Arrington 1958.

4. Ostling and Ostling 1999: 118. The Ostlings point out that if the LDS Church were a corporation, it would rank 243rd on the *Fortune* 500 list, between Paine Webber and Union Carbide (p. 124).

5. Ostling and Ostling 1999: 113–129. A more detailed but less recent study is John Heinerman and Anson Shupe, *The Mormon Corporate Empire,* Boston: Beacon Press, 1985. The LDS Church's policy of extreme secrecy regarding its finances makes any accurate assessment very difficult.

6. The Church officially prefers to restrict the term 'Mormon' to its scriptural usage. However, as believers commonly employ it in self-reference it will be used as such in this paper. See the terminology note in Ostling and Ostling, *Mormon America,* p. xii.

7. David O. McKay, who was LDS Church President from 1951 to 1970, once said that birth control put marriage on a level with 'the panderer and the courtesan.' In 1987 then-President Ezra Taft Benson instructed Mormons: 'Do not curtail the number of children for personal or selfish reasons.' (Ostling and Ostling 1998: 168.)

8. Rodney Stark, a non-Mormon sociologist, has predicted that LDS membership will reach 265 million members by 2080, making it 'the most important world religion to emerge since the rise of Islam some fourteen centuries ago' (Stark 1998).

9. The Quaker Neck dam in North Carolina was torn down in December 1998, and the Edwards dam in Maine is scheduled for removal in 2000. At present a dozen major dams in the U.S. are marked for dismantling. See Robbins 1999.

10. The semi-official *Encyclopedia of Mormonism* (1992) contains no entries for 'ecology', 'environment', or even 'nature'. The article on 'Stewardship' makes no explicit reference to the natural world.

11. This incident resulted in an investigation by the American Association of University Professors (AAUP), which concluded in BYU being censured for violations of academic freedom. Other ideologically-related BYU firings over the previous decade included professors David P. Wright, David Knowlton, Cecilia Konchar Farr, and Brian Evenson.

12. Name withheld, private communication, 1 December 1999.

REFERENCES

Alder, G. Michael 1991. 'Earth: A Gift of Gladness'. *The Ensign,* 21 (7): 27–28.

Alexander, Thomas G. 1998. 'Latter-day Saints, Utahns, and the Environment: A Personal Perspective'. In Williams et al., *New Genesis,* pp. 204–210.

—— 1994. 'Stewardship and Enterprise: The LDS Church and the Wasatch Oasis Environment, 1847–1930'. *Western Historical Quarterly* 25 (3): 341–366.

American Association of University Professors (AAUP) 1997. 'Academic Freedom and Tenure: Brigham Young University' (committee report). *Academe: Bulletin of the American Association of University Professors* 83 (5): 52–71.

Arnold, Marilyn 1998. 'A Descant of Praise and Thanksgiving'. In Williams et al., *New Genesis,* pp. 26–34.

Arrington, Leonard 1958. *Great Basin Kingdom: An Economic History of the Latter-day Saints, 1830–1900,* Cambridge, MA: Harvard University Press.

Ball, Terry B. and Jack D. Brotherson 1999. 'Environmental Lessons from Our Pioneer Heritage'. *BYU Studies* 38 (3): 63–88.

The Book of Mormon, Salt Lake City: Church of Jesus Christ of Latter-day Saints, 1981.

Budiansky, Stephen 1994. '10 Billion for Dinner, Please'. *U.S. News and World Report,* 12 Sept., pp. 57–62.

Doctrine and Covenants, Salt Lake City: Church of Jesus Christ of Latter-day Saints, 1981.

Ehrlich, Paul R. and Anne H. Ehrlich, 1996. *Betrayal of Science and Reason: How Anti-Environmental Rhetoric Threatens Our Future,* Washington: Island Press.

Ellsworth, Homer S. 1992. 'Birth Control'. In Daniel H. Ludlow, ed., *Encyclopedia of Mormonism,* 5 vols., New York: Macmillan, vol. 1, pp. 116–117.

England, Eugene 1998. 'Gooseberry Creek: A Narrative of Hope'. In Williams et al., *New Genesis,* pp. 82–89.

ESA Today 1995. Washington, D.C.: Endangered Species Coalition, 22 May.

Eurick, Janelle 1999. 'Outrageous Acts in Escalante'. *The Salt Lake Tribune,* 8 August sec. A, p. 6.

Faust, James E. 1995. 'Serving the Lord and Resisting the Devil'. *The Ensign* 25 (9), pp. 2–7.

Forbes, Malcolm S. Jr., 1994. 'The True Character of Health Care Reform'. *Forbes,* 12 Sept., p. 25.

Gibbon, Donald L. 1998. 'Conservation vs. Conservatives: How the Gospel Fits'. In Williams et al., *New Genesis,* pp. 130–137.

Heinerman, John and Anson Shupe 1985. *The Mormon Corporate Empire,* Boston: Beacon Press.

Journal of Discourses. On *New Mormon Studies* CD-Rom, Salt Lake City: Smith Research Associates and Signature Books, 1998.

Kay, Jeanne and Craig J. Brown 1985. 'Mormon Beliefs about Land and Natural Resources, 1847–1877'. *Journal of Historical Geography* 11 (3): 253–267.

Kellert, Stephen R. 1996. Letter to *New Scientist,* 7 January.

Kennedy, Kelly 1999. 'Home of Escalante Environmentalists Is Vandalized; LDS Bishop Calls Couple "Lucky"'. *The Salt Lake Tribune,* 27 July, sec. B, p. 2.

Kimball, Spencer W. 1976. "The False Gods We Worship'. *The Ensign* 6 (6): 4.

Korten, David 1995. *When Corporations Rule the World,* San Francisco: Kumarian Press.

League of Conservation Voters (LCV) 1999. Congressional voting record on environmental issues website: <http://www.scorecard.lcv.org>.

Ludlow, Daniel H., ed. 1992. *Encyclopedia of Mormonism,* 5 vols., New York: Macmillan.

Mander, Jerry and Edward Goldsmith 1996. *The Case Against the Global Economy,* San Francisco: Sierra Club Books.

Massey, Marshall 1991. 'Where Are Our Churches Today? A Report on the Environmental Positions of the Thirty Largest Christian Denominations in the United States'. *Firmament* 2 (4): 4–15.

Mayfield, James B. 1998. 'Poverty, Population, and Environmental Ruin'. In Williams et al., *New Genesis,* pp. 55–65.

Molen, Ron 1998. 'The Mormon Village: Model for Sustainability'. In Williams et al., *New Genesis,* pp. 42–48.

Nibley, Hugh W. 1978. 'Subduing the Earth'. In *Nibley on the Timely and Timeless: Classic Essays of Hugh W. Nibley,* Provo, UT: Religious Monograph Series, pp. 85–89.

—— 1972. 'Brigham Young on the Environment'. In Truman G. Madsen and Charles D. Tate, Jr., eds., *To the Glory of God: Mormon Essays on Great Issues,* Salt Lake City, pp. 3–29.

Owens, Stephen W. 1999. 'Disgusting Remarks by Bishop'. *The Salt Lake Tribune,* 6 August, sec. A, p. 16.

Owens, Wayne 1998. 'Wilderness in the Hand of God'. In Williams et al., *New Genesis,* pp. 222–227.

Ostling, Richard N. and Joan K. Ostling, 1999. *Mormon America: The Power and the Promise,* San Francisco: Harper.

The Pearl of Great Price, Salt Lake City: Church of Jesus Christ of Latter-day Saints, 1981.

Rauber, Paul 1999. 'Smoke Signals'. *Sierra.* January/February issue, p. 16.

Reisner, Marc 1993 [1986]. *Cadillac Desert,* New York: Penguin.

Robbins, Elaine 1999. 'Damning Dams: Is One Of The Greatest Engineering Marvels Of The Industrial Age Becoming Obsolete?' *E magazine*online <http://www.edf.org/pubs/emagazine/1999/dams.html>.

Robinson, Jeff 1999. 'Poor Theology'. *The Salt Lake Tribune,* 13 August sec. A, p. 12.

Rogers, Kristen 1990. 'Stewards of the Earth'. *This People* (Spring issue): 12–16.

Shipps, Jan 1998. "The Mormon Image Since 1960," paper presented at the Sunstone Symposium, Salt Lake City, August 1.

Skabelund, Shawn 1999. Personal communication, 10 November.

Smart, William B. 1998. 'The Making of An Activist'. In Williams et al., *New Genesis,* pp. 1–6.

Smith, Dennis 1998, 'Watermasters'. In Williams et al., *New Genesis,* pp. 74–81.

Southern Utah Wilderness Alliance (SUWA) 1996, 'Counties Blade Illegal Roads'. *Southern Utah Wilderness Alliance Newslette.* Winter issue.

Stark, Rodney 1998. 'The Rise of a New World Faith'. In James T. Duke, ed., *Latter-day Saint Social Life: Social Research on the LDS Church and its Members,* Provo, UT: Religious Studies Center, pp. 9–27.
Watkins, T.H. 1998. 'Paradise Found'. *Sierra*. November/December issue, pp. 44–49.
Watts, Ardean 1998. 'A House of Mud: Living Lightly on the Land'. In Williams et al., *New Genesis,* pp. 49–54.
White, Lynn, Jr. 1967. 'The Historical Roots of Our Ecologic Crisis', *Science* 155 (10 March): 1203–1207.
Williams, Terry Tempest, William B. Smart, and Gibbs M. Smith, eds. 1998. *New Genesis: A Mormon Reader on Land and Community,* Salt Lake City: Gibbs Smith Publisher.
Wilson, Ted L. 1998. 'The Truth of Granite: A Canyon Conversion', In Williams et al., *New Genesis,* pp. 7–15.

Theology and Ecology at the Birthplace of Kṛṣṇa

BRUCE M. SULLIVAN

INTRODUCTION

THE RELIGIONS OF THE WEST HAVE OFTEN been criticized for their theologies in which humanity is given "dominion" over nature, but they also include the conception of humanity's "stewardship" of nature, which may be more conducive to an ecological ethic. Indic religious traditions are often cited as possibly providing a corrective to the widely perceived lack of regard for nature in Western religions.[1] But Christianity and Hinduism are both extremely diverse traditions, in each of which a variety of views may be found. Theists may tend to value the world because it is the work of the divine Creator, seeing in nature a reflection of God. On the other hand, world-renouncing ascetics may regard the natural world very differently, seeing it as a source of temptations and distractions, their priorities lying elsewhere.

Hindus of theistic traditions in which Kṛṣṇa is the object of worship have recently initiated a program of reforestation and ecological activity with international support. The program is centered in the town of Vrindavan (Vṛndāvana in Sanskrit) in the state of Uttar Pradesh in north-central India, regarded as sacred because it is the site of Kṛṣṇa's early life. Devotees have begun an ecological movement in the region of Kṛṣṇa's birth—known as Braj in the vernacular Hindi, Vraja in Sanskrit—motivated largely by religious concerns and ideals.

HISTORICAL AND THEOLOGICAL BACKGROUND

A brief passage from the *Bhāgavata Purāṇa* will highlight themes to be encountered throughout this [essay].

> The glorious Lord [Kṛṣṇa], the son of Devakī, accompanied by Balarāma and surrounded by cowherds, went a distance from Vṛndāvana, grazing the cattle.
>
> Observing that the trees served as parasols by spreading their shade in the scorching heat of the sun, Kṛṣṇa addressed his cowherd friends, the residents of Vraja:
>
> "Look at these great blessed souls, who live only for the welfare of others, suffering stormy winds, heavy rains, heat and frost, sparing us.
>
> "The birth of trees is truly the most blessed in the world, for they contribute to the well-being of all creatures. Just as no one needy returns disappointed from generous persons, so too one who approaches trees for shelter.
>
> "They meet the needs of others with their leaves, flowers, fruits, shade, roots, bark, wood, fragrance, sap, ashes, and charcoal.
>
> "Offering life, wealth, intellect and speech to benefit others is the height of service of embodied beings for fellow creatures."
>
> Praising the trees in this way, the Lord pro-

Sullivan, Bruce M., "Theology and Ecology at the Birthplace of Kṛṣṇa," in Lance E. Nelson, Ed., *Purifying the Earthly Body of God: Religion and Ecology in Hindu India*, pp. 247–261.

> ceeded to the Yamunā, passing between rows of trees whose branches were bent low with clusters of sprouts, foliage, bunches of fruits, and flowers.
>
> Having made their cattle drink of the sweet, cool, healthy water of the Yamunā, the cowherds themselves drank that sweet water to their hearts' content.[2]

So ends a chapter of the *Bhāgavata Purāṇa* describing the environment around Vrindavan, Kṛṣṇa's home.

Vrindavan is important in the worship of Kṛṣṇa, and has been for centuries, precisely because Kṛṣṇa lived there. Bengali (or Gauḍīya) Vaiṣṇavism has been very prominent and influential in Vrindavan as well as Bengal for five centuries now.[3] The importance attached to Vrindavan by this tradition is indicated by the fact that Caitanya, reviver of Vaiṣṇavism in Bengal in the sixteenth century, sent several of his most trusted disciples there to establish a presence in the area, and himself made the long pilgrimage west some eight hundred miles to see the sites associated with Kṛṣṇa's youth. Similarly, in the twentieth century Swami Bhaktivedanta Prabhupada, the founder of the International Society for Krishna Consciousness (ISKCON, also popularly known as the "Hare Krishnas"), lived for a decade in Vrindavan before coming to America in 1966; he returned periodically until his death there in 1977, and his tomb is on the grounds of the large ISKCON temple he founded in Vrindavan (Brooks 1989a, 95). As will be shown below, the town itself, as a sacred center regarded as spiritually efficacious, plays a crucial role in the religious thought of devotees of Kṛṣṇa.

In the distinctive theology of this variety of Vaiṣṇavism, systematized in Vrindavan after the death of Caitanya by six scholarly theologians known collectively as the Gosvāmins, Kṛṣṇa is the object of worship and is regarded as the true form of Ultimate Reality. He is not an *avatāra,* or divine manifestation, of Viṣṇu not a portion of God on earth, but Ultimate Reality embodied. One of the most important ideas in this tradition is its emphasis on the eternal *līlā* (play, sport) of Kṛṣṇa in Vrindavan;[4] the tradition's most distinctive practice is the visualization of oneself as a participant in that divine play.

The Gosvāmin theologians drew upon the aesthetic theory of *rasa* to articulate their devotional system. In the *rasa* theory, a dramatic or poetic work of art is a precondition, presentation of which allows the audience member to experience, not merely a personal emotional state (*bhāva*) tied to specific personal experiences, but a generalized state of emotional consciousness (*rasa*) that is joyful aesthetic appreciation. Eight or nine *rasas* can be experienced, though aesthetic theorists had long regarded *śṛṅgāra* (love) as the most effective primary *rasa* for a work of art.[5] The Gosvāmins utilized the terminology of this aesthetic theory, but in important ways changed its purpose. For them, Kṛṣṇa became the only hero (*nāyaka*), and his life story the only play; moreover, the spectator was transformed from a passive observer relishing the state of consciousness evoked to an active participant in the drama itself. And while the aesthetic theorist Abhinavagupta had written that the *rasa* experience was analogous to the attainment of *mokṣa* but only temporary, lasting as long as the drama that was its catalyst, Rūpa Gosvāmin wrote that the attainment of *rasa* through Kṛṣṇa *bhakti* (devotion) was equivalent to *mokṣa* (Gerow 1981, 239–43; Larson 1976; Wulff 1986, 679–81). Associates of Kṛṣṇa depicted in the scriptures are taken as the models for loving relationships to him, and one is to identify oneself with one of these associates. Four positive relationships with Kṛṣṇa are enumerated: (1) servant (*dāsa*), (2) parent (*vatsālya*), (3) friend (*sākhya*), and (4) lover (*madhurya*).[6] All four relationships are regarded as varieties of love; indeed, the objective is to develop loving devotion to Kṛṣṇa in one or another of these ways.

The milkmaids (*gopīs*) of Braj embody the ideal of selfless devotion to the beloved, and are regarded as the model devotees. Chief among them is Rādhā, who, although not specifically named in the *Bhāgavata Purāna,* is celebrated as Kṛṣṇa's beloved some two hundred years later in a Sanskrit poem from Bengal, the *Gītagovinda.* She is sometimes regarded as the symbolic representation of the human soul, displaying in her relationship to Kṛṣṇa the devotional ideal; and she is sometimes regarded as the divine feminine principle, inseparable from Kṛṣṇa, the two together constituting Ultimate Reality.[7] The highest religious goal is the perfection of selfless devotion to and love for God, and the afterlife is conceived as a continuation of that *līlā* in Kṛṣṇa's paradise, known variously as Vaikuṇṭha ("free from misery," though the name is often used for the paradise of Viṣṇu) or Goloka ("realm of cows") or Vṛndāvana or Vraja

(De 1961, 333–39). As Kinsley (1979, 113) observes, Kṛṣṇa's heaven "is nothing else but the idyllic forest town of Vṛndāvana [Vrindavan] unabashedly magnified," and "Kṛṣṇa's heavenly sporting ground is identical with the scene of his earthly life as a youth." The heavenly paradise and the earthly town of the texts are often not distinguished, as they are regarded as identical; the earthly town of Vrindavan today is regarded by devotees as the site of Kṛṣṇa's eternal *līlā*. In short, one is to visualize oneself in Vrindavan during this lifetime imitating the paradigmatic actions of devotees of Kṛṣṇa, attaining liberation from rebirth through pure loving devotion so that one's service and devotion to Kṛṣṇa may continue eternally in the celestial Vrindavan.

The worshippers of Kṛṣṇa particularly revere the tenth book of the *Bhāgavata Purāṇa* for what it reveals about Kṛṣṇa's human life, especially his youth in and around Vrindavan. This *Purāṇa* was so important for the Gosvāmin theologians of Gauḍīya Vaiṣṇavism that they rejected all other sources of knowledge (*pramāṇa*) except for divine revelation (*śabda*), and regarded this work as the quintessential revelation and the ideal text for this era.[8] The *Bhāgavata Purāṇa*, other texts, and devotional songs make references to deeds of Kṛṣṇa in specific places in the vicinity of Vrindavan: Mount Govardhana, the Yamuna River, and others. Devotees are strongly encouraged to go to such places where they can feel a special closeness to Kṛṣṇa and Rādhā because of their actions there, and many will imitate certain of their actions at particular sites. The texts also refer to the beauty of Vrindavan and the surrounding land of Braj (as in the *Bhāgavata Purāṇa* passage above), with cattle grazing contentedly among flowering trees and clear waters—a land made perpetually lovely by Kṛṣṇa. The region of Braj is even said to be identical with the body of Kṛṣṇa himself, a topographic form of God, a physical manifestation of the love of Rādhā and Kṛṣṇa (Haberman 1994, 125–27). Specific sites are identified with specific body parts of Kṛṣṇa, such that Mathura is his heart, Vrindavan his brow, and so on. Hence, pilgrims may regard the very dirt of the area as sacred for having been walked on by God, even non-different from God, and will rub handfuls on their heads and ingest some, taking it as *prasāda* (Brooks 1989a, 6), an edible substance infused with God's grace. As Brooks (1989b, 185; cf. 1989a, 56) has observed, "every place in the town has some sacred significance," and "it cannot be said that there is a secular part and a sacred part." Specificity adds value, however, and while every molecule of dust may be sanctified, certain sites are regarded by devotees as more sacred than others because of particular deeds of Kṛṣṇa and Rādhā there.

Numerous Vaiṣṇava texts extoll the beauties of Braj, where leaves and fruits are envisioned as gleaming like jewels; indeed, the loveliness of nature has been seen as evidence that this spot was blessed with a divine presence (Kinsley 1979, 117–19). The *Gītagovinda* is a particularly vivid example of a Vaiṣṇava poet employing all his eloquence to describe the beauty of nature in the land of Rādhā and Kṛṣṇa. Other texts also present the region as inspiringly beautiful. For example, the *Harivaṃśa*, an appendix (*khila*) to the *Mahābhārata*, perhaps composed about five centuries before the *Gītagovinda* in the fifth century C.E., refers to the beauty of the forests of Braj as the reason the cowherds had chosen to live there.[9] The theme of the beauty of Braj is a constant in the literature devoted to the life of Kṛṣṇa. This paradise on earth was the scene of Kṛṣṇa's *līlā*, and is regarded as identical with his celestial paradise, where the *līlā* is eternal.

THE ECOLOGICAL PROGRAM

But there is trouble in paradise today, on earth if not in heaven. The town of Vrindavan has become badly deforested, and the area is rapidly turning into a desert such as is found just to the west in Rajasthan. Studies are said to indicate that the water table is falling by as much as five feet a year, and the quality of the available water is deteriorating (Dasa 1992, 27). The Yamuna River is also heavily polluted by industrial runoff from factories upriver and from sewage, some of which comes from Vrindavan itself. Raw sewage flows over the *parikrama* pilgrimage path and discharges directly into the Yamuna in many places. The problem is so serious that the Government of India has declared the Yamuna unfit for drinking or bathing.[10] One might think that such a pronouncement would affect the activities of devotees and pilgrims, but apparently it has not so far. A large oil refinery in Mathura, only about seven miles downriver, pollutes the air throughout the region. Sadly, ecological damage is not unique to this area.

Large tracts of India have been deforested due to the need for housing, farmland, and firewood by a rapidly increasing population. And sewage treatment is a widespread problem as well; it is estimated that only 10 percent of India's cities have sewage systems that could be described as "adequate."[11] The highly publicized deaths by plague in 1994, while not numerous, emphasize the point. But Vrindavan is unusual, and faces special ecological problems, because it receives over two million pilgrims per year. Modern transportation and the big business of guiding pilgrims to the sacred sites have increased traffic greatly, straining the capacity of municipal services such as water and sewage treatment.

The environment in and around Vrindavan has also suffered from an influx of people coming to live there. Relatively well-to-do Vaiṣṇavas want to retire to the scene of Kṛṣṇa's earthly activities, there to live out their days in the setting most conducive to worship and the liberation from rebirth that is its reward. Some of Delhi's wealthy devotees maintain second homes here. For them to live in Kṛṣṇa's land requires the building of new houses and flats in large number; the sign of one real estate developer in Vrindavan read:

> Welcome to this holy land of Lord Krishna. Holy forest plots for sale. Freehold residential complex in very peaceful and tranquility [*sic*] atmosphere.[12]

Ironically, the atmosphere of tranquility and peace that is advertized so persuasively will be destroyed with the bulldozing of the "holy forest" at the site. When sacredness is a marketable commodity, can any other outcome be expected? Perceiving this entrepreneurial activity as a problem, the devotees of ISKCON have raised money to purchase a forested plot called Ramaṇa Retī, famed as a place where Kṛṣṇa and his brother Balarāma played in their youth, and recently the target of real estate developers.[13] Thus one grove has been saved, but in a large region—all of which devotees regard as sacred—not all the forests of Kṛṣṇa are being saved. Many once forested areas are already treeless, or are being covered with buildings and roads as the town grows.

Obviously the degradation of the environment is an ecological problem for the Vrindavan area, and a problem for the quality of life, but it is also a specifically religious problem for the devotee of Kṛṣṇa. Pilgrims come to Vrindavan with the hope of seeing Kṛṣṇa's land, that is, having *darśana* of God in the form of his ponds and forests. Devotees want to bathe in the Yamuna to gain merit, but as already noted, to do so could now be dangerous to one's health; observers have commented that parasites and illnesses are often the result of prolonged exposure to the Yamuna, and skin rashes from even brief exposure (Prime, 108). Deforestation and desertification are also a religious problem because one is to visualize oneself as a participant in Kṛṣṇa's *līlā* in the beautiful setting he creates for devotees eternally, but the earthly manifestation of Kṛṣṇa's *līlā* is not as inspirational or conducive to a sense of wonder as could be desired. Devotees have cited the appearance of the region as causing despair (Dasa 1992; WWF 1993; WWF 1995), so that a pilgrimage now might occasion loss of faith instead of deepening it. The conflict between descriptions in ancient devotional texts and the reality of Vrindavan today is stark.

The response to the ecocide in Vrindavan has been led by devotees of Kṛṣṇa, both Western converts and Indians. The general approach could be described by the following slogan, used to generate support: "one who cares for Kṛṣṇa cares for His land" (Dasa 1992, 30). Indeed, as noted above, for many worshippers of Kṛṣṇa, the region of Braj with Vrindavan at its center is seen as identical with Kṛṣṇa, the land being his physical manifestation. One well-known Indian devotee instrumental in the effort is Shrivatsa Goswami, who points to Kṛṣṇa as the paradigm of reverence for nature; not only did he defeat the river-polluting demon Kāliya, but the only two occasions on which Kṛṣṇa worshipped were when he led the cowherds in worshipping Mount Govardhana and when he worshipped the Sun God to cure his son of leprosy (Prime 1992, 54–56). In short, Goswami maintains that Kṛṣṇa worshipped nature.

A major effort to reforest the area began as follows. Ranchor Prime, an English member of ISKCON, who is known also as Ranchor Dasa and is familiar with the situation in Vrindavan, conceived a plan with Sewak Sharan, longtime resident of the area, to plant trees along the eleven-kilometer *parikrama* path that encircles the town. The importance of the pilgrimage path in Vrindavan is indicated by the fact that, upon his death on November 14, 1977, the body of Swami Bhaktivedanta Prabhupada of ISKCON was taken on a final *pari-*

krama around the town, allowing fellow Vaiṣṇavas to honor him (Brooks 1989a, 95). Its importance is indicated, too, by the fact that it is traveled by over two million pilgrims per year.[14] But the path is no longer the sylvan and pastoral setting for envisioning Kṛṣṇa's *līlā* which it once apparently was. Now the path is highly urbanized and suffers from the problems of deforestation and pollution already mentioned. Ranchor Prime prepared a report to the World Wide Fund for Nature (WWF) in Geneva, an international ecological agency that gives grants for environmental projects. WWF especially wants to highlight the ecological values of the cultures and religious traditions where projects are funded, and this seemed to them an opportunity to do so. Funding was granted for three years, to run from mid-1991 through mid-1994, some $40,000 per year. ISKCON donated use of one and a half acres beside the pilgrimage path for a nursery to raise some 10,000 trees of local origin to be planted in succeeding months (WWF 1993; Prime 1992, 104–18).

Ranchor Prime (or Dasa) was a consultant and a major influence from the outset in the Vrindavan Forest Revival Project. The project was formally initiated on November 21, 1991, the festival day of Vṛndā Devī, the goddess regarded as representing the local flora. All present took the following pledge:

> The forest of Vrindavan is the sacred playground of Rādhā and Kṛṣṇa. However, we, the people of this region, have cut its trees, polluted its Yamunā River, and spoilt its sacred dust with our rubbish and sewage. I pledge that from now on I will do all within my power to protect Vrindavan from further destruction and to restore it to its original beauty.[15]

Stage One of the project was to encourage community involvement so that the trees planted would be protected and would survive. Planting began with some two thousand trees and shrubs along a two-kilometer segment of the path. Stage Two has included further planting along the entire pathway, and continued outreach efforts to involve the populace. Assorted eyesores and environmental problems have been dealt with along the way also.

A more serious problem, and one that is even more difficult to solve, is presented by the sewage system of Vrindavan. Prior to 1970 the traditional latrine method was employed, waste being recycled into fields as fertilizer. At that time work began on a modern system that was designed to treat sewage so that it could be safely dumped into the Yamuna. Some underground pipes were laid and toilets were connected all over town, but the main line was never completed! Blockages and breaks in the lines occurred almost immediately and have never been fixed. Worse still, the treatment plant was never built! Now sewage that does not overflow into the streets and gather in low spots, polluting the groundwater supply, is simply dumped untreated into the river, and most of the municipal water supply is drawn from that same river. Ranchor Prime argues that the traditional method worked and should be implemented again, abandoning the inadequate and inappropriate sewage system. In making his case, he marshals religious arguments, citing the ancient Sanskrit religio-legal text *Manu Smṛti* as follows:

> One should not cause urine, stool, or mucus to enter water. Anything mixed with these unholy substances, or with blood or poison, should never be thrown into water. (4.56)

Ranchor Prime accuses Indians of becoming enamored of new Western technology and of applying the technology inappropriately, in the process forgetting their own ancient and time-tested technology which is appropriate to the situation, and ignoring the venerable injunctions such as those found in *Manu Smṛti*. He offers the view that the Western lifestyle is overly materialistic, consumption oriented, not ecological, and therefore must be abandoned both by Indians who have adopted it and by Westerners themselves. He also cites the words of Mahatma Gandhi, warning Indians against mechanization and technology and advocating a simple lifestyle.[16]

Ranchor Prime (1992, 112) points to underlying causes of the widespread abandonment of traditional Hindu values and technology, citing centuries of Muslim and British rule as detrimental to traditional Hindu culture and practices:

> For 800 years Muslims ruled from Delhi. The whole surrounding region, including Vrindavan, bears the deep impression of this rule, which did nothing to foster Hindu culture, and at times bitterly suppressed it. Then the British, with their more subtle form of tyranny, made Hindus second-class citizens in their own land. The effect of this subjugation has been to drain the enterpris-

> ing spirit, the self-determination and inner resourcefulness from a people who had their affairs run for them by outsiders for longer than most nations or cultures have endured. This is why Gandhi stressed that India would not be able to have true independence until her people discovered *swaraj*—the power of self-rule—within themselves. This day has not yet come.

He concludes his discussion of the water pollution problems of the area by referring—like Shrivatsa Goswami above—to the myth of Kṛṣṇa overcoming the demon Kāliya, who was poisoning the Yamuna, with the result that trees and animals were dying. Finally the cowherds themselves drank the water and fell ill. Kṛṣṇa wrestled with the demon and subdued it, saving the region from the effects of poisoned water; for this, he is seen by an activist-devotee as "Kṛṣṇa the environmentalist" (Dasa 1992, 31). For many devotees of Kṛṣṇa, Vrindavan's problems are linked with a worldwide environmental crisis, the solution to which lies in the adoption of traditional Hindu values and practices. Clearly, the deforestation and water pollution in the Vrindavan region are not being caused by the widespread raising of cattle for slaughter, for their meat, as is the case in other parts of the world such as Brazil or the United States, where similar ecological problems abound. Indeed, in Vrindavan, because of the importance of vegetarianism to the Hare Krishna movement and to other Vaiṣṇavas, it is almost impossible to find meat or even eggs for sale, a rare situation even in India. For the same reason, devotees are writing works in which meat-eating is identified as a serious, worldwide ecological problem (Prime 1992; Cremo and Goswami 1995). They state that a meat-based diet causes tremendous petroleum usage, and creates many polluting waste products. The *Manu Smṛti* (5.51) is cited as prohibiting the eating of meat, saying that the butcher, vendor, cook and consumer all are murderers and reap bad karmic consequences.[17] Nonviolence (*ahiṃsā*) is cited as a traditional Hindu value, adherence to which is conducive to the well-being of the individual and the world as a whole. In this way, Vaiṣṇavas are advocating a lifestyle based on traditional Hindu religious ideals of *ahiṃsā* and vegetarianism as a solution to modern environmental crises.

Those who worship Kṛṣṇa see his divine example, recounted in ancient myths, as still relevant today, and as the paradigm for human action that is desperately needed. As Sewak Sharan observed, "Krishna didn't kill the *nāga* [Kāliya]—if he had he would have eliminated pollution forever. No, he just banished the pollution dragon. All we can do is try to manage the dirt better" (Sochaczewski 1994). Swami Raman Das, a forest-dwelling ascetic, similarly sees God's actions on earth as indicative of humanity's task: "Krishna shows that a two-armed, flesh-and-blood mortal, when energized by the spirit of the highest god Vishnu, can stand up to myriads of multi-armed demons. Every human being can perform miracles" (Sochaczewski 1994). These leaders hope that Kṛṣṇa will be the inspiration for this environmental program.

Hindu religious ideas, values, and practices are being marshalled to support a program, funded both by the Government of India and internationally, to restore the natural beauty of a Hindu pilgrimage site. The effort to save Vrindavan from ecocide by deforestation and polluted water, an undertaking that is essentially religious in inspiration and intent, is based on the hope that people will love the Earth just as they love Kṛṣṇa.

CONCLUSIONS

For devotees of Kṛṣṇa, the earthly Vrindavan is identical with Kṛṣṇa's heavenly paradise. To those who are truly devoted, everything is beautiful because it is God's creation, and they may have developed an interior life in which participation in the divine sport is continuous; for them, one might think that the visible world in which we live is irrelevant. However, it seems that precisely those who are most devoted are taking the lead in the environmental cleanup of Braj. And for those who have not yet matured in their devotion, the beautification of the environment may be an aid to devotional practice. Certainly it can be regarded as service of Kṛṣṇa and an appropriate way of caring for Kṛṣṇa's creation.

The World Wide Fund for Nature (WWF) is hopeful that a successful project in Vrindavan will encourage others throughout India to examine their environment and find ways of improving the situation. Indeed, it has already had an effect internationally; residents of the English city of Leicester, with a large community of South Asian heritage, by July 1993 had donated some £8000 to the project in Vrindavan, and residents have been motivated to plant over 22,000 trees in Leicester (Friends of Vrindavan 1993). The project in Vrindavan has completed the three years of its original funding period and has been renewed by WWF for an additional three years, though there have been many changes in the project's leadership. Ranchor Prime, the ISKCON devotee who wrote the original grant proposal to WWF and was a major figure in the project's leadership from the outset, is no longer affiliated with this program; in fact, ISKCON itself, so instrumental in the early stages of the effort, is not now involved with it.[18] Leadership has passed to other devotees of Kṛṣṇa, Indians who are not members of ISKCON, while ISKCON concentrates its efforts on other sacred sites in the region of Braj outside of town, such as near Mount Govardhana. It remains to be seen whether this one project will have an effect throughout India, helping to create a view of the world as sacred and to be protected from pollution. But Hindus do not view all places with the same reverence as they do Vrindavan. And even in Vrindavan itself not everyone is a devotee of Kṛṣṇa who for that reason can be convinced to love the land; some of the trees so recently planted have already been bulldozed for a new road.[19] While the Vrindavan region would benefit from solving its sewage problem and planting trees, can the nation as a whole be said to have benefited if pollution is simply shifted to other regions that are not viewed with the same degree of reverence?

WWF wants this project to serve as a means to increase awareness throughout India of the importance of protecting the natural world. The main purpose of the program according to WWF India has been "to promote an awareness and understanding of environmental values contained in the [Hindu] community's religious tradition, and to actively have them care for their environment" (WWF 1994, 1). WWF India reports that from mid-1993 through mid-1994, "cultural activities by children were an important instrument for influencing parents and the community," including the staging of four folk dramas on Kṛṣṇa and Rādhā's love for the environment (WWF 1994, 6; cf. WWF 1995, with picture). The report goes on to state that at the end of three years of work the program has successfully "evoked the people's collective religious conscience; previously they had no answer to the drastic decline in their environment, and the quiet abandonment of religious conservation practice is now being slowly reversed" (WWF 1994, 7). One practical outcome is that traditional religious views of nature are to be included in the official curriculum of Uttar Pradesh state: "This is partly due to WWF's helping to increase visibility about the importance of nature," according to Dr. Vinod Banerjee, spokesperson for the state teachers association (WWF 1995). Reports from Vrindavan on All-India Radio and the national television network Doordarshan have enabled WWF to take to the entire nation its message on the vital need for ecological action.

Other environmental movements exist in South Asia: the Chipko movement in the Himalayas, where people are protecting trees from clear-cutting by loggers (Gruzalski 1993; Shiva and Bandyopadhyay 1988), and the Trees for Life organization, which has given out over a million saplings for planting all over India (Prime 1992, 80–89). Sunderlal Bahuguna of Chipko tells stories of the life of Kṛṣṇa in his ceaseless efforts to better the environment: "There are people in India who are very devoted to religion and that is the secret of success of the Chipko movement" (Prime 1992, 96). Bahuguna himself has fasted repeatedly to combat deforestation, a technique of nonviolent non-cooperation he learned as a young follower of Mahatma Gandhi (Gruzalski 1993, 104–19; Shiva and Bandyopadhyay 1988, 231–34), and a tactic with a religious heritage in the idea of *ahiṃsā* and ascetic practices. Balbir Mathur of Trees for Life has his fruit tree saplings blessed by someone popularly regarded as possessing spiritual power, then gives the saplings as *prasāda* from a temple (Prime 1992, 85–87). Both these movements draw upon traditional Hindu religious ideas, values, and practices, to which they owe a considerable proportion of their popularity and success. And although none of these sources cites this example, there is a long tradition in India of state-sponsored protection of trees in public areas such as parks, sacred places, and along boundaries and highways (*Arthaśāstra* 3.19.28–30); one can only wonder whether respect for nature, fear of the king, or the perception of the practical value of trees played the greatest role in such a policy.

The World Wide Fund for Nature has established an office called the Conservation and Beliefs Network to coordinate their programs with the teachings of ecological significance in the religions of the world. WWF has also sponsored publication of a

World Religions and Ecology series, of which Prime's book is one. A new international organization called the Alliance of Religions and Conservation (ARC) has been established with WWF sponsorship to fund ecological projects based on religious ideals.[20] Emphasizing the religious significance of nature in India seems an especially effective approach to encourage ecological activity. As the case of the Ganges indicates, many Hindus are skeptical of scientific justifications for ecological programs and might be more receptive to programs that have religiously sensitive approaches and religiously significant outcomes (see Alley, this volume). Hence, a government pronouncement that the water of the Yamuna or Ganges River is not sanitary for bathing does not deter a pilgrim who places greater value on its salvific power than its cleansing ability.

Nonetheless, it is also apparent that an ecological program based on traditional religious values can be successful only to the extent that people adhere to and continue to honor those traditional values. Many in India have expressed the view that their traditional values are being abandoned, and that the younger generation is being inculcated with Western culture, particularly through communications media, a potential problem for ecology programs based on traditional religious values. And it must be noted that ascetic and monistic traditions, which are very strong in India, tend to see the natural world as a realm of suffering from which to escape, not as an environment to be cared for in the way Vrindavan's Kṛṣṇa worshippers do; such ascetic worldviews may undercut ecological efforts. Even within movements as thoroughly theistic as ISKCON or others devoted to Kṛṣṇa such as those that derive from Nimbārka or Vallabha, there are elements that may vitiate ecological action. After all, if one successfully visualizes an alternative reality (or as devotees would have it, true reality), and experiences oneself as dwelling within it blissfully serving God, mundane reality with its shortcomings, environmental or otherwise, might seem irrelevant or merely a distraction.

In India, where numerous religious traditions coexist, both Hindu and non-Hindu, finding the most ecologically useful of many available traditional value systems will be a challenge for those who want to preserve or restore the natural world.

Paganism and the Environment

GRAHAM HARVEY

WHAT IF I FELL IN A FOREST: WOULD A TREE hear? (Dillard 1974: 89).

Pagans have only recently begun to participate in Inter-Faith Dialogue (though they have significant contributions to make) and when they do participate it has largely been in discussions about ecology. This paper is offered as a contribution to Dialogue though its primary focus is on environmental debates and actions. Before looking at Paganism's contributions to this theme, perhaps an introduction to contemporary Paganism would be useful.

PAGANISM TODAY

Paganism is a spirituality in which Nature (the Earth and the body) is central and celebrated. It is fundamentally 'Green' in its philosophy and its practice, taking seriously the understanding that 'everything that lives is holy' (Blake 1795: 2.366). People who chose to name themselves Pagan associate the name with 'countryside'. They are aware that originally the term was derogatory, a 'country-dweller' was not honoured as living closer to nature, but vilified as a

Harvey, Graham, "Paganism and the Environment," in *Faiths and the Environment: Conference Papers* (Faith in Dialogue, no. 1), London: Center for Inter-Faith Dialogue, 1996, pp. 71–85. Reprinted by permission.

'bumpkin', an uneducated clod with no appreciation for the splendour of urban Rome and its varied expressions of spirituality. Christianity added to these associations that of 'civilian', or 'one not enlisted in God's army'. This too was an insult, not a celebration of pacifism. With the very recent Christian recognition of some religions as at least partially acceptable, 'Pagan' continues as a derogatory epithet for people outside of the 'World Religions' club. Except, that is, to people who chose to use it as a self-definition. For them, the choice is dictated by an honouring of the countryside as a possible place of closer contact with Nature.

Paganism encourages a greater intimacy with Nature, primarily through the inculcation of awareness of the seasons. Most Pagans celebrate the seasonal cycle in a round of eight annual festivals—the solstices and equinoxes and four quarter days. This eight-fold calendar is a recent creation of Pagans drawing on traditions about ancient and traditional festival days. Some of the feast days were known to the Pagan Irish, others to the Pagan Anglo-Saxons. Other Pagans, especially those who prefer self-designations associated with Pagan English, Germanic or Scandinavian traditions (e.g. Heathens, Odinists, Asatru) celebrate different calendar festivals expressive of the same themes. Many Pagans also celebrate lunar festivals (new, quarter and full moons). Some of the customs incorporated into Pagan festivals are known either in ancient literature or from more recent folk customs. Almost every Pagan book outlines these festivals and their associations. They are significant in our present context in being a cycle in which the participant is confronted not with the demands and claims of a 'spiritual' after-life or deity, but with the significance of everyday life on Earth. Birth, growth, sexuality, fecundity, creativity, death, decay, vitality, beginnings, endings, joy, sadness, and other mundane affairs are found to be meaningful and sacred. It would be misleading to see these 'themes' (or a 'quest for meaning') as the prime focus of the festivals. They are certainly significant but Pagans celebrate the festivals with the much simpler understanding that they are honouring the seasons and the land. Pagan calendar celebrations are about time and space: this time, the present, now, and this space / place, here. They encourage and inculcate an awareness of being 'at home' here and now in the mundane and therefore sacred Earth. In short, the festivals teach 'ecology'.

Whilst non-human beings are encountered at festival times, such encounters are not the primary focus of the celebration. Deities are honoured but rarely given the kind of attention that monotheists would call worship. Other other-than-human people (Hallowell 1960) are equally significant. They include beings drawn from ancestral traditions (the Faerie, elves, dwarves, land-spirits, brownies, etc.) as well as ancestors and more readily encounterable (but no less important) sharers of this world (trees, hedgehogs, midges, herons, etc.). The Otherworld ('as near as your shadow') is of great interest to many Pagans but it is not more significant that This World. It is this ordinary, mundane, physical, everyday world which Pagans honour as sacred and worthy of honour.

At the risk of over-stressing the significance of deities, it is important to note that despite a variety of ways of conceptualising the nature and number of deities, Pagans agree that deity is essentially immanent rather than transcendent. Goddess(es) and God(s) are met within this world, they are manifest in ordinary physical life. Paganism shares with many other religious traditions a comparative lack of interest in theology as a distinct discourse. Its 'God-talk' occurs in far less abstract contexts: story-telling, ritual drama, invocation, evocation and other ways of expressing honour. What is said about deities (their character and actions), in any religion, however, casts light (perhaps accidentally) on the speaker's view of Nature and life. While the language used by some Pagans might seem to imply monotheism ('the Goddess') the way in which even this seemingly singular deity is approached reveals a deep polytheism (Long 1994). The majority of Pagans are in fact explicitly polytheists. Such polytheism both expresses and encourages the honouring of those 'ordinary' things significant in life as it is lived (Green 1989; Bowes, 1977). Pagan deities are not expected to 'save' or 'forgive' people because people do not need forgiveness or salvation. Sin, guilt, salvation, eternal reward or punishment have no place in Paganism. Pagan ethics are not derived from Pagan theology, but from the understanding that we are part of a complex web of relationships which bring with them various demands, obligations, rights and responsibilities. Paganism is not simply a contemporary exhortation to 'know thyself' (though this is important, especially within Wicca) but is also concerned with the honouring of those with whom we share life on Earth.

Paganism is a spirituality which draws sustenance from ancient roots but is consciously exploring contemporary understandings of the world. This contemporaneity is part of Paganism's openness to life as it is lived rather than 'life as it is meant to be' according to some revelation or dogma. Paganism has grown and changed in relationship with insights gleaned from anthropology, ecology, feminism, religious studies, politics and other seemingly disparate areas of life and study.

The historical roots of contemporary Paganism have been revealed by Ronald Hutton in his explorations of ancient Paganism (1991, 1994, 1996). He has identified 'four direct links between the old religions and the present'. These are high ritual magic, traditional village witchcraft, folk rites and customs and the 'whole tremendous love affair of Christian Europe with the art and literature of the ancient world' (Hutton 1994: 29). He also notes the important influence of academic writings in various disciplines on the recreation of Paganism in this century. Howard Eilberg-Schwartz has also noted that the Enlightenment provided a context in which 'Neopaganism and Goddess Worship' were nurtured (Eilberg-Schwartz 1989). He notes that the Enlightenment was not only a precursor of the rise of Paganism, but that Paganism completes the movement of the Enlightenment by a criticism that moves from modernity into post-modernity (e.g. away from the deification of 'Rationality' and towards the celebration of pluralism). My own concern is with the various expressions of Paganism existing and growing in Britain today (Harvey 1996). Origins are interesting but are rarely the most significant aspect of a religion's formation, identify or character (Smart 1991). The fruits of a tradition (as those of a tree) are not found in its roots but at the end of its many branches and present manifestations.

THE GREENING OF RELIGION

Inter-Faith Dialogue is considerably easier (for Pagans at least) now that a near universal agreement on the goodness of 'Greenness' is established. Perhaps, however, we should refuse (for a while at least) to wear these Green-tinted glasses. If dialogue between religions is to be honest perhaps we should ask difficult questions and face difficult facts.

The Greening of western religion is an attempt to catch up with a secular vision of the world. The literatures of the monotheistic Faiths can be read as instructing us to look after God's world. Such stewardship is only lightly tinted with Green. It is the 'conservation' of the great landowner's gamekeeper looking after grouse and their habitats so that the 'great and good' can shoot their prey for which they will pray their gratitude. The concern of St Francis for the animals is also an expression of concern for divine and human rights, responsibilities and relationships. The animals are expected to praise the God whose judgement and salvation of 'the world' are centred on humanity, 'God's image'.

For anything more than these Green tints we must look to secular scientists like Darwin. Their careful look at the world has enabled us to refuse the human-centred and even the God-centred vision of the world. We can see that we are not the 'pinnacle and goal of creation' but one part of an elaborate and evolving community of living beings, a web of life, an ecosystem. The continuing work of ecologists and other such scientific observers of our planet teaches us to see ourselves as part of Nature. It is this work and not religious responses to the world which has enabled both popular concern about the ecological crisis and the articulation of that concern.

Once that is clear, it is possible to clarify the role of religions in this area. One of the abiding difficulties of policy making about the environment is not knowing what people want. The articulation of deep seated personal attitudes is something religions are good at. Their focus on the environment might therefore enable some deeper understanding of what people really want the world to be like. Secondly, perhaps more problematically, people often express 'concern' for the environment but are less willing to express such attitudes by changes in lifestyle, especially where such changes might cost money. Public transport is popular as an idea, but people are addicted to their cars. Lead-free fuel is acceptable because it seems to do something positive and its economic cost is equivalent to leaded fuel. Very few people are willing to pay more (for goods or in taxes) in order to clean up factories and power-stations. Nor are we willing to halt our exploitation of the environment, preferring the illusory 'sustainable development'. Rational argument alone will not motivate the required changes. Self-interest is more effective—this might explain the popularity of the idea that 'if we destroy the rainforest we destroy ourselves'. That something more positive is required is suggested by the wide-ranging debate on environmentalism by many academic disciplines and by conferences such as this. Perhaps the 'Greening' of religions might inspire a move beyond concern into its expression in effective action—it must not allow us the opiate of thinking 'concern' or 'ecological thinking' is enough (Bordo 1992).

My argument in brief is that contemporary Paganism is both inspired by environmentalism and inspirational of deeper more active participation in environmental action. It moves beyond the Enlightenment and has anticipated Post-modernism. It has already gained much from Feminism and I will suggest that it is currently benefiting from the insights of Eco-feminism and from Feminist critiques of environmentalist positions (including Deep Ecology).

INTIMACY AND SOMATIC ECOLOGY

I have noted elsewhere (Harvey 1994) that Paganism has Green roots and encourages a diversity of ecological actions. There are various levels (none necessarily better than another) of Pagan involvement with ecology. Some Pagans meditate for the good of the planet, some use the 'energy' raised in ritual drama to benefit rain forests, some lie in front of bulldozers, some spike threatened trees. In a forthcoming book on contemporary Paganism (Hardman, Harvey 1996) there are powerful contributions by Adrian Harris and Gordon MacLellan (Harris 1996; MacLellan 1996). Adrian Harris, a founding member of Dragon (a Pagan environmental network) argues eloquently for a Somatic (embodied) approach to ecological action and knowledge. Gordon MacLellan's chapter on Shamanism exemplifies one role of the contemporary shaman: that of 'Patterner—one who helps people listen to / relate to the world around them'. (This is especially useful as a counter to the sort of 'shaman' discussed by Leslie Jones [1994]). I want now to build on that discussion and suggest that the everyday life of Pagans valuably contributes to the ecological debate.

Deep Ecology encourages us to think deeply about our interrelationships with the rest of Nature. It provides a necessary critique of dominant ideologies of the west which permit and perhaps demand the mastery and exploitation of Nature. However, its critique is flawed by the inhibiting presence of both a dualistic dynamic and 'a heavily masculine presence' (Plumwood 1993: 2). It reiterates the dominance of people over Nature by an exhortation to see the Self as extended beyond the reality of spatiality, or embodiment (Jung 1988) into a vision in which threatened rain-forests are neither 'It' nor 'Thou' but in fact 'Me'. While an appeal to self-interest will certainly encourage many people to use more-energy-efficient light bulbs ('they are cheaper in the long run'), this is an inadequate response to the problems the Earth now faces because of human activity. The frequent pantheism of Deep Ecology, some Pagans and others, is also subjected to a powerful critique by Val Plumwood (1993: 127–8) though it gains eloquent support elsewhere (Wood 1985).

Many Pagans would recognise (and have to some degree anticipated) the value of Plumwood's suggestion that

> *a different and improved basis for environmental politics and philosophy might be constructed by taking better account of the ethics and politics of mutuality as developed by a number of feminist thinkers* (Plumwood 1993: 2).

While many Pagans do talk about 'connecting with' and 'tuning in' to something in Nature, I believe this language of radio better represents the 'New Age'. Talk of 'Harmony' with Nature is an improvement but might again suggest the merging of the individual's lived reality with some greater, more real, Reality. Such a loss of identity is disrespectful both of the individual's own embodied self and of the multiplicity of those with whom we relate. 'Mutuality', however, brings us firmly within the realm of relationships (Grey 1991) and ordinary experience and is thus more fundamentally Pagan.

Paganism is concerned with expressing, encouraging and developing intimacy between human people and all other-than-human people. It values all these people as 'beings in their own right' with their own rights, relationships, responsibilities, significance, agency, autonomy, and meaning (see Plumwood 1993: 128). While many Pagans do consider that all things are manifestation of deity, often of 'the Goddess' (Long 1994), this usually goes beyond the valuing of things only as manifestations of deeper spiritual realities to a more polytheistic celebration of the multiplicity of living things. Paganism encourages intimacy with oneself (especially in its most feminist influenced branches), with other human people and with other-than-human persons.

The Pagan stress on the countryside as a location for significant encounters with Nature, with 'spirituality' (without the dualistic separation of 'spirit' from 'matter') could be decried as 'mere Romanticism'. It is, however, a more positive experience and vision. The city too is part of Nature (and many Pagans do regularly and easily celebrate seasonal festivals in their urban environment) but the countryside is a place of greater bio-diversity. There are more types of living being, more life, 'out there' in the woods, moors, rivers, and hills of the countryside. There may be no wildwood, no wilderness, few remaining areas of semi-natural woodland left in Britain. But even in a city park or a working wood (not including plantation forest) it is possible to encounter a less human centred, more varied manifestation of the profligate abundance of life (Dillard 1976). It is possible to 'speak with' trees and hedgehogs, flowers and trout, robins and snakes. It is possible also to listen to oneself. The 'speaking with' and the 'hearing' may not be a pursuit of information, though some Pagans assert that trees are willing to communicate (in some way) things that we would otherwise be unaware of. Erazim Kohák argues that a philosopher and a tree can converse, neither exchanging information nor 'decorating a putative harsh reality with poetic gingerbread' but communicating respect and exploring a

> *manner of speaking which would be true to the task of sustainable dwelling at peace for humans and the world alike, a manner of speaking that would be true in the non-descriptive sense of being good* (Kohák 1993: 386).

Perhaps the trees have taught philosophers what they have been teaching Pagans and children for many years: the virtue of respect and the pleasure of intimacy. Sadly, children are soon removed from tutelage of trees by adults—perhaps because of a deeply suppressed and feared knowledge that

> *we are not bounded objects in orbit around each other, but we create ourselves in relationships with each other. We are the outcome of the intersections of our conflicts and cooperations and the influences we exert on each other* (McKay 1993 quoting Linda Gordon).

Recognising that even mystical experiences are both gendered and embodied (Raphael 1994) we can more easily become open to the diverse experiences which could enable us to celebrate the diversities of life. Even more easily we can celebrate everyday life, an integral part of polytheistic, feminist Paganism.

The Earth's ecological problems are not abstract, distant, philosophical problems. Nor are they only economic or technological problems. They are not to be left either to politicians, scientists or even philosophers. Just as such problems are largely caused by everyday life (the cars we drive, the trucks which deliver our foods, the rainforests destroyed to make way for our fields, etc.) so the responses must involve everyday life.

The final section of my discussion suggests one example of a Pagan life-style, an animist one, which takes a step further than Blake's 'everything that lives is holy' to the perception that 'everything that exists lives'.

HEDGEHOGS AND VEGANS

Ordinary human living threatens ordinary other-than-human living. Sometimes it does this intentionally (e.g. fox hunting, meat production, whaling, pest-control, leather production, badger baiting, vivisection). Equally often it does it unintentionally and just by-the-way. Our cars frequently run over hedgehogs, for example. I do not intend to give this unnecessary slaughter 'meaning' but it can help us to understand the relationship between ecological thinking, animist Paganism and neighbourly living.

If a driver stops their car to move a hedgehog from the middle of a road this is not because the hedgehog was praying for salvation. Nor would the rescued hedgehog go on to develop a religion praising and thanking that human (or all humankind). It would just carry on with its ordinary life. This is very much the same approach as Pagan might take to those other-than-human people which our tradition teaches us are more powerful than we are: deities and the Faerie. It might be a great pleasure to know that such beings share our delight in certain places and times. Their presence at festive occasions is invited (by some) but is not necessary or central to the celebration of that festival. By and large, humans get on with their lives, hedgehogs get on with theirs, deities with theirs. Sometimes our paths cross and this can be dangerous. Not necessarily because humanity is thought ill of (though that might be understandable) and only sometimes because, so our tradition teaches, the Faerie do things which are harmful to us (Pratchett 1992). What they consider to be entertaining is, for us, as dangerous as our relaxing drive in the country is dangerous to hedgehogs. Awareness of these dangers can enable us to adjust our lives to be less dangerous. We can become more ecological by enhancing the diversity of life. However, we will never be able to live without taking life, doing violence to those with whom we share this planet home.

A Maori writer, speaking from within his people's tradition, says that religion is 'doing violence with impunity' (Tawhai 1988). It is absolutely wrong to take life. It is also wrong to leave your guests unsheltered and unfed. So you must go into the forest and cut down a living tree to make a shelter, you must dig up a tuber to make food. These violent acts deserve a response and a recognition. The fact that they are necessary does not negate or mitigate their violence. So the tradition provides ways of enabling the 'doing violence with impunity'. I leave the reader to explore Tawhai's own work, acknowledging the violence that could be done by setting him up as another golden age, ecological, noble savage (Bowman 1994), which he is not.

If 'everything that exists lives' and 'everything that lives is holy' eating becomes a problem. When you eat, you eat souls. What you eat has been killed. Even vegans eat things that were once alive, once participated in more or less complex relationships with their neighbours, had rights, meaning and value. In the contemporary world it is perhaps not possible to go into a supermarket and address a can of beans in a way that expresses the recognition of the violence done and the need to do violence, or the mutuality, relatedness and neighbourliness of our shared lives. Some other, perhaps ceremonial, perhaps mystical, means must be found to address this problem.

Whilst the vegan and the carnivore both do violence in their eating, the vegan has made an ecological decision in lessening the amount of violence done. The carnivore eats a pound of meat produced by an animal eating ten pounds of grain. Thus in the pyramid of damage done, the meat eater does more damage. In an age of plenty this would be a neutral fact. In an age where the level of damage is so severe, so threatening, it becomes an ethical question. Can we justify this level of damage? When is it necessary? When rainforests are being destroyed to make way for cattle and coffee production, is it justifiable to eat and drink these 'products'? Of course, British woods have been and are being destroyed to make way for prairie sized grain fields, which are no more ecologically worthwhile than plantation forests (or perhaps denuded semi-deserts). I have deliberately put this rather starkly and provocatively (I hope!). My intention is to say that something must be done, 'and when all is said and done, more is often said than done'. Such a luxury of words is hardly affordable or sustainable.

CONCLUSION

We did not chose [*sic*] to be neighbours with those 'others' with whom we share our planet home. Yet here we are, surrounded by many neighbours (only some of them human). If other religionists are passing through this place on the way to some more spiritual afterlife (heaven, nirvana, enlightenment) Pagans are discovering that they are 'at home'. They are therefore in agreement with their more secular neighbours that something must be done now to halt the devastation and to increase the diversity of life. This needs doing not on behalf of some deity, nor because it will benefit our 'deep green' Self, but primarily as an act of neighbourliness (Finn 1992).

Paganism discourages the phallic view that we are dominant on Earth and therefore entitled to exploit its resources. It does not permit the equally phallic though potentially less damaging view that we are stewards of God's Earth, caring for it even as we rule over it. Paganism is not a phallic quest for a place in the world. Some Pagans do celebrate a more uterine view, chanting,

> *the Earth is our Mother, we will take care of her*
> *the Earth is our Mother, she will take care of us.*

On the other hand, Paganism encourages us to go beyond the return to the womb for comfort and nourishment. It certainly refuses to give us a rebirth in any way discontinuous with our current embodiedness, our actual temporal and spatial gendered reality. Paganism is not a uterine rebirth into connected harmony with the cosmos.

Paganism has a more ecological view. This is the clitoral affirmation of life in its physicality, its ordinariness, its diversity and its excess (Bell 1992: 199, quoting Spivak 1987: 82). This being at home in the body and in Nature is Paganism's greatest contribution to ecological debates today. The Earth is our only home and the only home of our many neighbours who we must learn to respect and live peacefully alongside. We have polluted the Earth, we must clean it, we must live ecologically.

BIBLIOGRAPHY

Bell, S. 1992, 'Tomb of the sacred prostitute: the Symposium' in Berry & Wernick, 1992: *Shadow of Spirit* 198–207.

Berry, P. & A. Wernick, 1992, *Shadow of Spirit: Postmodernism and Religion* (London: Routledge).

Blake, W. 1795, 'Vala or the Four Zoas' in G. Keynes, (ed.) 1972 *Blake: Complete Writings* (Oxford: OUP).

Bordo, J. 1992, 'Ecological peril, modern technology and the postmodern sublime' in Berry & Wernick *Shadow of Spirit* 1992: 165–180.

Bowes, P. 1977, *The Hindu Religious Tradition: a philosophical approach* (London: Routledge and Kegan Paul).

Bowman, M. 1994, 'The Commodification of the Celt: New Age / Neo-Pagan Consumerism in *Folklore in Use 2:* 143–52.

Dillard, A. 1976, *Pilgrim at Tinker Creek* (London: Picador).

Eilberg-Schwartz, H. 1989, 'Witches of the West: Neopaganism and Goddess Worship as Enlightenment Religions' in *Journal of Feminist Studies in Religion* 5.1: 77–95.

Finn, G. 1992, 'The politics of spirituality: the spirituality of politics' in Berry & Wernick 1992 *Shadow of Spirit:* 111–21.

Green, D. 1989, 'Towards a Reappraisal of Polytheism' in *Polytheistic Systems'* , G. Davies (ed.) *Cosmos 5,* Edinburgh: Edinburgh University Press, 3–11.

Grey, M. 1991, 'Claiming Power-in-Relation: exploring the ethics of connection' in *Journal of Feminist Studies in Religion* 7.1: 7–18.

Hallowell, A. I. 1960, 'Ojibwa Ontology, Behavior and Worldview' in S. Diamond, (ed.) *Culture in History: Essays in Honor of Paul Radin* (New York: Columbia University Press).

Hardman, C. & G. Harvey, 1996 *Paganism Today* (London: Aquarian Press). Harris, A. 1996, 'Sacred Ecology' in Hardman & Harvey, 1996 *Paganism Today.*

Harvey, G. 1994, 'The Roots of Pagan Ecology' in *Religion Today* 9.3: 38–41.

Harvey, G. 1996, *Paganism in Britain* (London: Hurst).

Hutton, R. 1991, *The Pagan Religions of the Ancient British Isles* (London: Blackwell).

Hutton, R. 1994, 'Neo-Paganism, Paganism and Christianity' in *Religion Today* 9.3: 29–32.

Hutton, R. 1996, 'The Roots of Modern Paganism' in Hardman & Harvey (1996) *Paganism Today.*

Jones, L. 1994, 'The Emergence of the Druid as Shaman' in *Folklore in Use 2:* 131–42.

Jung, L. S. 1988, 'Feminism and Spatiality: Ethics and the Recovery of a Hidden Dimension' in *Journal of Feminist Studies in Religion* 4.1: 55–71.

Kohák, E. 1991, *Speaking to Trees,* Filosoficky Casopis 39(6): 903–13.

Long, A. 1994, 'The Goddess Movement in Britain Today' in *Feminist Theology* 5: 11–39.

MacLellan, G. 1996, 'Dancing on the Edge: shamanism in modern Britain' in Hardman & Harvey, 1996 *Paganism in Britain.*

McKay, N. Y. 1993, 'Acknowledging the Differences: can women find unity through diversity?' in James, S. M. & A. P. A. Busia, *Theorizing Black Feminisms: the visionary pragmatism of black women* (London: Routledge): 267–282.

Plumwood, V. 1993, *Feminism and the Mastery of Nature* (London: Routledge).

Pratchett, T. 1992, *Lords and Ladies* (London: Corgi).

Raphael, M. 1994, 'Feminism, Constructivism and Numinous Experience' in *Religious Studies* 30: 511–26.

Smart, N. 1993, 'The formation rather than the origin of a tradition' in *Diskus* 1.1: 1

Spivak, G. C. 1987, 'Feminism and Critical Theory', in *In Other Worlds: Essays in Cultural Politics* (London: Routledge) 77–92.

Tawhai, T. P. 1988, 'Maori Religions' in Sutherland, S., L. Houlden, P. Clarke, & F. Hardy, (eds.), *The World's Religions* (London: Routledge): 854–63.

Wood, H. W. 1985, 'Modern Pantheism as an Approach to Environmental Ethics' in *Environmental Ethics* 8: 151–163.

Discussion Questions

1. How does the Baha'i view resolve the paradox between humans' unity with nature and their detachment from it? Is this explanation convincing?

2. Is the overdevelopment of sacred spaces inevitable? How can one avoid "loving a place to death"?
3. Does Paganism hold a special claim to being an ecological religion? Does this claim make it a viable form of expression in today's world?
4. Are new religions more likely than long-established ones to demonstrate adaptability to ecological doctrines?

Further Reading

Adler, Margot, *Drawing Down the Moon: Witches, Druids, Goddess-worshippers, and Other Pagans in America Today,* rev. ed., Boston: Beacon Press, 1986.

Albanese, Catherine L., *Nature Religions in America: From the Algonkian Indians to the New Age,* Chicago: University of Chicago Press, 1990.

Berger, Helen A., *A Community of Witches: Contemporary Neo-paganism and Witchcraft in the United States,* Columbia: University of South Carolina Press, 1999.

Brooks, Charles R., *The Hare Krishnas in India,* Princeton, N.J.: Princeton University Press, 1989.

Cremo, Michael, and Mukunda Goswami, *Divine Nature: A Spiritual Perspective on the Environmental Crisis,* Los Angeles: Bhaktivedanta Book Trust, 1995.

Griffin, Wendy, Ed., *Daughters of the Goddess: Studies of Healing, Identity, and Empowerment,* Walnut Creek, Calif.: Alta Mira Press, 2000.

Haberman, David L., *Journey Through the Twelve Forests: An Encounter With Krishna,* New York: Oxford University Press, 1994.

Hardman, C., and G. Harvey, Eds., *Paganism Today,* London: Aquarian Press, 1996.

Harvey, Graham, *Contemporary Paganism: Listening People, Speaking Earth,* New York: New York University Press, 1997.

Hutton, Ronald, *The Triumph of the Moon: A History of Modern Pagan Witchcraft,* New York: Oxford University Press, 1999.

Lewis, James R., Ed., *Magical Religion and Modern Witchcraft,* Albany, N.Y.: SUNY Press, 1996.

Prime, Ranchor, *Hinduism and Ecology: Seeds of Truth,* London: Cassell, 1992.

Seow, Jimmy, *Environment: Our Common Heritage,* Atlanta: Baha'i Distribution Service, 1994.

Starhawk, *The Spiral Dance: A Rebirth of the Ancient Religion of the Great Goddess,* New York: Harper & Row, 1979.

Williams, Terry Tempest, William Smart and Gibbs Smith., Eds., *New Genesis: A Mormon Reader on Land and Community,* Salt Lake City: Gibbs Smith, 1998.

Part Three

Contemporary Perspectives

If we define *religion* broadly as a worldview that informs our attitudes about where we belong in the universe and how we should live in it, it becomes apparent that not all such worldviews can be placed within the rubric of established religions. As the essays in Chapter 2 demonstrate, modernist frameworks such as humanism, capitalism, and rationalism can also be understood as faith systems, complete with their own beliefs and rituals. These modern worldviews and their offshoots are often blamed for bringing us to the present state of global environmental crisis.

Many have acknowledged that modernist worldviews have failed to provide us with a way of living as responsible citizens of the global biosphere community. As seen in the essays in Part 2, people of all cultural backgrounds around the world today are seeking reinterpretations of their existing cultural traditions that promise a healthier way of living on the Earth. Some, however, feel that mere reinterpretations are not enough. Many of these people hold that the existing worldviews have hopelessly failed us and need not to be reworked but rather to be replaced with something different. Others see existing systems as containing possibly salvageable elements but hold that these systems need to be approached and restructured from entirely new points of view, such as the historically marginalized standpoints of women, the poor, the colonized, or the otherwise disempowered.

In short, the chapters in this section present *alternatives* to the frameworks offered by historically mainstream worldviews. Some of these alternatives have emerged from attempts to break out of established frameworks; other proposed frameworks appear almost entirely new. If these diverse new worldviews have anything in common, it is that they each adopt and promote a system of values. These ethical systems are here described by their proponents in terms of their application to environmental problems.

Chapter 12

Ecocentrism and Radical Environmentalism

WORLDVIEWS THAT SEEM TO justify the exploitation and the resulting destruction of nature, such as Western Christianity in Lynn White Jr.'s example, are often accused of *anthropocentrism*—that is, treating human needs as if they were the primary or the only considerations to be taken into account. The advocates of this critique point out that humans do not exist in isolation from natural systems and, in fact, depend on them for survival, even though their choices and behavior often do not seem to take this reality into account. Decision makers today often see environmental problems through a lens of fragmentation, dealing with them on a case-by-case basis, as if they were discrete issues, and not taking into consideration the broader networks and patterns into which all human activities fit.

Humans are social beings; we are socialized to understand that our actions affect others and that we, likewise, depend on others to fulfill many of our needs. Even in a highly individualistic society such as the United States, we usually recognize that we are part of a community and that we should on some level accept that the welfare of that community is connected with our own.

But how do we define the boundaries of the community of which we are a part? Who has membership rights in our community? Who doesn't? Only a generation or two ago, non-Whites and women were denied many of the membership rights claimed by White male Americans. Although racism and sexism have not disappeared from our culture, they are no longer the accepted norm. As a society, we have agreed that the boundaries that excluded women and racial minorities from full civil rights were arbitrary; there was (and is) no legitimate justification for these boundaries. Critics of anthropocentrism argue that our continuing refusal to include the nonhuman world within the bounds of moral considerability is equally arbitrary.

Together with such figures as John Muir, Gifford Pinchot, and Theodore Roosevelt, Aldo Leopold was among the founding fathers of the North American conservation movement during the first half of the twentieth century. In his well-known work *A Sand County Almanac,* which has become something close to sacred scripture among conservationists, Leopold made the case that humans are part of a community that includes soil, water, plants, and animals—in short, the land. This idea, of course, closely resembles the worldviews of first peoples described in Chapter 3. The implications are that until we recognize that we are part of the land and act accordingly, we will continue to negatively affect the health of the land and, by extension, our own health.

In 1973, the Norwegian philosopher Arne Naess published the highly influential essay titled, "The Shallow and the Deep, Long-Range Ecology Movements," in which he contrasted conservation efforts aiming to manage natural resources only for human benefit with a position he named *deep ecology,* based on biospheric egalitarianism rather than human dominance. The American scholars Bill Devall and George Sessions developed Naess's ideas throughout the 1970s and became two of the leading expositors of the deep ecology movement, which remains influential today. The essay excerpted from their 1985 book *Deep Ecology* outlines some of the basic principles on which the movement is founded.

Naess began his long career as a scholar of Gandhi, and Eastern thought plays a large role in deep ecology thinking. Joanna Macy is both a deep ecologist and a practicing Buddhist. She is the cofounder, together with Australian rain forest activist John Seed, of the Council of All Beings, which seeks to give a voice to nonhuman nature in ecological discussions. Drawing on Buddhist ontological theory and on Naess's call for individual self-realization, Macy advocates cultivating an "ecological self"; in other words, an expanded notion of self that transcends the limits of our individual bodies to include the broader ecological networks of which we are a part.

In recent decades, some people have applied their broadened identification with nature to various forms of environmental activism that are occasionally perceived by mainstream society as extreme. One such activist organization is Earth First!, founded in 1980 by a small group of environmental activists who had become disillusioned by the compromising methods of existing environmental organizations such as the Wilderness Society and the Sierra Club. Rallying behind the slogan "No compromise in defense of Mother Earth," Earth First!ers sometimes practiced "monkeywrenching," a term borrowed from Edward Abbey's 1975 novel about an anarchic group of nature lovers who take to sabotaging various tools of environmental destruction such as bulldozers, billboards, and bridges. For many Earth First!ers, environmental protection has taken on religious aspects; they have adopted many aspects of pagan ritual associated with ancient societies that are seen as more reverent toward the Earth. Bron Taylor discusses the religious dimension of contemporary radical environmentalism, focusing on Earth First!'s example.

Excerpts from *A Sand County Almanac*

ALDO LEOPOLD

GOOD OAK

THERE ARE TWO SPIRITUAL DANGERS IN NOT owning a farm. One is the danger of supposing that breakfast comes from the grocery, and the other that heat comes from the furnace.

To avoid the first danger, one should plant a garden, preferably where there is no grocer to confuse the issue.

To avoid the second, he should lay a split of good oak on the andirons, preferably where there is no furnace, and let it warm his shins while a February blizzard tosses the trees outside. If one has cut, split, hauled, and piled his own good oak, and let his mind work the while, he will remember much about where the heat comes from, and with a wealth of detail denied to those who spend the week end in town astride a radiator.

• • •

ON A MONUMENT TO THE PIGEON[1]

We have erected a monument to commemorate the funeral of a species. It symbolizes our sorrow. We grieve because no living man will see again the onrushing phalanx of victorious birds, sweeping a path for spring across the March skies, chasing the defeated winter from all the woods and prairies of Wisconsin.

Men still live who, in their youth, remember pigeons. Trees still live who, in their youth, were shaken by a living wind. But a decade hence only the oldest oaks will remember, and at long last only the hills will know.

There will always be pigeons in books and in museums, but these are effigies and images, dead to all hardships and to all delights. Book-pigeons cannot dive out of a cloud to make the deer run for cover, or clap their wings in thunderous applause of mast-laden woods. Book-pigeons cannot breakfast on new-mown wheat in Minnesota, and dine on blueberries in Canada. They know no urge of seasons; they feel no kiss of sun, no lash of wind and weather. They live forever by not living at all.

Our grandfathers were less well-housed, well-fed, well-clothed than we are. The strivings by which they bettered their lot are also those which deprived us of pigeons. Perhaps we now grieve because we are not sure, in our hearts, that we have gained by the exchange. The gadgets of industry bring us more comforts than the pigeons did, but do they add as much to the glory of the spring?

It is a century now since Darwin gave us the first glimpse of the origin of species. We know now what was unknown to all the preceding caravan of generations: that men are only fellow-voyagers with other creatures in the odyssey of evolution. This new knowledge should have given us, by this time, a sense of kinship with fellow-creatures; a wish to live and let live; a sense of wonder over the magnitude and duration of the biotic enterprise.

• • •

I now suspect that just as a deer herd lives in mortal fear of its wolves, so does a mountain live in mortal fear of its deer. And perhaps with better cause, for while a buck pulled down by wolves can be replaced in two or three years, a range pulled down by too many deer may fail of replacement in as many decades.

So also with cows. The cowman who cleans his range of wolves does not realize that he is taking over the wolf's job of trimming the herd to fit the range. He has not learned to think like a mountain. Hence we have dustbowls, and rivers washing the future into the sea.

• • •

We all strive for safety, prosperity, comfort, long life, and dullness. The deer strives with his supple legs, the cowman with trap and poison, the statesman with pen, the most of us with machines, votes, and dollars, but it all comes to the same thing: peace in our time. A measure of success in this is all well enough, and perhaps is a requisite to objective thinking, but too much safety seems to yield only danger in the long run. Perhaps this is behind Thoreau's dictum: In wildness is the salvation of the world. Perhaps this is the hidden meaning in the howl of the wolf, long known among mountains, but seldom perceived among men.

• • •

THE COMMUNITY CONCEPT

All ethics so far evolved rest upon a single premise: that the individual is a member of a community of interdependent parts. His instincts prompt him to compete for his place in that community, but his ethics prompt him also to co-operate (perhaps in order that there may be a place to compete for).

The land ethic simply enlarges the boundaries of the community to include soils, waters, plants, and animals, or collectively: the land.

This sounds simple: do we not already sing our love for and obligation to the land of the free and the home of the brave? Yes, but just what and whom do we love? Certainly not the soil, which we are sending helter-skelter downriver. Certainly not the waters, which we assume have no function except to turn turbines, float barges, and carry off sewage. Certainly not the plants, of which we exterminate whole communities without batting an eye. Certainly not the animals, of which we have already extirpated many of the largest and most beautiful species. A land ethic of course cannot prevent the alteration, management, and use of these 'resources,' but it does affirm their right to continued existence, and, at least in spots, their continued existence in a natural state.

In short, a land ethic changes the role of *Homo sapiens* from conqueror of the land-community to plain member and citizen of it. It implies respect for his fellow-members, and also respect for the community as such.

In human history, we have learned (I hope) that the conqueror role is eventually self-defeating. Why? Because it is implicit in such a role that the conqueror knows, *ex cathedra,* just what makes the community clock tick, and just what and who is valuable, and what and who is worthless, in community life. It always turns out that he knows neither, and this is why his conquests eventually defeat themselves.

THE OUTLOOK

It is inconceivable to me that an ethical relation to land can exist without love, respect, and admiration for land, and a high regard for its value. By value, I of course mean something far broader than mere economic value; I mean value in the philosophical sense.

Perhaps the most serious obstacle impeding the evolution of a land ethic is the fact that our educational and economic system is headed away from, rather than toward, an intense consciousness of land. Your true modern is separated from the land by many middlemen, and by innumerable physical gadgets. He has no vital relation to it; to him it is the space between cities on which crops grow. Turn him loose for a day on the land, and if the spot does not happen to be a golf links or a 'scenic' area, he is bored stiff. If crops could be raised by hydroponics instead of farming, it would suit him very well. Synthetic substitutes for wood, leather, wool, and other natural land products suit him better than the originals. In short, land is something he has 'outgrown.'

Almost equally serious as an obstacle to a land ethic is the attitude of the farmer for whom the land is still an adversary, or a taskmaster that keeps him in slavery. Theoretically, the mechanization of farming ought to cut the farmer's chains, but whether it really does is debatable.

One of the requisites for an ecological comprehension of land is an understanding of ecology, and this is by no means co-extensive with 'education'; in fact, much higher education seems deliberately to avoid ecological concepts. An understanding of ecology does not necessarily originate in courses bearing ecological labels; it is quite as likely to be labeled geography, botany, agronomy, history, or economics. This is as it should be, but whatever the label, ecological training is scarce.

The case for a land ethic would appear hopeless but for the minority which is in obvious revolt against these 'modern' trends.

The 'key-log' which must be moved to release the evolutionary process for an ethic is simply this: quit thinking about decent land-use as solely an economic problem. Examine each question in terms of what is ethically and esthetically right, as well as what is economically expedient. A thing is right when it tends to preserve the integrity, stability, and beauty of the biotic community. It is wrong when it tends otherwise.

It of course goes without saying that economic feasibility limits the tether of what can or cannot be done for land. It always has and it always will. The fallacy the economic determinists have tied around our collective neck, and which we now need to cast off, is the belief that economics determines *all* land-use. This is simply not true. An innumerable host of actions and attitudes, comprising perhaps the bulk of all land relations, is determined by the land-users' tastes and predilections, rather than by his purse. The bulk of all land relations hinges on investments of time, forethought, skill, and faith rather than on investments of cash. As a land-user thinketh, so is he.

I have purposely presented the land ethic as a product of social evolution because nothing so important as an ethic is ever 'written.' Only the most superficial student of history supposes that Moses 'wrote' the Decalogue; it evolved in the minds of a thinking community, and Moses wrote a tentative summary of it for a 'seminar.' I say tentative because evolution never stops.

The evolution of a land ethic is an intellectual as well as emotional process. Conservation is paved with good intentions which prove to be futile, or even dangerous, because they are devoid of critical understanding either of the land, or of economic land-use. I think it is a truism that as the ethical frontier advances from the individual to the community, its intellectual content increases.

The mechanism of operation is the same for any

ethic: social approbation for right actions: social disapproval for wrong actions.

By and large, our present problem is one of attitudes and implements. We are remodeling the Alhambra with a steam-shovel, and we are proud of our yardage. We shall hardly relinquish the shovel, which after all has many good points, but we are in need of gentler and more objective criteria for its successful use.

NOTE

1. The monument to the Passenger Pigeon, placed in Wyalusing State Park, Wisconsin, by the Wisconsin Society for Ornithology. Dedicated 11 May 1947.

Principles of Deep Ecology

BILL DEVALL AND GEORGE SESSIONS

THE TERM *DEEP ECOLOGY* WAS COINED BY Arne Naess in his 1973 article, "The Shallow and the Deep, Long-Range Ecology Movements."[1] Naess was attempting to describe the deeper, more spiritual approach to Nature exemplified in the writings of Aldo Leopold and Rachel Carson. He thought that this deeper approach resulted from a more sensitive openness to ourselves and nonhuman life around us. The essence of deep ecology is to keep asking more searching questions about human life, society, and Nature as in the Western philosophical tradition of Socrates. As examples of this deep questioning, Naess points out "that we ask why and how, where others do not. For instance, ecology as a science does not ask what kind of a society would be the best for maintaining a particular ecosystem—that is considered a question for value theory, for politics, for ethics." Thus deep ecology goes beyond the so-called factual scientific level to the level of self and Earth wisdom.

Deep ecology goes beyond a limited piecemeal shallow approach to environmental problems and attempts to articulate a comprehensive religious and philosophical worldview. The foundations of deep ecology are the basic intuitions and experiencing of ourselves and Nature which comprise ecological consciousness. Certain outlooks on politics and public policy flow naturally from this consciousness. And in the context of this book, we discuss the minority tradition as the type of community most conducive both to cultivating ecological consciousness and to asking the basic questions of values and ethics addressed in these pages.

Many of these questions are perennial philosophical and religious questions faced by humans in all cultures over the ages. What does it mean to be a unique human individual? How can the individual self maintain and increase its uniqueness while also being an inseparable aspect of the whole system wherein there are no sharp breaks between self and the *other*? An ecological perspective, in this deeper sense, results in what Theodore Roszak calls "an awakening of wholes greater than the sum of their parts. In spirit, the discipline is contemplative and therapeutic."[2]

Ecological consciousness and deep ecology are in sharp contrast with the dominant worldview of technocratic-industrial societies which regards humans as isolated and fundamentally separate from the rest of Nature, as superior to, and in charge of, the rest of creation. But the view of humans as separate and superior to the rest of Nature is only part of larger cultural patterns. For thousands of years, Western culture has become increasingly obsessed with the idea of ***dominance:*** with dominance of humans over nonhuman Nature, masculine over the feminine, wealthy and powerful over the poor, with the dominance of the West over non-Western cultures. Deep ecological consciousness allows us to see through these erroneous and dangerous illusions.

Devall, Bill, and George Sessions, excerpts from *Deep Ecology: Living as if Nature Mattered.* Salt Lake City: Gibbs Smith, Publisher, 1985. Used with permission.

For deep ecology, the study of our place in the Earth household includes the study of ourselves as part of the organic whole. Going beyond a narrowly materialist scientific understanding of reality, the spiritual and the material aspects of reality fuse together. While the leading intellectuals of the dominant worldview have tended to view religion as "just superstition," and have looked upon ancient spiritual practice and enlightenment, such as found in Zen Buddhism, as essentially subjective, the search for deep ecological consciousness is the search for a more objective consciousness and state of being through an active deep questioning and meditative process and way of life.

Many people have asked these deeper questions and cultivated ecological consciousness within the context of different spiritual traditions—Christianity, Taoism, Buddhism, and Native American rituals, for example. While differing greatly in other regards, many in these traditions agree with the basic principles of deep ecology.

Warwick Fox, an Australian philosopher, has succinctly expressed the central intuition of deep ecology: "It is the idea that we can make no firm ontological divide in the field of existence: That there is no bifurcation in reality between the human and the non-human realms . . . to the extent that we perceive boundaries, we fall short of deep ecological consciousness."[3]

From this most basic insight or characteristic of deep ecological consciousness, Arne Naess has developed two *ultimate norms* or intuitions which are themselves not derivable from other principles or intuitions. They are arrived at by the deep questioning process and reveal the importance of moving to the philosophical and religious level of wisdom. They cannot be validated, of course, by the methodology of modern science based on its usual mechanistic assumptions and its very narrow definition of data. These ultimate norms are *self-realization* and *biocentric equality*.

I. SELF-REALIZATION

In keeping with the spiritual traditions of many of the world's religions, the deep ecology norm of self-realization goes beyond the modern Western *self* which is defined as an isolated ego striving primarily for hedonistic gratification or for a narrow sense of individual salvation in this life or the next. This socially programmed sense of the narrow self or social self dislocates us, and leaves us prey to whatever fad or fashion is prevalent in our society or social reference group. We are thus robbed of beginning the search for our unique spiritual/biological personhood. Spiritual growth, or unfolding, begins when we cease to understand or see ourselves as isolated and narrow competing egos and begin to identify with other humans from our family and friends to, eventually, our species. But the deep ecology sense of self requires a further maturity and growth, an identification which goes beyond humanity to include the nonhuman world. We must see beyond our narrow contemporary cultural assumptions and values, and the conventional wisdom of our time and place, and this is best achieved by the meditative deep questioning process. Only in this way can we hope to attain full mature personhood and uniqueness.

A nurturing nondominating society can help in the "real work" of becoming a whole person. The "real work" can be summarized symbolically as the realization of "self-in-Self" where "Self" stands for organic wholeness. This process of the full unfolding of the self can also be summarized by the phrase, "No one is saved until we are all saved," where the phrase "one" includes not only me, an individual human, but all humans, whales, grizzly bears, whole rain forest ecosystems, mountains and rivers, the tiniest microbes in the soil, and so on.

II. BIOCENTRIC EQUALITY

The intuition of biocentric equality is that all things in the biosphere have an equal right to live and blossom and to reach their own individual forms of unfolding and self-realization within the larger Self-realization. This basic intuition is that all organisms and entities in the ecosphere, as parts of the interrelated whole, are equal in intrinsic worth. Naess suggests that biocentric equality as an intuition is true in principle, although in the process of living, all species use each other as food, shelter, etc. Mutual predation is a biological fact of life, and many of the world's religions have struggled with the spiritual implications of this. Some animal liberationists who attempt to side-step this problem by advocating vegetarianism are forced to say that the entire plant kingdom including rain forests have no right to their own existence. This evasion flies in the face of the basic intuition of equality.[4] Aldo Leopold expressed this intuition when he said humans are "plain citizens" of the biotic community, not lord and master over all other species.

Biocentric equality is intimately related to the all-inclusive Self-realization in the sense that if we harm the rest of Nature then we are harming ourselves. There are no boundaries and everything is interrelated. But insofar as we perceive things as individual organisms or entities, the insight draws us to respect all human and non-human individuals in their own right as parts of the whole without feeling the need to set up hierarchies of species with humans at the top.

The practical implications of this intuition or norm suggest that we should live with minimum rather than maximum impact on other species and on the Earth in general. Thus we see another aspect of our guiding principle: "simple in means, rich in ends." . . .

A fuller discussion of the biocentric norm as it unfolds itself in practice begins with the realization that we, as individual humans, and as communities of humans, have vital needs which go beyond such basics as food, water, and shelter to include love, play, creative expression, intimate relationships with a particular landscape (or Nature taken in its entirety) as well as intimate relationships with other humans, and the vital need for spiritual growth, for becoming a mature human being.

Our vital material needs are probably more simple than many realize. In technocratic-industrial societies there is overwhelming propaganda and advertising which encourages false needs and destructive desires designed to foster increased production and consumption of goods. Most of this actually diverts us from facing reality in an objective way and from beginning the "real work" of spiritual growth and maturity.

Many people who do not see themselves as supporters of deep ecology nevertheless recognize an overriding vital human need for a healthy and high-quality natural environment for humans, if not for all life, with minimum intrusion of toxic waste, nuclear radiation from human enterprises, minimum acid rain and smog, and enough free flowing wilderness so humans can get in touch with their sources, the natural rhythms and the flow of time and place.

Drawing from the minority tradition and from the wisdom of many who have offered the insight of interconnectedness, we recognize that deep ecologists can offer suggestions for gaining maturity and encouraging the processes of harmony with Nature, but that there is no grand solution which is guaranteed to save us from ourselves.

The ultimate norms of deep ecology suggest a view of the nature of reality and our place as an individual (many in the one) in the larger scheme of things. They cannot be fully grasped intellectually but are ultimately experiential. We encourage readers to [further] consider . . . the psychological, social and ecological implications of these norms. . . .

As a brief summary of our position thus far, [the list below] summarizes the contrast between the dominant worldview and deep ecology.

Dominant Worldview	*Deep Ecology*
Dominance over Nature	Harmony with Nature
Natural environment as resource for humans	All nature has intrinsic worth/biospecies equality
Material/economic growth for growing human population	Elegantly simple material needs (material goals serving the larger goal of self-realization)
Belief in ample resource reserves	Earth "supplies" limited
High technological progress and solutions	Appropriate technology; nondominating science
Consumerism	Doing with enough/recycling
National/centralized community	Minority tradition/bioregion

III. BASIC PRINCIPLES OF DEEP ECOLOGY

In April 1984, during the advent of spring and John Muir's birthday, George Sessions and Arne Naess summarized fifteen years of thinking on the principles of deep ecology while camping in Death Valley, California. In this great and special place, they articulated these principles in a literal, somewhat neutral way, hoping that they would be understood and accepted by persons coming from different philosophical and religious positions.

Readers are encouraged to elaborate their own versions of deep ecology, clarify key concepts and think through the consequences of acting from these principles.

Basic Principles

1. The well-being and flourishing of human and nonhuman Life on Earth have value in themselves (synonyms: intrinsic value, inherent value). These values are independent of the usefulness of the non-human world for human purposes.

2. Richness and diversity of life forms contribute to the realization of these values and are also values in themselves.

3. Humans have no right to reduce this richness and diversity except to satisfy *vital* needs.

4. The flourishing of human life and cultures is compatible with a substantial decrease of the human population. The flourishing of nonhuman life requires such a decrease.

5. Present human interference with the nonhuman world is excessive, and the situation is rapidly worsening.

6. Policies must therefore be changed. These policies affect basic economic, technological, and ideological structures. The resulting state of affairs will be deeply different from the present.

7. The ideological change is mainly that of appreciating *life quality* (dwelling in situations of inherent value) rather than adhering to an increasingly higher standard of living. There will be a profound awareness of the difference between big and great.

8. Those who subscribe to the foregoing points have an obligation directly or indirectly to try to implement the necessary changes.

Naess and Sessions Provide Comments on the Basic Principles

RE (1). This formulation refers to the biosphere, or more accurately, to the ecosphere as a whole. This includes individuals, species, populations, habitat, as well as human and nonhuman cultures. From our current knowledge of all-pervasive intimate relationships, this implies a fundamental deep concern and respect. Ecological processes of the planet should, on the whole, remain intact. "The world environment should remain 'natural'" (Gary Snyder).

The term "life" is used here in a more comprehensive nontechnical way to refer also to what biologists classify as "nonliving"; rivers (watersheds), landscapes, ecosystems. For supporters of deep ecology, slogans such as "Let the river live" illustrate this broader usage so common in most cultures.

Inherent value as used in (1) is common in deep ecology literature ("The presence of inherent value in a natural object is independent of any awareness, interest, or appreciation of it by a conscious being.")[5]

RE (2). More technically, this is a formulation concerning diversity and complexity. From an ecological standpoint, complexity and symbiosis are conditions for maximizing diversity. So-called simple, lower, or primitive species of plants and animals contribute essentially to the richness and diversity of life. They have value in themselves and are not merely steps toward the so-called higher or rational life forms. The second principle presupposes that life itself, as a process over evolutionary time, implies an increase of diversity and richness. The refusal to acknowledge that some life forms have greater or lesser intrinsic value than others (see points 1 and 2) runs counter to the formulations of some ecological philosophers and New Age writers.

Complexity, as referred to here, is different from complication. Urban life may be more complicated than life in a natural setting without being more complex in the sense of multifaceted quality.

RE (3). The term "vital need" is left deliberately vague to allow for considerable latitude in judgment. Differences in climate and related factors, together with differences in the structures of societies as they now exist, need to be considered (for some Eskimos, snowmobiles are necessary today to satisfy vital needs).

People in the materially richest countries cannot be expected to reduce their excessive interference with the nonhuman world to a moderate level overnight. The stabilization and reduction of the human population will take time. Interim strategies need to be developed. But this in no way excuses the present complacency—the extreme seriousness of our current situation must first be realized. But the longer we wait the more drastic will be the measures needed. Until deep changes are made, substantial decreases in richness and diversity are liable to occur: the rate of extinction of species will be ten to one hundred times greater than any other period of earth history.

RE (4). The United Nations Fund for Population Activities in their State of World Population Report (1984) said that high human population growth rates (over 2.0 percent annum) in many developing countries "were diminishing the quality of life for many millions of people." During the decade 1974–1984, the world population grew by nearly 800 million—more than the size of India. "And we will be adding about one Bangladesh (population 93 million) per annum between now and the year 2000."

The report noted that "The growth rate of the human population has declined for the first time in human history. But at the same time, the number of people being added to the human population is bigger than at any time in history because the population base is larger."

Most of the nations in the developing world (including India and China) have as their official government policy the goal of reducing the rate of human population increase, but there are debates over the types of measures to take (contraception, abortion, etc.) consistent with human rights and feasibility.

The report concludes that if all governments set specific population targets as public policy to help alleviate poverty and advance the quality of life, the current situation could be improved.

As many ecologists have pointed out, it is also absolutely crucial to curb population growth in the so-called developed (i.e., overdeveloped) industrial societies. Given the tremendous rate of consumption and waste production of individuals in these societies, they represent a much greater threat and impact on the biosphere per capita than individuals in Second and Third World countries.

RE (5). This formulation is mild. For a realistic assessment of the situation, see the unabbreviated version of the I.U.C.N.'s *World Conservation Strategy*. There are other works to be highly recommended, such as Gerald Barney's *Global 2000 Report to the President of the United States*.

The slogan of "noninterference" does not imply that humans should not modify some ecosystems as do other species. Humans have modified the earth and will probably continue to do so. At issue is the nature and extent of such interference.

The fight to preserve and extend areas of wilderness or near-wilderness should continue and should focus on the general ecological functions of these areas (one such function: large wilderness areas are required in the biosphere to allow for continued evolutionary speciation of animals and plants). Most present designated wilderness areas and game preserves are not large enough to allow for such speciation.

RE (6). Economic growth as conceived and implemented today by the industrial states is incompatible with (1)–(5). There is only a faint resemblance between ideal sustainable forms of economic growth and present policies of the industrial societies. And "sustainable" still means "sustainable in relation to humans."

Present ideology tends to value things because they are scarce and because they have a commodity value. There is prestige in vast consumption and waste (to mention only several relevant factors).

Whereas "self-determination," "local community," and "think globally, act locally," will remain key terms in the ecology of human societies, nevertheless the implementation of deep changes requires increasingly global action—action across borders.

Governments in Third World countries (with the exception of Costa Rica and a few others) are uninterested in deep ecological issues. When the governments of industrial societies try to promote ecological measures through Third World governments, practically nothing is accomplished (e.g., with problems of desertification). Given this situation, support for global action through nongovernmental international organizations becomes increasingly important. Many of these organizations are able to act globally "from grassroots to grassroots," thus avoiding negative governmental interference.

Cultural diversity today requires advanced technology, that is, techniques that advance the basic goals of each culture. So-called soft, intermediate, and alternative technologies are steps in this direction.

RE (7). Some economists criticize the term "quality of life" because it is supposed to be vague. But on closer inspection, what they consider to be vague is actually the nonquantitative nature of the term. One cannot quantify adequately what is important for the quality of life as discussed here, and there is no need to do so.

RE (8). There is ample room for different opinions about priorities: what should be done first, what next? What is most urgent? What is clearly necessary as opposed to what is highly desirable but not absolutely pressing?

Interview With Arne Naess

The following excerpts are from an interview with Arne Naess conducted at the Zen Center of Los Angeles in April 1982. It was originally published as an interview in *Ten Directions.*[6] In the interview, Naess further discusses the major perspective of deep ecology. . . .

"The essence of deep ecology is to ask deeper questions. The adjective 'deep' stresses that we ask why and how, where others do not. For instance, ecology as a science does not ask what kind of a society would be the best for maintaining a particular ecosystem—that is considered a question for value theory, for politics, for ethics. As long as ecologists keep narrowly to their science, they do not ask such questions. What we need today is a tremendous expansion of ecological thinking in what I call ecosophy. *Sophy* comes from the Greek term *sophia,* 'wisdom,' which relates to ethics, norms, rules, and practice. Ecosophy, or deep ecology, then, involves a shift from science to wisdom.

"For example, we need to ask questions like, Why do we think that economic growth and high levels of consumption are so important? The conventional answer would be to point to the economic consequences of not having economic growth. But in deep ecology, we ask whether the present society fulfills basic human needs like love and security and access to nature, and, in so doing, we question our society's underlying assumptions. We ask which society, which education, which form of religion, is beneficial for all life on the planet as a whole, and then we ask further what we need to do in order to make the necessary changes. We are not limited to a scientific approach; we have an obligation to verbalize a total view.

"Of course, total views may differ. Buddhism, for example, provides a fitting background or context for deep ecology, certain Christian groups have formed platforms of action in favor of deep ecology, and I myself have worked out my own philosophy, which I call ecosophy. In general, however, people do not question deeply enough to explicate or make clear a total view. If they did, most would agree with saving the planet from the destruction that's in progress. A total view, such as deep ecology, can provide a single motivating force for all the activities and movements aimed at saving the planet from human exploitation and domination.

". . . It's easier for deep ecologists than for others because we have certain fundamental values, a fundamental view of what's meaningful in life, what's worth maintaining, which makes it completely clear that we're opposed to further development for the sake of increased domination and an increased standard of living. The material standard of living should be drastically reduced and the quality of life, in the sense of basic satisfaction in the depths of one's heart or soul, should be maintained or increased. This view is intuitive, as are all important views, in the sense that it can't be proven. As Aristotle said, it shows a lack of education to try to prove everything, because you have to have a starting point. You can't prove the methodology of science, you can't prove logic, because logic presupposes fundamental premises.

"All the sciences are fragmentary and incomplete in relation to basic rules and norms, so it's very shallow to think that science can solve our problems. Without basic norms, there is no science.

". . . People can then oppose nuclear power without having to read thick books and without knowing the myriad facts that are used in newspapers and periodicals. And they must also find others who feel the same and form circles of friends who give one another confidence and support in living in a way that the majority find ridiculous, naive, stupid and simplistic. But in order to do that, one must already have enough self-confidence to follow one's intuition—a quality very much lacking in broad sections of the populace. Most people follow the trends and advertisements and become philosophical and ethical cripples.

"There is a basic intuition in deep ecology that we have no right to destroy other living beings without sufficient reason. Another norm is that, with maturity, human beings will experience joy when other life forms experience joy and sorrow when other life forms experience sorrow. Not only will we feel said when our brother or a dog or a cat feels sad, but we will grieve when living beings, including landscapes, are destroyed. In our civilization, we have vast means of destruction at our disposal but extremely little maturity in our feelings. Only a very narrow range of feelings have interested most human beings until now.

"For deep ecology, there is a core democracy in the biosphere. . . . In deep ecology, we have the goal not only of stabilizing human population but also of reducing it to a sustainable minimum without revolution or dictatorship. I should think we must have no more than 100 million people if we are to have the variety of cultures we had one hundred years ago. Because we need the conservation of human cultures, just as we need the conservation of animal species.

". . . Self-realization is the realization of the potentialities of life. Organisms that differ from each other in three ways give us less diversity than organisms that differ from each other in one hundred ways. Therefore, the self-realization we experience when we identify with the universe is heightened by an increase in the number of ways in which individuals, societies, and even species and life forms realize themselves. The greater the diversity, then, the greater the self-realization. This seeming duality between individuals and the totality is encompassed by what I call the Self and the Chinese call the Tao. Most people in deep ecology have had the feeling—usually, but not always, in nature—that they are connected with something greater than their ego, greater than their name, their family, their special attributes as an individual—a feeling that is often called oceanic because many have it on the ocean. Without that identification, one is not easily drawn to become involved in deep ecology. . . .

". . . Insofar as these deep feelings are religious, deep ecology has a religious component, and those people who have done the most to make societies aware of the destructive way in which we live in relation to natural settings have had such religious feelings. Rachel Carson, for example, says that we *cannot* do what we do, we have no religious or ethical justification for behaving as we do toward nature. . . . She is saying that we are simply not permitted to behave in that way. Some will say that nature is not man's property, it's the property of God; others will say it in other ways. The main point is that deep ecology has a religious component, fundamental intuitions that everyone must cultivate if he or she is to have a life based on values and not function like a computer.

". . . To maximize self-realization—and I don't mean self as ego but self in a broader sense—we need maximum diversity and maximum symbiosis. . . . Diversity, then, is a fundamental norm and a common delight. As deep ecologists, we take a natural delight in diversity, as long as it does not include crude, intrusive forms, like Nazi culture, that are destructive to others."

Now I see the secret of the making of the best persons.
It is to grow in the open air, and to eat and sleep
with the earth.

—Walt Whitman, *Leaves of Grass*

NOTES

1. Arne Naess, "The Shallow and The Deep, Long-Range Ecology Movements: A Summary," *Inquiry* 16 (Oslo, 1973), pp. 95–100.

2. Theodore Roszak, *Where the Wasteland Ends* (New York: Anchor, 1972).

3. Warwick Fox, "Deep Ecology: A New Philosophy of Our Time?" *The Ecologist,* v. 14, 5–6, 1984, pp. 194–200. Arnie Naess replies, "Intuition, Intrinsic Value and Deep Ecology," *The Ecologist,* v. 14, 5–6, 1984, pp. 201–204.

4. Tom Regan, *The Case for Animal Rights* (New York: Random House, 1983). For excellent critiques of the animal rights movement, see John Rodman, "The Liberation of Nature?" *Inquiry* 20 (Oslo, 1977). J. Baird Callicott, "Animal Liberation," *Environmental Ethics* 2, 4, (1980); see also John Rodman, "Four Forms of Ecological Consciousness Reconsidered" in T. Attig and D. Scherer, eds., *Ethics and the Environment* (Englewood Cliffs, N.J.: Prentice-Hall, 1983).

5. Tom Regan, "The Nature and Possibility of an Environmental Ethic," *Environmental Ethics* 3 (1981), pp. 19-34.

6. Stephen Bodian, "Simple in Means, Rich in Ends: A Conversation with Arne Naess," *Ten Directions* (California: Institute for Transcultural Studies, Zen Center of Los Angeles, Summer/Fall 1982).

The Ecological Self
Postmodern Ground for Right Action

JOANNA MACY

IN A RECENT LECTURE ON A COLLEGE CAMPUS, I gave examples of actions being undertaken in defense of life on Earth—actions in which people risk their comfort and even their lives to protect other species. The examples included the Chipko, or "tree-hugging," movement among North Indian villagers to fight the lumbering of their remaining woodlands, and the Greenpeace organization's intervention on the open seas to protect marine mammals from slaughter. A student, Michael, wrote me afterwards:

> I think of the tree-huggers hugging my trunk, blocking the chainsaws with their bodies, I feel their fingers digging into my bark to stop the steel and let me breathe.
>
> I hear the bodhisattvas[1] in their rubber boats as they put themselves between the harpoons and me, so I can escape to the depths of the sea. . . .
>
> I give thanks for your life and mine . . . and for life itself. I give thanks for realizing that I, too, have the powers of the treehuggers and the bodhisattvas.

What strikes me in his words is the shift in identification. Michael is able to extend his sense of self to encompass the self of tree, of whale. Tree and whale are no longer removed, separate, disposable objects pertaining to a world "out there" but intrinsic parts of his own vitality. Through the power of his caring, his experience of self is expanded far beyond what Alan Watts termed the "skin-encapsulated ego."

I quote Michael's words not because they are unusual. On the contrary, they express a desire and a capacity arising in many people today as, out of deep concern over what is happening to our world, they begin to speak and act on its behalf.

Among those who are moving beyond conventional notions of self and self-interest, shedding them like an old skin or confining shell, is John Seed, director of the Rainforest Information Center in Australia. I asked him one day how he managed to overcome despair and sustain the struggle against the giant lumber interests. He said, "I try to remember that it's not me, John Seed, trying to protect the rainforest. Rather, I am part of the rainforest protecting myself, I am that part of the rainforest recently emerged into human thinking."

This ecological sense of selfhood combines the mystical and the pragmatic. Transcending separateness and fragmentation, in a shift that Seed calls a "spiritual change," it generates an experience of profound interconnectedness with all life. This has in the past been largely relegated to the domain of mystics and poets. Now it is, at the same time, a motivation to action. The shift in identity serves as ground and resource for effective engagement with the forces and pathologies that imperil planetary survival.

A variety of factors converge in our time to promote such a shift in the sense of self and self-interest. Among the most significant are 1) the psychological and spiritual pressures exerted by current dangers of mass annihilation, 2) the emergence from science of the systems view of the world, and 3) a renaissance of nondualistic forms of spirituality.

This essay explores the role of these three factors—planetary peril, systems thinking, and nondualistic religion, specifically Buddhist teachings and practice—in promoting this shift. It is written from a conviction that a larger, ecological sense of self will characterize the postmodern world, and that without it there simply may *be* no postmodern world.

I. PERSONAL RESPONSE TO PLANETARY CRISIS

The shift toward a wider, ecological sense of self is in large part a function of the dangers that threaten

Macy, Joanna, "The Ecological Self: Postmodern Ground for Right Action," in Mary Heather MacKinnon and Moni McIntyre, Eds., *Readings in Ecology and Feminist Theology,* 1995, pp. 259–269. Reprinted by permission of Sheed and Ward, an Apostolate of the Priests of the Sacred Heart, 7373 S. Lovers Lane Rd., Franklin, WI 53132.

to overwhelm us. Given accelerating environmental destruction and massive deployment of nuclear weapons, people today are aware that they live in a world that can end. For example, public opinion polls indicate that over half the population expects nuclear weapons to be used, and two thirds believe that once they are used, the resultant nuclear war cannot be limited, won, or survived.[2] The loss of certainty that there will be a future is, I believe, the pivotal psychological reality of our time.

Over the past ten years my colleagues and I have worked with tens of thousands of people in North America, Europe, Asia, and Australia, helping them confront and explore what they know and feel about what is happening to their world. The purpose of this work, known as Despair and Empowerment Work, is to overcome the numbing and powerlessness that result from suppression of painful responses to massively painful realities.[3]

As their grief and fear for the world is allowed to be expressed without apology or argument and validated as a wholesome, life-preserving response, people break through their avoidance mechanisms, break through their sense of futility and isolation. And generally what they break through *into* is a larger sense of identity. It is as if the pressure of their acknowledged awareness of the suffering of our world stretches, or collapses, the culturally defined boundaries of the self.

It becomes clear, for example, that the grief and fear experienced for our world and our common future are categorically different from similar sentiments relating to one's personal welfare. This pain cannot be equated with dread of one's own individual demise. Its source lies less in concerns for personal survival than in apprehensions of collective suffering—of what looms for human life and other species and unborn generations to come. Its nature is akin to the original meaning of compassion—"suffering with." It is the distress we feel on behalf of the larger whole of which we are a part. And when it is so defined, it serves as trigger or gateway to a more encompassing sense of identity, inseparable from the web of life in which we are as intricately interconnected as cells in a larger body.

This shift is an appropriate, adaptive response. For the crisis that threatens our planet, be it seen in its military, ecological, or social aspects, derives from a dysfunctional and pathogenic notion of the self. It is a mistake about our place in the order of things. It is the delusion that the self is so separate and fragile that we must delineate and defend its boundaries, that it is so small and needy that we must endlessly acquire and endlessly consume, that it is so aloof that we can—as individuals, corporations, nation-states or as a species—be immune to what we do to other beings.

Such a view of the human condition is not new, nor is the felt imperative to extend self-interest to embrace the whole in any way novel to our history as a species. It has been enjoined by many a teacher and saint. What is notable in our present situation, and in the Despair and Empowerment Work we have done, is that the extension of identity can come directly, not through exhortations to nobility or altruism, but through the owning of pain. That is why the shift in the sense of self is credible to those experiencing it. As poet Theodore Roethke said, "I believe my pain."

Despair and Empowerment Work draws on both General Systems Theory and Buddhist teachings and practice. Both of these approaches inform our methods and offer explanatory principles in the move beyond ego-based identifications. Let us look at them in turn to see how they serve the shift to the ecological self.

II. CYBERNETICS OF THE SELF

The findings of twentieth-century science undermine the notion of a separate self, distinct from the world it observes and acts upon. As Einstein showed, the self's perceptions are shaped by its changing position in relation to other phenomena. And these phenomena are affected not only by location but, as Heisenberg demonstrated, by the very act of observation. Now contemporary systems science and systems cybernetics go yet further in challenging old assumptions about a distinct, separate, continuous self, showing that there is no logical or scientific basis for construing one part of the experienced world as "me" and the rest as "other."

As open, self-organizing systems, our very breathing, acting, and thinking arise in interaction with our shared world through the currents of matter, energy, and information that flow through us. In the web of relationships that sustain these activities, there are no clear lines demarcating a separate, continuous self. As postmodern systems theorists aver, there is no categorical "I" set over against a categorical "you" or "it."

Systems philosopher Ervin Laszlo argues,

> We must do away with the subject-object distinction in analyzing experience. This does not mean that we reject the concepts of organism and environment, as handed down to us by natural science. It only means that we conceive of experience as linking organism and environment in a continuous chain of events, from which we cannot, without arbitrariness, abstract an entity called organism and another called environment.[4]

The abstraction of a separate "I" is what Gregory Bateson calls the "epistemological fallacy of Occidental civilization." He asserts that the larger system of which we are a part defies any definitive localization of the self. That which decides and does can no longer be neatly identified with the isolated subjectivity of the individual or located within the confines of his or her skin. "The total self-corrective unit which processes information, or, as I say, 'thinks' and 'acts' and 'decides,' is a *system* whose boundaries do not at all coincide with the boundaries either of the body or of what is popularly called the 'self' or 'consciousness'."[5]

"The self as ordinarily understood," Bateson goes on to say,

> is only a small part of a much larger trial-and-error system which does the thinking, acting and deciding. This system includes all the informational pathways which are relevant at any given moment to any given decision. The 'self' is a false reification of an improperly delimited part of this much larger field of interlocking processes.[6]

The false reification of the self is basic to the planetary ecological crisis in which we now find ourselves. We have imagined that the "unit of survival," as Bateson puts it, is the separate individual or the separate species. In reality, as throughout the history of evolution, it is the individual *plus* environment, the species *plus* environment, for they are essentially symbiotic. Bateson continues:

> When you narrow down your epistemology and act on the premise "What interests me is me, or my organization, or my species," you chop off consideration of other loops of the loop structure. You decide you want to get rid of the by-products of human life and that Lake Erie will be a good place to put them. You forget that the eco-mental system called Lake Erie is a part of your wider eco-mental system—and that if Lake Erie is driven insane, its insanity is incorporated in the larger system of your thought and experience.[7]

Although we consist of and are sustained by the currents of information, matter, and energy that flow through us, we are accustomed to identifying ourselves with only that small arc of the flow-through that is lit, like the narrow beam of a flashlight, by our individual perceptions. But we do not *have* to so limit our self-perceptions. It is as logical, Bateson contends, to conceive of mind as the entire "pattern that connects." It is as plausible to align our identity with that larger pattern and conceive of ourselves as interexistent with all beings, as it is to break off one segment of the process and build our borders there.

Systems Theory helps us see that the larger identification of which we speak does not involve an eclipse of the distinctiveness of one's individual experience. The "pattern that connects" is not an ocean of Brahman where separate drops merge and our diversities dissolve. Natural and cognitive systems self-organize and interact to create larger wholes precisely through their heterogeneity. By the same token, through the dance of deviation-amplifying feedback loops, the respective particularities of the interactive systems can increase. Integration and differentiation go hand in hand. Uniformity, by contrast, is entropic, the kiss of death.

The systems view of the world, unfortunately, has not characterized or informed the uses our society has made of systems science. The advances permitted by its perceptions of pattern and its models of circuitry have been mainly employed to further values and goals inherited from a mechanistic, reductionistic interpretation of reality. Systems thinker Milady Cardamone hypothesizes that it is the feminine-like quality of the systems approach that has kept our society from fully grasping this wholistic style of perceiving the universe.[8]

Molecular biologist and Nobel Prize winner Barbara McClintock reveals, however, how practical and revolutionary the results can be when science is done from the perspective of the ecological self. Her discovery of the interactive nature of the cell, as opposed to the previously accepted master control theory, came out of her ability to see the cell and feel herself as part of the system. "I actually felt as if I were down there and these [internal parts of the chromosomes] were my friends."[9]

THE BOUNDLESS HEART OF THE BODHISATTVA

In the resurgence of nondualistic spiritualities in our postmodern world, Buddhism in its historic coming to the West is distinctive in the clarity and sophistication it offers in understanding the dynamics of the self. In much the same way as General Systems Theory does, its ontology and epistemology undermine any categorical distinctions definitive of a self-existent identity. And it goes further than systems cybernetics, both in revealing the pathogenic character of any reifications of the self and in offering methods for transcending them,

Dependent co-arising (*pratitya samutpada*), the core teaching of the Buddha on the nature of causality, presents a phenomenal reality so dynamic and interrelated that categorical subject-object distinctions dissolve. This is driven home in the doctrine of *anatman* or "no-self," where one's sense of identity is understood as an ephemeral product of perceptual transactions, and where the experiencer is inseparable from his or her experience. The notion of an abiding individual self—whether saintly or sinful, whether it is to be protected, promoted or punished—is seen as the foundational delusion of human life. It is the motive force behind our attachments and aversions, and these in turn exacerbate it. As portrayed symbolically in the center of the Buddhist Wheel of Life, where pig, cock, and snake pursue each other endlessly, these three—greed, hatred, and the delusion of ego—sustain and aggravate each other in a continuous vicious circle, or positive feedback loop.

We are not doomed to a perpetual rat-race; the vicious circle can be broken, its energies liberated to more satisfying uses by the threefold interplay of wisdom, meditative practice, and moral action. Wisdom (*prajna*) arises, reflected and generated by the teachings about self and reality. Practice (*dhyana*) liberates through precise attention to the elements and flow of one's existential experience—an experience which reveals no separate experience, no permanent self. And moral behavior (*sila*), according to precepts of nonviolence, truthfulness, and generosity, helps free one from the dictates of greed, aversion, and other reactions which reinforce the delusion of separate selfhood.

Far from the nihilism and escapism often attributed to Buddhism, the path it offers can bring the world into sharper focus and liberate one into lively, effective action. What emerges, when free from the prison cell of the separate, competitive ego, is a vision of radical and sustaining interdependence. In Hua Yen Buddhism it is imaged as the Jeweled Net of Indra: a cosmic canopy where each of us—each jewel at each node of the net—reflects all the others and reflects the others reflecting hack [*sic*]. As in the holographic view in contemporary science, each part *contains* the whole.

Each one of us who perceives that, or is capable of perceiving it, is a *bodhisattva*—an "awakening being"—the hero model of the Buddhist tradition. We are all *bodhisattvas,* able to recognize and act upon our profound interexistence with all beings. That true nature is already evident in our pain for the world, which is a function of the *mahakaruna,* great compassion. And it flowers through the *bodhisattva's* "boundless heart" in active identification with all beings.

Christina Feldman, like many other women Buddhist teachers today, points out that this bodhisattva heart is absolutely central to spiritual practice. It is more transformative of ego and more generative of connection than the desire to be perfect, pure, or aloof from suffering. It is already within us, like a larger self awaiting discovery.

> We find ourselves forsaking the pursuit of personal perfection and also the denial of imperfection. To become someone different, to pursue a model of personal perfection is no longer the goal. . . . Learning to listen inwardly, we learn to listen to our world and to each other. We hear the pain of the alienated, the sick, the lonely, the angry, and we rejoice in the happiness, the fulfillment, the peace of others. We are touched deeply by the pain of our planet, equally touched by the perfection of a bud unfolding. . . . We learn to re-

spect the heart for its power to connect us on a fundamental level with each other, with nature and with all life.[10]

The experience of interconnection with all life can sustain our social change work far better than righteous partisanship; that is the teaching of Vietnamese Zen monk Thich Nhat Hanh. In Vietnam during the 1960s, he founded Youth for Social Service, whose members rescued and aided homeless, hungry, and wounded villagers on both sides of the war. From their ranks he created a nonmonastic Order called Tiep Hien, now gradually spreading in the West under the name Interbeing. . . .

IV. BEYOND ALTRUISM

What Bateson called "the pattern that connects" and Buddhists image as the Jeweled Net of Indra can be construed in lay, secular terms as our deep ecology. "Deep ecology" is a term coined by Norwegian philosopher Arne Naess to connote a basic shift in ways of seeing and valuing. It represents an apprehension of reality that he contrasts with "shallow environmentalism"—the band-aid approach applying technological fixes for short-term human goals.

The perspective of deep ecology helps us to recognize our embeddedness in nature, overcoming our alienation from the rest of creation and regaining an attitude of reverence for all life forms. It can change the way that the self is experienced through a spontaneous process of self-realization, where the self-to-be-realized extends further and further beyond the separate ego and includes more and more of the phenomenal world. In this process, notions like altruism and moral duty are left behind. Naess explains:

> Altruism implies that ego sacrifices its interests in favor of the other, the *alter*. . . . The motivation is primarily that of duty. . . . What humankind is capable of loving from mere duty or more generally from moral exhortation is unfortunately very limited. . . . Unhappily the extensive moralizing within the environmental movement has given the public the false impression that we primarily ask them to sacrifice, to show more responsibility, more concern, and better morals. . . . The requisite care flows naturally if the self is widened and deepened so that protection of free nature is felt and conceived of as protection of ourselves.[11]

Please note: Virtue is not required for the emergence of the ecological self! This shift in identification is essential to our survival at this point in our history precisely because it can serve in lieu of ethics and morality. Moralizing is ineffective; sermons seldom hinder us from pursuing our self-interest as we construe it. Hence the need to be more enlightened about what our real self-interest is. It would not occur to me, for example, to exhort you to refrain from sawing off your leg. That would not occur to me or to you, because your leg is part of you. Well, so are the trees in the Amazon Basin; they are our external lungs. We are just beginning to wake up to that, gradually discovering that the world *is* our body.

Economist Hazel Henderson sees our survival dependent on a shift in consciousness from "phenotype" to "genotype." The former, she says, springs from fear of the death of the ego and the consequent conflict between the perceived individual will and the requirements of society or biosphere.

> We may be emerging from the "age of phenotype," of separated ego awareness, which has now become amplified into untenable forms of dualism. . . . The emerging view is rebalancing toward concern for the genotype, protection of species and gene pools and for the mutagenic dangers of nuclear radiation, chemical wastes and the new intergenerational risks being transferred to our progeny, about which economists say little.[12]

V. GRACE AND POWER

The ecological self, like any notion of selfhood, is a metaphoric construct, and a dynamic one. It involves choice. Choices can be made to identify at different moments with different dimensions or aspects of our systemically interconnected existence—be they hunted whales or homeless humans or the planet itself. In so doing, this extended self brings into play wider resources—resources, say, of courage, wisdom, endurance—like a nerve cell opening to the charge of fellow neurons in the neural net. For example, in his work on behalf of the rainforest, John Seed felt empowered *by* the rainforest.

There is the experience then of being acted

"through" and sustained "by" something greater than oneself. It is close to the religious concept of grace, but, as distinct from the traditional Western understanding of grace, it does not require belief in God or supernatural agency. One simply finds oneself empowered to act on behalf of other beings—or on behalf of the larger whole—and the empowerment itself seems to come "through" that or those for whose sake one acts.

This phenomenon, when approached from the perspective of Systems Theory, is understandable in terms of synergy. It springs from the self-organizing nature of life. It stems from the fact that living systems evolve in complexity and intelligence through their interactions. These interactions, which can be mental or physical, and which can operate at a distance through transmission of information, require openness and sensitivity on the part of the system in order to process the flow-through of energy and information. The interactions bring into play new responses and new possibilities. This interdependent release of fresh potential is called "synergy." And it is like grace, because it brings an increase of power beyond one's own capacity as a separate entity.

As we awaken, then, to our larger, ecological self, we find new powers. We find possibilities of vast efficacy, undreamed of in our squirrel cage of separate ego. Because these potentialities are interactive in nature, they are the preserve and property of no one, and they manifest only to the extent that we recognize and act upon our interexistence, our deep ecology.

As David Griffin wrote of the emerging postmodern world in his introduction to an earlier volume, "the modern desire to master and possess is replaced in postmodern spirituality with a joy in communion."[13] That joy in communion is, I believe, a homecoming to our natural interexistence with all life forms, home to our deep ecology, home to the world as Dharmabody of the Buddha. And it brings with it the capacity to act with courage and resilience.

NOTES

1. A term in Buddhism for a compassionate being.

2. See *Voter Options on Nuclear Arms Policy* (Public Agenda Foundation, 1984).

3. See my *Despairwork* (Philadelphia: New Society Publishers, 1982) and *Despair and Personal Power in the Nuclear Age* (Philadelphia: New Society Publishers, 1983, 1988).

4. Ervin Laszlo, *Introduction to Systems Philosophy* (New York: Harper & Row Torchbook, 1973), 21.

5. Gregory Bateson, *Steps to an Ecology of Mind* (New York: Ballantine Books, 1972), 319.

6. *Ibid.*, 331.

7. *Ibid.*, 484.

8. Milady Cardamone, "The Feminine Aspect of the Systems Approach," *Proceedings of the Annual Meeting of the Society of General Systems Research* (Louisville, Ky.: Society for General Systems Research, 1987), F-44.

9. Evelyn Fox Keller, "Women, Science and Popular Mythology," in Joan Rothschild, ed., *Machina Ex Dea* (London: Pergamon Press, 1983), 143.

10. Christina Feldman, "Nurturing Compassion," in Fred Eppsteiner, ed., *The Path of Compassion* (Berkeley, Calif.: Parallax Press, 1988), 31.

11. Fred Eppsteiner, ed., *The Path of Compassion* (Berkeley, Calif.: Parallax Press, 1988), 31.

12. From an unpublished brochure by John Seed. See also Arne Naess, "Identification as a Source of Deep Ecological Attitudes," and "Self Realization: An Ecological Approach to Being in the World," in John Seed, Joanna Macy, Arne Naess, and Pat Fleming, ed., *Thinking Like A Mountain: Toward A Council of All Beings* (Philadelphia: New Society Publishers, 1988).

13. See Hazel Henderson, "Beyond the Information Age," *Creation*, March/April 1988: 34–35.

14. "Introduction: Postmodern Spirituality and Society," David Ray Griffin, ed., *Spirituality and Society: Postmodern Visions* (Albany: State University of New York Press, 1988), 1–31, esp. 15.

Earth First!
From Primal Spirituality to Ecological Resistance

BRON TAYLOR

FLIGHT IN THE DESERT

THE DARKNESS OF THE HIGH-DESERT NIGHT retreated into the shadows as the FBI's flares launched skyward.[1] The light signaled thirty heavily armed agents to descend on the three ecological saboteurs—and one FBI infiltrator—huddled below the giant electrical towers. Two of the saboteurs were quickly seized. The third disappeared into the shadows. Running with the wild abandon of all prey, pausing to catch her breath, she began to feel herself mystically descend into Earth, sensing it merging with her, surrounding her, protecting her. She had become invisible—ghost-like. When the helicopters passed overhead, she hugged a tree or pressed herself into the ground, invisible. She had become like the ringtail cat, her totem animal. "The ringtail consciousness was in me that night," she recalls. "I ran through cactus gardens without getting stuck. I could feel the ringtail, like it was a part of me, encircling me. I felt its presence." Secure in this sacred mind-space they could never find her. Several hours later, she slipped past her pursuers guarding a road on the edge of town, still imperceptible. Back at work the next day, back in the mundane world, Peg Millett was seized and arrested—but she was not surprised—she had become separated from the Earth's protective intention by the impermeable concrete of the building's foundation.

Mark Davis had been quickly apprehended that night. He was soon charged with several different acts of "ecotage" (a term meaning sabotage defending ecosystems, also known as "monkeywrenching" in movement parlance) including an effort designed to thwart the expansion of a ski resort in Arizona's San Francisco Mountains—an area considered sacred by the Hopi and Navajo tribes. In a letter from a federal penitentiary, he explained this particular action:

> Certainly there was some outrage involved at the blatant disregard of agreements with the Hopi and Navajo tribes, anger at the destruction of hundreds of acres of irreplaceable old growth forest for the new ski runs, and indignation that the Forest Service was subsidizing a private company with public dollars. But the bottom line is that those mountains are sacred, and that what has occurred there, despite our feeble efforts, is a terrible spiritual mistake.

When arrested in May 1989 in the Arizona desert, both Millett and Davis were involved with Earth First!, the self-described "radical environmental" movement. Also snared in the FBI's net were Earth First! co-founder Dave Foreman, the lead author of *Ecodefense: A Field Guide to Monkeywrenching* (Tucson, Arizona: Ned Ludd, 1987), which described how to destroy logging equipment and otherwise thwart those who would destroy "sacred wilderness ecosystems." The arrest, trial, and eventual conviction of these activists—combined with the 1990 bombing that permanently disabled and nearly killed ancient forest activist Judi Bari—helped catapult Earth First! into the public eye, especially in the western United States. But the sensational headlines that followed rarely mentioned the spiritual perceptions underpinning these tactics, or for that matter, the competing religious perceptions animating their most ardent opponents.

Many Earth First!ers, sympathizers and their opponents, however, recognize the importance of spiritual premises in contemporary environmental conflicts. One extreme example can be found in a letter purportedly from Judi Bari's bomber, who, quoting Genesis 1:26 (the "dominion" creation story), wrote that "this possessed [pagan] demon Judy Bari . . . [told] the multitude that trees were not God's gift to man but that trees were themselves

Taylor, Bron, "Earth First!: From Primal Spirituality to Ecological Resistance," in Roger S. Gottlieb, Ed., *This Sacred Earth,* New York: Routledge, 1996, pp. 545–557. Reprinted by permission of the author.

gods and it was a sin to cut them. [So] I felt the Power of the Lord stir within my heart and I knew I had been Chosen to strike down this demon." The letter concludes warning other tree worshipers that they will suffer the same fate, for "I AM THE LORD'S AVENGER." The letter's authenticity is in doubt. Some view it as an authentic, hard-to-fabricate synthesis of Christian fundamentalism and mental illness. Some Earth First!ers believe the letter is an FBI hoax—patterned after similar letters authorities received after abortion clinic bombings—designed to cast suspicion away from law enforcement agencies involved in the assassination attempt. But whether authentic or a ploy designed to divert attention from the actual perpetrator(s), this remarkable letter illustrates dramatically how competing religious values can underlie environmental controversies. Indeed, expressions of distaste and intolerance for the "pagan" spirituality of the radical environmentalists are increasingly expressed by anti-environmentalists and even by some conservationists.[2] Should we fear and suppress, tolerate, or join the radical environmentalists in their spirituality and politics? A fair evaluation depends on accurate description of their spiritual politics.

EARTH FIRST! RELIGION: A TRADITION EMERGING IN MYTH, SYMBOL AND RITE

Before proceeding, it is helpful to iterate a few preliminary points about religion, especially because many Earth First! militants reject organized religion, some do not view themselves as "religious," and others are uncomfortable with the explicitly religious rituals and songs that have become popular in the movement. With such discomfort in mind, why should we consider Earth First! a religious movement? Because it manifests all the elements that constitute an emerging religious movement.

All religious traditions, whether newer or long established, involve myth, symbol, and ritual. The myths delineate how the world came to be (a cosmogony), what it is like (a cosmology), what people are capable or incapable of achieving (a moral anthropology), and what the future holds (an eschatology). Religious ethics are directly informed by these very mythic elements. Yet religious traditions are plural, they are neither monolithic nor static, they are characterized by ongoing controversies over who owns, interprets and performs the myths, rituals, and rites. Nevertheless, despite great internal plurality, certain core beliefs, behaviors, and values unify and make it possible to speak of a diverse religious movement as a *tradition*. Close observation of Earth First! and of the wider deep ecology movement shows an emerging corpus of myth, symbol, and rite that reveals the emergence of a dynamic, new religious movement.

The theory of evolution provides a primary cosmogony that promotes the *ecocentric ethics* of the movement—namely the notion that all species ought to be able to fulfill their evolutionary destinies, and that ecosystem types should be allowed to flourish. This idea, that all ecosystems and species are intrinsically (or inherently) valuable, apart from their usefulness to human beings, is also the central idea of deep ecology. As Earth First! philosopher Christopher Manes notes in *Green Rage,* if all species evolved through the same process, and none were specially created for any particular purpose, the metaphysical underpinnings of anthropocentrism are displaced, along with the idea that human beings reside at the top of a "Great Chain of Being," ruling over all on Earth. "Taken seriously," he concludes, "evolution means that there is no basis for seeing humans as more advanced [or valuable] than any other species. Homo sapiens is not the goal of evolution, for as near as we can tell evolution has no telos—it simply unfolds, life-form after life-form . . ." The ethical significance of this cosmogony is that since evolution gives life in all its complexity, the evolutionary process itself is of highest value. Consequently, the central moral priority of Earth First! is to protect and restore wilderness because undisturbed wilderness provides the necessary genetic stock for the very continuance of evolution.

This still does not answer the question: Why should we care about evolution, or wild places, in the first place? Manes' argument, where an evolutionary cosmogony displaces human beings as the most valuable creatures, does not explain where *value* actually resides. This is why so much spirituality gets pulled into the Earth First! movement—some form of spirituality is logically needed to provide a basis for valuing the evolutionary process and the resulting life forms—evolutionary theory, as a descriptive cosmogony, cannot provide a reason for valuing the evolutionary process. Manes himself roots Deep Ecology and Earth First! in "the profound spiritual attachment people have to nature." Earth First!ers often speak of the need to "resacralize" our perceptions of nature. Interestingly, Earth First!ers believe that all life is sacred and interconnected, whether or not they consider themselves religious. Even those drawn to an ecocentric ethic based largely on an evolutionary cosmogony eventually rely on metaphors of the sacred to explain their feelings.[3]

Some of the diverse tributaries of the Earth First! movement are *explicitly* religious, tracing their ecocentric sentiments to such diverse religions as Taoism, Buddhism, Hinduism, Christian nature mysticism, witchcraft, and pagan earth-worship. Few Earth First!ers, however, become radical environmentalists due to socialization in or conversion to these traditions. The ecological consciousness uniting Earth First!ers usually begins early in life—in experiences I cannot here typify—long before exposure to these religious traditions. It is usually as young adults or later that many of the activists discover religious traditions sharing affinity with their religious sentiments. Most Earth First!ers are first "generic" nature mystics. Although they appreciate nature-grounded spiritual traditions—few identify exclusively with any particular religious tradition.

With this qualification in mind, we can explore the influences of various nature-sympathetic religious traditions upon the emerging, plural religion of Earth First!. Probably least important is Christian nature mysticism. Two radical environmentalist Christians told me that they no longer directly participate with Earth First! because its members refuse to unequivocally renounce tactics which involve risks to human beings, and because of the anti-theistic attitudes of many members. But I have also found several Earth First!ers who consider themselves Christians. Nevertheless, given the general hostility within Earth First! to Christianity, only once at an Earth First! gathering have I heard anyone argue that Christianity is compatible with deep ecology.

A few Earth First!ers consider themselves Hindu. Yet a much more significant affinity is found in neopaganism, including wicca or witchcraft. For example, one pagan Earth First!er, speaking at the 1991 Earth First! rendezvous in Vermont, asserted that modern people can no longer experience the world as enchanted because they have paved over wilderness, muting its sacred voices. He proclaimed that Earth First!ers are among the few who can still perceive the sacredness of the Earth, adding that "Gnomes and elves, fauns and faeries, goblins and ogres, trolls and bogies . . . [today must infiltrate our world to] effect change from the inside . . . [These nature-spirits are] running around in human bodies, . . . working in co-ops, . . . spiking trees and blowing up tractors, . . . starting revolutions, . . . [and] making up religions."

Until the early 1990s, the most important spiritual home for Earth First! activists seemed to be in Native American Spirituality, and some activists were appropriating aspects of such spirituality in their own ritual lives, and during wilderness gatherings. By the mid 1990s, however, as a result of increasing alliances between Native American activists and Earth First!ers in defense of areas considered sacred by both groups, the overt expression of such spirituality declined because the appropriation of native American Indian spiritual practices had become controversial.[4]

I have previously referred to the religious perceptions shared by most Earth First!ers as *primal spirituality* and to the movement at large as *pagan environmentalism*.[5] Such labels express the pantheistic and animistic experiences (including shamanistic beliefs and experiences of interspecies communication)[6] that many of these activists share, as well as their common belief that we should emulate the indigenous lifeways of most primal peoples, not just those in North America. Many of these activists call themselves pagans, and believe they are reconstructing nature spiritualities that have been violently suppressed by the world's monotheistic traditions. Others among them express affinity with the holistic religions originating in the Far East, which tend to view the world as metaphysically interconnected and sacred. Generally speaking, these activists consider the natural world to be sacred, especially where it remains wild and undefiled. Through their activism, ritualizing, and efforts at ecological restoration, they venerate wild nature and attempt to re-consecrate it wherever it has been desecrated.

Earth First!ers often call themselves tribalists, and many deep ecologists believe that primal tribes can provide a basis for religion, philosophy, and nature conservation that is applicable to our society. Moreover, Earth First!ers generally agree on the importance of ritual for any tribal "warrior society." At meetings held in or near wilderness, they sometimes engage in ritual war or "tribal unity" dances, sometimes howling like wolves. Indeed, wolves, grizzly bears, and other animals function as totems, symbolizing a mystical kinship between the tribe and other creature-peoples.

Native Americans often conceive of non-human species as kindred "peoples" and through "rituals of inclusion" extend the community of moral concern beyond human beings. Some Earth First!ers have developed their own rituals of *inclusion,* called "Council of All Beings" workshops, which provide a ritual means to connect people spiritually to other creatures and the entire planet. Diverse exercises are employed to help people experience their "ecological self"—namely—the self as embedded within the entire web of life, and therefore not superior to other life forms. During these workshops, rituals are performed where people allow themselves to be imaginatively possessed by the spirits of non-human entities—animals, rocks, soils and rivers, for example—and verbalize their hurt at having been so poorly treated by human beings. As personifications of these non-human forms, participants cry out for fair treatment and harmonious relations among all ecosystem citizens. In the final phase of the Council, the humans seek personal transformation and empowerment, through the gifts of special powers from the non-human entities present in their midst. Ecstatic ritual dance, celebrating inter-species and even inter-planetary oneness, may continue through the night. Such rituals enhance the sense that all is interconnected and sacred. The Council itself has become something of a rite of passage within the movement, or at least a vehicle fostering solidarity among movement participants. Sooner or later most Earth First!ers take part.

THINKING LIKE MOUNTAINS

One of the central myths of the emerging Earth First! tradition has been borrowed from Aldo Leopold's 1949 "Thinking Like a Mountain" essay, in *A Sand County Almanac.* He begins with the Pantheistic suggesting that perhaps mountains have knowledge superior to ours. Then he tells of an experience he once had of approaching an old wolf he had shot, just "in time to watch a fierce green fire dying in her eyes. I realized then," Leopold wrote, "and have known ever since, that there was something new to me in those eyes—something known only to her and to the mountain. I was young then . . . I thought that because fewer wolves meant more deer, that no wolves would mean hunters' paradise. But after seeing the green fire die, I sensed that neither the wolf nor the mountain agreed with such a view."

Among Earth First!ers, this story has evolved into a mythic moral fable in which the wolf communicates with human beings, stressing inter-species kinship. (Of course, animal-human communication is a common theme in primal religious myth, and animal-human and human-animal transmogrification and communion are often involved in Shamanism. Many Earth First!ers themselves report shamanistic experiences.) The wolf's "green fire" has become a symbol of life in the wild, incorporated into the ritual of the tradition. Soon after its founding, several Earth First! activists went on "green fire" road shows that were essentially biocentric revival meetings. "Dakota" Sid Clifford, a balladeer in these road shows, referred to them as "ecovangelism." At Earth First! wilderness gatherings, Jesse "Lone Wolf" Hardin, to the sound of pulsating drums and guitars, recounts Leopold's now mythic story, urging participants to dig down deep, discover the wild green fire within them, and use this power to fight the destroyers of life on this planet. In the road shows and wilderness gatherings, the personified wolf of the green fire narrative calls humans to repent from their destructive ways and defend the Earth.

Earth First!ers symbolically express their identification with other creatures through a variety of songs, such as Dana Lyon's sensual affirmation in "I am an animal" (sung to primal chant-rhythms). Sometimes at their wilderness gatherings, innovative and elaborate theatrical performances recount a state of primal innocence when people lived as foragers in harmony with nature, falling from this state with the advent of agriculture and anthropocentric, patriarchal attitudes, eventually experiencing the current period of industrial genocide. The pageant generally ends with a guerilla army of monkeywrench waving children dismantling the industrial machine and resurrecting the remnant animals, including humans, to a new life of natural harmony and ecstasy. At this point, virtually the entire assembly joins in a night of ecstatic dancing, characterized by, as described in the *Earth First!* journal, "pounding drums, naked neanderthals, and wild creatures." Commenting on the scattering of the tribe's warriors after one such gathering in, this article exclaimed, "the green fire is still running wild and free [as] we are once again scattered across the country." The centrality of primal spirituality in the movement can be discerned in such song and ritualized performance, as well as the notion that an authentic human nature is lived wildly and spontaneously in defense of Earth.

Ecotage, of course, is not merely acted out *symbolically* in ritual dance. Ecotage and civil disobedience are real-life ritual actions. Many Earth First!ers have come to recognize this. Dave Foreman, for example, although sometimes claiming to be an atheist, speaks nevertheless of ecotage as ritual worship: monkeywrenching is "a form of worship toward the earth. It's really a very spiritual thing to go out and do." Religious rituals function to transform ordinary time into sacred time, even to alter consciousness itself. Earth First! rituals are no different. A volume edited by Australian Earth First!er John Seed and several others, *Thinking Like a Mountain* (Philadelphia: New Society, 1988), describes how to orchestrate a Council of All Beings. In it, Graham Innes describes "a slow dawning of awareness of a hitherto unknown connection—Earth bonding"—that occurred when he was buried up to his neck while blockading a logging road. The Earth's "pulse became mine," he exclaimed, "and the vessel, my body, became the vehicle for her expression. . . . it was as though nature had overtaken my consciousness to speak on her behalf . . ." Such communion has been reported by more than one Earth First! activist. (For example, several activists, when sitting in trees to prevent logging, have experienced communication with them. One young woman told me that, previous to this experience, she had been a vegetarian. But after sensing that this tree had its own consciousness, she knew that animals were not superior to plants.)

John Davis, an editor of the *Earth First!* journal during much of the 1980s, suggested that tribal rites of passage should be developed that require direct action: "Rites of passage were essential for the health of primal cultures . . . so why not reinstitute initiation rites and other rituals in the form of ecodefense actions? Adolescents could earn their adulthood by successful completion of ritual hunts, as in days of yore, but for a new kind of quarry—bulldozers and their ilk." This is not mere rhetoric. One activist invented a rite of passage to manhood for his son. It included monkeywrenching a bulldozer.

Ecofeminism provides another tributary to Earth First!'s nature-revering spirituality. Many of its ideas have been incorporated into Earth First! liturgy. Songs like *Burning Times* and *Manley Men* satirize macho-hubris and patriarchal domination of nature and women, decry the massacres of witches, and praise various pagan earth-Goddesses.

Ecofeminism and other forms of primal spirituality have a close affinity with yet another tributary to Earth First!—bioregionalism. Bioregionalism is a countercultural movement that envisions self-governing communities living harmoniously and simply within the boundaries of distinct ecosystems. It critiques growth-based industrial societies preferring locally self-sufficient and ecologically sustainable economies and decentralized political structures. Bioregionalists generally share Earth First!'s ecological consciousness regarding the intrinsic value and sacred interconnection of all life. The earth-spirituality of bioregionalists parallels the primal spirituality prominent among Earth First!ers. In some cases their Earth-spirituality is tied to the Gaia hypothesis, a theory which conceives of Earth as a living spirit, a self-regulating organism—named after Gaia, goddess of the Earth.

Before bioregionalism can flourish, however, many Earth First!ers believe that industrial society must first collapse under its own ecologically unsustainable weight. The theory that society is creating an ecological catastrophe containing the seeds of its own destruction introduces another key part of Earth First!'s mythic structure: its apocalyptic eschatology. Earth First! is radical largely due to this apocalyptic worldview: There will be a collapse of industrial society, because this society is ecologically unsustainable. After great suffering, if enough of the genetic stock of the planet survives, evolution will resume its natural course. If human beings also survive, they will have the opportunity to re-establish tribal lifeways compatible with the evolutionary future. The late Edward Abbey, whose novel *The Monkeywrench Gang* helped forge the movement, provides a typical example of Earth First! eschatology:

> Whether [industrial society is] called capitalism or communism makes little difference . . . [both] destroy nature and themselves . . . I predict that the military-industrial state will disappear from the surface of the Earth within fifty years. That belief is the basis of my inherent optimism, the source of my hope for the coming restoration of higher civilization: scattered human populations modest in number that live by fishing, hunting, food-gathering, small-scale farming and ranching, that assemble once a year in the ruins of abandoned cities for great festivals of moral, spiritual, artistic and intellectual renewal—a people for whom the wilderness is not a playground but their natural and native home.

So while bioregionalism focuses on developing models for the future, many Earth First! activists think bioregionalism is impossible without the prior catalyst of an industrial collapse. For this reason, Earth First!ers tend to have a different priority than most bioregionalists, prioritizing ecodefense for now, while awaiting this collapse. Many Earth First!ers believe it is impossible to live sustainably in an industrial society. Thus, Foreman criticizes the priorities of those bioregionalists who become "mired in . . . composting toilets, organic gardens, handcrafts, [and] recycling." Although, "these . . . are important," Foreman concludes, "bioregionalism is [or should be] more than *technique,* it is resacralization [of the Earth] and self-defense."

A good example of Earth First! eschatology and strategy can be seen in Foreman's thoughts about bioregionalism. Bioregionalists should work toward reinhabiting natural preserves.

> That is where the warrior society of Earth First! comes into the bioregional world. In reinhabiting a place, by dwelling in it, we become that place. We are *of* it. Our most fundamental duty is self defense. We are the wilderness defending itself . . . We develop the mangement plan for our region. We implement it. If the dying industrial empire tries to invade our sacred preserves, we resist its incursions. In most cases we cannot confront it head to head because it is temporarily much more powerful than we are. But by using our guerrilla wits, we can often use its own massed power against itself. Delay, resist, subvert using all the tools available to us: file appeals and lawsuits, encourage legislation . . . demonstrate, engage in non-violent civil disobedience, monkeywrench. Defend . . . Our self-defense is damage control until the machine plows into that brick wall and industrial civilization self-destructs as it must. Then the important work begins [namely, the building of an ecologically sustainable tribal society].

Stopping here would leave a misleading portrait. Certainly ecocentric and evolutionary premises, primal spirituality, Eastern religions, and a panoply of other spiritual tributaries contribute to Earth First!'s worldview. Certainly Earth First!ers often distrust reason, deriving their fundamental premises from intuitions and feelings: their love for wild, sacred places, and their corresponding rage at the ongoing destruction of such places. Certainly the tradition has evolved by appropriating and creating a fascinating variety of myths, symbols, and rituals. But reason is not abandoned: ecological sciences and political analysis is essential to Earth First! praxis. Many within the movement worry about excessive preoccupation with spirituality, with what they musingly call "woo woo." In 1989 John Davis, who was himself responsible for much discussion of spirituality and ritual, cautioned:

> Spiritual approaches to the planet seem to be of growing concern these days. The last issue of the Journal reflects this trend. We ran many articles on sacred sites, rituals, and such, but very few articles pertaining to specific wild lands. (Almost we replaced "No Compromise in Defense of Mother Earth" on the masthead with "All Aboard the Woo Woo Choo Choo.") This is not all to the good. Sacred sites, ritual, and matters of personal growth are important . . . However, Earth First! may lose effectiveness if it promotes these matters while neglecting the time-worn practices of presenting wilderness proposals . . . and other such largely left-brain activity.

THREE PILLARS OF EARTH FIRST!'S ETHICS

Thus far we have focused on the essentially religious perceptions that underlie the *moral claim* advanced by Earth First!, that all parts of the intrinsically valuable and sacred natural world be allowed to fulfill their evolutionary destinies. This premise constitutes the first pillar of Earth First!'s ethics. But Earth

First!'s ethics also depends on two additional claims, this time empirical ones, the first based on the ecological sciences, the second on political analysis.

Based on their reading of the ecological sciences, Earth First!ers add the *ecological claim* that we are in the midst of an unprecedented, anthropogenic extinction crisis, caused most importantly by human overpopulation, greed, and overconsumption; consequently, many ecosystems are presently collapsing. This is the second pillar of Earth First!'s ethics. Without this claim there is no basis for urgency—no reason for people with deep ecological moral sentiments to risk their freedom or disrupt their private lives. If accurate, such ecological analysis reveals a wide gap between fact and value, between what is and what ought to be: ecosystems that *ought* to be flourishing are being destroyed by human action. This introduces the realm of politics, the necessary arena for strategy over how to bridge gaps between what "is" the relationship between humans and nature, and what such relations "ought" to be like.

POLITICAL ANALYSIS AND THE CALL TO RESISTANCE

Deep ecological moral perceptions combined with ecological urgency do not by themselves enjoin specific political strategies or tactics. The argument for such tactics requires political analysis. The heart of Earth First!'s *political claim* is either: democracy in the U.S. is a sham, thoroughly thwarted by corporate economic power; or, even if not a complete sham, the democratic political system is so distorted by corporate power and regressive human attitudes that it cannot respond quickly enough to avert the escalating extinction catastrophe. Moreover, Earth First!ers would argue that, in light of nature's intrinsic value, governing processes that disregard the interests of non-humans are illegitimate.

Many Earth First!ers add to such critique the ecofeminist contention that androcentrism and patriarchy play important roles in ecological destruction. Many agree that human hierarchy is also a key factor, drawing on Social Ecology or other anarchistic critiques. Few Earth First!ers would suggest, however, that androcentrism or hierarchy alone fully explain environmental degradation. Nevertheless, virtually all of today's Earth First!ers believe patriarchy, hierarchy and anthropocentrism reflect related forms of domination that destroy the natural world. Most Earth First!ers agree that ultimately all such domination must be overcome if humans are to reharmonize their lifeways within nature.

Such political analysis provides the third essential pillar of Earth First!'s radicalism. Without it, in a formally democratic society, it is difficult to argue that illegal tactics are morally permissible. By asserting either that democratic procedures never existed, or that they have broken down, or that they camouflage domination, these activists justify their illegal tactics.

Taken together, these three claims suggest that the current situation—morally, ecologically, and politically—is so grave that tactics usually considered to be wrong are instead obligatory. Such analysis, in turn, leads to a continuum of tactics that parallel these three claims. Some Earth First!ers prioritize efforts to change anthropocentric human attitudes by developing ritual processes that are believed to reawaken nature-spirituality in humans. Others prioritize the use of scientific knowledge to argue for biological diversity in legal and policy making venues. Still others prioritize even more aggressive political action, using a variety of provocative tactics to directly resist destructive enterprises and to publicize ecological injustices. Still others, especially those most influenced by anarchist ideas, now theorize about "revolutionary ecology," thereby emphasizing their desire to overturn what they consider to be an inherently destructive, capitalist-industrial state.

SCHISMS AND FACTIONALISM

Differences about priorities and tactics, along with related ideological and cultural differences, have contributed to many tensions within the movement. In 1990, such tensions led a number of prominent Earth First!ers to disassociate themselves from the movement. Dave Foreman and John Davis relinquished control of the *Earth First!* journal and began publishing *Wild Earth* in 1991. They founded, with conservation biologist Reed Noss and several others, The Wildlands Project, which as been designed to promote wilderness conservation in the Americas based on sound ecological science.

Throughout the early 1990s, battles continued among those still conducting their activism under the Earth First! banner. Meanwhile, during the first half of the 1990s, many activists spent less time organizing civil disobedience and ecotage, and more time using "paper monkeywrenching" techniques—namely vigilance and appeals of timber harvesting plans, scientific status reviews of species viability and computer mapping of the habitat requirements for endangered species, combined with appropriate lawsuits, when funds are available. They are doing so because, as one of these activists recognized, "When it's time to sit down in front of the bulldozers, we've already lost."

Differences between and among Earth First!ers—both past and present—are likely to continue over the same divisive issues that consumed much of their time over the first fifteen years of Earth First! activism: Is ecological restoration dependent on anarchistic bioregionalism, or must we be more pragmatic, accepting nation-states as givens while resisting their destructive impulses? Is a countercultural and spiritual reformation of all society top priority and our only hope, or rather is preoccupation with, or overt expression of, spirituality counterproductive to movement aims?[7] Is an ecological collapse that precipitates the collapse of industrial society, concomitant with a drastic reduction of human numbers, an unfortunate prerequisite to the restoration of natural evolution? Is ecotage (especially tree-spiking) effective or counterproductive? Should movement activists prioritize building a mass movement through outreach and civil disobedience, or rather work to thwart commercial incursions into biologically sensitive areas through monkeywrenching, and should ecotage be public (more like civil disobedience) or clandestine? Finally, there have been debates over whether violence against humans can ever be a legitimate tactic, and whether this issue should be debated in movement journals.

Despite such factionalism, far more unites than divides these radical environmentalists. They are all animated by a deeply spiritual ecocentrism and they generally share or respect the plural myths, symbols, and rituals of the emerging Deep Ecology worldview. They are cynical about the system's willingness to respond to the ecological catastrophe they see unfolding. They all endorse extra-legal direct action, at least when they judge it to be a reasonable and heartfelt effort to protect biological diversity. Moreover, the majority believe that the struggle for biodiversity must be fought on the three fronts that parallel their ethical pillars: promoting spiritual awakening, ecological education about the biodiversity crisis and the requirements for ecosystem health, and fundamental political change. Despite sometimes profound differences regarding strategic priorities, most past and present Earth First!ers respect the work of those whose priorities differ from their own.

The preceding analysis interprets how Earth First!ers move *from primal spirituality to ecological resistance,* and explains why, in spite of disagreements, it is possible to speak of this diverse movement as a spiritual tradition. Through their activism and spirituality Earth First!ers pose an important challenge to Western civilization, dramatically suggesting that the well being of Earth and her creatures requires a widespread resacralization of human perceptions of nature. They ask us to join them in defending and restoring the natural world to wildness, basing our actions on reverence, love, and sometimes rage.

NOTES

1. This [essay] is a revised and updated amalgamation of several articles published previously, including: "Earth First!'s Religious Radicalism" in Christopher Chapple (ed.) *Ecological Prospects: Scientific, Religious, and Aesthetic Perspectives* (Albany, New York: State University of New York Press, 1993), which can also be found in an abbreviated version as "The Religion and Politics of Earth First!" in *The Ecologist,* 21(6):258–266, Nov/Dec 1991.); "Resacralizing Earth: Pagan Environmentalism and the Restoration of Turtle Island" in David Chidester and Edward Linenthal (eds.), *American Sacred Space* (Bloomington: Indiana University Press, 1995); and in chapters two and nineteen in my edited volume, *Ecological Resistance Movements: The Global Emergence of Radical and Popular Environmentalism.* (Albany: State University of New York Press, 1995). "Earth First!'s Religious Radicalism" provides more detail than the present [essay] about the rituals of the movement and the 1990 schism. "Resacralizing Earth" argues that "pagan environmentalism" is nothing new in North American history, and provides a contemporary case study religious conflict over a wilderness considered sacred by Earth First!ers and native Americans, at the site of the Mount Graham International Observatory in Southeastern Arizona. The final section of *Ecological Resistance Movements* has the most extensive analysis currently in print of the political impacts of radical environmentalism.

In this [essay], to save space, I have only reproduced citations not recorded in the above mentioned articles.

For additional information about the north American deep ecology movement see also my "Evoking the Ecological Self: Art as Resistance to the War on Nature" in *Peace Review: The International Quarterly of World Peace,* 5(2):225–230, June 1993, and my forthcoming book, *Once and Future Primitive: The Spiritual Politics of Deep Ecology* (Boston: Beacon Press, 1996)

This [essay] is based on archival research of movement documents, and intensive field-based observations and interviews conducted between August 1990 and November 1994.

2. See especially David Helvarg's *War Against the Greens* (San Francisco: Sierra Club Books, 1994), pp. 142, 279, 281, 224, 414 and 436).

3. On this point, see especially "Resacralizing Earth . . ."

4. For a detailed discussion of this controversy, see "Empirical and Normative Reflections on the Appropriation of Native American Spirituality in the North American Deep Ecology Movement," a paper I presented at the National Meeting of the American Academy of Religion in November 1993.

5. In "Earth First!'s Religious Radicalism" and "Resacralizing Earth . . .", respectively.

6. Such notions are commonly what most people discussed in this article mean by animism. I use the term non-pejoratively to refer to the belief that the natural world is inspirited, and that communication with non-human entities is possible.

7. Since founding *Wild Earth,* Foreman and Davis have paid less attention to spirituality.

Discussion Questions

1. Is it possible for humans to be non-anthropocentric?
2. What would be the implications of extending our notions of community to include the nonhuman world? Where should we draw the boundaries?
3. How do we define self? How might we define it more broadly, and what would be the implications of doing so?
4. Is humanity analogous to a cancer on the Earth?
5. Does Earth First! qualify as a religious movement?

Further Reading

Barnhill, David, and Roger S. Gottlieb, Eds., *Deep Ecology and World Religions,* Albany, N.Y.: SUNY Press, 2001.
Bradford, George, *How Deep Is Deep Ecology?,* Hadley, Mass.: Times Change Press, 1989.
Capra, Fritjof, *The Turning Point,* New York: Simon & Schuster, 1982.
Devall, Bill, and George Sessions, *Deep Ecology: Living As if Nature Mattered,* Salt Lake City: Peregrine Smith, 1985.
Drengson, Alan, and Yuichi Inoue, Eds., *The Deep Ecology Movement: An Introductory Anthology,* Berkeley, Calif.: North Atlantic, 1995.
Fox, Warwick, *Toward a Transpersonal Ecology,* Albany, N.Y.: SUNY Press, 1995.
Foreman, Dave, *Confessions of an Eco-Warrior,* New York: Harmony, 1991.
Katz, Eric, and David Rothenberg, Eds., *Beneath the Surface: Critical Essays on Deep Ecology,* Cambridge, Mass.: MIT Press, 2000.
Lee, Martha F., *Earth First!: Environmental Apocalypse,* Syracuse, N.Y.: Syracuse University Press, 1995.
Leopold, Aldo, *A Sand County Almanac,* New York: Oxford University Press, 1949.
Macy, Joanna, *World as Lover, World as Self,* Berkeley, Calif.: Parallax Press, 1991.
Manes, Christopher, *Green Rage,* Boston: Little, Brown, 1990.
Matthews, Freya, *The Ecological Self,* London: Routledge, 1991.
Naess, Arne, *Ecology, Community, and Lifestyle,* Cambridge, U.K.: Cambridge University Press, 1989.
Prigogine, Ilya, *Order Out of Chaos: Man's New Dialogue with Nature,* New York: Bantam, 1984.
Scarce, Rik, *Eco-Warriors: Understanding the Radical Environmental Movement,* Chicago: Noble Press, 1990.
Sessions, George, Ed., *Deep Ecology for the 21st Century,* Boston: Shambhala, 1995.
Spretnak, Charlene, *The Spiritual Dimension of Green Politics,* Santa Fe, N.Mex.: Bear, 1986.
Tobias, Michael, Ed., *Deep Ecology,* San Diego: Avant Books, 1985.

Chapter 13

Ecofeminism

Ecofeminism is a branch of feminist critique that locates the source of environmental degradation in the structure of dualist thinking (male/female, nature/culture, and so on) and patriarchal systems. According to this critique, *patriarchy* is a male-oriented set of values that seeks to dominate, control, and manipulate for its own ends. Ecofeminism (especially the variant known as cultural ecofeminism) therefore links the historical subordination of nature with that of women. Hierarchies and authoritarianism are seen as basic structural problems within society that need to be eliminated.

Ecofeminists have at times referred to issues ranging from Third World development to technology itself as patriarchal projects. By contrast, some (though not all) ecofeminists have seen the feminine principle as being more in touch with nature and natural cycles and rhythms. A distinction is made here between *sex* (female/male) and *gender* (feminine/masculine), because one may be male and still possess feminine qualities and vice versa. Individual ecofeminists have taken diverse positions about whether such gender identifications are culturally constructed or biologically determined.

Many ecofeminists associate the feminine principle with the giving and nurturing of life. By contrast, they see patriarchal culture as arising from a fear of death, which thus ultimately creates a culture of death. Attempts by patriarchal figures to monumentalize, memorialize, and otherwise glorify themselves through their accomplishments reflect their frustration at being unable to produce life and are really simply attempts to flee, deny, or overcome their own mortality. The historical displacement, demotion, or elimination throughout the world of ancient, nurturing goddess figures by powerful, dominating male deities has been interpreted as a massive war of the sexes, which women have lost.

If for the past 4,000 years, patriarchy has waged a war against women, it has waged one against nature as well, and just as successfully. In a bestselling book, Bill McKibben bemoans the end of nature, whereas others, like Gregg Easterbrook (see Chapter 2), would seem to celebrate it. To many ecofeminists, it is no accident that environmentally destructive technologies and policies in the overwhelming majority of cases have been invented by men, seeking to control and dominate nature by forcing "her" to unveil her secrets and to submit to "his" will.

This critique is not aimed at men per se, but rather at masculine attitudes, which individual men may or may not hold, just as individual men may or may not choose to acknowledge their own feminine side. So-called social ecofeminists have pointed out that what is called for is not a war against men, or the replacement of patriarchy with matriarchy, but rather a rejection of patriarchal values such as hierarchies and ideologies of domination and submission. Others have noted that gender is also related to issues of class, because women and poor people bear a disproportionately large share of the costs of environmental degradation, and poor women doubly so.

Ynestra King outlines the argument that links the critiques of feminism and ecology together and asserts that they are, in fact, inseparable. She proposes that the domination of men over women is the model for other forms of oppression, whether social or ecological. She concludes by calling for ecofeminist direct action to confront militarism and other forms of domination and violence.

Feminist theologian Rosemary Radford Ruether turns the ecofeminist discussion to religion, specifically to Christianity. She states that the ecofeminist critique presents the Christian tradition with some hard questions about its patriarchal heritage. Ruether examines the mythical cosmologies of the ancient Near East to uncover the stories of patriarchal domination that they contain. The creation by a male god *ex nihilo* (that is, from the void, without the participation of a maternal figure), the concept of the Fall and of sin, and the separation of spirit and matter are all seen by Ruether as expressions of masculine anxieties. Finally, she suggests some ways in which an ecofeminist theology could reshape basic Christian beliefs.

Shamara Shantu Riley brings to our attention the special relevance of environmental issues to African and African-American women. Her essay highlights the importance of ecojustice, a perspective that recognizes that the poor are disproportionately burdened with the costs of environmental degradation ("environmental apartheid"). Riley shows how Black women have begun to overcome the historical forms of oppression that linked them to nature and provides inspiring examples of how they are getting involved—and often taking the lead—in environmental protection and restoration movements in Africa and the United States.

Mary Mellor raises some critical issues pertaining to ecofeminism using a Marxist approach. Specifically, she notes the dilemma of reconciling essentialist arguments (for example, that women have unique connections to natural processes) with materialist ones (for example, that all constraints are socially, not naturally constructed). In response, Mellor suggests a compromise position that acknowledges both perspectives.

The Ecology of Feminism and the Feminism of Ecology

YNESTRA KING

> [Woman] became the embodiment of the biological function, the image of nature, the subjugation of which constituted that civilization's title to fame. For millennia men dreamed of acquiring absolute mastery over nature, of converting the cosmos into one immense hunting ground. It was to this that the idea of man was geared in a male-dominated society. This was the significance of reason, his prouded boast.
>
> —Horkheimer and Adorno, *Dialectic of Enlightenment*[1]

King, Ynestra, "The Ecology of Feminism and the Feminism of Ecology," in Mary Heather MacKinnon and Moni McIntyre, Eds., *Readings in Ecology and Feminist Theology*, 1995, pp. 150–159. Reprinted by permission of Sheed and Ward, an Apostolate of the Priests of the Sacred Heart, 7373 S. Lovers Lane Rd., Franklin, WI 53132.

ALL HUMAN BEINGS ARE NATURAL BEINGS. That may seem like an obvious fact, yet we live in a culture that is founded on the repudiation and domination of nature. This has a special significance for women because, in patriarchal thought, women are believed to be closer to nature than men. This gives women a particular stake in ending the domination of nature—in healing the alienation between human and nonhuman nature. This is also the ultimate goal of the ecology movement, but the ecology movement is not necessarily feminist.

For the most part, ecologists, with their concern for nonhuman nature, have yet to understand that they have a particular stake in ending the domination of women. They do not understand that a central reason for woman's oppression is her association with the despised nature they are so concerned about. The hatred of women and the hatred of nature are intimately connected and mutually reinforcing. Starting with this premise, this article explores why feminism and ecology need each other, and suggests the beginnings of a theory of ecological feminism: ecofeminism.

WHAT IS ECOLOGY?

Ecological science concerns itself with the interrelationships among all forms of life. It aims to harmonize nature, human and nonhuman. It is an integrative science in an age of fragmentation and specialization. It is also a critical science which grounds and necessitates a critique of our existing society. It is a reconstructive science in that it suggests directions for reconstructing human society in harmony with the natural environment.

Social ecologists are asking how we might survive on the planet and develop systems of food and energy production, architecture, and ways of life that will allow human beings to fulfill our material needs and live in harmony with nonhuman nature. This work has led to a social critique by biologists and to an exploration of biology and ecology by social thinkers. The perspective that self-consciously attempts to integrate both biological and social aspects of the relationship between human beings and their environment is known as *social ecology*. This perspective, developed primarily by Murray Bookchin,[2] to whom I am indebted for my understanding of social ecology, has embodied the anarchist critique that links domination and hierarchy in human society to the despoliation of nonhuman nature. While this analysis is useful, social ecology without feminism is incomplete.

Feminism grounds this critique of domination by identifying the prototype of other forms of domination: that of man over woman. Potentially, feminism creates a concrete global community of interests among particularly life-oriented people of the world: women. Feminist analysis supplies the theory, program, and process without which the radical potential of social ecology remains blunted. Ecofeminism develops the connections between ecology and feminism that social ecology needs in order to reach its own avowed goal of creating a free and ecological way of life.

What are these connections? Social ecology challenges the dualistic belief that nature and culture are separate and opposed. Ecofeminism finds misogyny at the root of that opposition. Ecofeminist principles are based on the following beliefs:

1. The building of Western industrial civilization in opposition to nature interacts dialectically with and reinforces the subjugation of women, because women are believed to be closer to nature. Therefore, ecofeminists take on the life-struggles of all of nature as our own.
2. Life on earth is an interconnected web, not a hierarchy. There is no natural hierarchy; human hierarchy is projected onto nature and then used to justify social domination. Therefore, ecofeminist theory seeks to show the connections between all forms of domination, including the domination of nonhuman nature, and ecofeminist practice is necessarily antihierarchical.
3. A healthy, balanced ecosystem, including human and nonhuman inhabitants, must maintain diversity. Ecologically, environmental simplification is as significant a problem as environmental pollution. Biological simplification, i.e., the wiping out of whole species, corresponds to reducing human diversity into faceless workers, or to the homogenization of taste and culture through mass consumer markets. Social life and natural life are literally simplified to the inorganic for the convenience

of market society. Therefore we need a decentralized global movement that is founded on common interests yet celebrates diversity and opposes all forms of domination and violence. Potentially, ecofeminism is such a movement.

4. The survival of the species necessitates a renewed understanding of our relationship to nature, of our own bodily nature, and of nonhuman nature around us; it necessitates a challenging of the nature-culture dualism and a corresponding radical restructuring of human society according to feminist and ecological principles. Adrienne Rich says, "When we speak of transformation we speak more accurately out of the vision of a process which will leave neither surfaces nor depths unchanged, which enters society at the most essential level of the subjugation of women and nature by men. . . ."[3]

The ecology movement, in theory and practice, attempts to speak for nature—the "other" that has no voice and is not conceived of subjectively in our civilization. Feminism represents the refusal of the original "other" in patriarchal human society to remain silent or to be the "other" any longer. Its challenge of social domination extends beyond sex to social domination of all kinds, because the domination of sex, race, and class and the domination of nature are mutually reinforcing. Women are the "others" in human society, who have been silent in public and who now speak through the feminist movement.

WOMEN, NATURE AND CULTURE: THE ECOFEMINIST POSITION

In the project of building Western industrial civilization, nature became something to be dominated, overcome, made to serve the needs of men. She was stripped of her magical powers and properties and was reduced to "natural resources" to be exploited by human beings to fulfill human needs and purposes which were defined in opposition to nature (see Merchant, who interprets the scientific revolution as the death of nature, and argues that it had a particularly detrimental effect on women.)[4] A dualistic Christianity had become ascendant with the earlier demise of old goddess religions, paganism, and animistic belief systems.[5] With the disenchantment of nature came the conditions for unchecked scientific exploration and technological exploitation.[6] We bear the consequences today of beliefs in unlimited control over nature and in science's ability to solve any problem, as nuclear power plants are built without provisions for waste disposal, and satellites are sent into space without provision for retrieval.

In this way, nature became "other," something essentially different from the dominant, to be objectified and subordinated. Women, who are identified with nature, have been similarly objectified and subordinated in patriarchal society. Women and nature, in this sense, are the original "others." Simone de Beauvoir has clarified this connection. For de Beauvoir, "transcendence" is the work of culture, it is the work of men. It is the process of overcoming immanence, a process of culture-building that is based on the increasing domination of nature. It is enterprise. "Immanence," symbolized by women, is that which calls men back, that which reminds man of what he wants to forget. It is his own link to nature that he must forget and overcome to achieve manhood and transcendence:

> Man seeks in woman the Other as Nature and as his fellow being. But we know what ambivalent feelings Nature inspires in man. He exploits her, but she crushes him, he is born of her and dies in her; she is the source of his being and the realm that he subjugates to his will; Nature is a vein of gross material in which the soul is imprisoned, and she is the supreme reality; she is contingence and Idea, the finite and the whole; she is what opposes the Spirit, and the Spirit itself. Now ally, now enemy, she appears as the dark chaos from whence life wells up, as this life itself, and as the over-yonder toward which life tends. Woman sums up Nature as Mother, Wife, and Idea; these forms now mingle and now conflict, and each of them wears a double visage.[7]

For de Beauvoir, patriarchal civilization is about the denial of men's mortality—of which women and nature are incessant reminders. Women's powers of procreation are distinguished from the powers of creation—the accomplishments through the vehicles of culture by which men achieve immortality. And yet this transcendence over women and nature can never be total: thus the ambivalence, the lack of self without other, the dependence of the self on the other both materially and emotionally. Thus develops a love-hate fetishization of women's bodies, which finds its ultimate manifestation in the sadomasochistic, pornographic displays of women as objects to be subdued, humiliated, and raped—the visual enactment of these fears and desires. (See Griffin, *Pornography and Silence,* for a full development of the relationship between nature-hating, women-hating, and pornography.)[8]

An important contribution of de Beauvoir's work is to show that men seek to dominate women and nature for reasons that are not simply economic. They do so as well for psychological reasons that involve a denial of a part of themselves, as do other male culture-making activities. The process begins with beating the tenderness and empathy out of small boys and directing their natural human curiosity and joy in affecting the world around them into arrogant attitudes and destructive paths.

For men raised in woman-hating cultures, the fact that they are born of women and are dependent upon nonhuman nature for existence is frightening. The process of objectification, of the making of women and nature into "others" to be appropriated and dominated, is based on a profound forgetting by men. They forget that they were born of women, were dependent on women in their early helpless years, and are dependent on nonhuman nature all their lives, which allows first for objectification and then for domination. "The loss of memory is a transcendental condition for science. All objectification is a forgetting."[9]

But the denied part of men is never fully obliterated. The memory remains in the knowledge of mortality and the fear of women's power. A basic fragility of gender identity exists that surfaces when received truths about women and men are challenged and the sexes depart from their "natural" roles. Opposition to the not-very-radical Equal Rights Amendment can be partially explained on these grounds. More threatening are homosexuality and the gay liberation movement, because they name a more radical truth—that sexual orientation is not indelible, nor is it naturally heterosexual. Lesbianism, particularly, which suggests that women who possess this repudiated primordial power can be self-sufficient, reminds men that they may not be needed. Men are forced into remembering their own dependence on women to support and mediate the construction of their private reality and their public civilization. Again there is the need to repress memory and oppress women.

The recognition of the connections between women and nature and of woman's bridge-like position between nature and culture poses three possible directions for feminism. One direction is the integration of women into the world of culture and production by severing the woman-nature connection. Writes anthropologist Sherry Ortner, "Ultimately, both men and women can and must be equally involved in projects of creativity and transcendence. Only then will women be seen as aligned with culture, in culture's ongoing dialectic with nature."[10] This position does not question nature-culture dualism itself, and it is the position taken by most socialist-feminists (see King, "Feminism and the Revolt of Nature")[11] and by de Beauvoir and Ortner, despite their insights into the connections between women and nature. They see the severance of the woman-nature connection as a condition of women's liberation.

Other feminists have reinforced the woman-nature connection: woman and nature, the spiritual and intuitive, versus man and the culture of patriarchal rationality.[12] This position also does not necessarily question nature-culture dualism or recognize that women's ecological sensitivity and life orientation is a socialized perspective that could be socialized right out of us depending on our day-to-day lives. There is no reason to believe that women placed in positions of patriarchal power will act any differently from men, or that we can bring about a feminist revolution without consciously understanding history and without confronting the existing economic and political power structures.

Ecofeminism suggests a third direction: a recognition that although the nature-culture dualism is a product of culture, we can nonetheless *consciously choose* not to sever the woman-nature connection by joining male culture. Rather, we can use it as a vantage point for creating a different kind of culture and politics that would integrate intuitive, spiritual, and rational forms of knowledge, embracing both science and magic insofar as they enable us to transform the nature-culture distinction and to envision and create a free, ecological society.

ECOFEMINISM AND THE INTERSECTION OF FEMINISM AND ECOLOGY

The implications of a culture based on the devaluation of life-giving and the celebration of life-taking are profound for ecology and for women. This fact about our culture links the theories and politics of the ecology movement with those of the feminist movement. Adrienne Rich has written:

> We have been perceived for too many centuries as pure Nature, exploited and raped like the earth and the solar system; small wonder if we now long to become Culture: pure spirit, mind. Yet it is precisely this culture and its political institutions which have split us off from itself. In so doing it has also split itself off from life, becoming the death culture of quantification, abstraction, and the will to power which has reached its most refined destructiveness in this century. It is this culture and politics of abstraction which women are talking of changing, of bringing into accountability in human terms.[13]

The way to ground a feminist critique of "this culture and politics of abstraction" is with self-conscious ecological perspective that we apply to all theories and strategies, in the way that we are learning to apply race and class factors to every phase of feminist analysis.

Similarly, ecology requires a feminist perspective. Without a thorough feminist analysis of social domination that reveals the interconnected roots of misogyny and hatred of nature, ecology remains an abstraction: it is incomplete. If male ecological scientists and social ecologists fail to deal with misogyny—the deepest manifestation of nature-hating in their own lives—they are not living the ecological lives or creating the ecological society they claim.

The goals of harmonizing humanity and nonhuman nature, at both the experiential and theoretical levels, cannot be attained without the radical vision and understanding available from feminism. The twin concerns of ecofeminism—human liberation and our relationship to nonhuman nature—open the way to developing a set of ethics required for decision-making about technology. Technology signifies the tools that human beings use to interact with nature, including everything from the digging stick to nuclear bombs.

Ecofeminism also contributes an understanding of the connections between the domination of persons and the domination of nonhuman nature. Ecological science tells us that there is no hierarchy in nature itself, but rather a hierarchy in human society that is projected onto nature. Ecofeminism draws on feminist theory which asserts that the domination of woman was the original domination in human society, from which all other hierarchies—of rank, class, and political power—flow. Building on this unmasking of the ideology of a natural hierarchy of persons, ecofeminism uses its ecological perspective to develop the position that there is no hierarchy in nature: among persons, between persons and the rest of the natural world, or among the many forms of nonhuman nature. We live on the earth with millions of species, only one of which is the human species. Yet the human species in its patriarchal form is the only species which holds a conscious belief that it is entitled to dominion over the other species, and over the planet. Paradoxically, the human species is utterly dependent on nonhuman nature. We could not live without the rest of nature; it *could* live without us.

Ecofeminism draws on another basic principle of ecological science—unity in diversity—and develops it politically. Diversity in nature is necessary, and enriching. One of the major effects of industrial technology, capitalist or socialist, is environmental simplification. Many species are simply being wiped out, never to be seen on the earth again. In human society, commodity capitalism is intentionally simplifying human community and culture so that the same products can be marketed anywhere to anyone. The prospect is for all of us to be alike, with identical needs and desires, around the globe: Coca Cola in China, blue jeans in Russia, and American rock music virtually everywhere.

Few peoples of the earth have not had their lives touched and changed to some degree by the technology of industrialization. Ecofeminism as a social movement resists this social simplification through supporting the rich diversity of women the world over, and seeking a oneness in that diversity. Politically, ecofeminism opposes the ways that differences can separate women from each other, through the oppressions of class, privilege, sexuality, and race.

The special message of ecofeminism is that when women suffer through both social domination and the domination of nature, most of life on this planet suffers and is threatened as well. It is significant that feminism and ecology as social movements have emerged now, as nature's revolt against domination plays itself out in human history and in nonhuman nature at the same time. As we face slow environmental poisoning and the resulting environmental simplification, or the possible unleashing of our nuclear arsenals, we can hope that the prospect of the extinction of life on the planet will provide a universal impetus to social change. Ecofeminism supports utopian visions of harmonious, diverse, decentralized communities, using only those technologies based on ecological principles, as the only practical solution for the continuation of life on earth.

Visions and politics are joined as an ecofeminist culture and politics begin to emerge. Ecofeminists are taking direct action to effect changes that are immediate and personal as well as long-term and structural. Direct actions include learning holistic health and alternate ecological technologies, living in communities that explore old and new forms of spirituality which celebrate all life as diverse expressions of nature, considering the ecological consequences of our lifestyles and personal habits, and participating in creative public forms of resistance, including nonviolent civil disobedience.

TOWARD AN ECOFEMINIST PRAXIS: FEMINIST ANTIMILITARISM

Theory never converts simply or easily into practice: in fact, theory often lags behind practice, attempting to articulate the understanding behind things people are already doing. *Praxis* is the unity of thought and action, or theory and practice. Many of the women who founded the feminist antimilitarist movement in Europe and the United States share the ecofeminist perspective I have articulated. I believe that the movement as I will briefly describe it here grows out of such an understanding. For the last three years I have been personally involved in the ecofeminist antimilitarist movement, so the following is a firsthand account of one example of our praxis.

The connections between violence against women, a militarized culture, and the development and deployment of nuclear weapons have long been evident to pacifist feminists.[14] Ecofeminists like myself, whose concerns with all of life stem from an understanding of the connections between misogyny and the destruction of nature, began to see militarism and the death-courting weapons industry as the most immediate threat to continued life on the planet, while the ecological effects of other modern technologies pose a more long-term threat. In this manner militarism has become a central issue for most ecofeminists. Along with this development, many of us accepted the analysis of violence made by pacifist feminists and, therefore, began to see nonviolent direct action and resistance as the basis of our political practice.

The ecofeminist analysis of militarism is concerned with the militarization of culture and the economic priorities reflected by our enormous "defense" budgets and dwindling social services budgets. The level of weaponry and the militaristic economic priorities are products of patriarchal culture that speak violence at every level. Our freedom and our lives are threatened, even if there is no war and none of the nuclear weapons are ever used. We have tried to make clear the particular ways that women suffer from war-making—as spoils to victorious armies, as refugees, as disabled and older women and single mothers who are dependent on dwindling social services. We connect the fear of nuclear annihilation with women's fear of male violence in our everyday lives.

For ecofeminists, military technology reflects a pervasive cultural and political situation. It is connected with rape, genocide, and imperialism, with starvation and homelessness, with the poisoning of the environment, and with the fearful lives of the world's peoples—especially those of women. Military and state power hierarchies join and reinforce each other through military technology. Particularly as shaped by ecofeminism, the feminist antimilitarist movement in the United States and Europe is a movement against a monstrously destructive technology and set of power relationships embodied in militarism.

Actions have been organized at the Pentagon in the United States and at military installations in Europe. The Women's Pentagon Action, originally conceived at an ecofeminist conference which I and others organized, has taken place at the Pentagon twice so far, on November 16 and 17, 1980, and November 15 and 16, 1981. It included about two thousand women the first year, and more than twice that the second. I took part in planning both actions and we took care to make the actions reflect *all* aspects of our politics. Intentionally there were no speakers, no leaders; the action sought to emphasize the connections between the military issue and other ecofeminist issues.

The themes of the Women's Pentagon Action have carried over into other actions our group has participated in, including those organized by others. At the June 12–14, 1982 disarmament demonstrations in New York City, the group's march contingent proclaimed the theme: "A feminist world is a nuclear free zone," the slogan hanging beneath a huge globe held aloft. Other banners told of visions for a feminist future, and members wore bibs that read "War is man-made," "Stop the violence in our lives," and "Disarm the patriarchy." There have been similar actions, drawing inspiration from the original Women's Pentagon Actions, elsewhere in the United States and in Europe. In California, the Bohemian Club, a male-only playground for corporate, government, and military elite, was the site of a demonstration by women who surrounded the club, enacting a life-affirming protest ritual (see Starhawk).[15] In England on December 12, 1982, thirty thousand women surrounded a US military installation, weaving into the fence baby clothes, scarves, poems and other personal-life symbols. At one point, spontaneously, the word *freedom* rose from the lips of the women and was heard round and round the base. Three thousand women nonviolently blocked the entrances to the base on December 13 (see Fisher.)[16]

The politics being created by these actions draw on women's culture: embodying what is best in women's life-oriented socialization, building on women's difference, organizing antihierarchically in small groups in visually and emotionally imaginative ways, and seeking an integration of issues.

These actions exemplify ecofeminism. While technocratic experts (including feminists) argue the merits and demerits of weapons systems, ecofeminism approaches the disarmament issues on an intimate and moral level. Ecofeminism holds that a personalized, decentralized life-affirming culture and politics of direct action are crucially needed to stop the arms race and transform the world's priorities. Because such weaponry does not exist apart from a contempt for women and all of nature, the issue of disarmament and threat of nuclear war is a feminist issue. It is the ultimate human issue, and the ultimate ecological issue. And so ecology, feminism, and liberation for all of nature, including ourselves, are joined.

NOTES

1. Max Horkheimer and Theodor W. Adorno, *Dialectic of Enlightenment,* Seabury Press, New York, 1972, p. 248.
2. Murray Bookchin, *The Ecology of Freedom: The Emergence and Dissolution of Hierarchy,* Cheshire Books, Palo Alto, 1982.
3. Adrienne Rich, *On Lies, Secrets, and Silence,* W. W. Norton, New York, 1979, p. 248.
4. Carolyn Merchant, *The Death of Nature: Women, Ecology, and the Scientific Revolution,* Harper & Row, New York, 1980.
5. Rosemary Radford Reuther, *New Woman/New Earth: Sexist Ideologies and Human Liberation,* Seabury Press, New York, 1975.
6. Merchant, *op. cit.*
7. Simone de Beauvoir, *The Second Sex,* Modern Library, Random House, New York, 1968, p. 144.
8. Susan Griffin, *Pornography and Silence: "Culture's" Revenge against Nature,* Harper & Row, New York, 1981.
9. Horkheimer, *op. cit.,* p. 230.
10. Sherry B. Ortner, "Is Female to Male as Nature is to Culture?" *Woman, Culture and Society,* Michele Zimbalist Rosaldo and Louis Lamphere, eds., Stanford University Press, Stanford, 1974, p. 87.
11. Ynestra King, "Feminism and The Revolt of Nature," *Heresies* 13: 12–16, Fall 1981.
12. Many such feminists call themselves ecofeminists. Some of them cite Susan Griffin's *Woman and Nature* (Harper & Row, San Francisco, 1978) as the source of their understanding of the deep connections between women and nature, and their politics. *Woman and Nature* is an inspirational poetic work with political implications. It explores the terrain of our deepest naturalness, but I do not read it as a delineation of a set of politics. To use Griffin's work in this way is to make it into something it was not intended to be. In personal conversation and in her more politically explicit works such as *Pornography and Silence* (1981), Griffin is antidualistic, struggling to bridge the false oppositions of nature and culture, passion and reason. Both science

and poetry are deeply intuitive processes. Another work often cited by ecofeminists is Mary Daly's *Gyn/ecology* (1978). Daly, a theologian/philosopher, is also an inspirational thinker, but she is a genuinely dualistic thinker, reversing the "truths" of patriarchal theology. While I have learned a great deal from Daly, my perspective differs from hers in that I believe that any truly ecological politics, including ecological feminism, must be ultimately antidualistic.

13. Adrienne Rich, *Of Woman Born,* W. W. Norton, New York, 1976, p. 285.

14. Barbara Deming, *We Cannot Live Without Our Lives,* Grossman, New York, 1974.

15. Starhawk, *Dreaming the Dark: Magic, Sex and Politics,* Beacon Press, Boston, 1982, p. 168.

16. Berenice Fisher, "Women Ignite English Movement," *Womanews,* Feb. 1983.

OTHER SOURCES

Daly, Mary. *Gyn/ecology: The Metaethics of Radical Feminism.* Boston: Beacon Press, 1978.

Griffin, Susan. *Woman and Nature.* New York: Harper & Row, 1978.

King, Ynestra. "All is Connectedness: Scenes from the Women's Pentagon Action USA." In *Keeping the Peace: A Women's Peace Handbook,* Lynne Johnes, ed., London: The Women's Press, 1983.

Ecofeminism
The Challenge to Theology

ROSEMARY RADFORD RUETHER

IT IS THE CONTENTION OF THIS PAPER THAT ecofeminism poses a profound challenge to classical Christian theology and, indeed, to all the classical religions shaped by the worldview of patriarchy. Here I am focusing on Christianity, with its roots in the worldviews of the ancient Near East and Greco-Roman worlds. Let me start with a brief definition of ecofeminism. Ecofeminism, or ecological feminism, examines the interconnections between the domination of women and the domination of nature. It aims at strategies and worldviews to liberate or heal these interconnected dominations through a better understanding of their etiology and enforcement.

There are two levels on which this relation between sexism and ecological exploitation can be made: on the cultural-symbolic level and on the socioeconomic level. My assumption is that the first is an ideological superstructure that reflects and ratifies the second. That is, social patterns developed, deeply rooted in the distortion of gender relations with the rise of patriarchal slavocracies in the ancient Near East, that subjugated women as a gender group. The system of domination of women itself was rooted in a larger patriarchal hierarchical system of priestly and warrior-king control over land, animals, and slaves as property, which monopolized wealth, power, and knowledge.

As this system of domination was shaped socially, ideological tools were constructed to ratify it as a reflection of the "nature of things" and the "will of God/the gods." Law codes were developed to define these relations of power of dominant men over women, slaves, animals, and land as property.[1] These law codes are described as handed down to an inspired lawgiver by God/the gods. Creation stories were spun out to depict this hierarchical social order as itself a reflection of the cosmic order.

In the ancient Near East and classical Athens several creation stories were constructed to ratify this design of society. In the Babylonian creation story, which goes back to the third millennium B.C.E., the story of cosmogony is told as a theogony of the gods that culminates in an intergenerational conflict between the old earth mother, Tiamat, and her great-

Ruether, Rosemary Radford, "Ecofeminism: The Challenge to Theology," in Dieter T. Hessel and Rosemary Radford Ruether, Eds., *Christianity and Ecology: Seeking the Well-Being of Earth and Humans,* Cambridge, Mass.: Harvard University Press, 2000, pp. 97–112. Reprinted by permission of the Center for the Study of World Religions, Harvard Divinity School.

grandson Marduk. A mother-dominated old world of primal energies is set against a new world order of city-states championed by Marduk.[2]

Marduk is seen as conquering chaos and creating the cosmos by conquering the primal mother, treading her body underfoot and splitting it in half, using one half to fashion the starry firmament above and the other half the earth below. Her subordinate male consort is then slain, and from his blood, mixed with the earth, are fashioned human beings to be the slaves of the gods so the gods can be at leisure. The elemental mother is turned into "matter" which can then be used to shape a hierarchical cosmos. The creation of humans as slaves to the gods within this cosmos defines the primary social relation as that of masters over slaves.

In both the Hebrew and the Greek creation stories this primal battle against the mother, that suggested an earlier, alternative world, is concealed. These stories begin with the presupposition of patriarchal dualism as the foundational nature of things. For the Greek philosophical story, told by Plato, the primal dualism of mind divided from matter was the first state of things. On the one side stood Mind, containing the archetypal ideas; on the other side, unformed matter, the receptacle, or "nurse," of things to be. Between the two stood disembodied male agency as the divine architect or Creator, who shapes matter into a cosmos by fashioning it after the intellectual blueprint of the divine ideas.[3]

The Creator shapes a circular and hierarchically ordered cosmos, with the fixed stars and the realm of the gods at the outer edge, the earth at the bottom, and the planetary spheres ranged in between. He then fashions the world soul to set this cosmos in motion. Taking the residue of the world soul, he cuts this into individual souls and places them in the stars. There they have a preincarnational vision of the eternal ideas. Then they are encased in bodies, fashioned by the planetary gods, and put on the earth.

The task of the soul is to control the passions that arise from the body and to cultivate the intellect. If the soul succeeds in this task, it will doff the body at death and return to its native star, there to live "a blessed and congenial existence." But if it fails to control the body, it will enter a cycle of reincarnation, entering the bodies of lower beings, women, lower social classes, and animals.[4] The fall into an animal is terminal for the soul, but from lower forms of humans women, and lower classes, the soul can rise through successive incarnations into the highest state, the elite Greek male, and be liberated into disembodied bliss.

Although Christianity would shed the ideas of the preexistence and reincarnation of the soul,[5] it followed key presuppositions of Plato's cosmology, reading the Genesis story through the lens of the *Timaeus.* It continued the presuppositions that the soul is an ontological substance separable from the body, living in an alienated state on Earth, whose true home lies in Heaven. It attempted to combine the Platonic eschatology of the soul's return to the stars with the radically different Hebrew eschatology of the resurrected body on a millennial earth by imagining a "spiritual body" stripped of its mortal components that would clothe the soul in its final heavenly state.[6]

Like Plato, Christianity imaged the soul in relation to the body a male controlling power over female-identified body and passions that are to be controlled. Although Christianity concedes that women also possess a redeemable soul in God's image, the classical Christian theological tradition sees this soul as nongendered. A genderless soul that can be redeemed through baptism into Christ is distinguished from women as female who are seen as inherently closer to the sin-prone bodily tendencies.

This lower nature demands that women be subordinated and kept under control by men, but it also means that women are prone to insubordination and subversion of male rational control. It is through this female tendency that the male was seduced into sin in the beginning and paradise was lost, ushering humanity into a fallen world.

In this story of original paradise, sin and fall Christianity drew on a very different cosmology and earth story from the Hebrews. The Genesis story posits a patriarchal God who shapes an original chaotic matter into cosmos through his word-command during a six-day work week, culminating in sabbatical rest. The human, created male and female on the sixth day and given the command to rule over the earth and its plants and animals, is not created as a slave, but as a royal servant, or administrator, of the earth as representative of God, or "in God's image."[7]

There is no explicit mandate for the domination of some humans over others, as male over female or master over slave, in the Hebrew story. This fact allowed the Genesis story to be used as a potent basis for an egalitarian view of all humans as equal in God's image in later Christian movements that sought to dismantle slavery and sexism. But this later Christian usage of Genesis 1 overlooks what was implicit in the Hebrew story, and explicit in Hebrew law and exegesis. Adam is a generic human who is assumed to be embodied by the male patriarchal class which represents dependent humans, women, slaves, and children and rules over God's creation.[8]

Moreover, in Genesis 2–3, as if to make the gender assumptions explicit, the male is identified with the original male human being, out of which the female is created by the male God and handed over to the male to be his wife-servant. Contrary to modern feminist apologetics, this is not an egalitarian relation, but one in which the male is the normative human and the female a derivative auxiliary.[9] This derivative female is then described as initiating disobedience to God's command, thus causing the pair to be thrown out of paradise to live an oppressive existence. His punishment is hard labor by the sweat of his brow, while hers is painful childbearing and subjugation to her husband.

Although the present fallen world is sunk in sin, Hebrew thought looks forward to a future time when paradise will be restored. When humans (Israel's patriarchal class) turn and obey God, God will restore them to an idyllic world where there will be no violence between man and man, alienation between man and nature will be overcome, harmonic relations will reign on a peaceful and prosperous earth. Originally, this Hebrew hope for a future paradise was earth- and mortality-bound. It assumed that redeemed humans would live a long, healthy, but mortal life on a peaceful and bountiful but mortal earth.[10]

Later contact with Persian eschatology and Platonism would reshape Hebrew futurism into apocalyptic scenarios in which the dead of past generations rise, are judged by a messianic king and the whole earth transformed into immortal conditions. It is this apocalyptic eschatology that is received by the Christian movement and fused with elements of Platonic cosmology to create the classic Christian story of creation, fall, and redemption.

Since Christianity dropped the ideas of the soul's preexistence and reincarnation, it also lost the explanation for women's inferiority based on the view that women are born through the failure of souls in past male incarnations to control their bodily passions. Some early Christian movements suggested a subversive liberation in Christ from all relations of subjugation—women to men, slaves to masters, subjugated to ruling nations. The original equality prior to sexual differentiation was seen as restored, drawing on the Galatians text, "In Christ there is no more male and female, Jew and Greek, slave and free."[11]

As Christianity was institutionalized in the patriarchal family and political order, however, it moved quickly to suppress these radical interpretations of redemption in Christ. Although equal access to heavenly redemption was conceded to women, this future hope was not allowed to subvert patriarchal relations on Earth in the newly forming Christian church and society. This was already expressed in the post-Pauline dicta in 1 Timothy, which declared that women were created second and sinned first and therefore are to keep silence and to have no authority over men in the Christian community.[12]

Augustine, in his late-fourth- and early-fifth-century commentaries on Genesis, would shape the theological rationale for women's subordination that would be followed by the dominant line of Christian theologians through the Reformation. For Augustine, woman, although given a nongendered soul by the Creator that enables her to be redeemed, was created in her female nature to be subordinate to the male in the sexual-social roles of wife and childbearer. For Augustine, femaleness itself represents the inferior bodily nature, while the male represents the intellect which is to rule over both his body and hers. He is the collective Adam made in God's image, while woman as woman does not possess the image of God in herself but images the subordinate body. She is "in the image of God" only when taken together with the male, "who is her head."[13]

Moreover, for Augustine, due to her inferior and more sin-prone nature, Eve initiated disobedience to God. The male, by assenting to her prompting, conceded to his lower self. Only thus does the whole human fall into sin.[14] Although humans as a whole are punished by a loss of original immortality that was the gift of union with God and have lost the free will that allowed them to choose God over their sinful self-will, women are punished for their special fault by coercive subjugation.[15]

For Augustine, woman was created subordinate but is now in a state of forced subjugation, to punish her for her original insubordination and to keep her in her place. Redemption does not liberate her from this subordination. Rather, through voluntary acceptance of it, she makes herself obedient to God and a fit subject of heavenly bliss. Then, finally, there will be no hierarchy of male over female, but all the blessed will live in gloriously spiritualized bodies freed from sin and death.

These patriarchal patterns that fused Hebrew and Greek thought reigned in Christian cosmology, anthropology, Christology, and soteriology until modern times, being taken up and renewed by the mainline Reformers, Luther and Calvin. In the sixteenth and seventeenth centuries a few maverick feminist humanists and the Quakers challenged the doctrine of male domination as the order of nature and punishment due women for their priority in sin. They returned to suppressed early Christian themes of radical egalitarianism and argued that all humans were made equal in the original creation.[16]

For these thinkers the domination over women, as well as other forms of domination, such as slavery, came about through sin; not women's sin, but the sin of dominant males who distorted the original harmony by usurping power over others. Christ came to overcome all such dominations and to restore the equality of women and men, but male church leaders have distorted the gospel into new rationales for sexism. Redemption means not just a promise of spiritual equality in heaven, but a social struggle to overcome unjust domination of men over women, masters over slaves, here on Earth.

This theology of original and redeemed equality over against patriarchal slavocracy was picked up and developed by abolitionist feminists of the nineteenth century, such as the Grimké sisters and Lucretia Mott. In the pithy words of Sarah Grimké, writing in 1837, "All I ask of my brethren is, that they take their feet from off our necks and permits us to stand upright on the ground which God designed us to occupy."[17] Sarah Grimké had no doubt that woman's ground is one of an autonomous human being created as man's peer and equal partner, not his subordinate.

This anthropology of original and restored equality was rediscovered by modern feminist theology and has been the basis for a critique of patriarchal anthropology in recent decades. But the nineteenth-century feminists did not question an anthropocentric worldview in which man and woman together were created to dominate and rule over the nonhuman creation. It is only with the deepening of feminist theology in ecofeminism that there has been a questioning of patriarchal cosmology and a recognition of the need to grapple with the whole structure of the Christian story, and not just with gender relations in its anthropology.

When I speak about the challenge of ecofeminism to theology, it is in the context of a radicalization that takes place as ecological consciousness is incorporated into feminist theology. One then realizes the need to question and reconstruct the cosmological framework out of which the Christian worldview grew from its ancient roots in the Hebrew and Greek worlds. A full treatment of the implications of these deeper questions is still very much in process. One awaits a full presentation of what an ecofeminist theology would look like. Here, I will only attempt a few suggestions about how the self, sin and redemption, God, cosmology, and eschatology are being rethought by ecofeminist theology.

I begin with a view of the self in ecofeminist theology as the starting point for a challenge to the Platonic construct of soul and body which still reigns officially in Christian thought, although with failing conviction. The basic assumption of ecofeminist theology (although seldom clearly articulated) is that the dualism of soul and body must be rejected, as well as the assumptions of the priority and controlling role of male-identified mind over female-identified body. This anthropology is at the heart of the distortion in Western thought of our relation to ourselves, as well as to our fellow earth creatures and the cosmos as a whole.

Humans are latecomers to the planet. The plants and animals existed billions of years before us. We are descendents of the long evolution of increasingly complex life-forms on Earth. Our consciousness does not set us radically apart from the rest of the life-forms on Earth; rather, there is a continuity of matter-energy dynamics on different levels of organization, moving from inorganic energy to life, then to awareness of life, and then to self-reflecting consciousness in organisms with progressively more complex brains. We were not created to dominate and rule the earth, for it governed itself well and better for millions of years when we did not exist or existed as nondominant mammals.

Only in very recent earth history, in the last few thousand years, has *Homo sapiens* emerged as an increasingly dominant species, using its special gifts for thinking and organizing to control and exploit the majority of humans and the nonhuman earth community. Stewardship is not a primal command, but an ex post facto effort of dominant males to correct overabuse and become better managers of what they have presumed to be their patrimony, namely, ownership of the rest of the world.

We need to recognize that our self-reflective consciousness is not a separable ontological substance but our experience of our own interiority, which is integral to our brain-body and dies with it. We are finite moments of self-conscious life which arose from the earth and return to it at death. Our consciousness did not fall from a heaven outside the earth and will not escape outside of it into an eternal life. Our destiny and calling is of and for this earth, our only and true home. Immortality lies not in the preservation of our individual consciousness as a separate substance but in the miracle and mystery of endlessly recycled matter-energy out of which we arose and into which we return. A better translation of the Ash Wednesday proclamation is: "we are earth; to earth we shall return."

This means we need to use our special capacities for thought, not to imagine ourselves as ruling over others, superior to them, and as escaping our common mortality, but rather to celebrate the wonder of the whole cosmic process and to be the place where this cosmic process comes to celebrative consciousness. We also need to use our capacities to contemplate and understand these processes so that we may harmonize our lives with the life of the whole earth community. This demands a spirituality and ethic of mutual limitation and of reciprocal life-giving nurture, the very opposite of the spirituality of separation and domination.

This ecological consciousness of self calls for a very different understanding of the nature of evil and its remedies. We need to give up the presuppositions of an original paradise, when there was no evil, and a future paradise, when evil and death are overcome. Rather, we need to look more closely at the etiology of our particular distortion of our relation to one another and to the earth through myths of separation and domination. Here, I find myself particularly instructed by Brazilian ecofeminist theologian Ivone Gebara.

In Gebara's view, evil, in the sense of finitude and tragedy, has always been with us and with all life-forms on Earth, and this will always be so. The primal sin is not a disobedience that caused us to fall into a mortality to which we were not originally subjected. Rather, the primal sin lies in the effort to escape from mortality, finitude, and vulnerability. The desire to escape from mortality may have long been a part of human fear of death, but it took organized, pernicious forms with the use of powerful males who sought to monopolize power over other humans, land, and animals. For them the ultimate power over others was to rise superior to death itself, to organize their power to assure themselves of an invulnerability to that finitude that is the common lot of earth creatures.[18]

This very effort to secure man's own invulnerability from want and death impelled an endless process of seeking to amass power at the expense of the rest of humans and the earth. These dominant men, seeking ultimate salvation from vulnerability, constructed systems of abuse and exploitation of other humans and the earth to achieve overweening wealth and power. Women became the particular targets of this flight from vulnerability because they represented man's finite origins and the realities of earth-bound pain and limits. To rule over and to flee from woman, the body, and the earth was to seek to conquer and flee from one's own denied finitude.

For Gebara it is this impulse to dominate and exploit in order to conquer want, imagining oneself to have transcended finite limitations, that has created the system of distortion that heaps excessive want and untimely death on the majority of humans. This system of exploitation threatens to undo the processes that maintain the life cycle of all earth beings in relation to one another, crafted by the earth over billions of years. It is this system of domination and distortion which is sin, as distinct from tragedy and death, which are natural and inevitable.

This understanding of the etiology of sin and the fall into domination also dictates how Gebara understands salvation. Just as we must give up the original paradise where there was no tragedy or death, so we must give up the future paradise where tragedy and death are overcome.[19] We need to recognize that these myths of immortal and perfect beginnings and ends not only falsify our real possibilities but are themselves projections of the escape from vulnerability which is at the heart of sin.

The real salvation that is available to us is of much more modest dimensions and yet is, nevertheless, of world historic and global proportions. We need to dismantle the system of distortion that gives a privileged class overweening wealth and power at the expense of most humans and that is destroying the life-sustaining balances of the earth. In so doing, we will not expect a paradise free from tragedy and death but a community of mutual life-giving where we can hold one another in the celebrative as well as the tragic moments of our common life as earth creatures.

This more modest redemptive hope was summed up in the conclusion of the women's creed written by Robin Morgan for the Women's Conference in Beijing, China:[20]

> Bread. A clean sky. Active peace. A woman's voice singing somewhere. The army disbanded. The harvest abundant. The wound healed. The child wanted. The prisoner freed. The body's integrity honored. The lover returned. . . . Labor equal, fair and valued. No hand raised in any gesture but greeting. Secure interiors—of heart, home and land—so firm as to make secure borders irrelevant at last.

This is the vision of an ecological hope freed from false escapism and content to make common joys abundant and available to us all in the midst of those tragedies of limits, failures, and accidents that also should be equally shared, rather than heaped upon some in excess so a privileged few may imagine themselves immortal.

The dismantling of an escapist self and salvation history that is the root of human sin and *han*[21] (victimization of others and the pain of victimization) also demands a dismantling of the view of cosmology, God, and Christ that has sustained this distortion. Instead of modeling God after male ruling-class consciousness, outside of and ruling over nature as its controlling immortal projection, God in ecofeminist spirituality is the immanent source of life and the renewal of life that sustains the whole planetary and cosmic community. God is neither male nor anthropomorphic. God is the font from which the variety of particular beings "co-arise" in each generation, the matrix that sustains their life-giving interdependency with each other, and also the judging and renewing insurgency of life that enables us to overcome the distortions that threaten healthy relations.

This understanding of God is leading several ecofeminist theologians to reconstruct the understanding of the Trinity as the sustaining matrix of immanent relationality. Ivone Gebara sees the Trinity, not as a separate, self-enclosed relation of two divine males with each other, mediated by the Spirit, but as the symbolic expression of the basic dynamic of life itself as a process of vital interrelational creativity. Life as interrelational creativity exists on every level of reality. As cosmos it reveals itself as the whole process of cosmic unfolding and interrelation of planets and galaxies. As Earth it shows us the dynamic interrelational process of life unfolding in the biosphere.[22]

Each species ramifies into many differences, including human beings with their many races and cultures. We should celebrate this diversity of humanness and affirm our interrelation with each other in one community on Earth. Likewise, interpersonal society and the person herself exists as a creative dynamic of expanding plurality and new interrelationality, of unity and diversity in interaction. The trinitarian dynamic of life is both creational and salvational; it both creates new life and seeks to correct distorted relations and re-establish life-giving, loving relationality. The name of the Trinitarian God as sustaining, redeeming matrix of cosmic, planetary, social, and personal life is Sophia: Holy Wisdom.

In the context of this understanding of the ecological self, good and evil, and the Trinitarian God, what does it mean to speak of Jesus as Christ? Can we still affirm this one historical figure as the unique incarnation of God's creating Logos, even reinterpreted as Sophia? In what way is he both Sophia and Messiah?

Gebara questions the messianic myth of a heroic warrior who will deliver victims from oppression, punish the oppressors, and create an ideal earth freed from sin and want. She sees this myth as the counterpart, from the victims' perspective, of the desire to escape from finitude, but now coupled with the thirst for revenge upon those who have secured their own privilege at the expense of others. Messianic myths, as revenge scenarios of victims, reproduce, rather than break, the cycle of violence and create new victims and new victimizers.

Jesus, for Gebara, is a very different prophetic figure who sought to break through the cycle of violence. Taking the side of the victims, he also called those in power to repent and enter into a new community of mutual service. The dominant system could not tolerate his message and killed him to silence his countervision. But his followers also betrayed him by turning his call to a community of shared love into a new messianism, making him into the warrior imperial savior who would secure the Christian system of dominating power.[23]

Thus, to ask how Jesus is the Christ, one must overturn the messianic myth. Jesus stands instead as an antimessiah calling us to rediscover the community of equals that appears when the system of sin and *han*, of victimizers and victims, of rich and poor, is dismantled. We enter, then, not a community of immortal blessedness freed from finitude and limits, but a community of shared joys and sorrows as earth creatures, former Pharisees and prostitutes, the lame and the blind, women and men on the edges of the dominant system breaking bread together.

Likewise, if Jesus reveals God, the God he reveals is not the split-off, dominating Logos of immortalized male sovereignty but the Holy Wisdom of mutual self-giving and life-sustaining love. Jesus the Christ embodies the Holy Wisdom that creates and renews the creation, not as its exclusive and unique representative, but rather as a paradigm of her presence, one among many other sisters and brothers, to recall us to our true selves and relations and away from the madness of escapism and domination. These are the "temptations" from which we ask to be delivered, even as we pray for those conditions of daily bread and mutual forgiveness that recreate God's will done on Earth.

Gebara's understanding of the immanent Trinitarian God of life's dynamic relationality places revelation within our experience of nature. We read (and critique) our historical scriptures in the light of the book of nature. All life, from the evolution of the galaxies to the dynamics of the self, manifests the presence of God as sustaining Wisdom of creation. But this does not mean a blissful world of idyllic conditions. Nature reveals how life sustains its precarious balances by painful and tragic means. Lion and lamb do not lay down together but keep one another's population within sustainable limits by a bloody process of eating and being eaten.

We are tempted, in speaking of nature as revelatory, to see nature through a paradisal lens, ignoring its violent and tragic face. We imagine it as Eden only by removing ourselves from it and viewing it through the plate glass window of our momentary havens of invulnerability, purchased at the expense of many other humans. But a tornado can shatter this glass and sweep away this shelter at any moment.

Two revelatory commands come, from "nature" and from "history," that are not easy to reconcile. Some in Christian thought even saw them as revealing different gods opposed to one another. I call these two commands the call to sustainability and the call to preferential option for the poor. When I garden, I would be foolish to make a preferential option for the weak and the diseased. I need to root out the excess growth of many plants so that a few, the healthiest, can grow well. In like manner, as Jay McDaniel agonized, nature gives the pelican two eggs so that one will survive: if the first hatches well, the second will be pecked to death and thrown from the nest.[24] This cruelty is necessary for a sustainable population of pelicans or tomatoes. Sentimentality for the second pelican or the excess plants would be misplaced.

Likewise, humans need to limit their own species proliferation at the expense of the other species of Earth, as much as possible by decisions not to conceive rather than to abort. But to deny the need for birth limitation in the name of life is no favor to children. It means that thousands die each day of malnutrition soon after birth. To refuse to limit ourselves rationally means that these limits are imposed cruelly and violently.

A different call comes from our history of sin and *han*, arising as a protest against the distortion of relations between humans and with other creatures that results in overweening wealth for a few and impoverishment for the many. This pattern is not, contrary to social Darwinism, an expression of a natural ethic of the survival of the fittest, for nature does not favor the large carnivore, precariously perched at the top of the food chain, over all the creatures on which it depends, but seeks dynamic balance through a combination of mutual limits and cooperation. The scurrying insects that compost the forest are far more important to its well-being than the lion.

Preferential option for the poor seeks to correct the destructive option for the rich at the expense of the well-being of the whole community of life. The ethic of preferential option for the poor calls us to feed and nurture the child of the poor dying from malnutrition and unclean water and to rectify the conditions that are causing this untimely death, while the ethic of sustainability calls us to help the mother of this child limit her childbearing.

The two ethics often stand in tragic tension, but they should not be allowed to fall into irreconcilable dualism, with a war God of victory of the strong over the weak, on the one hand, and, on the other, a God of compassion for the weak distorted into a defense of fetuses against women. We need to seek a right balance between justice and sustainability. The challenge of ecological theology and ethics is to knit together, in the light of both earth knowledge and the crisis of human history, a vision of divine presence that underlies and sustains natural processes and struggles against the excesses of the powerful while reaching out to the victimized to create communities of mutual flourishing.

NOTES

1. For these relations of patriarchal domination in Ancient Near Eastern and Greek law codes, see Rosemary Ruether, *Gaia and God: An Ecofeminist Theology of Earth Healing* (San Francisco: HarperSanFrancisco, 1992), 174–80.

2. See "The Creation Epic" in *Religions of the Ancient Near East: Sumero-Akkadian Religious Texts and Ugaritic Epics,* ed. Isaac Mendelsohn (New York: Liberal Arts Press, 1955), 17–46.

3. Plato *Timaeus* 49, from *The Dialogues of Plato,* trans. B. Jowett (New York: Random House, 1937), 2:29.

4. Plato *Timaeus* 42, ibid., 23. See also Plato's *Phaedrus,* where he adds the idea that the fallen soul will enter into various upper or lower class people depending on the extent of its fall into the passions; *Dialogues of Plato,* 2:248.

5. See Origen *On First Principles* 2.2.2 (New York: Harper and Row, 1966), 81–82: also Ruether, *Gaia and God,* 133.

6. Gregory Nyssa describes the risen body as stripping off all that has made it mortal; see his "On the Soul and the Resurrection," in *Nicene and Post-Nicene Fathers,* 2d ser. (New York: Parker, 893), 5: 464–65.

7. Gen. 1:26–27.

8. See Phyllis Bird, "'Male and Female He Created Them': Gen 1:27b in the Context of the Priestly Account of Creation," in *Image of God and Gender Models in Judaeo-Christian Tradition,* ed. Kari Borresen (Minneapolis: Fortress Press, 1995), 11–34.

9. See Phyllis Trible, "Depatriarchalizing in Biblical Interpretation," *Journal of the American Academy of Religion* 46, no. 1 (March 1973): 30–48.

10. See Rachel Zohar Dulin, "Old Age in the Hebrew Scriptures" (Ph.D. diss., Northwestern University, 1982).

11. Gal. 3:28. See Rosemary R. Ruether, *Women and Redemption: A Theological History* (Minneapolis: Fortress Press, 1998), chap. 1.

12. 1 Tim. 1:11–15. See Dennis R. MacDonald, *The Legend and the Apostle: The Battle for Paul in Story and Canon* (Philadelphia: Westminster Press, 1983).

13. Augustine *De Trinitate* 10.10.7. See Ruether, *Women and Redemption,* chap. 2.

14. Augustine *City of God* 14.11.

15. Augustine *On Genesis: Two Books on Genesis against the Manichees* 2.19; *The Fathers of the Church,* trans. Roland J. Teske, vol. 84 (Washington, D.C.: Catholic University of America Press, 1991). See Ruether, *Women and Redemption,* chap. 2.

16. Particularly the tract of Agrippa von Nettesheim (1509), *De Nobilitate et Praecellentia foeminei Sexus,* ed. Charles Béné (Geneva: Librairie Droz, 1990). See Ruether, *Women and Redemption,* chap. 4.

17. Sarah Grimké, "Letters on the Equality of the Sexes and the Condition of Women" (1837), in *Feminism: The Essential Historical Writings,* ed. Miriam Schneir (New York: Vintage, 1992), 38.

18. Ivone Gebara, *Teología a Ritmo de Mujer* (Madrid: San Pablo, 1995), 146–56. Ruether, *Women and Redemption,* chap. 8.

19. Gebara, *Teología a Ritmo de Mujer,* 146–56.

20. This women's creed, written by Robin Morgan for the United Nations Conference on Women in Beijing, China, in September 1995, was sent to me by Catherine Keller of Drew Theological Seminary in Madison, New Jersey.

21. The term *han* comes from Korean Minjung theology that discusses the experience of victimization. For a theology that interconnects the Western Christian emphasis on sin with the Minjung emphasis on *han,* see

Andrew Sung Park, *The Wounded Heart of God: The Asian Concept of Han and the Christian Doctrine of Sin* (Nashville: Abingdon Press, 1993).

22. Ivone Gebara, "The Trinity and Human Experience," in Rosemary Radford Ruether, *Women Healing Earth: Third World Women on Ecology, Feminism, and Religion* (Maryknoll, N.Y.: Orbis Books, 1996), 13–23.

23. Gebara, *Teología a Ritmo de Mujer,* 146–56.

24. Jay B. McDaniel, *Of God and Pelicans: A Theology of Reverence for Life* (Louisville: Westminster/John Knox Press, 1989), 19–21.

Ecology Is a Sistah's Issue Too
The Politics of Emergent Afrocentric Ecowomanism

SHAMARA SHANTU RILEY

Black womanists, like everyone in general, can no longer overlook the extreme threat to life on this planet and its particular repercussions on people of African descent.[1] Because of the race for increased "development," our world continues to suffer the consequences of such environmental disasters as the Chernobyl nuclear meltdown and Brazil's dwindling forests. Twenty percent of all species are at risk of extinction by the year 2000, with the rate of plant and animal extinction likely to reach several hundred per day in the next ten to thirty years (Worldwatch 1987, 3). Manufacturing chemicals and other abuses to the environment continue to weaken the ozone layer. We must also contend with the phenomenon of climate change, with its attendant rise in sea levels and changes in food production patterns.

Along with these tragic statistics, however, are additional environmental concerns that hit far closer to home than many Black people realize. In the United States, poor people of color are disproportionately likely to be the victims of pollution, as toxic waste is being consciously directed at our communities. The nation's largest hazardous-waste dump, which has received toxic material from 45 states, is located in predominantly black Sumter County, Alabama (de la Pena and Davis 1990, 34). The mostly African-American residents in the 85-mile area between Baton Rouge and New Orleans, better known as Cancer Alley, live in a region which contains 136 chemical companies and refineries. A 1987 study conducted by the United Church of Christ's Commission for Racial Justice found that two-thirds of all Blacks and Latinos in the United States reside in areas with one or more unregulated toxic-waste sites (Riley 1991, 15). The CRJ report also cited race as the most significant variable in differentiating communities with such sites from those without them. Partly as a result of living with toxic waste in disproportionate numbers, African-Americans have higher rates of cancer, birth defects, and lead poisoning than the United States population as a whole.[2]

On the African continent, rampant deforestation and soil erosion continue to contribute to the hunger and poverty rates in many countries. The elephant population is rapidly being reduced as poachers kill them to satisfy industrialized nations' ivory trade demands (Joyce 1989, 22). Spreading to a dozen African nations, the Green Belt Movement is seeking to reverse the environmental damage created by the European settlers during colonialism, when the settlers brought nonindigenous trees on the continent. As with United States communities of color, many African nations experience "economic blackmail," which occurs when big business promises jobs and money to "impoverished areas in return for these areas' support of or acquiescence to environmentally undesirable industries" (Meyer 1992, 32).

The extinction of species on our ancestral continent, the "mortality of wealth," and hazardous-

Riley, Shamara Shantu, "Ecology Is a Sistah's Issue Too: The Politics of Emergent Afrocentric Ecowomanism," in Carol J. Adams, Ed., *Ecofeminism and the Sacred,* New York: Continuum, 1992, pp. 191–203. Reprinted by permission of The Continuum International Publishing Group.

waste contamination in our backyards ought to be reasons enough for Black womanists to consider the environment as a central issue of our political agendas.[3] However, there are other reasons the environment should be central to our struggles for social justice. The global environmental crisis is related to the sociopolitical systems of fear and hatred of all that is natural, nonwhite, and female that has pervaded dominant Western thought for centuries.[4] I contend that the social constructions of race, gender, class and nonhuman nature in mainstream Western thought are interconnected by an ideology of domination. Specific instances of the emergent Afrocentric eco-womanist activism in Africa and the United States, as well as West African spiritual principles that propose a method of overcoming dualism, will be discussed in this paper.

THE PROBLEM OF NATURE FOR BLACK WOMANISM

Until recently, few Black womanists gave more than token attention to environmental issues. At least in the United States, the origins of such oversight stem from the traditional Black association of environmentalism as a "white" concern. The resistance by many United States Blacks to the environmental movement may partly originate from a hope of revenge. Because of our acute oppression(s), many Blacks may conclude that if the world comes to an end because of willful negligence, at least there is the satisfaction that one's oppressors will also die. In "Only Justice Can Stop a Curse," author Alice Walker discusses how her life experiences with the Eurocentric, masculinist ideology of domination have often caused her to be indifferent to environmental issues:

> I think . . . *Let the earth marinate in poisons. Let the bombs cover the ground like rain. For nothing short of total destruction will ever teach them anything.* (Walker 1983b, 341)

However, Walker later articulates that since environmental degradation doesn't make a distinction between oppressors and the oppressed, it should be very difficult for people of color to embrace the thought of extinction of all life forms simply for revenge.

In advocating a reformulation of how humans view nonhuman nature, eco-feminist theorist Ynestra King states that from the beginning, women have had to grapple with the historical projection of human concepts onto the natural, which were later used to fortify masculinist notions about females' nature (King 1989, 118). The same problem is applicable to people of color, who have also been negatively identified with the natural in white supremacist ideologies.

Black women in particular have historically been associated with animality and subsequently objectified to uphold notions of racial purity. bell hooks articulates that since the 1500s, Western societies have viewed Black women's bodies as objects to be subdued and controlled like nonhuman nature:

> From slavery to the present day, the Black female body has been seen in Western eyes as the quintessential symbol of a "natural" female presence that is organic, closer to nature, animalistic, primitive. (hooks and West 1991, 153)

Patricia Hill Collins asserts that white exploitation of Black women as breeders during the Slave Era "objectified [Black women] as less than human because only animals can be bred against their will" (Collins 1990, 167). Sarah Bartmann, an African woman also known as the Hottentot Venus, was prominently displayed at elite Parisian parties. While being reduced to her sexual parts, Bartmann's protruding buttocks were often offered as "proof' that Blacks were closer to animals than whites. After her death in 1815, Bartmann was dissected, and her genitalia and buttocks remain on display in Paris (Gilman 1985). Bartmann's situation was similar to the predicament of Black female slaves who stood on auction blocks as masters described their productive body parts as humans do cattle. The historical dissection of Black women, be it symbolic or actual, to uphold white supremacist notions is interconnected with the consistent human view of nonhuman animals as scientific material to be dissected through an ideology that asserts both groups are inferior.

Because of the historical and current treatment of Blacks in dominant Western ideology, Black womanists must confront the dilemma of whether we should strive to sever or reinforce the traditional association of Black people with nature that exists in dominant Western thought. However, what we need is not a total disassociation of people from nature, but rather a reformulation of *everyone's* relationship to nature by socially reconstructing gender, class, and ethnic roles.

Environmentalism is a women's issue because females (especially those of color) are the principal farm laborers around the world, as well as the majority of the world's major consumers of agricultural products (Bizot 1992, 36). Environmentalism is also an important issue for people of color because we disproportionately bear the brunt of environmental degradation. For most of the world's population, reclaiming the Earth is not an abstract state of affairs but rather is inextricably tied to the survival of our peoples.

Womanism and ecology have a common theoretical approach in that both see all parts of a matrix as having equal value. Ecology asserts that without each element in the ecosystem, the biosphere as a whole cannot function properly. Meanwhile, womanism asserts the equality of races, genders, and sexual preferences, among other variables. There is no use in womanists advocating liberation politics if the planet cannot support people's liberated lives, and it is equally useless to advocate saving the planet without addressing the social issues that determine the structure of human relations in the world. If the planet as a whole is to survive, we must all begin to see ourselves as interconnected with nonhuman nature and with one another.

THE POLITICS OF NATURE-CULTURE DUALISM

At the foundation of dominant Western thought exists an intense ambivalence over humankind's place in the biosphere, not only in relation to one another, but also in relation to nonhuman nature. The systematic denigration of men of color, women, and nonhuman nature is interconnected through a nature-culture dualism. This system of interconnectedness, which bell hooks labels "the politic of domination," functions along interlocking axes of race, gender, species, and class oppression. The politic of domination "refers to the ideological ground that [the axes] share, which is a belief in domination, and a belief in the notions of superior and inferior, which are components of all those systems" (hooks 1989, 175). Although groups encounter different dimensions of this matrix based on such variables as species or sexual orientation, an overarching relationship nevertheless connects all of these socially constructed variables.

In discussing the origins of Western dualism, Dona Richards articulates the influence of dominant Jewish and Christian thought on Western society's conceptions about its relationship to nonhuman nature:

> Christian thought provides a view of man, nature, and the universe which supports not only the ascendancy of science, but of the technical order, individualism and relentless progress. Emphasis within this world view is placed on humanity's dominance over *all* other beings, which become "objects" in an "objectified" universe. Humanity is separated from nature. (Richards 1980, 69)

With dualistic thinking, humans, nonhuman nature, and ideas are categorized in terms of their difference from one another. However, one part is not simply deemed different from its counterpart; it is also deemed intrinsically *opposed* to its "Other" (Collins 1990, 69). For instance, speciesists constantly point to human neocortical development and the ensuing civilization that this development constructs as proof of human superiority over nonhuman animals. Women's position as other in Western patriarchies throughout the histories of both psychological theory and Christian thought has resulted in us being viewed as defective men.

Women, the nonelite, and men of color are not only socially constructed as the "Others," but the elite, white, male-controlled global political structure also has the power—through institutions such as the international media and politics—to extensively socialize us to view ourselves as others to be dominated. By doing so, the pattern of domination and subjugation is reinforced. Objectification is also central to the process of oppositional difference for all entities cast as other. Dona Richards claims that in dominant Western thought, intense objectification is a "prerequisite for the despiritualization of the universe and through it the Western cosmos was made ready for ever increasing materialization" (Richards 1980, 72). Since one component is deemed to be the other, it is simultaneously viewed as an object to be controlled and dominated, particularly through economic means.

Because nature-culture dualism conceives of nature as an other that (male) human undertakings transcend and conquer, women, nonhuman nature, and men of color become symbolically linked in Eurocentric, masculinist ideology. In this framework, the objectification of the other also serves as an escape from the anxiety of some form of mortality. For instance, white supremacists fear that it will be the death of the white race if people of color, who comprise the majority of the world's population, successfully resist the current global relations of power. Objectifying nonhuman nature by technology is predicated on an intense fear of the body, which reminds humans of death and our connection with the rest of nature. By making products that make tasks easier, one seeks to have more opportunities to live one's life, with time and nature converted into commodities.

World history can be seen as one in which human beings inextricably bind the material domination of nonhuman nature with the economic domination of other human beings. The Eurocentric, masculinist worldview that dominates Western thought tends to only value the parts of reality that can be exploited in the interest of profit, power and control. Not only is that associated with nature deemed amenable to conquest, but it is also a conquest that requires no moral self-examination on the part of the prospective conqueror. For instance, there is very little moral examination by research laboratories that test cosmetics on animals, or by men who assault women. There was also very little moral examination on the part of slave owners on the issue of slavery or by European settlers on colonialism in "Third World" nations.

By defining people of color as more natural and animalistic, a political economy of domination has been historically reinforced. An example of this phenomenon is the founding of the United States and the nation's resultant slave trade. In order for the European colonialists to exploit the American land for their economic interests, they first needed to subjugate the Native American groups who were inhabiting the land. While this was being accomplished, the colonists dominated Blacks by utilizing Africans as slave labor (and simultaneously appropriating much of Mexico) in order to cultivate the land for profit and expand the new capitalist nation's economy. Meanwhile, the buffalo almost became extinct in the process of this nation building "from sea to shining sea."

A salient example of the interconnectedness of environmental degradation and male supremacy is the way many societies attach little value to that which can be exploited without (economic) cost. Because nonhuman nature has historically been viewed by Westerners as a free asset to be possessed, little value has been accredited to it. Work traditionally associated with women via cultural socialization has similarly often been viewed as having little to no value. For instance, in calculating the Gross Domestic Product, no monetary value is attached to women's contributions to national economies through reproduction, housework, or care of children.

THE ROLE OF THE ENVIRONMENTAL-ISMS IN PROVIDING THE FOUNDATION FOR AN AFROCENTRIC WOMANIST AGENDA

While serving as executive director of the United Church of Christ's Commission for Racial Justice in 1987, Reverend Benjamin Chavis, Jr., coined the term *environmental racism* to explain the dynamics of socioeconomic inequities in waste-management policies. Peggy Shephard, the director of West Harlem Environmental Action, defines United States environmental racism as "the policy of siting potentially hazardous facilities in low-income and minority communities" (Day and Knight 1991, 77). However, environmental racism, which is often intertwined with classism, doesn't halt at the boundaries of poor areas of color. Blacks in Africa and the United States often have to contend with predominantly white environmental groups that ignore the connection between their own values and the struggles of people of color to preserve our future, which is a crucial connection in order to build and maintain alliances to reclaim the earth. For instance, because the Environmental Protection Agency is often seen as another institution that perceives elite white communities' complaints as more deserving of attention than poor communities of color, many United States social activists are accusing the EPA of "environmental apartheid" (Riley 1991, 15).

In "Granola Boys, Eco-Dudes and Me," Elizabeth Larsen articulates how race, class, and gender politics are interconnected by describing the overwhelmingly white middle-class male leadership of mainstream United States environmental groups. In addition to being indifferent to the concerns of people of color and poor whites, the mainstream organizations often reinforce male supremacy by distributing organizational tasks along traditional gender roles (Larsen 1991, 96). The realization that only we can best represent our interests, an eco-identity politics, so to speak, lays the foundation for an Afrocentric ecowomanist agenda.[5] Even though many Black women have been active in the environmental movement in the past, there appears not to be much *published* analysis on their part about the role of patriarchy in environmental degradation. The chief reason for this sentiment may stem from perceiving race as the "primary" oppression. However, there is an emergent group of culturally identified Black women in Africa and the United States who are critically analyzing the social roles of white supremacy, patriarchy, and classism in environmental degradation.

EMERGENT AFROCENTRIC ECOWOMANISM: ON THE NECESSITY OF SURVIVAL

There are several differences between ecofeminism and Afrocentric ecowomanism. While Afrocentric ecowomanism also articulates the links between male supremacy and environmental degradation, it lays far more stress on other distinctive features, such as race and class, that leave an impression markedly different from many ecofeminists' theories.[6]

Many ecofeminists, when analyzing the links between human relations and ecological degradation, give primacy to gender and thus fail to thoroughly incorporate (as opposed to mere tokenism) the historical links between classism, white supremacy, and environmental degradation in their perspectives. For instance, they often don't address the fact that in nations where such variables as ethnicity and class are a central organizing principle of society, many women are not only viewed in opposition to men under dualism, but also to other women. A salient example of this blind spot is Mary Daly's *Gyn/Ecology,* where she implores women to identify with nature against men and live our lives separately from men. However, such an essentialist approach is very problematic for certain groups of women, such as the disabled and Jews, who must ally themselves with men (while simultaneously challenging them on their sexism) in order to combat the *isms* in their lives. As writer Audre Lorde stated, in her critique of Daly's exclusion of how Black women use Afrocentric spiritual practices as a source of power against the *isms* while connecting with nonhuman nature:

> to imply, however, that women suffer the same oppression simply because we are women, is to lose sight of the many varied tools of patriarchy. It is to ignore how these tools are used by women without awareness against each other. (Lorde 1983, 95)

Unlike most white women, Black women are not limited to issues defined by our femaleness but are rather often limited to questions raised about our very humanity.

Although they have somewhat different priorities because of their different environments, Afrocentric ecowomanists in the United States and Africa nevertheless have a common goal—to analyze the issues of social justice that underlie environmental conflict. Not only do Afrocentric ecowomanists seek to avoid detrimental environmental impacts, we also seek to overcome the socioeconomic inequalities that led to the injustices in the first place.

Emergent United States Afrocentric Ecowomanist Activism

Contrary to mainstream United States media claims, which imply that African-Americans are not concerned about ecology, there has been increased environmental activism within Black communities since the early 1980s. Referred to as the environmental equity movement by Robert Bullard, predominantly Black grass roots environmental organizations tend to view environmentalism as an extension of the 1960s civil rights movement. In *Yearning,* bell hooks links environmentalism with social justice while discussing Black radicals and revolutionary politics:

> We are concerned about the fate of the planet, and some of us believe that living simply is part of revolutionary political practice. We have a sense of the sacred. The ground we stand on is shifting, fragile, and unstable. (hooks 1990, 19)

On discussing how the links between environmental concerns and civil rights encouraged her involvement with environmentalism, arts writer and poet Esther Iverem states:

> Soon I began to link civil rights with environmental sanity. . . . Because in 1970 Black folks were vocally fighting for their rightful share of the pie, the logical question for me became "What kind of shape will that pie be in?" (Iverem 1991, 38)

Iverem's question has been foremost in many African-American women's minds as we continue to be instrumental in the Black communities' struggle to ensure that the shape of the social justice pie on our planet will not be increasingly carcinogenic. When her neighborhood started to become dilapidated, Hattie Carthan founded the Magnolia Tree Earth Center of Bed-Stuy in Brooklyn in 1968, to help beautify the area. She planted more than 1,500 trees before her death in 1974. In 1986, the city council of Los Angeles decided that a 13-acre incinerator, which would have burned 2,000 tons of city waste daily, was to be built in a low-income Black and Latino neighborhood in South Central Los Angeles. Upon hearing this decision, residents, mostly women, successfully organized in opposition by forming Concerned Citizens of South Central Los Angeles. While planning direct actions to protest the incinerator, the grass roots organization didn't have a formal leadership structure for close to two years. Be it a conscious or unconscious decision, Concerned Citizens accepted a relatively nonhierarchical, democratic process in their political activism by rotating the chair's position at meetings, a form of decision making characteristic of many ecofeminist groups.[7]

The Philadelphia Community Rehabilitation Corporation (PCRC), founded by Rachel E. Bagby, operates a village community to maintain a nonhierarchical relationship between human and nonhuman nature for its working-class-to-poor urban Black residents. About 5,000 reside in the community, and there is communalistic living, like that of many African villages. PCRC has a "repeopling" program that renovates and rents more than 50 previously vacant homes and also created a twelve-unit shared house. PCRC also takes vacant lots and recycles them into gardens to provide food, and oversees literacy and employment programs. Hazel and Cheryl Johnson founded People for Community Recovery (PCR), which is operated from a storefront at the Altgeld Gardens housing project, after they became aware that their community sits atop a landfill and has the greatest concentration of hazardous waste in the nation. In its fight against environmental racism, PCR has insisted that the Chicago Housing Authority remove all asbestos from the Altgeld homes and has helped lobby city government to declare a moratorium on new landfill permits. PCR also successfully prevented the establishment of another landfill in Altgeld Gardens.

One Black women's organization that addresses environmental issues is the National Black Women's Health Project. The NBWHP expresses its Afrocentric ecowomanist sentiment primarily through its SisteReach program, which seeks to connect the NBWHP with various Black women's organizations around the world. On urging African-American women to participate in the environmental movement and analyze the connections between male supremacy and environmental degradation, Dianne J. Forte, the SisteReach coordinator, makes the following statement:

> At first glance and with all the major problems demanding our energy in our community we may be tempted to say, "this is not my problem." If however, we look at the ominous connection being made between environmental degradation and population growth; if we look at the same time at trends which control women's bodies and lives and control the world's resources, we realize that the same arguments are used to justify both. (Forte 1992, 5)

For instance, women are increasingly being told that we should not have control over our own bodies, while the Earth is simultaneously deemed feminine by scientists who use sexual imagery to articulate their plans to take control over the Earth. Meanwhile, dominant groups often blame environmental degradation on overpopulation (and with their privileged status, usually point at poor women of color), when industrial capitalism and patriarchal control over women's reproduction are among the most pronounced culprits.

The most salient example of practical United States Afrocentric ecowomanism combating such claims is Luisah Teish, a voodoo priestess. In connecting social justice issues with spiritual practices rooted in the West African heritage, Teish articulates the need for everyone to actively eliminate patriarchy, white supremacy, and classism, along with the domination of nonhuman nature. Members of Teish's altar circle have planned urban gardening projects both to supply herbs for their holistic healing remedies and to assist the poor in feeding themselves. They have also engaged in grass roots organizing to stop gentrification in various communities.

Emergent Afrocentric Ecowomanist Activism in Africa

On the African continent, women have been at the forefront of the movement to educate people about environmental problems and how they affect their lives. As with much of the African continent, environmental problems in Kenya particularly influence rural women's lives, since they comprise 80 percent of that nation's farmers and fuel gatherers (Maathai 1991, 74). Soil erosion directly affects the women, because they depend on subsistence agriculture for their families' survival. The lack of firewood in many rural areas of Kenya because of deforestation disproportionately alters the lives of women, who must walk long distances to fetch firewood. The lack of water also makes a negative imprint on Kenyan women's lives, because they have to walk long distances to fetch the water.

However, many Kenyan women are striving to alter these current realities. The most prominent Afrocentric ecowomanist in Africa is Wangari Maathai, a Kenyan microbiologist and one of Africa's leading activities on environmental issues. Maathai is the founder and director of the Green Belt Movement (GBM), a fifteen-year-old tree-planting project designed to help poor Kenyan communities stop soil erosion, protect their water systems, and overcome the lack of firewood and building materials.

Launched under the auspices of the National Council of Women of Kenya, the majority of the Green Belt Movement's members are women. Since 1977, these women have grown 10 million trees, 80 percent of which have survived, to offset Kenya's widespread deforestation.[8] Although the Green Belt Movement's primary practical goal is to end desertification and deforestation, it is also committed to promoting public awareness of the relationship between environmental degradation and social problems that affect the Kenyan people—poverty, unemployment, and malnutrition. However, one of the most significant accomplishments of the GBM, Maathai asserts, is that its members are "now independent; had acquired knowledge, techniques; had become empowered" (Maathai 1991, 74).

Another Kenyan dedicated to environmental concerns is Wagaki Mwangi, the founder and coordinator of the International Youth Development and Environment Network. When she visited the University of Illinois at Urbana-Champaign, Mwangi discussed how Kenya suffers economic and environmental predicaments primarily because her homeland is trying to imitate Western cultures. "A culture has been superimposed on a culture," Mwangi said, but there are not enough resources for everyone to live up to the new standards of the neocolonial culture (Schallert 1992, 3). She asserted that in attempts to be more Western, "what [Kenyans] valued as our food has been devalued, and what we are valuing is what they value in the West" (Schallert 1992, 3). For instance, Kenyans used to survive by eating a variety of wild foods, but now many don't consider such foods as staples because of Western influences. In the process, many areas of Kenya are deemed to be suffering from food shortages as the economy has been transformed to consumer capitalism with its attendant mechanization of agriculture.

In Kourfa, Niger, women have been the primary force behind preventing the village from disappearing, a fate that many surrounding villages have suffered because of the Sahel region's desertification. Reduced rainfall and the drying up of watering places and vegetation, combined with violent sandstorms, have virtually deprived Kourfa of harvests for the past five years. As a result, the overwhelming majority of Kourfa's men have had to travel far away for long periods of time to find seasonal work.

With the assistance of the Association of Women of Niger and an agricultural advisor, the women have laid out a small marketgarden around the only well in Kourfa. Despite the few resources at their disposal, the Kourfa women have succeeded in supporting themselves, their children, and the village elders. In response to the survival of the village since these actions, the Kourfa women are now calling for increased action to reverse the region's environmental degradation so "the men won't go away" from the village (Ouedraogo 1992, 38).

Afrocentric Ecomotherists: Ecowomanist Potential?

The environmental activism of some Black women brings up the question of whether community-oriented Black women who are addressing environmental issues are genuinely Afrocentric ecowomanists or possibly Afrocentric ecomotherists.[9] According to Ann Snitow, motherists are women who, for various reasons, "identify themselves not as feminists but as militant mothers, fighting together for survival" (Snitow 1989, 48). Snitow also maintains that motherism usually arises when men are absent or in times of crisis, when the private sphere role assigned to women under patriarchy makes it impossible for the collective to survive. Since they are faced with the dictates of traditional work but face a lack of resources in which to fulfill their socially prescribed role, motherists become a political force.

Since they took collective action to secure the survival of the village's children and elders only after the necessary absence of Kourfa's men, the activism of the Kourfa women may possibly be based on a motherist philosophy. One can only conjecture whether the Kourfa women criticized the social role of motherhood in Niger as they became a political force, or if womanist consciousness emerged after their political experiences. Because of their potential to transform into ecowomanists after they enter the political realm, Afrocentic ecomotherists shouldn't be discounted in an analysis of Black women's environmental activism. For instance, Charlotte Bullock contends that she "did not come to the fight against environmental problems as an intellectual but rather as a concerned mother" (Hamilton 1990, 216). However, she and other women in Concerned Citizens of South Central Los Angeles began to notice the sexual politics that attempted to discount their political activism while they were protesting. "I noticed when we first started fighting the issue how the men would laugh at the women . . . they would say, 'Don't pay no attention to them, that's only one or two women . . . they won't make a difference.' But now since we've been fighting for about a year the smiles have gone" (Hamilton 1990, 215). Robin Cannon, another member of Concerned Citizens, asserts that social relations in her home, specifically gender roles on caretaking, were transformed after she began participating in the group's actions (Hamilton 1990, 220).

MOVING BEYOND DUALISM: AN AFROCENTRIC APPROACH

In utilizing spiritual concepts to move beyond dualism, precolonial African cultures, with their both/and perspectives, are useful forms of knowledge for Afrocentric ecowomanists to envision patterns toward interdependence of human and nonhuman nature. Traditional West African cultures, in particular, which also happen to be the ancestral roots of the overwhelming majority of African-Americans, share a belief in nature worship and view all things as being alive on varying levels of existence (Haskins 1978, 30). One example of such an approach in West African traditions is the *Nyam* concept. A root word in many West African languages, *Nyam* connotes an enduring power and energy possessed by all life (Collins 1990, 220). Thus, all forms of life are deemed to possess certain rights, which cannot be violated at will.

In *Jambalaya,* Luisah Teish writes of the *Da* concept, which originates from the Fon people of Western Africa. *Da* is "the energy that carries creation, the force field in which creation takes place" (Teish 1985, 61). In the Fon view, all things are composed of energy provided by *Da.* For example, "the human is receptive to the energy emanating from the rock and the rock is responsive to human influence" (Teish 1985, 62). Because West Africans have traditionally viewed nonhuman nature as sacred and worthy of praise through such cultural media as song and dance, there is also a belief in *Nommo. Nommo* is "the physical-spiritual life force which awakens all 'sleeping' forces and gives physical and spiritual life" (Jahn 1961, 105).

However, with respect for nonhuman nature comes a different understanding of *Ache,* the Yoruba term for human power. *Ache* doesn't connote "power over" or domination, as it often does in mainstream Western thought, but rather power *with* other forms of creation. With *Ache,* Teish states that there is "a regulated kinship among human, animal, mineral, and vegetable life" (Teish 1985, 63). Humans recognize their *Ache* to eat and farm, "but it is also recognized that they must give back that which is given to them" (Teish 1985, 63). In doing so, we respect the overall balance and interdependence of human and nonhuman nature.

These concepts can be useful for Afrocentric ecowomanists not only in educating our peoples about environmental issues, but also in reclaiming the cultural traditions of our ancestors. Rachel Bagby states the positivity of humans connecting with nonhuman nature, a view that is interwoven in her organization's work:

> If you can appreciate the Earth, you can appreciate the beauty of yourself. The same creator created both. And if I learned to take care of that I'll also take care of myself and help take care of others. (Bagby 1990, 242)

Illustrating an outlook of planetary relations that is parallel to the traditional West African worldview, Bagby simultaneously reveals the continuous link between much of the African-American religious tradition and African spirituality.

In light of the relations of power and privilege that exist in the world, the appropriation of indigenous cultures by some ecofeminists must be addressed. Many womanists, such as Andy Smith and Luisah Teish, have criticized cultural feminists for inventing earth-based feminist spiritualities that are based on the exploitation of our ancestral traditions, while we're struggling to reclaim and defend our cultures from white supremacy. In "For All Those Who Were Indian in Another Life," Smith asserts that this appropriation of non-Western spiritual traditions functions as a way for many white women to avoid taking responsibility for being simultaneously oppressive as well as oppressed (see her article, pp. 168–71). White ecofeminists can reclaim their own pre-Christian European cultures, such as the Wiccan tradition, for similar concepts of interconnectedness, community, and immanence found in West African traditions.[10]

Adopting these concepts would transform humans' relationship to nonhuman nature in a variety of ways. By seeing all components of the ecosystem affecting and being affected by one another, such a world perspective demonstrates a pattern of living in harmony with the rest of nature, instead of seeking to disconnect from it. By viewing ourselves as a part of nature, we would be able to move beyond the Western disdain for the body and therefore not ravage the Earth's body as a result of this disdain and fear. We would realize that the Earth is not merely the source of our survival, but also has intrinsic value and must be treated with respect, as it is our elder.

The notion of community would help us to appreciate the biological and cultural diversity that sustains life. Because every entity is viewed as embodying spirituality under immanence, culture wouldn't be viewed as separate from, and superior to, nature, as it is seen in mainstream Western religions. Communalism would also aid us in reformulating the social constructions of race, gender, species, class (among other variables), which keep groups separate from one another. And finally, the environmental movement in particular would view politics as rooted in community and communally take actions to reclaim the Earth and move toward a life of interdependence for generations to come.

NOTES

I would like to acknowledge the help that Carol Adams has given me with this essay. Her reading suggested valuable changes in the structure of the paper as well as clearing up minor flaws in writing. She also suggested some references that would augment my claims.

1. Alice Walker's definition of womanist is a feminist of color who is "committed to the survival and wholeness of entire people, male *and* female" (Walker 1983a, xi–xii). University of Ibadan (Nigeria) English senior lecturer Chikwenye Okonjo Ogunyemi contends that "black womanism is a philosophy that celebrates black roots . . . It concerns itself as much with the black sexual power tussle as with the world power structure that subjugates blacks" (Ogunyemi 1985, 72). Since feminism often gives primacy to gender, and race consciousness often gives primacy to race, such limitations in terminology have caused many women of color to adopt the term *womanist,* which both Walker and Ogunyemi independently coined in the early 1980s. Although some of the women in this paper refer to themselves as feminists rather than womanists, or use both terms interchangeably, I am using the term *womanist* in an interpretative sense to signify a culturally identified woman of color who also critically analyzes the sexual politics within her respective ethnic group.

2. For a discussion of how toxic waste has affected the environmental health of United States Black communities, see Day and Knight (1991).

3. Robert Bullard (1990) contends that the mortality of wealth involves toxic-waste dumping to pursue profits at the expense of others, usually low-income people of color in the United States. Because this demographic group is less likely to have economic resources

and political clout, it can't fight back as easily as more affluent communities that possess white skin privileges. I think this term is also applicable to the economic nature of toxic dumping in "Third World" countries, which are basically disempowered in the global political process.

4. For an ecofeminist text that makes a similar claim, see King (1989).

5. My definition of an Afrocentric ecowomanist is a communalistic-oriented Black woman who understands and articulates the interconnectedness of the degradation of people of color, women, and the environment. In addition to articulating this interconnectedness, an Afrocentric ecowomanist also strives to eradicate this degradation. For an extensive discussion of Afrocentrism, see Myers (1988).

6. An example of this distinction can be seen in Davies (1988). In her article, Davies only discusses the interconnections between gender and nature and completely avoids analyzing how such variables as ethnicity and class influence the experience of gender in one's life.

7. For several descriptions of the political decision making within feminist peace organizations, see the essays in Harris and King (1989).

8. It is noteworthy that the seedlings come from over 1,500 tree nurseries, 99 percent of which are operated by women. In addition, the women are given a small payment for the trees that survive.

9. In comparison to an Afrocentric ecowomanist, I define an Afrocentric ecomotherist as a communalistic-oriented Black woman who is involved in saving the environment and challenging white supremacy, but who does not challenge the fundamental dynamics of sexual politics in women's lives.

10. For instance, Starhawk, a practitioner of the Wiccan tradition, has written about her spiritual beliefs (1990).

Ecofeminism and Ecosocialism
Dilemmas of Essentialism and Materialism

MARY MELLOR

INTRODUCTION

THE RETHINKING AND RECASTING OF HISTORICAL materialism from an ecological perspective only takes account of one of the so-called "new social movements" of the late twentieth century. Another new, but in fact very old movement, feminism, must also be addressed. This certainly has been the intention of eco-Marxists such as the founders of the journal *Capitalism, Nature, Socialism (CNS)*.[1] However, the integration of women as contributors to this debate in substantial numbers, or as theoretical subjects, has yet to be achieved. I hope that this [essay] will contribute to what will necessarily be a long and complex debate. The core of my argument here is that it will prove impossible to construct an ecosocialist/ecofeminist revolutionary theory and practice unless we can finally break out of the laager of economic analysis to embrace women and nature not as objects of the economic system, but as subjects in their own right, an argument I have addressed more fully elsewhere.[2]

This endeavor raises the critical issue of the relationship between the seemingly ahistoric universals of biological sex and nature as "essential" features of human existence and the historical materialism of class analysis. Historical materialism asserts that the constraints on, and potential for, collective human development and creativity are socially constructed, and thereby capable of being socially resolved. The dilemma between essentialism and materialism is whether the socially materialist analysis of historical materialism can integrate the physically material reality of women and nature, that is, can we bring women in without their biology, or nature in without the constraint of its "natural" limits? These problems are inherent in the debate between ecofeminism and ecosocialism.

Mellor, Mary, "Ecofeminism and Ecosocialism: Dilemmas of Essentialism and Materialism," in Ted Benton, Ed., *The Greening of Marxism*, New York: Guilford Press, 1996, pp. 251–267.
Reprinted by permission of the author.

The debate in *CNS* was opened in response to the very cursory treatment of ecofeminism by Faber and O'Connor in their discussion of the environmental movement in the United States where they dismissed ecofeminism as fused with "neo-Romantic nature ideologies."[3] While agreeing that this criticism of some kinds of ecofeminism was valid, Lori-Ann Thrupp responded by claiming that ecosocialism was in danger of missing the "rich theoretical and historical analysis" of ecofeminism.[4] She pointed to the common exploitation that women and nature have received at the hands of patriarchy and the role that women have played in labor, antimilitary, and environmental struggles. Drawing on the work of Carolyn Merchant, Thrupp distinguished between the radical feminist grounding of human nature in human biology with its evocation of ancient rituals and goddess worship and socialist ecofeminism that sees both "nature and human nature as historically and socially constructed." While radical ecofeminist philosophy embraces intuition, an ethic of caring, and weblike human-nature relationships, socialist ecofeminism would seek to give both production and reproduction a central place in materialist analysis.[5]

Faber and O'Connor responded by apologizing for giving limited attention to ecofeminism but went on to affirm their criticism of "romantic" ideas such as intuition as against science and technology, the privileging of the human body over "mind," and "organic theories emphasizing emotional ties to the community ('caring')."[6] I do not think these ideas can be so easily dismissed; in particular, we cannot ignore emotional ties and caring if we are to theoretically integrate reproduction and production.

A central difficulty in discussing this relationship is that neither ecofeminism nor ecosocialism can be easily defined, reflecting the fact that the former draws on many feminisms and the latter on many socialisms. Ecofeminists range from New Age thinkers to socialists, and ecosocialists range from Marxists to anarchists.[7] However, it has become plain in the context of *CNS* that the debate is between a reading of ecofeminism that sees it as embodying variants of cultural or radical feminism and a neo-Marxian socialism:

> In the U.S., *radical* ecofeminism means more or less an "essentialist" view of women and men, not a "materialist" view of human nature as socially and historically (as well as naturally) constructed, as in the socialist traditions that we associate ourselves with.[8]

The core of this argument is whether an analysis and programme for change based on sex/gender (reflecting relations of both reproduction and sexuality) stand independent of a programme for change based on production relations. Despite the best efforts of many theorists, far too numerous to list, a "marriage" between Marxism and radical feminism has not been achieved. Ariel Salleh is quite right to be concerned that a debate between ecofeminists and eco-Marxists might end up in a similar barren theoretical quagmire.[9] It is clear that Marxist socialism cannot "take account" of women-as-subjects and feminist theory generally without seriously threatening the male and productivist basis of Marxist theory.

At the same time, ecosocialists such as Faber and O'Connor who draw on a Marxist base quite rightly are concerned about any analysis, green or feminist, that threatens to divert attention from the massive and corrupting power of capital. The dilemma between essentialist readings of women and nature versus a materialist analysis of economic relations is that feminist and ecological concerns will undermine historical materialism by positing essentialist limits to human activity (ecological or biological) or by claiming an intuitive source of knowledge that draws on biological or ecological dynamics. From the perspective of historical materialism such a course would trap human societies in a reified naturalism whereby social relationships are presented as ordained by biology or by nature. The green arguments that there are "natural" limits to growth or that nature contains within it a "natural" balance, or claims by some feminists that they are "naturally" more peace loving and cooperative, risk presenting constructs of human society as constructs of nature.

I would argue that we will not overcome this dilemma by denying the *material* issues at the basis of the feminist and ecological critique. Rather, we should move to the central question of how we theorize the very real question of the finite nature of the planet and the biological differences between men and women. To maintain that there is a biological and ecological limit to human activity and our capacity for social reconstruction is not to revert to essentialism but to begin to theorize the conditions of our material existence.

GETTING DOWN TO ESSENTIALS

The extent to which the accusation of essentialism can be laid against ecofeminism depends on the way in which the relationship between women and nature is defined. Is it a relationship of affinity, of a unity of spirit/biology between women and nature, or the sharing of a socially constructed relationship of exploitation? Petra Kelly clearly expressed the affinity of women with nature:

> Women are the "ombudsmen" [*sic*] of future generations . . . because only [a woman], I feel, can go back to her womb, her roots, her natural rhythms, her inner search for harmony and peace, while men, most of them anyway, are continually bound in their power struggle, the exploitation of nature, and military ego trips.[10]

As Cynthia Enloe has remarked, the overwhelming predominance of men in international politics and the violent relations that ensue has meant that there is scarcely a woman who "on a dark day" has not been attracted by essentialist arguments about the inherently violent nature of men, if not the inherently peaceful nature of women.[11] The same is probably true for those women, like myself, whose political history lies in socialist movements. On my dark days I wonder if male-dominated structures are irredeemably bureaucratic and sex/gender-blind. Given the very real experience of women at the hands of men and the institutions they control, it is inevitable that essentialist ideas tremble beneath the surface of most feminist thought. This is particularly true of ecofeminism, one of whose primary roots is in the women's peace movement.[12]

Do women have a privileged role in the "intricate web of life" through the nurturing experience they share with the planet? Do they have more peace-loving, intuitive, and caring characteristics? Green writings that lean toward New Age thinking proclaim the existence of feminine and masculine "principles."[13] The feminine principle associated with women exhibits the "soft/yin" qualities of cooperation, empathy, holistic thinking, emotion, and intuition, while the masculine principle associated with men displays the hard/yang qualities such as competitive assertiveness, rationalism, aggression, and materialism. These principles are seen as timeless and universal but not essentially limited to either sex. Ideally, each human being should be a balance of yin and yang, of the masculine and feminine principles. Advocates of the feminine principle seek a change of values so that we all become "balanced" in a "cultural transformation" whereby men recover the "feminine" side of themselves and women become more assertive. Cultural feminists have also proclaimed the superiority of women's culture, rooted in her "nature"—although without any optimism about men's ability to respond to women's "healing" powers.[14]

This form of analysis is clearly unacceptable to socialists. It returns to exactly the kind of essentialist idealism that Marx and Engels opposed. Historical materialism rejects such ahistorical universals and the claim that changing (or recovering) values will change society. However, we are still left with a problem: while it is easy to reject idealist essentialism, the question of the relationship between the biological/ecological and the social remains. In the original "Prospectus" of *CNS* the "human-nature" puzzle is set out as one that has to be theoretically resolved.[15] This is a biological as well as an ecological puzzle. Murray Bookchin has proposed that we recognize a dialectical relationship between ecology and society in the concept of a "social ecology," but the idea of a "social biology" has a very different ring, largely because of the reactionary work of sociobiologists. However, the dangers of essentialism, and the reactionary nature of previous analysis, should not blind us to the need to incorporate the reality of biology and ecology into our theory and practice.

Not only socialists have been reluctant to open discussion about the "human-nature" puzzle; feminists also have only hesitatingly addressed the question of biology. As Ariel Salleh points out, the primary task of second-wave feminism was to overthrow the limitations that male-dominated conceptions of women's biology had placed upon them, and to deny that biology was destiny. At the same time, she points out that "the biological" cannot be thrust aside.[16] Motherhood, in particular, is being reassessed within feminist thought and forms a substantial basis of feminist analysis of the issues of ecology and peace.[17] Heather Jon Maroney argues that the failure to address the "presocial reality" of motherhood reflects a continuing desire on the part of men to maintain the separation of the public from the private.[18] Mary O'Brien sees it as a male-dominated urge to separate (social) life from (biological) necessity: "an ideological separation, a yearning and a dream of the sweet sunshine always outside the cave of the contradications of carnality."[19]

Salleh draws our attention to the danger of socialists perpetuating the Judeo-Christian, Baconian-Cartesian division between mind and body in ignoring the reality of women's biological experience: or "the *masculine* will to disconnect from and transcend our earthly condition: what Marx called 'necessity.' . . . the rationalist thrust to transcend bodily embeddedness in place and relationships."[20] Martin O'Connor points to the "inescapable materiality of pregnancy and childbirth."[21] O'Brien argues that the separation of production and reproduction that runs right through the work of Marx and the Marxists translates what is specifically a male experience of that separation into a false universal truth. I would argue that the claim that biology/ecology can be subsumed within the human determination of the social is unrealistic and male-oriented in its prioritizing of the economic over all other aspects of human and nonhuman existence. In effect, Marxian socialism is presenting us with a *normative* theory that represents the experience and ideology of men. In this it *shares* rather than opposes the perspective of capital.

WHAT IS MATERIAL ABOUT HISTORICAL MATERIALISM?

If we are to synthesize ecosocialism and ecofeminism we must be clear about the relationship between historical materialism and the material relationship between men and women. More contentiously, perhaps, we need to theorize the way in which biological differences are reflected in male–female relations. This brings us to the crux of the question of the relationship between what we might call physical materialism and social materialism. This is caught in Marx's epithet that "[men] make history, albeit not under conditions of their own choosing." How far are human biological differences (and ecological limits) not "conditions of our own choosing"? The foundation of Marxist historical materialism is the primacy of economic relations. Under capitalism, these are primarily relations among men and, despite valiant efforts from Engels onward, the position of women has never been adequately theorized within historical materialism.[22]

In Marxist theory, economic relations are based on the primary need of human beings to produce the means of their survival. In particular eras this takes the form of a particular mode of production of which the most world-dominant has been capitalism. However, what does it mean to say that economic relations are "determinant in the last instance," to use Althusser's phrase? Is this not in itself an essentialist statement? To Marxists this question is sacrilege, but from a feminist point of view a challenge must be made. In *The German Ideology,* in Marx's discussion of the social relations of production, he talked first of "the production of life, both of one's own labor and of fresh life by procreation." Why should the means of survival (a biological imperative) be allowed into historical materialism but not the means of reproducing life itself? Further, if the means of survival produced definite social relations and particular forms of consciousness, why not the means of procreation?

I would argue that there are three interlinked material bases to human society: the forces/relations of production, the forces/relations of reproduction, and the relations between human society and nature. In the case of the first two the distinction between them is in itself socially constructed. What is incorporated in the sphere of "production" does not just represent the interests of capital, it represents the interests of men. By separating production from both reproduction and from nature, patriarchal capitalism has created a sphere of "false" freedom that ignores biological and ecological parameters. It is a sphere that can exploit nature without paying attention to what O'Connor has called the "second contradiction of capital," the conditions of production itself.[23] However, unlike O'Connor, I do not think this is a contradiction just for capital: it is a contradiction for men as well.

The integration of ecofeminism with ecosocialism cannot be achieved by trying to add women onto a male-dominated productivist socialism; that has been tried many times and failed lamentably. Marxian socialism must be reconstructed to take account of the reality of women's lives and the way in which the male/capitalist sphere of production is materially dependent upon women and nature. The reality of women's lives is not only sexual and reproductive, but productive, particularly in the struggle for livelihood by the women of the South. As the women of the Development Alternatives with Women for a New Era (DAWN) point out, "In food production and processing, in responsibility for fuel, water, health care, child-rearing, sanitation and the entire range of so-called basic needs, women's labor is dominant."[24] The invisibility of women's work and its existence outside of formal economic relations still has to be placed on the (male) political agenda.[25] However, capitalism has found women's caring and domestic work and builds upon preexisting patriarchal structures to produce appalling hardship where women are exploited as workers and as women, to the point of "superexploitation" where even their basic subsistence is denied.[26]

In women's lives, particularly in subsistence economies, it is impossible to separate productive and reproductive work. It is this work of producing the means of life and of survival, ecofeminists argue, that establishes the close relations between women and the planet. Vandana Shiva claims that in their subsistence work women have been guardians of the ecological sustainability of the planet, and that woman-based sustainability is now threatened by the cash-cropping and genetic engineering of patriarchal capitalism.[27] It is in women's lives that the relationship between the social/biological is constructed and it is this underlaboring work that women do that is not incorporated into the "material" world of men as represented in the theoretical framework of historical materialism. By that token, overthrowing capital will not resolve the "second contradiction" of the conditions of production for either women or nature. In fact, the theory of historical materialism based on the primacy of (formal) economic relationships as defined by capitalism has produced the catastrophe of the command economies which, by mimicking the productive power of capital, continued to deny the reality of much of women's lives and produced ecological devastation.

WOMEN'S LIVES: NURTURING THE WORLD

Feminists are increasingly focusing on the sexual divisions that surround mothering and nurturing and the role of women in sustaining human physical and emotional existence as a means of understanding our relationship with the natural world and as the basis of a reconstructed socialism:

> Because of the way it mediates between the biology of procreation and historical institutionalization, motherhood provides a prime site for exploring and constructing boundaries between nature and culture. Historically, the division in Western thought has been dichotomous and drawn in such a way as to exclude women from the social and the historical.[28]
>
> The world of nurturance and close human relationships is the sphere where the basic human needs are anchored and where models for *humane* alternatives can be found. This world, which has been carried forward mainly by women, is an existing alternative culture, a source of ideas and values for shaping an alternative path of development for nations and all humanity.[29]

This is not to return to an essentialist idealization of "women as mothers." Not all women are mothers or want to be mothers. Not all mothers enjoy that role. Moreover, "mothering" is a role that can be carried out by men. The potentially positive values of mothering attach to the performance of the task, not to the biology of the performer.[30] The fact that women biologically can and do give birth does not imply any particular adoption of feminine/feminist values. Women who have borne children do go to war and do embrace militaristic nationalism, racism, and fascism. However, with Ann Ferguson and Sara Ruddick, I would argue that mothering/nurturing is a biological/social task that has to be carried out if human society is to survive and that in a patriarchal society that task is carried out, willingly or unwillingly, by women.

Women's work as mothers and nurturers, or their identification with that role, has justified their marginalization within economic relationships to the extent that their work, quite literally, does not count. Throughout history this work has led to the association of women with nature rather than with culture,[31] constraining them to the private sphere of unfreedom, while men colonize the public "sphere of freedom" untrammeled by domestic necessities. Although sexual and reproductive relationships have been constructed differently across history and across cultures, in their domestic, nurturing, and subsistence work women have been held almost universally responsible for meeting the immediate emotional and material needs of their families and for sustaining relationships within the community.

The main characteristic of women's work, as Charlotte Perkins Gilman pointed out, is its "immediate altruism." Women's work is altruistic in the sense that it is carried out for only incidental personal gain (the pleasure of close personal relationships), and it is immediate in the sense that it cannot be "put off" or slotted into a work schedule. Immediate emotional and physical care cannot be "logically" ordered or "rationally programmed." The needs to which women respond are demands that cannot be ignored; if they are ignored, the social fabric of society begins to disintegrate: "The main distinction of human virtue is. . . altruism [and] 'otherness'. . . to love and serve one another, to feel for and with one another. . . . The very existence of humanity is commensurate with [the] development [of them]."[32]

While the work that women do is both socially and biologically essential, women's responsibility for meeting the immediate needs of both family and community is not a biological given, nor is it freely chosen: it is an "altruism" imposed on women by men. I would argue that this is the most fundamental division in society, that women are primarily (but not all and not always) responsible for meeting the immediate needs of others, while men (again, not all and not always) are not. In industrial or market economies, a great deal of women's subsistence work and some caring work is incorporated within the economic system, but, if that system fails, women once more begin the long struggle of "holding the family together" and maintaining the relationships that create "humanity." In doing this work, women produce a substantial proportion of the material basis of men's lives, but perhaps more importantly give men that most precious asset: time.[33] Ignoring women's role in the production of time produces a public world that does not take account of the reality of women's lives. As feminists have pointed out, the division between the public and the private world is a false one that reflects male interests and male experience. It is a world that can compartmentalize human existence into categories of space and time, where decisions can be made that do not take account of the complexities of human existence. It is a world where military, scientific, or economic "logic" can be pursued regardless of its impact on human relationships or even human existence.

The combined and uneven development of men's and women's lives was exacerbated by industrial capitalism, but it was not created by it. Patriarchal society has a long history whose origins are still obscure.[34] Failure to recognize women's work means that male-dominated capitalism is constructed on a false premise, that of the independently functioning individual. This reflects not only bourgeois individualism but patriarchal individualism, reflected in economic terms (Marxist and non-Marxist) as "free" labor. Only a small minority of men, and an even smaller minority of women, actually achieve sufficient power to function independently, but that does not prevent the public world from being constructed on that basis. Women who enter the public world have to operate according to the principles of male/bourgeois individualism, that is, they must deny any domestic responsibilities or pass them on to someone else (usually another woman). Men who undertake caring responsibilities must also be available to work long hours and be ready to uproot themselves and their families according to political/economic or military demands.

Insofar as Marxist theory shares its definition of economic relations with patriarchy and capitalism, it will be unable to break through the theoretical barriers of its own construction. Marxist socialism rejects the capitalist economic relations that exploit workers, peoples of the South, women, and the planet, but it does not recognize that it shares with these relations the artificial boundaries of male-dominated productivism, so that women's lives become theoretically a leftover category, the "sphere of reproduction." The differences in men's and women's approaches to life are not defined by some biological "essentialism," nor do they reflect universal male or female "principles"; rather, they reflect the very real differences in life experience of men and women, male-experience-reality (ME-reality) as against women's-experience-reality (WE-reality). By the same token, a feminist analysis that focuses upon women's experience is no more essentialist than the Marxist emphasis on the predominantly male experience of the public world of production. We are not talking about a distinction between essentialist versus materialist theories, but rather a particular dynamic between the essential needs of human existence and the material construction that is put upon them. The essentialism-materialism dichotomy is, in fact, a contradiction. It *appears* as a dichotomy if viewed through male-defined reality; but when viewed from the perspective of women's lives, the dichotomy can clearly be seen as a contradiction. The male construction of a social world presupposes its material base in women's time and work. When women try to articulate a perspective that reflects their social condition, they are accused of essentialism, or at least of detracting from the "primary" economic struggle with capital.

In the debate between essentialism and materialism we must be sure whose reality we are representing. A socialism that starts from ME-reality prioritizes public relationships, in particular, economic relationships. A socialism constructed on the basis of ME-reality will be *essentially* limited. It will establish itself on a limited material base, an economic system defined by both patriarchy and capitalism.

A FEMINIST REALITY

Like Ariel Salleh, I was concerned to see Faber and O'Connor from an eco-Marxist perspective dismiss "organic theories emphasizing emotional ties to the community ('caring')" as "romantic" radical feminism.[35] Women's lives are caught in a network of interconnected relationships not as an essentialist ideal, but as a material reality. Their thinking has to be feeling, intuitive, and multifaceted because that is the structure of their lives. Dubbing ecofeminism "essentialist" means that it can be easily marginalized and rejected by socialists without a real engagement with feminist theory and practice. There is no question but that both women and the planet have suffered abominably at the hands of men, and that men have a case to answer. The problem is to explain the dominance of men in destructive practices without collapsing into an equally one-sided feminism.

The answer lies in the material limitations of the need to secure human reproduction and survival and the parameters it places upon human (in practice, women's) activity. Failure to acknowledge these limitations masks the material benefit that men gain, as men, from women's work.[36] A feminist ecosocialism must not dodge the fact that there is a direct connection between the biological differences between men and women and the social construction that is put upon them: between the forces and the relations of reproduction. Biological differences of sex do not determine human behavior; they are the forces of reproduction that have to be accommodated in relations of reproduction. To put it more simply, in the absence of the reproductive technology that Firestone envisaged (and many feminists fear men are trying to create), women will continue to bear children and be primarily responsible for them, at least in the early years.[37]

This is not to say that biology determines the power relationships between men and women, but it does constrain them. To resolve those power relations will not mean that biological differences between the sexes will wither or be "willed away." I would agree with Pat and Hugh Armstrong that the distinction between sex and gender, while helpful in many ways, ultimately can be misleading. Women will continue to be subordinated under socialism "unless socialist women and men are prepared to take their biological differences into account."[38] As Ynestra King put it, there is a "masculinist mentality which would deny us our right to our own bodies and our own sexuality, and which depends on multiple systems of dominance and state power to have its way."[39] Recent concern about reproductive engineering reminds us that scientific developments are not just about creating profits by genetic engineering, they are also about men controlling women through their biology.[40] It is also not essentialist to point to the implications of the fact that men, as a rule, do not mother. Dorothy Dinnerstein and Nancy Chodorow have both warned convincingly about the dangers of mothering being assigned exclusively to women.[41] From a psychoanalytic perspective, they argue that girls respond to female mothering by becoming dependent on emotional relationships and continue to identify with the mothering role, while boys have to distance themselves from emotional relationships in order to follow the distant father into the public world where, in their emotionally truncated state, they can wreak havoc. Carol Gilligan has argued that the differences in male and female development have created two different moral universes where "male and female voices typically speak of the importance of different truths, the former of the role of separation as it defines and empowers the self, the latter of the ongoing attachment that creates and sustains the human community."[42] Elizabeth Spelman has quite rightly pointed out that Freudian theory, from which Dinnerstein and Chodorow draw their inspiration, is historically and culturally specific and cannot be assumed to apply universally to family and child-rearing, but this does not detract from its applicability to male and female development in Western cultures.[43]

There is no biological reason why men should not nurture children after birth, and many do. However, the reason most men do not "mother" is not purely social; it is far too universal a phenomenon for that to be the case. I would suggest that a possible explanation is social inertia resting on a biological phenomenon. If women give birth, and in most cultures suckle, what is there to encourage men to take over nurturing at some later stage? I would argue that only a socialism that recognizes the *fact* of biological difference, and constructs a political response to it, will be able consciously to take control of human history and found a society based upon WE-reality. Feminists have argued that their biological/social position in society has given women a specific standpoint that enables them to produce an alternative view of the world, one that "can overcome the old, oppressive dichotomy between the natural and the social," that can "represent a more complete materialism, a truer knowledge."[44] As Nancy Hartsock has pointed out, "The lived realities of women's lives are profoundly different from those of men." It is from the perspective of women that we can transcend the false boundaries between the natural and the social and accept that "as embodied humans we are. . . inextricably both natural and social."[45]

A feminist standpoint would lead us away from the ME-reality of the male-oriented public world and toward a WE-reality society that would find space and time not only for our physical needs, but also for emotional sustenance and the development of nonmaterial aspects of human development. Only a socialism that not only incorporates, but prioritizes, women's experience will be able to create the kind of society that will relieve women of the imposed altruism of their nurturing and caring work. By reintegrating the divided worlds of men and women, such a society will pull men back to the pace of biological time in which women live. It will create a society in which political and economic decisions will be local and accountable. It will equalize the resource of time, so that we can begin to slow down the pace of human development to sustainable levels. This is not to deny the present overwhelming dominance of capitalist economic relations. Theory or practice based on WE-reality will not of itself confront multinational companies, end the nuclear arms race, or prevent the exploitation of workers. An ecofeminism that does not embrace socialism would be as theoretically and politically limited as an ecosocialism that does not embrace feminism.

TOWARD A FEMINIST GREEN SOCIALISM

A feminist green socialism would not assume that human society is so exclusively determined by its mode of production that all other social/biological/ecological structures will "fall into line" if that mode of production is changed. It would accept that while there is no predetermined destiny in biology or ecology, we need to come to terms politically with their reality. It is true that to see aspects of human existence as a "given" prevents us from realizing that, through collective struggles, we can reconstruct our *social* world on egalitarian principles. And, quite rightly, to defend this principle socialists have waged a fierce battle against all forms of naturalism and essentialism, against all claims that certain aspects of human existence are beyond social control, and can only be "discovered," not constructed. However, in defense of the social we must not overly socialize the natural. To do so obscures the ecological framework of our existence and leads to a mystification of the material conditions of women's lives. The dominance of economic relationships in Marx and Engels's thought was, to say the least, unfortunate given the importance of feminist analysis in early French and British socialism.[46] Marx and Engels were well aware of the embeddedness of humanity in nature and of nature in humanity, as well as of women's inequality, but neither were incorporated into Marx's critique of capital. Engels attempted to construct a dialectics of nature and explain the origins of the patriarchal family, but neither subject has been substantively taken up by the legions of predominantly male, middle-class, and white Marxist theorists, nor have they formed part of the structure of socialist theory.

Faber and O'Connor criticize "some self-described ecofeminist practice" for opposing "some self-described ecosocialist practice as irredeemably 'patriarchal.'"[47] I see this as something male ecosocialists must refute, rather than as something ecofeminists should justify. Socialism, particularly in its Marxist form, has been "irredeemably" patriarchal for most of its existence. A feminist ecosocialism will need to expand historical materialism to explain relationships other than economic ones. Moreover, it will need to question the reification of the economic. It will have to recognize that economic relationships are not just defined by capitalism, but are also defined by patriarchy. Look, for example, at production decisions in Eastern Europe, guns and heavy machinery, but no adequate contraception, anesthetics for abortions, and limited domestic equipment and cleaning materials. A feminist green socialism would also recognize that men have very real interests in controlling women's sexuality and the domestic relations of production and reproduction, with their reflection in occupational segregation, inequalities, and sexual harassment.

By reifying economic relations, Marxian socialist theory has been limited by the boundaries of the capitalist mode of production. It has itself suffered from essentialism. A feminist ecosocialism would insist that the socially constructed "economy" should not be seen as the sole determining "material reality." Other realities are equally important, especially those of women and nature, and cannot be accommodated without reconstructing the whole socialist project. Socialists must realize that the boundaries of women's lives are not defined by economic relations: women cross and recross the so-called public–private world. Most important for women is the fact that the boundaries of their lives are policed by male violence, which also crosses the public–private divide. This is something that male-dominated socialism has not even begun to take on board.

At present, Marxist theory reflects the historically specific structure of Western patriarchal capitalism which prioritizes the interests of some men (and a few women) against the remaining men, exploited and oppressed by race and class, and the vast majority of women. For women, overthrowing those structures means accepting the biological materialism of sex differences and building a society that prevents social inertia starting the whole destructive process all over again, with men colonizing the "public" world and confining women to "inferior" work. A feminist ecosocialism would not deny the exploitative reality of capitalist economic relations or class politics, but would see it as one aspect of a much wider set of material relations.[48] A socialism conceived in the industrial center of a colonial power, based on a dominant race and sex, is not equipped to transport us to a feminist or a green future. If we have a socialism that only recognizes and embraces the male-dominated world of trade, war, and politics, a socialist revolution will do nothing to reconstruct those priorities. Men will continue to "take women's time," relying on women to be available for the twenty-four-hour responsibility of creating the framework of physical, emotional, and social relationships that make human society possible. They will be able to continue designing weapons of war, economic structures, and political systems that discount the needs of the majority of the world's peoples. A socialism that does not challenge the economic and sexual domination of women by men will never achieve an egalitarian society, nor one that is ecologically sustainable.

ACKNOWLEDGMENTS

The author wishes to thank Nancy Folbre for her superbly helpful editorial support, and Dr. Barbara Holland-Cunz, Jack Kloppenburg, Jr., Ropo Sekoni, and Arun Agrawal for their many useful comments.

NOTES

1. "Discussion" between Lori-Ann Thrupp, Daniel Faber, and James O'Connor, in *CNS,* Issue 3, November, 1989; "Discussion" between Ariel Salleh, Martin O'Connor, James O'Connor, and Daniel Faber, *CNS,* 2(1), Issue 6, February, 1991.

2. Mary Mellor, *Breaking the Boundaries: Towards a Feminist, Green Socialism* (London: Virago, 1992); see also Brinda Rao, *Dominant Constructions of Women and Nature in Social Science Literature* (Santa Cruz, Calif.: *CES/CNS* Pamphlet 2, 1991); Mary Mellor, *Feminism and Ecology* (Polity Press), forthcoming.

3. Daniel Faber and James O'Connor, "The Struggle for Nature: Environmental Crisis and the Crisis of Environmentalism in the United States," *CNS,* Issue 2, 1989, 32.

4. Thrupp, "Discussion," November, 1989, 170.

5. Ibid., 172–173.

6. Faber and O'Connor, "Discussion," February, 1991, 177.

7. See, for example, the myriad themes and visions woven into two recent ecofeminist anthologies: Irene Diamond and Gloria Feman Orenstein, eds., *Reweaving the World* (San Francisco: Sierra Club Books, 1990); and Judith Plant, ed., *Healing the Wounds: The Promise of Ecofeminism* (London: Green Print, 1989). For a review of socialist perspectives, see Martin Ryle, *Ecology and Socialism* (London: Radius, 1988).

8. Faber and O'Connor, "Discussion," February, 1991, 138; italic in original.

9. Salleh, "Discussion," February, 1991, 134.

10. Petra Kelly, *Fighting for Hope* (London: Chatto and Windus, 1984), 104.

11. Cynthia Enloe, *Bananas, Beaches, and Bases* (London: Pandora 1989), 5.

12. Leonie Caldecott and Stephanie Leland, eds., *Reclaim the Earth* (London: Women's Press, 1983).

13. Fritjof Capra, *The Turning Point* (London: Flamingo, 1982); Dorothy and Walter Schwarz, *Breaking Through* (Bideford, U.K.: Green Books, 1987). Ecofeminists have also expounded the idea of a feminist principle; see, for example, Stephanie Leland, "Feminism and Ecology: Theoretical Considerations," in Caldecott and Leland, eds., *Reclaim the Earth.*

14. Mary Daly, *Gyn/Ecology: The Metaethics of Radical Feminism* (London: Women's Press, 1989); Andree Collard, with Joyce Contrucci, *Rape of the Wild* (London: Women's Press, 1988); Susan Griffin, *Woman and Nature* (London: Women's Press, 1984).

15. *CNS,* Issue 1, 1988, 3.

16. Salleh, "Discussion," February, 1991, 130.

17. Sara Ruddick, *Maternal Thinking* (London: Women's Press, 1989).

18. Heather Jon Maroney, "Embracing Motherhood: New Feminist Theory," in *Politics of Diversity,* eds. Roberta Hamilton and Michele Barret, (London: Verso, 1986).

19. Mary O'Brien, *The Politics of Reproduction* (London: Routledge and Kegan Paul, 1981), 141.

20. Salleh, "Discussion," February, 1991, 134; italic in the original.

21. Martin O'Connor, "Discussion," February, 1991, 136.

22. Zillah Eisenstein, ed., *Capitalist Patriarchy and the Case for Socialist Feminism* (New York: Monthly Review Press, 1979); Heidi Hartmann, "The Unhappy Marriage of Marxism and Feminism: Towards a More Progressive Union," in *Women and Revolution* ed. Lydia Sargent (London: Pluto Press, 1981); Michelle Barrett, *Women's Oppression Today* (London: Verso, 1980); Annette Kuhn and AnnMarie Wolpe, *Feminism and Materialism* (London: Routledge and Kegan Paul, 1978); Lise Vogel, *Marxism and the Oppression of Women* (London: Pluto Press, 1983).

23. James O'Connor, "The Second Contradiction of Capitalism: Causes and Consequences," in *Conference Papers* (Santa Cruz, Calif.: *CES/CNS* Pamphlet 1, 1991).

24. Gita Sen and Caren Grown, *Development, Crises, and Alternative Visions* (New York: Monthly Review, 1987), 23–24. See also Vandana Shiva, *Staying Alive* (London: Zed Press, 1989); and Brinda Rao, "Struggling for Production Conditions and Producing Conditions of Emancipation: Women and Water in Rural Maharashtra," *CNS,* Issue 2, Summer, 1989.

25. Marilyn Waring, *If Women Counted* (London: Macmillan, 1989).

26. Maria Mies, *Patriarchy and Accumulation on a World Scale* (London: Zed Press, 1986).

27. Shiva, *Staying Alive,* 96ff.

28. Maroney, "Embracing Motherhood," 398.

29. Hilkka Pietilä, "Alternative Development with Women in the North" (Paper given to Third International Interdisciplinary Congress of Women, Dublin, July 6–10); also published in John Galtung and Mars Friberg, eds., *Alternativen Akademilitteratur* (Stockholm, 1986).

30. Ann Ferguson, *Blood at the Roots* (London: Pandora, 1989); O'Brien, *Politics of Reproduction,* 22; Ruddick, *Maternal Thinking,* 52.

31. Sherry Ortner, "Is Female to Male as Nature Is to Culture?," in *Woman, Culture and Society,* ed. Michele Z. Rosaldo and Louise Lamphere (Stanford, Calif.: Stanford University Press, 1974).

32. Charlotte Perkins Gilman, *Women and Economics* (London: G. P. Putnam's Sons, 1915), 523.

33. Frieda Johles Forman, ed., *Taking Our Time* (Oxford: Pergamon, 1989); Mellor, *Breaking the Boundaries,* 249ff.

34. Mies, *Patriarchy,* 44ff.

35. Faber and O'Connor, "Discussion," February, 1991, 138.

36. Christine Delphy, *Close to Home* (London: Hutchinson, 1984).

37. Shulamith Firestone, *The Dialetic of Sex* (London: Women's Press, 1979).

38. Pat Armstrong and Hugh Armstrong, "Beyond Sex-less Class and Classless Sex: Towards Feminist Marxism," in *Politics of Diversity,* ed. Roberta Hamilton and Michele Barret (London: Verso, 1986), 252.

39. Ynestra King, "The Ecofeminist Imperative," in Caldecott and Leland, *Reclaim the Earth,* 10.

40. Gena Corea, *The Mother Machine: Reproductive Technologies from Artificial Insemination to Artificial Wombs* (New York: Harper and Row, 1985).

41. Dorothy Dinnerstein, *The Mermaid and the Minotaur* (New York: Harper and Row, 1976); Nancy Chodorow, *The Reproduction of Mothering* (Berkeley and Los Angeles: University of California Press, 1976).

42. Carol Gilligan, *In a Different Voice: Psychological*

Theory and Women's Development (Cambridge, Mass.: Harvard University Press, 1982), 156.

43. Elizabeth V. Spelman, *Inessential Woman* (London: Women's Press, 1988).

44. Hilary Rose, "Beyond Masculinist Realities: A Feminist Epistemology for the Sciences," In *Feminist Approaches to Science,* ed. Ruth Bleier (London: Pergamon Press, 1986), 72.

45. Nancy Hartsock, "The Feminist Standpoint: Developing the Ground for a Specifically Feminist Historical Materialism," in *Feminism and Methodology,* ed. Sandra Harding (Milton Keynes, U.K.: Open University Press, 1987).

46. B. Taylor, *Eve and the New Jerusalem* (London: Virago, 1983).

47. Faber and O'Connor, 1989, "Struggle for Nature," 177.

48. See, for example, Ariel Salleh, "Nature, Woman, Labor, Capital: Living the Deepest Contradiction," in *Is Capitalism Sustainable?,* ed. Martin O'Connor (New York: Guilford Press, 1994).

Discussion Questions

1. Are women closer to nature than men?
2. What is patriarchy? Is it inherently ecologically destructive?
3. Would seeing God as feminine have ecological repercussions?
4. Is Christianity a misogynistic religion? Where do its misogynistic elements come from?
5. Would improving the status and the rights of women lead to improvements in how we treat nature?
6. To what extent are ecological and biological constraints inherent, and to what extent are they socially constructed?

Further Reading

Adams, Carol, *The Sexual Politics of Meat: A Feminist-Vegetarian Critical Theory,* New York: Continuum, 1990.

Adams, Carol, Ed., *Ecofeminism and the Sacred,* New York: Continuum, 1993.

Berger, Pamela, *The Goddess Obscured: The Transformation of the Grain Protectress from Goddess to Saint,* Boston: Beacon Press, 1985.

Biehl, Janet, *Rethinking Ecofeminist Politics,* Boston: South End Press, 1991.

Diamond, Irene, and Gloria Feman Orenstein, Eds., *Reweaving the World: the Emergence of Ecofeminism,* San Francisco: Sierra Club Books, 1990.

Easlea, Brian, *Science and Sexual Oppression: Patriarchy's Confrontation with Women and Nature,* London: Weidenfeld & Nicolson, 1981.

Gaard, Greta, Ed., *Ecofeminism: Women, Animals and Nature,* Philadelphia: Temple University Press, 1993.

Griffin, Susan, *Woman and Nature: The Roaring Inside Her,* San Francisco: Sierra Club Books, 2000 [1978].

McFague, Sallie, *Models of God: Theology for an Ecological, Nuclear Age,* Philadelphia: Fortress, 1987.

MacKinnon, Mary Heather, and Moni McIntyre, Eds., *Readings in Ecology and Feminist Theology,* Kansas City, Mo.: Sheed and Ward, 1995.

Mellor, Mary, *Feminism and Ecology,* New York: NYU Press, 1997.

Plant, Judith, *Healing the Wounds: The Promise of Ecofeminism,* Philadelphia: New Society, 1989.

Plumwood, Val, *Feminism and the Mastery of Nature,* London: Routledge, 1994.

Rothschild, Joan, Ed., *Machina ex Dea,* New York: Pergamon Press, 1983.

Ruether, Rosemary Radford, *Gaia and God,* San Francisco: Harper, 1992.

Sandilands, Catriona, *The Good-Natured Feminist: Ecofeminism and the Quest for Democracy,* Minneapolis: University of Minnesota Press, 1999.

Shiva, Vandana, *Staying Alive: Women, Ecology and Development,* London: Zed Books, 1989.
Sjöö, Monica, and Barbara Mor, *The Great Cosmic Mother: Rediscovering the Religion of the Earth,* San Francisco: Harper, 1987.
Stone, Merlin, *When God Was a Woman,* New York: Harcourt Brace Jovanovich, 1976.
Strange, Mary Zeiss, *Woman the Hunter,* Boston: Beacon Press, 1997.
Sturgeon, Noel, *Ecofeminist Natures,* New York: Routledge, 1997.
Warren, Karen, Ed., *Ecofeminism: Women, Culture, Nature,* Bloomington: Indiana University Press, 1997.
Zimmerman, Michael, *Contesting Earth's Future: Radical Ecology and Postmodernity,* Berkeley: University of California Press, 1994.

Chapter 14

Voices from the Global South

FOLLOWING THE DISINTEGRATION of the Soviet bloc in 1989–1991, the tendency to dichotomize the communist East from the capitalist West has been giving way to the paradigm of the industrial North as opposed to the developing nations of the global South. Whereas the global South includes what used to be referred to as the Third World, it also includes societies that have only recently come to claim a voice on the world stage. These are the so-called Fourth World or first peoples covered in Chapter 3—small-scale societies that are not represented by (and typically do not identify with) the nation states within whose boundaries they live. Of course, given the current scale of migration and the integration of economies, the accuracy and usefulness of retaining any dichotomous framework may not be entirely appropriate, but the essays in this chapter at least continue to speak in these terms.

As of this writing, the industrial countries of the global North still produce the bulk of the world's pollution, and the United States is still the world's single largest polluter. This trend is changing, however, as the countries of the global South industrialize at a pace exceeding even that of Europe during the Industrial Revolution. Within a few years, China is expected to surpass the United States as the world's most polluting nation, and India is not far behind. Expensive pollution control technologies have tended to be low on the priority list for developing nations, most of which are facing problems such as overpopulation and widespread poverty that they see as more immediately pressing. Indeed, there is a widespread sense among the governments of developing societies that a clean, healthy environment is a luxury that they cannot at present afford. As several of the essays in this chapter indicate, however, these official positions do not always represent the will or the interests of the people themselves.

Of course, even in the global North, there has not been a consensus to treat environmental issues as being more important than economic growth. Thus, Northern calls for developing nations to be more environmentally sensitive (as happened at several international meetings during the 1990s) often come across as hypocritical. Northern nations have already industrialized and are responsible for most of the environmental degradation that has so far occurred. Having enjoyed the benefits of their own industrialization with little regard for the cost to the global environment, are Northern nations now in a position to demand that other countries follow a different path?

Furthermore, signals from the industrial countries of the global North to the developing world are decidedly mixed. Even as countries like the United States insist that poorer nations take better care of their environments, control their population growth rates, and so on, Northern businesses (with the strong support of many Northern governments) are actively seeking to export high-consumption economies and lifestyles throughout the world. For example, even while some in the North argue that we need to reduce our consumption of fossil fuels, Northern industries aim to make private car ownership the norm for Chinese, Indians, and others.

Likewise, although Northerners bemoan the ongoing obliteration of tropical rain forests, it is principally their demand for fast-food beef that incites tropical ranchers to turn forest land into pasture. Northern efforts to save endangered species—usually charismatic megafauna such as tigers, panda bears, and the like—often result in the creation of preserves from which indigenous human groups, many of whom live at subsistence level, are expelled. And although most Northern populations are stable, their consumption rates per capita are many times higher than in the South, suggesting that in terms of ecological impact, it is actually the wealthy countries that are overpopulated.

How do the worldviews of citizens of the global South relate to those of the religious traditions we have been analyzing, especially given that most of these global Southerners are also practitioners of these established religions? As noted in the Introduction, the worldviews that shape individual and group attitudes and decisions are really composites, consisting of religious, cultural, and other considerations and influences. Among these other dimensions, poverty, dispossession, and the colonial experience can be particularly strong. Someone raised in, say, a Roman Catholic background in a wealthy U.S. suburb is likely to hold a very different worldview from a Roman Catholic in a Brazilian *favela* (urban slum) or rural village. A movement known as Liberation Theology, which has been especially influential in Latin America, places a strong emphasis on social justice and has a special appeal among the poor.

In sum, the wealthy societies of the global North often possess a markedly different perspective on environmental issues than the poor ones of the global South, stemming from differing sets of needs and priorities. In an essay originally addressed to representatives attending the so-called Earth Summit in Rio de Janeiro in 1992, Indian rural advocate B. D. Sharma highlights some of these differences. Sharma illustrates how the process of constructing a national economy—and now a global economy—almost invariably entails the destruction of local economies, as resources and benefits are transferred from the periphery to the center (and, most often, from the poor to the rich). Laws protect distant commercial interests at the expense of local residents, even to the point of threatening their survival. Development often benefits only the elite, while the majority lose what little they have. Development policies as they are carried out in the world today reflect the priorities of only a small segment of the societies concerned.

In addressing the issue of how development can alleviate world poverty and hunger, Brazilian theologian Leonardo Boff criticizes what he calls the "providentialist and assistentialist solution" of "technological messianism." Such an approach, he argues, only intensifies relationships of inequality and dependency. Boff does not reject science and technology but calls for their application to serve all people and not just those in power.

Marthinus L. Daneel looks at a very different kind of local ecological movement, that of indigenous Christian organizations in Zimbabwe. As with most other local initiatives in the global South, however, the issues are food, water, fuel, and the ravages of deforestation on subsistence economies. Daneel describes the African Independent Churches, which combine Christian and indigenous beliefs and practices, as a force serving to mobilize grassroots environmental preservation and restoration in southern Africa. Counting as many as two million members, this homegrown movement of African "earthkeepers" offers a compelling alternative to the kind of conservationist model frequently imposed by the North.

Eliane Potiguara describes yet another indigenous perspective, that of the native peoples of Brazil. Although the empowerment of Brazilian Indians is seen as vital for their survival and that of their environment, Potiguara insists that the dominant society must also come to respect Indians on their own terms. Her critique of capitalist values is set against the backdrop of 500 years of violent domination and prejudice that the Amazonian peoples have suffered at the hands of Europeans. Potiguara's themes echo those of the Indian case described by Sharma; native Amazonians have seen and continue to see their lands and livelihoods taken away by outside commercial interests that threaten their very survival as small-scale societies living in a reciprocal relationship with their ancestral lands.

On Sustainability

B. D. SHARMA

DHORKATTA, BASTAR, MADHYA PRADESH, India—May 1, 1992. Honorable Members of the Earth Summit, Rio, Brazil: We, the residents of this small village republic, deep in the luxuriant subtropical forests of the Indian sub-continent, wish to invite the attention of your august assembly to some vital issues concerning "the future viability and integrity of the Earth as a hospitable home of human and other forms of life," the main theme of your deliberations at Rio. Before we begin, however, we profoundly compliment you on your bold initiative in holding the Earth Summit. At this end of the globe, in our small forest habitats, we too share your fears for Spaceship Earth.

You should know that in our villages we have stopped, totally, the commercial exploitation of our forests. The government of our country, of course, may not appreciate the spirit behind our decision. They have, in fact, taken it to be defiance of the law. For the forests formally belong to the state. We are, accordingly, treated as intruders in our own abodes where we have been living through the ages. Consequently, according to the law, we cannot even dig for root and tubers, pluck fruits, or even breathe freely the nectar of earth. We cannot pick bamboo to cover our huts, or cut a pole to mend our plough. "That will destroy the forests," they say. And when magnificent tall trees of all varieties are mercilessly felled and carted away, leaving the earth naked and bare, we are told that is scientific management. That such acts are performed in the service of the nation. The little sparrow and owl meanwhile desperately flutter about searching for a place to perch. But even the hollow trunks of dried trees have not been spared!

This perception of national economy which the state today represents is not the perception of the people for whom forest, land, and water together comprise a primary life-support system. The legal fiction of the state's suzerainty over natural resources was created during the colonial era and has been continued and even reinforced after independence, in the name of development. This is not acceptable to us. It is a denial of the very right to life with dignity—the essence of a free democratic society. We are confident that this perception of ours is shared by the people similarly placed across the globe.

We, therefore, respectfully submit that the honorable representatives of governments at the Earth

Sharma, B. D., "On Sustainability," *Sanctuary Magazine* (Mumbai, India) (1991). Reprinted by permission.

Summit are not competent to speak for the disinherited among us. Your perceptions and therefore your stand will be that of estate managers keen to exploit resources on the lines already set by the North. In the past this has invariably implied deprivation of the masses to benefit small elite groups. Frankly, we fear that even though the honorable representatives of Non-Government Organizations (NGOs)—notable exceptions apart—may differ in their views with the state, they are, by and large, bound to share such common basic frameworks as are necessary for their acceptance as partners in the negotiating process. It will not surprise us, therefore, if deliberations at the Summit turn out to be partial. In which case the conclusions will almost certainly be one-sided. This fear is amply borne out in the way the agenda has been framed and also by the Prepcon discussions.

The rich countries are justifiably keen that natural tropical forests be preserved. We too feel the same way, but for different reasons. You require "sinks" for the carbon dioxide emitted by your automobiles which are vital for your "civilization on wheels." We hear about a queer proposal for the declaration of our forests as "global commons." Forests as wilderness would be ideal for this purpose, though you would not mind enjoying usufructory rights. But our paddy fields will be out of place, for they produce CO_2 and thus compete with your cars for that sink. So your basic position as far as we can see is identical to that of our governments. In both cases the people themselves are dispensable. In truth, the two are virtually one as the modern sector of our country, for all practical purposes, is a mere extension of the Western economic system. Of late, in fact, even the thin veneer of national identity has been blown away by the gusty winds of globalization. Discussions at the Summit are bound to be in the nature of bouts for booty rather than for responsible handling of a sacred trust of humankind—generation after generation. But this can be avoided. Please give what follows a patient and considered hearing.

Friends, we are surprised at the casual and parochial vein in which grave issues concerning the survival of life itself have been taken up. If you fail, nothing will remain. If nothing remains, what will be there to share and fight about? But this is the way of all estate managers. They must assume they are always right. Our own experience, a very bitter one, bears this out. In the name of preservation of forests, for instance, our ancestors were mercilessly driven out. And what followed in the name of scientific management was catastrophic. Luxuriant natural forests which sustained us were replaced by teak, which does not even provide us shade in summer. Then came eucalyptus under which not even grass can grow! After that, it was the turn of vast plantations of pine, which would burn like a torch in high summer. But each of these decisions was proclaimed as *the* right way. And to question such projects was blasphemous. Tragically for us, the estate-managers never recognized that the true worth of the magnificent sal, *Shorea robusta,* was far, far greater than the cash recovered from a dead log. The sal is *Kalpavriksha,* the tree that fulfills all desires. Once sal vanished from our forests the struggle of forest dwellers became reduced to physical survival—the evening meal. You see the irony. You worry about how your cars and air-conditioners can continue to operate for a hundred, or a thousand years. Our concern is the next meal that has to be procured at any cost. How can these two perceptions ever meet unless *you* see things from our end of the world and set your own perspectives in order. Friends, can you really not see how far such trivial priorities as air-conditioning and aerosol, with all they represent, have pushed the earth? Yet, you continue to talk about business as usual, of development through your lens, fueled by the same ecological system which has pushed us to the brink of an ecological abyss. Worse, you pose poverty as the worst pollutant and dedicate most of your agenda to eradicating this "environmental hazard."

On the face of it your endeavor might well sound laudable, but consider the hackneyed prescriptions you have chosen to tackle poverty—management of capital, technology, and resource flows. There are two reasons why this framework does not sit well with us. Nor, incidentally, can it help you in the long run. Let's first take the economic frame. Be clear that the phenomenon you are talking about has little to do with poverty. The issue is one of deprivation and denial. You seem ignorant of the fact that we have been robbed of not only our resources, but the great wealth of our life-sustaining skills acquired over millennia. Seen from your horizon, ordinary people are ignorant. Even despised.

Why are we despised? Because we live closer to nature, we do not don many clothes, nor do we have much use for your kind of energy options. We are, therefore, "poor" in your book. And since you, with missionary zeal, wish to "eradicate poverty" we must be enabled to acquire more commodities, consume more. Is this not why the czars of your ecological system incessantly bombard us with visuals of the glittering life? Making our simple ways look ridiculous by contrast to your own may well whip up new demands and expand your markets, but can you seriously suggest this to be the way to eradicate poverty? Such approaches have been directly responsible for the phenomenal inequality we see around us today. These are also the very reasons that the ecology of vast portions of the globe has been so terribly fractured. Yet, the estate managers of the world continue to wrangle for inflated entitlements and deflated obligations, indulging in reckless brinkmanship in dealing with the commons.

This, friends, is the law of the market. Little wonder that the focus of the Earth Summit has already shifted from land, water, and air, to the illogical issue of money! This drift, to our minds, is contemptible.

Those who have crossed the Rubicon of consumerism must point out at this stage that the Summit debate seems poised to miss the main point. You are no doubt talking about the quality of life, but *within* the consumerist paradigm of development and bounded inescapably by an economic framework. Other aspects of life have not even been brought up. We do not blame you for this lapse, for as leaders of the "modern" economic world, you have no experience of the "real life." In a bid to make the system produce more, for that is what decides its competitiveness in the market and its ranking in the world, all that is human is squeezed out, bit by tiny bit. Human concerns and relationships are dispensable, or at best market-convertible. Rushing to the faraway home to be by the side of an ailing mother, leaving the working machine unattended, is not rational. "Do not get emotional, you are not a doctor, send money instead," counsels the manager, worried by the high incidence of absenteeism in his production unit. To us this is the advice of an eccentric. To you it is the cold logic of your economic system. The machine *must* be used round the clock or else you lose your competitive edge. And people? They are but extensions of the machine! For them, even sleeping at night represents lost opportunities! But you have designed ways for the rattled living robot to enjoy "perfect equaniminity." A variety of vintage spirits, or still more modern aids such as heroin, cocaine, and LSD are on hand. At the end of the day, the market determines the cost of life and living.

Look again at your world. The community has already been sacrificed on the altar of productivity. The family now is the last impediment in the way of achieving "perfect rationality" and highest levels of productivity. But even here solutions were at hand. Within the family you dispensed with the burden of dead wood by packing your elders, where necessary, to senior citizen's homes. Now only the nucleus of husband-wife remains, at best. But this too appears to be haunted. Why should a man and a woman remain tied by emotional bonds for life? They too must subjugate themselves to the dictates of the economic system, each one serving the system at points most suited to it. Thus, marriage must break. Living together is good enough for sex. And sex, of course, can be rationally negotiated in a free market. The recent trend towards cynicism about motherhood and about women having eternally to carry the cross of procreation is really the culmination of the challenge of reason against human emotion. Such are the compulsions of perfectly rational beings.

Can you recognize the ugly, twisted logic of your economic system? Perhaps it is too much to ask. For you are clearly dazzled by its benign aura. You have surrounded yourselves and studded your abodes with all sorts of gadgets—surrogates for human concerns, relationships, and emotions. Even your moments of leisure, acquired at heavy financial costs, are determined once again by the market. You are no longer able even to laugh and dream unaided! Having lobotomized the soul from your neighborhoods you now take refuge in the mirage of telecommunications and rapid transport to create the illusion of "one earth."

But let us, for the moment, set aside human concerns and relations. Instead, let us consider the implications of this market-substitution which the economic system is coercing the rest of us to emulate as a lifestyle model. Given the proclamations of your scientists and even some of your world leaders, you obviously admit that we are poised on the brink—even before one in five people (who command four-fifths of the earth's resources) have been able to attain the desired standard of life. How much further must we continue to tread the same lethal path before the final collapse? This is the question the Earth Summit must ponder. Can you really not see the catastrophe you have set into motion? Having "co-opted" your own elite, you state that poverty alleviation is now your objective. This is the mirage we are condemned to chasing in vain, endlessly. Meanwhile you content yourself in tinkering with buttons, watching us follow in your footsteps even as a void engulfs us and our communities and families shatter. The writing is on the wall. The omnipotent, omnipresent market is turning living, breathing men and women into commodities-in-trade.

Honorable members of the Summit: it is in the face of this deluge that we earnestly call upon you to put your agenda, indeed your houses, in order. The development and associated lifestyles you chase are a hallucination. There is nothing sustainable about your ambitions. Your blueprint of sustainability will not even nourish a tiny section of humankind. Ironically, even as the bulk of humanity suffers hitherto unthinkable indignities and hardships, even the few who do manage to monopolize resources will be condemned to a veritable hell, as they stand bereft of the small innocent pleasures of life, the security and the warmth of their community, and the assurance of a family bond.

The basic question then, even before those who represent privileged groups at the Summit, is how long and how far can you afford to ignore and barter away the human face of existence. Such basic human values cannot be taught through lectures and books, nor can they be nurtured in formal systems which at best treat them as naive and irrelevant aspirations. Such values can only be imbibed in human institutions—small face-to-face communities and families where they are assiduously practiced and lovingly cultivated. We must caution you that this great heritage of mankind can be lost to posterity even if one generation trips and thus causes the chain to be broken. Are we prepared for that cataclysm?

Time is of the essence, friends. We, the disinherited of the earth, particularly in India, wish to make our position clear. The tide of "development" which started rising with the industrial revolution and gained huge momentum during the colonial phase of human history, has now run its full course. The allocation of benefits and costs of this development have been oppressively unfair and iniquitous. The more profitable and amenable activities at every stage have been reserved for themselves by the captains of development—the *Brahmins* (the highest caste) of the new order. The drudgery and the sloth was passed over to the *shudras* (outcasts) comprising the rest. Thus, the creation of a Third World was a precondition of your model. And a Fourth World is in the making, now that the Third World countries have accepted your prescription for their economies. This is the cold logic that must sit in the many minds that deliberate ways and means to save the world. The tide, thus, has reached the furthest shore and has begun to turn menacingly inward. The machine must now feed on itself.

We in Dhorkatta, Bastar, Madhya Pradesh, India are a fragment of this newly created Fourth World. As a logical unfolding of your paradigm, the modern economy of our country, a mere extension of the Western system, has misappropriated our resources. On the principle that you cannot make an omelet without cracking an egg, our little world must disintegrate. It cannot be allowed, of course, to stake any claim to the fruit enjoyed by the estate managers. We either get absorbed in the more powerful system, to the extent possible, or get exhumed and expelled. This logic, if accepted, will not remain circumscribed to one area like ours. It will inform all the disinherited of the Third World and also the deprived of the First and the Second Worlds. The prevailing conditions in the erstwhile Eastern Block and among the non-white minorities in the U.S. and Europe are clear pointers in this direction.

We cannot possibly accept these inevitable consequences of your paradigm as our ordained fate. We do not believe in any iron laws of history, or of economics—free, planned, or mixed in any hue. Man is the maker of history and can chart his own path. Accordingly, after careful consideration, we have rejected outright your paradigm, and its associated lifestyle. It is not only socially unjust, but ecologically unsustainable, besides being devoid of human concerns.

A new paradigm—ecologically viable, socially equitable, and rich in human content—is the historical need of our time. You, at the Summit, have missed the human element totally and considered the social issue only superficially. The outcome of your deliberations will therefore be biased and slanted—perversions which we will have to carefully guard ourselves against. In rejecting your paradigm and raising these issues about the Summit, we are not alone. We echo the deepest feelings of ordinary people across the globe. In doing so, we unwittingly accept a historic role for ourselves, which so far you have refused even to consider. But we are, for all the reasons enumerated above, perhaps better placed in this regard, for we in our system still rank human concerns high. As you can see we have questioned and rejected some of the most fundamental elements of your paradigm. The quality of life cannot be measured by how much we consume or how much energy we utilize. It must, instead, be defined in terms of personal accomplishment of individuals, and the richness of interpersonal relationships within the family and community. A precondition naturally is the fulfillment of basic physical needs for a reasonable living. Accepting this should be the first decisive step towards dismantling the unbearable burden created in the name of so-called development at the cost of earth's fragile ecology. Obviously, human concerns and relationships are non-negotiable. The scope of market, on the other hand, must be circumscribed to the bare minimum. Some areas of life such as enjoyment of leisure must be out of bounds for market, in the interest of a sane society recreating conditions for absorbing dialogue and spontaneous laughter.

Contrary to what the ignorant believe of us, we heartily celebrate advances in science and the expanding horizons of man's universe. But we reject technological regimes built up with an eye on centralization of economic and political power. Technology in such hands has "de-skilled" humans and pushed us from the center to the periphery of the stage. While drudgery can and should be erased through harnessing of technology, it must be remembered that honest physical labor is an essential condition of human life and happiness. In this scheme of things production must be non-centralized in units of human dimension, keeping the master-labor relations to the minimum and slashing heavily on trade, advertisements, and transport. These are the devices of distribution wielded by the haves, whose burden our earth can no longer carry. These are clearly wasteful luxuries created as a sequel to a massive usurpation spree. We reject the production system which has depleted even our non-renewable capital resource-base (subsoil water) for frivolous, temporary gains. By casting this heavy burden on ecology such resources have been rendered out of the reach of ordinary people, forever. Thus, not only do we reject the perceptions and the paradigm, but also the legal framework of the estate-managers which seeks to legitimatize wanton destruction of natural resources and prey even on tomorrow's children of nature.

It should be clear that we are not for the negation of life and progress. What we insist on is that development must have a human face, or else it is tantamount to destruction. Towards this end we wish to announce that a beginning has already been made here in our small corner of the globe. We are clear about our goals, our rights, and our responsibilities. We are establishing village republics (*Nate-na-raj*) in the true spirit of democracy, equity, and fraternity following Gandhian tenets to the extent possible. Our village-republics are not islands in the wilderness, but they encompass even the smallest amongst the ever-expanding circles of the-human canvass. We believe that life and vivacity in its totality can be perceived, experienced, and realized only in the microcosms of community and family. It is the community and community alone—not the formal state—which can save the earth for humankind and other forms of life.

So, friends, we have taken upon ourselves a great challenge, with humility yet fully cognizant of the historic role we are playing in one of the most bewildering eras of history. We do not await the advent of a messiah or the conclusion of a revolution—white or red—to move ahead and achieve our goal. The radical structural change associated with the formation of village-republics is a concomitant of the people's struggle. A corollary objective is to assert their will and right of self-governance in the short run and work for a new world order based on equity, fraternity, and democratic values in the long run.

We may, of course, appear momentarily to be moving against the current of history. But that is what it is. We have made a conscious choice that way. But it should be noted, and noted well, that the tide has changed its course. We, therefore, call upon the nations of the world to acknowledge this change, break from the past, and chart out a new path at the Summit for the establishment of a more humane, sustainable, and equitable world.

Science, Technology, Power, and Liberation Theology

LEONARDO BOFF

LIBERATION THEOLOGY REPRESENTS THE mind of the parts of the church that have adopted the people's struggle so that they can make sure that society changes sufficiently to satisfy fundamental needs and allow the exercise of basic human rights. It arose, and continually arises, from the confrontation of human misery with the gospel, and of collective injustice with a thirst for justice; and it starts from a definite practice of liberation focused on the poor themselves as subjects of change.

THE DEPENDENT CAPITALIST SYSTEM AND UNSATISFIED NEEDS

The specific and cruel experience of organized popular groups from the 1960s onward, which has been shared by many Christians (including bishops, priests, theologians, and pastoral workers), is that the thrust of the present socio-economic system has hindered (as it continues to hinder) the satisfaction of basic needs and respect for the person, and the social rights of the vast majority of the population.

Development may follow one of three models: that of an alliance between the bourgeoisie of a certain country with its people (populism); that of a pact between national groups and multinational trusts (alliance for progress); or, more recently, that of a modern, transnational, and populist neo-liberal state (modernization). In each case it takes place at the cost of an increasing impoverishment of the masses. If they are part of the system, they are exploited by it; if not, they are excluded from it.

In Latin America today the most crucial problem is not that of the poor within the dominant system, but that of the 30 to 40 percent of the population, the mass of the urban proletariat, who are excluded from it. They count for nothing economically, for their production and consumption are marginal in GNP terms. They do count politically, for they can vote and decide the outcome of elections, as happened recently in Argentina, Peru, Brazil, and Mexico. They vote for the candidates who speak to their profound awareness, and who can articulate fundamental deficiencies with the myth of a great father (with the characteristics of a protective mother), or of a hero, the savior of his country, who can give them bread, a roof over their heads, health care, and leisure. That is how the new populism is born; it manipulates these desires cleverly, but its ability to put them into effect is weak.

The non-satisfaction of basic needs is seen as oppression. It not only seems unlikely but has been shown to be impossible for the present socio-economic system applied in the Third World to satisfy the fundamental demands for life—and ongoing life—of most of the population.

Experience shows that within the dependent liberal-capitalist system (the capitalism, that is, of the Third World, of former colonies), there is no salvation for the poor, no respect for basic rights, and no satisfaction of basic needs. Therefore we have to abandon this system. The alternative may not be clear, but there is irrefutable evidence that we can expect no solution within the logic of capitalism for wage-earners or for those excluded from the system.

The pope's recent statement in *Centesimus annus* that the alternative to capitalism in the Third World should be sought not in socialism but in an improved form of capitalism (no. 42) has dashed the hopes of the oppressed. With the papal blessing, capitalists can now calmly condemn the poor of the world to another hundred years (*centesimus annus!*) of blood, sweat, and tears. The papal magisterium has never been so far from the truth and from compassion with the wretched of the earth.

The iron logic that constitutes the secret power of capitalism is that of the greatest profit in the shortest possible time. Any business that does not observe this law runs the risk of failing in competition with those that do. This logic can soften only if the stabil-

Boff, Leonardo, "Science, Technology, Power, and Liberation Theology," in *Ecology and Liberation,* Maryknoll, N.Y.: Orbis Books, 1995, pp. 123–130. Reprinted by permission.

ity of the market is guaranteed, or under exceptional circumstances, such as temporary collaboration to bring down the rate of inflation. Today, with continental economies and a global market, this law remains in force; it is absolutely necessary to observe it. Those who are not successful in the marketplace go under. What is not in the marketplace does not exist.

Faced with this bleak prospect for the poor, we seek liberation. Liberation is real only if political conditions for exercising justice are created. Social justice presupposes power and a different quality in its exercise. We therefore seek power for the people in order to obtain social justice and to satisfy people's basic needs efficiently and effectively. Otherwise, what freedom can we achieve for society as a whole?

POPULAR POWER TO SATISFY NEEDS AND ENSURE FREEDOM

Liberation theology locates science and technology within the triangle formed by the satisfaction of basic needs, justice for society, and power. In other words, it seeks power for the people, so that it can guarantee that basic needs are satisfied and that justice is obtained for society as a whole.

Consequently, science and technology are seen not as neutral elements standing alone (instrumental rationalization), but as dependent on the way in which society, politics, economics, and culture are organized. From the viewpoint of the poor of the Third World, science and technology today are the new caravelles, the main weapons for upholding political dependence and ensuring economic dominance over nations and their populations that do not control the production, distribution, and sale of goods. This statement does not amount to a rejection of science and technology. We need them to satisfy present-day basic human needs on a global scale. But we want to see them politically integrated in a society that sets itself better goals than unlimited growth (with the ecological violence this entails) and the greatest profit in the shortest time (leading to the marginalization and exclusion of the masses).

Liberation theology is in communion with the political aspirations of many social groups that seek a society concentrated on the dignity of the human person and on a form of participation that, through labor, satisfies the basic needs of food, shelter, health, education, and leisure, and opens up areas of freedom for creativity and the collective building up of society. Because of this, liberation theology is opposed to the technological messianism (the gospel of technocracy) of the ruling system. This claims to resolve the problems of underdevelopment, and its failed solution, which produced libertarian thinking in politics and in the churches. It seeks to do this by making intensive use of science and technology to produce food and everything else necessary for human sustenance, and by distributing them to those who are without them. Biotechnology has set itself such a goal.

This is the providentialist and assistentialist solution on a world scale. It is an agenda for guaranteeing survival (by providing food), but not for promoting life (by creating conditions for people to produce their food). Liberation theology is opposed to this kind of erroneous good will.

TECHNOLOGICAL MESSIANISM VERSUS PARTICIPATORY POLITICS

The problem cannot be reduced to guaranteeing survival, as though human beings were simply hungry animals (beings full of needs). Instead, it supposes an adequate vision of what human life is (human beings are beings made for freedom, for solidarity, for unlimited relationships, and with a capacity for communication, even with God). The logic of human life does not merely obey the instinct to reproduce, but seeks the advancement and expansion of systems of life. This logic is built on freedom, participation, communication, and creativity.

It is not enough, therefore, to distribute bread, which can be done by technological messianism. If we want to respect human nature, we have to create the appropriate conditions for producing food. That is, we have to provide work by means of participatory politics. Through work and the creativity it involves, human beings share in food production, build their houses, take care of their health, advance their education, organize their free time, and create conditions for communicating and expressing their world. They do not want to be simply creatures helped by the decisions of others, in a history made by others. They want to share in decision making and in a history which they themselves have helped to shape. That is, they want to construct their own individualities and their collective subjectivity. Only thus will they feel human and build up their own historical, ecological, and social humanity.

Finally, liberation theology seeks to throw light on society's agenda. In doing so it reflects on the power expressed through science and technology, which is deeply problematical. In effect, it is exercised with a capitalist agenda that produces a bad quality of life, both in the so-called First World and in the world in which two-thirds of the population live in poverty. The current process of globalization is being pursued within the capitalist ambit, yet not by means of religion, ethics, or ideology, but through the global market (in general, the needs of the market are not those of human beings).

Left to its own devices, the market eventually puts a price on everything and sets aside everything that is not profitable. Therefore, even if the great trusts, with their masses of technicians and technostructures, were to succeed in satisfying basic needs, the question of the nature of human beings, their freedom, creativity, sharing, and the meaning of their lives, which goes well beyond material needs, would remain unanswered.

REQUISITES OF A NEW GLOBAL POLITICAL ECONOMY

Liberation theology insists on this orientation: Technological globalization should be directed toward a worldwide political agenda (a new political economy), including a minimum of humanization, citizenship, equity, human and ecological welfare, and respect for cultural differences and openness to cultural reciprocity and complementarity. I shall examine each of these elements briefly.

A minimum of humanization. All human beings should have the basic right to existence. This means that they should be able to eat at least one a meal a day, have a roof over their heads, and be helped with basic health care. Present regimes do not focus on whole persons, but only on their work effort (muscles, brains, the athlete's feet, and so on). It is revolutionary nowadays to say that we have to nourish love and friendship for human persons as such, beyond their ethnic, religious, or cultural attributes. The novelty of human rights movements in the Third World consists in reclaiming them primarily for the victims, and in taking as their motto: "Serve life, beginning with the most threatened."

Citizenship. Social systems should not tend to exclude people. All people should feel themselves to be potentially citizens of the world, used to thinking globally while acting locally in their own countries (with their own cultural roots). Citizenship implies anti-authoritarianism and the intrinsic acceptance of plurality.

Equity. This implies the certainty of being able to enjoy social benefits and of being able to overcome an established relationship between the contribution which certain citizens can make and what they receive in exchange. Equity seeks a greater realization of the political ideal of equality, which becomes a utopian goal in the positive sense of the term (a reference that makes relative all embodiments and continually invokes new ones). Solidarity among groups and nations alleviates the harshness of social inequalities.

Human and ecological welfare. The best projects, practices, and organizations are those that do not aim exclusively at the quality of goods and services, but at the quality of life, in order to make that life truly human. Society as a whole should make a life of this kind its goal. The alliance that is in the course of establishment between men and women and nature, in terms of brother-sisterhood and veneration, also forms part of human well-being. Another component is spirituality, in the sense of the capacity to communicate with the deepest subjectivity of other persons, and all other entities, including the otherness of all created beings and the absolute Otherness of God. Another, final, component is the pluralist expression of the values and visions of life, of history, and the ultimate goals and confines of the universe.

Respect for cultural differences. Human beings live in history. They have worked out their responses to the meaningful questions about their passage here on earth in different ways. Just as we have an external archeology (environmental and social ecology), so we have an internal ecology (profound ecology). We interpret, evaluate, and dream our existence on the basis of our cumulative experience. All this diversity reveals the richness of the venture and adventure that being human is. We have been able to communicate this, to the enrichment of all. In spite of the tendency of science and technology to homogenize everything, new singularities are constantly emerging from specific cultural appropriations of such processes. Each culture has a different way of expressing solidarity, of celebrating, of combining work and leisure, and of articulating great dreams with harsh reality. Science and technology are stages in this mode of inhabiting the earth and experiencing our integration in a greater ecological whole.

Cultural reciprocity and complementarity. It is not sufficient to recognize otherness. This act of respect is truly fulfilled when we accept the values of others, develop reciprocity (the exchange of experience and understanding), and reciprocally complement others. No one culture expresses the entire human creative potential. This means that one culture can complement another. All cultures together demonstrate the versatility of human beings and our various ways of fulfilling our humanity. In this way, every culture proffers an inestimable richness of language, philosophy, religion, and arts, as well as techniques and technologies—a whole way of living in the world. This is true whether we speak of a simple culture, such as that of the Amazonian tribes, or the "modern" scientific-technological form of culture.

In conclusion, liberation theology sees science, technology, and power as part of the program of redemption, construction, consolidation, and expansion of human life and freedom, starting with those who have the least life and freedom. Life and freedom are the greatest and most desirable goods in existence, without which we always feel enslaved to needs, but with which we can feel that we are sons and daughters of happiness.

Earthkeeping Churches at the African Grass Roots

MARTHINUS L. DANEEL

"The church is the keeper of creation," said Bishop Nhongo of the Zion Christian Church. "All churches now know that they must empower their prophets to expose the wizards [*varoyi*] who kill the land. These people who wilfully defile the church through their destruction of the earth should be barred from participation in the holy communion. If I was the One who owned heaven I would have barred them from entry. The destroyers of the earth should be warned that the "blood" they cause to flow will be on their own heads. . . ."

The Bishop's son, evangelist Samuel Nhongo, concurred: "Jesus said to Simon Peter: 'I give you the keys to lock and unlock!' It is in this light that I see the earth-destroyers whom we expel from the church. . . . The tree-fellers who persist in their evil ways should be locked out of the church. . . . This war [of the trees] must be fought on all fronts and with severity. The church's new ecological laws should be universally known and respected. Otherwise we will be merely chasing the wind."[1]

To a casual passerby the conversation between father and son would appear like any other between two peasants in an African village. Clad in plain khaki clothes, seated in their courtyard in the shade of a *muchakata* tree, next to a couple of nondescript mud-and-pole huts, the two men are likely

Daneel, Marthinus L., "Earthkeeping Churches at the African Grass Roots," in Dieter T. Hessel and Rosemary Radford Ruether, Eds., *Christianity and Ecology: Seeking the Well-Being of Earth and Humans,* Cambridge, Mass.: Harvard University Press, 2000, pp. 531–552. Reprinted by permission of the Center for the Study of World Religions, Harvard Divinity School.

to be talking about their crops or livestock, the source of their livelihood. At least so one would think. Surely this is not the context for profound statements on ecotheology, statements that would be taken note of in the distant halls of fame where much of the business of the world church is being conducted. After all, these are the radical statements of only barely literate leaders of the African Independent Churches,[2] considered by some of the so-called mainline churches in Africa as heretical splinter groups of dubious Christian nature, if not syncretistic throwbacks to traditional religion. To propose the purging of the church of the wizards of the land and debarring such evildoers from heaven, sound rather like the idiom of the witch-hunt and the imposed legalism of medieval patriarchs. Until, of course, one sees the devastation of deforestation in the immediate vicinity of Bishop Nhongo's village; until one feels the helplessness of villagers observing the mindless onslaught on the remaining trees by those who have no hope of earning the necessary school fees for their children unless they sell firewood; until one listens to the sighs of tired village women who have to walk miles each day to gather firewood and fetch water! Then the radical and irritated attitudes of earthkeepers in relation to those who refuse to heed the environment—and, by implication, their communities—start making sense.

The conversation between father and son obtains even more meaning in the light of their earthkeeping ministry. For, like thousands of their fellow believers in Zimbabwe's peasant society, they have decided to stand up and fight the war of the trees, to combat soil erosion, deforestation, the depletion of wildlife, and the misuse of wetlands. Although they did not have the benefit of listening to Joseph Sittler's call for united action in the face of earth destruction, at the third assembly of the World Council of Churches in New Delhi in 1961,[3] or have access to subsequent ecumenical literature on the development of an ethic which integrates ecology, liberation, justice, and peace, they did respond to their own intuition and reading of scriptures in relation to the deteriorating conditions of their own local environment. Empowered by ZIRRCON—the Zimbabwean Institute of Religious Research and Ecological Conservation[4]—they formed a green force of some 150 African Independent Churches with a total combined membership of an estimated two million followers. This body is called the AAEC—Association of African Earthkeeping Churches. From the outset it collaborated with its traditionalist counterpart, AZTREC—Association of Zimbabwean Traditionalist Ecologists—comprising a host of chiefs, headmen, and spirit mediums who engage in the environmental liberation struggle in terms of their traditional religious worldviews and ritual praxis. During the past decade this ecumenical peoples' movement, comprising two distinct green armies, Christian and traditionalist, has succeeded in establishing tree nurseries throughout the Masvingo Province of Zimbabwe and planting between three and four million trees, exotic and indigenous, in the country's central and southeastern regions. Currently, this is probably the largest grassroots ecological movement in all of Southern Africa, operating on the basis of religious motivation and mobilization.

In this paper I shall attempt to trace briefly the profile of a grass-roots ecclesiology as it emerges or lies dormant in a green ministry which seeks to establish eco-justice in accordance with local African insights and convictions. African earthkeepers keep turning out in hundreds and thousands year after year, to perform their *maporesanyika*—earth-healing—ceremonies of tree planting at the behest of Mwari, the creator, keeper, and savior of creation. This they do regardless of the disheartening, repeated losses in tree seedlings wiped out by black frost, the low rate of tree survival in years of drought, the monotony of repetition, and many more setbacks encountered in the green struggle. This they do, too, as the poor and relatively underprivileged members of society, dependent on an oft capricious subsistence economy, yet deriving meaning and pride from sustained ecological service.

AIC theology at best eludes written definition and the industry of bookmaking. Enacted and lived, it finds expression in the throb of celebration, spontaneous proclamation, holistic cleansing of body, spirit, and earth, in rousing song and the rhythm of dancing feet. The attraction and relevance of this theology in the local setting derives from a literal, if at times fragmented, reading of scriptures, which allows for uninhibited and direct identification with biblical characters. At the same time it allows for in-depth interaction between the world of the Bible and the cosmologies of Africa without the interference of Western ecclesial leadership or dogmatism.

Hence it is with some hesitation that I, as fellow earthkeeper yet as a privileged white missiologist, attempt to unravel and analyze the ecotheology underlying the activities of an essentially black African peoples' movement.

THE MISSION OF AN EARTHKEEPING CHURCH

> Bishop Wapendama, leader of the Signs of the Apostles Church, defined the mission of AAEC churches, during a tree-planting Eucharist, as follows: "Mwari saw the devastation of the land. So He called his envoys [ZIRRCON/AAEC leaders] to shoulder the task of delivering the earth. Together with you, we, the Apostles, are now the *deliverers of the stricken land*. . . . We, the deliverers were sent by Mwari on a sacred mission. . . . Deliverance, Mwari says, lies in the trees. Jesus said: 'I leave you my followers, to complete my work!' And that task is the one of healing! We, the followers of Jesus, have to continue with his healing ministry. So, let us all fight, clothing and healing the earth with trees! It is our task to strengthen this mission with our numbers of people. If all of us work with enthusiasm we shall clothe and heal the entire land with trees and drive off affliction. I believe we can change it."

Taken together with Bishop Nhongo's statement above, Wapendama's portrayal of the church's mission illuminates two dominant themes which are evolving from the AAEC's tree-planting ministry. First, the mission of the church comprises earth healing as an extension of Christ's healing activities (Wapendama); and second, the church, in so doing, functions as the keeper or guardian of creation (Nhongo). The good news proclaimed and enacted by the earthkeeping church clearly extends beyond and complements soul salvation and the healing of human beings, as formerly envisaged by the AICs. However, this trend does not supersede or replace the rich evangelistic tradition within the prophetic AICs which focused the church's outreach in conversion, the promise of salvation to converts both in this existence and in a kingdom of heaven yet to come and the baptism of converts in the name of the triune God, as prescribed in the classic missionary text of Matthew 28:18–19.[5] For the AICs involved in the AAEC continue with their missionizing strategies of old. Yet, decidedly new is the preoccupation with the inclusion of the deliverance of Mwari's stricken land in the church's mission. Bishop Wapendama, as many other church leaders, is neither a naïve optimist nor an opportunist, merely riding the wave of the latest fad. A surprising amount of his time is spent in the cultivation and planting of tree seedlings at the church headquarters. Moreover, his interpretation of conversion as condition for church entry increasingly includes an emphasis on individual change from earth-destructive to earth-care activity.

Although Wapendama did not specifically mention Holy Communion in his call to mission, his message in the context of a tree-planting Eucharist implies that at the point where the union between Christ and his disciples (cutting across denominational boundaries) is sacramentally confirmed, the mission of earth healing integral to it, is visibly acknowledged and revitalized. In this view the dialectic between summoning and mandating God and responding human earth-keepers remains focal. God certainly takes the initiative to deliver and restore his ravaged earth, in what remains essentially *missio Dei*. Wapendama, in the same sermon quoted above, repeatedly reminded his audience that they were facing a formidable task, one which could only be accomplished in full recognition of dependence on God. "I beseech you," he said, "to place yourselves in the hands of Mwari. He alone can give us the strength to endure in this struggle." But the responsibility to deliver the stricken earth from its malady here and now lies with the Christian body of believers, the church. Membership to this institution, the head of which extends his healing ministry through grace to the entire cosmos, therefore implies active earth stewardship.

Wapendama's understanding of the church's mission may be limited. Yet, it signals one of the ways in which ecologically active AICs update their sacramental-cum-missionary tradition in the face of environmental needs.[6] It also hints at Africa's understanding of the church's comprehensive missionary task in this world, not as a privileged community of mere soul-savers, but in terms of Bishop Anastasios of Androussa's vision that "the whole world, not only humankind but the entire universe, has been called to share in the restoration that was accomplished by the redeeming work of Christ."[7]

The function of the church as guardian of creation, as depicted by Bishop Nhongo, hinges on an emergent Christology which increasingly interacts with Shona cosmology. Christ in a sense absorbs for the Christian earthkeepers that part of the spirit world which traditionally provided the sanction and incentive for customary conservationist laws and practice. This is the domain of the founder ancestors of tribes and clans popularly referred to as the "guardians of the land" (*varidzi venyika*). They are the protectors of the holy groves and sanctuaries in the territories they once ruled. Their environmental commands are mediated through spirit mediums and implemented by the local chief's court. These are the senior ancestors who, during Zimbabwe's liberation struggle, were considered to operate in unison in the "council of war" (*dare rechimurenga*), providing spirit guidance and support to the guerrilla fighters in their quest to retrieve the "lost lands" from the colonial power. These, too, are the spirit forces considered by the chiefs and mediums of AZTREC—the AAEC's counterpart—as the inspiration and sanction behind the "war of the trees."

Although the AAEC earthkeepers refrain from calling Christ *mudzimu*, or ancestor, the tendency to proclaim his lordship over all creation and to envisage him as the controller of all cosmic and life-giving forces strengthens the perception of an earthkeeper who, as part of the human family of necessity, also relates to the ancestral world. And the analogy which immediately comes to mind in such interrelatedness is that Christ is the universal *muridzi venyika* (guardian of the land). I have myself, in a number of tree-planting ceremonies, compared Christ's earth care with that of the Shona guardian ancestors. The theological assumption behind such portrayal is that the traditional guardian ancestors have through the ages sensed and accepted their responsibility for the land politically under their jurisdiction through their closeness and response to Mwari, the Creator. As such, they prefigured as earthkeeping prototypes of Christianity among the Shona. Christ's role as *muridzi venyika* therefore fulfills and transforms the old guardianship. Christ, the earth guardian, somehow inspires and holds sway through his Spirit over generations of Shona *varidzi*. Through them he appeals to *all* their living descendants, whatever their religious persuasion, to share and extend their responsibility for the earth. As John Pobee would say, Christ shares ancestorship with the living dead on account of his *kra* (soul) linking him to God.[8] However, he also transcends the regional and kinship limitations of the African senior ancestors in linking the local Shona environmental and kingroup with the universal cosmos and family of humankind. Such extension is already manifest in AAEC praxis: widening ecumenical horizons and financial and moral support from the Christian earthkeeping community inhabiting the global village.

This contextualized Christology undergirds in AIC circles the image of the church as guardian of the land, locally, and keeper of creation in the more universal sense. The proximity of the ancestral guardians also broadens the understanding of a people-oriented redemption to include salvation of all the earth. Sundkler has correctly pointed out that Africans invariably understand redemption and the forgiveness of sins in terms of Christ's revelation of such truth both to the living and the living dead.[9] Christ's *descensio* into the spirit world, to the Shona believer, not only signifies salvific proclamation to the entire human community—the living, the dead, and the unborn—but it also validates and absorbs for them the ecological concerns of the guardian ancestors into the ministry of the church, where it finds expression in liberative environmental activity, symbolizing the holistic concreteness of God's salvation in this existence.

It is at this point, in the emergence of the church as guardian or keeper of creation, that an understandable and realistic ethic of the environment takes shape. Bishop Nhongo's preoccupation with earth destruction as a form of wizardry, *uroyi*, reflects the new idiom. Sin no longer concerns only the antisocial acts committed directly against fellow human beings or against God, but also and particularly offenses against the environment. These include the indiscriminate felling of trees, refusal to participate in curative conservationist activities, riverbank cultivation and related agricultural activities, such as the use of sledges, which promote soil-erosion, pollution and misuse of water resources, and so forth. The dire implications of such activities for the entire earth community—people, animals, vegetation, and all animate or inanimate objects belonging to creation—are considered in such a serious light that willful perpetrators are indeed branded as destroyers, or wizards, of the land. Prophets of earthkeeping AICs are becoming "guardians of the land" in their own rights, in that they are instrumental in detecting environmental sins in fellow church members and urging public confessions prior to church services and a variety of earthkeeping rituals. Their green ministry enables the church to identify the enemy outside and within its own ranks. Identification of the wrongdoers illuminates the church's concern for eco-justice and concretizes its ethical code and control system. This development is reminiscent of the *chimurenga* struggle prior to Zimbabwean independence, during which the counterrevolutionaries and collaborators with the Smith regime were branded as wizards. The task of the AIC war prophets, alongside the traditionalist spirit mediums, was to elicit confessions from suspects during the secret *pungwe* vigils as part of the process of exposing the wizard-traitors and singling them out for punitive measures.

> "Earthkeeping is part of the body of Christ," the Reverend Davison Tawoneichi of the Evangelical Ministry of Christ Church told his followers in a sermon. "It is so because we as humans are part of his body and the trees are part of us; they are essential for us to heal to breathe. So trees, too, are part of Christ's body. Our destruction of nature is an offense against the body of Christ. . . . It hurts Christ's body. Therefore the church should heal the wounded body of Christ."

This view complements Bishop Wapendama's assertion about mission as an extension of Christ's healing ministry. Only, in this instance, Christ's body is understood as being itself afflicted by the abuse of nature.[10] This statement underscores the growing tendency in AAEC tree-planting Eucharists to view Christ's body in both its ecclesiastic and its cosmic connotations: first, through partaking in the elements of the sacrament the earthkeepers witness to their unity in Christ's body, the church, and derive from it strength, compassion, and commitment for their environmental struggle; second, they subsequently set out on their healing mission of tree planting to restore the cosmically wounded body of Christ.

An earthbound Christology of this nature cannot but have far-reaching implications for the structure and program of the church. The prophetic AICs have all along communicated a gospel message of wholeness in healing, whereby the people of God could find well-being, peace, and belonging in a hostile world. The black "Jerusalems" and "holy cities" epitomized the presence of God where prophetic leaders and their bands of healers mirrored as icons the healing powers of Christ and of the Holy Spirit. Healing in this context encompassed all of human life. Not only were assailing spirits exorcised, wizardry banished, barren women cured and socially reinstated, and all kinds of ailments treated, but those without spouses or jobs were taken care of, entire congregations in drought-ridden areas were fed, and the mediation of rain and sound farming methods secured. Hence, from the outset a comprehensive healing ministry turned the predominant image of the Spirit-type churches, mainly the Zionists and Apostles, into that of a "hospital" (*hospitara*).

Preoccupation with Christ, both as earthkeeper and as the broken earth, introduces a revolutionary new dimension. With this in mind Wapendama's call to mission aims at mobilizing the entire church membership as active earth healers, instead of only a number of specialized evangelizers and/or healers. It is as if he and the Reverend Tawoneichi anticipate in the healing of creation and of Christ's body the liberation of the church itself—liberation from an overriding preoccupation with the human condition. In healing the earth, by reaching out beyond the vexing physical and mental ailment of human beings and by setting aside internal leadership and interchurch conflicts—the very illness of the church itself—for a higher, God-given purpose, the earthkeeping church, and the earthkeeper, is healed. In such liberation unto earth service, the apostolate of the church obtains prominence and meaning.

SACRAMENTS OF HEALING

> Look at the stagnant water
> where all the trees were felled
> Without trees the water-holes mourn
> without trees the gullies form
> For, the tree-roots to hold the soil—
> are gone!
>
> There were forests
> abundance of rain
> But in our ignorance and greed
> we left the land naked.
> Like a person in shame
> our country is shy
> in its nakedness.

Our planting of trees today
is a sign of harmony
between us and creation
We are reconciled with the earth
through the body and blood of Jesus
which brings peace.
He who came to save
All creation.

[Col. 1:17–20]

In these excerpts, taken from the liturgy of the AAEC's tree-planting Eucharist, we find the themes of confessing ecological guilt, recognizing the plight of landscapes stripped bare, anticipating the cosmic dimension of Christ's atoning death, and the determination of celebrant earthkeepers to relate the salvific message within the sacrament to the cosmos as a form of therapeutic restoration through tree planting. Rousing sermons usually underscore the significance of confessing ecological guilt, implicit in the liturgy. Christ is proclaimed as the One, who in the midst of ecological devastation, holds everything together (Col. 1:17), as the one who atones for ecological sins. "As the recipients of Christ's salvation," Bishop Marinda, author of the liturgy, would repeatedly insist, "*humans have the duty to extend salvation to all of creation as Christ's co-workers!*" (my italics). What this imparting of salvation essentially means in the earthkeeping church is the symbolic fusion of healing humans and healing earth in the sacramental reenactment of Christ's death and resurrection as found both in baptism and Holy Communion.[11]

Baptism in the green movement is preceded by the kind of conversion which highlights the relationship between humans and Mother Earth. The individual's change of heart in rebirth will remain incomplete if it does not include a deliberate move from earth destruction to earth care. Acceptance of this responsibility surfaces in the novice's public confession of ecological *uroyi* (wizardry) against the Creator and the earth community, immediately before entry into "Jordan" (any dam or river where baptism is conducted). Baptism thus acquires the meaning of rejecting illicit exploitation of the environment and obtaining Christian discipleship in a community of earth healers. Subsequently, spiritual growth of the individual believer no longer derives exclusively from worship, Bible study, and prayer in the conventional sense. It also results from the encounter with God in the protective stewardship of his garden.

It makes sense for novices to confess ecological guilt and obtain earthkeeping discipleship at "Jordan," where a barren landscape, erosion gullies, and unprotected riverbanks will in most cases be in full view. With its focus on Christ the wounded healer, the earthkeeping church is rendering the broken environment that "holds" the baptismal pool or river party to the sacrament of baptism, in similar fashion as the trees to be planted are made to participate as brothers and sisters in the Eucharist. The barren plains and erosion gullies, so to speak, enter the waters of life to be baptized into a future of healing and recovery, in the person of the novice who, in crossing "Jordan," gives witness to his or her transition from earth abuser to earthkeeper.

To most Independents, baptism has always held the connotation of healing. Here, the life-giving water of "Jordan," filled for the occasion according to popular belief by the power and presence of the Holy Spirit, is drunk by the baptisands and afflicted church members for cleansing and curative purposes. Thus, the ceremony offers a unique opportunity for interpreting the Holy Spirit as healer of both the people and the land. In this instance the drinking of "Jordan" water symbolizes the shift from personal, individual benefit of the baptisand by the Holy Spirit's healing and salvific powers to a ritual statement of divine and human solidarity with all creation; an affirmation of new commitment through conversion to a vocation aimed at eco-justice. As the Spirit-filled water of "Jordan" heals and empowers the newly converted earthkeepers, it also touches the wounded earth where it courses down a riverbed troubled by siltation—in itself a reminder to those with eyes to see that they have to be more than mere spectators in the realization in this existence of the new heaven and new earth.

The sequence of activities in the healing tree-planting Eucharist is briefly as follows:

Preparation starts with the digging of holes in the vicinity of AIC headquarters of the hosting church. The prospective woodlot may be fenced, named "the Lord's Acre," and placed under the surveillance of a church committee responsible for watering the newly planted seedlings and for general aftercare. While the communion table is being prepared near to the new woodlot, robed dancers, representing the region's ecumenically united churches, dance around the seedlings stacked nearby. Dance and song bring praise to Mwari, the Creator, recognize his presence, encourage the green fighters and even exhort the young trees to grow well. The sermons of AAEC bishops and ZIRRCON staff members are augmented by speeches delivered by government officials and representatives of the Forestry Commission, Parks and Wildlife, or other ecological institutions. Thus, the outdoor setting, religiously pluriform audience, and varied sermons and speeches cause the tree-planting Eucharist to be an open-ended, inclusive rather than strictly exclusive, in-group event.

The opening to the Sacrament itself is the public confession of sins. All the celebrants, church leaders and dignitaries included, line up behind a band of prophesying prophets to confess their guilt in earth destruction. The idea is that the Holy Spirit reveals through the prophets the still-hidden sins of communicants lest they partake of the bread and wine in an unworthy manner. Thus, divine intervention and opposition to wanton exploitation of the earth is vividly enacted in a ceremony which recognizes no individual status or privilege. My own position as founder of the movement, for instance, does not exempt me from public admission of the excesses I have committed as a big game hunter in my youth.

After confession each communicant picks up a tree seedling and carries it to the communion table as if to draw all the members of the earth community symbolically into the inner circle of communion with Christ, the Redeemer. Establishing communion with Christ in this manner gives recognition to his role as Healer-earthkeeper and is a way of focusing the sacramental union between him and his disciples, the church, on the earth-healing activity to follow. Meanwhile, one of the AIC bishops blesses the stretch of land to be healed by trees, by sprinkling holy water and scattering holy soil over it—yet another way of drawing the earth community into sacramental participation. Subsequently, all the tree planters converge on the new woodlot where they "converse" with their "fellow communicants"—the seedlings—as they plant and water them. The liturgical formula for communication with the trees at this juncture is as follows:

You, tree, my brother . . . my sister
today I plant you in this soil
I shall give water for your growth
Have good roots
to keep the soil from eroding
Have many branches and leaves
So that we can:
—breathe fresh air
—sit in your shade
—and find firewood.

In conclusion, many of the tree planters themselves kneel in queues in front of the prophetic healers for the ceremony of laying on of hands and prayer, in the hope of a cure of their own afflictions. Thus, the healing of barren earth and of a crippled humanity blend into a single sacramental ceremony which witnesses poignantly to the reign of Christ, crucified and resurrected Savior of all the earth.

The AAEC's tree-planting Eucharist paves the way for significant developments in local African theologies and interreligious dialogue. I mention but a few aspects worthy of consideration.

First, the AAEC tree-planting Eucharist is in itself the witnessing event, the proclamation of good news unto all the earth! It is enacted in and with nature and in the presence of non-Christian fellow-fighters of the war of the trees. In a sense this is the Christian equivalent of the attendance of the traditionalist high-god oracles, when Christian representatives of the AAEC accompany their AZTREC counterparts to the distant shrines in the Matopo Hills near Bulawayo, to observe them commune with their creator-god and receive directives for the further conduct of the war of the trees. Likewise, the traditionalist earthkeepers at the Eucharist do not partake of the sacramental elements—bread and wine—but they assimilate the message, observe the proceedings, and assist with the tree planting. In treading the holy ground of their Christian friends, as the latter are allowed to approach the ancient oracular holy of holies, where Christians normally will not venture, a new tone for interreligious tolerance and dialogue is set. The traditionalist earthkeeping brother or sister is no longer an "opponent" but a fellow-pilgrim in the joint quest for eco-justice, someone whose religiosity is seen and respected in the reverencing of creation and creator. Not that ecological endeavor supersedes the call for repentance, conversion, human salvation, and church formation—the essential missionary dynamic of all prophetic AICs! For the tree-planting Eucharist, in essence, also highlights the difference between Christian sacrament and traditional beer libation for the ancestors. Yet, it is as if the green struggle through the newly planted trees breathes the message: you cannot afford the luxury of religious conflict if it causes the wounded earth to suffocate! Ultimately, therefore, the Christian *maporesanyika* (earth-healing) and the traditionalist *mafukidzanyika* (earth-clothing) ceremonies, for all their religious differentiation, hold hands in the greening of God's earth.

Second, the christological significance of the tree-planting Eucharist lies in its ritualized blending of the wide-ranging tenets of Christ's healing ministry. Observations of villagers of different religious persuasions, who participate in the *maporesanyika* ceremonies, reflect a growing awareness of the comprehensive nature of this ministry. Said a villager during one of these ceremonies: "The protection of trees is a holy matter. The land is barren. The blanket of vegetation which should cover it has been torn away. In its nakedness the land is ill. We too, the people of Mupakwa, are ill. We have come to be healed, together with the land. In Jesus' time you only needed to touch his garment to be healed. In clothing the land with trees we, too, are being healed." Here an unpretentious peasant shows understanding of the fact that Christ had come to heal the sickness of the entire world and that care for the environment is part of the therapy of one's own malady. Such observations not only illustrate the effectiveness of the *maporesanyika* event as a means of communicating the good news of Christ's incarnation in current peasant society, but they also corroborate Aylward Shorter's views that all healing, sacramental healing in particular, is directed toward eternal life and wholeness, and that healing facilitates harmony with the natural environment as condition for human well-being.[12]

Third, the *maporesanyika* Eucharist convincingly qualifies the uniqueness of Christ's image as healer in its adaptation to transformatory fulfillment of the African *nganga*—traditional healer—paradigm.[13] During the tree-planting confession, for example, the prophetic healer, as icon of Christ, probes for and exposes the perpetrators of wizardry as the traditional *nganga* does in his or her witchcraft eradication practice. In this instance, however, the self-confessed, or divinely exposed, ecological offender, the *muroyi venyika* (wizard of the earth), is not ostracized from the community or permanently stigmatized, as the *nganga* would tend to recommend. In the event of an unrepentant spirit, the person may be temporarily barred from sacramental participation. But, despite the calls for the excommunication of willful tree fellers by such radicals as Bishop Nhongo and his son, the green prophet opens the door of reconciliation by keeping the *muroyi* in the church community. Hence, the prospect remains of Christ's forgiveness and grace being enacted in the *muroyi*'s eventual change of heart. Holistic healing in this respect seeks to establish respect for life and mercifully stays final judgment of the as yet heartless exploiters of creation.

Fourth, Christ's healing of the land also contains a spiritual and ecumenically empowering dimension, because his cross and resurrection transcend the barriers of rivalry between ancestral guardians of the land, opposing churches, Christians and non-Christians, and related societal afflictions. The concern for the traditional spirit provinces and the conflicts associated with histories of conquest of the land are, for the duration of the *maporesanyika* Eucharist at least, pushed into the background. The presence and cordial interaction of chiefs and headmen, together with a wide range of AIC members, all from the surrounding territories and all of them representing different and oft conflicting histories, myths, and ancestral bonds with the soil, point at a spirit of mutuality and reconciliation at the expense of recurrent land feuds of the past. It is at this juncture that Christ, who mends things fallen apart (Col. 1:17), interacts with the ancestral guardians of the land. His lordship over all creation relativizes territorial divisions as the contesting representatives of those divisions are drawn into united action for environmental restoration.

Fifth, the incarnation of Christ as healing earthkeeper in his fellow healers at the African grass roots goes a long way in overcoming the image of an alien, white Christ belonging to the Western world. Cécé Kolié complains about Christologies in the mission churches of Africa, which do not function convincingly in the existential reality of African believers.[14] "Our liturgies" he contends, "do not celebrate human beings fighting disease, or struggling so hard to get up on their feet, or striving to be free. . . . To give Christ the face of the healer in Africa will not be feasible until the manifold gifts of healing possessed by all of our Christian communities have begun to manifest themselves." Kolié's criticism correctly signals a serious limitation in Western-oriented Christianity in Africa. However, the AAEC's blending of a ministry of human and environmental healing illustrates that in liturgy, sacraments, and individual experience the healing features of Christ are being unmasked and revealed. The "manifold gifts of healing" *are* in fact emerging forcefully and understandably in the African context where Christ encounters and guides his fellow "wounded healers." He does so in the prophetic diagnosis of all afflictions, cleansing confessionals, tree-planting hands, exorcising hands—much of which follows the rhythm of dancing feet and song, where the inner struggle for life, dignity, and wholeness is fierce and relentless.

THE GOOD NEWS OF JUSTICE AND LIBERATION

> "There is absolutely no doubt about the connection [between our war of the trees and the former liberation struggle, *chimurenga*]," said Zionist Bishop Machokoto, first president of the AAEC. "I will go so far as to say that this is the most important war, following the first *chimurenga*. We are all committed to this struggle to restore the vanquished land through afforestation. . . . *Trees are our life-line!* We say, 'A ward with dense forests knows no death!' Even President Mugabe and the government know that the earth cannot be the earth, and we cannot be people without trees."

Bishop Machokoto's assertion about the connection between the country's erstwhile political liberation struggle and the current war of the trees is no coincidence. The quest for justice and liberation in colonial Zimbabwe has always been integral to the good news propagated by the AICs. Soul salvation and eternal life for believers in heaven as antithesis to "the pit of fire" remained focal in the drive for conversion and church growth. Yet, one of the major characteristics of AIC eschatology is its emphasis on a *visible salvation* in the present dispensation. This requires the realization of God's saving grace in this existence, in the creation of black "holy cities," or "Jerusalems," where security, health, and well-being can be experienced tangibly in closely knit communities of believers. Salvation, therefore, to many Independents has strong connotations of holistic healing, as suggested above, and of justice and liberation.

The good news of eco-justice in the tree-planting Eucharist signals much more than environmental care. It repeatedly underscores social justice in the empowerment of the poor and marginalized people—two-thirds of the world—to make a contribution which will be of such significance that it captures, for once, the imagination of the nation, the recognition of the government. To a large extent, the earthkeepers engaged in these ceremonies are similar to those in Brazil who flock to the popular religious movements and are described by Leonardo Boff as:

> Impoverished people who are of no account socially, who are wanted by no one, not even by the politicians whom they have elected; people who are anonymous, disoriented in a society that ejects and marginalizes them . . . [those] who discover in these popular celebrations some measure of dignity, as well as a purpose in continuing to live, hope and struggle.[15]

Probably the most convincing example of the comprehensive nature of eco-justice evolved in ZIRRCON praxis is to be found in the movement's Women's Desk, with its seventy-five rural women's clubs. Less rigidly organized along lines of religious affiliation than AZTREC and the AAEC, the women's clubs—each comprising on average thirty to forty adult women—combine the objectives of earth care, socioeconomic advancement through income-generating projects, and the promotion of female emancipation. In compliance with ZIRRCON policy, women's clubs develop their own nurseries and woodlots as a condition for some form of sponsorship for their community development programs, such as sewing, bakeries, soap-production, agricultural projects, vocational training, and water schemes.

The combination of ecological repair and economic advancement in a poverty-ridden peasant society, is especially good news for women who bear the brunt of collecting firewood and attempt to keep their households going in an abused countryside. Considering, in addition, that some 80 percent of all adults in the AICs are women and that the majority of them have little or no access to the top leadership offices of bishop, priest, or minister in their respective churches, then the magnitude of relatively unfettered opportunity in their new clubs becomes apparent. Ms. Raviro Mutonga, chairperson of the Women's Desk, comments on the changed status of ZIRRCON women as follows: "They [the women] still constitute the bulk of marginalized and oppressed people in rural society. . . . They were deprived of the basic rights of self-determination, co-responsibility and shared authority. Here in ZIRRCON the women are now redefining their status. . . . They are treated as equals by the men and they have their own insights and plans in the movement without interference or domination from the side of men." The relief felt by women, to be engaged in and to receive recognition for their own struggle against poverty and ecological degradation without interference from their male counterparts in the movement, is reflected in Mutonga's address to club members during a women's tree-planting ceremony. "We women have our own things [green activity] here. I am so happy because we know these things are really ours. How satisfying to know that no human being will be coming here to interfere, to ask what it is we are doing. You fathers, who have come here today are in support of *our* endeavors. You have come here because of genuine interest."

Mutonga's words confirm feelings of self-worth, dignity, and commitment in the ranks of neatly uniformed female tree planters as they set an example of orderly, emancipated militancy in the green struggle. Ms. Mangombe, one of the local club leaders, concluded the ceremony with a prayer that summed up the good news for women in rural peasant society:

> "We thank you Lord for mercy, bestowed on us women. You have bestowed a seven-fold grace on us. We were an oppressed "tribe" [*rudzi*], always criticized, even to the end of our days. A woman was given little space, even within her own home. A woman was not allowed to undertake a journey, without her father or husband following with a *tsvimbo* [club]. A woman was not allowed to attend court proceedings. A woman was never allowed to hold high position [lit., "to sit on high seats"]. But, we now see with our own eyes, Lord, that you change all this; as you yourself have said: 'Let the old things go by. Set your minds on the new things that will appear these days!' We place these new things in your hands, Lord, as we ask you to bless the Women's Club at 'Wadzanai Doroguru.' You have allowed us to plant trees and vegetables as you have planted in your own garden, Eden, where you allowed your representatives to live. We thank you that you have reintroduced that privilege for us women; we, the stewards of your creation. We thank you for male support, for the good men who have dug the holes for our trees. Bless the people [of ZIRRCON] whom you have sent here. Bless them as they traverse *all of Zimbabwe* to plant trees. Mwari, let this task have your full endorsement. . . . Strengthen us in our earthkeeping quest and let the message within the sermons keep motivating us. Amen."

In this prayer Mwari is not explicitly called "Mother," but in the thought world of the women tree planters he or she certainly is the "God of the mothers," the One who liberates women from bondage and sets them free to serve "Eden," the earth, from a position of dignity and equality with males. There is no overt militancy here, as if all existing patriarchal structures should be destroyed before women can come into their own—but assertive, courageous activity born of the conviction that Mwari is near and that he or she guides the struggle of restoring the earth in a new mode of equality and justice. The prayer includes a vision for earthkeeping throughout the entire country and is suggestive of gender harmony in a cause which ideally should transcend oppressive hierarchical authority in a new communion of all important yet humble service.

I have been able here to highlight only one or two features of what could be termed a contextualized form of "African ecofeminism." As yet, the story of women earthkeepers is lived at the grass roots by the growing numbers of women's clubs. Hopefully, the creative theology implicit in such development will yet be documented by the women concerned themselves to enrich and give impetus to the crucial labors of the "healing mothers of Eden" worldwide.

CHALLENGE IN ACTION

The strength of the earthkeeping churches of Zimbabwe lies in their willingness to respond to the needs of the earth community. They work in a spirit of sacrificial yet celebratory service despite discouraging ecological set-backs. Eco-justice in these churches takes shape as a life-style rather than a written code of conduct. We have briefly traced how this life-style in Zimbabwean peasant society translates into a spontaneous reinterpretation of the church's mission. Attempts at realizing this mission of earth care lead to structured, ritual, and symbolic change within the church. Here, the Gospel finds expression in wholeness, therapy, and liberation relevant to the needs of African society. It is based, moreover, on an incarnational Christology, conversant with and easily understood within the framework of indigenous African worldviews. In the development of their earth-healing ministry, which includes the struggle against poverty, the AICs promote eco-justice as a process which seeks balance rather than competition in the treatment of both human and ecological afflictions. Eco-justice thus stands as the sign of a deliberate shift in emphasis from human dominion over to human service of nature.

In pioneering new forms of ecological outreach, as an integral part of church life, the AAEC is challenging the world church to put its earthkeeping mission into practice. This means giving substance to ecotheological theories and ethical considerations which abound in the literature on creation of recent years. The AAEC derives its mandate for earthkeeping from an intuitive reading of scriptures on themes dealing with environmental stewardship. Scriptural truths are applied literally to the locally observed condition of an ailing earth community. This dialectic stimulates calls for mobilization of the entire church in earth care. As an instrument of earthkeeping the church is obviously better placed to revision its task, institutional shape, worship, and service from within the struggle rather than from a position of discreet, controversy-free distance.

Sacramental healing in an African earthkeeping church includes, as we have seen, afforestation as therapy for a denuded and soil-eroded landscape. Should the urban church in the global village accept its environmental responsibility, it could fruitfully celebrate the sacraments in confrontation with the evils of the urban context: water and air pollution, toxic waste, mountains of garbage and the need for proper recycling procedures. Remedial action in the urban situation is bound to be more complex than tree planting in rural wastelands. Nevertheless, inventive, city-cleansing pastorates could contribute substantially toward the protection and quality of life in the metropolis.

Regional ecumenism between Christian communities undoubtedly strengthens combined ministries of earth care. The Zimbabwean case study also illustrates that interchurch ecumenism in ecological stewardship is complemented and enriched by a broadened form of interreligious ecumenism that includes traditional religious collaboration and dialogue. Interfaith encounter in this instance does not lead to religious relativism, as some Christians may fear. For, the co-operation between Christian and traditionalist earthkeepers in the Zimbabwean war of the trees illustrates quite clearly that pluriform religious identities obtain clarity and tolerant acceptance where diverse religious partners direct their activity at the well-being of God's earth. Conflicts do arise at times. However, Christian witness on the whole is kept in a healthy and creative tension with the goodwill and respect shown the ecological partner of a different faith.

NOTES

1. This and the other narratives derive from my interview discussions with ZIRRCON participants or are quotes from tree-planting sermons. They will appear in a forthcoming publication: M. L. Daneel, *African Earthkeepers*, vol. 2, *Environmental Mission and Liberation in Christian Perspective* (Pretoria: Unisa Press, 1999).

2. The African Independent Churches, also known as the African Initiated Churches (AICs), are found in large numbers throughout sub-Saharan Africa. In Southern Africa they represent vigorous, fast-growing movements varying in size from a few relatives in a small family church to several million adherents in the largest churches (e.g., the Zion Christian Church of Bishop Lekganyane, with its headquarters at Pietersburg, South Africa, and the African Apostolic Church of John Maranke, centered near Mutare in eastern Zimbabwe). Leadership in these churches is based on spiritual experience, charisma, a sense of vocation, and kinship ties, rather than on educational qualifications and theological training. To date, theological training programs for the AICs have barely touched the tip of the proverbial iceberg.

Typologically, the AICs can be classified in two main categories: the Ethiopian-type, or nonprophetic, churches whose patterns of worship and doctrines reflect those of the Western-oriented Protestant mission churches from which they have evolved; and the Spirit-type, or prophetic, churches (the vast majority)—mainly Zionist or Apostolic movements—with indigenized Pentecostal traits, focused on Holy Spirit manifestations, glossolalia, and prophetic healing. Some of the latter churches develop leadership patterns with "messianic" or "iconic" features. See Marthinus L. Daneel, *Quest for Belonging: Introduction to a Study of African Independent Churches* (Gweru: Mambo Press, 1987), 38–42.

3. Joseph Sittler's call for the integration of ecology, justice, and Christian faith in his significant address, "Called to Unity," to the third assembly of the WCC, marked the beginning of intensified ecotheological reflection in the Christian ecumenical movement. Sittler considers a doctrine of redemption meaningful only when it swings within the larger orbit of a doctrine of creation. Joseph Sittler, "Called to Unity," *Ecumenical Review* 14 (1962): 178.

4. ZIRRCON evolved from an empirical research unit which facilitated my study of the religious factor in Zimbabwe's liberation struggle. As founder of the movement, I have admittedly influenced its religio-ecological activities. Yet, my contribution at the outset was more that of stimulating motivation for environmental reform and providing financial empowerment through fund-raising than attempting to provide a theological blueprint for all activities. Instead, I encouraged local initiative and contextualization. Consequently, there was no question of the imposition of ecological models from above.

5. In Bishop Mutendi's Zion Christian Church, for instance, the celebration of the Eucharist during the Easter paschal festivities became the pivot for an annual reconsideration of the classic mission command as found in Matthew 28:18–19. Zionist identification with this text stimulated country-wide missionary campaigns involving the majority of ZCC officeholders and resulting in consistent church expansion; Marthinus L. Daneel, "Missionary Outreach in African Independent Churches," *Missionalia* 8, no. 3 (1980).

6. John Carmody, *Ecology and Religion: Toward a New Christian Theology of Nature* (New York: Paulist Press, 1983), 78.

7. Quoted in Donald E. Messer, *A Conspiracy of Goodness: Contemporary Images of Christian Mission* (Nashville: Abingdon Press, 1992), 69–70.

8. John S. Pobee, *Toward an African Theology* (Nashville: Abingdon Press, 1979), 81–98.

9. Bengt Sundkler, *The Christian Ministry in Africa* (London: SCM Press, 1960), 292.

10. See also the attempts of ecotheologians to describe the world as God's or Christ's body; Sallie McFague, *Models of God: Theology for an Ecological, Nuclear Age* (London: SCM Press, 1987), 69f.; Messer, *A Conspiracy of Goodness,* 67f.

11. Aylward Shorter considers the Eucharist to be "the pre-eminently healing sacrament," the symbolism of which heralds social healing and reconciliation. "The Eucharist," he correctly suggests, "also brings about our organic involvement with the physical environment and the interaction of every level of our existence. If human beings are the synthesis of the universe, the Eucharist makes them even more clearly the priests of creation." Aylward Shorter, *Jesus and the Witchdoctor: An Approach to Healing and Wholeness* (Maryknoll N. Y.: Orbis Books, 1985), 206.

12. Charles Nyamiti, "African Christologies Today," in *Faces of Jesus in Africa,* ed. Robert J. Schreiter (Maryknoll, N. Y.: Orbis Books, 1991), 10.

13. Several African theologians have pointed out that the traditional African healer, the *nganga,* has provided the primary paradigm for an indigenous Christology since the inception of African Christianity. Gabriel Setiloane believes that an authentic Christology should be sought in the healing practices of the *bongaka;* Gabriel M. Setiloane, *The Image of God among the Sotho-Tswana* (Rotterdam: Balkema, 1979), 64. According to John Pobee, the similarity between the *nganga* and Christ lies in both being "ensouled" by God during the process of healing; Pobee, *Toward an African Theology,* 93. Buana Kibongo in turn describes Christ's ministry as the fulfillment of *nganga*'s work. He stated that "*Ngangas* willed to save man, but did not succeed in doing so; Christ did so fully once for all. Christ has therefore accomplished the work of *Nganga*"; Buana Kibongo, "Priesthood," in *Biblical Revelation and African Beliefs,* ed. Kwesi A. Dickson and Paul Ellingworth (London: Lutterworth, 1969), 55. For a detailed discussion of the *nganga*-Christ paradigm, see J. Matthew Schoffeleers, "Christ in African Folk Theology: The *Nganga* Paradigm," in *Religion in Africa: Experience and Expression,* ed. Thomas D. Blakely, Walter E. A. van Beek, and Dennis L. Thomson (London: James Currey; Portsmouth, N.H.: Heinemann, 1994), 72–88.

14. Cécé Kolié, "Jesus as Healer?" in *Faces of Jesus in Africa,* ed. Robert J. Schreiter (Maryknoll, N.Y.: Orbis Books, 1991), 141–42.

15. Leonardo Boff, *Ecology and Liberation: A New Paradigm* (Maryknoll, N.Y.: Orbis Books, 1995), 66.

The Earth Is the Indian's Mother, Nhãndecy

ELIANE POTIGUARA
TRANSLATED BY LELAND ROBERT GUYER;
EDITED BY KAREN J. WARREN

IN THE PROPOSAL BY GRUMIN (GRUPO Mulher-Educação Indígena, or Women's Group for Indigenous Education), the work directed toward village-based education is unique in its contribution to the indigenous movement's struggle to reclaim its history, its culture, even its identity within the regions where the process of colonization has been most destructive. It is also unique in its work to preserve those cultures as yet untouched.

In this reconstructive effort, education and health emerge as the pillars of the work to be done. It is perfectly realistic in that it is in step with the consciousness-raising process of indigenous peoples toward the defense of their land rights, their environment of which they are courageous defenders and, in the end, their lives. For this to happen, it is not enough that the Indian be aware of his or her problems in terms of the reality of the encroaching society. The encroaching society must also become aware that the Indian is not a quaint or incapable being. Throughout the last five centuries, circumstances have forced Indians to be warriors in defense of their people and their lands in the longest war in the world's memory.

By publishing the pamphlet from which this [essay] is edited, GRUMIN aspires only to summarize the efforts of brother and sister Indians seeking their goal to convey their support of education officials, indigenous health care givers, and urban professors to help in the understanding of the social, political and economic reasons that have caused the oppression and social and racial discrimination that have always encroached upon them and the natural world.

THE INDIGENOUS POPULATION: WHO ARE WE?

Science continues to study the origins of primitive peoples. What we already know, however, is that Indians inhabited America for many centuries prior to the European invasion.

Before 1500, Brazilian Indians numbered five million, forming nine hundred indigenous nations. The extermination wrought by the invaders reduced the population to the current level of little more than 200,000, forming 180 nations and speaking 120 languages.

The capitalist economic model transformed the indigenous way of life as the Indian encountered the notions of the accumulation of wealth, products, metals, currency, and private property. They succumbed to this for the most part, transforming their customs and traditions in the same way as, for example, the Iroquois in the United States, whose matriarchal system ceased to exist.[1]

In the new society, as men accumulated money and goods, they became the proprietors of wealth, which their names and surnames guaranteed. Previously honored and respected, women and their families went to work for the holders of money—an acquaintance, a brother, even the husband. Indigenous cultures are rich. Nevertheless, the white people's attempts to acculturate them to serve their own needs puts the purity of their customs at risk. If we were allowed to continue to exist in our traditional ways, we would forever have stories as beautiful as the ones which follow, as told by the Amazonian Toyucas.

Potiguara, Eliane, "The Earth Is the Indian's Mother, Nhãndecy," in Karen J. Warren, Ed., *Ecofeminism: Women, Culture, Nature,* Bloomington: Indiana University Press, 1997, pp. 140–151. Reprinted by permission.

Possessing its own beliefs, mythology, customs and traditions, the Toyuca tribe was part of the indigenous nations long before Brazil ever existed. Today the Toyuca tribe is reasonably conservative, in the sense that it conserves its culture. We celebrate nature, manioc and fish. We observe *Dabucuri,* a festival in which we gather fish and fruit to offer to our relatives. It is a traditional festival for which we make *caxiri,* a drink prepared from grated manioc. A woman prepares the drink. She chews the manioc and then spits into a bowl, believing that the process fortifies the cairi and helps ferment the drink. Without *caxiri* the festival is not lively. We smoke natural *sorocaba* tobacco which we form into a long, thick rolled cigar which must remain lit throughout the night. We do not smoke the way city dwellers do. We smoke seldom and only in rituals. *Epadu* is a plant that must not disappear. Used only in our rituals, it helps enhance the ideas of our elders, our shamans and our thinkers. This plant helps us communicate with the spirits. Our parents and grandparents also use it as a stimulant on long journeys to ward off hunger.

We pray for the health of nature, for the phenomenal power of the rains and of lightning, and we pray to the God of Summer. It is our thinker who prays for us, and if I also wish to pray I must be near him.

Indigenous Participation

Up until now Indians have been warriors in a struggle for their life. Today, as a consequence of this struggle, we have a constitution that was written in recognition of their historical rights. Nevertheless, a lot of work must still be done to guarantee these rights. Toward this end, Indians are publicizing their rights on television, in newspapers, on radio, and in conferences held at schools, universities, and union halls.

Others have gone to international congresses at the United Nations where they have denounced the grand governmental projects that have assaulted our ecology, attacked our social structure, and upset the ecosystem.

In local assemblies or regional conferences held in our villages we have discussed the problems affecting Indians. Our leaders demand discussion of these problems with the government. We have won many battles, each one the result of the heightened awareness of indigenous people.

Customs and Traditions

Food and drink prepared by women and children permeate dances, festivals, and music. The people celebrate their harvests, the rain, the sun, the birds, and an endless number of natural phenomena in their festivals.

The community makes its day-to-day utensils. These include baskets, hammocks or sleeping nets, weaving, individual or collective home construction, and the production of canoes, adornments, and feathered crafts.

The division of labor in the areas of weaving, painting, and tattooing varies from village to village. Some allow men to paint; in others painting is the exclusive domain of the women. The paints, derived from the genipap and annatto trees, are used on the occasion of festivals, wars, death, and sickness.

Kinship forms the social and political organizations of the indigenous communities, with some variation from group to group. Some people, the Marubo as an example, divide themselves into clans, and the ancestry of each clan is matrilineal, that is, based on the ancestry of the mother.

The *pajés,* or shamans, care for the sick. They are the tribe's wise old men who know secret herbal cures and invoke the protection of the spirits through ritual.

Before the arrival of the Europeans, the tribal council would gather the wisest and most experienced of the collective. The Europeans introduced the "little despotic king" concept of subregional tribal chief.

Indigenous Society

Indigenous society has five key features. First, barter, not money, is the basis for the exchange of staple foodstuffs and objects of necessity. Second, indigenous society is classless. Since the collective is the basis of land and produce, there are neither rich people nor poor people. Third, indigenous society is communal. Labor is communal. Having no basis in power, relations between parents and children, husbands and wives, etc. are harmonious, and cooperative effort and mutual solidarity are everywhere present. Fourth, Indians do not accumulate material goods. They produce only that which they need to survive. Lastly, indigenous society is different from the encroaching society in customs, traditions, history, economy, social politics, and religion.

Misunderstanding and Prejudice

When the Portuguese came to the land that is now called Brazil they did not understand indigenous life and society. The letters to Portugal sent by Pero Vaz de Caminha to Aspilcueta Navarro reflect misunderstanding and ignorance about the realities of indigenous people. Following are quotations which show this misunderstanding and prejudice: "Everything about them reveals a culture of the most abject backwardness." "They were deceitful, disloyal, untrustworthy and, in a word, barbarous." "This Indian language is the only one along the length of the Brazilian coast. Lacking the three phonemes F, L and R, it follows that the Indians have neither Faith, Law nor Royalty, and for this reason they exist in a state of chaos and anarchy."

When the Spanish encountered indigenous civilization they raised doubt as to whether the Indian belonged to the human race. They came to consider the Indian as *casi mono,* "nearly monkeys." European morality, troubled by the religious notion of sin in the Indian settlements, brought in the Jesuits to dress the Indian women in white from head to toe. In Gorotire, a missionary interpreted indigenous culture as having absurd customs.

"Indians are synonymous with the past." In what may appear to be nothing more than harmless jokes there hides a legacy of prejudice that the colonists have nurtured through the centuries. Its intent is to destroy indigenous culture with misinformation. It is an oppressor's game where we find an attempted sense of humor in quips such as the following: "Indians know that if there's nothing else to eat, at least they've got their whistles." "Those lazy Indians just won't work." "Indians are drunken, thieving savages." "He's an Indian, but at least he's clean." "The Indian's a relic from the past." "How did the Indians live?" (as if they were not alive today). The year 1759 marks the official beginning of paternalism toward the Indian: Francisco Xavier, brother of the Marquis of Pombal and responsible for the expulsion of the Jesuits from Brazil, created the office of "Director of Indians" in response to the inherent savagery and manifest ignorance of the Indian.

"Indians wear no clothes. They're depraved; they're indecent." There are seven cardinal concepts about indigenous peoples:

1. Indians are minors, lazy and incompetent.
2. Blacks are slum dwellers, marginal.
3. Rural workers are people without land rights; they are lunch pailers, low-paid manual laborers.
4. Women are inferior and incompetent.
5. Children are ignorant.
6. Elders are obsolete, useless as workers.
7. The disabled are crippled and incompetent.

The exercise of these concepts by the elite and the powerful has done violence against human beings, especially indigenous peoples. They allege that the masses have limited education, then turn around and deny them education. Ignoring these problems and devaluing its very self, Brazilian society perpetuates its prejudicial underpinnings. It adopts a holier-than-thou attitude toward others and ultimately within its own arena. It is repressive and misinformed about health and nutrition. All of this reveals a feature of our educational system that is distinctly out of touch.

The prejudice of a whole era and centuries of paternalism have had powerful effects. The Indian cultures have been decimated, leaving virtually no mark upon the register of history.

Education and the Indigenous Family

The education of the indigenous child is very wise and simple. Children accompany their parents in their daily tasks, such as hunting, working in the field, preparing food and drink, producing arts and crafts, and participating in festivals and dances. In this way the child learns from an early age to be independent and enjoy working. This relationship does not allow violence or repression to intrude. It develops a link with the collective sentiment for the earth, a feeling of solidarity, the lifestyle and experience of the parents, grandparents, and extended family, and leads to a natural and healthful education of all children and young people.

Brazil Was Not Discovered; Brazil Was Invaded

People oppressed and discriminated against throughout the world, including those in Africa, Asia, Latin America, Central America, and Australia, have suffered centuries of subordination, inflicted upon them by European domination. During the fifteenth and sixteenth centuries in Brazil, the colonizers enslaved indigenous people. However, Indians refused to accept this slavery and many of them, such as the Guarani in the south of Brazil, would throw their wives, elders, and children from cliff tops prior to killing themselves. This was a comprehensible manner of protest.

The Indians would never accept subordination, racism, or violence against their people in their own land. They would never work hours of forced labor on behalf of the invaders whose culture, language, and lives were different from their own. Yet from the perspective of the colonizer of that era, indigenous resistance, struggle, dignity, and culture were synonymous with indolence and incompetence.[2]

Despite resistance to forced labor, slavery of the indigenous people was imposed by force of arms, and many deaths resulted. Sadly, the history of Brazil does not recognize this. At the same time, there are hundreds of books and documents that tell of the heroic deeds of the colonial explorers and pioneers, the work of the Jesuits and the first regional governors. History is written to mark the trajectory of human lives and truth. Employing these factors, we would have a history that gave birth to the Brazilian people: whites, mestizos, blacks, and the Indians who were already here.

In 130 years, two million Guarani Indians from the basins of the Paraná, the Paraguay, and the Uruguay rivers were killed or enslaved. We know that in a single year Indians harvested two thousand tons of the invaders' cotton and that, through the eyes of slavery, Indians watched over a million head of cattle in the Guara region.

The colonial explorers and pioneers, about whom history records glorious deeds, were nothing more than large paramilitary bands engaged in the capture and enslavement of Indians. Every manner of degenerate who had come to the New World or to Brazil formed these Indian hunting parties.

After illness, massacres, and the inhuman treatment of slavery eliminated 90 percent of the Indian population, the enslavement of blacks began in Brazil. Indians no longer served a function. They were "indolent and incompetent," according to the Portuguese.

The differences between indigenous society and the encroaching society can be represented by the following table:

Indigenous Society	Encroaching Society
1. Sense of collective land holding	1. Private property
2. Economy of subsistence	2. Economy of acquisition
3. Egalitarian society	3. Discriminatory society
4. Barter system	4. Cash-based system
5. Respect for life and environment	5. Predatory behavior

THE NORTHEASTERN INDIANS: FIVE HUNDRED YEARS OF RESISTANCE

The invasion of Brazil began in the northeast and moved eastward along the coast. For this reason the Indians of this region suffered the most. With a coalition of several tribes, the Tamoio Confederation waged the best-known armed conflict.

With lies and treachery the Portuguese defeated but did not subjugate these tribes. They preferred death to slavery, and for this reason the Tupinambá Kaete, Goiataká, Aymoré, and Tomiminó exist only in our memory.

Through all this the surviving Indians of the northeast and east assimilated the colonial culture. Many lost their native language, adopted mud and wattle construction for their homes, and began wearing clothing as they worked. In addition, many adopted the colonial economic system of work for pay.

Even the fashions, customs, and cherished dances, symbols of indigenous origins, sustained change as a consequence of the acculturation process, suffered for nearly five centuries in which the people confronted the Portuguese, the Dutch, the French, and the *sertanejos*.[3] Throughout these centuries they also confronted pressures to stop being Indian: the missions with their religious instruction, the Pombaline emancipation, the scorn and prejudice of the sertanejos and, today, the capitalist society.

Despite these pressures, they remain united with

the same conviction: they continue being Indians with a powerful sense of solidarity, founded upon the beliefs that explain nature, their origins, and a common destiny that unifies them as a people. From this they derive their organization as well as their political and cultural work toward the restoration of their traditions, the reaffirmation of their ethnic identity, and the recovery of their lands. This is the struggle of the Potiguara, of the Kukuru, of the Fulni-ô, of the Pankakaru, of the Tupiniquim, of the Xocó, and of others.

Against this backdrop they confront multinational corporations that covet their lands and natural resources, as well as local plantation owners, lumber companies, even gold miners, not to mention our traditional politicians.

THE TWENTIETH CENTURY

Nowadays the invasions of our lands by large landholders, the constant threats to indigenous families by gunmen, the huge mining, hydroelectric, highway, and lumber concerns are responsible for death, violence, and aggression against indigenous people. Just as in the past, indigenous leaders still combat these invasions of their lands, these attacks upon Mother Nature, this violence against their people. They are our twentieth-century warriors.

Going beyond the examples through history of social and racial prejudice against Indians, we can now demonstrate the consequences of the behavior of the people in power. They possess national and foreign capital, control the means of production and retain all profits, possess advanced technology and do not extend its benefit to others, possess money but do not distribute its earnings, possess land for their private use, and possess firearms and use them to repress.

The colonizers have employed violence to subjugate indigenous people. In the following table, one can compare the differences between whites and Indians. These differences have determined the outcomes of each.

Whites	Indians
1. Superiority in firearms	1. Bows and arrows, spears, snares, and bolas
2. Ships and horses for transportation	2. Canoes and feet
3. Use of steel and other metals	3. Traditional crafts
4. Imposition of psychological, racial, intellectual, and religious sense of superiority	4. Misunderstood indigenous culture and traditions
5. Climate of violence, injustice, and hypocrisy	5. Climate of struggle and resistance against slavery

Other factors have also contributed to the annihilation of the indigenous society by the whites: biological devastation (illnesses, premature aging), economic devastation (forced Indian labor with no recourse), psychological devastation (the Indians' sense of inferiority), and social devastation (social maladjustment).

The social disintegration of indigenous people affects even more the acculturated indigenous communities and the displaced and marginalized Indians who live in the city, with the following results: illegal ghettos, deaths and suicides, rapes, massacres, alcoholism, insecurity, timidity, discouragement, and mental illness. The first contacts with white people brought the school-based concept to the village, an idea that had both positive and negative aspects, given the indigenous population's lifestyle.

ENERGY: A CHALLENGE TO NATURE

"These lands belong to us now. You have twenty-four hours to clear out." The politics of development in Brazil evolved in the second half of the twentieth century. In 1964, the military government then in power, in an effort to transform a Third World country into a First World country overnight, put into action a development plan financed with foreign loans that we'll be paying off until who knows when. This resulted in the impoverishment of the entire Brazilian nation.

With the implementation of these grand projects, we have witnessed enormous assaults upon nature and the environment. The powers that be have flooded lands, poisoned rivers and seas, devastated whole regions, and spread sickness and ethnic and social disorder. Mercury and sugarcane waste products have contaminated the Indians' rivers, and their flora and fauna have died. The Indians have suffered the most from the authorities' neglect of their future and the disrespect with which they deal with their issues.

Development, yes. Massacre, no!

There are four types of energy available to us. First, there is hydroelectric energy. Dams built on large rivers generate energy for lights for factories, for cities, and so on. When they flood the areas behind the dams, cities, indigenous settlements, and riverbank populations must leave. The flora and fauna of the flooded areas die and decompose, and the results are diseases like malaria and leishmaniasis. More than ninety hydroelectric projects are planned in the Amazonian basin and in the south.

Second, there is mineral energy. Petroleum is the basis for this energy source. Gasoline and other thousands of derivatives (plastics, foam rubber, diesel fuel, kerosene, etc.) come from petroleum. The national petroleum conglomerate Petrobras is responsible for the exploration for and production of petroleum. In addition, there are other subsidiary concerns that operate refineries and conduct research (Shell, Esso, British Petroleum, Ida Mitsu, and Elf Equitaine).

Third, there is energy derived from the atom, from matter itself, nuclear energy. This source is highly controversial because it is a powerful and dangerous form of energy that, if it escapes, can contaminate the population with its radioactivity. A disaster of this type occurred in Goiânia, where many people died.

Finally, there are alternative sources of energy. One is energy derived from sugarcane. It appeared in response to the gasoline shortage. The Pro-Alcohol Program was created for the development of this source of energy. Now, tons of *vinhoto* (a sugarcane waste product) poison the rivers.

> When the sugar refineries appeared, everything began to die. They drained the wetlands, and the black and green chameleon, the freshwater turtle and the cayman died off. The snakes also died. I remember them—the maracatifa, the salamantabois, the howling snake and the rattlesnake. The river fish. . . . What can I say? Today everything's polluted. The camurim, the saúna, the traira and the pitu are gone.
>
> Our land used to give us everything: fruits and nuts like capi, mango, mangaba, guava, pine nuts, graviola, jack fruit, bananas, cana-caiana and pineapple. The sweet potato and the yam would grow to an immense size in the earth. With the sugarcane residue from the refineries, together with deforestation, the Potiguara lands diminished. Now we must rebuild what remains. It's a shame.

Brazilian society will respect Indians only when it recognizes them as a part of its own culture, language, and traditions. When Brazilian society, in a nonpaternalistic way, looks upon the Indian as a brother, as the head of a family, and not as an indigent but as a Brazilian in need like anyone else, then Indians will have respect. After all, they have the great fortune of nature and all the wealth that it encompasses.

WHAT SHOULD WE DO?

If we want to undergo a social transformation in our country it is not enough to criticize. Besides criticizing, we must present solutions in pursuit of change. All the struggles undertaken up to now on behalf of indigenous peoples have been very valuable. We won a new constitution. Now we must find new ways to struggle, work programs, and suggestions to guarantee the rights we have established.

This is why we need the Organization of Indigenous Movements. The National Indigenous Union, other indigenous organizations, and legal counsel exist. The GRUMIN Project appeared as an offshoot to sensitize and strengthen and communicate the work that the women and children have been doing. This is how we'll get to where we're going. It is through unity that the prophecy will come true and indigenous people will survive, and it is through hard work and persistence that we will build unity.

We must suggest—no, demand—of the powers that be that we have a Program of Health, Education, and Agriculture, backed by state and municipal administrations. We can seek solutions with the Department of Education, Health, and Agriculture. Indigenous leadership has already opened lines of communication and has done a lot of work. We need to get moving.

But how? By organizing workers' groups within or outside the village by the labor that they perform. The groups would focus on five key areas:

1. The right to land and the observance of its boundaries. How do we guarantee these lands? Have an attorney. The National Indigenous Union has a nucleus of indigenous rights.

2. Education. We must be convincing when we say that we need a hearing on education—its professionalization and salary, research into the indigenous reality, teaching materials, school supplies, guarantees with respect to our culture, traditions, and language. School-based education in the villages is still unrealistic, despite best efforts. This kind of education has harmed our customs and indigenous languages, and therefore we need a radical change in this area.

3. Health. We must be convincing when we say that we need a hearing on health—its professionalization and salary, medicines that don't conflict with indigenous culture, the restoration of natural medicine, and the use of hospitals only in extreme cases.

4. The organization of position papers and how to advance them. These papers can be done on each topic (education, health, agriculture, etc.).

5. To advance projects that solicit funds, we must establish work groups in legal terms, have bank accounts, and truly work with the community.

There are people, present, absent, and anonymous, who have contributed greatly to GRUMIN, or Women's Group for Indigenous Education. Some are present in the strength they've given, others in the critiques that have helped put this work together.

Our work was born in our consciousness, in the blood that runs in our veins, and in the struggle against all forms of oppression or discrimination. It's there, ready for our discussion.

We will continue our project because our scope is enormous. Earth, nature and Tupã have been witness to our spilled blood, our pain, and the prejudice indigenous people have suffered.

Few know our true history. Many of our grandparents have responded to distress with silence, which, as much as struggling and persistence, represents wisdom. With this wisdom they have passed to us, we must dive deeply into the depths of the rivers and the sea, climb mountains, and enter the heart of the forests and the cataracts, and feel the origins of indigenous people and struggle with and for them.

It is the deliverance and the conservation of our identity. Nature cannot be conserved if its guardians—the Indians—exist no more.

So, let us live!

AFTERWORD

"A Prayer for the Liberation of Indigenous People"
To Marçal Tupã-Y (Guarani Chief Nhandewa, murdered in 1983)

Stop stripping my leaves and give me back my hoe.
Quit drowning my beliefs and chopping up my roots.
Cease tearing out my lungs and smothering my reason.
It's time to stop killing my songs and silencing my voice.
You cannot dry out the roots of those who possess seeds
Cast upon the earth to sprout.
You cannot extinguish the fertile memory of our grandparents—
Ancestral blood, rituals to remember.
No one clips our broad wings
For the sky is liberty,
And we have faith in finding it.
Pray for us, our Father Xamã,
That the evil forest spirit
Not create weakness, misery, and death in us.
Pray for us, our Mother Earth,
That these torn clothes
And that these evil men
Withdraw before the rattle of maracas.
Deliver us from sorrow, cane liquor, and strife,
Help unite our nations.
Enlighten our men, women, and children,
Obliterate ingratitude and envy among the strong.
Give us light, faith, and life in our healing ceremony,
Avoid, oh Tupã, violence and bloodshed.
In a sacred spot near the river's edge,
On full moon nights, oh Marçal, invoke
The spirits of the stones so we can dance the Toré
Bring the life force
To our shamans and our celebrations of the manioc
After we drink our chicha in faith.
Pray for us, our heavenly bird,
That jaguars, peccaries, crested cranes, and capybaras
Line our rivers Jurena, São Francisco, and Paraná,
Line the shores of the Atlantic.
After all, we are pacific.

Show us our way like the freshwater dolphin,
Illuminate our star for our future.
Help us play the magic flutes
To sing to you a song of offering
Or dance our ritual lamakó
Pray for us, our bird-Xamã,
In the northeast and in the south all morning.
In the Amazon wilds or in the heart of the back-woods woman.
Pray for us, macaws, armadillos, or speckled catfish,
Come to us,
Our god that we call Nhendiru!
Make happy our children
Who from Indian bellies will be reborn.
Give us hope each day
For all we wish is earth and peace
For our poor people—our wealthy children.

NOTES

Editor's Note: I met Eliane Potiguara at an International Seminar on Ecofeminism, held in conjunction with the Earth Summit, in Rio de Janeiro, Brazil, during May 1992. I was impressed by her passion and commitment, her work in GRUMIN, and the pamphlet she wrote, *A Terra É A Mã Do Índio,* translated here as "The Earth Is the Indian's Mother, Nhãndecy." With Potiguara's permission, Macalester College Professor of Spanish and Portuguese Leland Guyer translated the pamphlet and then I edited it to produce this essay-length version. Anyone interested in the Portuguese version may write Eliane Potiguara at GRUMIN, Rua da Quitanda, 185 s/503-CEP 20.091, Rio de Janeiro, Brasil; anyone interested in the English version may contact Leland Guyer at Macalester College, 1600 Grand Avenue, St. Paul, MN 55105. Eliane Potiguara dedicates this work "to Vo Maria de Lourdes, for her awareness; to Mother Elza, for her life; to my children, Moina, Tajira, and Potiguara, for their strength, and to the indigenous peoples of Brazil, for their claws and for their struggle."

1. Many indigenous societies continue to resist the influence of the encroaching capitalist society. An example of this are the Yanomami, who preserve their culture, customs, and traditions. There are 20,000 Yanomami Indians living in Amazonia, in the Surucucus Mountains. They have managed to resist the ever-present threats of the gold miners and mining companies attracted by the richness of their soil. They live as protectors of their environment, in a struggle for which their great leader David Yanomami won the Global 2000 award, conferred by the United Nations.

2. Ângelo Kretã, Chief Kaigang, was the first Indian to exercise politics in the country, believing that this would accrue positive results to the war Indians waged for their lands. Speaking as a councilman, he said: "Brazil was not discovered. It was invaded."

3. *Sertanejo* is the name given to those who live in the *sertão,* a harsh region of the northeastern part of Brazil, of sparse population and vegetation, beset by periodic and extended droughts, regularly followed by sudden and devastating floods. Curiously, the sertão is the locale of many of the most powerful social movements in the last two hundred years of Brazilian history. We also know the sertão as the inspiration of much of Brazil's recent literature and film. (Translator's note.)

Discussion Questions

1. Who should decide how to manage natural resources in developing countries, inhabitants or trained experts?
2. Must developing countries choose between addressing environmental issues or addressing social problems?
3. What is the relationship between overpopulation and overconsumption in terms of environmental degradation?
4. Will developing nations inevitably follow Western models of consumption? What alternatives are available?
5. Is a high standard of living the same as a high quality of life? What defines each?

Further Reading

Boff, Leonardo, *Ecology and Liberation: A New Paradigm,* Maryknoll, N.Y.: Orbis, 1995.
Burger, Julian, *Report from the Frontier: The State of the World's Indigenous Peoples,* London: Zed Books, 1987.

Dankelman, Irene, and Joan Davidson, *Women and the Environment in the Third World,* London: Earthscan Publications, 1988.
Gebara, Ivone, *Longing for Running Water: Ecofeminism and Liberation,* Minneapolis: Augsburg Fortress, 1999.
Guha, Ramachandra, *The Unquiet Woods : Ecological Change and Peasant Resistance in the Himalaya,* New Delhi: Oxford University Press, 1989.
Hallman, David G., Ed., *Ecotheology: Voices from South and North,* Maryknoll, N.Y.: Orbis, 1994.
McDonagh, Sean, *The Greening of the Church,* Maryknoll, N.Y.: Orbis, 1990.
Rothenberg, David, and Marta Ulvaeus, Eds., *The World and the Wild,* Tucson: University of Arizona Press, 2000.
Ruether, Rosemary Radford, Ed., *Women Healing Earth: Third World Women on Ecology, Feminism and Religion,* Maryknoll, N.Y.: Orbis, 1996.

Chapter 15

New Cosmologies and Visions

WITH THE MOMENTUM OF HUMAN activities seeming to hurtle us collectively toward the brink of planetary disaster, there have been calls for a whole new way of looking at life and our place in the universe—a *metanoia* or change of consciousness, a paradigm shift away from prevailing models. It is argued that much of the prevailing worldview and the environmentally disruptive behavior it justifies is based on outdated models, cosmologies that are no longer accepted by mainstream science.

Just as physics has come to abandon the Newtonian, mechanistic model of describing the universe in favor of a relational one, the very nature of life itself is now coming to be understood in new ways. Likewise, long-held social norms pertaining to class, race, and gender have given way to revised understandings of how human societies should be constituted and how they operate. Indeed, today we may be living through a transition on a par with or exceeding the great historical transformations brought about by agriculture, the Renaissance, the Industrial Revolution, and the civil rights movement.

Thomas Berry defines a worldview as a story, a tale, or even a myth that tells us who we are and how we should live. Given the magnitude of the changes going on all about us, Berry argues that we need a new story to account for and make sense of these changes as none of our old stories is able to do. Trained as a historian of religion in the Roman Catholic tradition, Berry (who now refers to himself as a *geologian*) sees the evolution of the universe as an ongoing revelation of the divine. In that sense, Berry suggests that this evolution itself can be the basis for the new story we need.

James Lovelock is an atmospheric scientist who stumbled on a new way of conceptualizing life while he was doing research for NASA in the 1960s. Observing that the composition of the Earth's atmosphere was different from what one would expect to develop through known trends in chemistry, Lovelock began to suspect that there were forces on Earth acting to maintain a chemical balance in the atmosphere that was conducive to the flourishing of life-forms. Eventually, with the collaboration of fellow scientist Lynn Margulis, Lovelock developed the hypothesis that the Earth's biosphere acted as a huge, self-regulating superorganism, which he called Gaia, after the ancient Greek goddess of the Earth. The notion of the Earth as a living being of which we all are but small components captured the imagination of many and, to some, held religious implications. Lovelock addresses such responses to his work in a chapter from his book *The Ages of Gaia*.

Riane Eisler shifts our focus to social norms. Observing that most human societies in historical memory have been based on paradigms of domination and control (which, as we have seen, ecofeminists associate with patriarchy), Eisler calls for a new way of envisioning social relations, based not on domination but on partnership. In fact, pointing out the reassessment of gender roles characteristic of modern societies and the growing trend toward seeking win–win conflict resolutions, she claims that such a transformation is already underway. However, Eisler cautions, we must not limit the discussion to social relations but allow it to encompass domains as diverse as science, spirituality, economics, and politics.

Philosopher Roger S. Gottlieb describes the search for peace in an unpeaceful world. Rejecting the option of simply shutting out the reality of suffering and injustice, Gottlieb argues that even in the face of daunting odds, one can find peace through the struggle for what is right and necessary. He calls this practice "a spirituality of resistance."

The New Story

THOMAS BERRY

It's all a question of story. We are in trouble just now because we do not have a good story. We are in between stories. The old story, the account of how the world came to be and how we fit into it, is no longer effective. Yet we have not learned the new story. Our traditional story of the universe sustained us for a long period of time. It shaped our emotional attitudes, provided us with life purposes, and energized action. It consecrated suffering and integrated knowledge. We awoke in the morning and knew where we were. We could answer the questions of our children. We could identify crime, punish transgressors. Everything was taken care of because the story was there. It did not necessarily make people good, nor did it take away the pains and stupidities of life or make for unfailing warmth in human association. It did provide a context in which life could function in a meaningful manner.

Presently this traditional story is dysfunctional in its larger social dimensions, even though some believe it firmly and act according to its guidance. Aware of the dysfunctional aspects of the traditional program, some persons have moved on into different, often new-age, orientations, which have consistently proved ineffective in dealing with our present life situation. Even with advanced science and technology, with superb techniques in manufacturing and commerce, in communications and computation, our secular society remains without satisfactory meaning or the social discipline needed for a life leading to emotional, aesthetic, and spiritual fulfillment. Because of this lack of satisfaction many persons are returning to a religious fundamentalism. But that, too, can be seen as inadequate to supply the values for sustaining our needed social discipline.

A radical reassessment of the human situation is needed, especially concerning those basic values that give to life some satisfactory meaning. We need something that will supply in our times what was supplied formerly by our traditional religious story. If we are to achieve this purpose, we must begin where everything begins in human affairs—with the basic story, our narrative of how things came to be, how they came to be as they are, and how the future can be given some satisfying direction. We need a story that will educate us, a story that will heal, guide, and discipline us.

Western society did have, in its traditional story of the universe, an agreed-upon functioning story up until somewhere around the fourteenth century. This religion-based story originated in a revelatory experience some three thousand years ago. According to this story, the original harmony of the universe was broken by a primordial human fault, and that necessitated formation of a believing redemptive community that would take shape through the course of time. Human history was moving infallibly toward its fulfillment in the peace of a reconstituted paradise.

This religious story was integrated with the Ptole-

Berry, Thomas, "The New Story," in *The Dream of the Earth* by Thomas Berry, pp. 123–137.

maic account of the universe and how it functioned, an abiding universe that endlessly renewed itself and its living forms through the seasonal sequence of time. The introduction of irreversible historical time onto this abiding cosmological scene is precisely the contribution of the Western religious tradition. However severe the turbulent moments of history through the late classical and early medieval periods, these at least took place within a secure natural world and within a fixed context of interpretation. Whatever the problems were, they were not problems concerning the basic human or spiritual values that were at stake. Those were clear.

The confusion and insecurity that we presently experience originated, to a large extent, in the fourteenth century when Europe experienced the plague known as the Black Death. Without making this event a simplistic explanation of all later history, we can say that it was a transition period. Even more, it was a central traumatic moment in Western history. It is estimated that this plague, which reached Europe in 1347, had by 1349 killed off perhaps one-third of the population. Almost half of the people of Florence died within a three-month period. Throughout the later fourteenth century there was a population decline in the whole of Europe. In London the last of the great plagues was in 1665.

In response to the plague and to other social disturbances of the fourteenth and fifteenth centuries, two directions of development can be identified—one toward a religious redemption out of the tragic world, the other toward greater control of the physical world to escape its pain and to increase its utility to human society. From these two tendencies the two dominant cultural communities of recent centuries were formed: the believing religious community and the secular community with its new scientific knowledge and its industrial powers of exploiting the natural world.

Since the people of these centuries had no knowledge of germs and thus no explanation of the plague, other than divine judgment on a wicked world, the answers most generally sought were in the moral and spiritual order, frequently outside the orthodox teachings of the church. The believing community in its various sectarian expressions had recourse to supernatural forces, to the spirit world, to the renewal of esoteric traditions, and sometimes to pre-Christian beliefs and rituals that had been neglected in their deeper dynamics since the coming of Christianity. Even within traditional Christianity there was an intensification of the faith experience, an effort to activate supernatural forces with special powers of intervention in the phenomenal world now viewed as threatening to the human community. The sense of human depravity increased. The need for an outpouring of influences from the higher numinous world was intensified. Faith dominated the religious experience. Redemption mystique became the overwhelming form of Christian experience.

Such excessive emphasis on redemption, to the neglect of the revelatory import of the natural world, had from the beginning been one of the possibilities in Christian development. The creed itself is overbalanced in favor of redemption. Thus the integrity of the Christian story is affected. Creation becomes increasingly less important. This response, with its emphasis on redemptive spirituality, continued through the religious upheavals of the sixteenth century and on through the Puritanism and Jansenism of the seventeenth century. This attitude was further strengthened by the shock of the Enlightenment and Revolution periods of the eighteenth and nineteenth centuries.

The American version of the ancient Christian story has functioned well in its institutional efficiency and in its moral efficacy, but it is no longer the story of the earth. Nor is it the integral story of the human community. It is a sectarian story. At its center there is an intensive preoccupation with the personality of the Savior, with the interior spiritual life of the faithful, and with the salvific community. The difficulty is that we came to accept this situation as the normal, even the desirable, thing.

The other response to the Black Death was the reaction that led eventually to the scientific secular community of our times. That reaction sought to remedy earthly terror not by supernatural or religious powers, but by understanding and controlling the earth process. Although those working in that trend were at first committed to the esoteric wisdom traditions and to Platonic idealism, they did emphasize the need for empirical examination of the phenomenal world and its expression in quantitative terms. Scientific inquiry became the controlling human preoccupation, pushed by obscure forces in the unconscious depths of Western culture. The telescope and microscope were invented. Calculus, the supreme instrument of modern science, was discovered. A scientific priesthood came to govern the thought life of our society. We looked at the earth in its physical reality and projected new theories of how it functioned. The celestial bodies were scrutinized more intently, the phenomenon of light was examined, new ways of understanding energy evolved. New sciences emerged. The *Novum Organum* of Francis Bacon appeared in 1620, the *Principia* of Isaac Newton in 1687, the *Scienza Nuova* of Giambattista Vico in 1725.

All of these led to an awareness that the human mind was advancing. This in turn led to the Enlightenment period of the eighteenth century and to the sense of absolute progress of the human mind as expressed by Condorcet in his 1793 volume entitled *Historical Survey of the Progress of the Human Mind.* In the nineteenth century the doctrines of social development appear with Fourier, Saint-Simon, and August Comte. Karl Marx brought this movement to its most realistic expression in his 1848 *Manifesto.*

While these changes in the mode of human perception and of social structure were taking place, evidence was appearing in the realms of geology and paleontology indicating that there was a time sequence in the very formation of the earth and of all lifeforms upon the earth. The earth was not the eternal, fixed, abiding reality that it had been thought to be. It suddenly dawned upon Western consciousness that earlier lifeforms were of a simpler nature than later lifeforms, that the later forms were derived from the earlier forms. The complex of life manifestations had not existed from the beginning by some external divine creative act setting all things in their place. The earth in all its parts, especially in its lifeforms, was in a state of continuing transformation.

Discovery of this life sequence, with an explanation of how it came about, found expression in Darwin's *Origin of Species* in 1859. After Darwin, the physicists in their study of light and radiation came almost simultaneously to an understanding of the infra-atomic world and the entire galactic system. Insight into both the microphase and macrophase of the phenomenal world was obtained, and the great unity of the universe became apparent both in its spatial expansion and its time sequence.

Just at that moment, however, a sudden shift in the mode of consciousness took place. The scientists suddenly became aware that the opaqueness of matter had dissolved. Science was ultimately not the objective grasping of some reality extrinsic to ourselves. It was rather a moment of subjective communion in which the human was seen as that being in whom the universe in its evolutionary dimension became conscious of itself.

Thus a new creation story had evolved in the secular scientific community, equivalent in our times to the creation stories of antiquity. This creation story differs from the traditional Eurasian creation stories much more than those traditional stories differ one from another. This new creation story seems destined to become the universal story taught to every child who receives formal education in its modern form anywhere in the world.

The redemptive believing community, first dazzled by this new vision of developmental time, then frustrated by an inability to cope with the new data, lapsed unenthusiastically into its traditional attitudes. In recent centuries, indeed, the believing community has not been concerned with any cosmology, ancient or modern, for the believing community has its real values concentrated in the Savior, the human person, the believing church, and a postearthly paradisal beatitude.

There is, however, a surviving cosmology in which the redemption story takes place and which to some extent still plays a role in the Christian story. According to this story the cosmos, and every being in the cosmos, reflects the divine examplar considered by Plato as the Agathon, the Good; by Plotinus as the One; by the Christian as God. All things are beautiful by this beauty. The supremely beautiful is the integrity and harmony of the total cosmic order, as Saint Thomas insists upon repeatedly.

The human mind ascends to the contemplation of the divine by rising through the various grades of being, from the physical forms of existence in the earth, with its mountains and seas, to the various forms of living things, and so to the human mode of consciousness, then to the soul, and from the inner life of the soul to God. This sequence, portrayed first in the *Symposium* of Plato, is presented in all its sublime qualities in the soliloquy of Augustine as he meditated with his mother by the window just prior to her death. So Bonaventure could write on the reduction of all the arts and sciences to theology, for all eventually depend upon the divine reference. So, too, the journey of Dante through the various spheres of reality up to the divine vision in itself. Initiation into the basic human and Christian values was initiation into this cosmology. Christian spirituality was built up in this manner. The mysteries of Christianity were integral with this cosmology.

The difficulty with this cosmology is that it presents the world simply as an ordered complex of beings that are ontologically related as an image of the divine. It does not present the world as a continuing process of emergence in which there is an inner organic bond of descent of each reality from an earlier reality.

Yet in their functional roles neither this traditional cosmology nor the new scientific cosmology has been of serious religious concern because of the shift in the Western religious tradition from a dominant creation mystique to a dominant redemption mystique. This Christian redemptive mystique is little concerned with the natural world. The essential thing is redemption out of the world through a personal savior relationship that transcends all such concerns. Even the earlier mystical experiences of ascending to the divine through the realms of created perfection are diminished.

Presently this excessive redemptive emphasis is played out. It cannot effectively dynamize activity in time because it is an inadequate story of time. The redemption story has grown apart not only from the historical story, but also from the earth story. Consequently an isolated spiritual power has eventuated that is being victimized by entropy.

If this is the impasse of the believing redemption community of America, the impasse of the secular scientific community, committed to a developmental universe, is the commitment to the realm of the physical to the exclusion of the spiritual. This has been the tough, the realistic, position. The Darwinian principle of natural selection involves no psychic or conscious purpose, but is instead a struggle for earthly survival that gives to the world its variety of form and function. Because this story presents the universe as a random sequence of physical and biological interactions with no inherent meaning, the society supported by this vision has no adequate way of identifying any spiritual or moral values.

We must not think that these two communities have no regard for each other. Extensive courtesies are extended; cooperation is offered. Persons in the scientific professions as well as in modern industrial and commercial pursuits have extensive regard for the religious dimension of life. Many are themselves religious personalities. Those in the religious community have their own esteem for scientific, technological, and commercial activities. Training in the professions takes place in religious schools and even dominates the curriculum. So what's the fuss about? The answer is that surface agreement is not depth communion or the basis of sound cosmic-earth-human values. The antagonisms are deeper than they appear. An integral story has not emerged, and no community can exist without a unifying story. This is precisely why the communication between these two is so unsatisfying. No sustaining values have emerged. Our social problems are not resolved. The earth continues to disintegrate under the plundering assault of humans.

Both traditions are trivialized. The human venture remains stuck in its impasse. Children who begin their earth studies or life studies do not experience any numinous aspect of these subjects. The excitement of existence is diminished. If this fascination, this entrancement, with life is not evoked, the children will not have the psychic energies needed to sustain the sorrows inherent in the human condition. They might never discover their true place in the vast world of time and space. Teaching children about the natural world should be treated as one of the most important events in their lives. Children need a story that will bring personal meaning together with the grandeur and meaning of the universe. The secular school as presently constituted cannot provide the mystique that should be associated with this story. Nor can the religious-oriented school that has only superficially adopted this new story of the universe evoke this experience in the child.

The tragedy of this situation is that schooling now fulfills a role in our society that is similar to the role of initiation ceremonies in earlier tribal societies. In those societies the essential mystery communicated to the youthful initiates was the story of the universe in its awesome and numinous aspects. The capacity for communing with and absorbing into their own beings these deeper powers of the natural world was bestowed on them. The pathos in our own situation is that our secular society does not see the numinous quality or the deeper psychic powers associated with its own story, while the religious society rejects the story because it is presented only in its physical aspect. The remedy for this is to establish a deeper understanding of the spiritual dynamics of the universe as revealed through our own empirical insight into the mysteries of its functioning.

In this late twentieth century that can now be done with a clarity never before available to us. Empirical inquiry into the universe reveals that from its beginning in the galactic system to its earthly expression in human consciousness the universe carries within itself a psychic-spiritual as well as a physical-material dimension. Otherwise human consciousness emerges out of nowhere. The human is seen as an addendum or an intrusion and thus finds no real place in the story of the universe. In reality the human activates the most profound dimension of the universe itself, its capacity to reflect on and celebrate itself in conscious self-awareness.

So far, however, spiritually oriented personalities have been pleased because the mechanistic orientation of the scientific world enables them to assume an aloof spiritual attitude that disdains any concern for the natural world. Scientists, on the other hand, are pleased since that attitude leaves them free to structure their world of quantitative measurements without the problem of spiritual values associated with human consciousness. Thus both scientists and believers remain disengaged from any profound understanding of the earth process itself. To remedy this situation, we need simply to reflect on the story itself.

The story of the universe is the story of the emergence of a galactic system in which each new level of expression emerges through the urgency of self-transcendence. Hydrogen in the presence of some millions of degrees of heat emerges into helium. After the stars take shape as oceans of fire in the heavens, they go through a sequence of transformations. Some eventually explode into the stardust out of which the solar system and the earth take shape. Earth gives unique expression of itself in its rock and crystalline structures and in the variety and splendor of living forms, until humans appear as the moment in which the unfolding universe becomes conscious of itself. The human emerges not only as an earthling, but also as a worldling. We bear the universe in our beings as the universe bears us in its being. The two have a total presence to each other and to that deeper mystery out of which both the universe and ourselves have emerged.

If this integral vision is something new both to the scientist and to the believer, both are gradually becoming aware of this view of the real and its human meaning. It might be considered a new revelatory experience. Because we are moving into a new mythic age, it is little wonder that a kind of mutation is taking place in the entire earth-human order. A new paradigm of what it is to be human emerges. This is what is so exciting, yet so painful and so disrupting. One aspect of this change involves the shift in earth-human relations, for we now in large measure determine the earth process that once determined us. In a more integral way we could say that the earth that controlled itself directly in the former period now to an extensive degree controls itself through us.

In this new context the question appears as to where the values are, how they are determined, how they are transmitted. Whereas formerly values consisted in the perfection of the earthly image reflecting an external Logos in a world of fixed natures, values are now determined by the human sensitivity in responding to the creative urgencies of a developing world. The scientist in the depths of the unconscious is drawn by the mystical attraction of communion with the emerging creative process. This would not be possible unless it were a call of subject to subject, if it were not an effort at total self-realization on the part of the scientists. As scientists, their taste for the real is what gives to their work its admirable quality. Their wish is to experience the real in its tangible, opaque, material aspect and to respond to that by establishing an interaction with the world that will advance the total process. If the demand for objectivity and the quantitative aspect of the real has led scientists to neglect subjectivity and the qualitative aspect of the real, this has been until now a condition for fulfilling their historical task. The most notable single development within science in recent years, however, has been a growing awareness of the integral physical-psychic dimension of reality.

The believing redemption community is awakening only slowly to this new context of understanding. There is a fear, a distrust, even a profound aversion, to the natural world and all its processes. It would be difficult to find a theological seminary in this country that has an adequate program on creation as it is experienced in these times. The theological curriculum is dominated by a long list of courses on redemption and how it functions in aiding humans to transcend the world, all based on biblical texts. Such a situation cannot long endure, however, since a new sense of the earth and its revelatory import is arising in the believing community. The earth will not be ignored, nor will it long endure being despised, neglected, or mistreated. The dynamics of creation are demanding attention once more in a form unknown for centuries to the orthodox Christian.

It is clear that the primordial intention of the universe is to produce variety in all things, from atomic structures to the living world of plant and animal forms, to the appearance of humans, where individuals differ from one another more extensively than in any other realm of known reality. This difference can be seen not only in individuals, but also in social structures and in historical periods of our development. But here, also, the difficulty in the human order, for there is no absolute model for the individual. Personal realization involves a unique creative effort in response to all those interior and exterior forces that enter into individual life. So, too, with each historical age and each cultural form, there is need to create a reality for which, again, there is no adequate model. This is precisely the American difficulty, a difficulty for which there is no complete answer, but only a striving toward. At each moment we must simply be what we are, opening onto a larger life.

Interior articulation of its own reality is the immediate responsibility of every being. Every being has its own interior, its self, its mystery, its numinous aspect. To deprive any being of this sacred quality is to disrupt the larger order of the universe. Reverence will be total or it will not be at all. The universe does not come to us in pieces any more than a human individual stands before us with some part of its being. Preservation of this feeling for reality in its depths has been considerably upset in these past two centuries of scientific analysis and technological manipulation of the earth and its energies. During this period, the human mind lived in the narrowest bonds that it has ever experienced. The vast mythic, visionary, symbolic world with its all-pervasive numinous qualities was lost. Because of this loss, we made our terrifying assault upon the earth with an irrationality that is stunning in enormity, while we were being assured that this was the way to a better, more humane, more reasonable world.

Such treatment of the external physical world, deprived of its subjectivity, could not long avoid also encompassing the human. Thus we have the most vast paradox of all—ourselves as free, intelligent, numinous beings negating those very interior qualities by our own objective reasoning processes and subserving our own rationalizations. Yet, finally, a reversal has begun, and the reality and value of the interior subjective numinous aspect of the entire cosmic order is being appreciated as the basic condition in which the story makes any sense at all.

Here we come to the further realization that the universe is coherent within itself throughout the total extent of space and the entire sequence of its time development. This web of relationships throughout the universe is what first impinges on our waking consciousness. It is this deepening association within the universe that enables life to emerge into being. The living form is more individuated, with greater subjectivity and more intensive identity within itself and with its environment. All these factors are multiplied on a new scale of magnitude in the realm of consciousness. There a supreme mode of communion exists within the individual, with the human community, within the earth-human complex. Increased capacity for personal identity is inseparable from this capacity for mutual presence. Together this distance and this intimacy establish the basic norms of being, of life, of value. It is the mission of our present and all future generations to develop this capacity for mutual presence on new and more comprehensive levels.

In transmitting values through the sequence of generations, we no longer have the initiation techniques whereby the vision and values of earlier generations were transmitted to succeeding generations. Yet there is an abiding need to assist succeeding generations to fulfill their proper role in the ongoing adventure of the earth process. In the human realm education must supply what instinct supplies in the prehuman realm. There is need for a program to aid the young to identify themselves in the comprehensive dimensions of space and time. This was easier in the world of the *Timaeus,* where the earth was seen as an image of the eternal Logos. In such a world Saint Thomas could compose his masterful presentation of Christian thought, and the place and role of the human within that context. This could then be summarized in catechetical form and taught to succeeding generations.

Now a new way of understanding values is required. We are returning to a more traditional context of story as our source of understanding and value. It is somewhat fascinating to realize that the final achievement of our scientific inquiry into the structure and functioning of the universe as evolutionary process is much closer to the narrative mode of explanation given in the Bible than it is to the later, more philosophical mode of Christian explanation provided in our theologies.

It is of utmost importance that succeeding generations become aware of the larger story outlined here and the numinous, sacred values that have been present in an expanding sequence over this entire time of the world's existence. Within this context all our human affairs—all professions, occupations, and activities—have their meaning precisely insofar as they enhance this emerging world of subjective intercommunion within the total range of reality. Within this context the scientific community and the religious community have a common basis. The limitations of the redemption rhetoric and the scientific rhetoric can be seen, and a new, more integral language of being and value can emerge.

Within this story a structure of knowledge can be established, with its human significance, from the physics of the universe and its chemistry through geology and biology to economics and commerce and so to all those studies whereby we fulfill our role in the earth process. There is no way of guiding the course of human affairs through the perilous course of the future except by discovering our role in this larger evolutionary process. If the way of Western civilization and Western religion was once the way of election and differentiation from others and from the earth, the way now is the way of intimate communion with the larger human community and with the universe itself.

Here we might observe that the basic mood of the future might well be one of confidence in the continuing revelation that takes place in and through the earth. If the dynamics of the universe from the beginning shaped the course of the heavens, lighted the sun, and formed the earth, if this same dynamism brought forth the continents and seas and atmosphere, if it awakened life in the primordial cell and then brought into being the unnumbered variety of living beings, and finally brought us into being and guided us safely through the turbulent centuries, there is reason to believe that this same guiding process is precisely what has awakened in us our present understanding of ourselves and our relation to this stupendous process. Sensitized to such guidance from the very structure and functioning of the universe, we can have confidence in the future that awaits the human venture.

God and Gaia

JAMES LOVELOCK

Gaia, mother of all, I sing, oldest of gods,
Firm of foundation, who feeds all creatures living
on Earth,
As many as move on the radiant land and swim in
the sea
And fly through the air, all these does she feed
with her bounty.
Mistress, from you come our fine children and
bountiful harvests,
Yours is the power to give mortals life and to take
it away.

J. Donald Hughes,
Gaia: An Ancient View of Our Planet

PHOTOGRAPHS, LIKE BIOGRAPHIES, OFTEN reveal more of the artist than of the subject. Maybe this is why passport photographs, taken in mechanically operated booths, look so lifeless. How could a mere machine capture the soul of its subject, stiffly sitting and gazing into the blind eye of the camera? Trying to write about God and Gaia, I share some of the limitations of a mechanical camera, and I know that this [essay] will show more about myself than about my subjects. So why try?

When I wrote the first book on Gaia I had no inkling that it would be taken as a religious book. Although I thought the subject was mainly science, there was no doubt that many of its readers found otherwise. Two-thirds of the letters received, and still coming in, are about the meaning of Gaia in the context of religious faith. This interest has not been limited to the laity; a most interesting letter came from Hugh Montefiore, then Bishop of Birmingham. He asked which I thought came first, life or Gaia. My attempts to answer this question led to a correspondence, reported in a chapter of his book, *The Probability of God*. I suspect that some cosmologists are similarly visited by enquiries from those who imagine them to be at least on nodding terms with God. I was naïve to think that a book about Gaia would be taken as science only.

So where do I stand about religion? While still a student I was asked seriously, by a member of the Society of Friends, if I had ever had a religious experience. Not understanding what he meant, imagining that it referred to a manifestation or a miracle, I answered no. Looking back from 45 years on, I now tend to think that I should have said yes. Living itself is a religious experience. At the time, however, the question was almost meaningless because it implied a separation of life into sacred and secular parts. I now think that there can be no such division. In any relationship there are high points of delight, as well as pitfalls in the great plain of contentment. For me one high point came when I was asked by Jim Morton, the Dean of the Cathedral Church of St. John the Divine in New York, to serve as a participant in a religious celebration. I still recall with wonder being part of that colorful procession, with him and other clerics, dressed in medieval costume. The music of the choir singing that lovely hymn "Morning Is Broken" seemed to take on a new significance in the ambience of that sacred place. It was a sensual experience, but to me that does not make it less religious.

My thoughts about religion when a child grew from those of my father and the country folk I knew. It was an odd mixture, composed of witches, May trees, and the views expressed by Quakers, in and outside the Sunday school at a Friends' meeting house. Christmas was more of a solstice feast than a Christian one. We were, as a family, well into the present century yet, still amazingly superstitious. So ingrained was my childhood conditioning about the power of the occult that in later life it took a positive act of will to stop touching wood or crossing fingers whenever some hazard was to be faced. Christianity was there not so much a faith, rather as a set of sensible directions on how to be good.

When I first saw Gaia in my mind I felt as must an astronaut have done as he stood on the Moon, gazing back at our home, the Earth. The feeling strengthens as theory and evidence steadily confirm the thought that the Earth may be a larger state of life. Thinking of the Earth this way makes it seem, on happy days, in the right places, as if the whole planet were celebrating a sacred ceremony. Being on the Earth brings that same special feeling of comfort that attaches to the celebration of any religion when it is seemly and when one is fit to receive. It need not suspend the critical faculty.

That is only what I feel about Gaia. What about God? I am a scientist and do not have faith, but neither am I the counterpart of those with faith, an atheist. I go along with E. O. Wilson who sees us as tribal carnivores who happened to have evolved to the point of forming civilizations. It takes a lot of hubris to imagine that we can ever reach the limits of our own intelligence; to think that we will ever be able to explain everything about the universe is absurd. For these reasons I am equally discomforted by religious faith and scientific atheism.

I am too committed to the scientific way of thinking to feel comfortable when enunciating the Creed or the Lord's Prayer in a Christian Church. The insistence of the definition "I believe in God the Father Almighty, Maker of Heaven and Earth" seems to anaesthetize the sense of wonder, as if one were committed to a single line of thought by a cosmic legal contract. It seems wrong also to take it merely as a metaphor. But I respect the intuition of those who do believe, and I am moved by the ceremony, the music, and most of all by the glory of the words of the prayer book that to me are the nearest to perfect expression of our language. When atheistic science can inspire anything as moving as Bach's St Matthew passion or as seemly as Salisbury Cathedral I will respect it but not be part of it.

I have kept my doubts in a separate place for too long. Now that I write this [essay], I have to try somehow to explain, to myself as well as to you, what is my religious belief. I am happy with the thought that the Universe has properties that make the emergence of life and Gaia inevitable. But I react to the assertion that it was created with this purpose. It might have been; but how the Universe and life began are ineffable questions.

At a meeting in London recently, a wise man, Dr. Donald Braben, asked me: "Why do you stop with the Earth? Why not consider if the Solar System, the Galaxy, or even the Universe is a self-organized system? My instant answer was that the concept of the Earth, as Gaia, is manageable. We know that there is no other life in this Solar System, and the nearest star is utterly remote. There must be other Gaias circling other docile long-lived stars but, curious though I may be about them and about the Universe, these are intangible—concepts for the intellect not the senses. Until, if ever, we are visited from other parts of the Universe we are obliged to remain detached.

Many, I suspect, have trodden this same path through the mind. Those millions of Christians who make a special place in their hearts for the Virgin Mary possibly respond as I do. The concept of Jahweh as remote, all-powerful, all seeing is either frightening or unapproachable. Even the sense of presence of a more contemporary God, a still, small voice within, may not be enough for those who need to communicate with someone outside. Mary is close and can be talked to. She is believable and manageable. It could be that the importance of the Virgin Mary in faith is something of this kind.

Gaia is a religious as well as a scientific concept, and in both spheres it is manageable. Theology is also a science, but if it is to operate by the same rules as the rest of science, there is no place for creeds or dogma. By this I mean theology should not state that God exists and then proceed to investigate his nature and his interactions with the Universe and living organisms. Such an approach is prescriptive, presupposes his existence, and closes the mind to such questions as: What would the Universe be like without God? How can we use the concept of God as a way to look at the Universe and ourselves? How can we use the concept of Gaia as a way to understanding God? Belief in God is an act of faith and will remain so. In the same way, it is otiose to try to prove that Gaia is alive. Instead, Gaia should be a way to view the Earth, ourselves, and our relationships with living things.

The life of a scientist who is a natural philosopher can be devout. Curiosity is an intimate part of the process of loving. Being curious and getting to know the natural world leads to a loving relationship with it. It can be so deep that it cannot be articulated, but it is nonetheless good science. Creative scientists, when asked how they came upon some great discovery frequently state, "I knew it intuitively, but it took several years work to prove it to my colleagues." Compare that statement with this one by William James, the nineteenth-century philosopher and psychologist, in *Varieties of Religious Experience:*

> The truth is that in the metaphysical and religious sphere, articulate reasons are cogent for us only when our inarticulate feelings of reality have already been impressed in favor of the same conclusion. Then, indeed, our intuitions and our reason work together, and great world ruling systems, like that of the Buddhist or of the Catholic philosophy, may grow up. Our impulsive belief is here always what sets up the original body of truth, and our articulately verbalized philosophy is but a showy translation into formulas. The unreasoned and immediate assurance is the deep thing in us, the reasoned argument is but a surface exhibition. Instinct leads, intelligence does but follow.

This was the way of the natural philosophers in James Hutton's time in the eighteenth century and is still the way of many scientists today. Science can embrace the notion of the Earth as a superorganism and can still wonder about the meaning of the Universe.

How did we reach our present secular humanist world? In times that are ancient by human measure, as far back as the earliest artifacts can be found, it seems that the Earth was worshipped as a goddess and believed to be alive. The myth of the great Mother is part of most early religions. The Mother is a compassionate, feminine figure; spring of all life, of fecundity, of gentleness. She is also the stern and unforgiving bringer of death. As Aldous Huxley reminds in his book *The Human Experience:*

> In Hinduism, Kali is at once the infinitely kind and loving mother and the terrifying Goddess of destruction, who has a necklace of skulls and drinks the blood of human beings from a skull. This picture is profoundly realistic; if you give life, you must necessarily give death, because life always ends in death and must be renewed through death.

At some time not more than a few thousand years ago the concept of a remote master God, an overseer of Gaia, took root. At first it may have been the Sun, but later it took on the form we have with us now of an utterly remote yet personally immanent ruler of the Universe. Charlene Spretnak, in her moving and readable book, *The Spiritual Dimensions of Green Politics,* attributes the first denial of Gaia, the Earth goddess, to the conquest of an earlier Earth-centered civilization by the Sun-worshipping warriors of the invading Indo-European tribes.

> Picture yourself as a witness of that decisive moment in history, that is, as a resident of the peaceful, artful, Goddess-oriented culture in Old Europe. (Don't think "matriarchy"! It may have been, but no one knows, and that is not the point.) It is 4,500 B.C. You are walking along a high ridge, looking out across the plains to the east. In the distance you see a massive wave of horsemen galloping towards your world on strange, powerful animals. (The European ancestor of the horse had become extinct.) They brought few women, a chieftain system, and only a primitive stamping technique to impress their two symbols, the sun and a pine tree. They moved in waves first into southeastern Europe, later down into Greece, across all of Europe, also into the Middle and Near East, North Africa and India. They brought a sky god, a warrior cult, and patriarchal social order. *And that is where we live today*—in an Indo-European culture, albeit one that is very technologically advanced.

The evolution of these horsemen to the modern men who ride their infinitely more powerful machines of destruction over the habitats of our partners in Gaia seems only a small step. The rest of us, in the cozy, comfortable hell of urban life, care little what they do so long as they continue to supply us with food, energy, and raw materials and we can continue to play the game of human interaction.

In ancient times, belief in a living Earth and in a living cosmos was the same thing. Heaven and Earth were close and part of the same body. As time passed and awareness grew of the vast distances of space and time through such inventions as the telescope, the Universe was comprehended and the place of God receded until now it hides behind the Big Bang, claimed to have started it all. At the same time, as population increased so did the proportion forced to lead urban lives out of touch with Nature. In the past two centuries we have nearly all become city dwellers, and seem to have lost interest in the meaning of both God and Gaia. As the theologian Keith Ward wrote in the *Times* in December 1984:

> It is not that people know what God is, and have decided to reject him. It seems that very few people even know what the orthodox traditional idea of God, shared by Judaism, Islam and Christianity is. They have not the slightest idea what is meant by the word God.
>
> It just has no sense or possible place in their lives. Instead they either invent some vague idea of a cosmic force with no practical implications at all; or they appeal to some half-forgotten picture of a bearded super-person constantly interfering with the mechanistic laws of Nature.

I wonder if this is the result of sensory deprivation. How can we revere the living world if we can no longer hear the bird song through the noise of traffic, or smell the sweetness of fresh air? How can we wonder about God and the Universe if we never see the stars because of the city lights? If you think this to be exaggeration, think back to when you last lay in a meadow in the sunshine and smelt the fragrant thyme and heard and saw the larks soaring and singing. Think back to the last night you looked up into the deep blue black of a sky clear enough to see the Milky Way, the congregation of stars, our Galaxy.

The attraction of the city is seductive. Socrates said that nothing of interest happened outside its walls and, much later, Dr. Johnson expressed his view of country living as "One green field is like another." Most of us are trapped in this world of the city, an everlasting soap opera, and all too often as spectators, not players. It is something to have sensitive commentators like Sir David Attenborough bring the natural world with its visions of forests and wilderness to the television screens of our suburban rooms. But the television screen is only a window and only rarely clear enough to see the world outside; it can never bring us back into the real world of Gaia. City life reinforces and strengthens the heresy of humanism, that narcissistic devotion to human interests alone. The Irish missionary Sean McDonagh wrote in his book *To Care for the Earth:* "The 20 billion years of God's creative love is either seen simply as the stage on which the drama of human salvation is worked out, or as something radically sinful in itself and needing transformation."

The heartlands of the great religions are now in the last bastions of rural existence, in the Third World of the tropics. Elsewhere God and Gaia that once were joined and respected are now divorced and of no account. We have, as a species, almost resigned from membership in Gaia and given to our cities and our nations the rights and responsibilities of environmental regulation. We struggle to enjoy the human interactions of city life yet still yearn to possess the natural world as well. We want to be free to drive into the country or the wilderness without polluting it in so doing; to have our cake and eat it. Human and understandable such striving may be, but it is illogical. Our humanist concerns about the poor of the inner cities or the Third World, and our near-obscene obsession with death, suffering, and pain as if these were evil in themselves—these thoughts divert the mind from our gross and excessive domination of the natural world. Poverty and suffering are not sent; they are the consequences of what we do. Pain and death are normal and natural; we could not long survive without them. Science, it is true, assisted at the birth of technology. But when we drive our cars and listen to the radio bringing news of acid rain, we need to remind ourselves that we, personally, are the polluters. We, not some white-coated devil figure, buy the cars, drive them, and foul the air. We are therefore accountable, personally, for the destruction of the trees by photochemical smog and acid rain. We are responsible for the silent spring that Rachel Carson predicted.

There are many ways to keep in touch with Gaia. Individual humans are densely populated cellular and endosymbiont collectives, but clearly also identities. Individuals interact with Gaia in the cycling of the elements and in the control of the climate, just like a cell does in the body. You also interact individually in a spiritual manner through a sense of wonder about the natural world and from feeling a part of it. In some ways this interaction is not unlike the tight coupling between the state of the mind and the body. Another connection is through the powerful infrastructures of human communication and mass transfer. We as a species now move a greater mass of some materials around the Earth than did all the biota of Gaia before we appeared. Our chattering is so loud that it can be heard to the depths of the Universe. Always, as with other and earlier species within Gaia, the entire development arises from the activity of a few individuals. The urban nests, the agricultural ecosystems, good and bad, are all the consequences of rapid positive feedback starting from the action of an inspired individual.

A frequent misunderstanding of my vision of Gaia is that I champion complacence, that I claim feedback will always protect the environment from any serious harm that humans might do. It is sometimes more crudely put as "Lovelock's Gaia gives industry the green light to pollute at will." The truth is almost diametrically opposite. Gaia, as I see her, is no doting mother tolerant of misdemeanors, nor is she some fragile and delicate damsel in danger from brutal mankind. She is stern and tough, always keeping the world warm and comfortable for those who obey the rules, but ruthless in her destruction of those who transgress. Her unconscious goal is a planet fit for life. If humans stand in the way of this, we shall be eliminated with as little pity as would be shown by the micro-brain of an intercontinental ballistic nuclear missile in full flight to its target.

What I have written so far has been a testament built around the idea of Gaia. I have tried to show that God and Gaia, theology and science, even physics and biology are not separate but a single way of thought. Although a scientist, I write as an individual and my views are likely to be less common than I like to think. So now let me tell you something of what the scientific community has to say on this subject.

In science, the more discovered, the more new paths open for exploration. It is usual in science, when things are vague and unclear, for the path to be like that of a drunkard, wandering in a zigzag. As we stagger back from what lastly dawns upon our befuddled wits is the wrong way, we cross over the true path and move nearly as far to the equally wrong, opposite side. If all goes well, our deviations lessen and the path converges towards, but never completely follows, the true one. It gives a new insight to the old tag *in vino veritas.* So natural is this way to find the truth that we usually program our computers to solve problems too tedious to do ourselves by setting them to follow the same trial-and-error, staggering, stumbling walk. The process is dignified and mystified by calling it "iteration," but the method is the same. The only difference is that, so quickly is it done, the eye never sees the fumbling.

We have lost the instinctive understanding of what life is and of our place within Gaia. Our attempts to define life are much in the stage of the drunkard's walk. The two opposing verges representing the extremes of iteration are illustrated by a splendid philosophical debate that has gone on for the past twenty years between the molecular biologists on the one side and the new school of thermodynamics on the other. Jacques Monod's *Chance and Necessity,* although first published in 1970, most clearly and beautifully conveys the clear, strong, and rigorous approach of solid science based firmly in a belief in a materialistic and deterministic Universe. The other verge is represented by those, like Erich Jantsch, who believe in a self-organizing Universe. It is concerned with the thermodynamics of the unsteady state of which dissipative structures such as flames, whirlpools, and life itself are examples. Although the participants are all well known and respected in the English-speaking world most of this entertaining debate has gone on in French, so many of us have missed the fun.

The essence of this contest is a rerun of the ancient battle between the holists and the reductionists. As Monod reminds us:

> Certain schools of thought (all more or less consciously or confusedly influenced by Hegel) challenge the value of the analytical approach to systems as complex as living beings. According to these holist schools which, phoenix like, are reborn in every generation, the analytic attitude (reductionist) is doomed to fail in its attempts to reduce the properties of a very complex organization to the "sum" of the properties of its parts. It is a very stupid and misguided quarrel which merely testifies to the holists' total lack of understanding of scientific method and the crucial role analysis plays in it. How far could a Martian engineer get if trying to understand an earthly computer, he refused on principle to dissect the machine's basic electronic components which execute the operation of propositional algebra.

These strong words were in the 1970 edition of *Chance and Necessity.* Maybe they are by now less extremely held, but they serve well to express what was and still is an important scientific constituency.

No one now doubts that it was plain, honest reductionist science that allowed us to unlock so many of the secrets of the Universe, not least those of the living macromolecules that carry the genetic information of our cells. But clear, strong, and powerful though it may be, it is not enough by itself to explain the facts of life. Consider Jacques Monod's Martian engineer. Would it have been sensible to have dashed in with a kit of tools and disassembled analytically the computer he found? Or would it have been better, as a first step, to have switched it on and questioned it as a whole system? If you have any doubts about the answer to this question then consider the thought that the hypothetical Martian engineer was an intelligent computer and the object he examined, you.

By contrast, in 1972 Ilya Prigogine wrote:

> It is not instability but a succession of instabilities which allow the crossing of the no man's land between life and no-life. We start to disentangle only certain stages. This concept of biological order leads automatically to a more blurred appreciation of the role of chance and necessity to recall the title of the well-known work by Jacques Monod. Fluctuation which allows the system to depart from states near thermodynamic equilibrium represents the stochastic aspect, the part played by chance. Contrariwise, the environmental instability, the fact that the fluctuations will increase, represents necessity. Chance and necessity cooperate instead of opposing one another.

I wholly agree with Monod that the cornerstone of the scientific method is the postulate that Nature is objective. True knowledge can never be gained by attributing "purpose" to phenomena. But, equally strongly, I deny the notion that systems are never more than the sum of their parts. The value of Gaia in this debate is that it is the largest ecosystem. It can be analyzed both as a whole system and, in the reductionist manner, as a collection of parts. This analysis need disturb neither the privacy nor the function of Gaia any more than would the movement of a single commensal bacterium on the surface of your nose.

Prigogine was not the first to recognize the inadequacies of equilibrium thermodynamics. He had many illustrious predecessors, among them the physical chemists J. W. Gibbs, L. Onsager, and K. G. Denbigh, who explored the thermodynamics of the steady state. But it was that truly great physicist, Ludwig Boltzmann, who pointed the way towards the understanding of life in thermodynamic terms. It was by reading Schrodinger's book *What Is Life?* in the early 1960s that I first realized that planetary life was revealed by the contrast between the near-equilibrium state of the atmosphere of a dead planet and the exuberant disequilibrium of the Earth.

When we cross from the sharp clarity of the real world into that nightmare land of dissipating structures, what do we learn that makes the next staggering lurch less erroneous than the last? I have gained from Prigogine's world view a confirmation of a suspicion that time is a variable much too often ignored. In particular, many of the apparent contradictions between these two schools of thought seem to resolve if viewed along the time dimension instead of in space. We have evolved from the world of simple molecules through dissipative structures to the more permanent entities that are living organisms. The further we go from the present, either into the past or the future, the greater the uncertainty. Darwin was right to dismiss thoughts about the origins of life; as Jerome Rothstein has said, the restrictions of the second law of thermodynamics prevent us from ever knowing about the beginning or the end of the Universe.

In our guts and in those of other animals, the ancient world of the Archean lives on. In Gaia also the ancient chaotic world of dissipating structures that preceded life still lives on. A recent and relatively unknown discovery of science is that the fluctuations at every scale from viscosity to weather can be chaotic. There is no complete determinism in the Universe; many things are as unpredictable as a perfect roulette wheel. An ecologist colleague of mine, C. S. Holling, has observed that the stability of large-scale ecosystems depends upon the existence of internal chaotic instabilities. These pockets of chaos in the larger, stable Gaian system serve to probe the boundaries set by the physical constraints to life. By this means the opportunism of life is insured and no new niche remains undiscovered. For example, I live in a rural region surrounded by farmers who keep sheep. It is impressive how adventurous young lambs, through their continuous probing of my boundary hedges, can find their way through onto the richer, ungrazed land on my side. The behavior of young men is not so different.

My reason for wandering onto the battlefield of the war between holists and reductionists was to illustrate how polarized is science itself. Let me conclude this digressionary visit and return to the theme of this [essay], God and Gaia, and let me start by reminding you of Daisyworld—a model which is reductionist and holistic at the same time. It was made to answer the criticism of Gaia, that it was teleology. The need for reduction arose because the relationships between all the living things on Earth in their countless trillions and the rocks, the air, and the oceans could never be described in full detail by a set of mathematical equations. A drastic simplification was needed. But the model with its closed loop cybernetic structure was also holistic. This also applies to ourselves. It would be pointless to attempt to disentangle all the relationships between the atoms within the cells that go to make up our bodies. But this does not prevent us from being real and identifiable, and having a life span of at least 70 years.

We are also in an adversary contest between our allegiance to Gaia and to humanism. In this battle, politically minded humanists have made the word "reductionist" pejorative, to discredit science and to bring contumely to the scientific method. But all scientists are reductionists to some extent; there is no way to do science without reduction at some stage. Even the analyzers of holistic systems, confronted with an unknown system, do tests, such as perturbing the system and observing the response, or making a model of it and then reducing that model. In biology it is impossible to avoid reduction, even if we wished. The material and relationships of living things are so phenomenally complex that a holistic view is seen only when it suits the biota to exist as an identifiable entity such as a cell, a plant, a nest, or Gaia. Certainly, the entities themselves can be observed and classified with a minimum of invasion, but sooner or later curiosity will drive an urge to discover what the entities are made of and how they work. In any case, the idea that mere observation is neutral is itself an illusion. Someone once said that the reason the Universe is running down is that God is always observing it and hence reducing it. Be this as it may, there is little doubt that a nature reserve, a wildlife park, or an ecosystem is reduced in proportion to the amount of time that we and our children perturb the wildlife by watching them.

In *The Self-Organizing Universe,* Erich Jantsch made a strong argument for the omnipresence of a self-organizing tendency; so that life, instead of being a chance event, was an inevitable consequence. Jantsch based his thoughts on the theories of those pioneers of what might be called the "thermodynamics of the unsteady state"—Max Eigen, Ilya Prigogine, Humberto Maturana, Francisco Varela, and their successors. As scientific evidence accumulates and theories are developed in this recondite topic, it may become possible to encompass the metaphor of a living Universe. The intuition of God could be rationalized; something of God could become as familiar as Gaia.

For the present, my belief in God rests at the stage of a positive agnosticism. I am too deeply committed to science for undiluted faith; equally unacceptable to me spiritually is the materialist world of undiluted fact. Art and science seem interconnected with each other and with religion, and to be mutually enlarging. That Gaia can be both spiritual and scientific is, for me, deeply satisfying. From letters and conversations I have learned that a feeling for the superorganism, the Earth, has survived and that many feel a need to include those old faiths in their system of belief, both for themselves and because they feel that Earth of which they are a part is under threat. In no way do I see Gaia as a sentient being, a surrogate God.

The philosopher Gregory Bateson expressed this agnosticism in his own special way:

> The individual mind is immanent but not only in the body. It is immanent also in pathways and messages outside the body; and there is a larger mind of which the individual mind is only a subsystem. This larger mind is comparable to God and is perhaps what some people mean by God, but it is still immanent in the total interconnected social systems and planetary ecology.

As a scientist I believe that Nature is objective but also recognize that Nature is not predetermined. The famous uncertainty principle that the physicist Werner Heisenberg discovered was the first crack in the crystalline structure of determinism. Now chaos is revealed to have an orderly mathematical prescription. This new theoretical understanding enlightens the practice of weather forecasting. Previously it was believed, as the French physicist Laplace had stated, that given enough knowledge (and, in this age, computer power) anything could be predicted. It was a thrill to discover that there was real, honest chaos decently spread around the Universe and to begin to understand why it is impossible in this world ever to predict if it will be raining at some specific place or time. True chaos is there as the counterpart of order. Determinism is reduced to a collection of fragments; like jewels that have fallen on the surface of a bowl of pitch.

Science has its fashions, and one thing guaranteed to stir interest and start a new fashion is the exploration of a pathology. Health is far less interesting than disease. I well recall as a schoolboy visiting the Museum of the London School of Hygiene and Tropical Medicine where there were on display life-sized models of subjects stricken by tropical illnesses. Although less well crafted, they were so strange and horrible as to make tame the professional horrors of Madame Tussaud's waxworks. The sight of full-sized models of the victims of elephantiasis or leprosy and the imagination of their suffering made bearable the adolescent agonies of a schoolboy. Contemporary science is similarly fascinated by pathologies of a mathematical kind. Theoretical ecology, as we have already discussed, is more concerned with sick than healthy ecosystems. The vagaries of weather are more interesting than the long-term stability of climate. Continuous creation never had a chance in face of the ultimate pathology of the Big Bang.

Interest in the pathologies of science has a curious link with religion. Mathematicians and physicists are, without seeming aware of it, into demonology. They are found investigating "catastrophe theory" or "strange attractors." They then seek from their colleagues in other sciences examples of pathologies that match their curious models. Perhaps I should explain that in mathematics, an attractor is a stable equilibrium state, such as a point at the bottom of a smooth bowl where a ball will always come to rest. Attractors can be lines, planes, or solids as well as points, and are the places where systems tend to settle down to rest. Strange attractors are chaotic regions of fractional dimensions that act like black holes, drawing the solutions of equations to their unknown and singular domains. Phenomena of the natural world—such as weather, disease, and ecosystem failures—are characterized by the presence of these strange attractors in the clockwork of their mathematics, lurking like time bombs as harbingers of instability, cyclical fluctuations, and just plain chaos.

The remarkable thing about real and healthy living organisms is their apparent ability to control or limit these destabilizing influences. It seems that the world of dissipating structures, threatened by catastrophe and parasitized by strange attractors, is the foreworld of life and of Gaia and the underworld that still exists. The tightly coupled evolution of the physical environment and the autopoietic entities of pre-life led to a new order of stability; the state associated with Gaia and with all forms of healthy life. Life and Gaia are to all intents immortal, even though composed of entities that at least include dissipative structures. I find a curious resemblance between the strange attractors and other denizens of the imaginary world of mathematical constructs and the demons of older religious belief. A parallel that goes deep and includes an association with sickness not health, famine not plenty, storm not calm. A saint of this fascinating branch of mathematics is the Frenchman, Benoît Mandelbrot. From his expressions in fractional dimensions it is possible to produce graphic illustrations of all manner of natural scenes: coastlines, mountain ranges, trees, and clouds, all startlingly realistic. But when Mandelbrot's scientific art is applied to strange attractors we see, in graphic form, the vividly colored image of a demon or a dragon.

Gaia theory may seem to be dull in comparison with these exotica. A thing, like health, to be taken for granted except when it fails. This may be why so few scientists and theologians are interested in it; they prefer to explore the origins of life, or the Universe instead of the natural world, here and now, that surrounds them. I find it difficult to explain to my colleagues why I prefer to live and work alone in the depths of the country. They think that I must be missing all the excitement of exploration. I prefer a life with Gala here and now, and to look back only to that part of its history which is knowable, not to what might have been before it came into being. A friend has asked why, if this is so, I chose to spend so much of this book on the history of the Earth. I find it easiest to explain my reasons for this apparent inconsistency as a fable.

Imagine an island set in a warm blue sea with sandy beaches. The lush forest in the foreground gives way to small rocky mountain peaks as sharp and clear as a line drawing on the distant horizon. There is no sign of habitation, human or other. What at first sight looks like a village of white stone houses turns out, on closer inspection, to be a chalk outcrop, laser bright in the sunlight. Something looks odd, though; you blink, for the light is very bright, and look again. It is not an illusion, the trees are not green, they are a dark shade of blue.

The island in view is somewhere on Earth 500 million years from now. The exact details are unpredictable and unimportant to this travel tale, but we can say it is hotter than any seaside place on Earth today, with a sea temperature near 30°C; and it often reaches 60°C in the desert inland. There is little or no carbon dioxide in the air, but otherwise it is much the same as now with just the right amount of oxygen for breathing but not so much as to make fires uncontrollable. There has been a major punctuation, and the dominant life forms on the land surface are of a structure no botanist or zoologist of our time would recognize.

In a small meadow near the shore, a group of philosophers is gathered for one of those civilized meetings hosted by a scientific society. A symposium that leaves ample time for swimming and walking and just talking idly. A participant has a theory that their form of life, so unlike that of many of the organisms in the sea and of the microorganisms, did not just evolve but was made artificially by a sentient life form living in the remote geological past. She bases her argument on the nature of the nervous system of the philosophers and of land animals generally. It operates by direct electrical conduction along organic polymer strands, whereas that of the ocean life operates by ionic conduction within elongated cells (which we, of course, would recognize as nerves). The brains of the philosophers operate by semiconduction, in contrast to the chemically polarized systems of the sea organisms. In this new form of life, males do not exist as mobile sentient organisms, merely as a vegetative form that supplies the necessary separate pathway for genetic information so that recombination can reduce the expression of error. Marriage is still a lifelong relationship, but with males rooted in the soil like plants it is more one of that between a loving gardener and the flowers. Our philosopher argues that such a system could never have originated by chance but must have been manufactured at some time in the past. Not surprisingly, her theory is not well received. Not only is it outside the paradigm of the science of those times, but the theologians and mythopoets find the notion repugnant to their view of a single spontaneous origin of a living planet. To bring back the Creationist heresy is unacceptable.

These occupants of a future Atlantis have no need for speech or writing. The possession of an electronic nervous system makes speech redundant; they are able to use radio frequencies to communicate directly a wide range of images and ideas. In spite of these advantages and their superior wisdom, they are, like the whales of today, neither mechanically adept nor interested in mechanisms. This being so, the very idea of making as anything as intricate as a brain or nervous system as an artifact is beyond their understanding, and therefore, in their minds, beyond the capabilities of a past life form.

The point of the fable is to argue that it is not necessary to know the intricate details of the origin of life itself to understand the evolution of Gaia and of ourselves. In a similar way, the contemplation of those other remote places before and after life, Heaven and Hell, may be irrelevant to the discovery of a seemly way of life. We may well have been assisted by the nature of the Universe to cheat chaos and evolve spontaneously, on some Hadean shore, into our ancestral form of life. It seems unlikely that we come from a life form planted here by visitors from elsewhere; or even arrived clinging to some piece of cometary debris from outer space. I like to think that Darwin dismissed enquiries about the origins of life not merely because, so sparse was the information available in his time, the search for life's origin would have had to remain speculative, but, more cogently, because he recognized that it was not necessary to know the details of the origin of life to formulate the evolution of the species by natural selection. This is what I have in mind when I talk of Gaia, as a concept, being manageable.

Breakthrough in Evolution
Toward a Partnership Future

RIANE EISLER

Science fiction writers' visions of the future are filled with incredible technological inventions. But by and large, theirs is a world singularly bereft of new social inventions. In fact, more often than not, what they envision takes us backward while seeming to go forward in time. Be it in Frank Herbert's *Dune*[1] or George Lucas's *Star Wars,* what we frequently find is actually the social organization of feudal emperors and medieval overlords transposed to a world of intergalactic high-tech wars.

After five thousand years of living in a dominator society, it is indeed difficult to imagine a different world. Charlotte Perkins Gilman tried in *Herland.*[2] Written in 1915, this was a tongue-in-cheek utopia about a peaceful and highly creative society in which the most valued and rewarded work—and the top social priority—was the physical, mental, and spiritual development of children. The catch was that this was a world where all the men had wiped themselves out in a final orgy of war, and the handful of surviving women had, in an amazing mutation, saved their half of humanity by learning to reproduce themselves all by themselves.

But as we have seen, the problem is not men as a

sex, but men and women as they must be socialized in a dominator system. There were men and women in the Neolithic and in Crete. There are men and women among the peaceful !Kung and Ba-Mbuti. And even in our male-dominated world not all women are peaceful and gentle, and many men are.

Clearly both men and women have the biological potential for many different kinds of behaviors. But like the external armor or shell that encases insects and other arthropods, androcratic social organization encases both halves of humanity in rigid and hierarchic roles that stunt their development. If we look at our evolution from the perspective of androcracy and gylany as the two possibilities for human social organization, we see that it is not by accident that the sociobiologists who are today trying to revitalize androcratic ideology with yet another infusion of nineteenth-century social Darwinism so frequently cite insect societies to support their theories. Neither is it accidental that their writings reinforce the view that the normative model for rigidly hierarchic social rankings—the male-dominator/female-dominated model of human relations—is preprogrammed in our genes.[3]

As many scientists have pointed out, evolution is not predetermined.[4] On the contrary, from the very beginning we have been active co-creators in our own evolution. For example, as Sherwood Washburn wrote, our invention of tools was both the cause and effect of the bipedal locomotion and erect posture that freed our hands to fashion ever more complex technologies.[5] And, as both technology and society have grown more complex, the survival of our species has become increasingly dependent on the direction, not of our biological, but of our cultural evolution.

Human evolution is now at a crossroads. Stripped to its essentials, the central human task is how to organize society to promote the survival of our species and the development of our unique potentials. In the course of this book we have seen that androcracy cannot meet this requirement because of its inbuilt emphasis on technologies of destruction, its dependence on violence for social control, and the tensions chronically engendered by the dominator-dominated human relations model upon which it is based. We have also seen that a gylanic or partnership society, symbolized by the life-sustaining and enhancing Chalice rather than the lethal Blade, offers us a viable alternative.

The question is how do we get from here to there?

A NEW VIEW OF REALITY

Scientists like Ilya Prigogine and Niles Eldredge tell us that bifurcations or evolutionary branchings in chemical and biological systems involve a large element of chance.[6] But as the evolutionary theorist Erwin Laszlo points out, bifurcations in human social systems also involve a large element of choice. Humans, he points out, "have the ability to act consciously, and collectively," exercising foresight to "choose their own evolutionary path." And he adds that in our "crucial epoch" we "cannot leave the selection of the next step in the evolution of human society and culture to chance. We must plan for it, consciously and purposefully."[7] Or as the biologist Jonas Salk writes, our most urgent and pressing need is to provide that wonderful instrument, the human mind, with the wherewithal to image, and thereby create, a better world.[8]

Initially this may seem an impossibly difficult task. But as we have seen, our views of reality—of what is possible and desirable—are a product of history. And perhaps the best proof that our ideas, symbols, myths, and behaviors can be changed is the evidence that such changes were in fact effected in our prehistory.

We have seen how the image of woman was once venerated and respected in most of the ancient world and how images of women as merely sexual objects to be possessed and dominated by men became predominant only after the androcratic conquests. We have also seen how the meaning of symbols such as the tree of knowledge and the serpent that sheds its skin in periodic renewal were completely reversed after that critical bifurcation in our cultural evolution. Now seemingly firmly associated with terrible punishment for questioning male dominance and autocratic rule, these same symbols were not so long ago in evolutionary time seen as manifestations of the human thirst for liberation through higher or mystical knowledge.

We have seen that even after the imposition of androcratic rule, the meaning of our most important symbols has often shifted radically through the impact of gylanic resurgence or androcratic regression. A striking example is the cross. The original meaning of the crosses incised on prehistoric figurines of the Goddess and other religious objects appears to have been her identification with the birth and growth of plant, animal, and human life. This was the meaning that survived into Egyptian hieroglyphics, where the cross stands for life and living, forming part of such words as *health* and *happiness.*[9] Later, after impaling people on stakes became a common way to execute them (as shown in Assyrian, Roman, and other androcratic art), the cross became a symbol of death. Later still, the more gylanic followers of Jesus again tried to transform the cross on which he was executed into a symbol of rebirth—a symbol associated with a social movement that set out to preach and practice human equality and such "feminine" concepts as gentleness, compassion, and peace.[10]

In our time, centuries after this movement was coopted by the androcratic/dominator system, the way we interpret ancient symbols and myths still plays an important part in how we shape both our present and our future. At the same time that some of our religious and political leaders would have us believe a nuclear Armageddon may actually be the will of God,[11] we are seeing a vast reaffirmation of the desire for life, not death, in an accelerated, and indeed unprecedented, movement to restore ancient myths and symbols to their original gylanic meaning.[12]

For instance, artists like Imogen Cunningham and Judy Chicago are for the first time in recorded history using female sexual imagery in ways that are strikingly reminiscent of Paleolithic, Neolithic, and Cretan symbolisms of birth, rebirth, and transformation.[13] Also for the first time in recorded history, images from nature, such as seals, birds, dolphins, and the green forests and grasses—in earlier times symbols of the unity of all life under the Goddess's divine power—are being used by the ecology movement to reawaken in us the consciousness of our essential link with our natural environment.[14]

Often unconsciously, the process of unraveling and reweaving the fabric of our mythical tapestry into more gylanic patterns—in which "masculine" virtues such as "the conquest of nature" are no longer idealized—is in fact already well under way.[15] What is still lacking is the "critical mass" of new images and myths that is required for their actualization by a sufficient number of people.

Perhaps most important is that women and men are increasingly questioning the most basic assumption of androcratic society: that both male dominance and the male violence of warfare are inevitable. Among studies by anthropologists bearing on this point, a cross-cultural study conducted by Shirley and John McConahay found a significant correlation between the rigid sexual stereotypes required to maintain male dominance and the incidence of not only warfare, but wife beating, child beating, and rape.[16] As will be detailed in a second book continuing our reports, these systems correlations are verified by a growing number of new studies undertaken precisely because scientists in many disciplines are beginning to question the prevailing models of reality.[17] Moreover, by studying *both* halves of humanity, scientists are today in ground-breaking ways expanding our knowledge about the possibilities for human society, as well as for the evolution of human consciousness.[18]

Indeed, from the perspective of Cultural Transformation theory, the much written about modern "revolution in consciousness" can be seen as the transformation of androcratic to gylanic consciousness.[19] An important index of this transformation is that, for the first time in recorded history, many women and men are frontally challenging destructive myths, such as the "hero as killer,"[20] They are becoming aware of what "heroic" stories ranging from those of Theseus to Rambo and James Bond actually teach us and demanding that children of both sexes be taught to value caring and affiliation instead of conquest and domination.[21] In Sweden, laws have already been enacted to phase out the sale of war toys, which have traditionally served to teach boys lack of empathy with those they hurt, as well as all the other attitudes and behaviors that men require for killing others of their kind.[22] And peace demonstrations by millions of people all over this planet are dramatic evidence of a renewed consciousness of our connectedness with all of humanity.

Women and men all over the world are, for the first time in such large numbers, frontally challenging the male-dominator/female-dominated human relations model that is the foundation of a dominator worldview.[23] At the same time that the idea of the "war of the sexes" is being exposed as a consequence of this model, its further result of seeing "the other" as "the enemy" is also being challenged.[24] There is, most significantly, a growing awareness that the emerging higher consciousness of our global "partnership" is integrally related to a fundamental reexamination and transformation of the roles of both women and men.[25]

As the psychiatrist Jean Baker Miller writes, in society as presently constituted only women are "geared to be carriers of the basic necessity for human communion"[26]—and to in fact value their affiliations with others more highly than even themselves. In contrast to men, who are generally socialized to pursue their own ends, even at the expense of others, women are socialized to see themselves primarily as responsible for the welfare of others, even at the expense of their own well-being.[27]

This dichotomization of human experience, as Miller extensively documents, creates psychic distortions in both women and men. Women tend to be so overidentified with others that the threatened loss, or even disruption, of an affiliation can be, as she writes, "perceived not as just a loss of a relationship but as something closer to a total loss of self." Men, on the other hand, often tend to see their human need for affiliation as "an impediment" or "a danger." Thus, they can perceive service to others not as something central but rather secondary to their self-image, something a man "may desire or can afford *only* after he has fulfilled the primary requirements of manhood."[28]

These views of gender roles and of reality are, as we have seen, fundamental to androcratic society. But, as Miller writes, "it is extremely important to recognize that the pull toward affiliation that women feel in themselves is not wrong or backward. . . . What has not been recognized is that this psychic starting point contains the possibilities for an entirely different (and more advanced) approach to living and functioning—very different, that is, from the approach fostered by the dominant culture. . . . It allows for the emergence of the truth: that for everyone—men as well as women—individual development proceeds *only* by means of affiliation."[29]

These new ways of imaging reality for both women and men are giving rise to new models of the human psyche. The older Freudian model saw human beings primarily in terms of elemental drives such as the need for food, sex, and safety. The newer model proposed by Abraham Maslow and other humanistic psychologists takes these elemental "defense" needs into account but also recognizes that human beings have a higher level of "growth" or "actualization" needs that distinguish us from other animals.[30]

This shift from defense needs to actualization needs is an important key to the transformation from a dominator to a partnership society. Hierarchies maintained by force or the threat of force require defensive habits of mind. In our type of society, the creation of enemies for man begins with his human twin, woman, who in prevailing mythology is blamed for nothing less than our fall from paradise. And for both men and women, this ranking of one half of humanity over the other, as Alfred Adler noted, poisons all human relations.[31]

Freud's observations bear out that the androcratic psyche is indeed a mass of inner conflicts, tensions, and fears.[32] But as we move from androcracy to gylany, more and more of us can begin to move from defense to growth. And as Maslow observed in studying self-actualizing and creative people, as this happens, rather than becoming more selfish and self-centered, more and more of us will move toward a different reality: the "peak-experience" consciousness of our essential interconnectedness with all of humanity.[33]

A NEW SCIENCE AND SPIRITUALITY

This theme of our interconnectedness—which Jean Baker Miller calls affiliation, Jessie Bernard calls the "female ethos of love/duty," and Jesus, Gandhi, and other spiritual leaders have simply called love—is today also a theme of science. This developing "new science"—of which "chaos" theory and feminist scholarship are integral parts—is for the first time in history focusing more on relationships than on hierarchies.

As the physicist Fritjof Capra writes, this more holistic approach is a radical departure from much of Western science, which has been characterized by a hierarchic, overcompartmentalized, and often mechanistic approach.[34] It is in many ways a more "feminine" approach, as women are said to think more "intuitively," tending to draw conclusions from a totality of simultaneous impressions rather than through step-by-step "logical" thinking.[35]

Salk writes of a new science of empathy, a science that will use both reason and intuition "to bring about a change in the collective mind that will constructively influence the course of the human future."[36] This approach to science—successfully used by the geneticist Barbara McClintock, who in 1983 won a Nobel Prize—will focus on human society as a living system of which all of us are a part.[37] As Ashley Montagu said, it will be a science congruent with the true, and original, meaning of education: to draw forth and cause to grow the innate potentialities of the human being.[38] Above all else, as Hillary Rose writes in "Hand, Brain, and Heart: A Feminist Epistemology for the Natural Sciences," it will no longer be a science "directed toward the domination of nature or of humanity as part of nature."[39]

Evelyn Fox Keller, Carol Christ, Rita Arditti, and other scholars point out how, under the protective mantle of "objectivity" and "field-independence," science has often negated as "unscientific" and "subjective" the caring concerns considered overly feminine by the traditional view.[40] Thus, science has until now generally excluded women as scientists and focused its study almost entirely on men. It has also excluded what we may call "caring knowledge": the knowledge that, as Salk writes, we now urgently need to select those human forms that are "in cooperation with evolution, rather than those that are antisurvival or antievolutionary."[41]

This new science is also an important step toward bridging the modern gap between science and spirituality, which is in large part the product of a worldview relegating empathy to women and "effeminate" men. Scientists are further beginning to recognize that—like the artificial conflict between spirit and nature, between woman and man, and between different races, religions, and ethnic groups fostered by the dominator mentality—the way we view conflict itself needs to be reexamined.

As Miller writes, focusing her research on actualization rather than defense, the question is *not* how to eliminate conflict, which is impossible. As individuals with different needs and desires and interests come into contact, conflict is inevitable. The question directly bearing on whether we can transform our world from strife to peaceful coexistence is how to make conflict productive rather than destructive.[42]

As a result of what she terms productive conflict, Miller shows how individuals, organizations, and nations can grow and change. Approaching each other with different interests and goals, each party to the conflict is forced to reexamine its own goals and actions as well as those of the other party. The result for both sides is productive change rather than nonproductive rigidity. Destructive conflict, by contrast, is the equation of conflict with the violence required to maintain domination hierarchies.

Under the prevailing system, Miller points out, "conflict is made to look as if it *always* appears in the image of extremity, whereas, in fact, it is actually the lack of recognition of the need for conflict and provision of appropriate forms for it that leads to danger. This ultimate destructive form is frightening, but it is also *not* conflict. It is almost the reverse; it is the end result of the attempt to avoid and suppress conflict."[43]

Although this suppressive dominator approach to conflict still overwhelmingly prevails, the success of less violent and more "feminine" or "passive" approaches to conflict resolution offers concrete hope for change. These approaches have ancient roots. In recorded history Socrates and later Jesus both used them. In modern times they are best known as embodied by men like Gandhi and Martin Luther King, Jr.—whom androcracy handled by killing and canonizing. But by far their most extensive use has been by women. A notable example is how in the nineteenth and twentieth centuries women nonviolently fought against unjust laws. For access to family planning information, birth control technologies, and the right to vote, they permitted themselves to be arrested and chose to go on hunger strikes, rather than using force or the threat of force to gain their ends.[44]

This use of nonviolent conflict as a means of attaining social change is not merely passive or nonviolent resistance. By refusing to cooperate with violence and injustice through the use of violent and unjust means, it is the creation of the positive transformative energy Gandhi called *satyagraha* or "truth force." As Gandhi said, the aim is to *transform* conflict rather than to suppress it or explode it into violence.[45]

Just as critical in recharting the course of cultural

evolution is the current reexamination of the way we define power. Writing about the still prevailing view of power, Miller notes how the so-called need to control and dominate others is psychologically a function *not* of a feeling of power but rather of a feeling of powerlessness. Distinguishing between "power *for* oneself and power *over* others," she writes: "The power of another person, or group of people was generally seen as dangerous. You had to control them or they would control you. But in the realm of human development, this is not a valid formulation. Quite the reverse. In a basic sense, the greater the development of each individual the more able, more effective, and less needy of limiting or restricting others she or he will be."[46]

A central motif of twentieth-century feminist literature has been the probing not only of existing power relations but also of alternative ways of perceiving and using power: of power as affiliation. This theme has been explored by Robin Morgan, Kate Millett, Elizabeth Janeway, Berit Aas, Peggy Antrobus, Marielouise Janssen-Jurreit, Tatyana Mamonova, Kathleen Barry, Devaki Jain, Caroline Bird, Birgit Brock-Utne, Diana Russell, Perdita Huston, Andrea Dworkin, Adrienne Rich, to name but a few.[47] Described in such phrases as "sisterhood is powerful," this nondestructive view of power is one that women are increasingly bringing with them as they move into the "men's" world from their "women's" place. It is a "win-win" rather than a "win-lose" view of power, in psychological terms, a means of advancing one's own development *without* at the same time having to limit the development of others.

In visual or symbolic terms, this is the representation of power as linking. It has from time immemorial been symbolized by the circle or oval—the Goddess's cosmic egg or Great Round—rather than by the jagged lines of a pyramid where, as gods or as the heads of nations or families, men rule from the top. Long suppressed by androcratic ideology, the secret of transformation expressed by the Chalice was in earlier times seen as the consciousness of our unity or linking with one another and all else in the universe. Great seers and mystics have continued to express this vision, describing it as the transformative power of what early Christians called *agape*. This is the elemental linking between humans that in the distortion characteristic of androcracy is called "brotherly" love. In essence, it is the kind of selfless love a mother has for her children, once mythically expressed as the divine love of the Great Mother for her human children.

In this sense, our reconnection with the earlier spiritual tradition of Goddess worship linked to the partnership model of society is more than a reaffirmation of the dignity and worth of half of humanity. Nor is it only a far more comforting and reassuring way of imaging the powers that rule the universe. It also offers us a positive replacement for the myths and images that have for so long blatantly falsified the most elementary principles of human relations by valuing killing and exploiting more than giving birth and nurturing.

[A]t the outset of our cultural evolution the feminine principle embodied in the Goddess was the image not only of the resurrection or regeneration of death into life, but also of the illumination of human consciousness through divine revelation. As the Jungian psychoanalyst Erich Neumann notes, in ancient mystery rites the Goddess represented the power of physical transformation of the "godhead as the whirling wheel of life" in its "birth-bringing and death-bringing totality." But she was also the symbol of spiritual transformation: "the force of the center, which within this cycle passes toward consciousness and knowledge, transformation and illumination—the higher goals of humanity from time immemorial."[48]

A NEW POLITICS AND ECONOMICS

In our time, a good deal is being said and written about transformation. Futurists like Alvin Toffler write of great technological transformations from "first wave," or agragrian, to "second wave," or industrial, and now to "third wave," or postindustrial society.[49] Indeed, we have in recorded history seen major technological transformations. But within the perspective of the Cultural Transformation theory we are developing, it can be seen that what have often been described as major cultural transformations—for example, the shift from classical to Christian times and more recently to the secular or scientific age—have only been changes within the androcratic system from one type of dominator society to another.

There have been other bifurcation points, points of social disequilibrium when a fundamental systems transformation could have occurred, when new fluctuations or more gylanic patterns of functioning appeared. But these have never gone beyond the nucleation thresholds that would signal a shift from androcracy to gylany. To use a familiar analogy, until now the androcratic system has been like a rubber band. During periods of strong gylanic resurgence, for example, in Jesus' time, the band has stretched quite far. But always in the past, when the boundaries or limits of androcracy were reached, it snapped back toward its original shape. Now, for the first time in recorded history, instead of snapping back this band may break—and our cultural evolution may at last transcend the confines that have for millennia held us back.

What, at our level of technological development, would be the political and economic implications of a complete shift from a dominator to a partnership society? We have the technologies that in a world no longer governed by the Blade could vastly accelerate our cultural evolution. As Ruth Sivard records in her yearly report *World Military and Social Expenditures,* the cost of developing one intercontinental ballistic missile could feed 50 million children, build 160,000 schools, and open 340,000 health care centers. Even the cost of a single new nuclear submarine—equal to the annual education budget of twenty-three developing countries in a world where 120 million children have no school they can go to and 11 million babies die before their first birthday—could open new opportunities for millions of people now doomed to live in poverty and ignorance.[50]

What we lack, as futurist writings stress again and again, is the social guidance system, the governing values, that would redirect the allocation of resources, including our advanced technological knowhow, to higher ends.

Willis Harman, who has headed major futurist studies at the Stanford Research Institute, writes that what is needed—and evolving—is a "metamorphosis in basic cultural premises and all aspects of social roles and institutions." He describes this as a new consciousness in which competition will be balanced with cooperation and individualism will be balanced with love. It will be a "cosmic consciousness," a "higher awareness," which "relates self-interest to the interests of fellow man and of future generations." And it will entail nothing short of a fundamental transformation of "truly awesome magnitude."[51]

Similarly, in the second Club of Rome report we read that in order "to avoid major regional and ultimately global catastrophe," we must develop a new world system "guided by a rational master plan for long-term organic growth," held together by "a spirit of truly global cooperation, shaped in free partnership."[52] This world system would be governed by a new global ethic based on a greater consciousness of and identification with future as well as present generations and will require that cooperation, rather than confrontation, and harmony with, rather than conquest of, nature become our normative ideals.[53]

A striking aspect of these projections is that these futurists do *not* see technology or economics as the main determinants of our future. They recognize instead that our roads to the future will be shaped by human values and social arrangement, in other words, that our future will be primarily determined by the way we human beings conceive its possibilities, potentials, and implications. In the words of the futurist John McHale, "Our mental blueprints are its basic action programs."[54]

But what is most remarkable is that what many futurists are actually saying—practically in so many words—is that we must leave behind the hard, conquest-oriented values traditionally associated with "masculinity." For is not the need for a "spirit of truly global cooperation, shaped in free partnership," "a balancing of individualism with love," and the normative goal of "harmony with rather than conquest of nature," the reassertion of a more "feminine ethos"? And to what end could "drastic changes in the norm stratum" or a "metamorphosis in basic cultural premises and all aspects of social institutions" relate if not to the replacement of a dominator with a partnership society?

The transformation from a dominator to a partnership society would obviously bring with it a shift in our technological direction: from the use of advanced technology for destruction and domination to its use for sustaining and enhancing human life. At the same time, the wastefulness and overconsumption that now robs those in need would also begin to wane. For as many social commentators have observed, at the core of our Western complex of overconsumption and waste lies the fact that we are culturally obsessed with getting, buying, building—and wasting—*things,* as a substitute for the satisfactory emotional relationships that are denied us by the child-raising styles and the values of adults in the present system.[55]

Above all, the shift from androcracy to gylany would begin to end the politics of domination and the economics of exploitation that in our world still go hand in hand. For as John Stuart Mill pointed out over a century ago in his ground-breaking *Principles of Political Economy,* the way economic resources are distributed is a function not of some inexorable economic laws, but of political—that is, human—choices.[56]

Many people today recognize that in their present form neither capitalism nor communism offers a way out of our growing economic and political dilemmas. To the extent that androcracy remains in place, a just political and economic system is impossible. Just as Western nations like the United States, where slates of candidates are financed by powerful special interests, have not yet reached political democracy, nations like the USSR, ruled by a powerful, privileged, and mostly male managerial class, are still far from economic democracy.

In particular, the politics of domination and the economics of exploitation are in *all* androcracies exemplified by a "dual economy" in which women's unpaid, or at best low paid, productive activities are systematically exploited. As the United Nations *State of the World's Women 1985* points out, globally women are half the population, perform two thirds of the world's work in terms of hours, earn one tenth as much as men earn, and own one hundredth the property that men own.[57] Moreover, the unpaid labor of women—who in Africa do most of the food growing and who worldwide provide as many health services for free as all formal health care sectors combined—is routinely excluded from calculations of national productivity.[58] The result, as the futurist Hazel Henderson points out, is global economic projections based on "statistical illusions."[59]

In *The Politics of the Solar Age,* Henderson describes a positive economic future in which the roles of women and men are fundamentally rebalanced. This will entail facing up to the fact that our "masculine" militarism is the "most energy-intensive entropic activity of humans, since it converts stored energy directly into waste and destruction without any useful intervening fulfillment of basic human needs." Following the present period "marked by the decline in systems of patriarchy," Henderson predicts neither economic nor ecological reality will be governed by the "masculinized" values "now deeply associated with male identity."[60]

Similarly, in *The Sane Alternative,* the British writer James Robertson contrasts what he terms the "hyper-expansionist" or HE future with a "sane, humane, ecological" or "SHE future."[61] And in Germany Professor Joseph Huber describes his negative economic scenario for the future as "patriarchic." By contrast, in his positive scenario, "the sexes are on a socially equal standing. Men and women share in paid positions, as well as household tasks, child rearing, and other social activities."[62]

The central theme unifying these and other economic analyses, though of critical importance for our future, still remains largely unarticulated. This is that traditional economic systems, be they capitalist or communist, are built upon what, borrowing from Marxist analyses, may be called the *alienation of caring labor.*[63] As this caring labor—the life-sustaining labor of nurturing, helping, and loving others—is fully integrated into the economic mainstream, we will see a fundamental economic and political transformation.[64] Gradually, as the female half of humanity and the values and goals that in androcracy are labeled feminine are fully integrated into the guidance mechanisms of society, a politically and economically healthy and balanced system will emerge. Then, unified into the global family envisioned by the feminist, peace, ecology, human potential, and other gylanic movements, our species will begin to experience the full potential of its evolution.

TRANSFORMATION

The move to a new world of psychological and social rebirth will entail changes we cannot yet predict, or even envision. Indeed, because of so many failures following earlier hopes for social betterment, projections of a positive future elicit skepticism. Yet we know that changes in structure are also changes in function. Just as one cannot sit in the corner of a round room, as we shift from a dominator to a partnership society, our old ways of thinking, feeling, and acting will gradually be transformed.

For millennia of recorded history, the human spirit has been imprisoned by the fetters of androcracy.

Our minds have been stunted, and our hearts have been numbed. And yet our striving for truth, beauty, and justice has never been extinguished. As we break out of these fetters, as our minds, hearts, and hands are freed, so also will be our creative imagination.

For me, one of the most evocative images of the transformation from androcracy to gylany is the caterpillar metamorphosed into the butterfly. It seems to me a particularly fitting image to express the vision of humanity soaring to the heights it can attain, as the butterfly is an ancient symbol of regeneration, an epiphany of the transformative powers attributed to the Goddess.

Two further books, *Breaking Free* and *Emergence,* will explore this transformation in depth. They will lay out a new blueprint for social actualization—not for a utopia (which literally means "no place" in Greek), but for a *pragmatopia,* a realizable scenario for a partnership future. Though a few pages obviously cannot even begin to cover what will be developed in two books, I would like to close this [essay] by briefly sketching some of the changes I envision as we resume our interrupted cultural evolution.[65]

The most dramatic change as we move from a dominator to a partnership world will be that we, and our children and grandchildren, will again know what it means to live free of the fear of war. In a world rid of the mandate that to be "masculine" men must dominate, and along with the rising status of women and more "feminine" social priorities, the danger of nuclear annihilation will gradually diminish. At the same time, as women gain more equality of social and economic opportunities—so that birthrates can come into better balance with our resources—the Malthusian "necessity" for famine, disease, and war will progressively lessen.[66]

Since they also are to a large extent related to overpopulation, to "man's conquest of nature," and to the fact that environmental "house-keeping" is not in androcracies a "masculine" policy priority, our problems of environmental pollution, degradation, and depletion should likewise begin to lessen during the years of transformation. So also should their consequences in shortages of energy and other natural resources and in health problems from chemical pollution.[67]

As women are no longer systematically excluded from financial aid, land grants, and modernization training, Third World economic development programs for advancing education and technology and raising standards of living will become much more effective. There will also be far less economic inefficiency and less of the terrible human suffering that is the lot of millions of people, in both the developed and developing world today. For, as women are no longer treated as breeding animals and beasts of burden and have greater access to health care, education, and political participation, not only the female half of humanity, but all of humanity will benefit.[68]

Along with more rational measures aimed at successfully reducing the poverty and hunger of the mass of the world's poor—women and children—the growing consciousness of our linking with all other members of our species should gradually also narrow the gulf between rich and poor nations. Indeed, as billions of dollars and work hours are rechanneled from technologies of destruction to technologies that sustain and enhance life, human poverty and hunger could gradually become memories of a brutal androcratic past.[69]

The changes in woman-man relations from the present high degree of suspicion and recrimination to more openness and trust will be reflected in our families and communities. There will also be positive repercussions in our national and international policies. Gradually we will see a decrease in the seemingly endless array of day-to-day problems that now plague us, ranging from mental illness, suicide, and divorce to wife and child battering, vandalism, murder, and international terrorism. As research to be detailed in the second book of our report shows, these types of problems in large part derive from the high degree of interpersonal tension inherent in a male-dominated social organization and from dominator child-rearing styles heavily based on force. Thus, with the move to more equal and balanced relations between women and men and the reinforcement of gentler, more pro-human and caring behavior in children of both sexes, we may realistically expect fundamental psychic changes. These, in a relatively short time, will in turn exponentially accelerate the tempo of transformation.

In the world as it will be when women and men live in full partnership, there will, of course, still be families, schools, governments, and other social institutions. But like the already now emerging institutions of the equalitarian family and the social-action network, the social structures of the future will be based more on linking than ranking. Instead of requiring individuals that fit into pyramidal hierarchies, these institutions will be heterarchic, allowing for both diversity and flexibility in decision making and action. Consequently, the roles of both women and men will be far less rigid, allowing the entire human species a maximum of developmental flexibility.[70]

In keeping with present trends, many of our new institutions will also be more global in scope, transcending national boundaries. As the consciousness of our linking with one another and our environment firmly takes hold, we can expect to see the old nation-state as a self-absorbed political entity wither away. However, rather than more uniformity and conformity, which is the logical projection from the dominator system viewpoint, there will be more individuality and diversity. Smaller social units will be linked in matrices or networks for a variety of common ends, ranging all the way from the cooperative cultivation and harvesting of oceans and space exploration to the sharing of knowledge and the advancement of the arts.[71] There will also be other, as yet unforeseeable, global ventures to develop more equitable and efficient ways of utilizing all our natural and human resources, as well as new material and social inventions that we at this point in our development cannot yet foresee.

With the global shift to a partnership society will come many technological breakthroughs. There will also be adaptations of existing techniques to new social requirements. Some of these may, as Schumacher, and others have predicted, be better, more labor-intensive technologies in areas of craft—for example, a return to the pride of creativity and individuality in weaving, carpentry, pottery, and other applied arts. But at the same time, since the goal is to free humanity from insectlike drudgery, this will *not* mean a return to more labor-intensive technologies in all fields. On the contrary, allowing us the time and energy to actualize our creative potentials, we can expect that mechanization and automation will play an even more life-supporting role. And both small- and large-scale methods of production will be utilized in ways that encourage, and indeed require, worker participation, rather than, as required in a dominator system, turning workers themselves into machines or automatons.

The development of safer and more reliable birth control methods will be a top technology priority. We will also see much more research on understanding and slowing down the aging process, ranging from already emerging techniques to replace worn-out body parts to means of regenerating body cells. We might also see the perfection of laboratory-created life. But rather than replacing women, or converting women into incubators for artificially developed cells, such new technologies of reproduction would be carefully evaluated by both women and men to ensure they serve to actualize both sexes' full human potential.[72]

Since technologies of destruction would no longer consume and destroy such a vast portion of our natural and human resources, as yet undreamed (and presently undreamable) enterprises will be economically feasible. The result will be the generally prosperous economy foreshadowed by our gylanic prehistory. Not only will material wealth be shared more equitably, but this will also be an economic order in which amassing more and more property as a means of protecting oneself from, as well as controlling, others will be seen for what it is: a form of sickness or aberration.

In all this, there will be a number of economic stages. The first of these, already emerging, will be what is termed a mixed economy, combining some of the best elements of capitalism and communism—and in the sense of a variety of decentralized cooperative units of production and distribution—also anarchism.[73] The socialist concept that human beings have not only basic political but basic economic rights will certainly be central to a gylanic economy based on caring rather than domination. But as a partnership society replaces a dominator one, we can also except new economic inventions.

At the heart of this new economic order will be the replacement of the presently failing "dual economy," in which the male-dominated economic sector that is rewarded by money, status, and power must in its industrial stages, as Henderson documents, "cannibalize both social and ecological systems." Instead we can expect that the non-monetized "informal" economy—of household production and maintenance, parenting, volunteer community service, and all the cooperative activities that permit the now "over-rewarded competitive activities to appear successful"—will be appropriately valued and rewarded.[74] This will provide the now-missing basis for an economic system in which caring for others is not just given lip service but is the most highly rewarded, and therefore most highly valued, human activity.

Practices like female sexual mutilation, wife beating, and all the other more or less brutal ways through which androcracy has kept women "in their place" will of course be seen not as hallowed traditions but as what they are—crimes spawned by man's inhumanity to woman.[75] As for man's inhumanity to man, as male violence is no longer glorified by "heroic" epics and myths, the so-called male virtues of dominance and conquest will also be seen for what they are—the brutal and barbaric aberrations of a species turned against itself.

Through the reaffirmation and celebration of the transformative mysteries symbolized by the Chalice, new myths will reawaken in us that lost sense of gratitude and the celebration of life so evident in the artistic remnants of the Neolithic and Minoan Crete. By reconnecting us with our more innocent psychic roots—before warfare, hierarchism, and male dominance became our ruling norms—this mythology will not move us back psychically to the world as it was in the technological childhood of our species. On the contrary, by intertwining our ancient heritage of gylanic myths and symbols with modern ideas, it will move us forward toward a world that will be much more rational, in the true sense of the word: a word animated and guided by the consciousness that both ecologically and socially we are inextricably linked with one another and our environment.

Along with the celebration of life will come the celebration of love, including the sexual love between women and men. Sexual bonding through some form of what we now call marriage will most certainly continue. But the primary purpose of this bonding will be mutual companionship, sexual pleasure, and love. Having children will no longer be connected with the transmission of male names and property. And other caring relationships, not just heterosexual couples, will be fully recognized.[76]

All institutions, not only those specifically designed for the socialization of children, will have as their goal the actualization of our great human potentials. Only a world in which the quality rather than the quantity of human life is paramount can have such a goal. Hence, as Margaret Mead predicted, children will be scarce, and thus highly valued.[77]

The life-formative years of childhood will be the active concern of both women and men. Not just biological parents, but many other adults will take various responsibilities for that most precious of all social products: the human child. Rational nutrition as well as physical and mental exercises, such as more advanced forms of yoga and meditation, will be seen as elementary prerequisites for healthy bodies and minds. And rather than being designed to socialize a child to adjust to her or his place in a world of rank orderings, learning will be—as we are already beginning to see—a lifelong process for maximizing flexibility and creativity at all stages of life.

In this world, where the actualization of our higher evolutionary potentials—our greater freedom through wisdom and knowledge—will guide social policy, a primary focus of research will be the prevention of personal and social illness, of both body and mind. Beyond this, our as yet untapped, but increasingly recognized, mind powers will be extensively researched and cultivated. The result will be that as yet undreamed of mental and physical potentials will be uncovered and developed.[78]

For above all, this gylanic world will be a world where the minds of children—both girls and boys—will no longer be fettered. It will be a world where limitation and fear will no longer be systematically taught us through myths about how inevitably evil and perverse we humans are. In this world, children will not be taught epics about men who are honored for being violent or fairy tales about children who are lost in frightful woods where women are malevolent witches. They will be taught new myths, epics, and stories in which human beings are good; men are peaceful; and the power of creativity and love—symbolized by the sacred Chalice, the holy vessel of life—is the governing principle. For in this gylanic world, our drive for justice, equality, and freedom, our thirst for knowledge and spiritual illumination, and our yearning for love and beauty will at last be freed. And after the bloody detour of androcratic history, both women and men will at last find out what being human can mean.

NOTES

1. Frank Herbert, *Dune* (Philadelphia: Chilton, 1965).
2. Charlotte Gilman, *Herland* (New York: Pantheon Books, 1979 reprint).

3. For example, E. O. Wilson illustrates "aggressive behavior" as a "form of competitive technique" in evolution by citing ant colonies, which he describes as "notoriously aggressive toward one another." See E. O. Wilson, *Sociobiology: The New Synthesis* (Cambridge: Harvard University Press, 1975), 244. He also uses insect societies to back up the theory of "intrasexual selection," which he writes "is based on aggressive exclusion among the courting sex," stating there is "rampant machismo" among some species of beetles (p. 320). He then goes on to some examples of violent male dominance among insects, for instance the yellow dung fly, where the male forcefully immobilizes the female for long periods of time to prevent rival males from mounting her (pp. 321–24). In some of his writings Wilson makes a point of distinguishing insect from human behavior. For example, he writes how "the mosquito is an automaton" in which "a sequence of rigid behaviors programmed by the genes" must "unfold swiftly and unerringly from birth," whereas "rather than specifying a single trait, human genes prescribe a *capacity* to develop a certain array of traits" (*On Human Nature* [Cambridge: Harvard University Press, 1978], 56, emphasis in original). But the overall import of what Wilson says is such that it is not hard to see why he is so often cited to prove notions of inevitable male aggression and male dominance. For instance, in explaining his evolutionary theory of "paternal investment," Wilson writes that since "males invest relatively little with each mating effort . . . it is to their advantage to tie up as many of the female investments as they can"—which presumably only the most aggressive males can do, thus eliminating the genes of "inferior" males (*Sociobiology,* 324–25). Again, he illustrates the sociobiological theory that evolution favors male aggression with an insect experiment that is a favorite of sociobiologists: the 1948 Bateman experiment involving the mating of ten *Drosophila melanogaster,* a species of fly (p. 325). This is followed by a discussion of how animals are fundamentally polygamous because the mating of the "fittest" males with more than one female gives an evolutionary advantage to the entire species (p. 327). Elsewhere Wilson contends that the "reproductive advantages conferred by dominance" extend to our species as well. To substantiate this, he cites one sole example: the Yanomama Indians of Brazil, a highly warlike, rigidly male-dominant tribe where female infanticide is practiced. Here, "the politically dominant males father a disproportionate number of children." And here, Wilson reports, the impression of the anthropologists describing what they termed a type of "natural selection" was that "the polygynous Indians, especially the headmen, tend to be more intelligent than the nonpolygynous." On this basis, Wilson implies that his hypothesis of "dominance advantage in reproductive competition" is founded on "persuasive" evidence (p. 288).

4. See, e.g., Vilmos Csanyi, *General Theory of Evolution* (Budapest: Akademiai Kiado, 1982); Ervin Laszlo, *Evolution: The Grand Synthesis* (Boston: New Science Library, 1987); Niles Eldredge, *Time Frames* (New York: Simon & Schuster, 1985). As Margaret Mead summed it up, "There were options and turning points throughout cosmic and biological evolution. If you look seriously at the process of evolution, it did not have to take the present course. It could have taken many others" ("Our Open Ended Future," *The Next Billion Years,* Lecture Series, UCLA, 1973).

5. Sherwood Washburn, "Tools and Human Evolution," *Scientific American* 203 (Sept. 1960): 62.

6. Ilya Prigogine and Isabel Stengers, *Order out of Chaos* (New York: Bantam, 1984), esp. 160–76; Eldredge, *Time Frames,* 189.

7. Ervin Laszlo, "The Crucial Epoch," *Futures* 17 (Feb. 1985): 16.

8. Jonas Salk, *Anatomy of Reality* (New York: Columbia University Press, 1983), 12–15.

9. See, e.g., Marija Gimbutas, *The Goddesses and Gods of Old Europe, 7000–3500* B.C. (Berkeley and Los Angeles: University of California Press, 1982), 91.

10. During the Crusades and the Inquisition, the cross again became associated with killing and torturing. A grisly modern use of the cross as a symbol of death and oppression is its use by the Ku Klux Klan in the United States.

11. See, e.g., *Liberty* 80 (Nov.–Dec. 1985): 4, quoting President Ronald Reagan, who on at least eleven occasions has suggested that the end of the world is coming—a sobering statement from a man who could bring this end on.

12. This re-mything is also being countered by the global regression to "fundamentalism"—a code word for androcratic religious mythology. This regression is so strong precisely because of the enormous movement worldwide to both create new myths and reinterpret old ones in more gylanic ways.

13. There is also a new genre of modern Goddess art. See, e.g., Gloria Orenstein, "Female Creation: The Quest for the Great Mythic Mother," slide lecture; and Gloria Orenstein, "Artist as Shaman," art exhibit at Women's Building Gallery, Los Angeles, California, Nov. 4–28, 1985.

14. It is also significant that the birth of the ecology movement is often said to have been the publication of a book by a woman: Rachel Carson's *The Silent Spring* (Boston: Houghton Mifflin, 1962). As former Secretary of the Interior James Udall wrote, "A great woman has awakened the nation by her forceful account of the danger around us."

15. See, e.g., Francoise D'Eaubonne, *Le Feminism ou La Mort (Feminism or Death)* (Paris: Pierre Horay, 1974); Elizabeth Dodson-Gray, "Psycho-Sexual Roots of Our Ecological Crises" (paper distributed by Round-

table Press, 1974); and Susan Griffin, *Woman and Nature* (New York: Harper Colophon, 1978), for analyses linking our ecological crises and our male and masculine values–dominated system.

16. Shirley McConahay and John McConahay, "Sexual Permissiveness, Sex Role Rigidity, and Violence Across Cultures," *Journal of Social Issues,* 33, (1977), 134–43.

17. This is detailed in Riane Eisler and David Loye, *Breaking Free.* See also Eisler, "Violence and Male Dominance: The Ticking Time Bomb," *Humanities in Society* 7 (Winter/Spring 1984): 3–18.

18. The term *consciousness raising* was a contribution of the women's liberation movement during the late 1960s when women came together in groups to share a growing understanding of how many of their supposedly personal problems are the common social problems of half of humanity in androcratic society.

19. This will be examined in depth in Eisler and Loye, *Breaking Free,* forthcoming.

20. See also Eisler and Loye, "Peace and Feminist Theory: New Directions," *Bulletin of Peace Proposals,* No. 1 (1986); Eisler, "Women and Peace," *Women Speaking* 5 (Oct.–Dec. 1982): 16–18; Eisler, "Our Lost Heritage: New Facts on How God Became a Man," *The Humanist* 45 (May/June 1985): 26–28.

21. For example, veterans of the Vietnam War were in December 1985 leafletting in front of toystores to raise consciousness about how destructive war toys are. As one veteran put it in a TV interview, if they sell Rambo and GI Joe dolls glamorizing war, they ought to at least make some of them amputees to show what war really is like.

22. *The Futurist,* Feb. 1981, 2.

23. The growth of the international women's movement has been enormously accelerated during the First United Nations Decade for Women (1975–1985), with more and more men also beginning to recognize that there can be no real social or economic development without major changes in the status of women. For instance, at the opening of the End of United Nations for Women Conference held in Nairobi, Kenya, in July 1985, Kenyan president Daniel Arap Moi said that "a twenty-first century of peace, development, and the universal observance of human rights will remain elusive without the full partnership of women." Kenya's vice-president Mwai Kibaki recently spoke of how African women, who now often give birth every thirteen months "are helpless, weak, and miserable in the difficult task of having to cook for and suckle three or four children . . . with yet another waiting . . . and must be liberated" (Moi and Kibaki quoted in David Loye, "Men at the U.N. Women's Conference," *The Humanist* 45 [Nov./Dec. 1985]: 28, 32).

24. See, e.g., Mary Daly, *Gyn/Ecology: The Metaethics of Radical Feminism* (Boston: Beacon, 1978); and Wilma Scott Heide, *Feminism for the Health of It* (Buffalo: Margaretdaughters Press, 1985).

25. See Louise Bruyn, *Feminism: The Hope for a Future* (Cambridge, MA: American Friends Service Committee, May 1981) for a forceful articulation of what Daly terms the "misogynistic roots of androcratic aggression" (*Gyn/Ecology,* 357). See also Eisler and Loye, "Peace and Feminist Theory: New Directions"; and "Peace and Feminist Thought: New Directions," *World Encyclopedia of Peace,* Laszlo and Yoo, eds. (London: Pergamon Press, 1986).

26. Jean Baker Miller, *Toward a New Psychology of Women* (Boston: Beacon, 1976), 86.

27. Ibid., 69.

28. Ibid. Quotations (in order) from 83, 87, and 69.

29. Ibid. Quotations (in order) from 95 and 83 (emphasis in original).

30. Abraham Maslow, *Toward a Psychology of Being* (New York: Van Nostrand-Reinhold, 1968).

31. Alfred Adler, *Understanding Human Nature* (Greenwich, CT: Fawcett, 1954).

32. Research bearing of the different characteristics of androcratic and gylanic personality types is reported in Eisler and Loye, *Breaking Free,* forthcoming.

33. Maslow, *Toward a Psychology of Being.*

34. Fritjof Capra, *The Turning Point: Science, Society, and the Rising Culture* (New York: Simon & Schuster, 1982).

35. It is ironic that only now, as male scientists are discovering how limited the traditional "masculine" linear approach is, there is more openness to the idea that both sexes probably have similar innate thinking capabilities. Although there are some biological differences, women's ability to process information more holistically is probably mainly due to sexually stereotyped socialization and roles. For instance, unlike men, women have been socialized to see their lives primarily in terms of relationships and to be more attuned to the needs of others.

36. Salk, *Anatomy of Reality,* 11–19.

37. The definitive work on McClintock is Evelyn Fox Keller, *A Feeling for the Organism: The Life and Work of Barbara McClintock* (San Francisco: W. H. Freeman, 1983).

38. Ashley Montagu, quoted in *Woodstock Times,* August 7, 1986.

39. Hillary Rose, "Hand, Brain, and Heart: A Feminist Epistemology for the Natural Sciences," *Signs* 9 (Autumn 1983): 81.

40. See, e.g., Evelyn Fox Keller, *Reflections on Gender and Science* (New Haven: Yale University Press, 1985); Carol Christ, "Toward a Paradigm Shift in the Academy and in Religious Studies," in Christie Farnham, ed., *Transforming the Consciousness of the Academy* (Bloomington, IN: Indiana University Press, 1987); Rita Arditti, "Feminism and Science," in *Science and Libera-*

tion, Rita Arditti, Pat Brennan, and Steve Cavrak, eds. (Boston: South End Press, 1979).

41. Salk, *Anatomy of Reality,* 22.

42. Miller, *Toward a New Psychology of Women,* chap. 11.

43. Ibid., 130.

44. For an overview of the nineteenth-century feminist struggle for the vote, see Eleanor Flexner, *A Century of Struggle* (Cambridge: Belknap Press of Harvard University Press, 1959). For an overview of the nineteenth-century struggle for access to higher education, see Mabel Newcomer, *A Century of Higher Education for Women* (New York: Harper & Brothers, 1959). Some sources on the twentieth-century women's liberation movement are Vivian Gornick and Barbara Moran, *Woman in Sexist Society* (New York: Basic Books, 1971); Robin Morgan, ed., *Sisterhood Is Powerful* (New York: Random House, 1970); Johnson, *From Housewife to Heretic* (Garden City, NY: Doubleday Anchor, 1983); Riane Eisler, *The Equal Rights Handbook* (New York: Avon Books, 1978).

45. For a discussion of Gandhi's approach, see Marilyn Ferguson, *The Aquarian Conspiracy: Personal and Social Transformation in the 1980s* (Los Angeles: Tarcher, 1980), 119–200. See also Louis Fisher, *The Life of Mahatma Gandhi* (New York: Harper & Brothers, 1950).

46. Miller, *Toward a New Psychology of Women,* 116. The distinction between power *for* and power *over* is the distinction symbolized by the Chalice and the Blade.

47. See, e.g., Morgan, ed., *Sisterhood Is Powerful;* Marilyn French, *Beyond Power: On Women, Men, and Morals* (New York: Ballantine, 1985); Adrienne Rich, *Of Woman Born* (New York: Bantam, 1976); Devaki Jain, *Woman's Quest for Power: Five Indian Case Studies* (Ghanziabad: Vikas Publishing House, 1980); Marielouise Janssen-Jurreit, trans. Verne Moberg, *Sexism: The Male Monopoly on History and Thought* (New York: Farrar, Straus & Giroux, 1982).

48. Erich Neumann, *The Great Mother* (Princeton, NJ: Princeton University Press, 1955), 333–34.

49. Alvin Toffler, *The Third Wave* (New York: Bantam, 1980).

50. Ruth Sivard, *World Military and Social Expenditures 1983* (Washington, D.C.: World Priorities, 1983), 5, 26.

51. Willis Harman, "The Coming Transformation," *The Futurist,* Feb. 1977, 5–11.

52. Mihajlo Mesarovic and Eduard Pestel, *Mankind at the Turning Point* (New York: Dutton, 1974), 157.

53. Ibid., 146–47.

54. John McHale, *The Future of the Future* (New York: Ballantine, 1969), 11.

55. See, e.g., T. W. Adorno, Else Frenkel-Brunswik, Daniel Levinson, R. Nevitt Sanford, *The Authoritarian Personality* (New York: Harper & Row, 1950), particularly the work of Frenkel-Brunswik on how individuals brought up in rigidly hierarchic families are particularly prone to substitute material acquisition for the emotionally satisfactory relations they are incapable of having. These social and personality dynamics are examined in depth in Eisler and Loye, *Breaking Free.*

56. John Stuart Mill, *Principles of Political Economy,* W. J. Ashley, ed., new edition of 1909 based on the 7th ed. of 1871 (New York: Longman, Green, 1929). See also Heilbroner, *The Worldly Philosophers* (New York: Simon & Schuster, 1961).

57. *State of the World's Women 1985* (compiled for the United Nations by New Internationalist Publications, Oxford, U.K.), 1.

58. Ibid.

59. Hazel Henderson, *The Politics of the Solar Age* (New York: Anchor Books, 1981), 171.

60. Ibid. Quotations (in order) are from 337, 364, and 373.

61. James Robertson, *The Sane Alternative* (St. Paul, MN: River Basin Publishing, 1979).

62. Joseph Huber, "Social Ecology and Dual Economy," an English excerpt from *Anders Arbeiten–Anders Wirtshaften* (Frankfurt: Fischer-Verlag, 1979).

63. I am indebted to Hillary Rose's "Hand, Brain, and Heart: A Feminist Epistemology for the Natural Sciences" for her forceful articulation of this central point. (See note 39.)

64. This economic transformation is discussed in more depth in Eisler and Loye, *Breaking Free* and Riane Eisler, *Emergence* (work in progress).

65. See Riane Eisler, "Pragmatopia: Women's Utopias and Scenarios for a Possible Future," paper presented at Society for Utopian Studies Eleventh Conference, Asilomar, California, October 2–5, 1986, for the first introduction of the concept of *pragmatopia* (which inGreek means a real place, and a realizable future, as contrasted to the conventional term *utopia,* which literally means "no place.")

66. Since present population growth rates cannot be sustained by the earth's ecological system, the issue is not whether population growth will stabilize, but how. See, e.g., Jonas Salk, *World Population and Human Values: A New Reality* (New York: Harper & Row, 1981). See also Riane Eisler, "Peace, Population and Women's Roles," in *World Encyclopedia of Peace,* Laszlo and Yoo, eds.

67. This issue will be discussed in more depth in Eisler, *Emergence.* See also D'Eaubonne, *Le Feminism ou La Mort;* Elizabeth Dodson-Gray, *Green Paradise Lost* (Wellesley, MA: Roundtable Press, 1979); and other eco-feminist works.

68. See, e.g., *The State of the World's Women 1985;* Barbara Rogers, *The Domestication of Women: Discrimination in Developing Societies* (New York: St. Martin's, 1979); Mayra Buvinic, Nadia Joussef, and Barbara Von

Elm, *Women-Headed Households: The Ignored Factor in Development Planning* (Washington, D.C.: International Center for Research on Women, 1978); May Rihani, *Development as if Women Mattered* (Washington, D.C.: Overseas Development Council, 1978); Riane Eisler, "The Global Impact of Sexual Equality," *The Humanist* 41 (May/June 1981).

69. See, e.g., Sivard, *World Military and Social Expenditures 1983;* Riane Eisler and David Loye, "The 'Failure' of Liberalism: A Reassessment of Ideology from a New Feminine-Masculine Perspective," *Political Psychology* 4 (1983): 375–91.

70. See, e.g., Luther Gerlach and Virginia Hine, *People, Power, Change: Movements of Social Transformation* (Indianapolis: Bobbs-Merrill, 1970).

71. See, e.g., E. F. Schumacher, *Small Is Beautiful* (New York: Harper & Row, 1973); Henderson, *The Politics of the Solar Age.*

72. For the androcratic scenario on new birth control technologies see, e.g., Wendy Faulkner and Erik Arnold, eds., *Smothered by Invention: Technology in Women's Lives* (London: Pluto Press, 1985); and Rita Arditti, Renate Duelli Klein, and Shelley Minden, eds., *Test Tube Women: What Future for Motherhood?* (London: Routledge & Kegan Paul, 1984).

73. For a work exploring some of these possibilities, see Martin Carnoy and Derek Sherer, *Economic Democracy* (New York: Sharpe, 1980).

74. Henderson, *The Politics of the Solar Age,* both quotations from 365.

75. Riane Eisler, "Human Rights: The Unfinished Struggle," *International Journal of Women's Studies* 6 (Sept./Oct. 1983): 326–35.

76. Riane Eisler, *Dissolution: No-Fault Divorce, Marriage, and the Future of Women* (New York: McGraw-Hill, 1977).

77. Mead, "Our Open-Ended Future"; Riane Eisler and David Loye, "Childhood and the Chosen Future," *Journal of Clinical Child Psychology* 9 (Summer 1980).

78. David Loye, *The Sphinx and the Rainbow: Brain, Mind, and Future Vision* (Boston: New Science Library, 1983).

A Spirituality of Resistance
Finding a Peaceful Heart and Protecting the Earth

ROGER S. GOTTLIEB

SPIRITUAL TEACHINGS OFFER US PEACE IN place of pain. Or at least they offer us a way to accept and be at peace with the inevitable distress that comes from being alive. After my first child died at the age of two months, I went through a period of shrinking from the sight of children. Yet I liked kids and didn't want to go through life feeling envious whenever I encountered them. I asked myself what I could do. *"It's simple,"* I realized; *"when I see a child and start to feel that gnawing bitterness, I will thank God that I have eyesight to see them. Some people, after all, are blind."* This was a spiritual approach: it made me a better person and made me happier. It took nothing away from anyone else, but instead increased the world's positive resources.

If we choose to follow a spiritual path, we face a dilemma. On the one hand, my awareness of the generalized suffering in the world—of the Holocaust and other genocides, and of the ecocide that threatens us all—makes me feel decidedly unpeaceful. I'd rather not be aware of them. Various forms of escape are so attractive, and seem so natural, in a world like ours. On the other hand, spiritual growth cannot be accomplished while I'm screening out the pains and dangers around me. This response will thwart my spiritual aspirations and leave me no better off than when I began. A way out of this dilemma requires that we face—and resist—that which frightens us the most. My own search for spiritual peace began as a child. I might come upon it unexpectedly on a brilliant spring afternoon, when instead of taking the bus home from elementary school I would walk the one and a half miles back to my house. Every tree, flowering bush, and blade of

Gottlieb, Roger S., "A Spirituality of Resistance: Finding a Peaceful Heart and Protecting the Earth," *Tikkun* 14/2 (March/April 1999), pp. 33–37, 68. Reprinted by permission of the author.

grass of this well-kept suburban setting seemed wonderfully, almost painfully, alive. And that almost-but-not-quite pain mixed with enough joy to float my little body back to my slightly anxious mother, home wondering why I hadn't gotten off the school bus.

As I got older I explored Mediterranean islands, hung out in tiny tribal settlements in northern Pakistan, and trekked through the Himalayas. Living as a young man with no responsibilities, far from the industrial madness that seemed to be driving everyone crazy, I discovered an ever-deeper experience of serenity: that same wonderful, almost painful, sense of being alive; a simple joy in every leaf, in the glow of stars and moon, in the touch of my lover's hand. I was also helped by psychedelic chemicals that were conducive to deep feelings of peace, belonging, and openness. Under their influence, my heart opened not just to this or that leaf or river, but to the entire cosmos.

So I have known these moments, treasured them, and thanked the spirits for them. Yet at the same time there has almost always been a little voice that comes in somewhere during the experience and starts to ask painful questions. *"Of course, this all feels wonderful. The world is beautiful: that tree, this piece of music, your lover's breast. But what about the Others? What about the people who aren't having such a great time?"* My awareness of the Others has taken many forms. It began, I suppose, on train rides to New York from my home in White Plains. The last few miles, before the cavernous confusion of Grand Central Station, the track ran through the middle of Harlem's black ghetto. The blocks of tenements riveted me. I peered at shabbiness, dirt, laundry drying on back porches, peeled paint, tired old cars, junk-filled yards. And the people glimpsed casually from the train window against which my boy's nose was pushed seemed tired, old at any age, and beaten down.

It all made such a contrast to the brilliant green lawns on my street, my friends' immaculate split-levels. I couldn't see any reason why my family and the other kids at school should be so much better off. It seemed obvious that the people in Harlem, crammed into those ugly buildings, lacking so much that I had, didn't deserve their fate. And it was simultaneously clear that my parents, my friends, and I didn't really deserve what we had either. As I passed through Harlem for those fleeting moments, I wondered if I was right to really enjoy what I had while these other people had so much less.

I couldn't figure out what I felt about a world that was set up this way; and I didn't know how to be thoroughly at home here, full of unmixed joy at all the goodies I enjoyed, when I couldn't help but see how different it was for others.

It reminded me of those who, having been spared in a car crash which killed four acquaintances, would say, *"It's a miracle that I wasn't killed." "Some miracle,"* I'd think, *"you weren't taken and all the Others are dead. What kind of miracle is that?"* We have feelings of peace or joy. These feelings, we want to say, prove how beautiful, how holy, the universe is. Or perhaps the feelings call up images of a more personal sense of the divine: of God the compassionate Father/Mother, of Jesus the Savior, of the Grace of Allah. The feelings then become signs of God's perfection and love, of the deep protectiveness with which a Guiding Force holds us. For me, in between these feelings of love or serenity and the assertion of perfection and God's love, there lies an often uncrossable gap: all I know about the pain, cruelty, and injustice that permeates this life, all the suffering for which I can find no justification, rationale, or excuse.

I am concerned that to achieve spiritual peace I will have to accept what should not be accepted: that I will be told to concentrate on myself, and forget about others; or that I will be reassured that all this pain is encompassed by Forces and Realities that somehow make up for it. I cannot respond in any of these ways. I seek to live on this earth, without having to rely on promises of aid and comfort from Cosmic Forces. And I cannot forget the Others, or the threats to myself and my children. I don't see how I can accept the world, or approve of it, when these other realities are as genuine as any experiences of mystical delight or tranquillity I might have. To find a peaceful heart, I need a spirituality in which the world's unjustified pain is not denied, avoided, or forgotten. For me, the spiritual challenge is to combine moral and political commitments that direct us to respond to injustice and needless suffering with spiritual teachings about serenity and wisdom. In the act of resistance, I believe, an answer to this challenge can be found.

In *Seeking the Heart of Wisdom,* the contemporary American Buddhist teachers Joseph Goldstein and Jack Kornfield put the spiritual challenge this way:

> Wisdom replaces ignorance in our minds when we realize that happiness does not lie in the accumulation of more and more pleasant feelings, that gratifying craving does not bring us a feeling of wholeness or completion. It simply leads to more craving and more aversion. When we realize in our own experience that happiness comes not from reaching out but from letting go, not from seeking pleasurable experience but from opening in the moment to what is true, this transformation of understanding then frees the energy of compassion within us. Our minds are no longer bound up in pushing away pain or holding on to pleasure. Compassion becomes the natural response of an open heart.

The question is: what am I letting in and what am I keeping out? Isn't there a difference between letting go of my own desires, and letting go of my concern for others? Give up my own desires—for fame, higher salary, some free time, more sex—this I understand. But what would it mean to "let go" of my hope that poor people might have a better life? or to "open my heart" to the realities of abused children or the dolphins suffocating in two-mile-long fishing nets? What might we have to screen out—and what might we have to add on top—to let go of them?

The well-known American spiritual teacher Ram Dass once said that for him the essential task of spiritual life, regardless of circumstances, is to "quiet my mind, open my heart, and relieve the suffering that I see around me." Supported by his belief that the universe is to be trusted, that it is worth our "faith," Ram Dass acts to end suffering while remaining unattached to the outcome of his actions. He writes:

> Somehow I have faith in the universe—I'm not sure where it comes from—even with all the horror and the torture and so on. This is hard to say because it's morally reprehensible to even think that the people who died in the Holocaust are, from a soul point of view, on an evolutionary path in which that experience was functional. That sounds too horrible to consider. But that's the part that isn't humanistic about the spiritual path. I have such a deep conviction about that, and it's part of what allows me to be in the presence of suffering. If somebody is suffering, even though I will do my best to relieve them, there's another part of me that trusts that the suffering is in the greater good and if I could see, I could understand.

The belief Ram Dass expresses here takes us far beyond the reality of the earth. He later admits that "certain things are not reversible—like what we're doing to the forests and species, which will disappear . . . ." In the case of the irreversibility of ecological damage it's clear that even Ram Dass' own metaphysical view cannot accommodate the slaughter of non-human innocents. The human-centered view that sees the entire universe as a learning ground for people is a little hard to apply to species made extinct and whole ecosystems poisoned.

What is more poignant is that this extremely intelligent and generous man admits quite candidly that the core of his teaching—the necessity to open the heart to the world's pain—depends on his belief that we (humans, anyway) are all on a cosmic trip of spiritual evolution.

THE PAIN IS REAL, BUT FOR THE "GREATER GOOD."

What would have happened, I wonder, if he had lost that faith? Would he still have opened to what was going on around him? Is it truly openness if to sustain it we have to believe that the pain is somehow justified? That, like the irritability of the teething infant or the distress of childbirth, the suffering is intimately connected to a Greater Good? Ram Dass is no escapist. He has set up foundations to help the blind and sat in rooms with dying AIDS patients. But when we believe suffering is "all to the good," then it is damped down—as we might do to a fire burning too fast when we toss some water on it and reduce the air flow—by a metaphysics which puts it all In Perspective.

Of course it takes a certain kind of deep strength to accept that the world is the way it is. Denials, avoidance, hysteria, numbness to the pain involved, we might say, are ways of not accepting the facts. That is, of not having the emotional courage to be with the dark truths of our time. But acceptance that something is going on is very different from accepting the thing itself, approving of it, or feeling that a universe in which it takes place deserves our blessing.

In place of an acceptance that is passive, or that hides from the facts, we can offer resistance. In a spirituality of resistance evil is not avoided, wished away, or neutralized by a metaphysics that promises that it will be All Right in the End. In this spiritual realm we can fully experience the deepest of joys because we engage directly with unjust suffering by opposing it. In the act of resistance, our acceptance of cruelty, injustice, and unnecessary death is made complete—we embrace them by seeking their end. Why is resistance so powerful? Because in the act of resistance we fully engage that which frightens and depresses us the most. What we would avoid, deny, submit to, or go along with is brought into full reality. We no longer have to feel that it is too much, that we cannot tolerate a world in which it exists, or that we have to let it command our obedience. We can open our hearts in full acceptance of the world, not by telling others or ourselves that there is some cosmic meaning for all this pain, but by seeking to do something about it.

JUST WHAT IS RESISTANCE?

To begin with, to resist is to oppose superior and threatening powers in a context of injustice, oppression, or violence. When we resist we cannot be neutral, or tolerantly accept that everyone's viewpoint is equally valid. When we fight back against rape, or concentration camps, or environmental ruin, the lines are drawn. Nevertheless, while resistance means we take a stand in the face of a painful reality, it is not always clear exactly what should be done. Nor does it mean that the people we oppose are unredeemably evil (though they sometimes are). People may take part in unredeemably evil activities, even though they are more frightened, numb, or weak than they are outright ethical monsters. What resistance does mean is that I answer my students' question—"But who is to judge what is right or wrong?"—by saying "We are; each and every one of us." We make the judgment, even though the situation may be terribly complex. We oppose the evil, even as we try to have compassion for the evildoers.

To resist is to act with the aim of lessening the collective injustice, oppression, and violence we face. We are not resisting if all we are trying to do is get the pain shifted somewhere else. Working to have the toxins stored in the next town over, or buying sun block when the thinning ozone makes the sunlight dangerous—these things might be prudent, or good for my health. But they do not really count as resistance to the massive forces of environmental destruction. Individual self-protection poses no threat to the powers-that-be, but seeks to accommodate those forces, to coexist with them.

Because the engines of environmental destruction, like many other types of evil, are strong, entrenched, and often mighty rich, and because we carry conflicting obligations, time pressures, and simple fatigue, it often seems easier or safer not to resist. Thus if we are to act, we will need to overcome the temptations of fear or laziness, of complacency and habit. These temptations, as I know very well from my own life, are continual. Unless we are in the throes of some extreme situation—the oil company at the gates of our little village, as it were; or unless we are heroes, or just plain tirelessly devoted—we will give in to those temptations.

But that is not what we always do. While the dominant social forces make it ever so easy to go along with business as usual, we may come to realize that these same forces are controlling, constraining, and limiting us. Since resistance involves throwing off limits, there can be an element of gladness, even joy, when we engage in it. Instead of conforming to the ways things are, living day to day with the gnawing feeling that something is not right, we refuse to go along. We attempt to halt or slow, if only in the most minuscule ways, the machinery of ruin. And when we do so we often experience the rush of feeling which comes from liberating the energy long buried by our suppressed awareness that we have been part of something we know to be wrong. In this light, the deep satisfaction expressed by some Jews who resisted the Nazis makes perfect sense. They chose to resist—and to just that extent, no matter what the forces arrayed against them, they had become free.

In fact, the emotional and spiritual meaning of the Holocaust can be profoundly changed when we think of it not solely as the history of how the Jews were slaughtered but also of how they fought back. The images of victimization remain, but along with the piles of dead bodies we see resistance fighters. Auschwitz is identified not only with the millions who were gassed, but also with the organized network of inmates who blew up one of the crematoria. Poring over the historical record, we see that the Jews sang songs to celebrate their survival, smuggled forbidden food into the ghettos, blew up Nazi troop trains and at times expended superhuman courage and determination just to stay alive. These resistors show us that despite all the pain inflicted by violent oppression, freedom is always possible. Not freedom from the situation, but freedom within it.

In the same way, the despair engendered by environmental destruction—the self-caused cancer plagues, the dying coral reefs, the newly dangerous sunlight—can be altered by our knowledge of the people throughout the world who are resisting that destruction; and our own spiritual life can reach its most profound point when we join our energies to theirs. Our sense of the ultimate meaning of the environmental crisis may change if we see it as a time of joyful resistance, a time when we can deeply penetrate the meaning of our existence.

In the freedom of resistance comes a unique and pure happiness. It may last for only a short while before it once again gets clouded by regrets for losses, confusion over strategy, and fear for the future. But for a precious time we are at one both with ourselves and the world. Life, usually so flawed, has become perfect. Feeding the world as it has fed us, we are at that moment like a bee pollinating an apple tree, like the salmon struggling upstream against the rapids to lay its eggs, like the hawk bringing back fresh kill for its chicks, like a maple tree offering soft red buds to the warming April sunshine.

Resistance takes many forms. In any given situation, we can see that there are choices to be made: between living in denial, and living in the truth; between accepting the way things are and saying "no" to them. We can speak up, act up, share our concerns with others, give money, teach our children the truth, confront political candidates, write letters to the editor, join groups to keep indigenous peoples from being slaughtered, hug trees to protect forests from bulldozers, shut down the local polluter, nationalize the oil industry, and overthrow the government. For a start.

Consider Diana Steck, a housewife from Yukon, PA, who confronted the relation between the chronic illnesses of her own and many of her friends' children and the nearby dump that contained chromium, cadmium, lead, arsenic, mercury, and other toxic chemicals. She struggled with condescending government officials who promised an investigation and did nothing; and health "experts" who told her she didn't know what she was talking about. Refusing to give up, she and some neighbors became a group with a name, received training in grassroots environmental politics, got arrested for sitting-in at a state office, and took over a crucial public meeting when public officials tried to dodge the issue. Friends and relatives were shocked when she was arrested or tried to stop trucks from going to the dump. But Diana had become a different person, one who wouldn't get stopped by her own fears or others' judgments. "All this," she said, referring to countless illnesses in her town, "happened for a reason. Otherwise we'd still be out here, just stupidly working and making money, oblivious to the world around us. We wouldn't be the people we are today. We wouldn't be as complete."

In my own community of Jamaica Plain, a racially and economically mixed section on Boston's southern edge, people banded together to protect our treasured Jamaica Pond: an actual lake—one and one-half miles around—within the city limits. The Pond is bordered by a thin belt of trees and graced by sea gulls, Canadian geese, ducks, exotic-looking cormorants, snapping turtles, and imported swans. Its marvelously clear water attracts joggers, strollers, baby carriages, dog-walkers, drummers on hot summer nights, old Chinese ladies doing Tai Chi, and couples of various sexual persuasions dreamily holding hands.

When you stand at the little boathouse where popsicles and popcorn are sold, you can look across the water and see the sun set over wooded hills. These hills, which border the park but are not actually part of it, were sold to a builder who wants to replace the old trees with luxury condos so that proud owners can enjoy the vista of the Pond while the rest of us can view the sun setting over expensive apartments.

A local social worker spearheaded the opposition, raising 4,000 signatures demanding that the local development board forbid the project and the city or state acquire the land. On the coldest night of the winter of 1998, 350 people jammed a local church to make their voices heard—to say that this spot was not only lovely, but also sacred. Each of us at the meeting could have found something else to do that evening; could have left the effort to others; could have felt, "Oh well, you can't fight the developers." But we didn't, and in the end the project was stopped.

As we resist, we look for allies, and sometimes find them in unlikely places. Melody Chavis, a writer and community activist in Berkeley, faced a neighborhood increasingly dominated by the drug trade. She watched local kids grow up to be pushers, junkies, and gang members, and offered something better. She connected them to a local organic gardening center, where they learned to work the land with their own hands, and to take deep pride in the ecological quality of what they were growing. For a number of kids the healthy connection to the soil meant a viable alternative to the polluted options that surrounded them. Our allies can be from the neighborhood, or from very far away. In an ecological age, "Love your neighbor" includes the whole world. Consider, for instance, the way international activity has been mobilized in response to the Narmada river valley project in India. Called by critics the "world's greatest planned environmental disaster," the project envisaged 30 major, 135 medium, and 3,000 minor dams throughout central India. If completed as planned, it would displace close to 400,000 people, destroy wildlife habitat, and flood some of the last remaining tropical forest in India. As early as 1977, local opposition formed when people realized that there was in fact no land available for the local people who were to be displaced—that they would simply join the millions of other "refugees from development." During the next decade and a half, opposition grew and took a variety of forms: road blockades, hunger fasts, demonstrations at state capitals, and massive gatherings at sites which were to be flooded. What is crucial here is the way a ring of international solidarity has formed around resistance to the Narmada valley project. Japanese environmentalists persuaded their government not to advance money to it, while American activists pressured the World Bank. In 1992, facing reports that the entire project was colored by fraud and incompetence, legislators in Finland, Sweden, and the United States asked the World Bank not to lend any more money. The International Rivers Project, located in San Francisco, organizes financial and technical aid to the continuing struggle.

Even though ozone depletion and acid rain make everyone "neighbors," we should remember that if the dam goes through, the writer and the readers of this book will not be displaced, and people in India will. We are not all affected equally by everything that takes place in the world. Martin Luther King's claim that we are bound by an "inescapable network of mutuality, tied in a single garment of destiny" must be read in the most general of ways, or else we will paper over the differences between the drowned and the saved. Yet it is also true, I believe, that similar forces are at work in crazy dam projects, unnecessary condo building, and leaking toxic dumps. Monoculture, big money, blind indifference, and shortsighted thoughtlessness carry their weight everywhere. For that reason, resistance to one is resistance to all.

At times acts of resistance will demand everything we have. Chico Mendes was murdered for defending the rainforest and the people who live there. Ken Saro-Wiwa was hung by the Nigerian government for resisting the toxic effects of oil extraction in Nigeria—these and countless unknown others have put their time, money, energy, and even their lives on the line.

However, some acts of resistance will involve doing just a little more than we are doing already. We can make one extra phone call, toss a few more dollars towards the organization that is doing good work, not buy the chemicalized food, take the trouble to ask the office manager to use the organic bathroom cleanser. Returns on such actions won't be as grand or dramatic as those times when we manifest a greater devotion. Still, they can be essential parts both of a worldwide environmental movement and our own, most personal, spiritual life. Like a short but heartfelt prayer, a daily ten minutes of meditation, a brief reading from Psalms, each act of resistance can be a small but loving acknowledgment of our yearning to join the best within us to the best for others.

Finally, in resistance we can keep up our hope. Optimism is not always easy to hold onto, especially as we become more and more knowledgeable about what is really going on. But our knowledge should include successes as well as failures, our moments of grace as a species and culture as well as our moments of degradation. We can read of Gaviotas, a tiny Colombian village that re-claimed seemingly barren land with sustainable agriculture, democratic decision making, and an inclusive economic structure. Its windmills convert mild breezes into energy, its solar collectors work in the rain, and children's seesaws power its water pumps. In the shelter of the Caribbean pines planted as a renewable crop, an ancient rain forest is regenerating. We can marvel at the growth of the organic food industry, the resurgent forests of the American northeast, the return of the wolves to Yellowstone. We can marvel at the growth, in about a decade, of an environmental justice movement that includes groups from Texas to Massachusetts, from California to Georgia. All these examples of resistance can inspire our own. They are precious opportunities to know, as deeply as we know anything, that the environmental crisis is a time of great courage as well as great loss.

If spirituality means, among other things, moving beyond my isolated ego (and this is, indeed, the way it is frequently portrayed) then resistance is that movement. For in acts of resistance I go beyond my isolation, my self-concern, my very sense of myself as fully separate. And that sense of moving beyond my ego takes me not only into connection with the suffering Others who are human, but with the more-than-human as well. I can walk over to Jamaica Pond, pat the trunk of a sugar maple tree I pass along the way and say, only half believing I won't be understood: "You and me pal—we're in this together. Best of luck to us both." I can know that my kinship with the beings of this earth is essential to who I am; and that I will not let them be wantonly destroyed without some defiance. Paradoxically, if I put some of my soul into resistance, I will occasionally be able to put down my burden of selfhood and responsibility, that searing sense that I must make it all better. There will be moments when I realize that I am merely a brief flower of mind and feeling in this vast meadow of existence. At my best I will try to be a true flower and not some plastic rose that doesn't bloom and will not wither for a hundred years. I will have offered myself to all the other flowers, to the life and health and blossoming of the rest of this garden we call the earth. Having done so I will then be able to feel the full sweetness of the springtime sun, the evening rain, and even the approach of the chill winter morning of my own natural, fitting and joyous death.

Discussion Questions

1. What is a myth? What are the myths that inform the dominant worldview at present? What sort of myth do we require in order to live successfully and sustainably in the future?
2. How have recent developments in the sciences challenged our view of the world? How are we adapting our worldviews to better accommodate the story science is telling us?
3. What are the implications of thinking of the Earth as a superorganism? How does this perception call upon us to live differently than we do at present?
4. What would a partnership society look like? How would it differ from the society we know? Is a partnership society a viable goal to work toward?
5. If facing tragedy makes us stronger, how far must the tragedy advance before we learn and grow from it? Can we, as a society, see danger coming in time to choose another path, or will we not react until disaster has struck?

Further Reading

Berry, Thomas, *The Great Work,* New York: Bell Tower, 1999.
———, *The Dream of the Earth,* San Francisco: Sierra Club Books, 1988.
Bunyard, Peter, and Edward Goldsmith, *Gaia: The Thesis, the Mechanisms, and the Implications,* Wadebridge, Cornwall, U.K.: Wadebridge Ecological Centre, 1988.
Gottlieb, Roger, *A Spirituality of Resistance,* New York: Continuum, 1999.
Lovelock, James, *The Ages of Gaia,* New York: W. W. Norton, 1988.
———, *Gaia: A New Look at Life on Earth,* Oxford, U.K.: Oxford University Press, 1979.
Macy, Joanna, *World as Lover, World as Self,* Berkeley, Calif.: Parallax Press, 1991.
Nollman, Jim, *Spiritual Ecology: A Guide to Reconnecting With Nature,* New York: Bantam, 1990.

Chapter 16

Globalization, Community, and Ecojustice

FOLLOWING THE FALL of the Soviet Union and the dissipation of the Cold War paradigm that had described world affairs since the end of World War II, throughout the 1990s there was talk of a new world order in which a global economy would bring the world's peoples together into a global village. Such optimistic language is now coming to be seen as masking a darker emerging reality, namely, a world in which transnational corporations grow ever larger and more powerful and operate under fewer and fewer restraints, jeopardizing national and local sovereignty even as the rich–poor gap widens and the environment suffers.

Even ostensibly communist nations such as China and Vietnam have now adopted forms of market capitalism as their economic model. Everywhere, the concentration of wealth in fewer and fewer hands is being accompanied by the adoption of high-consumption lifestyles for national elites and by increasingly uniform cultural standards, from fast food and cell phones to Hollywood films and baseball caps. Meanwhile, the increasing mobility of labor and capital leads to the disintegration of local communities and families, and traditional value systems are watered down or abandoned altogether. Contrary to promises that free trade would raise the living standards of all, the past thirty years have seen a dramatic widening of the gap between rich and poor along with a huge increase in absolute poverty, which now affects 2.5 billion people. Is this the natural course of human evolution that we all must accept, or are there alternatives?

Economist David C. Korten traces the roots of these recent changes and highlights how they may not be changes for the better. In Korten's view, the beneficiaries of globalization are large corporations. Virtually everyone else, he suggests, stands to lose. Our economic system is flawed, he argues, because it fails to include all manner of negative impacts in its accounting, from the impoverishment of landless peasants to the ecological costs of industrial production. In a full world, Korten says, the notion of unlimited economic growth must be abandoned.

Swedish philosopher Helena Norberg-Hodge addresses the question of cultural homogenization, drawing on her observations of Ladakhi Tibetan culture over the course of three decades. Only with the coming of Western influence, she writes, did Ladakhis come to feel economically poor and culturally inferior. As Ladakh has been integrated into the national economy of India, its formerly self-sufficient local economy has been virtually destroyed. Likewise, Ladakhi society has become increasingly fragmented and violent.

Kentucky farmer Wendell Berry applies a similar analysis to the rural United States. Arguing that the modern American system no longer accords value to maintaining the stability and integrity of a community, Berry notes some of the benefits that Americans have lost as a result. He concludes that rural Americans are the victims of a kind of internal colonization that is not unlike international colonialism in its detrimental effects.

Theologian Larry Rasmussen points out that within the industrial economy, rural societies are not the only ones that suffer from exploitation and fragmentation; urban societies suffer as well. Rasmussen notes that the issues of social justice have converged with those of environmental degradation, and both should now be addressed in terms of global ecojustice. Rasmussen takes the Christian churches to task for being late in recognizing how these problems are interconnected, but he suggests that churches have an important role to play in bringing about a more just and sustainable society for the future.

The Failures of Bretton Woods

DAVID C. KORTEN

This essay is adapted from David C. Korten's keynote address at the 1994 convention of the Environmental Grantmakers Association of America, held at the Mt. Washington Hotel, Bretton Woods, New Hampshire, on the fiftieth anniversary of the famous Bretton Woods conference that created the World Bank, the International Monetary Fund, and, soon after, the General Agreement on Tariffs and Trade (GATT).

Korten has emerged as one of the world's clearest critics of the economic philosophies and practices that drive our system. He formerly worked in Asia for the United States Agency for International Development (AID) and the Ford Foundation's development programs. He holds a Ph.D. from Stanford University's Business School and served on the faculty of Harvard University's Business School. He is president of the People-Centered Development Forum in New York, and author of *When Corporations Rule the World* (1995).

THE FAME OF BRETTON WOODS AND OF THIS hotel dates from July 1944, when the United Nations Monetary and Financial Conference was held here. The world was in the throes of World War II. Mussolini had been overthrown. The Allies had landed at Normandy, but Hitler would last another ten months. War also continued to rage in the Far East, and Japan would not surrender for another thirteen months. The United Nations Charter was still a year away. In that context, the economic leaders who quietly gathered at this hotel were looking beyond the end of the war with hopes for a world united in peace through prosperity. Their specific goal was to create the institutions that would promote that vision.

The Bretton Woods meeting did create new institutions that have shaped and controlled the world's economic activity since that time, but some theorists will say that the plans for these institutions go back still further, to the 1930s and to the U.S. Council on Foreign Relations. A meeting ground for powerful members of the U.S. corporate and foreign policy establishments, the council styled itself as a forum for the airing of opposing views, an incubator of leaders and ideas unified in their vision of a global economy dominated by U.S. corporate interests.

Members of this group assessed early on that, at a minimum, the U.S. national interest required free access to the markets and raw materials of the Western Hemisphere, the Far East, and the British Empire. On July 24, 1941, a council memorandum outlined the concept of a *grand area:* the part of the world that the United States would need to dominate economically and militarily to ensure materials for its industries. The council also called for the creation of worldwide financial institutions for "stabilizing currencies and facilitating programs of capital investment for constructive undertakings in backward and underdeveloped regions." (Sklar 1980) President Franklin D. Roosevelt was duly apprised of the council's views.

Three years later, at the opening session at Bretton Woods, Henry Morgenthau, then U.S. Secretary of the Treasury and president of the conference, read a welcoming message from Roosevelt and gave his own opening speech, which set the tone and spirit of the gathering. Morgenthau envisaged "the creation of a dynamic world economy in which the peoples of every nation will be able to realize their potentialities in peace and enjoy increasingly the fruits of material progress on an earth infinitely blessed with natural riches." He called on participants to embrace the "elementary economic axiom . . . that prosperity has no fixed limits. It is not a finite substance to be diminished by division."

Thus Morgenthau set forth one of several underlying assumptions of the economic paradigm that guided the work of the architects of the Bretton Woods system. Many of these assumptions were reasonably valid, but two of the most important were deeply flawed. The first erroneous assumption is that economic growth and enhanced world trade would benefit everyone. The second is that economic growth would not be constrained by the limits of the planet.

By the end of this historic meeting, the World Bank and the International Monetary Fund (IMF) had been founded, and the groundwork had been laid for what later became GATT. In the intervening years, these institutions have held faithfully to their mandate to promote economic growth and globalization. Through structural adjustment programs (SAPs), the World Bank and the IMF have pressured countries of the South to open their borders and change their economies from self-sufficiency to *export* production. Trade agreements negotiated through GATT have reinforced these actions and opened economies in both North and South to the increasingly free importation of goods and money.

As we look back fifty years later, we can see that the Bretton Woods institutions have indeed met their goals. Economic growth has expanded fivefold. International trade has expanded by roughly twelve times, and foreign direct investment has been expanding at two to three times the rate of trade expansion. Yet, tragically, while these institutions have met their goals, they have failed in their purpose. The world has more poor people today than ever before. We have an accelerating gap between the rich and the poor. Widespread violence is tearing families and communities apart nearly everywhere. And the planet's ecosystems are deteriorating at an alarming rate.

Yet the prevailing wisdom continues to maintain that economic growth offers the answer to poverty, environmental security, and a strong social fabric, and that *economic globalization*—erasing economic borders to allow free flow of goods and money—is the key to such growth. Indeed, the more severe the economic, environmental, and social crises, the stronger the policy commitment to these same prescriptions, even as evidence mounts that they are not working. In fact, there is a growing consensus outside of official circles that they cannot work, for reasons I will explain.

ECOLOGICAL LIMIT TO GROWTH

As the founder of ecological economics, Herman Daly, regularly reminds us, the human economy is embedded in and dependent on the natural ecosystems of our planet. Until the present moment in human history, however, the scale of our economic activity relative to the scale of the ecosystems has been small enough so that, in both economic theory and practice, we could, up to a point, afford to ignore this fundamental fact.

Now, however, we have crossed a monumental historical threshold. Because of the fivefold economic expansion since 1950 the environmental demands of our economic system have filled up the available environmental space of the planet. In other words, we live in a "full world." . . .

The first environmental limits that we have confronted and possibly exceeded are not the limits to nonrenewable resource exploitation, as many once anticipated, but rather the limits to renewable resources and to the environment's *sink functions*—its ability to absorb our wastes. These are limits related to the loss of soils, fisheries, forests, and water; to the absorption of CO_2 emissions; and to destruction of the ozone layer. We could argue whether a particular limit was hit at noon yesterday or will be passed at midnight tomorrow, but the details are far less important than the basic truth that we have no real option other than to adapt our economic institutions to the reality of a "full world."

The structure and ideology of the existing Bretton Woods system is geared to an ever-continuing expansion of economic output—*economic growth*—and to the integration of national economies into a seamless global economy. The consequence is to intensify competition for already overstressed environmental space. In a "full world," this intensified competition accelerates destruction of the regenerative capacities of the ecosystem on which we and future generations depend; it crowds out all forms of life not needed for immediate human consumption purposes; and it increases competition between rich and poor for control of ecological resources. In a free market—which responds only to money, not needs—the rich win this competition every time. We see it happening all over the world: Hundreds of millions of the financially disenfranchised are displaced as their lands, waters, and fisheries are converted to uses serving the wants of the more affluent.

As long as their resources remain, the demands of the rich can be met—which may explain why so many of the rich see no problem. The poor experience a very different reality, but in a market economy their experience doesn't count.

The market cannot deal with questions relating to the appropriate scale of economic activity. There are no price signals indicating that the poor are going hungry because they have been forced off their lands; nor is there any price signal to tell polluters that too much CO_2 is being released into the air, or that toxins should not be dumped into soils or waters. Steeped in market ideology and highly responsive to corporate interests, the Bretton Woods institutions have demonstrated little capacity to give more than lip service either to environmental concerns or to the needs of the poor. Rather, their efforts have *de facto* centered on ensuring that people with money have full access to whatever resources remain—with little regard for the broader consequences.

A new Bretton Woods meeting to update the international system would serve a significant and visionary need—if its participants were to accept that economic growth is no longer a valid public policy priority. Indeed, whether the global economy grows or shrinks is largely irrelevant. Having crossed the threshold to a full world, the appropriate concern is whether the available planetary resources are being used in ways that: (1) meet the basic needs of all people; (2) maintain biodiversity; and (3) ensure the sustained availability of comparable resource flows to future generations. Our present economic system fails on all three counts.

ECONOMIC INJUSTICE

In *How Much Is Enough?* (1992), Alan Durning divided the world into three consumption classes: overconsumers, sustainers, and marginals. The overconsumers are the 20 percent of the world's people who consume roughly 80 percent of the world's resources—that is, those of us whose lives are organized around automobiles, airplanes, meat-based diets, and wastefully packaged disposable products. The marginals, also 20 percent of the world's people, live in absolute deprivation.

If we turn to measurements of *income* rather than *consumption,* the figures are even more stark. The United Nations Development Program (UNDP) *Human Development Report* for 1992 introduces the champagne glass as a graphic metaphor for a world of extreme economic injustice. The bowl of the champagne glass represents the abundance enjoyed by the 20 percent of people who live in the world's richest countries and receive 82.7 percent of the world's income. At the bottom of the stem, where the sediment settles, we find the poorest 20 percent of the world's people, who barely survive on 1.4 percent of the total income. The combined incomes of the top 20 percent are nearly sixty times larger than those of the bottom 20 percent. Furthermore, this gap has doubled since 1950, when the top 20 percent enjoyed only thirty times the income of the bottom 20 percent. And the gap continues to grow.

These figures actually understate the true inequality in the world, because they are based on national averages rather than actual individual incomes. If we take into account the very rich people who live in poor countries and the very poor people who live in rich countries, the incomes of the richest 20 percent of the world's people are approximately 150 times those of the poorest 20 percent. That gap is growing as well.

Robert Reich, the U.S. Secretary of Labor in the Clinton administration, explained in his book *The Work of Nations* (1991), that the economic globalization the Bretton Woods institutions have advanced so successfully has served to separate the interests of the wealthy classes from a sense of national interest and thereby from a sense of concern for and obligation to their less fortunate neighbors. A thin segment of the super rich at the very lip of the champagne glass has formed a stateless alliance that defines *global interest* as synonymous with the personal and corporate financial interests of its members.

This separation has been occurring in nearly every country in the world to such an extent that it is no longer meaningful to speak of a world divided into northern and southern nations. The meaningful divide is not geography—it is class.

Whether intended or not, the policies so successfully advanced by the Bretton Woods institutions have inexorably empowered the super rich to lay claim to the world's wealth at the expense of other people, other species, and the viability of the planet's ecosystem.

FREEING CORPORATIONS FROM CONTROL

The issue is not the market per se. Trying to run an economy without markets is disastrous, as the experience of the Soviet Union demonstrated. However, there is a fundamentally important distinction between markets and free markets.

The struggle between two extremist ideologies has been a central feature of the twentieth century. Communism called for all power to the state. Market capitalism calls for all power to the market—a euphemism for giant corporations. Both ideologies lead to their own distinctive form of tyranny. The secret of Western success in World War II and the early postwar period was not a free market economy; it was the practice of democratic pluralism built on institutional arrangements that sought to maintain balance between the state and the market and to protect the right of an active citizenry to hold both accountable to the public interest.

Contrary to the claims of ideologues who preach a form of corporate libertarianism, markets need governments to function efficiently. It is well established in economic theory and practice that markets allocate resources efficiently only when markets are competitive and when firms pay for the social and environmental impact of their activity—that is, when they *internalize* the costs of their production. This requires that governments set and enforce the rules that make cost internalization happen, and, since successful firms invariably grow larger and more monopolistic, governments regularly step in to break them up and restore competition.

For governments to play the necessary role of balancing market and community interests, governmental power must be equal to market power. If markets are national, then there must be a strong national government. By expanding the boundaries of the market beyond the boundaries of the nation-state through economic globalization, the concentration of market power moves inevitably beyond the reach of government. This has been a most important consequence of both the structural adjustment programs of the World Bank and IMF and the trade agreements negotiated under GATT. As a result, governance decisions are transferred from governments, which at least in theory represent the interests of all citizens, to transnational corporations, which by their nature serve the interests only of their dominant shareholders. Consequently, societies everywhere on the planet are no longer able to address environmental and other needs.

Enormous economic power is being concentrated in the hands of a very few global corporations relieved of constraints to their own growth. Antitrust action to restore market competition by breaking up the concentrations is one of the many casualties of globalization. Indeed, current policy encourages firms to merge into ever more powerful concentrations to strengthen their position in global markets.

The rapid rate at which large corporations are shedding employees has created an impression in some quarters that the firms are losing their power. It is a misleading impression. The Fortune 500 firms shed 4.4 million jobs between 1980 and 1993. During this same period, their sales increased 1.4 times, assets increased 2.3 times, and CEO compensation increased 6.1 times. Of the world's one hundred largest economies, fifty are now corporations, not including banking and financial institutions.

Any industry in which five firms control 50 percent or more of the market is considered by economists to be highly monopolistic. The *Economist* recently reported that five firms control more than 50 percent of the global market in the following industries: consumer durables, automotive, airlines, aerospace, electronic components, electricity and electronics, and steel. Five firms control over 40 percent of the global market in oil, personal computers, and—especially alarming in its consequences for public debate on these very issues—media.

FORUMS FOR ELITE DOMINATION

It is worth adding here that the forums within which corporate and government elites shape the global policies of the Western world were not limited to Bretton Woods. In May 1954, a powerful group of North American and European leaders also began meeting as an unofficial, low-profile group with no acknowledged membership. Known simply as Bilderberg, the group played a significant role in advancing the European Union and shaping a consensus among leaders of the Atlantic nations on key issues facing Western-dominated transnational systems. Participants included heads of state, other key politicians, key industrialists and financiers, and an assortment of intellectuals, trade unionists, diplomats, and influential representatives of the press with demonstrated sympathy for establishment views. One Bilderberg insider had observed that "today there are very few figures among governments on both sides of the Atlantic who have not attended at least one of these meetings."

As Japan assumed an increasing powerful and independent role in the global economy, the need became evident for a forum that included the Japanese and that had a more formal structure than Bilderberg.

In response, the Trilateral Commission was formed in 1973 by David Rockefeller, chair of Chase Manhattan Bank, and Zbigniew Brzezinski, who served as the commission's director/coordinator until 1977 when he became national security advisor to President Jimmy Carter.

The members of the Trilateral Commission include the heads of four of the world's five largest nonbanking transnational corporations; top officials of five of the world's six largest international banks; and heads of major media organizations. U.S. presidents Jimmy Carter, George Bush, and Bill Clinton were all members of the Trilateral Commission, as was Thomas Foley, former speaker of the House of Representatives. Many key members of the Carter administration were both Bilderberg and Trilateral Commission members. Many of President Clinton's cabinet and other appointments are former members of the Trilateral Commission.

Both Bilderberg and the Trilateral Commission have provided forums in which top executives from the world's leading corporations meet regularly, informally, and privately with top national political figures and opinion leaders to seek consensus on immediate and longer-range problems facing the most powerful members of the Western Alliance.

To some extent, the meetings help maintain "stability" in global policies, but they also deprive the public of meaningful participation and choice—as some participants explicitly intend. Particularly significant about these groups is their bipartisan political membership. Certainly, the participation of both George Bush and Bill Clinton in the Trilateral Commission makes it easier to understand the seamless transition from the Republican Bush administration to the Democratic Clinton administration with regard to U.S. commitment to pass GATT and NAFTA. Clinton's leadership in advancing what many progressives saw as a Bush agenda won him high marks from his colleagues on the Trilateral Commission.

INSTRUMENTS OF CONTROL

Corporations have enormous political power, and they are actively using it to reshape the rules of the market in their own favor. The GATT has now become one of the corporations' most powerful tools for reshaping the market. Under the new GATT agreement, a World Trade Organization, the WTO, has been created with far-reaching powers to provide corporations the legal protection they feel they need to continue expanding their far-flung operations without the responsibility to serve any interest other than their own bottom line. . . .

The WTO will hear disputes brought against the national or local laws of any country that another member country considers to be a trade barrier. Secret panels made up of three unelected trade experts will hear the disputes, and their rulings can be overturned only by a unanimous vote of the member countries. In general, any health, safety, or environmental standard that exceeds international standards set by industry representatives is likely to be considered a trade barrier, unless the offending government can prove that the standard has a valid scientific basis.

As powerful as the large corporations are, they themselves function increasingly as agents of a global financial system that has become the world's most powerful governance institution. The power in this system lies within a small group of private financial institutions that have only one objective: to make money in massive quantities. A seamless electronic web allows anyone with proper access codes and a personal computer to conduct instantaneous trade involving billions of dollars on any of the world's financial markets. The world of finance itself has become a gigantic computer game. In this game the smart money does not waste itself on long-term, high-quality commitments to productive enterprises engaged in producing real wealth to meet real needs of real people. Rather, it seeks short-term returns from speculation in erratic markets and from simultaneous trades in multiple markets to profit from minute price variations. In this game the short-term is measured in microseconds, the long-term in days. The environmental, social, and even economic consequences of financial decisions involving more than trillion dollars a day are invisible to those who make them.

Joel Kurtzman, former business editor of the *New York Times* and currently editor of the *Harvard Business Review*, estimates that for every $1 circulating in the productive economy today, $20 to $50 circulates in the world of pure finance. Since these transactions take place through unmonitored international computer networks, no one knows how much is really involved. The $1 trillion that changes hands each day in the world's international currency markets is itself twenty to thirty times the amount required to cover daily trade in actual goods and services. If the world's most powerful governments act in concert to stabilize exchange rates in these same markets, the best they can manage is a measly $14 billion a day—little more than pocket change compared to the amounts mobilized by speculators and arbitrageurs. . . .

The corporations that invest in *real* assets (as opposed to ephemeral financial assets), are forced by the resulting pressures to restructure their operations in order to maximize immediate short-term returns to shareholders. One way to do this is by downsizing, streamlining, and automating their operations, using the most advanced technologies to eliminate hundreds of thousands of jobs. The result is jobless economic growth. Contemporary economies simply cannot create jobs faster than technology and dysfunctional economic systems can shed them. In nearly every country in the world there is now a labor surplus, and those lucky enough to have jobs are increasingly members of a contingent work force without either security or benefits. The resulting fear and insecurity make the jobs-versus-environment issue a crippling barrier to essential environmental action.

Another way to increase corporate profits is to externalize the cost of the firm's operations on the community, pitting localities against one another in a standards-lowering competition to offer subsidies, tax holidays, and freedom from environmental and employment standards. Similarly, workers are pitted against one another in a struggle for survival that pushes wages down to the lowest common denominator. This is the true meaning of *global competitiveness*—competition among localities. Large corporations, by contrast, minimize their competition through mergers and strategic alliances.

Any corporation that does not play this game to its limit is likely to become a takeover target by a corporate raider who will buy out the company and profit by taking the actions that the previous management—perhaps in a fit of social conscience and loyalty to workers and community—failed to take. The reconstruction of the global economic system makes it almost impossible for even highly socially conscious and committed managers to operate a corporation responsibly in the public interest.

• • •

We are caught in a terrible dilemma. We have reached a point in history where we must rethink the very nature and meaning of human progress; yet the vision and decisions that emerged some fifty years ago catalyzed events that have transformed the governance processes of societies everywhere such that the necessary changes in thought and structure seem very difficult to achieve. It has happened so quickly that few among us even realize what has happened. The real issues are seldom discussed in a media dependent on corporate advertising.

Nonetheless, the fact is that sustainability in a growth-dependent globalized economy is what Herman Daly calls an impossibility theorem. What is the alternative? Among those of us who are devoting significant attention to this question, the answer is the opposite of globalization. It lies in promoting greater economic localization—breaking economic activities down into smaller, more manageable pieces that link the people who make decisions in ways both positive and negative. It means rooting capital to a place and distributing its control among as many people as possible.

Powerful interests stand resolutely in the way of achieving such a reversal of current trends. The biggest barrier, however, is the limited extent of public discussion on the subject. The starting point must be to get the issues on the table and bring them into the mainstream policy debates in a way that books like this may help to achieve.

The Pressure to Modernize and Globalize

HELENA NORBERG-HODGE

For thirty years, on three continents, Swedish philosopher, teacher, and activist Helena Norberg-Hodge has been fighting the excesses of today's economic development models, particularly their effects on traditional societies and local culture. She was the first foreigner accepted to make her home in the Himalayan province of Ladakh (Kashmir). There, over three decades, she learned the native language and helped people study and resist the hidden perils and culturally destructive effects of modernization. Meanwhile in Europe, she was a leading campaigner in the Norwegian vote opposing entry into the European Economic Community, and is now codirector of the International Forum on Globalization-Europe. In the United States, her organization, the International Society for Ecology and Culture, runs educational campaigns on globalization issues. She is the author of *Ancient Futures: Learning from Ladakh* (1991), and coauthor of *From the Ground Up* (1993).

LADAKH IS A HIGH-ALTITUDE DESERT ON THE Tibetan Plateau in northernmost India. To all outward appearances, it is a wild and inhospitable place. In summer the land is parched and dry; in winter it is frozen solid by a fierce, unrelenting cold. Harsh and barren, Ladakh's land forms have often been described as a "moonscape."

Almost nothing grows wild—not the smallest

Norberg-Hodge, Helena, "The Pressure to Modernize and Globalize," in Jerry Mander and Edward Goldsmith, Eds., *The Case Against the Global Economy,* pp. 33–46.

shrub, hardly a blade of grass. Even time seems to stand still, suspended on the thin air. Yet here, in one of the highest, driest, and coldest inhabited places on Earth, the Ladakhis have for a thousand years not only survived but prospered. Out of barren desert they have carved verdant oases—terraced fields of barley, wheat, apples, apricots, and vegetables, irrigated with glacial meltwater brought many miles through stone-lined channels. Using little more than stone-age technologies and the scant resources at hand, the Ladakhis established a remarkably rich culture, one that met not only their material wants but their psychological and spiritual needs as well.

Until 1962, Ladakh, or "Little Tibet," remained almost totally isolated from the forces of modernization. In that year, however, in response to the conflict in Tibet, the Indian Army built a road to link the region with the rest of the country. With the road came not only new consumer items and a government bureaucracy but, as I shall show, a first misleading impression of the world outside. Then, in 1975, the region was opened up to foreign tourists, and the process of "development" began in earnest.

Based on my ability to speak the language fluently from my first year in Ladakh, and based on almost two decades of close contact with the Ladakhi people, I have been able to observe almost as an insider the effect of these changes on the Ladakhis' perception of themselves. Within the space of little more than a decade, feelings of pride gave way to what can best be described as a cultural inferiority complex. In the modern sector today, most young Ladakhis—the teenage boys in particular—are ashamed of their cultural roots and desperate to appear modern.

TOURISM

When tourism first began in Ladakh, it was as though people from another planet suddenly descended on the region. Looking at the modern world from something of a Ladakhi perspective, I became aware of how much mere successful our culture looks from the outside than we experience it on the inside.

Each day many tourists would spend as much as $100—an amount roughly equivalent to someone spending $50,000 per day in America. In the traditional subsistence economy, money played a minor role and was used primarily for luxuries—jewelry, silver, and gold. Basic needs—food, clothing, and shelter—were provided for without money. The labor one needed was free of charge, part of an intricate web of human relationships.

Ladakhis did not realize that money meant something very different for the foreigners; that back home they needed it to survive; that food, clothing, and shelter all cost money—a lot of money. Compared to these strangers, the Ladakhis suddenly felt poor.

This new attitude contrasted dramatically with the Ladakhis' earlier self-confidence. In 1975, I was shown around the remote village of Hemis Shukpachan by a young Ladakhi named Tsewang. It seemed to me that all the houses we saw were especially large and beautiful. I asked Tsewang to show me the houses where the poor people lived. Tsewang looked perplexed a moment, then responded, "We don't have any poor people here."

Eight years later I overheard Tsewang talking to some tourists. "If you could only help us Ladakhis," he was saying, "we're so poor."

Besides giving the illusion that all Westerners are multimillionaires, tourism and Western media images also help perpetuate another myth about modern life—that we never work. It looks as though our technologies do the work for us. In industrial society today, we actually spend more hours working than people in rural, agrarian economies, but that is not how it looks to the Ladakhis. For them, work is physical work: ploughing, walking, carrying things. A person sitting behind the wheel of a car or pushing buttons on a typewriter doesn't appear to be working.

MEDIA IMAGES

Development has brought not only tourism but also Western and Indian films and, more recently, television. Together they provide overwhelming images of luxury and power. There are countless tools, magical gadgets, and machines—machines to take pictures, machines to tell the time, machines to make fire, to travel from one place to another, to talk with someone far away. Machines can do everything; it's no wonder the tourists look so clean and have such soft, white hands.

Media images focus on the rich, the beautiful, and the mobile, whose lives are endless action and glamour. For young Ladakhis, the picture is irresistible. It is an overwhelmingly exciting version of an urban American Dream, with an emphasis on speed, youthfulness, super-cleanliness, beauty, fashion, and competitiveness. "Progress" is also stressed: Humans dominate nature, while technological change is embraced at all costs.

In contrast to these utopian images from another culture, village life seems primitive, silly, and inefficient. The one-dimensional view of modern life becomes a slap in the face. Young Ladakhis—whose parents ask them to choose a way of life that involves working in the fields and getting their hands dirty for very little or no money—feel ashamed of their own culture. Traditional Ladakh seems absurd compared with the world of the tourists and film heroes.

This same pattern is being repeated in rural areas all over the South, where millions of young people believe contemporary Western culture to be far superior to their own. This is not surprising: looking as they do from the outside, all they can see is the material side of the modern world—the side in which Western culture excels. They cannot so readily see the social or psychological dimensions: the stress, the loneliness, the fear of growing old. Nor can they see environmental decay, inflation, or unemployment. This leads young Ladakhis to develop feelings of inferiority, to reject their own culture wholesale, and at the same time to eagerly embrace the global monoculture. They rush after the sunglasses, walkmans, and blue jeans—not because they find those jeans more attractive or comfortable but because they are symbols of modern life.

Modern symbols have also contributed to an increase in aggression in Ladakh. Young boys now see violence glamorized on the screen. From Western-style films, they can easily get the impression that if they want to be modern, they should smoke one cigarette after another, get a fast car, and race through the countryside shooting people left and right.

WESTERN-STYLE EDUCATION

No one can deny the value of real education—the widening and enrichment of knowledge. But today in the Third World, education has become something quite different. It isolates children from their culture and from nature, training them instead to become narrow specialists in a Westernized urban environment. This process has been particularly striking in Ladakh, where modern schooling acts almost as a blindfold, preventing children from seeing the very context in which they live. They leave school unable to use their own resources, unable to function in their own world.

With the exception of religious training in the monasteries, Ladakh's traditional culture had no separate process called education. Education was the product of a person's intimate relationship with the community and the ecosystem. Children learned from grandparents, family, and friends and from the natural world.

Helping with the sowing, for instance, they would learn that on one side of the village it was a little warmer, on the other side a little colder. From their own experience children would come to distinguish different strains of barley and the specific growing conditions each strain preferred. They learned how to recognize and use even the tiniest wild plant, and how to pick out a particular animal on a faraway mountain slope. They learned about connection, process, and change, about the intricate web of fluctuating relationships in the natural world around them.

For generation after generation, Ladakhis grew up learning how to provide themselves with clothing and shelter: how to make shoes out of yak skin and robes from the wool of sheep; how to build houses out of mud and stone. Education was location-specific and nurtured an intimate relationship with the living world. It gave children an intuitive awareness that allowed them, as they grew older, to use resources in an effective and sustainable way.

None of that knowledge is provided in the modern school. Children are trained to become specialists in a technological rather than an ecological society. School is a place to forget traditional skills and, worse, to look down on them.

Western education first came to Ladakhi villages in the 1970s. Today there are about two hundred schools. The basic curriculum is a poor imitation of that taught in other parts of India, which itself is an imitation of British education. There is almost nothing Ladakhi about it.

Once, while visiting a classroom in Leh, the capital, I saw a drawing in a textbook of a child's bedroom that could have been in London or New York. It showed a pile of neatly folded handkerchiefs on a four-poster bed and gave instructions as to which drawer of the vanity unit to keep them in. Many other schoolbooks were equally absurd and inappropriate. For homework in one class, pupils were supposed to figure out the angle of incidence that the Leaning Tower of Pisa makes with the ground. Another time they were struggling with an English translation of *The Iliad*.

Most of the skills Ladakhi children learn in school will never be of real use to them. In essence, they receive an inferior version of an education appropriate for a New Yorker, a Parisian, or a Berliner. They learn from books written by people who have never set foot in Ladakh, who know nothing about growing barley at 12,000 feet or about making houses out of sun-dried bricks.

This situation is not unique to Ladakh. In every corner of the world today, the process called *education* is based on the same assumptions and the same Eurocentric model. The focus is on faraway facts and figures, on "universal" knowledge. The books propagate information that is believed to be appropriate for the entire planet. But since the only knowledge that can be universally applicable is far removed from specific ecosystems and cultures, what children learn is essentially synthetic, divorced from its living context. If they go on to higher education, they may learn about building houses, but these "houses" will be the universal boxes of concrete and steel. So too, if they study agriculture, they will learn about industrial farming: chemical fertilizers and pesticides; large machinery and hybrid seeds. The Western educational system is making us all poorer by teaching people around the world to use the same global resources, ignoring those that the environment naturally provides. In this way, Western-style education creates artificial scarcity and induces competition.

In Ladakh and elsewhere, modern education not only ignores local resources but, worse still, robs children of their self-esteem. Everything in school promotes the Western model and, as a direct consequence, makes children think of themselves and their traditions as inferior.

Western-style education pulls people away from agriculture and into the city, where they become dependent on the money economy. Traditionally there was no such thing as unemployment. But in the modern sector there is now intense competition for a very limited number of paying jobs, principally in the government. As a result, unemployment is already a serious problem.

Modern education has brought some obvious benefits, such as improvement in the literacy rate. It has also enabled the Ladakhis to be more informed about the forces at play in the world outside. In so doing, however, it has divided Ladakhis from each other and the land and put them on the lowest rung of the global economic ladder.

LOCAL ECONOMY VERSUS GLOBAL ECONOMY

When I first came to Ladakh the Western macroeconomy had not yet arrived, and the local economy was still rooted in its own soils. Producers and consumers were closely linked in a community-based economy. Two decades of development in Ladakh, however, have led to a number of fundamental changes, the most important of which is perhaps the new dependence on food and energy from thousands of miles away.

The path toward globalization depends upon continuous government investments. It requires the buildup of a large-scale industrial infrastructure that includes roads, mass communications facilities, energy installations, and schools for specialized education. Among other things, this heavily subsidized infrastructure allows goods produced on a large scale and transported long distances to be sold at artificially low prices—in many cases at lower prices than goods produced locally. In Ladakh, the Indian government is not only paying for roads, schools, and energy installations but is also bringing in subsidized food from India's breadbasket, the Punjab. Ladakh's local economy—which has provided enough food for its people for two thousand years—is now being invaded by produce from industrial farms located on the other side of the Himalayas. The food arriving in lorries by the ton is cheaper in the local bazaar than food grown a five-minute walk away. For many Ladakhis, it is no longer worthwhile to continue farming.

In Ladakh this same process affects not just food but a whole range of goods, from clothes to household utensils to building materials. Imports from distant parts of India can often be produced and distributed at lower prices than goods produced locally—again, because of a heavily subsidized industrial infrastructure. The end result of the long-distance transport of subsidized goods is that Ladakh's local economy is being steadily dismantled, and with it goes the local community that was once tied together by bonds of interdependence.

Conventional economists, of course, would dismiss these negative impacts, which cannot be quantified as easily as the monetary transactions that are the goal of economic development. They would also say that regions such as the Punjab enjoy a "comparative advantage" over Ladakh in food production, and it therefore makes economic sense for the Punjab to specialize in growing food, while Ladakh specializes in some other product, and that each trade with the other. But when distantly produced goods are heavily subsidized, often in hidden ways, one cannot really talk about comparative advantage or, for that matter, "free markets," "open competition in the setting of prices," or any of the other principles by which economists and planners rationalize the changes they advocate. In fact, one should instead talk about the unfair advantage that industrial producers enjoy, thanks to a heavily subsidized infrastructure geared toward large-scale, centralized production.

In the past, individual Ladakhis had real power, since political and economic units were small, and each person was able to deal directly with the other members of the community. Today, "development" is hooking people into ever-larger political and economic units. In political terms, each Ladakhi has become one of a national economy of eight hundred million, and, as part of the global economy, one of about six billion.

In the traditional economy, everyone knew they had to depend directly on family, friends, and neighbors. But in the new economic system, political and economic interactions take a detour via an anonymous bureaucracy. The fabric of local interdependence is disintegrating as the distance between people increases. So too are traditional levels of tolerance and cooperation. This is particularly true in the villages near Leh, where disputes and acrimony within close-knit communities and even families have dramatically increased in the last few years. I have even seen heated arguments over the allocation of irrigation water, a procedure that had previously been managed smoothly within a cooperative framework.

As mutual aid is replaced by dependence on faraway forces, people begin to feel powerless to make decisions over their own lives. At all levels, passivity, even apathy, is setting in; people are abdicating personal responsibility. In the traditional village, for example, repairing irrigation canals was a task shared by the whole community. As soon as a channel developed a leak, groups of people would start shoveling away to patch it up. Now people see this work as the government's responsibility and will let a channel go on leaking until the job is done for them. The more the government does for the villagers, the less the villagers feel inclined to help themselves.

In the process, Ladakhis are starting to change their perception of the past. In my early days in Ladakh, people would tell me there had never been hunger. I kept hearing the expression *tungbos zabos:* "enough to drink, enough to eat." Now, particularly in the modern sector, people can be heard saying, "Development is essential; in the past we couldn't manage, we didn't have enough."

The cultural centralization that occurs through the media is also contributing both to this passivity and to a growing insecurity. Traditionally, village life included lots of dancing, singing, and theater. People of all ages joined in. In a group sitting around a fire, even toddlers would dance, with the help of older siblings or friends. Everyone knew how to sing, to act, to play music. Now that the radio has come to Ladakh, people do not need to sing their own songs or tell their own stories. Instead, they can sit and listen to the *best* singer, the *best* storyteller. As a result, people become inhibited and self-conscious. They are no longer comparing themselves to neighbors and friends, who are real people—some better at singing but perhaps not so good at dancing—and they never feel themselves to be as good as the stars on the radio. Community ties are also broken when people sit passively listening to the very best rather than making music or dancing together.

ARTIFICIAL NEEDS

Before the changes brought by tourism and modernization, the Ladakhis were self-sufficient, both psychologically and materially. There was no desire for the sort of development that later came to be seen as a "need." Time and again, when I asked people about the changes that were coming, they showed no great interest in being modernized;

sometimes they were even suspicious. In remote areas, when a road was about to be built, people felt, at best, ambivalent about the prospect. The same was true of electricity. I remember distinctly how, in 1975, people in Stagmo village laughed about the fuss that was being made to bring electric lights to neighboring villages. They thought it was a joke that so much effort and money was spent on what they took to be a ludicrous gain: "Is it worth all that bother just to have that thing dangling from your ceiling?"

More recently, when I returned to the same village to meet the council, the first thing they said to me was, "Why do you bother to come to our backward village where we live in the dark?" They said it jokingly, but it was obvious they were ashamed of the fact they did not have electricity.

Before people's sense of self-respect and self-worth had been shaken, they did not need electricity to prove they were civilized. But within a short period the forces of development so undermined people's self-esteem that not only electricity but Punjabi rice and plastic have become needs. I have seen people proudly wear wristwatches they cannot read and for which they have no use. And as the desire to appear modern grows, people are rejecting their own culture. Even the traditional foods are no longer a source of pride. Now when I'm a guest in a village, people apologize if they serve the traditional roasted barley, *ngamphe,* instead of instant noodles.

Surprisingly, perhaps, modernization in Ladakh is also leading to a loss of individuality. As people become self-conscious and insecure, they feel pressure to conform, to live up to the idealized images—to the American Dream. By contrast, in the traditional village, where everyone wears the same clothes and looks the same to the casual observer, there seems to be more freedom to relax, and villagers can be who they really are. As part of a close-knit community, people feel secure enough to be themselves.

A PEOPLE DIVIDED

Perhaps the most tragic of all the changes I have observed in Ladakh is the vicious circle in which individual insecurity contributes to a weakening of family and community ties, which in turn further shakes individual self-esteem. Consumerism plays a central role in this whole process, since emotional insecurity generates hunger for material status symbols. The need for recognition and acceptance fuels the drive to acquire possessions that will presumably make you somebody. Ultimately, this is a far more important motivating force than a fascination for the things themselves.

It is heartbreaking to see people buying things to be admired, respected, and ultimately loved, when in fact the effect is almost inevitably the opposite. The individual with the new shiny car is set apart, and this furthers the need to be accepted. A cycle is set in motion in which people become more and more divided from themselves and from one another.

I've seen people divided from one another in many ways. A gap is developing between young and old, male and female, rich and poor, Buddhist and Muslim. The newly created division between the modern, educated expert and the illiterate, "backward" farmer is perhaps the biggest of all. Modernized inhabitants of Leh have more in common with someone from Delhi or Calcutta than they do with their own relatives who have remained on the land, and they tend to look down on anyone less modern. Some children living in the modern sector are now so distanced from their parents and grandparents that they don't even speak the same language. Educated in Urdu and English, they are losing mastery of their native tongue.

Around the world, another consequence of development is that the men leave their families in the rural sector to earn money in the modern economy. The men become part of the technologically based life outside the home and are seen as the only productive members of society. In Ladakh, the roles of male and female are becoming increasingly polarized as their work becomes more differentiated.

Women become invisible shadows. They do not earn money for their work, so they are no longer seen as "productive." Their work is not included as part of the Gross National Product. In government statistics, the 10 percent or so of Ladakhis who work in the modern sector are listed according to their occupations; the other 90 percent—housewives and traditional farmers—are lumped together as non-workers. Farmers and women are coming to be viewed as inferior, and they themselves are developing feelings of insecurity and inadequacy.

Over the years I have seen the strong, outgoing women of Ladakh being replaced by a new generation—women who are unsure of themselves and extremely concerned with their appearance. Traditionally, the way a woman looked was important, but her capabilities—including tolerance and social skills—were much more appreciated.

Despite their new dominant role, men also clearly suffer as a result of the breakdown of family and community ties. Among other things, they are deprived of contact with children. When men are young, the new macho image prevents them from showing any affection, while in later life as fathers, their work keeps them away from home.

BREAKING THE BONDS BETWEEN YOUNG AND OLD

In the traditional culture, children benefited not only from continuous contact with both mother and father but also from a way of life in which different age groups constantly interacted. It was quite natural for older children to feel a sense of responsibility for the younger ones. A younger child in turn looked up to the older ones with respect and admiration and sought to be like them. Growing up was a natural, noncompetitive learning process.

Now children are split into different age groups at school. This sort of leveling has a very destructive effect: By artificially creating social units in which everyone is the same age, the ability of children to help and to learn from each other is greatly reduced. Instead, conditions for competition are automatically created, because each child is put under pressure to be just as good as the next one. In a group of ten children of quite different ages, there will naturally be much more cooperation than in a group of ten twelve-year-olds.

The division into different age groups is not limited to school. Now there is a tendency to spend time exclusively with one's peers. As a result, a mutual intolerance between young and old has emerged. Young children nowadays have less and less contact with their grandparents, who often remain behind in the village. Living with many traditional families over the years, I have witnessed the depth of the bond between children and their grandparents. It is clearly a natural relationship that has a very different dimension from that between parent and child. To sever this connection is a profound tragedy.

Similar pressures contribute to the breakdown of the traditional family. The Western model of the nuclear family is now seen as the norm, and Ladakhis are beginning to feel ashamed about their traditional practice of polyandry, one of the cultural controls on population growth. As young people reject the old family structure in favor of monogamy, the population is rising significantly. At the same time, monastic life is losing its status, and the number of celibate monks and nuns is decreasing. This too contributes to population increase.

VIOLENCE

Interestingly, a number of Ladakhis have linked the rise in birth rates to the advent of modern democracy. "Power is a question of votes" is a current slogan, meaning that in the modern sector, the larger your group, the greater your access to power. Competition for jobs and political representation within the new centralized structures is increasingly dividing Ladakhis. Ethnic and religious differences have taken on a political dimension, causing bitterness and envy on a scale hitherto unknown.

This new rivalry is one of the most painful divisions that I have seen in Ladakh. Ironically, it has grown in proportion to the decline of traditional religious devotion. When I first arrived, I was struck by the mutual respect and cooperation between Buddhists and Muslims. But within the last few years, growing competition has actually culminated in violence. Earlier there had been individual cases of friction, but the first time I noticed any signs of group tension was in 1986, when I heard Ladakhi friends starting to define people according to whether they were Buddhist or Muslim. In the following years, there were signs here and there that all was not well, but no one was prepared for what happened in the summer of 1989, when fighting suddenly broke out between the two groups. There were major disturbances in Leh bazaar, four people were shot dead by police, and much of Ladakh was placed under curfew.

Since then, open confrontation has died down, but mistrust and prejudice on both sides continue to mar relations. For a people unaccustomed to violence and discord, this has been a traumatic experience. One Muslim woman could have been speaking for all Ladakhis when she tearfully told me, "These events have torn my family apart. Some of them are Buddhists, some are Muslims, and now they are not even speaking to each other."

The immediate cause of the disturbances was the growing perception among the Buddhists that the Muslim-dominated state government was discriminating against them in favor of the local Muslim population. The Muslims for their part were becoming anxious that as a minority group they had to defend their interests in the face of political assertiveness by the Buddhist majority.

However, the underlying reasons for the violence are much more far-reaching. What is happening in Ladakh is not an isolated phenomenon. The tensions between the Muslims of Kashmir and the Hindu-dominated central government in Delhi; between the Hindus and the Buddhist government in Bhutan; and between the Buddhists and the Hindu government in Nepal, along with countless similar disturbances around the world, are, I believe, all connected to the same underlying cause: The intensely centralizing force of the present global development model is pulling diverse peoples from rural areas into large urban centers and placing power and decision making in the hands of a few. In these centers, job opportunities are scarce, community ties are broken, and competition increases dramatically. In particular, young men who have been educated for jobs in the modern sector find themselves engaged in a competitive struggle for survival. In this situation, any religious or ethnic differences quite naturally become exaggerated and distorted. In addition, the group in power inevitably tends to favor its own kind, while the rest often suffer discrimination.

Most people believe that ethnic conflict is an inevitable consequence of differing cultural and religious traditions. In the South, there is an awareness that modernization is exacerbating tensions; but people generally conclude that this is a temporary phase on the road to "progress," a phase that will only end once development has erased cultural differences and created a totally secular society. On the other hand, Westerners attribute overt religious and ethnic strife to the liberating influence of democracy. Conflict, they assume, always smoldered beneath the surface, and only government repression kept it from bursting into flames.

It is easy to understand why people lay the blame at the feet of tradition rather than modernity. Certainly, ethnic friction is a phenomenon that predates colonialism, modernization, and globalization. But after nearly two decades of firsthand experience on the Indian subcontinent, I am convinced that "development" not only exacerbates tensions but actually creates them. As I have pointed out, development causes artificial scarcity, which inevitably leads to greater competition. Just as importantly, it puts pressure on people to conform to a standard Western ideal—blond, blue-eyed, "beautiful," and "rich"—that is impossibly out of reach.

Striving for such an ideal means rejecting one's own culture and roots—in effect, denying one's own identity. The inevitable result is alienation, resentment and anger. I am convinced that much of the violence and fundamentalism in the world today is a product of this process. In the industrialized world we are becoming increasingly aware of the impact of glamorous media and advertising images on individual self-esteem: problems that range from eating disorders such as anorexia and bulimia to violence over high-priced and "prestigious" sneakers and other articles of clothing. In the South, where the gulf between reality and the Western ideal is so much wider, the psychological impacts are that much more severe.

COMPARING THE OLD WITH THE NEW

There were many real problems in the traditional society, and development does bring some real improvements. However, when one examines the fundamentally important relationships—to the land, to other people, and to oneself—development takes on a different light. Viewed from this perspective, the differences between the old and the new become stark and disturbing. It becomes clear that the traditional nature-based society, with all its flaws and limitations, was more sustainable, both socially and environmentally. It was the result of a dialogue between human beings and their surroundings, a continuing coevolution that meant that, during two thousand years of trial and error, the culture kept changing. Ladakh's traditional Buddhist worldview emphasized change, but that change occurred within a framework of compassion and a profound understanding of the interconnectedness of all phenomena.

The old culture reflected fundamental human needs while respecting natural limits. And it worked. It worked for nature, and it worked for people. The various connecting relationships in the traditional system were mutually reinforcing and encouraged harmony and stability. Most importantly, having seen my friends change so dramatically, I have no doubt that the bonds and responsibilities of the traditional society, far from being a burden, offered a profound sense of security, which seems to be a prerequisite for inner peace and contentment. I am convinced that people were significantly happier before development and globalism than they are today. The people were cared for, and the environment was well sustained—which criteria for judging a society could be more important?

By comparison, the new Ladakh scores very poorly when judged by these criteria. The modern culture is producing environmental problems that, if unchecked, will lead to irreversible decline; and it is producing social problems that will inevitably lead to the breakdown of community and the undermining of personal identity.

Does Community Have a Value?

WENDELL BERRY

COMMUNITY IS A CONCEPT, LIKE HUMANITY or peace, that virtually no one has taken the trouble to quarrel with; even its worst enemies praise it. There is almost no product or project that is not being advocated in the name of community improvement. We are told that we, as a community, are better off for the power industry, the defense industry, the communications industry, the transportation industry, the agriculture industry, the food industry, the health industry, the medical industry, the insurance industry, the sports industry, the beauty industry, the entertainment industry, the mining industry, the education industry, the law industry, the government industry, and the religion industry. You could look into any one of these industries and find many people, some of them in influential positions, who are certifiably "community spirited."

In fact, however, neither our economy, nor our government, nor our educational system runs on the assumption that community has a value—a value, that is, that *counts* in any practical or powerful way. The values that are assigned to community are emotional and spiritual—"cultural"—which makes it the subject of pieties that are merely vocal. But does community have a value that is practical or economic? Is community necessary? If it does not have a value that is practical and economic, if it is not necessary, then can it have a value that is emotional and spiritual? Can "community values" be preserved simply for their own sake? Can people be neighbors, for example, if they do not need each other or help each other? Can there be a harvest festival where there is no harvest? Does economy have spiritual value?

Such questions are being forced upon us now by the loss of community. We are discouraged from dealing with them by their difficulty in such a time as this, and yet these questions and others like them are indispensable to us, for they describe the work that we must do. We can only be encouraged to see that this work, though difficult, is fascinating and hopeful. It is homework, doable in some part by everybody, useful to everybody—as far as possible unlike the massive, expensive, elitist projects that now engross virtually every government of the world.

But, before I go any farther, let me make clear what I mean by community. I will give as particular an example as I know.

• • •

My friends Loyce and Owen Flood married in October 1938, and moved to a farm in hilly country near Port Royal, Kentucky. She was seventeen; Owen was eighteen.

Loyce had graduated from high school and had been to college for a short while. Although she had been raised on a farm she did not know a great deal about being a farmer's wife on a small, poor, hillside

Berry, Wendell, "Does Community Have a Value?" in *Home Economics*, pp. 179–192.

place. She and Owen had little money, and she had to learn quickly the arts of subsistence.

Fortunately, they were living in a neighborhood of households closely bound together by family ties or friendships and by well-established patterns of work and pleasure. This neighborhood included, in varying degrees of intimacy and interdependence, nine households, all more or less within walking distance. The women kept house individually, but all the big jobs they did together: housecleaning, wallpapering, quilting, canning, cooking for field crews. Though Loyce looked up to these women and called them "Miss Suzy," "Miss Berthy," and so on, most of them were still fairly young, in their late thirties or early forties. They were a set of hearty, humorous, industrious women, who saw whatever was funny and loved to make up funny names for things.

They became Loyce's teachers, and now, nearly fifty years later, she remembers with warmth and pleasure their kindness to her and their care for her. They helped her to learn to cook and can, to work in the hog killing and in the field (for, at planting and harvest times, the women went to the field with the men); they looked after her when she was sick; they taught her practical things, and things having to do with their mutual womanhood and community life. Although she had more formal schooling than any of them, she says now, "Everything I know I learned from those people." And the men were as kind and useful to Owen as the women were to Loyce. "They took us under their wing," she says.

The men farmed their own farms, but, like the women, they did the big jobs together. And when they worked together, they ate together. They always had a big dinner. "They never shirked dinner," Loyce says, "that was one thing sure." In hot weather, chicken would be the only fresh meat available, and they ate a lot of chicken. The women were perfectionists at making noodles.

By our standards now, these people were poor. The farms ranged in size from thirty-seven to perhaps a hundred acres. But only the thirty-seven-acre farm was entirely tillable. The others included a lot of "hill and holler." Then, as now, most of the money made on the produce of that place was made by manufacturers and merchants in other places; probably no household grossed more than $1,000 a year. The subsistence economy was necessarily elaborate and strong. The people raised and slaughtered their own meat, raised vegetable gardens, produced their own milk, butter, and eggs. They gathered the wild fruit as it ripened. They canned and dried and cured and preserved. They spent little money. The cash for the household came mainly from the sale of cream, and each farm kept three or four milk cows for that purpose. Loyce remembers that her weekly cream check was three dollars; they budgeted half of that for groceries and gasoline for the car and half for payment on a debt.

These people worked hard, and without any modern conveniences or labor savers. They had no tractors, no electricity, no refrigerators, no washing machines, no vacuum cleaners. Their one luxury was the telephone party line, which cost fifty cents a month. But their work was in limited quantities; they did not work at night or away from home; they knew their work, they knew how to work, and they knew each other. Loyce says, "They didn't have to do a lot of explaining."

Their work was mingled with their amusement; sometimes it *was* their amusement. Talk was very important: They worked together and talked; they saw each other in Port Royal on Saturday night and talked; on Sunday morning they went to church early and stood around outside and talked; when church was over, they talked and were in no hurry to go home.

In the summer they would get fifty pounds of ice and make ice cream, and eat the whole freezer full, and sometimes make another, and eat that. In the winter they would all go to somebody's house at night and pop corn, and the men would play cards and the women would talk. They played cards a lot. One of the households had books that could be borrowed. Loyce's private amusements were reading and embroidery. She does not remember ever getting lonesome or bored.

• • •

There are, as I see it, two salient facts about this neighborhood of 1938:

1. It was effective and successful as a community. It did what we know that a good community does: It supported itself, amused itself, consoled itself, and passed its knowledge on to the young. It was something to build on.
2. It no longer exists. By the end of World War II, it was both reduced and altered, and the remnants of its old life are now mainly memories.

The reasons why it no longer exists are numerous and complexly interrelated. Some of them are: increased farm income during and after the war; improved roads and vehicles; the influence of radio and then of television; rising economic expectations; changing social fashions; school consolidation; and the rapid introduction of industrial technology into agriculture after the war. And so the disappearance of this community into the modern world and the industrial economy is both a fact and, to a considerable extent, an understandable fact.

But we must take care not to stop with the mere recognition and understanding of facts. We must go ahead to ask if the fact exists for our good, if it can be understood to our good, and if its existence is necessary or inescapable. After establishing that a community has died, for example, we must ask who has been served by its death.

Such a community as I have described has often been caricatured and ridiculed and often sentimentalized. But, looked at in its facts, as my friend recalls them, it escapes both extremes. The people were manifestly equal to their lot; they were not oafish or stupid. On the other hand, they were not perfect; they were not living an idyll. The community was not immune either to change or to the need to change. Anyone familiar with the history of farming on Kentucky hillsides knows its practices could always have been improved.

But another fact that we must now reckon with is that this community did not change by improving itself. It changed by turning away from itself, from its place, from its own possibility. Somehow the periphery exhausted and broke the center. This community, like thousands of similar ones, was not changed by anything that *it* thought of, nor by anything thought of by anybody who believed that community had a practical or an economic value. It was changed, partly to its own blame, by forces, originating outside itself, that did not consider, much less desire, the welfare or the existence of such communities. This community, like any other, had to change and needed to change, but what if its own life, its own good, had been the standard by which it changed, rather than the profit of distant entrepreneurs and corporations?

We are left with questions—that one and others.

Is such a community desirable? My answer, unhesitatingly, is yes. But that is an answer notoriously subject to the charge of sentimentality or nostalgia. People will ask if I "want to turn back the clock." And so I am pushed along to another question, a more interesting one: Is such a community necessary? Again, I think, the answer must be yes, and here we have access to some manner of proof.

For one thing, the place once occupied by that community is now occupied by people who are not, in the same close, effective sense, a community. The place is no longer central to its own interest and its own economy. The people do not support themselves so much from the place or so much by mutual work and help as their predecessors did; they furnish much less of their own amusement and consolation; purchasing has more and more replaced growing and making; and less and less of local knowledge and practical skill is passed on to the young. In 1938, the community and its economy were almost identical. Today, the community is defined mostly by the mere proximity of its people to one another. The people belong, often to their own detriment, to a *national* economy whose centers are far from home.

For another thing, we now have before us the failure of the industrial system of agriculture that supplanted the community and the ways of 1938. There is, so far as I am aware, no way of denying the failure of an agricultural system that destroys both land and people, as the industrial system is now doing. Obviously, we need a way of farming that attaches people to the land much more intimately, carefully, and democratically than the industrial system has been able to do, and we can neither establish good farming nor preserve it without successful communities.

It is easy to suppose, as many powerful people apparently have done, that the principle of subsistence on family farms and in rural communities will be bad for the larger economy, but this supposition has proved to be a dangerous and destructive error. Subsistence is bad for the industrial economy and for the paper economy of the financiers; it is good for the actual, real-world economy by which people live and are fed, clothed, and housed. For example, in 1938, in the time of subsistence, there were three thriving grocery stores that were patronized by the neighborhood I have been talking about—one at Drennon's Lick and two at Port Royal. Now there is only one, at Port Royal. The "standard of living" (determined, evidently, by how much money is spent) has increased, but community life has declined, economically and every other way. In the neighborhoods around Port Royal, we now have many modern conveniences, but we buy and pay for them farther and farther from home. And we have fewer and fewer people at home who know how to maintain these conveniences and keep them running. Port Royal, in other words, now exists for "the economy"—that abstract accumulation of monetary power that aggrandizes corporations and governments and that does not concern itself at all for the existence of Port Royal.

• • •

For many years, I think, the people of rural America have been struggling with the realization that we are living in a colony. It is an irony especially bitter for Americans that, having cast off the colonialism of England, we have proceeded to impose a domestic colonialism on our own land and people, and yet we cannot deny that most of the money made on the products that we produce in rural America—food and fiber, timber, mineable fuels and minerals of all kinds—is made by other people in other places. We cannot deny that all of these fundamental enterprises, as now conducted, involve the destruction of the land and the people. We cannot deny that there is no provision being made and no thought being taken in any segment of the rural economy for the long-term welfare of the people who are doing the work. Indeed, we cannot deny that our leaders appear to take for granted that the eventual destruction of lives, livelihoods, homes, and communities is an acceptable, though not a chargeable, cost of production. The washed-out farm and bankrupt farmer, the strip-mined mountain and the unemployed or diseased miner, the clear-cut forest and the depressed logging town—all are seen as the mere natural results of so-called free enterprise. The pattern of industrial "development" on the farm and in the forest, as in the coal fields, is that of combustion and exhaustion—not "growth," a biological metaphor that is invariably contradicted by industrial practice.

The fault of a colonial economy is that it is dishonest; it misrepresents reality. In practice, it is simply a way of keeping costs off the books of an exploitive interest. The exploitive interest is absent from the countryside exactly as if the countryside were a foreign colony. The result of this separation is that the true costs of production are not paid by the exploitive interest but only suffered by the exploited land and people. The colony, whether foreign or domestic, becomes unstable, both as an ecosystem and as a community because colonialism does not permit the development of strong local economies. The economy of a colony exports only "raw material" and imports only finished goods. It buys and sells on markets over which it has no control; thus, both markets drain value from the colony. The economy of a colony is thus as far as possible from E. F. Schumacher's just (and safe) ideal of "local production from local resources for local use."

The way that a national economy preys on its internal colonies is by the destruction of community—that is, by the destruction of the principle of local self-sufficiency not only in the local economy but also in the local culture. Thus, local life becomes the dependent—indeed, the victim—not just of the food industry, the transportation industry, the power industries, the various agribusiness industries, and so on, but also of the entertainment, the education, and the religion industries—all involving change from goods once cheap or free to expensive goods having to be bought.

That the economy of most of rural America is a colonial economy became plain as soon as the local economies of subsistence lapsed and were replaced by the so-called "consumer economy." The old local economies of subsistence, which in America were often incomplete and imperfect, were nevertheless sources of local strength and independence, and, as I have suggested, they were a beginning on which we could have built. Their replacement by the "consumer economy" has brought a helpless dependence on distant markets, on transported manufactured goods, on cash, and on credit.

• • •

Even so cursory a description of one of the old local subsistence economies as I gave at the beginning of this essay reveals that its economic assets were to a considerable extent intangible; culture-borne knowledge, attitudes, and skills; family and community coherence; family and community labor; and culture or religious principles such as respect for gifts (natural or divine), humility, fidelity, charity, and neighborliness. Such economies, furthermore, were mainly sun-powered, using plants and the bodies of animals and humans as "solar converters." By means of neighborhood, knowledge, and skill, they were turning free supplies to economic advantage. Theirs was an economy that took place, largely, off the books. The wonderful fact, then, is that those emotional and spiritual values that are now so inconsequentially associated with the idea of community were economic assets in the old communities, and they produced economic results.

This finding can be corroborated by an example that is contemporary, though somewhat more removed from my own acquaintance and culture. David Kline and his family, who are members of one of the Amish communities in the hilly country of eastern Ohio, have a farm of 123 acres that, even in the present hard times, is successful, both economically and agriculturally. It is one of the farms that, in my thinking about agriculture, I have used as a standard.

• • •

Of the Klineses' 123 acres, seventy-five are arable, twenty-nine are in permanent pasture, ten are forested, five are in orchard and gardens, and four are occupied by buildings. The major money-making enterprises of the farm are a dairy of twenty-three Guernsey cows (with about an equal number of heifers), and seven brood sows and a boar. The field crops, raised mainly to be fed on the place, are hay, corn, oats, and wheat. There are also the orchard and gardens, fifty laying hens, fifty pullets, fifty roosters for the table, and seven hives of bees. The farm combines commercial and subsistence enterprises, and its subsistence or household economy is obviously strong, producing some marketable surplus. In addition to the family's subsistence, this farm has been grossing about $50,000 a year and netting $25,000 to $30,000. In 1985, the gross was $47,000, and the net $25,000. In the midst of an agricultural depression, this is a startling accomplishment. Again, it is an economic result that is only somewhat computable; it is accounted for, in part, by the religious, cultural, family, and community coherence that is still maintained by the Old Order Amish, whose way of life, including their technology, makes possible the maximum utilization of natural (and therefore cheap or free) energy and fertility. A *full* accounting of David and Elsie Kline's economy would have to consider, as well, the extensive substitutions of natural and cultural gifts for purchased supplies.

That David Kline is also an excellent conservationist and a naturalist, who may delay a hay-cutting in order to allow bobolink fledglings to leave the nest, makes him even more useful to us as an example. For a part of the Amish understanding of good work, built into their technology and their methods, is this respect for nature. Farming, to the Klines, is the proper husbanding of nature, a stewardly care for the natural integrities and processes that precede and support the life of the farm.

David once attended a conference on the subject of community. What is community, the conferees were asking, and how can we have it? At some point, late in the proceedings, they asked David what community meant to him. He said that when he and his son were plowing in the spring he could look around him and see seventeen teams at work on the neighboring farms. He knew those teams and the men driving them, and he knew that if he were hurt or sick, those men and those teams would be at work on his farm.

Conditioned as we all are now by industrial assumptions, we must be careful not to miss or to underestimate the point of David's reply: It is a practical description of a spiritual condition. With the Amish, economy is not merely a function of community; the community and the economy are virtually the same. We might, indeed, call an Amish community a loving economy, for it is based on the love of neighbors, of creatures, and of places. The community accomplishes the productive work that is necessary to any economy; the economy supports and preserves the land and the people. The economy cannot prey on the community because it is not alienated from the community; it *is* the community. We should notice, too, that David has described the economic helpfulness, the charity, that is natural to the life of a community—and free to members—that has been replaced, among most of the rest of us, by the insurance industry.

• • •

But let us go a little further and speculate on the relation between a subsistence-based family economy, such as the Klineses', and a local—say, a county—economy. It is easy to assume, as I have said, that a subsistence-based family economy would be bad for the larger economy of the locality or county. But let us put beside the Kline farm an industrial Ohio farm of 640 acres (or one square mile), and let us say that this farm grosses $200,000 and nets $20,000. (I think that those are safe figures for our purpose, for midwestern industrial farmers have often found it impossible to net 10 percent of gross.) This square mile of land is one farm, farmed by one family, and therefore dependent on large-scale equipment. For years, as the people have been leaving the farms and the farms have been getting larger, the suppliers and servicers of farm machines, which have also been getting larger, have been withdrawing toward the larger towns. Now industrial farmers must sometimes drive astonishing distances for parts and repairs. For the farmer of a large industrial farm, the economic center has thus moved far beyond the local community, and we must suppose that a large percentage of his operating costs goes outside the local community.

But a square mile of even reasonably good land would contain five farms more or less the size of the Klineses'. If we suppose that the families would average three children each, this would increase the human population of the square mile from five to twenty-five. Such an increase in population implies a reduction in the scale of equipment, which in turn implies an increase of business for local suppliers and mechanics. Moreover, the population increase implies an increase of business for local shops and businesses of all kinds. If we use the Klines' farm economy as a base and suppose that the five farms average $50,000 a year gross and $25,000 a year net, then we see that they increase the gross income of the square mile by only $50,000. But, individually, the five farms each would net $5,000 a year more than the large farm, and together they would increase the net income on the square mile to $125,000, an increase of net over the large single farm of $105,000.

This comparison is not entirely speculative; Marty Strange says, for instance, that in Iowa, in the years 1976–1983, small farms achieved "*more* output per dollar invested" than large farms. "In fact," he says, "the larger the farm, the lower the output per dollar invested." However, since my comparison must be at least partly speculative, I can hope only to suggest a possibility that has been ignored: that strong communities imply strong local economies and vice versa—that, indeed, strong communities and strong local economies are identical.

Does this mean that, as local economies grow strong, there must be a concomitant weakening of the national economy? I do not think so. Strong local economies everywhere would, it seems to me, inevitably add up to strong national economies and to a strong world economy. The necessary distinction here is between temporary and permanent economic strength. A national economy may burgeon at the expense of its local economies, as ours has been doing, but, obviously, it can do so only for a while. The permanence of a national economy, we may be sure, would not be measurable by "gross national product," which may, after all, involve local net deficits of, say, topsoil or underground water. It would have to be measured by the health of its communities, both human and natural.

If these communities are given no standing in the computations, then all costs and benefits to and from the community are "externalized," and a business may show a profit to everybody else's loss. The cost of community to each of its members is restraint, limitation of scale. Its benefits, within acceptance of that limitation, are the many helps, human and natural, material and otherwise, that a community makes freely or cheaply available to its members. If an appropriate limitation of scale is not accepted, then the community is simply replaced by large-scale operators who work in isolation and by the dispossessed and excluded poor, who do not stay in place but drift into the cities where they are counted, no longer as "surplus" farmers (or miners or woods workers), but as "unemployed."

If the human and natural communities are given no standing in the computations, then the large farm or other large enterprise acts as a siphon to drain economic and other values out of the locality into the "gross national product." This happens because its technology functions on behalf of the national economy, not the local community.

The bait that has opened communities to exploitation and destruction has always been ready cash for local people. But there has never been as much cash forthcoming to the local people as to people elsewhere—not by far. The supply of ready cash has tended to be undependable or temporary, and it has usually come as a substitute for things more permanent and dearer than cash, and harder to replace, once lost.

The only preventive and the only remedy is for the people to choose one another and their place, over the rewards offered them by outside investors.

The local community must understand itself finally as a community of interest—a common dependence on a common life and a common ground. And because a community is, by definition, *placed,* its success cannot be divided from the success of its place, its natural setting and surroundings: its soils, forests, grasslands, plants and animals, water, light, and air. The two economies, the natural and the human, support each other; each is the other's hope of a durable and a livable life.

Global Eco-Justice
The Church's Mission in Urban Society

LARRY RASMUSSEN

There is a middle-aged book by a city pastor who addressed the rancid conditions of a neighborhood on my little island. The neighborhood was "Hell's Kitchen," just west of Times Square. The pastor was Walter Rauschenbusch. The book is *Christianity and the Social Crisis,* published in 1907. A remarkable passage in that book leads off this [essay].

CENTENNIAL SPIRITS

The passage portrays a gathering of centennial spirits. Imagine yourself gathering at century's close, and listen in.

"When the Nineteenth Century died," Rauschenbusch writes, "its Spirit descended to the vaulted chamber of the Past, where the Spirits of the dead Centuries sit on granite thrones together."[1] There the Spirit of the Eighteenth Century asks for the mandated report: "Tell thy tale, brother. Give us word of the human kind we left to thee."[2] The Spirit of the Nineteenth Century obliges.

> I am the Spirit of the Wonderful Century. I gave men mastery over nature. Discoveries and inventions, which lighted the black space of the past like lovely stars, have clustered in the Milky Way of radiance under my rule. One man does by the touch of his hand what the toil of a thousand slaves never did. Knowledge has unlocked the mines of wealth, and the hoarded wealth of today creates the vaster wealth of to-morrow. Man has escaped the slavery of Necessity and is free.
>
> I freed the thoughts of men. They face the facts and know their knowledge is common to all. The deeds of the East at even are known in the West at morn. They send their whispers under the seas and across the clouds.
>
> I broke the chains of bigotry and despotism. I made men free and equal. Every man feels the worth of his manhood.
>
> I have touched the summit of history. I did for mankind what none of you did before. They are rich. They are wise. They are free.[3]

The Spirits of the dead Centuries sit in silence for awhile, "with troubled eyes." Eventually the Spirit of the First Century speaks. It poses a series of searing questions about the Nineteenth Century claims that "You have made men rich. . . . You have made men wise. . . . You have set them free. . . . You have made them one."[4] The Spirit of the Nineteenth Century listens carefully. Soon its head sinks to its breast. Then it says:

> Your shame is already upon me. My great cities are as yours were. My millions live from hand to mouth. Those who toil longest have the least. My

Rasmussen, Larry, "Global Eco-Justice: The Church's Mission in Urban Society," in Dieter T. Hessel and Rosemary Radford Ruether, Eds., *Christianity and Ecology: Seeking the Well-Being of Earth and Humans,* pp. 515–529. Reprinted by permission of the Center for the Study of World Religions, Harvard Divinity School.

> thousands sink exhausted before their days are half spent. My human wreckage multiplies. Class faces class in sullen distrust. Their freedom and knowledge has only made men keener to suffer.[5]

Pensive, and now with troubled eyes of its own, the Spirit of the Nineteenth Century can only issue a request: "Give me a seat among you, and let me think why it has been so."[6]

Thinking "why it [was] so" for the Nineteenth Century was the work of many. Rauschenbusch and his colleagues in the Social Gospel joined to give voice in the final third of that century to what Ernst Troeltsch at about the same time called "the social question" or "the modern social problem." Troeltsch's own rendition of that is among the conclusions of his opus, *The Social Teaching of the Christian Churches* (1911).

> This social problem is vast and complicated. It includes the problem of the capitalist economic period and of the industrial proletariat created by it; and of the growth of militaristic and bureaucratic giant states; of the enormous increase in population, which affects colonial and world policy, of the mechanical technique, which produces enormous masses of materials and links up and mobilizes the whole world for purposes of trade, but which also treats men and labour like machines.[7]

"The social question" or "the modern social problem" was the effort to name the exploitative character and massively dislocating effects of rapidly developing industrial society. Troeltsch himself found Marx's treatment descriptively powerful and persuasive even though he rejected Marx's conclusion that economic forces created religious consciousness in such degree that religious impulses could not be considered independent, culturally creative forces in their own right. But Marx had the upending and downside effects of modernity largely right. I cite a passage now one hundred fifty years old (1848):

> Modern industry has established the world market. . . .
>
> The need of a constantly expanding market for its products chases the bourgeoisie over the whole surface of the globe. It must nestle everywhere, settle everywhere, establish connections everywhere.
>
> The bourgeoisie has through its exploitation of the world market given a cosmopolitan character to production and consumption in every country. . . . In place of the old wants, satisfied by the productions of the country, we find new wants, requiring for their satisfaction the products of distant lands. . . . In place of the old local and national seclusion and self-sufficiency, we have intercourse in every direction, universal inter-dependence of nations. And as in material, so also in intellectual production.[8]

To Marx's mind this dynamism means a tumultuous, permanently destabilized world and an epoch that sets modernity apart from all preceding ones.

> Constant revolutionizing of production, uninterrupted disturbance of all social conditions, everlasting uncertainty and agitation distinguish the bourgeois epoch from all earlier ones. All fixed, fast-frozen relations . . . and opinions are swept away, all new-formed ones become antiquated before they can ossify. All that is solid melts into air, all that is holy is profaned, and man is at last compelled to face, with sober senses, his real conditions of life and his relations with his kind. . . . The bourgeoisie, during its rule of scarce one hundred years, has created more massive and more colossal productive forces than have all preceding generations together. Subjection of Nature's forces to man, machinery, application of chemistry to industry and agriculture, steam-navigation, railways, electric telegraphs, clearing of whole continents for cultivation, canalization of rivers, whole populations conjured out of the ground—what earlier century had even a presentiment that such productive forces slumbered in the lap of social labor?[9]

Marx was wrong in his prophecy that the proletariat would dig the graves of the bourgeoisie and the coming socialist revolution would upend global capitalism itself. But he was right, as were Troeltsch and Rauschenbusch, that society was being atomized by the new economics of capitalism and that industrialized orders were humanly exploitative and alienating.

Still, the initial point here is that the last third of the nineteenth century gave voice to "the modern social problem," graphically reported by the otherwise triumphalist Spirit of the Nineteenth Century.

The social question persists. Indeed, the most

extraordinary fact a century later may well be the simplest one; namely, that both the tally of unprecedented accomplishment and the litany of steady shame that Rauschenbusch penned could simply be repeated in 2007, adjusted for extremes at certain notable points. After all, the Twentieth Century both promised more than the Nineteenth and delivered on it. Goods and services increased fiftyfold. Lifetimes for millions, even billions, doubled. Equal numbers—millions and billions—were lifted from misery. Children lived better than their parents. Education became a common treasure, as did better health. And the gifts of innumerable cultures, together with the amazing discoveries of science and inventions of technology, moved far beyond their home borders and at higher velocity.

At the same time, the Nineteenth Century's domestic problems of industrializing nations have now gone global with a vengeance. Mass unemployment, the bumpy ride of casino capitalism's rapid-fire investment and mobile business, the spreading distance between rich and poor in a confrontation of limousine plenty and homelessness, and limited revenues for limitless needs now afflict most societies, albeit in drastically different proportion. Not least, violence has been both common and extreme, and the twentieth century stands as easily the deadliest to date—something like 187 million lives lost to the waste of warfare alone, not to mention intimate violence and periodic spasms of genocide.

So perhaps the gathering of centennial spirits now would only rachet up the tally of weal and woe this particular immigrant urban pastor witnessed as he walked the streets of his Hell's Kitchen parish.

SOMETHING OLD, SOMETHING NEW

But I think not. There is a new dimension. The Spirit of the Twentieth Century would have to testify to a reality about which the spirits of previous dead centuries were silent. To put that in perspective, we must of needs return briefly to Rauschenbusch and the Social Gospel.

As noted, in the nineteenth century, progressive clergy and social theorists in the West joined popular movements of reform, especially workers' movements, to voice "the modern social problem" as one way of naming the results of the exploitative character of rapidly developing industrial society. These allies developed an extensive critique of the capitalist order and the political and economic efforts to govern it, envisioned the outlines of a more just and humane civilization, and took on an array of interlocking issues: the use and abuse of wealth, racial reform, tenement housing, women's rights, "machine" politics, police corruption, taxes, immigration policy, and political reform. Such issues were all matters of rapidly growing cities and industrial relations.

The chief difference from its nineteenth-century form is that the social question has now gone both global and urban. Indeed, one of the most stunning shifts in human demographics in history has happened in this century. For the very first time since we stood upright to sniff the air somewhere on the savannahs of East Africa, the majority of human beings now live in urban centers. As recently as a century ago, the vast majority lived in rural environments dominated by village and small town life.

Yet, the second salient point is not the global and urban dimensions of the social question, important as that is. The new factor is that, in the final third of the twentieth century, "the social question" has been joined by "the ecological question." The degradation of Earth's life-forms and life systems threatens the habitats of human and other creatures, habitats all of us depend upon for every breath we take, every morsel we chew, every song we sing, every right we claim, every enjoyment we cherish. While the causes are multiple, "the ecological question" is chiefly the result of the destructive downside of modern industrialized society, whether in the form of corporate capitalism or state socialism.

The social question is essentially the social justice question. The ecological question is essentially the question of sustainability. They must now be addressed together as the global eco-justice question.

GLOBALIZATION

The effort of these pages is to argue that global eco-justice—addressing the social and ecological questions together for the sake of comprehensive sustainability[10]—is the proper frame for the churches' urban mission. To put the normative concerns in the proper historical framework we will identify the ecosocial consequences arising from three consecutive waves of globalization, consequences largely ignored by dominant cultures and most churches.

"Globalization," as awkward a term as we can muster, is associated with many things: the information society, the erosion of borders and national sovereignty itself, footloose corporations hopscotching the planet, growing premiums for skilled workers and a growing plight for unskilled ones, and the free flow of finance capital.

But this late-twentieth-century rendition is too narrow a gauge. Globalization as it impacts cities and the biosphere itself and as it creates the need for global eco-justice has long been underway. It has been underway in the three waves of colonialism, development, and free trade global capitalism. These successive waves deeply altered not only human society, to give us "the social question" in its modern and largely urban form; they also upended the biotic community locally, regionally, even globally, to give us the present "ecological question." And (we will return to this) these waves largely sucked away any remaining sense of Earth itself as a living community in the churches' theology, liturgy, and mission. The present point, in short, is that all life's communities, human and nonhuman alike, have been and are being dramatically recast, not separately but together, as a single, enormously complex Community of Life comprised of the socio-communal, the biophysical, and the geoplanetary simultaneously.

The major outcome of all three waves of globalization, then, is not only what social scientists have documented from the rise of the new economy of the bourgeoisie to the present; namely, that globalization has been and is disruptive of intact local community and corrosive of settled traditions and ways of life. The waves of globalization have always been transformative, and sometimes destructive, of lifeforms themselves, together with the ecosystems that comprise their lifelines and matrix. Moreover, the waves of globalization continue to institutionalize the conquest of nature as the key to progress, just as they continue to live off nature's capital for the sake of human well-being, rather than off nature's income only.

We need not tarry long with the first wave of globalization: conquest, commerce, and Christianity as a mission faith self-identified by its (European) bearers as the "spread of civilization." If your genes are "Euro," you are part of by far the highest population growth rates and by far the largest and most dispersed emigration in recorded history—fifty million people left Europe in the long century, 1820–1930. You are also part of the greatest upending of both culture and nature in history, the greatest exchange and transformation of flora and fauna and crops and diseases the planet has experienced. That happened over the centuries trailing in they wake of Columbus's embarkation from Cadiz.

To underscore the matter again: globalization is about the socio-communal, biophysical, and even geoplanetary simultaneously in an upending of nature and culture together. Yet, the churches' urban mission has never taken account of this, preferring only the domain of the social question in the realm of the sociocommunal. This conceives justice in intrahuman terms only and circumscribes the moral world in a way that excludes human power's effects on the more-than-human world. Any church urban mission now that is not about the sociocommunal, biophysical, and geoplanetary together is truncated, blinded by its own anthropocentrism, and ignorant of its actual historical legacy.

Conquest and colonization in the name of a globalizing civilization effected chiefly through commerce is far from dead. But it merged some time ago with the second wave, development.

Consider a citation from the newspaper, *Perfil de la Jornada*, Mexico City, January 27, 1994. The date is important. The North American Free Trade Agreement went into effect at midnight, January 1 of that year. That very day, and by design, a hitherto unknown movement emerged from the forests of the state of Chiapas to challenge the Mexican government. But not only the national government; it intended—and still intends—to challenge the whole process by which Earth is now unified. The leader, Subcommandante Marcos, wrote a letter to the editor. It begins as follows:

> Suppose you want to travel to the South East of the country, and suppose you find yourself on one of the three roads which lead to the state of Chiapas. . . . Our wealth leaves this land not just on these three roads. Chiapas is bleeding to death in a thousand ways: through oil and gas pipelines, power supply lines, railway cars, banking accounts, trucks, ships and air planes, clandestine paths and paved roads. This land continues to pay its tribute to the empire: oil, electricity, cattle, coffee, maize, honey, tobacco. . . . Primary resources, several billion tons with various destina-

tions, flow out to . . . the USA, Canada, Holland, Germany, Italy, Japan, but always with the same destination: the empire.[11]

The citation from *Perfil de la Jornada* moves us from globalization as colonization to globalization as development. The message from Chiapas was a call, says Gustavo Esteva, for an end "to 500 years of oppression and 40 years of development."[12] An end to "40 years of development?" What's behind *that* Indian demand?

"Development" once meant "evolution from within." It was "synonymous with evolution as self-organization,"[13] a process in the hands of those who were developing. It was internally rather than externally guided. But, at least since President Harry Truman's inaugural address of 1949, development has come to mean the way of life of capitalist democracies as defined by modern economic progress and advanced science and technology. In Wolfgang Sachs's words: "The degree of civilization in a country could from now on be measured by its level of production. This new concept allowed the thousands of cultures to be separated into the two simple categories of 'developed' and 'underdeveloped.' [Modulated somewhat, 'developed' and 'developing'; or, to use the present term of the International Monetary Fund, "societies in transition."] Diverse societies were placed on a single progressive track, more or less advancing according to the criteria of production."[14] So, on one winter day in 1949, two-thirds of the planet's space and two billion of its peoples became "underdeveloped" and in need of another way of living, whether or not they had considered themselves so or not.

Globalization's third wave is post–Cold War free trade liberalization. Here, globalization is effected less by nation states, including those "societies in transition" in the South, than by global economic powers mastering global markets. I mention one characteristic only, the extension and intensification of market society in a capitalist mode. The market is not only the place of economic exchange now; it is a model of society itself and a logic for it, a determiner of relationships of all kinds. In that form it continues to do what colonization and development did; namely, further modernity's assault on intact local community and transformation of the land. People are largely shorn of "their self-organizing, self-governing, and self-provisioning capacities" in the places they live and on the terms and with the resources indigenous to those places, peoples, and traditions.[15]

But beyond this expanded reach there is corporate capitalism's deeper reach into nature, to life's fundamental building blocks themselves, and into the world of ideas and the knowledge banks of cultures. There is also the spectacular growth of global financial markets in which vast sums of financial capital change hands (about 1.4 trillion U.S.$ daily as of this writing), not in the interests even of development or any real exchange of goods and services, but in the search for speculative profits.[16]

Nature itself is increasingly colonized by capital. Life-forms are more and more the organic plastic of engineering and patents as rights *to* nature are favored over the rights *of* nature, if indeed the rights *of* nature get any hearing at all. And biodiversity, the source of all future life possibilities, is under assault most everywhere—by bioprospecting, biotechnology, the spread of global monoculture and mass production and consumption, not to mention the habitat intrusions of an expanding human economy. Third world, not only first world, agriculture is drawn into the orbit of colossal agribusiness firms. Farmers may in fact lose the right to produce and use their own seeds to commercial capitalism and governmental allies.[17]

In a closely related manner, information and knowledge itself are increasingly rendered commodities in a kind of enclosure of the intellectual commons. Intellectual property rights have become private rights rather than common rights as international trade talks, pushed by corporate interests and their governmental allies, proceed.

In short, the vertical reach of global free trade capitalism into nature, knowledge, and culture matches its intensified and extended horizontal one.

Allow a summary and commentary from the *Nation*. Recent economic globalization is arguably the most far-reaching redesign and centralization of the planet's political and economic arrangements since the Industrial Revolution itself. Yet the profound implications are not given genuine public airing by elected officials, by educational institutions, by the media, or by faith communities. So the advocates of globalization have free reign at the same time that they lump the dissenters together as "protectionists" and dismiss them as out-of-touch throwbacks to pre-1989 worlds. But, of course, what we really have is corporate protectionism that fails to protect jobs, communities, effective democracy, and nature.[18] We have the triumph on a new scale of the mobility and investment of corporations and banks, the technologically enhanced acceleration of global development and commerce, a profound, rather abrupt shift in political power that "liberates" even currency from many nations' control, and, in fact, the elimination of most regulatory controls over global corporate activity.[19]

The point above, and Jerry Mander's in the *Nation,* is not only the dimensions of the new; it is the failure of corporations, elected officials, educators, media powers, and faith communities to see and air critical connections among issues. These issues—crowded urban megapolises, accelerated climate change, the growth of global poverty amidst unprecedented wealth, the stagnation and sometimes lowering of wages while stocks soar, the privatization and sometimes elimination of social services, the destruction of plants, wildlife, wilderness, wetlands, and vast amounts of habitat, and the protests of Chiapan Indians—are not presented as complex outcomes of interacting global policies. They are not understood as part of the vast transformation of nature and society together on this end of three cumulative waves of globalization. So the *New York Times* can carry two front-page stories side by side, "As Boom Fails, Malaysia Sends Migrants Home"[20] and "One in Every 8 Plant Species Is Imperiled, a Survey Finds,"[21] and can spell out the terms of the largest merger in history to that date ($70 billion), of Citibank and the Travellers Group, without a hint of any kind in these stories, on the editorial or the op-ed page, that they belong together in any way. Eyes to see and ears to hear Earth as factually a comprehensive community without an exit seem utterly to fail us. We don't recognize the linkages, from the inside out, of the social and the environmental.

A PROPOSED FRAMEWORK

Given these waves of globalization, the task of addressing the social question (social justice) and the ecological question (sustainability) simultaneously as the global eco-justice question requires far-reaching changes. These changes frame any consideration of Christianity itself as a positive force for the next period of history. The changes are those that move us from a presently unsustainable Earth to a sustainable one. The changes entail eight transitions: an *economic* transition that lives off nature's "income" instead of "capital" and builds into all economic activity, including the cost of goods, that which is required for nature's regeneration and renewal indefinitely; a *social* transition to a far broader sharing of nature's income and human wealth, together with increased opportunities for sustaining and sustainable livelihoods for all; an *institutional* transition that combines greater cross-national cooperation in order to address global problems with greater attention to what makes for sustainable local and regional communities; an *informational* transition in which research, education, and global monitoring allow large numbers of people to understand the interrelated problems they face and offer them the means to address these problems; a *demographic* transition from an unprecedented population explosion to a roughly stable world population; a *technological* transition which effectively means minimal environmental impact per person; a *moral* transition to a framework that includes the societal, the biophysical, and the geoplanetary—the whole Community of Life—as the arena of responsibility; and a *religious* transition to earthkeeping as the religious calling and vocation common to all the world's religions.[22]

These transitions in turn require their own institutional and policy vision and framework. That vision and framework should not be that of "sustainable development," if by that is meant what most people mean; namely, how to "green" the growing global economy so as to make it environmentally sustainable. Such a course assumes, and leaves, the powerful forces of centuries-deep globalization in command. The result will likely be a hard, brown world tinged with soft, green edges for the rich and aspiring-rich. Trying to wrap the besieged environment around the ever-expanding global economy is not the way to go.

The way to go is "sustainable community." Its basic question is how we wrap both economy and environment around healthy local and regional communities. The proper goal of an economy is not increased production and consumption as such. It is materially healthy communities, for the long haul. To this end, sustainable community in our kind of world requires a considerable devolution of economic and political power as well as strengthening certain international networks and institutions. It requires a heightened status and respect for all life and a sphere of responsibility that includes the whole Community of Life. In the phrase of one author, this is "cosmopolitan localism." It refers to "new ways of revitalizing and protecting local communities while participating in wider associations to check the growing domination of economic globalization"[23] and offer politically acceptable ways for the social protection of land, labor, local capital, and culture.

CLOSING

Too little has been said in these pages. The discussion has only now brought us to the proper query: What presently makes for sustainable community in the great urban areas that presently form a global necklace, and what roles might churches play in alliances that would help create sustainable cities? Instead of answering that question, I have framed it. I have conceptually staked out an ungainly territory encompassing the sociocommunal, the biophysical, and the geoplanetary together. While that is necessary, it is only a beginning.

The specific roles churches and other religious communities might play is being addressed in several metropolitan areas.[24] This brings me to the topic mentioned in passing and postponed: the churches' loss—in theology, liturgy, and mission—of Earth itself as a living community.

The constructive ecclesial task is both long-term and immediate. The pressing immediate task is to address, one by one, the downside effects in city neighborhoods of the global economy's impacts and to try to find, in practice and policy, those incremental changes that slowly build toward sustainable communities. The closely related long-term task—give it a century or so—is liturgical, theological, educational, and practical (referring here to church-institutional practices). The long-term task, succinctly put, is the conversion of Christianity to Earth. That means overcoming, in an urban setting, the collective estrangement from the numinous powers that create, sustain, and, yes, extinguish human life itself. It means recovering in new forms, fitted to urban living, of deep genetic and ancestral reciprocity with the animate earth. It means sensing in our own senses that all forms of life are *experiencing* forms that have their own indispensable agency in the wonder and mystery we call life.[25]

It means experiencing the presence and power of none other or less than God incarnate in the more-than-human universe that surrounds and surpasses the burning mysteries of our own fragile and precious lives, wherever they are lived. It means the embrace of Earth as the providing ground that is bone of our bone and flesh of our flesh and the only habitat for living the lives we can and desire to have. It means the vision of the city where, though the temple is no longer there, fruited trees of life line the banks of rivers of crystal water flowing from the throne of God located right downtown. It means a practical everyday mysticism, an aesthetic, and an ethic that knows in gut and heart as well as head that the redemption of each creature is required for the redemption of all and that the borders of all life, indeed of inorganic being and the galaxies themselves, all leak into the presence of God and bespeak the power of the same. It means conversion to urban ground, and all ground, as holy ground and the land of promise. It means cities that are green and are, in fact, food-producing regions.

Finally, then, conversion to Earth on this end of the waves of globalization is the church's eco-justice urban mission, both short- and long-term.

NOTES

1. Walter Rauschenbusch, *Christianity and the Social Crisis* (New York: Macmillan Co., 1907), 211.
2. Ibid.
3. Ibid.
4. Ibid., 212.
5. Ibid.
6. Ibid.
7. Ernst Troeltsch, *The Social Teaching of the Christian Churches* (Chicago: University of Chicago Press, 1960), 2:1010.
8. Karl Marx, *The Communist Manifesto* (Chicago: Henry Regnery Co., 1954), 20–21.
9. Ibid., 20, 23.
10. The subject of my book, *Earth Community, Earth Ethics* (Maryknoll, N.Y.: Orbis Books, 1996).
11. Cited in Wolfgang Sachs, *The Political Anatomy of "Sustainable Development,"* The Wuppertal Institute, Occasional Papers, no. 35, May 1995: 23. The translation is Sachs's.
12. Gustavo Esteva, "Basta!" *Ecologist* 24, no. 3 (May/June 1994): 83.

13. I draw here from Vandana Shiva, *Biopiracy: The Plunder of Nature and Knowledge* (Toronto: Between the Lines Press, 1997), 107.

14. Wolfgang Sachs as cited by Wesley Granberg-Michaelson, *Redeeming the Creation: The Rio Earth Summit: Challenges for the Churches* (Geneva: WCC Publications, 1992), 1.

15. Shiva, *Biopiracy,* 115.

16. David Korten, "Economic Globalization: The War against Markets, Democracy, People, and Nature," in *A World That Works: Building Blocks for a Just and Sustainable Society,* ed. Trent Schroyer (New York: Bootstrap Press, 1997), 232.

17. Hans Leenders, former secretary general of the International Association of Plant Breeders for the Protection of Plant Varieties, argues for this: "Even though it has been a tradition in most countries that a farmer can save seed from his own crop, it is under the changing circumstances not equitable that farmers can use this seed and grow a commercial crop out of it without payment of a royalty; the seed industry will have to fight hard for a better kind of protection." Cited from Shiva, *Biopiracy,* 53.

18. Jerry Mander, "The Dark Side of Globalization: What Media Are Missing," *Nation* 263, no. 3 (15/22 July 1996): 10.

19. Mander, "The Dark Side of Globalization," 10.

20. To Indonesia, chiefly. "If we must grow calluses on our hearts, so be it," an editorial in the *Straits Times* of Singapore responded. Reported in the *New York Times,* 9 April 1998, A1.

21. *New York Times,* 9 April 1998, A1.

22. An adaptation from the discussion in M. Mitchell Waldrop, *Complexity: The Emerging Science at the Edge of Order and Chaos* (New York: Simon and Schuster, 1992), 350–51.

23. Trent Schroyer, "Introduction: Working Alternatives for a World That Works," in *A World That Works: Building Blocks for a Just and Sustainable Society,* ed. Trent Schroyer (New York: Bootstrap Press, 1997), 1.

24. E.g., see *One Creation, One People, One Place,* a statement of the Interreligious Sustainability Project of Metropolitan Chicago, initiated by Stephen A. Perkins, Center for Neighborhood Technology, 2125 W. North Ave., Chicago, IL 60647. In New York City, I coteach seminary courses entitled "Ecology and Ethics in the 'hood" and "Environmental Racism" that explore local/global eco-justice.

25. These lines are suggested by David Abram's *The Spell of the Sensuous: Perception and Language in a More-Than-Human World* (New York: Random House, 1997), 7–11.

Discussion Questions

1. Are there limits to growth? What determines these limits?
2. Why is there such enthusiasm throughout the world for emulating the American way of life? How might different cultures retain their pride and ensure their survival in the face of cultural homogenization?
3. Why have countries that have opened up their economies to foreign investment seen increases in poverty?
4. Is globalization a threat to community? How? What exactly is at risk?
5. What is a colonial economy? How do colonial economies hide certain kinds of costs? What alternative systems can you envision?

Further Reading

Barber, Benjamin R., *Jihad vs. McWorld,* New York: Times Books, 1995.

Berry, Wendell, *The Unsettling of America,* San Francisco: Sierra Club Books, 1977.

Hirst, Paul, and Grahame Thompson, *Globalization in Question: The International Economy and the Possibilities of Governance,* Cambridge, U.K.: Polity Press, 1996.

Karliner, Joshua, *The Corporate Planet: Ecology and Politics in the Age of Globalization,* San Francisco: Sierra Club Books, 1997.

Korten, David, *When Corporations Rule the World,* West Hartford, Conn.: Kumarian Press, 1995.

LaFeber, Walter, *Michael Jordan and the New Global Capitalism,* New York : W. W. Norton, 1999.

Mander, Jerry, and Edward Goldsmith, Eds., *The Case Against the Global Economy and for a Turn Toward the Local,* San Francisco: Sierra Club Books, 1995.

Ritzer, George, *The McDonaldization of Society,* Thousand Oaks, Calif.: Pine Forge Press, 2000.

Sale, Kirkpatrick, *Dwellers in the Land: The Bioregional Vision,* San Francisco: Sierra Club Books, 1985.

Sassen, Saskia, *Globalization and Its Discontents: Essays on the New Mobility of People and Money,* New York: New Press, 1999.

Sivaraksa, Sulak, and Chandra Muzaffar, *Alternative Politics for Asia: A Buddhist Muslim Dialogue,* New York: Lantern Books, 2000.

Appendix: The Earth Charter

PREAMBLE

We stand at a critical moment in Earth's history, a time when humanity must choose its future. As the world becomes increasingly interdependent and fragile, the future at once holds great peril and great promise. To move forward we must recognize that in the midst of a magnificent diversity of cultures and life forms we are one human family and one Earth community with a common destiny. We must join together to bring forth a sustainable global society founded on respect for nature, universal human rights, economic justice, and a culture of peace. Towards this end, it is imperative that we, the peoples of Earth, declare our responsibility to one another, to the greater community of life, and to future generations.

Earth, Our Home

Humanity is part of a vast evolving universe. Earth, our home, is alive with a unique community of life. The forces of nature make existence a demanding and uncertain adventure, but Earth has provided the conditions essential to life's evolution. The resilience of the community of life and the well-being of humanity depend upon preserving a healthy biosphere with all its ecological systems, a rich variety of plants and animals, fertile soils, pure waters, and clean air. The global environment with its finite resources is a common concern of all peoples. The protection of Earth's vitality, diversity, and beauty is a sacred trust.

The Global Situation

The dominant patterns of production and consumption are causing environmental devastation, the depletion of resources, and a massive extinction of species. Communities are being undermined. The benefits of development are not shared equitably and the gap between rich and poor is widening. Injustice, poverty, ignorance, and violent conflict are widespread and the cause of great suffering. An unprecedented rise in human population has overburdened ecological and social systems. The foundations of global security are threatened. These trends are perilous—but not inevitable.

The Challenges Ahead

The choice is ours: form a global partnership to care for Earth and one another or risk the destruction of ourselves and the diversity of life. Fundamental changes are needed in our values, institutions, and ways of living. We must realize that when basic needs have been met, human development is primarily about being more, not having more. We have the knowledge and technology to provide for all and to reduce our impacts on the environment. The emergence of a global civil society is creating new opportunities to build a democratic and humane world. Our environmental, economic, political, social, and spiritual challenges are interconnected, and together we can forge inclusive solutions.

Universal Responsibility

To realize these aspirations, we must decide to live with a sense of universal responsibility, identifying ourselves with the whole Earth community as well as our local communities. We are at once citizens of different nations and of one world in which the local and global are linked. Everyone shares responsibility for the present and future well-being of the human family and the larger living world. The spirit of human solidarity and kinship with all life is strengthened when we live with reverence for the mystery of being, gratitude for the gift of life, and humility regarding the human place in nature.

We urgently need a shared vision of basic values to provide an ethical foundation for the emerging world community. Therefore, together in hope we affirm the following interdependent principles for a sustainable way of life as a common standard by which the conduct of all individuals, organizations, businesses, governments, and transnational institutions is to be guided and assessed.

PRINCIPLES

I. Respect and Care for the Community of Life

1. Respect Earth and life in all its diversity.
    a. Recognize that all beings are interdependent and every form of life has value regardless of its worth to human beings.
    b. Affirm faith in the inherent dignity of all human beings and in the intellectual, artistic, ethical, and spiritual potential of humanity.
2. Care for the community of life with understanding, compassion, and love.
    a. Accept that with the right to own, manage, and use natural resources comes the duty to prevent environmental harm and to protect the rights of people.
    b. Affirm that with increased freedom, knowledge, and power comes increased responsibility to promote the common good.
3. Build democratic societies that are just, participatory, sustainable, and peaceful.
    a. Ensure that communities at all levels guarantee human rights and fundamental freedoms and provide everyone an opportunity to realize his or her full potential.
    b. Promote social and economic justice, enabling all to achieve a secure and meaningful livelihood that is ecologically responsible.
4. Secure Earth's bounty and beauty for present and future generations.
    a. Recognize that the freedom of action of each generation is qualified by the needs of future generations.
    b. Transmit to future generations values, traditions, and institutions that support the long-term flourishing of Earth's human and ecological communities.

In order to fulfill these four broad commitments, it is necessary to:

II. Ecological Integrity

5. Protect and restore the integrity of Earth's ecological systems, with special concern for biological diversity and the natural processes that sustain life.

a. Adopt at all levels sustainable development plans and regulations that make environmental conservation and rehabilitation integral to all development initiatives.

b. Establish and safeguard viable nature and biosphere reserves, including wild lands and marine areas, to protect Earth's life support systems, maintain biodiversity, and preserve our natural heritage.

c. Promote the recovery of endangered species and ecosystems.

d. Control and eradicate non-native or genetically modified organisms harmful to native species and the environment, and prevent introduction of such harmful organisms.

e. Manage the use of renewable resources such as water, soil, forest products, and marine life in ways that do not exceed rates of regeneration and that protect the health of ecosystems.

f. Manage the extraction and use of non-renewable resources such as minerals and fossil fuels in ways that minimize depletion and cause no serious environmental damage.

6. Prevent harm as the best method of environmental protection and, when knowledge is limited, apply a precautionary approach.

a. Take action to avoid the possibility of serious or irreversible environmental harm even when scientific knowledge is incomplete or inconclusive.

b. Place the burden of proof on those who argue that a proposed activity will not cause significant harm, and make the responsible parties liable for environmental harm.

c. Ensure that decision making addresses the cumulative, long-term, indirect, long distance, and global consequences of human activities.

d. Prevent pollution of any part of the environment and allow no build-up of radioactive, toxic, or other hazardous substances.

e. Avoid military activities damaging to the environment.

7. Adopt patterns of production, consumption, and reproduction that safeguard Earth's regenerative capacities, human rights, and community well-being.

a. Reduce, reuse, and recycle the materials used in production and consumption systems, and ensure that residual waste can be assimilated by ecological systems.

b. Act with restraint and efficiency when using energy, and rely increasingly on renewable energy sources such as solar and wind.

c. Promote the development, adoption, and equitable transfer of environmentally sound technologies.

d. Internalize the full environmental and social costs of goods and services in the selling price, and enable consumers to identify products that meet the highest social and environmental standards.

e. Ensure universal access to health care that fosters reproductive health and responsible reproduction.

f. Adopt lifestyles that emphasize the quality of life and material sufficiency in a finite world.

8. Advance the study of ecological sustainability and promote the open exchange and wide application of the knowledge acquired.

a. Support international scientific and technical cooperation on sustainability, with special attention to the needs of developing nations.

b. Recognize and preserve the traditional knowledge and spiritual wisdom in all cultures that contribute to environmental protection and human well-being.

c. Ensure that information of vital importance to human health and environmental protection, including genetic information, remains available in the public domain.

III. Social and Economic Justice

9. Eradicate poverty as an ethical, social, and environmental imperative.

a. Guarantee the right to potable water, clean air, food security, uncontaminated soil, shelter, and safe sanitation, allocating the national and international resources required.

b. Empower every human being with the education and resources to secure a sustainable livelihood, and provide social security and safety nets for those who are unable to support themselves.

c. Recognize the ignored, protect the vulnerable, serve those who suffer, and enable them to develop their capacities and to pursue their aspirations.

10. Ensure that economic activities and institutions at all levels promote human development in an equitable and sustainable manner.

a. Promote the equitable distribution of wealth within nations and among nations.

b. Enhance the intellectual, financial, technical, and social resources of developing nations, and relieve them of onerous international debt.

c. Ensure that all trade supports sustainable resource use, environmental protection, and progressive labor standards.

d. Require multinational corporations and international financial organizations to act transparently in the public good, and hold them accountable for the consequences of their activities.

11. Affirm gender equality and equity as prerequisites to sustainable development and ensure universal access to education, health care, and economic opportunity.

a. Secure the human rights of women and girls and end all violence against them.

b. Promote the active participation of women in all aspects of economic, political, civil, social, and cultural life as full and equal partners, decision makers, leaders, and beneficiaries.

c. Strengthen families and ensure the safety and loving nurture of all family members.

12. Uphold the right of all, without discrimination, to a natural and social environment supportive of human dignity, bodily health, and spiritual well-being, with special attention to the rights of indigenous peoples and minorities.

a. Eliminate discrimination in all its forms, such as that based on race, color, sex, sexual orientation, religion, language, and national, ethnic or social origin.

b. Affirm the right of indigenous peoples to their spirituality, knowledge, lands and resources and to their related practice of sustainable livelihoods.

c. Honor and support the young people of our communities, enabling them to fulfill their essential role in creating sustainable societies.

d. Protect and restore outstanding places of cultural and spiritual significance.

IV. Democracy, Nonviolence, and Peace

13. Strengthen democratic institutions at all levels, and provide transparency and accountability in governance, inclusive participation in decision making, and access to justice.

a. Uphold the right of everyone to receive clear and timely information on environmental matters and all development plans and activities which are likely to affect them or in which they have an interest.

b. Support local, regional and global civil society, and promote the meaningful participation of all interested individuals and organizations in decision making.

c. Protect the rights to freedom of opinion, expression, peaceful assembly, association, and dissent.

d. Institute effective and efficient access to administrative and independent judicial procedures, including remedies and redress for environmental harm and the threat of such harm.

e. Eliminate corruption in all public and private institutions.

f. Strengthen local communities, enabling them to care for their environments, and assign environmental responsibilities to the levels of government where they can be carried out most effectively.

14. Integrate into formal education and life-long learning the knowledge, values, and skills needed for a sustainable way of life.

a. Provide all, especially children and youth, with educational opportunities that empower them to contribute actively to sustainable development.

b. Promote the contribution of the arts and humanities as well as the sciences in sustainability education.

c. Enhance the role of the mass media in raising awareness of ecological and social challenges.

d. Recognize the importance of moral and spiritual education for sustainable living.

15. Treat all living beings with respect and consideration.

a. Prevent cruelty to animals kept in human societies and protect them from suffering.

b. Protect wild animals from methods of hunting, trapping, and fishing that cause extreme, prolonged, or avoidable suffering.

c. Avoid or eliminate to the full extent possible the taking or destruction of non-targeted species.

16. Promote a culture of tolerance, nonviolence, and peace.

a. Encourage and support mutual understanding, solidarity, and cooperation among all peoples and within and among nations.

b. Implement comprehensive strategies to prevent violent conflict and use collaborative problem solving to manage and resolve environmental conflicts and other disputes.

c. Demilitarize national security systems to the level of a non-provocative defense posture, and convert military resources to peaceful purposes, including ecological restoration.

d. Eliminate nuclear, biological, and toxic weapons and other weapons of mass destruction.

e. Ensure that the use of orbital and outer space supports environmental protection and peace.

f. Recognize that peace is the wholeness created by right relationships with oneself, other persons, other cultures, other life, Earth, and the larger whole of which all are a part.

THE WAY FORWARD

As never before in history, common destiny beckons us to seek a new beginning. Such renewal is the promise of these Earth Charter principles. To fulfill this promise, we must commit ourselves to adopt and promote the values and objectives of the Charter.

This requires a change of mind and heart. It requires a new sense of global interdependence and universal responsibility. We must imaginatively develop and apply the vision of a sustainable way of life locally, nationally, regionally, and globally. Our cultural diversity is a precious heritage and different cultures will find their own distinctive ways to realize the vision. We must deepen and expand the global dialogue that generated the Earth Charter, for we have much to learn from the ongoing collaborative search for truth and wisdom.

Life often involves tensions between important values. This can mean difficult choices. However, we must find ways to harmonize diversity with unity, the exercise of freedom with the common good, short-term objectives with long-term goals. Every individual, family, organization, and community has a vital role to play. The arts, sciences, religions, educational institutions, media, businesses, nongovernmental organizations, and governments are all called to offer creative leadership. The partnership of government, civil society, and business is essential for effective governance.

In order to build a sustainable global community, the nations of the world must renew their commitment to the United Nations, fulfill their obligations under existing international agreements, and support the implementation of Earth Charter principles with an international legally binding instrument on environment and development.

Let ours be a time remembered for the awakening of a new reverence for life, the firm resolve to achieve sustainability, the quickening of the struggle for justice and peace, and the joyful celebration of life.

Resources

Au Sable Institute of Environmental Studies
7526 Sunset Trail NE
Mancelona, MI 49659
http://www.ausable.org/

Coalition on the Environment and Jewish Life
443 Park Avenue South
New York, NY 10016
(212) 684-6950 ext.210
info@coejl.org
http://www.coejl.org/

EarthCare, Inc.
P.O. Box 23291
Chattanooga, TN 37422
http://www.alltel.net/~jrossing/ecare.html

Earth Sangha
10123 Commonwealth Boulevard
Fairfax, VA 22032-2707
(703) 764-4830
info@earthsangha.org
http://www.earthsangha.org/index.html

Ecojustice Working Group
National Council of Churches
475 Riverside Drive, #812
New York, NY 10115
(212) 870-2385/2386
fax (212) 870-2265
ecojustice@ncccusa.org
http://www.webofcreation.org/ncc/Workgrp.html

Ecunet
http://www.ecunet.org/

Evangelical Environmental Network
10 E. Lancaster Avenue
Wynnewood, PA 19096-3495
http://www.esa-online.org/een/

Forum on Religion and Ecology
P.O. Box 380875
Cambridge, MA 02238-0875
phone/fax (617) 332-0337
fore@environment.harvard.edu
http://www.environment.harvard.edu/religion/

Franciscan Ecological Project "Stoutenburg"
Stoutenburgerlaan 5
NL 3835 PB Stoutenburg
The Netherlands
+ 31 33 494 55 00
fax + 31 33 432 55 22
stoutenburg@hetnet.nl
http://www.stoutenburg.nl/engelsNF.htm

Friends Committee on Unity with Nature in the Americas
fcun@fcun.org
http://www.fcun.org/

Islamic Foundation for Ecology and Environmental Sciences
93 Court Road
Birmingham B12 9LQ, UK
+ 44 121 440 3500/8218
fax + 44 121 440 8144
ifees@ctv.es
http://www.ifees.org/

National Religious Partnership for the Environment
1047 Amsterdam Avenue
New York, NY 10025
(212) 316-7441
fax (212) 316-7547
nrpe@nrpe.org
http://www.nrpe.org/

North American Coalition on Religion and Ecology/International Consortium on Religion and Ecology
nacre@earthlink.net
http://www.caringforcreation.net/

Presbyterians for Restoring Creation
P.O. Box 70170
Louisville, KY 40270
http://www.pcusa.org/prc/

Religion and Ecology Program
Boston Theological Institute
mainoffice@bostontheological.org
http://www.bostontheological.org/rae/

Seventh Principle Project
Unitarian Universalist Association
board@uuaspp.org
http://www.uuaspp.org/

USCC Environmental Justice Program
National Conference of Catholic Bishops
3211 4th Street NE
Washington, DC 20017-1194
(202) 541-3000
http://www.nccbuscc.org/sdwp/ejp/index.htm

Web of Creation
1100 E. 55th Street
Chicago, IL 60615
webofcreation@lstc.edu
http://www.webofcreation.org/